The Origin and Character of God

The Origin and Character of God

Ancient Israelite Religion through the Lens of Divinity

THEODORE J. LEWIS

OXFORD
UNIVERSITY PRESS

Oxford University Press is a department of the University of Oxford. It furthers the University's objective of excellence in research, scholarship, and education by publishing worldwide. Oxford is a registered trade mark of Oxford University Press in the UK and certain other countries.

Published in the United States of America by Oxford University Press
198 Madison Avenue, New York, NY 10016, United States of America.

© Oxford University Press 2020

All rights reserved. No part of this publication may be reproduced, stored in a retrieval system, or transmitted, in any form or by any means, without the prior permission in writing of Oxford University Press, or as expressly permitted by law, by license, or under terms agreed with the appropriate reproduction rights organization. Inquiries concerning reproduction outside the scope of the above should be sent to the Rights Department, Oxford University Press, at the address above.

You must not circulate this work in any other form
and you must impose this same condition on any acquirer.

Library of Congress Cataloging-in-Publication Data
Names: Lewis, Theodore J., author.
Title: The origin and character of God : ancient Israelite religion through the lens of divinity / Theodore J. Lewis.
Description: New York, NY : Oxford University Press, 2020. |
Includes bibliographical references. |
Identifiers: LCCN 2020015308 (print) | LCCN 2020015309 (ebook) |
ISBN 9780190072544 (hardback) | ISBN 9780190072568 (epub) |
ISBN 9780190072575
Subjects: LCSH: God (Judaism) | Judaism—History—To 70 A.D. |
Palestine—Religion—History. | Palestine—Religious life and customs.
Classification: LCC BM610 .L494 2020 (print) |
LCC BM610 (ebook) | DDC 296.3/11—dc23
LC record available at https://lccn.loc.gov/2020015308
LC ebook record available at https://lccn.loc.gov/2020015309

For Dawn

Contents

Acknowledgments	ix
Abbreviations	xiii
1. Introductory Matters	1
2. The History of Scholarship on Ancient Israelite Religion: A Brief Sketch	17
3. Methodology	48
4. El Worship	73
5. The Iconography of Divinity: El	119
Section I: *Methodology and Iconography*	119
Section II: *Ancient Near Eastern Iconography and Divine Images*	128
Section III: *The Iconography of Ugaritic ʾIlu*	142
Section IV: *The Iconography of Israelite El*	155
6. The Origin of Yahweh	209
Section I: *The Meaning and Revelation of the Name Yahweh in the Hebrew Bible*	210
Section II: *The Name Yahweh in Extra-Biblical and Epigraphic Sources*	227
Section III: *The Geographic Origins of Yahwistic Traditions and the Debate Concerning Northern (Canaanite) Versus Southern (Midianite) Origins*	252
7. The Iconography of Divinity: Yahweh	287
Section I: *The Iconography of Yahweh: Anthropomorphic and Theriomorphic Traditions*	287
Section II: *The Iconography of Yahweh: Aniconic and Abstract Traditions*	333
8. The Characterization of the Deity Yahweh	427
Part One: Yahweh as Warrior and Family God	427
Section I: *Yahweh as Divine Warrior*	428
Section II: *Yahweh the Compassionate and Family Religion*	473
9. The Characterization of the Deity Yahweh	495
Part Two: Yahweh as King and Yahweh as Judge	495
Section I: *Yahweh as King*	495
Section II: *Yahweh as Judge*	513

10.	The Characterization of the Deity Yahweh	575
	Part Three: Yahweh as the Holy One	575
	Conclusion	674
Notes		701
Works Cited		905
Subject Index		1019
Citation Index		1045

Acknowledgments

Producing this volume was only possible due to a large support system of many people over many years. I was taught by stellar teachers who have left their imprint on my work more than they know. As the onomastic portions of the present work will illustrate, it is important to leave a record of the names of such giving people. I am deeply thankful for the efforts and the humanity of teachers from the University of Wisconsin–Madison (Michael Fox, Menahem Mansoor, Norman Roth, Keith Schoville, Barbara Fowler, Barry Powell), the Hebrew University in Jerusalem (Shraga Assif, Moshe Greenberg, Sarah Groll, Victor Avigdor Hurowitz, Rafi Kutscher, Alexander Rofé), and Harvard University (Michael Coogan, Frank Moore Cross, Paul Hanson, Thomas Lambdin, Patrick Miller, William Moran, Piotr Steinkeller). I also learned much from Douglas Gropp and Choon-Leong Seow, my classmates at Harvard, and from Marc Brettler and Bernard Levinson, my classmates at Hebrew University.

I found supportive colleagues helping me to grow at the University of Georgia in its Department of Religion (Alan Godlas, Kenneth Honerkamp, George Howard, Russell Kirkland, Sandy Martin, William Power, Shanta Ratnayaka, Thomas Slater, David Williams), in Athens, Georgia (Howard and Linda Abney, Chris and Cheryl Cornwell, Ed and Lucy Larson, William and Amburn Power, Henry F. and Karen Schaefer), and at Johns Hopkins University in its Department of Near Eastern Studies (Betsy Bryan, Jerry Cooper, Paul Delnero, Marian Feldman, Mike Harrower, Richard Jasnow, Jake Lauinger, Alice Mandell, P. Kyle McCarter, Glenn Schwartz, and Ray Westbrook). I am a historian of religion who was blessed to have been trained in Near Eastern languages and civilizations (not theology, as close readers will see) and even more so to have made my home for the past eighteen years in a Near Eastern studies department with colleagues in Assyriology, Egyptology, and Northwest Semitics as well as in Near Eastern archaeology and art history. I have had the privilege of editing *Near Eastern Archaeology* for the American Schools of Oriental Research (thanks are due especially to Billie Jean Collins), and serving with dedicated board members promoting the amazing work of the W. F. Albright Institute of Archaeological Research in Jerusalem. For years I have also had the privilege of editing the Writings from the Ancient World series (SBL Press). Thanks to working with stellar WAW authors and editors, I have enjoyed learning of the entire ancient Near East broadly through a wide variety of literary genres. Special thanks for this endeavor go to Bob Buller and Simon B. Parker. I also thank the members of the Biblical Colloquium, who have provided rigorous feedback to my work for many years.

The list of scholars and researchers from whom I have learned is endless, as documented throughout the volume and in the lengthy bibliography. I fear I will leave so many out should I begin to list their names. Hopefully the citations of their work can underscore my indebtedness. I must mention five scholars who graciously read portions of my manuscript and provided me with substantial feedback: Daniel Fleming, David Noel Freedman, Peter Machinist, Kathryn Medill, and Sara Milstein. Taking the time to go through another's work and offer incisive feedback is a hallmark of collegiality. Thank you. Those who know Daniel Fleming's extraordinary investments to improve the research of others (faculty and students alike) will not be surprised to read of my deep indebtedness to him for covering my drafts at every turn with probing historical challenges to rethink my approach and the very categories of my analysis. I am also indebted to the numerous students who have pushed me in my thinking, especially those graduate students who read earlier drafts of the present work in seminars on ancient Israelite religion at Johns Hopkins University.

On an institutional level, I am indebted to Johns Hopkins University. The importance of strong institutional support for the humanities is needed more than ever, and I thank the numerous leaders who make this a reality at Johns Hopkins day after day, year after year. A special thanks to the Blum family for endowing the Blum-Iwry Chair, which I have the honor of holding, as it celebrates the life of Samuel Iwry. (See the oral history of his life, *To Wear the Dust of War: From Bialystok to Shanghai to the Promised Land.*) For the current volume, I also owe a large debt to fellowship support from the John Simon Guggenheim Memorial Foundation, from the Center for Advanced Judaic Studies at the University of Pennsylvania, and from the National Endowment for the Humanities.

Words cannot begin to express my appreciation of Oxford University Press for agreeing to publish a manuscript of such length and with so many images. Special thanks to Steve Wiggins (truly a scholar and a gentleman), Drew Anderla, Amy Whitmer, Melissa Yanuzzi, the typesetting team at Newgen, and especially Sue Warga, who took on the herculean task of copy-editing such a large and technical manuscript. I am deeply indebted too to WordCo Indexing Services for producing the subject index and to Noah Crabtree for producing the citations index. I am delighted to give thanks to the many individuals who kindly helped in securing permissions for the images that occur in the volume, and in some cases the images themselves, as noted in the various credit lines. These thoughtful individuals include Susan Allison, Yael Barshak, Robert D. Bates, Adam L. Bean, Amnon Ben-Tor, Nelly Beyman, Stephen Bourke, Edward F. Campbell, Felicity Cobbing, Billie Jean Collins, Stefanie P. Elkins, Yosef Garfinkel, Garth Gilmour, Joseph A. Greene, Ze'ev Herzog, James K. Hoffmeier, Kathryn Hooge Hom,

Sarah Horowitz, Jean-Baptiste Humbert, David Ilan, Yael Klein, Kay Kohlmeyer, Marilyn Lundberg, Valérie Matoïan, Amihai Mazar, Nadine Meouchy, Michael Moore, Dick Osseman, Jaimie Owen, Nava Panitz-Cohen, Alan Paris, Zev Radovan, Seth Richardson, Lucia Rinolfi, David Schloen, Olaf Tausch, Gary Lee Todd, Christoph Uehlinger, Andrew Vaughn, Kim Walton, Ziony Zevit and Bruce Zuckerman. A special word of thanks goes to Kim Walton (of Walton Image Supply) for her heroic efforts in tracking down and organizing the many possible sources for images. I am indebted to Kim for her efficiency and many hours on my behalf. I also need to express a special word of appreciation to Amnon Ben-Tor and the Selz Foundation Hazor Excavations, as I use more images from Hazor than from any other site.

I close with deep thanks to my family. One of the chapters in this volume articulates the vital importance of family religion. So too the importance of family in every aspect of life. Though they have both passed, I honor the lives of my father, Harland Richard Lewis, and my mother, Jean Margaret Van Den Heuvel Lewis, whose love, concern, and work ethic were formative. The poignancy of life without them finds solace only in the memory of their devoted caring. And where would I be without the love and supportive prayers of my in-laws, Jess and Jan Daniels? My siblings (Sally, Michael, Martin, Andrew, Matthew) have always provided the deepest bonds of support. My children (Eric, Meghan, Hannah, Liam) have been the richest of blessings. One of my greatest delights and honors is to be a father to such amazing individuals.

To Dawn Tierney Lewis, wife, lover, best friend, intellectual, musician, companion, and contemplative soul-mate: I am ever thankful for the depths and joys of love we share. You have lived with this book for so long, ever patient, ever supportive, ever wise in your counsel. I dedicate this book to you, my love.

Acknowledgments combine acts of recognition and expressions of gratitude. How then could I do any other than to close by giving all thanks and honor to the subject of this volume, "the God who holds in his hand our every breath and every path" (Dan 5:23)?

Abbreviations

1Q	Dead Sea Scroll text number from Qumran Cave 1
4Q	Dead Sea Scroll text number from Qumran Cave 4
11Q	Dead Sea Scroll text number from Qumran Cave 11
A.	Tablet signature of texts from Mari
Akk	Akkadian
ANEP	*The Ancient Near East in Pictures Relating to the Old Testament.* Edited by James B. Pritchard
ANET	*Ancient Near Eastern Texts Relating to the Old Testament.* Edited by James B. Pritchard
Arb	Arabic
Arm	Aramaic
BDB	Brown, Francis, S. R. Driver and Charles A. Briggs. *A Hebrew and English Lexicon of the Old Testament*
C stem	causative stem (e.g., Hiphil in Hebrew)
CAD	*The Assyrian Dictionary of the Oriental Institute of the University of Chicago*
Chr	Chronicler
CIS	*Corpus Inscriptionum Semiticarum*
CoS	*The Context of Scripture.* Edited by William W. Hallo and K. Lawson Younger
CT	*Cuneiform Texts from Babylonian Tablets in the British Museum*
CTH	*Catalogue des textes hittites.* Emmanuel Laroche
CWSS	*Corpus of West Semitic Stamp Seals.* Nahman Avigad and Benjamin Sass
D	Deuteronomy-related source (of the Pentateuch)
D stem	doubled stem (e.g., Piel in Hebrew)
DN	deity name
DNWSI	*Dictionary of the North-West Semitic Inscriptions.* Jacob Hoftijzer and Karen Jongeling
DSS	Dead Sea Scrolls

DtrH	Deuteronomistic History
Dtr1	Deuteronomistic History (Josianic edition)
DULAT	*A Dictionary of the Ugaritic Language in the Alphabetic Tradition.* Gregorio del Olmo Lete and Joaquín Sanmartín
E	Elohist source (of the Pentateuch)
EA	El-Amarna tablets
G stem	ground or simple stem (e.g., Qal in Hebrew)
Gen rab	Genesis Rabbah
GKC	*Gesenius' Hebrew Grammar.* Edited by Emil Kautzsch. Translated by Arther E. Cowley
GN	geographic name
HALOT	*The Hebrew and Aramaic Lexicon of the Old Testament.* Ludwig Koehler, Walter Baumgartner and Johann J. Stamm
H	Holiness source/code (of the Pentateuch)
Heb	Hebrew
Impf	imperfect or prefixal verbal form
J	Jahwist/Yahwist source (of the Pentateuch)
JPS	Jewish Publication Society Translation of the Hebrew Bible
KA	Kuntillet 'Ajrud
KAI	*Kanaanäische und aramäische Inschriften.* Herbert Donner and Wolfgang Röllig
KAR	*Keilschrifttexte aus Assur religiösen Inhalts.* Edited by Erich Ebeling
KB	Koehler, Ludwig and Walter Baumgartner. *Lexicon in Veteris Testamenti libros*
KH	Ketef Hinnom
KTU	*Die keilalphabetischen Texte aus Ugarit.* Edited by Manfried Dietrich, Oswald Loretz and Joaquín Sanmartín
KUB	*Keilschrifturkunden aus Boghazköi*
LB	Late Bronze Age
LXX	Septuagint
MHeb	Medieval Hebrew
MT	Masoretic Text (of the Hebrew Bible)
N stem	N-prefix stem (Niphal in Hebrew)
NAB	New American Bible
NEB	New English Bible

NIV	New International Version
NJPS	*Tanakh: The Holy Scriptures: The New JPS Translation according to the Traditional Hebrew Text*
Non-P	The non-Priestly writings in the Pentateuch that included J and E in the documentary hypothesis
NRSV	New Revised Standard Version
OG	Old Greek
OL	Old Latin
P	Priestly source (of the Pentateuch)
Pf	perfect, perfective or suffixal verbal form
PN	personal name
RES	Répertoire d'Épigraphie Sémitique
RIH	Ras Ibn Hani (excavation number)
RS	Ras Shamra (excavation number)
RSV	Revised Standard Version
Syr	Syriac
Syr-Hex	Syro-Hexapla, translation of Origen's six-column edition of the Hebrew and Greek texts into Syriac
Sum	Sumerian
TAD	*Textbook of Aramaic Documents from Ancient Egypt*. Bezalel Porten and Ada Yardeni
tD/Dt stem	doubled stem with infixed t (e.g., Hitpael in Hebrew)
Tg	Targum
TUAT	*Texte aus der Umwelt des Alten Testaments*. Edited by Otto Kaiser
Ugr	Ugaritic
V	Vulgate
VAT	Vorderasiatische Abteilung Tontafel. Vorderasiatisches Museum, Berlin
WAW	Writings from the Ancient World. SBL Press

1

Introductory Matters

This volume is a reference work about God—the god who comes to be understood in different ways by Jews, Christians, and Muslims through the ages. Can you imagine a more daunting challenge? Hence the length of this book. And its brevity. One would have to write endlessly to cover such a topic, only to realize that any treatment would remain incomplete. Immediately one must choose how to approach the material and selectively what to cover. My approach is that of a historian of religion rather than that of a theologian. Specifically, I write as a historian of the religion of ancient Israel as it is understood within its ancient Near Eastern context, primarily the societies of ancient Syria, Iraq, Jordan, Lebanon and Egypt. These ancient cultural and sociological contexts gave birth to fundamental understandings of God that would come to be foundational to Judaism, Christianity, and Islam. Prior to articulating the selective scope of the present volume, it is worth pausing to ponder the vastness of the task before us.

The Scope of a Comprehensive Volume on Ancient Israelite Religion

Deciding on the scope of the present work presents a challenge. As a reference volume, it should present a resource for readers who seek to delve into the subjects it treats, presenting the issues at hand as well as the primary and secondary sources to which the reader may turn for additional study. Yet the subject of the present volume, ancient Israelite religion, is far too large to be covered in a single volume. This is especially true if one desires to probe its various topics with the depth of research they deserve and to present readers with the primary texts and secondary literature where they can dig deeper still. Consider what a comprehensive volume on ancient Israelite religion should entail.

History of Scholarship and Methodology

Foundationally, the reader should be introduced (but briefly) to the history of scholarship and the present state of the field such that she appreciates the river into which she is stepping. There are a number of ways to approach the topic, so ideally the reader should also be presented with the author's methodological principles (whether she agrees with them or not). Articulating a thoughtful methodology is a desideratum, for today's analyses of Israelite religion (indeed, of the academic study of religion in general) are dramatically different from those of past generations. So far, so good. The two chapters that cover this are Chapter Two, "A Brief History of Scholarship," and Chapter Three, "Methodology."

Divinity

The overwhelming task of articulating ancient Israelite religion comes into sharper focus when one ponders the lengthy list of topics that must be addressed. Surely the gods must be given their due (within Israel and within its broader cultural context), yet cracking the door to divinity invites a plethora of the preternatural. Even if we restrict ourselves to only the male gods of the Levant and only those of the Iron Age, we still face dealing with Athtar, Baal, Baal Hammon, Bethel, Chemosh, Dagan, El, Elyon, Eshmun, Gad, Hadad, Horon, Melqart, Milcom, Molek, Mot, Qadosh, Qaus, Reshep, Shamash, Yahweh, Yam, and Yarikh. Even this list is partial, as it does not include the various local and regional manifestations of the same deity.[1] Obviously, female divinity needs a similar full and nuanced treatment, and here too the list is lengthy, including named deities (Anat, Anat-Yahu, Asherah,[2] Ashtart/Astarte,[3] Ashtarot, Baalat, Ishtar, Qedeshet, Qudshu, Tanit) and those known through titles and iconography (e.g., Queen of Heaven, Dea Nutrix, Mistress of Animals). Fleshing out divinity further would have to include the plural gatherings known as divine councils and assemblies. Examining the preternatural in ancient Israel more broadly would necessitate looking at entities linked to the heavens and the angelic as well as the netherworld and the demonic.

Sacred Time, Sacred Space

Israelite religion took place in sacred time and sacred space, and these too would have to be studied fully for a comprehensive understanding. Even the briefest of surveys of the former would have to work through reams of calendrical sources, and surveys of the latter with volumes of archaeological data. Ziony Zevit's (2001) masterful study of Israelite religions reveals the daunting task of articulating the many and varied forms of sacred architecture with ever increasing examples coming from each new season of excavations. That sacred trees and sacred waters—even agrarian threshing floors—were also places of cult increases the level of difficulty.⁴ Of course, the religious paraphernalia filling such sacred spaces would need attention as well (e.g., apotropaic objects, censers, cultic jewelry, cultic symbols, incense, lampstands, the Nehushtan, *mĕzûzôt*).

The Practice of Religion

Clearly, one would soon need to address cult per se, and here too there is a staggering amount of material about the actual practice of religion. Hopefully one could settle on an organizing principle (political? sociological? economic? ideological? theological?) that could facilitate articulating the varieties of royal cult, family and household religion, priestly tenets, prophetic and mantic practices, the daily religion of the sages writing reflective literature, and last but not least apotropaia thought to be effectual. Reform movements would need to be juxtaposed with counterreform measures. While certain rituals and religious festivals would take center stage (e.g., Sabbath observance, circumcision, sacrifice, Passover, *yôm kippur*), the comprehensive treatment we are envisioning would have to include a wide array of rituals (birth rituals, healing rituals, funerary rituals, ritual bathing, clothing, anointing, purification rituals, dedications, fasting, oaths, vows, temple rituals, etc.) and the full calendar of festivals and feasts (*ḥag maṣṣôt, ḥag haqqāṣîr, ḥag hāʾāsîp, ḥag šābûʿôt, ḥag hassukkôt, bikkûrîm, pesaḥ,* New Year's festivals, New Moon, Sabbatical Year, Jubilee Year, etc.). Dare we mention cults of the dead, cultic prostitution, and child sacrifice? The finely tuned differences of offerings (*zebaḥ, šĕlāmîm, ʾāšām, ḥaṭṭāʾt, ʿōlâ, tĕrûmâ*) would have to be scrutinized diachronically and synchronically, as would dietary regulations and rationales.

With the manipulation of blood seen as particularly distinctive in Israelite religious practice, one would have to examine whether blood was used symbolically and/or instrumentally, whether Passover blood should be understood as apotropaic, whether daubing blood on the right ear, thumb, and big toe is best seen as purificatory or as an indexical sign.⁵ And once we start to consider the human body, Catherine Bell's voice in our head urges us to consider the "ritual body" and the "socialized body." How does ritual performance (e.g., garbing, anointing) reveal how Israelite religion was used ideologically to construct and reinforce hierarchy?

Religious Personnel: Kings, Priests, and Prophets

Once humans enter the picture, the scope enlarges still further to include the different personnel involved in the various types of religion. Israelite religion broadly construed includes the king as a (the) primary cultic officiant together with a wide variety of priestly functionaries and various intermediaries associated with prophecy in its many forms. For a comprehensive look, each of these would have to be addressed for their religious components. Kings were closely associated with divinity and often perceived as the primary cultic actor who provides access to the gods. They were involved in the performance of cult, such as making burnt offerings (ʿōlôt) as well as the so-called peace offerings (šĕlāmîm) and, in King Ahaz's case, even blood manipulation. In addition to the performance of cult, Israelite and Judean rulers were the primary sponsors of religion, building and maintaining altars, sanctuaries, and temples. A glance at the remarkable finds at Kuntillet ʿAjrud (a remote site on the Darb el-Ghazza caravan route under royal control) reminds us to include well-trained scribes in any scenario of royal cult, as they were the ones used by monarchs to pen poetic theophanies (KA 4.2) similar to what we find in the Hebrew Bible's oldest war poems.

Ideologically, some have claimed divinity for the Judean king, and this too would need to be thoroughly examined. Were kings thought to be divine, or merely elevated leaders, or perhaps "infused with divinity" just short of being deified? A look at royal cult would also have to include the king's role in judicial affairs, as earthly kings were to be righteous in imitation of the Divine Judge, who gifted them with discernment. Righteousness (ṣĕdāqâ), as the prophet Amos underscores, is parallel to justice (mišpāṭ).

Just as royal cult was a mainstay of Israelite religion of the monarchic period, so too priestly cult was an ever-present reality. The pages of the Hebrew Bible present us with Aaronids, Levites, Levitical priests, Mushites, the priests of Nob, Shilohnites, and Zadokites, not to mention groups known as "priests of the second order," "the priests of the high places," and the kĕmārîm priests. Even David's sons are called priests. Yet another category are the male *and female* Nazirites who, in the formulation by the Priestly Source (P), vow a temporary threefold abstinence: refraining from cutting their hair, avoiding intoxicants and unclean food, and avoiding any contact with a corpse.

Though an arduous undertaking, a comprehensive treatment would have to unpack the Hebrew Bible's descriptions of ongoing negotiations over sacerdotal power, status, and cultic privilege. This is true particularly for understanding holiness in the biblical tradition. For, in addition to holiness being about cultic purity (i.e., cleanness void of moral, social, and/or ritual pollution), holiness also served as an indicator of rank among cultic personnel. For example, the P traditions advocate that *only* Aaronid priests (in contrast to the non-Aaronid Levites) are called holy. Analogously, just as holiness served as an indicator of rank among priestly personnel, so too holiness served as an indicator of Yahweh's supremacy over the gods. Aged Israelite lore proclaimed:

Who is like you among the gods, Yahweh?	*mî-kāmōkâ bā'ēlim yhwh*
Who is like you, feared in holiness?	*mî kāmōkâ ne'dār baqqōdeš*
	(Exod 15:11)

Again, God must be given his due.

A third group of religious personnel central to our task would be intermediaries best known from the Hebrew Bible's prophetic corpus but now expanded to encompass the divinatory arts (see Kitz 2003; Nissinen et al. 2003, 2019; Hamori 2015). Prophetic perspectives have always had their appeal to historians of Israelite religion due to the prophets' varying modes of experience (visionary, auditory, audiovisual, dreams, ecstasy, omens, etc.) and modes of communication (verbal and nonverbal symbolic acts). Wide-ranging religious viewpoints come from their different chronological, geographic, and sociological contexts. The last is particularly needed for revealing how prophetic engagement with royal and priestly cult was tied to one's sociological setting (see Wilson 1980). Indeed, the roles of prophets and priests could be symbiotic (cf. Ezekiel the *kōhēn*) as much as they could be adversarial. Prophets cannot simply be reduced to outsiders speaking truth to religious power, as they themselves could be practitioners of cult. Elijah may never have been called a priest, yet he builds an altar "in the name of Yahweh," procures a bull and fuel source, cuts the sacrificial animal into pieces, and invokes the deity through petitionary prayer—all resulting in divine visitation. Moreover, "cult" should not be reduced to the sacrificial. That Elisha, "a holy man of God" (*'îš 'ĕlōhîm qādôš hû'*), was thought to resurrect the dead is just as much a part of Israelite religious belief. That a variety of divinatory procedures—those legitimized and those branded illicit—are attested (belomancy, cleromancy, extispicy, necromancy, oneiromancy) urges us to expand our definition of how divine intermediaries functioned (see Kitz 2003; Hamori 2015). That the primary medium used by the high priest to seek the will of God was the divinatory, binary Urim and Thummim once again shows how the priestly blends with the prophetic.

Other Religious Actors

The three groups of personnel just described (royal, priestly, and prophetic intermediates) scratch only the elite surface of religious actors. Ancient Israelite religion encompassed far more than the elite preoccupation of using religion to obtain, secure, and bequeath power, be it the throne's or the temple's. The non-elite religion of private individuals, families, and households was of abiding concern, as it addressed the transitions of life (birth, marriage, death). Thus our panoramic look at Israelite religion should treat the petitioning of the

Divine Parent for safe births, fit children, and sturdy livestock; for snakebite remedies and sexual potency; for good weather, adequate water, and abundant crops. Lest we draw dichotomous categories too rigidly, we should remember the porous boundaries between elite and non-elite religion: kings, priests, high-ranking officials, elite merchants, and the like shared similar concerns with commoners, as they all petitioned the divine for personal health and prosperity.

During desperate times, certain individuals regardless of social standing turned yet elsewhere to seek succor. Though the precise literary genre of incantations is missing from the pages of the Hebrew Bible (contrast, for example the Ugaritic ritual texts), the Hebrew Bible nonetheless knows of such activity—activity that was certainly at home within ancient Israel (though often deemed illicit) (see Lewis 2012). Thus a comprehensive coverage of the religion that was practiced in ancient Israel would have to explore the following incantation specialists: *ḥōvēr ḥāver* "enchanter of spells" (Deut 18:11; Isa 47:9,12); *ḥōvēr ḥăvārîm mĕḥukkām* "expert enchanter of spells" (Ps 58:6); *mĕnaḥēš* "omen interpreter" (Gen 44:5,15; Deut 18:11); *mĕkaššēp* "sorcerer" (Exod 7:1; 22:17; Deut 18:11; Mic 5:11); *mĕʿônēn* "cloud watcher?" (Deut 18:11; Mic 5:11; cf. Arslan Tash II); *ḥăkam ḥărāšîm* "skilled enchanter" (Isa 3:3; cf. Deir Alla I.36); *nĕvôn lāḥāš* "expert incantation specialist" (Isa 3:3); *mĕlaḥăšîm* "incantation specialist" (Ps 58:6); *baʿal hallāšôn* "master of the tongue" (Qohelet 10:11); *ʾōrĕrê-yôm* "those who curse the day" (Job 3:8); *ʾōrēr livyātān* "those who (are skilled at) rousing Leviathan" (Job 3:8); *ʾaššāpîm/ʾāšĕpîn/ʾāšĕpayyāʾ* "exorcist" (Dan 1:20; 2:27, 4:4; cf. Akk *ʾāšipu*). As we learn from the presence of amulets in the archaeological record, the prevalence of apotropaia thought to be effectual should not be underestimated.

The Reflective Side of Israelite Religion

Also among the religious actors were those who sought to reflect on society, divinity, and the human condition, the sages who have left us with probing remarks that scholars have called "wisdom literature." Wisdom (*ḥôkmâ*) in biblical tradition is grounded theistically: "The fear of Yahweh is the beginning of wisdom, and the knowledge of the Holy One is understanding" (Prov 9:10). It has a great respect for the elderly and a strong sense of community: "Ask your ancestor, and he will tell you; Your elders, and they will inform you" (Deut 32:7). It privileges collective truths, accrued over time: "Indeed, inquire of bygone generations, Ascertain the insights of their ancestors; For we are but of yesterday and know nothing; Our days on earth are but a shadow. Will they not teach you and tell you, Utter words out of their understanding?" (Job 8:8–10).

Thus a comprehensive treatment of Israelite religion would need to articulate the "wisdom perspective"—that religion had better be about how to make the right choices in life, how to get along with people, how to live life decently, how to avoid personal disaster, how to drink deeply of God. For these concerns, about religion in its applied form, the historian of religion would have to turn his focus away from the grand affairs of state, history, politics, and law. Wisdom's goal is personal holiness, marked by honesty, self-control (especially in speech), diligence, and morality, and dedicated to securing a life of well-being, decency, and dignity. Godly wisdom stands in contrast to "folly" (*'iwwelet*), a term used to encapsulate self-destructive behaviors focusing on oneself apart from God.[6]

The thorough treatment we are envisioning would have to appreciate the variety of literary forms used to express these perspectives (axioms, disputation speeches, exhortations, folk wisdom, maxims, pithy expressions, precepts, proverbs, reflections, theodicies) together with how wisdom is personified as a woman bidding one to dine (Prov 9:1–3). It would have to explore religious reflections on suffering (see Job) and on finding order among the absurdities and perceived randomness of life (see Qoheleth) as it probed questions of theodicy. It would need to be attuned to the ways in which authors were self-referential as they included descriptions of "interiority" (see Niditch 2015). In short, it would have to "look at life honestly, as the sages of Israel surely did," in order to "see goodness, beauty, and justice" along with life's "evil, ugliness, and injustice" (Fox 2000: 3).

Aesthetic Presentations of Israelite Religion: Literature, Music, Art, and Dance

Many readers of a volume on Israelite religion who have a passion for the humanities would want to see substantial coverage of the ways in which literature, the visual arts, music, dance, and drama were used by the ancients to express their religious beliefs. In this desire they stand in good company, for text (the Hebrew Bible and the epigraphic record) and material culture reveal that the ancients widely embraced the humanities. One need look no further than the many examples of literary craftsmanship (puns, double entendres, storytelling, etc.),[7] melodious psalms, the large percentage of the Hebrew Bible that was written in poetry, David's ritual dance (2 Sam 6:12–16), Elisha's music-induced prophecy (2 Kgs 3:15; cf. 1 Sam 10:5–6), Job's morning stars singing (Job 38:7), or the tradition that God gifted Bezalel and his craftsmen with superior artistic skills to be used in his service (Exod 31:1–11; 35:30–35).

The Priestly Tradition offers the strongest apology for how God desires the best of the humanities to be used in religious service—in the creation of sacred architecture (Tent of Meeting, Ark, *kappōret*, altar, basin), religious furnishings (incense stands, lampstands, tables, utensils), and the paraphernalia of cult (from priestly vestments to anointing oil and incense). P elaborates on how God called Bezalel personally, how he filled him with his divine spirit (*rûaḥ ʾĕlōhîm*), with ability, intelligence, and knowledge in every kind of craft (*bĕḥokmâ ûbitĕbûnâ ûbĕdaʿat ûbĕkol-mĕlāʾkâ*; Exod 31:3; 35:31). God desires and empowers his artisans to work skillfully in a variety of media and with various artistic techniques (Exod 31:4; 35:32–35).

There are aesthetic reasons why the Hebrew Bible is chanted (Jacobson 2017: 4–10), why its psalter is the hymnbook of the church, why its pages are vital to the canon of English (and non-English) literature curricula, and why its stories are a canvas for the history of art, not to mention the worlds of theater and film. Turning again to religion, when the great English humanist and apologist G. K. Chesterton (1908: 60, 63–64) mused about his "ultimate attitudes toward life; the soils for the seeds of doctrine," he quipped: "I had always felt life first as a story: and if there is a story, there is a story-teller."

Conclusion to the Scope of a Comprehensive Volume on Ancient Israelite Religion

The preceding survey articulates the breadth of scope that a comprehensive volume should entail, together with the daunting task of carrying out such an endeavor. To make matters even more challenging, Chapter Three will address the academic disciplines and methodologies needed to write a history of Israelite religion. Obviously, a single volume of manageable length cannot cover all of the aforementioned features unless one chooses to present a brief flyover, and then one ends up with an introduction rather than a reference volume. The best approach, then, is to be selective in choosing several broad areas of concentration that are representative of the whole.

Taste and see that Yahweh is good . . . (Ps 34:9 [Eng 34:8])

The Scope of the Present Volume

The present volume is a synthetic presentation of core elements of ancient Israelite religion. The varied topics mentioned earlier have undergone a distillation process that hopefully, as with an aged Scotch, brings out the intense flavors, colors, and aromas of the remarkable past without being reductionist. Israelite religion must be understood through texts (the Hebrew Bible and the epigraphic record) and material culture, yet also within its broader ancient Near Eastern cultural and historical context. Synthesizing so much material runs the risk of oversimplifying, yet in our age of narrowing specializations there remains a great benefit in looking at the broad picture.

An Organizing Principle: Studying Ancient Israelite Religion through the Lens of Divinity

There are many options for organizing our material, as varied as the many topics just mentioned. Ziony Zevit (2001: 79) wisely uses the materiality of cult, especially the variety of sacred architecture and the epigraphic record, "as a matter of research strategy" in order to appreciate the multiplicity of Israelite religions. Rainer Albertz uses a sociological lens to view the history of Israelite religion from small family groups to a centralized state, but also with a keen eye on personal piety (Albertz 1978, 1994; Albertz and Schmitt 2012). Susan Niditch (2015) looks to descriptions of self-representation and self-contemplation to view the individualistic experience of religion. Debra Ballentine (2015) looks afresh at how religious myths of combat functioned ideologically as much as they delightfully entertained. Mark Smith (2001b, 2002a, 2004, 2008, 2016) repeatedly turns to divinity as a conceptual category to organize his multifaceted studies of Israelite religion. Karel van der Toorn's (2018b) varied essays on Israelite religious beliefs and practices are now collected under the title *God in Context*.

Similar to the work of Smith and van der Toorn, the present volume looks to divinity as an organizing principle, though this book will include a variety of theoretical perspectives, including those of the historians of religion already listed. By using divinity, I do not mean to narrow the topic theologically; rather, writing as a historian of religion, I intend to explore divinity as a window to the historical, the sociological, the performance of cult, the ideological, and the aesthetic. I have chosen to look at literary and iconographic portrayals to see how humans represented their deities and in so doing represented themselves and their religious world.

Why the lens of divinity? Daniel Schwemer (2016: 1–3) articulates the divine orientation of Hittite cult in ways that resonate with the religions across the ancient Near East, including (with certain adjustments) ancient Israel:

> The sphere of the divine forms part of the Hittite landscape; mountains, rivers and rocks are regarded as numinous powers, as are the sea, the sun and the storm. The gods inhabit the various regions of the cosmos and the land, but, at the same time, they reside in houses built for them by mortals whose relationship to their divine lords is conceived in analogy to that of a

slave to his master. The people take care of and provide for the gods whose contentment and favorable presence are considered to be essential for the prosperity of the land.

The basic patterns of how and when mortals provide [for] and honour the gods are . . . shaped by the conceptualisation of divine beings in analogy to human authorities (anthropomorphism). . . . The observance of the cult is regarded as a prerequisite of the gods' favour; it thus plays a central role in establishing and preserving the exclusive relationship between the Hittites and their gods.

James Kugel (2011: 28–30) concurs lucidly:

The peoples [of the ancient Near East] had always deferred, and *referred*, to God or the gods in all things, going back to time immemorial. . . . The gods' looming presence in the ancient Near East has, of course, some practical consequences. . . . [H]ow someone thinks about God . . . has very much to do with how that person conceives of himself or herself, and more precisely, how such a self conceives of itself fitting into the world.

Mark Smith (2001b: 103) poignantly adds:

To understand divinity is to extrapolate from the human condition to express reality that cannot be entirely described; and to understand humanity is in turn to make some sense of divinity that can be sensed only in part. . . . [D]ivinity is not simply humanity writ large. . . . The ancients struggled with the limits of their understanding of divinity. . . . It was a mystery of something beyond themselves.

Seven Tastings

The distillate before you has seven flavors. As a first taste, Chapter Four considers the worship of El, the deity who appears in the name of the eponymous ancestor Israel. Sociologically, the flavors here are those of ancestral traditions, the so-called God of the Fathers, and family religion—standing apart from the religion of a centralized state and hierarchical priestly cult. The literary portrayals of El worship must be complemented by a look at the aesthetically physical. Was El imagined in the form of an enthroned, benevolent patriarch, a majestic bull, or even a solid block of stone? Chapter Five, our second taste, blends in the iconography of El situated within a comparative study of ancient Israel's neighbors, especially the robust 'Ilu religion of Late Bronze Age Syria (Ugarit). The numerous cults of standing stones (known elsewhere as betyls or "houses of El") attested archaeologically throughout Iron Age Israel's history will also be sampled.

Yahweh is far and away the dominant deity of Israelite religion, such that Patrick Miller (2000: xviii) can assert that "the centrality of this deity" and his "nature and character" are "at the heart of *all the practices* of Israelite religion" (my emphasis). Thus our remaining five tastings will probe the historical question of the origin of Yahweh and the various ways in which he was characterized.[8] Chapter Six provides a third tasting with an emphasis on the historical. Readers can evaluate the Hebrew Bible's foundation stories about Yahweh (and vis-à-vis El worship) juxtaposed next to the epigraphic record, with datable texts ranging from Egyptian geographical lists of the fourteenth and thirteenth centuries BCE to a ninth-century BCE Moabite inscription and multiple ninth-and eighth-century BCE Yahwistic inscriptions from a remote site on the Darb el-Ghazza caravan route just south of Qadesh-Barnea (Tell el-Qudeirat), a site with a long biblical pedigree. Anyone who enjoys hypothesizing about the identity of Moses's father-in-law or connections to Midianites and Kenites will find an array of theories that can be sampled alongside archaic Hebrew poetry (biblical and epigraphic) describing militaristic wilderness theophanies.

Chapter Seven offers yet another tasting (our fourth) of the ways in which divinity was represented, with a detailed exploration of Yahweh's image in text and object. Whether Yahweh was embodied anthropomorphically, theriomorphically (with bulls and lions), or as taking up residence in solid stone is situated within the broader philosophical debate coming from ancient Israel's well-known aniconic traditions, which advocated that the image of God cannot and must not be fashioned. Anthropologically, here we come up against Rudolph Otto's theories that humans can be fascinated by the irresistible appeal of the numinous while at the same time standing in utter dread of the danger, even lethality, of the sacred.

The ubiquity of anthropomorphic language used of Yahweh resides on the pages of the Hebrew Bible alongside multiple traditions that represented Yahweh abstractly. With its ethereal qualities, fire was consistently chosen as representing Yahweh's presence, from Moses' burning bush and Elijah's "proof of divinity" contest on Mt. Carmel to fiery anthropomorphisms where Yahweh's mouth breathed fire and his nostrils snorted smoke. The ancients also developed a notion of abstract "radiance" that they assigned to their gods (e.g., Akkadian *melammu*), and for several biblical authors (e.g., the Priestly Source and Ezekiel) Yahweh was best conceptualized as *kābôd*, a term that we will do our best to define. A third attempt at portraying the divine abstractly was developed by Deuteronomic/Deuteronomistic scribes. They asserted that the very Name (*šēm*) of Yahweh could capture his essential nature and represent his presence "residing" in the Jerusalem Temple in a way that avoids (humanlike) limitations such as sitting on a throne. Yet other thinkers imagined that Yahweh might manifest as an invisible presence, and here they were echoing their neighbors to the north (in Ayn Dara, Syria) who carved a series of gigantic footprints representing an invisible deity of enormous size walking into his (or her) inner sanctum.

The remaining chapters correlate the ways in which Yahweh was characterized with the practice of cult, and with a variety of ideologies, religious expressions, and understandings throughout society. The plurality of religious actors described earlier in our panorama (kings, priests, prophetic intermediaries, sages, and the non-elite) will be addressed—though, again, through a representative sampling and without any attempt at an exhaustive coverage. Chapter Eight (our fifth taste of Israelite religion) intentionally juxtaposes two extremes: Yahweh as warrior and Yahweh as parent. Our intent is to provide a corrective for those who choose to view religion (especially biblical religion) narrowly, asserting that "the God of the Old Testament" is militaristic and thus they want nothing to do with him. In the ancient world (known for its brutality no more than ours) gods had to fight for their adherents. For whatever reason (the desperate petitions of the victims of brutality crying out for justice, or the aggrandizing and legitimizing of a self-serving monarch), gods were perceived as and needed to be powerful—to right wrongs, protect crops, and vanquish enemies. As a shock to our modern perspective, to say that a god is "holy" can emphasize that he is militarily powerful. *Ḥērem* battles are cultic as much as they are military. A soldier "consecrates" himself for the sacrality of war. Moreover, the notion of Yahweh as divine warrior transcended the mundane to include what has been labeled "cosmic" warfare, where a superendowed deity was able to vanquish seven-headed dragons that threatened society at large.

Yet as we see with all societies, alternative voices were at the ready to provide a counternarrative that God is a force of peaceful existence. Thus Chapter Eight balances tales of divine warfare with powerful rhetorical aspirations of disarmament. People can choose to beat their swords into plowshares, to learn of war nevermore. Surprisingly, we come across juxtaposed similes that depict Yahweh as both "like a warrior" and "like a woman giving birth" (Isa 42:13–14). Such language gives us a thirst for the ways in which Yahweh was portrayed as a compassionate family god. The rest of Chapter Eight then explores the non-elite religious actors sketched in the panorama. How is it that the warrior God can stoop to dry one's tears? Using the language of family religion (what Saul Bellow called "kitchen religion"), we will see that Yahweh is portrayed as a caring father to his child Israel, like a mother nourishing her newborn.

Another blended (sixth) taste is found in Chapter Nine: it intentionally juxtaposes God as king and God as judge. Just as pondering Yahweh as a family god provided a window into domestic cult, so viewing Yahweh as king helps us to peer into royal cult, and seeing Yahweh as judge provides an avenue into ancient

INTRODUCTORY MATTERS   13

Israel's judiciaries. Some scholars advocate that the metaphor of Yahweh as king was the primary way in which the ancients understood their god. Reciprocally, the way they conceptualized kingship was informed by the actions of their monarchs and the ideology of royal power and prestige. As already noted, both actions and ideologies were wrapped in theocentric garb, as kings were the primary cultic actors and, at least for the Davidides, occupied their thrones because of divine providence. Chapter Nine then looks at royal cult, including the religious lives of Israelite and Judean monarchs and their putative divinity, all set against the backdrop of ancient Near Eastern royalty. As Yahweh was the Eternal King, so the anointed monarch sat on Yahweh's eternal throne (*wayyēšeb ʿal-kissēʾ yhwh lĕmelek*; 1 Chr 29:23; Ps 45:7 [Eng 45:6]). As Yahweh was the king par excellence, so "incomparable" language was used of certain kings (e.g., Solomon, Hezekiah, Josiah), as they were linked to the divine especially via cult. Some kings receive considerable attention for their sponsoring and performance of cult—not just the favored David and Solomon, but also Ahaz, whose blood manipulation is unparalleled among all the other kings of the Bible. (Elsewhere such activity is solely the prerogative of priests.)

Ideologically, while Judean kings were not considered to be divine (nowhere do they ever receive cult), they nonetheless were infused with divine qualities. As Yahweh was seen as the chief magistrate and divine lawgiver, so Judean monarchs were ordained of God to ensure justice (*mišpāṭ*), equity (*mîšōr*), and righteousness (*ṣedeq, ṣĕdāqâ*). Chapter Nine thus rounds out our look at royal religion by considering Judean kings, who were viewed as "kings of justice," to borrow a phrase from their Mesopotamian neighbors. It articulates judicial ideals found across the Near East that sound quite contemporary, as they provide legal safeguards for the disadvantaged of society (especially widows, orphans, and the *gērîm*, or non-Israelite residents). It also explores whether kings actually enacted laws, in light of the poor documentation for royal legislation within the Hebrew Bible.

Considering ancient Israelite societies at large, over long chronological and geographical spans, Chapter Nine also looks at non-royal judiciaries. Understanding the origin and organization of early Israelite judiciaries is fraught with challenges, yet this need not stop us from exploring what can be said about the roles of the paterfamilias, fathers and mothers, kinsmen, tribal "heads" (*rāʾšîm*), tribal "officials" (*šōṭĕrîm*), judges (including the female Deborah), town elders, and priests. A theocentric constant is again in full view: the notion of God as judge permeates all social levels. So too we find the divinely inspired judicial ideal of rendering decisions without partiality, providing justice for native and non-native resident alike, with all social rungs (*kaqqāṭōn kaggādōl*) receiving equal treatment.

Chapter Nine also considers the abuse of judicial power by documenting, albeit briefly, prophetic voices speaking out against injustice. Sociologically, it mattered not if prophets commissioned by Yahweh stood within the power structure or without. Advocating for justice was their vocation. As will be detailed later, they employed a variety of literary genres (e.g., judicial parables, judgment oracles, covenant lawsuits) to advocate change for the disenfranchised.

Finally, Chapter Nine focuses attention on the reflective nature within Israelite religion, where sages probed the nature of the judicial ideal as it applies to divinity. The theodicies left for us to ponder are nuanced and existential. They include affirmations that Yahweh is indeed just (Leibniz's *théodicée*), but that lessens not the absurd and maddening ways in which divine retribution plays out (thus Qoheleth). Boldly, the reflective side of Israelite religion also made space for direct challenges to the Almighty. One need not only imagine taking God to court, says Job; an actual legal case can be filed. Yet with litigation comes a verdict, and likely not what the litigant Job had in mind when he first strove to put God in the dock.

For our final tasting we offer a holiness blend. Using divinity once again as an organizing principle, Chapter Ten explores the notion of Yahweh as the Holy One to speak primarily about priestly religion. When many people think of the practice of Israelite religion, they imagine priestly cult, and with good reason. As previously mentioned, a wide variety of sacerdotal personnel and their activities are ubiquitously documented. The sheer volume of this material and its unparalleled relevance for understanding Israelite religion can be daunting, even paralyzing. Surely one must have the brilliance and constitution of a Jacob Milgrom or a Baruch Levine to understand this material fully. True enough. But this need not keep us from appropriating their insights (and those of other dogged researchers) to sketch a partial picture. Still, the reader should be forewarned: even the partial picture presented in Chapter Ten is not for the timid. Yet exploring priestly cult in detail is essential for understanding Israelite religion—hence the bulk of our chapter even as a distillate.

Chapter Ten examines the concept of holiness broadly construed within ancient Israelite religion. Perhaps counterintuitively, it begins with an overview of non-cultic understandings of holiness. Again, this is intentional, in order to awaken the reader cross-culturally, to bring the reader to consider that within the Levant to call a god holy can likely be an affirmation of power, especially military power. Surprisingly, here there is no hint of what comes to define holiness in priestly and Deuteronomic traditions (e.g., sacerdotal rank, cultic purity, social and ethical behaviors, and being withdrawn from common use). The earliest passages of the Hebrew Bible on holy divinity resonate with what we see in Late Bronze Age Levantine antecedents and from the ninth-/eighth-century BCE epigraphic record at Kuntillet ʿAjrud: to say that Yahweh is holy is to say that he is powerful. All such passages—including archaic poetry and the lethal holiness of the Ark narrative (with poor Uzzah as an object lesson matched only by the deaths of Nadab and Abihu), not to mention Hosea's and Isaiah's "Holy One of Israel"—are examined in turn.

The cultic management of holiness takes up the core of Chapter Ten. One text after another reveals how the actions of individuals within a sacred location and the delimiting of sacred space correlate with social and cultic status. It is easy to see how the concept of holiness is used ideologically to construct and reinforce rank, power, and privilege. This is especially true in the promotion of Moses, Aaron, and the Aaronid priests. And yet curious oddities will jump out to the reader. For example, though Moses is the preeminent authority throughout this material (and though we use the exclamatory "Holy Moses!"), the verb *qdš* is never used of Moses throughout the Hebrew Bible apart from a single (late) reference. Moreover, though the inaugurator of cult, Moses is never explicitly called a priest and never undergoes any type of consecration ritual. The discussion in Chapter Ten probes why this may be so.

Building on the work of Catherine Bell and others on ritual performance and the ritual body, Chapter Ten examines two particular ritual acts (clothing and anointing) that serve to construct and reinforce social realities and hierarchies. It is shown how the ritual clothing of Aaron is an act of investiture that formally bestows and confirms the authority due his rank as high priest. Vestments are used to mark both his subservience before God and his elevated status before humans. The ritual substances (oil and blood) and manner (pouring versus sprinkling) of anointing similarly mark sacerdotal rank.

Chapter Ten also devotes special attention to cultic actors ("holy" personnel) per se and across a wide swath of literature. As Saul Olyan (2000: 35) perceptively notes, there is nothing more fascinating than to see how "among the ranks of the cultic elite, distinctions of status . . . are often expressed through the idiom of holiness." One need probe no further than P's adamant assertion, mentioned previously, that only Aaronid priests (*kōhănîm*) are holy. In this volume the reader will see how each tradition (e.g., Priestly Source, Holiness Code, Ezekiel, Deuteronomy, Deuteronomistic History, and Chronicles) has its own nuances and terminology about who can be holy and why it vitally matters for the control and exercise of cult. Readers not familiar with this material should gain a new appreciation for how the Hebrew Bible preserves opposing voices with regard to restricting and expanding holiness. Of special interest for the latter are P's traditions about temporary Nazirites who were able to achieve a higher level of sanctity, especially women who have no other cultic role in P's scheme. Even more striking is the Holiness Code's (H's) comprehensive notion of holiness that includes the entire community (not only priests) and covering a wide array of cultic, economic, judicial, moral, and social parameters.

Conclusion

I never imagined that I would begin a book on religion (and on God!) by talking about Scotch. Hopefully the distillate before you has the maturity to capture a taste of Israelite religion with all its complexities. Hopefully it is robust yet supple, offering something for every palate with surprising notes, layered aromas, and intricate coloring. And hopefully it is well balanced, able to warm the soul as on a wintry day and linger long with a smooth finish.

2
The History of Scholarship on Ancient Israelite Religion: A Brief Sketch

Introduction: Schematizing Intellectual History

Schematizing the history of human thought into categories is always risky, yet pedagogically necessary in order to focus discussion. Dividing history into periods usually predisposes us to treat them as antithetical. When C. S. Lewis gave his inaugural lecture as professor of medieval and Renaissance literature at Cambridge in 1954, he remarked that the opposite is often preferable. In his field of study, he noted, following Jean Seznec, "as the Middle Ages and the Renaissance come to be better known, the traditional antithesis between them grows less marked" (1955: 1–3). The same could be said of the history of human thought presented in this chapter as one realizes the degree to which thinkers (ancient and modern) are indebted to their predecessors. On the other hand, one could adopt Thomas Kuhn's (1970) well-known "paradigm shift" model and assert that the major advances that have propelled fields of study are not at all gradual or linear, but revolutionary in character. Here too one could easily demonstrate insights gained because certain scholars stepped outside of accepted dogma and saw things in a new light (cf. Rendtorff 1993b).

Clearly, the best reconstructions of intellectual history resist such binary oppositions, realizing that continuity and novelty can coexist. Out of necessity one must provide structures within which to view the vast sweep of human thought as it pertains to the study of religion. To quote Lewis again, "We cannot hold together huge masses of particulars without putting into them some type of structure.... All divisions will falsify our material to some extent; the best one can hope is to choose those which will falsify it least" (1955: 3–4). With this hope in mind, the following brief outline of the history of scholarship is presented for heuristic purposes. Not all aspects of biblical scholarship are treated, only those with direct impact on the study of ancient Israelite religion. Even so restricted, the secondary literature is vast and can only be sketched.

The Growth of the Critical Study of the Bible: The Enlightenment

It is common to find introductory books that assert that the critical study of the Bible began with the Enlightenment in eighteenth-century Europe (e.g., Fohrer 1972: 17; Frei 1974: 51; Oden 1987: 19). To be sure, traditional beliefs regarding the Bible were already being questioned prior to this time. As early as the late medieval period Ibn Ezra (1092–1167) was intimating that portions of the Pentateuch were incompatible with Mosaic authorship, as were the latter chapters of Isaiah with the eighth-century BCE Isaiah ben Amoz.[1] Yet the late seventeenth and early eighteenth centuries do represent an increase in direct challenges against the traditional views of the church and synagogue. Richard Simon (1638–1712) would contest the Mosaic authorship of the Pentateuch based on his literary studies, while Jean Astruc's (1684–1766) isolation of divine names and duplicate narratives would mark the beginnings of source criticism (cf. Knight 1973: 39–58).

Thus, for our purposes, the Enlightenment is a convenient place to start the story of intellectual history as it influenced the study of the Bible. And yet, if a personal caveat may be permitted, I would argue that in choosing this period we need to be careful not to imply even subtly the denigration of pre-Enlightenment intellectual activity (due to the unstated view that scholarship must be skeptical to be critical). Working backward in time from the Enlightenment, one can appreciate biblical insights (even critical in nascence, although rarely skeptical) coming from many avenues of inquiry (philosophical, theological, exegetical) from diverse groups, including Jewish (e.g., Spinoza, Maimonides, the Qimḥis, Ibn Ezra, Rashi), Catholic (e.g., Thomas Aquinas, Anselm), and Protestant (e.g., the sixteenth-century reformers) scholars.

Though often hailed as monolithic, the Enlightenment period was certainly not uniform in its expression. At various points one finds intellectualism as well as anti-intellectualism, belief in progress as well as pessimism, theism as well as deism and atheism, credulity as well as skepticism. Nonetheless, the Enlightenment spirit in general placed emphasis on human reason, experience, and autonomy as it rebelled against external authority. "Sapere aude! [Dare to be wise!] Have courage to use your own reason!—that is the motto of enlightenment," opined Immanuel Kant (1959: 85). As epitomized in the work of Kant, Enlightenment thought is a product of seventeenth-century Rationalism and eighteenth-century British Empiricism. In rejecting Rationalism (which wanted to argue for the existence of God but from reason instead of revelation), Kant argued that one simply cannot have a scientific theology. The human mind is capable of wrestling with the material world; it is powerless for speculating theologically. Following David Hume, he denied the necessity (non-contingency) of

God, the classic doctrine of previous historical theology, thereby reducing "religion" to human morality. For Kant, future historical researchers could no longer appeal to any truth claims that a biblical author may make. They must be satisfied with describing only religious people, their beliefs, and their morality. One cannot theorize about God.

The empirical spirit of the Enlightenment did not go unchallenged. As the eighteenth century drew to a close, poetic writers who yearned for passion and aesthetics rather than scholasticism revolted against rationalism and Kantian skepticism. Some Romantics followed in the footsteps of Jean-Jacques Rousseau in their emphasis of feelings, imagination, intuition, and a return to nature. The Romantic who left his mark on the study of ancient Israel more than any other was the prolific Johann Gottfried von Herder (1744–1803), himself a student of Kant.[2] "The historian, Herder said, must loathe metaphysical abstractions and purely rational constructs. The proper historian must rather work as does an artist or a poet" (Oden 1987: 9). And thus Herder did, as he emphasized the *Volkspoesie* of the early Hebrews (see his two-volume *The Spirit of Hebrew Poetry*).

Such was the world of intellectual thought when the history of biblical scholarship was entering its most pivotal century, the nineteenth. It is hard to overestimate the impact of nineteenth-century German intellectual culture on the critical study of the Bible. Oden (1987: 5–6) has rightly noted how the German intellectual paradigm would become infectious elsewhere on the Continent as well as in England and the United States, often unconsciously, as academic institutions modeled their program of biblical studies after that of their German counterparts.

The Biblical Scholarship of Germany in the Nineteenth Century

German scholars of the nineteenth century inherited the Enlightenment's emphasis that the individual should prefer his own reasoning over institutional religion (tradition and dogma) when it comes to interpreting the Hebrew Bible. At the same time, many were still wrestling with the theology of the church.[3] Helping bridge the gap was Johann Gabler, who advocated that one should demarcate between articulating the religion of the Bible in its historical context and using the biblical texts to formulate a systematic theology to be used for dogmatics.[4] The former is a descriptive task that concerns itself with historically and culturally conditioned material, while the latter amounts to theology proper with its aim of instructing believers. In so doing, Gabler helped chart a course for his fellow German historians of religion as they tried to free their discipline from the strictures of dogmatic theology (although Gabler himself saw his work as benefiting dogmatic theology).

The stage was set. Over the next century German scholars would reconstruct (for better and for worse) the development of Israelite religion in ways that were decidedly different from those that had been handed down by the synagogue and church over hundreds of years. They did this through a variety of approaches indebted to (1) Gabler's views on the proper method for describing biblical religion (historical, language-based studies), (2) continued source criticism (e.g., Gabler's contemporary J. G. Eichhorn, who built on the work of Astruc), (3) the philosophical spirit of the times, which celebrated the individual exercise of reason, and which was soon to face Hegelian Idealism and social Darwinism, and (4) the Romantic spirit, typified by the work of Herder. Along with these approaches, and in part through Martin Luther's animosity toward the Jews, came a disturbing trend to treat Judaism (especially the post-exilic period) in a very derogatory manner. Thus it was that the data of the Hebrew Bible were transformed into remarkably different syntheses.

Wilhelm de Wette (1780–1849), a pupil of both Gabler and Herder, is known in biblical circles primarily for his contribution to Pentateuchal studies, which at the time were being done mostly along literary levels (see Dozeman 2017: 53–62; Rogerson 1992). De Wette made his mark in 1806 when he equated the literary strand known as D with the "book of the Law" found during Josiah's reform in the eighteenth year of his reign (621 BCE). By advocating that D was in fact authored *at the time* of Josiah's reform, de Wette made 621 BCE the benchmark for reanalyzing the history of ancient Israelite religion. D's central thesis is the centralization of worship. Thus de Wette argued that those literary strands that were ignorant of centralization were prior to 621 BCE, while those that presupposed centralization were later than 621 BCE.[5]

The ramifications of de Wette's work went far beyond literary analysis. In the words of Robert Morgan and John Barton, "Theories about the dating of the Pentateuchal sources ceased to be primarily solutions to a literary puzzle and became a tool for rewriting the history of Israel, and especially its religious institutions and theological ideas" (1988: 78). De Wette divided his material into the pre-exilic period, which he called "Hebraism," and the post-exilic period, which he called "Judaism." He then drew a caricature of the latter that reflected his low opinion of Judaism: "Judaism is the unfortunate reinterpretation of Hebraism. . . . [W]hereas Hebraism was a matter of life and enthusiasm, Judaism is a matter of the concept and literalism" (Albertz 1994: 4). In the spirit of Herder's poetics, de Wette made "Hebraism" soar as it burst into life, while Ezra's Judaism was dying on the vine, without "life and animation" (Hayes and Prussner 1985: 100).

Like de Wette,[6] Johann Karl Wilhelm Vatke (1806–1882) is also known for his contribution to Pentateuchal studies, in particular his insight that P was later than D, although much of the credit for this was to be given to the later treatments by Karl Heinrich Graf (1815–1869) and Julius Wellhausen (1844–1918).[7] Also similar to de Wette is the degree to which Vatke's overall construct of Israelite religion owes more to his philosophical understandings and speculations. In place of de Wette's Romantic Herder, Vatke turned to German Idealism in the person of G. W. F. Hegel (1770–1831). Vatke adopted Hegel's dialectical process (thesis, antithesis, synthesis) as his own philosophy of history, with the prophetic material forming the antithesis between the pre-prophetic (thesis) and post-prophetic (synthesis) stages. In contrast to older notions that Israelite religion emerged as a full-fledged monotheistic system during the time of Moses, Vatke argued that early Hebraic worship was primitive and astral in nature (Yahweh being identified with Saturn). Moses, in contrast, tried to spiritualize this nature religion and argued for Yahweh as the solitary national deity. Yet for Vatke it was only with the prophets and the wisdom tradition (and ultimately with Christianity) that the religion reached its spiritual climax.

With Graf's further elaboration of P presupposing centralization and thus being later than D, the new paradigm had arrived in nascent form.[8] It broke away from the old paradigm, the traditional view (the law prior to the prophets) of an early Mosaic monotheism and an Israel that battled the polytheism of the nations throughout its history with the law functioning as a national constitution and theological conscience. The new paradigm, based on the law coming after the prophets, was dramatically different.[9] It argued for the evolutionary nature of Israelite religion, which grew out of a primitive beginning, with monotheism arriving on the scene late and through the insights of the prophets rather than Moses.

All the new paradigm needed to win the allegiance of the next generation was an eloquent spokesperson, and such was to be found in Wellhausen, whose name has become synonymous with German source criticism. Every reader of Wellhausen's superbly crafted *Prolegomena to the History of Ancient Israel* (1878) is struck not by its originality (cf. de Wette, Vatke, Graf) but by its brilliant synthesis. There is little wonder why it became the dominant statement of the German position. Key to the splendid simplicity and symmetry of Wellhausen's reconstruction was his introductory chapter on the centralization of worship.[10] If the literary strand known as D is associated with Josiah's reforms and the insights of the prophets, then the material that lacks a central sanctuary (JE) must represent the earliest phase of Israelite religion (a primitive one at that), while the material that presupposes centralized worship (P) must represent the law codes of the post-exilic Judaic community and its Temple. Similarly, the development of monotheism follows suit and only evolves late, once again with the insights of the prophets and centralization. In Wellhausen's famous remark: "One God one sanctuary, that is the idea" (1965: 34).

Thus for Wellhausen, Israelite religion is unilinear and evolutionary in nature, progressing in positive fashion from primitive, animistic origins to the ethical monotheism of the prophets. Yet once it reached such heights, it would lose its ability to grow and became a static, mechanical abstraction in post-exilic Judaism (cf. Oden 1987: 23). As Stephen Geller has pointed out, Wellhausen contrasted the primitive youth of JE and the maturity of the Deuteronomic reform with the "lifeless" Priestly Code of the "Jewish" stage. According to Wellhausen's caricature of "Judaism," "the warm pulse of life no longer throbbed in it to animate it ... the soul was fled, the shell remained" (Geller 1985: 43).

There are those who choose to ignore Wellhausen's philosophical underpinnings. For example, Morgan and Barton argue that Wellhausen advocated literary criticism in order to be "free from contamination by *any* particular philosophical theory." In their opinion, Wellhausen worked in the spirit of the German historian Hans Mommsen to achieve "research free of presuppositions" (Morgan and Barton 1988: 79–86). Yet most assessments, especially any that incorporate Rudolf Bultmann's (1957) famous essay on the impossibility of doing exegesis without presuppositions, have not ignored the theoretical framework through which Wellhausen filtered his work.[11] While he may not have been a fan of Hegel (cf. Morgan and Barton 1988: 79–80), Wellhausen nonetheless was a product of his time. In the words of Rudolf Smend, "Wellhausen stood at as great a remove from Hegelian speculation as a German historian of the nineteenth century could without falling right out of context."[12] In addition, it is no mere coincidence that 1859 saw the publication of Charles Darwin's (1809–1882) *The Origin of Species*. Geller (1985: 43) is right to see Wellhausen refracting his view of Israelite history and religion through the optimistic evolutionary lenses of social Darwinism.[13]

Finally, from the Romantic Herder and Heinrich Ewald (1803–1875), Wellhausen inherited his high view of "the prophetical party" that brought about "the great metamorphosis of the worship" (1965: 368). Ewald, Wellhausen's teacher at Göttingen, taught with great conviction[14] that the prophets possessed "the divine spark of the true knowledge [that] was brought to consciousness by the spirit of God."[15] Thus for Wellhausen, who harbored an antipathy for the post-exilic phase of Israelite religion, the prophets were geniuses "resting on nothing outside themselves ... They do not preach on set texts; they speak out of the spirit" (1965: 398). For Wellhausen, the prophets were the great innovators of Israelite religion: their individual awakenings brought about the ethical reform that culminated in monotheism.

Even though Wellhausen saved his greatest praise for the prophets, it was his attempts to understand the earliest (what he called primitive) stages of Hebrew religion that was to mark the next great methodological phase of scholarship, the comparative approach. In 1887, almost a decade after writing his famous *Prolegomena*, Wellhausen published *Reste arabischen Heidentums, gesammelt und erläutert* (Remnants of Arabic paganism collected and explained), which attempted to flesh out primitive Hebrew religion through the use of pre-Islamic Arabian parallels, even though more relevant ancient Near Eastern texts had been published for some time prior (e.g., portions of the Gilgamesh Epic were published as early as 1873; cf. George Smith's so-called Deluge Tablet [1873: 213–234]). Today, with our wealth of comparative material coming from the Late Bronze and Iron Ages, turning to the pre-Islamic material looks rash, and it is little wonder that it produced such poor results. In the end, despite his noble attempt at using extra-biblical materials, Wellhausen's theories remained essentially literary, and it was up to William Robertson Smith and Hermann Gunkel to chart new methodological paths.

William Robertson Smith: A Sociological Approach to Biblical Studies

William Robertson Smith's *Kinship and Marriage in Early Arabia* (1885) and *Lectures on the Religion of the Semites* (1889)[16] marked a new yet short-lived direction in understanding religion as a social phenomenon.[17] According to Robertson Smith's famous dictum, "religion did not exist for the saving of souls but for the preservation and welfare of society."[18] Sociologists (e.g., Émile Durkheim and Max Weber) were indebted to Robertson Smith's pioneering work in studying societal evolution, as was Sir James G. Frazer of *Golden Bough* fame. Yet this was not to be the case among biblical scholars of his time.

Like his contemporary Wellhausen, Robertson Smith's appeal to "comparative religion" looked to pre-Islamic Arabian Bedouin tribalism to illuminate Israelite religion rather than the more relevant texts coming from ancient Egypt and Mesopotamia. This was due to Robertson Smith's prejudice that Semitic peoples were primitive in nature. Because Mesopotamian religion was not primitive in nature but, rather, "complex" (a result of, he said, "a large pre-Semitic element" of its population), one must not use these ancient texts for purposes of comparison, because "ancient and primitive are not synonymous terms; and we must not look for the most primitive form of Semitic faith in a region where society was not primitive" (1972: 13). Robertson Smith then underscored what he deemed the primitive nature of Arabian tribalism ("destitute of ethical motives" and without "any spiritual conception of the deity or any lofty conception of man's chief end") in order to heighten the superiority of ancient Israel's worship, with its "entirely different spirit and meaning."[19]

Robertson Smith's approach backfired. Despite his apologies, he did not convince large numbers of biblical scholars (certainly not those with theological interests) to embrace a sociological method.[20] Too much suspicion lingered that Robertson

Smith's approach was not "safe or advantageous" for the training of ministerial students, and thus he was removed from his chaired professorship in the Free Church College in Aberdeen (Johnstone 1995: 19–20). In the words of Norman Gottwald (1979: 293), "After W. R. Smith and J. Wellhausen studied the applicability of bedouin tribalism to early Israelite tribalism, so headlong was the retreat away from any further sustained anthropological and sociological studies of Israel that biblical study has been almost totally divorced from the social sciences for half a century."

Hermann Gunkel and the Rise of the History-of-Religion Method

Thanks in part to the growth of the emerging field of Assyriology, the comparative method lived on as the nineteenth century turned to the twentieth, especially through the works of Hermann Gunkel (1862–1932) and the history-of-religion school. The origin of the history-of-religion school has rightly been traced back to Albert Eichhorn, but it was Gunkel who gave it a compelling voice together with his students Hugo Gressman and W. Baumgartner.[21] Gunkel recognized early in his career the importance of myth as a category of religious thought. In particular, Gunkel isolated the combat myth (*Chaoskampf*) in the Mesopotamian sources (e.g., Enuma Elish), which he then compared to similar combat myths in both the Hebrew Bible and the New Testament, from Genesis' creation accounts to Revelation's apocalyptic narratives (1895, 1901).[22] Such comparative sources inspired Gunkel to advocate that it was possible to get beyond Wellhausen's literary approach to the prehistory of the text and the process by which the stories grew over time. Through studying the literary forms (*Gattungen*) of contiguous cultures one would be in a better position to sketch the history of Israel's literature and the life settings (*Sitze im Leben*) in which they were produced. Whereas Wellhausen was transfixed by internal source criticism, Gunkel argued that the biblical texts were the result of a long process of growth that can be traced through oral tradition.[23] Finally, Gunkel argued that the historian of ancient Israelite religion must be able to participate in the feelings of the ancients in order to achieve historical understanding. Here, once again, we feel the influence of Herder's idealism and romanticism.

The "Babel-Bibel" Controversy

Soon after the appearance of two of Gunkel's primary works (1895, 1901), Friedrich Delitzsch, a professor of Assyriology from Berlin University, gave a lecture to the German Oriental Society that resulted in what came to be known as the "Babel-Bibel controversy" (Babel being the Hebrew name for Babylon).[24] The basic data that formed the basis of Delitzsch's lecture were well known by this time.[25] Yet rarely has a single lecture had such an impact on intellectual history. The year was 1902, and this was no ordinary academic meeting. Surrounded by an aura of German nationalism, Delitzsch addressed the elite of German society, including Emperor Wilhelm II, a patron of ancient Near Eastern exploration for personal satisfaction and national aggrandizement.[26]

In the course of his lecture, Delitzsch emphasized not only that stories between the biblical narratives and the Mesopotamian texts were parallel but also that the former were dependent on the latter for their origin. This was nothing new; indeed, it was similar to Gunkel's comparative method.[27] Yet the high-profile nature of the lecture, Delitzsch's preference for the ethical superiority of Babylonian civilization to Israelite, and several putative parallels that bordered on the sensational turned this "Babel-Bibel" talk into a national and international debate. At stake was the uniqueness of biblical revelation and the preeminence of Israelite culture, and thus Delitzsch drew the ire of the majority of the religious community both in Germany and abroad. After a follow-up lecture the next year that was significantly more heretical theologically, Delitzsch lost the support of the emperor, which in turn resulted in his third lecture being given outside of the Oriental Society.[28] Nonetheless, the gauntlet had been thrown down.

Four reactions typified the times and lived on into the new century. Delitzsch's approach came to be known as the "pan-Babylonian school."[29] As already mentioned, the majority of those with religious or theological interests rejected Delitzsch quite summarily due to his denigration of the superiority and uniqueness of the biblical witness. A third group continued Gunkel's and Gressman's use of comparative material with their intent of "uplifting us and bearing us onward [to] the Religion of the Bible in all its glory and dignity." Thus for these scholars, the history-of-religion approach freely utilized the comparative ancient Near Eastern texts but was opposed to "a dragging down of what is Biblical to the level of the non-Biblical."[30] The fourth group were Assyriologists who went about their work (not always relating it to the Bible) while staying out of the fray created by Delitzsch.[31] This group would ultimately find a voice in later scholars who argued for the autonomy of Assyriology apart from biblical studies.[32]

Because three of the four responses embraced the use of ancient Near Eastern material, setting the Bible in its larger cultural context and looking at its prehistory outweighed theological approaches at the end of the nineteenth century and the beginning of the twentieth. The steady influx of newly discovered Mesopotamian texts (especially Hammurabi's code, newly published by Jean-Vincent Scheil in the same year as Delitzsch's first lecture) continued to fuel a raging thirst to know more about the ancient Near East and to see the Bible in the light shed by these new discoveries.

The Theological Rejoinder and the Biblical Theology Movement

At the turn of the century the theological approach to the Bible was in eclipse for several reasons. Ongoing historical-critical analysis questioned the chronology of the biblical story line (e.g., the law was seen as late and not early, as the Bible depicts). The history-of-religion approach asserted that one needed to look outside the Bible for illumination. Enlightenment philosophies that questioned traditional beliefs persisted as new disciplines emerged, of which sociology had the greatest impact. The latter is best characterized by the works of Émile Durkheim (who was born into a rabbinical family), the most notable being *The Elementary Forms of the Religious Life*, published in 1912. Durkheim gave functional, non-theological explanations (e.g., social imperatives, division of labor, promotion of group solidarity and renewal) for what was once derived solely from the religious and metaphysical realms. Religious rituals are not the by-product of beliefs and ideas; rather, the opposite is the case. Societal needs create sacred institutions and rituals. In addition to being functional, Durkheim's method was also reductionist: "Religion has *only* a social function."[33]

Though their discipline was not in vogue, it would be a mistake to portray early twentieth-century theologians as being in mass retreat. Most continued pressing the contributions and relevance of theology. It was not so much that theologians rejected historical critical scholarship in toto (although some conservative theologians did just that) than that they felt critical methodologies were incomplete because they ignored theology and the prominent role the Bible played in the life of the church. The atmosphere would soon become more adversarial with the advent of World War I, which dealt a crushing blow to the optimism and progressivism that underlay most critical methods of the post-Enlightenment era. Suddenly theology found a new voice of relevance. Theologians stressed the centrality of divine revelation and the supernatural, concepts that had been sidetracked by the then current anthropocentric methods.

This resurgent interest in biblical theology was led by Karl Barth and Emil Brunner and went under various names (e.g., neo-orthodoxy, dialectical theology, theology of crisis, theology of the Word). This rejoinder was so appealing to a postwar populace searching for theological assurance that, according to Rainer Albertz, "academic interest in history-of-religions accounts had been paralysed." It is true that some scholars (E. König, E. Sellin, G. Fohrer) keep a foot in both worlds by writing both Old Testament theologies and treatments on Israelite religion. But for the most part theologians had won the day. Albertz writes harshly of the lack of method of those who attempted works on Israelite religion:

The histories of Israelite religion ... which have continued to appear since the First World War are largely uninteresting résumés which in method and historical system hardly go beyond those of Wellhausen and the beginnings of the history-of-religions school. . . . [T]he few "histories of Israelite religion" which were written after the Second World War under the domination of Old Testament theology mark more of a step back in method and system. (Albertz 1994: 8–9)

The theological revolution was exported to America in the late 1920s and 1930s, where it coincided with American particularities (e.g., the fundamentalist-modernist controversies, the Scopes trial, the stock market crash in October 1929, the migration of universities away from church affiliations), leading Brevard Childs to advocate distinguishing an American "Biblical Theology Movement" distinct from—although related to—its European counterparts.[34] Childs chronicled the growth of the movement especially in the late 1930s and 1940s and underscored that "although the challenge to recover the essential message of the Bible was often couched in polemical language, it was also clear that the basic assault was not directed against historical criticism as such. . . . [T]he major thrust was directed against the misuse of historical criticism by the theological liberals . . . having lost themselves in the minutiae of literary, philological, and historical problems." Childs (1970b: 15) deemed this "an exercise in trivia, in which tragic process the profound theological dimensions were overlooked."

The Myth-and-Ritual Approach

In England and Scandinavia the situation was different from the 1930s through the 1950s.[35] The contributions of Samuel Henry Hooke (1874–1968; University of London) and Sigmund Mowinckel (1884–1965; University of Oslo) stand out and are often referred to as the "myth-and-ritual" or "patternist" approach.[36] This method has also been described pejoratively as "excessive forms of comparative religion" (Albertz 1994: 244 n. 4). Foundational to the biblical myth-and-ritual approach was the work of the Scottish social anthropologist James G. Frazer (1854–1941), whose famous work on mythology and religion, *The Golden Bough: A Study in Magic and Religion*, had grown from its two-volume first edition (1890) to twelve volumes in its third edition (1915).[37]

John W. Rogerson (1974: 66–73), who described Hooke as the theoretician of the myth-and-ritual position, argued that Hooke was primarily influenced by three factors: the ritual theory of myth from such scholars as Frazer and the classicists Jane Harrison and Gilbert Murray, the publication of Mesopotamian texts describing the New Year's festival by Heinrich Zimmern and François

Thureau-Dangin, and the diffusionist method in vogue among English anthropologists in the 1920s. For his part, Mowinckel was influenced by his teachers Gunkel and V. P. Gronbech (University of Copenhagen); the latter's essays on ritual drama were published as *The Culture of the Teutons* in 1912. Svend Aage Pallis, who wrote *The Babylonian Akîtu Festival* (1926)—which was used extensively by Hooke—was also a student of Gronbech.

The myth-and-ritual approach assumed a more or less homogenous culture throughout the ancient Near East. In contrast to Robertson Smith's and Wellhausen's reliance on "primitive" Arabian parallels, Hooke looked to Mesopotamia as an advanced culture whose myths and rituals permeated the ancient Near East, including ancient Israel. Moreover, for Hooke the Mesopotamian texts clearly showed that myth and ritual were inseparable and integrated at a deep level, because the texts themselves mentioned the recitation of the Enuma Elish myth during the Akitu festival. In addition, inferences from the texts could be used to establish a "pattern" that could be replicated throughout the ancient Near East. In particular, the myth-and-ritual approach hypothesized that the myth of a dying and rising god was acted out in ritual by human participants, especially kings. Together with the divine combat myth, these stories pointed toward the triumphal procession of the deity (= the king) leading to coronation (cf. Hooke 1933: 8). Because the cognate cultures were formed around the same basic skeleton, it is not surprising that similar myth-ritual "patterns" were created for ancient Israel through the works of Hooke and Mowinckel's followers, who included over the next decades Aubrey Johnson (1935, 1955), Julian Morgenstern (1917, 1938a, 1938b, 1938c), Theodore Robinson (1933), R. de Langhe (1958), Ivan Engnell (1943, 1969), and Theodor H. Gaster (1961, 1969). Even though textual data were lacking, some of these scholars saw enough hints in the Hebrew Bible to reconstruct for ancient Israel an Akitu-type New Year festival out of the feast of Asiph, a seven-day New Year festival corresponding to the seven days of the Genesis creation story (Hooke 1963: 121), the death and resurrection of Yahweh, the pairing of Yahweh and the goddess Anath (Robinson), a sacred marriage from the booth (= a divine bridal chamber) of the Feast of Tabernacles, and an extensive sacral kingship where the king is a "*divine* being . . . a powerful, superhuman being . . . He is a god" (Mowinckel 1956: 62, emphasis his).[38] A trend emerging from the myth-and-ritual approach was to look at the phenomenology of religion. Engnell, and the Uppsala school associated with him, argued for getting away from a "book mentality" and a strictly literary approach to reconstructing ancient Israelite religion so that one may appreciate how religious communities weave rituals and myths into a seamless garment that defines their existence.

The myth-and-ritual school suffered from insufficient data, conjectural reconstructions, and methodological imprecision.[39] Yet even devastating critiques did little to slow the fascination with such a grand theory. Harold Louis Ginsberg (1950: 157) eviscerates Gaster, noting how "no philological dragon has ever stood in the way of the recognition of a single halfway tenable hypothesis of the metasemasiologists [the "meaning-behind-the-meaning" school], but their dogmas have more than once barred their way to an understanding of the sound observations of others." More recently, their misinterpretation of the Mesopotamian texts has been even more noticeable.[40] Bruce Lincoln (2008: 221), in critiquing the "staunch devotees of the 'Myth and Ritual School' [who] continued to espouse Frazerian positions even into the 1960s," levels his critique squarely at Frazerian theory due to "the breadth of its popularity." Of Frazer he writes:

> Like all grand theorists, however, and especially those of the armchair variety, he was guilty of distortion, pretentiousness, procrusteanism, selective blindness, cultural condescension, and a host of other failings. As each of his errors was identified, his project slowly deflated, with the result that his theories not only lost their power to transport, they began to look a bit pathetic. . . . At present, Frazer stands alongside Friedrich Max Müller as one of the ancestors remembered with more embarrassment than gratitude, let alone reverence, by several interrelated disciplines that once hailed him as one of their founders (anthropology, folklore, history of religion).[41]

A telling sign of the decline of the myth-and-ritual approach in Israelite religion—at least in its excesses—was the work of Helmer Ringgren. Though Ringgren stated that he was "consciously allied with the so-called Uppsala school" (indeed, he succeeded Engnell at the University of Uppsala), his moderate approach distanced him from his predecessors, especially in his restrictions of "patternism" and his rejection of the divine kingship paradigm.[42] Despite devastating critiques, many facets of the myth-and-ritual comparative approach still linger today due to large degree to the discovery of the Ugaritic texts, to which we now turn.

The Ugaritic Discoveries

In 1928 a Syrian plowman accidentally ran over a tomb, setting in motion events that would change forever our understanding of ancient Syrian (referred to by many as Canaanite) religion. Through the efforts of Claude F. A. Schaeffer, the principal archaeologist, and Charles Virolleaud, the primary epigrapher, an ancient kingdom came to life, and hundreds of alphabetic cuneiform texts came to be published in record time.[43] It soon became clear that the tell from which the tablets came (Ras Shamra) was none other than the ancient city of Ugarit, a city known from its mention in texts from Mari, Bogazköy, and Tell Amarna. The new texts were written in a previously unknown language that was, appropriately, called Ugaritic.

It is hard for us today—with multiple editions of the texts to study, a mushrooming literature including journals and series devoted to the study of Ugaritic culture, and subsequent excavations by the French Mission to Ras Shamra under the direction of Jean Margueron and Marguerite Yon and the Syrian-French Mission work of Yves Calvet, Bassam Jamous, Jamal Haydar, and Valerie Matoïan—to imagine the constraints facing scholars at the birth of a discipline. What was clear to early interpreters was that Ugaritic was a Northwest Semitic language remarkably close to Hebrew with a Canaanite religious vocabulary and mythology akin to that of the Hebrew Bible with regard to deities (ʾIlu/ ʾEl, Baʿlu/Baʿal, Dagan/Dagon, Rashpu/Reshep, ʾAthiratu/ʾAsherah, ʿAnatu/ ʿAnat, ʿAthtartu/ʿAstarte), cosmic "monsters" (Yammu/*yām*, Litanu/Leviathan, Tunnanu/*tannin*, Motu/*māwet/môt*), shades of the dead (Rapiʾūma/Rephaʾim), cultic terminology (especially that related to sacrifices and offerings), and cultic personnel.[44] Thus early studies of Ugaritic language and religion were juxtaposed with Hebrew and ancient Israelite religion from the outset, with several scholars adapting Ugaritic religion into a myth-and-ritual scheme.[45]

Over time the Ugaritic texts would come to have the most profound impact on the study of ancient Israelite religion of any manuscript discovery of the twentieth century (far more than even the Dead Sea Scrolls).[46] Furthermore, the value of these texts for Northwest Semitic philology, linguistics, and prosody was considerable. My intent is not to trace such influence here but to point out how the archaeological discoveries at ancient Ugarit, combined with continuing archaeological finds throughout the entire ancient Near East (temples, temple paraphernalia, cultic figurines, tombs, letters, onomastica, seals, inscriptions, etc.), reinvigorated the history-of-religion approach to biblical studies from the 1930s to the present. The Ugaritic texts provided so many new points of contact with ancient Israel that a revolution in biblical studies soon got under way as scholars debated once again how ancient Hebraic culture related to its Near Eastern environment. Once again, polar positions occupied the debates.

Ancient Israel's Distinctiveness Vis-à-Vis Its Environment

The biblical theology movement flourished even more during and after World War II, as once again its emphasis on revelation resonated with a restless audience. Coinciding with this robust interest in the relevance of the theological enterprise were new assertions of the distinctiveness of ancient Israel coming from unlikely allies: archaeologists and Near Eastern specialists. One would have thought that all those involved in unearthing and studying the comparative material of cognate cultures would naturally ally themselves with a history-of-religion approach. The opposite was true for such noted archaeologists and Semitists as William Foxwell Albright, Henri Frankfort (1946, 1951; see too Frankfort and Groenewegen-Frankfort 1949: 241–248), and Thorkild Jacobsen (1976: 164), all of whom spoke of the uniqueness of Israel's faith.[47] Even against the amazing finds coming from Mesopotamia, Egypt, and Syria, Albright especially firmly held to the distinctiveness of ancient Israel's religious and intellectual achievements.

William Foxwell Albright

Between the 1930s and the 1960s, especially in America, one could not find a more influential scholar than William Foxwell Albright (1891–1971), whose work in "Oriental studies" and archaeology (cf. Albright 1935, 1940, 19571966b, 1968a, 1968b) would almost single-handedly shape an entire generation of scholarship.[48] Albright wrote his 1916 dissertation, "The Assyrian Deluge Epic," under the guidance of Paul Haupt and devoted a significant amount of his early research to Mesopotamia.[49] When the Ugaritic discoveries were coming to light, Albright (along with Ginsberg) offered some of the earliest analyses of these texts from ancient Syria and their relevance for ancient Israelite religion (Smith 2001a: 24–25).[50] Compare, for example, how the Ugaritic texts form a core of Albright's *Yahweh and the Gods of Canaan: A Historical Analysis of Two Contrasting Faiths* and *Archaeology and the Religion of Israel*.[51] Albright expanded his scholarly repertoire even further when in 1926 he undertook the first major excavation of his career at Tell Beit Mirsim. Over time Albright would come to be known as the dean of biblical archaeology and a pioneer in the subfields of epigraphy, paleography, and ceramic typology.[52] Albright insisted that archaeology was indispensable for turning biblical studies into a "scientific discipline."[53]

Albright's overarching purpose was to reconstruct the cultural and intellectual history of the ancient Near East in a way that would highlight biblical religion as its crowning achievement. As much as he genuinely appreciated the civilizations of the ancient Near East, he reserved his highest praise for the intellectual and spiritual accomplishments of ancient Israel and the majesty of its literature as found in the Hebrew Bible.[54] Albright (2006: 17–21) articulated "the sublimity and the poignancy" as well as the "delicacy" of the affective literature of Mesopotamia and Egypt. He was frank in stating that "the literature of Israel seldom rises to emotional heights which cannot be paralleled somewhere in the ancient Near East outside of Palestine." And yet for Albright (2006: 22–23),

"Hebrew literature [being] much younger . . . could select the choicest motifs and situations from its folkloristic and literary inheritance, and could transform them by passing them though the crucible of Israelite affective and spiritual genius." Moreover, wrote Albright (2006: 115), the nature of the god Yahweh (one "without sexuality or mythology"; "invisible . . . [with] no graphic nor plastic representation"; "not restricted to any part of His creation") "was radically different from all figures of pagan mythology . . . He remained uniquely superior to all possible competitors."[55]

Yehezkel Kaufmann

Yet even Albright's effusive language could not match the rhetoric of Yehezkel Kaufmann (1889–1963), who was, without doubt, the strongest proponent of ancient Israel's distinctiveness. Kaufmann is commended by some and ridiculed by others, often misunderstood, and even ignored.[56] His challenge to classical criticism deserves close attention.

Kaufmann's most significant work was an eight-volume history of Israelite religion, appearing between 1937 and 1956.[57] Some have failed to appreciate how Kaufmann differs from the Christian biblical theology movement.[58] Kaufmann emphasized, as did the biblical theology movement, the sharp divergence of monotheistic Israelite religion from the polytheistic religions of the rest of the ancient Near East. But Kaufmann went even further. He asserted categorically that "the Bible is utterly unaware of the nature of and meaning of pagan religion" (1972: 7). Similarly, he wrote that "Israelite religion was an original creation of the people of Israel. It was absolutely different from anything the pagan world ever knew" (1972: 2). This new way of looking at the world "was created," said Kaufmann, "by the impact of the monotheistic revolution which occurred at Israel's birth as a nation in the days of Moses."[59] Had Kaufmann lived later in time, he might have borrowed Kuhn's phrasing to label such a revolution in thinking a "paradigm shift."

Benjamin Sommer (2017: 205) astutely summarizes: "For Kaufmann . . . monotheism is about the nature of divinity, not about the number of divinities; it is a matter of quality, not quantity." The sovereignty of the biblical God who was transcendent and utterly distinct from his creation became an overriding theme for Kaufmann. His comment on the absence of myth in the biblical legends reads:

> The store of biblical legends lacks the fundamental myth of paganism: the theogony. All theogonic motifs are similarly absent. Israel's God has no pedigree, fathers no generations; he neither inherits or bequeaths his authority. He does not die and is not resurrected. He has no sexual qualities or desires and

shows no need of or dependence upon powers outside himself. (Kaufmann 1972: 60–61)

The absence of divine sex and death in the ancient Near Eastern context was startling for Kaufmann. Indeed, it was Kaufmann who wrote that "the Hebrew of the Bible possesses no word to designate a feminine deity: it has no ʾēlā, ʾelīlā, or ʾelōhā" (1951: 181). The key to the biblical riddle, said Kaufmann (1951: 193), was the Israelite concept of idolatry, "which was lifeless, without gods or mythology." Kaufmann (1972: 61) did admit that "we do find vestiges of Israel's ancient mythology imbedded in the Bible, and there was 'idolatry' in Israel; yet the biblical God has no mythological features" and the vestigial idolatry that is represented is merely fetishistic.

Kaufmann's preoccupation with the absence of myth can also be seen in his remarks about how various West Semitic deities are presented in biblical literature:

> We know today that these deities [Baal, Chemosh, Milcom, Dagan, etc.] were both bound up with natural phenomena and the subjects of mythical accounts. Not so in the Bible. Here there is no allusion to the natural functions of any god, nor to other of his mythological qualities. Gods are identified only by the nation which serves them: thus there are gods of Egypt, Sidon, etc. But there is no god of the sun, earth, or sea. Nor is there any indication of cosmogonic activity, genealogical descent, generations and matings, wars and victories. Most amazing is the absence of sexual differentiation among the gods of the gentiles. . . . In no Biblical story does any of the heathen gods appear as actor or acted upon, as conscious or perceptive, as speaking, moving, eating, etc. (Kaufmann 1951: 180–181, 183)

The nature of divinity in ancient Israel will be discussed in detail in the following chapters. On the macro level, it is easy to see how Kaufmann's use of strong categorical language evokes a charge of naiveté, although Moshe Greenberg cautions us not to overreact to Kaufmann's use of hyperbole.[60] Yet, as pointed out by Jon Levenson, Kaufmann failed to recognize how the biblical polemics themselves are hyperbolic in nature. Levenson criticizes Kaufmann's imprecise definition of myth (especially as applied to Israelite kingship) and his misunderstanding of interreligious polemics (as applied to divine icons) that are satirical and reductionist by nature (Levenson 1985: 107–111). "We cannot conclude from the inaccuracy of the Israelite poet's satire that he had no understanding of the spiritual life of his Canaanite neighbor and nothing in common with it," writes Levenson. "To do so would be to miss entirely the situation out of which interreligious polemics grow . . . Syncretisms do not form between things that have nothing in common" (Levenson 1985: 110). Sommer (2017: 239) concurs: "Kaufmann's approach is deeply unrealistic insofar as he insists that monotheism and polytheism are worlds apart."

Kaufmann's rhetoric was also undercut by Albright's emphasis on the ancient Near Eastern setting in which Israelite religion emerged. Whereas Albright shared Kaufmann's passion for the uniqueness (and superiority) of ancient Israelite religion, his command of Levantine material culture as well as cognate language and literature (especially Ugaritic) compelled him to write that "the early Hebrews' . . . borrowings and adaptations from Canaanite culture" did not support Kaufmann's "extreme" position. Even more forcefully, Albright (2006: x) would exclaim that "there was so much exchange of cultural influences between Israel and its neighbors on all sides of its tiny territory . . . that the ignorance presupposed by Kaufmann's view is simply incredible." Further dialogue with Kaufmann's philosophical challenge would next come from one of Albright's most influential students, Frank Moore Cross.

Frank Moore Cross

One of the most substantive works on Israelite religion in the 1970s was a collection of programmatic essays by Frank Moore Cross entitled *Canaanite Myth and Hebrew Epic* (1973).[61] Cross, a scholar known especially for his work in Northwest Semitic epigraphy and the Dead Sea Scrolls, was of the firm opinion (instilled by his teacher Albright) that achievements in analyzing epigraphic material were due to a well-defined typological method of dating the historical change of alphabetic scripts and pottery. Yet for Cross (1982: 123–124), "all human artifacts are amenable to typological study." Thus we see Cross applying his typological method to the study of ancient Israelite religion and even ideas in general. He writes:

> Are we not to expect the breaking in of the *sui generis*, the radically new, in poetry, in religious ideas, in philosophical speculation? I do not think so. I believe it is as illegitimate methodologically to resort to the category of the *sui generis* in explaining historical sequences, as it is contrary to scientific method to resort to the category of miracles in explaining natural occurrences. (Cross 1982: 130)

Cross followed Albright in critiquing Kaufmann's position, which acted as his foil. Cross would assert:

> The religion of Israel has been conceived as a unique, isolated phenomenon, radically or wholly discontinuous with its environment. In extreme form these

views are rooted ultimately in dogmatic systems, metaphysical or theological, and often serve an apologetic purpose.... The claim that Israelite religion "was absolutely different from anything the pagan world ever knew" to quote the late, great Yehezkel Kaufmann is now being swept away under an avalanche of archaeological evidence. But this claim should never have been made. It violates fundamental postulates of scientific historical method. The empirical historian must describe novel configurations in Israel's religion as having their origin in an orderly set of relationships which follow the usual typological sequence of historical change. (Cross 1982: 131)

In short, whereas Kaufmann (1972: 60) asserted that the notion of God's sovereignty "first appeared as an insight, an original intuition," Cross retorted in his defense of the typological method that there are no new ideas (cf. Qoheleth 1:9–10). Nevertheless, Cross (1982: 131) stated that his approach was intended "not to denigrate the importance or majesty of Israel's religious achievement." With greater nuance than Albright (and with less of Albright's stringency), Cross wrote: "Characteristic of the religion of Israel is a perennial and unrelaxed tension between the mythic and the historical." Cross preferred the term "epic," rather than "myth," to characterize Israel's lore.[62] "This epic," wrote Cross, "rather than the Canaanite cosmogonic myth, was featured in the ritual drama of the old Israelite cultus.... Israel's choice of the epic form to express religious reality, and the elevation of this form to centrality in their cultic drama, illustrates both the linkage of the religion of Israel to its Canaanite past and *the appearance of novelty* in Israel's peculiar religious concern with the 'historical'" (1973: viii–ix; emphasis mine).

Cross (1973: 143) was of the firm opinion that "Israel's religion in its beginning stood in a clear line of continuity with the mythopoeic patterns of West Semitic, especially Canaanite myth." At the same time Cross could speak of the "radical differentiation" of the Yahweh cultus in the Proto-Israelite league, which split off from the El cult (1973: 71). "[Ancient Israel's] religion did emerge from the old matrix, and its institutions were transformed by the impact of formative historical events ... which came together in the days of Moses and in the era of the Conquest" (1973: 143).

Newer Studies of Myth

As seen from the history of scholarship just traced, the study of Israelite religion is intimately tied to the study of mythology in general. Having looked at how scholars such as Hooke wedded myths and rituals, how Kaufmann completely rejected the presence of myth in the Bible (as did Albright), and how Cross widened the dialogue to include epic as well as myth, it is best to pause to survey briefly how the larger scholarly community has wrestled with new definitions of myth.[63] Several surveys on the topic, some of which have been written by historians of Israelite religion, can allow our sketch to be brief.[64]

The modern study of mythology, which is often traced to post-Enlightenment thought, frequently takes as its point of departure how modern readers have inherited from the Grimm brothers an overly simplistic notion of myths as stories about the gods and how, in popular vernacular, myths are equated with falsehood.[65] In contrast, contemporary mythologists define myths in various ways consistent with their chosen fields of study. Sociologists, in the wake of Durkheim, underscore how myths mirror social structures or how they function to validate social order. Anthropologists try to personalize mythology by describing the cultural context of modern storytellers, as opposed to the notion that myths come from nowhere and have existed since the beginning of time. Historians have largely replaced the myth-and-ritual model with a myth-and-politics paradigm that posits political backgrounds and historical referents underlying the tales. Scholars of narrative structure emphasize that myth has more to do with the plot of a tale than with the tale itself. To many folklorists, myths are just one type of lore that can be traced throughout disparate cultures with amazing similarity. Ever since Claude Lévi-Strauss, structuralists would go even further to see underneath myths a "deep structure" of shared humanity and its dichotomies (Niditch 1993: 22). Psychologists view myths as products of the human unconscious in either a Freudian or Jungian sense. Modern historians of world religions like to show how myths describe universal themes of human existence and ask ultimate religious questions. Some (e.g., Joseph Campbell) homogenize myths into comforting mystical storytelling that celebrates humanity's shared mysteries, while others (e.g., Wendy Doniger) point out how myths can be subversive and far from soothing to the status quo. Yet others (e.g., Debra Scoggins Ballentine) concentrate on how myths are ideological productions.[66] For example, conflict myths (see Chapter Eight) are primarily used to legitimize gods and humans alike (and to delegitimize their rivals), not to mention broader sociopolitical structures. According to Ballentine, conflict myths encode hierarchical taxonomies, marking dominant versus subservient characters and establishing which behaviors are "natural" ("given," "universal," "foundational") and which are errant. The recasting and revising of myths function similarly as ideologically charged productions.

A universal definition of "myth" that would cover all facets of ancient Israelite religion (and that of the rest of the ancient Near East) is neither attainable or desirable.[67] Some historians of religion have gone so far as to argue that the word "myth" is so overworked that it has lost its communicative value and we should instead speak of "original tales." I do not favor abandoning the use of the word "myth," because it carries with it cultural weight (e.g., conveying the religious imaginations of a society) that transcends the simple narration of a story. It is also best not to delimit the genre of myth as if it marked a discrete boundary; literary genres commonly overlap, so we should not be surprised if stories of the gods also involve human characters and vice versa.

Scholars have debated whether the biblical material is better described as mythopoeic or mythopoetic. The mythopoeic has to do with "myth making"— though often recasting older Near Eastern myths in Israelite dress rather than creating new myths. To borrow the words of the folklorist Stith Thompson (1965: 175–176): "It is always easier to borrow a myth or tale than it is to construct one."[68] In contrast, the mythopoetic describes the use of "mythic imagery," where only echoes of myths are preserved in attenuated form. I have suggested elsewhere that this is analogous to vestigial features documented in the archaeological record (Lewis 1998: 47). Arguing for mythopoeic over mythopoetic, Bernard Batto (1992: 1) writes that "myth permeates virtually every layer of biblical tradition from the earliest to the latest." In contrast, Mark Smith (1994c: 299) contends that " 'mythic imagery' . . . is more prevalent in biblical texts than myth." In the material that follows I will argue that ancient Israel contained both mythopoeic and mythopoetic material on a continuum, with a larger concentration of the latter.

The Fribourg School of Iconographic Study

The 1970s saw the use of a new tool for the study of the Syro-Palestinian world: iconography. In 1972 Othmar Keel's *The Symbolism of the Biblical World: Ancient Near Eastern Iconography and the Book of Psalms* (now in its fifth German edition) offered a massively detailed study of how visual symbols could supplement the written text. Biblical scholars had utilized iconography prior to this time, especially those with knowledge of Mesopotamian glyptic art.[69] Yet systematic studies were rare in a discipline that preferred philology and theology to the worlds of archaeology and art history.

Keel's work on the Psalms was a systematic attempt at blending literary symbols and visual symbols to unpack the conceptual world of the biblical author. Moreover, as keenly as Keel recognized the contributions of iconography, he was aware of its limitations and the chance of misinterpretation. Keel (1997: 9) would write: "We constantly run the risk of reading these pictures too concretely, or having avoided that risk, of treating them too abstractly." Of course, the same can be said of analyzing a text. At least iconographic representations are easier to fix in historical context than the biblical material, which emerges from a long editorial process.

Keel continued his impact in the subsequent decades. Scholars associated with his Fribourg school (e.g., Urs Winter, Silvia Schroer, Thomas Staubli, Izak Cornelius, and especially Christoph Uehlinger) have turned out numerous volumes (mostly in the Orbis Biblicus et Orientalis series), including exhaustive studies of the previously overlooked seals and amulets.[70] Whereas Keel's initial offering was broadly construed (covering conceptions of the cosmos, destructive forces, the temple, conceptions of God, the king, and humans before God), his later work, including several coauthored works, thoroughly documented divine images, both male and female. Especially noteworthy in this area is Keel and Uehlinger's *Gods, Goddesses and Images of God in Ancient Israel* (1998; German 1992). Female divine iconography is especially relevant now that studies are reassessing ancient Israelite religion in light of the archaeological finds at Kuntillet ʿAjrud and Khirbet el-Qom and their mention of the Canaanite goddess Asherah and/or her symbol (asherah). The most comprehensive work here is the iconographic study by Cornelius (2004).

It is a very good sign indeed when one now finds articles on art and iconography in standard reference works such as the *Anchor Bible Dictionary*, *Civilizations of the Ancient Near East*, and the *Handbook of Ugaritic Studies*, and textbooks devoted to using iconography for biblical exegesis.[71] Extensive new databases such as Schroer's four-volume *Die Ikonographie Palästinas/Israels und der Alte Orient* (2005–2018) provide researchers with unparalleled resources that would have been rare just a generation ago. The future holds great promise, especially as the Fribourg school continues its amazing productivity. Even more encouraging, iconographic study is no longer restricted to the Fribourg school.[72]

Revising Historical Hermeneutics

The mid-1970s also ushered in a vibrant discussion that continues into the present—often with heated rhetoric—regarding Israelite historiography.[73] The newer hermeneutical schools of thought have been called "revisionist" and "minimalist," the latter term referring to skepticism regarding to the historical veracity of the biblical text. Like German criticism of the nineteenth century, these discussions are not restricted to historical matters and impact how the biblical text can be used to reconstruct ancient Israelite religion (see Chapter Three, on methodology).[74]

While certainly not monolithic, as its critics often make it out to be, the overall approach of these historians is to date the majority of biblical texts to the post-exilic periods. Works that have contributed to or are associated with this paradigm shift include those by Thomas L. Thompson, John Van Seters, Niels Peter Lemche, Gösta Ahlström, Keith Whitelam, Robert Coote, Giovanni Garbini,

Philip Davies, and Margaret Gelinas.[75] By lowering traditional dating into the Persian and even Hellenistic periods, these scholars overturned frameworks derived from Albrecht Alt (e.g., settlement hypothesis) and Albright (the biblical archaeology approach). The historiography offered in these works is derived from newer sociological and anthropological models as well as studies of the Bible as literature. As a result, new avenues of research addressed social and ideological history along with a reexamination of questions of ethnicity.

The revisionist approach has been portrayed by Thompson (1992: 383) as a return to "the dictum of Wellhausen that a biblical document reflects the historical context of its own formation rather than the social milieu of its explicit referents to a more distant past." For Thompson, "the essential thrust of Wellhausen's axiom continues to haunt us." Such methodological assumptions of the revisionist approach have prevented it from winning wide acceptance among historians and the many archaeologists and epigraphists who have weighed in on the debate.[76] Lemche (1996a: 9) overstated the movement's influence when he pronounced that extracting historical information from the biblical text is "an old-fashioned endeavor . . . considered a thing of the past by many of today's scholars." On the contrary, many historians of Israelite religion continue to emphasize that the biblical witness is *not* "a theological fiction of later utopians" (Albertz 1994: 24). Moreover, it is still possible to seek out a "critically assured minimum" (Mettinger 1988: 56) from which we may reconstruct ancient Israelite religion, at least partly (see Chapter Three). Smith's (2014a: 42–43, 211–283) study of early biblical warrior culture carefully argues that there are "texts that reflect traditions or even textual composition in the tenth century (or perhaps ninth century) or earlier." Nonetheless, the revisionist hermeneutic proved valuable for chastising those who analyzed the biblical text uncritically (although what constitutes proper criticism is in the eye of the practitioner). It is clear that the text must be studied in conjunction with modern approaches to extra-biblical ancient Near Eastern texts and archaeology, to which we now turn.

Archaeology Reasserts Its Influence

The biblical archaeology movement that flourished from the 1930s through the 1960s, and which became synonymous with the names William Foxwell Albright and G. Ernest Wright, focused on using archaeology to demonstrate the uniqueness of ancient Israelite religion. The Albrightian model has often been labeled biblicist in nature even though Albright wrote widely disseminated works that showcased extra-biblical material, such as *Archaeology and the Religion of Ancient Israel* and *Yahweh and the Gods of Canaan*. In addition, Albright's lack of interest in using the archaeological realia to unpack the actual practice of ancient

Israelite religion has led William Dever (1987: 217) to describe his era of archaeology as "the 'revolution' that failed to materialize." In the time since Albright's generation of archaeologists (the majority being biblical scholars), the discipline of Syro-Palestinian archaeology has taken pride in extracting itself from the Bible and theology and turning to the social sciences.[77] The archaeology of ancient Israel is no longer seen as a branch of biblical studies or as the handmaiden of biblical history; rather, it is a multidisciplinary field that aims at describing socioeconomic and cultural histories through studying environmental forces, the development of technology, food production, population growth, materiality, monumentality, and so on.

In the years that followed, some Syro-Palestinian archaeologists embraced trends in processual archaeology (also known as "New Archaeology") and post-processual archaeology that arose in the wake of Fernand Braudel's theoretical framework of *la longue durée* and the rise of the French *Annales* school (see Levy and Holl 1995: 3–8). As historians turned their focus from political, military, and diplomatic history to long-term perspectives (*la longue durée*) that included geography and climate, economic cycles, and large-scale social and cultural factors, so too archaeologists turned their focus from the material culture of great people and grand events to "the archaeology of society," with its fascination for everyday life. An early example can be seen in Thomas Levy's edited volume *The Archaeology of Society in the Holy Land* (1995).[78] No longer do these scholars write only of stratigraphy and pottery typology; theoretical frameworks from the likes of Lewis Binford, Colin Renfrew, and Ian Hodder are well integrated into their analyses.[79] Older processual archaeology prided itself in being ahistorical, which made it a welcome companion for the revisionist historians previously mentioned (cf. Whitelam 1996: 9–10, 66–67). Thankfully, the post-processual archaeology that started in the mid-1980s has brought a welcome correction to some of the more doctrinaire versions of the New Archaeology.[80]

In the last three decades, archaeology has reasserted its influence as an independent discipline capable of unearthing the practice of Israelite religion without being subservient to biblical studies.[81] Some archaeologists such as John Holladay part ways with the biblical text entirely, reconstructing Israelite religion from an explicitly archaeological approach.[82] In contrast, Dever, through a series of methodological essays dating back to 1983, called for a true dialogue between archaeology and text (which he calls a "curated artifact")—even though his latest work is entitled *Beyond the Texts* (Dever 2017). Only by combining the realia of religious practice (both legitimate and illegitimate, public and private) as seen from the archaeological record with a sophisticated reading of the biblical text can historians of Israelite religion achieve their goal. The following aspects of Israelite religion (staggering in scope) have greatly benefited from recent archaeological research: altars (large and small), burials, cultic paraphernalia, cultic figurines, cultic stands (incense and other), divine images, domestic/household religion, ethnohistory, gate shrines, gendered archaeology, Iron Age I cult centers (e.g., the "Bull Site," Hazor, Mt. Ebal, Shechem), Iron Age II cult centers (e.g., Arad, Bethsaida, Kuntillet ʿAjrud, Lachish, Megiddo, Tell Dan), magic of all sorts (amulets, incantations, magic bowls, etc.), the Midianite hypothesis and Qurayya ware, model shrines, non-elite religion, religious architecture, religious inscriptions, scarabs and seals, sacrificial practices, standing stones, and votives. Scholars have been responding to Dever's call, yet such a huge undertaking will take some time to be realized by biblical scholars, who are predominantly trained as philologians, and by archaeologists who prefer fieldwork (or pure theory) to such syntheses.[83]

The Social Sciences Rejoined

The interface of the social sciences and biblical studies has been traced by others and need not detain us here.[84] As has been mentioned, the use of sociological and anthropological applications for biblical studies waned after the initial experimentations by Robertson Smith and Wellhausen. Nonetheless, these fields continued to mature independently and eventually were applied to biblical studies with such enthusiasm that today their influence is everywhere. One scholar stands out from all others as the pioneer and most articulate voice of modern social-science biblical criticism: Norman Gottwald. Gottwald's *The Tribes of Yahweh*, published in 1979, carried with it the subtitle *A Sociology of the Religion of Liberated Israel*. A collection of Gottwald's articles entitled *The Hebrew Bible in Its Social World and in Ours* (1993) shows that Gottwald's concerns (and those of many of his followers) were not restricted to the sociology of the ancient world but also encompassed our present context, including the hermeneutics of class welfare, liberation theology, Marxist thought, peace studies, and economic ethics. Thus it is not surprising that even though social science criticism cuts across the full spectrum of ancient Israelite society (including the archaeological and historiographic material just mentioned), the majority of early scholarship concentrated on the sociopolitical and socioeconomic rather than cultic studies per se. To be sure, there is a continuity between the former and the latter (see again the work of Gottwald), and ethnographic research has taught us to see societies as total systems.[85]

In subsequent years more works were devoted to ancient Israelite religion. These included general studies (e.g., Cook 2004) and specialized analyses such as the works of Mary Douglas (1966, 1993), Howard Eilberg-Schwartz (1990), Frank Gorman (1991), Walter Houston (1993), Jonathan Klawans (2000, 2006), and Isabel Cranz (2017) on purity codes and rituals; those of Gary Anderson

(1987), Bruce Malina (1996), and William Gilders (2004) on sacrifices and blood rituals; those of Robert Wilson (1980), Thomas Overholt (1989), and Jonathan Stökl (2012) on prophecy; those of Carol Meyers (1983, 1988, 1991, 2002, 2003a), Phyllis Bird (1997a, 1991, 1987), and Hennie Marsman (2003) on the socioreligious roles of women; and those of Kristine Garroway (2014) on the social roles of children, Ronald Hendel (1988, 1992) on the aniconic traditions, Mark Smith on cultural memory (2004) as well as cross-cultural discourse with respect to divinity (2008), C. L. Crouch (2014) on the role of religion in identity formation, and Brian Schmidt (2016) on the social history of magic. New analyses of the Hebrew Bible's priestly hierarchies (see Chapter Ten) have benefited from the work of Michel Foucault, Pierre Bourdieu, Caroline Bell, and others on ritual performance and the socialized body.

The landmark attempt at integrating a social analysis across the full spectrum of ancient Israelite religion is the work of Albertz (1994) and more recently with Rüdiger Schmitt (Albertz and Schmitt 2012) (their onomastic approach is described in Chapter Three).

From Ze'ev Meshel to Rainer Albertz: Personal Piety and Family Religion

There were three scholars working independently in the mid- to late 1970s, two of them archaeologists, the other a historian of religion, whose work would serve as harbingers of the next decades. Through three seasons of excavations in 1975–1976, Ze'ev Meshel excavated the Iron Age site of Kuntillet ʿAjrud (also referred to as Ḥorvat Teman) on the Darb el-Ghazza caravan route.[86] The inscriptions (mentioning "Yahweh and his A/asherah") and iconography (thought by some to represent the divine pair) revolutionized the field of Israelite religion. Each of these will be treated in detail in this book (see Chapter Six, pp. 236–241; Chapter Seven, pp. 325–330). Suffice it to say that the field has never been the same since. Every treatment now incorporates this material, as it demonstrates how Israelite religion was far more pluralistic than one might have guessed from a cursory reading of the Hebrew Bible. Whereas the Hebrew Bible has notable passages disparaging the abominable Canaanites, here we have Yahweh paired with one of the best-known Canaanite goddesses. The amount of secondary literature debating whether we have here a god and his consort ("Yahweh and his Asherah") or, more likely, a god and a cultic object of some sort ("Yahweh and his asherah") is staggering.[87]

A few years later, two paleo-Hebrew inscriptions (dating to the end of the seventh century BCE or the beginning of the sixth) were found at Ketef Hinnom in Jerusalem in excavations under the direction of Gabriel Barkay. Their discovery in 1979 set the field ablaze, as they constituted our oldest attestations of a biblical passage: the famous priestly benediction of Numbers 6:24–26. Yet for Israelite religion, it was not merely the paleographic value of these inscriptions (on which see Chapter Six, pp. 247–250) but the medium on which they were written (two silver amulets) together with their context (both texts were found in close proximity in a "repository" of a grave complex that totaled five burial chambers). The study of this material presented early analyses of what would later come to be known as the study of the "materiality" of texts (see Barkay et al. 2004). Here we have written evidence of the name of Yahweh (and a biblical passage) being used apotropaically (see Lewis 2012). Moreover, "the use of the confessional statement in Ketef Hinnom I ... introduces a context associated with *personal piety and family life*—that of family tomb and burial of an individual. The blessing itself [i.e. Numbers 6:24–26], which is found in a cultic context in the MT, is thus shown by these inscriptions also to have been used in *personal and family context*" (Barkay et al. 2004: 68; my emphasis).

This new window into personal piety occurred at the same time as the appearance of Rainer Albertz's groundbreaking work *Persönliche Frömmigkeit und offizielle Religion: Religionsinterner Pluralismus in Israel und Babylon* (1978). Key to Albertz's understanding is how personal piety relates to the religion of the family, especially in contrast to what he terms "official" religion. By the latter, Albertz (2008: 92) means the religion that "claims to be ... valid for the whole society" and thus includes "not only the state religion of kings and priests but also the opposing preaching of the prophets." In contrast, "the degree of institutionalization in family religion was very low," as its "target group ... was that face-to-face community that lived together in the house of the family head, the center of its everyday life."[88]

While disparate in nature, the works of these three scholars contributed to the growing trend we have been sketching—from the French *Annales* school (mentioned earlier) and its impact on history and archaeology to the use of the social sciences to study of marginalized groups. The focus was now firmly fixed on non-elite (e.g., non-royal, non-priestly) communities that were slighted in the past in favor of the religion of the privileged. Family religion, ancestral cults, and patrimonialism received close analysis, especially from comparative perspectives using cognate ancient Near Eastern cultures (e.g., van der Toorn 1996b, 2008; Schloen 2001; Fleming 2008; Lewis 2008a). Key works on the archaeology of the family and domestic cults also appeared (e.g., Stager 1985a; Daviau 2001; Schmitt 2008). Evidence of the flowering of this interest can be seen in how Sarah Iles Johnston's edited volume *Religions of the Ancient World* (2004) contains a dedicated section on "Religious Practices of the Individual and the Family." Compare too *Household and Family Religion in Antiquity* (2008), edited by John Bodel and Saul M. Olyan, and the landmark *Family and Household Religion in Ancient Israel and the Levant*, by Albertz and Schmitt (2012). The latter contains an impressive collection of archaeological data covering domestic ritual assemblages and Iron Age cult places as well as a comprehensive analysis of personal names.[89]

In the study of family religion, the religious lives of ancient women started to emerge as scholars willed themselves to look for them (cf. Meyers 2002, 2005, 2010; Marsman 2003; Ackerman 2006, 2008a, 2016; Olyan 2010). Here feminist criticism led the way.

Feminist Contributions

Much of the early history of scholarship on Israelite religion was male-dominated. Intellectual historians can debate the best place to pick up the study of feminist contributions as they impact biblical study, but surely a watershed event came in 1895 with the publication of the first volume of Elizabeth Cady Stanton's (1895–1902) *The Woman's Bible*, followed by the second volume in 1898. Though Stanton assembled a "revising committee" to complete the task, by far the bulk of the work bears her imprint.[90] One should situate Stanton's achievement historically by remembering that Wellhausen's prolegomena was published just some twenty years earlier, in 1878, with Robertson Smith's *Lectures on the Religion of the Semites* only a decade removed, in 1889. Gunkel's *Schöpfung und Chaos* was of the same vintage (1895), with the first edition of his *Genesis* (1901) right around the corner. Thus we find in *The Woman's Bible* references to source criticism (especially the work of Astruc and Graf) and even Norse mythology. Yet Stanton's undertaking is best understood within the women's suffrage and abolitionist movements. And here she is ever so bold. She starts her introduction as follows:

> From the inauguration of the movement for woman's emancipation the Bible has been used to hold her in the "divinely ordained sphere." ... The Bible teaches that woman brought sin and death into the world, that she precipitated the fall of the race, that she was arraigned before the judgment seat of Heaven, tried, condemned and sentenced. Marriage for her was to be a condition of bondage, maternity a period of suffering and anguish, and in silence and subjection, she was to play the role of a dependent on man's bounty for all her material wants, and for all the information she might desire on the vital questions of the hour, she was commanded to ask her husband at home. Here is the Bible position of woman briefly summed up.

The vital need, wrote Stanton, was "to issue a Woman's Bible, that we might have women's commentaries on women's position in the Old and New Testaments."

Understandably, the pioneering work of Stanton received mixed receptions among readers based on whether they felt her work to be liberating or threatening. The full flowering of her contributions would not be realized for biblical studies until decades later, when the second wave of feminist scholarship would emerge. Yet the field has consciously looked back to Stanton's groundbreaking work, as evident in the intentionally titled *The Women's Bible Commentary*, edited by Carol A. Newsom and Sharon H. Ringe, which was first published in 1992 (with a revised and updated third edition issued with Jacqueline E. Lapsley in 2012).

The so-called second wave of feminist biblical studies emerged in the mid-twentieth century. Ever since Phyllis Trible's *God and the Rhetoric of Sexuality* (1978), gender studies have produced a staggering volume of research on biblical topics.[91] Surveys of the field and comprehensive bibliographies are easy to find, though they are hard pressed to remain current due to the rapid pace of publications.[92] In addition to the *The Women's Bible Commentary*, subsequent years have seen such highly visible publications as the Feminist Companion to the Bible series, edited by Athalya Brenner and Carole Fontaine; *Women in Scripture*, edited by Carol Meyers, Toni Craven, and Ross Shepard Kraemer; *Women in the Hebrew Bible: A Reader*, edited by Alice Bach; *Feminist Biblical Interpretation*, edited by Luise Schottroff and Marie-Theres Wacker; and the three-volume *Feminist Interpretation of the Hebrew Bible in Retrospect*, edited by Susanne Scholz—not to mention a plethora of books and detailed articles on literature, theory, and ideology (e.g., Brenner 1985; Bach 1997; Bird 1997; Exum 1993, 1996; Fuchs 2000; Shectman 2009; Ackerman 2016; Gafney 2017). These studies impact the way in which the biblical text is used (or jettisoned, as some prefer) in today's communities, both scholarly and lay-oriented.[93] It is now commonplace to come across volumes that articulate how women's voices, though marginalized in our androcentric texts, can be resurrected even though the nature of our sources makes many aspects unrecoverable.[94]

Of special relevance for the practice of religion are those studies that go beyond literary analysis by integrating insights gained from archaeology and cognate ancient Near Eastern cultures.[95] In particular, the field of feminist scholarship has advanced through such works as those of Meyers on archaeology (discussed at greater length in the following section), Brenner (1985), Bird (1987, 1989, 1991), Susan Ackerman (1989, 1998a, 2003, 2008), Marsman (2003), Deborah Rooke (2007, 2009), Jennie Ebeling (2010), and Cynthia R. Chapman (2016) on the sociological roles of women in religious institutions; Erin Fleming on the politics of sexuality (2013); Jo Ann Hackett (1989) on the methodology of studying "fertility" religion; Tikva Frymer-Kensky (1992) and Joan Westenholz (1989; Asher-Greve and Westenholz 2013) on Mesopotamian religion; Jessie DeGrado (2018) on applying cognitive linguistics to understand Hosea's *qĕdēšâ*; and Wilda

Gafney (2017) on critiquing the Bible's enslavement of women. Feminist criticism has also led to a renewed interest by scholars, both female and male, in the presence of goddesses in Israelite religion (see the Conclusion).[96]

Over the past decades, Silvia Schroer (1987, 2005–2018), Elizabeth Bloch-Smith (1992a, 1992b, 2005, 2006, 2015), Susan Ackerman (1992, 1998a, 2003, 2008a, 2016), Ann Jeffers (1996), Diana V. Edelman (1996), Susan Niditch (1997, 2015), Elizabeth Larocca-Pitts (2001), Beth A. Nakhai (2001), Hennie J. Marsman (2003), Francesca Stavrakopoulou (2004; Stavrakopoulou and Barton 2010), Tallay Ornan (2005a, 2006, 2011, 2016), Deborah Rooke (2007, 2009), Anne Marie Kitz (2014), Marian Broida (2014), Erin Darby (2014), Kristine Garroway (2014), Esther Hamori (2008, 2015), Debra Scoggins Ballentine (2015), Cynthia R. Chapman (2016), and Isabel Cranz (2017) have produced some of the most vibrant volumes on Israelite religion. A lasting benefit of such scholarship is that historians of Israelite religion are now more prone to look beyond the public and elite face of religion (e.g., royal or state-sanctioned religion; the central sanctuary of priestly cult) to address domestic and private worship (e.g., local sanctuaries, family rituals). They are now more likely to attempt to reconstruct not only normative religion (i.e., that which has been unduly privileged as normative) but also non-sanctioned (non-privileged) elements of religious expression that powerfully shaped Israelite society. As was noted earlier in this chapter, these emphases fit extremely well with trends in the sociological analysis of family and domestic cults.

Carol Meyers: Engendering Archaeology

One feminist scholar's work on Israelite religion stands out among all others: that of Carol Meyers. Over a lengthy career, Meyers has successfully blended writing on both archaeological and textual aspects of Israelite religion.[97] A particular focus of her work examines the agrarian basis of the majority of the population of Iron Age Israel and Judah vis-à-vis the urban elites that produced the ethnohistorical sources (primarily the Hebrew Bible) that we use to reconstruct Israelite religion. Her focus on agrarian culture naturally includes a study of the household, especially the gendered qualities of its social space. Meyers articulates how ethnographic and ethnohistorical data have underscored the central role of women in food preparation and textile production (see the Conclusion). In premodern societies, argues Meyers, each of these roles had considerable economic value.[98] Moreover, when one factors in the central role of women in household/family religion, one may conclude that "women were *not* much more disadvantaged in their participation of *communal* religious activities than were non-priestly males" (Meyers 2002: 279).

Obviously, the study of material culture plays a vital role in articulating agrarian and household religion. It is regrettable that, even decades after the second wave of feminist scholarship reset scholarly agendas, Meyers (2003a: 429) would have to write that "identifying gendered social space is a project that has received very little attention in traditional Syro-Palestinian archaeology." In response, Meyers has boldly critiqued the way archaeological data are recovered and published. "Gender archaeology," she writes, "should be incorporated into the conceptual framework of all projects. Anything less represents a bias that should be deemed as ethically intolerable as tossing away the remains of periods that do not interest the excavator."[99]

Conclusion

The history of scholarship presented in this chapter is the briefest of sketches, yet it allows the reader an appreciation of various ways in which our subject matter has been addressed. The current state of scholarship on ancient Israelite religion (and Hebrew Bible studies) is growing exponentially and cannot be easily synthesized, though it will be addressed at every turn in the chapters that follow. One could argue that there has never before been such an age of scholarly productivity, as new source material becomes available and as vibrant theoretical models address the challenges of our postmodern age (see J. Collins 2005; Stavrakopoulou and Barton 2010; Schmidt 2016). Much of this scholarship wrestles with one's methodological approach, to which we now turn.

3
Methodology

Introduction

The aim of this volume is to present a work that is worthy of the ideas imagined by the people who lived in ancient Judah and Israel, ideas that should captivate a modern audience for their intrinsic quality and for their historical relevance. Its goal is also to present a synthetic volume that can be used as a reference work for readers of varying backgrounds. In order for readers to contextualize what they find before them, they should be presented with the methodological choices that one faces when reconstructing ancient Israel's past.

How should a historian of religion attempt to address ancient Israelite religion given the inherent difficulties involved in such a task? What methods should be employed when one stands at such a great distance from the culture in question and when the source material (textual and archaeological) is so sparse? Even with great advances in literary and redactional analysis, more nuanced applications of the social sciences, and the growing sophistication in handling the archaeological record, we still come back to a haunting question: What percentage of the information is available to the historian? The nature of our source material and the necessary scholarly tool kit need to be squarely addressed in order to articulate the methods that have the best potential for discovery.

The Disciplines Needed

The academic disciplines needed to write a history of ancient Israelite religion and not just a history of biblical religion (discussed later) are many. Ideally the investigator would possess the skills needed to work with texts, including epigraphy, onomastica, textual criticism, Northwest Semitic philology, comparative Semitics, linguistics, exegesis, source criticism, redaction criticism, genre theory, and a wide array of literary analyses, modern and postmodern. Ideally, the researcher of the Hebrew Bible would have an appreciation of diachronic and synchronic perspectives. Additionally, the researcher's tool kit would include training in archaeology, both as a field archaeologist and as a theorist, not to mention a knowledge of landscape archaeology, which asks new questions about the effects of water pathways and climate on culture. Art history must be privileged as well, for visual representations have their own complex narratives that complement as much as challenge textual narratives and stretch the study of objects into questions of identity, networks of cultural exchange, and collective memory. Obviously, the social sciences must be included, as no tapestry about texts and objects can be woven without the fabric of society. From sociolinguistics to ritual performance to gender to ethnicity to spatial theory, the social sciences are imperative for understanding the ideological nature of cult, where social actors negotiated status, power, and prestige. Lastly, the historian of religion must embrace, not shun, the discipline of philosophy of religion/theology.[1] Properly employed, it explores the varieties of religious experience regarding the nature of divinity and the preternatural as well as the nature of humanity. Questions of metaphysics are on the table as much as questions of theodicy and ethics; questions of human aspirations as much as those of human frailties. Philosophical explorations of "the ideal" can be examined, whether judicial, political, or societal. The relevance of these past musings for the present is profound. In Philip Davies' (2011: 152, 164) words, "The Bible is rich in philosophy.... The claim that much of the Bible is an intellectual product permeated with philosophical reflection should manage to attract some dinner-party interest."

The present volume does not pretend to be comprehensive. Yet it attempts to dabble seriously enough here and there in the scholarly enterprises just discussed that readers can imagine what would be required to undertake a thorough analysis combining the many requisite disciplines. If readers come away with a renewed appreciation for the difficulty of reconstructing an ancient religion when we stand at such a great distance, are so removed culturally, and have such meager data, then one of the author's preliminary goals will be achieved. Yet it is the hope that the reader will persevere (despite scholarly reservations at every turn) with the ultimate goal of appreciating the fascinating world that is ancient Israelite religion.

Preliminary Matters: Defining "Religion"

Scholars have a tendency to search for the ideal definition, even though Catherine Bell's (2007: 283) quip is well known: "No field ever moves forward because a good number of people agree on the definition of some central concept that then allows them to get down to work."[2] Our colleagues who work within religious studies departments or are involved otherwise with the American Academy of Religion know all too well how every new school year brings with it new examination copies of the latest textbooks wrestling with the definition of "religion," including "insider" and "outsider" perspectives. Seven theories of religion (Tylor and Frazer, Freud, Durkheim, Marx, Eliade, Evans-Pritchard, Geertz) are not enough (Pals 1996); we must have at least eight (Pals 2006), for how could one not include Max Weber? Make that nine (Pals 2015) with William James. Opposing theories are easily set at odds under the rubrics of substantive-phenomenological versus functionalist-explanatory perspectives. Where Mircea Eliade (1949: xiii) asserts that religion must be studied "at its own level ... *as* something religious" due to the sacred being essentially irreducible, Edmund O. Wilson (1998: 266) opines that "all tangible phenomena, from the birth of stars to the workings of social institutions, are based on material processes that are ultimately reducible, however long and tortuous the sequences, to the law of physics."[3]

In view of the academic disciplines needed for such a study, it is obvious that many and varied theoretical models are likewise necessary for the investigation of ancient Israelite religion. Because we now take for granted the necessity of interdisciplinary work, especially in the humanities and social sciences, we are as astonished as Pals (1996: 9; 2015: 8) to read of the "naive overconfidence" and "vaulting ambition" of past scholars who assumed that a single theory of religion was attainable, much less desirable. Even Eliade (1949: xiii), with his narrow definition, conceded that "because religion is human it must for that very reason be something social, something linguistic, something economic—you cannot think of man apart from language and society."[4]

Defining Israelite Religion: Two Notable Developments

Bringing the discussion into the present—inheriting trends that emerged in the 1970s (see Chapter Two, pp. 42–44)—we find two notable developments in defining Israelite religion. The first has to do with the pluralistic nature of religious experience within any society. For ancient Israel, Rainer Albertz (1978: 3; 1994: 19; Albertz and Schmitt 2012: 3) deserves credit for using Günter Lanczkowski's phrase "internal religious pluralism" to describe the religious differences within varying layers of society (e.g., royal religion vs. household religion). Ziony Zevit (2001) makes the point explicit by titling his magisterial study *The Religions of Ancient Israel*—note the plural. (Let the reader understand that the singular "religion" in the subtitle of the current volume is used collectively.) Studies such as Francesca Stavrakopoulou and John Barton's *Religious Diversity in Ancient Israel and Judah* (2010) are now common. Even within a single tradition (e.g., Yahwism) we find a plurality of opinions. Compare the diversity of thought about divine representation—from Yahweh's dominant manifestation by fire to P's and Ezekiel's *kābôd* presence, from Deuteronomic/Deuteronomistic "name theology" to Zion traditions that have Yahweh invisibly enthroned. Others envision the Almighty residing aloft and bowing the heavens to descend to earth (Ps

18:10 [Eng 18:9]; Ps 144:5). (See Chapter Seven, pp. 333–426.) Aniconic physical representation resides beside bold literary anthropomorphisms. (See Chapter Seven, pp. 287–290.) Sociologically, note the diverse notions about sacerdotal status and which individuals are hierarchically marked by "holiness." (See Chapter Ten, pp. 616–643.) Theologically, Yahweh is held by some as the fiercest of warriors, issuing calls to holy war, and by others as the tenderest of fathers and mothers, making pleas for compassion. (See Chapter Eight.) Politically, to some Yahweh is the ever-just monarch and judge, while others deem it proper to haul him into court. (See Chapter Nine, pp. 545–557.)

With diversity in mind, modern historians of Israelite religion are a world apart from their past counterparts, who often sought to define the *essence* of particular aspects of ancient Israelite religion. Sacrifice is a case in point, with its blood symbolism. As early as 1956 E. E. Evans-Pritchard (1956: 281) listed at least fourteen underlying motivations for sacrifice, but it was not until 1980 that M. F. C. Bourdillon (Bourdillon and Fortes 1980: 23) would write that "any general theory of sacrifice is bound to fail." The work of Ronald Hendel and Jacob Milgrom resonated similarly for biblical studies. Writing on sacrifice as a cultural system, Hendel (1989: 369) cautions that we should not be under the illusion that "there is necessarily some essential idea that underlies the history of ritual practice," and adds, "The primary locus of meaning is the system of religious concepts, not a single postulated essence that guides a rite through history." Milgrom (1991: 442) is succinct: "No single theory can encompass the sacrificial system of any society." As for blood symbolism, the theoretical and contextual studies at our disposal today (e.g., Gilders 2004; Lewis 2006a; Feder 2011), not to mention studies on the archaeology of sacrifice (e.g., Porter and Schwartz 2012), make A. Leo Oppenheim's (1964: 192) musings about "the 'blood consciousness' of the West" and "the magic power of blood" appear quaint. Thus when we turn to examine the priestly anointing ritual that uses blood and oil (see Chapter Ten, pp. 627–629), we will necessarily look to contextual data from the ancient city of Emar along with considering how blood functioned as an indexical medium of priestly prerogative, status, and power.

The second development is related to the first, as scholars underscored that defining the diversity of Israelite "religion" must include the lives of the non-elite. Here I quote from the summary in Lewis 2008a: 60:

> Over the last century, many historians in the wake of the French *Annales* school turned away from what they saw to be a narrow study of political, military, and diplomatic history (i.e., "traditional event-based narratives") to articulating long-term perspectives (what the French termed *la longue durée*) tied more to geography and climate, economic cycles, large-scale social and cultural factors, even the history of perception ("mentalities"). Archaeologists

went from focusing on the material culture of great people and grand events to "the archaeology of society" with its fascination for the mundane and ordinary. Textual scholars "read between the lines" of texts written (and edited) by those who wielded power to glimpse the lives of the semi-literate who held less or none at all. In particular, the lives of ancient women started to emerge as scholars willed themselves to look for them. Thus it is that we find ourselves, historians of religion of the present generation, focusing on non-elite (e.g., non-royal, non-priestly) communities that were slighted in the past in favor of the religion of the privileged.

This reexamining and redefining of Israelite "religion" focused particularly on the cultic activities of families and households. (See Chapter Eight, pp. 473–494.) Suffice it here to quote Saul Bellow's *The Adventures of Augie March*:

> Grandma, all the same, burned a candle on the anniversary of Mr. Lausch's death, threw a lump of dough on the coals when she was baking, as a kind of offering, had incantations over baby teeth and stunts against the evil eye. It was kitchen religion and had nothing to do with the giant God of the Creation who had turned back the waters and exploded Gomorrah, but it was on the side of religion at that.[5]

Preliminary Matters: Defining "Israelite" Religion

If the subtitle of the present work, *Ancient Israelite Religion*, necessitates pondering the definition of "religion," it might also call for a defense of using the term "Israelite" vis-à-vis geography, chronology, ethnicity, linguistics, and culture. In short, the term "Israelite" is used here heuristically, according to scholarly convention, to designate the religions of ancient Israel and Judah (from the Iron Age, Persian, and Hellenistic periods) found in textual sources such as the Hebrew Bible (what could be termed "biblical religion") together with that gleaned from other written sources (e.g., inscriptions, onomastica) and with what can be inferred from material culture. The geographic and chronological scope includes widespread ancestral traditions as well the religions of the northern (Israelite) and southern (Judean) kingdoms, not to mention the religions of the exilic and post-exilic periods. By following the convention of using the name "Israelite" as an umbrella term, I do not mean to homogenize distinctly different Israelite and Judean religions into a unified whole. The impossibility of so doing should be obvious. (The Israelite religion and cultic apparatus at Tel Dan in the north simply cannot be homogenized with the Judean religion of the south, as can be seen in the Jerusalem Temple.) Yet this is not to imply that there are no particulars (e.g., belief in the god Yahweh) that would be shared by disparate groups. Such shared beliefs would have been facilitated by a shared scribal tradition (Rollston 2006; Sanders 2009: 126–133; Carr 2008: 120–121).

The umbrella term "Israelite" is simply an acknowledgment that our textual sources are a nightmare for the historian of religion who thinks she/he can separate northern/Israelite traditions from texts (i.e., the Hebrew Bible) that have been transmitted, reimagined, and even reworked by southern/Judean hands. To borrow Daniel Fleming's (2012: 32) wording, "All of [the Bible's] contents have been filtered through Judahite assumptions," so the final product exhibits the ubiquitous overlay of Judahite revision. Sociolinguistically, northern (Israelian Hebrew) dialectic and cultural features were "collected, edited, and [re-]written in Jerusalem and Judah" using standardized Judean Hebrew (Schniedewind 2013: 77–78). If one were to write a history of religion only from material culture, then one could be site-specific and talk about Israelite versus Judean religions. Yet once one incorporates the Hebrew Bible (our best textual witness), the entire dataset changes and so too must our approach.

While there are exciting new attempts at teasing out traditions about "the legacy of Israel in Judah's Bible" (Fleming 2012), acute methodological problems remain that are hard to overcome. These include (1) how to distinguish "genuine" traditions about Israel from "reused" and "invented" traditions, especially when all three types have been mixed together in what has come down to us in the Hebrew Bible,[6] and (2) how to determine the mechanism for the transmission of genuine traditions about Israel as well as the geographical and chronological parameters for such transmission.[7] The future of historical research along Fleming's lines when combined with new archaeological data holds great promise. Yet at present the hurdles remain high. Thus, with regret, we default to the heuristic convention of speaking of ancient "Israelite" religion.

The Nature of Our Source Material, Part I: Texts

Textual sources are central to reconstructing any religion, and for ancient Israel we have the Hebrew Bible, epigraphic material, and onomastica. The nature of epigraphy and onomastica will be dealt with first, followed by an exploration of the parameters of using the Hebrew Bible as a historical source. In recent years the importance of using textual sources has experienced a renaissance due to technological and hermeneutical advances. In addition, the growing interest in materiality and monumentality (Osborne 2014) throughout the social sciences and humanities has resulted in textual scholars moving beyond philological study to examine how physical objects (including texts) provide windows into human behavior and cognition. History adheres to material objects. Consider, for example, how excavations at Tell Tayinat reveal how a copy of Esarhaddon's Succession Treaty was placed in the inner recesses of a dark temple for its symbolic and communicative value (see Deut 31:24–26; Exod 25:16; Josh 24:26). Similarly, the Ketef Hinnom amulets inscribed with a priestly blessing can be taken into the tomb, where the apotropaic power of a biblical text facilitates Yahweh rebuking the Evil One (Lewis 2012). In the years ahead, the study of the dynamic nature of texts and their life cycles will certainly generate new understandings of religion as scholars go beyond treating texts as passive objects.

Textual Sources: Epigraphy

In many ways, the field of epigraphy has rewritten the history of ancient Israelite religion.[8] The discovery of new epigraphic sources of information arrived at a time when the historical study of the Hebrew Bible was undergoing a crisis as a result of the collapse of analytical literary models of the past that no longer proved convincing (e.g., the documentary hypothesis) and the application of a variety of postmodern theories from the broader humanities and social sciences. It is thus quite understandable that Zevit (2001: 75–79), who views himself "as modern, not post-modern," argues: "Israelite religion is most approachable through its manifestations in physical evidence discovered in archaeological excavations [including] inscriptions and drawings." For Zevit, the "specialized discipline[s]" of archaeology and paleography provide the needed "hermeneutics" of interpretation.

Restricting our tally here to Israelite male divinity, in the pages to follow readers will find that epigraphic sources have played a key role in discussions of the identity of El (Proto-Sinaitic, Ugarit, Deir ʿAlla, Kuntillet ʿAjrud), El Elyon (Sefire), El-Elyon, "Creator of Heaven and Earth" (Elkunirsha, Karatepe, Jerusalem, Hatra, Leptis Magna, Philo of Byblos), El Shaddai (Ugarit, Deir ʿAlla), Baal/baal (Ishbaal, Kuntillet ʿAjrud), Yahweh (Shasu, Mesha stela, Kuntillet ʿAjrud, Khirbet el Qom, Khirbet Beit Lei, Ein Gedi, Arad, Ketef Hinnom, Lachish), and Yahweh, the Holy One (Ugarit, Kuntillet ʿAjrud).

As readers will see, epigraphic sources are also integral to larger questions such as whether the god El virtually disappears in the Iron Age (decidedly not, in our opinion); whether Albrecht Alt was correct about his notion of "the God of the Fathers"; whether there existed a Transjordanian "El repertoire"; whether El was the original God of Israel and/or the original god of the Exodus; whether El and Yahweh are distinct deities and/or syncretized into one; whether one should look geographically to the north or to the south for the origin of Yahweh; whether Judean *Chaoskampf* traditions (e.g., Yahweh's battle at the sea and with Sea) are different from their Near Eastern counterparts; whether Yahweh and Asherah are equally worshipped at Kuntillet ʿAjrud; whether a proper name can be used in a construct chain in Hebrew (i.e., the meaning of Yahweh Sebaʾot in light of Yahweh of Teman); whether the name of Yahweh could be used apotropaically (e.g., Ketef Hinnom); whether ḥrm, "holy war," is found outside of the Bible (e.g., Ugarit KTU 1.13, Moabite inscription, Sabaean texts RES 3945 and DAI Ṣirwāḥ 2005-50); whether family religion is integral to Yahwistic theology (e.g., Khirbet Beit Lei's mention of "god the compassionate"); whether Job's complaint against Yahweh resonates with known examples of a plaintiff accusing a superior of abusing power (e.g., Meṣad Ḥashavyahu); whether cultic objects are designated as "holy" in the archaeological record and how early (Hazor, Beersheva, Arad, Tel Miqne); and whether Yahweh is attested as "the Holy One" apart from the Bible (e.g., Kuntillet ʿAjrud). The simple fact alone that the earliest attestation of the divine name Yahweh comes from the ninth-century BCE Moabite inscription of King Mesha underscores the need for historians of Israelite religion to control the Northwest Semitic epigraphic record.

This is not to say that the use of epigraphy has been without its missteps. In Chapter Four (p. 97) readers will find my critique of one of the world's leading epigraphists (and a beloved teacher) with regard to three inscriptions used to understand the deity El Olam. A heavily relied-upon reading of "El, the Ancient One" (ʾl ḏʿlm = ʾil ḏū ʿōlami) in an inscription from Serabit el-Khadim can no longer be sustained. Two other epigraphic sources that were used for comparative purposes (Ugarit KTU 1.108 and one of the Arslan Tash amulets) are now interpreted quite differently and can thus no longer carry the weight once placed on them.

The field of epigraphy is also beset with the real possibility that any inscription that does not come from a controlled excavation could very well be a forgery. Where past miscreants did not have either the technology or the economic incentive to produce forgeries that could fool the trained epigrapher, today's forgers have both. As a result, certain epigraphic finds of the past that were once thought to be genuine (e.g., the Moussaieff Ostraca, the Ivory Pomegranate inscription) are now called into question to such an extent that they cannot be used. Other, more recent forgeries (e.g., the so-called Jehoash inscription) have been unmasked more quickly and thus have not entered into the secondary literature to much degree.[9]

A clear benefit of using the epigraphic record is the ability to date inscriptions (using archaeological context when available together with script typology), in contrast to the inability to date most biblical texts with any certainty. In contrast to the post-monarchic dating of many biblical texts, a good deal of the epigraphic record relating to ancient Israelite religion dates as early as the eighth century BCE, with a few examples dating to the ninth century BCE (the Mesha inscription, Kuntillet ʿAjrud), and, rarely, the late eleventh or tenth century BCE (the Ishbaal inscription). Granted, the amount of epigraphy that we possess is a drop in the bucket.

Textual Sources: Onomastica

Because of its complicated nature as well as its vital importance for reconstructing ancient Israelite religion, the onomastic record has been a mainstay in the field ever since the publication of Martin Noth's *Die israelitischen Personennamen* in 1928 followed by the appearance of approximately ten thousand Amorite personal names (PNs), especially from Mari (Huffmon 1965; Streck 2000).[10] Israelite onomastics has benefited from a plethora of insightful analyses by scholars such as Rainer Albertz, Richard Hess, and Ran Zadok. The academic discipline of onomastic research has continued to grow ever since, with an ever-expanding database from all cognate fields of study, especially Akkadian (Zadok 1997: 93). Modern treatments of Israelite religion frequently address the onomastic record and the parameters of its use for historical reconstruction.[11] Seth Sanders (2015: 59) optimistically writes: "Despite their limits, inscribed names provide our single clearest source of evidence for early Israelite religion because, unlike edited literary texts, they can be precisely dated and confidently connected with society beyond Judahite scholarly circles."

Onomastics, simply defined, is the study of names and their meanings, origins, and history. Various types of names include personal names (anthroponyms), place names (toponyms), and, especially important for the current study, divine names and theophoric elements in anthroponyms and toponyms.[12] Specialists also investigate prosopography, the science of identifying particular individuals, which for ancient Israel is gleaned mostly from seals, seal impressions, ostraca, letters, votive inscriptions, and graffiti. Many of these sources present epigraphic challenges, especially when correlated with the ever-complicated biblical record.[13] Broadly construed, onomastic science is a part of anthropological linguistics, where in addition to the etymology and history of names ethnographers examine how names reveal ethnicity, settlement patterns, and acculturation; how naming practices can reveal insights into society; and how names encode linguistic features. Obviously, historians of ancient religions stand at such a historical and cultural distance from their subject that some of these analyses are beyond their ability. Yet the growth of onomastics within ancient Near Eastern studies and related fields (e.g., the Helsinki Neo-Assyrian Text Corpus Project's *The Prosopography of the Neo-Assyrian Empire* and Oxford University's Lexicon of Greek Personal Names, now expanded into Anatolia) over the past few decades has been astonishing.

The primary methodological hurdle with onomastics is the same hurdle we have with other types of information: the lack of a large enough dataset. As Hess (2009: 11) writes regarding the provisional nature of the enterprise: "Since we have no complete census of all the names in any city or region in the Ancient Near East, it is always possible that names relevant to our comparative study may have been present but are now missing due to the vicissitudes of the preservation, discovery, and publication of the names." Equally concerning is lack of scholarly control in selecting only provenanced material to study. Sanders (2014: 222) writes of "a naïve tendency to prefer statistically friendly quantity over archaeological and epigraphic quality" despite repeated calls by epigraphists challenging the authenticity of many seals, seal impressions, and inscriptions.[14] Yet such appropriate cautions should not minimize the provisional contributions that onomastics can make. Moreover, the database of provenanced material, though relatively small, has shown steady growth in recent years.

Other methodological difficulties with our raw data include the inability of writing systems to indicate telling linguistics features such as vowels (Canaanite, Aramaic, and Ugaritic apart from its system of three alephs), vowel length (Akkadian, Amorite), and the doubling of consonants (cf. Zadok 1997: 93–94).[15] When we do have writing systems that can mark such linguistic features, as with the Masoretic Text (MT), other complications arise, such as late developments (e.g., the segolation one finds in names such as ʾĕlîmelek, ʾăbîmelek, ʾăḥîmelek) that historically would not reflect the pronunciation of a name in Iron Age Israel (*-malk; cf. PNs such as malkîʾēl). Layton (1990: 19) summarizes: "The end product is a unified language that tends to mask or eliminate altogether genuine dialectal differences of temporal and/or local origin." Moreover, in the Masoretic Text, foreign names are often represented in Hebrew form: "The Aramaic PN br hdd occurs in the Bible under the Canaanite form ben-hădad, and the Aramaic PN *Hadad-ʿidrī appears in Hebrew guise as hădadʿezer."

As for using the onomastic record to understand Northwest Semitic divinity, Jeffrey Tigay (1986), Dennis Pardee (1988b), Roger Callaway (1999), and Rainer Albertz (1978, 2012) have offered additional methodological cautions. Almost every scholar notes the elite nature of most of our data (and connections to the state) and how this can skew our understanding. Pardee's (1988b: 144) study argues for contextualizing Hebrew onomastic patterns and variations within the broader ancient Near East (using Phoenician-Punic, Ugaritic, and Eblaite sources for comparison). He points out how "different divine names will occur in different genres." Note the markedly different distribution of deities occurring in the Ugaritic onomastic record when compared to mythological texts, deity lists, and ritual texts (Pardee 1988b; 2002a: 222–224). For example, where the latter three sources would attest to a vibrant cult dedicated to the goddess ʾAṯiratu (Asherah), we have but one attestation of her name as the theophoric element in a personal name. The god Motu (Death) may have captured one's attention in myth, yet not in the ritual texts, where he is never the recipient of offerings.[16] Turning to Israelite material, Pardee (1988b: 124–126) notes how the Hebrew Bible's long list of "proper and acceptable designations of Hebrew deity . . . ʾēl, ʾĕlōah, ʾĕlōhîm, yāh, Yahweh, ʿelyôn, šadday" together with compound names (ʾēl

ʿelyôn, ʾēl šadday, ʾēl bĕrît, ʾēl ʿôlām, ʾēl rīʾî, yahweh ṣĕbāʾôt) does *not* correspond to the much smaller set of divine names in the onomastic record. A case in point is Pardee's startling observation that "never does a person bear [the full name Yahweh], neither in the Bible, nor in extrabiblical sources."

Methodologically, the interpreter must also factor in how certain terms (e.g., ʾil, bʿl) are inconclusive when it comes to representing a divine name (El, Baal) or a simple noun (god, lord). Appellatives that substitute for a divine name (e.g., Father, Brother, King, Rock, Light, Lord) are not explicit as to the god in question. Some original names may be subsequently altered along ideological lines, as with MT examples of changing *baʿal* names to *bōšet* names (cf. Tigay 1986: 8; Rollston 2013b: 377–382). Moreover, writes Tigay (1986: 17), "onomastic habits change slowly," so a family can hold on to a theophoric naming practice well after their devotion has changed.[17] Due to social pressures, those of a certain faith (e.g., polytheists such as Ahab, Jezebel, and Athaliah) may give their children names (e.g., Yahwistic names) that do not align with their religious practice. Among the population at large, one can easily imagine the reasons (e.g., political motivation, fear of repression) where one would adopt the name of the national deity yet in practice worship a different deity.

Rainer Albertz and the Social Context of Personal Names

The most revolutionary methodological change with regard to Israelite onomastica has come from Rainer Albertz. Chapter Two (pp. 43–44) noted how over the past three decades we have witnessed the study of family and household religion (variously defined) grow from a small subdiscipline within ancient Israelite religion and gender studies to today's maturing discipline, a field of study in its own right. At the center of this paradigmatic change was Albertz, and at the center of his research was a new approach to studying Israelite personal names.

The study of Israelite personal names and their theophoric elements has often focused on distribution patterns and percentages in an effort to document the breadth of Yahweh worship (especially in the eighth and seventh centuries BCE) as part of a process of pantheon reduction. (For such statistics, see Chapter Six, note 5.) Historians of Israelite religion typically used onomastica to globalize about the nature of religion (e.g., Israelite vs. Canaanite; Israelite vs. Judahite; polytheistic vs. monotheistic) and the prevalence of Yahweh (over against El, Baal, Asherah, Bes, etc.). Diachronically, onomastica were sometimes sifted to demarcate the percentage of Yahweh names according to historical period (pre-monarchy, united monarchy, divided monarchy, exilic, and post-exilic; e.g., Fowler 1988: 365–370). In short, frequently scholars looked to articulate "the dominance of a deity in the religion of the people" and the degree to which "the Yahwistic names outnumber the non-Yahwistic divine names" (Hess 2007a: 306, 308, 310).

As important as such questions may be, Albertz argued that they were sorely misguided, as they largely ignored the social context of personal names. In three defining works spanning three decades, the last of which was co-authored with Rüdiger Schmitt, Albertz underscored the importance of social context for uncovering ancient Israelite religion (see Albertz 1978; 1994; Albertz and Schmitt 2012). In particular, Albertz (Albertz 1978: 49–77; Albertz and Schmitt 2012: 245–367) studied how the verbs and nouns in the large majority of personal names were expressions of personal piety. Rather than reflecting matters of state and priestly cult, the petitions, thanksgivings, hopes for salvation, confessions, and concerns about the birth process that are found in names had more to do with personal religion and life cycle events. Such sentiments, argued Albertz, were similar to what we find in non-royal psalms and oracles of salvation. Moreover, similar expressions of personal piety could be found throughout the onomastica from the Levant (Ammonite, Aramaic, Moabite, Phoenician), such that a cross-cultural comparison was not only a possibility but a desideratum.[18]

A Survey of Onomastica in the Present Volume

In the present volume, readers will see how onomastica have played a significant role in many different discussions. For El worship (see Chapter Four), the name Jacob-el (*yaʿqub-ilu*, "May El Protect"), from the toponym lists of Thutmose III, Ramses II, and Ramses III, and the name "Israel," in the Merneptah victory stela, tease the historian trying to reconstruct the worship of El in the Late Bronze Age, whereas West Semitic anthroponyms with El anchor the deity's presence in the Iron Age, contrary to some scholarly reconstructions. In the Hebrew Bible, we find El present in the name of the eponymous ancestor Israel. An etiological tale involving Hagar's distress and a sacred spring connects the deity El Roi to the name of a well (Beer-Lahai-Roi). Other well-known toponymic references to El worship occur in the narratives about Bethel and Peniel. As for understanding the intriguing deity El Shadday, here too we find scholars referencing onomastic sources that range from Late Bronze Age Egypt to P's fascinating list of (archaic or archaizing) El and Shadday personal names in Numbers 1:5–15. From this list and elsewhere, the nature of Israelite El as a benevolent provider resonates with onomastica attesting to the deity as a stable "rock" (ʾElî-ṣûr, Ṣûrî-ʾēl, Ṣûrî-šadday) guiding and protecting his flock.

Turning to Yahweh (see Chapter Six), onomastica have been at the center of determining the pronunciation of the tetragrammaton (Yhwh) as well as speculations about the deity's origin. Due to the Masoretic tradition's lack of historically accurate vowels, scholars have turned to the onomastic record (together with other avenues) to reconstruct both vowels of the name *Yahweh. As readers will see, anthroponyms from the Hebrew Bible (e.g., Nērî-yāh, Něṭan-yāh) as well as sentence names from Amorite onomastica (e.g., *yawi-ila, yahwi-Dagan, yawi-Addu*) together with Greek transcriptions of the divine name (Iaoue and Iabe) have proved crucial for historical reconstruction. As for the meaning of the name Yahweh, the well-documented use of sentence names in Akkadian and especially Amorite onomastica lies behind one of the dominant proposals that reconstructs Yahweh as originally a cultic name of El (i.e., "El who creates the heavenly armies" was *ʾēl zū yahwī ṣabaʾōt).[19] (For exposition and critique, see Chapter Six, pp. 220–222.)

As for the historical origin of Yahweh, Egyptian toponyms from the Shasu texts as well as the Book of the Dead give us our very earliest data (Eighteenth and Nineteenth Dynasties, fourteenth and thirteenth centuries BCE) but are surrounded by murky questions of their own and have thus generated volumes of research. (See Chapter Six, pp. 229–233.) For definitive Northwest Semitic epigraphic sources documenting Yahweh, we have the Mesha stela, Kuntillet ʿAjrud, and Khirbet el-Qom, which bring the discussion down to the ninth and eighth centuries BCE. Kuntillet ʿAjrud, as readers will see, is especially tantalizing not only for its Yahwistic anthroponyms (e.g., ʿObadyaw, Yawʿasah) but also for toponyms that locate Yahweh in the north (Yahweh of Samaria) and the south (Yaweh of Teman). Bridging the gap between the thirteenth-century BCE Egyptian material and the ninth-/eighth-century BCE Kuntillet ʿAjrud material is the late eleventh-/early tenth-century BCE Ishbaʿl Inscription from Khirbet Qeiyafa. Once again it is an anthroponym that drives the discussion. And once again the methodological hurdles we have noted prove how hard it is to work with such data: does Ishbaʿl refer to Baal or Yahweh? (See Chapter Six, pp. 234–235.)

As for the merging of El and Yahweh, the many literary traditions that reinforce the seamless wedding of the two (e.g., Yahweh is El Olam; *yhwh ʾēl ʿôlām*) find corroboration in the onomastic phenomenon of "equating names," where El is Yahweh and Yahweh is El (e.g., *ʾlyhw, yhwʾl*). (See Chapter Six, note 1.) Sociologically, the ways in which both El and Yahweh were involved in family religion are strongly echoed by our onomastic data. (See Chapter Eight, pp. 480, 493–494.) When it comes to the Hebrew Bible's other literary characterizations of Yahweh, one sees both the strengths and the limitations of the onomastic record. The notions of Yahweh as warrior, as king, and as judge are reflected in the onomastic record, biblical and epigraphic. (See Chapters Eight and Nine.) Yet, quite curiously, there is no evidence that people used personal names to express their devotion to Yahweh as holy. (See Chapter Ten.) That such a core aspect of Yahweh's character is not reflected in personal names provides yet another methodological caution. For it reveals that even one of our greatest resources for reconstructing ancient Israelite religion can nonetheless come up empty.

Textual Sources: The Hebrew Bible and Textual Criticism

If historians of religion speak about their methodology, they are more likely to talk about theory (anthropological, archaeological, literary, ritual, social). Rarely do they delve into the necessity of textual criticism (or, for that matter, philology and comparative Semitics). Theory is sexy; the nut and bolts of a text, not so much. For the historian of ancient Israelite religion, the situation is the very opposite, as the Hebrew Bible, an artifact with multiple layers of textual transmission, constitutes a (perhaps the) primary source of information.

The importance of the field of textual criticism for biblical studies needs no justification, and no apology will be presented here. Biblical exegetes are adamant about the need, as all serious commentary series attest. Even newer series concentrating on reception history (e.g., the Eerdmans Illuminations series) or those wedding diachronic and synchronic approaches (e.g., Kohlhammer's International Exegetical Commentary on the Old Testament) do not do so at the expense of textual criticism. Granted, space restraints may mean that only certain series will give textual criticism the full attention it deserves. Thankfully, newer text editions (such as the Biblia Hebraica Quinta series and the series The Hebrew Bible: A Critical Edition) that provide commentaries on textual variants and reconstructions fill these gaps. Ideally, for the historian, the two fields of textual criticism and exegesis must go hand in hand if we are to have any hope of reconstructing the religion of Israel from the Iron Age, Persian, and Hellenistic periods.

Textual Sources: The Hebrew Bible and Source Criticism, a Limited Dataset

As we saw in Chapter Two, since the nineteenth century source criticism has played a large role in Pentateuchal interpretation and not merely for solving questions of literary cohesion. As Morgan and Barton (1988: 78) astutely observed: "Theories about the dating of the Pentateuchal sources ceased to be primarily solutions to a literary puzzle and became a tool for rewriting the history of Israel, and especially its religious institutions and theological ideas." Thus historians of Israelite religion must be attuned methodologically to how different literary strands present quite different portrayals (remembrances, imaginations) of Israelite and Judean cults. Moreover, unlike our nineteenth-century counterparts, today's historians face an even greater challenge: the field of source criticism has undergone such scrutiny in recent decades that there is little consensus on key issues such as the existence, content, and dating of certain sources. There are serious debates over scribal models of formation (documentarian, fragmentary, supplementarian) and, with respect to Pentateuchal law collections, genuine methodological differences between "supersessionist" and "complementarian" approaches (see Berman 2016). The lack of consensus has led to a general sense that Pentateuchal studies is "parochialized," with only rare instances of productive dialogue (Dozeman, Schmid, and Schwartz 2011: xi), "fractured" (Erisman 2013: 552), and, in the mind of some (e.g., Berman 2014a), "a field in crisis."[20] Alternatively, one could argue that the revitalized field of source criticism has never been stronger, as the weaknesses of older models give way, even if a replacement consensus is quite unlikely.

Rehearsing the particularities of today's source critics is beyond the scope of the present volume, and readers have plentiful resources (introductory and technical) to help wade through the various and nuanced positions.[21] The heuristic challenge for the present work (on reconstructing ancient religion) is to adopt a model that is sensitive to the nature of our data and has descriptive terminology that is inclusive enough for readers of varying approaches. Three strategies immediately present themselves as options. The first strategy is to agree that today's source criticism is in crisis and to retreat from its use as an analytical tool. A second is to favor strongly one of our current models over another—for example, using classical nomenclature (JEDP) though with revised understandings, or advocating for alternative terminology (P, non-P) together with specific notions of scribal formation and historical context. A third strategy, adopted here, has four components:

1. Using source criticism as a helpful (though limited) analytical tool that reveals parallel streams of tradition showcasing how ancient Israelite religion was not static
2. Using classical nomenclature (JEDP), though not dogmatically (non-P is used as well) and with heuristic intent
3. Insisting that we do not have a large enough dataset to make the type of statistical evaluations that are so common in our field
4. Admitting our limitations—that often the literary presentation of cult may be all we have, with the realia of cult no longer recoverable

These four components deserve further comment.

Source Criticism as a Helpful (Though Limited) Analytical Tool for Looking at Non-Static Cult

Given the widely different conclusions of today's source critics and the massive amounts of minutiae, pondering a retreat from using source criticism is understandable. Yet such a flight is neither wise nor helpful. For source criticism, even with all its flaws and irreconcilable debates, is the best mechanism to show

how the Hebrew Bible is not static.[22] The cultural memories that we read on the pages of the Hebrew Bible were written by individuals from a wide variety of backgrounds who learned of their traditions from a wide variety of sources (written and oral). They also added to and subtracted from their inherited traditions and reshaped them to address the needs of their own quite different historical contexts. The notion that individuals would reshape, revise, or even rewrite their inherited traditions based on their own historical and sociological contexts should not be surprising, even for today's most conservative reader holding a high view of Scripture. Listening to any modern sermon or homily easily reveals how even canonical Scripture is not static. It can be orally updated (sometimes faithfully, sometimes co-optatively) to speak afresh to the present. Reading any of today's many volumes that apply the teaching of the Hebrew Bible to our human dilemma readily shows how Scripture is regularly re-presented in written form (sometimes faithfully, sometimes co-optatively) to speak afresh to the present.

The updating and reframing of an inherited text—though maddening to the historian interested in the indigenous context that occasioned a text's initial writing—is an indicator of the significance of the text in subsequent tradition. Appropriating a given text is a sure indicator of the social power of that text. Writers rarely appropriate something that has minimal cultural importance. Rather, we appropriate significant texts that we agree or disagree with in order to increase or to lessen the text's influence.

When modern believers appropriate Scripture, they are following their biblical counterparts. For example, consider one of the most well-known traditions in Judaism: the prohibition against "boiling a goat in its mother's milk" (lō'-tĕbaššēl gĕdî baḥălēb 'immô). The prohibition is found in three sources: (1) in Exodus 23:19, a part of what source critics have called "the Covenant Code" (Exod 20:19–23:19); (2) in Exodus 34:26, a part of the so-called Ritual Decalogue found in Exodus 34:11–26; and (3) in Deuteronomy 14:21.[23] The minimal words here bear little relation to the subsequent, expansive *kashrut* on meat and dairy.

Regardless of how one defines and dates these three sources, and regardless of how they relate to one another (whether they are complementary or supersessionist), it is clear that these three sources provide differing presentations of a singular practice. Two of the three align, having a surrounding context of a festal calendar, sacrifice, and the presentation of first fruits within a temple context (Exod 23:19 and Exod 34:26). In contrast, the third source (Deut 14:21) situates our text within a dietary context: the prohibition of eating non-slaughtered meat, the social and economic benefits from non-Israelites' eating of such, and identity formation (via consecration). As for the historian of religion, with such minimal and conflicting data he is hard pressed to recover historical details about such a practice, though many have tried.[24] What one can conclude is that our divergent sources do point to varying streams of tradition reflecting different understanding of this singular practice. These different understandings (remembrances) developed and coexisted in dialogue over a long duration. In the cultural memory that the ancients handed down (and eventually canonized), it was important to preserve each of these streams of tradition.

For a more helpful diachronic application, consider the streams of Pentateuchal traditions regarding the practice of child sacrifice and how they were inherited by later authors. Here we benefit from Heath Dewrell's (2017) perceptive analysis. Dewrell argues that the Covenant Code's law of child sacrifice without a redemption clause is early: "The firstborn of your sons you shall give to me" (*běkôr bānêkā titten-lî*; Exod 22:28b–29 [Eng 22:29b–30]). Ezekiel inherits this tradition and thus, regrettably, must deal with it by having God admit that he himself "gave his people statutes that were not good [*'ănî nātatî lāhem ḥuqqîm lō' ṭôbîm*] and by which they could not live" (Ezek 20:25–26; cf. 16:19–21; 23:37–39). In contrast, other streams of tradition (J's Ritual Decalogue [Exod 34:17–26] and P [Exod 13:12a–13]) added a redemption clause such that no children are actually sacrificed. Yet other streams of tradition (e.g., Deuteronomy's Law of the Firstborn [Deut 15:19–23]) dealt with the matter by replacing the Covenant Code outright. Their own legislation omitted humans from the list of firstborn sacrifices, which then apply only to animals. Jeremiah, closely agreeing with Deuteronomy, seems to be speaking directly to Ezekiel 20:25–26 when he asserts three times that Yahweh never commanded child sacrifice, for it is an abomination that "never even entered his mind" (Jer 7:31; 19:5; 32:35).

The value here of source criticism and intertextual analysis is that it can give us a partial look at cultic practice and suggest plausible (though tentative) diachronic scenarios. In the present case, once again, the day-to-day realia of child sacrifice are irrecoverable, and comparative studies and archaeology have yet to provide clarification.[25] Yet our literary sources reveal an incredibly vibrant cultural memory. While the practice of child sacrifice was eventually eradicated, its memory lived on for hundreds of years—provoking later authors who strongly objected to such practices (rightly so!) to have to deal with how to frame their inherited authoritative traditions. That they chose dramatically different approaches underscores the diversity of the various forms of Yahweh worship in ancient Israel. Source criticism, with its focus on diverging information and presentation, forces a close reading of texts. By grappling with contradictions (real and apparent) and mixed evidence, we can better account for (and better appreciate) the diversity of testimony on cultic practice (here child sacrifice) as it now resides in the pages of the Hebrew Bible. Older treatments of our discipline narrowed the discussion, either viewing "ancient Israelite religion" as a static, monolithic tradition or treating it as a simple dichotomy between "official" (= "orthodox") Yahwism and a "popular religion" that was cast as heterodox in nature.

Instead it makes much more sense to argue for multiple streams of traditions where different Yahwistic groups held a variety of positions with regard to cultic practice. The field of source criticism, despite its "fractured parochialization," remains a viable analytical tool for the historian of religion.

Using Classical Nomenclature (JEDP), Though Not Dogmatically (non-P is used as well) and with Heuristic Intent

Heuristically, the current analysis uses classical source critical nomenclature of JEDP (together with non-P vocabulary) to engage the widest audience (for example, current advocates of an E source). Pragmatically, it is easier for advocates of alternative models/nomenclature to make the necessary adjustments when they read long-standing classical nomenclature than the other way around. It is easier for a non-documentarian to frame this material within his understanding than for a documentarian to take broader terminology (e.g., non-P) and determine if it was classically defined as J or E.[26] Yet the reader should not impute to our use of classical terminology a rigid understanding of any of these four sources, especially when the jury is still out as to their existence, dating, nature, and content. For example, even though we refer to the J source, the reader should not conclude that we are backtracking to the days of Gerhard von Rad with his "great personality" ingeniously working during a period of "Solomonic Enlightenment." As can be seen in our critique of the Graf-Wellhausen source paradigm in Chapter Two, we certainly would eschew any attempt to chart a linear (evolutionary) course for a monolithic Israelite religion.

Readers will also find that unless there is a secure context (historically and/or linguistically), the presentation here is intentionally vague when it comes to the dating of source material, preferring broad categories such as "ancient lore" or "late material."[27] Our sources give us windows into "streams of tradition." These are ongoing traditions that inherit older material. As active traditions, they regularly update or revise this material with later layers of tradition. (See the discussion of child sacrifice texts earlier in this chapter.) Thus any source, even in a later incarnation, can preserve earlier tradition. (For example, compare the onomastica in Num 1:5–15, discussed in Chapter Four.) It goes without saying, then, that dating a tradition is a difficult endeavor, for a late updated/revised feature in a text may reside alongside genuinely early material. Here I am in agreement with Benjamin Sommer (2011: 106) when he advocates: "For most biblical texts, general rubrics [e.g., archaic, pre-exilic, post-exilic, Hellenistic] are the best we can apply with any intellectual honesty." My preference for "streams of tradition" also resonates with Sommer's (2011: 106–108) critique of "pseudo-historicist reductionism" that fails to appreciate how "literature that endures for millennia does so precisely because it transcends its setting," especially when it grapples with ideas of "deep humanistic significance."

The Size of Our Dataset and Statistical Evaluations: Limited Data and the "Propp Principle"

All too commonly scholars make evaluations (regarding dating, source, semantic range of a word, etc.) based on the number of occurrences and distribution patterns of a specific lexeme. There is a lot to be said for the statistical study of our material, yet our conclusions need to be measured. Often biblical scholars make assessments that statisticians would challenge due to the nature of our dataset. Often the assumption is that we have a complete or nearly complete dataset of lexemes, rendering our assessments statistically valid. In truth, we have a *very small* dataset with which to work, and it is minimally representative of language use both chronologically (across the entire Iron Age and later) and spatially (across the southern Levant).

In addition to a limited linguistic dataset, consider too how often writers of the Hebrew Bible are silent on matters of cult that were out of their purview. I have written elsewhere (Lewis 2012) of how incantations were certainly used in ancient Israel (cf. the early sixth-century BCE Ketef Hinnom amulets), yet apotropaia are absent from the pages of the Hebrew Bible. Incantations are often associated with domestic/family/local religion (see Chapter Eight) that addresses personal concerns such as safe births, healthy children, the treatment of illness (including snakebite remedies), marriage rites, sexual potency, mourning rites, and burial rituals. Much of this activity is not recorded by the individuals who come to articulate the "normative" biblical perspective (e.g., Priestly, prophetic, Deuteronomistic, wisdom-school parties), as their interests lie elsewhere. In addition, these individuals were prone to ignore and/or condemn practices they deemed unworthy for various reasons that were linked to their control of cult.

Narrowing our material even further, consider how our texts can even be silent on normative cultic practices. A good illustration of this is the lack of any mention of cultic singers and musicians in the Pentateuch and their relative absence in the Deuteronomistic History in contrast to the Chronicler's portrayal of their prominent roles (2 Chr 29: 25–30). Situating the discussion within its broader historical context, Gary Knoppers (2004: 619–620) notes how "musicians and singers were a constituent feature of temple worship" throughout the ancient Near East. Thus rather than Chronicles inventing fictional scenarios, "the complete absence of singers from the Pentateuch and from most of the Deuteronomistic work tells us more about the limitations of these sources than it does about the conditions of the Jerusalem Temple during the monarchy."

Lastly, William Propp (2006: 793) objects strenuously to how we use the meager data that we have; I hereby label his argument "the Propp Principle." Propp challenges the "scholarly axiom" that "*we are obliged to adopt as provisional truth the most likely and parsimonious reconstruction, based on the evidence available*" (italics Propp's). In response Propp boldly writes:

No doctrine could sound more innocuous but be so pernicious. What obliges us? Who? Given the gaps in our knowledge, the complexity of historical processes and our inability to conduct proper experiments, we should aim rather for multiple, parallel hypotheses, as complex as the events they purport to explain. We can and must take into account the 95 percent of information hidden from our view, the sea bottom connecting solitary islands of data. The only sensible response to fragmented, slowly but randomly accruing evidence is radical open-mindedness. A single, simple explanation for a historical event is generally a failure of imagination, not a triumph of induction.

In short, historians of religion need to ponder the sober reality that our dataset is extremely limited. (Is saying that we possess even 5 percent too generous?) We need to be appropriately agnostic. In addition, we need to be appropriately humble with our conclusions given our cultural and historical distance. At the same time, we should be adventurous enough to articulate measured statements about which scenarios are more likely to be on the right path.

Admitting Our Limitations Regarding the Realia of Cult

A significant percentage of the present volume has to do with the deity Yahweh and various representations of Yahwistic cult. Readers then may be concerned to read the conclusion of one of the most respected historians of religion in our field. Mark Smith (2001b: 146) soberly remarks that it may very well be that "the original profile of Yahweh may be permanently lost." When combined with the mere 5 percent of the data that we have to work with for reconstructing cultic practice (the Propp Principle), we could begin to wonder whether there is just too much uncertainty to the endeavor.

As we hope to show in the pages that follow, measured judgments can be made. Some archaeological, epigraphic, and linguistic data can situate our biblical source material within more confined parameters. Ancient Near Eastern comparanda can underscore the undeniable cultural continuum within which ancient Israel's religious culture is perfectly at home.

Yet readers will also see admissions that sometimes all we have is the literary portrayal of cult (what could be called "biblical religion"), with the realia of cultic practice being irrecoverable. This was noted already regarding our inability to probe deeper into the realia behind the prohibition regarding "boiling a goat in its mother's milk." This was due in part to its minimal treatment (a few verses). In contrast, we could examine the extremely well attested data we have for Passover (*pesaḥ*) and unleavened bread (*maṣṣôt*) traditions. These include (1) narrative texts from various sources (Exod 12:1–20 [P]; Exod 12:21–27 [traditionally J]; Exod 12:43–50 [P]; Exod 13:3–10 [traditionally E]; Josh 5:10–15; 2 Kgs 23:21–23; Ezra 6:19–22; 2 Chr 30:1–27; 2 Chr 35:1–9); (2) non-narrative regulations (Exod 23:10–19 [Covenant Code]; Exod 34:18–26 [so-called Ritual or J Decalogue]; Lev 23:4–8 [H]; Num 9:1–15 [P]; Num 28:16–25 [P]; Deut 16:1–8; Ezek 45:21–25); and even (3) extra-biblical material in the "Passover Letter" from fifth-century BCE Elephantine (TAD A 4.1; P. Berlin 13464). Even with such detailed sources and an overwhelming amount of secondary literature, we are still hard pressed when it comes to describing the realia of cultic practice for the two festivals over time. We are faced with a diverse array of cultic actors, social contexts, technical vocabulary (ḥag, môʿēd, miqrāʾ qōdeš, ʿăṣārâ, ʿăbōdâ), cultic offerings, temporal markers, and guiding rationale (social bonding, social regulation, construction of cultural memory, pilgrimage, regulation of cult, legitimization of a centralized cult place, etc.). Substantive questions remain murky: How, when, and why did two discrete types of rituals (sacrificial/apotropaic versus harvest/rite of riddance) become linked? Historians of religion must acknowledge that the literary presentation of religion (e.g., incorporating pesaḥ into the narrative about the plague of the firstborn) is mostly what we are able to describe, not a diachronic analysis of the realia of ritual practice.

The Nature of Our Source Material, Part II: Material Culture

Archaeology uses the physical remains (material culture) of the past to reconstruct how humans interacted with their physical world, from human subsistence and social organization to economic realities and cultural experiences—all of which intersected with religion. Today's discipline is a highly interdisciplinary enterprise combining the social sciences (especially anthropology) and the humanities (especially history), with the natural sciences playing a key role in the study of skeletal remains (human and animal), biodiversity, artifacts, architecture, and physical environments. Landscape archaeology is particularly adept at using newer technologies (GIS applications) to reconstruct ancient societies (e.g., water pathways, human settlement patterns, travel networks).

For proto-historic and historic periods (in contrast to the prehistoric), scholars integrate archaeological data with textual materials. As widely acknowledged, the field is marked by an unevenness, with archaeologists having less (sometimes little) training in ancient languages and textual scholars having less (sometimes little) training in archaeology. As each discipline has become more sophisticated and more specialized, the gulf has grown wider. As I have explored elsewhere with respect to reconstructing mortuary activities and afterlife beliefs (Lewis 2002), each discipline has inherent strengths and weaknesses. Our best historical reconstructions emerge from both disciplines working critically and independently, yet informing each other when integrated.

In recent years archaeology and cultural anthropology have contributed to theoretical constructions of identity formation, gender, and ethnicity as well as cognitive issues of beliefs and ideologies. The cognitive issues are particularly relevant for the study of religion, yet the hurdles are many. As my archaeologist colleague Glenn Schwartz has quipped, "It is easier to learn from ancient physical evidence about what people ate than what they thought."[28]

The limited nature of the present work will not use archaeology to address the varied forms of sacred architecture, as they have been well covered by Zevit's (2001) magisterial treatment.[29] Yet when it is appropriate additional discussion will be added either where such treatment is lacking (e.g., the fascinating Ayn Dara Temple) or in light of more recent research (e.g., assessing the religious nature of the important site of Kuntillet ʿAjrud now that the final report has been published). With the focus of the present work on divinity, we will address three primary ways in which archaeology has entered the debate, all having to do with divine representation. These include discussing anthropomorphic and theriomorphic artifacts as well as "standing stones" (*masseboth,* sing. *massebah*) that represent a type of "material aniconism." (See Chapters Five and Seven.) In those chapters we will also provide methodological comments about the misuse of material culture, the nature of our limited dataset, and the criteria for determining whether a specific artifact can be categorized as divine.

The Nature of Our Source Material, Part III: The Ancient Near Eastern Context and Comparanda

Now and then a scholar turns a phrase in a memorable way. At a lecture in the early 1980s I heard Peter Machinist quip that a phrase such as "the Bible *and* the ancient Near East" assumes that the former was not a part of the latter. This short, incisive remark called for comparativists to ponder how our terminology can reveal subconscious understandings. Scholars who have used the phrase "the Bible *and* the ancient Near East" (rather than "the Bible *in* the ancient Near East") are typically biblicists who actively promote studying the Hebrew Bible within its ancient Near Eastern cultural contexts. Yet the phrase has also been found within the broader humanities ever since the discoveries of the Rosetta Stone, the Gilgamesh Epic, Enuma Elish, and the Ugaritic texts (cf. Chapter Two) forced humanists to realize that the core text of Western civilization had antecedents.

As Machinist observes, underlying such a phrase is a failure to embrace fully the reality that the Hebrew Bible is an ancient Near Eastern production. Ancient Israel and ancient Judah are fully Near Eastern cultures, and their literary productions are fully Near Eastern. That the Hebrew Bible has lived on as a scriptural text to the present (and been domesticated by modern people to address their situations) does not erase its essence as a product of the ancient Near East. For all its sociological and theological uses in later Judaism and Christianity (and Islam as well), the Hebrew Bible is at its core an ancient Near Eastern text that emerged out of an ancient Near Eastern world. It is thus essential for all interpreters (historian, rabbi, minister, imam, philosopher, English professor, lay teacher, general humanist) to situate the Hebrew Bible firmly within its West Asian historical and cultural context. It would seem that such an obvious hermeneutic would need no defense. Yet a glance at the way in which the Hebrew Bible is taught within religious institutions and secular universities reveals how little this hermeneutic is embraced. For various reasons, even religious institutions require less and less Hebrew and Aramaic of their students, not to mention facility with the other languages of the ancient Near East (e.g., Akkadian, Egyptian, Phoenician, Sumerian, Ugaritic) and their many dialects. It is understandable how our culture requires that the Hebrew Bible be studied with post-historical-critical approaches (especially the important fields of feminist and post-colonial interpretation). Yet the growth of these disciplines need not come at the expense of studying the emergence of the Hebrew Bible as an ancient Near Eastern production. Indeed, contextualizing the Hebrew Bible in its world can provide important correctives to its misuse in reception history and safeguards against its misapplication for our modern context.

The present work is not exhaustive, yet it is intentional about looking at features of ancient Israelite religion through an ancient Near Eastern lens. Obviously, there is the dilemma of how much comparanda to include. The amount of relevant ancient Near Eastern material is staggering, as one can see from perusing the contents of the four volumes of *The Context of Scripture* (edited by Younger and Hallo), the numerous titles in the Writings from the Ancient World series (published by SBL Press), and similar collections (e.g., ANET, LAPO, TUAT, Dalley 2008, J. Foster 2001, B. Foster 2005, LAS, Chavalas 2007, Hays 2014, Walton 2018), including electronic databases (e.g., CDLI, CCP, ETCSL, Oracc).[30] I hope to have struck the right balance, with some readers wishing I had included more and others wishing I had included less.

What distinguishes modern comparative analysis from earlier attempts as discussed in Chapter Two? Today's comparativists shun the "parallelomania" of old, where—according to Samuel Sandmel (1962: 1), who coined the term in his SBL Presidential Address—a scholar extravagantly "overdoes the supposed similarity in passages and then proceeds to describe source and derivation as if implying literary connections flowing in an inevitable or predetermined direction." Instead today's scholars are much more prone to follow Shemaryahu Talmon's (1978b) acclaimed essay on comparative method. Where past scholars went in search of similarities (parallelomania) and homogenizing cultures (e.g.,

Ugarit and Israel), Talmon (1978b: 345) urges that "our concern should be with difference as much as with likenesses."

Yet in avoiding homogenizing "parallelomania," one should not slip into a naive contrastive approach using categorical language, as we saw with Kaufmann in Chapter Two. Today's comparativists, for the most part, work as cultural historians rather than as apologists arguing for the uniqueness of a given "pure" trait. Machinist (1991: 197) has written insightfully on the question of distinctiveness in ancient Israel:

> There has been a determined search for clear concepts and behaviors which would neatly separate Israel from the cultures being compared with it. ... The goal here has been a kind of "trait list" ... in which "x" could be marked as present in Israel but absent elsewhere in the ancient Near East, or vice-versa. But establishing such traits is an elusive business ... Indeed, as the increasing volume of archaeological discoveries makes clear, some correspondence always seems to be waiting to be found somewhere in the ancient Near East ... for what is proposed to be a distinctive concept or behavior in ancient Israel.

Instead, argues Machinist (1991: 200), the modern historian needs to study the configurations of traits and ideas to understand the distinctiveness of ancient Israel—or, for that matter, any culture. This is not to say that the Hebrew Bible itself is not apologetic, for it does indeed contain assertions of distinctiveness, beginning with its earliest literature (Exod 15:11 proclaims: "Who is like you O Yahweh?"). Yet such passages need to be studied for their internal rhetoric. Machinist (1991: 202, 210–212) is certainly correct to situate these in the context of identity formation. As we will explore in Chapter Six, Israel's preference for the supremacy of Yahweh aligns with how surrounding cultures used divinity in their own identity formation (e.g., Tyre's selection of Melqart and Baal/Baal-Shamem, Sidon's recognition of Eshmun as their chief god, Moab's elevation of the god Chemosh, the Edomite choice of Qos, and the Ammonite adoption of Milcom).

Today's comparativists recognize the failures of past approaches that drew simplistic comparisons of similarities between Israel and another culture without factoring in differences in literary genres and historical settings. Again, see Talmon's (1978: 351–356) remarks on *Gattungen* and *Sitz im Leben*. Historians of religion are now quite wary of drawing any *direct* comparisons between cultures unless one can defend the mechanisms of cultural transmission with attention to scribal culture and sociolinguistics.[31] Instead, today's comparativists underscore the broad cultural continuum of ancient Near Eastern societies in every period starting with the Middle Bronze Age. For our purposes, Chapter Six (pp. 256–269) will unpack the Canaanite and Aramean cultural continuum, especially from the Late Bronze Age through the Iron Age and from the northern Levant to Egypt. Today's comparativists rarely argue for one-to-one comparisons between cultures and, due to the past errors of grand theorists, they refrain from describing a meta-narrative in which every ancient Near Eastern culture adopted a singular story. Instead, they advocate the shared cultural continuum painted with broad strokes while respecting how each society wove its stories in culturally specific ways.

Conclusion

With respect for the disciplines needed to carry out the present endeavor (see pp. 48–49), and acknowledging the present author's limitations, we begin our study with an examination of El, the deity who appears in the name of the eponymous ancestor Israel. The limitations of our data and methodological challenges will be addressed in due order, yet hopefully readers will gain an appreciation for this exciting aspect of ancient Israel's religious experience.

4
El Worship

Conceptualizing divinity is difficult, even for those of us with ample exposure to a particular theistic tradition. Occasionally we are successful in understanding how contemporaries outside our frame of reference conceptualize the divine, but only through substantial exposure and dialogue. How then are we to understand the religious mindset of people (both individual persons and collective groups) living in the ancient Near East in the Late Bronze and Iron Ages, from whom we stand at so great a distance?[1] All that we can hope for is a general impression derived from the words and objects they have left behind. In ancient Israelite religion divinity was dressed in predominantly male language, and thus we begin with this here.[2]

The Deity El

The logical place to begin looking at ancient Israelite divinity is with El, the deity whose name is found in the designation of the eponymous ancestor "Isra<u>el</u>." This variant name for the patriarch Jacob is usually taken to mean "El reigns supreme" or "El contends."[3] It is often argued that the absence of Yahweh in this name, together with the name of the Shechemite deity "El, the god of (the patriarch) Israel" (Gen 33:20) and the absence of Yahweh (and Baal) in anthroponyms and toponyms in early literature, indicates the antiquity of El worship over Yahweh worship. This too makes a discussion of the deity El a proper launch point for examining Israelite divinity.

How did West Semites of the Iron Age conceptualize the deity El in word and object? What traditions did they inherit about this deity from their Late Bronze Age predecessors? What functional role did they ascribe to El in their various societal structures? Immediately we run into ambiguity in text and artifact. The etymology of the common Semitic (apart from Ethiopian) word *ilu/ʾel* is beyond our grasp.[4] It was used both as a generic appellative ("god") and as a proper name ("El"), but often our texts are anything but clear about which usage is being employed.[5] The iconography of male figures in bronze and stone is equally vague due to the lack of accompanying inscriptions that could ascertain identity. As for inherited traditions, we run up against the problems of comparative methodology articulated in Chapter Three. It would be foolish to assert that conceptions of a deity are homogenous transhistorically and transculturally, yet a brief sketch of the deity El in contiguous cultures can be instructive for painting a broad religious picture against which one can situate Israelite El worship.

What did the divine name El connote in Canaan and its environs in the Late Bronze Age? How did such connotations live on, and how were they transformed in the Iron Age to influence an Israelite cult that came to be dominated by the worship of the deity Yahweh? F. M. Cross, following Ignace Gelb, J. J. M. Roberts, and Herbert Huffmon, argues that El had a long Semitic pedigree dating back to the Pre-Sargonic period and was especially popular during the Amorite period of the eighteenth century BCE.[6] Yet in many cases the use of *ilu/ilum* (and the logogram DINGIR) reflects the ambiguity mentioned earlier. Thus we cannot always determine whether names such as Ilum-bānī mean "the god is my creator" or "El is my creator."[7]

El in the Late Bronze Age Levant

Broadly speaking, the word *ilu* is used in East Semitic (Mesopotamian) culture more as an appellative for deity and as a designation of spirits good and evil than as the proper name of a deity.[8] In any event, the Late Bronze West Semitic material is more relevant for painting the backdrop that we desire. Here we are blessed with a substantial corpus of material that comes from the land of Canaan itself: the Amarna letters, a collection of 382 tablets from the fourteenth century BCE. These letters represent diplomatic and administrative correspondence between local rulers in Canaan and Egyptian pharaohs, primarily Amenophis III and Akhenaten (see Moran 1992; Rainey 2015). Even though the Amarna tablets are written in (peripheral) Akkadian, the language of diplomacy at the time, they reflect a distinct Northwest Semitic morphology and syntax (and occasionally vocabulary), which is attributed to their native Canaanite setting.

If we were able to step back into Canaan in the Amarna period, we would find, in the words of William L. Moran, "largely a provincial and, in many respects, a very heterogeneous culture, the product of a long, complex history, of which we know but a very small part" (1992: xviii). The same would seem to apply for their religious culture if it is valid to put any stock in the theophoric elements in personal names found in the Amarna correspondence. (See Chapter Three, pp. 56–60, on the methodology of using onomastica.) Richard Hess's (1989; 1993: 233–242) catalogue of divine names shows a pluralistic religious environment, including Egyptian (Amon, Api, Horus, Hu, Ḫaʿpi, Jah, Ptah, Rēʿ, Seth), Mesopotamian (Anu, Aššur, Baštu, Ninurta), Kassite (Ḫarbe, Šugab), Hurrian (Ḫebat, Iršapppa, Teššub), and Indo-Aryan (Índraḫ, Rta, Yamáḫ) deities alongside general Semitic ([H]addu, Dagan, ʿAmmu) and West Semitic deities (ʿAnat, ʾAsherah, ʿAštart, Baʿlu, Beltu, El, Milku/Malik, Ṣaduq, Yamm).

There is no indication of any superiority of the deity El from this catalogue of names. The ruler of Ḫasi may assert through his name Ildayyi ("El is my sufficiency")[9] that El meets his every need (EA 175: 3), to which a Tyrian messenger named Ilumilku could add that "El is king" (EA 151: 45).[10] Ben-Elima (EA 256: 15), if he could convince his contemporaries to believe in enclitic *mems* as much as some modern Hebraists do, might even claim that he was "the Son of El" like a famous Syrian king named Kirta. But the majority of those living in Canaan at this time would beg to differ, as they looked to deities other than El for personal protection and blessings such as the birth and well-being of children.[11]

To be fair, we should not weigh the Amarna letters very heavily. They are straightforward correspondence of a fairly stereotypical nature. While they may be full of international tension, political intrigue, and administrative detail, they have precious little comment on religion in general and meager data on the nature of the deities reflected in the personal names. Once again, we see that it is hard to reconstruct religion solely from onomastica. At least the plethora of different divine elements should give us pause about being too narrow in our reconstructions.

Clearly, the Amarna letters do nothing to assert the preeminence of El in Late Bronze Canaan, and there is little hint that he gains any prestige in the Ramesside period that follows, where the elite of society are engaged in emulating high Egyptian culture (Higginbotham 1996; cf. Tazawa 2009). What is truly fascinating and intriguing from this time period, especially for determining the deity associated with the eponymous ancestor Israel, is the occurrence of the name Jacob-el ("May El protect") in toponym lists of Thutmose III, Ramses II, and Ramses III.[12] Gösta Ahlström (1993: 230 n. 8) answers Thomas L. Thompson's (1974: 49 n. 229) charge that we "are dealing with place names and not tribal names" by reminding us that "in the Semitic world, geographical names and names of people could often be the same, for instance, Ephraim, Assur." Nonetheless, these occurrences are far too meager to glean much about the worship of El in the Bronze Age, not to mention their use for reconstructing patriarchal religion.

Where then can we turn if texts from Canaan itself fall short in describing the deity El in West Semitic religion of the Late Bronze Age? Some scholars have emphasized the Semitic worship at Serabit el-Khadim as reconstructed from the Proto-Sinaitic inscriptions. These texts are notoriously difficult to decipher. Though putative epithets derived from these texts (*ḏ ṭb*, "the Merciful One"; ʾ*El ḏū ʿōlam*, "the Eternal One") have played a large role in previous reconstructions of the deity El (Albright 1966a: 24; Cross 1962a; 1973: 18–20), they are now so much in question that they must be set aside.[13] In any event, the Canaanite pantheon at Serabit el-Khadim (Baʿlat, El, Lady of the Serpent(s), Resheph(?), and ʿAnat) is so syncretized with Egyptian deities (Baʿlat = Hathor, El = Ptah) that it is difficult to distinguish Canaanite from Egyptian elements (cf. Tazawa 2009). In short, Meindert Dijkstra's (1997: 92) conclusion that "the character of El at Serabit is not at all clear" is apt and prevents us from going any farther with this material.

'Ilu (= El) at Ugarit

Leaving the Egyptian sphere of influence and looking north to the Syrian coast, we come to the Late Bronze Age kingdom of Ugarit, a West Semitic culture that shares close religious affinities with ancient Israel and which has the fullest representation of the deity 'Ilu (= El) both in word and object of any ancient Near Eastern society.[14] Our intent at reviewing this material is to sketch the West Semitic backdrop, not to equate Ugaritic religion with early Israelite religion.[15]

The deity 'Ilu occurs at Ugarit in a wide array of literary genres (mythological texts, epics, deity lists, ritual texts, etc.), and his role of the head of the pantheon was sketched early in Ugaritic research (see Eissfeldt 1951; Pope 1955). Ritual texts refer to a "temple of 'Ilu" (*bt 'il*, e.g., KTU 1.119.14; cf. too *qdš 'il* in 1.119.6), and it may be that the acropolis temple usually designated "the temple of Dagan" (based on the nearby discovery of the Dagan stela; cf. KTU 6.13, 6.14) was in reality 'Ilu's. 'Ilu invites both gods and shades to his "house"//"palace" (*bt*//*hkl*) for banquets (KTU 1.20–22; 1.114). In other texts his abode is watery, being situated "at the sources of the two rivers, at the confluence of the double-deep" (*mbk nhrm b'dt thmtm*, KTU 1.100.3) or "the channels/fountains of the double-deep" (*'apq thmtm*, KTU 4.4.20–24, etc.).[16]

'Ilu's epithets describe him as "father" (*'ab*) to both gods (cf. *'ab bn 'il*, KTU 1.40) and humans (*'ab 'adm*), and in discourse both groups frequently refer to "Bull 'Ilu" (a sign of power and virility) as their father. Family metaphors (*bn il, dr il, dr bn il*) are used to describe deities and humans as his children.[17] 'Ilu is designated "the father of years" (*'ab šnm*), which seems to be a positive description of his eternity and seniority rather than a stage of advanced old age.[18] Similarly, the description of his gray hair and beard should be understood positively, as the gray is associated with 'Ilu's wisdom (KTU 1.4.5.3–4; though compare the reference to it in the context of 'Anatu's threats against 'Ilu [KTU 1.3.5.24–25; 1.18.1.11–12]).

Along with being the father of gods and humans, 'Ilu also plays the role of creator, though this conclusion is drawn more from inference rather than from explicit references.[19] Marvin Pope concluded that "it is altogether probable that El was a Creator God, but the Ugaritic evidence is by no means explicit. [Virtually] all the Ugaritic allusions to El's creativity are in terms of generation and paternity."[20] To date we have found no Ugaritic myth celebrating 'Ilu's creation of the world. One text (KTU 1.16.5.25–41) does mention how ʾIlu magically creates an exorcist named Shaʿtiqatu by "pinching off clay" (*rṯ* + *yqrṣ*), an expression used elsewhere of Enki's and Yahweh's creation of humanity.[21] The one explicit text preserved regarding ʾIlu's "creative" powers is KTU 1.23, where he engenders the deities Dawn and Dusk (*šḥr wšlm*) in very human fashion:[22]

ʾIlu's "hand"* grows long as the sea,   [* a euphemism for phallus]
ʾIlu's "hand" as the ocean.

ʾIlu's "hand" is long as the sea,
ʾIlu's "hand" as the ocean.

ʾIlu takes a pair of brands,*   [* representing two goddesses]
Twin brands from atop the firestand.

He takes them into his house.

ʾIlu lowers his scepter,
ʾIlu is generous with the "staff" in his hand . . .[23]

Lo! the maiden pair cries out:

"O husband! husband!
Lowered is your scepter,
Generous the 'staff' in your hand.

Look! a bird roasted on the fire,
Basted and browned on the coals."

The pair became his wives,
Wives of ʾIlu, his wives forever.

He bows down to kiss their lips,
Ah! their lips are sweet,
Sweet as succulent fruit.

In kissing, conception,
In embracing, pregnant heat.

The two travail and give birth
to the gods Dawn and Dusk.

Some have argued that ʾIlu is a *deus otiosus* who suffers from impotency.[24] Such a view is difficult to maintain in view of his ribald behavior in this text and elsewhere (cf. KTU 1.4.4.38–39, where ʾIlu brazenly brags: "Does the *yd* [a play on words meaning both "hand" and "love"] of ʾIlu the King excite you, the love of the Bull arouse you"). ʾIlu is repeatedly portrayed in KTU 1.23 as an amorous kisser who successfully impregnates two females.[25] Nowhere else in Ugaritic myth does the creator of the gods have any problems with impotency. Consider, for example, ʾIlu's epithet *ṯr*, "the bull" (KTU 1.1.4.12; 1.2.1.16; 1.3.4.54; 1.3.5.10, 35; 1.4.1.4, 1.4.2.10, 1.4.4.47, etc.), connoting virility, strength, and dignity—a fitting title for the head of the pantheon in a society well acquainted with herds (see Curtis 1990: 31).[26] As already noted by Wesley Toews (1993: 55–56), ʾIlu's "bull" epithet "has a close association with the concept of El as progenitor." A bronze bull may even have functioned as ʾIlu's divine symbol (see Chapter Five).

ʾIlu is known for his wisdom; an astute person in the Kirta Epic can be referred to as "being wise like ʾIlu" (KTU 1.16.4.1–2). Elsewhere, the goddess ʾAthiratu proclaims:

Your decree is wise, O ʾIlu,
Your wisdom is eternal,
A fortunate life is your decree . . .

You are great, ʾIlu, you are so wise,
Your gray beard instructs you. (KTU 1.4.4.41–43; 1.4.5.3–4)

ʿAnatu uses the same speech in KTU 1.3.5.30–31, perhaps less than sincerely, and both her words and ʾAthiratu's (which take place in the context of trying to secure a house for Baʿlu) could be sheer flattery for purposes of manipulation. Rhetorically speaking, some tradition of ʾIlu's wisdom (consider the formulaic pattern in both texts) must stand behind such usage for the words to have their desired effect—whatever may be the intent of the goddesses. The Ugaritic behind the translation "a fortunate life" is *ḥyt ḥẓt*, which designates ʾIlu's governing of one's fate (if Arabic cognates for *ḥẓt* are preferred) or a connection with divination (if *ḥẓt* is to be connected to Northwest Semitic cognates designating "arrows" and hence belomancy; cf. Smith and Pitard 2009: 353).[27] There is some indication that ʾIlu was associated with the divinatory arts. In the story about ʾIlu healing the mortally ill King Kirta, ʾIlu uses magic and clay to create an apotropaic figure known as Shaʿtiqatu (*ʾank ʾiḥtrš w ʾaškn*; KTU 1.16.5.25–28).[28] We may even have a reference to "the house of ʾIlu" as "the house of magic/the magician" (*bt ḥrš*; KTU 1.12.2.60–61).

Even more prominent is ʾIlu's beneficence, which can be seen in his frequently used title *lṭpn ʾil d pʾid*, "the Gracious One, the Benevolent God."²⁹ Another of his titles associates his beneficence with his holiness (*lṭpn wqdš*, "the Gracious and Holy One").³⁰ Thus we find ʾIlu beseeched by gods and humans looking for his blessings, especially the granting of children. In response to a request from Baʿlu, ʾIlu blesses Daniʾilu with a son in the tale of ʾAqhatu (KTU 1.17.1.24ff). In the Kirta Epic, ʾIlu blesses King Kirta with a wife and children (revealed through a dream and also in conjunction with a request from Baʿlu; KTU 1.14.1.26ff; 1.15.2.12ff); one of those children, Yassibu, later stages a revolution against his father. The same story also tells of ʾIlu's beneficence in healing an ailing Kirta by magically creating an exorcist who expels the disease (KTU 1.16.5.10ff).³¹ ʾIlu's beneficence is familial, yet the emphasis on securing Kirta's royal office underscores (at least for Ilimilku, the scribe of this text) ʾIlu's divine parentage of the king. According to Simon Parker (1977: 173–174), the Kirta Epic demonstrates "the virtues of El as the incomparable savior," for it is ʾIlu alone who delivers Kirta from his various dilemmas, not the gods in general. Thus "the poem in effect makes El the one and only reliable object of faith." "El is the unrivalled master of specifically royal affairs, but by extension of human affairs in general."

Some Ugaritians celebrated ʾIlu's benevolent provision of something that, according to Judges 9:13, cheers the hearts of gods and people: wine. A social institution reputed for its drinking, known as the *marzeaḥ*, is attested throughout the ancient Near East (including the Bible).³² At Ugarit it is particularly associated with ʾIlu, who invites the gods (and even the shades of the dead in KTU 1.20–22) to his banquets and presides over vintage rites (cf. KTU 1.41; 1.39; 1.23).³³ At one of these banquets (KTU 1.114), ʾIlu, the patron of drinking, drinks to excess, the results of which are described in very human language:

> ʾIlu slaughters game in his house,
> Butchers beasts in his palace,
> Bids gods to the cuts of beef.
>
> The gods eat and drink,
> Drink wine till sated,
> Vintage till inebriated . . .
>
> ʾIlu sits . . .
> ʾIlu settles into his bacchanal [*mrzḥ*]
>
> ʾIlu drinks wine till sated,
> Vintage till inebriated.

'Ilu staggers to his house,
Stumbles in to his court.

Thukamuna and Shunama carry him,[34]
Habayu then berates him,
He of two horns and a tail.

He slips in his dung and urine,
'Ilu collapses like one dead
'Ilu like those who descend to Earth.[35]

The text ends with two goddesses presenting what seems to be a cure for individuals ('Ilu included) suffering from hangovers. In many ways, then, 'Ilu is all too human in his frailties. Some scholars even question whether 'Ilu was deprived of his authority as head of the pantheon as a result of a conflict with Ba'lu (e.g., Kapelrud, Oldenburg). There is nothing explicit in the Ugaritic texts to support such a notion (Mullen 1980: 92–109), and according to David Schloen, the tension in these texts may have to do more with sibling rivalry (between Ba'lu and both Yammu and Môtu) than with a rebellion to overthrow 'Ilu.[36] The deity lists found at Ugarit (KTU 1.47, 1.102, 1.118, 1.148; cf. RS 20.024)[37] are not all uniform in their presentation (a fact further complicated by what may be hierarchical listings of deities elsewhere in a variety of formats).[38] Nonetheless, the prominent position of 'Ilu in these lists is "fairly stable" (cf. de Moor 1970: 219). See too KTU 1.65, which describes the "family of 'Ilu" as well as attributes of 'Ilu's grace and constancy.[39] Another text, reflecting the fusion of Hurrian elements in Ugaritic society (KTU 1.28), praises 'Ilu as an exalted high god (Dijkstra 1993). Note too in this vein the common epithet of "king" (*mlk, mlk ab šnm, mlk dyknnh*) applied to 'Ilu in the mythological texts and his royal portrayal in KTU 1.23 (cf. Lewis forthcoming a).[40] It is perplexing to see scholars who, despite evidence to the contrary, say that the "title ['king'] is not applied to El in the Ugaritic inscriptions but to Baal."[41] Rather than seeing Baal's kingship as replacing 'Ilu's, most scholars assert that the two kingships work in tandem but on different levels. Mark Smith summarizes well:

> Both El and Baal are called "king" (*mlk*)[42] though in complementary ways: El remains the executive order of the universe and Baal is the sustainer of the cosmos. El is not deposed in an active struggle with Baal; nor is El degraded or demoted by Baal. El retains his dignity in a way comparable to Ea in Enuma Elish.... El and Baal differ more in function than in realm.[43]

This is not to say that 'Ilu is omnipotent, though some have suggested his role as a divine warrior (cf. KTU 1.6.6.27–29).[44] He does show signs of weakness, and any reflex of a warrior tradition is minimized in light of the battle prowess of ʿAnatu and Baʿlu. In addition, cultic prayers, such as the one embedded in the ritual text KTU 1.119, show us that when faced with a crisis many Ugaritians looked to Baʿlu for military help. In the ritual section of this text, which precedes a description of the city under siege, offerings are presented to Baʿlu-Ugarit, that is, Baʿlu who was seen to be the protective deity of the city. Despite the royal theology of the Kirta Epic, where ʾIlu is the patron of kings (cf. too KTU 1.23), it seems that Baʿlu was more prominent as the dynastic god, to judge from the use of *(h)addu* as the only divine element occurring in royal names (Smith 1994b: 90).

The Hittite Elkunirsha Myth

Before leaving the Late Bronze Age, one should mention traces of the Semitic deity El in the Hittite myth of Elkunirsha and Ashertu, preserved only in fragments from approximately the thirteenth century BCE.[45] While native Hittite myths are found imbedded in ritual texts, many Hittite myths are of foreign (primarily Mesopotamian) origin. From the basic outline and divine persona of the Elkunirsha myth, scholars typically conclude that Hatti also imported this "Canaanite" tale from the northern Syrian coast even though the detailed storyline is not preserved in any extant Ugaritic text. In contrast, Itamar Singer (2007: 637; cf. Dijkstra 2013: 83) refers to this imported myth as "West Semitic/ Amorite" (without christening it as "Canaanite"), arguing for its origin "from inner Syria and beyond" due to its mention of "the abode of Elkunirsha [being located] at the source of the Euphrates."

Elkunirsha, the husband of the goddess Ashertu, is described as living in a tent (from which Röllig [1999a: 280] infers a nomadic cultural setting). The name Elkunirsha is evidently the Hittite translator's rendering of "El, the Creator of Earth" (*ʾl qn ʾarṣ*),[46] an epithet known elsewhere: (1) in the eighth-century BCE Phoenician-Luwian inscription from Karatepe (KAI 26A III: 18); (2) in a partially restored eighth-/seventh-century BCE Jerusalem inscription ([*ʾl*] *qn ʾrṣ*);[47] (3) in late Aramaic texts from Palmyra (cf. too *bʿ[l]šmwn qnh dy rʿh* from Hatra; KAI 244:3); and (4) in a Neo-Punic text from Leptis Magna (Miller 1980). A reflex is also to be found in Genesis 14:19, 22, which mentions "El Elyon, Creator of Heaven and Earth" (*ʾēl ʿelyôn qōnēh šāmayim wāʾāreṣ*).[48] If *qnh* refers to creation, as seems almost certain despite dissenting voices, then reference to El here as "creator" (*qn*) nicely pairs with Ugarit's ʾAthiratu, who bears the epithet *qnyt ilm*, "creatress of the gods."[49]

In 2013 Dijkstra published a fragmentary Hittite prayer to Elkunirsha that is even more tantalizing. What we have preserved of the text refers to a libation ritual petitioning the deity as "Lord of the Dream/Sleep, Son of the Dark Earth [i.e., the netherworld], husband [or brother?] of the Sun Goddess of the Earth [i.e., the netherworld], Deliverer." In addition, Elkunirsha is referred to as "Lord of the Dream, evil dreams, evil shortened years, shortened months, shortened days" (see Dijkstra 2013: 79–80). It seems clear here that the deity Elkunirsha was perceived to be able to counter ominous dreams (born of the netherworld?) that afflicted the sufferer. At Ugarit we read of the deity 'Ilu appearing to King Kirta in a dream (even providing him with ritual instructions) in order to secure a wife and an heir (KTU 1.14.1.35–1.14.3.51). In the Baal Cycle, 'Ilu himself has a dream (yes, even the gods dream!) that portends the return of Baal from the netherworld (KTU 1.6.3.1–21). All these data are fragmentary, yet there is a clear indication that in the Late Bronze Age supplicants of the Northern Levant looked to an El figure (Hittite Elkunirsha; Ugaritic 'Ilu) to address their worries, from familial concerns to chthonic perils. Comparatively, Dijkstra (2013: 86–87) concludes that such broadly attested notions of an El figure as "the Lord of Sleep and Dreams" exhibit a deeply rooted tradition that lies behind the notion of "Yhwh as the El who neither slumbers nor sleeps and is able to deliver the worshipper from all perils of the night." To assess such a claim, one must determine the vibrancy of El worship in the Iron Age.

El in the Iron Age

Some scholars assert that the deity El virtually disappears as one approaches the Iron Age except for Israel, where El loses his independent nature as he is conflated with Yahweh. Such reconstructions are based in part on misunderstandings of the Ugaritic texts that assume (1) that there was a major conflict between 'Ilu and Ba'lu (Oldenburg 1969) and (2) that 'Ilu/El was a *deus otiosus*. Karel van der Toorn (1992a: 87) says as much when he writes the following: "El is a common Northwest Semitic god to whom the devotion is largely rhetoric in the first millennium B.C.E. Having turned into a *deus otiosus*, his place was gradually taken by Baal-shamem or Baal-shamayin." Once scholars assume that El has lost his status, they argue that the Ugaritic evidence is irrelevant for understanding the nature of El in the Syro-Cannanite religions of the Iron Age (see Rendtorff 1966; 1993a; 1994; Niehr 1990: 3–6, 7–22; 1996: 46). As noted earlier, 'Ilu was not dethroned or castrated by Ba'lu at Ugarit nor was he thought to be impotent.

Even though the Northwest Semitic inscriptional material we have at our disposal does not constitute a large corpus, it nonetheless underscores El's presence in the Iron Age and cautions against reducing El worship to mere rhetoric.[50] El is regularly positioned in the second slot (after Hadad) in the eighth-century BCE Sam'alian (Aramaic) pantheon (cf. KAI 214.2–3, 11, 18–19; KAI 215.22).

In another eighth-century BCE Old Aramaic text, El (paired with Elyan) is one of the gods invoked to witness a treaty (discussed later). According to Edward Lipiński (2000: 614), "The name ʾIl is the commonest theophorous element in the Aramaic personal names of the first millennium B.C. and it certainly reflects the importance of the cult of ʾIl among the early Arameans."[51] Walter Aufrecht (1999) argues that El, and not Milcom, was the chief deity of the Ammonites.[52] Rainer Albertz and Rüdiger Schmitt (2012: 341) write that "all selected Levantine onomasticons show a considerable portion of El-names."[53] Concurring with the conclusions of Ingo Kottsieper's analysis (1997: 25–50), they note how "El still played a significant role in the Levant of the 1st millennium. . . . El was still regarded as a high god, but his activity was seen to be particularly focused on the protection of individuals, whereas Hadad, Baal, and other deities gained more prominence in political realms." Albertz and Schmitt (2012: 354–355) go on to suggest that "the Hebrew Bible presents a similar picture" (with El being tied especially to family religion and Yahweh to the political sphere), and our analysis will largely bear this out.[54] Such analyses would also be buttressed by the study of Ryan Thomas (2019) if he is correct that in the first millennium BCE the god El is to be equated with the god Gad as the deity responsible for one's personal good fortune and fate (cf. the common noun *gad*).

In short, when placed alongside the El worship attested in the biblical corpus (not to mention later Phoenician and Old South Arabic material) and the presence of bull iconography in the archaeological record (see Chapter Five), one concludes along with Alberte Naccache (1996: 255) that "our perception of a change [in El's status] might simply be due to the randomness of the available data, and that the Canaanite/'Phoenician' and Aramaic conception of El's nature had remained basically the same as that held by the Amorites." Thus it makes more sense to side with those scholars who argue for the ongoing cult of El in the Iron Age.[55]

El and the God of the Fathers

In the biblical corpus, the origin of El worship is concentrated in the patriarchal narratives that have occasioned well-worn debates regarding their historicity. Past scholarship has seen the likes of John Bright (1981: 97), who argued, in the spirit of his teacher William Foxwell Albright, that "the patriarchal religion as depicted in Genesis is no anachronism, but represents a historical phenomenon." In contrast, Thomas Thompson (1974: 314), in the spirit of Julius Wellhausen, countered that "the quest for the historical Abraham is . . . fruitless," and it is this view that has been widely embraced by historians and archaeologists alike in the generations that followed, including up to the present. Along with such historical debates, we find a substantial reassessment of Pentateuchal source criticism. Once built upon the sure foundation of the documentary hypothesis, with subsequent work being variations on its theme, it has for the last few decades been characterized by considerable instability (cf. Chapter Three).

Nonetheless, modern historians of Israelite religion insist that one can uncover a "critically assured minimum" (Mettinger 1988: 56) from which to work. David N. Freedman, in a series of seminal articles[56] building on earlier work with Frank Moore Cross,[57] argues that truly archaic poetry (e.g., Exod 15, Ps 29, Judg 5, Num 23–24, Gen 49) can be identified through orthographic, prosodic, and linguistic analysis.[58] Smith (2002a: 54–57) uses such poetry to show how a variety of Canaanite deities converge in "Israel's earliest history."[59] More recently, Albertz's sociological approach asserts that though the patriarchal traditions suffer from inaccuracies, their historical value remains an open question. He contends that though "the cultural milieu of Palestine presupposed by the patriarchal narratives . . . does not go back beyond the conditions of Iron Age I," the tradition about patriarchal religion "differs markedly at a series of points from Yahwistic religion." Thus he insists that "it is hardly possible to regard the view of the beginnings of the religion of Israel as a whole projected in the Pentateuch as a theological fiction of later utopians" (1994: 24, 28; cf. Albertz and Schmitt 2012: 52–56). Similarly, van der Toorn's study concludes that "early Israelite religion consisted of a variety of local forms of family religion" (1996b: 255; see Ackerman's [2008a] analysis of Judg 17–18, building on the work of Stager [1985a]). According to van der Toorn (1996b: 65), this religion provided "the ground from which national religion eventually sprang" but also had to be reconciled with "a new type of religion, promoted and patronized by the state, and focusing on Yahweh as the god of the Israelite nation."

The point of departure for many historians of religion has been Albrecht Alt's study of the "the God of the Fathers," originally published in 1929. Alt made a clear distinction between the El deities mentioned in the patriarchal sagas (El Bethel, El Olam, El Roi, El Elyon, El Shadday)—to which he added El Berit from Judges 9:4, 46—and the deities referred to as "the god of my/your/their father" or "the god of Abraham/Isaac/Jacob." The former, which Alt (1968: 6, 19, 37) called "the Elim," represented "a very ancient type of religious practice" involving minor deities (numina) associated with local Palestinian sanctuaries. The latter, the *theoi patrōoi*, were nameless and siteless. In other words, "the god of the father" did not bear a personal name, but was identified by the name of the person (the head of the clan or tribe) who first encountered the deity. Thus we come across "the Shield of Abraham" (Gen 15:1; see Alt 1968: 37–38, 85 n. 179), "the Fear of Isaac" (Gen 31:42, 53), and "the Mighty One of Jacob" (Gen 49:24). Such a personal encounter did not occur at a particular site, underscoring for Alt the nomadic character of the religion. Only at a later point were these three individual cults woven into an artificial worship of "the god of the father*s*" (cf. Exod 3:13, 15–16; 4:5)—that is, "the God of Abraham, Isaac, and Jacob" (cf. Exod 3:6, 15–16; 4:5). For support, Alt drew upon late Nabatean, Palmyrene, and Greek inscriptions that attested nomadic peoples who worshipped deities named after individuals.

It is ironic that the very year that Alt's treatment appeared was the same year that the Ugaritic tablets were first discovered, with their rich documentation of El worship. This material, as well as the proliferation of discoveries from the ancient Near East such as texts documenting Mesopotamian personal gods, has led to a major reassessment of Alt's work. Critics have faulted Alt on many grounds, especially his overall notion of a nomadic ideal and his reliance on late comparative material (Cross 1973: 3–12; Mettinger 1988: 53–74; Albertz 1994: 28, 250 n. 19). In contrast to Alt's schema, personal gods and clan deities from Mesopotamia were not restricted to nomadic groups, nor were they nameless (indeed, they could even be high gods) or siteless. The weakest part of Alt's construction was his demotion of the deity El to a numen whose only purpose was to legitimize a local shrine. Rather, Alt's so-called Elim actually bore the proper name of El, and all of them (with the lone exception being El Shadday) were associated with a particular site. What remains of Alt's insights is the personal character of these deities, which has been underscored by more recent studies on the familial and kinship ties of the patriarchal deities.

Who, then, are these biblical El deities, and how should we characterize El worship in ancient Israel? According to biblical tradition, El deities are associated with specific locales. The deity associated with the eponymous ancestor Isra*el* (= Jacob) is localized at Shechem. El Elyon is associated with Salem (Gen 14:18–22), El Roi with Beer-Lahai-Roi (Gen 16:13), El Olam with Beer-Sheba (Gen 21:33), and El Bethel with Bethel (Gen 31:13; 35:7). El Shadday is the only El deity without locale, the relevance of which will be addressed later in this chapter.

Shechemite El/El Berith

The clearest evidence of the worship of an El deity from Israelite tradition is Genesis 33:20, which mentions the worship of the Shechemite deity called ʾēl ʾĕlōhê yiśrāʾēl. This name refers to "El, the god of (the patriarch) Israel" rather than a redundant generic expression: "god, the god of Israel." Pope (1955: 15) comments that "mere comparison of the unique formula ʾēl ʾĕlōhê yiśrāʾēl with the common one YHWH ʾĕlōhê yiśrāʾēl should convince one that ʾēl in this case is as much a proper name as is YHWH." Similarly, "I am El, the god of your father" in Genesis 46:3 is preferable to a redundant alternative. This is corroborated by other references to Shechemite religion mentioning the worship of El Berith in his temple (*bêt ʾēl bĕrît*; Judg 9:46; cf. 8:33, 9:4). I have argued elsewhere that the expression *baʿal bĕrît* in Judges 8:33; 9:4 most likely refers to El's epithet as "the lord of the covenant," who was viewed as the patron of the city (Lewis 1996a).[60] Thus one may plausibly suggest, following Cross (1973: 49), that there once existed the full epithet "El, the lord of the covenant" (*ʾēl baʿal bĕrît*), similar to "El, the god of Israel" (*ʾēl ʾĕlōhê yiśrāʾēl*) at Shechem. Possible iconographic representations of Shechemite El include two Late Bronze Age figurines, yet their identity is far from certain. One is a benign standing bronze from Tell Balâṭah (see Fig. 7.4), the other an enthroned (but beardless) figurine with a cup in his right hand that is without provenance yet was said to have come from Nablus (see Fig. 5.42; Lewis 1996a: 416–422). See too the presence of standing stones (*masseboth*) within the (Iron I?) Temple 1 at Shechem that may also be symbolic of El worship. (See Chapter Five, pp. 172–174, and Stager 1999, 2003.)

El Elyon

The composite title of the deity known as El Elyon (an alternative translation being "God the Most High") is used only in Genesis 14:18–22 and Psalm 78:35. In the former we read of Melchisedek, king of Salem, who was also "priest of El Elyon." Melchisedek blesses Abram with the following blessing:

> Blessed be Abram to El Elyon [*lĕʾēl ʿelyôn*][61]
> Creator of heaven and earth [*qōnēh šāmayim wāʾāreṣ*],
> Blessed be El Elyon [*ʾēl ʿelyôn*],
> Who has delivered [*miggēn*] your enemies into your hand.

The supremacy of El Elyon is emphasized by attributing to him the title "the creator of heaven and earth" (*qōnēh šāmayim wāʾāreṣ*), a variant of which (*ʾl qn ʾrṣ*) was well known in the West Semitic environs of the Late Bronze and Iron Ages (see the earlier discussion of the Elkunirsha myth). Psalm 78:34–35 recounts past divine deeds in the following way (according to the MT):

> When he slew them, they sought him;
> They repented and sought El [*ʾēl*] earnestly.

> They remembered that God [*ʾĕlōhîm*] was their rock,
> El Elyon [*ʾēl ʿelyôn*] their redeemer.

El and Elyon: Two Distinct Deities or One and the Same?

Scholars debate whether El and Elyon are distinct deities or one and the same with ʿelyôn ("the Most High") functioning as an epithet of El. And if these problems were not enough, we also have to wrestle with the identification of Elyon with Yahweh.

To help sort through these questions, scholars have used extra-biblical occurrences of the name Elyon to reconstruct the history of El Elyon in the Bible. Regrettably, this has been done in an uneven fashion without much concern for epigraphy and comparative methodology. For example, Johannes de Moor suggests that if his reading of KTU 111.17–18 is correct (he reads ʾly[n] ʾil mlk, "Elyon, El the King"), "this would be the first confirmation that in Ugarit too El and Elyon were one and the same divine being" (1979: 652–653; 1980: 185 n. 73a). Yet this reading is not confirmed by KTU³, which reads .l. il mlk. Nowhere else at Ugarit do we have reference to the deity El Elyon. In contrast, it is Baʿlu who is twice called "the Most High" (ʿly), as he provides rain (KTU 1.16.3.4–8).

G. Levi Della Vida (1944), followed in part by Rolf Rendtorff (1967), argues that El Elyon is not an original title and "corresponds to no actual deity in the Canaanite pantheon." Rather, the term is an artificial combination resulting from "theological speculation." To prove the independent status of Elyon, they rely on two extra-biblical sources, Philo of Byblos and one of the Sefire inscriptions, each of which is problematic upon closer examination. Other scholars have followed suit, with Philo of Byblos serving as the point of departure. Thus Claus Westermann (1985: 204) writes that Philo of Byblos is "the closest parallel" to biblical El Elyon with its mention of "Elioun, called Most High."

A detailed discussion of Philo of Byblos (ca. 70–160 CE) can be found in Chapter Six (pp. 255–256). We agree with those scholars who call into question the degree to which this material can be used to recover accurate Canaanite lore of the Late Bronze and Iron Ages. Thus Eric Elnes and Patrick Miller (1999: 294) are correct when they assert that "closer inspection of Philo's account betrays a conflation of traditions that may not be true to their earlier forms.... His understanding of Elioun as an independent deity may reflect first century influences."

The Sefire material (Old Aramaic inscriptions coming from the mid-eighth century BCE) is far more relevant, yet it has been overinterpreted by those using it to prove an independent status of Elyon. Della Villa (1944) and Rendtorff (1967) state that El and Elyon are mentioned as two distinct deities in Sefire I A (KAI 222) line 11 based on numerous pairs of deities mentioned in the preceding and following lines. Thus for Rendtorff ʾl wʿlyn is a pair of deities, not the double name of a single deity, as we have elsewhere. Yet the context is far more complicated. As pointed out by Cross (1973: 51), Choon-Leong Seow (1989: 52 n. 146), and Elnes and Miller (1999: 294–295), the pairing is not uniform. Most of the pairs are natural pairs (binary opposites such as Heaven and Earth, Abyss and Springs, Day and Night) or god and consort (e.g., Marduk and Zarpanit, Nergal and Las). Clearly, El and Elyon are neither binary opposites nor husband and wife. In addition, El and Elyon occur after a structural break mentioning a single deity (Hadad of Aleppo) and the *sbt* (Sibitti, a group of seven gods known from Mesopotamian texts). Thus while *'l w'lyn* could refer to two distinct (but closely associated deities), the term could also be the double name of a sole deity (cf. such frequent use at Ugarit, perhaps for the option of writing synonymously parallel bicola; cf. KTU 1.17.5.10–11). Compare what may be a similar double name, Shamash-and-Nur, in Sefire I A (KAI 222) line 9.[62] In short, both Sefire and Philo of Byblos provide inconclusive data for the independent status of Elyon.

When we then come to the Bible, we see that there is minimal evidence here too for Elyon standing alone. Rendtorff (1967: 168) states that "in the Old Testament we find a number of passages mentioning *'lywn* as an independent divine name," yet he gives no citations. Pope (1955: 55) cites Psalm 9:3 and Isaiah 14:14. The former is explicitly linked with Yahweh in Psalm 9:2 (see the text listed later). In Isaiah 14:14 Elyon does stand alone, yet the expression "the stars of El" (*kôkĕbê 'el*) is in close proximity in the previous verse, making one lean toward El associations.[63] The same may be true for the independent use of Elyon in Deuteronomy 32:8 (discussed later). Likewise, in Psalm 78 we have reference to rebelling against Elyon, yet the double name El Elyon soon follows (Ps 78:17, 34–35). In light of Elyon frequently being attached to both El and Yahweh in the Hebrew Bible (cf. too *bêt ḥôrôn 'elyôn* in Josh 16:5) and the use of *'ly* for Baal in KTU 1.16.3.4–8, it seems reasonable to conclude, along with Elnes and Miller (1999: 295), that Elyon "was a common epithet in the West Semitic region, applied at different times and in different cultures to any god thought to be supreme."[64]

Elyon Traditions Associated with El

The associations of Elyon with El traditions are many. We have already listed the two occurrences of the joint name "El Elyon" (Gen 14:19–20 and Ps 78:34–35) and the collocation of Elyon with the "stars of El" in Isaiah 14:13–14.

Excursus: Elyon Traditions in The Elohistic Psalter

It should be noted that Psalm 78 is a part of the so-called Elohistic Psalter, a scholarly designation referring to Psalms 42–83 that may have undergone an editorial process that systematically replaced the name of Yahweh with that of *'ĕlōhîm*.[65] Some scholars (see, for example, Kraus's commentaries [1988, 1989]) try to reflect a more original text by translating Yahweh wherever *'ĕlōhîm* occurs in the MT of Psalms 42–83.

Thus the Elyon tradition in Psalm 78:34–35 may refer to Yahweh rather than ʾĕlōhîm. Nonetheless, the double name El Elyon in Psalm 78:35 clearly exhibits an (earlier?) association of the Elyon epithet with El. The same could be concluded about Psalm 57:3, where presumably Yahweh Elyon parallels El (MT reads ʾĕlōhîm ʿelyôn// ʾēl; discussed later).[66]

If the Elohistic Psalter substitution hypothesis is correct, we also have a psalmist crying out to Yahweh (MT ʾĕlōhîm) as he reflects back on "the days of old, the years long past" (yāmîm miqqedem šĕnôt ʿôlāmîm; Ps 77:6 [Eng 77:5]). In this prayer of affliction he continues:

> Has El [ʾēl] forgotten to be gracious?
> Has he in anger shut up his compassion?
> I say: "It is my sickness[67]
> That the right hand of Elyon has changed." (Ps 77:10–11 [Eng 77:9–10])

Even if the word ʾĕlōhîm in Psalm 77:2, 4, 14 (Eng 77:1, 3, 13) originally read Yahweh, El traditions seem to be clear, to judge from the Ugaritic texts where the god El is known for his compassion and healing. Compare also the echo of El and Yahweh in Psalm 77:14 (Eng 77:13), which asks, "Who is a great god [ʾēl] like Yahweh [MT mî ʾēl gādôl kēʾlōhîm]?"

A fourth text coming from the Elohistic Psalter is Psalm 82:1, which contains El and Elyon in descriptions of the divine council. In this fascinating text (which is treated in detail in Chapter Nine), Yahweh (MT ʾĕlōhîm) takes his place among the gods (ʾĕlōhîm) who are assembled in "the council of El" (ʿădat ʾēl; Ps 82:1). Several verses later these same gods (ʾĕlōhîm) are addressed as "the sons of Elyon" (bĕnê ʿelyôn). Thus, even if this psalm comes from a Yahweh tradition, the association of Elyon with an El tradition is clear to see. David Frankel (2010) goes so far as to argue that El is the speaker of Psalm 82:6–8, playing the role of the high judge, in which he condemns the gods and appoints Yahweh to rule in their place.

The oldest El Elyon tradition in the Bible seems to be the synonymously paired terms in one of the Balaam oracles:

> The oracle of him who hears the words of El [ʾimrê ʾēl],
> who knows the knowledge [daʿat] of Elyon [ʿelyôn],
> who sees [yeḥĕzeh] the vision [maḥăzēh] of Shadday [šadday].
>   (Num 24:16; cf. 24:4)[68]

This remarkable triplet, which has "the earmarks of early Hebrew poetry" (Levine 1993: 74; cf. Milgrom 1990: 476), has been dated as early as the eleventh/

tenth century BCE by some (Albright 1944; Freedman 1976: 66–67; 1980: 88–90; Seow 1989: 48 n. 132; cf. Toews 1993: 45) and to the ninth/eighth century by others (Coogan 1987a: 116–118). The triplet contains three of the patriarchal designations for the deity (El, Elyon, Shadday). Though the prose narrative into which this pericope is placed is a Yahweh tradition, the poetry reflects clear El traditions (cf. El Shadday and the identical *'imrê 'ēl* in Psalm 107:11; see too the archaic expression *'ēl dē'ôt* in the Song of Hannah [1 Sam 2:3]). A similar couplet is found in Psalm 73:11, where a negative protagonist is heard to say:

"How can El know [*yāda' 'ēl*]?
Is there knowledge [*dē'â*] with Elyon ['*elyôn*]?" (Ps 73:11)

Baruch Levine has argued that the poetry of the Balaam pericope in Numbers 22–24 actually stems from an "El repertoire" relating the experience of Israelites in Transjordan.[69] This is further underscored by the possibility of El worship found in the extra-biblical Balaam story from Deir 'Alla (eighth century BCE).[70] In the Deir 'Alla texts, which seem to contain parallel vocabulary, we read of a seer named Balaam who "saw a vision like an oracle of El" (*wyḥz mḥzh kmś' 'l*; Combination I.1–2).[71] Later in the text we find reference to the Shaddayyin, which have been plausibly connected to the god Shadday (discussed later).

A common motif found in several El traditions is an association with visions and dreams. In addition to the references just mentioned in the Balaam oracles and the Deir 'Alla texts, we are reminded of El's dream revelation to Kirta at Ugarit (discussed earlier). Cross (1973: 177–186), followed by Tryggve Mettinger (1982a: 130–131) and Seow (1984; 1989: 30–31), has noted how dreams and visions (often in conjunction with the language of the divine council) characterize El's mode of self-revelation, as opposed to that of Baal, which is found in the storm theophany.

Elyon Traditions Associated with Yahweh: A Later Tradition?

Elyon traditions are also frequently found in association with Yahweh. Theoretically, the El Elyon traditions and the Yahweh Elyon traditions could date to the same time. Some have even argued for Yahweh being an epithet of El (Cross 1973: 71). It seems more likely that Yahweh's origin is to be found in the south (south/southeast of the Dead Sea; see Chapter Six) and that Yahweh worship was aligned in its earliest phases with the religion of storm gods. Although one cannot be certain, it seems that only at a later time did Yahweh worship coalesce with that of El Elyon. The notion that El worship predates that of Yahweh is reflected in El anthroponyms and toponyms (van der Toorn 1996b: 240–241) as well as Exodus 6:3, which, even though it comes from the late P source, seems to be an accurate reflection of ancient lore: "I am Yahweh. I appeared to Abraham, to Isaac, and to Jacob as El Shadday, but by my name Yahweh I did not make myself known to them."

This is supported by the Song of Moses in Deuteronomy 32:6b–9, which in its original form described a stage of tradition where Yahweh was seen as subordinate to El Elyon.[72] As it now stands in the MT, the El Elyon traditions have been fused onto Yahweh. Readers have already been prepared in Deuteronomy 4:19 to view Yahweh as the one who allots deities to all the nations (McClellan 2011: 70). As many scholars have recognized, the older El Elyon tradition imbedded here refers to the deity as both father (*ʾāb*) and creator (*qn*), both of which are El epithets (cf. the *ʾl qn ʾrṣ* discussion earlier).

Is not he [Yahweh] your father, who created you [*ʾābîkā qānekā*].
Who made you and brought you into existence [*yěkōněnekā*]?[73]

Remember the days of old,
Consider the years of many generations;

Ask your father, and he will tell you;
Your elders, and they will inform you.

When Elyon [*ʿelyôn*] allotted the nations,
When he divided the human race,

He fixed the boundaries of peoples,
Equal to the number of divine beings [*běnê ʾělōhîm*].[74]

Lo, his [Elyon's] people became Yahweh's portion,[75]
Jacob his allotted heritage ...

According to the reconstruction, which restores Deuteronomy 32:8 based on the Qumran readings from 4QDeut[j] and the Septuagint, (El) Elyon as god most high demonstrated his supremacy by establishing national boundaries and assigning land and people to various divine beings.[76] Where nations lived and the deities they worshipped did not come about by chance but were ordered by the sovereignty of the Most High (El Elyon).[77] The poem celebrates how Israel is especially fortunate because not only were they (El) Elyon's own special people, but they were assigned to Yahweh, who is presented as the divine heir apparent. Yahweh starts out in the telling of this story as one of the divine sons (*běnê ʾělōhîm*), and yet he ends up preeminent, ruling over Elyon's people and bearing the creator's epithets (*'āb, qn*). A similar story of "monolatry-in-process" is found in Psalm 82, which describes Yahweh condemning the unjust rulings of the gods (*'ĕlōhîm*) seated at the divine council (*'ădat 'ēl*).[78] These "sons of Elyon" (*bĕnê 'elyôn*) are then stripped of their immortality, as Yahweh (see the earlier discussion of the Elohistic Psalter) becomes sovereign over all the nations (Ps 82:7–8).[79] It is little wonder that we see widespread use of the epithet Elyon (which seems to be original with El) applied to Yahweh by adherents wishing to underscore his claim to supremacy.

Using Yahweh Elyon Traditions to Uncover El Elyon Motifs

When Yahweh came to be viewed as the preeminent deity, he was naturally assigned the epithet Elyon ("the Most High"). Hans-Joachim Kraus refers to the "archaic-hymnic quality" of this honorific appellation (1988: 175), and it is noteworthy that we find it concentrated in the psalter. It is instructive to assemble some of the Yahweh Elyon traditions in order to see if they can tell us anything about the character of El Elyon worship.[80] As with most biblical material, we are faced with the dilemma of uncovering earlier traditions through a later overlay. The precariousness of our enterprise must be underscored. Nonetheless, there are a few motifs in the Yahweh Elyon traditions that resonate with independent El Elyon traditions as well as with extra-biblical El worship.

Excursus: Psalmody Celebrating Yahweh as Elyon

(The Elohistic Psalter material [Psalms 42–83] is listed between the two sets of ***.)

I will praise Yahweh according to his righteousness,
I will sing the name of Yahweh Elyon.[81] (Ps 7:18 [Eng 7:17])

I will praise Yahweh with all my heart,
I will tell of all your wonders,
I will rejoice and exult in you,
I will sing of your name, Elyon. (Ps 9:2–3 [Eng 9:1–2])

Yahweh thundered in the heavens,
Elyon uttered his voice. (Ps 18:14 [Eng 18:13] = 2 Sam 22:14)[82]

The king trusts in Yahweh,
By the loyalty of Elyon he will not be moved. (Ps 21:8)

***

There is a river whose streams gladded the city of Yahweh [MT *ĕlōhîm*)],
the holy dwellings of Elyon. (Ps 46:5 [Eng 46:4])

Indeed, Yahweh is the awesome Elyon,
The great king over all the earth. (Ps 47:3 [Eng 47:2])

Offer a sacrifice of thanksgiving to Yahweh [MT *ĕlōhîm*],
Pay your vows to Elyon. (Ps 50:14)

I cry to Yahweh Elyon [MT *ĕlōhîm 'elyôn*],
To El, who avenges me. (Ps 57:3)

How good is Yahweh [MT *ĕlōhîm*] . . . ,
Yet they say, "How can El know?
Is there knowledge with Elyon?" (Ps 73:1, 11)

. . . the right hand of Elyon . . .
I will recall the deeds of Yah[weh] . . .
O Yahweh [MT *ĕlōhîm*], your ways are holy,
Who is a great god [*'ēl*] like Yahweh [MT *kē'lōhîm*]? (Ps 77:11–14 [Eng 77:10–13])

. . . rebelling against Elyon in the desert,
They tested El in their heart . . .
They spoke against Yahweh . . .
When he slew them, they sought him;
They repented and sought El [*'ēl*] earnestly.
They remembered that Yahweh [MT *ĕlōhîm*] was their rock,
El Elyon [*'ēl 'elyôn*] their redeemer . . .
Yet they tested and rebelled against Yahweh Elyon [MT *ĕlōhîm 'elyôn*]. (Ps
    78:17–18, 34–35, 56)

And may they know that you[83] alone Yahweh,
Are Elyon over all the earth. (Ps 83:19 [Eng 83:18])

***

Of Zion it will be said:
"This one and that one were born in her."
For Elyon himself will establish her;

> Yahweh records as he registers the peoples,
> This one was born there. (Ps 87:5–6)
>
> For you, Yahweh, are my refuge.
> You have made Elyon your haven. (Ps 91:9)[84]
>
> It is good to praise Yahweh,
> To sing praises to your name, Elyon. (Ps 92:2 [Eng 92:1])
>
> Indeed you, Yahweh,[85] are Elyon over all the earth
> You are greatly elevated above all the gods. (Ps 97:9)
>
> Give thanks to Yahweh . . .
> They cried to Yahweh in their trouble . . .
> Let them thank Yahweh . . .
> . . . for they had rebelled against the words of El ['imrê 'ēl],
> Spurned the counsel of Elyon ['ăṣat 'elyôn].
> . . . they cried to Yahweh in their trouble . . . (Ps 107:1, 11)

A review of this psalmody shows that the application of the title Elyon to Yahweh was ubiquitous. Many of the actions and features associated with Elyon are so generic that they could be applied to any deity (e.g., praises, sacrifices, vows, greatness, holiness). The wedding of older El traditions with Yahweh worship is so thorough that it is almost impossible to separate El Elyon attributes from Yahweh Elyon attributes. Nonetheless, there are a few motifs that were known to be used particularly of El. For example, Psalm 107:11 contains what looks like an independent couplet celebrating El Elyon, whose counsel is unwisely forsaken:

> They rebelled against the words of El ['imrê 'ēl],
> They spurned the counsel of Elyon ['ăṣat 'elyôn].

As presented in the full text, it is clear that Yahweh is the intended referent throughout Psalm 107 (so already Elnes and Miller 1999: 296). Yet the similar couplet ('imrê 'ēl//da'at 'elyôn) coming from the Balaam oracles (Num 24:16) argues for a more archaic El Elyon tradition that has been taken over and applied to Yahweh. We are reminded of stories from Ugarit celebrating El's decrees, wisdom, and counsel.

Seow has pointed out how Hebraic psalmody regularly uses Elyon to designate Yahweh "as the supreme deity in the divine council, with YHWH functioning like 'Ēl" (Seow 1989: 50–52, referring to Ps 97:9; 47:3; 83:19). The three occurrences of Elyon's rule "over all the earth" ('al kol hā'āreṣ) are fitting for El, the Creator of the Earth (*'l qn 'rṣ*). That this title, known to be used exclusively for El elsewhere (cf. the earlier description of its attestation in the Elkunirsha myth and the Karatepe inscription), is applied secondarily (in its fuller form) to Yahweh is clear from Genesis 14:18–22. In Genesis 14:19, we read of an older poetic blessing mentioning "El Elyon, Creator of Heaven and Earth" (*'ēl 'elyôn qōnēh šāmayim wā'āreṣ*). The later prose account that follows in 14:22 praises "Yahweh El Elyon, Creator of Heaven and Earth" (*yhwh 'ēl 'elyôn qōnēh šāmayim wā'āreṣ*). The secondary nature of the divine title—we would expect Yahweh Elyon—is clear to see (cf. LXX, Syr).

Even some Elyon associations listed earlier that are closely related to Yahweh need not be restricted to him. Thus the title of "king" (Ps 21:8; 47:3) is also at home in El traditions (cf. again Ugarit, where the title "king" [*mlk, mlk ab šnm, mlk dyknnh*] is regularly applied to El, who has a special regard for the earthly king Kirta, who was portrayed as his son). The mention of birth in the royal city (Ps 87:5–6) reminds us of El's involvement in granting children, especially to the royal line, at Ugarit. Even the notion of Elyon being one's redeemer and warrior (Ps 78:35; 57:3) is not out of the question for an El figure, although this may stem from Yahweh tradition, where it is far better attested.

El Roi

The El deity known as El Roi (*'ēl rŏ'î*), commonly translated "God of seeing," needs only brief comment due to its single occurrence in Genesis 16:13.[86] There is no attestation of this divine name in any cognate culture, although the notion of deities "seeing" the predicaments of their worshippers and then providing for their needs is common. Due to the lack of ancient Near Eastern background, scholars concentrate their efforts on the redactional character of this material and on the exact meaning of the name, with attention being paid to who saw whom. Did El see Hagar or did Hagar see El?[87]

The context is one of a surrogate wife's childbirth, specifically the promised birth of Ishmael to Hagar.[88] The promise is delivered through a divine messenger who speaks to Hagar, yet her response assumes that the messenger and the deity are one and the same (on the *mal'ak yhwh*, see Chapter Seven). The narrative in its present form stems from a Yahweh tradition, but scholars have long recognized that an El tradition lies behind the pericope both because of the name El Roi and because the expression "you shall call his name *yišmā'-'ēl* ['may El hear']" requires that El (and not Yahweh) be the deity who heard (*šāma'*) Hagar's distress in 16:11.[89] Some scholars even reconstruct El's name in place of Yahweh's in 16:11, although without textual warrant.[90] Mitchell Dahood (1968b) ingeniously translates it as "For Yahweh has heard you//El has answered you," yet his repointing of the text (and reliance on a resumptive double-duty suffix) adds up to an unlikely scenario. It seems far easier to assume that, like the Yahweh Elyon material, this is an El tradition that has been fused with Yahweh tradition.[91] When such a blending took place is hard to say. Albert de Pury (1999: 292), following John Van Seters (1975: 193, 288), argues that Genesis 16:13–14 is secondary and "could therefore be nothing more than the invention of the redactor" who created El Roi as "a pseudo-archaic divine name in the style of El Olam and El Shadday whom he probably knew from written or oral traditions about the Patriarchs." Yet the etiological character of 16:11–14 could reflect an older Ishmaelite tradition where a child (Ishma_el_) was named by his mother after a "god of seeing" (El Roi) who was worshipped at a sacred spring ('*ayin*) named Beer-Lahai-Roi.[92] The connection between El Roi as "a god who sees" and El's connections with visions elsewhere (cf. Num 24:16 and the Deir 'Alla text, both mentioned earlier) could suggest that this is genuinely archaic and perhaps part of an ancient "El repertoire," as envisioned by Levine. Compare too the etymology of the name of the well (*bĕʾēr laḥay rōʾî* = "the well [dedicated] to the living one who sees me"), which could designate an authentic toponym where an El figure was worshipped. The toponym seems to reflect a mixture of the name El Roi and the divine title *ʾel ḥay* known elsewhere (cf. Josh 3:10; Hos 2:1 [Eng 1:10]; Ps 84:3 [Eng 84:2]; etc.).[93]

As for who saw whom, most scholars assert that El Roi designates El "seeing" Hagar in the sense of seeing one's needs and rescuing one from a predicament. Many interpreters have deferred to Klaus Koenen (1988: 472), who concludes his analysis by translating the original text of Genesis 16:13 as follows: "You are 'the God who has seen/delivered me.' . . . Truly here have I seen [in the sense of met] the one who sees/delivers me." This analysis is in accord with traditional commentators, dating back at least as early as the medievals, who have rationalized that there is little difference between the *rōʾî* that occurs in the middle of the verse and the *rōʾî* that is at the end of the verse.

Yet there is the possibility that *rōʾî* could have referred to an older tradition wherein Hagar saw the deity (Hagar is clearly the subject of *rāʾîtî*). This is the understanding behind the RSV's rather free translation "Have I really seen God and remained alive after seeing him?" (See too NRSV, NEB.) Such translations show the lasting impact of Wellhausen on the field. It was Wellhausen (1957: 326 n. 1) who without textual warrant read *ʾĕlōhîm* for *hălōm* and inserted *wāʾeḥî*, "and I lived," prior to *ʾaḥărê* (see the BHS apparatus). Suffice it to say that the corrupt state of the text will prevent us from resolving this passage.[94] That seeing the deity can be lethal is a motif well attested in biblical lore (cf. *kî lōʾ yirʾanî hāʾādām wāḥay*, "a person cannot see me and live," in Exod 33:20; see Hendel 1997: 220–224 and Chapter Seven). At the same time, in special instances a favored person is allowed to see the divine without dying (see the discussion later in this chapter regarding Jacob seeing El at Peniel). In our passage, we clearly have God seeing (favoring) Hagar and Hagar seeing God in some sense of the word, whether it be physical sight (a non-lethal God sighting) or an experience of God's protection (see Koenen 1988). Nahum Sarna (1989: 121) argues that the vocalization El-rŏ'î demonstrates "a marvelous ambiguity" where "the several meanings are intended to be apprehended simultaneously."

El Olam

El Olam, which can be translated "the god of eternity," "the ancient god," or "El, the Eternal One," occurs only in Genesis 21:33.[95] Like most of our El traditions, it comes to us imbedded in a Yahweh tradition. Thus, as Yahweh–El Elyon (Gen 14:22) is secondary to El Elyon (Gen 14:19), so in Genesis 21:33 Yahweh–El Olam is secondary to an original El Olam, although the latter is not attested independently. The narrative itself—whose source-critical discussion has been called a "scholarly merry-go-round" by Westermann (1985: 346)—describes a treaty made between Abraham and Abimelech at a well at Beersheba and Abraham's planting of a sacred tree ('ešel).

Cross has stated that "the evidence ... is overwhelming to identify the epithet [El Olam] as an epithet of [Canaanite] 'El" (1973: 50). His argument (see Cross 1962a: 236–241; 1973: 18–20) was based in part on cognate evidence from Serabit el-Khadim, Ugarit, and Arslan Tash, all of which is now disputed. As mentioned previously, the reading of "El, the Ancient One" ('l ḏ'lm = 'il ḏū 'ōlami) in the proto-Sinaitic inscriptions is questionable.[96] Soon after the Ugaritic text KTU 1.108 was published, Cross suggested that rpu mlk 'lm (KTU 108.1) referred to El as "the Hale One, the eternal King" (1973: 16–17; 1974a: 245–246; so too L'Heureux 1979: 169–172). In contrast, today most scholars argue that the epithet refers to a deity other than El, with suggested candidates being Baal, Rapiu, Reshep, or Milku.[97] Finally, the phrase krt ln 'lt 'lm (KAI 27.8–10), which Cross and Saley (1970: 44–45; Cross 1973: 17) read as "The Eternal One [El] has made a covenant with us," is more regularly translated with the adjective "eternal" modifying the covenant and not the deity, as in Ziony Zevit's (1977: 11–12) translation: "Assur has established an eternal covenant with us."[98]

Nonetheless, there is good documentation that El was thought to be an ancient ("eternal") deity in the Late Bronze Age, a notion that then became a part of Iron Age Israelite lore. Late Bronze Syrian traditions include the description of 'Ilu at Ugarit as "the father of years." His elder status is also portrayed in both text and iconography with depictions of his gray hair and beard. We read twice that 'Ilu's wisdom is everlasting (ḥkmk 'm 'lm; KTU 1.3.5.30–31, 1.4.4.41–42). H. L. Ginsberg (1938a: 9; so too Pope 1955: 51; Cross 1962a: 240) also restored 'lm in KTU 1.10.3.5–7, so the text reads: "that our creator ['Ilu] is eternal ... unto all generations, is he who fashioned us" (*kqnyn 'l[m] kdrd<r> dyknn*). Even though 'Ilu's seniority and eternity fit well with his supremacy over the pantheon, other deities were also thought of as ancient or eternal—albeit for other reasons. Though Ba'lu doesn't bear the title *'lm*, in KTU 1.2.4.10 it is he who assumes "eternal kingship" (*tqḥ mlk 'lmk*).[99] Two deities who do bear the title *'lm* are *rpu* and Shapshu. While the exact identification of *rpu* eludes us, the deity's association with death makes the title "King of Eternity" (*rpu mlk 'lm*) a fitting one (KTU 1.108.1).[100] Similarly, the notion of the sun being eternal occasions the use of *'lm* as an epithet for the goddess Shapshu (*špš 'lm*, KTU 2.42).[101] From the Iron Age, compare the attestation of the deity "the Eternal Sun" (*špš 'lm*) in the Phoenician Karatepe inscription alongside two other senior deities, Baalshamem and El-Creator of Earth (KAI 26.A III.19; cf. A IV.2-3; on *'l qn 'rṣ*, see earlier discussion).[102]

In addition to the El Olam reference in Genesis 21:33, some scholars have suggested that Olam, as a substantivized adjective, occurs as an independent deity ("the Eternal One") in the Bible (Dahood 1968a: 215–216; Van den Branden 1990: 36).[103] In most of the cases suggested (especially those Dahood purported to have found in the Psalms), it is more likely that we have *'lm* referring to "eternity" rather than "the Eternal One."[104] And even though Dahood's overenthusiasm for advocating *'lm* referring to the deity has not met with acceptance, two of his suggestions retain some plausibility.[105] The syntax of the MT of Psalm 75:10 (Eng 75:9) (*'aggîd lĕ'ōlām*, "I will tell *to* eternity") has often been regarded as problematic.[106] Thus many scholars change the text to *'āgîl lĕ'ōlām*, "I will rejoice forever" (cf. LXX), and assume that a textual error led to a confusion between *'āgîl* and *'aggîd*. In 1964, Dahood suggested that the tradition of the MT suffered not from a textual error (mistaking *d* for *l*) but merely from a misdivision of the consonants. Thus he reconstructed the original text as *'agaddēl 'ōlām* by redividing the consonants. If Dahood is correct, we have an abbreviated title of El Olam parallel to the God of Jacob.

> I will extol [*'agaddēl*][107] the Eternal One [*'ōlām*],
> I will praise the God of Jacob [*'ĕlōhê ya'ăqōb*]. (Ps 75:10; cf. Ps 89:2)

Similarly, Psalm 73 contains the parallel El//Elyon in verse 11 followed by *'ōlām* in the next verse. But it is very unclear whether the phrase *šalwê 'ōlām*, a hapax legomenon, refers to the actions of the wicked ("eternally carefree") or to their negligence of the deity ("the Eternal One").[108]

Many scholars have seen a reflex of the deity El Olam in Deuteronomy 33:26–27.[109] That text reads:

> There is none like El, O Jeshurun,[110]
> Riding through the heavens to help you,[111]
> Through the skies in his majesty.

The God of Old [*'ĕlōhê qedem*] is a refuge,
Under [him?][112] are the arms of the Ancient One [*zĕrō'ōt 'ōlām*].

In particular, scholars note how the description of El here as an ancient deity (*'ĕlōhê qedem*) accords well with his nature elsewhere. El is he who existed "from everlasting to everlasting" before the mountains were born (Ps 90:2, *mē'ōlām 'ad 'ōlām 'attâ 'ēl*). The El Elyon tradition in Psalm 77:10-11 (Eng 77:9-10) is set back in "the days of old, the years long past" (*yāmîm miqqedem šĕnôt 'ôlāmîm*, Ps 77:6; Eng 77:5). While the translation "everlasting arms" is possible for Deuteronomy 33:27, a divine name forms a better parallel with "the God of Old."[113] Other reflexes of El's age may lie behind Isaiah 9:5 (Eng 9:6), which describes the illustrious king as "El, the Warrior, Eternal Father" (*'ēl gibbôr 'ăbî 'ad*).

As has already been pointed out, it seems clear from the name Yahweh-El-Olam in Genesis 21:33 that the name El Olam was appropriated by Yahweh worshippers. It is easy to see Yahweh as the "Rider of the Clouds" being referred to in Deuteronomy 33:26.[114] In this light, compare too the expression "Yahweh is an Eternal God" (*'ĕlōhê 'ôlām yhwh*) in Isaiah 40:28 (cf. Ps 90:1-2) and "Yahweh . . . is an Eternal King" in Jeremiah 40:10 (*yhwh . . . melek 'ôlām*). Though not using the word *'ôlām*, Psalm 102:25b-28 (Eng 102:24b-27) expresses the notion that Yahweh's years endure through all generations (*bĕdôr dôrîm šĕnôtêkā*) and thus have no end (*šĕnôtêkā lō' yittāmmû*). At an even later time, apocalyptic literature would pick up on the archaic El titles "The Most High who lives forever . . . whose dominion is eternal" (*'illāyā' . . . ḥay 'ālmā' . . . šālṭānēh šālṭān 'ālam/ḥē hā'ôlām*; Dan 4:31 [Eng 4:34]; 12:7) and "the Ancient of Days" (*'attîq yômayyā'*; Dan 7:13) to evoke memories of a distant past (Collins 1993: 231).

El Bethel

The biblical traditions about El worship and Bethel are concentrated in the Jacob narratives in Genesis 28:10-22; 31:1-17; and 35:1-16. Traditional source critics see these texts (apart from the P material in 35:9-15) to be mostly a mixture of J and E material, as evidenced by the varying names for the deity, Yahweh and Elohim.[115] The composite text in its fused state functions to underscore the cult of Yahweh. Nonetheless, vestiges of earlier El tradition remain in the text. These are visible not only in the name Beth*el* but also in P's storyline, which culminates in Genesis 35:10 with the renaming of Jacob as Isra*el* (cf. J's name change at Peni*el* ["the face of El"] in Gen 32:31). In Genesis 35:11, P goes on to identify the God (*'ĕlōhîm*) of these passages with another El figure, El Shadday (discussed later). In other biblical texts, Bethel is one of the locales of Jeroboam's bull shrines (1 Kgs 12:28–33), which have been connected to El worship (Cross 1973: 198–199; Toews 1993; see iconography discussion in Chapters Five and Seven).

The meaning of the name Bethel (*bêt-ʾēl*) is ambiguous, able to refer to "the house/temple of a god" or to "the house/temple of El," but in light of similar place names such as Beth Anat, Beth Horon, Beth Dagan, Beth Shemesh, Beth Baal-Meon, and so on, it seems more likely that Bethel (at least originally) contained a reference to the deity El (Sarna 1989: 399).[116] Similarly, the expression *ʾēl bêt-ʾēl* in Genesis 35:7, referring to the naming of an altar site, more likely refers to "El of Bethel" than to a generic alternative, "the god of the house of a god" (see Gen 33:20 and the naming of another altar site *ʾēl ʾĕlōhê yiśrāʾēl*, "El, the god of Israel"). Having argued here for El's presence, which is in accord with other biblical El traditions, we should note that there was a tendency in the later Masoretic tradition to tone down the appearance of El.[117] Thus in Genesis 31:13 we read of "*the god* of Bethel" (*haʾēl bêt-ʾēl*). Similarly, Genesis 35:3, which most likely originally read "Let us rise and go up to Bethel [*bêt-ʾēl*] so that I can build there an altar to El [*mizbēaḥ lĕʾēl*] who answered me," is presented in the Masoretic pointing as "so that I can build there an altar to *the god* [*lāʾēl*] who answered me" (cf. 35:1).

If the El material in these three narratives was not overcoated with later Yahweh tradition, we would be able to point out a number of ways in which El was seen to function. Due to the nature of the data at hand, the most we can do is suggest motifs that seem to be consistent with other El traditions and less so with later Yahweh traditions. Yet such a method can quickly become circular, and thus the tentativeness of such an endeavor needs to be stressed.

The deity portrayed in these Bethel traditions is associated with sacred space on a smaller scale (stones [Gen 28:11, 18, 22; 35:14],[118] *masseboth* [28:18–19, 22; 31:13; 35:14],[119] altars [35:1, 3, 7; cf. 12:8], terebinths [35:4], oaks [35:8]). He is portrayed as intimately involved in Jacob's life and his sustenance. He travels with Jacob wherever he goes (Gen 35:3), protects him on the way (Gen 28:15, 20), and keeps him from harm (Gen 31:7; 35:5). He provides him with children (Gen 28:14), flocks (Gen 31, passim), land (Gen 28:13, 15; 31:13), food, and clothing (Gen 28:20). This is in accord with one of the oldest passages in the Hebrew Bible, which describes El as "the Mighty One of Jacob" and "Shepherd" whose blessings are abundant (Gen 49:25; discussed later). Genesis 48:15 (traditionally E) also portrays Jacob describing his god as the one who has been his shepherd from the very day of his birth (*hārōʿeh ʾōtî mēʿôdî*). Jacob/Israel also refers to *seeing* (*rʾh*) his deity (identified as El in the place name Peniel) face-to-face in Genesis 32:31. This reminds us of Hagar's encounter with El Roi (previously mentioned).

The association of two additional motifs from the Bethel narratives, dreams and divine presence, with El are harder to isolate. The divine manifestations in these passages frequently accompany dreams (Gen 28:12; 31:10–11).[120] Even though Yahweh is frequently associated with dream revelation elsewhere in the Hebrew Bible, we shouldn't forget El's connection to such revelation. As noted, the characteristic association of dreams and visions with El occurs in the Ugaritic texts, the Balaam oracles, and the Deir ʿAlla texts. Granted, visions are not mentioned here in the Bethel narratives, but the collocation of dreams and visions elsewhere (cf. Isa 29:7; Dan 1:17) suggests that they are variant terms. Similarly, the promise of the presence of the deity ("I am/will be with you") that dominates Yahweh worship (e.g., Exod 4:12), and which has even been linked etymologically with the name Yahweh, occurs in our Bethel narratives to underscore the protection of the shepherding deity (Gen 28:15, 20; 31:3). Although it cannot be proved, who is to say that such a notion could not have originated with an El figure prior to it being absorbed for Yahweh?

El Shadday

Of all the El figures, El Shadday has received by far the most attention from scholars because of an ample supply of puzzling questions. What is the ancient etymology of Shadday and how does this square with the translations of the Septuagint (*pantokratōr*, "all-powerful") and Vulgate (*omnipotens*, "omnipotent"), which elevate the deity to preeminent status? Why does the literary strand known as the Priestly Source (P) use this title in Exodus 6:3 to sum up the worship of the patriarchs prior to the revelation of the name Yahweh in Moses' time? Is P's account a late fiction or does it preserve ancient memories? Does the fact that Shadday occurs most frequently in the book of Job, widely acknowledged to be a late book, argue against the antiquity of the name? If so, then how can some scholars assert that El Shadday is the oldest deity in the Bible? Finally, why is this El deity not associated with a particular locale, a characteristic feature of the other El figures?

Even though most scholars recognize the pitfalls of reconstructing religion out of etymological speculation, this has not deterred them when it comes to the nature of El Shadday. A glance at standard treatments reveals that far more attention has been given to the etymology of the name El Shadday than to the deity himself. Modern translations, which almost universally translate El Shadday as "God Almighty," reveal that the Septuagint's understanding has won the day—at least in practical use—despite its near total rejection by historians of religion. These philologians assume that the Septuagint translators' understanding of God as *pantokratōr* arose far later than the biblical period. L. F. Hartman (1971: 677; cf. BDB; Mettinger 1988: 70) suggests that this rendering is "based on ancient rabbinic interpretation" that divided Shadday into two parts (*še*, "who" + *day*, "enough"), resulting in "He who is self-sufficient." Yet there is no evidence of the antiquity of this etymology. Even the Talmudic tractate to which Hartman refers (Ḥagigah 12a) does *not* contain the use of *day* as a statement by the divine about his own self-sufficiency, but rather treats it as a rebuke ("Enough!") limiting the expansion of the world at the time of creation.[121]

What then does the name El Shadday mean, and are our translations based on the Septuagint anachronistic? The numerous and lengthy etymological discussions (which include debates about the inconsistent use of sibilants in the various cognate languages) cannot detain us here; readers are directed to the many treatments of the topic.[122] Three possible etymologies are worthy of consideration.

El Shadday as "the God of the Mountain"

The etymology that has been most widely adopted views El Shadday as "the God of the Mountain," linking Shadday with Akkadian *šadû*, "mountain," and *šaddûʾa/šaddāʾu* "mountain dweller, highlander" (cf. CAD). Though first proposed by Franz Delitzsch in 1896, this etymology gained popularity through the work of Albright (1935), Cross (1962: 244–250; 1973: 52–60), and the various lexica of their time (BDB, KB). Lest one object to a Mesopotamian origin of the lexeme, adherents of this view promptly add that the underlying root is *ṯdy*, "breast," which is common in Hebrew and related metaphorically to mountains (cf. Cross 1973: 55 n. 44). El is associated with mountains in the lore of both ancient Syria and Israel, but this is hardly unique in the ancient Near East, where "we are embarrassed with the plenitude of deities associated with mountains" (Cross 1973: 57).[123] Shadday is used alongside divine mountains (particularly "[Mt.] Salmon" and "Mt. Bashan") in Psalm 68:15–17 (Eng 68:14–16) and is combined with a similar motif in the proper name *ṣûrî-šadday*, "Shadday is my Rock."[124]

While proponents of this etymology point out the way in which El functions on mountains (as head of the divine council, making decrees, etc.), others note that El Shadday in the biblical tradition is more involved in providing the blessings of offspring and fertility (Gen 17:1–2; 28:3–4; 35:11; 49:25; see Mettinger 1988: 72; Albertz 1994: 33–34). For example, Genesis 28:3 tells of Isaac blessing Jacob with the following words: "May El Shadday bless you, make you fruitful, and multiply you that you become a congregation of peoples." To these scholars, it is far more fitting to think of a more literal etymology where *ṯdy* refers to "breast" and not, by extension, to "mountain." Thus El Shadday should be viewed in accord with Genesis 49:25 as the one who brings "the blessings of breasts [*šādayîm*] and womb" (discussed later).

El Shadday as "the God of the Steppe Lands"

Other scholars, some unnecessarily having a problem associating a male deity with breasts (e.g., Albertz 1994: 31), argue that El Shadday refers to "El of the Wilderness/Steppe" and should be equated with Hebrew *śādeh*, "field" (e.g., Weippert 1961a; de Vaux 1978: 276–278; Wifall 1980; Knauf 1999; Albertz 1994: 31). These scholars overcome the objection that the initial sibilants of *šadday* and *śādeh* are not identical by arguing that Shadday preserved a pronunciation that predated Hebrew. For support they note that the Ugaritic texts refer to the deities *'il šd(y)*, "El of the Steppe," and *'ttrt šd*, "Athtartu/Astarte of the Steppe."[125] In addition, one of the Amarna letters from Jerusalem contains the Canaanite gloss *ša-de₄-e* on the Akkadian word for field, *ugāru* (EA 287: 56; Rainey in Cross 1973: 54 n. 41; de Vaux 1978: 277).

The Ugaritic text KTU 1.108 has been used to provide a possible origin for the name El Shadday that connects the deity to the steppe lands (see Loretz 1980; Knauf 1999). The line in question is written without a word divider following the term suggested for Shadday. Thus one can read either *'il šd yṣd mlk* or *'il šdy ṣd mlk*. Dennis Pardee (1988a: 110) is inclined toward the latter on stylistic grounds. Some scholars truncate the phrase when they translate "El Shadī is hunting" or "El, in the wilderness he is hunting" (Knauf 1999: 750). The text is incomplete, and thus we should not build grand theories based on a single occurrence lacking adequate context. Nonetheless, the previous line seems to refer to "the god Ġanatu, the calf of El" (*'il ġnṯ 'gl 'il*), and thus structurally we would expect "the god Shadday, the hunter of Milku." That we have a deity Shadday seems clear, but his association with Milku (cf. too the god "Rapiu, the eternal king" in this text) makes one wonder if there are chthonic (and not animal) notions behind Shadday's hunting in this text (cf. *šēdu* and the PN Šadrapha; see Pardee 1988: 110).

A much better Ugaritic text for underscoring the connection between 'Ilu and fields or steppe lands is KTU 1.23 (see Lewis forthcoming a). In this text, the multivalent word *šd* can designate both fertile fields (KTU 1.23.13, 28) as well as steppe lands (parallel to *p'at mdbr* in KTU 1.23.68). Steppe lands, though lacking in rainfall, provided seasonal "shrub steppe" and "dry" vegetation that led to the predominance of sheep and goat pastoralism, supplemented by hunting activity. Such a scenario is depicted in KTU 1.23.67b–68, which has the ravenous "gracious gods" roaming the steppe lands and desert fringes in their hunting activity only to find hunting insufficient when compared to sustainable agricultural production. Coming to the rescue is 'Ilu as the guardian of the sown land (*nġr mdr'*), who provides bounty to his children. KTU 1.23 is an 'Ilu-centric text that celebrates how 'Ilu is the provider of cultivated agriculture, even viticulture. Arable fields are divine fields (cf. *šd 'ilm* in KTU 1.23.13).[126] Analogously, one could call to mind the Deuteronomic tradition—noted for its father/mother birthing language (see pp. 110–111)—whose vocabulary echoes that of KTU 1.23, with El protecting (*nṣr*) his child in the wilderness (*midbār*) as he nurses (*ynq*) him with honey and feeds him with the produce of the field (*śāday*), where he drinks fine wine (*tišteh ḥāmer*) made of grapes (*'ēnāb*) (Deut 32:6, 10, 13–14).

El Shadday as "the Destroyer"

A third etymology for Shadday is the most securely based in the Hebrew language, yet its greatest support stems more from folk etymology rather than from historical development. The Hebrew *šādad*, "to destroy," is common and even refers to divine destruction, but as a finite verb it is not used with the name Shadday. Yet two identical prophetic passages describe Yahweh's impending day of judgment as *kešōd miššadday*, "like destruction from Shadday" (Isa 13:6; Joel 1:15; cf. Job 5:17, 21). Folk etymologies, while not correct historically on linguistic grounds, are nonetheless reflective of popular understanding. On some popular level the god Shadday could be seen as a warrior deity. (The verbatim vocabulary in these two passages [cf. too Ezek 30:2–3], whether the result of literary borrowing or stemming from colloquial discourse, shows the popularity of the alliterative saying.) Jeremiah frequently uses the expression *šōdēd yhwh* to refer to Yahweh destroying his enemies (Jer 25:6; 47:4; 51:55; cf. Jer 12:12; 48:1, 8; 51:56; cf. Hos 10:2; Isa 33:1). Ezekiel's use of Shadday (1:24; El Shadday in 10:5) pictures a storm god's military theophany (*qôl* = thunder; *maḥăneh* = army), as pointed out by Cross.[127]

Some of those who object to this etymology do so apologetically. To their ear it seems harsh to worship a god whose etymology refers to him as "the destroyer." Yet such sensitivities were not felt by the ancients, who took great pride in celebrating God as the Divine Warrior who vanquished one's enemies. (See Chapter Eight.) Others object to this etymology for El Shadday because he is portrayed as a deity of blessing, especially granting progeny. Yet compare 'Ilu at Ugarit, who granted children and yet may have had warrior traits, though they were not central to his functions.[128] A closer look at the distribution of El Shadday in biblical texts shows that relatively few have to do with progeny, though those that do are concentrated in the patriarchal narratives and thus have been privileged in scholarly discourse. The book of Job, where the name Shadday occurs the most often, speaks of the "chastening," the "arrows," and the "wrath" of Shadday (Job 5:17; 6:4; 21:20). It is Shadday who brings terror (Job 23:16) and is even called Job's adversary (31:35). Granted, the subject of the book of Job is suffering, but the author did not shy away from associating the divine with such vocabulary. It is little wonder that the Greek rendering of El Shadday as *pantokratōr* occurs sixteen times in the book of Job.

El Shadday: Early or Late?

What then can be concluded about the etymology of El Shadday? Each of the three suggestions is plausible, and no preference will be listed here, allowing the reader to decide. As for dating, the name El Shadday is concentrated in the late material (P and Job) and so has been described as a late artificial construct. Yet because of its association with the patriarchal narratives, scholars working out of various confessional heritages have frequently wished the divine title into antiquity. Thus dates for El Shadday range from the very early to the very late. How do we evaluate whether P and Job are being creative or nostalgic? How do we distinguish between archaic and archaizing?

Extra-biblical evidence attests that a deity Shadday was known in Late Bronze Age Syria (see KTU 1.108, described earlier). Cross (1973: 53–54) and Ernst Knauf (1999: 750) argue that the name is also attested in the Late Bronze Age Egyptian name *š3-d-i-ʿ-m-y*, "Shadday is my paternal relative" (cf. ʿ*ammišadday* in Num 1:12; 2:25). Even closer in proximity and chronology are the Transjordanian Deir ʿAlla texts, which date to the eighth century BCE. These texts, discovered in 1967 and remarkable in their own right, are fascinating for the study of Israelite religion because they refer to a host of characters that have biblical counterparts. In addition to finding the presence of a seer called Balaam, we run across what seems to be an attestation of El (see p. 90) and the divine tandem Sheger and Ashtar (cf. the demythologized *šeger* and ʿ*aštĕrôt* in Deut 7:13; 28:4, 38, 51). A group of generic gods (*ʾlhn*) are also mentioned along with deities called the Shaddayyin (*šdyn*). These Shadday deities meet together in the divine council (*mwʿd*), presumably under the headship of El. Jo Ann Hackett (1980: 87) extrapolates from this to describe the function of El Shadday: "If the gods in the council were known . . . as *Šaddayyīn*, there is good reason to suspect that *Šadday* is applied as an epithet of El in his position as chief of the council."[129]

To these extra-biblical attestations we could add three biblical passages that seem archaic in nature and thus able to anchor Shadday in the early Iron Age.

A. By the hands of the Mighty One of Jacob,
   By the . . . Shepherd, the Rock of Israel,[130]

By El, your Father,* who helps you,   [*or "the God of your father"]
By Shadday,[131] who blesses you

> With blessings of heaven above,
> Blessings of the deep that couches below,
> Blessing of breasts and womb.[132]
>
> The blessings of your father . . .
> The blessings of the ancient mountains,
> The bounty of the eternal hills. (Gen 49:24–25)

B. The oracle of him who hears the words of El,
Who knows the knowledge of Elyon,
Who sees the vision of Shadday. (Num 24:16; cf. 24:4)

C. 'Elî-ṣûr ["The Rock is my god"/"El is a Rock"]
Šĕdê-'ûr ["Shadday is/gives light"]
Šĕlumî-'ēl ["El is my friend/ally"]
Ṣûrî-šadday ["Shadday is my Rock"]
'Ammî-nādāb ["My (divine) kinsman has been generous"]
Nĕtan-'ēl ["El has given"]
'Elî-'āb [El is the (divine) father"/"the (divine) father is my god"] (cf. Ugr. Ilib)
'Elî-šāma' ["My god/El has heard"]
'Ammî-hûd ["My (divine) kinsman is the majestic one"]
Gamlî-'ēl ["El has been gracious to me"]
Pĕdāh-ṣûr ["The Rock has redeemed me"]
'Abî-dān ["My (divine) father judges/is strong"]
'Aḥî-'ezer ["My (divine) brother is a help"]
'Ammî-šadday ["Shadday is my (divine) kinsman"]
Pag'î-'ēl ["My entreaty? (= the child I asked?) of El"]
'El-yāsāp ["El has added"]
Rĕ'û-'ēl ["the companion of El"] (cf. 2:14/MT: Dĕ'û-'ēl ["Know O El"])
(Num 1:5–15; cf. 2:3–29)[133]

It is interesting to note that in the texts just mentioned Shadday occurs as an independent element. This can be analyzed as documenting the deity Shadday in his own right (as in the cognate material), but it is more likely that here Shadday functions already as an epithet of El. In other words, the MT of Genesis 49:25 suggests that the full name El Shadday was divided into its two constituent parts in order to achieve a poetic parallelism. The same notion is suggested by Numbers 24:16, where both Elyon and Shadday would be epithets describing El. In addition to an early wedding of El and Shadday traditions in ancient Israelite religion, Genesis 49:25 also attests to an early union of El Shadday and the "god of the father" (originally "El, the father") traditions.[134]

The first two passages, from the Testament/Blessing of Jacob and the Oracles of Balaam, have often been dated among the earliest poems in the Hebrew Bible. Freedman (1987: 315), for example, includes both of these in the five poems he considers to be the oldest literature in the Hebrew Bible "and hence the best available source for recovering a valid contemporary account of the religion of Israel in its earliest phases."[135]

The third selection contains an abbreviated list of personal names from Numbers 1:5–15 (cf. 2:3–29). Three of the names bear the theophoric element Shadday (Šĕdê-ʾûr, Ṣûrî-šaddāy, ʿAmmî-šaddāy). Although they are imbedded in a P narrative, some scholars view the list as genuinely archaic. Jacob Milgrom (1990: 6) remarks that it "betrays evidence of great antiquity" (see Ringgren 1966: 22; Mettinger 1988: 69; Wenham 1997: 86). Other scholars are more circumspect. Albertz says that it was "meant deliberately to depict archaic traditions."[136] Levine (1993: 138) asserts that "it would be reasonable to conclude that the list is more traditional than historical as regards biblical Israel." Cross (1973: 54) notes that "whatever their history," these lists (Num 1:5–15; 2:3–29) "actually reflect characteristic formations of the onomasticon of the second millennium." Of special note is the wealth of El and Shadday names, together with kinship terms, and the complete lack of Yahweh and Baal names. All of this makes one lean toward viewing this list as genuinely archaic. The other option would be to stand in admiration of P's archaizing artistry.[137]

In conclusion, the extra-biblical attestations of Shadday together with these three biblical passages make it unwise to view P's and Job's use of Shadday as fictitious creations from a late (exilic/post-exilic) period. Likewise, Genesis 49:25, which parallels Shadday and the god of the fathers, underscores the veracity of P's famous statement about associating El Shadday with patriarchal tradition: "I am Yahweh. I appeared to Abraham, to Isaac, and to Jacob as El Shadday, but by my name Yahweh I did not make myself known to them." (Exod 6:3)

Albertz (1994: 31) is correct when he states that P "is hardly sheer invention." P has a motive to structure his religious history so that the revelation of divine names in the Pentateuch (Elohim → El Shadday → Yahweh) culminates with Mosaic Yahwism and Sabbath observance as the sign of the eternal covenant.[138] (See Chapter Six.) Nonetheless, he appears to be quite accurate in describing the worship of El Shadday as archaic. Here, Cross's (1998: 21) words, lifted from another context on kinship and covenant, are quite apt: "The Pentateuchal tradents . . . were more successful in their reconstructions of . . . early Israel than we critical historians have supposed, and . . . their traditionalist approaches are often less doctrinaire and closer to historical reality than the unilinear historical schemes imposed by scholars of yesteryear."

Finally, why isn't El Shadday associated with a particular place and sanctuary, as are other El deities? Some scholars suggest a historical occasion. Roland de Vaux (1978: 277) says that El Shadday, as the god of the steppe, was "brought by the ancestors of the people of Israel from Upper Mesopotamia," and that "this would . . . explain why, unlike El Roi or El Olam, El Shadday was not linked to a special sanctuary." Similarly, Mettinger links El Shadday to the Amorites (Amurru or "westerners" living in mostly northern Mesopotamia)[139] who worshipped a deity *bēl šadê*, "the lord of the mountain.[140] If El Shadday was "already used by patriarchal groups prior to settlement in Canaan," then it "would be one of the oldest names in the Bible" (Mettinger 1988: 71). Other scholars look to an editorial solution and suggest that El Shadday is P's term to summarize all of the patriarchal El deities (Exod 6:3). P's El Shadday can better function inclusively if he is not restricted to a specific site.

Of these two suggestions, the former, which suggests a foreign origin, seems more likely (especially if we are correct in concluding that P's El Shadday is more a reflection of ancient lore than a literary creation). At the same time, in light of the last decades of work on the patriarchal narratives, it is impossible to revive the specificity associated with the detailed "Amorite hypothesis" of old.[141] Nonetheless, if this mountain god were native to Canaan, we might expect the El Shadday traditions to be linked with any number of mountains in Palestine, given "the Israelite predilection for locating 'sacred space' on mountains" (Talmon 1978: 442). There is, however, one text that does locate biblical El's cosmic mountain in the north, although there is no mention of Shadday in the passage. Isaiah 14:13 reads:

> I will ascend to heaven,
> Above the stars of El [*kôkĕbê ʾēl*]
> I will set my throne on high;
> I will dwell on the mount of the [divine] council [*har môʿēd*],
> On the recesses of Saphon [*yarkĕtê ṣāpôn*];
> I will ascend above the heights of the clouds,
> I will make myself like Elyon [*ʿelyôn*].

This passage associates El with the divine council, which takes place on a mountain in the far north.[142] It is tempting to hear the echo of Ugaritic myth and its majestic Mt. Saphon. Ugaritic 'Ilu has a mountainous divine council of similar name (*puḫru môʿidi*), although it is Baal who is most intimately associated with Mt. Saphon.[143] Such grand lore might appeal to those worshippers in Palestine whose geography, while mountainous, lacked the commanding presence of Jebel al-Aqra. In the final analysis, all that remains is speculation. Any archaic El/Shadday mountain traditions were absorbed by Yahweh, whose theophanies were localized on a southern mountain (Mt. Sinai/Horeb). This deity eventually came to dominate Mt. Saphon as his holy mountain, renamed Mt. Zion (*har qodšô . . . har ṣiyyôn yarkĕtê ṣāpôn*; Ps 48:2–3 [Eng 48:1–2]).

The Functions of El Deities and the Wedding of El Traditions

Having documented that there was El worship in Iron Age Israel, it is natural to ask how the various El deities were seen to function. Occasionally we can get a glimpse of El functioning in a particular way at a specific locale, such as his involvement in the cult at Shiloh (Seow 1989: 11–54). But for the most part, uncovering the function of a particular El deity is near impossible because biblical tradition has fused all of the El deities into one. Thus, even in an ancient text such as Numbers 24:16, we have El, Shadday, and Elyon as parallel equivalents. Israelite worshippers did not have two deities in mind when they sought refuge "in the shelter of Elyon . . . in the shadow of Shadday" (Ps 91:1). The biblical texts, written and edited in retrospect, present patriarchal religion as monolatrous El worship, but we have few clues as to how this came to be so.[144] Was the historical reality underlying the literary presentation a rapid process or one of gradual accretion? What we see is only the end of the affair, where all El titles are represented as manifestations of a lone deity.

Now that we have acknowledged such limitations in the nature of our data, it would be a mistake to stop here. Little attention has been paid to the wedding of El traditions even though it is a common textual reality. Most treatments of El worship are isolationist and atomistic—an El Elyon here, an El Olam there —perhaps because we are unnecessarily fixated on origins as the key to understanding the nature of a deity. Yet for theists ancient and modern, the understanding of one's deity grows over time. Later conceptions of El worship, even if they are composite in nature and wed traits that were originally distinct, are equally (perhaps more) important for understanding ancient Israel's religious devotion.

A brief composite sketch of El worship shows that El was seen to be eternal (*'ōlām*) both in the sense of being an ancient individual and in the sense of being one who lives forever. Thus El was viewed as existing "from everlasting to everlasting" (Ps 90:2; *mē'ōlām 'ad 'ōlām 'attâ 'ēl*). His eternal status was a sign of his preeminence (there is no hint of a *deus otiosus* in biblical tradition), and thus the join with those traditions that celebrated the deity as "Most High" (*'elyôn*) was a natural one. The supremacy of El was also underscored by absorbing for him the title "the creator of heaven and earth" (*qōnēh šāmayim wā'āreṣ*), a variant of which (*'l qn 'rṣ*) was well known in the West Semitic environs of the Late Bronze and Iron Ages. Where there is creation, there is sovereignty. He who created the world was seen as exercising his authority over the affairs of nations. In particular, (El) Elyon, who, according to the psalmist's praise, rules "over all the earth," gave countries their respective divine patrons (Deut 32:6b–9). All four of these themes (eternity, supremacy, creativity, and sovereignty) are central to the biblical El traditions. Their latest articulation in the Hebrew Bible, coming from an apocalyptic voice, celebrates the "Ancient of Days" (ʿattîq yômayyāʾ; Dan 7:13), who lives forever, exercising his eternal dominion over the cosmos (ʿillāyāʾ . . . ḥay ʿālmāʾ . . . šālṭānēh šālṭān ʿālam/hê hāʿôlām; Dan 4:31 [Eng 4:34]; 12:7).

El as Father

There is no reflex of Israelite El's creative powers being celebrated with the language of human intercourse (contrast Ugaritic ʾIlu in KTU 1.23, discussed earlier) or employed in a theogonic context (see Kaufmann 1972: 60–61). Nor is the attribute of El as creator ever developed into a fully articulated cosmic creator.[145] Granted, we have reflexes of this role, especially the reference to the "stars of El" (kôkĕbê ʾel) in Isaiah 14:14. The role that functioned more prominently for the cult of El was that of the creator as father. Just as Ugaritic tradition pays more attention to ʾIlu's role as father (ʾab) than as cosmic creator, so too our extant biblical texts, which, while affirming El's role of "creator of heaven and earth," exert more energy discussing El as a father figure.[146] Note again Deuteronomy 32:6b, 18:

> Is not he your *father*, who created you [ʾābîkā qānekā].
> Who made you and brought you into existence?
> . . .
> You neglected the Rock [ṣûr] who bore you,
> You forgot El [ʾēl] who gave you birth.

In this remarkable passage celebrating El's creative powers, the cosmos takes a backseat to children. The masculine gender of El necessitates the description of his parentage as that of a father (ʾāb), and yet the language of god as a mother giving birth is unmistakable.[147] This accords well with other El traditions that identified with the lives of women. El Shadday is he who provides "the blessings of breasts and womb" (Gen 49:25). As Ugaritic ʾIlu was looked to for progeny, so too women and men sought Israelite El for the blessings of offspring and their nurturing.[148] He was the deity who brought fecundity (Gen 17:1–2; 28:3–4; 35:11; 49:25). When Hagar encounters El Roi and receives his blessing, it is in the context of childbirth (Gen 16:11–14). Feminist scholars have argued that the religion of the pre-state period may have been where women's roles were the greatest and most unrestricted (contrary to the state periods with their centralized cultus under royal control; see Bird 1987). On the social level, Carol Meyers argues that "the house of the mother" (*bêt 'ēm*) may have functioned as a counterpart to "the house of the father" (*bêt 'āb*) as the basic unit of society (1991; cf. Stager 1985a; Chapman 2016), but here our texts are not as forthcoming as we would like.

The metaphor of "father" used to describe religious devotion came full circle, from the womb to the tomb. Van der Toorn argues that early Israelite religion "consisted of a variety of local forms of family religion," including cults of deceased ancestors.[149] At birth, both the divine father and one's human father gave one life—yet with women doing the actual labor! Upon death a person did not simply return to his divine father alone but was "gathered to his deceased kin" and "slept with his *fathers*."[150]

El as Divine Kinsman

All of this is consistent with studies emphasizing that Israelite religion in the pre-state period is family oriented (e.g., Albertz 1994: 25–39; van der Toorn 1996b: 236–265; Albertz and Schmitt 2012). Albertz (1994: 30) argues that "the idea of God" is grounded in the metaphor of god as father or forefather and that the family cult is led by a father figure rather than an institutionalized priesthood. The divine father is also the kinsman par excellence. A direct line of kinship with one's deity was reinforced each time El as the divine father was referred to as "the god of the [human] father" (Gen 33:20, *'ēl 'ĕlōhê yiśrā'ēl*; Gen 46:3, *'ēl 'ĕlōhê 'ābîkā*).

El's connection with kinship metaphors is also reflected in the concept of "covenant" or "treaty." At Shechem we come across the deity El Berith, who played the role of a treaty partner and was thus likely understood to be "El, the lord of the covenant" (Lewis 1996a). Cross (1998: 3–21) has underscored the function of the patron deity within the sociological framework of tribal relationships. He concludes that the role of divine covenant partner is an extension of the role of a deity as divine kinsman. This is particularly true of the West Semitic tribal organizations, asserts Cross, in which the clan was seen as kin of the deity. This is "especially vivid in the West Semitic onomasticon," which reflects a great number of divine kinsman names (e.g., Ammi-Shadday; cf. Cross 1973: 6, 14). Cross concludes that such tribal organizations are typologically patriarchal, with the proper divine kinsman being an El figure.

El as Benevolent Protector

El as the dominant family member and head of the clan was seen to be the benevolent provider not just of fertility but of all sustenance and protection (cf. the

Bethel narratives). Most scholars understand the fuller name Jacob-El (*yaʿqub-ilu*) to mean "May El protect" (e.g., Hamilton 1995: 178–179).[151] In the Hebrew Bible there is no formal epithet attesting to El's benevolence such as Ugaritic ʾIlu's *lṭpn ʾil d pʾid*, "the Gracious One, the Benevolent God." One could speculate that Yahweh's attribute *ʾēl raḥûm*, "a compassionate god," was once El's, but there is no explicit evidence of such other than El's associations with womb imagery (*raḥam*) and compassion (*raḥămîm*) elsewhere.[152] Nonetheless, El is portrayed as compassionate in early as well as late texts. Genesis 49, which contains womb imagery in verse 25, pictures El as a shepherd (49:24) and "rock" guiding and protecting his flock. The deity Jacob encounters at Bethel is explicitly described as a benevolent shepherd (Gen 48:15) providing subsistence and safety. Onomastica referring to El as the "rock" (ʾElî-ṣûr, Ṣûrî-ʾēl, Ṣûrî-šadday) also evoke notions of stability and protection (see Ps 78:34–35). Such notions of security led the author of Deuteronomy 33:27 to seek his den of refuge (*mĕʿōnâ*) in the arms of (El) Olam. Similarly, the language of shelter and protection was used of Elyon//Shadday by the psalmist (Ps 91:1).

Benevolence brings us back once more to Hagar's encounter with El Roi. The birth of a child is central to the narrative, yet Hagar's desperation in the desert and her affliction (*ʿŏnî*) cry out from each line. El is portrayed as the one who restores her life. In turn, she dedicates the well at which the theophany occurred to "the living one who sees me." Her divine benefactor is "living," actively engaged in her predicament. He is anything but a passive or disinterested deity. El's concern for the afflicted becomes such a well-fixed concept that we read of a psalmist who (though his misery tempts him to think otherwise) affirms that it is inconceivable that El could have forgotten his compassion (*hăšākaḥ ḥannôt ʾēl//raḥămāyw*) in his anger (Ps 77:10 [Eng 77:9]). Who is such a great god (*mî ʾēl gadôl*)?[153]

A father's benevolence must entail physical protection of his family and clan, and thus we should not be surprised to see references to El's ability as a warrior. The notion of El fighting for his people may stand behind the etymology of "Israel," and, as I have argued, at least in a folk understanding, Shadday was understood to bring destruction.[154] Granted, this is not the predominant focus of El's nature, yet it would be rare in an ancient Near Eastern context for people to look for protection from a deity who did not have some military prowess. Thus Albertz (1994: 36, 253 n. 49) overstates the situation when he insists that the god of family religion is "completely unwarlike" and the religion itself pacifist in nature. Similarly, Westermann (1985: 110) exaggerates when he writes that the god of the fathers "has no connection with the waging of war. He is not a God of war and does not assist in battle." In general terms these scholars are correct. El is not a national deity who engages in wars of imperial conquest nor a storm deity who thunders and has the power of lightning. El's protective nature is not the same as Yahweh's combative persona.

On the other hand, El, according to Genesis 14, is not only the most high god who creates the universe but also "he who has delivered [*miggēn*] your enemies into your hand" (Gen 14:20). Abram's deity can only be his "shield" (*māgēn*; Gen 15:1) if he has the ability to defend (*miggēn*) him in armed conflict. Jacob's deity at Bethel protects him on the way and keeps him from harm, even casting "terror" (*ḥittat*) on any potential pursuers (Gen 35:5). Similarly, El Elyon's function as "redeemer" (*gō'ēl*; Ps 78:35) does not function only on a spiritual level. Some scholars argue that some reflex of El's warrior side can be reconstructed from personal names (e.g., *'ēl gibbôr*), bull imagery (*'ăbîr ya'ăqōb*), extra-biblical inscriptions (e.g., El at Kuntillet ʿAjrud), and cognate cultures.[155] Traditions that seem to describe El riding through the heavens[156] or even bringing Israel out of Egypt as a horned ox (*'ēl môṣî'ām mimmiṣrāyîm*)[157] are more complex because such language may very well be reflecting the storm language of Yahweh and/or Baal.

El and the Divine Council

El's role in the "the council of El," as reflected in texts such as Psalm 82:1 (*'ădat 'ēl*) and Isaiah 14:13 (*har môʿēd*), has already been mentioned. The Israelite tradition of having El at the head of this governing body made up of his "sons" is remarkably similar to that seen in Ugaritic religion, where ʾIlu plays a like role in a comparably named and constituted institution. So consistent is this motif that it has become paradigmatic for describing ʾIlu's mode of revelation (in contrast to that of Baʿlu, who appears in storm theophanies) (Cross 1973: 177–186). Cross goes so far as to say that "the functions of Canaanite ʾEl [= Ugaritic ʾIlu] and his modes of manifestation are virtually the same as those of the god of the Israelite patriarchs" (1973: 183; see Mullen 1980).

Particularly notable in both Ugaritic and Israelite lore is the wisdom ascribed to ʾIlu/El and the sagacity of his decrees. At Ugarit, the bard celebrates: "Your decree is wise, O ʾIlu, your wisdom is eternal; a fortunate life is your decree" (KTU 1.4.4.41–43; 1.4.5.3–4; see p. 78). Similarly, in one of the oldest biblical passages, a poet praises the one who receives "the words of El, the knowledge of Elyon, and the vision of Shadday" (Num 24:16; 24:4). Similar texts elsewhere (including the Deir ʿAlla texts from Transjordan and Ps 73:11; 107:11) show that the respect for El's decrees was affirmed widely. That the council members are called "shaddays" at Deir ʿAlla underscores the connection between the divine council and the deity El Shadday. (El) Elyon's "elevation over all the gods" (Ps 97:9) is another indicator of El's headship over the divine council. It is thus easy to see how several El titles could be wed with little difficulty (cf. again Num 24:16, which contains the three names El, Elyon, and Shadday as parallel terms).

Summary: Who El Was Not

Having painted a composite picture of Israelite El gleaned from the wedding of various traditions, we need to conclude by balancing this portrait with an acknowledgment of our inability to articulate the full reality of ancient Israel's religious devotion to El. As mentioned in Chapter Three, societies are complex and often more pluralistic than our texts lead us to believe. Thus it is impossible to be able to assign a percentage to the number of people in ancient Israel who were El worshippers or who embraced the composite picture of El we have drawn. With our data, which are unlike those culled from a modern poll, we cannot track how El was perceived throughout the Iron Age from one locale to the next or whether one of his traits received more emphasis than another due to any number of reasons (economic, political, cultural, theological, etc.). On the individual level, we can no more find out if an ancient Israelite held a view of El that unified all of these characteristics than we can tell if a modern theist is consistently holding at once all of the classical attributes of God. In short, we need to avoid homogenizing ancient Israelite society into a monolithic entity that never existed. To the degree that El worship is particularly characteristic of the pre-state period, we need to affirm Westermann's (1985: 107–108) recognition of "layers and distinctions within ... patriarchal religion" and our naiveté if we "accept uncritically every religious trait as characteristic of patriarchal religion as a whole."

Nonetheless, such reservations should not keep us from sketching who El was not, for in so doing we can demarcate manifestations of El from those of Yahweh. I have freely admitted the problem of deriving older El traditions from a corpus that has been passed down through later hands. It is all too likely that we have later Yahweh features retrojected into earlier El narratives. It is less precarious to point out who El was not. Yet methodologically it should be noted that we still run the risk that our sources may have stripped El of certain features in an effort to restrict them to Yahweh. The fact that Yahweh was fully wedded with El traditions lessened any sense of impropriety by transmitters who may have done so.

Israelite El is not portrayed as a national deity whose worship is entwined with the support of a royal hierarchy.[158] Contrast Ugaritic 'Ilu's multiple wives in KTU 1.23 (paralleling those of the king) with Israelite El having no royal spouse.[159] Contrast Ugaritic 'Ilu's parentage of King Kirta and Yahweh's (not El's) role as father to the Davidic line (2 Sam 7:11–16). The El names and their association with particular people and places seem to point to a deity with a regional character, rather than one involved in a centralized city-state system of governance. Metaphors associated with El point to the locus of family and clan, not monarch and court (but cf. Melchisedek, a kingly priest of El Elyon and the language of the divine council).[160] Similarly, the sacred space associated with El worship (altars, wells, springs, standing stones, trees, etc.) is presented on a smaller scale (humanly speaking; mythically, a cosmic mountain can be ever so majestic), not the grand scale of a temple with its attendant priesthood.

El is not a combat deity who slays cosmic creatures the likes of Leviathan and Yam, nor a vegetative deity who battles the forces of Death (Mot). Nor is he a storm deity who uses the voice of lightning to manifest his nature (but cf. Deut 33:27). Israelite El is not associated with human sacrifice.[161] His origin is never said to have been from the lands south/southeast of the Dead Sea (Seir, Teman, Paran, Midian), although some traditions localize him in the vicinity (e.g., El Roi at Beer-Lahai-Roi "between Qadesh and Bered," El at Kuntillet ʿAjrud).[162]

El narratives do not exhibit the intolerance that comes to characterize later Yahwism (note the ease with which El and Shadday traditions are wed, and see Albertz 1994: 32). We do have a patriarchal text (Gen 35:2) that articulates an exclusivism, but the hand of a late editor seems apparent (Westermann 1985: 551). Here we could compare Yahweh's epithet *ʾēl qannāʾ*, "a jealous god."[163] At the same time, when we compare the regional pantheon reconstructed from Iron Age inscriptions of the Levant, we are struck by the monolatrous El worship presented in patriarchal tradition.[164] In this tradition, there is a striking absence of some manifestation of Hadad/Baal as well as female deities (e.g., Asherah, Ashtart) functioning on their own or as El's consort.[165]

Conclusion: El as the Original God of Israel

The conclusion to be drawn from this chapter is that there is ample evidence that El was the original god worshipped by the ancient Israelites. El was well known in the Levant in both the Late Bronze and Iron Ages, and thus it is not surprising to find his name (and not Yahweh's) in the name Israel. The date and origin of Yahweh worship will be treated in Chapter Six. The way in which Yahweh becomes a national deity will also be explored. The biblical tradition ascribes much of Yahweh's rise to fame to his ability as a warrior, with emphasis on his liberation of the Hebrew slaves from the land of Egypt. Yet, prior to exploring this material, we need to examine the thesis put forth by several scholars that El may have been the original god of the exodus tradition.

El as the God of the Exodus?

At several points in this analysis I have commented on hints in both Ugaritic and biblical texts that El was associated with warrior traditions.[166] As noted, this should not be surprising in light of the obvious desire in the ancient Near East to worship a deity powerful enough to be able to provide protection (even if that deity functions sociologically on the level of the clan rather than the state). The ability of a deity to provide protection does not necessarily make him a warrior or national deity. Nevertheless, some scholars have pieced together some of these traditions to argue that El was a warrior deity.[167]

As for the exodus tradition, we have to wrestle with the intriguing expressions of "El bringing Israel out of Egypt like the horns of a wild ox" (*'ēl môṣî'ām/môṣî'ô mimmiṣrāyîm kĕtô'ăpōt rĕ'ēm lô*) in Numbers 23:22 and 24:8 (cf. 23:8). As noted by Hans-Peter Müller (2004: 246), the use of the bull imagery (*rĕ'ēm*) here (as in Deut 33:17, where *rĕ'ēm//šôr*) portrays invincibility and superiority in battle. In the past, Mettinger pointed out the possible association of El with the exodus tradition and translated the relevant passages as follows:

> How can I curse whom El has not cursed?
> How can I denounce whom JHWH has not denounced?
>
> JHWH, his God, is with him . . .
> El brought him out of Egypt,
> he is like the wild ox's horns to him. (Mettinger 1979: 19)[168]

In Mettinger's (1979: 17) framework, these passages, while associating El with the exodus from Egypt, are a reflection of "an early assimilation between JHWH and El, who had the bull as his symbol." Similarly, Toews (1993: 46) described the bull symbolism of El at length and concluded that "at least some components of earliest Israel could confess that it was El who had brought Israel out of Egypt." As for assimilation, Toews (1993: 65) underscored the cultic activities of Jeroboam I, who "intended the calf-iconography to re-present El = Yahweh's strength as displayed in the battle against the Egyptians."[169] (See Chapters Five and Seven on bull representation of El and Yahweh, respectively.)

In 1985, motivated by the fascinating texts from Deir 'Alla, Levine argued that these inscriptions, when combined with El literature in the Bible, are evidence of an "El *repertoire*, a body of literary creativity originally composed at various centers of El worship on both sides of the Jordan; in biblical Israel, as well as in Gilead of Transjordan" (Levine 1985: 337; 1991: 58). This repertoire included the references to El as the god of the exodus in Numbers 23:22 and 24:8. Several years later, Nick Wyatt wrote a more detailed treatment of El and the exodus tradition (1992; 1996: 170, 245; 1999a). In addition to translating Numbers 23:22 and 24:8 similarly to Mettinger and Levine, with *'ēl* designating a proper name ("El brought him out of Egypt"), Wyatt argued for the relevance of Exodus 32:4, 8 and Psalm 106:19–22, which concern the golden calf incident. Yet each of these passages is inconclusive. Wyatt's (1992: 79) interpretation is based on changing Exodus 32:4, 8 to read "El [*ʾēl*] is your god, Israel, who brought you up out of the land of Egypt," as opposed to the MT's "*These* [*ʾēlleh*] are your gods, O Israel, who brought you up out of the land of Egypt." In Psalm 106:21 Wyatt translates *ʾēl* as a proper name rather than a generic noun: "They forgot El [*ʾēl*] who had saved them" (cf. JPS's "God who saved them"). While such a translation is possible (Wyatt appeals to the "kerygma" of El association), especially in light of the word "bull" (*šôr*) in verse 20 (cf. Ugaritic *tr ʾil*), one must retain reservations due to the completely Yahwistic context of the psalm (the name Yahweh/Yah occurs eleven times in Psalm 106). Another scholar arguing for the possible association of El with exodus tradition, but from another avenue, is Smith (1994a: 207–208; 2001b: 146–148). Smith builds on the work of Seow (1989), who argues for an El cult at Shiloh, by noting that personal names of the Shilonite priesthood are Egyptian in origin. He concludes that it would stand to reason "that El was the original god of the Israelites who came out of the land of Egypt and not Yahweh" (1994a: 208).

One last bit of evidence is found in Habakkuk 3:3, which mentions "Eloah marching forth from Teman" (*ʾĕlôah mittēmān yābôʾ*) in a passage referring to the exodus that is markedly militaristic and fully celebrating the god Yahweh as the driver of his war chariot (3:8) with Deber and Reshep at his side (3:5).[170] According to Francis Andersen (2001: 289), "the ancient names for God used in [Hab 3:3; i.e., Eloah and Qadosh] point to a stage before the widespread or at least dominant use of Yahweh."[171]

What should we make of such tantalizing evidence? Its fragmentary character recommends caution. The fusion of earlier El traditions with those of Yahweh makes it likely that El's divine warrior motifs are, if one may use a linguistic term, back-formations. If El had such strong divine warrior traditions (not just those of a family deity protecting his clan), one wonders, why did he not become the national deity? Why were cosmic combat myths (e.g., the fighting of Leviathan and Yam) assigned to Yahweh rather than to El?[172] It seems that the portrayals of El and Yahweh are the result of underlying social realities for which we have only partial evidence. The majority of the biblical traditions at our disposal point to El as more of a regional and familial deity than Yahweh, who functioned as the national deity and the patron deity of the monarch, and whose worship was supported by a hierarchical priesthood. Thus it would have been necessary to portray Yahweh not just as a deity able to provide protection for one's clan but also as the warrior par excellence who founded the nation by delivering his people from a primordial enemy (historicized as Egypt).

If, for the sake of argument, one assumes that El was the original god of the exodus, one then wonders how Yahweh was welcomed into the fold. What function would Yahweh have provided if worshippers looked to El to fight their battles? Maybe two gods were thought to be better than one (although biblical tradition says that El and Yahweh are one and the same, not two separate deities).

Or perhaps El's strength was waning (although there is no evidence of such) and a successor to the divine throne was needed. Perhaps Ugaritic 'Ilu provides an analogy. As we have seen, 'Ilu is described at the end of the Ba'lu Cycle by the goddess Shapshu as being able to "overturn the seat of Mot's kingship" by "breaking the scepter of his rule" (KTU 1.6.6.27–29). At the same time, any further development of 'Ilu's capacity as a warrior is minimized in Ugaritic tradition due to the military prowess of Ba'lu and 'Anatu. This is clear both from the myths celebrating their battles as well as from ritual texts in which Ugaritians turned to Ba'lu for military help when their city was under siege (KTU 1.119). Perhaps just as Ba'lu comes to the fore and 'Ilu recedes when it comes to a dynastic deity who fights for the nation, so the traditions of Yahweh as divine warrior come to the fore over those of El as the needs of the society changed from those of a small family group to those of a nation (cf. Albertz 1994: 23–138). Perhaps popular sayings that mentioned Yahweh as divine warrior were spoken with a voice inflection: "It is *Yahweh* [implying "and not El"] who delivered you from Egypt."

5
The Iconography of Divinity: El

Ancient Israel's aniconic tradition has a long history. The notion of not portraying the divine in concrete/physical reality appears as early as the Decalogue (if not earlier) and has been reinforced in subsequent Jewish and Christian traditions up to and including the present.[1] Yet prior to exploring this fascinating and enduring tradition (and its underlying abstract theology), it is best first to situate ancient Israel firmly in its ancient Near Eastern context. Moreover, pluralistic expressions of worship demand that we explore how some parts of ancient Israelite society conceptualized divinity within a firmly held and time-honored iconic tradition. Indeed, Christoph Uehlinger (1993: 281; 2006: 84) boldly states: "On the whole, the notion of 'Ancient Israel' as an 'aniconic nation' is erroneous," for "had 'Israel' not known images, no veto would ever have been conceived." And he adds, "The prohibition [of cultic images] presupposes the knowledge and practice of iconolatry in at least some circles of Judahite society."

Historians of religion have ignored iconography at their own peril. I will briefly sketch in Section I the pitfalls inherent in using iconography, followed in Section II by a general description of how divine images were viewed in the ancient Near East. Sections III and IV will narrow the analysis to the iconography of Ugaritic ’Ilu and Israelite El. I will restrict my remarks to the iconography of divine images. Therefore, the survey of the Israelite material in this chapter does not treat cultic images in general, such as golden mice (1 Sam 6:4, 11), a bronze sea (1 Kgs 6:23), Jachin and Boaz (1 Kgs 7:21), kernoi and zoomorphic vessels, or even pomegranate scepters from Jerusalem.[2]

Section I: Methodology and Iconography

A brief introduction to the Fribourg school of iconography (led by Othmar Keel and Christoph Uehlinger) is found in Chapter Two, pp. 37–38. Prior to the 1970s systematic treatments of Syro-Palestinian iconography were rare. Ever since that time, iconographic studies have been one of the most productive subfields of ancient Near Eastern scholarship. Yet the considerable advances that have been achieved have not been without their pitfalls.[3]

Pitfalls

Lack of Use of Material Culture

The primary hazard continues to be textual scholars who do not take iconography seriously. With regard to cultic images, Keel and Uehlinger's quote is apt: "Anyone who prefers to work exclusively with texts . . . ought to get little or no hearing."[4] Current analysis of Syro-Palestinian deities is uneven, and without accompanying inscriptions, identifications will remain uncertain. Thanks to renewed interest in the goddess Asherah, many female figurines are now attributed to her, including her alleged presence on the Taanach cult stand, on the Lachish ewer, and at Kuntillet ʿAjrud.[5] Thankfully, more attention has recently been given to other Canaanite goddesses such as Anat, Ashtart/Astarte, and Qudshu/Qedeshet. Of special note is Izak Cornelius' *The Many Faces of the Goddess* (2004), Keiko Tazawa's *Syro-Palestinian Deities in New Kingdom Egypt* (2009), Silvia Schroer's *Die Ikonographie Palästinas/Israels und der Alte Orient* (2005–2018), and the forthcoming reference work *Iconography of Deities and Demons in the Ancient Near East*.[6] The iconography of other Syro-Palestinian deities gets far less attention. We study the role of (pre-)Israelite El in text, yet pay little attention to possible reflexes in archaeology such as the enthroned male figurines in benedictory pose coming from sites such as Beth Shemesh, Megiddo, Beth Shean, Tel Kinneret, and Tell Balatah. The rich documentation of Ugaritic ʾIlu can serve as a proper backdrop for both anthropomorphic and theriomorphic speculation, as we will see.

When textual scholars do attempt to study iconography, often they cannot extract themselves from a textual myopia.[7] Suffering from textual fixation, we ignore some deities due to their absence in written sources, yet we know that they are present in material culture. Bes figurines are ubiquitous and had a significant impact upon domestic religion (see Chapter Seven, pp. 325–330), yet they are understudied because we are so text-centered. Similarly, Reshep appears rarely in the Ugaritic mythological texts or the Hebrew Bible. Yet his presence is well attested in the ritual texts (see Pardee 2000, 2002a), and, as Cornelius (1994) has shown, there were many private stelae devoted to him, not to mention the inscribed lion-headed mug offered to Rashap-Guni.[8] The Canaanite god Mekal appears on an inscribed stela from Beth Shean (Mazar 1990: 289) but not in our mythic repertoire. The Bethsaida stela (as shown in Bernett and Keel 1998) reveals a greater presence for the moon god (note too that not all bulls are El, Hadad, or Baal).

Limitations of What We Possess

Yet using iconography has its own pitfalls, such as the limitations inherent to the nature of material culture. Archaeology does not document everything.

Biblical writers speak of dragons yet to be found in the drawings of Iron Age Israel.[9] To what degree can iconography represent actual cult? Can iconography adequately reflect ritual activity? Note Cornelius' (1994: 264) claim that iconographic depictions "can fulfill a role comparable to the texts from Ugarit." Victor Hurowitz (1997: 69) rightly challenges this by noting that whereas "purely iconographic analysis" shows that a raised hand is a symbol of power, "only the texts describing Reshef as a god who listens to prayers and who heals inform us that Reshef's power is an apotropaic power—an ability to ward off disease."

Iconography complements texts; it cannot replace them. The portrait of *transcendent* Baal (to use the wording of Wyatt [1998: 388]) in KTU 1.101 cannot be crafted in stone or metal. Yet neither is iconography "impotent" (Hurowitz 1997: 69). See Chapter Seven for the transcendence achieved by the artists at the Iron Age temple at Ayn Dara, Syria.

Misuse of Material Culture

The misuse of material culture is legendary. Why must every item coming out of the ground be cultic rather than domestic in nature? One need only remember failed past attempts at turning house pillars and stone tables into cultic *masseboth*. Tryggve Mettinger's *No Graven Image?* (1995) and the work of Elizabeth Bloch-Smith (2005, 2006, 2015) are splendid corrections. And yet, according to Mettinger, *masseboth* are cultic in nature, representing divine images (cf. the many articles by Uzi Avner). While some standing stones may indeed represent divine images, such as one at Arad (Figure 5.1), most were probably commemorative or even functional in nature—for example, an olive press installation at Tirzah (Figure 5.2; see Stager and Wolff 1981: 99–100). Nowhere in Mettinger's treatment does one come across *masseboth* functioning as tombstones (for Rachel; Gen 35:19–20), as boundary markers (between Jacob and Laban; Gen 31:44–49), as markers for twelve tribes (Exod 24:3–8); and as surrogates for a male heir (2 Sam 18:18).[10] Every group of standing stones does *not* necessarily document a pantheon. (A full discussion of *masseboth* that may have been used to represent the deity El can be found on pp. 169–196. For the association of Yahweh and *masseboth*, see Chapter Seven, pp. 333–336.)

Misidentifications

Methodologically, one must ask whether anthropomorphic figures are deities or humans. As P. R. S. Moorey and Stuart Fleming (1984: 79) point out, without accompanying inscriptional evidence there is no way of knowing for certain, and the safest methodology would argue that "no metal statuette may be taken to represent a divinity until arguments for a mortal have been discounted." Sometimes headdresses (especially those with horns), standards, gold or silver sheathing, fine workmanship, and cultic context can tip the scales in favor of the divine.

Figure 5.1 A standing stone and incense altars in the temple at Arad, stratum IX, as reconstructed.
Courtesy of Ze'ev Herzog, Tel Aviv University.

(A fuller discussion of criteria for determining divine images may be found on p. 142.)

In contrast to inscribed Egyptian material (such as the Anat, Astarte, and Qedeshet material touched on earlier and the Winchester plaque mentioning Qudshu-Astarte-Anat [Figure 5.3]), rarely do inscriptions accompany Syro-Palestinian figures. That the Judean pillar figurines were consistently labeled "Astarte" figurines in the past should give us pause when today people regularly call them "Asherah" figurines.[11] Despite Carol Meyers' work to the contrary, scholars persist in labeling the so-called tambourine figurines as Asherah.[12] The desire is strong to interpret every object coming out of the ground as cultic. The ancients had domestic lives too.

Misidentification is a problem even when we are relatively certain that we are dealing with cultic items. Note, for example, the drinking mug (Figure 5.4) from the southern acropolis at Ugarit portraying an enthroned bearded figure (arguably the deity 'Ilu). The offering scene depicts an attendant holding

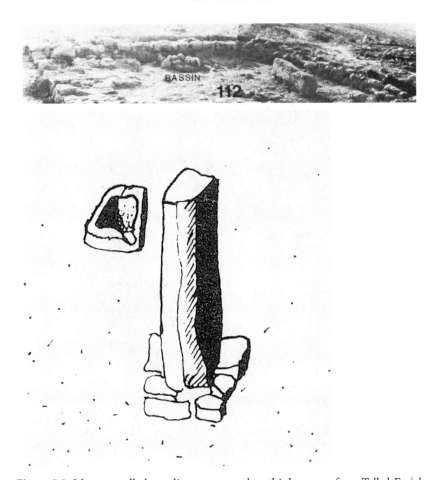

Figure 5.2 Many so-called standing stones, such as this large one from Tell el-Farʿah North (biblical Tirzah), functioned in ways other than that of a divine symbol.

Photo and line drawing from A. Chambon, *Tell El-Farʿah I: L'âge du fer* (Paris: ERC, 1984), pl. 8, 27. Courtesy École biblique et archéologique française de Jérusalem.

a libation jug. Due to the ritual nature of the scene, it is not surprising that C. F. A. Schaeffer, Marvin Pope, and others equated the scene with ʾIlu's *marzēaḥ*. Yet Pope (1994: 21–23) did not stop there. He argued (prior to the line drawing restoration) that the personage to the left was the goddess ʾAthiratu. The horse, fish, and fowl represented the donkey of ʾAthiratu, the watery domain of ʾIlu, and the bird-like character of ʿAnatu. It makes more sense to follow Marguerite Yon in seeing the personage to the left to be a human male (perhaps the king).[13] The horse, fish, and fowl more likely represent land, sea, and air, according to Yon.[14]

Figure 5.3 The Winchester limestone plaque mentioning Qudshu-Astarte-Anat, presumably from Deir el-Medina.

From I. E. S. Edwards, "A Relief of Qudshu-Astarte-Anat in the Winchester College Collection," *Journal of Near Eastern Studies* 14 (1955): 49–51, Pl. III. Courtesy of the *Journal of Near Eastern Studies*.

Figure 5.4 A drinking mug from Late Bronze Age Ugarit found in the so-called House of the Magician-Priest in the south acropolis.

Reproduced by permission of Mission archéologique de Ras Shamra–Ougarit.

THE ICONOGRAPHY OF DIVINITY: EL   125

Some scholars would include the female seated lyre player on Kuntillet ʿAjrud pithos A (mid-ninth to mid-eighth century BCE) as representing the goddess Asherah (Figure 5.5).[15] This seems inadvisable. There is no association of Asherah with music, nor would one expect to find the great mother goddess off center, facing away from the central figures. Those who reason that we have Asherah on the throne do so because of the inscription, which mentions "Yahweh of Samaria and his asherah." (For discussion, see Chapter Six, pp. 236–240; Chapter Seven, pp. 325–330.) Yet there is no need to equate the drawings with the inscription, especially if they come from two separate times, as seems likely.[16] If the drawings and the inscription are contemporaneous and thus represent the same subject matter, how would those who place Asherah on the throne account for the presence of *three* figures?

Figure 5.5 A depiction of two standing Bes-like figures and a seated lyre player that some scholars (questionably) see as the goddess Asherah. From the Iron Age II site of Kuntillet ʿAjrud.
Courtesy of the Israel Exploration Society, Jerusalem.

126 THE ORIGIN AND CHARACTER OF GOD

Misdating

Other pitfalls involve misdating. Gösta Ahlström (1970–1971; 1975) made much of the Hazor figurine (Figure 5.6) from Area B, calling it "an *Israelite* god figurine" (my italics) that represented "Yahweh or Yahweh-El." As noted by several scholars, a closer look at the archaeological picture shows that this figurine was a part of a hoard of Late Bronze Age (i.e., thirteenth century BCE) implements. Thus they represent earlier, pre-Israelite material culture.[17]

Almost every other treatment of Israelite divine images shows the stick figure on a miniature limestone altar from Gezer (Figures 5.7, 5.8) and *notes its tenth-century BCE date*. Its fame comes from William Dever's (1983: 574) often-used quote that "no representations of a *male* deity in terra cotta, metal, or stone have ever been found in clear Iron Age contexts" except for this stick figurine. (To his credit, Dever added that it is unclear whether it represents a human or a deity.) Yet a glance at Gezer Plan VIII raises questions about whether it should indeed be dated to the tenth century BCE. It is found in

Figure 5.6 Late Bronze Age figurine from Hazor (Area B, stratum XI) that some scholars have misidentified as Yahweh.
Courtesy of the Selz Foundation Hazor Excavations in Memory of Yigael Yadin.

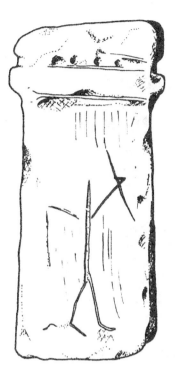

Figure 5.7 A line drawing of a miniature limestone altar from Gezer thought to date to the tenth century BCE.
Courtesy of the Nelson Glueck School of Biblical Archaeology.

destruction debris that includes later intrusive material from trenches 3044 and 3113. Each of these trenches contains late (even Persian) material.[18] Thus the central role that this figurine has played in scholarly reconstructions needs to be nuanced.

Misinterpretations from the Drawing Process

Misinterpretations can also be "read into" iconography in the drawing process. The first lesson one learns as an epigraphist is never to trust anyone else's script chart. Yet such care (and appropriate skepticism) has not been a part of line drawings and the study of iconography.

For example, compare the bearded statuette from Ugarit (Figure 5.9) (often thought to be 'Ilu) with Schaeffer's often-used drawing (Figure 5.10). The line drawing (perhaps unduly influenced by the mistaken view that 'Ilu was a *deus otiose*) adds many wrinkles.[19] 'Ilu, no more than we in our vanity, certainly did not appreciate our adding in wrinkles he didn't have. Or compare the creature in

Figure 5.8 A miniature limestone altar from Gezer thought to date to the tenth century BCE.
Courtesy of the Nelson Glueck School of Biblical Archaeology.

the attendant's hand on the serpentine stela from Ugarit (Figure 5.11) with a line drawing (Figure 5.12). Is it really a happy snake?

Section II: Ancient Near Eastern Iconography and Divine Images

Promises and New Directions

Enough about pitfalls. What promising new directions lie ahead? The impact of the Fribourg school is remarkable, especially with its influential Orbis Biblicus et Orientalis series. The future will continue to produce more valid syntheses than the past. Most importantly, our expectations are higher. No longer will scholars of ancient religion be allowed to get away with a narrow text-centered approach with a few token illustrations of a god here or a goddess there. Now

Figure 5.9 A bearded statuette from Ugarit often thought to be 'Ilu.
Reproduced by permission of Mission archéologique de Ras Shamra–Ougarit.

that we have seen the fruits of full-length iconographic treatments, the bar has been raised.

Comparative Insights from the Ancient Near East

Any advance in understanding Syro-Palestinian images will directly benefit from the study of cultic images in cognate cultures.[20] As recently as 1964, A. Leo Oppenheim lamented that "the role and the function of the divine image in [Mesopotamian] civilization have never been considered important enough to merit a systematic scholarly investigation"; "they have received a modicum of the attention they deserve."[21] The same could have been said of the iconography of ancient Egypt, Anatolia, Syria, and Israel in the mid-1960s. Yet not anymore.

Today, thanks to recent studies of cultic images in Mesopotamia, Egypt, and Anatolia, we have a new set of questions to ask of the Syro-Palestinian world: (1) What materials were used to craft a deity? (2) What was the role of the artisan?

Figure 5.10 A line drawing of the Ugaritic deity ʾIlu (published by Shaeffer) to be compared with the photograph in Figure 5.9.

Drawing from C. F. A. Schaeffer, "Nouveaux témoignages du culte de El et de Baal à Ras Shamra–Ugarit et ailleurs en Syrie-Palestine," *Syria* 43 (1966): 7, fig. 3. Reproduced by permission of Institut français du Proche-Orient and Mission archéologique de Ras Shamra–Ougarit.

(3) How was the image actually made? (4) How was it quickened and consecrated for use? (5) Finally, and perhaps most importantly, how was the image used in ritual performance and in theology? In the space remaining in this brief introduction, I will explore some of the answers that can be found in Syro-Palestinian sources (textual, archaeological, and iconographic).

Materials Used

Mesopotamian and Egyptian texts (in genres of myth and ritual) reveal the materials used to make statues (e.g., gold, silver, bronze, copper, precious stones, worked stone, and wood).[22] Archaeology is less helpful due to the reuse of costly goods in antiquity and their inability to withstand the ravages of time.

A New Kingdom text describes Re: "his bones being silver, his flesh gold, his hair from true lapis lazuli." Inanna's statue is described in cuneiform literature

THE ICONOGRAPHY OF DIVINITY: EL 131

Figure 5.11 From C. F. A. Schaeffer, "Les fouilles de Ras Shamra–Ugarit huitième campagne (printemps 1936): rapport sommaire," *Syria* 18, no. 2 (1937): pl. 17. Reproduced by permission of Institut français du Proche-Orient and Mission archéologique de Ras Shamra–Ougarit.

as made of metal, lapis lazuli, and boxwood. Of special note is the Erra Epic's mention of *mēsu* wood, the preferred material for statues, for it is "the flesh of the gods."[23] Images were then dressed with various accessories such as crowns, standards, clothing, insignia, and decorative jewelry. Occasionally we have textual references to less costly goods such as clay, wood, and wax.[24]

In contrast, we have few textual references of the materials used by artisans in ancient Syria to form a cult statue (although we do read of "Nergal of Stone" at Emar).[25] Here we must rely on material culture to stock the inventory of the workman's shop. As one would suspect, similar materials were used, including gold, bronze with gold overlay, silver, finely worked limestone, ivory, and terra-cotta.[26]

Similarly, we have artisans working in gold and bronze at places such as MB Gezer, LB Lachish, LB Hazor, Megiddo, and Shechem/Tel Balatah; silver at Iron Age Tel Miqne; stone at Iron Age Arad, Hazor, and Dan; terra-cotta at Taanach

Figure 5.12 An artist's drawing of Figure 5.11. Note, by comparing the line drawing to the photograph (esp. the creature in the attendant's hand), how interpretation (and the possibility of misrepresentation) is involved in the drawing process.
Image from T. N. D. Mettinger, *In Search of God*, © Fortress Press. Reproduced by permission.

and Qitmit; and ivory at LB Megiddo.[27] Whether the Judean pillar figurines designate goddesses or "prayers in clay" to a deity remains unsettled (see Darby 2014).

Though we have no inventory lists of materials used, we do have occasional mention in our written sources.[28] In EA 55, Akizzi, the mayor of Qatna, tells his lord (Namhurya; prenomen of Amenophis IV) that to refashion the statue of Shimigi (= Hurrian sun god), the god of his father (which was taken away by the king of Hatti), he will require "a sack of gold, just as much as is needed." Tushratta's lust for solid gold images—in contrast to wooden images with gold overlay—is well documented (EA 27:33; 26:41).

Biblical tradition mentions Aaron's golden bull (Exod 32:4), Moses' bronze serpent (Num 21:8–9), Micah's mother's silver image (Judg 17:1–5), the iron image of Deutero-Isaiah's foes (Isa 44:12), and stone *masseboth* of Baal (2 Kgs 3:2; 10:26–27), not to mention wooden images (Isa 40:20; 44:13–17) and wooden

ʾăšērîm (e.g., Judg 6:26). Ezekiel notes the fine jewelry used for divine images (Ezek 7:20; 16:17). The so-called image ban texts are replete with mentions of gold, silver, and wood (Jer 10:3–4; Isa 40:19–20; 41:7; 46:6; Hos 8:4; 13:2; Hab 2:19; Ps 115:4; 135:15; Exod 20:23). As for the choice of materials, the most surprising reference is Jeremiah 44:19, which implies the making of cakes bearing the image of the Queen of Heaven.

As noted by Hurowitz (2006: 21, 23; cf. Dick 1999a: 41–43), "the narrators indicate that illegitimate cult images are made of tainted materials." Curiously, especially in light of the Judean pillar figurines, the Bible includes no polemic against the making and worshipping of clay images.[29] Was clay thought to be used for subordinate beings, such as humans (Gen 2:7; Jer 18:6; Job 10:9; 33:6)?[30]

Artisans' Role

Our fullest description of the role of artisans in crafting a divine image comes from Mesopotamia, especially the *mīs pî* rituals published by C. B. F. Walker and Michael Dick (2001). These rituals were elaborate affairs involving extensive divination to locate a time for the task, to select the many different artisans, and to determine the place of refurbishing (the *bīt mummi*). Various craftsmen are listed in detail, as are the costly materials (e.g., red gold, precious stones) used to make the statue, together with its crown and decorative jewelry, so that the gods could be ceremoniously "born."[31] The cult image was the joint product of human and divine artisans.[32] Human artisans were acting on behalf of the gods in fashioning the statues, and any skill displayed was ultimately that of specific craft deities. It is clear that the statues could not "become divine" through mere human activity. The "opening of the mouth" was a magical act enabling the statue to serve as a vessel for the deity. We end up with human artisans even disavowing that they have crafted the deity, for, in Esarhaddon's words, "the making of (images of) the gods and goddesses is your [i.e., Aššur's and Marduk's] right, it is in your hands" (Walker and Dick 1999: 65).

In contrast, the Levant gives only hints of the artisans, their role, and their techniques. We do have documented (at least for Ugarit) mention of specialized craftsmen, including metalworkers (*nsk*), goldsmiths, silversmiths (*nsk ksp*), coppersmiths (*nsk ṯlṯ*), sculptors and carvers (*psl, zadimmu*), engravers and polishers (*mly*), borers (*sḥl*), specialists in lapis lazuli (*qnuym*), and so on.[33]

The actual crafting of the divine image goes unmentioned. As noted earlier, Akizzi, the mayor of Qatna, reminds Amenophis IV that he "knows what the fashioning of divine statues is like." Perhaps it was such common knowledge that it went without saying. Yet when Akizzi says that he will require "a sack of gold, just as much as is needed," to refashion the statue of his father's god, one wonders how honest he was with any leftovers.

The ʾAqhatu story at Ugarit implies that in certain circumstances one need not go to a specialist. It describes a son setting up a stela for his divine ancestor. Yet we have no image-making texts preserved from ancient Syria comparable to the *mīs pî* texts from Mesopotamia. Here we must look to the material culture, which speaks loudly of the craft of metalworkers and stonecutters. Perhaps these artisans gave credit for their ability to Kothar-wa-Hasis (as did Mesopotamian artisans to their craft deities: Ea, Ninildu, Kusibanda, Ninkurra, and Ninzadim).[34]

Ironically, in biblical tradition it is the polemical image ban texts that give our best insight into the various artisans. We read of metalworkers (goldsmiths and silversmiths) and carpenters. Despite the polemical tone, we still read of their technique and skill. Deutero-Isaiah mentions ironsmiths working over coals and carpenters working with hammers, lines, pencils, compasses, and planes. Others speak of the technique of gold and silver overlay (Isa 40:19; Jer 10:3–4; Hab 2:19). Hosea speaks of "idols *skillfully* made of silver" (13:2; cf. the "*skilled* craftsman" in Isa 40:20). Nonetheless, emphasis is placed not on the skills of the human artisans but on how human hands taint the final product (e.g., Ps 115:4).

In contrast to these unnamed artisans, Moses, Aaron, and Gideon are portrayed as craftsmen (Moses and the bronze serpent; Aaron and the golden bull; Gideon and the ephod), yet one wonders to what degree they would have relied on the expertise of fellow craftsman.[35] In the situation with Micah's mother, we can see that she was the patron who employed the silversmith (Judg 17:4).

Of special note is the association of royalty with divine images. Carl Evans (1995: 192), following Ahlström, has astutely pointed out how "kings set up or removed cult images whenever they engaged in cultic organization or reorganization." He is certainly correct that "religious iconography was … an important aspect of the national cult which the king administered." Yet our texts are often silent. In 1 Kings 11:5–8 Solomon makes shrines for Chemosh, Molech, Ashtart, Milcom, and others. One could posit that he had divine images crafted for each, yet the text is silent. Elsewhere the text is more forthcoming. In 1 Kings 12:28 there is the famous story of Jeroboam making two bulls of gold (El images?) in his attempt to "out-archaize" David (see pp. 198–200). Several kings (Ahab in 1 Kgs 16:33; Manasseh in 2 Kgs 21:3, 7; cf. 2 Chr 33:3, 7) and one queen (Maacah in 1 Kgs 15:13) made *ʾăšērāh* images. Ahab's making of a *massebah* of Baal seems to be referring to a divine image (2 Kgs 3:2).

Finally, in late apocalyptic literature we have the account of King Nebuchadrezzar making a colossal golden image (*ṣĕlēm dî dĕhab*) for cultic purposes (Dan 3:1).[36] This golden image contrasts with Nebuchadrezzar's "large image" (*śaggîʾ*) in Daniel 2:31–32, which, though exhibiting an awesome brightness (*zîwēh yattîr*) (similar to *melammu*?), had literal "feet of clay." That the image in Daniel 3 is that of a deity seems almost certain (cf. 3:12, 14, 18, "they do not serve your gods or worship the golden image which you have set up").[37] Similarly, compare Nabonidus' erection of a statue for the moon god Sin.[38]

Rituals of Quickening and Consecration (and Purification?)

Texts are often better than archaeology when it comes to articulating ritual performance. Elaborate rituals of the quickening and the consecration of cult statues, of their "(re)vivification" and "mouth opening," are well attested in Mesopotamia and Egypt. In Anatolia we even read of a newly constructed golden cult image being smeared with blood in a purification rite.[39]

In the Hebrew Bible there are no texts mentioning a quickening ritual for a divine image, and as far as I know there are only three brief mentions of any consecration ritual.[40] In Judges 17:3, Micah's mother "wholly consecrated" (haqdēš hiqdaštî) silver "to Yahweh" prior to giving it to the silversmith. In Daniel 3:1-7, we read of the royal making of the golden image and its erection (3:1). An elaborate dedication ritual follows (ḥănukkat ṣalmāʾ), attended by royal, judicial, and administrative officials (3:2-3). We then hear of proclamations and commands to worship the image along with a large variety of musical accompaniment (3:4-7).[41]

We may have a third example in the Bethel narratives where Jacob pours oil on a *massebah* (wayyiṣōq šemen, Gen 28:18; 35:14) that "shall be God's house" (bêt ĕlōhîm, Gen 28:22). Does this imply a ritual whereby the deity takes up residence in stone, or is the *massebah* a marker of sacred space?[42] In either case, it is apparent that while the anointing with oils and pouring of libations denote sacral effectiveness, they fall far short of the elaborate "(re)vivification" and "mouth opening" rituals accorded Mesopotamian and Egyptian cult statues.

Once Made/Consecrated/Purified

In the ancient Near East (especially in Mesopotamia), once images are fashioned, vivified, and consecrated they become the focus of attention.[43] Our extant evidence for the Levantine world preserves nothing so elaborate, yet our data are ever increasing. Common sense tells us that those who fashioned divine statues then erected them in their temples and sanctuaries, yet we have no explicit ritual in our extant texts. It has been commonly asserted that "Azatiwada placed the statue of the god *Krntryš* in the midst of his city,"[44] yet K. Lawson Younger has convincingly shown that this is not supported by the Hieroglyphic Luwian of this bilingual text.[45]

Two economic texts from Ugarit (KTU 4.168, 4.182) mention clothes for divine statues.[46] The large number of garments mentioned in the ritual texts is also telling. Dennis Pardee concludes: "The fact that so many textile products were presented to the deities in the Ugaritic cult would seem to indicate either that the cult statues were clothed and that these garments were changed fairly often or that the clothing of their priestly representatives was provided by this divine fiction."[47] Note especially the mention of garments (and possible clothing ritual?) in one of the so-called entry rituals (KTU 1.43.4, 22; see the next section).[48]

Even the biblical tradition preserves the dressing of an image. We read that "women wove hangings for the Asherah" (2 Kgs 23:7) and that the divine image of the Ammonite god Milcom wore a crown with a precious stone.[49] We also have allusions to clothes associated with Yahweh. Herbert Niehr (1997: 89) writes:

> Some passages in the Old Testament say that YHWH is clothed. Isa 6:1 mentions the fringes of YHWH's garments; Ezek 16:8 the clothing of YHWH; Dan 7:9 the garment of the Olden One; and Isa 63:1–3 the blood-stained garments of YHWH. Ps 60:10 and 108:10 list YHWH's sandals. Allusions to jewels adorning YHWH's cult statue and his throne are made in Exod 24:10 and Ezek 1:22, 26.

Yet, in contrast to Niehr's assertion, there is no explicit mention of a cult statue of Yahweh (on which see Chapter Seven) or an explicit clothing ritual. Niehr adds that "clouds, justice, strength and light as YHWH's clothes" are used as metaphorical expressions. Such could also be the case with the passages just cited if there was indeed no image of Yahweh used in the Jerusalem Temple.

Reverence for images is evident in Hosea's mention that "men kiss bull image[s]" (13:2; cf. 1 Kgs 19:18).[50] When Ahaz sacrifices to "the gods of Damascus who had defeated him" (2 Chr 28:23), one could posit that he did so in front of their cult images (although the text is silent). When the Judean king Amaziah brings divine images from Edom, he "installs them as his gods, bows down to them, and offers incense to them" (2 Chr 25:14–16). The "Queen of Heaven" text in Jeremiah 44 mentions cakes made in the goddess' image in conjunction with burning incense and pouring libations (Jer 44:17–19).

Rituals of Procession and Travel

The ritual procession and traveling of divine images is well documented in the texts and iconography of the ancient Near East (Figure 5.13). The reasons for their travel vary: pilgrimage, installation, ritual banquets, marriage rites, and ritual warfare.[51] In Enuma Elish we read that when the gods travel their cult images stay at the hotel Babylon (a terrestrial counterpart created by Marduk to parallel the Esharra, the abode of the gods in heaven).[52] Kuntillet ʿAjrud comes to mind as well as a way station for travelers (and their gods?).

As noted by Jean-Michel de Tarragon, Paolo Xella, Gregorio del Olmo Lete, Dennis Pardee, and others, several ritual texts from Ugarit seem to indicate ritual processions of divine images.[53] KTU 1.43 mentions (the cult statues of) ʿAthtartu and the Gatharuma "entering" the royal palace, followed by offerings and a

THE ICONOGRAPHY OF DIVINITY: EL   137

Figure 5.13 A procession of deities wearing horned headdresses and mounted on various animals coming before an Assyrian king. From Maltai, located approximately 43 mi. (70 km) north of Mosul. Illustration from V. Place, *Ninive et l'Assyrie* vol 3 (Paris, Imprimierie impériale, 1867) pl 45.

banquet.[54] The king has a prominent role in the procession, welcoming the gods and walking in procession seven times after their statues.[55] KTU 1.91 mentions ʿAthtartu of the Steppe Land and (two?) Rashap (statues) entering the royal palace in conjunction with royal sacrifices.[56] In KTU 1.148.18–22, after ʿAthtartu of the Steppe Land enters the royal palace, numerous offerings are presented.[57] KTU 1.112.6–8 mentions the king's sons and daughters going up seven times to the "ḫmn sanctuary," followed by the divine statues doing likewise.[58]

In EA 164 Aziru has his divine images travel with his messenger in order to properly secure an oath.[59] In biblical tradition the Philistines send messengers throughout the land "to proclaim the good news [of Saul's defeat] to their images" (LXX 1 Sam 31:9).

Biblical writers also acknowledge that gods travel (*ĕlōhîm ʾăšer yēlĕkû lĕpānênû*, Exod 32:1; cf. Deut 1:30; 20:4; 31:6) and occasionally speak of the processions of deities. That Rachel hid the *tĕrāpîm* images (also referred to as *ʾĕlōhîm*) in the saddlebag of her camel (Gen 31:34) implies their portability (as does the small size of many extant figurines). Other divine images (such as Jeroboam's bulls) are sites of pilgrimage to which humans do the traveling.

Pilgrimage passages are presented both positively and negatively based on Yahwistic criteria. The processions that the biblical editors favored were those of "the Ark of Yahweh's covenant" (on which see Chapter Seven, pp. 364–366, 388–390, 395–397, 408; Chapter Ten, pp. 595–599). In contrast, Amos takes the positive notion of a solemn ritual procession of divine images and reverses it by noting that people will have to carry the images they made into exile (Amos 5:26). The procession of Babylonian deities is referred to in Isaiah 46:1–7 in a pejorative context:[60]

> Bel is bowed, Nebo is cowering,
> Their images are a burden for beasts and cattle;
> The things you would carry [in procession]
> Are now piled as a burden
> On tired [beasts]. (Isa 46:1; JPS)

Similarly, the polemic in Jeremiah 10:5 mocks how (illegitimate) images "have to be carried, for they cannot walk."

Use in Magic Rituals (Nurturing, Healing, Protecting)

From texts we know that gods and demons were thought to heal illnesses or inflict diseases. Similarly, cultic images were used for each of these purposes.[61] Occasionally the lines between apotropaic images and divinity become blurred. For example, the dozens of Bes amulets reflect a "personal piety" not often found in textual pantheons.[62]

At Ugarit we read of gods and royalty being suckled by 'Athiratu.[63] Such nurturing is reflected in iconography as well, as depicted in Figure 5.14.[64] Elsewhere we read of an apotropaic figure/exorcist named Shaʿtiqatu, who is fashioned by 'Ilu acting as a craftsman:

> 'Ilu fills his hands [with clay],
> With the very best clay fills his [right hand].
> He pinches off some clay. (KTU 1.16.5.25–30)

Such language is very suggestive of a clay figurine.[65] Perhaps potters at Ugarit (imitating 'Ilu) crafted figurines of Shaʿtiqatu to be used in healing rituals.

Similarly, at Ugarit we read of snake incantations mentioning gifts of snakes (KTU 1.100.73–76).[66] Were these apotropaic figurines such as those mentioned in Mesopotamian *namburbi* rituals or those attested in the archaeological record?[67]

Hector Avalos (1995a: 339–343) has documented the many metallic snakes found at various archaeological sites in Israel and its environs, such as the one from Timna. As for biblical texts, one need look no further than the Nehushtan crafted by Moses as a therapeutic ritual to cure snake bites (Num 21:8). That such an image was a threat to the Hezekian reform (2 Kgs 18:4) shows that apotropaic figurines could be viewed by some as objects of worship.[68] The suggestion that the Nehushtan was a divine image of the goddess Asherah (see Olyan 1988: 71) is speculative.

Three other biblical examples may denote cultic/divine images being viewed magically. In 1 Samuel 5, the Ark is portrayed as afflicting humans (Philistines) and deities (Dagon) alike with evil. In turn, those afflicted make even more cultic

Figure 5.14 An ivory panel from LB Ugarit showing a winged goddess with bull's horns and a Hathor-style headdress surmounted by a disk. She is suckling two (royal?) individuals.

Photo from J. Gachet-Bizollon, "Le panneau de lit en ivoire de la cour III du palais royal d'Ougarit," *Syria* 78 (2001): 29, fig. 7, pl. 2/H. Reproduced by permission of Institut français du Proche-Orient and Mission archéologique de Ras Shamra–Ougarit.

images (five golden mice and five golden tumors in 1 Sam 6:4–15) to ward off the ill effects. In Jeremiah 44:15–19, the Queen of Heaven brings prosperity (e.g., plenty of food) when proper cult such as incense and libations is presented, presumably to her statue, and tragedy (sword and famine) when left unattended. In Malachi 3:20 (Eng 4:2), the "sun of righteousness will rise with *healing* in its wings" (cf. the winged sun disks on the seals mentioned earlier).

In short, the fact that Jeremiah 10:5 urges people to

> be not afraid of [illegitimate images],
> for they cannot do evil
> neither is it in them to do good

suggests that some people thought they could do both.

Images Taken in Battle: The Exile of Statues

Capturing divine images in battle and exiling them is well attested in text and archaeology. Year after year the Old Hittite king Ḫattušili I bragged about carrying off the deities of the lands he conquered.[69] Consider too an inscription from Sargon II's palace in Dūr-Šarrukīn (= modern Khorsabad) noting that after he besieged and conquered the cities of Ashdod, Gi[mtu] (= Gath), and [Ashdod-Yam], he declared the divine images to be booty.[70] For iconography, consider the famous depiction from Nimrud of Tiglath-Pileser III's soldiers carrying away the statues of the gods of the conquered city (Figure 5.15).[71]

The Levant has not preserved any such reliefs and very few texts. Nonetheless, the texts we do have show that the practice was well known. In EA 134 we read: "From time im[memorial] the g[ods] have not gone aw[ay] from Gubla. [N]ow Aziru has sent troops t[o sei]ze it [Gubla] so that we must give up our gods a[nd they have gone for]th." In EA 252 we read Lab'ayu speaking: "The city, along with my god, was seized. . . . I will guard the men that seized the city [and] my god. They are the despoilers of my father, but I will guard them." William Moran (1992: 215, 305–306) notes that "by taking the statue or image of the family god, Lab'ayu's enemies had violated his family."

In Judges 18:24, the Danites steal Micah's cult images, prompting him to lament, "You have taken away my gods." Jeremiah 48:7 notes how the Moabite deity Chemosh (i.e., his statue) will go forth into exile. In the only explicit occurrence of its kind in the Bible, we read of the Judean king Amaziah, after defeating

Figure 5.15 Tiglath-Pileser III's soldiers carrying away captured statues of gods of a conquered city.
Kim Walton, taken at the British Museum.

the Edomites, transporting their divine images back to Judah: "He installs them as his gods, bows down to them, and offers incense to them" (2 Chr 25:14–16).[72]

The Destruction or Ritual Mutilation of Statues

At other times, the divine statue was destroyed rather than exiled. The spoliation and mutilation of statues is well known in the ancient Near East, especially in Assyrian texts, as shown by Morton Cogan.[73] And yet, as shown by Amnon Ben-Tor (2006: 11), "the intentional destruction of statues goes back to the third millennium B.C.E." Israel preserved its own paradigmatic event in the story of Moses' destruction of the so-called golden calf (specifically referred to as ʾĕlōhîm) in Exodus 32:20 (on which see pp. 198–200).[74]

Taking his clue from Deuteronomy 7:25 ("The graven images of their gods you shall burn with fire"),[75] the Deuteronomist chronicles the destruction of cultic images by numerous kings.[76] David carries off and burns the images of retreating Philistines (2 Sam 5:21; cf. 1 Chr 14:12).[77] In 2 Samuel 12:30, David takes the crown off the image of Milcom, the Ammonite god.[78] Asa removes the "images that his fathers had made," cuts down an Asherah image (mipleṣet lāʾăšērāh), and burns it at the brook of Kidron (1 Kgs 15:12–13). Similarly, Hezekiah and Josiah break masseboth and cut down the asherah (hāʾăšērāh, 2 Kgs 18:4; 23:6, 14–15). Hezekiah also breaks the Nehushtan into pieces (2 Kgs 18:4). Baal images are destroyed by the kings Joram (2 Kgs 3:2) and Jehu (2 Kgs 10:26–27), as well as the priest Jehoiada (2 Kgs 11:18).

Yet the Deuteronomist's greatest delight is in relating a story that needs no king to smash the enemy's deity (1 Sam 5:1–5). Rather, it is a battle of divine images punching it out, so to speak: in one corner is "the Ark of God," in the other the image of Dagon. Ben-Tor (2006: 14) has noted how "in all the cases of mutilation" of statues at Hazor, "the heads and hands of the statues were the primary targets." He notes how the literary image of Dagon suffers the same fate: "Dagon's head and both his hands were lying broken off upon the threshold; only his trunk was left intact" (1 Sam 5:4).

The Burial of Statues

The burial of statues (and other cult objects) is well attested in the archaeological record but rarely attested in texts. For archaeology one thinks of favissae, with examples ranging from the Ain Ghazal statues to the bronze hoard at Hazor (see Figures 5.54 and 5.55). The rationale of such burials still needs further unpacking. Are cultic images buried out of respect because they are sacral, or out of disdain because they have lost some efficacy?[79] Are the Hazor items heirlooms or scrap metal? Our best textual reference is Genesis 35:4: "So they gave to Jacob all the foreign gods that they had, and the rings that were in their ears; and Jacob hid them under the oak which was near Shechem" (cf. Keel 1973).

Section III: The Iconography of Ugaritic 'Ilu

Having rehearsed how divine images were perceived in the ancient Near East in general, one can now look closer at the iconography associated with Ugaritic 'Ilu and then with Israelite El and Yahweh. It is helpful to summarize at the outset the criteria for determining whether a specific object can be categorized as divine.

Criteria for Determining Divine Images

Ideally, one would hope to have an object that had a sufficient number of divine markers to remove all doubt about its divine status. Preferably, to identify a divine image one would like to see the use of precious metals and fine workmanship (investment of resources can correlate with prestige),[80] headdresses with divine markers (e.g., horns,[81] "Hathor" hairdo), a body posture combined with standards and/or other objects that in turn correlate with known functions (e.g., striding warrior gods wielding maces), and the use of attendant animals (e.g., bulls, lions, horses) or other motifs (e.g., sacred trees, snakes, caprids) associated with the divine in neighboring cultures. When we find such an object in a cultic assemblage, in a location designated to be cultic by some other means (see Zevit 2001: 81–266), or in a locus that indicates that the object was the clear focus of cult, we rest even more certain about assigning a divine label. Yet even here one must still search for nuances in order to determine whether the object functioned as an attribute symbol directly representing the deity or as an object associated with the paraphernalia surrounding the deity's cult. Finally, most of our doubts could be removed if only a figure could be accompanied by a clear identifying inscription such as we have for deities in Egypt.[82] Of course, meeting the ideal criteria is nearly impossible for Levantine figurines. At every turn there are a number of considerations, and scholars have been known both to rush to judgment and to be overly circumspect.

Bronze Statuary of Ugaritic 'Ilu?

Iconography from Ugarit helps us understand how artisans visualized 'Ilu using a mixture of mediums (bronze metallurgy and stone sculpture) and styles (Syrian, Egyptian, and Anatolian).[83] At the outset of studying such figurines, we need to acknowledge once again that they could represent humans or deities (most scholars see them as divine). Moreover, identifying a figurine with a specific deity is precarious when there is no accompanying inscription, a dilemma for studying most anthropomorphic metal statuary (Moorey and Fleming 1984).

THE ICONOGRAPHY OF DIVINITY: EL   143

Nonetheless, in general, we can distinguish typologically at least two distinct categories. The first category represents male deities usually striding and in a smiting position. It is the better-attested of the two and often thought to represent a warrior or storm deity (= Negbi's Type III).[84] The second category deals with "enthroned-benedictory" deities, represented as seated figures that "do not carry weapons, but hold scepters, standards, cups, bowls and goblets ... [They] are usually depicted with their right hand raised in a gesture of benediction" (Negbi 1976: 46). The latter group is attested at Ugarit in the four well-known examples seen in Figures 5.16, 5.18, 5.19, and 5.20.[85]

For all its majesty, Figure 5.16 comes not from where one might expect (from the area of the two acropolis temples or from the House of the Magician-Priest), but rather from the South City Trench at Ugarit, a densely populated residential area. This once again underscores the need to appreciate family and community religion.[86] The figurine was once horned, to judge from the drill holes

Figure 5.16 Bronze statuette with gold foil from Ugarit likely depicting the enthroned god 'Ilu. Drill holes appear above the ears, giving evidence that the figure originally had horns, a common symbol of divinity in the ancient Near East.
Reproduced by permission of Mission archéologique de Ras Shamra–Ougarit.

Figure 5.17 A divine image from Late Bronze Age Hama.
Courtesy Dick Osseman.

located above the ears.[87] Its right hand is raised in a benedictory pose, while its left hand once held an object that is now missing. It was found along with an exquisite bronze figurine of the god Baʻlu. A similar figurine can be found in the enthroned male from Late Bronze Age Hama (Figure 5.17).

Other Anthropomorphic Representations of Ugaritic ʾIlu?

A serpentine stela (Figure 5.18) depicts a cultic scene with an attendant engaged in a ritual act (holding a libation jug in his left hand and a staff of some kind in his right). He is standing before an enthroned bearded figure with a horned crown and elaborate garment, his feet resting on a footstool. This stela also comes from a crowded residential quarter, this one to the south of the acropolis temples.[88] A similar scene can be found on the drinking mug (Figure 5.19) already mentioned (see pp. 122–124). Because this mug was found in the so-called House of the Magician-Priest, Yon (2006: 147) argues that "the religious and magical

Figure 5.18 Serpentine stela from Ugarit likely depicting the god 'Ilu.
Drawing from C. F. A. Schaeffer, "Les fouilles de Ras Shamra–Ugarit huitième campagne (printemps 1936): rapport sommaire," *Syria* 18, no. 2 (1937): pl. 17. Reproduced by permission of Institut français du Proche-Orient and Mission archéologique de Ras Shamra–Ougarit.

Figure 5.19 A drinking mug from Late Bronze Age Ugarit found in the so-called House of the Magician-Priest in the south acropolis.
Reproduced by permission of Mission archéologique de Ras Shamra–Ougarit.

context in which the vase was discovered confirms that this is a cultic scene with symbolic elements."[89] Here too an officiant (bearded) is standing before an offering table that is in front of an enthroned bearded male. In his right hand he holds a libation (rhyton?) vessel. Breakage keeps us from knowing what was in his left hand. Yon's identification of the officiant as the king makes good sense here (and would equally apply to our Figure 5.18, from what we know of the royal cult, especially through the ritual texts).[90] Alternatively, the officiant could be a priestly figure. The names of elite male cultic personnel that we happen to know include ʾAttānu-purulini (diviner?);[91] the chief priest (*rb khnm*), who was also the chief of the cultic herdsmen (*rb nqdm*; KTU 1.6.6.55–56); Ḫurāṣānu, the chief priest (*ḫrṣn rb khnm*; KTU 6.10);[92] and ʾAgaptarri, a diviner mentioned in liver models used for divination (KTU 1.141; RS 24.325).[93]

Figure 5.20 comes from the so-called Rhyton Sanctuary, one of the best examples in the ancient Near East of a local sanctuary positioned in the heart of the domestic sections of the city (the Center City at Ras Shamra).[94] The religious

Figure 5.20 A limestone statuette depicting an enthroned male (ʾIlu?) from the so-called Rhyton Sanctuary at Ugarit, located in a residential district.
Reproduced by permission of Mission archéologique de Ras Shamra–Ougarit.

activities practiced within this residential cult complex (which included an oil press) were thriving at the same time as those taking place within the two acropolis temples, the palace, and the royal sacred space known as the Hurrian temple. Yet, as Yon (1996: 416) underscores, the rhyton "temple did not have the status of those of the acropolis: this can be observed both in the mediocre quality of the architecture and the common quality of the offerings and furnishings found associated with it. There are no royal aspects."

The handsome statuette is carved from limestone. The enthroned male once looked even more regal with arms and inlaid eyes (now lost through the ravages of time).[95] We cannot be certain whether this individual is a human being of high rank or a deity. Most if not all scholars argue for the latter, especially because of the exquisite workmanship, yet the absence of horns (a common symbol of divinity) gives us slight pause.

Figures 5.16, 5.18, 5.19, and 5.20, while not uniform in all respects (note, for example, the unusual raised left hand in Figure 5.18 and the absence of horns in Figure 5.20), seem to represent the deity 'Ilu (a consensus among scholars) because their physical representations coincide with the description of 'Ilu we find in Ugaritic literature (bearded, aged, bull [= horned], benevolent, enthroned with footstool, etc.). One would be hard pressed to find another Ugaritic deity whose textual description comes anywhere close to combining all of the features that we see depicted graphically in these figurines. Ba'lu, for example, has horns (Curtis 1990), and there is also mention of his footstool (KTU 1.6.1.59–60), but nowhere at Ugarit is he depicted as an aged deity wearing a beard. Thus 'Ilu is the obvious choice for the deity in these representations. One is tempted to compare the bare feet (though with exquisite sandals in Figure 5.16) in the iconography with KTU 1.4.4.29–30, where 'Ilu seems to be tapping his toes with delight at the approach of 'Athiratu![96]

Excursus on a Seal from Mari

For practical purposes we have restricted our study of the Late Bronze Age backdrop of Israelite divinity (especially El worship) to Ugarit, with its rich documentation in text and object. Yet in the present case, one other exemplar needs to be mentioned because of the extensive argument made by one of the world's leading specialists in Near Eastern iconography, Othmar Keel (1997: 47–49; 1986: 309), who in turn was building on the work of Pierre Amiet (1960).[97] A well-known cylinder seal from Mari (Figure 5.21) depicts a deity enthroned on a mountain from which flow rivers (out of serpents' heads) that blend with two flanking goddesses who in turn produce tree branches. Though the image presents obvious connections to Ea and Anu, Keel suggests that because of Mari's geographic location "the god on the mountain could

Figure 5.21 A cylinder seal from Mari depicting a deity enthroned on a mountain from which flow rivers (out of serpents' heads) that blend with two flanking goddesses who in turn produce tree branches.

From Helene J. Kantor, "Landscape in Akkadian Art," *Journal of Near Eastern Studies* 25.3 (1966) Plate XV, Fig. 4. Courtesy of the *Journal of Near Eastern Studies*. Drawing by Helene J. Kantor.

therefore be taken as the Canaanite El or some related figure." Using the Ugaritic reference to 'Ilu's mountain abode being located "in the midst of the sources of the two oceans" (see Chapter Four, p. 76), Keel concludes that "El, like the god of the mountain [in this figure], unites in himself aspects both of Anu and Ea."

As tempting as this interpretation is, it should be noted that the seal in question comes from circa 2350–2150 BCE.[98] While religious motifs can be long-lasting, such a large gap in time between the date of this seal and the Late Bronze Age should prompt caution.

Theriomorphic Representations of Ugaritic 'Ilu?

In agrarian societies it is not surprising that gods were associated with animals, as we can clearly see in the well-attested iconographic motifs of "the lord of the animals" and "the mistress of animals."[99] Deities were also commonly associated with majestic animals in the ancient Near East, thereby absorbing metaphorically the beast's strength, virility, and power. Evidence can be found in the animal epithets used of deities in literary texts and onomastica.[100] In material culture we find both divine images of the deity in theriomorphic form and small votive statuettes of a particular animal that were given as a fitting offering to a deity. Though fluctuations could occur, including what Tallay Ornan (2001, 2006: 303)

THE ICONOGRAPHY OF DIVINITY: EL   149

Figure 5.22 A Hittite king worshipping before a bull image of the storm god from the city gate at Alaca Höyük.
Photograph courtesy of Billie Jean Collins.

terms "visual syncretism," many deities had one particular animal with which they were associated, such as Ishtar's lion, Marduk's *mušḫuššu* dragon, Hathor's cow, Anubis' jackal, Bastet and Sekhmet's lion, Khnum's ram, Hadad's bull, Astarte's horse, and so on. Such animals were attribute animals that represented the deity in a tangible way. Compare, for example, the bull image (Figure 5.22) on the orthostat relief from the city gate at Alaca Höyük, which clearly represented the Hittite storm god receiving worship from the king.[101]

One of the most common artistic motifs was to depict deities mounted on the backs of such animals.[102] Examples abound, such as the procession of the gods pictured in Figure 5.13. In this relief from Maltai, we see various gods standing on dragons, bulls, lions, and horses. Artisans commonly pictured warrior deities and storm deities riding on the backs of bulls (and occasionally lions; cf. ANEP §486). The widespread nature of this motif can be seen through the examples coming from Jekke (Figure 5.23), Arslan Tash (Figure 5.24), Tell Ahmar (Figure 5.25), Ahmar/Qubbah (Figure 5.26), Hazor (Figure 5.27), and Byblos (Figure 5.28). A variant theme has a bull pulling the storm god's chariot (Figure 5.29).[103]

Of special note are deities mounted on the hybrid or composite animals sometimes referred to as *Mischwesen* (see Figure 5.30).[104] *Mischwesen* show up in biblical tradition in a variety of dragon creatures (cf. Lewis 1996b) as well

Figure 5.23 A mid-eighth-century BCE stela from Jekke, Syria, depicting the storm god standing on the back of a bull.
Courtesy Theodore J. Lewis.

as in the cherubim, beings that mix together, at least according to the prophet Ezekiel, features of humans, lions, birds, and bulls. The appearance of such fantastic beasts complemented mythological texts that described otherworldly creatures. In one particular genre (the so-called *Chaoskampf* traditions), we read of divine battles that were elevated to a cosmic scale because of the nature of such foes. Warrior gods (e.g., Marduk in Enuma Elish or Baʿlu in the Baʿlu Cycle) demonstrated their sovereign majesty by defeating overwhelming powers (often labeled "chaos monsters") that made even other gods shudder in fear. (See the detailed discussion of *Chaoskampf* traditions in Chapter Eight, pp. 430–461.)

In light of this, it is easily within the realm of consideration to interpret animal images as describing the deity ʾIlu at Ugarit, and especially to nominate bull figurines because of the divine epithet "the Bull," which ʾIlu alone bears. However, even though bronze bulls have been found in Ugarit's archaeological record, it is difficult to determine whether they were used as divine symbols. One

THE ICONOGRAPHY OF DIVINITY: EL   151

Figure 5.24 A stela from Arslan Tash (eighth century BCE) depicting a striding god wielding two double tridents (lightning?) and standing on a bull.
Kim Walton, taken at the Louvre.

cannot judge merely by craftsmanship. For example, one splendidly fashioned recumbent bronze bull found at Ugarit (see Yon 2006: 171 §65) has the figure "20" carved into its side, representing twenty units of measurement, and thus it is surely a weight. Even if a cultic context can be demonstrated, such items may be votive offerings *to* a deity rather than representations *of* a deity in theriomorphic form. Indeed, an exquisitely fashioned bull from third-millennium Iran (Figure 5.31) shocks our culturally based assumptions when we realize that the ancients could even depict bulls in human posture and clothes lifting up hooves in an act of supplication. With these cautions in mind, we can suggest Figure 5.32 as the best candidate for representing "Bull 'Ilu" at Ugarit.

Olivier Callot (1994: 187, 224) has documented how this figurine was found together with two very well-known divine images, one of 'Ilu (Figure 5.16), the other of Baal.[105] This context, together with the bronze's superb craftsmanship and features ("a powerful bull with strongly emphasized sexual organs"), may suggest 'Ilu (so too Schaeffer [1966: 4–5], who equated it with

Figure 5.25 A basalt stela from Tell Ahmar depicting a smiting storm god with axe, trident, and sword standing on the back of a bull.
Courtesy Theodore J. Lewis.

our Figure 5.16).[106] Compare again "Bull 'Ilu," who brags about his sexual nature in KTU 1.4.4.38–39 (cf. KTU 1.23). A. H. W. Curtis (1990: 31) argues that "Bull" is a fitting epithet for 'Ilu even if he is not strongly connected to fertility at Ugarit because the term can equally refer to the qualities of strength and dignity. Less likely, the bronze figurine here could refer to Baʿlu, who is also associated with bulls (although he does not bear the epithet *tr*, "bull")[107] and fertility, yet his iconography (a striding storm/warrior figurine sometimes portrayed with horns) is strikingly different.[108] It would seem prudent to distinguish between freestanding bull figurines and the common representation of the storm deity riding on top of a bull (see Figures 5.23–5.28). Cornelius (1994: 165, 228) goes so far as to say that "the title 'bull' is the prerogative of 'Ilu." He concludes that "Baʿal is never represented as a bull" and that "Baʿal is never depicted as a *bull* in (old) Canaanite iconography . . . although he has bull horns [with an anthropomorphic body]."[109]

THE ICONOGRAPHY OF DIVINITY: EL   153

Figure 5.26 A stela from northern Syria depicting a smiting storm god with axe, trident, and sword standing on the back of a bull. It was found in 1999 between the modern village of Qubbah and the site of Tell Ahmar.

Photo from G. Bunnens, *A New Luwian Stele and the Cult of the Storm God at Til Barsip* (Peeters, 2006), 140, fig. 7. Courtesy Peeters Publishers.

Though our focus has been on Ugaritic ʾIlu, it should be noted that Levantine bull images within cultic contexts appear elsewhere and they too should be examined when considering theriomorphic images of Canaanite ʾIlu/El. Three freestanding bulls are of particular note.[110] A bronze statuette of a mature zebu bull acquired by the Ashmolean museum in 1889 is of particularly fine workmanship. Moorey (1971) dates it to the eighth century BCE and notes North Syrian and Urartian stylistic influences. Regrettably, the statuette (which Moorey considers "a miniature version of a monumental votive statue of a bull") is unprovenanced, and thus any attempt to relate it to a deity would be speculative. A small bronze bull statuette (Figure 5.33) once coated with silver was found at Middle Bronze Age II Ashkelon (ca. 1600 BCE). This superbly fashioned statuette (4 in. [10 cm] high, 4 in. [10 cm] long) was found together with a pottery model

154 THE ORIGIN AND CHARACTER OF GOD

Figure 5.27 A statue of a storm god adorned with a crescent-and-disc emblem and sword standing on a bull from Hazor Temple H, stratum 1B (fourteenth century BCE).
Courtesy of the Selz Foundation Hazor Excavations in Memory of Yigael Yadin. Photo by Kim Walton, taken at the Israel Museum.

shrine complete with miniature doorway (Stager 2008: 577–580). Consider too the bronze bull statuette (Figure 5.34) from the Phoenician temple of "the Lady of Byblos" (nineteenth/eighteenth century BCE). Yet a simple, astute observation by Daniel Fleming gives us pause: these two images are of slender young bull calves, not muscular, fully grown bulls.[111] Fleming (1999a: 23*) argues that "El's identity as bull, not calf, is inseparable from his position as head of the gods. He stands in the generation of the divine parents and cannot equally be treated as a calf." In order to support this thesis, Fleming notes how the description of the young bull calf is not used of senior members of pantheons in the ancient Near East such as Anu, Enlil, Taru, Teššub, and 'Ilu. A term such as "calf," designating offspring, would naturally be inappropriate for heads of the pantheons. Thus we agree with Fleming (1999a: 25*) when he concludes: "Surely, then, the calves from Middle Bronze Ashkelon and Byblos do not represent El or a god of

THE ICONOGRAPHY OF DIVINITY: EL 155

Figure 5.28 A male figure astride a bull from Byblos.
© Philippe Maillard/akg-images.

equivalent status." The best alternative is to see the god Baʿlu/Haddu represented by such young bull calves.[112]

Section IV: The Iconography of Israelite El

Iconography: What Did Israelite El Look Like?

One might think that it would be easy to find pictures of the divine in ancient Israel's material culture. A glance at the wall paintings and statuary of ancient Egypt or the kudurru stones, clay figurines, and glyptic art from Mesopotamia (not to mention the Ugaritic material previously rehearsed) shows a celebration of divinity in all types of artistic media. Divine symbols in all shapes and sizes (anthropomorphic, theriomorphic, astral, vegetative, emblems, standards, etc.) were woven into the fabric of ancient Near Eastern societies. In contrast, Iron Age Israel, with its lack of physical representations of male divinity, is

Figure 5.29 A bull pulling the storm god's chariot from the temple on the Aleppo Citadel.
Mission Archéologique d'Alep/Kay Kohlmeyer.

exceptional. (The rationale for the aniconic tradition in ancient Israel is taken up on pp. 333–426.) In contrast to the absence of concrete representations, literary texts freely employ anthropomorphic language for El and Yahweh. There are, however, certain depictions for which we have no evidence even here. For example, in contrast to Ugaritic ʾIlu, Israelite El is never portrayed imbibing to the point of inebriation (cf. KTU 1.114) or engaging in sexual intercourse (cf. KTU 1.23).

Bronze Statuary of Pre-Israelite/Israelite El?
This is not the place to interact with the numerous studies on Syro-Palestinian bronze statuary.[113] As with the figures from ancient Syria, we can distinguish typologically two distinct categories in ancient Israel: (1) male storm/warrior deities, usually striding and in a smiting position, and (2) enthroned benedictory deities, who do not brandish a weapon but rather hold a variety of objects, often those involved with banqueting. The second category is relevant for Israelite El, who was seen to be a sovereign yet benevolent father. A gesture of benediction from an enthroned patriarch would fit what we know of his character from textual sources. Though Israelite El was able to fight to protect his kinsmen, the lack

Figure 5.30 A Neo-Assyrian depiction of Aššur riding on the back of a *Mischwesen* creature.
Kim Walton, taken at the Vorderasiatisches Museum, Berlin.

of textual descriptions of him as a striding storm/warrior deity makes the first category unlikely.

In the second category (enthroned males in benedictory pose) there are several candidates to consider for unpacking the possibility of El worship. Most of the male figurines to be discussed here come from the Late Bronze Age, and those that have been found in later Iron Age contexts have been seen to be heirlooms of the Late Bronze period by most scholars.

A bronze figurine from Hazor (Figure 5.35; from Area B, stratum XI, found in a jar under the floor of locus 3283) is a case in point. As we have seen, Dever wrote in 1983 that "no representations of a *male* deity in terra cotta, metal, or stone, have ever been found in clear Iron Age contexts, *except possibly for an El statuette in bronze from 12th-century Hazor*."[114] Dever wisely questioned whether the context was "necessarily Israelite."[115] In contrast, much was made of the figurine by Ahlström, who called it "an *Israelite* god figurine" (my italics); rather

Figure 5.31 A silver bull in human posture and dress holding a Proto-Elamite spouted vase, ca. 2900 BCE.
Courtesy The Metropolitan Museum of Art.

than seeing a reference to El, Ahlström suggested that here we have "Yahweh or Yahweh-El."[116]

A closer look at the archaeological picture shows that Ahlström was mistaken, as Keel and William Hallo surmised early on.[117] According to Dever, much of this interpretation can be traced back to Yigael Yadin's interest in showing an Israelite presence at Hazor. But what Yadin and Ahlström call a "foundation deposit" is in reality a hoard of Late Bronze Age (thirteenth century BCE) implements (cf. the hoard of such material at Byblos). Today most if not all scholars identify this bronze and the other objects found alongside as remnants of earlier, pre-Israelite material culture.[118] (See pp. 180–184 on the cultic space in which this bronze figurine was found.) Thus Ahlström's identification with Yahweh is impossible. As a seated figurine in benedictory pose (cf. Negbi 1976: 46), the figure would be analogous to the four Ugaritic 'Ilu figures mentioned earlier, but note the lack of a beard.[119] The lack of horns makes Ronald Hendel wonder whether it might be human rather than divine (Hendel

Figure 5.32 A bronze figurine of a muscular bull ('Ilu?) standing on a plinth found in the south city of Ugarit together with several statuettes of deities, including Figure 5.16.

From C. F. A. Schaeffer, "Nouveaux témoignages du culte de El et de Baal à Ras Shamra–Ugarit et ailleurs en Syrie-Palestine," *Syria* 43 (1966): pl. I. Reproduced by permission of Institut français du Proche-Orient and Mission archéologique de Ras Shamra–Ougarit.

1997: 212; Negbi 1989: 358–359; cf. Moorey and Fleming 1984; see Figures 5.20 and 5.36, 5.38–5.43, all without horns).

A 13.75-in. (35 cm) bronze figurine once coated with precious metal (Figure 5.36) was found in the 1996 excavations at Hazor directed by Ben-Tor.[120] Ornan (2011: 255) observes that we have here "the largest seated statue known so far from the preclassical Levant." This meticulously made figurine was found in a Late Bronze context, deliberately buried ("to protect from desecration by marauders," suggest Ben-Tor and Rubiato [1999: 36]) in one of the side rooms next to the throne room of Area A of the acropolis in the heart of the upper city. Presumed to be a deity because of his elaborate dress and crown, this figure is seated in a benedictory pose and thus is similar to enthroned figures thought to designate the deity El. At the same time, the raised right hand of this figurine is turned to the side and parallel to the chest, and the figure is beardless.[121]

160 THE ORIGIN AND CHARACTER OF GOD

Figure 5.33 A bronze bull calf statuette with silver overlay from Ashkelon and its model shrine (Middle Bronze Age IIC, ca. 1600 BCE).
Kim Walton, taken at the Israel Museum.

Ornan sees this figurine as representing Baal because of the depiction of the "tree and horned animals" motif that appears on the statue's crown (Figure 5.37). This motif is well known, especially in the Levant, to illustrate the connection of female divinity with the abundance of flora and fauna (Ornan 2011: 267–269).[122] Ornan (2011: 268, 271) argues that the motif of the abundance of nature is significant for identifying the deity in question and concludes (based especially on Ugaritic parallels) "that the Hazor statue can be identified as Baʿal, who was strongly associated with the fertility of the land by virtue of his patronage of rains and storms." Ornan is certainly correct to point to other iconography that associated Baal with plant life, such as the vegetation growing out of his lance on the famous Ugaritic *Baal au foudre* stela or the god with a plant-like (or feather-like?) crown on a stela found west of the temple of Baʿlu.[123] And yet for another male deity who is better situated as the patron of abundance of flora *and* fauna, one must consider the deity El. This is especially underscored

THE ICONOGRAPHY OF DIVINITY: EL   161

Figure 5.34 A bronze bull statuette from the Phoenician temple of the "Lady of Byblos" (nineteenth–eighteenth century BCE).
Wikimedia Commons. Photo courtesy of Tangopaso.

in the Ugaritic text KTU 1.23, where 'Ilu is "the Guardian of the sown land" (*nǵr mdrʿ*), who provides bounty with respect to both fertile fields and steppe lands, where sheep and goat pastoralism was supplemented by hunting activity.[124] The synergy between god ('Ilu) and king as being responsible for agricultural sustenance in KTU 1.23 would parallel the divine/royal profile of Hazor Area A. In short, Baal does not have a corner on fertility and other agrarian concerns, nor on royal cult.

Rather than positing a new style type for this Hazor bronze (Ornan's [2011: 279] "the Reigning Baʿal"), one could argue that if El is designated in Figure 5.36, it would be a good fit for the general typology, where more often than not Baal figures are striding with arm raised whereas El-type figures are seated in benedictory pose. The striding male figurine (Baal?) in smiting pose (Figure 5.38) found in the palace courtyard could suggest that the artisans at Hazor held to this general typology. On the other hand, Ornan (2011: 276–277) makes the astute observation that at Ugarit Baal certainly sits enthroned, and this is tied to his royal nature. Yet as we have seen in Chapter Four, 'Ilu too is king, and he too exercises his royal (and lifegiving) sovereignty over Motu, whose rule was

Figure 5.35 A bronze figurine from Hazor from Area B, stratum XI, found in a jar under the floor of Locus 3283.
Courtesy of the Selz Foundation Hazor Excavations in Memory of Yigael Yadin.

characterized by drought and death (KTU 1.6.6.27–29; KTU 1.23.8–9; see Lewis forthcoming a).

Firmer conclusions will be possible only with the final excavation reports, when these figurines are understood within their broader cultic context, which also included an enthroned ruler and three small bronze bull figurines (Ben-Tor and Rubiato 1999: 35–36; Ben-Tor 2016: 105–106, 109–110; cf. Ornan 2011: 253–254).[125] Hazor's well-developed cults that centered around standing stones must also be factored into our considerations (see pp. 176–183).

Hazor's expansive economic base and relations with countries far and wide—consider the mention of Hazor in Egyptian and Mari texts (cf. Ben-Tor 1997) as well as the fifteen cuneiform inscriptions found at Hazor (including two texts from the Amarna period),[126] not to mention an ivory box with Hathor images (Ben-Tor and Rubiato 1999: 35)—warn against looking only at Northwest Semitic deities for the identity of these bronze figurines. On the other hand, whereas Mari personal names contain both eastern and western theophoric

Figure 5.36 A large seated bronze figurine from Hazor (Area A) with elaborate dress and crown (Late Bronze Age).
Courtesy of the Selz Foundation Hazor Excavations in Memory of Yigael Yadin.

names, to date the Hazor cuneiform archive yields no clear example of an eastern deity. Those names that we do possess argue, once again, for El and Adad, with Ruhama Bonfil (1997: 101, followed by Hesse 2008: 163) privileging El as the primary deity worshipped in Hazor Area A.[127]

There are other examples of enthroned male figurines. See Ora Negbi's convenient compilation, which includes bronzes from Beth-Shemesh (Figure 5.39; loc. 135, str. III; Negbi #1450), Megiddo (Figure 5.40; loc. 2048; str. VII–VI; Negbi fig. 59, #1453),[128] Beth-Shean (Figure 5.41; level V southern temple; Negbi #1448), and Tel Kinneret (Figure 5.42), as well as an unprovenanced bronze housed in the Harvard Semitic Museum that is said to have come from Nablus (Figure 5.43; Negbi #1449).[129]

All of these figurines seem to be representative of the Late Bronze Age. The Beth-Shemesh bronze (Figure 5.39) was labeled Iron I by Negbi, following Donald Hansen.[130] G. E. Wright had noted that this bronze was out of context and probably belongs to stratum IV (= LB).[131] Dever has noted that this too is

Figure 5.37 A "tree and horned animals" motif that appears on the crown of the male figure from Hazor depicted in Figure 5.36.

From Tallay Ornan, "'Let Baʿal Be Enthroned': The Date, Identification, and Function of a Bronze Statue from Hazor," *Journal of Near Eastern Studies* 70, no. 2: 253–280. Courtesy of the *Journal of Near Eastern Studies*. Drawing by Helena Bitan.

an LB heirloom.[132] Similarly, even though the Tel Kinneret (Tell el-ʿOreimeh) figurine (Figure 5.42) was found in an Iron Age (eighth-century BCE) context, Volkmar Fritz (1993: 300), who identifies it with El, states that "according to its style it was manufactured in the Late Bronze Age." The Iron Age dating suggested for the Harvard Semitic Museum bronze (Figure 5.43) said to have come from Nablus has no foundation. Hansen (1957: 15) prefers the fourteenth century for this figurine, dating it "with the Palestinian group of the Late Bronze and *Iron I* Ages" (my emphasis). Without a provenance, any assignment to the Iron Age is baseless (Lewis 1996a: 418–422). Thus it seems best to conclude, along with Hendel (1997: 216–217), that these bronzes

> are Late Bronze Age types that represent what P. R. S. Moorey and S. Fleming (1984: 73) define as "the end of the Canaanite tradition in the region to be occupied by the kingdoms of Judah and Israel." These types were no longer produced after the eleventh and tenth centuries BCE. . . . Some of these figurines may have been objects of cult, while others may have been kept as heirlooms or antiquities.

As with the Hazor bronzes, we cannot be sure of the identity of these figurines. Given the relatively large size (approx. 9.8 in. [25 cm]) of the Megiddo bronze, its gold-leaf covering, its headdress, its pose, and its find spot (Temple 2048),

Figure 5.38 A striding male figurine (Baal?) in smiting pose found at Hazor in the palace courtyard.
Courtesy of the Selz Foundation Hazor Excavations in Memory of Yigael Yadin.

scholars readily identify it as a divine image. The other bronzes, while not as well marked for divinity, have some combination of indicators such that scholars regularly identify them as divine figurines. If these figurines do indeed represent deities (which seems likely), they are of the subgroup that includes El but is not restricted to him. Signs of foreign influence (e.g., the *w3s*-scepter on the Beth-Shean figurine [Figure 5.41]) caution us not to restrict our identifications to the West Semitic realm.[133] All we can conclude with some certainty is that these figurines do not seem to represent storm and/or warrior figures, so such deities known from the regional pantheon as Baal, Hadad, Reshep, and Rakib-el need to be set aside.[134] We cannot be certain that these figurines represent El. Even in those instances where one might wish to align the material record with biblical tradition (the Nablus/"Shechem" figure with pre-Israelite El Berith?), we cannot extrapolate any firm evidence that would help us understand how El was portrayed in Iron Age Israel.[135] The closest we would come would be the Tel Kinneret bronze because of its use in the Iron IIB period (Fritz 1990: 115).

166 THE ORIGIN AND CHARACTER OF GOD

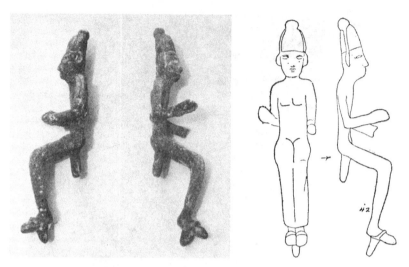

Figure 5.39 A seated male bronze figurine from Beth Shemesh. Courtesy Haverford College.

The Beth Shean Seal

Keel and Uehlinger have argued in detail that a cylinder seal from Beth Shean (Figure 5.44) helps document the importance of El worship, especially in the Iron Age IIC period.[136] Using epigraphic data such as the 'l qn 'rṣ inscription from Jerusalem (see Chapter Four, p. 81) and the Khirbet Beit Lei inscriptions (see Chapter Six, p. 245) combined with the biblical El-Elyon traditions, they go so far as to assert that "*El*-aspects advance into the foreground of the Palestinian religious symbol system during Iron Age IIC, especially in the central parts of the country" (1998: 311, fig. 308; Uehlinger 1997: 142).

The seal appears in two registers and represents, in Keel and Uehlinger's (1998: 312) words, "an iconographic anthology of deities and other numinous beings." The primary figures in the upper register include a winged "Lord (?) of the Animals" and a kneeling archer in a hunting scene together with a standing caprid in the middle and a winged composite animal on the right below the archer and his prey. According to Keel and Uehlinger, the lower register stands in "remarkable contrast." From left to right we have another (but different) winged composite animal, a tall jar, a stylized tree, a caprid, an upright male holding an object (a fan?), a small figure with a long pointed object, a seated bearded male wrapped in a lengthy garment and holding a jug, another (but different) stylized tree, and an armed man.

Such a complex symbol set urges caution. The multiplicity of images and scenes makes a uniform interpretation difficult. Yet Keel and Uehlinger (1998: 313) conclude that the lower register portrays "*one* complex constellation." Moreover, "the

Figure 5.40 A seated Late Bronze Age II male bronze figurine gilded with gold leaf from Megiddo.
Courtesy of the Oriental Institute of the University of Chicago.

juxtaposition of the . . . enthroned male figure and the . . . cultic symbol, which mediates the blessing of the god in the form of a stylized tree, points clearly to the fact that this is *a representation of El and 'his asherah'*" (1998: 314, italics theirs, underlining mine).[137] They conclude by noting that here we have a "completely independent confirmation for the interpretation of the meaning 'Yahweh . . . and his *asherah*'" in the inscriptions from Kuntillet ʿAjrud and Khirbet el-Qom (on which see Chapter Six, pp. 236–243, and Chapter Seven, pp. 325–330).

Yet the difficulties in interpreting the evidence from this cylinder seal provide enough reasonable doubt that such a certain verdict cannot be rendered. Who, for example, is the "armed man" behind the seated figure, and how does he function? The royal images in the bottom register also present problems. Keel and Uehlinger write:

> In front of the [seated figure] stands a servant with fan or brush.[138] A comparable figure *never* appears in front of a god in contemporary glyptic art; one

Figure 5.41 A seated Late Bronze Age male bronze figurine from Beth-Shean holding a w3s-scepter.
Kim Walton, taken at the Israel Museum.

does appear, however, in the Neo-Assyrian cultic scenes in front of a standing or seated king. . . . Aspects that are connected with a king's display of his royalty that appear frequently in Neo-Assyrian cylinder seal glyptic art (a servant with a brush, a cup being raised) appear here as well, in the royal imagery. (Keel and Uehlinger 1998: 313–314, emphasis mine)

In light of these data, Keel and Uehlinger's solution, that the royal imagery "portrays a local deity," is not convincing.[139] In addition, they argue that the *asherah* is represented here by a "conflation" of two separate motifs associated with the goddess elsewhere, the winged creature and the caprid, who appear to the left and right, respectively, of the stylized tree. Granted, the goddess Asherah may be portrayed elsewhere by flanked caprids and lions, yet as we saw with Figure 5.37, so is the male deity from Hazor Area A. The use of single creatures here and the unexplained tall jug (to the left of the tree), which interrupts such a clean portrayal, when added to the royal imagery that suggests a human king

THE ICONOGRAPHY OF DIVINITY: EL   169

Figure 5.42 A bronze seated figure from Tell el-ʿOreme (Tel Kinneret), likely Late Bronze Age II.
Kim Walton, taken at the Israel Museum.

(not to mention the unexplained armed man), add up to too much uncertainty to confirm their assertion that this seal "clearly" depicts "El and '*his asherah*.'" Lastly, while ʾIlu and ʾAthiratu are attested as a pair at Late Bronze Age Ugarit, our Iron Age Judean sources (i.e., epigraphic material and the biblical tradition) suggest the pairing of Baal and/or Yahweh with the *asherah*, not El.

Masseboth as Representations of El?

The etymological origin of cultic stones known as betyls or baetyls (from *bēt-ʾel*, "the house of God/El") predisposes us to look for ways in which sacred stones were envisioned as physical representations of the deity El.[140] Primarily as a result of research by Mettinger (esp. 1995), who builds much of his foundation on the work of the archaeologist Uzi Avner, scholars have been reanalyzing how standing stones known as *masseboth* (sing. *massebah*) may represent divine

Figure 5.43 An unprovenanced seated male bronze figure that is said to have come from Nablus. Harvard Semitic Museum 1907.3.1.

Courtesy of the Semitic Museum, Harvard University.

Figure 5.44 A cylinder seal from Beth Shean with two registers depicting numerous scenes including a "lord of the animals" and kneeling archer (top) as well as a stylized tree and seated bearded male (bottom).

Image from O. Keel and C. Uehlinger, *Gods, Goddesses, and Images of God*. © Fortress Press. Reproduced by permission.

symbols.[141] As for a *massebah* representing a divine symbol of El, Mettinger looks to the description of worship at Bethel found in Genesis 28. He writes: "The pre-Yahwistic cult at Bethel was focussed on an El deity (with a standing stone as the major manifestation of his presence)" (1997b: 192; cf. 1995: 140-141). Similarly, Marjo Korpel (1999a: 819) equates standing stones with ancestor cults, which are—"at least at Hazor"—associated with a cult of El (cf. de Moor 1995a; Bonfil 1997: 100-101).

The interpretation of the *masseboth* material (archaeological and textual) is tricky business, with pitfalls everywhere. One need only remember failed past attempts where architectural pillars were mistakenly viewed as divine because of the strong desire to interpret every object coming out of the ground as cultic (Shiloh 1979: 147). In addition, archaeologists must decide whether to interpret a fallen slab as a *massebah*, a house pillar, a table, or an altar. As for textual interpretation, Carl Graesser (1969: 1-25; 1972) has documented a long history of scholarship that introduced extraneous items (e.g., primitive stone worship, phallic symbols, sacred mountains) into the reading of a text.

Mettinger (1995: 32, 37) concludes too strongly that "the cultic function seems to me to be predominant" and, with even less justification, that the "cultic *masseboth* must be regarded as aniconic representations of the divine." Even if he were correct with the first claim, this by no means implies the second. The archaeological record is simply replete with standing stones in all shapes, sizes, and number, and it would be naive to think that every grouping documents a pantheon.[142] The same can be said of the textual material. There are two passages that do indeed indicate that a *massebah* could represent a divine symbol. (Unfortunately for the present discussion, neither is associated with El.) 2 Kings 3:2 specifically mentions "the *massebah* of Baal which his father made," and in 2 Kings 10:26-27 we read of "the *massebah* of Baal," which resided in "the temple of Baal," demolished during Jehu's purge (cf. 2 Kgs 23:14).[143] It is equally clear that there are standing stones that did *not* mark the deity's presence. *Masseboth* could function as tombstones (for Rachel, Gen 35:19-20), as boundary markers (between Jacob and Laban; Gen 31:44-49), as markers for twelve tribes (Exod 24:3-8), and as a surrogate for a male heir (2 Sam 18:18).[144] In none of these passages is a *massebah* symbolic of a deity. None of the four biblical passages that Mettinger (1995: 140) proposes to show "*masseboth* as representations of the deity" is explicit (cf. Lewis 1998).

What makes matters even more difficult are the clear indications that *masseboth* could be used to mark encounters with a deity and not the deity per se. Here it is instructive to look at the related verbal root *nṣb/yṣb*, where the deity acts as subject. As Joseph Reindl (1998: 528) has observed, in the Hebrew Bible there are eight occurrences of Yahweh/Elohim in this capacity, with an additional four occurrences that have the quasi-divine *mal'ak*-Yahweh as subject (on which see Chapter Seven, pp. 349–353). In several of these episodes, God "stands" before an individual in a dream or a vision (e.g., with Jacob in Gen 28:23; with Amos in Amos 7:7; 9:1; with the boy Samuel in 1 Sam 3:10). In yet another, Yahweh "stands" before Moses via a cloud (Exod 34:5). In Psalm 82:1, God "stands" among the deities who make up the divine council (cf. Job 1:6; 2:1). In the Balaam oracles, the *mal'ak*-Yahweh "stands" in the road, visible to the donkey but not to the human Balaam (Num 22:22–23, 31, 34). It is clear from all of these passages that the authors are *not* speaking of a physical entity that one could see in real (non-dream, waking, non-mystical) space. If the same notion of the root meaning (i.e., √*nṣb/yṣb*, used of divinity) is operative in the noun pattern (*maṣṣēbâ/maṣṣēbôt*, used of divinity), then perhaps we should view some of the standing stones more anthropologically. In other words, individuals may have desired to use a "standing stone" (*maṣṣēbâ*) to mark physically in space and time what they perceived to be a mystical encounter with the deity "standing" before them. (Analogously, yet in the non-mystical realm, stones were used to commemorate all sorts of social encounters, such as treaties, boundary negotiations, and funerals.) Such a commemorative marking may or may not imply that the deity was thought to inhabit the stone. (For further exploration of this conceptualization, see Chapter Seven, pp. 333–336).

Returning to archaeology, according to Bloch-Smith's (2005, 2006, 2015) synthetic treatments, we do have clear examples of *masseboth* in both public space and cultic contexts from the Iron I and Iron II periods. Bloch-Smith (2006) categorizes what she calls "questionable or mistakenly identified *masseboth*" (Megiddo, Tell Ta'anach, Lahav, Jerusalem, a basalt saddle quern at Lachish, Beth Shemesh), as opposed to "the best candidates for *masseboth*." The latter she categorizes by either "public space" (Tell el-Far'ah N, Lachish, Tel Dan) or "sacred space" (Shechem, the Bull Site, Hazor, Arad). When the *masseboth* occur in clear cultic contexts, they may very well represent the deity/deities.[145] Let us briefly examine Bloch-Smith's last four examples as well as additional examples coming from Hazor Area A and Area M, the gate complex at Tel Dan, and a stela from Khirbet Ataruz.[146]

Masseboth at Shechem

According to Lawrence Stager, three *masseboth* in the vicinity of Temple 1 functioned well into the Iron I period.[147] A huge *massebah* (Figure 5.45) of worked limestone (with a corresponding stone socket) stood 6.5 ft. (2 m) southeast of the temple. Though broken, its current measurements are impressive: 5.4 ft. (165 cm) tall × 4.75 ft. (145 cm) wide × 1.4 ft. (42 cm) thick. Graesser (1969: 181) called it "perhaps the most striking of all Palestinian *maṣṣēbôt*." Estimates of its original height put it twice as high. Two small standing stones (with stone sockets)

Figure 5.45 What remains of an impressively large standing stone of worked limestone at Shechem. The original is estimated to have been approximately 10 ft. (3 m) in height.
Zev Radovan/Bible Land Pictures.

flanked the entrance to the temple in its later phases, according to Stager.[148] The huge *massebah* has the classic attention-focusing characteristics needed to indicate cult and is located next to a large rectangular open-air altar in the forecourt of the temple. Its great size can mark divinity, if not directly then at least by association, as we see elsewhere with the huge Molten Sea, which also stood in a temple courtyard. Yet seeing this large stela as a divine image is complicated in that it is not located in a cultic niche in the inner sanctum of the temple, where one would like to have a divine image reside (contrast Arad and Hazor, discussed later). Moreover, Stager (1999: 233; 2003: 33) even suggests that it may have been plastered and "once bore an elaborate inscription."[149] If this proves true, its communicative value may have been more didactic in nature. Stager is influenced by Deuteronomy 27's preservation of memories of a ritual involving "large stones" (*'ăbānîm gĕdōlôt*) erected on Mt. Ebal (overlooking Shechem).[150] Here Moses and the elders instruct the people to erect and plaster over (*wĕśadtā 'ōtām baśśîd*) multiple large stones on which teachings (*dibrê hattôrâ hazzō't*) are inscribed. Mention is also made of the erection of an altar together with various types of sacrifice (*wĕha'ălîtā 'ālāyw 'ôlōt . . . wĕzābaḥtā šĕlāmîm*) and a ritual banquet (*wĕ'ākaltā*) (Deut 27:1–8).

Two other traditional accounts (Josh 24; Judg 9) place cultic stones directly at Shechem. In neither of these traditions do the stones function explicitly as a divine image. In Joshua 24:26–27 a "great stone" (*'eben gĕdōlâ*) is erected "under the oak in the sanctuary [*miqdaš*] of Yahweh" to serve as a witness to treaty obligations. One is immediately reminded of how deities typically play the role of witnesses in ancient Near Eastern treaties. In contrast, the author of Joshua 24 seems consciously to use a large stone in the place of the deity. Yet one wonders to what degree this is a later updating by the Deuteronomist. Perhaps without the layer of Deuteronomistic editing, there once stood a tradition where the huge stela represented the Israelite deity witnessing the treaty obligations.[151]

In Judges 9:6 the citizens of Shechem make Abimelech king "by the oak [and] the pillar [*'ēlôn muṣṣāb*] at Shechem."[152] Both Wright (1965: 123–138) and Stager (1999, 2003) connect the physical temple (Temple 2 for Wright; Temple 1 for Stager) with the temple of the god El-Berit (*bêt 'ēl bĕrît*) at Shechem, mentioned in Judges 9:46. In Stager's (1999: 242; 2003: 31–33) words, "the likeliest place for the anointing of Abimelech would have been on the acropolis of Shechem, in the courtyard of the most prominent building in the city and the region, the 'Temple of El-Berith'; that is, in the courtyard of Temple 1, beside the great slab stela (*Maṣṣēbāh* 1)." It is anyone's guess as to how the ancients would have viewed the stela in such a coronation ceremony. It is conceivable that it could have represented the very presence of the deity giving his sanction to the activity.

If the huge *massebah* did represent divine presence, it is likely that its earliest referent at Shechem was El. Compare again how Stager (2003: 31) argues that "Temple 1 was the Temple of El-berith, that is, El, the Lord of the Covenant" (see Lewis 1996a). El traditions at Shechem have a long heritage, as one sees in the divine epithet "El, the god of [the patriarch] Israel" (*'ēl 'ĕlōhê yiśrā'ēl*), used of the Shechemite deity in Genesis 33:20. *Masseboth* traditions are also associated with the god El at Bethel (Gen 28:18–19, 22; 31:13; 35:14; also see Chapter Four, pp. 99–101.) Although it uses different vocabulary, compare too the archaic El tradition found in Genesis 49:24–25, where, in addition to being referred to as "The Mighty One of Jacob" and El Shadday, the deity is also referred to as "the Rock [*'eben*] of Israel."[153]

The *Massebah* at the Bull Site

As its name implies, the so-called Bull Site, located on the top of a mountain ridge in northern Samaria (Daharat et-Tawileh), is most famous for the discovery of an exquisitely fashioned bronze bull statuette dated to the Iron Age I period (see pp. 200, 202 and Figure 5.70). Equally intriguing at this one-period site (apparently an open-air cult center) is the presence of a large (4 ft. [122 cm] long × 3 ft. [91 cm] high × 1.75 ft. [53 cm] thick), rough, slightly worked stone

(Figure 5.46), in front of which lies a pavement of rough flat stones. Scholars are quick to note that the large stone is wider than it is high and thus not typical of other examples of *masseboth*. Nonetheless, due to various associated items (two bowl fragments, a small bronze object, a corner of a cult vessel) and especially the bull statuette, most conclude that the installation was cultic, with the "conspicuous" stone designating a *massebah* of some sort (Mazar 1982: 34–37; 1983: 36–37; 1993: 267; Mettinger 1995: 153–155; Zevit 2001: 178; Bloch-Smith 2006: 75; contrast Coogan 1987b).[154] Doron Ben-Ami (2006: 129) argues that despite the exquisitely made bull figurine, it was nevertheless the "standing stone that served as the focal point in this cult place."

If the Bull Site is indeed cultic in nature, and if its bronze bull represents El worship rather than a cult of Baal or even Yahweh (as will be discussed later), then perhaps El is also associated with the large stone found at the site.[155] The paved area in front of the large stone has been interpreted as a place for offerings (Mazar 1982: 35; Zevit 2001: 179; Bloch-Smith 2006: 75). Amihai Mazar (1982: 35, 41

Figure 5.46 A large, slightly worked stone from the Iron Age I Bull Site (so called due to Figure 5.70), located on the top of a mountain ridge in northern Samaria.
Photo: Amihai Mazar, The Hebrew University of Jerusalem.

n. 5) notes a suggestion by Menahem Haran that "the stone and the floor in front of it served as a simple altar." If offerings were indeed placed on the flat stone pavement, then the *massebah* stone would occupy the position typically reserved for the divine image. Mazar (1983: 37; 1982: 36) refers to "a few remains of some animal bones, possibly from sacrificial animals," though Ziony Zevit (2001: 180) remarks that "no archaeological evidence supports [the] conjecture" that "sacrifice was part of the ritual performed at this place." Mazar (1982: 35) also refers to the analogy of Genesis 35:14, where Jacob pours out a drink offering (*nesek*) and oil (*šemen*) on a *massebah* to El Shadday, who had spoken to him about his name being changed to Israel (Gen 35:9–15).[156] Obviously, such liquids would leave little if any archaeological traces.

Masseboth at Hazor

Several *masseboth* installations have been excavated at Hazor, the largest (more than 225 acres [91 ha]) and most important site in the southern Levant, located on strategic trade routes in the Upper Galilee. These installations range from the Middle Bronze Age to the Iron Age, underscoring the long-standing tradition at Hazor of using such stones in a symbolic and even cultic manner. From the Middle Bronze Age we have the Standing Stone Precinct (Figure 5.47), located in the ceremonial precinct in the Upper City (Area A), which contained approximately thirty standing stones. According to Ben-Tor (2013: 82; 2016: 52–54), these stones together with "several offering tables" and "a round stone basin" indicate "that, in addition to the cultic activities held in the [nearby] roofed Southern Temple, cultic rituals were also carried out a short distance away under the open sky."[157] Late Bronze Age evidence for the symbolic use of standing stones at Hazor is well known because of the Stelae Temple (Figure 5.48), in Area C of the Lower City, which contained several small stelae, including one stela with two hands raised toward a lunar symbol.

Turning to the early Iron Age, excavators found an eleventh-century BCE installation (termed a "cultic corner") in Area A approximately 65 ft. (20 m) east of the ruins of the Ceremonial Palace (Ben-Tor 2016: 130–131, 139). A single medium-sized basalt standing stone (Figure 5.49) (measuring approx. 2.3 ft. [70 cm] × 1.6 ft. [0.5 m]) was found in situ. The standing stone was roughly dressed and clearly the focal point of the area, which contained several flat stones—described by Ben-Tor (2016: 130–131) and Ben-Ami (2006: 123) as "offering tables"—and a "circular installation" of ten small stones. According to Ben-Ami (2006: 125), the only remarkable additional find was "a horned head of a zoomorphic vessel, most probably a bull . . . found buried in a pit dug approximately 2 m to the east of the paved area." Regrettably, "no signs of ash or organic material could be traced inside or in the immediate vicinity of the [circular] installation, thus its actual function remains unclear." We are therefore in

Figure 5.47 The Middle Bronze Age standing stone precinct that contained approximately thirty standing stones. Located in Hazor's ceremonial precinct in the Upper City (Area A).
Courtesy of the Selz Foundation Hazor Excavations in Memory of Yigael Yadin.

Figure 5.48 Several small stelae (including one stela with two hands raised toward a lunar symbol) from Hazor's Late Bronze Age Stelae Temple in Area C of the Lower City.
Courtesy of the Selz Foundation Hazor Excavations in Memory of Yigael Yadin.

Figure 5.49 A prominent basalt standing stone from Hazor Area A together with a circular installation of ten small stones and several flat stones seen as offering tables.
Courtesy of the Selz Foundation Hazor Excavations in Memory of Yigael Yadin.

no position to make any definitive remarks other than that the standing stone was an attention-focusing device that seems to have been "intentionally located at high elevation" with pavement that seems to have been a place for offerings. One particular feature that does stand out, as noted by Sharon Zuckerman (2011: 387–388), is how this cult area was intentionally "dug into the destruction layers of the Late Bronze Age ceremonial precinct," seemingly as an act of "conscious appropriation."

Preliminary reports of Area M (on the northern slope of the acropolis) give us additional information for understanding *masseboth* as we come down to the tenth century BCE. In the vicinity of the ruins of the Late Bronze Age administrative palace, archaeologists uncovered four limestone standing stones together with their bases (Figure 5.50). Ben-Tor (2016: 139–140) considers this additional "*masseboth* precinct" to be "a small cultic installation" dating the tenth century BCE. Both Zuckerman (2011) and Ben-Tor (2016: 131) wonder if these two Iron Age installations (Figures 5.49 and 5.50)—together with another installation in Area B (discussed next)—constituted "ruin cults."[158] With such installations, worshippers marked sacred space and offered cult in response to the "awe" and "fear" that were occasioned by "the fierce conflagration that brought Bronze Age Hazor to its end and whose ruins were still visible in the tenth century BCE."

Figure 5.50 A series of four standing stones with their bases from Hazor Area M, dating to the tenth century BCE.
Courtesy of the Selz Foundation Hazor Excavations in Memory of Yigael Yadin.

When one considers the impressive architectural glory that once was Hazor, prominently visible remains of its dramatic destruction certainly occasioned a cultic response (to whom we do not know), much as ruined Egyptian remains occasioned Percy Shelley's famous poem of the shattered Ozymandias or, better yet, Horace Smith's of a destroyed London: "What powerful but unrecorded race / Once dwelt in that annihilated place."[159]

The cultic area known as the Iron Age I "high place" at Hazor (coming from stratum XI, Area B) represents another "value-laden landscape" whose placement, according to Zuckerman (2011: 399), was another "undoubtedly intentional" act of "conscious appropriation." This installation was excavated by Yadin in the 1950s and restored during the 1996 season by Orna Cohen under the direction of Ben-Tor.[160] Zuckerman's (2011: 387–388) "ruin cult" theory underscores how its location on the higher western entrance of the tell gave its Iron Age inhabitants a perfect view of the remains of the once illustrious and now violently destroyed Late Bronze Age ceremonial precinct. What is preserved of the Iron Age area are four partial rooms with the southern part higher than the northern. As can be seen from Zevit's (2001: 204) isometric drawing (Figure 5.51), Locus 3283 constituted the primary room, with a tall, curved basalt standing stone functioning certainly as an attention-focusing device—especially with its curvature—and, according to Ben-Ami (2006: 127), "as the prime focus of the cult practiced in Area B." The stone can be seen lying horizontally prior to restoration in (Figure 5.52) (middle, rear) yet vertically in (Figure 5.53) (middle), as conservators stood it erect in a plaster socket that was found during the 1996 restoration.

This room also contained a cultic stand, a lamp, a store jar, multiple basalt objects (bowls, pestles, mortar, scraper), and, most importantly, a jar under the floor filled with bronze objects (Figures 5.54, 5.55). One of these bronzes was the divine image (seated, in benedictory pose) discussed in Figure 5.35. Those commenting on this deposit of bronze objects have expressed radically different opinions of its nature: a foundation deposit, a favissa, a hoard, offerings, heirlooms, and even scrap metal. As noted on pp. 157–158, the jug and its objects are not foundation deposits from the Iron Age I but rather are of Late Bronze Age vintage.

As for the character of the jar and its contents, judicious comments can be found by Bloch-Smith (2006: 76) and David Ilan (1999: 156). Bloch-Smith summarizes:

> While the figurine supports cultic continuity, the aggregate bronzes require explanation. In addition to the figurine, the jug contained an axe, two swords, two javelin butts, a needle, a wire, two javelin heads, two possible fibula, a bracelet, a bent rod, and a lump. The bronzes are arguably scrap metal to be smelted and cast anew.

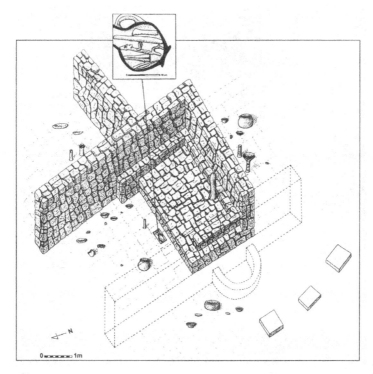

Figure 5.51 An isometric drawing reconstructing Hazor Area B, Locus 3283, with its tall, curved basalt standing stone and related assemblage of various bronze objects including a divine image (Figure 5.35).
From Ziony Zevit, *The Religions of Ancient Israel: A Synthesis of Parallactic Approaches* (London: Continuum, 2001), with permission.

In the end, after considering the rest of the four-room area (which contained a total of five cult stands), Bloch-Smith (2006: 76) concludes that "this aggregate assemblage likely served a cultic function."[161] Rather than adopting a binary model (cultic or mundane), Ilan (1999: 156) wisely concludes:

> Assuming that the deposit does belong to Stratum XI, what we have is a group of scavenged LB metal objects placed in a scavenged LB jug, left as either an offering of sorts or socked away for future commercial exchange or remelting. As we have seen in the discussion of the Tel Dan Sanctuary 7082, cultic behavior, metallurgy and metal hoarding frequently go together in this period.

In short, the cultic function of the standing stone in Area B at Hazor makes good sense and seems to be the emerging consensus (Zevit 2001: 202; Ben-Ami

Figure 5.52 The location of the standing stone in Hazor Locus 3283 prior to restoration.
Courtesy of the Selz Foundation Hazor Excavations in Memory of Yigael Yadin.

Figure 5.53 The location of the standing stone in Hazor Locus 3283 after restoration.
Courtesy of the Selz Foundation Hazor Excavations in Memory of Yigael Yadin.

Figure 5.54 The various bronze objects included in a jar that was buried under the floor of the main room of Locus 3283, including Figure 5.35.
Courtesy of the Selz Foundation Hazor Excavations in Memory of Yigael Yadin.

2006: 125–127; Zuckerman 2011: 389–390).[162] Given its Late Bronze Age–Iron Age I cultural context, if the standing stone marked the presence of a deity, El would certainly be a candidate, as would Addu. Even though archaeologists have yet to find Late Bronze or Iron Age archives at Hazor, there is a tradition of Semitic deities attested from the Middle and Late Bronze Ages in a handful of administrative documents and letters. A Middle Bronze Age disbursement (payroll?) tablet contains theophoric elements in personal names with close affinities to Old Babylonian Mari. Among these are the names ʾIlu-Kayyanum, Ishme-El, Ḫinni-El, Iblut-El, Ishput-Addu, Yanṣur-Addu, and Yadâda.[163] A poorly preserved vessel seems to contain the personal name Ishme-Addu together with what may be a forked lightning symbol (Horowitz, Oshima, and Sanders 2006: 65–66). As noted previously, typologically the bronze figurine could designate El.

Masseboth at Arad

Arad is our best example of *masseboth* found in the inner sanctum (*děbîr*/"holy of holies") of a temple, where one usually locates the cult statue.[164] It should be noted that the dating and character of this material are much debated, and we do not have clear archaeological reports to help us reconstruct the history of the *masseboth* in the temple.[165] Even though most photographs (Figure

Figure 5.55 The jar with the deposited bronze objects (from Hazor Area B, Locus 3283).
Courtesy of the Selz Foundation Hazor Excavations in Memory of Yigael Yadin.

5.56) show two neatly reconstructed *masseboth* side by side—which some scholars are overly quick to identify with Yahweh (the taller) and Asherah (the shorter)—according to Yohanan Aharoni's initial report (1967) there were three stones. Two rough "slabs of flint stone" were found "located near the walls" (cf. Figure 5.57). According to Graesser (1972: 52, fig. 6), these two flint stones "were built into the right and rear walls." A third well-dressed stone—a 3.2 ft. (1 m) limestone stela with rounded top—that contained traces of red pigment was found "lying on the floor of the shrine" (visible in Figure 5.57). Aharoni concluded that this taller stone was used separately from the other two and at a later stage. According to Aharoni, the two flint stones "probably belong to an earlier phase of the building, and only the last stone was used in stratum IX" (1967: 248; 1968: 19). Ze'ev Herzog also emphasizes that only the single "rounded stele" (3.3 ft. [1 m] high) originally stood in the niche of the stratum IX temple (cf.Figure 5.58).[166] If it is indeed correct that the tall red-painted stela comes from a different time than both the two stone slabs (and the two small incense altars), then the commonly used picture of the tall stela

Figure 5.56 A common portrayal of dual standing stones at Arad that belies the difficulty of our evidence and varying interpretations.
Kim Walton.

juxtaposed with one of the stone slabs and both incense altars (Figure 5.56) is very misleading.

Scholars are of one mind when it comes to the single large red-painted stela, seeing it as a marker or symbol of divinity. Herzog (2013: 40) identifies it as a *massebah*, "symbolizing the presence of the deity in the temple." Bloch-Smith (2015: 112) concurs: "The Arad stone occupied the place where the deity resided and was manifest" in the late ninth- to eighth-century BCE temple. The character of the two "slabs of flint stone" is debated. Nadav Na'aman (1999a: 405; 2006a: 324–325), following Herzog (1997b: 192), argues that "the two stone slabs differ in work and dimension from the well dressed *maṣṣebah* and were apparently part of the construction of the temple, one serving as a door post and the other support[ing] the sanctuary's western wall. Only one *maṣṣebah* stood in the sanctuary and served as the central symbol of the deity's presence in the place." Zevit (2001: 166–167, 169) agrees that only a single red-painted stela stood in the temple in strata X–IX (which he dates to the eighth century BCE). In contrast,

Figure 5.57 The temple niche at Arad during excavations showing a 3.3-ft. (1 m.) limestone stela with rounded top in its original location lying on the floor.
Courtesy of Ze'ev Herzog, Tel Aviv University.

Figure 5.58 Only a single stela originally stood in the niche of the stratum IX temple at Arad.
Courtesy of Ze'ev Herzog, Tel Aviv University.

Zevit (2001: 166–168) argues that Na'aman's two stone "slabs" (which Zevit calls "stele-shaped slabs" and then simply "stelae") stood in the niche during stratum XI (which he dates to the first half of the ninth century BCE). That the "two-by-two" slabs parallel the "two-by-two" small incense altars "suggests strongly that two deities were worshipped in the stratum XI temple." If the two stones were not merely a part of the construction, then Zevit's suggestion is an interesting possibility. But even here, Graesser's comments about the duality of stones used elsewhere to mark symmetry should caution us not to rule out artistic conventions.[167] The most recent treatment of the two flint stones by Bloch-Smith (2015: 101) favors the interpretation of Na'aman and Herzog: "The variant type of stone, their rough contours compared to the worked limestone example, and their placement in the niche walls favor the constructional interpretation."

Masseboth at Tel Dan

Tel Dan is one of the richest sites when it comes to documenting religious expressions in ancient Israel in both text and archaeology. The most famous textual tradition involves King Jeroboam setting up major cult centers in Dan and Bethel to rival the Jerusalem Temple (see 1 Kgs 12:28–33 and pp. 198–200 on his use of bull images). The most famous archaeological discovery at Tel Dan is surely its Area T, which contains an impressive temple complex containing (1) a large podium (the so-called *bamah* platform), (2) a large central altar area with temenos wall and double stairs, (3) an olive press installation, and (4) a smaller cultic area in T-West as documented by a small square sacrificial altar of five travertine blocks, two incense altars, three iron shovels, a carinated bronze bowl, and a deposit of animal bones.[168]

Yet for our present purpose, what is most remarkable is the attestation of multiple standing stone installations at Tel Dan in the Area A–AB gate complex (mostly dating to Iron Age IIB, prior to the destruction by the Assyrian king Tiglath-Pileser III in 733 BCE).[169] Preliminary reports document at least four such installations, including three areas of five stones and one with three stones (Biran 1998). One of the installations of five stones (Figure 5.59) also included items (e.g., sheep and goat bones, incense burners, lamps) and a bench/table in front that caused the excavator to assert: "That these are *maṣṣebot*, or sacred pillars, there is no question ... sacrificed animals had been offered or eaten here" (Biran 1998: 44). The installation with three stones (labeled the "sacred enclosure") has been dated to the seventh century BCE after the destruction by Tiglath-Pileser III. Here we find an elevated structure with three (or four?) basalt stones standing side by side (Figure 5.60). Most notable is the presence of a bowl in front of the tallest of the standing stones (Figure 5.61) in which were found ashes. According to Avraham Biran (1998: 42, 45), "the monoliths marked a place of cultic worship" and gave evidence that "the religious practices hallowed

Figure 5.59 One of the installations of five stones at Tel Dan from the Iron Age II Area A–AB gate complex.
Kim Walton.

Figure 5.60 A seventh-century BCE installation of three stones in the gate complex at Tel Dan (labeled "the sacred enclosure") with an offering bowl in front of the tallest of the stones.
Kim Walton.

THE ICONOGRAPHY OF DIVINITY: EL   189

Figure 5.61 A close-up of Figure 5.60 showing the bowl, in which was found ash residue.
Courtesy of the Nelson Glueck School of Biblical Archaeology.

in previous generations obviously persisted" despite the Assyrian destruction. Though Bloch-Smith (2006: 74) discusses the Dan *masseboth* in the context of public space, she too concludes that while "it is not certain that all these stones [from Area A] served cultic purposes," a cultic function for the stones that make up the so-called sacred enclosure is "confirmed." Bloch-Smith also notes how these stones in what seems to be a gate shrine at Tel Dan finds support in the well-documented gate shrine at Bethsaida (the Iron Age capital of Geshur), which has a standing stone carved with a bull-headed deity (see the following discussion and Figure 7.18).[170]

In addition to the material just discussed, we should note an additional area in the Area A gate complex. A single large basalt stone (Figure 5.62) was found next to a canopied or baldachin-like structure (with a raised platform) between the outer and inner gates. Biran (1998: 42, 44) wondered whether the stone should be interpreted as a *massebah* symbolizing a deity. Arguments against this proposal would be its position relative to the canopied structure (a divine symbol

Figure 5.62 On the left is yet another standing stone at Tel Dan in the Area A gate complex next to a canopied structure (Figure 5.64).
Kim Walton.

should be in the center of the canopy, not to the side) and the ninth-century BCE Bethsaida gate shrine (Figure 5.63), where a pair of standing stones mark the passageway to the immediate left of the shrine. Perhaps the standing stone at Tel Dan was one of two, the other stone (now missing) marking the other side of the Tel Dan passageway. Compare the two small standing stones that flanked the entrance to the temple at Shechem (see pp. 172–173 and n. 148 in this chapter).

As for the canopied structure itself (Figures 5.62, 5.64), the platform with a large stone block featuring a depression has been interpreted as once housing either a statue of the king or a divine image.[171] For an example of the former, compare a relief (Figure 5.65) from the ninth-century BCE Balawat gates that has Shalmaneser III receiving booty after the battle of Qarqar. For an example of the latter, compare the relief (Figure 5.66) of the enthroned god Shamash from the ninth-century BCE Sippar Tablet of Nabu-apla-iddina II (cf. T. Ornan 2005a: 63–65; Hurowitz 2000). The Ba'lu Cycle from Late Bronze Age Syria contains a description of a divine throne (*kattu 'ili// kaḫtu 'ili*), footstool (*hudumu 'ili*), and canopied structure (*ḥayamu wa-tabṭuḫu*) made by the craftsman god Kotharu-wa-Hasisu as a gift for the goddess 'Athiratu (cf. KTU 1.4.1.29–35).

Figure 5.63 Dual standing stones at the Bethsaida gate complex marking a passageway next to the shrine.
Kim Walton.

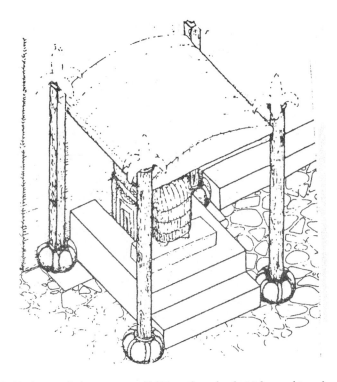

Figure 5.64 A canopied structure at Tel Dan, though what it housed is unknown.
Courtesy of the Nelson Glueck School of Biblical Archaeology.

Figure 5.65 A relief from the ninth-century BCE Balawat gates that has Shalmaneser III receiving booty after the battle of Qarqar.
Kim Walton, taken at the British Museum.

Figure 5.66 The enthroned god Shamash from the ninth-century BCE Sippar Tablet of Nabu-apla-iddina II.
Kim Walton, taken at the British Museum.

A *Massebah* from Khirbet Ataruz

Finally, to round out the broader Iron Age *masseboth* picture, one must bring in a remarkable temple from Khirbet Ataruz (Ḥirbet ʿAṭārūs, 8.7 mi. [14 km] northwest of Dhiban, Jordan) that combines a prominent standing stone with a significant bull cult (on which see pp. 202–205).[172] Excavations at Khirbet Ataruz have documented an early Iron Age II multi-chambered temple complex with several cultic installations (Ji 2012; Ji and Bates 2014). Hundreds of cultic objects were found, including a storage jar decorated with seven bulls and one ibex (see Figures 5.71 and 5.72). The storage jar was found in the Main Sanctuary Room and was filled with ashes including the remains of animal bones (Ji 2012: 207, 211, fig. 2). Significantly, the jar was located 16 ft. (5 m) in front of a prominent standing stone (4.9 ft. [1.5 m] high) that stood atop a pedestal (4.3 ft. [1.3 m] high) within a cultic niche and next to an offering table (Figure 5.67). According to Chang-Ho Ji (2012: 206), the cultic assemblage found in association with the pedestal suggests that it "was erected not only to hold the standing stone but also to support a terracotta altar and the lamps and cups for burning incense and oil."[173] As for interpreting the standing stone, the excavators (Ji 2012: 212; cf. Ji and Bates 2014: 51) argue that "given its size and location . . . [it] is most likely to have represented the main deity that was worshiped in the Ḥirbet ʿAṭārūs temple."

Concluding Remarks About *Masseboth* as Representations of El

When one considers the six sites that have been described (Shechem, Bull Site, Hazor, Arad, Tel Dan, and Khirbet Ataruz), it is abundantly clear that standing

Figure 5.67 On the right, a prominent standing stone (4.9 ft. [1.5 m] high) that stood atop a pedestal (4.3 ft. [1.3 m] high) within a cultic niche and next to an offering table. Photograph courtesy of Adam L. Bean.

stones (*masseboth*) were regularly used in cultic settings from every time period. At Hazor, standing stones were in use for hundreds of years, long before any Israelite presence at the site—underscoring their *longue durée* and the respect with which they were viewed by subsequent generations. As Mettinger (1995: 140) observes, "*Masseboth* simply belonged to the normal cultic paraphernalia of such shrines." Here archaeology and text (i.e., descriptions of *masseboth* in the Hebrew Bible) are fully compatible. We need not rehearse once again the multiple uses of *masseboth*. Any comprehensive study of the data acknowledges the multifaceted functions of impressive monoliths (see pp. 171–172). Among these functions is to focus attention in sacred space, whether to mark a past memorable experience with a deity/deities (e.g., a theophany), to signify the place where cult (offerings, libations, prayer) to a deity/deities took place, and/or to mark the ongoing presence of the deity residing in (or symbolized by) a standing stone.[174] Our present concern here is whether the deity in question at these six sites was El. (On Yahweh being represented by *masseboth*, see Chapter Seven, pp. 333–336.)

Though the word "betyl" (which, as we have seen, derives from *bēt-'el*, "the house of El"), used of cultic stones, predisposes us to look for El's presence, no inscriptions or iconography accompanies the *masseboth* described here. We have no *explicit* archaeological indicators that would help us to determine the deity or deities to whom cult was given at these Iron Age sites.[175] The following speculations can be put forth. Of the Iron Age standing stone installations, some are plural in nature (Hazor Area M, Tel Dan), yet a significant number are singular in focus (Shechem, the Bull Site, Hazor Area B, Hazor Area A, Arad [i.e., its well-dressed 3.3-ft. (1 m) *massebah*], Khirbet Ataruz). It seems plausible that these could mark monolatrous worship. The clearest markers of the plurality of divinity would be the standing stones at Tel Dan and Tel Hazor (discussed later), with the two flint stones at Arad possibly being an additional example, although this is less likely, as we have seen.

The only *explicit* indicator of divinity associated with *masseboth* are the texts of the Hebrew Bible. Granted, many references are generic in nature, such the Deuteronomic/Deuteronomistic traditions denouncing the *masseboth* of the nations (e.g., Deut 7:5; 12:3; 16:22; 1 Kgs 14:23; 2 Kgs 17:10; cf. 2 Kgs 18:4; 23:14; 2 Chr 14:2; 31:1) and similar generic pronouncements in the Priestly material (Exod 23:24 [cf. Exod 34:13, traditionally J]; Lev 26:1) and certain prophets (Micah 5:12 [Eng 5:13]; Isa 6:13 [cf. Iwry 1957]). Yet in a handful of references *masseboth* are associated with specific deities: El (Gen 28:18, 22; 31:13; 35:6–15; cf. Gen 49:24); Baal (2 Kgs 3:2; 2 Kgs 10:26–27); seemingly Re, the sun god in Heliopolis (Jer 43:13); and Yahweh (Isa 19:19–20; Hos 3:4; 10:1–2; see Chapter Seven, pp. 335–336).

Regrettably, none of these specific biblical passages contains traditions related to the six sites studied here.[176] We can say in general terms that the deity El is associated with *masseboth* in ancestral traditions, especially those at Bethel. Moreover, as has been noted, the strong connection of the Shechemite cult to El traditions (e.g., El Berith, El, Elohe Israel) makes El's association with the material cult at Shechem (including its majestic *massebah*) quite plausible. Moreover, as discussed in Chapter Four, pp. 100, 114–115, Israelite El worship was typically associated with sacred space on a smaller scale, with traditions commonly centering on clan and family. (Contrast Ugaritic 'Ilu worship, associated with the power and prestige of the Late Bronze Age city of Ugarit, and the worship of Yahweh as a national deity with state support.) Thus to have a *massebah* in a smaller cult space that is less impressive architecturally (e.g., the Bull Site and the so-called ruin cults at Hazor Area A and Area B) would be appropriate for El worship. Lastly, one can at least say that, typologically, the bronze figurine in Hazor Area B (Figure 5.35)—if it is related in a meaningful way to the *massebah* site (Figures 5.51–5.53)—would fit what we know of El. Yet in the end, all such musings are speculative and we would likely be surprised at which god was being worshipped at a specific site were we able to walk back in time.

A final note needs to be made about multiple standing stone installations at Tel Hazor and Tel Dan. As seen with the thirty-some Middle Bronze Age standing stones found at Hazor (Figure 5.47), correlating this large number of stones with any list of named deities has proven impossible. We see no indication of there ever being thirty deities worshipped at Hazor.[177] Thus one wonders if these thirty standing stones marked multiple encounters with a deity (or deities) that were thought to be especially noteworthy, or perhaps episodes where the god(s) acted in a particularly benevolent way. Alternatively, these thirty stones could commemorate humans (rulers? ancestors?) and their achievements.

Can we be more successful in correlating multiple groupings that are smaller in number? As noted, at Hazor we have four large standing stones in Area M (Figure 5.50) and a circle of ten small stones in Area A (Figure 5.49). At Tel Dan we have three groupings of five stones (Figure 5.59) and one installation of three stones (Figures 5.60, 5.61). No satisfying proposal has yet been offered for identifying a cluster of deities with the ten, five, four, or three stones at these two sites. We have a wide distribution of numbers of standing stones from the Southern Negev (singles, pairs, and triads as well as groups of five, seven, and nine), yet their dates (sixth through third millennia BCE) are far removed from our material (see Avner 2018). More significant is Shua Kisilevitz's (2015: 151) mention of "five medium sized field stones" in the Iron IIA sacred complex at Tel Moza that "were clearly placed in the temple intentionally and probably served as sacred stones, or *maṣṣēbôt*." A far-afield reference is the mention of five pillars ('*mwdy*') being offered to the single god Baal-Shamem in a Palmyrene votive inscription.[178] Yet these pillars seem to be support pillars for a sacred construction (cf. the 'ammudîm in the Solomonic Temple in 1 Kgs 7:21), not stand-alone pillars as with the *masseboth*. George Athas (2003: 315) and Bob Becking (2011: 413–414) have suggested that the stone pillars in the Temple of Yahô in fifth-century BCE Elephantine document divine images. No specific number of pillars is given, yet Athas suggests that they are five in number, which he correlates with Yahô, Anath-Bethel, Eshem-Bethel, and Bethel. Though this is tantalizing material (and would further confirm the long duration of this practice), the context refers to the demolition of the temple by describing various architectural features that were destroyed (e.g., hewn stone gateways, standing doors, bronze hinges, cedarwood roof).[179] Thus it is hard to discern whether the stone pillars (*'mwdy'* is used rather than *mṣb'* or *mṣbt'*) are indeed divine images or non-cultic architectural features.

To my knowledge, the only clear Iron Age Levantine examples come from two archaic Aramaic inscriptions from the city-state of Sam'al (Zincirli). These two eighth-century BCE inscriptions (the Hadad Inscription = KAI 214 and the Panamuwa Inscription = KAI 215) are contemporaneous with the Iron IIB gate complex at Tel Dan. The Hadad inscription contains four attestations of a near-fixed list of five deities (Hadad, El, Rashap, Rakib-El, and Shamash).[180] The Panamuwa inscription (line 22) contains four of these five deities (Hadad, El, Rakib-El, Shamash) and a reference to "all the gods of Y'dy," a substitute for the god Rashap. It would be extremely rash to make an equation of these five deities with the five standing stones at Tel Dan.[181] And yet Andrew Davis (2013: 174) has noted that Tel Dan's "location at Israel's border with Aram made it susceptible to religious fluctuations, as it alternated between Israelite and Aramean hegemony." In other words, it seems likely that the cult celebrated by the inhabitants at Tel Dan incorporated elements from both Israelite and Aramean spheres. A variety of deities would also be appropriate for meeting the "religious needs" of "merchants and travelers many of whom were not indigenous inhabitants at Dan."[182]

Possible Theriomorphic Representations of Israelite El in Textual Sources

As we have seen, in the ancient Near East majestic animals often served as symbols of gods or pedestals on which the deities were mounted. As we saw with depictions from Ugarit, the mature bull was the animal of choice to render the virility and power of "Bull 'Ilu." (See pp. 150–152 and Figure 5.32.) Nowhere are there any references to Ugaritic 'Ilu being represented by other majestic animals, such as lions, dragons, or even horses.

El and Lions
In this light it is curious to come across the occurrence of the name ʾAriel (ʾărîʾēl; "El is a lion"?, "the lion of El"?) and its variants attested in the Hebrew Bible and the Mesha inscription and used to designate a proper name (Ezra 8:16), the city Jerusalem (Isa 29:1–2, 7), and an altar hearth (Ezek 43:15–16).[183] At first glance we might assume that El was portrayed as a lion both in literary texts and in material culture. While we could turn to a great number of lions in the archaeological record (from the large Hazor lions to numerous seal impressions),[184] some of which even occur in temple complexes (e.g., Hazor, Arad),[185] on cult stands (especially the two from Tell Taanach),[186] and even in amulets,[187] we have no clear example of any of them functioning as an attribute animal that was the object of cult.

For example, the numerous lions on the Taanach cult stand are interpreted by Keel and Uehlinger (1998: 155) as guardian animals rather than divine symbols. Even if lion images are associated with the divine, they need not refer to El, with other West Semitic deities being more likely candidates, especially the god Baal-Seth and the goddess Qedeshet (see Cornelius 1994: 195–208; 2004; Strawn 2005: 193, 196–197) or even Yahweh (discussed later).[188] In contrast to the use of lions as divine epithets elsewhere in the ancient Near East (Lewis 1996b: 34–45; Strawn 2005: 200–214), the closest we come to a similar usage in biblical literature are the descriptions of El crouching *like* a lion (Num 24:9). Yet we have no hints, apart from the name ʾAriel, that El was ever referred to with lion epithets in ancient Israel.

El and Bulls
Let us return to consider whether bull imagery was used of Israelite El. At the outset we should note that nowhere does Israelite El ever bear the epithet *tr/šôr*, as does Ugaritic ʾIlu. Scholars have long debated possible bull imagery for El in three cases: (1) lying behind the phrase ʾăbîr yaʿăqōb in Genesis 49:24, which some scholars translate as "the Bull of Jacob"; (2) in the description of El acting like a horned ox in the Balaam oracles; and (3) in the description of Jeroboam's bull images in 1 Kings 12:28–33. We will treat each of these passages in turn.

El, the Mighty One/Bull of Jacob
Determining the precise connotations of ʾăbîr yaʿăqōb, "the Mighty One of Jacob," is complicated. The expression occurs five times (Gen 49:24; Isa 49:26; 60:16; Ps 132:2, 5). Of these, Genesis 49:24–25 is a distinctly El tradition that resonates with the theophoric element in the similar ʾăbîr yiśrāʾēl, "the Mighty One of Israel," occurring in Isaiah 1:24. Some scholars such as Sarna (1989: 343) argue that this title "corresponds to the Akkadian divine title *bel abāri*, 'endowed with strength,' and is to be distinguished from ʾabbir, which is used of stallions,

bulls, and warriors." Other scholars admit that *'abbîr* can be used of stallions (cf. Judg 5:22; Jer 8:16; 47:3) but underscore its clear reference to bulls elsewhere (Isa 34:7; Ps 50:13 [cf. 50:9]; 68:31 [Eng 68:30]). They then conclude that the Masoretes consciously and artificially omitted the doubling of the *b* in *'ăbîr ya'ăqōb* "to avoid any suspicion that Yahweh [or El in our case] was to be identified with the bull" (Kapelrud 1974: 42). Setting aside such hairsplitting, it is easy to see how ancient hearers of the divine epithet *'ăbîr ya'ăqōb* could use the vocabulary and imagery of a bull as they tried to describe the strength of Jacob's deity. This would line up nicely with the agrarian imagery used in the Jacob narratives regarding El-Bethel (see p. 100). To borrow the words Curtis (1990: 31) used to describe Ugaritic 'Ilu and apply them here: "The 'bull' imagery would suit . . . admirably in the eyes of people who were familiar with herds. The bull was the head of the herd, the strongest and most fearsome of the group. . . . [Bull] horns primarily symbolize strength and dignity."

El as Victorious Bull
As mentioned earlier (pp. 116–118), the description of "El bringing Israel out of Egypt" (*'ēl môṣî'ām mimmiṣrāyîm*) "like the horns of a wild ox" (*kětô'ăpōt rě'ēm lô*) in Numbers 23:22; 24:8 leaves no doubt about bull imagery being used of El. Most scholars see *rě'ēm* referring here to *Bos primigenius*, the auroch, but our textual evidence is mixed.[189] Note how *rě'ēm* is parallel to *šôr* ("bull") in Deuteronomy 33:17 and to *'ēgel* ("young bull") in Psalm 29:6. Yet there is no doubt that the bull here is a mature, muscular beast who (as in Deut 33:17) is aggressively victorious in battle (Num 24:8). What is still open to debate is whether this expression indicates a parallel (earlier?) tradition where El (and not Yahweh) was seen to be the God of the Exodus. Indeed, the conflation of these two traditions could have been facilitated if bull imagery was used of both El and Yahweh (see the next section).

El and Jeroboam I's Bull Images
Our third passage involves King Jeroboam I's erection of two bull images at Bethel and Dan as described in 1 Kings 12:25–33. We need not rehearse the details of this passage or the many theories on how it relates to the famous passages centering on the "golden calf" incident (Exodus 32, Deut 9:7–21, Hosea 8), for they are well known.[190] (For Hosea 8:5–6, see Chapter Seven, pp. 320–321.) The material culture probably associated with the event (especially the Area T North podium in Str III at Tel Dan) will be taken up in a subsequent chapter. The prominence and success of Jeroboam I's cultic activity can easily be inferred from the amount of attention devoted to it in the Deuteronomist's polemic against it. Gary Knoppers (1995b: 94–95) writes well: "Like the authors of Exodus 32, the Deuteronomist implicitly concedes the antiquity and appeal of Jeroboam's cultus, including his

tauromorphic iconography.... Moreover, if the sanctuaries at Bethel and Dan were not popular and well established, there would be no need to privilege them with such critical coverage."

What is at issue is the deity being represented by Jeroboam I's bull images. Some scholars interpret Jeroboam's acts as part of either a Yahweh cult or a Baal cult (see Chapter Seven for details).[191] Other scholars point out that had Jeroboam initiated a Baal cult with his bull images, he would have had little hope of winning over Israelite Yahwists; furthermore, had he tried to introduce such a cult, "tradition should have preserved [that] fact, in vivid invective."[192] Thus they assume that Jeroboam I's cult was devoted to the deity El as he wooed the people away from the Jerusalemite worship of Yahweh to his version of a venerated El worship, especially at Bethel, an old El sanctuary.[193] (Note too that the passage begins by mentioning how Jeroboam I rebuilt Shechem and Penuel [1 Kgs 12:25], both associated with El worship [see pp. 85–86].) With this strategy Jeroboam I was attempting to "out-archaize" David, who was so skillful in his use of the Ark of the Covenant, a venerated symbol of divine presence from the days of the tribal league (Cross 1973: 74).[194] The people need not make a pilgrimage to the Solomonic temple, with its worship of an aniconic Yahweh, when they could instead venerate El as the Mighty One of Jacob at locales with their own history of divine visitation. According to this theory, "Jeroboam I's real sin [according to the Deuteronomist] was in establishing a rival to the central sanctuary in Jerusalem, not in the introduction of a foreign god or pagan idol" (Cross 1973: 75).

Though I lean toward this interpretation, it must be admitted that all interpreters are forced into a good deal of speculation, for in the attempt to reconstruct Jeroboam's true intentions all we have to work with is the Deuteronomist's polemical language. The Deuteronomist goes out of his way to discredit Jeroboam I's ritual actions not only in the passage discussed here but also throughout his history, where Jeroboam I is held up as a negative role model of apostasy. Indeed, his actions are portrayed as leading to the fall of the Northern kingdom (2 Kgs 17:7–23, esp. vv. 16, 21–23). By equating Jeroboam I's apostasy with that of Aaron's perversions of the "golden calf" and then making his objects of worship dyotheistic, the Deuteronomist attempts to delegitimize the Bethel and Dan cults through slander.[195] One cannot overemphasize the Deuteronomist's passion for centralizing worship in Jerusalem. Such fervor could very likely have motivated his negative portrayal of Jeroboam I's "high place sanctuaries" (*bāttê habbāmôt*, 1 Kgs 13:32; cf. 1 Kgs 12:31).

Support for this thesis depends on the meaning of the noun *'ēgel* and how it came to be used in the Jeroboam and Exodus 32 passages.[196] The term can indeed be used of a young bull calf, even one suckling. Obviously, such a dependent offspring would not be the most appealing visual for a divine image, especially one designating a senior or sovereign deity (see Fleming 1999a and the remarks earlier in this section). If this is the meaning of ʿēgel in our passages, then one can only conclude that the biblical authors or editors substituted a pejorative term in order to discredit even further Jeroboam's and Aaron's activities.[197]

Yet the term ʿēgel can also designate a young bull in its prime, and thus we find it used in parallel to šôr (Ps 106:19–20) and rěʾēm (Ps 29:6), two terms for grown bulls.[198] Even our pejorative sources suggest that a young bull image was crafted by those who deemed it an adequate representation of the divine. The young bull (ʿēgel) is specifically and repeatedly referred to as ʾĕlōhîm. Moreover, it is treated as a divine image in ways that resonate with practices elsewhere in the ancient Near East (see pp. 136–141), including being a focal point in sacred space involving sacrifice and the burning of incense (Exod 32:5–6; 1 Kgs 12:29–33), traveling in procession (Exod 32:1; cf. 1 Kgs 12:28), being surrounded by ritual dance (Exod 32:19), and eventually being ritually destroyed (Exod 32:20; cf. Num 5:23–28). The bull images could then either designate divine bull images of El or (if Jeroboam I felt threatened by Jerusalem's more innovative abstract theology of aniconsim) serve as pedestals on which El could have been invisibly mounted.[199]

Possible Theriomorphic Representations of Israelite El in Material Culture

As for physical representation, the same cautions stated with respect to identifying bronze bull figurines at Ugarit apply to bull figurines found in Israel. From the Late Bronze Age temple of Area H at Hazor (stratum 1A; thirteenth century BCE) we have a 2-in. (5.5 cm) bronze statuette of a bull (Figure 5.68).[200] Three miniature (approx. 1.5–3 in. [4–8 cm] in length) bronze bull figurines, one of them silver-plated, were found in the Late Bronze Age throne room of Area A's Ceremonial Palace (Figure 5.69).[201]

The best candidate for a theriomorphic representation of Israelite El (Figure 5.70) would be from the Bull Site, published by Mazar in 1982, which included a standing stone (see Figure 5.46).[202] Mazar attributed the bronze zebu bull (*Bos indicus*) from this site to "Israelite settlers of the 12th ct. B.C.," "dated to the period of the Judges."[203] In contrast, Ahlström (1990: 79–81) argues that the bull represents a non-native religious tradition brought by "an intrusive group" from the north. This is suggested, argues Ahlström, by the nature of the figurine, which represents a type of bull not native to Canaan. Yet the Hazor bronze bull from Area H (with which Ahlström is familiar), as well as the new Hazor bronze bulls, would seem to suggest otherwise.

Figure 5.68 A bull statuette from the Late Bronze Age temple of Area H at Hazor.
Courtesy of the Selz Foundation Hazor Excavations in Memory of Yigael Yadin.

Figure 5.69 Three miniature bronze bull figurines from the Late Bronze Age throne room of Hazor Ceremonial Palace in Area A.
Courtesy of the Selz Foundation Hazor Excavations in Memory of Yigael Yadin.

Figure 5.70 An exquisitely made bronze bull from the Iron Age I Bull Site in northern Samaria, where a large worked stone was also found (see Figure 5.46).
Kim Walton, taken at the Israel Museum.

Mazar (1982: 32) further commented that "the size of our figurine, the great care taken in its manufacture, and the inlayed eyes that are unusual in simple votive offerings suggest . . . . an actual cult object in itself." Ahlström (1990: 79) concurs that it "is most certainly a ritual object," but adds that "its precise function cannot be established . . . [the bull] can . . . be considered the deity's attribute animal." Even Michael Coogan, who questions the cultic (public) context of the site, argues for a ritual function of the bull figurine.[204] Thus most scholars see the figurine representing either El, Baal, or Yahweh. At the same time, the cautions we have mentioned keep us from knowing definitively. If Baal's bovine iconography is to be equated with riders on top of bulls only, then perhaps we should consider El. Though Yahweh remains a possibility, Dever (1990: 130; cf. 2017: 178) states that "it is irresistible to connect this [the bull figurine] with the worship of the god El."[205]

To round out the broader picture, one should also note two Jordanian sites with bull representations.[206] The excavations at Iron Age II Khirbet Ataruz

THE ICONOGRAPHY OF DIVINITY: EL   203

have already been mentioned (p. 193) with respect to the large standing stone within sacred space (Figure 5.67). Among the hundreds of cultic objects also found in the Main Sanctuary Room was a storage jar decorated with seven bulls and one ibex (Figures 5.71, 5.72). East of the Main Sanctuary Room excavators found five altars with a nearby courtyard. West of this courtyard was a rectangular building (whose function has yet to be identified) with an assortment of cultic objects including a splendid terra-cotta bull figurine (14.2 in. [36 cm] long × 6.5 in. [16.5 cm] wide × 15.2 in. [38.5 cm] high) (Figure 5.73). Ji (2012: 211) notes the conspicuously large horns on the seven bull reliefs and on the terracotta figure (to judge from the disproportionate thickness of the broken remains). Extrapolating from the statue's "superbly sculpted head and neck and slightly rippling muscles," Ji (2012: 211–212) infers that these are indicators of "the deity's power, prowess, and supremacy." Ji further posits "that the iconography and practice of bull cult was truly embedded in the religion of Ḥirbet ʿAṭārūs during the early Iron Age II era."[207] Ji's conclusion was underscored when

Figure 5.71 An image of a bull on a storage jar from the Main Sanctuary Room at Iron Age II Khirbet Ataruz.
Photo by Robert D. Bates.

Figure 5.72 An image of a bull and ibex on a storage jar from the Main Sanctuary Room at Iron Age II Khirbet Ataruz.
Photo by Robert D. Bates.

Figure 5.73 A terra-cotta bull figurine from Iron Age II Khirbet Ataruz.
Photo by Robert D. Bates.

yet another bull image was discovered, this time carved/plastered on the wall of the entrance shaft of a cistern located near the Western Courtyard. Preliminary remarks describe a bull image that is 1.6 ft. (50 cm) × 2.0 ft. (60 cm) (Figure 5.74) with a face shape "nearly identical to those on the bull storage jar from the Main Sanctuary Room . . . [and] reminiscent of the [terra-cotta] bull figurine" (Ji and Bates 2014: 57–58, figs. 23, 24, 26).

The University of Sydney's excavations at ancient Pella (modern Ṭabaqāt Faḥil) in the north Jordan Valley have documented temple architecture with six distinct phases from MB I through Iron Age IIA. Using the MB temple at Shechem as an analogue, Stephen Bourke (2012: 165) tentatively suggests that the MB "Hollow-Box" architecture of the MB Pella temple may have been associated with the deity El and that El may have been worshiped as "a numinous aniconic deity."[208] Due to the architectural change that occurred with the Late Bronze Age IIB longroom temple as well as the mention of the ruler Mut-Baal ruling from Pella in the Amarna letters (EA 255, 256), Bourke (2012: 170)

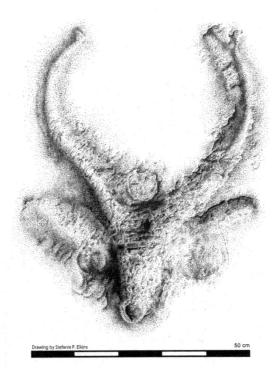

Figure 5.74 An artist's rendering of a bull that was carved/plastered on the wall of the entrance shaft of a cistern located near the Western Courtyard at Khirbet Ataruz. Drawing by Stefanie P. Elkins; published by permission. All rights reserved, Robert D. Bates.

suggests a change in cult from the god El to the deity Baal. One could also note the presence of a Late Bronze Age male bronze figurine with raised arm (identified as a "Resheph" figure in Bourke 2012: 175, 177, fig. 12.4) that could also point toward the god Baal.

As for the presence of bull images, a fragment of a Late Bronze Age IIA cult stand depicts a painted "bull-man" figure (Figures 5.75, 5.76) that has tentatively been identified as a man wearing a bull mask (Bourke 2012: 183 fig. 18). A model shrine with five bull heads (Figure 5.77), termed the "bull box," was discovered in the courtyard east of the remodeled Iron IIA "bent-axis" temple construction. Bourke's (2012: 184–191; figs. 21–22; Tafel 42A, 42B) preliminary publication of this material documents "extensive evidence" of burning in the bottom and lower sides of the bull box, with chalices and incense cups in the vicinity as well as large storage jars, one of which was decorated "with ceramic bulls-head protomes associated with a ceramic pomegranate."

Figure 5.75 A photograph of a painted bull-man figure on a Late Bronze Age IIA cult stand from ancient Pella in the north Jordan valley.
© Pella Excavation Project, University of Sydney.

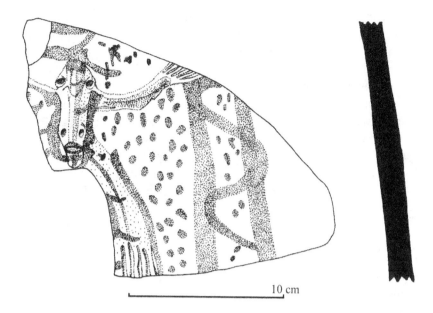

Figure 5.76 A line drawing of Figure 5.75.
© Pella Excavation Project, University of Sydney.

Figure 5.77 A model shrine with five bull heads from the courtyard east of the remodeled Iron IIA "bent-axis" temple construction at Pella.
© Pella Excavation Project, University of Sydney.

The preliminary nature of both of these Jordanian finds cautions against anything but tentative speculation. We can confidently say that bull symbolism was a part of the religious vocabulary at each of these sites, and speculate that the Pella bull-man figure could point to ritual performance where a religious officiant wore bull attire (yet for what purposes we do not know).[209] The identity of the deity behind these various bull images is nearly impossible to secure. One would have to have much more data about the Moabite religion practiced at Khirbet Ataruz to suggest the deity depicted by (or associated with) the terra-cotta bull figurine (Figure 5.73).[210] From the Mesha inscription alone one could posit Kemosh, a syncretistic Ashtar-Kemosh, Baal, or even Yahweh.[211] As for the religion practiced at Pella, we are once again faced with the methodological criteria for identifying divinity, and the degree to which it is diagnostic to use the theophoric element in a ruler's name (Mut-Baal) or the presence of a nearby bronze figurine to extrapolate about the overall cult practices at such a complex religious site. Caution is in order. Moreover, from what we know of the presence of El worship at Deir ʿAlla and the religious activities of Israelites in the Transjordan (cf. Levine's "El repertoire" in Chapter Four, p. 90), one would not want to rule El out as a possible candidate for Transjordanian bull symbolism.

6
The Origin of Yahweh

Introduction

It was logical to start our examination of Israelite religion with the deity El, whose worship predates that of Yahweh. Admittedly, Chapter Five was largely an effort in gleaning El traditions imbedded in later narratives. It was necessary to caution readers that our El traditions have been handed down and preserved by worshippers who came to identify El with Yahweh. In writing and editing their material in retrospect, they have collapsed a good deal of material. The ancients were less interested in the historical development of religion than a modern historian is. To them it was more important to present a unified storyline that underscored Yahweh's preeminence as a time-honored tradition. They did this by applying El's epithets and attributes to Yahweh (e.g., Yahweh-El-Elyon and Yahweh-El-Olam). Even personal names seemingly attest how Yahweh was El (see Elijah, Joel, and the names *'lyw, 'lyhw, yhw'l* and *yw'l* in the onomastic record).[1] These authors (especially the P literary strand) thought it equally crucial to emphasize an ancestral connection. The deity whom the patriarchs worshipped as an El figure was in reality Yahweh (Exod 6:3; Gen 17:1). According to biblical writers, their ancestors never worshipped two *separate* deities under the names El and Yahweh, however much a historian of religion might like to suggest otherwise.[2] Rather, Yahweh is El (cf. Ps 118:27; 150:1). All of the themes associated with El articulated earlier (eternity, supremacy, creativity, sovereignty, fatherhood, kinsman, benevolent protector, and head of the divine council) are applied to Yahweh without reservation.

New chapters were added to the story to announce Yahweh's additional abilities. In particular, worshippers told of a powerful divine warrior who fought on their behalf, a liberating deity who battled on a cosmic scale, and a god of national stature who favored the establishment of the monarchy. Yahweh was a divine king, the nation's patron deity who bonded with "his people" in a special covenant relationship. Yahweh was the supreme judge of a society that required an organized judiciary. Such a deity could no longer be worshipped only at the family level with a minimal cultic apparatus. It was fitting that a deity of such stature should have an elaborate priesthood, an intricate cult, and a great house of worship.[3]

So even though the name Isra<u>e</u>l bears witness to El as the founding deity, when Yahweh became Israel's national god the foundation story was updated. In addition, it is only natural to find his royal presence retrojected into the remote past, even when there was no nation at that time over which one could rule. Thus prophet and psalmist alike assert that Yahweh is the "king from of old" (*malkî miqqedem*; Ps 74:12) who battled cosmic forces "in days of old, generations long ago" (*yĕmê qedem dōrôt ʿôlāmîm*; Isa 51:9; cf. Isa 45:21; Hab 1:12; Prov 8:22).[4] Not only was his throne established "from antiquity," but so was his very origin (*nākôn kisʾăkā mēʾāz mēʿôlām ʾāttâ*; Ps 93:2). Yahweh is El Olam (*yhwh ʾēl ʿôlām*; Gen 21:33) but in royal dress.

Section I: The Meaning and Revelation of the Name Yahweh in the Hebrew Bible

Who Is Yahweh?

Who is this deity who won the allegiance of ancient Judeans and Israelites and the subsequent worship of Jews and Christians? Who is this god whose name is overwhelmingly attested in the onomastic record of Iron Age Israel?[5] What was so appealing about his nature that he supplanted not only El but also all of the deities attested in the various regional pantheons of the Iron Age Levant? A betting person in the Late Bronze Age would certainly have placed his money on El, Baal, Hadad, Dagan, or even Reshep as the male deity who would capture the devotion of the people living in the land of Canaan. What was it about Yahweh that proved so inviting? Where should one look for his origin? Is he found in any Late Bronze Age literature? Is his representation fashioned in bronze or stone elsewhere in the Levant? How was Yahweh seen to function in ways similar to and different from those of El?

Prior to searching for answers to these questions, we need to establish the basic meaning of the name Yahweh (*yhwh*). This is no small task even though we are dealing with only four consonants (often referred to as the Tetragrammaton) of a most common verb ("to be"). The vast literature on the topic attests to the passion that scholars have brought to the investigation. Indeed, so much attention has been paid to the etymology of Yahweh that one would think unlocking its meaning is the key to understanding the nature of Israelite religion as a whole.[6] Such lofty hopes are deflated by Frank Moore Cross' (1973: 60) assessment that the many articles are more likely "a monumental witness to the industry and ingenuity of biblical scholars." All the wind could go out of our sails if the difference of opinion among scholars leads one to conclude, as does H. O. Thompson

(1992: 1011), that "the meaning of the name is unknown" or if we are overly critical of the value of the etymological enterprise, as when Karel van der Toorn (1999b: 913) concludes that "even if the meaning of the name could be established beyond reasonable doubt, it would contribute little to the understanding of the nature of the god." Thankfully, there is enough of a consensus in the field that one need not become agnostic, and there remains a return for investing time in etymological study. While van der Toorn (building on the work of James Barr) is certainly correct that "it is much more important to know the characteristics which worshippers associated with their god, than the original meaning of the latter's name," there remains nonetheless a great value to be gained from understanding the meaning of the name of Yahweh. The ancients—who had a far greater appreciation for the significance of names (see Mettinger 1988: 6–13)— certainly understood and respected the denotation and connotation of the name Yahweh, and they were fully aware that the name constituted a prefixal form of a verb.[7]

The Pronunciation of the Name Yahweh

A common assertion in introductory textbooks and even in more scholarly treatments is that we do not have a firm hold on the pronunciation of *yhwh*. It is common to read that "the pronunciation of *yhwh* as Yahweh is a scholarly guess" (Thompson 1992: 1011) or "uncertain" (Baker 2003: 362) or "unknown" (Grabbe 2010: 175 n. 1; 2017: 193). Such statements are overly circumspect and reflect a long-standing agnosticism born out of the post-rabbinic tradition that one ought not to pronounce the divine name at all.[8] In contrast, historians of Israelite religion have confidently vocalized *yhwh* as Yahweh for years, and rightly so. Numerous lines of evidence both internal and external can be marshaled for such a pronunciation. That the first vowel is an *a*-class is clear from the abbreviated form Yah that occurs independently (e.g., Exod 15:2; Ps 68:5, 19 [Eng 68:4, 18]; Ps 89:9 [Eng 89:8]; cf. also *yh yhwh* at Khirbet Beit Lei), as a theophoric element in personal names (e.g., Nērî-yāh = "Yah is my light"; Nĕtan-yāh = "Yah has given"), and in liturgical expressions such as *hallĕlû-yāh*, "Praise Yah." That the second vowel is an *i*-class is clear due to the regular formation of third-*he* verbs in Hebrew (the precise stem form—causative or non-causative—will be discussed later). External evidence concurs. In Amorite personal names we find *yaqtil* forms such as *yawi-ila*, *yahwi-dagan*, *yawi-addu* ("DN lives/exists" or "DN brings life/causes to exist"). In Greek transcriptions we find both *iaoue* and *iabe*.[9]

Excursus: The Putative Name Jehovah

Despite numerous scholarly treatments to the contrary, one can still find in popular discourse those who speak of the name "Jehovah" as the original name of "the LORD." Historically, the name Jehovah never existed in antiquity. It is an artificial construct based on an erroneous understanding of the Masoretic pointing of the Hebrew text.

Due to the reverence for the divine name Yahweh (written in pre-Masoretic manuscripts without vowel indicators as *yhwh*), which was perceived to be holy, the tradition developed early to read a substitute whenever it was encountered. This tradition continues into the present, with observant Jews utilizing a variety of substitutes (e.g., Adonay, Lord, Ha-Shem, The Name, Adoshem, Lo[rd] + Name) rather than pronounce the name Yahweh. The tradition crosses over into English, where we find the Jewish tradition of substituting "G-d" for "God" and where most translations render Yahweh as "the LORD" rather than as a proper name (cf. too the proper names of El, such as El Shadday, usually rendered "God Almighty").

The Masoretes who pointed the Hebrew text in the second half of the first millennium CE continued a tradition of reading the noun *adonay*, "Lord," as a substitute for Yahweh. Similarly, the Septuagint and the Vulgate usually render Yahweh by "Lord" (*kurios, dominus*). The Masoretes guaranteed the continued use of the practice by graphically rendering the consonants of Yahweh's name (*yhwh*) with the vowels taken from the word *ʾădōnay*. A similar substitution system, known as the Ketiv-Qere practice, was used by the Masoretes to indicate a preferred oral reading (Qere) in contrast to what was written in the received consonantal text (Ketiv), especially when dealing with textual corruptions.

The result of this activity was an artificial hybrid form ("Yehovah") that was never intended to be read. The vowels were merely perpetual indicators to signal readers to read "*ʾădōnay*" rather than "Yahweh." Graphically, the situation can be represented as follows:

Original:	**yahweh*
Substitution Process:	*yhwh* + vowels from *ʾădōnay*
Result:	**Yehowah* [written, but to be read as *ʾădōnay*]

YHWH + vowels from ᵃdᵒnᵃy ("lord")

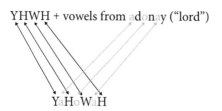

YᵃHᵒWᵃH

Clarifications:

1. The earliest texts are not written with vowel indicators. Thus by "original" we mean the form as reconstructed from the lines of evidence noted earlier.
2. The word *'ădōnay*, due to its first letter being a guttural consonant ('), contains a composite or hateph-shewa (ă). The first letter of the Tetragrammaton (*yhwh*) is not a guttural consonant. Thus when the reduced vowel *ă* is applied to *y* it takes the form of a regular shewa (*ĕ*).
3. The Hebrew letter *waw* was originally pronounced as a *w* (thus scholars reconstruct "Yah<u>w</u>eh"), though later Hebrew (including modern Hebrew) came to pronounce it as a *v* (thus Yeho<u>v</u>ah).
4. English normalizes *j* for Hebrew *y*. Thus, as English writes "Jerusalem" for Hebrew "<u>Y</u>erushalayim," so too it renders Jehovah (not <u>Y</u>ehovah).

Again, it must be stressed that the Masoretes were *not* intending for readers to pronounce the hybrid form as written (*yĕhōwāh). There is no evidence of such a pronunciation until the Middle Ages, when the Masoretes' pointing system was misunderstood.[10] The hybrid form (with the consonants of the original word combined with the vowels from a substitute reading) is purely artificial.[11] The Qere vowels were simply indicators for the pious to pronounce *'ădōnay* rather than Yahweh to avoid possible profanation of the holy name. The same practice (reading *'ădōnay* even though the written consonants are *yhwh* [= Yahweh]) continues today when reading the Hebrew text in synagogues, yeshivas, seminaries, and even secular universities.

The Meaning of the Name Yahweh

The aphorism "etymology is not destiny" is certainly true in that the meaning of a word can change over time. In and of themselves, words have no inherent meaning and can be redefined by different communities with the passage of time. Yet it is just as true that the denotation and connotation of a word can be reinforced over time, and this may hold true for the way in which divinity was conceived and passed down, especially if a deity's specific nature continued to resonate with societal needs. Thus conceptualizing a deity as a mighty "lord" (*baʿal*) could be reinforced continually, as the need for a dominant/warrior god was an ever-present reality in the Late Bronze and Iron Ages.

There have been so many suggestions for the etymology of the name Yahweh that one could devote an entire monograph to the subject.[12] Yet there are only a handful of serious possibilities, and thus our treatment can be brief. William

F. Albright's (1968a: 168) assessment that "the most incredible etymologies are still advanced by otherwise serious scholars" is as true today as when he penned it some fifty years ago. One need not devote time to non-Semitic proposals such as (1) an Egyptian moon god named *Yah* + *we3*, "one"; (2) a Proto-Indo-European **Dyau-s*, which comes down into Greek as Zeus, into Latin as Jupiter, and into Hebrew as Yaw; (3) the Hurrian *ya*, "god," plus a *-ha* or *-wa* suffix; (4) and a putative deity Yae/Yaue from an undeciphered third-millennium BCE inscription from the Indus Valley.[13] Also unlikely is Sigmund Mowinckel's (1961: 131) argument that the name should be analyzed as a cultic shout, *ya-huwa* ("O He!"), similar to "the ecstatic cries of the Islamic dervishes 'Allah hu!'" Mowinckel suggests, on analogy with the Arabic, that *ya-* is an interjection and *huwa* the archaic third-person singular masculine pronoun. This view has won few adherents.[14] Rather, the consensus of scholarship is certainly correct that *yhwh* represents a verbal form, with the *y-* representing the third masculine singular verbal prefix of the verb *hyh* "to be."[15]

The foundation for this consensus is the revelation of the divine name in Exodus 3:14, a notoriously difficult passage where God declares "I am who I am" (*'ehyeh 'ăšer 'ehyeh*). Despite the various ways in which the passage can be interpreted, scholars unanimously assert that the Hebrew *'ehyeh* is the first person prefixal form of the verb "to be" with God as the speaker. (This verb is necessarily reformulated into *yhwh* by worshippers when they speak to or of God in the third person. Cf. Exod 3:15.) This is corroborated by the nearby context in which God assures Moses by saying "I will be [*'ehyeh*] with you" (Exod 3:12) and "I will be [*'ehyeh*] with your mouth" (Exod 4:12, 15). Dennis McCarthy (1978: 316) argues that "the repeated assonance *'ehyeh*—*'ehyeh*—*'ehyeh*—*yahweh*" in Exodus 3:14–15 has "tied Yahweh to *hyh* irrevocably." Compare too the wordplay in Hosea 1:9, which can be translated as either "I am not Ehyeh to you" or "As for me, I will no longer be[long] [*'ehyeh*] to you."[16] Such references and the oral traditions and transmission histories that preserved them argue against Rainer Albertz's (1994: 51) view that the *'ehyeh* tradition in Exodus 3:14 is a "speculative allusion" that "stands in almost complete isolation."

The Interpretation of Exodus 3:14

The difficulties associated with the enigmatic expression *'ehyeh 'ăšer 'ehyeh* (durative verbs usually translated "I am who I am" or "I will be who I will be") are many. The unusual syntax (where the same verb is repeated before and after a relative pronoun) has led some scholars to insinuate a "suspicion of haziness" in which God is deliberately sidestepping the question. They suggest that the tautology is dismissive in nature; God would rather people *not* know the meaning of his sacred name (cf. Mettinger 1988: 33–34; Albertz 1994: 50). Yet the examples of this *idem per idem* construction are not uniform and are too few in number to be relevant for our passage, especially in light of the context where God is portrayed as willingly revealing his name. Elsewhere the hiddenness of the divine name plays a thematic narrative role (e.g., Gen 32:29–30; Judg 13:17–18), but in the present passage God is anything but evasive when it comes to divulging his name.[17]

Yahweh: "He Who Is"?

One of the most common suggestions for the etymology of Yahweh can be traced back as early as the Septuagint translators who construed the name Yahweh in terms of being.[18] Thus Exodus 3:14 refers to "I am the one who is" or "I am the existing one" (*egō eimi hō ōn*). Similar understandings can be found in the Wisdom of Solomon 13:1 (where God is *ton onta*, "the one who is") and in the Qumran Community Rule (where God is *hww' 'wlm*, "Eternal Being"; 1QS XI:4–5). Critics have argued that such an etymology is secondary, reflecting Greek philosophical language that is incompatible with the original Hebrew.[19] Yet the element *yahwi-* (*ia-wi*) in Amorite personal names (noted by many to be the semantic equivalent of the Akkadian *ibašši*-DN, designating that the deity is present) cautions against relegating all such notions to Hellenistic thought.[20] Roland de Vaux (1978: 353) agreed that we should not import "the [Greek] metaphysical idea of Being in itself or Aseity," yet he retained the etymology, which fits "the biblical view of God, according to which 'being' was first and foremost 'existing.'" Still, one wonders whether an etymology having to do with existence would appeal to an ancient Semite. According to ancient Near Eastern lore, do not the gods exist immortally by definition? Numerous myths (e.g., Adapa, the Gilgamesh Epic, Aqhatu) illustrate the mortality of humans in contrast to undying gods (cf. Genesis 3:22; Ps 82:6–7). The Gilgamesh Epic (a fragment of which was even found at Megiddo [George 2003: 339–347]) reminded humans that they are fragile, "snapped off like a reed" (Tablet X, 301 [Column VI.10]; George 2003: 505, 696–697). The divine Alewife in the story reminds Gilgamesh: "When the gods created humans, they established death for humans, Eternal life they kept just for themselves."[21] Even the brash Gilgamesh knows in his heart that "only the gods dw[ell] forever along with the sun" and that humans, whose days are numbered, cannot scale heaven (cf. George 2003: 200–201).[22] Thus what sense would it make to say that one's deity "exists" if gods were thought to be immortal?

On the other hand, such myths do not tell the whole story. Occasionally we see clear indications that gods can and do die.[23] There are the well-known stories of the deaths of Osiris in Egypt and Ba'lu at Ugarit, yet their emergence later in

Figure 6.1 A god cuts the throat of another god. From a cylinder seal of the Akkadian period.
Courtesy the Trustees of the British Museum, and the British Museum Press.

the myths erases the fear that they remained dead. Dumuzi's descent into the underworld evokes ritual mourning, reflected in Mesopotamian literature and in the Bible (Ezek 8:14). Occasionally we can point to religious iconography of one deity killing another (e.g., Figure 6.1), which comes as no surprise to anyone familiar with the creation myth *Enuma Elish* (where Ea kills Apsu and Mummu, Marduk kills Tiamat, etc.). Other tales, both East and West Semitic, that tell of the death of the gods include those in the *Chaoskampf* traditions (see Chapter Eight), those dealing with rebellious gods, and those that describe the killing of individuals who were deemed guilty of some offense (cf. Qingu in Enuma Elish VI). Compare especially the tale of Atrahasis (1.4.223–226), which tells of the slaughter of the rebel god Geshtu-e (formerly read as We-ila), whose flesh, blood, "spirit" (*eṭemmu*), and "intelligence" (*ṭēmu*) are then used as ingredients for making humans.[24]

Yet the musings found in Ugarit's Kirta Epic may be more telling. It is hard not to feel the uncertainty voiced as Kirta's son weeps for his ailing father and wonders: "Do gods die after all?" (KTU 1.16.I.20–23; 1.16.II.43). Perhaps there was enough instability in the Levant regarding the permanence of the divine that it would have been appealing for the ancient Israelites to name their deity "the (permanently) existing one." Is it just a coincidence that Yahweh (a divine name written with a prefixal verbal form that can designate past durative as well as future durative) comes to bear the "Olam" epithet of El, who exists "from everlasting to everlasting" (mēʿôlām ʿad ʿôlām ʾattâ ʾēl; Ps 90:2)?[25] Similarly, what prompted Israelite authors to describe Yahweh as "the living god" (cf. Mettinger 1988: 82–91) if all gods were by definition immortal? One advantage of understanding Exodus 3:14's etymological puzzle as dealing with eternal existence is that it would be in concert with the following verse. Together the two verses underscore that "the god who is" bears a name that reflects the permanency of his character.

Yahweh has sent me ...
This shall be my name *forever*,   zeh šĕmî lĕʿôlām
This is my appellation *for all eternity*.   zeh zikrî lĕdōr dōr
                                                    (Exodus 3:15)

Instability among the gods was not restricted to their deaths. Because of their own ill-fated behaviors, gods could be viewed as less than dependable. Consider the heavy drinking by Ugaritic ʾIlu (see Chapter Four, pp. 79–80), where he collapses dead drunk like those who descend to the underworld. Dennis Pardee (1997b: 304 n. 16) notes how this is "a rather striking image for an immortal." At other times gods simply disappeared. Turning again to ancient Near Eastern lore, we find considerable mention of gods who vanish, some forever, others for only a period of time. Anatolia is our richest resource for tales about gods disappearing (cf. Beckman 1997: 566–567; Archi 1995: 2375), often in anger and often with drastic ramifications for humans' crops, especially if the god in hiding is the storm god or the sun god. The most famous Hittite myth tells of the disappearance of the storm god Telepinu (Hoffner 1990: 14–20; cf. also 20–29). The result of a deity disappearing is often the same as if the deity had died: anxiety and distress, especially in agrarian-based societies that attributed stagnation, drought, and sickness to the god's absence. Mark Smith (2001a: 121–122), building on the work of Jonathan Z. Smith (1969, 1987a) and Simon Parker (1989a), has argued that the category of "disappearing gods" is more appropriate than the "dying and rising god" motif promoted ubiquitously ever since Sir James George Frazer's *The Golden Bough*. If the notion that gods could be in hiding, sleeping, or occupied elsewhere was widely known in the Levant (cf. KTU 1.16.III and 1 Kgs 18:27 [Parker 1989a]), then perhaps such uncertainty prompted the choice of the name Yahweh to designate a deity who existed permanently. In short, "the existing one" is he who will not angrily disappear and leave the worshipper alone with his drought and/or personal illness.[26]

Yahweh as Actively Present?

This brings us back to de Vaux's suggestion that we should add an existential dimension to our understanding of the etymology of Yahweh as the existing god. McCarthy (1978: 317) concurs that "he who is" is a statement about the deity actively participating in the life of his worshippers: "Yahweh *is* above all others and this means active and helping, for being and acting effectively were not separated. . . . He is Yahweh. . . . The one who is acts." Similarly, Nahum Sarna (1991: 17–18) writes that Yahweh's name expresses eternal being along with "dynamic presence" and "unvarying dependability." Albertz (1994: 50) adds that "Yahweh is the god who is with his people and works for them."

A volume on ancient Israelite religion is not the proper place for a discourse on the Hebrew verbal system, yet for understanding the full significance of the name Yahweh one needs to know that the form *yhwh* is a prefixal (non-perfective or "imperfect") conjugation that designates an incomplete or durative (even habitual) action. Thus 'ehyeh can equally designate "I am" or "I will be," and most translations that render Exodus 3:14 as "I am who I am" also footnote the alternative translation "I will be who I will be." The ancients—not being preoccupied with our modern compulsion to form dichotomies—may have held both ideas simultaneously. But in what sense was "the existing one" also the one who "will be"? McCarthy (1978: 316) has humorously noted that a true future meaning without a predicate ("I shall be") "used absolutely means that the speaker is not yet in existence, a very unstable platform from which to speak."

Indeed, the verb 'ehyeh is consistently used with a predicate (often the preposition "with") denoting the active presence of Yahweh. One need turn no further than the present context. As already mentioned, the exact verbal form 'ehyeh occurs immediately before (Exod 3:12) and after (Exod 4:12, 15) the enigmatic 'ehyeh 'ăšer 'ehyeh expression in Exodus 3:14. It is hard to ignore the significance of such a juxtaposition.[27] In each instance, 'ehyeh is used to emphasize that God will be "with" Moses, in both speech and action, to bring about the liberation of the Hebrew slaves. This is not the only place where biblical authors employ this particular vocabulary. Deuteronomistic authors used the language of "Yahweh being with a person" to show divine favor (e.g., Josh 1:5, 9; Judg 2:18, 6:12; see a more complete listing in Cross 1973: 252). In particular, the expression is used as a "theological leitmotiv" of the Davidic royal ideology (McCarter 1984: 201–202). Consider the parade example in 2 Samuel 7:3–14:

Nathan said to the king . . .
Yahweh is with you . . .   y̲h̲w̲h̲ ʿimmĕkā . . .

Yahweh of Hosts says . . .
I was with you wherever you went,   wā ʾe̲h̲y̲e̲h̲ ʿimmĕkā . . .
clearing all your enemies from your path . . .

Yahweh declares to you . . .
For my part, *I will be* for him as a father,   ʾănî ʾe̲h̲y̲e̲h̲ lô lĕʾāb
For his part, *he will be* for me as a son.   wĕ hûʾ y̲i̲h̲y̲e̲h̲ lî lĕbēn

Here the notion of Yahweh's presence (*ʾehyeh*)—mixed with adoption language (cf. Ps 2:7; Ps 89:27–28 [Eng 89:26–27])—is used to legitimize the institution of the monarchy and its dynastic succession, in contrast to the tribal league's theocratic ideal with its emphasis on temporary leadership. Yahweh was "with" David in a military way, cutting down the enemies in his path, similar to the way Yahweh dispatched Pharaoh for Moses (note how 2 Sam 7:6 alludes to the exodus from Egypt). Yet not only is Yahweh actively present, but his relation to the king is presented as kinship, with God being the father. Similarly, the king bears an active role as a son, not merely as a divinely appointed ruler. Indeed, the divine election language of Yahweh *being with* the Davidides is so strong and obvious in this passage (cf. 1 Sam 16:18; 17:37; 18:14, 28; 2 Sam 5:10; 1 Kgs 1:37; 11:38; Ps 89:21; Isa 7:14) that one wonders whether the *ʾehyeh/yahweh* etymology originated as a part of the Davidic apology (cf. McCarter 1980b: 494, 503–504; Knapp 2015: 222) or whether it was brilliantly adapted from earlier traditions. The vocalization of *yahweh*, to which we now turn, may point to the latter.

"Ya̲hweh": An Archaic Vocalization?

If the etymology of Yahweh has to do with his eternal and active presence, the verbal form would be in a non-causative (Qal) stem. (For a possible etymology involving the causative stem, see the next section.) What accounts then for the *a*-class vowel in *ya̲hweh*? The normal non-causative form would be *yi̲hweh*. Tryggve Mettinger (1988: 32), following de Vaux (1978: 348), suggests that this vocalization "may be understood as an archaism . . . a survival from an earlier stage in the history of the language." The *ya*- prefix (if non-causative) would argue that *yahweh* stems from a dialect other than classical biblical Hebrew prose (usually identified by linguists with the time of the monarchy). The use of *w* as the middle radical would point in the same direction. That Hebrew's *yiqtol/yiqtel* forms are secondary to older *yaqtul/yaqtil* forms is supported by evidence from Ugaritic and Amarna Canaanite.[28] The existence of *yaqtul/yaqtil* forms in these two languages, which date from the Late Bronze Age II, would suggest that the vocalization of *yahweh* (if non-causative) is pre-monarchic. One could argue that the biblical tradition is archaizing, yet this would be peculiar especially in light of the *yawi-/yahwi-* forms occurring in Amorite personal names.[29]

Yahweh: "He Who Causes to Be"?

Another way of sifting much of the same data has been advocated by Albright (1924: 370–378; 1948; 1968a: 168–172) and his students David N. Freedman (1960; Freedman and O'Connor 1986) and Cross (1962a; 1973: 60–71).[30] This view argues on several lines of evidence that *yahweh* is a causative, "he who causes to be," a reference to the ability of the deity as creator. Freedman (Freedman and O'Connor 1986: 513) argues that "*yahweh* must be a causative, since the dissimilation of *yaqṭal* to *yiqṭal* did not apply in Amorite, while it was obligatory in Hebrew. The name *yahweh* must therefore be a hiphil [= causative]." Such an analysis is perfectly logical, but it allows for no dialectical variation and ends up analyzing the morphology of *yahweh* according to the standards of classical biblical Hebrew prose. Yet the *ya-* prefix as reconstructed for the earliest stage of Hebrew (a *yaqtil* form for III weak verbs; cf. Ugaritic and Amarna Canaanite)—which predates classical biblical Hebrew—does not require a causative meaning (cf. Kitz 2019). In addition, the root in question (*hwy, hwh,* or *hyh*) never occurs in Hebrew as a causative—a remarkable fact given the commonness of the root. Mettinger (1988: 32) tallies 3,561 attestations of the verb *hyh* ("to be") in Hebrew with "not a single example . . . construed in the causative stem."

Having said this, one needs to acknowledge the elegance and economy of the Albright-Freedman-Cross hypothesis, which offers one of the best explanations for why the name of the deity Yahweh is a verbal form to begin with (cf. the noun *baʿal*, "lord," to describe Baal).[31] In addition, it accounts for the epithet Yahweh Sebaoth, exquisitely relates all of this to the worship of the deity El, and even yields a theory to solve the crux of Exodus 3:14. No wonder it has been so appealing.

The foundation to the theory is to see *yahweh* as a verbal element of a "sentence name" whose other constituent element was the name of a deity. Appealing especially to the Amorite onomastica, this theory noted that personal "sentence names" (e.g., *yahwi-addu*) reflected the deity worshipped by an individual combined with a verb describing the deity in action. Such names were thought to be "formulas" derived from cultic liturgies and litanies.[32] Over the course of time, such "transparent appellations" typically shorten rather than lengthen. In Cross'

(1962a: 252; 1973: 62) colorful wording, West Semitic divine epithets and names, like personal names in general, go through a process of shortening and disintegration: "They do not begin in numinous grunts or shouts and build up into liturgical sentences or appellations."

Thus *yahweh* was originally the verbal element of a sentence name. An additional building block for this theory was found in the phrase Yahweh Sebaoth. Rather than rendering it in the traditional way as "Yahweh of Hosts," Albright advocated translating it as "a perfectly good sentence meaning, 'He brings armies into existence.'" Cross (1973: 65) buttressed Albright with a grammatical argument: "*yahwê ṣĕbāʾôt* . . . cannot be read 'Yahweh of hosts,' that is, as a construct chain. A proper name cannot be put into the construct state (as a *nomen regens*) according to grammatical law." Similarly, Cross (1973: 70) translated this as "he creates the (divine) hosts," a fitting liturgical title for a divine warrior/creator worshipped by tribes of the League militia, which advocated a holy war ideology. Freedman (1960: 152–156; 1997: 86–88) and Cross (1973: 69) underscored such an epithet in the Ark narrative, where "The One Enthroned upon the Cherubim creates the hosts (of Israel)" (*yhwh ṣĕbāʾôt yōšēb hakkĕrubîm*; 1 Sam 4:4). In addition, Freedman and O'Connor (1986: 515) pointed out that *yahweh ṣĕbāʾôt* is not the only use of *yahweh* in a sentence name. Other examples include *yahweh šālôm*, "he creates peace" (Judg 6:24); *yahweh qannāʾ*, "he creates zeal" (Exod 34:14); and *yahweh nissî*, "he creates my refuge" (Exod 17:15).

The final piece of the puzzle turned out to be the most elegant. Cross simply probed the identity of the deity who once stood behind the sentence name. El, the creator god best known from Ugarit, was the irresistible choice. Thus Yahweh was "originally a cultic name of ʾEl," whose full epithet was *ʾēl zū yahwī ṣabaʾōt*, "El who creates the heavenly armies" (Cross 1962a: 256; 1973: 71). This is why biblical tradition shows no animosity between El and Yahweh (in contrast to the friction between Yahweh and Baal). In addition, this theory would account for why Yahweh came to bear many of the traits and functions of El (Cross 1973: 72).

Finally, according to Cross (1973: 71), when Yahweh became the principal cult name of the Israelites' deity at a later stage (most likely through the shortening process previously described), Yahweh would have been substituted for El, resulting in the sentence name hypothetically reconstructed as **yahwê zū yahwê ṣabaʾōt*, "Yahweh who creates the heavenly armies." Once one recognizes *zū* as an older relative pronoun, one sees how this reconstruction is the third-person approximation of God's first-person declaration *ʾehyeh ʾăšer ʾehyeh* in Exodus 3:14 (especially if one follows Cross [1973: 68 n. 94] in revocalizing the original form of both verbs as causatives: *ʾahyê ʾăšer ʾahyê*, "I create what I create").[33]

As elegant and economical as this theory is, it is not without its drawbacks. At the outset we mentioned how the verb "to be" (*hwy, hwh*, or *hyh*) never occurs in Hebrew as a causative despite a large statistical sampling. Nor is the verb *hyh* ever explicitly used for creation.[34] Hebrew instead uses the verbs *brʾ*, *ʿśh*, and *yṣr* to denote creative activity (Eichrodt 1961: 189). These criticisms can be overcome if one hypothesizes that the choice of the verb in the causative to denote the deity was itself the reason behind the statistics. In other words, because the verb *hyh* in the causative stem (i.e., Yahweh) came to denote the sacred, the same usage was restricted from denoting the profane. But this seems forced. Would not Hebrew poets, with their love of alliteration, have celebrated Yahweh's creative activity by artistically juxtaposing his name next to *hyh*?

The grammatical difficulty that Cross used to support Albright's hypothesis (that *yahweh ṣĕbāʾôt* could not be in a genitive relationship) is weakened due to inscriptions that have come to light since Cross' treatment. The inscriptions from Kuntillet ʿAjrud attest, in contrast to Cross' statement, that a proper name *can* be used in a construct state in Hebrew (Emerton 1982). In particular, we read of the divine name *yhwh* used in construct with geographical locations: Yahweh of Samaria, Yahweh of Teman (Meshel 1992: 107; 1993: 1462; 2012: 130). In addition, even if we agree to reconstruct the necessary hypothetical liturgical formulas (**ʾēl zū yahwī ṣabaʾōt* is never actually attested), we run into logical difficulties. It seems circular to posit a shortened liturgical phrase in order to procure the name Yahweh independently (**ʾēl zū yahwī ṣabaʾōt* → *yahwī ṣabaʾōt* → *yahwê*) while at the same time needing the full liturgical formula to be operational in order to substitute (an already independent) Yahweh for El (**ʾēl zū yahwī ṣabaʾōt* → **yahwê zū yahwê ṣabaʾōt*). Perhaps there was a fluid process of shortening appellations while at the same time retaining their fuller form as functioning heirlooms. Coexisting modernizing and conservative tendencies are common in all religions. Yet to advocate this line of thinking feels like special pleading.

Finally, there is the fundamental critique voiced by de Vaux: "The most serious objection to this hypothesis is that it insists on a correction to the text of Ex 3:14, which provides [the biblical] explanation of the name Yahweh."[35] Not only would one be rewriting the "obvious wordplay" in this verse (Mettinger 1988: 32), but one would be ignoring the immediate context as well. As has been noted, the triple occurrence of the exact verbal form (*ʾehyeh*) in Exodus 3:12 and 4:12, 15 argues for keeping the vocalization of 3:14 as it is represented in the Masoretic text. Thus the non-causative etymology of *yahweh* must be preferred if our aim is to understand the *biblical* interpretation of the name Yahweh. This conclusion does not rule out the hypothesis that a different (causative) understanding of the name could have existed in pre-Israelite times or in extra-biblical material. If this was the case, the biblical texts would be witnesses to a reformulation. But until some newly discovered inscriptions cause us to think otherwise, it is prudent to retain the biblical witness as the best window into the ancient Israelite understanding of the etymology of Yahweh.

Yahweh: "He Who Blows"? "He Who Fells with Lightning"?

As will be shown, many biblical and extra-biblical sources point to a locale for the origin of Yahweh in the area south or southeast of the Dead Sea. This has prompted some scholars, building on older work of defenders such as Julius Wellhausen, to look to Arabic etymologies for *hwy*, meaning "to blow (wind)" or "to fell (with lightning)."[36] Such an etymology, they argue, would be fitting for Yahweh as a storm god and would help explain "why Yahweh could assume various of Baal's mythological exploits" (van der Toorn 1999b: 916). There is no denying that Yahweh shares many qualities of a storm god, as does Baal, but one need not argue that this aspect of his nature was derived from an Arabic theonym. Furthermore, it is difficult to posit a verbal meaning ("to blow" or "to fell") that was never productive in the language used to worship the deity.[37] One could, I assume, envision an archaic frozen epithet (Yahweh = "he who blows") that the ancient Israelites inherited from their southern neighbors. Yet again, would we not expect to find punning or alliterative poetry (i.e., using *hwy* in this sense alongside *yhwh*) celebrating Yahweh as he who blows with the wind and fells with his lightning, especially when Hebrew bards have left behind such a great deal of literature containing storm imagery?[38] Finally, the same critique leveled against the causative use of *hyh* and its relation to Exodus 3:14 applies here. The meaning of a verb denoting blowing or felling cannot be reconciled with the wordplay of Exodus 3:14, which reveals the etymological understanding of at least one segment of ancient Israelite society. Until we are able to secure more complete information, this segment's understanding will have to serve for the whole.

The Revelation of the Name Yahweh in the Hebrew Bible

When was the name Yahweh revealed, according to the various literary presentations that have come down to us in the Hebrew Bible as we now have it? The Hebrew Bible presents different answers to this question, and source critics have long used this material to define various literary strands. In Chapter Five, on the deity El, we looked at P's famous assertion—placed on the lips of the divine— that the patriarchs worshipped God under the name of El Shadday. To clarify more precisely, P has God declare: "But I did not make myself known to them by my name Yahweh" (Exod 6:2-3). This coincides with the passage we have just visited (Exod 3:14) where the name Yahweh was revealed during the time of Moses as a part of the story of liberation from Egypt. Traditional source critics who analyze Exodus 3:14-15 as the E literary strand point out that this source affirms the same timetable of revelation as P. God speaks to Moses and identifies himself as "Yahweh, the god of your fathers." In contrast to these to sources, J assumes that the name Yahweh was known prior to the Mosaic period. For J, the worship of Yahweh goes back to the earliest times; it was in the days of Enosh that people "began to call upon the name of Yahweh" (Gen 4:26). However one understands source criticism (traditional J and E sources or non-P), it is obvious that we are dealing with variant streams of tradition that coexisted in antiquity without any need to harmonize their differences. Nonetheless, the literary critic can still probe to see which of these traditions is a more dominant reflection of the *biblical* understanding of the time when the worship of Yahweh commenced, an understanding that the historian can then juxtapose with the first attestations of the name Yahweh in the extra-biblical inscriptions.

Let us look at both streams of traditions and assume for our first test case that the name Yahweh was thought to be known in patriarchal times (= J's view). In support of this view one can marshal approximately ninety occurrences of the name Yahweh spread across the patriarchal narratives (e.g., Gen 4:1–7; 7:1, 5; 8:20–21; 12:1, 4, 7–8; 15:1, 6–7; 17:1; 18; 21:1; 24:1; 25:21–23; 26:12, 24–25; 28:13, 16; 29:31–35; 30:24; 30:27; 39:23). Indeed, for traditional source critics, the name Yahweh helps demarcate the J literary strand. Adam's grandson Enosh was not a lone voice calling upon the name of Yahweh. Despite the statement in Genesis 4:26 that people *began* to call upon the name Yahweh, the deity was already known to Adam and Eve as well as Cain and Abel (Gen 4:1–7). Many who came after Enosh and yet prior to Moses (including Noah, Abraham, Sarah, Isaac, Rebekah, Jacob, Leah, Rachel, and Joseph) also had a relationship with the deity Yahweh, to whom they prayed, brought offerings, and built altars (Gen 8:20; 12:7–8; 13:4, 18; 26:25), not to mention engaging in other cultic activity such as Laban's use of divination (Gen 30:27; cf. 44:5, 15). Even the name of Moses' own mother (Jochebed) could be used to prove that Yahweh was worshipped prior to his advent.[39]

How does this view handle P's bold contradiction in Exodus 6:2–3 that the name Yahweh was unknown in patriarchal times? One could assume, along with more conservative scholars (who are generally dismissive of source criticism in the first place), that the name Yahweh was understood in patriarchal times and that Exodus 6 is not stating that the appellation itself was unknown; rather, it was the covenantal nature of the name that was kept secret prior to Moses.[40] Thus the author meant for his audience to be able to read between the lines. Yet relying on an ellipsis to communicate such an important concept hardly makes for an attractive hypothesis. Other, more critical scholars find their solution in the nature of P. All source critics agree that well-ordered structures and patterns are characteristic of P. Fastidiousness is one of P's defining characteristics. In looking at how P structures his history, we see a sequential progression in the revelation of God's name. In a three-stage process P shows how God's name was revealed in a

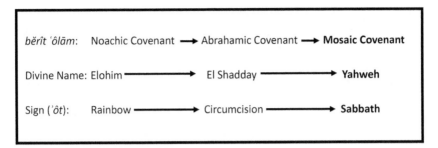

Figure 6.2 P's structure of covenantal history.
Illustration by Theodore J. Lewis.

step-by-step fashion coinciding with three "eternal covenants" (*bĕrît ʿôlām*) and three particular "covenant *ʾôt*-signs" (*ʾôt bĕrît, ʾôt lĕʿôlām*) (Gen 9:16–17; 17:7, 11; Exod 31:16–17; see Figure 6.2).[41]

P emphasizes how the fullness of God's self-disclosure comes only through the revelation of the name Yahweh to Moses. P uses Elohim for the primeval history, then El Shadday for the patriarchs, reserving his most special name for the foremost covenant, which culminates with the priest and lawgiver Moses. The priestly interests of P here are easy to see. Not only is Moses' covenant celebrated as the zenith of this historical timeline, but so too is sabbath observance. It is not just a coincidence that P tells the creation story to teach a cultic lesson. After the heavens and the earth were finished, God observed a sabbath and hallowed the seventh day so that humans could do likewise (Gen 2:2–3). By designating the sabbath as the *eternal* covenant sign (*ʾôt lĕʿôlām*) and combining it with the unique revelation of the name Yahweh, P is going out of his way to underscore the preeminence of the Sinaitic covenant.

In other words, P may have had an ulterior motive in presenting his scenario as he does. His rationale would have been to give credibility to Mosaic legislation and to underscore the need for sabbath observance. What better way to accomplish this than to have Yahweh self-disclose to Moses in Exodus 6:2–3 and to make apparent the sabbath sign that was foreshadowed in creation (Exod 16:22ff.; 31:12–18)? If J's account that Yahweh was already worshipped since the time of Enosh is to be believed, then P's omission of such a fact in Exodus 6:2–3 would be intentional editing on his part. In sum, P's assertion that the name Yahweh comes into use after the patriarchal period could be discounted due to his concealed motive.

The alternative option, our second test case, assumes that P and E are correct in their "unanimous witness" (Mettinger 1988: 20) that the name Yahweh was revealed at the time of Moses and not beforehand. There may be a possible allusion to a Mosaic timetable in the self-presentation formula "I am Yahweh your

God, from the land of Egypt" (*'ānōkî yhwh 'ĕlōhêkā mē'ereṣ miṣrāyîm*), found twice in the book of Hosea (12:10 [Eng 12:9]; 13:4). Several translations and commentators treat the preposition *min* as temporal. Thus JPS, NEB, NRSV, and NAB translate Hosea 13:4 as "I have been Yahweh your God *ever since* the land of Egypt." While such a grammatical usage expressing the *terminus a quo* is possible (Joüon and Muraoka 1991: §133e; Waltke and O'Connor 1990: §11.2.11c) and fits the context of Hosea 13:4, there is always the possibility that the Hebrew is elliptical in nature (cf. LXX) and expresses the notion that Yahweh is the god (who brought the people out) from the land of Egypt (cf. Hos 11:1; Exod 20:2; Andersen and Freedman 1980: 617, 634).

Offering better support is the preponderance of El names in the patriarchal narratives. In fact, Mettinger (1988: 20–21) points out that "in the patriarchal narratives there is not a single name . . . in which the Name [Yahweh] is a constitutive element, as we would have expected if the patriarchs had actually known this divine Name." Dana Marston Pike (1990: 35) concurs, writing that "a simple survey of the Biblical onomastic evidence yields no Yahwistic PN preserved from the time prior to the Israelite bondage in Egypt, nor do such names appear in significant numbers until well into the period of the Judges."[42] This statistical evidence resonates with what we learned of Israelite El in the Chapter Four. There we saw, through several lines of converging evidence, that El worship is attested in the earliest biblical narratives (e.g., Gen 49:25). Set against a Late Bronze Age backdrop (such as the Ugaritic texts that celebrate the prominence of a deity also named 'Ilu), the biblical tradition that El worship preceded Yahwism makes perfect sense. The name Isra*el* (with El as the theophoric element) is just what we would expect for groups of people who looked back to El and not Yahweh as their founding deity (cf. again the name "El, the god of Israel" in Gen 33:20).

How then does our second test case account for J's own bold contradiction that the worship of Yahweh began in the days of Enosh? And how does this view account for the presence of the ninety occurrences of Yahweh in the patriarchal narratives? For the first question, many scholars doubt whether the meaning of Genesis 4:26 refers to the beginning of Yahweh worship, for if it does, J would be contradicting his own reference to Eve calling on Yahweh in Genesis 4:1. Rather, they assert, this is simply a reference to the beginning of public worship, or worship in a general sense.[43] Gordon Wenham (1987: 116) draws Sumerian parallels where worship is established in the pre-flood era. As for the many occurrences of the name Yahweh prior to the advent of Moses, scholars argue that these are anachronistic and reflect the writing and editing of these texts in retrospect. In other words, all of these texts were written and/or edited at a later point in time when Yahweh was worshipped as the preeminent Israelite god. Thus it was natural for editors holding this belief to retroject Yahweh's worship to the earliest time—indeed, even back to Eve and Adam.[44]

In support of this anachronistic theory are the clear signs of editing that show a mixture of older notions and more recent updating. For example, in Genesis 16:11 Hagar is told, "You will bear a son and you will call his name Ishmael [*yišmāʿ-ʾēl*, "May El hear/El hears (my cry)"] because *Yahweh* has heard your cry." The obvious wordplay here presupposes that El and not Yahweh was the original name of the deity mentioned in the second half of the verse. Hagar's son was named Ishma-El and not Ishma-Yah or Shama-Yah. This is also supported by the broader context of this pericope where the deity is named El-Roi (Gen 16:13; see Chapter Four, pp. 95–97). Similarly, El is the deity who is associated with the place Bethel (*bêt-ʾēl* even means "house/temple of El") in the patriarchal narratives (and later in Jeroboam's bull cults). In Genesis 35:7 we read of the deity "El of Beth-El," after whom Jacob names an altar site at Bethel. So when we come across Abram building an altar to *Yahweh* at Beth-*El* (Gen 12:8; cf. 28:16, 19) one again suspects that the hand of a later (Yahweh-worshipping) editor is at work updating his inherited (El) sources. Thus the answer offered by proponents of our second option (that the many occurrences of Yahweh names in the patriarchal narratives are the result of anachronistic editing) has good precedent.[45]

Section II: The Name Yahweh in Extra-Biblical and Epigraphic Sources

The Name Yahweh in Extra-Biblical Sources

In recent years archaeologists and epigraphists, by finding and deciphering extra-biblical inscriptions, have grounded our discussions about the origin of Yahweh with more empirical evidence. I do not mean to imply that biblical texts are unreliable—they exhibit internal criteria (morphology, syntax, prosody, etc.) that give us clues as to when and where the texts were penned. And while it is safe to say that such criteria do not support the notion that all we have are late Hellenistic retrojections, we are, nonetheless, presented with *traditional* accounts, and this complicates our task. Traditional texts, due to their reuse (which can entail updating and rewriting), are hard to anchor in space and time. Thus when we find extra-biblical inscriptions (especially those found in situ) mentioning Yahweh, it does constitute a significant advancement for reconstructing the origin of the deity.

False Leads: Yahweh at Ebla and Ugarit, Moses as Beya

There have been missteps along the way where scholars alleged that the name Yahweh could be found in certain ancient Near Eastern texts. The most famous of these, which made headlines and even carried political repercussions,[46] was the announcement in 1976 by Giovanni Pettinato that a "specific divinity," Ya (a shortened form of Yaw), was mentioned in the third-millennium BCE texts from Ebla (Tell Mardikh in northern Syria).[47] Even though Pettinato hedged, noting that the -yà ending in question could just be hypocoristic, commentators hastily rushed to equate Ebla's Ya with the patriarchs' Yahweh.[48] Anson Rainey (1977: 38) feared non-specialists becoming "too enthusiastic about the value of a 'parallel,'" thereby tending "to overdramatize the relevance of the comparative evidence." And dramatize they did, despite an article by the epigraphist Alfonso Archi in 1979 that poured cold water on the equation (see too Archi 1981: 153). For example, Mitchell Dahood (1981: 277) wrote that, based on personal names at Ebla, "the evidence for the pre-Israelite existence of Ya for a Canaanite deity grows ever more impressive." Elsewhere, Dahood (1978: 107) referred to the "pre-Abrahamic designation of God as Ya" at third-millennium Ebla and then stated that this seemed "to be in accord" with Genesis 4:26, where "in the second generation after Adam 'man began to call upon the name of Yahweh.'" Today, with the benefit of hindsight, scholars no longer draw such sensationalistic parallels—what Manfred Krebernik (2017: 61) categorized as "wishful thinking lead[ing] to premature conclusions." All of the past excitement was based on the interpretation of a single cuneiform sign (NI) in personal names, such as mi-ga-NI, en-na-NI, and iš-ra-NI. In contrast to reading NI as ià, a theophoric element, most scholars today would read NI as either a hypocoristic ending or, following Hans-Peter Müller (1980, 1981), an abbreviation for ì-lí, "my god."[49] Van der Toorn (1999b: 911) deals a final blow to the Yahweh-at-Ebla theory by pointing out that "in no list of gods or offerings is the mysterious god *Ya ever mentioned; his cult at Ebla is a chimera."

Ebla is not the only Syrian site where scholars have thought that they found Yahweh. Four decades before Ebla was discovered, Charles Virolleaud published a Ugaritic text (VI AB IV = KTU 1.1.4) which mentioned a deity *yw*. René Dussaud and Cyrus Gordon were two of the major Semitists who followed Virolleaud's lead in identifying *yw* with Yahweh.[50] In the years since, few scholars have embraced this view, with critics (see especially Gray 1953) pointing out the total absence of the deity *yw* elsewhere in the Ugaritic corpus. In addition, the mention of the well-known deity Yammu in the next line caused most scholars to conclude that "*Yw* may be a different way of writing *Ym* or else part of a title of the same god" (de Vaux 1978: 342; cf. Smith 1994b: 148–152). The relevant text is a cryptic section in KTU 1.1.4.13–14 that reads as follows:

wy'n lṭ<p>n 'il d[p'id] 'Ilu the gracious and be[neficent] replies:
[. . .] (14) šm bny yw 'ilt . . . the name of my son is Yw, O goddess,
[. . .] (15) wp'r šm ym [. . .] . . . and he pronounced the name Yammu.

Despite his own earlier rejection of the Yw = Yahweh hypothesis, Johannes C. de Moor revived the theory.[51] It is clear to de Moor that "the people of Ugarit equated Yawê with Yam, the sea-god," for "Yawê/Yam is a *deliberate* Ugaritic caricature of YHWH" (1995b: 221–222, emphasis mine). De Moor based most of his argument on a comparative analysis in which he tried to show how there are parallels between Yammu in the Ugaritic texts and Yahweh in the Bible. Yet the motifs and epithets suggested by de Moor (Yammu and Yahweh both bear the titles of King, Lord, Master, Judge, etc.) are so generic that they could apply to any number of ancient Near Eastern deities.

While the identification of *yw* in KTU 1.1.4 with Yahweh is tantalizing, it must be rejected as too conjectural, especially when based on such a fragmentary text. The Ugaritic pantheon is well attested in deity lists, sacrificial lists, and ritual texts, not to mention the better-known myths, legends, and epics. There is *no* evidence of Yw as a distinct deity in any of this material. The only attestation is in the broken text presented earlier, and it strains credulity to base such a grand thesis on such little evidence. In addition, there are other solutions (see Hess 1991: 182–183) to explain the name *yw*, which seems to be an alternative designation (a by-form?) of Yammu. There is no hint that the Late Bronze Age Ugaritic scribes are making a caricature of the Israelite deity Yahweh, and de Moor's appeal to "a historical association of the proto-Israelites with certain Sea peoples" is special pleading.

The third false lead for identifying Yahweh in extra-biblical inscriptions prior to the Iron Age can also be traced to de Moor. In *The Rise of Yahwism* de Moor popularized a bold thesis (following Knauf 1988: 135–141) that an Egyptian vizier from the New Kingdom who bore the name of Beya was actually Moses.[52] The name Beya, suggested de Moor (1990: 149), might mean "In Yh (is my trust)." Critiquing this theory would take us too far afield, and Richard Hess has done a splendid job in pointing out the weaknesses of such speculation. Even if de Moor is correct in pronouncing this personal name as Beya (the Egyptian reads *B3i*) based on RS 86.2230 from Ugarit, Hess (1991: 182) is nonetheless correct that "the presence of a hypocoristic suffix in the name Beya seems a much more probable interpretation than its identification as a shortened form of the divine name Yahweh."

Three Possible Leads: Shasu Nomads, a Shepherd of Yah, and Yahweh in Hamath, Syria?

In contrast to the three attempts just described, there are three more promising possibilities for finding the name Yahweh in extra-biblical inscriptions, two from

Egypt (the Shasu material and a proper name found in a Book of the Dead manuscript), and one from northern Syria (Stephanie Dalley's Hamath theory). If these three possibilities are correct, they would constitute dramatic evidence. The first two from Egypt would represent the earliest mention of Yahweh—indeed, as early as the fourteenth century BCE. The third would document Yahweh in inland Syria in the eighth century BCE, a previously unattested instance and one that could contrast with the view of most scholars who look to a southern locale for the deity's origin. Moreover, it would challenge the claims of some biblical authors that "Yahweh was worshipped solely by the people of Israel and Judah, through the institution of the Covenant" (Dalley 1990: 23).

Egyptian geographical lists from the time of Amenophis III (first half of the fourteenth century BCE) and Ramses II (thirteenth century BCE) refer to "the land of the Shasu[-nomads?] of Yhw," *t3 š3sw yh(w)/yhw3*, and "the Shasu[-nomads?] of Seir," *š3sw sʿrr*.[53] Some scholars have seen in this material not only the earliest mention of the divine name Yahweh but also solid proof that the deity originated in the area of the Arabah.

Who were these Shasu (or Shosu), who crop up in texts from the Eighteenth Dynasty through the Third Intermediate Period? They are known pictographically from the reliefs of battle scenes at Karnak, where they wear short kilts and turban-like headdresses.[54] The term *š3sw* comes from a root (*š3s*) that refers to traveling or wandering (cf. Coptic *šōs*, "shepherd, herdsman"), and so most scholars see them as nomads or semi-nomads, although Lawrence Stager (1985b: 59*) is correct that the texts "reveal very little about their mode of livelihood." Lester Grabbe (2017: 55, 128) cautions that we should not assume that all Shasu were exclusively nomadic: "Although we know that pastoralism was characteristic of some or possibly even most Shasu, we cannot say that this was the sole means of livelihood of all of them." Writing more generally, he adds: "Nomadic pastoralism covers a wide-ranging spectrum and can include those who raise crops, engage in trade, or even go raiding or robbing caravans, alongside their livestock husbandry."

Donald Redford (1992: 271–272) notes how the Egyptians shaded the term *š3sw* to mean "lawless malcontents" (cf. Hebrew *šāsâ*, "to plunder"; Lambdin 1953: 155). They are described as military foes in texts at Seti I's Karnak temple in Thebes (CoS 2:23–25), and in Papyrus Anastasi I, a text filled with West Semitic loanwords (Wente 1990: §129; CoS 3:9–14; ANET 475–479). Yet in Papyrus Anastasi VI they are portrayed as serene pastoralists, "clans of the Shasu of Edom," traveling to the Delta region in search of the "pools [*brkt*, a West Semitic loanword] of the House of Atum" (Per-Atum = biblical Pithom?) for their livestock (CoS 3:16–17; ANET 259).[55]

Though they are to be found throughout Syria-Palestine, Redford (1992: 272) argues, based on the geographical lists previously mentioned, that the "original concentration of Shasu settlements lay in the southern Transjordan in the plains of Moab and northern Edom." This is in concert with the view of many scholars that Seir (its connection with the Shasu will be discussed shortly) is to be located *east* of Wadi Arabah. Moshe Weinfeld (1987: 304), using the same lists, argues that Seir "should not be sought in Edom of Transjordan... because the mountain of Seir denotes also the range of mountains to the west of Arabah and to the south of the Dead Sea" (cf. Deut 1:2; Josh 11:17; 12:7; EA 288:26).[56] Nadav Na'aman's (1992: 74) conclusion unifies both theories: "The names Seir and Edom originally referred to the entire area south of the Dead Sea, on both sides of Wadi Arabah."[57] Tantalizing evidence from the Faynan region in southern Jordan (especially the Wadi Fidan 40 cemetery) has also been related to the activity of the Shasu. Erez Ben-Yosef and colleagues (2010: 743) write: "The evidence from Faynan indicates that the resumption of copper production at the very end of the Late Bronze–Early Iron Age, was opportunistically initiated by local semi-nomadic tribal societies. These may be the 'Shasu' tribes" (cf. Levy, Adams, and Muniz 2004; Levy 2008, 2009b).

The Shasu are tantalizing for historians of Israelite religion due to their mention in conjunction with the term *yh(w)/yhw3* (pronounced ya-h-wí?), which seems to be a toponym rather than a theonym, to judge from parallel expressions that refer to the various encampments of the Shasu.[58] Raphael Giveon (1964: 415–416) speculates that the fuller form of the toponym might have been Beth Yahweh. Nevertheless, the term is still relevant for tracing the origin of Yahweh because, as Michael Astour (1979: 25) reminds us, "in the ancient Near East many anthroponyms could serve as toponyms" (cf. the GN and DN Aššur). In fact, it may very well be that the name of the territory was derived from the deity or vice versa (Giveon 1964; van der Toorn 1999b: 911–912). Thus many scholars conclude that these Shasu are nomads worshipping a god named Yahweh as early as the fourteenth century BCE. Redford (1992: 280) even goes so far as to speak of "the religious life of the Shasu/Israelites." In contrast, Frank Yurco (1978; 1986; 1990) and Stager (1985b) argue that the two are distinct based on the Karnak battle reliefs (from the western wall of the Cour de la Cachette), where the dress of the Israelites is portrayed quite differently from that of the Shasu. Yet the interpretation of this iconography is debated (Rainey 1991, 1992, 2001a; Rainey and Notley 2006: 103; Yurco 1991, 1997; Hasel 2003; Faust 2006: 185–186). In particular, Rainey (1992: 74; 2001a: 69–70) notes the presence of chariots in the relief (attributed by Yurco to the Israelites) and counters that "the status of the chariot warrior and the maintenance of chariot forces, not to mention the need for training and logistics to support a chariot force, were hardly commensurate with Israelite social structure until the age of the monarchy." Instead, for Rainey (1991: 59), "Yurco has probably found the long-sought missing link between Israel and the Shosu/Shasu pastoralists known from Egyptian inscriptions." In

Rainey's (1991: 93; cf. Rainey and Notley 2006: 111–112) opinion, "The Israelites were part of the Shosu pastoral elements in Canaan (especially in the hill country, in the steppe land of Mt. Seir/Edom in Transjordan and in the Sinai) during the 13th and 12th centuries BCE." Yurco (1997: 41–42) also believes that some of the Israelite pastoralists (cf. Judg 5:16) originated as Shasu, but that "nowhere do the Egyptians call the Shasu Israelites." This is not the place to survey competing theories about the emergence of Israel and its ethnogenesis, especially with regard to pastoral and sedentarizing nomadism and agrarianism as well as the role of nomads in the Transjordan (cf., for example, Finkelstein 1988; Faust 2006: 17–19, 167–187; Dever 2017: 200–257). Yet every theory leaves room for some of the Shasu groups becoming a part of what eventually constitutes the peoples of Israel. Thus the association of the Shasu with the term *yh(w)/yhw3* remains tantalizing.

The expression *š3sw s'rr* has served as the linchpin connecting these texts with the biblical tradition.[59] Many scholars have interpreted *s'rr* as Seir and noted that Yahweh marching from Seir (*śē'îr*) is featured in archaic biblical poetry (Judg 5:4; Deut 33:2) along with other southeastern locales such as Edom, Teman, Mt. Paran, and Midian (addressed later). Several dissenting voices, such as Manfred Weippert (1972: 491 n. 144), Michael Astour (1979), Gösta Ahlström (1986: 59–60), and Johannes de Moor (1990: 111), have argued that *s'rr* is not to be equated with Seir. In addition, some of these critics argue that the toponym Yhw is to be located in Lebanon and Syria, in the Beqa'-Orontes districts. Redford calls such skepticism "wholly unwarranted."[60] He argues that the doubled *r* of *s'rr* does indeed designate Seir and "is thoroughly in keeping with Late Egyptian orthography." In addition, the Shasu and Seirites are mentioned together in Papyrus Harris I (as objects of Ramses III's destruction), and Papyrus Anastasi VI speaks of the Shasu from Edom.[61] In this light, compare Judges 5:4, which uses Seir and Edom as parallel terms designating the place from which Yahweh marches as a divine warrior.

After decades of scholars writing about the *yh(w)/yhw3* toponym in the Shasu texts, the Egyptologist (and onomastic specialist) Thomas Schneider (2007) entered the discussion with what he proposed to be "the first historical evidence of the god" associated with the land of Yah.[62] The reference in question comes from the late Eighteenth or Nineteenth Dynasty and thus is a perfect fit to relate to the pharaohs mentioned earlier, with Amenophis III being in the Eighteenth Dynasty and Ramses II in the Nineteenth Dynasty. Schneider's evidence comes from the name of "an acculturated foreigner" who owned a copy of the Book of the Dead that preserved his name as "My lord [Yahweh] is the shepherd of [the land of] Yah" (*'adōnī rō'ē-yāh*). The interrelationships of Egypt with the Levant during these two dynasties is well documented, including the presence of West Semitic "émigré gods" (Baal, Reshef, Astarte, Anat, Horon, Qedeshet) in text and iconography.⁶³ Yet here for the first time, argues Schneider, appears a reference to the god of the land of Yah (*yh*), whose shepherding resonates with the nomadic Shasu, also of the land of Yah (*yh(w)/yhw3*). Can such references have any connection to biblical traditions that tell of both El and Yahweh being shepherds of their ancestors, who were also shepherds (e.g., Gen 48:15; 49:24; Num 27:17; Isa 63:11; Ps 78:52; 80:1)?

Jumping hundreds of years forward, we turn to a theory by the Oxford Assyriologist Stephanie Dalley, who concluded, based on three personal names, that "in the late 8th century both before and after the fall of Samaria, Yahweh was worshipped as a *major* god in Hamath and its vicinity" (1990: 28, emphasis mine). Dalley (1990: 24) started out by noting that scholars in the past have worked with "the unspoken assumption that a person with a Yahweh-bearing name is automatically considered to belong to Israel and Judah." She then analyzed three royal names associated with Hamath (in northern Syria) or its vicinity and argued that they contained Yahweh as a theophoric element: (1) Azri-Yau of the vicinity of Hamath (Hatarikka?), mentioned in Tiglath-pileser's annals (Cogan and Tadmor 1988: 165)—though not to be confused with the putative Azriyau of Yaudi, whose existence, based on a false reading, has now been disproven; (2) Yau-biʾdi, a king of Hamath who led an anti-Assyrian coalition in 720 BCE; and (3) Yôrām, mentioned as son of Toi, the king of Hamath, in 2 Samuel 8:9–10.⁶⁴ Specialists in the field are well acquainted with the debates swirling around these names, and Dalley is by no means original in using this material to look for signs of Yahweh worship among the North Syrian Arameans (e.g., Murtonen 1951). Nonetheless, her theory that we are dealing with *indigenous* Syrian rulers breathed new life into the thesis and met with some acceptance (cf. Zevit 1991; Keel and Uehlinger 1998: 314 n. 35; Grabbe 2010: 178–179).

As enticing as this theory is—especially the association of three royal names with Hamath, which at first glance seems hardly coincidental—it is not without difficulties that are significant enough to cripple its plausibility (van der Toorn 1992a: 88–90; cf. too Krebernik 2017: 61–63). First, given the comments on the use of onomastica to reconstruct religion (see Chapter Three), should we draw such a grand conclusion (that Yahweh was a *major* god in North Syria) based on a mere three examples, two of which (Azri-Yau and Yau-bidi) may indeed refer to usurpers of Israelite/Judean lineage? Despite Dalley's rebuff, would it not be more likely to find Idri-Yau (rather than Azri-Yau) if the king bore an indigenous Aramaic name?⁶⁵ In addition, there is the possibility that Yau-bidi does not even contain Yahweh as a theophoric element. According to Edward Lipiński's (1971b) and Karel van der Toorn's (1992a: 89–90) analyses, Yau-bidi occurs in six different spellings, including ^{m}i-lu-$ú$-bi-$ʾ$-di and $^{m}dingir$-bi-$ʾ$-di. This may indicate that the name was pronounced Iluyu-biʾdi or that the full name ʾIlu-$yahū$-bi-$ʿīdī$, "El/god will appear as my witness," may have contained *yahū* as a verbal element, rather than a reflex of the deity Yahweh. In addition, if Yahweh was a major deity, why is he absent from native inscriptions that mention the deities Ba'lat, Baalshamayin, Elwer, Shamash, and Shahar (van der Toorn 1992a: 89)?

In short, of these possible leads, the Shasu texts and Schneider's notion of Yah as another example of a West Semitic "émigré god" are more likely to contain attestations of Yahweh worship than Dalley's Hamath theory. As will be seen, the Shasu material is also more in accord with archaic poetic passages in the Hebrew Bible that point to a southern rather than northern locale for Yahweh's origin.[66] But first it is necessary to turn from false and possible leads to epigraphic sources that are not in doubt and solidly attest the worship of Yahweh in pre-exilic, extra-biblical inscriptions.

Epigraphic Sources from the Ninth and Eighth Centuries BCE

Due to the traditional nature of our biblical sources (and challenges to their early dating and/or historicity), it is important to underscore that there is a substantial body of extra-biblical epigraphic evidence documenting the presence of the deity Yahweh that is not in doubt. All of it is West Semitic. None of our epigraphic evidence that explicitly names Yahweh predates the ninth century BCE. And yet Yahweh's presence may indeed be documented in the late eleventh-/tenth-century BCE epigraphic record—though under another name/title. The Ishba'l inscription (Figure 6.3) from controlled excavations at Qeiyafa (found in 2008) is dated radiometrically to circa 1020–980 BCE. As others have pointed out, the DN *b'l* in the personal name Ishba'l ("man of *b'l*," *'šb'l*) can attest to

Figure 6.3 The late eleventh-/tenth-century BCE Ishba'l inscription from Khirbet Qeiyafa containing the earliest reference to *b'l* in a Judean site.

Courtesy of the Khirbet Qeiyafa Expedition, Institute of Archaeology, The Hebrew University of Jerusalem. Photographer Tal Rogovski.

the presence of Yahweh worship as easily as that of the Canaanite god Baal.⁶⁷ Albertz's (Albertz and Schmitt 2012: 348–359, 576–581) study of "equating names" such as *baʿalyāh* ("Baal is Yah[weh]"/"Yah[weh] is Baal/lord") shows the overlap of the two deities, as does Hosea 2:18 (Eng 2:16).

The earliest uncontested explicit occurrence of the name Yahweh comes from the Moabite stone, also known as the Mesha stela (Figure 6.4), the earliest and longest royal inscription from the southern Levant.⁶⁸ Its inscription, which dates to the mid-ninth century BCE, mentions how Mesha, the king of Moab, at the direction of his god Chemosh, engaged the king of Israel in battle. As a part of his successful campaign he brags that he dragged "the [ve]ssels of Yahweh" ([k]*ly yhwh*) from (a sanctuary at) the Reubenite town of Nebo before his god Chemosh.⁶⁹ In this type of divine *ḥrm*-warfare, the captured enemy cult objects would have been understood as war booty presented to the divine warrior who enabled the victory, in this case Chemosh (Rainey 2001b: 304).⁷⁰

Figure 6.4 The mid-ninth-century BCE Moabite Stone (also known as the Mesha Inscription) containing the earliest uncontested explicit occurrence of the name Yahweh.
Kim Walton, taken at the Louvre.

In the late 1990s, Pierre Bordreuil, Felice Israel, and Dennis Pardee published two Hebrew ostraca (sometimes referred to as the "Moussaieff Ostraca" after the name of their collector), one of which mentions the giving of "silver of Tarshish to the House/Temple of Yahweh" (*lbyt yhwh*).[71] The other ostracon opens with the blessing formula "May Yahweh bless you in peace" (*ybrkk yhwh bšlm*). They have been dated on paleographic grounds to the late ninth or early eighth century BCE by Frank Moore Cross and P. Kyle McCarter (Shanks 1997c: 31). In contrast, the authors of the *editio princeps* assign the ostraca to the latter part of the seventh century BCE (Bordreuil, Israel, and Pardee 1996: 57–59). Unfortunately, the ostraca are unprovenanced, and while there have been strong assertions regarding their authenticity, counterarguments suggesting that they are forgeries render them too questionable to use.[72] The most detailed of these is the analysis by Christopher Rollston (2003: 173), who was once in favor of their authenticity but now is "confident beyond a reasonable doubt that both of the Moussaieff Ostraca ... are modern forgeries."

Inscriptions from the site of Kuntillet ʿAjrud have become more famous for reconstructing the presence of the goddess Asherah in Israelite religion than for documenting early occurrences of the name Yahweh.[73] According to the final report, the corpus includes fifty-five mostly fragmentary texts written on various media (incised in stone and pottery as well as being written in ink on pottery and on plastered walls). The consistent use of northern theophoric names (*-yw* as opposed to *-yhw*) as well as the reference to Yahweh of Samaria in KA 3.1 buttresses the view that Kuntillet ʿAjrud was closely associated with the northern Kingdom of Israel. Based on epigraphy, pottery, and C-14 dates, a common view is that the findings of Kuntillet ʿAjrud, a single-period site, should be dated to the end of the ninth century BCE or the first half of the eighth century BCE and correlated with the reign of Jeroboam II (ca. 787–748 BCE) or perhaps Jehoash (ca. 801–787 BCE). In response to this consensus, William Schniedewind (2017) has argued that we have at least three different scribal hands, and thus a case can be made that Kuntillet ʿAjrud is a multigenerational site "ranging from the late 10th century through the late eighth century BCE."[74]

Strategically situated on the Darb el-Ghazza caravan route, the site of Kuntillet ʿAjrud (located in the northeast Sinai Desert 30 mi. [50 km] south of Qadesh-Barnea) reveals signs of a religious presence including inscribed names of various deities, prayers for blessings, a military theophany, dedicated vessels, and sacred iconography. Though the architecture and the absence of altars give no evidence of a temple,[75] Ziony Zevit concludes that we have a "dedicated structure, i.e., one planned in advance for a certain purpose, and that its raison d'être was cultic."[76] Zeʾev Meshel (2012: 65–69, esp. 68, 307) also writes of "the religious nature of the site." For Meshel, the presence of linen suggests a sacerdotal wardrobe, and he extrapolates that "the inhabitants comprised a group of priests and

Levites who were supplied by the provision of offerings and tithes that were sent to them from Jerusalem." As a result, he subtitles the final report *An Iron Age II Religious Site on the Judah-Sinai Border* (emphasis mine).

Other scholars suggest that Kuntillet ʿAjrud was more likely a desert way station (a caravanserai) where weary travelers thanked their god(s) for sustenance and prayed for safety on the open road (e.g., Hadley 1993).[77] After surveying the various options, Nadav Naʾaman and Nurit Lissovsky (2008: 189) conclude that "neither the royal caravanserai hypothesis, nor the 'religious centre' one (with all its variants), fully resolve the problems entailed in the interpretation of the site." Nonetheless, Naʾaman and Lissovsky (2008: 190) still see a religious function as being primary. They offer a "daring hypothesis," speculating that the site "was chosen because of a prominent sacred tree (or a sacred grove) grew in its vicinity" and was dedicated to the goddess Asherah.[78] Schniedewind (2014: 273–274) offers a substantive critique of Naʾaman and Lissovsky's putative sacred tree as well as Meshel's priestly wardrobe. Instead, he argues for the military function of this strategic "state-sponsored fortress" together with significant scribal activity that "underscores the economic and administrative function ... as opposed to a religious interpretation." Alice Mandell (2012: 137) offers a mediating view: "The 'fortress-like' design of Building A, the site's location at the nexus of desert routes coupled with the unique décor and inscriptions suggest that Kuntillet ʿAjrud was originally built as a military installation to monitor the regions, but over time developed into a religious attraction—two functions which are not mutually exclusive." See too Tallay Ornan's (2016: 3) conclusions about the royal nature of the iconography: "The combination of ... themes typifies state-run official buildings ... and does not support the suggestion that Kuntillet ʿAjrud served as a 'religious' building or centre, although the state sponsored site at Kuntillet ʿAjrud included a small cultic architectural space."

The full name Yahweh occurs several times at Kuntillet ʿAjrud in a variety of contexts. In shortened form, the name Yaw (*-yw, yw-*) dominates the onomastica coming from the site.[79] A stone basin (Figure 6.5) (whose weight, approx. 330 lbs. [150 kg; *pace* Naʾaman and Lissovsky 2008: 199], argues for it being native to the site rather than brought from elsewhere) contains the inscription "[Belonging] to ʿObadyaw, son of ʿAdnah. Blessed be he of Yahweh" (*lʿbdyw bn ʿdnh brk hʾ lyhw*).[80]

Two large pottery storage jars (pithoi) also contained inscriptions written in red ink. The inscription on Pithos A (= Pithos #1 in other publications) is brief and partially missing. (On the iconography of three figures depicted alongside and even overlapping this inscription and the possible representation of Yahweh and the goddess Asherah, see Chapter Seven, pp. 325–330.) The text that is preserved describes an unknown person asking for blessings for two other individuals (Yehal[ʾel] and Yawʿasah) from "Yahweh of Samaria and his asherah" (*lyhwh šmrn wlʾšrth*) (Figure 6.6).[81] Mention of the god Yahweh in conjunction

Figure 6.5 A stone basin (approx. 330 lbs. [150 kg]) at Kuntillet ʿAjrud containing the name Yahweh (*yhw*).

Courtesy of the Israel Exploration Society, Jerusalem.

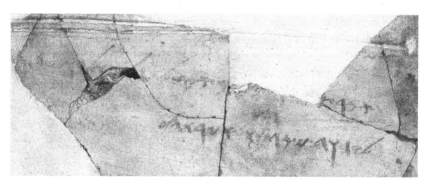

Figure 6.6 An inscription from Kuntillet ʿAjrud Pithos A mentioning "Yahweh of Samaria and his asherah" (*lyhwh šmrn wlʾšrth*).

Courtesy of the Israel Exploration Society, Jerusalem.

THE ORIGIN OF YAHWEH 239

with the northern capital (or region) of Samaria is quite significant since it was found at the southern site of Kuntillet ʿAjrud. (Elsewhere in the Kuntillet ʿAjrud inscriptions, as we will see, Yahweh is connected to Teman, a locale that is much closer geographically.)[82] One is tempted to extrapolate the widespread prestige of the northern Yahwistic cult and/or the syncretistic nature of religious expression at Kuntillet ʿAjrud that combined northern and southern expressions of Yahwism, not to mention the worship of other Canaanite deities (El, Baal, and Asherah) also appearing in this epigraphic record.[83] At the least, we have evidence that this author had exposure to Yahweh of Samaria and preferred to use this divine name as the effectual element in this blessing.[84]

There are various inscriptions on pottery fragments of what once constituted Pithos B (= Pithos #2 in other publications).[85] The largest of the three (Figure 6.7), by a certain Amaryaw, asks for blessings for his (unnamed) lord from "[Ya]hweh of Teman and his asherah" (*lyhwh tmn wlʾšrth*). Note here the designation of Yahweh by a regional geographic locale (as opposed to "Yahweh of Samaria" on Pithos A) and by either the goddess Asherah or, more likely, a cult symbol representing her presence. Amaryaw then beseeches of Yahweh: "May

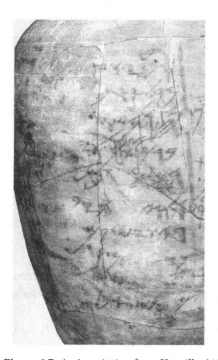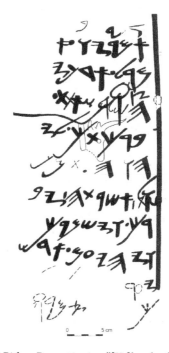

Figure 6.7 An inscription from Kuntillet ʿAjrud Pithos B mentioning "[Ya]hweh of Teman and his asherah" (*lyhwh tmn wlʾšrth*).
Courtesy of the Israel Exploration Society, Jerusalem.

he bless and keep you and be with my lord" (*ybrk wyšmrk wyhy ʿm ʾdny*).[86] As noted by commentators, this blessing resonates with letter formulae and finds close parallels in the priestly blessing found in Numbers 6:24 (*yĕbārekĕkā yhwh wĕyišmĕrekā*) and the divine promise to Jacob (*ʾānōkî ʿimmāk ûšĕmartîkā*) in Genesis 28:15.[87] As astutely noted by Zevit (2001: 396) and Jeremy Smoak (2015), it is also found in the amulets from Ketef Hinnom (*ybrk yhwh wyšmrk*; discussed later).

What is particularly noteworthy is the clear presence of *third-person masculine singular* verbs (*ybrk wyšmrk*) in this blessing.[88] The presence of "Yahweh and his asherah" has been used repeatedly to suggest an active divine pair, or, in the words of Garth Gilmour, it helps provide "overwhelming evidence" for "a well established religious *dualism* in ancient Judah in the 8th and 7th centuries and that the two deities involved are best identified as Yahweh and Asherah" (2009: 100, emphasis mine). Naʾaman and Lissovsky even mistakenly speak of the "remarkable appearance [of Asherah] in the inscriptions *as a source of blessings, side by side with YHWH*."[89] More accurate would be the carefully worded conclusion of Zevit (2001: 397), who writes that our author here records "a prayer that YHWH, not YHWH and Asheratah, will bless, guard and be with his lord."[90] This focus on Yahweh as the sole blessing agent is also found in the stone basin described earlier.

Another inscription from Pithos B is similar.[91] Its blessing formula also mentions the regional "Yahweh of the Teman" together with "his asherah" (*lyhwh htmn wlʾšrth*).[92] Similar to the other inscription on Pithos B, it too contains a third-person masculine singular verb (*ntn*) mentioning Yahweh alone as the deity who will grant the supplicant his desire (lit. "according to what is in his heart," *wntn lh yhw klbbh*).[93]

In addition to the inscriptions on the pithoi, multiple fragments of inscriptions originally written in ink on white plaster walls were found among the floor debris.[94] One of these (KA 4.1.1; Figure 6.8) twice refers to "Yahweh of Teman/the south" ([*y*]*hwh tymn*; *yhwh hty*[*mn*]) together with three third-person masculine singular verbs remarking on the god's lengthening of days ([*y*]*ʾrk ymm*) and making things go well (*hyṭb*, used twice) for the worshipper.[95] Note once again how these verbs underscore Yahweh as the sole agent of blessing.[96] Yet another plaster text (KA 4.2) stands out as truly remarkable, as it describes a militaristic wilderness theophany couched within what has been called "the oldest known Hebrew poem" outside of the Hebrew Bible.[97] This text is discussed in detail in Chapter Ten, pp. 583–587 (see too Lewis 2020). It mentions El (*ʾl*) and Baal (*bʿl*), terms that some scholars understand to represent independent Canaanite deities worshipped at Kuntillet ʿAjrud, while others see these two terms as indicators of the syncretistic nature of worship at Kuntillet ʿAjrud, where overall a single deity, Yahweh, was prominent.

Figure 6.8 A part of the plaster inscription (KA 4.1.1) from Kuntillet ʿAjrud.
Courtesy of the Israel Exploration Society, Jerusalem.

Yet another inscription dated on paleographic grounds to the first half of the eighth century BCE appears on an exquisite miniature seal carved from jasper gemstone (Figure 6.9). It reads "Belonging to Miqneyaw, servant of Yahweh" (*lmqnyw ʿbd yhwh*).[98] While the epithet "servant of Yahweh" is known from the Hebrew Bible, the Miqneyaw seal is the only occurrence of the title in a seal or extra-biblical inscription and may designate an official title (a *terminus technicus*). Because there is only one other mention of a person with the name Miqneyahu (in 1 Chr 15:18, 21), Cross (1983: 56, 62–63), followed by Nahman Avigad and Benjamin Sass (1997: 25–26), suggested that the Miqneyaw mentioned in this seal may have been a functionary of the Jerusalem Temple, perhaps a temple musician. Sadly, this seal is unprovenanced, and so it must be discounted.

From the late eighth century BCE we have Yahweh documented at the site of Khirbet el-Qom (probably biblical Makkedah), located approximately eight and a half miles (13.7 km) west of Hebron.[99] In 1967, William Dever became aware of a three-line inscription, robbed from a tomb, that contained a Yahwistic

242 THE ORIGIN AND CHARACTER OF GOD

Figure 6.9 An exquisite miniature seal carved from jasper gemstone that reads: "Belonging to Miqneyaw, servant of Yahweh." Harvard Semitic Museum 1959.1.2

Photograph by Bruce Zuckerman, West Semitic Research. Courtesy of the Semitic Museum, Harvard University.

personal name, Netanyahu. Dever, "after considerable intrigue," quickly traced the inscription to the modern village of Khirbet el-Qom. As a part of a "salvage operation" to prevent further looting, Dever excavated two Iron Age tombs. Another inscription (Figure 6.10) soon emerged; it had been looted, but thanks to Dever's detective work, it too was identified as coming from Khirbet el-Qom (from the "butterfly-shaped" Tomb II).[100] Indeed, Dever (1969–1970: 146) writes that "a recess in the east pillar revealed where [the inscription] had recently been removed; the lateral dimensions and the smoothly dressed sides of the inscription fit this hole perfectly." The inscription is accompanied by a deeply carved upside-down human hand, the relevance of which was most likely apotropaic.[101] At first the decipherment of the inscription proved difficult. Through subsequent study[102] it came to be seen as a petition asking that a person bearing a Yahwistic name, ʾUriyahu, be blessed and saved by Yahweh (*brk*[103] *ʾryhw lyhwh . . . hwšʿ lh*). The remainder of the inscription is quite hard to read, though the presence of the reading *asherah* is certain (occurring two and perhaps three times). The context seems to mention ʾUriyahu's enemies, but the legibility is uncertain (*wmṣryh? lʾšrth hwšʿ lh*). Thus the Khirbet el-Qom inscription closely parallels those found

Figure 6.10 A late eighth-century BCE inscription from Khirbet el-Qom accompanied by a deeply carved and upside-down human hand, most likely used apotropaically.
Kim Walton, taken at Israel Museum.

at Kuntillet ʿAjrud in attesting the worship of Yahweh in the eighth century BCE both in the south and in the Judean hills, not to mention the possible worship of Asherah. Yet once again, the verb for saving is in the masculine singular (*hwšʿ lh,* "he saved him"), underscoring, in Othmar Keel and Christoph Uehlinger's (1998: 239–240) words, how "only one divine power, namely Yahweh, is considered as the active agent who provides freedom from enemies." While this is undeniably true, given the many masculine singular verbs, the juxtaposition of *ʾšrth* with Yahweh makes one wonder whether what we have both here and at Kuntillet ʿAjrud is a reinterpretation of what some viewed as a divine pair.[104]

Epigraphic Sources from the Seventh and Sixth Centuries BCE

The independent use of the divine name Yahweh is amply attested in the seventh century BCE and later. From the first half of the seventh century BCE we have

244 THE ORIGIN AND CHARACTER OF GOD

several cave inscriptions/graffiti published by Joseph Naveh in 2001 (Figures 6.11, 6.12). Though these are of unknown provenance, epigraphists have noted that the script is quite close to that of the Khirbet el-Qom inscriptions and a certain named individual ('Ofay son of Netanyahu) may occur in both texts (cf. Khirbet el-Qom #1–2 and Naveh #2–3).[105] In the Naveh inscriptions the name Yahweh is invoked for blessing (*brk*) and cursing (*'rr*) a total of four times. Of

Figure 6.11 An unprovenanced seventh-century BCE cave inscription mentioning Yahweh Sebaoth. Line drawing by Joseph Naveh.

Courtesy of the Israel Exploration Society, Jerusalem.

Figure 6.12 An unprovenanced seventh-century BCE cave inscription mentioning Yahweh.
Courtesy of the Israel Exploration Society, Jerusalem.

particular note is the use of Yahweh Sebaoth (*yhwh ṣbʾt* in inscription #1 [Figure 6.11]), a divine name well known from the Hebrew Bible yet only attested here in the epigraphic corpus.[106]

Several inscriptions dating from circa 700 BCE were found in a burial cave at Khirbet Beit Lei, a short distance east of Lachish.[107] Epigraphers (e.g., Naveh, Cross, Lemaire, McCarter, Zevit, Suriano)[108] all agree that these inscriptions attest to the worship of Yahweh by supplicants who prayed that he would save them from their dire straits ("Save, O Yahweh!" *hwšʿ [y]hwh*)[109] as well as curse (*ʾrr*) their detractors/enemies. Sociolinguists (e.g., Mandell and Smoak 2016: 234) argue that Yahweh's salvation was particularly "germane to the context of concerns over death and the status of the deceased in the tomb." There is disagreement when it comes to interpreting the two longest inscriptions coming from this cave, yet most scholars see a confession affirming that Yahweh, "the God of Jerusalem" (*ʾlhy yršlm*), is also "the God of the entire earth" (*yhwh ʾlhy kl hʾrṣ*), whose sovereignty includes "the highlands of Judah" (*hry yhdh*).[110] What follows next is a plea for a "compassionate" Yahweh (*ʾl ḥnn* or *yhwh ḥnn*) to "intervene" (*pqd*) in the present crisis and absolve (*nqh*) the petitioner.[111]

From a similar date (ca. 700 BCE) we have an enigmatic tomb inscription (Figure 6.13) from a cave in the Judean desert near Ein Gedi, what Zevit refers to

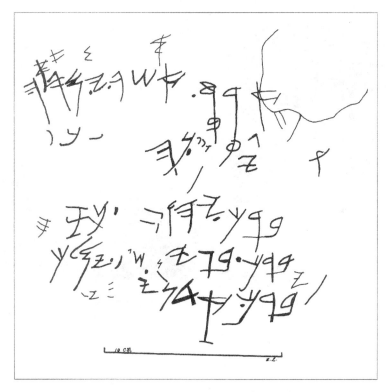

Figure 6.13 Ziony Zevit's line drawing of a tomb inscription from a cave in the Judean desert near Ein Gedi.

From Ziony Zevit, *The Religions of Ancient Israel: A Synthesis of Parallactic Approaches* (London: Continuum, 2001), with permission.

as "an ad hoc cult place ... used by a Jerusalemite refugee."[112] The word for curse (*'rr*) occurs at the beginning and end of the extant inscription.[113] In the middle one can read the phrase "Blessed is Yahweh" (*brk yhwh*) followed by an appeal in the next line for Yahweh to reign (*ymlk*).[114] An acknowledgment of Yahweh being blessed "among the nations" (*brk bgy[m]*) has also been reconstructed by Zevit (2001: 352–356).

Inscriptions on ostraca coming from Arad (dating from the late seventh/early sixth centuries BCE) were first published by Yohanan Aharoni.[115] The most important of these for the present purpose (ostracon #18, Figure 6.14) petitions Yahweh for health (lines 2–3: *yhwh yš'l lšlmk*) and makes mention of "the house/temple of Yahweh" (line 9: *byt yhwh*).[116] Another inscription (ostracon #21) describes Yahweh restoring a person to his master (*yšlm yhwh l'dn[y]*). Prior to the discovery of the inscriptions from Kuntillet ʿAjrud and Khirbet el-Qom,

Figure 6.14 A inscription from late seventh-/early sixth-century BCE Arad (ostracon #18) mentioning "the temple of Yahweh."
Courtesy of the Israel Exploration Society, Jerusalem.

scholars had restored similar blessing formulas in two Arad ostraca (ostraca #40.3: *brktk [lyhw]h*; cf. #21.2).

Next we turn to the two Ketef Hinnom inscriptions dating to the end of the seventh or the beginning of the sixth century BCE.[117] These texts have received much attention since their discovery in 1979 because they constitute our oldest attestations of a biblical passage—namely, the famous Priestly Benediction of Numbers 6:24–26. That these two "mini-scrolls" were etched in silver and were found in an elaborate burial complex shows that their owners were elite by most standards.[118]

The two inscriptions (designated KH I [Figure 6.15] and KH II [Figure 6.16]) are notoriously difficult to analyze because of their small size and poor state of preservation. Yet from the outset the benediction could be clearly read with minor reconstructions. KH 1:14–18 reads "May Yahweh bless you and [may he] keep you. [May] Yahweh make [his face] shine [upon you]" (*ybrk yhwh [wy]šmrk [y']r yhwh pn[yw 'lyk]*), while KH II:5–12 contains the fuller benediction "May

Figure 6.15 One of the two inscriptions etched on silver scrolls from Ketef Hinnom (dating to the end of the seventh or the beginning of the sixth century BCE) that constitute our oldest attestations of a biblical passage (Numbers 6:24–26).

Photograph by Bruce and Kenneth Zuckerman, West Semitic Research. Courtesy Israel Antiquities Authority.

Yahweh bless you [and] may he keep you. May Yah[we]h make his face shine [upon] you and grant you p[ea]ce" (*ybrk yhwh yšmrk y'r yh[w]h pnyw ['l]yk wyśm lk š[l]m*). Considering that we have exactly the same vocabulary attested at late ninth- or early eighth-century BCE Kuntillet ʿAjrud (*ybrk wyšmrk*; discussed previously), not to mention its presence in Numbers 6:24–26, we can confidently underscore a long standing (for at a minimum more than two hundred years) and geographically widespread tradition of associating Yahweh with protection and well-being.

Many other readings in these two inscriptions are often overlooked. Using vocabulary well known from biblical literature, Yahweh is celebrated as the deity "who [keeps] the covenant" (*[šmr] hbryt*) and is "gracious toward those who love [him]" (*[h]ḥsd l'hb[w]*).[119] He is also looked to as the petitioner's "restorer" (*[m]šybnw*) and "rock" (*ṣwr*) "in whom there is redemption" (*ky bw g'l*).

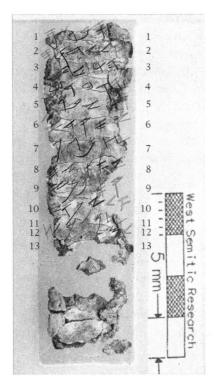

Figure 6.16 One of the two inscriptions etched on silver scrolls from Ketef Hinnom (dating to the end of the seventh or the beginning of the sixth century BCE) that constitute our oldest attestations of a biblical passage (Numbers 6:24–26).
Photograph by Bruce and Kenneth Zuckerman, West Semitic Research. Courtesy Israel Antiquities Authority.

Additionally, new readings confirmed by the 2004 edition by Gabriel Barkay and colleagues have dramatically contributed to our understanding of how Yahweh was viewed at this time in this locale. For the first time, we have clear Iron Age evidence of the power of the divine name Yahweh, as well as the power of the written word (i.e., using a biblical passage) being used for apotropaic purposes, similar to the well-attested practices of Late Jewish antiquity. Specifically, Yahweh is described in KH II.2–5 as "the warrior [or helper] and the rebuker of [E]vil" (*lyhw[h] (3) hʿzr w (4) hgʿr b(5)[r]*ʿ; cf. also *hrʿ* in KH I.10). Indeed, this occasions little surprise when one remembers that the two "mini-scrolls" were in fact small amulets that would have been worn as talismans around the neck.[120]

One should also note how these texts contribute to our understanding of Yahweh and family/domestic religion. The Ketef Hinnom inscribed amulets were found in close proximity in a "repository" of a grave complex that totaled five

250   THE ORIGIN AND CHARACTER OF GOD

burial chambers (Barkay 1992: 139–147). Similarly, the Khirbet el-Qom inscription with its apotropaic character was found in a burial context.[121] Even though the prayers invoked at Ketef Hinnom share with the prayers from Kuntillet ʿAjrud exact vocabulary seeking Yahweh's assistance (*ybrk yhwh wyšmrk*), the former's domestic/familial/burial context contrasts with the latter's cultic structure, which focused on Yahweh's protection of its regional inhabitants and travelers seeking safety on the open road.[122]

Lastly, from early sixth-century BCE Lachish, we have letters that use a series of formulaic greetings invoking Yahweh's blessings.[123] These letters were written by a subordinate to his administrative and/or military superior.[124] They include full blessing formulas such as "May Yahweh cause my lord to hear reports of peace and goodness/prosperity" (ostracon #3.2–4: *yšmʿ yhwh [ʾt] ʾdny šmʿt šlm w[š]mʿ[t] ṭb*; cf. #5.1–2) and shortened variants asking for either peace (ostracon #2.2–3) or prosperity (ostracon #4.1–2). Yahweh is also implored to "cause my master to see this season in good health" (ostracon #6.1–2: *yrʾ yhwh ʾt ʾdny ʾt hʿt hzh šlm*; cf. #5.7–8). In addition to such introductory salutations, we also find in the Lachish letters two examples of the oath formula "As Yahweh lives" (ostracon #6.12: *ḥy yhwh*; cf. #3.9) so well known from biblical texts and elsewhere (cf. Ringgren 1980: 339–340) (Figure 6.17). Finally, Yahweh also occurs

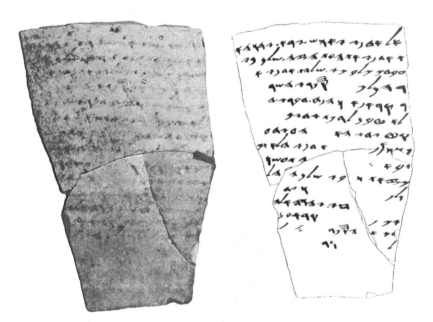

Figure 6.17 An inscription from early sixth-century BCE Lachish (ostracon #6) containing the oath formula "As Yahweh lives."
Zev Radovan/Bible Land Pictures.

independently in an enigmatic broken text that reads *ybkr yhwh* . . . (ostracon #2.5). If the text is correct, it may refer to Yahweh giving priority to someone (Aḥituv 2008: 62), with the verb being analyzed as a denominative of *bĕkôr*, "firstborn." In contrast, it has been suggested that *ybkr* is a scribal metathesis for an original text that referred to Yahweh blessing (*ybrk*) someone.

Conclusions from Epigraphy

Setting aside the Shasu material, extra-biblical inscriptions document that the deity Yahweh was known as early as the mid-ninth century BCE, the date of the Mesha stela. Both of the most common reconstructions for the broken text (either "[ve]ssels of Yahweh," [*k*]*ly yhwh*, or "the a[ltar-hea]rths of Yahweh," ʾ[*rʾ*]*ly yhwh*) assume that some type of cultic activity was devoted to Yahweh by the inhabitants of Nebo (cf. Mesha stela lines 14–18). Cross (1998: 57–58) surmises we have "every reason to believe that there was a Reubenite shrine beneath Mount Nebo" that was "reestablished in the time of Omri."[125] If the Moabite king and his scribes were cognizant of the existence of the god Yahweh by the ninth century BCE, one can posit (totally apart from the Hebrew Bible) that Yahweh was known across a wide geographic region even earlier and even in northern Israel (to judge from the mention of Omri).[126] Such geographic breadth is precisely what we have attested soon afterward at Kuntillet ʿAjrud, which makes mention of both Yahweh of the south/Teman (*yhwh htmn/yhwh tmn*) and Yahweh of Samaria (*lyhwh šmrn*).

Obviously, there is a large gap between the putative mention of Yahweh in the thirteenth-century BCE Shasu texts and the firm mention of Yahweh in the ninth-century BCE Mesha stela. This is not the place to engage the "tenth-century question" or discussions of state formation. Yet if we are looking at a southern origin for Yahweh (see Section III in this chapter), Thomas Levy (2009a: 258), in writing on Edomite ethnogenesis, has plausibly filled the gap:

> The Egyptian scarabs and stamp seal found at Khirbat en-Nahas and the Wadi Fidan cemetery indicate that nomads had connections with Egypt from the late fifteenth century to the tenth century BCE, providing archeological evidence for the "tribes" or Shasu nomads known from Papyrus Harris, Papyrus Anastasi, and other biblical sources.

Epigraphically, Seth Sanders (2009: 120) and others have noted that "a state is not a prerequisite of scribal production." Suffice it here to quote Schniedewind (2013: 69) on the "active [though non-standardized] writing tradition [of the] decentralized . . . small polities" of the early Iron Age, and McCarter's (2008b: 48) comment that "inland Canaan had a long history of alphabetic literacy prior to the 10th century BCE." Here McCarter has in mind the "substantial corpus of Old Canaanite epigraphic materials" from the "13th through the 11th centuries."[127] Regrettably, none of these texts makes mention of Yahweh[128] (though the Canaanite deities Anat, Astarte, Baal, Dagan, Elat and Ṣidqu do appear in the fuller corpus).[129] More recent epigraphic finds such as the Tel Zayit abecedary[130] and the inscription from Khirbet Qeiyafa attest to literate culture in tenth-century BCE Canaan (though not universal literacy)[131] and, according to McCarter, to a distinctively South Canaanite (or Proto-Hebrew) scribal tradition whose heir will be found in the Hebrew national script (McCarter 2008b: 49; Tappy et al. 2006: 26–28, 40–42; contrast Rollston 2008: 82). Though Yahweh has yet to be found in these tenth-century BCE inscriptions, it would seem (to judge from the attestation of Yahweh in the ninth-century BCE Mesha inscription, whose scribe certainly did not invent Yahweh de novo) that finding such an epigraphic attestation in this "nascent Old Hebrew script" is just a matter of time.[132]

Section III: The Geographic Origins of Yahwistic Traditions and the Debate Concerning Northern (Canaanite) Versus Southern (Midianite) Origins

The Geographic Origins of Yahweh

These discussions have set the stage for the debate surrounding the geographic origin of Yahwistic traditions and whether we should be looking to the north or to the south. Chapters Four and Five detailed the cultural heritage of northern Canaanite religion as it pertains to the Israelite deity El. In particular, textual references from the kingdom at Ugarit illustrated points of similarity and difference between how 'Ilu was conceptualized at Late Bronze Age Ugarit and how El was depicted at Iron Age Israel. Material culture emphasized remarkable continuity with regard to enthroned bronze figurines, standing stones, and bull figurines of the Late Bronze Age–Iron Age I Levant.

Proper methodology argues strongly against homogenizing such data into any type of one-to-one correspondence, especially when hundreds of years and a vast distance separate the two cultures, whose societies were distinctly different. Yet a cultural continuum with regard to Canaanite religious concepts is clearly evident, and this phenomenon deserves further elaboration. Moreover, it is especially appropriate to explore the northern Canaanite continuum at this point in our study, for it has played a vital role in unpacking the possible northern origin of Yahwism. At the same time, and in direct contrast, the best extra-biblical parallels for exploring the possible origin of the deity Yahweh are the texts describing the Shasu Bedouin with mention of Yh and Seir (see pp. 229–232). These sources point not north but south. In what follows, we will document why a synthetic description of the origin of the deity Yahweh and the religious culture of Yahwism must include *both* southern and northern traditions.

A Desideratum: The Study of Pre-Israelite Canaanite Lore

For decades scholars have thoroughly documented the presence of pre-Israelite Canaanite lore, which is vital for reconstructing a synthetic treatment of ancient Israelite religion. Yet in spite of this rich cultural heritage there remains, as Cross (1973: vii) would bemoan, "the tendency of scholars to overlook or suppress continuities between the early religion of Israel and the Canaanite ... culture from which it emerged." Understanding pre-Israelite Canaanite religious concepts remains a desideratum for the study of ancient Israel's religious expressions. The simple fact that Hebrew falls within the Canaanite language family (one of two branches of Northwest Semitic, the other being Aramaic) should rivet attention on the Canaanite world of the Hebrew Bible.[133] Similarly, a desire for understanding the nuances of Canaanite religion should be quickened once one recognizes that the religion practiced in ancient Israel was situated geographically in a part of what was termed "the land of Canaan" in biblical and extra-biblical sources (e.g., the Amarna letters).[134]

"Canaanite Religion": A Modern Scholarly Construct

At the outset, we need to underscore that there never existed a unified "Canaanite" religion. "Canaanite" religion never existed in a single locale such that we can speak of it as we speak of Egyptian or Mesopotamian religion. (Yet even here, the widespread geographic religious influence of these two major cultures can complicate any attempt at tidy definitions.) As such, any notion of a one-size-fits-all "Canaanite" feature or practice simply belies the data. The designation "Canaanite religion" that appears so often in scholarly and popular literature is merely a scholarly construct. It has been used (more often by the past generation than the present) to describe shared religious traditions found in the Levant in the geographic areas occupied today by Syria, Lebanon, Israel, and Jordan.[135] Ideally, it would be preferable to find a neutral geographical designation such as "Levantine" to describe such regional continuity, a term that would not carry the polemical baggage that comes with the term "Canaanite." And yet, as we will be demonstrating, the broad term "Levantine" does not adequately differentiate between Canaanite and Aramean divinity. Thus we are left with the term "Canaanite." Yet hopefully the following discussion will help readers rehabilitate the term.

The Biblical Polemic and Sketching Canaanite Religion from Phoenician Inscriptions

Prior to the modern discovery of the remains of the ancient kingdom of Ugarit (at Ras Shamra and at neighboring Ras Ibn Hani) along the coast of Syria, most people's impression of "Canaanite" religion came from the Iron Age biblical texts, many of which were polemical in nature. The portrait was decidedly skewed—like having your worst enemy write your obituary. It is not that the biblical writers were ignorant of the multitude of Canaanite deities in their midst. On the contrary, biblical texts contain numerous references to the likes of Asherah, Ashtoreth (Ashtart, Astarte), Baal, Baal-Zebub, Chemosh, Dagan, Milcom, and the Queen of Heaven (cf. too references to *yām, nāhār, liwyātān, tannin, môt,* and *rĕpā'îm*). Yet the biblical writers and/or editors chose not to flesh out the natures and characteristics of these deities. Sometimes they serve as mere foils to the biblical deity. From the mocking portrayal of Dagon in 1 Samuel 5 one would never guess that he was a major deity in Syria, with a temple at Ugarit and his principal residence at Tuttul on the Balih River.

The modern misperception of Canaanite religion was not due to a lack of non-polemical sources that were linguistically Canaanite. Indeed, thousands of Phoenician inscriptions (many of which are contemporaneous with authors of the Hebrew Bible) have been known for decades.[136] Yet their nature was such that the Canaanite religion they espoused had to be teased out of non-literary references. (I am not considering here secondary references to Phoenician religion found in Classical Greek and Roman authors.) The large collection of Phoenician inscriptions does not consist of lengthy mythological tales of banqueting with the gods, lamenting dying gods and celebrating rising ones, embarking on grand quests for eternal life, or fearing a descent through the gates of the netherworld.[137] We have no elaborate liturgies from which to describe the movement of assorted religious paraphernalia by consecrated religious officiants. Rather, the bulk of our epigraphic sources is made up of royal inscriptions, dedicatory stela, funerary inscriptions, votive texts, sacrificial tariffs, temple expenses, building inscriptions, personal names, and graffiti.[138]

Sergio Ribichini (1997: 120) bemoans the fact that "although Phoenician epigraphic sources at present amount to a total of over 6,000 inscriptions, for the most part they provide no information on religion." This is certainly an overstatement (contrast Peckham 1987, 2014; Clifford 1990; Schmitz 1992; Markoe 2000: 115–142; Quinn 2018: 78–79, 91–131). Consider the lengthy list of cultic personnel associated with the fifth-century BCE temple to ʿAštart at Kition (cf. KAI 37; see the Conclusion, p. 685). Yet the point is made nonetheless. By gleaning references from our textual, onomastic, and archaeological sources we can document the presence of numerous Canaanite deities including Anat, Ashtart, Baal, Baal-Hammon, Baal-Shamem, Baalat, Bes, El, Eshmun, Horon, Kushor, Melqarth, Reshep, Shamash, Tanit, and Yarih, not to mention various divine ancestors.[139] Indeed, the rich data gathered by Rainer Albertz and Rüdiger Schmitt (2012: 343, 512–513, table 5.12) reveal a "striking diversity" of divinity. Yet for the general reader, and even many scholars, such gods never fully captured the imagination because of the lack of compelling stories. It was far easier to reiterate the pejorative caricature of Canaanite religion that had been inherited and reinforced through hundreds of years of confessional teachings. Even the documentation of religious expression in excavations at Byblos (ancient Gubla), Sidon, Tyre, Kition (eastern Cyprus), Sarepta, and Umm el-ʿAmed and their environs did little to rewrite the biblical portrait (cf. the Conclusion, pp. 685–689). If anything, the tophet sanctuary at Carthage was used to reinforce the demonizing accusation that all Canaanites engaged in widespread child sacrifice (cf. Lev 18:21; Deut 12:31; 2 Kgs 3:27; 21:6; 23:10). In contrast, today scholars debate whether ritual infanticide among the Carthaginians was an exceptional and localized custom used in extreme circumstances or a regular and systematic practice.[140]

Philo of Byblos

The use of Phoenician epigraphic sources has been limited. In contrast, some hope for reconstructing Canaanite religion was thought to be found in the so-called Phoenician History by Philo of Byblos. Here one's imagination is captured by Philo's accounts "Cosmogony," "History of Culture," "History of Kronos" (*hon oi phoinikes ʾĒl* "whom the Phoenicians call El"), "On Human Sacrifice," and "On Snakes." For the past generation of scholars, the then new discovery of the Ugaritic texts breathed new life into the possibility that Philo of Byblos might indeed preserve authentic Canaanite traditions. Yet over the past three decades such enthusiasm has waned considerably as scholars have called for a sober reassessment.

What we have in Philo of Byblos (ca. 70–160 CE) is third- or fourth-hand material that is polemical in nature (Baumgarten 1992; L'Heureux 1979: 40–45). Philo's Phoenician History only comes down to us through Eusebius of Caesarea's (ca. 260–340 CE) *Praeparatio Evangelica*. As for the source of Philo's information, he supposedly used a learned scholar named Sanchuniathon (Sakkunyaton), who presumably antedated Hesiod and tracked down the records of Taautos, yet none of this can be confirmed (cf. Barr 1974: 33–40; Baumgarten 1992: 342–344). While there are touchpoints between the mythology of Philo of Byblos and the Canaanite/Israelite lore of the Late Bronze and Iron Ages, it is far from what we know from other Northwest Semitic sources closer in time and proximity. For but one example, Elioun dies in an encounter with wild beasts, a motif without reflex in the West Semitic Elyon traditions (but cf. the death of Adonis and Apollodorus; see Attridge and Oden 1981: 86 n. 83).[141]

Albert Baumgarten (1992: 343) asserts that "Philo's claims are now ... regarded with considerable skepticism. ... Philo does present Phoenician traditions ... but he has not discovered and somehow preserved unaltered texts from hoary antiquity. Rather he has retold contemporary versions of Phoenician myths, modified them to suit his pet theories, and presented the results as true ancient versions. We therefore do not read relatively unaltered Bronze Age or early Iron Age sources in Philo."[142] Even scholars who are more charitable about using Philo are nonetheless cautious. For example, Grabbe (1994: 115) acknowledges that "whatever Philo's sources, his version has taken in many elements known from Greek cosmogonic accounts, whether added by him or already present in his source(s). . . . Philo [may] include native Phoenician elements. The problem is sorting them out."

The Canaanite Cultural Continuum: The Middle Bronze Age, Late Bronze Age, and Iron Age

Where then shall we turn for our best archive of pre-Israelite Northwest Semitic lore? As will become clear, the elevated reputation of the material coming from Late Bronze Age Ugarit is justly deserved. Yet it would be premature to start there without a few comments about even earlier periods that reveal cultural contacts from north to south. One could of course start at the very beginning, following Richard Steiner's (2011: 10) admonition that "trade between Egypt and the Levant is attested not only in the Old Kingdom but also in the Predynastic and Early Dynastic periods." Steiner's 2011 work on the early Northwest Semitic serpent spells in the Old Kingdom Pyramid texts provides written documentation from the oldest of our Egyptian sources. Or one could follow the lead of Keel and Uehlinger (1998: 16ff.), who settled on the Middle Bronze Age for a starting point to survey the religious landscape for their *Gods, Goddesses and Images of God in Ancient Israel*. Their reasoning is instructive to read at length:

> Whereas Egypt grew noticeably weaker at the end of the Twelfth Dynasty, the Palestinian cities grew even stronger during the eighteenth century, at the

beginning of Middle Bronze IIB. Strong influences came from the north, specifically from Syria. The powerful Canaanite influence reached even as far as the Nile Delta and led there to the establishment of a Canaanite dominated dynasty about 1650 [BCE], the Fifteenth Dynasty that is often identified by using the term "Hyksos" (a hellenization of the Egyptian ḥq3.w ḫ3ś.wt, "ruler from foreign lands").[143]

One can justify beginning our survey at this point, when the urban culture of Palestine begins to flourish, because from this point on we can deal with a cultural continuum in Palestine that extends all the way to the time of the emergence of the Hebrew Bible.... [B]oth the Canaanite and the Egyptian cultures had begun to exert considerable influence *on each other* already during the Middle Bronze Age. It is also likely that the same ethnic groups continued to maintain their cultural system from the Middle Bronze Age right into the Iron Age. (Keel and Uehlinger 1998: 17, emphasis theirs)

This is not the place to examine the many historical and archaeological questions associated with the renaissance of complex society in Middle Bronze Age IIA nor the flowering of Canaanite culture in Middle Bronze Age IIB–C.[144] Nor is it appropriate here to explore the current stage of research on the Hyksos rulers, their capital at Avaris, and their Levantine origins.[145] And space does not allow us to explore the presence of Canaan in Egyptian literature such as the Tale of Sinuhe and the Execration Texts or the particulars of the New Kingdom Legend of Astarte and the Tribute of the Sea—not to mention the Canaanite pantheon attested in the Proto-Sinaitic inscriptions at Serabit el-Khadim.[146] (Though we will single out gleanings from the fourteenth-century BCE Amarna texts shortly.)

What must be underscored is the "cultural continuum" of which Keel and Uehlinger write, with points of mutual contact and influence from north (Syria) to south (Egypt) and south to north.[147] The two-way influence between Egyptian and Canaanite religious cultures is easily underscored by the presence of each culture's deities in the other's material culture and textual sources. Compare, for example, the presence in Egypt of Canaanite gods such as Baal (equated with Seth), Reshep, Anat, Astarte, Qudshu/Qedeshet, and Horon (cf. Tazawa 2009; Zivie-Coche 1994, 2011; Schneider 2003, 2006) and, in turn, the presence in the Levant of Egyptian gods such as Hathor, Horus, Bes, Ptah, Amun, and Re. Of particular note, consider the number of Egyptian amulets that abound in the archaeological record.[148] As for textual sources, Zevit (2001: 117 n. 51; cf. Ayali-Darshan 2015) has remarked how "local versions of myths widely circulated through the Middle Bronze period in the Levant" such that "the goings-on of the deities in Ugaritic myths were most likely local versions [thereof]." Similarly, he continues, "the presence of Canaanite deities in the Egyptian pantheon from the reign of Amenophis II (1436–1413 BCE) to the Roman period suggests that myths about these gods were circulated widely."

Let us focus particularly on the Late Bronze Age. Canaanite religious culture of this time period is remarkably widespread and thus influenced by and integrated with adjacent cultures. That there is a cultural continuum of certain West Semitic religious practices from the Late Bronze period through the Iron Age and beyond is easily demonstrated through the institution known as the *marzeaḥ*.[149] Pondering such enduring traditions—even if we cannot easily articulate mechanisms of transmission—is instructive.[150] Sociolinguists have demonstrated how language and writing are vehicles of such cultural transmission and integration, and with regard to Canaanite culture, the development and spread of alphabetic writing was key (Schniedewind 2013: 53–66). For the material culture of the Late Broze Age Levant, consider the various descriptive categories used by Ora Negbi (1976) for the bronze figurines she analyzes in her *Canaanite Gods in Metal*. Negbi arranges her many figurines into categories based on physical features (male/female warriors in smiting pose, male/female deities in benedictory pose, enthroned male/female figures, joined figurines, divine couples). Though they are clearly Canaanite (originating mostly "in the Levantine coast and its immediate hinterland"), the presence of well-defined cultural identifiers results in Negbi using descriptors that reflect the mixing of cultural styles (esp. Syro-Egyptian, Syro-Anatolian, Syro-Phoenician, and Syro-Palestinian). Negbi (1976: 2) concludes that "various considerations may enable us to demonstrate that the Levantine metalsmiths evolved a certain style of their own," yet "it is true that many figurines found in the Levant depend largely on Egyptian, Mesopotamian and Anatolian counterparts."

As for the presence of religion in Late Bronze Age textual sources, we have already noted the rich pluralistic attestations of divinity exhibited in the Amarna letters, where theophoric elements attest to Egyptian (Amon, Api, Horus, Hu, Haʿpi, Jah, Ptaḥ, Rēʿ, Seth), Mesopotamian (Anu, Aššur, Baštu, Ninurta), Kassite (Ḫarbe, Šugab), Hurrian (Ḫebat, Iršapppa, Teššub), and Indo-Aryan (Índraḫ, Rta, Yamáḫ) deities alongside broadly attested Semitic deities ([H]addu, Dagan, ʿAmmu) and deities known from West Semitic sources (ʿAnat, ʾAsherah, ʿAštart, Baʿlu, Beltu, El, Milku/Malik, Ṣaduq, Yamm). In short, there is substantial evidence of a widespread and enduring Canaanite religious influence from Syria to Egypt from the Middle Bronze Age on and especially so in the Late Bronze Age.

This brings us to the religious culture of Ugarit, a city on the Syrian coast whose discoveries have already been noted, especially with regard to the deity ʾIlu/El (Chapter Two, pp. 29–30; Chapter Four, pp. 76–81; Chapter Five, pp. 142–155). To emphasize the point: *The Late Bronze Age civilization of Ugarit* (with its some 1,550 mythological, ritual, and administrative alphabetic cuneiform texts—not to mention approximately 2,500 texts in seven other languages, especially

Akkadian, and the impressive material culture of Tell Ras Shamra) *is without rival for articulating the northern Canaanite religious lore that resonates with later Iron Age Israelite belief and ritual.* Whereas earlier decipherers (e.g., Virolleaud) dated the texts in the fourteenth century BCE, new textual discoveries (RS 92.2016 = KTU 1.179) suggest that Ugarit's most famous scribe, Ilimilku, lived in the last decades of the thirteenth century BCE (cf. Pardee 2007b: 186–189; Dalix 1997a, 1997b).

Why Ugarit?

The discovery of ancient Ugarit changed everything. Its importance for reconceptualizing Canaanite religion cannot be underscored enough. Since the modern discovery of Tell Ras Shamra in 1928 (and especially since the publication of the mythological texts coming from the first three seasons of excavations), every new treatment of Canaanite religion has looked to Tell Ras Shamra first and foremost—and with good reason. For here we have a richly documented religious culture evidenced by the royal complex, the two acropolis temples, the residential "rhyton sanctuary," numerous tombs, a host of cultic objects, and—last but certainly not least—hundreds of religious texts. And while the mythological texts have garnered past attention, the fuller spectrum of Ugaritic religion has been emerging as scholars explore the wide range of literary genres, especially the ritual texts (see Pardee 2000, 2002a).

Early Ugaritic Studies: Parallelomania Versus Demonization

At the outset, apart from those studies devoted to linguistics and archaeology, many scholars filtered these amazing discoveries through two distinctly different (and sometimes polar opposite) lenses, both equally narrow and colored.[151] Their respective glasses may be labeled "parallelomania" and "demonization." Showing little concern for differences in *Sitz im Leben*, chronology, function, and literary *Gattung*, the "parallelomania" approach rushed to propose putative similarities between Ugarit and various ancient Near Eastern cultures. Parallel Akitu festivals, myths of dying and rising gods, rituals of child sacrifice, and cultic prostitution were thought to be everywhere. A wide variety of religious concepts and practices were thought to be homogenous transhistorically and transculturally.

The "demonization" approach was employed most often by biblicists who used the Ugaritic texts as just another platform to continue the Deuteronomistic tradition of ridiculing the Canaanites in order to underscore the supremacy of biblical religion. The rhetoric was so pejorative that Delbert Hillers (1985: 253–254) wrote in response that biblical scholars were "singularly ill-suited" to articulate the wonders of ancient Ugarit, for they "are committed in advance to finding it inferior, puerile, barbarous, retarded, or shocking"—merely an "abomination" to be ridiculed. Mark Smith characterized the early years of Ugaritic studies as being dominated by the "contrastive approach," where the stereotype of the depraved Canaanites was everywhere.[152] Such an approach reduced a magnificent culture to the status of a handmaid of biblical studies. Ugarit's fame was as merely a "Canaanite" foil to the biblical viewpoint.[153] Yet that was more than ninety years ago. To be charitable, those scholars of the past who wrote polemically against Canaanite (i.e., Ugaritic) culture did so with only a fraction of the texts we have available today, and with only a partial understanding of what we now know of the Late Bronze Age kingdom of Ugarit.[154]

What has happened in the years since? The independent discipline of Ugaritic studies that was always at the core of the French Mission to Ras Shamra has continued to flourish fully apart from the field of biblical studies. Note in particular the many volumes published in the Ras Shamra–Ougarit series (Éditions Recherche sur les Civilisations, Paris). Comparative study between Ugaritic and biblical studies goes on apace, yet with only a rare hint (if any) that a major civilization like Ugarit should function in a subservient handmaid role. While current studies emphasize the shared cultural legacy between ancient Ugarit and ancient Israel, most are cognizant of not drawing overreaching conclusions that would ignore the wide geographical, chronological, and societal divides.

Ugarit as "Canaanite": The Linguistic and Religious Continuum
Most notably for our discussion, the relation between Ugaritic language and religious culture and that of the "Canaanites" has been significantly clarified thanks in part to the work of Rainey, Na'aman, Pardee, Joseph Tropper, and others. As pointed out by Rainey (1963, 1964, 1996) and Na'aman (1994, 1999), if one desires a narrow geographical definition, then it is clear from the texts themselves that the people of Ugarit viewed Canaanites as foreigners (cf. KTU 4.96)![155] One text (RS 20.182A+B = *Ugaritica V* #36) even mentions a payment by the "sons of Ugarit" to the "sons of Canaan." Thus geographically, the people of Ugarit are not Canaanites.

What about a linguistic definition? Is Ugaritic a Canaanite language? The answer to this age-old question is "it depends." That is, whether Ugaritic is Canaanite depends on the criteria used for assessment. Those in favor point to certain linguistic features that would support their case, while those in opposition tally their own list.[156] The current writer would side with Tropper (1994) in the affirmative because of the simple fact that Ugaritic is in the Northwest Semitic family, which is divided into two main branches, Canaanite and Aramaic. Whatever Ugaritic is, it is clearly not Aramaic. It is either a Northern Canaanite dialect (so Tropper) or a direct descendant from a Levantine "Amorite" dialect (so Bordreuil and Pardee).[157]

Finally, and most importantly for the present discussion, we come to a cultural and religious definition. Without doubt, the vast corpus of literature (and iconography) from Ugarit presents us with the clearest picture of "Canaanite" religious culture as it has been customarily defined. For example, thanks to texts of varying genres (mythological, ritual, administrative) and numerous divine figurines and other cultic artifacts, Ugarit presents us with the fullest assemblage of Canaanite deities universally recognized as Canaanite from other sources (i.e., Phoenician, Punic, Egyptian, Amarna Canaanite, the Hebrew Bible, epigraphic Hebrew, Moabite, Edomite, Ammonite).[158] These Ugaritic deities (which have direct etymological counterparts in the surrounding civilizations) include the male figures ʾIlu (El), Baʿlu (Baal), Athtar, Dagan, Rashpu (Reshep), Yarihu, and Horanu (Horon); the goddesses ʾAthiratu (Asherah), ʿAnatu, ʿAthtartu (Ashtart, Astarte), and Shapshu; the negative protagonists (i.e., combat figures) of Yammu, Motu, and Litanu (Leviathan); the shades of the dead, known as the Rapiʾuma (Rephaim); ancestral gods (ʾIlu-ʾibi; cf. the Hebrew Bible's *ʾĕlōhê ʾăbôt*, "the god of fathers"); and divine assemblies (*pḫr ʾilm; pḫr mʿd; ʿdt ʾilm*).

When we compare the pantheon in Late Bronze Age Ugaritic religion with the West Semitic deities mentioned in Late Bronze Age Egypt and Amarna Canaanite and the various Iron Age religious cultures (Phoenician, Israelite, Moabite, Edomite, Ammonite), we see a cultural continuum that warrants the label "Canaanite." This is not to say that each of these cultures did not develop their own preferences (and novelties) with regard to the makeup of their regional pantheons and which deities played which roles. To do so would be to ignore empirical data about cultural preferences such as Israel's insistence on the supremacy of Yahweh, Tyre's selection of Melqart, Baal/Baal-Shamem, and ʿAštart, Sidon's recognition of Eshmun as their chief god, Moab's elevation of the god Chemosh, the Edomite choice of Qos, and the Ammonite adoption of Milcom.

Moreover, recent research on divinity at Ugarit has led to a nuancing of traditional understandings of Levantine pantheons. Thanks to the variety of literary genres within the Ugaritic textual corpus, we are now able to recognize different types of pantheons, each with different rankings. In the past, the "mythological" (or "narrative") pantheon (assembled from the literary texts KTU 1.1–1.24) dominated every publication of Ugaritic religion. Scholars today round out the picture by drawing attention to how several deity lists reveal synthetic attempts at documenting a "canonical" pantheon (for lack of a better term).[159] Yet another view of divinity is the "functional" pantheon, which includes the various gods that actually receive cult and in what quantity (thus designating rank).[160] Here ritual texts, administrative texts, and personal names play a central role, not to mention the expenditure of resources devoted to certain gods, as ascertained through archaeology. In short, though we have a cultural Canaanite continuum throughout the Levant, any attempt at synthesizing divinity within even a single culture must be appropriately nuanced.

In addition to describing divinity, Ugaritic religion is of paramount importance for sketching many of the religious themes and motifs that dominate the Canaanite religion found in the Hebrew Bible. Many of these themes will be treated in Chapters Eight through Ten, and thus our treatment here will be very brief. Chief among these has been the combat myth (or *Chaoskampf* traditions), where the divine storm/warrior god defeats enemies described as the Sea or a related cosmic dragon creature. Such traditions are widespread in the ancient Near East (especially Mesopotamia), as recognized long ago in Hermann Gunkel's (1895) famous volume *Schöpfung und Chaos in Urzeit und Endzeit*. Yet, as John Day (1985: 4) has underscored, "since the discovery of the Ugaritic texts from 1929 onwards, it has become clear that the immediate background of the Old Testament allusions to the sea monster is not Babylonian but Canaanite." Consider how the Ugaritic texts' Baʻlu and the Hebrew Bible's Yahweh (both designated "Rider of the Clouds") fight the very same foes (*ym*/Yammu—*yām*; *nhr*/Naharu—*nāhār*; Litanu—*liwyātān*/Leviathan; Tunnanu—*tannîn*; Motu—*māwet/môt*). Multiheaded dragons of the same name are slain by each culture's divine warrior. There may be minor disagreement among historians of religion about the precise literary genre used by writers to convey these stories (e.g., mythopoeic vs. mythopoetic), yet all scholars are in agreement about the ubiquitous presence of pre-Israelite Canaanite *Chaoskampf* traditions within the pages of the Hebrew Bible as well as in Iron Age epigraphic Hebrew (cf. the Kuntillet ʻAjrud plaster fragment described later). These widespread Canaanite tales are also marked by longevity. To borrow Sanders' (2009: 58) words, "Ugaritic literature drew on old traditions that were widely known: the Baal epic's theme of the battle between the storm god and the sea appears in West Semitic cultures five hundred years earlier at Mari and a thousand years later in the biblical book of Daniel."

Equally remarkable are poetic conventions (parallelism, phraseology, poetic formulae) and stock literary type-scenes. Groundbreaking work by scholars such as Harold Louis Ginsberg, Umberto Cassuto, and Albright provided a foundation for subsequent work such as that of Parker (1989b), whose identification of shared stock type-scenes in the Kirta and Aqhat poems (e.g., the birth announcement, the vow, the marriage blessing) led him to assert that the Ugaritic texts constitute a "pre-biblical narrative tradition."[161] Parker (1989b: 225) asserts that "Ugaritic represents better than any other second millennium language or literature the antecedents of the language and literature of ancient Israel."[162] See too the work of Frank Polak (1989, 2006) on the linguistic and stylistic aspects of poetic formulae.[163]

Finally, a brief remark needs to be made about the phenomena of sacrifice and religious personnel. It goes without saying that the entire ancient Near East developed temple economies that constituted the core of religious ritual. Few if any historians of religion would assert a direct line of dependence between Late Bronze Age Ugaritic and Iron Age Israelite sacrifice and cultic personnel. (What would be the mechanisms?) Yet the specific linguistic vocabulary used by these two cultures is so exact and precise etymologically that one cannot deny a shared cultural legacy.[164] Pardee (2002a: 233) calls the etymological similarities "striking."

The Ugaritic ritual texts attest to the following sacrifices with exact etymological parallels to Israelite sacrifice: (1) the general term *dibḥu* (Hebrew *zebaḥ*), (2) the term for altar, *madbiḥu* (Hebrew *mizbēaḥ*), (3) the "peace" or "communion" offering known as the *šalamūma* (Hebrew *šĕlāmîm*), (4) the presentation offering known as the *šanūpatu* (cf. Hebrew *tĕnûpāh*), and (5) the *nidru* offering of a vow (Hebrew *neder*).[165] The many types of offerings in the Ugaritic ritual texts also have direct etymological correlates in Hebrew (e.g., male bovid, *ʾalpu/ʾelep*; ram/sheep, *šû/śeh*; donkey, *ʿeru/ʿayir*; lamb, *ʾimmiru/ʾimmēr*; dove, *yônatu/yônâ*; liver, *kabidu/kābēd*; silver, *kaspu/kesep*; wine, *yēnū/yayin*; neck, *napšu/nepeš*; wheat, *kussumu/kussemet*).

Ugaritic religious officiants with etymological parallels in the Hebrew Bible include (1) priests (Ugaritic *kāhin/kāhinūma*; Hebrew *kōhēn/kōhănîm*), (2) chief priests (Ugaritic *rabbu kāhinīma*; Hebrew *hakkōhēn haggādôl*), (3) the king as religious officiant (Ugaritic *malku*; Hebrew *melek*), (4) cultic scribes (Ugaritic *sāpiru*; Hebrew *sōpēr*), (5) cultic herdsmen (Ugaritic *nāqid*; Hebrew *nōqēd*), (6) undefined "holy" cultic functionaries (Ugaritic *qdš*; Hebrew *qdš*), and (7) various incantation specialists (Ugaritic *mulaḫḫišu*; Hebrew *mĕlaḥăšîm*).

The various locales of sacred space also resonate etymologically: (1) temple, *bētu/bayit*; (2) sanctuary, *qidšu/qodeš*; (3) altar, *madbiḥu/mizbēaḥ*; (4) palace, *hêkalu/hêkāl*; (5) threshing floor, *gurnu/goren*; (6) vineyard, *karmu/kerem*; (7) meeting place, *marziḥu/marzeaḥ*; and (8) tomb, *qibru/qeber*.

Once again we must underscore Pardee's (2002a: 233) caveat that "identity or similarity of vocabulary may not be taken as indications that practice and ideology were the same" (similarly Smith 2002a: 24). Returning to divinity, we could cite Ribichini's (1997: 124) caution that "the same divine name . . . cannot be accepted as proof that the morphological and functional features of the deity of that name remained unchanged." In fact, such truisms should be stated even more strongly. It is *certainly* the case that each of these cultures developed different religious practices and imbued many of these religious terms and deities with different ideologies. Israelites, according to the Hebrew Bible, never sacrificed donkeys, as we have in KTU 1.40 (but cf. Lewis 2006a: 347–348). As demonstrated by the location of tombs under their houses, Ugaritians did not share the same notions about corpse contamination and ritual pollution that we find in Numbers 19 (see Pitard 2002: 150; Lewis 2002: 182). The royal cult of Judean kings never comes close to matching the pageantry of the Ugaritic king as chief religious officiant (e.g., KTU 1.41, 1.119). Israel's preoccupation with blood as a purificatory substance is entirely absent from the Ugaritic ritual texts (cf. Lewis 2006a: 346–347). Nonetheless, the point has been clearly made: *Even with a wide array of culture-specific practices factored in, and the religious autonomy of each culture, there was nonetheless a demonstrable and overarching linguistic and religious Canaanite continuum between Late Bronze Age Ugarit and Iron Age Israel.*[166] The "larger Canaanite cultural continuum" in which Israel found itself led J. Andrew Dearman (2006: 535) to conclude that "indeed, Israel could hardly be anything else than Canaanite, culturally speaking." For the historian of religion in search of data, Smith's (2014a: 41) words ring true: "The Ugaritic texts . . . often represent a more proximate resource for understanding themes and concepts expressed in early Israelite literature or society than many biblical texts that date to the eighth century or later."

Aramean Religion

Ugarit is not the only Syrian culture to contribute to our understanding of ancient Israel's religious heritage. Discoveries such as finding an Old Aramaic memorial inscription mentioning the god Hadad at Tel Dan, one of the most important religious sites in Israel, remind us of the presence of Aramean religion at this multiethnic hybrid site, even if its primarily religious affiliation was Yahwistic (cf. Thareani 2016; Greer 2017). Similarly, the bull-headed warrior deity discovered in the elaborate gate shrine of Bethsaida (in Geshur of Aram) likely designates the Aramean god Hadad and/or the Aramean moon god Śahr (see Chapter Seven, pp. 330–333). Biblical tradition notes how Rebekah, the mother of Jacob and Esau, is "the daughter of Bethuel, the Aramean of Paddan-Aram" (Gen 22:23; 25:20; 28:5).[167] Deuteronomy 26:5 contains the famous reference to Jacob as an *ărāmî ʾōbēd* (Deut 26:5), "a wandering" (RSV) or "fugitive" (JPS) Aramean. Absalom makes a vow to Yahweh while in Geshur of Aram (2 Sam 15:8). The boldest story in the Hebrew Bible about a king officiating in the cult, specifically with regard to blood manipulation, is that of the Judahite king Ahaz in 2 Kings 16:10–16. The king admires an altar (in what is presumably an Aramean temple complex) in Damascus and has a replica built in Jerusalem; on this altar he engages in various religious rituals. While the god of the Damascus altar is never explicitly mentioned, it could very well have been the Aramean god Hadad (cf. Greenfield 1999: 380; 1987: 70).

In light of this, one would think that Aramean religion would be a focal point of historians of Israelite religion, especially as providing another portrait to balance (or rival) the Canaanite backdrop. (After all, according to J's account in Gen 24:2–4, Abraham's search for an Aramean wife for Isaac was specifically intended to avoid his marriage to a Canaanite!) As yet another northern source, should not Aramean religion too be mined as a possible wellspring for religious concepts that become central to Iron Age Israelite Yahwism?

Once again methodological caution is in order. Just as one recognizes the impossibility of defining a unified "Canaanite religion," so too one needs to underscore that there never existed anything approaching a single Aramean religion or culture. Attempts to define Aramean identity face significant hurdles (Sergi, Oeming, and de Hulster 2016; Berlejung, Maeir, and Schüle 2017). Moreover, the terms "Aramaic/Aramean" themselves are imprecise and inadequate as classifying terms, as they can refer to languages and dialects that are not easily grouped together as well as distinctly different sociopolitical polities.[168] Yet we have no alternative. Caveat lector.

Nonetheless, we do have a few synthetic treatments of Aramean religion (e.g., Niehr 2013, 2014a; Lipiński 2000: 599–640). Like the various Canaanite civilizations, Aramean cultural expressions (though of murky origin) have a long legacy during the late second and especially the first millennium BCE.[169] Because Aramaic was used as a sort of lingua franca throughout the Fertile Crescent, Aramean language spread much further abroad than the political or military reach of any of its minor polities (active mostly in the tenth through the late eighth centuries BCE). Regrettably for the historian of religion, the vast amount of Aramaic literature was not written by Arameans and thus is of little use for articulating indigenous Aramean religion. Caution is in order to guard against reconstructing Aramean religion via inaccurate non-Aramean portrayals (which could even redefine or appropriate certain elements). Consider as but one example how Neo-Assyrian theologians during the time of Sennacherib (704–681 BCE) took it upon themselves to portray the god Amurru as an Aramean deity riding beside Aššur in his chariot as he sets off to battle the cosmic monster Tiamat.[170]

As for uncovering the various forms of indigenous Aramean religion, the relevant source material is primarily epigraphic, onomastic, and sparse. Yet from this material we can at least sketch Aramean divinity (albeit imperfectly due to the small statistical sampling), acknowledging at the outset that "there never was a pan-Aramean religion . . . any more than there was an overall Aramean kingdom" (Niehr 2014a: 127). Restricting ourselves to the most important Archaic Aramaic inscriptions (ninth/eighth centuries BCE) as a control group, we can come up with an impressive list of named deities, half of which are not Aramean![171] Once we set aside the distinctly Mesopotamian deities ('Inurta, Ir,

Laṣ, Marduk, Nabu, Nergal, Nikkal, Nusk, Shala, Sibitti, Sin, Tashmet, Zarpanit) as well as the Phoenician Melqart, the Anatolian Kubaba, and the Urartian Ḫaldi, we are left with a core list.[172]

If we then remove generic references to the gods (e.g., *'lhy/'lhn/'lhyn; 'lhy byt 'by*), references to (deified?) natural phenomena (Heaven and Earth; Abyss and Springs; Day and Night), and the gods of a certain locale (the gods of Arpad, the gods of KTK, the gods of Yʾdy), a primary list of Aramean deities comes into focus.[173] This list includes Hadad (and his manifestation in Aleppo and Sikkan), Baʿl-Shamayn, El, ʿElyan, Ilu-Wer/El-wer, Rashap (and the seemingly related ʾArqu-Rashap), Rakib-El, Shahar/Śahr, and Shamash.[174] As noted earlier, five of these deities occur in multiple near-fixed lists in the two Samʾalian Aramaic texts from Zincirli: Hadad, El, Rashap, Rakib-El, and Shamash. (See Chapter Five, pp. 196 and 750, n. 180.)

Hadad is clearly the most preeminent deity in Aramean religion. As nicely summarized by Daniel Schwemer (2001; 2008: 135–168), Alberto R. W. Green (2003: 166–175), and Alan Lenzi (2011: 85–86), the West Semitic/Amorite deity Adad is attested in Sumerian and Akkadian sources as early as the third millennium BCE. His cult was centered in the Middle Euphrates and Syria and "diffused not only southward throughout Babylonia, but also to the north, affecting the Anatolian Plateau, and to the northeast, in the Urartian regions" (Green 2003: 169). A fascinating prophecy text from eighteenth-century BCE Mari gives us a peek into what must have been a rich *Chaoskampf* mythology surrounding this storm/warrior god. A prophet of Adad, lord of Aleppo, by the name of Abiya mentions (speaking for the deity in first-person discourse) how the god Adad let King Zimri-Lim use his divine weapons, the very weapons Adad used to defeat the cosmic monster Tiamat.[175] Compare too the Iron Age orthostat discovered at the citadel of Aleppo that depicts the storm god of Aleppo being pulled in a chariot by a majestic bull (Figure 5.29; cf. Kohlmeyer 2000, 2009). Surely similar myths circulated about Hadad in Aramean religion, which inherited this cultural background. The Old Aramaic royal inscription from Bukan speaks of Hadad thundering with language (*ytn ql*) reminiscent of Adad (*rigim Adad*), not to mention Yahweh-Elyon (*yittēn qōlô*; e.g., Ps 18:14 [Eng 18:13]).[176] The cultural continuum is also reflected in biblical texts where a reference to the god Hadad-Ramman (Hadad the Thunderer) is reflected in 2 Kings 5:18. Here in a single verse the Syrian army commander Naʾaman thrice mentions a temple of Rimmon (*bêt rimmôn*) seemingly in Damascus. Yet another tradition in Zechariah 12:11 is particularly fascinating. It mentions "the mourning of Hadad-Rimmon" (*mispad hădad-rimmôn*), a likely reference to stories about Hadad as a dying (and later rising) god (cf. Greenfield 1976; 1999: 380–381).

The use of the name Hadad to designate this storm/warrior god remained central in Aramean religion, in contrast to the name Baʿlu/Baal, which came to label the equivalent deity in Canaanite culture. The texts from Ugarit reflect the change in process. In the mythological texts Baʻlu and Haddu can serve as synonymous, parallel terms, yet notably with Baʻlu always functioning in the dominant A position parallel to Haddu in the B position (A//B).[177] The ritual texts are even more instructive. Hadad is never the recipient of cult, in contrast to Baʻlu Ṣapunu/Baʻlu, who receives the majority of offerings (cf. Pardee 2002a: 222–224). Baʻlu appears prominently and in multiple manifestations in the various deity lists (and corresponding to ^{d}IŠKUR), whereas the writing of Hadad/Haddu (*hd*) in alphabetic cuneiform is virtually absent.[178] Commenting on the later Iron Age, Jonas Greenfield (1987a: 68) argues that "in the first millennium a functional bifurcation had taken place—Baʻlu/Baal became a Canaanite god and Hadad an Aramaic one."[179]

According to Lipiński (2000: 599–636), who includes the onomastic data, in addition to Hadad the other most prominent Aramean deites would include ʼIl/ʼEl, ʻAttar, Reshep, Shamash, and the moon god Śahr; there were also vibrant cults of betyls and ancestors. As for quantifying the onomastic evidence, Lipiński (2000: 614) notes that "the name ʼIl is the commonest theophorous element in the Aramaic personal names of the first millennium B.C. and it certainly reflects the importance of the cult of ʼIl among the early Arameans." One example is Matîʻʻēl (*mtʻʻl*), the king of Arpad (an Aramean kingdom 19 mi. [30 km] north of Aleppo), whose name means "protected [or saved] by [the god] El."[180]

To date there is no comprehensive study of the iconography of Aramean divinity (cf. Schwemer 2008: 31–36; Gilibert 2011; Yadin 1970). Hadad was certainly depicted as a storm/warrior god riding a bull (cf. Figures 5.23, 5.24). With the discovery of the bull-headed stela at Iron Age Bethsaida, Keel has studied the iconography of the Aramean moon god Śahr, the equivalent of Sin. After documenting "typically Aramean phenomena" with regard to the "astral deities of the night," Keel (1998: 101) concludes:

> The numerous anepigraphic seals with symbols of the astral deities of the night from the Palestinian eighth and seventh centuries [BCE], as well as the evidence given in the Old Testament of the widespread cult of the "host of heaven" in seventh-century Judah, are compelling evidence for the heavy impact of Aramean culture on Judah as well as on the whole of the Levant at the end of the eighth and, mainly, in the seventh century [BCE].

In conclusion, the several points of contact between Aramean culture and ancient Israelite culture noted at the outset of this discussion (e.g., the Tel Dan stela, the bull-headed stela from Bethsaida, King Ahaz's replication of a Damascus altar, the numerous references to the Arameans in biblical tradition) as well as the names of various Aramean deities that resonate (at least etymologically) with gods appearing in Israelite religion (e.g., Hadad, 'Il/'El, 'Elyan, Reshep, Shamash) make a compelling case for factoring in Aramean influence throughout Israelite religion.

Mixed Texts: Deir ʿAlla and Arslan Tash

Prior to leaving the Canaanite and Aramean backdrop to ancient Israelite religion, we must briefly note two texts that do not fit easily into tidy linguistic categories: the eighth-century BCE Transjordanian Deir ʿAlla texts and two seventh-century BCE incantations coming from Arslan Tash (ancient Hadatu). Though it is the later of the two, we will treat the Arslan Tash material first due to geography (i.e., dealing first with north Syria, close to the present-day Turkish border, prior to heading south to the eastern Jordan valley).

The two small seventh-century BCE limestone plaques from Arslan Tash are well known for being our best examples of Levantine incantations (*lḥšt*) complete with graphic iconography.[181] The language of the inscriptions seems to be Phoenician (or a local dialect) with possible Aramaisms, while the script is Aramaic.[182] As for divinity, we read of common generic references (*kl bn 'lm*, "all the sons of the gods"; *dr kl qdšn*, "the assembly of all the Holy Ones") and deified natural phenomena (*šmm w'rṣ*, Heavens and Earth). Named deities include the Assyrian Aššur and the Canaanite gods Baal (*bʿl*),[183] who hitches his chariot (*bʿl ʾsr mrkbty*; cf. Figure 5.29), and Hawron/Horon (*ḥwrn*), who seems to be called "the lord of holiness" (*bʿl q[d]š*).[184] The presence of the Assyrian god Aššur is expected given Hadatu's role as a seat of Assyrian administration (Akkermans and Schwartz 2003: 382–384). As for the two other deities, they are Canaanite, not Aramean. Note how an eighth-century BCE basalt stela (Figure 5.24) also documents a striding storm god atop a charging bull at Arslan Tash a century earlier than our two incantations. Stylistically, the figure depicts the Assyrian Adad, and the stela was found in the temple of the goddess Ishtar. Yet given the overlap of Adad with Aramean Hadad and Canaanite Baal, the identity for the dwellers at eighth-century BCE Arslan Tash likely depended on the eye (and ethnic background) of the beholder.

The Transjordanian Deir ʿAlla plaster texts that date to the eighth century BCE have been discussed with regard to how their "El repertoire" (Baruch Levine's terminology) might shed light on the Hebrew Bible's El Elyon and El Shadday (see Chapter Four, pp. 89–90, 96, 116). Jeremy Hutton (2010a: 166–167; 2006) nuances Levine's treatment to describe a "literary appropriation of sacred geography ... [the] reclamation of the very physical ... pilgrimage paths along which the covenant community of the biblical Israel purportedly received its identity." The precise language of the texts has been debated at length because of their admixture of Aramaic and Canaanite traits. Many scholars view the language as an Aramaic dialect and account for certain linguistic distinctives and oddities by appealing to its peripheral or regional nature as well as its literary or archaistic character (Hoftijzer and van der Kooij 1976; McCarter 1980b: 50). Material culture complicates such conclusions. According to Aren Maeir (2017: 59–60), "There is very little, if at all archaeological evidence of an Aramean connection [at Deir ʿAlla] . . . the pottery styles and technologies are of local Southern Levantine character . . . the overall evidence makes it hard to accept an Aramean 'story' behind the Deir Allā texts." Others argue for the language being Canaanite, specifically a South Canaanite dialect, in order to account for similarities with Moabite and Hebrew (Hackett 1984: 109–125; Pat-El and Wilson-Wright 2015). Holger Gzella (2017: 23–24; 2015: 72–77, 87–91) suggests a hybrid approach where "a local, and perhaps oral, tradition in a Transjordanian language was then recorded in a basically Aramaic grammatical code or literally translated into Aramaic." Some linguists assert that the "Deir ʿAlla dialect is . . . neither Canaanite nor Aramaic" (Huehnergard 1995: 276) or that it is simply "a dead-end, peripheral dialect" (Kaufman 1980: 73). McCarter (1991: 97) notes how "the Deir ʿAlla dialect resists classification as Aramaic or Canaanite in categorical terms" yet is perfectly understandable in terms of dialect geography (remote from Phoenician, strongly linked to Hebrew and Moabite with their communities nearby as well as to Aramaic with the considerable political and cultural influence of Damascus).

A great deal of the subject matter of these texts directly resonates with traditions recorded in the Hebrew Bible, particularly the mention of the seer called Balaam (cf. Num 22–24).[185] Aramean, Canaanite, and Israelite conceptions of prophecy and divination (vis-à-vis practices at eighteenth-century BCE Mari and Neo-Assyrian Nineveh) will be treated elsewhere (cf. Nissinen et al. 2003, 2019). What concerns us here are the various references to divinity that include a group of generic gods (ʾlhn) and the specific mention of a divine assembly (mwʿd) wherein we meet the Shaddayyin (šdyn) gods. Named deities include El, Sheger, and Ashtar. However one parses the linguistic character of the Deir ʿAlla texts, the family of the gods here is decidedly Canaanite, with clear etymological reference points to ancient Israelite religion (i.e., El Shadday; the demythologized šeger and ʿaštĕrôt in Deut 7:13; 28:4, 38, 51; and P's Tent of Meeting [ʾōhel môʿēd]). Levine (2000b: 141) argues that "given what is known of the immediate region in the early to mid-eighth century BCE, it is likely that Israelites constituted the principal element in the Gileadite population."

Yahweh from the North: An Insurmountable Problem?

The shared cultural heritage of northern Canaanite religion (best exemplified by Ugaritic religion) as well as certain features of Aramean religion could argue strongly for a northern origin of many of the key components of Israelite religion—*except for its most vital ingredient: the god Yahweh!* Thanks to the Ugaritic texts we know of a robust "Canaanite" pantheon with hundreds of named deities, from 'Adamma to Zizzu-wa-Kamatu. Yet the god Yahweh is not attested in any of our several deity lists nor in any ritual or mythological texts, even the ones that mention deities of surrounding nations. (As has been remarked, the putative notion that Yahweh is found in KTU 1.1.4 has met with near universal rejection. See pp. 228–229.)

Where does this leave us as to the geographic origin of Yahweh? Whereas the majority of scholars would join Cross (1973: 72) in asserting that "the early cultic establishment of Yahweh and its appurtenances... all reflect Canaanite models," they would at the same time wonder how such a cult of Yahweh could be established without any antecedent for its chief (and eventually national) deity. That Yahweh rides on the clouds like Baʿlu and fights the very same cosmic foes almost begs for his presence in Ugaritic lore. Or, if Ugarit cannot come through, surely his presence might be found at Late Bronze Age Emar or Iron Age Damascus or Phoenicia. To further complicate matters, we have no imported divine image of Yahweh (in metal, stone, or even terra-cotta) coming from an Iron Age I find spot in Israel that could be assessed for chemical composition in hopes of locating its place of origin.

Despite these daunting hurdles, those who argue for Yahweh emerging from northern traditions assert that there is a "general religious-historical constellation, according to which *YHWH belongs to the North Levantine-Syriac type of the kingly weather-god Adad-Baal*" (Leuenberger 2017: 165; emphasis his).[186] The only (allegedly) explicit solutions for a northern origin of Yahweh were the two noted earlier, and neither is without its problems. The weaker of the two solutions is that of Dalley, who tried to use three royal names to assert that "Yahweh was worshipped as a major god in Hamath" (Syria) in the eighth century BCE. Not only are there significant obstacles to this theory (see pp. 233–234), but it still would not account for the *origin* of the god Yahweh. There are many ancient Yahwistic traditions and actual poems (or at least portions thereof) in the Hebrew Bible that predate the eighth century BCE (e.g., Gen 49, Exod 15, Deut 33, Judg 5, 2 Sam 22 = Ps 18, Ps 29, Ps 68, Hab 3). The mention of Yahweh on the mid-ninth-century BCE Moabite stone (i.e., the Mesha stela) is also earlier than Dalley's Hamath references.

The more promising of the two solutions is the Albright-Cross-Freedman theory that Yahweh's origins are indeed to be found in the northern Canaanite traditions surrounding the god ʾIlu/El (cf. Green 2003: 246, 254). (The theory and its weaknesses have already been discussed at length [see pp. 220–222], but to summarize: Cross [1973: 169] writes that "Israel used traditional Canaanite language in early descriptions of Yahweh's theophany"—that is, authors drew on traditions with "highly imaginative poetry of the storm god's epiphany" inspired by "the northern storms of Lebanon, Cassius, or the Amanus"; the independent name Yahweh resulted from a shortened sentence name; and a full cultic expression describing El as "the god who creates the heavenly armies" [*ʾēl zū yahwī ṣabaʾōt] over time came to emphasize its creator epithet ["he who creates"] alone, so what was once a verbal element (yahwê) was isolated to become the name of the deity [Yahweh].) In addition to the critiques already listed, one could add the lack of any reference to this new creator god in any northern sources. In order for this theory to be salvaged, the process of differentiating Yahweh from El as a separate deity would have to have taken place in the Iron I period and in the land of Israel. Indeed, Cross (1973: 71) advocated that "the god Yahweh split off from ʾEl in the radical differentiation of his cultus in the Proto-Israelite league."

And yet for Cross the "traditional poetic language" that was inspired by Late Bronze Age northern storms was used in "the Epic accounts of the revelation at Sinai." Indeed, Cross places a great deal of emphasis on ancient poems in the Hebrew Bible that speak of Yahweh marching from the south (to be discussed later). In his earlier work, Cross (1973: 71) suggested how the wedding of northern and southern traditions could be facilitated: "If Yahweh is recognized as originally a cultic name of ʾEl, perhaps the epithet of ʾEl as patron deity of the Midianite League in the south, a number of problems in the history of the religion of Israel can be solved." Granted, no explicit mechanism is articulated for such a wedding. Yet as we will see, Cross (1988, 1998) later developed these ideas by reworking the well-known Midianite hypothesis.

Southern Origins of Yahwism: A Brief Overview of the Midianite Hypothesis

The earliest references to what has come to be known as the Midianite hypothesis (aka the Kenite hypothesis and the Midianite/Kenite hypothesis) have been traced back to Friedrich Wilhelm Ghillany writing under the pseudonym Richard von der Alm (1862), C. P. Tiele (1872: 558–560), Bernhard Stade (1887), and Karl Budde (1899). Daniel Fleming has argued convincingly that Tiele should get credit as the innovator of the hypothesis.[187] Two of the ways the theory came to be viewed can be seen in the contrasting portrayals by H. H. Rowley (1950: 149–160) in the affirmative and by Theophile James Meek (1950: 93–98) in opposition. In its briefest exposition, the hypothesis asserts that Moses first learned of Yahweh through contact with his father-in-law Jethro, who was a priest in Midian (Exodus 3:1; 18:1). Albertz (1994: 52) summarizes: "We may suppose that the Midianites or Kenites were already worshippers of Yahweh.... [T]he god Yahweh is older than Israel; he was a southern Palestinian mountain god before he became the god of liberation for the Moses group." In the more elaborate formulation that we find today, the hypothesis integrates the extrabiblical references to the Shasu texts mentioned earlier, ties to the tribe of Reuben (Cross 1988, 1998), the archaeology of Midian and "Midianite/Hijaz painted pottery" (also known as Qurayyah ware; cf. the work of Peter J. Parr and others),[188] references to caravan economy in Judges 5 (Schloen 1993), the underpinnings of King Saul's reign (van der Toorn 1996b: 281–286), and southern geographical traces in "ancient Yahwistic poetry."

The Hebrew Bible's Differing Portrayals of the Midianites and Kenites

It is helpful at the outset to sketch the ways in which the Midianites and Kenites are portrayed in the Hebrew Bible. According to ancestral tradition, the Midianites are an Abrahamic people whose eponymous ancestor was one of six sons born to Abraham and his wife Keturah (Gen 25:2). This underlying understanding of kinship will be reflected in the material discussed later, especially when it comes to mitigating the hostility felt toward the Midianites (cf. too the ambivalence toward the Edomites). Some understanding of kinship, some recognition of intimacy, lies behind the portrayal of brothers and cousins (even with sibling rivalry) and, in contrast, the completely negative representation of those with whom there are no kinship bonds (e.g., the alien Philistines).

A cursory glance at various biblical traditions could easily lead to the most negative of assessments about the two related tribal groups known as the Midianites and Kenites. According to the J/non-P literary strand, Cain (*qayin*), the eponymous ancestor of the Kenites (*qênî*), is the first murderer of the human race, and he is cursed with banishment from the soil he once tilled (Gen 4:1–16).[189] This same tradition tells of Abram's descendants being granted the land of the Kenites along with that of the Canaanites and other dispossessed peoples (Gen 15:19). Midianite traders play a role in selling Joseph into slavery (Gen 37:28 [cf. 37:36], traditionally labeled as E). The P(riestly) Tradition contains an extensive holy war narrative in Numbers 31 where Yahweh commands Moses to bring about the full destruction of the Midianites (including "the five kings of Midian" and the prophet Balaam) as a result of the famous Baal Peor incident (Num 25:6–18).[190] Finally, consider the Gideon narrative (Judg 6:1–8:12), which portrays the Midianites (along with the Amalekites) as a marauding enemy whom Gideon defeats through God-given instruction and ability. The lore about this defeat lived on such that Isaiah could simply refer to divine conquering "as on the day of Midian" (kĕyôm midyān) (Isa 9:3 [Eng 9:4]; cf. 10:26).[191]

In this light it is most intriguing to read of parallel traditions that portray extremely positive relations with the Midianites and Kenites. In these traditions (which are used to support the Midianite hypothesis), Moses has very good relations with the Midianites (Exod 2:15b–22 = J/non-P)—so good, in fact, that he marries Zipporah, a Midianite, and tends her father's herds (Exod 3:1). Moses' father-in-law is a priest of Midian who is passionate in his praise of Yahweh's deliverance of Moses and Israel from the hand of the Egyptians (Exod 18:9–12; = E/non-P). "Yahweh is greater than all gods!" (gādôl yhwh mikkol-hāʾĕlōhîm) he exclaims in response, together with presenting burnt offerings and sacrifices (ʿōlâ ûzĕbāḥîm). Furthermore, this Midianite priest is depicted as a wise and trusted advisor to Moses in the subsequent narrative, instructing him in how best to structure his judicial administration (Exod 18:13–26).[192] Later still in the storyline, Moses begs his Midianite father-in-law to travel with them to the promised land, for Moses views him as an expert guide in traversing the wilderness, someone "who can serve as eyes for us" (wĕhāyîtā llānû lĕʿênāyim; Num 10:29–32 = J/non-P). There is no hint here of P's directives that Moses should instead be annihilating any and all Midianites. As for the Kenites, 1 Samuel 15:6 mentions how the Kenites dealt kindly with all the Israelites when they came out of Egypt (wĕʾattâ ʿāśîtâ ḥesed ʿim-kol-bĕnê yiśrāʾēl baʿălōtām mimmiṣrāyim)—an "obvious reference," asserts Levine (1993: 335), "to Exodus 18 and to Num 10:29–32." The most celebrated poem dealing with Kenites is Judges 5, one of the oldest passages in the Hebrew Bible.[193] Here we read of the actions of Jael, a "tent dwelling woman" (minnāšîm bāʾōhel). Her stature as eventual heroine is implied at the outset of the drama, as the stage is set with the laudatory phrase "in the days of Jael" (Judg 5:6).[194] The climatic event has Jael, "the wife of Heber the Kenite," dealing the death blow to the enemy general Sisera (Judg 5:24–26).[195] This Kenite woman is hailed as "most blessed of women" (<u>tĕbōrak minnāšîm yāʿēl</u> ʾēšet ḥeber haqqênî <u>minnāšîm bāʾōhel tĕbōrāk</u>) for her heroic actions, which are then recounted in detail with exquisite poetry. In the later prose account of the tale (Judg 4:17–22), Jael's defeat of Sisera is foretold in Deborah's prophecy as an event that Yahweh will bring about (Judg 4:9, 15).[196]

Moses' Father-in-Law: A Complicated Textual Tapestry

The Hebrew Bible also contains a complicated portrayal of Moses' father-in-law that must have resulted from varied textual traditions and literary strands that were used to weave the final tapestry that appears in the Hebrew Bible.[197] The heuristic chart that follows illustrates the situation as we find it in classical source criticism.[198]

Passage/ Source	Name of Individual +	Relation to Moses	Occupation/Tribal Association
Exod 2:16, 18, 21 [J]	Reuel "friend of El"	father-in-law (ø but cf. v. 21)	priest of Midian (*kōhēn midyān*)
Exod 3:1 [E]	Jethro	father-in-law (*ḥōtēn*) *ḥōtnô*	priest of Midian (*kōhēn midyān*)
Exod 4:18 [E]	Jeter/Jethro	father-in-law (*ḥōtēn*) *ḥōtnô*	ø [setting = Midian 4:19]
Exod 18:1–27 [E]	Jethro	father-in-law (*ḥōtēn mōšeh*)	priest of Midian (*kōhēn midyān*)
Num 10:29 [J]	Hobab Son of Reuel	father-in-law (*ḥōtēn mōšeh*)	Midianite *hammidyānî*
Judges 1:16	ø [LXX^A Hobab]	father-in-law (*ḥōtēn mōšeh*)	Kenite *qênî*
Judges 4:11	Hobab	father-in-law (*ḥōtēn mōšeh*)	Kenite *qênî/qayin*

In light of this confusion, Ernst Knauf (1992: 693; 1988) posits that "in the most ancient tradition, Moses' father-in-law seems to have been without a name." Unless harmonized, the data could imply that three different individuals (possibly four if Jeter in Exod 4:18 is separate from Jethro) were named as Moses' father-in-law or, following Rashi, that one individual simply went by multiple names. Of these three, two (Reuel and Jethro) bear the title "priest," while the other (Hobab) does not. Two (Reuel and Jethro) are distinctly identified as Midianite (and never as Kenite), while the other (Hobab) is associated with both Midianites and Kenites. Most problematic, both Reuel and his own son Hobab (according to Num 10:29) were Moses' father-in-law. In light of this, Albertz's (1994: 51) comment that "the tradition fluctuates a little" is somewhat of an understatement.

The various streams of tradition that underlie these data are no longer fully recoverable. Were one to harmonize the passages, the easiest route would be to identify Reuel and Jethro as the same individual, who is known by different names in variant traditions. An editor would have been responsible for conflating these variant traditions into the storyline as we have it. The most obvious discrepancy in the list is Hobab not being identified as a priest, a title of prestige that one would expect to be listed had an individual actually served in such a capacity. Albright (1963: 6) noted how the social roles of Jethro (elderly with seven daughters) and Hobab (a seemingly younger, vigorous wilderness guide) are distinctly different. Repointing *ḥōtēn* to the more generic *ḥātān* ("related by marriage") would result in Hobab being the *brother-in-law* of Moses.[199] This suggestion would have the advantage of erasing the conflict between Exodus 2 and Numbers 10:29 (both J) previously noted.

Who Taught Whom?

At the core of the Midianite hypothesis is that Jethro instructed Moses about Yahweh. Some adherents of the theory would even assert that Moses was trained in priestly functions by his father-in-law.[200] The theory is based on the "Jethro tradition" found in Exodus 18. This (traditionally E) account is privileged over J's "Reuel tradition," to which we will return.

It is easy to see why the proponents of the Midianite hypothesis chose to privilege Exodus 18 and ignore Exodus 2. It is not because Moses' father-in-law is identified as "a priest of Midian," since both traditions contain this designation (Exod 2:16 [J]; Exod 18:1 [E]). Rather, it is primarily due to Jethro's cultic activities. Upon hearing of Yahweh's deliverance of the Israelites from the Egyptians, he breaks out in superlative praise of Yahweh (Exod 18:9–11). Immediately thereafter, he presents burnt offerings and sacrifices (*'ōlâ ûzĕbāḥîm*) followed by partaking in a meal with Aaron and the elders of Israel (Exod 18:12). Herein lies the strength of the Midianite hypothesis. Adherents of the theory (e.g., Rowley 1950: 151) point out how such sacrifice can hardly be the action of a new initiate into the faith of Yahweh. Rather, asserts Rowley, Jethro was formerly "a properly initiated priest [of Yahweh]" who would not be "presid[ing] at the sacred feast unless his own God was being approached."

Critics of the hypothesis are quick to point out that nowhere is there any explicit reference to Jethro being "a priest of Yahweh" even in the three explicit references to his priestly office (Exod 2:16; 3:1; 18:1). A straightforward reading of Exodus 18:8 (as well as the logical function of the "recognition formula" of *'attâ* ["now, as a result"] in Exod 18:11) more likely implies that Moses, as the evangelist, helped bring about Jethro's conversion to Yahwism.[201] After all, the intent of Exodus 18:11 is apologetic in nature. As for Jethro's cultic acts, we are so far removed from ancient tribal norms that even with our best anthropological models it is sheer hubris to assert that we understand what priests, converts, and initiates could or could not do. Meek (1950: 95) adds that had Jethro been a priest of Yahweh "who initiated the Hebrew into his cult, it would surely have been on that ground that Moses would have invited him to join their journey" rather than "solely on the ground that he knew the desert and its camping places, and so would prove an efficient guide (Num. 10:29–32)."

Moreover, the name of Moses' mother, Yochebed, contains a Yahwistic theophoric element (not to mention the Levitical lineage in J's account in Exod 2).[202] Most importantly, at least for understanding the Hebrew Bible's ancestral (i.e., E) traditions, is the narrative in Exodus 3 (cf. too Exod 6:3 [P]) that describes the revelation of the name Yahweh to Moses as being intimately connected to the God of the three patriarchs (Exod 3:6, 13, 15–16). It would be hard to describe what the E tradition would be up to if it had Yahweh (speaking in the first person) saying that he was "the God of your fathers, the God of Abraham, of Isaac, and of Jacob" (wayyōʾmer ʾānōkî ʾĕlōhê ʾābîkā ʾĕlōhê ʾabrāhām ʾĕlōhê yiṣḥāq wēʾlōhê yaʿăqōb; Exod 3:16) while at the same time affirming the contradictory notion that Jethro's Midianite clan was the true originator of Yahwism, with Jethro being a pre-Mosaic priest of Yahweh. (Like Exod 3:16, Exod 18 is also traditionally assigned to the E literary strand.)

In the end, it is hard to reconstruct Jethro as the originator of Yahwism from the Hebrew Bible, which combines various traditions that all celebrate Yahweh's unique revelation to Moses. (On Moses as priest, see Chapter Ten, pp. 617–619.) This is not to assert that there could not have been extra-biblical traditions that preserved hagiographic traditions about Jethro as a "priest of Yahweh." Yet such traditions are not to be found in the Hebrew Bible, which does not accord Jethro such a title even though he is portrayed as a passionate Yahwist (Exod 18:9–12). Elsewhere the Hebrew Bible (i.e., the Deuteronomist) will assign the title "priest of Yahweh" (kōhēn yhwh) to the ill-fated priesthood at Shiloh (1 Sam 14:3). But the title is never accorded to Jethro, even in the J literary tradition. (E's reluctance to use Yahweh for Jethro's deity [e.g., Exod 18:19, 21, 23] is understandable.) Perhaps here is an appropriate time to revisit J's "Reuel tradition" (Exod 2:15b–22). Is it relevant that J's version of Moses' father-in-law has him bearing an El name? What does J have in mind when he speaks about this rēʿû-ʾēl ("friend of El" or "El is [my] companion") being a priest of Midian?[203] If anything, this would suggest, as Meek (1950: 95) observed long ago, that Moses' father-in-law "was originally a worshiper of the god El" and not Yahweh.

Updated Versions of the Midianite Hypothesis

In a series of works culminating in 1998, Cross (1973, 1983, 1988, 1998) argued for a "reformulated" Midianite hypothesis (see esp. 1998: 66ff). Central to Cross' theory is *not* the role of Moses' father-in-law but rather the role of Reuben as the firstborn of the patriarch Jacob and the conduit of archaic southern Yahwistic traditions. Cross (1998: 53) states an anthropological truism and then asks a simple question. The truism is that the placement of a person (and his tribe) at the head of a tribal list designates more than mere birth order, for "genealogies serve social, political, or religious functions" (sometimes more than one) and can "shift to meet new circumstances or changed social realities." If this is true, what accounts for Reuben's preeminence as the firstborn of Jacob? When we survey the reality of which tribes hold power, authority, and leverage, it is obvious that Judah and Levi hold the reins of royal and priestly power for most of Israel's history after the advent of the monarchy. Cross (1998: 53, 56) asserts that there was indeed a time when "Reuben once played a role in Israelite society, even a dominant one."[204] This "era of preeminence was early in the history of the tribes, perhaps in the formative era of Israel's religious and political self-consciousness." A hint can be found in the archaic poetry of Genesis 49:3, the Blessing of Jacob. Though it too speaks of Reuben's later demise (cf. Gen 49:4; Deut 33:6), it begins with his dominance:

Reuben, my firstborn,	*rĕʾûbēn bĕkōrî*
You are my strength,	*ʾattâ kōḥî*
The prime of my vigor,	*rēʾšît ʾônî*
Preeminent of rank,	*yeter śĕʾēt*
Preeminent of power.	*yeter ʿāz*

Cross' theory is too elaborate and detailed to rehearse here.[205] In the end Cross (1998: 68) argues that "there is good reason to believe that the religious traditions and military institutions that inspired and shaped the league stemmed from those elements of Israel who came from the southern mountains and entered Canaan from the lands of Reuben." This "migration or incursion from Reuben [contained] elements of Israel who came from the south, with ties to Midian, and whose original leader was Moses" (Cross 1998: 70). Yet over time, "Reuben's time of greatness [became] hidden . . . overlain by a patina of traditions stemming from later centers of power and prestige, in Joseph and Judah," as well as "the triumph of the Aaronids and the Zadokite house in Jerusalem" (1998: 56, 70).

Another scholar updating the Midianite hypothesis with the use of archaic poetry and southern caravan routes is David Schloen (1993a). Schloen bases his study on Judges 5, the archaic text we earlier noted that celebrates the heroism of Jael the Kenite woman, who kills the oppressive Canaanite general Sisera in her tent. Building on the work of Stager (1988), Schloen asks "why *any* of the Israelite tribes [mentioned in Judg 5] found it necessary to fight" a battle with an enemy of such superior force. After ruling out several motives (territorial conquest, countering Canaanite raids, asserting political hegemony), Schloen argues that Israelite highlanders had "a powerful incentive" to protect Midianite caravans and the lucrative trade upon which they were dependent. Schloen looks to hints in Judges 5:6–7 that mention caravan traffic being stifled by "Sisera and his Canaanite allies . . . through extortion of exorbitant tolls, or even outright plunder."[206] To buttress his arguments, Schloen (1993a: 26–27) reads *midyān* in Judges 5:10 as an explicit reference to the Midianites, who, given their joint economic interests, "celebrate the victories of Yahweh and his villagers in Israel" in the verse that follows.[207] As for the attention given by the poet to Jael, Schloen (1993a: 30–32) notes how "it is striking that at the climax of the narrative, it should be a Kenite and not an Israelite who vanquishes the foe." Such attention may hint at "some sort of alliance" between the Kenites and the Israelites, "symboliz[ing] the common cause [Jael's] people had made with the villagers of Israel." Finally, Schloen's theory attempts to solve the notable problem of "how the kings of Canaan expected to garner luxury goods [i.e., the silver, slaves, and textiles noted in Judg 5:19, 30] when they met the ["decidedly impoverished"] Israelite militia at Taanach." As Schloen (1993a: 30) notes, if these sought-after spoils are "typical caravan commodities, the difficulty vanishes." In summation, Schloen (1993a: 38) argues that Judges 5 provides "a glimpse" at how "a new ethnic identity involves the making of boundaries—inclusion and exclusion, alliance and enmity," fleshed out in particular as "the villagers of Yahweh [being] allied with caravan-trading Midianites (including Kenites and Amalekites) against a common enemy."

A decade later Schloen (2002: 59) would embrace Cross' 1998 formulation that "situates the original cult of Yahweh in northwest Arabia, where the theophanic mountain of Sinai should properly be located."[208] For Schloen, "Midianite caravans moving through inland Palestine in the early Iron Age were the carriers and proselytizers of this southern faith." Schloen briefly mentions "the intrinsic appeal of the new religion and its symbolization of the cosmos," yet he clearly places heavier weight on the political-economic incentives that led to the forging of Israel's Yahwistic identity: "The wealth and prestige of the first Arabian Yahwistic preachers, and the common political and economic interests of southern traders and highland villagers over against the lowland Canaanites may have played a role in fostering conversion to Yahwism."

In contrast to Cross, Stager, and Schloen, van der Toorn (1996b: 281) thinks it erroneous to assume "that the Israelites as an ethnic group honoured Yahweh as their common god well before the Monarchic Era." Instead, van der Toorn (1996b: 281–286) argues for "a modified form" of the Kenite hypothesis that tries to answer the question of why Saul, with links to the Gibeonites, would have chosen Yahweh to be his national deity instead of Baal or some other more prominent West Semitic deity. For van der Toorn (1996b: 284), it is "highly plausible that the Kenites introduced Israel to the worship of Yahweh, [yet] unlikely that they did so outside the borders of Palestine." More likely is that such beliefs were "brought to Transjordan and Central Palestine by traders along the caravan routes from the south to the east." Here van der Toorn (1996b: 284 n. 89) briefly and cautiously cites Schloen's caravan hypothesis. Van der Toorn (1996b: 286) admits that his case is "circumstantial," yet he is convinced that links between the Gibeonites and the Edomites are sufficient to claim that Saul's reign was the "turning point in both the political and religious history of Israel."[209] "Henceforth (with Saul's choice of Yahweh), the Israelites would be 'the people of Yahweh.'"

Topographic Allusions to Yahweh Coming from the South/Southeast

Most of these scenarios make mention of how archaic poetry in the Hebrew Bible (as well as the late ninth-/early eighth-century BCE inscriptions from Kuntillet ʿAjrud, also known as Ḥorvat Teman) connect Yahweh to southern locations.[210] It is best to assemble all of these references in a single place. Consider the following passages:

Judges 5:4–5

O Yahweh, when you set out from Seir,	*yhwh běṣēʾtěkā miśśēʿîr*
When you marched from the steppe of Edom,	*běṣaʿděkā miśśědēh ʾědôm*
The earth quaked,	*ʾereṣ rāʿāšâ*
Yea, the heavens rained,	*gam-šāmayim nāṭāpû*
Yea, the clouds rained water,	*gam-ʿābîm nāṭěpû māyim*
The mountains shuddered,	*hārîm nāzělû*
Before Yahweh, the one of Sinai,	*mippěnê yhwh zeh sînay*[211]
Before Yahweh, the God of Israel.	*mippěnê yhwh ʾělōhê yiśrāʾēl*

Psalm 68:8–9, 18 [Eng 68:7–8, 17]

O Yahweh, when you set out at the head of your army	*yhwh*[212] *běṣēʾtěkā lipnê ʿammekā*
When you marched in/from the wilderness,	*běṣaʿděkā bîšîmôn*
The earth quaked	*ʾereṣ rāʿāšâ*
Yea, the heavens rained	*ʾap šāmayim nāṭěpû*

Before Yahweh, the one of Sinai,	*mippĕnê yhwh zeh sînay*[213]
Before Yahweh, the God of Israel.	*mippĕnê yhwh ʾĕlōhê yiśrāʾēl*
...	
Yahweh's chariotry [numbers in] the myriads,	*rekeb yhwh ribbōtayim*
Thousands upon thousands;	*ʾalpê šinʾān*
Yahweh comes from Sinai ...	*yhwh bāʾ missînay* ...[214]

Deuteronomy 33:2[215]

Yahweh came from Sinai	*yhwh missînay bāʾ*
He dawned from Seir ...[216]	*zāraḥ miśśēʿîr lāmô*
He beamed forth from Mt. Paran.	*hôpîaʿ mēhar pāʾrān*

With him were myriads of holy ones,	*ʾittô-m*[217] *ribĕbōt qōdeš*
At/From his right hand fire flies forth,	*mîmînô ʾešdāt*[218] *lāmô*
Yea, the [???] of the troops.	*ʾap ḥōbēb ʿammîm*

Habakkuk 3:2a, 3–7

| O Yahweh, I heard of your fame, | *yhwh šāmaʿtî šimʿăkā* |
| I was frightened, Yahweh, by your deeds ... | *yārēʾtî yhwh pāʿālēkā* ... |

| Eloah came from Teman, | *ʾĕlôah mittêmān yābôʾ* |
| Qadosh [the Holy One] from Mt. Paran. | *qādôš mēhar-pāʾrān* |

His glory covered the heavens,	*kissâ šāmayim hôdô*
His splendor filled the earth	*tĕhillātô*[219] *mālĕʾâ hāʾāreṣ*
[his] radiance was like light.	*nōgah kāʾôr tihyeh*

| He had horns/rays [coming out] from his hand | *qarnayim miyyādô lô* |
| There he cloaked [?] his power | *šām ḥebyôn ʿuzzōh* |

| Before him went Pestilence, | *lĕpānāyw yēlek dāber* |
| Plague marched at his feet. | *yēṣēʾ rešep lĕraglāyw* |

He stood, and spanned the earth	*ʿāmad wayĕmōded ʾereṣ*
He scrutinized, and made the nations tremble,	*rāʾâ wayyattēr gôyim*
Ancient mountains crumbled	*yitpōṣĕṣû harĕrê-ʿad*
Age-old hills collapsed.	*šaḥû gibʿôt ʿôlām*
His ancient paths [were destroyed].	*hălîkôt ʿôlām lô*

...²²⁰

The tents of Cushan quaked,²²¹	'ohŏlê kûšān yirgĕzûn
Tent curtains of the land of Midian.	yĕrî'ôt 'ereṣ midyān

Kuntillet ʿAjrud, Pithos B²²²
Utterance of ʾAmaryaw: "Say to my lord: 'Is it well with you? I bless you by Yahweh of Teman and his asherah. May He bless you and may He keep you, and may He be with my lord.'"
'mr 'mryw 'mr l 'dn[y] hšlm 't brktk lyhwh tmn wl'šrth ybrk wyšmrk wyhy 'm 'd[n]y

Kuntillet ʿAjrud, Pithos B²²³
To Yahweh of the Southland and His asherah ... all which he asks from the compassion god [a compassionate man?] ... and may Yahw[eh] give him according to what is in his heart
[ ] lyhwh htmn wl' šrth [ ]kl 'šr yš'l m 'l ḥnn ('š ḥnn?) ... wntn lh yhw klbbh

Kuntillet ʿAjrud, plaster fragment 4.1.1²²⁴
May he prolong [their] days and may they be sated ... may they give to [Y]ahweh of Teman and His asherah ... Yahweh of the Southland has made things go well ...
[y']rk .ymm . wyśb'w ... ytnw l[y]hwh tmn wl'šrth ... hyṭb.yhwh. hty[mn]

Kuntillet ʿAjrud, plaster fragment 4.2²²⁵
... second time/years* ...
... with/during the earthquake, when El shines forth (or buffets?) [with fire?]; [Ya]hwe[h]* ...
... The mountains melt, the hills are crushed ...
... earth. The Holy One at/against the ever-flowing waters. He gazes like ...
  [Or: From/In] the land of Qadesh at the ever-flowing stream he looked upon [with favor]
... [??] to bless the (war-)lord [El? Yahweh?] on a day of war ...
... [to prai]se the name of El on a day of wa[r] ...
... šnt* ...
... brʾš.wbzrḥ. [or wbyrḥ] 'l b[ʿš] [y]hw[h]* ...
... r.wymsn. hrm. wydkn. pbnm
... [ ]ʾrṣ.qšdš.ʿl°y.ʾtʿnʿ/mʿ. ḥz.kr/s[
  Or: ... [m/b]ʾrṣ.qšdš.ʿl°y.ʾtʿnʿ/mʿ. ḥz.kr/s
... °kn lʿbrk. bʿl. bym. mlḥ[mh] ...
... [lhl]l šm 'l. bym. mlḥ[mh] ...

As seen in the archaic material, the Hebrew Bible contains enduring poetic traditions about Yahweh's presence in the south that resonate with the blessing texts and the militaristic wilderness theophany coming from the late ninth-/early eighth-century BCE Kuntillet ʿAjrud. One of the most fascinating narrative traditions in the Hebrew Bible is the ninth-century BCE prophet Elijah's flight to Mt. Horeb in the south, a healthy distance away from Mt. Carmel in the north, where the Gileadite prophet had his most glorious and triumphant public experience (1 Kgs 18). That Elijah heads to Mt. Horeb for his personal theophany blatantly underscores his connection to the southern locale where Moses too experienced Yahweh. According to 1 Kings 19, this mountain site (where Yahweh came to the prophet amidst wind, earthquake, fire, and voice) was located in the wilderness, a far-off journey in the steppe lands south of Beer-sheba. (Cogan [2001: 452] rightly notes that the reference to a forty-day and forty-night journey south lends a legendary feel to the story.)

Yet whereas 1 Kings 19 is written polemically against the use of storm god imagery (here Yahweh is *not* in the wind, earthquake, fire), the ancient poetry celebrates precisely Yahweh's march as a victorious warrior and storm god. Over and over again, the setting for his military march is from the south with respect to Judah (Seir, the steppe of Edom, Sinai, *yĕšîmôn*, Mt. Paran, Teman, Cushan, and Midian).[226] Indeed, Kuntillet ʿAjrud's reference to "*the* Teman" (*hty[mn]*) refers to "the Southland." While the precise southern locale of two of these places (*yĕšîmôn* and Cushan) is uncertain, the other places are more precisely known and point to areas south of the Dead Sea in and around the Wadi Arabah as it stretches southward to Midian.

Conclusions

The best conclusion with regard to the origin of the deity Yahweh would be one that is appropriately agnostic and yet adventurous enough to articulate which data and which scenarios are more likely to be on the right path.[227] It should be appropriately humble given our cultural and historical distance from Iron Age Israel, and it should also be appropriately complex, taking into account the complicated nature of our data.

Agnosticism comes easily. We simply do not know the historical origin of the deity Yahweh. Here Stager's (1998: 148) well-balanced conclusion strikes the right tone:

> Circumstantial evidence of time and place suggests Midianite antecedents and contributions to Yahwism. . . . [We have several] tantalizing hints about the relationship. But until more is known about Midianite religion, these connections will remain tentative at best.

As for the complex nature of any conclusion, the Propp Principle deserves to be referenced again:[228]

> Given the gaps in our knowledge, the complexity of historical processes and our inability to conduct proper experiments, we should aim rather for multiple, parallel hypotheses, as complex as the events they purport to explain. We can and must take into account the 95 percent of information hidden from our view, the sea bottom connecting solitary islands of data. The only sensible response to fragmented, slowly but randomly accruing evidence is radical open-mindedness. A single, simple explanation for a historical event is generally a failure of imagination, not a triumph of induction. (Propp 2006: 793)

What Can We Posit?

Given the Propp Principle, what can we posit from the approximately 5 percent of information that we possess? We submit that the uniform witness (of ancient poetic biblical sources and the inscriptions from Kuntillet ʿAjrud) to a southern tradition is telling. Moreover, not only does Yahweh march from the region of Seir, Edom, and Teman, but he is also consistently portrayed as "the one of Sinai" (*yhwh zeh sînay*).[229] Compare especially the nearly identical wording found in Judges 5:4–5 and Psalm 68:8–9 (see translations on pp. 279–280). The endurance of Mt. Sinai traditions (also found ubiquitously in narrative texts such as 1 Kgs 19) is significant, especially when it goes against expectations of Judean Yahwism (and in particular its royal cult), as McCarter (1992: 128) has pointed out:

> The persistence of the Sinai tradition is remarkable, because there was a natural tendency to eliminate it. That is, there was an understandable tendency to transfer the mountain location of the theophany of Yahweh to some place *within* the Promised Land, and specifically to Jerusalem. And, in fact, in the royal theology that grew up after the establishment of the Davidic dynasty, Mt. Zion was the sacred mountain. According to the Zion tradition, the Solomonic Temple was Yahweh's dwelling place forever (1 Kings 8:13). Why, then, didn't Mt. Zion displace Sinai altogether? The only explanation I know is that the old Sinai tradition was so venerable and well known, that it was so persistent and authentic, that it couldn't be suppressed.

In short, even in later Judean royal religion, Sinai remained as the paradigmatic locale of sacred revelation, reaching legendary status.

The 95 percent of information that Propp suggests is "hidden from our view" would include all the ways in which the tantalizing data discussed earlier might suggest "multiple, parallel hypotheses" for both the origin of Yahweh (through the heroism of a Moses? via Midianite clans? mediated through Kenite oral traditions?) and the possible locale of Mt. Sinai (in southern Edom? in northern Midian?), not to mention a Reubenite sanctuary on Mt. Nebo. Propp's "radical open-mindedness" would have us explore the mechanism for how such origin traditions traversed trade routes (via Shasu nomads? whose material culture lay in the Faynan region in southern Jordan? whose copper production may be reflected in the *nĕḥaš nĕḥōšet* lore of Num 21:9?),[230] ultimately ending up in southeastern territories (Edomite and Moabite) that came into contact with people groups (e.g., Reubenite clans) that in turn embraced Yahweh as their ancestral deity. Mechanisms for transmitting Yahwistic traditions from the Transjordan into tribal areas north and south of the Jezreel valley may very well have involved external economic interests and alliances (via Midianite caravans coming from the south?) as well as bards singing or writers inscribing religious lore (cf. the Deir ʿAlla texts, the narratives of Elijah the Tishbite from Gilead, and the strange case of Mt. Ebal).[231] In addition, surely one should be open to how the continuity of traditions about Yahweh could be maintained at non-state religious festivals (cf. 1 Sam 1) and perhaps even via "military muster ... [which could be an] occasion for contacts across greater distances."[232]

Similarly "hidden from our view" is how trade routes passing through strategic southern locales (such as at Kuntillet ʿAjrud but earlier) would have facilitated the transfer of Yahwistic origin traditions into inland Canaan, where they might have been written down by scribes using a distinctly South Canaanite (or Proto-Hebrew) scribal tradition. Though we cannot determine precisely the medium, eventually these origin-of-Yahweh traditions would be wed with the royal cult of David and Solomon in Jerusalem as well as that of northern kings proclaiming allegiance to "Yahweh of Samaria." Finally, Propp's "complexity of historical processes" would also include the decidedly different ways in which some later groups (reflected in the P literary tradition) emphasized the unique self-disclosure of this god Yahweh to the Moses of Exodus fame (Exod 6:2–3), while others (reflected in the J tradition) imagined Yahweh's origin to be even older, going all the way back to the days of Enosh (Gen 4:26).

Ethnic Self-Identification

At the same time, we should juxtapose Propp's "multiple, *parallel* hypotheses" with hypotheses that run counter-parallel.[233] Just as messy to discern, if not messier, this line of thinking would underscore how the origin of Yahweh was a part of a multifaceted process of ethnic self-identification and boundary marking.[234] As we will see in the following chapters, identity formation and complex processes of legitimization and differentiation—the defining of oneself and one's group against others (often polemically), which includes the construction and maintenance of boundaries—are constants throughout ancient Israel's history. As Carly Crouch (2014: 114) has emphasized, "the definition and protection of Israelite identity" arise "out of social, economic and political circumstances"—and religion is integral at every turn.²³⁵ Perhaps an early reflex of the use of religion is found in Judges 5:8, where mention is made of tribes "choosing new gods" (*'ĕlōhîm ḥădāšîm*), especially in a heightened battle context, "when war was at the gates."

Though certain groups may have had an underlying understanding of kinship (see the earlier discussion of the Midianites as an Abrahamic people), they nonetheless defined themselves against even their closest of kin (real or fictive). Thus even though etiological tales were told of Moab being the son of Abraham's nephew Lot (Gen 19:30–38), Moabites came to be identified as those who worshipped the god Chemosh. Ammonites, descended from the other son of Lot, worshipped the deity Milcom. Jacob's brother Esau, "red/ruddy and hairy" (*'admônî, śē'ār/śā'îr*; Gen 25:25; 27:11), moves (appropriately so) "to the land of Seir, the country of Edom" (*'arṣâ śē'îr śĕdēh 'ĕdôm*; Gen 32:3; 36:8–9), whence marched Yahweh. Nonetheless, Esau's heirs, the Edomites, were known as those who worshipped the god Quas/Qos. As for Jacob/Israel, his people were self-identified and recognizably marked (especially in the archaic poetry noted earlier) as those who chose to worship the storm god Yahweh, who was thought to fight on their behalf. Granted, alternative traditions would describe the decision in more theological terms. In this perspective, cast in remote antiquity, it was El Elyon who made the choice for them.²³⁶

> Remember the days of old,
> Consider the years of many generations;
>
> Ask your father, and he will tell you;
> Your elders, and they will inform you.
>
> When Elyon [*'elyôn*] allotted the nations,
> When he divided the human race,
>
> He fixed the boundaries of peoples,
> Equal to the number of divine beings [*bĕnê 'ĕlōhîm*].²³⁷
>
> Lo, his [Elyon's] people became Yahweh's portion,²³⁸
> Jacob his allotted heritage ... (Deut 32:7–9)

The boundary marking that is concomitant with ethnic self-identification can be seen in texts early and late. As early as Exodus 15 we read of (the then new and revised) boundary marking, which gives no hint that the deity who was praised for vanquishing the Edomites and Moabites "with terror and dread" once marched from a homeland in Edom or dwelt in a sanctuary on Mt. Nebo.

They were dismayed	ʾāz nibhălû
the clans of Edom,	ʾallûpê ʾĕdôm
the rams of Moab	ʾêlê môʾāb
seized by terror,	yōʾḥăzēmô rāʿad
melted	nāmōgû
all Canaan's inhabitants.	kōl yōšĕbê kĕnāʿan
You fell on them	tippōl ʿălêhem
[with] terror and dread,	ʾêmātâ wāpaḥad
By your great power	bigdōl zĕrôʿăkā
they were still as stone.	yiddĕmû kāʾāben (Exod 15:15–16)

The late Deuteronomy 2:1–6 acknowledges that the people had "traversed Mt. Seir for many days" (Deut 2:1). Yet once again there is no hint of celebrating Yahweh as victoriously "dawning" from this region, as we have in the archaic poetry (Deut 33:2), or of being blessed by Yahweh of Teman/the Southland, as mentioned in the inscriptions from Kuntillet ʿAjrud. Rather, this territory is divinely marked as Edomite ("I have given Mt. Seir to Esau as a possession"; Deut 2:5). The boundary lines could not be drawn more dramatically: "I will not give you of their land so much as a foot can tread on" (Deut 2:5).

The Northern Canaanite Cultural Continuum Redux

We have emphasized that there is substantial evidence (linguistic data, geographic determinants, and material culture) of a widespread and enduring Canaanite cultural continuum between Syria and Egypt from the Middle Bronze Age on and especially in the Late Bronze Age (e.g., the Ugaritic texts and the Amarna letters; the data we are able to glean from Phoenician sources coincide). *That this Canaanite cultural continuum continues into the Iron Age is especially apparent in the realm of religion, except for a single datum: the complete absence of Yahweh.* Here the historian of Israelite religion must again remain agnostic. We simply do not know the social settings and mechanisms by which the widespread pre-Israelite Canaanite lore (e.g., both the family religion of El traditions and the storm and warrior themes associated with Baal) was woven on to the god Yahweh of southern, southeastern, and Transjordanian fame.[239] What we can assert was that it was—and so thoroughly that it is unmistakable. Yahweh's origin seems to be southern, yet many of the garments put onto Yahweh are sewn from northern and inland Canaanite cloth. And yet over time the deity Yahweh would become central to the differentiation process whereby Israel's ethnic boundaries were constructed and maintained.[240]

7
The Iconography of Divinity: Yahweh

Section I: The Iconography of Yahweh: Anthropomorphic and Theriomorphic Traditions

Currently there is no consensus as to whether Yahweh was represented in either anthropomorphic or theriomorphic form. As will become apparent in the discussions that follow, literary and archaeological challenges will offer discomfort for scholars no matter what position they hold. On the literary side, one reads of an aniconic Yahweh being enthroned invisibly above the winged cherubim or described with "Name" (*šēm*) and "Glory" (*kābôd yhwh*) theologies. Other voices add commandments against graven images (Exod 20:4, 23), divine pronouncements that "one cannot see God's face and live" (Exod 33:20, 23), and prophetic parodies mocking the fashioning of the divine in material substance (e.g., Jer 10:1–6, Isa 40:19–20; 41:5–14; 44:6–22). Yet at the same time, and in striking contrast, one reads of various body parts of Yahweh on almost every other page of the Hebrew Bible, not to mention the erection of bull images for "the Mighty One of Jacob."

In the field of archaeology, we come across first-rate scholars asserting that we have never found any image of Yahweh alongside other premier scholars who claim the very opposite. The former assert that "the perennial search for . . . Yahweh-statues goes on apace but it is as unlikely as ever to produce results" (Hallo 1988: 54). The latter counter that archaeology attests not just one but multiple examples of divine images of Yahweh (Uehlinger 1997). Moreover, they add, because these figures come from a variety of sites, logic would posit that a divine image once stood in the Jerusalem Temple as well. The following analysis will sketch various arguments and data (text and object) relevant to the debate.

Anthropomorphic Representations of Yahweh in Textual Sources

When analyzing the Hebrew Bible's viewpoint on representing the deity Yahweh, it is helpful once again to remember that while biblical tradition may speak with a uniform voice on a particular topic, it nonetheless includes a variety of nuances, the certain outcome of literary traditions growing over hundreds of years and voiced by authors and editors of different perspectives. Thus even within the aniconic tradition's assertion that Yahweh is not to be portrayed in concrete form, we see diversity. Strikingly different portrayals are woven together in the Hebrew Bible's composite picture. Consider how the picture of Yahweh majestically (though invisibly) enthroned above the winged cherubim contrasts with the altogether different abstract notion of him taking up divine residence via his sacred "Name" (*šem*), which is itself conceptually quite distinct from the notion that Yahweh's "Glory" (*kābôd yhwh*) represents his tangible presence.

The Hebrew Bible challenges all these portrayals. It has no qualms about describing Yahweh in human terms and with human body parts (apart from genitalia).[1] Archaic poetry celebrates Yahweh as a "*man of war*" (*'îš milḥāmāh*) whose right *hand* shatters his enemies and whose *nostrils* blast waters into a pile (Exod 15:3, 6, 8). The highly anthropomorphic representation of Yahweh is one of the defining characteristics of the Yahwist's (J's) literary style. In contrast to P's more transcendent picture, the Yahwistic source presents a God who *fashions* a man from clay (Gen 2:7), *plants* a garden (Gen 2:8), *walks* in the garden of Eden (Gen 3:8), *makes* clothes (Gen 3:21), is grieved in his *heart* (Gen 6:6), *seals* the door of the Ark (Gen 7:16), *smells* the pleasing aroma of Noah's sacrifice (Gen 8:21), visits Sodom and Gomorrah to *see* what is happening (Gen 18:21), and even *bargains* with Abraham (Gen 18:22–32). Exodus 33:11 is most explicit in describing how Yahweh "*speaks* with Moses *as a man speaks* to his friend" (*ka'ăšer yĕdabbēr 'îš 'el rē'ēhû*; cf. Deut 34:10).[2] Additional examples can be found throughout the Hebrew Bible (in various literary genres and from all periods) by simply noting the various human features (e.g., face, head, eyes, arms, hands, legs, feet), human occupations, and social relations used to describe the divine.[3]

In dealing with hundreds of years of literary activity, we see that there were certainly lesser degrees of emphasis, as well as multiple voices emphatically underscoring that Yahweh is God and not human. Consider the nuances within the priestly traditions. H is comfortable speaking of offerings as a type of "food" for God, as they are transformed through fire into a *rêyaḥ nîḥōaḥ lĕyhwh*, a phrase usually translated as "a pleasing aroma for Yahweh" or a "soothing, appeasing odor for Yahweh."[4] In either case, the notion implies that the deity has nostrils. In contrast, as Knohl has emphasized, P "systematically attempts to remove all anthropomorphisms from the name of Yahweh."[5] In particular, "the description of the Presence [*kābôd*] of God, as it is revealed to all of Israel, lacks all human dimension."[6] Turning elsewhere, the prophet Hosea has Yahweh proclaim "I am God and not human" (*kî 'ēl 'ānōkî wĕlō'-'îš*) to underscore divine compassion (Hos 11:9), as does Balaam (*lō' 'îš 'ēl wiykazzēb*) to underscore divine honesty (Num 23:19). The Deuteronomist proclaims that "Yahweh sees not as humans see" (*kî lōʾ ʾăšer yirʾeh hāʾādām... wayhwh yirʾeh lallēbāb*) because he can perceive the human heart (1 Sam 16:7). Job complains that God is not human, as Job is (*kî lōʾ ʾîš kāmōnî*), and so Job would not stand a chance at trial in a case against him (Job 9:32), while at the same time using God's lack of human properties to argue his complaint against him (Job 10:4-6).

Yet overall, anthropomorphic descriptions of Yahweh are ever present. In Genesis 32, God shows up as a man (*ʾîš*) with whom Jacob wrestles at a place he then calls "the Face of God" (*pĕnîʾēl*). Yahweh uses the palm of his hand (*kap*) to shield Moses from his glory, but then allows him to see his back (*ʾāḥōr*; Exod 33:23). Isaiah seats Yahweh on a throne, as does the Deuteronomist (Isa 6:1-2; 1 Kgs 22:19). Jeremiah takes a cup from the very hand of Yahweh (Jer 25:15-17), while the divine hand in Ezekiel 8:2 grabs the prophet by a lock of his hair. Job's divine slayer gnashes his teeth and pierces with his eyes (Job 16:9). Apocalyptic literature mentions a disembodied hand (of God) (Dan 5:5; cf. Exod 31:18; Deut 9:10) and will even dress the "Ancient of Days" with the appropriate white raiment and matching hair (Dan 7:9). Conceptually, the editors of the Hebrew Bible found it perfectly acceptable to juxtapose an embodied Yahweh in literature with denouncements of anyone attempting to craft such a body in physical form.

There are occasional pauses where authors were more reflective about how they used anthropomorphic language to describe Yahweh. The author of Numbers 12 describes Moses as privileged[7] to see the *tĕmunāh* ("form, semblance, likeness") of Yahweh, which, though evidently not a full manifestation, is nonetheless of a higher order than a "vision" (*marʾeh*).[8] Similarly, in Exodus 33:23 Yahweh declares that Moses may see his "back" (*ʾāḥōr*) rather than his "face" (*pānîm*).

Yet it is Ezekiel who excels all others in the cautious use of anthropomorphic language to describe Yahweh. In his description of the theophany (Ezek 1:26-28; cf. 8:2), he uses the words for "human being" (*ʾādām*) and "loins" (*motnayîm*) to describe, as Moshe Greenberg (1983: 52) put it, "an effulgent human figure... all brilliant and fiery, and encased by a rainbow radiance... the Majesty of God." Yet the priest-prophet qualifies his depiction with explicit words of restraint that occur so frequently, his intention cannot be missed. In particular, he uses three words for comparison (*marʾeh, dĕmût, ʿên*) a total of fourteen times in three verses! In language befitting a vision or dream (cf. *marʾôt ʾĕlōhîm* in 1:1), he portrays the human-like divine figure opaquely. Only by analogy is a given property of the divine articulated to have the "appearance" or "likeness" of something tangible. Ezekiel's rhetoric of circumvention (what Greenberg called "buffer terms") will be unpacked together with his preoccupation with describing Yahweh through multiple "radiant" images (see pp. 373-379).

Yet such circumvention is rare and surely the product of Ezekiel's desire as a priest to differentiate the Most Sacred from the profane, even if the profane objects of comparison are gleaming metals (*kěʿên ḥašmal*), fire (*ʾēš*), and radiant brightness (*nōgah*).⁹ Ezekiel's description of the divine in 1:26–28 is the axiomatic exception that proves the rule. The norm was to use anthropomorphic language to describe Yahweh.

There is no attempt in the Hebrew Bible to circumvent literary anthropomorphism of the divine, as we have with later traditions such as those found in the Aramaic Targums. There we find "a general tendency towards the transcendentalization of God" (Grossfeld 1988: 19) that avoids anthropomorphic language when speaking of Yahweh's presence. The use of paraphrases and/or substitutes such as the Memra ("command, word"), the Yeqara ("majesty, honor"), and the Shekinta ("residing presence") of God try to avoid expressing the corporeality of God.¹⁰ Yet we see no such circumvention in the Hebrew Bible. The closest we come is P's suppression of anthropomorphic language used of God and Ezekiel's unique formulation.¹¹

Do Anthropomorphisms and Metaphors Indicate a Divine Image of Yahweh?

Unpacking the abstract ideas behind aniconism requires considerable discussion. How did the various biblical authors and editors handle the antinomy of not representing Yahweh as corporeal in metal, stone, and wood while freely mentioning his body parts in their literary compositions? Equally important is Herbert Niehr's (1997: 74) double query: How would Yahweh have been perceived as being vitally present in the Jerusalem Temple, and how would actual temple ritual have worked without a divine image?

Yet first one should consider the thesis of several scholars who solve such tensions by claiming that they are based on false assumptions. They argue that the physical descriptions of Yahweh are precisely that: physical descriptions. And divine images of Yahweh were indeed fashioned, especially for rituals that took place in the Jerusalem Temple; the production of such images was a regular practice elsewhere in the ancient Near East. After looking at this thesis, we will turn our attention to archaeology to see how it squares with the various literary positions.

Excursus: Was There an Anthropomorphic Divine Image of Yahweh in the Jerusalem Temple?

The Argument
Scholars who have argued that there were divine images of Yahweh (and especially an anthropomorphic statue of Yahweh as a focal point in the Jerusalem Temple) include Manfried Dietrich and Oswald Loretz (1992: 158–172),

Christoph Uehlinger (1993, 1996, 1997, 2006), Brian Schmidt (1996), Bob Becking (1997, 2006), Herbert Niehr (1997, 2003), and Karel van der Toorn (1997b, 2002); cf. Berlejung (2017: 75–77). Seven key concepts are central to this argument.

1. The cultures of ancient Israel's neighbors were uniform in that they *all* emphasized the need for divine images of their deities. All types of ritual activity (processions, sacrifices, offerings, prayers) had the gods' divine images as their focus. The divine image (usually crafted of precious material) took center stage in the inner sanctums of ancient Near Eastern temples and sanctuaries. This is amply documented in text and archaeology. Thus, asserts this thesis, it makes perfect sense to start here and assume that ancient Israel is part and parcel of the ancient Near East, with past claims for the uniqueness of aniconism being more the fruit of the history of scholarship than the realia of Iron Age cult. In Niehr's (1997: 93) words: "There is no reason to assume that the cult of the First Temple deviated from the predominant ancient Near Eastern practice."
2. Reading between the lines, we can infer from the various injunctions against the use of divine images that such images were indeed a reality. Here Uehlinger's (1993: 281; 2006: 84) succinct words are apt: "Had 'Israel' not known images, no veto would ever have been conceived." "The prohibition of cultic images . . . presupposes the knowledge and practice of iconolatry in at least some circles of Judahite society."
3. The various texts describing the aniconic tradition "should not be read as mirrors of factual reality" (Uehlinger 2006: 84). Here one can easily document past historians of ancient Israelite religion who uncritically parroted the Deuteronomistic, prophetic, or priestly viewpoints. Instead, readers should treat the texts at our disposal as "collective memory struck by a kind of amnesia, as a result of which the once flourishing worship of images was now remembered as a foreign intrusion into the religion of the fathers. The authors responsible for the metamorphosis . . . are the Deuteronomists" (van der Toorn 1997b: 240). In Niehr's words, the Hebrew Bible presents the "strong ideological bias" of certain exilic and post-exilic theologians. What we have is a "completely misleading picture," the product of a Deuteronomistic "coalition" of concealment (Niehr 1997: 74, 82).

Other scholars nuance the debate differently by suggesting that there were a variety of Yahwisms, of which aniconic Yahwism was only one option. "Concrete depictions of animals, humans, and the greater and lesser lights were eliminated as acceptable symbols and receptacles of YHWH by biblical writers," remarks

Schmidt (1996: 96), "although they undoubtedly served as images in the competing versions of Yahweh religion." Similarly, Becking (1997: 158) writes that "the aniconic Yahwism in its monotheistic form was only one of a variety of Yahwisms." Uehlinger (1997: 153) argues that future researchers should address "competing Yahweh iconographies by not only differentiating the Israelite from the Judahite traditions . . . but also rivaling traditions within Israelite and/or Judahite society."

4. Some biblical passages *explicitly* mention a divine image for Yahweh. According to Niehr (1997: 89), "the original *Sitz im Leben* of [the] anthropomorphic mode of speaking about YHWH is evident in the cult surrounding his statue in the First Temple." Descriptions of Yahweh's garments, sandals, and jewels are not mere metaphorical expressions (1997: 89). "The most simple and most plausible explanation of the phrase 'to see the face of YHWH'" is "the existence of a divine statue" (1997: 84; cf. Uehlinger 1997: 148).
5. Some biblical passages *implicitly* mention a divine image for Yahweh. That the Jerusalem Temple is referred to as the "House of Yahweh" suggests a resident inhabitant: "This locution implies that gods dwelt in their temples as humans did in their houses" (Niehr 1997: 75; cf. van der Toorn 2002: 48–49).

Becking (2006) argues that the motif of the "return of the deity" in the Hebrew Bible is best understood in its ancient Near Eastern context to refer to the return of the divine image. In particular, Becking (2006: 57) uses the Ketiv of Jeremiah 31:21 ("the road that I [= Yahweh] will go") to conclude the following: "Because ancient Israelite tradition was one part of a greater ancient Near Eastern whole, we may presume that the return of the Israelite divine from Exile should be construed as the carrying home of a tangible object."

Lastly, consider how the erection of Asherah images by Queen Maacah and King Manasseh prompts van der Toorn (1997b: 239; 2002: 50) to suggest the following: "Since an image of Asherah was present in the temple in Jerusalem (1 Kgs 15:13; 2 Kgs 21:7; 2 Kgs 23:6), there is every reason to suspect that her consort also was represented by an image."

6. Two identical hexagonal cuneiform prisms from Nimrud contain a description of the booty Sargon II derived from his conquest of Samaria. Among the items mentioned are "the gods in whom they trusted" (DINGIR.MEŠ [*ilāni*] *tiklīšun*). This text is mentioned by several scholars advocating the theory of a divine image of Yahweh, with detailed analyses appearing in Becking 1997 and in Uehlinger 1997: 123–128; 1998 (and, in opposition,

Na'aman 1999, 2006a: 311–338).[12] Becking (1997: 166) concludes that the phrase "the gods in whom they trusted" is not a mere literary topos and that "the divine images taken away were most probably not theriomorphic, but anthropomorphic." The mention of "Yahweh of Samaria" in the Kuntillet 'Ajrud inscription has led some scholars of this thesis to identify Yahweh and Asherah as "the gods in whom they trusted." Becking (1997: 166) finds such a suggestion "attractive, but [it] remains to be proven." After positing a divine image of Yahweh in a temple in Samaria, some scholars by analogy then assert that a similar divine image resided in the Jerusalem Temple and was similarly taken away by Nebuchadrezzar.

7. A driving force behind the theory (if not *the* driving force) is the presence of various archaeological figures thought to represent Yahweh. The fullest collection can be found in Uehlinger 1997: 152. Uehlinger concludes that his vast catalogue of data is "definitely sufficient to make the hypothesis [of an anthropomorphic divine image of Yahweh] more reasonable and probable than its opposite."

The Response
How can one respond to these points?

1. It makes perfect sense to assume for the sake of argument that there was a divine image in the Jerusalem Temple. The rest of the current chapter will test various exemplars to see if such a hypothesis can be proven empirically. It is an altogether different and misguided methodological step to assume in one's comparative method that all ancient Near Eastern cultures were uniform. See the comments on comparative methodology in Chapter Three, pp. 69–72.
2. It is a truism that the existence of laws reflects an underlying social reality to which those laws correlate. References to cultic images (divine and otherwise) are common in the Hebrew Bible. Yet their existence must be analyzed on a passage-by-passage basis with an eye toward determining the reality they signified and for whom they signified it (see, for example, the discussion of Jeroboam's bull images on pp. 198–200, 318–322).
3. As with all literature, a variety of perspectives, ideologies, and motives are in play. Biblical texts both can and cannot mirror reality. Rather than positing blanket statements assuming large-scale "coalitions of concealment" meant to misrepresent *all* "factual reality," it is more likely that the views of ancient writers were multidimensional. The study of individual texts (again on a case-by-case basis) must articulate the multiple nuances of authors and editors alike. It is agreed that ancient Israelite religion was more pluralistic than our texts lead us to believe

4 and 5. Contra Niehr, there is no reason metaphorical expressions of Yahweh's body cannot be "the most simple and most plausible explanation."[13] Either view (physical or literary representation) can be valid (cf. Schwartz 2010).[14] Neither should be privileged from the outset. Referring to the Jerusalem Temple as being "God's house" need not imply a physical divine image in residence any more than how God is thought to reside in various "houses" of worship today. As van der Toorn (2002: 48) admits: "That [a god] was believed to inhabit [a house] ... need not imply that this presence took the form of an image." Moreover, as Tryggve Mettinger (2006: 277) underscores in light of West Semitic cults of standing stones, it certainly does not require an anthropomorphic image.

Even passages such as Isaiah 6:1 (where the prophet says that he "saw the Lord sitting upon a throne, high and exalted") need not imply a divine image, even though the vision is based on the physical Jerusalem Temple and not a heavenly sanctuary (so Williamson 2007: 124–126). Williamson's careful study shows how the phrase is a part of the narrative structure (cf. 1 Kgs 22:19) and is similar in phraseology to Amos 9:1 ("I saw the Lord standing beside the altar"). Equally important, Isaiah 6:1–4 envisions a deity of enormous size. Williamson (2007: 129) concludes: "That he exceeds by far the confines of the sanctuary ... seems easier conceptually to derive from the presence of an empty throne than from one on which there was a cult statue of *ex hypothesi* limited size."

While divine images do indeed travel in the ancient Near East (see Chapter Five, pp. 136–138), metaphorical travel is common as well. Becking even acknowledges the well-known literary motif of the *eschatologische Wundersstrasse* (especially prominent in Deutero-Isaiah) that promises the return of Yahweh to Jerusalem.

The existence of Asherah images in the Jerusalem Temple need not imply coexisting Yahweh images. After all, our knowledge of the existence of Asherah images comes from the pejorative portrayal of them by the Deuteronomists, who, one would have to assume, would have heaped vitriolic criticism on Manasseh had he also erected a divine image of Yahweh contrary to the Deuteronomistic "Name" (*šem*) theology (2 Kgs 21:7). Likewise, the same Deuteronomists who mention Josiah's destruction of the Asherah images associate her vessels with those of the god Baal, not Yahweh as consort (2 Kgs 23:4–6).

6. A detailed discussion of the Nimrud prisms is beyond the scope of this study. Suffice it to say that the interpretation put forth by Becking and others has not gone without challenge. In particular, Nadav Na'aman (1999, 2006a) challenges the historical reliability of its claim about Sargon's removal of divine images because the episode is missing from the almost identically worded Khorsabad annals. According to Na'aman (1999: 398;

2006a: 317–318), "the analysis of the Nimrud Prism indicates that it is an inferior source compared with Sargon's earlier inscriptions, and that its author felt free to manipulate his sources and write his own version of Sargon's campaigns." Specifically, "in his effort to magnify the Assyrian conquest of Samaria, [he] inserted the motif of the spoliation of divine images into his account . . . the statement ["the gods in whom they trusted"] is a literary embellishment by the later author and does not reflect a genuine historical memory of the captivity of the cult images of Samaria."

Whatever the final analysis of the historicity of the Nimrud prisms' remark, the notion of there being divine images in Samaria should occasion little surprise, especially in light of the bull images erected by Jeroboam (see Chapter Five, pp. 198–200, and pp. 318–322 in this chapter). Indeed, Na'aman (1999: 414; 2006a: 332) concludes: "It is not impossible that anthropomorphic images of YHWH were also set in some Israelite sanctuaries, although no conclusive evidence for such statues has been found." In addition, divine and other cultic images of Samaria are mentioned in the Lucianic rendering of 2 Kings 18:34 ("where are the gods/is the god of Samaria?") as well as in Isaiah 10:11, where Samaria's images (*ĕlîlîm*) are found in parallel to Jerusalem's (*ăṣabbîm*).[15] Yet the nature of our source material renders any attempt to identify these Samarian deities highly precarious. Consider the pejorative language being used by the author of Isaiah 10:11, who thinks of these images as worthless idols (*ĕlîlîm, ăṣabbîm*).[16] We may add to this the Deuteronomists' theological lens, whereby we read that Sargon's capture of Samaria was a result of the people sinning against Yahweh by fearing other gods (*ĕlōhîm ăḥērîm*), not to mention a catalogue of other acts deemed illegitimate, with special mention of Jeroboam's bull images and the deities Baal, Asherah, and the "host of heaven" (2 Kgs 17:16). If the images were of Yahweh, we would never know it explicitly from this source material, which if anything points in the other direction. The only clear hint is the Deuteronomist's refracted notion that the king of Assyria returned a Samarian priest to teach Yahwistic faith to the foreigners he settled in Bethel (2 Kgs 17:24–28).

Yet the discussion of a supposed image of Yahweh in Samaria is off-topic for the present excursus. If Yahweh was represented in anthropomorphic or, more likely, theriomorphic form in Samaria, this need not imply anything about whether there was a divine image of Yahweh in the Jerusalem Temple (cf. Mettinger 2006: 280–281). Though "ancient Israelite religion" is the rubric used among historians of religion, historically one must clearly differentiate "Israelite" religion from "Judean" religion (cf. Uehlinger 1997: 153; Na'aman 1999: 394–395; 413–415; 2006a: 313–314, 331–333).

There is no mention of any divine image of Yahweh in the Jerusalem Temple in the biblical corpus or in Mesopotamian literature. Nebuchadrezzar carried off "all the treasures of the temple of Yahweh" and "cut in pieces all the vessels of gold in the temple of Yahweh" (2 Kgs 25:13–17; cf. Jer 52:17–23; 2 Chr 36:18–19). If the divine image of Yahweh was such a preeminent focal point, would not we expect its specific mention? When these vessels are enumerated, they include bronze pillars, the bronze sea, cult stands, pots, shovels, snuffers, gold and silver basins and bowls, incense dishes, firepans, lampstands, and "other vessels" of even lower importance (2 Kgs 25:13–17; Jer 52:17–23; Ezra 1:7–11). No mention is made of a divine image.

Neither does Jeremiah or any other author refer to the divine image in the delivery of temple vessels in 597 BCE (Jer 27:16–18; 28:3; cf. 2 Kgs 24:13; 2 Chr 36:7, 10). The Babylonian Chronicle mentions "heavy tribute" (Millard 1997: 468). That no mention is made in a Mesopotamian source, with that culture's emphasis on divine images being taken in battle, is telling.

Other biblical texts concur. Earlier, King Ahaz dismantles the bronze altar, cult stands, the laver, the bronze sea, and the bronze oxen (2 Kgs 16:14, 17; cf. 16:8; 2 Chr 28:24). No mention is made of the destruction of any image of Yahweh. When the Judean king Amaziah installs Edomite divine images (*ĕlōhîm*), there is no mention of him setting them next to an image of Yahweh in a cult niche (2 Chr 25:14–16).[17] Finally, if there was a divine image of Yahweh in the Jerusalem Temple that functioned as the focal point of worship, why are there no ritual texts describing its making and consecrating (similar to the texts noted on pp. 129–136)?

Admittedly, these are answers from silence and from texts that have been edited by those sympathetic to aniconic theology. Yet Na'aman (1999: 404–408; 2006a: 323–327) suggests that the historical and archaeological pictures from Lachish and Arad may provide useful analogies. Sennacherib's destruction of Lachish and deportation of its booty is depicted in great detail in the iconographic record of his palace in Nineveh. Na'aman notes that the cultic vessels that are carried off are bronze incense stands, not the prized statue of the deity of the city. The Arad sanctuary's image was that of a standing stone, not an anthropomorphic statue (see pp. 183–187). Following Mettinger, Na'aman (1999: 413; 2006a: 331) concludes that "all the available evidence from the Kingdom of Judah supports the assumption of the image of YHWH in the eighth-seventh centuries BCE as aniconic and that YHWH was represented in the cult places by a standing stone (*maṣṣebah*)."

Finally, Ronald Hendel (1997) has provided corroboration from an anthropological perspective. Hendel, blending the insights of James Barr and Mary Douglas, has drawn new attention to the leitmotif of "lethal God sightings" found in non- and pre-Deuteronomistic stories of theophanies (e.g., those of Jacob, Moses, Gideon, Manoah, and Isaiah).[18] A handful of blessed individuals note with surprise that despite seeing God "face-to-face," they escaped death. According to Exodus 33:20, "one cannot see God and live." According to Hendel (1997: 221–222), the belief in "deadly God-sightings" is "best understood as a motif of Israelite folklore, rooted in popular conceptions concerning purity and danger." Moreover, he asserts (correctly in my opinion) that "the lethal danger of seeing God is . . . related to the problem of anthropomorphic representation of deity and to the de facto aniconism of the Yahwistic cult."

If proponents are correct that Yahweh had a cult statue and that his adherents regularly viewed Yahweh's image in cult processions similar to those in Mesopotamia and Egypt, how does one account for the traditions of lethal God sightings? If adherents saw God on a regular basis (and viewed the image in Israel as the full embodiment of divinity similar to Mesopotamia), then what would make one think that (1) seeing God was an unusual privilege according only to the blessed few, and (2) it was in any way lethal? In short, it seems more likely that we should take the biblical tradition at face value in its assertion that there was *not* an anthropomorphic statue of Yahweh in the Jerusalem Temple.

7. Archaeology is indeed key to resolving the issue at hand and will occupy a good deal of the discussion that follows. Though Uehlinger (1997: 152) sometimes refers to his large catalog of evidence as "clear," "indisputable," and "definitely sufficient," he wisely modulates his conclusion, affirming that "our picture still remains awkwardly fragmentary." In particular, he admits that "we are still unable to identify beyond a doubt a Yahweh image as such, either from Israel or from Judah." Nonetheless, though using cautionary words, Uehlinger certainly advocates that "his main thesis . . . that Yahweh was worshipped in the form of an anthropomorphic cult statue both in the central state temples of Israel (Samaria) and Judah (Jerusalem), is basically correct."

Other scholars strongly disagree. Na'aman (1999: 394; 2006a: 313) writes: "Examining the large corpus of 'cult objects' collected by Uehlinger, I cannot find a single object that was found in a cultic site in the kingdoms of Israel or Judah and that could be unequivocally interpreted as an anthropomorphic cult statue of a god." Mettinger's (2006: 279, 281) latest statement on the subject is similar: "The essential question is this: do we have even one three-dimensional representation of YHWH in metal or terracotta that may be classified as a cultic image? The answer is no." Mettinger goes on: "At the present state of research, the presence of a cultic image of YHWH in the First Temple has not been proved. The arguments adduced simply do not hold weight."[19]

Anthropomorphic Representations of Yahweh in Material Culture?

If they were made, what type of anthropomorphic figurines would best represent Yahweh? What should we look for? What markers of divinity would help us differentiate Yahweh from other gods with similar attributes? Is there a specific typology we should use in evaluating the pose, headdress, garments, standards, and so forth, one that would be telling? In short, the answer is no. To judge from the textual representations of Yahweh, no narrow typology would do. Yahweh fully incorporates the qualities of El such that an enthroned male in benedictory pose would be fitting (see Chapter Five). Yet the distinctive military portrayal of Yahweh as a divine warrior would make striding males with raised weapon equally appropriate. Could an artisan perhaps craft a striding figure that was nonetheless benign (as we will see with the Tell Balâṭah bronze figurine to be discussed shortly)? Such speculations are examining species of trees prior to recognizing the contours of the forest. A wide-angled view of anthropomorphic male figures from the Iron Age demands attention.

In 1983, after noting the hundreds of examples of female figurines attested in the archaeological record of ancient Israel, William Dever made a side comment that he thought "may be significant":

> No representations of a *male* deity in terra cotta, metal, or stone have ever been found in clear Iron Age contexts, except possibly for an El statuette in bronze from 12th-century Hazor and a depiction of an El-like stick figure on a miniature chalk altar from 10th-century Gezer, and neither is necessarily Israelite. (Dever 1983: 574).

Ever since, this remark has become the starting point for all scholars wrestling with the iconic/aniconic debate. Those asserting that there were representations of Yahweh and El set out to prove Dever wrong, while those asserting the aniconic tradition hailed his remarks as a vindication of their position.

The two exceptions Dever noted have been eliminated from consideration (see pp. 126–128 and 157–158). What remains are two questions: (1) Why is it that there are no Iron Age male figurines, especially when we consider the Late Bronze Age evidence? (2) Has archaeology produced examples since 1983 that would now invalidate Dever's observation?

What Accounts for the Absence of Male Divine Figurines in the Iron Age Archaeological Record?

On pp. 156–170 we had our pick of numerous male bronze figurines coming from the Late Bronze Age to nominate as candidates for the presence of pre-Israelite El. These seated figures in benedictory pose included figurines from Hazor, Beth Shemesh, Megiddo, Beth Shean, Tel Kinneret, and "Shechem." If we turn our attention to striding figures (often depicted with weapon in hand and in smiting position), we could add three well-known examples from Megiddo.[20]

The first figurine (Figure 7.1) comes from Tomb 4 (Late Bronze Age II), the second (Figure 7.2) from strata IX–VII, Area BB (Late Bronze Age I–Iron Age I), and the third (Figure 7.3) from stratum VB, Area BB (Iron Age I).[21] Due to the combination of pose, weapon, and especially shield, Figures 7.1 and 7.3 are thought to designate the Canaanite god Reshef (Cornelius 1994: 126–127, 130–131; Keel and Uehlinger 1998: 60, 116). Figure 7.2 lines up with typical striking warrior (e.g., Baal) typologies, yet due to the absence of the left arm as well as the object that was once in his right hand, definitive identification is impossible.[22] As with the bronze from eighth-century BCE Tel Kinneret (Figure 5.42), scholars view Figure 7.3 as being inherited from the Late Bronze Age rather than actually being fashioned in the Iron Age (Keel and Uehlinger 1998: 116, 135; cf. Hendel 1997: 216–217). Othmar Keel and Christoph Uehlinger add that even if such bronzes were produced in Iron Age I, "they were still following in the Late Bronze Age tradition nonetheless."

Figure 7.1 A striding male bronze figurine in smiting position with weapon and shield. From Megiddo Tomb 4 (Late Bronze Age II).
Kim Walton, taken at the Israel Museum.

Figure 7.2 A striding male bronze figurine in smiting position from Megiddo strata IX–VII, Area BB (Late Bronze Age I–Iron Age I).
Courtesy of the Oriental Institute of the University of Chicago.

Figure 7.3 A striding male bronze figurine in smiting position with weapon and shield. From Megiddo stratum VB, Area BB (Iron Age I).
Courtesy of the Oriental Institute of the University of Chicago.

THE ICONOGRAPHY OF DIVINITY: YAHWEH   301

One could also add a Late Bronze Age IIA figurine (Figure 7.4) from Tell Balâṭah (Field VII, stratum XIII) that defies categorization in either of the two typologies mentioned.[23] The figure, which has been commented on frequently, is a typical "Baal" figurine that was once coated with silver (cf. the grooves for tucking the metal foil and the remnants of sheet silver sheathing).[24] It wears a conical headdress usually described as analogous to the white crown of Upper Egypt. It stands 7.2 in. (18.4 cm) high in a striding position with bent arms that originally grasped either a weapon, staff, or a standard. Edward Campbell (1965a: 24) described the fists as follows: "Both fists are clenched around a core of silver-colored metal; conceivably the right hand held a spear or staff in vertical position while the left hand held a dagger."[25]

Ora Negbi (1976: 165) suggested that the right arm was once in the upraised position, typical of warrior figurines, but has since dropped down due to the pegged armpit construction. But Campbell tested such a hypothesis from the start

Figure 7.4 A Late Bronze Age IIA figurine from Tell Balâṭah (Field VII, stratum XIII) that defies categorization.

Photo by Lee C. Ellenberger; reproduced by permission of the Joint Expedition to Tell-Balâṭah and E. F. Campbell, Publication Director.

and concluded that it was simply impossible: "The peg is of a slightly off-square shape and will not permit setting the arm 180 degrees differently. Even if the arm were forced into that position, it would be in a grotesque backward bend... the fist would be away up behind the head and by no means in the smiting position.... The only position the arm can take is the benign one on the photograph."[26]

In light of the prevalence of male bronze figurines in the Late Bronze Age, their near-total absence in the Iron Age is indeed striking.[27] Equally striking is what seems to be the near absence of male divine figurines in other media such as stone, terra-cotta, and wood (especially in contrast to known examples of goddesses).[28] In dealing with metal statuary, two basic options are available: (1) for some reason, few if any male metal figurines were produced, or (2) male figurines were produced in the Iron Age from precious metals, yet for some reason we do not have them.

Let us briefly probe each of these options. At the outset, one must underscore the tentative nature of such an enterprise. The finding of male divine figurines in next season's excavations could overturn our entire analysis in one fell swoop. Consider, for example, how the finds at Kuntillet ʿAjrud necessitated a rewrite of all previous histories of ancient Israelite religion.

Option 1: Few if Any Male Metal Figurines Were Produced in Iron Age Israel

Uehlinger (1997: 111) suggests that "the fact that metal statuary production receded during the early Iron Age is most probably due to economic factors, such as the limited availability of raw materials and technical expertise." Depending on how early one dates the aniconic tradition and how widespread its influence, one could also posit an ideological motivation underlying such a lack of production.

While each of the factors could be true, various data lessen their impact. For example, the Iron Age I bronze zebu bull figurine from the Bull Site (see Figure 5.70 Five, p. 202) shows evidence of both raw materials and expertise, as does the ninth- to eighth-century BCE bronze plaque with an inscribed bull rider from Tel Dan, though its execution is decidedly less sophisticated (see Figure 7.12, p. 319). Technical craftsmanship with regard to divine (but not male) images elsewhere and in other media include the terra-cotta Taanach cult stands (see Figures 7.10, 7.11, pp. 315–316) and the eighth-century BCE stone bull-headed stela from Bethsaida (see Figure 7.18, p. 331). Yet the small amount of data we possess overall makes Uehlinger's point well taken. As for ideological suppression of the making of images in the first place, one could note the inhospitable environment for such production during the reigns of the kings Asa (1 Kgs 15:12–13), Hezekiah (2 Kgs 18:4), and Josiah (2 Kgs 23:4–15). Yet it is empirically impossible to judge how widespread such activities were and how long they lasted, even with archaeological correlates such as the covering over of the sanctuary at Arad (cf. Herzog 1997: 202–203; 2002: 35; 2013: 40; Bloch-Smith 2015: 101, 105–106, 114).[29]

Option 2: Male Figurines Were Produced in the Iron Age from Precious Metals, Yet for Some Reason We Do Not Have Them
As noted by Silvia Schroer (1987: 164–177) and Keel and Uehlinger (1998: 136), biblical tradition preserves memories of anthropomorphic representations of male deities of neighboring societies. The most famous of these is the (pejorative) depiction of the god Dagon in 1 Samuel 5:1–5 that describes the statue's head, trunk/back, and hands.[30] The passage 2 Samuel 12:30 almost certainly refers to a golden crown sitting on top of a large statue of the Ammonite god Milkom (*milkōm*).[31] The so-called image ban texts (though most are admittedly late in date) are replete with mentions of images being made of gold, silver, and wood (Jer 10:3–4; Isa 40:19–20, 41:7, 46:6; Hos 8:4, 13:2; Hab 2:19; Ps 115:4, 135:15; Exod 20:23). Such passages reveal without doubt that divine images were well known in biblical times and seemingly produced in considerable numbers.

Given that images were made and yet are not in our possession, we could assume some were destroyed in the royal religious reforms. Others could have been buried and archaeologists have simply yet to come upon them. The practice of burying precious metals has already been noted, with examples coming from archaeological and textual sources. The bronze hoard from Hazor (see Chapter Five, pp. 180–184) contained a divine figurine (Figure 5.35) and was buried in a jar in a sacred context. As for texts, in Genesis 35:2–4, Jacob is described as burying "all the foreign gods" (*kol ʾĕlōhê hannēkār*) under a tree, with specific mention of the "rings that were in their ears." The author's specific vocabulary has Jacob "hiding" (*yiṭmōn*) the "foreign" divine images together with insisting that the people rid themselves of them (*hāsirû*). Though the language is pejorative, the images were nonetheless not destroyed nor merely cast away with the rubbish. Thus we seem to have a type of desacralizing of cultic paraphernalia. An archaeological parallel would be the desacralizing of the Arad temple by those who chose consciously to bury (rather than pulverize) both the standing stone and the incense altars.[32]

Yet the most likely scenario is a purely pragmatic one: the metal was melted down and reused for other purposes. While we have no real way of knowing the extent of this practice, it makes common sense. An argument can be made by analogy with similar practices elsewhere in the ancient Near East.

Divine Images and the Reuse of Precious Metals
In 1981, Naʾaman published a fascinating text from the Alalakh VII archive that records what he called the "recycling" of a silver statue. Two lists of silver (ornamental silver cups and silver used for plating or settings) are tallied, with the

total value adding up to the large sum of 685 shekels; Na'aman estimates that silver of that value would weigh more than 12 lbs. (5.5 kg). There are two notes mentioning "the silver of the divine statue" (^{d}ALAM), one occurring after each individual tally of silver. At first glance one could think we have here a parallel to Exodus 32:2–4, where various items of gold were gathered together for Aaron to use in making his divine bull image (see Chapter Five, pp. 198–200). Yet the Alalakh texts twice mention that some of the silver was used to fashion burial gifts for a deceased king and hence buried in his grave. Thus Na'aman (1981: 48) concludes: "The context makes it clear that this statue [of a god] was the source of the silver, and it appears that the statue was melted down in order to manufacture the objects recorded in the text."

Realizing the indispensable role of the divine image in ancient Near Eastern ritual, Na'aman conjectures "that a new statue of the god was already fashioned and that the old statue, too expensive to be buried in the ground, was melted down for raw material . . . Our ancestors were quite rational in their attitude toward divine objects. While statues of stones or figurines were buried after they became obsolete, they saved the more expensive divine objects in order to reuse their precious metal."

Conclusion on Absence of Male Divine Figures

A reasonable scenario for the absence of male divine figurines in Iron Age Israel and Judah would combine the factors we have discussed. If we were only talking about precious metals (gold, silver, bronze), then we could make an economic argument: figurines were too expensive to make, so fewer were produced (due to lack of raw materials and expertise), and those that were fashioned were either desacralized (i.e., buried) or melted down at some point for reuse.[33] But the fact that older Late Bronze Age divine images were not melted down for reuse (seemingly out of respect) together with the absence of male figures in affordable terra-cotta shows that an economic answer cannot be the sole reason. That we have female divine figures in terra-cotta but not male ones suggests some degree of ideological motivation driving the latter's absence. Rainer Albertz and Rüdiger Schmitt (2012: 379) suggest that this is a part of a broader trend: "There appears to have been a definite aversion to anthropomorphic representation of major deities in national panthea, including Israelite/Judean YHWH, Moabite Chemosh, Ammonite Milkom, and Edomite Qauš, as well as the major deities of Philistia, Phoenicia, and the Aramean states."[34]

An Anthropomorphic Divine Couple?

William Hallo (1988: 54–55) once remarked that it was "possible that an essentially aniconic ethos (as applied to Israel's God) coexisted with a more tolerant attitude toward other icons from Mosaic to Deuteronomic times." As for Israel's God, he also remarked: "The perennial search for Yahweh-idols and Yahweh-statues goes on apace, but is unlikely as ever to produce results." Little did Hallo realize that after the publications of the Kuntillet ʿAjrud inscriptions (see Chapter Six, pp. 237–241) and iconography (see pp. 325–330) the perennial search for Yahweh would indeed go on apace, but now combined with a quest to document the goddess Asherah at his side. Four such searches are of particular note: the famous Kuntillet ʿAjrud standing figures (which we will treat with the theriomorphic images because of their facial features), a pair of winged deities on a seal with a Hebrew inscription, a pair of figurines on a terra-cotta vessel published by Jörg Jeremias, and a potsherd from Jerusalem that depicts two geometric/anthropomorphic figures.

The *Aladlammu* Seal from the Seyrig Collection

A well-known (but unprovenanced) seal from the Seyrig collection of the Bibliothèque Nationale in Paris includes a Hebrew inscription (*y[h?][y]hw [š]lm*) as well as a portrayal of a two-winged male deity on top of an *aladlammu* (*lamassu*) creature with a divine headdress facing a four-winged figure above a stylized Phoenician volute tree (Figure 7.5). Though the male figure "depicts

Figure 7.5 An unprovenanced seal that includes a Hebrew inscription (*y[h?][y]hw [š]lm*) as well as a portrayal of a two-winged male deity on top of an *aladlammu* (*lamassu*) creature with a divine headdress.

Image from O. Keel and C. Uehlinger, *Gods, Goddesses, and Images of God*, © Fortress Press. Reproduced by permission.

an Assyrian-style male deity," the Hebrew inscription leads Albertz and Schmitt (2012: 379) to "tentative[ly]" suggest that "the representations most likely corresponded to YHWH and his consort Asherah in Ishtar-like appearance." Compare the analysis by Keel and Uehlinger (1998: 340), who point out the "Assyrian, Urarturian and Phoenician" stylistic features and assume that the Hebrew inscription reflects "a local *interpretatio judaica* by a Judahite owner" who may have made a connection between Yahweh and Asherah because of the "constellation of images" with the cherub and the stylized tree.

Other studies of the seal were more circumspect, noting especially the unique nature of the seal. Benjamin Sass (1993: 236–237) remarked upon a "cluster of enigmas" that at first led him to doubt the authenticity of the scaraboid, whose complex composition was more typical of cylinder seals. Uehlinger (1993: 275–276) tones down his and Keel's earlier inference, saying that the seal's "Judean owner *might* have recognized Yahwe and the 'Queen of Heaven,' possibly identified with Asherah" (emphasis Uehlinger's). He contextualizes his comment in a methodological discussion (building on the work of André Lemaire) in which he notes that inferring any "religious significance" is complicated, for it must take into account the engraver's cultural symbol system as well as the owner's, whose name would have been added later "only as a result of the [economic] transaction." In his final summation about the seal representing Yahweh and Asherah, Uehlinger writes: "But as the seal remains unique for the time being, we have no other documentary evidence to test such an hypothesis against other documentary evidence ... [Its] weight for religious history is thus limited in comparison to other seals [that are] more conventional."[35] Moreover, the seal's unprovenanced nature limits its use even more.

Jeremias' Terra-Cotta Figurines

The terra-cotta vessel pictured in Figure 7.6 and depicting two individuals side by side is fraught with so many problems that it would be preferable to bypass it altogether. Regrettably, it has entered the canon of objects celebrated for possibly depicting Yahweh and Asherah, and thus it requires attention.

The vessel in question was published by Jeremias (1993), who acknowledged that it came from the Jerusalem antiquities market. It now resides in the Bible and Orient Museum at the University of Fribourg, Switzerland (inv. no. VFig 2000.11). Though broken in areas significant for interpretation, it has been celebrated as a "unique" find representing "what scholars have tried, in vain, to find for so long: an 8th-century Judahite figural representation of 'Yahweh and his Asherah'" (Uehlinger 1997: 149, 151).

Emotions run high about the ethics of publishing and using such items, as evidenced in the formal denunciations coming from almost every archaeological journal.[36] Scholars must nuance their treatments, for to shy away from discussing

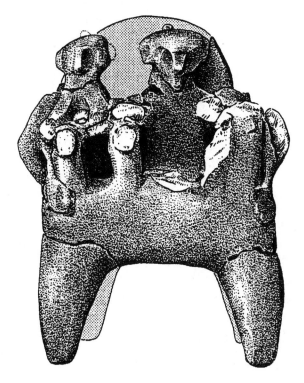

Figure 7.6 An unprovenanced terra-cotta vessel published by Jeremias showing two seated individuals.
Courtesy Orbis Biblicus et Orientalis.

such objects unconditionally would mean to set aside such finds as the Amarna tablets, the Dead Sea Scrolls, and the Nag Hammadi Codices, not to mention tens of thousands of cuneiform tablets, especially those that became known in the spring of 2003, after the Iraq War. Yet all scholars agree that unprovenanced objects void of context are seriously flawed for use in drawing most inferences. The current object is a case in point.

Even though *lmlk*-stamped jar handles (for which we have secure dates) were among the approximately fifty items that were acquired at the same time as the terra-cotta in question, we cannot be certain that they constituted a unified, uncontaminated group from the same find spot.[37] We certainly do not have data that would support Uehlinger's firm assertion that "we can be *confident* that the group has a Judahite provenance and should be dated to the late 8th or early 7th century BCE" (Uehlinger 1997: 150, my emphasis), not to mention any connection with Tell Beit Mirsim, where the various items were said to have been found. In addition to problems having to do with substantiating chronology and geography, without context we have no way of knowing whether the object was part of a cultic assemblage or from a find spot with some other indicators of cult.

As for its interpretation, there is no clear marker of divinity for either figure (see Chapter Five, p. 142). A "conspicuous hairdo" led to the tentative identification of the figure on the right as representing a god. Jeremias tentatively suggested Baal Hammon, and Uehlinger identified Yahweh (Jeremias 1993: 54–57; Uehlinger 1997: 151). There is no such marker for the presumably female figure to the left, though Uehlinger argues that "the spatial and generic relationship of the two figures is apparently a paredros relationship which could be perfectly transcribed by the syntagm 'DN1(male) and DN2(female) + suffix(3.m.sg.)'"[38] It is clear that this suggestion is being driven by the Kuntillet ʿAjrud inscriptions.

Without any cultic context or usual markers of divinity, we could very well have human figures represented here, not deities. Indeed, pairs of male and female elites seated side by side are ubiquitous in ancient Egypt. Uehlinger (1997: 151–152) tries to support the claim that we have deities here by noting that Jeremias "tentatively identified [the partially preserved animals on the object] as lions or sphinxes" and then concluding: "Sphinxes and cherubim were naturally related to major state deities in the Phoenician-Palestinian art of the late Iron and Persian periods." Yet a look at the sphinxes/cherubim used on the Idrimi statue, the Ahiram sarcophagus, and the Megiddo ivory (which we will discuss later) shows that this artistic motif can just as easily be associated with royalty.

Lastly, Jeremias suggested that rather than a male and female on a throne, these could be two chariot riders, a notion he derived from Cypriot terra-cotta figurines. Publishing his article in 1993, Jeremias did not have at his disposal Nancy Winter's (1996) extremely detailed report of the terra-cotta chariot groups from the excavations of the archaic precinct of the sanctuary of Appollo Hylates at Kourion.[39] While the material from Kourion is later than the putative date assigned to the Jeremias terra-cotta, the number of finds there is staggering, especially when added to the previously published Cypriot data. According to Winter (1996: 100), "More than 700 horse riders and 110 chariot groups were reconstructed ... in addition, over 1,000 unjoined heads and 500 horses" were documented, such that "riders can be estimated to have numbered ca. 1,000 and chariot groups less than 300." While there is, regrettably, only a handful of pictures of the chariot groups in Winter's publication, the presence of two individuals side by side, pillar-like legs for the horses, and a box-like frame for the chariot argues for reconsidering Jeremias' alternative explanation that we may have chariot riders here.

If we have riders here driving a schematic chariot (and this remains a big if), one would still have to debate whether the pair of figures represents humans or deities. *If* the latter, one would then have to debate whether the primary chariot driver would be Baal or Yahweh, both known to be "Riders on the Clouds" (cf. too Rakib-El; see Niehr 2014a: 158–159). *If* the latter could be substantiated, it would make more sense, judging from Habakkuk 3:5, to see the god Reshep at Yahweh's side (or, if the second figure is female, a war goddess associated with horses, such as ʿAštart/Astarte, rather than the non-warrior Asherah. And yet, according to Habakkuk 3:8, Yahweh alone drives his chariot!

When such substantial interpretive doubt is added to an already suspect unprovenanced object, we can only conclude that this terra-cotta is of no help in documenting whether Yahweh was represented in material culture.

A Geometric Pair from Jerusalem

As a result of the Shelby White–Leon Levy Program for Archaeological Publications, Garth Gilmour worked through the material produced by excavations at the Ophel in Jerusalem in the 1920s carried out by R. A. S. Macalister and J. G. Duncan. A highlight of his research has been the rediscovery of a sherd from an Iron Age II jug that was engraved with two geometric (triangular) humanoid figures (Figure 7.7). Gilmour (2009: 93) understands this engraving "to represent two deities to be identified as Yahweh and Asherah, with the male figure, Yahweh, striding over the natural world."

The two figures here do not meet many of the criteria for determining whether a specific object can be categorized as divine (see Chapter Five, p. 142). On the positive side, Gilmour (2009: 95) points out that "the naked frontal view with prominent pubic triangle [of the figure on the left] is a definitive element." He

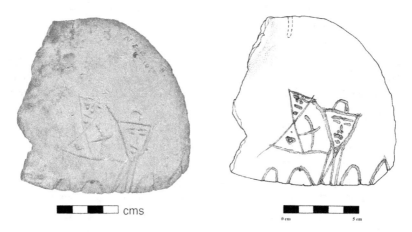

Figure 7.7 Two geometric (triangular) humanoid figures portrayed on a sherd from an Iron Age II jug excavated at the Ophel in Jerusalem in the 1920s.

Garth Gilmour, "An Iron Age II Pictorial Inscription from Jerusalem Illustrating Yahweh and Asherah," *PEQ* 141, no. 2 (2009). 87–103, © Palestinian Exploration Fund.

argues, based on comparisons with similar iconography from Late Bronze Age Lachish, Gezer, and Tel Batash, that it represents "the most common type of female religious iconography." As for the male figure on the right, Gilmour notes parallels for the conical headdress among Middle Bronze through Early Iron Age bronze figures thought to be divine (cf. Figures 7.1–7.4). Yet Gilmour concedes: "Humanoid deity figures with triangular shapes carved into pottery are unprecedented in Iron Age Israel and Judah." The closest parallels are several male warriors with upper bodies represented by inverted triangles coming from two sherds from Late Bronze Age Megiddo (cf. Keel and Uehlinger 1998: figs. 58–59). Yet the Megiddo figures are decidedly militaristic (wielding weapons and holding shields), which the Jerusalem sherd figure is not. Moreover, because they are grouped in sets of three (or more—one sherd is broken), they likely represent humans rather than an array of deities posed for battle.[40]

All other diagnostic criteria for determining divinity are lacking. The sherd was not found together with a cultic assemblage or in any type of sacred precinct. There are no other clear markers of divinity (horns, hairdo, garb, insignia, symbolic animal, body posture combined with standards and/or other correlates of cult, precious metals) and no inscriptional evidence (apart from what could be the letter *taw*).

This is not to say that the sherd is not cultic. Though it fails to meet the criteria needed to designate divine images (and hence should not have been published with such certainty), we could have here an expression of domestic religion. In commenting on the famous Judean pillar figures, Carol Meyers (2002: 286) remarks: "Even if the figurines are meant to represent a deity, the focus on identifying the deity detracts from a consideration of their function."[41] It is wise to apply the same corrective to analysis of the Jerusalem sherd. The current fixation with identifying another example of "Yahweh and his asherah" can keep us from considering why this sherd was engraved in the first place and how its owner used it. When viewed through the lenses of non-elite cult and the materiality of cult, one might conclude that this engraving on a small terra-cotta sherd from a spouted jug was meant to address a medical or social concern.

What is the significance of the X mark that dominates the center of the relief? Gilmour (2009: 95) comments: "Clearly it may represent a *taw* sign, but in the absence of any obvious significance it may be more prudent to interpret it simply as a space filler, filling in the open area created by the lines joining the two figures." If the X is indeed the letter *taw*, perhaps clues to its significance can be found in the two passages in the Hebrew Bible that mention the letter. In Job 31:35, the letter *taw* designates Job's signature. An X signature can signify agreement with the contents of a "signed" document or even ownership, but more importantly, it represents and validates a person's presence. Studies on materiality (e.g., Mandell and Smoak 2016) have underscored the performative nature of inscriptions, and perhaps we should look here to help us understand its iconography. The other use of such a mark in Ezekiel 9:4–6 is more explicit with regard to functionality. Here the X mark serves as a divinely given protective (apotropaic?) symbol assigned to the righteous to avert destruction. In particular, it is given to those who grieve over the cultic "abominations" that were taking part in the Jerusalem Temple (as depicted in Ezekiel 8). If the X on the Jerusalem sherd functioned in any way similar, then the two individuals "marked" by the X here would be humans. In this sense, the owner of the sherd could have kept it as a mark of his (and his wife's?) righteous standing and/or as an apotropaic object to ward off perceived evil.

To factor in the nudity of the female, perhaps the talisman was perceived to ward off any threat to the woman's fecundity. Here Meyers' comments on domestic cult deserve to be quoted at length:

> For any pre-modern agrarian people, the production of offspring is essential for maintaining the household's food supply and thus its survival and also in securing care for aging adults. In such a context, infertility, childbirth complications resulting in the death of the mother or child, difficulty in lactation, and high infant mortality rates are constant threats to the durability of the family household. Women's religious practices can be seen as strategies akin to preventative and restorative medical procedures of the modern world, to intervene with the divine forces believed to impact the well-being of mother and child and to influence them in order to assure their benevolent and protective presence or to avert their destructive powers. (Meyers 2002: 283)

As noted by Gilmour, the iconography of the female figure (an inverted triangle on the top of a triangle) is without precedent. The following material from a much later time period (and with as many differences as similarities) is introduced heuristically to help us think in new categories.

Joseph Naveh and Shaul Shaked (1993, 1998) have published collections of magic spells and formulae written on various media and coming from Late Antiquity. They include several instances of people engraving broken potsherds that were then used in rituals for various family and social remedies. Because our Jerusalem sherd depicts a male and a female, it might be useful to note that some of the texts documented by Naveh and Shaked functioned as love spells. The following two rituals using potsherds are recorded in a collection of magic spells:

> Write on unbaked clay. . . Just as this piece of clay burns in the fire, so shall the heart of PN son of PN and his kidneys burn after me, and after my fortune

and after my lot. His heart shall not sleep. (Naveh and Shaked 1993: 216–217 = Geniza 22, §1.8ff.)

For a man to return to his wife. Wr[ite] on an unbaked piece of clay, and throw it in an oven or fire, and this is what you shall write: In the name of TSN WP [further magic words]. (Naveh and Shaked 1993: 196, 202 = Geniza 18, §17:9)

An actual engraved potsherd from the excavations at Horvat Rimmon contains just such a love spell (see Naveh and Shaked 1998: 84–89). It too mentions a sympathetic magic ritual asking for the heart and desire of a person to burn after the petitioner. It should be noted, but only in passing, that the second love charm (from Geniza 18) also contains two schematic drawings (Figure 7.8) of an inverted triangle on the top of a triangle complete with small circles (cf. the same triangle orientation of the female figure on the Jerusalem sherd together with small circles denoting facial features) together with additional magic symbols (Naveh and Shaked 1993: pl. 54).

In conclusion, we do not have enough information to interpret the iconography of the Jerusalem sherd with any degree of confidence. Any suggestion—whether "it is the earliest picture of Yahweh ever found" (Gilmour 2009: 100), an

Figure 7.8 Two schematic drawings of an inverted triangle on the top of a triangle with small circles from a love charm drawn on a potsherd from Late Antiquity.
Courtesy The Hebrew University Magnes Press.

apotropaic symbol of divine favor, or an apotropaic object to secure love—is speculative. Given the fact that domestic religion has largely been unexplored, it seems best to conclude with P. R. S. Moorey and Stuart Fleming (1984: 79) that no figure should "be taken to represent a divinity until the arguments for a mortal have been discounted." There are certainly other instances where an inscribed X must occur, and these must be discovered (by combing through the archaeological record) and explored first in order to help contextualize the Jerusalem sherd.[42]

Possible Theriomorphic Representations of Yahweh

Yahweh and Lions

As has been noted, there are no explicit examples of an Israelite deity (El or Yahweh) being referred to with the epithet of a lion in the Hebrew Bible or extrabiblical sources.[43] This may come as a bit of a surprise to Christians, whose New Testament celebrates Jesus as "the Lion of the tribe of Judah, the Root of David" (Rev 5:5). Yet this picture comes from a particular genre that weds the anointed Davidide material (e.g., Isa 9:2–7; 11:1–10; Jer 23:5–6; 33:14–16) with the mention of the eponymous ancestor Judah as a lion in Genesis 49:9–10.

Yet leonine metaphors and literary images in the Hebrew Bible are so numerous that Brent Strawn (2005: 58) notes that "the Deity is frequently compared to a lion . . . more so than with any other animal."[44] Indeed, various prophets describe Yahweh "roaring like a lion" (Amos 1:2, 3:8; Joel 4:16 [Eng 3:16]; Hos 5:14; 11:10, 13:7–8; Jer 25:30), a simile used to describe divine ferocity so intense that even the heavens and earth shake in response (Joel 4:16 [Eng 3:16]). Such explicit references to Yahweh behaving like a lion lead Strawn (2005: 250) to conclude that "Yahweh might well be described as a Lion-God." Be that as it may, a literary trope need not indicate that lions ever served as emblematic animals in actual religious rituals where they would have been objects receiving cult (e.g., sacrifices, adoration). An analogy would be the ubiquitous anthropomorphic imagery used of Yahweh in the Hebrew Bible, and yet there is no indication that an anthropomorphic statue ever served as a divine image of Yahweh in the inner sanctum of the Jerusalem Temple. Indeed, our extant texts argue the opposite, as we will see.

Keel and Uehlinger (1998: 190–191) go beyond the Hebrew Bible's literary references to Yahweh and lions by adding iconographic data such as the famous Megiddo "Shemaʿ-servant-of-Jeroboam" seal with its majestic roaring lion (see too Strawn 2005: 102–104). After sifting the various data, they conclude: "As in the Northern Kingdom, Yahweh could also be depicted in Judah by means of a roaring lion. But these images can hardly be interpreted as symbols or attribute animals of Yahweh." In contrast, Tallay Ornan and colleagues (2012: 5*–8*) collect several additional seals (from the City of David, Tell en-Nasbeh, and an unprovenanced CWSS 1098) to argue that "lions in both Israelite and Judahite seals symbolize Yahweh. . . . If this proposal is accepted, the lion will join other Yahwistic emblems." In another article, Ornan (2012: 17*) refers to the lion here as "a stand-in for Yahweh." Going even further, Ornan and colleagues (2012: 11* n. 12) argue that a ninth-/eighth-century BCE seal (Figure 7.9) from the City of David that shows a striding lion together with a (perpendicularly aligned) human with a raised right arm depicts "a gesture of veneration, *signifying the beast as a focus of worship*" (my emphasis).[45]

The terminology in these discussions (symbol, attribute, emblem) is murky from a semiotic perspective. At the least, all would agree to a metonymic designation where the glyptic record aligns well with the literary record of the Hebrew Bible to underscore that Yahweh was frequently associated with lions. Moreover, Yahwistic leonine associations fit well within the larger ancient Near Eastern context, where divine warriors were juxtaposed with lions over which they were seen to be victorious (Ornan et al. 2012: 6*–7*; Lewis 1996b: 33–45). Beyond this we simply do not have enough data. While the City of David seal published

Figure 7.9 A ninth-/eighth-century BCE seal from the City of David depicting a striding lion with lifted tail and a human with raised right arm.
Courtesy Institute of Archaeology, The Hebrew University of Jerusalem.

by Baruch Brandl is enticing, it stops short of proving that a statue of a lion ever served as a divine image used in cult—that is, a lion image served as an attention-focusing device to which cult would have been offered, similar to what can be said of bull images (to be discussed shortly).

Yet as for cult, it should be emphatically underscored that lion images appear on cultic objects (apart from divine images). That the enigmatic term "'Ariel" (see Chapter Five, p. 197) seems to have been used for Yahwistic altar hearths in Ezekiel 43:15–16 and presumably in the Mesha inscription suggests that lion images were used as symbols on Yahwistic cult objects.[46] Note the presence of the three lion heads on a libation tray from Tell Beit Mirsim that Ruth Amiran, in contrast to William F. Albright, dated "to the 8th or at the earliest, to the 9th century B.C."[47] Lions together with bulls and cherubim (not to mention date palm trees [timōrōt]) were used to decorate cultic stands in the Solomonic temple complex devoted to Yahweh (1 Kgs 7:29, 36).[48]

It is quite fascinating that the collocation of these animal and tree motifs appears on the two tenth-century BCE cult stands from Taanach.[49] The first of these stands (Figure 7.10) was found by Ernst Sellin in 1902 and depicts

Figure 7.10 A cult stand from Taanach (discovered in 1902) depicting alternating lions and cherubim/sphinxes (one on top of the other) and two caprids flanking a tree.

Courtesy Ziony Zevit, *The Religions of Ancient Israel: A Synthesis of Parallactic Approaches* (London: Continuum, 2001), 318, fig. 4.8.

alternating lions and cherubim/sphinxes one on top of the other. Two caprids appear on both sides of a tree, a timeless motif in the ancient Near East attested as early as the third millennium BCE and very popular in Late Bronze Age Palestine (Beck 1994: 363).

Similarly, the second cult stand (Figure 7.11) from Taanach (discovered by Paul Lapp in 1968) also contains alternating lions and cherubim/sphinxes, although with a distinctly different arrangement. As noted by Pirhiya Beck (1994: 360), these two "cult stands from Taanach are the only ones in Palestine on which lions and winged sphinxes appear together."[50] Like the first stand, the second register of the second stand contains two caprids flanking a tree, presumably a sacred symbol. The top register of the second stand contains another animal as well, but scholars are divided on whether it is a bull or a horse. If

Figure 7.11 A cult stand from Taanach (discovered in 1968) depicting alternating lions and cherubim/sphinxes and two caprids flanking a tree—as well as an animal under a winged sun disk in the top register and a naked female with lions in the lower register.

Courtesy Gary Lee Todd WorldHistoryPics.com. https://www.flickr.com/photos/101561334@N08/42312681665/in/album-72157698086736974.

it is the former, the second stand would have all four motifs (lions, cherubim, bulls, trees) that are used in the description of the Yahwistic cult stands in 1 Kings 7:29, 36.[51] John Holladay (1987: 296) boldly suggests that "it is not impossible that the Ta'anach . . . 'Cult Stands' might be exactly such provincializing substitutes for the bronze wheeled stands of 1 Kgs 7:27–37."[52] The bovine/equine and cherubim images (along with the empty space on register three) will be addressed later.

Yahweh and Bulls
Painting with a broad brush, it is easy to see why certain worshippers fully embraced using bull imagery for Yahweh, for, in William Henry Propp's (2006: 580) words, "in ancient iconography and myth, the wild male bovine in its maturity represents untrammeled masculinity and fecundity. The domestic bull represents masculinity civilized—powerful, potentially violent, but under restraint." Yet imagery is one thing, and a direct one-to-one representation of Yahweh by a bull image is quite another. Thus it is equally easy to understand how those holding to an aniconic theology would have rejected a physical image if they perceived it as reducing ultimate Reality to an object.

From the biblical narrative, it is clear that bull symbols were used by artisans in their depictions of the accoutrements used in the worship of Yahweh. The extremely large cast metal basin described in 1 Kings 7:21–26—the so-called Molten Sea (*yām mûṣāq*)—stood in the Temple courtyard (1 Kgs 7:39) and was supported on the backs of twelve huge bull statues (1 Kgs 7:25, 44). Arranged in four triads with each group facing a different point of the compass and with their faces oriented outward, the spectacle of these twelve colossal bulls would have been impressive. Indeed, so much bronze was used that Jeremiah 52:20 says it was "beyond weighing." Elizabeth Bloch-Smith (1994: 20–21, 25), in noting the "unusually great size" of the basin complex (as well as the magnitude of the cherubim throne), concludes: "The enormous size symbolized the spatial and temporal magnitude of the deity."

As we have noted, bulls, together with lions and cherubim, were used as decorative elements engraved on side frame panels of the ten cultic wheeled stands used in the Temple (1 Kgs 7:29, 36). Finally, Solomon's magnificent ivory and gold throne was also said to have bull imagery (royal cult mimicked the divine), with a bull head carved on its back and set against the backdrop of fourteen lions (so LXX's Vorlage *'ēgel* for MT's term *'āgôl*; 1 Kgs 10:19–20).

More mystically, consider Ezekiel's "visions of God" (*mar'ôt 'ĕlōhîm*).[53] Here the winged cherubim that made up Yahweh's flying throne were part human and part composite animals (cf. the *Mischwesen* discussion in Chapter Five, pages 149–150), one of which was the bull (*šôr*). The composite creature also possessed bull hooves (*kĕkap regel 'ēgel*) (Ezek 1:7, 10; but cf. 10:14).[54]

Bull Traditions About El Applied to Yahweh

As for bull epithets used of Yahweh, much of what we discussed earlier is relevant here, for the authors and editors of the Hebrew Bible sewed descriptions of El together with those of Yahweh into a single seamless garment. Thus if the epithet "the Mighty One of Jacob" (*ăbîr yaʿăqōb*) evoked bull imagery for El (Gen 49:24–25), which seems likely, then it equally did so for Yahweh, to whom the title was enthusiastically applied without qualification (Isa 49:26; 60:16; Ps 132:2, 5). See also the PN ʾAbbiryāhû, "[my] strength is Yahweh" (Albertz and Schmitt 2012: 313). The similar epithet "the Mighty One of Israel" (*ăbîr yiśrāʾēl*) in Isaiah 1:24 is used unreservedly to describe "the Sovereign, Yahweh of Hosts" (*hāʾādôn yhwh ṣĕbāʾôt*). While El may have been the god who was thought by some to have "brought Israel out of Egypt like the horns of a wild ox" (*ʾēl môṣîʾām mimmiṣrāyim kĕtôʿăpōt rĕʾēm lô*), it was Yahweh who was celebrated with this bovine imagery as the tradition was handed down (Num 23:21b–22; 24:8).[55] As has been suggested, perhaps the ease with which bull symbols and imagery could be used of both El and Yahweh helped facilitate this weaving process.

Yahweh and Jeroboam I's Bull Images

Once again we must return to Jeroboam's bull images and the related golden calf traditions (see pp. 198–200). It is here that many advocates find the clearest bull imagery used of Yahweh, a claim that sounds counterintuitive from a straightforward reading of Exodus 32 and its apostasy.

In summing up previous scholarship on Jeroboam I's (and Aaron's) bull images, Lloyd Bailey (1971: 97) wrote, "The consensus is that they were intended to be variations upon the cherubim, *pedestals upon which the invisible Yahweh rode*" (emphasis mine).[56] He cited scholars such as Walter Harrelson (1962: 488–489), who proclaimed that "the connection of the bull with Yahweh is unmistakable." While the nominations for the intended bull deity increase each decade (current suggestions include El, Yahweh, Baal, Sin, Apis, Hathor, Mnevis, and Moses), the consensus that the god in question is Yahweh remains firm.[57] And there is good reason. Both Exodus and Jeroboam traditions describe the bull image as representing "the god(s) who brought the people out of Egypt," and biblical tradition affirms Yahweh to be that very god, from the earliest texts to the latest. The thesis is secured by mention of Aaron proclaiming a "feast to Yahweh" (*ḥag lyhwh*) in the very context in which he fashioned the young bull and built an altar before it (Exod 32:5).[58]

What is left to debate is whether the bull image was a direct representation of Yahweh or whether it served as a pedestal for an aniconic Yahweh. As noted, in Bailey's generation scholars firmly embraced the latter. Yehezkel Kaufmann (1960: 271) wrote: "[Jeroboam's bulls] were not conceived of as representations of YHWH—such a notion would have been too blasphemous for the biblical

THE ICONOGRAPHY OF DIVINITY: YAHWEH   319

historian to have passed over in silence." Albright (1957: 299) was of the same mind when he penned: "Direct representation of Yahweh as bull-god" is a "gross conception" that is "not only otherwise unparalleled in biblical tradition, but is contrary to all that we know of Syro-Palestinian iconography in the second and early first millennia B.C." Yet today the former option is back in play, especially because of new iconographic data. The following discussion, though not exhaustive, will bring the history of scholarship up to date.

As a representative of modern scholars who support the "pedestal" option, consider Mettinger, one of the most prolific scholars in the study of aniconism in ancient Israel. With regard to Jeroboam I's cult images, he concludes:

> There are examples [in the ancient Near East] where the deity is represented as standing on the back of a bull. The male figure above the bull then symbolizes the god. But the animal itself is only the god's pedestal or socle animal. Similarly, Jeroboam's bull image is thus only the visible pedestal over which JHWH stands unseen. We are confronted by the Northern Kingdom's counterpart to the empty divine throne in the Holy of Holies of the Jerusalem temple.[59]

Similarly, Zevit (2001: 317) believes that "YHWH was considered to be the invisible deity standing on the back of the calf/young bull pedestal."[60] In addition to the numerous examples of deities riding on bulls from elsewhere in the ancient Near East (cf. Chapter Five, pp. 149–155, Figures 5.23-5.28), the 1998 excavations at Tel Dan provided us with a ninth- to eighth-century BCE divine bull rider at one of the very cities where Jeroboam had earlier set up his bull images.[61] Granted, what we have in Figure 7.12 is a small bronze plaque, not big

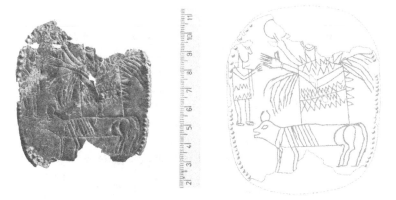

Figure 7.12 A divine bull rider (Ishtar?) depicted on a small bronze plaque from Tel Dan (ninth to eighth century BCE).
Courtesy of the Nelson Glueck School of Biblical Archaeology.

enough to be a divine image that could have functioned as the focal point of religious ritual. Moreover, it most likely represents a goddess (Ishtar?) rather than a god, and it is decades later than Jeroboam I's reign. Nonetheless, this artifact underscores the presence of the long-enduring motif of divine bull riders.[62]

The fact that some of the bull images on which gods rode were composite animals (*Mischwesen*) would have made them a close parallel with the cherubim in the Jerusalem temple. Compare, for example, the winged lion with the head of a bull in Figure 5.30 with the composite cherub of Ezekiel 1:10 that is also a winged beast—part lion, part bull.[63] Years ago scholars asserted that "Jeroboam's calves were perhaps of the winged type and thus no more than a variation on the theme of the cherub. In essence, then, there is no difference between the calves and the cherubs" (Kaufmann 1960: 271; cf. Albright 1957: 300).

In order to sustain this interpretation of Jeroboam I's (and Aaron's) original intention being to create a version of an invisible Yahweh astride a bull (rather than cherub), one must posit that aniconic theology is quite old. Indeed, Mettinger (2006: 290) concludes that "the Israelite cult was aniconic from the beginning." While some aniconic traditions are in fact ancient—judging from Elijah's intolerant monolatry within a pre-Deuteronomistic setting (note the positive use of a Yahwistic sanctuary outside of Jerusalem)—it should be noted that many of the prophetic parodies against making a divine image, not to mention the Deuteronomistic sanctions, are quite late (cf. Dohmen 1985).[64]

Hosea's Portrayal of Jeroboam I's Bull Images

Alongside the Elijah material, Wesley Toews (1993: 151–172), Michael Dick (1999a: 10–11), and other scholars point to the role of Hosea 8 as a precursor to the extensive image polemics that were to follow. In Hosea 8:5–6 (cf. too Hosea 13:2), the prophet speaks out against what he considers to be an illegitimate cult in Samaria. In his anti-image polemic he refers to the "bull of Samaria" (*'ēgel šōmrôn*) that will be destroyed.[65] Here Hosea is directing his words against Jeroboam I's two golden bull (*šĕnê 'eglê zāhāb*) shrines at Dan and Bethel (1 Kgs 12:25–33). Yet Hosea's take on the matter is altogether different from what we have seen previously. Unlike Elijah, Elisha, Jehu, and Amos, Hosea does not pass over Jeroboam I's bull images without comment. And unlike the Deuteronomists in 1 Kings 12:25–33, Hosea's concern about Jeroboam I is not merely about condemning him for setting up rival sanctuaries to Jerusalem's centralized worship.[66]

In Hosea 8:5–6, the prophet gives no indication that Jeroboam might have been finessing his theology to compete against Jerusalem. For Hosea it is a matter of making an illegitimate graven image of the divine. The bull of Samaria (whether it designates El or Yahweh, and whether the deity is directly or invisibly enthroned) should be rejected outright (*zanāḥ*), for as the product of human workmanship (*hû' ḥārāš 'ăśāhû*), "it is not God" (*lō' 'ĕlōhîm hû'*).⁶⁷ Elsewhere in the book (13:1–2) the making of the bull images is juxtaposed with Baal worship, damning any of Jeroboam I's possible good intentions with guilt by association and mockery (*'ăgālîm yiššāqûn*).⁶⁸

Yahweh Represented Through a Bull Image?
This has led some scholars to deny the hypothesis that Jeroboam was engaged in his own brand of competitive aniconic theology. Instead, they assert that Jeroboam set up bull images as actual representations of Yahweh. Niehr (1997: 82) writes: "The calf, as YHWH's divine image, is not only a pedestal for an invisible deity, as is so often claimed, but is itself a theriomorphic cult image."⁶⁹ Similarly, Na'aman writes: "The calves were considered both statues and pedestals of YHWH, and theriomorphic divine images were part of the official cult in Israel."⁷⁰ In this line of thinking, Hosea's description of Jeroboam's bull of Samaria should be taken at face value as designating a bull image of Yahweh.

A circumstantial case can be built to support this hypothesis by piecing together scattered data. It is indeed interesting that Samaria ostracon #41 (though broken) preserves the PN *'glyw*, "Yah[weh] is a bull." One could compare the name *'glhdd*, "Hadad is a bull," that appears on an unpublished scaraboid currently housed in Boston's Museum of Fine Arts.⁷¹ Though unprovenanced, a quadruped (bovine?) is depicted on a ninth-century BCE seal (Figure 7.13)

Figure 7.13 A quadruped is depicted on an unprovenanced ninth-century BCE seal along with the name "Shema'yahu son of 'Azaryahu."

Charles Jean Melchior de Vogüé, *Mélanges d'archéologie orientale* (Paris: Imprimerie impériale, 1868), 131, fig. 34.

along with an individual's name that contains Yahwistic theophoric elements ("Shemaʿyahu son of ʿAzaryahu").[72] Yet it should be noted that the theophoric element in personal names on seals does not always correspond to the depiction of the deity on the same seal (cf. Bregstein 1993).

Mark Smith (2002a: 84, following Steiner 1997a: 318) notes that Yahweh (together with Horus) is described as a bull in the syncretistic religion portrayed in the Egyptian Papyrus Amherst 63.[73] Yet this interpretation has been debated. The Demotic contains the fixed spelling of a divine name ($ḥr_2w_2$ or divine determinative), followed by $yhw_2\ tʾr_2ʾn$ (col. xii, 17).[74] Richard Steiner initially read the name as Horus and the second series as two words, Yaho followed by $t(w)rn$, "our bull." In contrast, Sven Vleeming and Jan-Wim Wesselius (1985: 51, 59) read the name of the fixed spelling as Yaho and the following letters as one word, $yhwtrn$ (literally "may he cause us to be left"), citing Ps 79:11 as a parallel. Steiner's 2017 edition (Steiner and Nims 2017) reads $YHW(H)\ tnṭr-(l)k$ and translates "LORD, may you protect [us]." Yet more recently both van der Toorn (2018a: 66, 166–168) and Tawny Holm (forthcoming) read $yhw(ʾ)\ trnʾ\ ʾymn$ and translate "May Yahu, our Bull, be with us."

Most intriguing is the mention of "Yahweh of Samaria" (*yhwh šmrn*) in one of the inscriptions coming from the southern site of Kuntillet ʿAjrud (on Pithos A; see Chapter Six, pp. 237–239). As will be seen, the standing figure drawn immediately below this inscription has caused some scholars (notably P. Kyle McCarter) to argue that the Kuntillet ʿAjrud artist was portraying Yahweh with bovine symbolism in precisely the way that would have led Hosea to speak out against the idolatrous bull of Samaria (*ʿēgel šōmrôn*).[75] The record from material culture deserves its own section, to which we now turn.

Possible Bull Representations of Yahweh in Material Culture

Can archaeology help us to determine whether Yahweh was portrayed using bull symbolism? Of the Iron Age evidence we possess, four bull images deserve mention: the Bull Site bronze, the top register of the Taanach cult stand, the largest of the two standing images on Kuntillet ʿAjrud Pithos A, and the bull-headed warrior from the gate shrine at Bethsaida.

Once Again: The Bull Site Bronze

As we have seen, our data from bronze figurines (be they anthropomorphic or theriomorphic) are frustratingly inconclusive because of the lack of accompanying inscriptions. Thus we simply do not know whether the Bull Site bronze (see Figure 5.70) depicted El, Yahweh, or even Baal. What is not to be lost in stating such objective uncertainty is the possibility that it could indeed represent a cultic statue of Yahweh used in a ritual in an Iron Age I cultic setting. It is possible. We just don't know for certain.

THE ICONOGRAPHY OF DIVINITY: YAHWEH 323

Once Again: The Taanach Cult Stand

The top register of the Taanach cult stand discovered by Lapp in 1968 portrays a quadruped underneath a winged sun disk (Figure 7.14). The quadruped has been taken as an animal associated with a deity, but not as a direct emblem of the deity (although at times these lines of distinction become blurred). If anything, the winged disk above the quadruped is seen as the divine symbol in this picture. As for the animal, scholars are quite divided on whether it is a bull or a horse. In surveying the secondary literature about the identity of the animal, Keel and Uehlinger (1998: 158) conclude that these two options are "irreconcilable ... both supported recently in opinions offered by zoologists."

The excavator of the cult stand interpreted it as a bovine (Lapp 1969: 44), and he has been followed by many interpreters (e.g., Dayagi-Mendels 1986: 163; Hestrin 1987: 67; Weippert 1988: 472; Smith 1990: 20; 2002a: 53; Bretschneider 1991: 82, 215; Beck 1994; Zevit 2001; King and Stager 2001: 343; Dever 2005: 219).[76] This line of thinking points out the lack of a mane if it was a horse and that the tail and

Figure 7.14 The top register of a Taanach cult stand (discovered in 1968), portraying a quadruped underneath a winged sun disk.
Kim Walton, taken at the Israel Museum.

possibly split hooves are more bovine than equine (e.g., Zevit 2001: 321). As for the deity here associated with the bull, some scholars insist on Baal, while others advocate Yahweh.

The strongest case for the animal being a horse has been made by J. Glen Taylor (1988: 561–564; 1993: 30–33; 1994: 57–58), whose view was buttressed by Keel and Uehlinger (1998: 158) when they wrote that "not a single bit of zoological evidence identifies the animal clearly as a bovine." Taylor further argued that the horse here is associated with Yahweh, who, as a solar deity, is represented by the sun disk. Furthermore, the empty space of tier three on the stand represents Yahweh's invisible presence (discussed later). To bolster his theory, Taylor noted how King Josiah's seventh-century BCE cult reforms specifically mention removing horses that Judean kings had dedicated to the sun at the entrance to the temple of Yahweh (2 Kgs 23:11). Similarly, Taylor argued that a terra-cotta horse figurine (with a disk on its forehead) from Hazor was fashioned to depict the animal drawing the sun god's chariot.[77] Other scholars who agree that the animal on the top register of the Taanach cult stand is a horse are Glock, Schroer, Keel and Uehlinger, Hadley, and Sommer.[78] Yet the identity of the animal as a horse need not necessitate its association with Yahweh. Keel and Uehlinger (1998: 160), for example, argue that "it is much more likely that the striding horse is to be interpreted … as an attribute animal of Anat-Astarte."[79] If we do have an association with ʿAshtart on the top register, it would resonate with Smith's (2014a: 208) suggestion that ʿAshtart is also the goddess being portrayed between the lions on the bottom register.[80]

Though artistic convention should be interpreted cautiously, perhaps a new factor to consider is how scholars often describe the animal in question as being "young" (e.g., Hestrin 1987: 67; Beck 1994: 356), "frolicking" (Taylor 1994: 58), or even "frisky" (Stager 2008: 580).[81] If the animal is a horse, its youthfulness contrasts with mature/stately horses that are well documented as prestige animals in iconography from Egypt to Assyria and the Levant.[82] For a cultic item such as we have in the Taanach stand, we could contrast its youthful colt with the mature horse on which a goddess stands coming from the Late Bronze Age acropolis temple at Lachish. If the animal is a bull calf, its youth would be underscored by its lack of horns. Lawrence Stager (2008: 579) suggests that the horned bull calf figurine at Ashkelon (see Figure 5.33) "depicts a male calf about a year old." The calf on the Taanach cult stand has not aged to the point of developing horns and would thus be extremely young.

Whether bull calf or colt/filly, would such a young creature be an appropriate animal to designate the status of a god such as Yahweh? (See Fleming 1999a.)[83] Because the other gods nominated (Baal for a calf; Anat/Astarte for a horse) are referred to elsewhere as offspring deities, they seemingly would be better candidates to be associated with the animal here in question. Granted, this may

THE ICONOGRAPHY OF DIVINITY: YAHWEH   325

be stretching Daniel Fleming's thesis thin, yet nowhere is Yahweh ever described as an offspring deity such that a young animal would be appropriately associated with him.[84] In contrast, the traditions we do have about Yahweh (biblical and extra-biblical) describe him as a senior/creator god and one who easily appropriated the epithets of an aged and sovereign El, together with divine warrior traditions in which he vanquishes others riding on horses with the "blast of his nostrils" (Exod 15:1, 8, 19, 21).

The Standing Figures from Kuntillet ʿAjrud Pithos A

Whether Yahweh is represented as a bull figure at Kuntillet ʿAjrud depends on (1) whether the standing figure to the left (illustration S) in Figure 7.15 does indeed have bovine features, as some scholars claim, and (2) whether that figure is then to be equated with the inscription that specifically mentions Yahweh.[85]

The notion that Yahweh was represented through bull imagery in the iconography drawn on Kuntillet ʿAjrud Pithos A was suggested from the outset by the

Figure 7.15 A depiction of two standing Bes-like figures and a seated lyre player from the Iron Age II site of Kuntillet ʿAjrud.
Courtesy of the Israel Exploration Society, Jerusalem.

excavator of the site, Ze'ev Meshel. Meshel (1979: 31; cf. 2012: 129–133), who wrote that it was "enticing to try to find a connection between the inscription [i.e., Inscription 3.1, mentioning "Yahweh and his asherah"] and the drawings below it," noticed that "the faces and ears of the two figures on the left resemble a cow or a calf." Without skipping a beat, he immediately mentioned Jeroboam's bull images and then concluded that the bovine presence was that of Yahweh and the goddess Asherah. In subsequent years, numerous scholars have reinforced Meshel's view that the two standing figures contain bovine imagery.[86] Scholars astutely pointed out how the use of Kuntillet 'Ajrud's bovine imagery with what they deemed a figure of Yahweh resonated with "theriomorphic aspects of the 'bull of Jacob'" (Coogan 1987a: 119) or Hosea's condemnation of the "young bull of Samaria" (Gilula 1979; McCarter 1987: 147).[87] Some of these scholars saw the bull imagery here as a part of Bes iconography (Meshel 1979: 30–31; Margalit 1990: 275, 288–289), while others saw such imagery as pointing away from Bes (Coogan 1987a: 123 n. 23; McCarter 1987: 154 n. 55).

Yet as certain as some of these scholars were that the features were bovine and hence not Bes (e.g., McCarter 1987: 154 n. 55: "the bovine features of both figures—the face of the larger is unmistakably that of a bull—exclude the Bes interpretation"), others were equally adamant that "there is simply nothing bovine in these figures" (Uehlinger 1997: 145) and that indeed we do have Bes represented here. For these scholars the animal characteristics are leonine, not bovine.

Those affirming that the two standing figures are Bes or Bes-like include the six scholars who have presented the most detailed analyses of the Kuntillet 'Ajrud iconography: Beck (1982, 2012), Keel and Uehlinger (1998: 210–225, 240–241), Hadley (2000: 136–155), Schmidt (2016: 59–90, esp. 84–90; 2013), and Ornan (2016).[88] Even if they disagree with her conclusions, all scholars defer to Beck's expertise when it comes to her detailed study of the Kuntillet 'Ajrud iconography. Beck (1982: 29–30; 2012: 168–169) acknowledges that "there are numerous problematic details in the depiction of these [two standing] figures" and that they are "unlike anything known so far in the Levant." Yet her conclusion is resolute: "There is no doubt that they represent the god Bes." Keel and Uehlinger (1998: 218) express an equally strong assertion: "The iconographic features (the head ornamentation that is probably a blossom and/or feather crown; the grotesque, lion-like, grimacing face with protruding ears; the beard or collar; the arms akimbo, turned outward and resting on the hips; the crooked legs that are relatively short by comparison with the upper body; the tail) and the formal characteristics (frontal representation) leave no doubt that these are representations of *Bes-type figures*." That Bes is commonly associated with music would provide a context in which the seated lyre player would make sense.[89]

As for there being two figures, because the male Bes is well documented with breasts, the second figure to the right (illustration T in Figure 7.15) need not designate the less-attested Beset, the female version of Bes.[90] In contrast, Schmidt (2016: 59–62, 65–66, 71–73; 2013) concludes from the absence of a phallus, the presence of nipple circles, and its smaller size—together with what he sees as "coherent, integrated scenes"—that our artisan is certainly gender-marking the Bes figure on the right as feminine (i.e., Beset). Yet this coherency has been called into question by Ornan (2016), who sees the "transient pottery drawings" as preliminary sketches in preparation for wall paintings. Ornan (2016: 17) even suggests that the reason for having two Bes images might correlate with their eventual destinations on two opposing door jambs, or that their differing size and design might simply be two artistic trials.

For our present discussion, it is important to point out that lion imagery lies behind the development and portrayal of the god Bes in his various manifestations, as nicely argued by James Romano (1980) in his study of the origin of the Bes image. Following Romano, Zevit (2001: 387) remarks how the various features found in typical Bes images "originated as Bes evolved iconographically in Egypt from a lion standing upright... into a more humanoid deity."[91] Similarly, Herman te Velde (1999: 173) notes that Bes "was represented... more precisely as a lion-man." Strawn (2005: 107) argues that we have seals depicting Bes as "Lord of the Lions" at ʿAtlit and Ashkelon. In critiquing Meshel's notion that the figures here are bovine, Keel and Uehlinger (1998: 217–218 n. 47; cf. Hadley 2000: 137; Schmidt 2016: 86) argue that "bovines... are almost never portrayed frontally on ancient Near Eastern two-dimensional artistic works."[92] After noting the absence of horns on our two figures, which we would expect to see if the creatures were bovine, they conclude that "Bes figures have human or lion-like heads or faces but never have bovine heads or faces."

In short, there is considerable doubt about whether the standing figures are bovine in nature. Most signs point to these being two Bes-like deities with probable leonine features, though admittedly our drawings are crude.

Acknowledging the two standing figures to be Bes or Bes-like, many scholars have abandoned Mordechai Gilula's original theory that tied the two images to the inscription and suggested that they represent Yahweh and the goddess Asherah.[93] Yet some scholars hold to both a Bes interpretation and to the notion that Yahweh and his consort Asherah are represented here. The most sophisticated of these syntheses are those of Zevit (2001: 387–392) and Schmidt (2016).[94] Though Bes is of Egyptian origin, Zevit (2001: 388) notes the remarkable frequency with which Bes amulets appear in the archaeological record of ancient Israel (cf. especially the catalogues by Christian Herrmann). Because Bes was used syncretistically with a variety of Egyptian deities, he could be viewed as "an icon expressing divinity... and not necessarily the representation of any given deity." Therefore, "in the ʿAjrud context, they signified, but did not necessarily represent a likeness of YHWH." Elaborating further, Zevit (2001: 392) concludes that "the big Bes was comprehended as an icon for YHWH ... and the little Bes either as a second icon for YHWH in some other aspect ... or for Asherata in some other guise." Schmidt (2016: 73, 84–90) argues that the two Bes figures form "a coherent scene" (see description on p. 327): "they complement each other in their respective husband-wife or ruler-consort positions." For Schmidt, the inscription mentioning Yahweh and his A/asherah would serve as "an inscribed caption in which case the respective illocutionary messages of text and figure were designed to mutually inform and complement each other and to convey a divinely-endowed and convergent aprotropaic driven semiotics: YHWH as Bes, through his mediatrix, or a female mediator, Asherah as Beset, will provide protection."

Schmidt is certainly correct to focus on the social context in which Bes figurines and amulets were used. According to Veronica Wilson (1975: 83), "In whatever guise, [Bes's] function was mainly apotropaic." It should be noted that rows of Bes deities standing next to each other (similar to the two we have at Kuntillet ʿAjrud) are attested (e.g., Altenmüller 1975: 721; Pinch 1994: 171). This underscores the protective nature of Bes in safeguarding the perimeter of a building (as did attendant lion statues in Egypt).[95] All scholars acknowledge that the numerous Bes amulets found throughout ancient Israel were apotropaic in function. Yet Judith Hadley was one of the first to make the astute observation that the Bes figurines at Kuntillet ʿAjrud fulfilled a protective function, "guarding those that were inside from harm as they rested during their perilous journey."[96] Though the dating is much later, compare the Bes figures placed on top of column capitals (Figure 7.16) and in the forecourt (Figure 7.17) of the temple dedicated to Hathor at Dendera "to act as magical defenders" (Pinch 1994: 129).

Returning to Schmidt's (and Zevit's) thesis, there is no indication that a figure of Yahweh (not to mention two) was ever used in an apotropaic function. Uehlinger (1997: 145) argues: "We can safely rule out the possibility of a state god such as Yahweh being officially represented as a Bes-like figure." Ornan (2016: 20) concurs, and elaborates: "Bes retained his lesser divine rank and apotropaic nature when appropriated into Levantine imagery and thus, his characteristics are not fitting of a major deity such as YHWH ... [M]ajor deities in the Levant, Syria and Mesopotamia were very rarely portrayed as hybrids comprised of theriomorphic and anthropomorphic features, as manifested by Bes."

The social function of apotropaism is especially relevant when one considers the fact that Judean writers (including biblical authors) were well aware of amulets and incantation specialists (Lewis 2012). That the seventh-century BCE Ketef Hinnom inscriptions were engraved as amulets is our primary example of how some Judeans turned toward Yahweh via the recitation of "effective words" (i.e., the divine name Yahweh and the so-called priestly blessing) to ward off evil.

Figure 7.16 The use of apotropaic Bes images on top of column capitals at the Temple of Dendera.

Olaf Tausch. https://commons.wikimedia.org/wiki/File:Dendera_R%C3%B6misches_Mammisi_13.JPG.

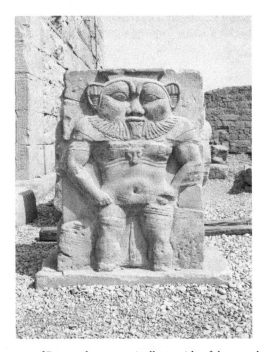

Figure 7.17 A statue of Bes used apotropaically outside of the temple dedicated to Hathor at Dendera.

Olaf Tausch. https://commons.wikimedia.org/wiki/File:Dendera_Bes_01.JPG.

Other Judeans used a wide variety of amulets. Yet the gods represented by the hundreds of amulets that have appeared in the archaeological record are never Yahweh but rather are distinctly Egyptian (Bes, Isis, Ptah, Sekhmet, Udjet; cf. Herrmann 1994, 2002, 2006). Keel and Uehlinger (1998: 350) even speak of "a continued . . . and even increased fascination" with Egyptian amulets in the Iron IIC period.

In conclusion, the Kuntillet 'Ajrud figurines cannot be used as evidence of Yahweh being portrayed through bull imagery. The two standing figures are best viewed as Bes or Bes-like figures, widely known throughout ancient Israel for their apotropaic function and apart from any association with Yahweh. Ornan (2016: 20) concludes: "Scholarly efforts to equate Bes images with YHWH and/or YHWH and Ashera are to be rejected."[97] This is not to say that the final compositional nature of the iconography (pottery drawings and wall paintings) was uniform in its theology. Furthermore, there are distinct royal themes that are only recently being emphasized with the work of Ornan (2016). Considering the various inscriptions and iconography found on in various media, it seems that multiple composers[98] (a number of them transient) hedged their bets, so to speak, with some appealing for blessings from "Yahweh [of Samaria and/or Teman] and his asherah," while others sought military aid from a divine warrior (El? Baal? Yahweh?),[99] and yet others sought protection from Egyptian Bes.[100] A certain number of residents likely employed a combination of all three.

The Bull-Headed Warrior from Bethsaida

Our last bull figure is admittedly not likely to represent Yahweh, yet it serves two purposes. First, it was found in a clear Iron Age context and in an installation (with its bull stela, raised platform, water basin, incense cups, and four more stelae of aniconic variety) that now represents the most elaborate and complete cultic gate site in the southern Levant (Figure 5.63). Second, a detailed examination of this bull figure should serve to disturb our sense of scholarly control if we think we have exhausted all possibilities for Levantine bull deities with El, Baal, and Yahweh.

A basalt stela on which was carved a bull-headed figure was found in 1997 during the excavations at Bethsaida (the Iron Age capital of Geshur) on the northern shore of the Sea of Galilee (Figure 7.18). The stela (45 in. [115 cm] high, 23 in. [59 cm] wide, and 12 in. [31 cm] thick), found in situ, quickly became the subject of scholarly interest because of what were initially thought to be unique features.[101] The bull figure is portrayed with two large curved horns, what looks like a stick figure's body with a sword strapped to its side, and four small circles in the shape of a rosette. The stela was part of a gate sanctuary that was destroyed in the latter half of the eighth century BCE (Figure 5.63).

THE ICONOGRAPHY OF DIVINITY: YAHWEH   331

Figure 7.18 A bull-headed warrior found in situ at Bethsaida on a stela that formed a part of a gate sanctuary.
Kim Walton, taken at the Israel Museum.

That the god represented here is a bull-headed warrior (complete with sword) immediately conjures descriptions of Hadad, Baal, and Yahweh as divine warriors. (See Chapter Eight.) Smith (2002a: 83–84) mentioned the Bethsaida stela in the context of his discussion of "the old northern tradition of bull iconography for Yahweh." Expectations for a Yahwistic connection could only increase with the comments by the excavators that "tenth-century B.C.E. Bethsaida allied itself with King David and his dynasty [and] (*as a result Bethsaida absorbed many Israelite cultural influences*)" (emphasis mine).[102] Absalom, when estranged from his father, fled to "Geshur of Aram," the birthplace of his mother, Maacah, one of David's queens. During his three-year exile there he is said to have made a vow to Yahweh (before a divine image?) (2 Sam 15:8). And yet any attempt to tie all these tidbits of information together to show that the Bethsaida stela presents evidence of a northern tradition of Yahweh being represented by a bull image is bound to fail.

From the very start a corrective was in place, as the excavators turned to art historians from the Fribourg school to interpret the bull iconography. Monika Bernett and Othmar Keel (1998; Keel 1998: 115–120) countered those scholars who thought that the stela was devoted to the Syrian warrior god Hadad or Baal by noting that the moon god is repeatedly associated with bull terminology in Syria and Mesopotamia.[103] In Bernett and Keel's opinion, the Syrian warrior god was more apt to be portrayed as *standing on* a bull, whereas the moon god was associated with the iconography of a bull's *head*. In addition, Bernett and Keel dispelled the notion that the moon god of South Anatolia and Syria was primarily a peaceful deity (and thus a poor fit for the Bethsaida stela with its sword).

So an initial consensus was in place that the Bethsaida bull figure owed its artistic heritage to Aramean rather than Phoenician-Canaanite influence and depicted the worship of a lunar deity, most likely Śahr, the equivalent of Sin. Subsequently, Ornan (2001: 2) wrote affirming Bernett and Keel's overall argument, yet she provided the following caution: "As the bull is a frequent symbol of the storm god in the ancient Near East in general and in the geographic area where the stelae were found in particular, one should not rule out the possibility that both gods—moon and storm deities—were alluded to on these monuments."[104] By developing her theory of "visual syncretism" through numerous examples (see too Ornan 2006), she posits "a deliberate dualism . . . according to which the features pertaining to moon imagery were oriented towards the moon worshippers, while signifiers referring to the storm god were aimed at the latter god's devotees" (2001: 25). Noting that neither set of features precludes the other, Ornan nonetheless favors the idea that we have at Bethsaida a storm god with lunar features rather than a lunar god with storm attributes. If Ornan's theory holds up under further scrutiny, then one would have to give preference to the Aramean god Hadad being represented by the bull stela at Bethsaida (together with the Aramean moon god Śahr), with a Yahweh/Śahr syncretism being only a remote possibility.

Conclusion: Possible Bull Representations of Yahweh in Material Culture

As a balance to our textual analysis, we nominated four bull images from Iron Age archaeological contexts (the Bull Site, Taanach, Kuntillet ʿAjrud, and Bethsaida) that could help us flesh out (1) whether a bull was used as Yahweh's attribute animal and (2) whether we have Yahweh associated with bovine imagery, as he clearly is with cherubim and leonine imagery. Our conclusion is mostly negative. This is regrettable, as one would hope that here archaeology would complement the textual record. Of the four possibilities, the Bes figures at Kuntillet ʿAjrud are almost certainly not bovine images of Yahweh. As for the Taanach cult stand, it would be much easier to see the quadruped as *associated* with Yahweh (it is certainly not an attribute animal) if it were a mature bull rather than a frisky calf or colt. A view of the Bethsaida bull stela as representative of Yahweh has little chance of being correct. That leaves only the exquisite Bull Site bull figure as a possibility, if it does not represent El (our preference) or Baal.

Section II: The Iconography of Yahweh: Aniconic and Abstract Traditions

The aniconic tradition has always been the subject of considerable reflection, from the curiosity of the Roman historian Tacitus to the voluminous writings of theologians wishing to probe the meanings of the first two commandments.[105] Thanks primarily to the in-depth work of Mettinger (1995), scholars now differentiate between types of aniconic traditions. In contrast to many previous works lacking such precision, Mettinger (1995: 18–20) refined our definitions of aniconism to distinguish between "de facto traditions" (indifference to icons, mere absence of images, tolerant aniconism) and "programmatic traditions" (repudiation of images, iconophobia, iconoclasm). He also introduced the terms "material aniconism" (no anthropomorphic or theriomorphic icon of the deity serving as the central cultic symbol) versus "empty space aniconism" (sacred emptiness such as Yahweh invisibly seated on the cherubim).

Material Aniconism/*Masseboth* as Representations of Yahweh

We have detailed (pp. 169–196) how material aniconism was portrayed through the use of a standing stone, what the Hebrew Bible refers to as a *massebah* (pl. *masseboth*). There we looked at the best exemplars of standing stones being used in sacred space, such as the sites of Shechem, the Bull Site, Hazor, Arad, Tel Dan, and Khirbet Ataruz. It was concluded that, at a minimum, such conspicuous standing stones constitute attention-focusing devices and are key determinants of cult, as noted by Colin Renfrew (1985: 19–20; cf. Renfrew and Bahn 2000: 408–409) and Ziony Zevit (2001: 81–82). Probing further, it was argued that such stelae can focus attention to mark a past memorable experience with a deity or deities (e.g., a theophany), to signify the place where cult (offerings, libations, prayer) to a deity or deities took place, and/or to mark the ongoing presence of the deity residing in (or symbolized by) a standing stone.

An archaeological discovery of an inscribed stela in 2008 may help the modern reader with an analogy for how the ancients might conceive of a stone that could mark both immanence and transcendence. At the end of the nineteenth century, German excavators found two large stelae (called $nṣb$, related etymologically to Hebrew *maṣṣēbâ*) in secondary contexts from the region of

Samʾal (Zincirli) in southeast Turkey. Both statues were funerary in nature and inscribed with eighth-century BCE Samʾalian Aramaic texts that mentioned the wish for a deceased person's post-mortem essence (*nbš*)[106] to eat and drink with the god Hadad in the afterlife (KAI 214.17, 21–22; cf. KAI 215.59; Lewis 2019: 359–371). In 2008 another inscribed stela (Figure 7.19) coming from the same period was found at Zincirli in controlled excavations by the University of Chicago.[107] Surprisingly, it describes how the deceased person's post-mortem essence (*nbš*) was envisioned as continuing to dwell *within the stela itself* (*bnṣb*). By analogy, if a deceased person's non-material, ongoing presence could be thought to reside in a physical stone (thereby localized in space and time), then so too could a deity's non-material presence be thought to reside in a *massebah*.[108] Zevit (2001: 257) describes *masseboth* phenomenologically as "either symbols evoking a presence, or objects engorged by the power of presence, and hence for all practical purposes en-theosed in some way."

Figure 7.19 An eighth-century BCE mortuary stela from Zincirli whose inscription mentions that the deceased person's "soul/essence" (*nabš*) was envisioned as continuing to dwell in the stela itself.
Courtesy of the Neubauer Expedition to Zincirli of the University of Chicago.

What about Yahweh? Could his presence be thought to dwell in (or be marked by) stone? Previously we focused on the possibility of El's presence being marked by standing stones, especially due to the explicit literary traditions about such stones in the Bethel narratives (Gen 28:18, 22; 31:13; 35:6–15; cf. Gen 49:24).[109] This fits well with what we know about the worship of El at Shechem as well as the deity's association with sacred space on a small scale (stones, altars, and trees, as opposed to temples of ashlar masonry), which finds a direct correlate with clan and family religion rather than the religion of the state.

The question of whether Yahweh was symbolized by standing stones is both easy and hard to answer. The easy (superficial) answer from the stylus of the author of Deuteronomy 16:22 strongly states that Yahweh hates (śānēʾ yhwh) *masseboth*, and therefore injunctions are made against their erection (wĕlōʾ-tāqîm lĕkā maṣṣēbâ). Such strong objections are echoed elsewhere—for example, in the Holiness Code (Lev 26:1), and by authors/traditions that associated *masseboth* with foreign gods (Exod 23:23–24; 34:11–14; Deut 7:5; 12:3; Jer 43:13; cf. Ezek 26:11). Several deities were mentioned by name, including Baal (2 Kgs 3:2; 10:26–27) and seemingly Astarte, Chemosh, and Milcom (2 Kgs 23:13–14). Reading between the lines, one can infer that segments of the ancient Israelite population were indeed engaged in using *masseboth* in non-Yahwistic cultic contexts, to the degree that they drew the ire of the writers just mentioned. The monolatrous author of Exodus 34:14 writes that *masseboth* should be smashed precisely because "Yahweh whose name is Jealous" (yhwh qannāʾ šĕmô) is "a jealous god" (ʾēl qannāʾ hûʾ) who tolerates no rivals (lōʾ tištaḥăweh lĕʾēl ʾaḥēr).[110]

And yet what we know of the Deuteronomistic emphasis on the transcendence of Yahweh (where Yahweh is localized in heaven with only his "Name" resident in the Jerusalem Temple) makes us wonder whether the injunctions against the *masseboth* are only due to fears of polytheism and/or syncretism. It seems that even *masseboth* used in the service of Yahweh were deemed tainted beyond legitimate use. As noted years ago by E. Stockton (1972: 18), "The high places (presumably with their associated *masseboth*) which were destroyed by Hezekiah and Josiah *belonged to the Yahwistic cult*. This is deduced from the Assyrian taunts about Hezekiah's reliance on [Yahweh] the God whose high places he had destroyed (2 Ki. xviii:22) and from Josiah's restraint against the priests of the provincial high places (2 Ki. xxiii:8–9)." Indeed, Hezekiah's destruction of the *masseboth* makes no mention of foreign gods (2 Kgs 18:4; cf. too 1 Kgs 14:23). Thus one can only conclude that certain segments of Israelite society were using *masseboth* in their worship of Yahweh just as they did with foreign gods. Such adherents could have used the heritage of a legitimate use of *masseboth* in the older El traditions as a counterweight to the injunctions coming from Deuteronomic (Deut 16:22) and Priestly (Lev 16:22) hands. An additional counterweight may have been a tradition such as the one preserved in 1

Samuel 7:12 where Yahweh is associated with "stone" imagery (i.e., the Ebenezer stone = "Yahweh has helped us"), as was El when he was described as "the Stone ['*eben*] of Israel" (Gen 49:24).[111]

Remarkably, we do have a single passage (but only one) that explicitly records a positive tradition of Yahweh with *masseboth*.[112] Isaiah 19:18–22 reads:

> In that day there will be five cities in the land of Egypt speaking "the language of Canaan" [*śĕpat kĕnaʿan*] and swearing allegiance to Yahweh of Hosts.... In that day there will be an altar to Yahweh in the midst of the land of Egypt, and a *massebah* to Yahweh at its border. They [lit. "it"] shall serve as a sign ['*ôt*] and a witness ['*ēd*] to Yahweh of Hosts in the land of Egypt, so that when [the Egyptians] cry out to Yahweh because of oppressors he will send them a savior, and will defend and deliver them. And Yahweh will make himself known to the Egyptians; and the Egyptians will know Yahweh in that day and worship with sacrifice and oblation, and they will make vows to Yahweh and fulfill them. Yahweh will first afflict Egypt and then heal; when they return to Yahweh, he will respond to their entreaties and heal them.

The specifics of the historical context behind this passage (and its genre as a possible *vaticinia ex eventu*) need not detain us here, although a significant amount of literature has been devoted to the presence of Yahwism in Egypt during the times of King Jehoahaz (818–802 BCE), the Persian period (as evidenced by the Elephantine papyri), and the time of the priests Onias III–IV from the Hellensitic period.[113] Suffice it to quote Hans Wildberger's (1997: 274) summation that "every attempt to arrive at a precise date for [Isaiah] 19:19 has come up short."

Though the *massebah* in Isaiah 19:19 marks a border (cf. Gen 31:44–49), Wildberger (1997: 275) is certainly correct when he writes that "the context here would only allow one to identify the *massebah* as a specific reference to a cultic object." In addition, note how the *massebah* (along with the altar) serves as "a sign ['*ôt*] and a witness ['*ēd*] to Yahweh of Hosts."[114] One could not ask for more apt words to designate what we have referred to as a conspicuous stone used as an attention-focusing device! Thus if we return to the six examples of standing stones in the archaeological record (detailed with pictures in Chapter Five, pp. 169–196), theoretically any one of these could have marked Yahweh's presence as easily as they could have marked the presence of El.

Other Abstract Traditions: From Sacred Stone to Sacred Emptiness

Among their archaeological indicators of cultic ritual, Renfrew and Bahn note that the association with a deity or deities may be reflected in the use of a cult [= divine] image, or *a representation of the deity in abstract form* (e.g., the Christian Chi-Rho symbol). [My emphasis][115]

The use of abstract symbols for ancient Near Eastern religions is well documented.[116] As we have just seen, abstract expressions can be conveyed through the most physical of objects (standing stones). At the same time, abstract thought (in every religious tradition) has produced "images" of divinity that go beyond the use of physical objects and symbols. Scholars—including biblicists, Assyriologists, and anthropologists—describing this type of presence often use Rudolph Otto's categories of *fascinans* and *tremendum* from his *The Idea of the Holy: An Inquiry into the Non-Rational Factor in the Idea of the Divine and Its Relation to the Rational*.[117] For example, van der Toorn (1999: 363), commenting on both Akkadian *melammu* and Hebrew *kābôd*, writes: "This glory is a luminosity which both frightens and fascinates; it is, in terms of Rudolph Otto, truly numinous." Similarly, we read from Benjamin Sommer's (2009: 97; cf. 2001: 59) treatment of the bodies of God:

> [A] duality . . . results from the tension between two religious impulses, neither of which is confined to a particular period, place, or culture. One impulse emphasizes what the theorist of religion Rudolph Otto called *fascinans*, the aspect of divinity that humans find alluring and appealing. This impulse produces a desire to approach the divine, and hence it reflects a hope that God is locatable, even in a physical sense. . . . The other impulse is rooted in what Otto calls the *tremendum*—the overwhelming, dangerous, and repelling aspects of the divine. From this viewpoint, the divine realm must be a realm of absolute freedom, and hence the divine cannot be confined to a single place and can never be confidently located by humans.

Sommer here sounds very much like the Yale theologian-ethicist H. Richard Niebuhr (1960: 120), who wrote of the difference between "visible and tangible" objects of adoration, "of whose reality our senses give us assurance," and objects of adoration, which are "essences, ideas, concepts, or images which are accessible only to abstract thought."

Perhaps one could say that humans hunger for the visible, ever desiring to picture the divine in material terms. Sculptors and painters both ancient and modern have satisfied this desire, as the examples given here attest.[118] Writers use anthropomorphisms to dress their gods in human clothes, deeds, and actions or theriomorphisms to describe superhuman power and virility. Yet for others, divine essence goes beyond such crafting. For them, abstract ideas "exercise a certain compulsion over the mind . . . known only by a kind of empathy or by an intuition that outruns sense [perception]."[119]

To keep our treatment anchored to the ancient Near East, it is best to consider briefly how other ancient writers used abstract images to depict the divine.[120] I have no intention of unpacking the various and widespread (geographically and chronologically) notions of "holiness," "transcendence," or "the sacred" throughout the ancient Near East.[121] For our purposes, three sample cases will do for reorienting our thoughts away from our modern categories and adjusting them to be more in line with how the ancients might have thought a god could take up real residence via a non-material presence. Our sampling will include (1) the use of *melammu* in Mesopotamia, especially in the Sargonid period, (2) the Aten cult in Egypt, and (3) the Iron Age Ayn Dara temple in Syria. Without any desire to make one-to-one comparisons (or be guilty of "parallelomania"), we will then turn our attention to corresponding references to divine radiance, light, and sacred emptiness in the Hebrew Bible. Attention must also be given to how the ancients personified particular aspects of a deity that then serve as a surrogate for the deity. Here scholars use the vocabulary of "hypostasis" to articulate how such personifications can function as the "cultically available presence" of a deity.[122] In particular, in order to understand Deuteronomistic Name Theology, we will examine whether the essence of a deity could be contained in his name to such an extent that it could function hypostatically in an effective way, especially as that name "resides" in the Jerusalem Temple.

The Use of Abstract Images in the Ancient Near East to Depict the Divine: A Brief Glimpse

The Sumerologist Thorkild Jacobsen (1976: 3) wrote of "a unique experience of confrontation with power not of this world" that Otto called "numinous" and that was "basic to all religion—and also to ancient Mesopotamian religion."[123] In Jacobsen's adaptation of Otto, this numinous power was "*terrifying*, ranging from sheer demonic dread through awe to sublime majesty," as well as "*fascinating*, with irresistible attraction" (my emphasis). Jacobsen (1976: 5–6, 14) went on to note the "tendency to experience the numinous as immanent" in Mesopotamian religion, especially with how "the fashioning of images of the god sought and achieved his lasting presence." At the same time, he used the language of *tremendum* to describe the sacred space where the deity took up residence:

> Unlike a human dwelling... the temple was sacred. The ancient Mesopotamian temple was profoundly awesome, sharing in the *tremendum* of the Numinous. It carried "awesome aura" (ni) and awesome "nimbus" (me-lam). The temple

of Nusku in Nippur was a "temple laden with great awesome aura and angry nimbus." Also in Nippur was Enlil's temple: "Ekur, the blue house, your (Enlil's) great seat, laden with awesomeness, its beams of awe and glory reach toward heaven, its shadow lies upon all lands." As it participated in the *tremendum* of the Numinous, so also in its *fascinosum* and its *mysterium*. (Jacobsen 1976: 16; my emphasis)

Thirty years later, the concept of *melammu* was studied in detail by Shawn Aster.[124] According to Aster (2006: 74), in the Sargonid period (starting in 720 BCE) *melammu* "acquires the meaning radiance . . . it can be used in a way that is identical to *girru* (fire), *birbirrū* (luminosity), *namrirrū* (radiance), *šarūru* (light), and *šalummatu* (radiance)." Nergal, for example is described as "fire, wearing *melammu*" (*girru lābiš melamme*), and Ishtar of Arba'il as "clothed in fire, bearing *melammu*" (*girru litbušat melamme našâta*) (Aster 2006: 75, 77). The moon god Nanna's *melammu* radiates luminosity; the sun god Shamash's *melammu* displays the brightness of sunshine (Aster 2006: 96–98). Above all, when used of divinity[125] *melammu* celebrates the god's power, an unseen[126] though irresistible force that overwhelms any enemy. Thus when an Assyrian king went to battle, he was assured of victory because he was thought to embody "the awe of the radiance (*pulḫu melamme*) of Aššur" that frightened enemies into submission even from afar.[127]

Anthropomorphic and theriomorphic representations of deities in ancient Egypt are ubiquitous. At the same time, Egypt presents a plethora of material for exploring abstract, aniconic representations of divinity, especially with the deity Amun and even more so with Aten (cf. Mettinger 1995: 49–56). Aten's self-origin is such an unknown mystery that it "cannot be captured by means of iconic representation" (Assmann 1992: 165). Aten is "the one who constructed himself with his own arms, the craftsman does not know him" (*p3 qd sw ḏs·f m'·wy·f bw rḫ sw ḥmw*).[128] Indeed, Aten never appears in the form of a statue; all that appears is a sun disk with rays ending in human hands—a "concession to anthropomorphism" (Figure 7.20).[129] Donald Redford (1984: 175) describes Akhenaten's iconography as "the most prominent act in a progressive move to rid concepts of the divine . . . of all anthropomorphic and theriomorphic forms." In Mettinger's (1995: 49) words, "The god's parousia in light suppresses and supersedes all forms of symbolic representation."

Of note here is how the Aten cult of Akhenaten (1352–1336 BCE) used the immaterial concept of light to depict the glorious essence and real presence of divinity.[130] Scholars (especially Assmann [1983, 1992]) have underscored how Aten was "not just another form of the sun god, or the sun disk, but the living sun best described as the light."[131] Note too John L. Foster's articulation of how Aten

340   THE ORIGIN AND CHARACTER OF GOD

Figure 7.20 The Egyptian god Aten depicted as a sun disk with rays ending in human hands extending down to Akhenaten, Nefertiti, and their children.
Kim Walton, taken at the Neues Museum, Berlin.

is "unseen" and at the same time a "visible incarnation" as the light of the sun shines on the earth:

> "Aten" is the name for the visible incarnation or manifestation of the unseen godhead . . . light is pervasive in the *Hymn* [to Aten] . . . The physical attributes of Aten are described by [abstract] words such as "lovely," "gleaming," or "dazzling." [Aten] is the light of day, which bathes every object in creation with its caressing and revealing rays . . . and everything is made visible by means of Aten, who actually "drives away" the darkness of light. (Foster 1995: 1757)

Lastly, to showcase abstract thought via material culture, consider the Iron Age temple at the site of Ayn Dara in northern Syria, discovered in 1955, excavated in the 1980s (Abou-Assaf 1990), and, sadly, severely damaged in 2018 by Turkish airstrikes. This temple has attracted the attention of Northwest Semitic scholars, in particular those who used it to understand architectural features and symbolism in the literary description of Solomon's temple (Bloch-Smith 1994: 21, 23; Monson 2000, 2006) and those who saw it as relevant to the study of aniconism (Lewis 1998: 40; 2005a: 105–107; Mettinger 2006: 284).

At Ayn Dara we have one of the most fascinating and profound depictions of the divine (Figures 7.21–22. Everything about its abstract (quasi-anthropomorphic) portrayal is majestic. The deity (god or goddess?) was dramatized as simultaneously transcendent and immanent by artisans who made him/her disappear and yet leave behind a trace of his/her presence.[132] As can be seen from the plans of the temple published by Ali Abou-Assaf (1990: Abb. 13–14) and John Monson (2000: 23), four huge footprints (of bare feet) were carved into three large limestone slabs that served as threshholds of the temple. That each of the footprints measures approximately 3.2 ft. (0.97 m) in length (Figure 7.22) shows that the imagined deity was portrayed as superhuman in size, with estimates (based on the length of stride) of 65 ft. (19.8 m) tall.[133]

The layout of the footprints depicts the deity entering the temple and walking back to the inner sanctum, where the statue of the deity would normally be found. At the portico entrance to the temple (Figure 7.21) we find two footprints represented side by side on the first stone slab, "as if some giant [deity] had paused at the entryway before striding into the building" (Monson 2000: 27). As one progresses forward, each of the next two limestone slabs has a single carved footprint: first the left foot, followed by the right.

The first two stone slabs are adjacent (Figure 7.21). The length between the second and third slabs (depicting the right leg stride of the deity) is about 30 ft. (9.1 m). The ancient artisans are portraying the deity standing at the entrance to the temple and then walking, right foot after the left, into the inner sanctum. One knows the deity was (and is still?) present, not because a physical, anthropomorphic statue embodies the deity but from a type of sacred emptiness (i.e., the footprints left behind). The intricate carving makes the viewer imagine that the god left his/her impression in rock as humans do in sand. Such artistry evoked feelings of intimacy and wonder about how the god was tangibly present and yet also invisibly transcendent.

Resetting our Iconoclastic Clock

I chose these three positive examples from the ancient Near East deliberately in order to reset our iconoclastic clock prior to turning to the Hebrew Bible, also a product of the ancient Near East. Aniconism is regularly associated with iconoclasm (though their pairing is not always appropriate). Because iconoclasm

Figure 7.21 The Iron Age Syro-Hittite temple at Ayn Dara in northern Syria showing a series of large footprints depicting the deity walking from the portico entrance into the inner chambers. Two large side-by-side carved footprints depict the deity standing still prior to striding into the inner sanctum, depicted with a single left footprint followed by, farther in, a single right footprint.
Courtesy Kathryn Hooge Hom and Kim Walton.

THE ICONOGRAPHY OF DIVINITY: YAHWEH 343

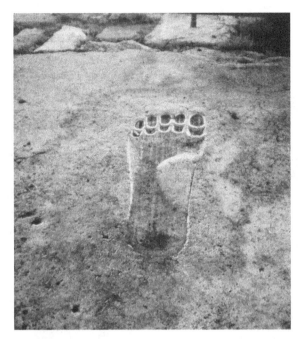

Figure 7.22 A close-up of the left footprint (3.2 ft [0.97 m] long) carved into the limestone threshold. The footprints depict a type of aniconic representation of divinity.
Courtesy Theodore J. Lewis.

involves the deliberate destruction of a culture's own religious icons, we cannot help but view it pejoratively—even more so if we think of the 2001 destruction of the giant Buddhas of Bamyan by the ultra-iconoclastic Taliban of Afghanistan or the numerous cultural atrocities of ISIS. The brutality of such acts should not be minimized. And yet some depictions of the divine as "unseen" (dare we even say some iconoclastic visions?) are born of poetry, artistry, and/or a philosophy that prefers abstract thought as the best way to depict divine essence.

Lastly, it should also be underscored that the ancients certainly thought that one could speak about a god's "unseen" or "transcendent" presence. To do so only enhanced the majesty and mystery of the divine. The examples we gave did not resort to the language of the ineffable to describe divinity. "Ineffable" (so well known via its later use with the name Yahweh) designates how adherents think that divinity is incapable of being expressed (because of the god's indescribable nature) and/or unutterable in nature (e.g., not to be spoken of because of the risk of misuse or irreverence). Rather, the poets strained the limits of language to describe the *tremendum* of divinity. They used text and material culture to celebrate manifestations of divine glory.

The Hebrew Bible's Use of Abstract Images to Depict the Divine

The Hebrew Bible uses many abstract images to depict the divine. It has even been argued by grammarians that the use of the plural noun *ĕlōhîm* to designate a singular deity may be due to the frequent use of grammatical plurals in Hebrew to designate abstract concepts and especially those of intensity and quality.[134] Despite the plethora of these abstract depictions, we will restrict the following treatment to only the primary pictures—namely, those that echo common ancient Near Eastern themes such as radiance, fire, light, and sacred emptiness. The aggregate of such multifaceted notions contributed to why certain individuals advocated the unseen, aniconic portrayal of Yahweh and as a result to the absence of any divine images in the inner sanctum of the Jerusalem Temple.

Radiance and Fire

As with the use of *melammu* in Mesopotamia, chief among the abstract pictures drawn of Yahweh was that (whatever his true essence was thought to be) his presence was manifested via radiance (*kābôd*) and fire (*'ēš*).[135] As the radiant Ishtar of Arba'il could be poetically described as "clothed in fire, bearing *melammu*" (*girru litbušat melamme našâta*), so too Yahweh's "radiance" (*kābôd*) is "like a devouring fire" (*kĕ'ēš 'ōkelet*; Exod 24:17; Deut 4:24; 9:3; Isa 10:17). He is one who "is clothed in glory and majesty, wrapped in a garment of light" (*hôd wĕhādār lābāštā 'ōṭeh-'ôr kaśśalmâ*; Ps 104:1–2), whose "radiance" (*kābôd*) is "encompassing brilliance" (*nōgah sābîb*; Ezek 1:28; 10:4). As "the awe of the radiance [*pulḫu melamme*] of Aššur" frightened enemies into submission even from afar, so too did "the terror of Yahweh" (*paḥad yhwh*) cause the unrighteous to flee into caves "from the radiance of his majesty" (*mēhădar gĕ'ônô*) when "Yahweh rises to terrify the earth" (*bĕqûmô la'ărōṣ hā'āreṣ*; Isa 2:10, 19, 21).[136]

Divine Fire

The Use of Fire to Depict the Presence of Yahweh
The numinous quality of fire is one of the most (perhaps *the* most) enduring of images used by the authors of the Hebrew Bible to depict divine presence. It

appears in every literary strand (i.e., Pentateuchal), in most literary genres, and throughout every period. For example, the "pillar of fire" (ʿammûd ʾēš) motif as a symbol of Yahweh's presence during the Exodus wanderings ("to give them light," lĕhāʾîr lāhem) is articulated in both J/non-P (Exod 13:21-22; 14:24; Num 14:14) and P (Num 9:15-16) literary strands, not to mention its use in Deuteronomy 1:33, in Psalm 78:14 ("with fiery light," bĕʾôr ʾēš), and as late as Nehemiah (9:12, 19). Should we narrow our focus to divine presence in battle via fire, in addition to a fiery Yahweh we would have a plethora of comparative material from elsewhere in the ancient Near East and Greece from which to choose (see Weinfeld 1983: 131–140).

Surely the *locus classicus* for divine fire is Yahweh's self-revelation, found in the burning bush episode in Exodus 3:1–6, a section that traditionally has been seen as a mixture of J and E literary strands.[137] On a thematic level, Propp (1999: 36) notes how fire as "the medium by which Yahweh appears on the terrestrial plane" is a recurring theme that serves "to unify the Book of Exodus." Similarly, Greenberg (1969: 16–17) suggests that "it is possible to epitomize the entire story of Exodus as the movement of the fiery manifestation of the divine presence." In Exodus 3:1–8 the divine revelation of Yahweh appears in a flame of fire (bĕlabbat-ʾēš).[138] Its qualities make it easy to understand why fire was chosen as a vehicle to articulate the numinous. Yet what we have here goes beyond even the wonders of natural fire. That the fire does not consume the bush (defying "nature's laws and all human experience") lends a preternatural aspect to the divine encounter.[139] The antiquity of this lore is underscored by a fragment of archaic poetry that mentions Yahweh's epithet as "He who dwells in the bush" (šōknî sĕneh; Deut 33:16).[140]

The use of fire to represent Yahweh appears in other memorable J/non-P passages as well. Fire depicts the divine presence as a "flaming torch" (lappîd ʾēš) moving between the cut animals in the Abrahamic covenant ceremony in Genesis 15:17. Yahweh descends on Mt. Sinai in fire and smoke, "like the smoke from a kiln" (yārad ... yhwh bāʾēš ... ʾăšānô kĕʿešen hakkibšān), in J's theophany in Exodus 19:18. The Priestly tradition uses distinctly different vocabulary (which we will treat later), yet its description of the divine theophany (i.e., the appearance of the radiance of Yahweh [marʾēh kĕbôd yhwh]) also emphasizes how its nature was akin to "devouring fire" (kĕʾēš ʾōkelet) on the top of the mountain (Exod 24:17). So too the Deuteronomic traditions describe the mountain of divine revelation as "ablaze with fire" (bōʿēr bāʾēš; Deut 4:11; 9:15).

A survey of other theophanies in the Hebrew Bible reveals that fire together with associated storm images are the norm for depicting the active presence of Yahweh. In the storm god theophany found in Psalm 18 (//2 Sam 22), Yahweh again descends (18:10 [Eng 18:9]; cf. Exod 19:18), but this time by "bowing the heavens" (*wayyēṭ šāmayim wayyērad*; cf. Ps 144:5). With "fiery transcendent anthropomorphisms" via "poetry of high antiquity"[141] we read:

The earth heaved and quaked,	*wattigʿaš wattirʿaš hāʾāreṣ*
foundations of mountains shook;	*ûmôsdê hārîm yirgāzû*
they reeled, because his [anger] burned.	*wayyitgāʿăšû kî-ḥārâ lô*
Smoke rose from his nostrils,	*ʿālâ ʿāšān bĕʾappô*
fire from his mouth devouring;	*wĕʾēš-mippîw tōʾkēl*
coals blazed forth from him . . .	*geḥālîm bāʿărû mimmennû* . . .
He bowed the heavens and came down	*wayyēṭ šāmayim wayyērad*
Dark clouds beneath his feet	*waʿărāpel taḥat raglāyw*
He mounted the cherub and flew	*wayyirkab ʿal-kĕrûb wayyāʿōp*
He flew on the wings of the wind . . .	*wayyēdeʾ ʿal-kanpê-rûaḥ* . . .
Out of the brilliance before him	*minnōgah negdô*
his clouds broke through,	*ʿābāyw ʿābĕrû*
fiery hail[142] and fiery coals.	*bārād wĕgaḥălê-ʾēš*
Yahweh thundered from the heavens,	*wayyarʿēm baššāmayim yhwh*
Elyon uttered his voice,	*wĕʿelyôn yittēn qōlô*
fiery hail and fiery coals.	*bārād wĕgaḥălê-ʾēš*
He loosed his arrows and scattered them;	*wayyišlaḥ ḥiṣṣāyw wayĕpîṣēm*
he discharged lightning and terrified them.	*ûbĕrāqîm rāb wayĕhummēm*[143]

(Ps 18:8–11, 13–15 [Eng 18:7–10, 12–14];
cf. 2 Sam 22:8–11, 13–15)

Notice the dramatic effect of the piling up of fiery images emanating from Yahweh: fire (*ʾēš*), coals (*geḥālîm*), brilliance (*nōgah*), fiery hail (*bārād*), lightning (*bĕrāqîm*), and verbs of burning (*ḥārâ*), devouring (*tōʾkēl*), blazing (*bāʿărû*), thundering (*yarʿēm*), and discharging (*rāb*). Isaiah 30:27–30 (also couched in storm language) expresses similar "fiery transcendent anthropomorphism" when it likens Yahweh's *tongue* to "devouring fire" (*lĕšônô kĕʾēš ʾōkālet*) or conveys Yahweh's "majestic *voice*" (*hôd qôlô*)[144] and "the descent of his *arm*" (*naḥat zĕrôʿô*) through "devouring flames of fire" (*lahab ʾēš ʾôkēlâ*).[145]

By noting the presence of divine fire in storm theophanies we are not suggesting that authors drew only upon tempests as sources of imagery. As Delbert Hillers (1964) has noted, divine fire plays a key role in mythological battles in ancient Near Eastern and classical traditions. In Hillers' analysis of

Amos 7:4, Yahweh is portrayed by the prophet as "summoning a rain of fire" (*qōrēʾ lirbîb ʾēš*) to consume the Great Deep (*wattōʾkal ʾet-těhôm rabbâ*).[146] "The text is thus to be understood as the prophet's vision of the conflict of Yahweh with the primordial monster of the deep, in which his weapon is lightning, or supernatural fire" (Hillers 1964: 222).[147] Surely each of these genres (storm theophanies and combat myths) blurred lines of distinction in their use of fiery images to depict the divine.

Fire representing the active presence of Yahweh is clearly seen in the famous trial by ordeal on Mt. Carmel between Yahweh and Baal (and their respective prophets, with Elijah taking center stage) in 1 Kings 18. The agreed-upon terms of the contest specifically state that "the god who answers via fire, he is god" (*hāʾělōhîm ʾăšer-yaʿăneh bāʾēš hûʾ hāʾělōhîm*; 1 Kgs 18:24). According to the Septuagint reading of 1 Kings 18:36 (which is preferable), Elijah cries out to the heavens, "Answer me, O Yahweh, answer me this day *in fire* [*en puri*] so that these people may know that you are Yahweh."[148] As one could have guessed from the outset, Baal's "voice" (*qôl*; a play on thunder?) never answers, whereas "the fire of Yahweh" (*ʾēš-yhwh*) falls from the heavens. In dramatic fashion, the conflagration consumes not just the bull offering but the altar complex as well (1 Kgs 18:38). As Volkmar Fritz (2003: 193) concludes, "The climax has to be seen as a self-revelation of Yahweh."

A countertrend (that serves to prove the same point) is preserved later in the Elijah narrative of 1 Kings 19. In this polemical narrative, the author states that Yahweh is *not* made manifest via the traditional features that accompany a storm theophany, even those found elsewhere in the Hebrew Bible (e.g., Exod 19:16–19; 20:18; Judg 5:4–5; 2 Sam 22:8–15//Ps 18:8–15 [Eng 18:7–14]; Ps 68:9; Hab 3:3–6). According to 1 Kings 19:11–12, Yahweh was not in the great and mighty wind (*rûaḥ gědôlâ wěḥāzāq*), the earthquake (*raʿaš*), or the fire (*ʾēš*). The polemical nature of this passage is easily seen, as it argues that Yahweh is not to be thought of as akin to the storm god Baal (Jeremias 1965: 73–90; Cross 1973: 194; contra Cogan 2001: 457 n. 2). Reading between the lines (and with widespread support from elsewhere in the Hebrew Bible), it is clear that—as much as the author advocates otherwise—Yahweh was indeed thought by many to be a storm god whose active presence was manifest via the travail of nature and especially via fire.[149]

From Fiery Accompaniment to Attendant Beings of Fire

As surely as there were those who viewed Yahweh as manifest in fire or by means of fire, there were others who felt more comfortable keeping Yahweh's essence distinct from fire, which served as an agent of the deity's will. Granted, here too the lines of distinction are blurry. How much the average Judean was interested in probing the so-called creator-creature difference is anyone's guess.

Alongside the passages just discussed (where fire is more intimately associated with the self-revelation of Yahweh) are other portions of Hebrew Bible that clearly demonstrate that fire was thought to be an entity that serves God's purposes more than a mode of divine revelation. Thus we read in Psalm 97:

> Yahweh is king! Let the earth exult!
> Let the many isles rejoice!
>
> Clouds and thick darkness enfold him;
> righteousness and justice are the base of his throne.
>
> Fire goes before him [*'ēš lěpānāyw tēlēk*]
> burning his foes on every side [*tělahēṭ sābîb ṣārāyw*].
>
> His lightnings lighten the world;
> the earth sees and trembles.
>
> The mountains melt like wax before Yahweh's presence,
> at the presence of the Lord of all the earth. (Ps 97:1–5)

Similarly, according to Isaiah 29:5–6, when "Yahweh of Armies" brings his divine visitation (*mēʿim yhwh ṣěbāʾôt tippāqēd*), he does so in an instant, with thunder, earthquake, and loud roar (*běraʿam ûbraʿaš wěqôl gādôl*)//with tumult, tempest, and blaze of devouring fire (*sûpâ ûsěʿārâ wělahab ʾēš ʾôkēlâ*). Such passages could be replicated elsewhere, for many other poets picked up on the motif of how "devouring fire preceded Yahweh" (*ʾēš-lěpānāyw tōʾkēl*; Ps 50:3).

With the specific vocabulary of "fire going before Yahweh," one wonders if fire was ever thought to be a member of Yahweh's divine entourage similar to Deber and Reshep, mentioned in Habakkuk 3:5.

| Before him went Pestilence, | *lěpānāyw yēlek dāber* |
| Plague followed close behind. | *yēṣēʾ rešep lěraglāyw* |

Perhaps a hint is to be found in the archaic yet very difficult poem found in Deuteronomy 33:2:[150]

> Yahweh came from Sinai
> He dawned from Seir . . .[151]
> He beamed forth from Mt. Paran.
>
> With him[152] were myriads of holy ones [*riběbōt qōdeš*],
> At/From his right hand fire flies forth [*'ēš dāt*],
> Yea, the consecrated [?] of troops [*ḥōbēb*[153] *ʿammîm*].

Of the enigmatic ʾēš dāt (and its anachronistic pointing "fire of law"), Patrick Miller (1964: 241) writes that it is "entirely unintelligible." Frank Moore Cross and David Freedman (1975: 72 n. 11; cf. Cross 1973: 101) write of "conjectures [that] are almost as numerous as scholars"—to which they then add their own ingenious conjectural reading. Scholars who try to salvage a reading from the consonants of the Masoretic text (though with emendation) include S. R. Driver's (1895: 393) "burning fire" (ʾēš dāt ēš [yōqe]det) and Jeffrey Tigay's (1996: 320) "blazing fire" (ʾēš dāt ēš d[ōleqe]t).[154] A breakthrough came with Steiner (1996), who keeps the consonantal text as is but reads dāt as a contraction of an archaic verbal form *dāʾāt—thus producing the translation "from his right, fire flew."[155] We have already documented the numerous occurrences of fiery images emanating from Yahweh in Psalm 18//2 Samuel 22. What should also be underscored is that the psalmist's picture of Yawheh coming with fire also involves him flying (yēdeʾ), with the same verb being used in Psalm 18:11 that Steiner posits for Deuteronomy 33:2! (On the iconography of a god flying with fire, see Figure 7.23.)

Perhaps mythopoeic layers of tradition lie behind the mythopoetic metaphors we read in Psalm 104:4. Here Yahweh is described as

He who makes the winds his messengers,	ʿōśeh malʾākāyw rûḥôt
fiery flames his ministers	měšārtāyw ʾēš lōhēṭ

Hendel (1985) explores just such ideas in his analysis of "the flame of the ever-whirling sword" (lahaṭ haḥereb hammithappeket) that guards the way to the tree of life in Genesis 3:24.[156] Building on the work of Miller (1965), Hendel cites Phoenician inscriptions bearing the epithet "Reshep of the Arrow" (ršp ḥṣ) and the mention of "a pair of fiery divine beings" wielding sharpened swords at Ugarit.[157] Hendel suggests that the "Flame" (lahaṭ) in Genesis 3:24, in similar fashion, represents "an independent fiery being, a divine being in service to Yahweh, in precisely the same mythological category as the cherubim." Similarly, it cannot just be a coincidence that Yahweh (who self-reveals by fire) is attended by seraphim (śěrāpîm), creatures whose name has an etymology (śrp = "to burn") that clearly has to do with their fiery nature (Isa 6:1–7).[158] That they are able to manipulate the burning coal (rispâ běmelqaḥayim) from the altar in the Jerusalem Temple thus comes as no surprise (Isa 6:6).

The most prominent being that attends Yahweh and carries out his wishes is the so-called Messenger/Angel of Yahweh, known in Hebrew as malʾak-Yahweh. This enigmatic figure is depicted as human yet also quasi-divine in nature and even a direct manifestation of Yahweh. For the present discussion, note the associations of the malʾak-Yahweh with fire. In the burning bush episode, it is the malʾak-Yahweh that appears "in a flame of fire" (bělabbat-ʾēš). In Judges 13:2–23 the appearance of the *malʾak*-Yahweh is cloaked in mystery, with his true identity not immediately recognized (13:16). He is portrayed as a human (*ʾîš*) at the outset and in the middle of the story (13:6, 8, 10–11). Yet because of his "extremely terrifying" (*nôrāʾ mĕʾōd*) appearance, his mysterious lack of a name (13:6, 17–18), and the supernatural events that follow, he is thought to be divine (*ʾĕlōhîm*) by Manoah and his wife (13:21–22). The climactic event that causes them to think they have seen the very presence of God (and thus are in danger of death) is the *malʾak*-Yahweh's ascent "in the very flame of the altar" (*bĕlahab hammizbēaḥ*).[159]

> Manoah took the kid and the meal offering, and offered them upon the rock to Yahweh, to him who works wonders. While Manoah and his wife looked on, as the flames ascended from the altar toward heaven, the *malʾak*-Yahweh ascended in the very flame of the altar (all while Manoah and his wife actually looked on). They flung themselves on their faces to the ground. The *malʾak*-Yahweh never appeared again to Manoah and his wife. Manoah then realized that the being was the *malʾak*-Yahweh. Manoah exclaimed to his wife, "We shall surely die, for we have seen God."[160] (Judg 13:19–22)

An older tradition that speaks of Yahweh fighting for his people (*yhwh yillāḥēm lākem/yhwh nilḥām lāhem*; Exod 14:14, 25) is found in Exodus 14. Similar to the fiery *malʾak*-Yahweh passages in Exodus 3:1–6 and Judges 13:19–22, this passage strongly implies that the divine messenger (here *malʾak hāʾĕlōhîm*) who goes before the armies of Israel was equated with the well-known pillar of fire (Exod 14:19, 24). Propp (1999: 549), following H. Holzinger, "renders *bĕʿammud* [*ʾēš*] (13:21[; cf. 14:24]) as '*in the form of* a pillar'—i.e., the pillar [of fire] *is* God or his angelic manifestation" (italics Propp's).

Yet another messenger of God, this time the prophet Elijah, also goes up in flames, so to speak. Granted, nowhere is Elijah explicitly referred to as a "messenger of Yahweh" (*malʾak yhwh*), as is the later prophet Haggai (Hag 1:13; cf. Mal 1:1; 3:1), yet 2 Chronicles 21:12 alludes to a tradition of Elijah sending a letter on behalf of Yahweh to King Jehoram.[161] According to 2 Kings 2:11–12, Elijah, at the end of his earthly life, ascends to the heavens with "a chariot of fire and horses of fire" (*rekeb-ʾēš wĕsûsê ʾēš*) that separate him from the earthbound Elisha (2 Kgs 2:11–12; cf. 2 Kgs 6:17).[162] As noted by Fritz (2003: 235), "The chariot of fire has to be interpreted as a divine vehicle, since fire usually signifies the manifestation of divine presence."

Hypostatic Fire? Hypostatic Anger?
We are forced to address whether fire was ever used hypostatically. In other words, was fire personified to the point that it functioned as a surrogate for Yahweh that might also act independently of Yahweh? Or are we working only

in the realm of figurative or metaphorical language, which we should not use to reconstruct a pseudo-mythology that never existed in the minds of the ancients?

A parallel phenomenon may help us decide. McCarter (2008a) has investigated the hypostatic use of "anger" (*'ap*) in the Hebrew Bible as set against notions of divine rage within the Ugaritic corpus. The relevance of this material for the portrayal of divine fire is obvious, for fire is the predominant image used to express Yahweh's wrath. E. Johnson (1974: 354, 358) has assembled the pertinent data:

> Although it was clearly connected originally with angry snorting, [*'aph*] often expresses the idea of anger as "fire." Of the 78 times *'aph* is used as a subject in the [Hebrew Bible], it appears as the subject of *charah*, "to glow," "to burn," 54 times (in fact, the verb *charah* is used only with *'aph* as subject). The expression *charon 'aph*, "burning anger," occurs 35 times, and *chari 'aph* is found 6 times. *'aph* is used as the subject of *ba'ar*, "to burn," and *'ashan*, "to smoke," twice each. *chemah*, which is derived from *yacham*, to be hot," is the word used most frequently in parallelism with *'aph* (33 times, of which *'aph* appears in the first line 25 times)....
>
> [The Hebrew Bible] speaks of the fire of Yahweh's wrath (Ezk. 21:36[31]; 22:21, 31; 38:19), or it says that the anger of Yahweh is like fire (Jer. 4:4; 21:12; Nah. 1:6; Ps. 89:47[46]; Lam. 2:4).[163] The anger of Yahweh can also be compared with a blazing oven (Ps. 21:10[9]). Several passages state that Yahweh's anger burns, smokes, or is kindled (Isa. 30:27; Ps. 2:12; Jer. 7:20; Isa. 42:25; Jer. 44:6; Dt. 29:19[20]; Ps. 74:1; 2 K. 22:13, 17).

McCarter (2008a: 86–91) discusses several passages (Exod 32:7–14; Ps 78:49–50; Josh 7; 2 Sam 6:6–7; Num 11:31–33; Num 25:3–4; Num 22:20–22, 31–35; 2 Sam 24; 1 Chr 21) that are central to the developing notion that Yahweh's anger (*'ap*) could function on an independent level. We will mention only two of them here.[164]

> He sent against them his burning anger [*ḥărôn 'appô*]
> rage [*'ebrâ*] and execration [*za'am*] and distress [*ṣārâ*],
> a band of evil messengers [*mal'ăkê rā'îm*].
> He cleared a path for his anger [*'appô*].
> He did not spare their lives from death.
> He surrendered their lives to plague.[165] (Ps 78:49–50)

As we saw with fire earlier (Ps 104:4; Exod 3:1–6; Judg 13:19–22), here "burning anger" (*ḥărôn 'appô*) and the other divine agents are called Yahweh's "messengers" (*mal'ăkîm*). Yahweh's anger, in nearly independent fashion, marches down a path of destruction much as Yahweh's fire advanced under divine orders to engage enemies in other passages (Ps 97:3; Isa 29:5–6; Deut 33:2). Commenting on Psalm 78:49–50, McCarter (2008a: 87) writes of "Yahweh's anger as a hypostatic or quasi-independent entity . . . something that can be dispatched as an agent of destruction." Johnson (1974: 359) concurs: "Here anger is on its way to becoming an independent power separated from the divine subject, and its presence is evident in concrete acts." Of these two scholars, McCarter uses the more precise vocabulary: "quasi-independent." Consider earlier in the psalm, where the poet writes:

> Yahweh heard and was infuriated [*yitʿabbār*]
> Fire [*ʾēš*] burned against Jacob,
> Anger [*ʾap*] flared up at Israel. (Ps 78:21; cf. 78:31)

This triplet with its splendid parallelism reveals how fire and anger (parallel concepts) are of Yahweh and yet act as agents to accomplish his will.

A fully developed use of anger (*ʾap*) as a hypostasis of Yahweh appears in 2 Samuel 24 (//1 Chr 21). Every reader of 2 Samuel 24 comes away perplexed at first glance. How can Yahweh's kindled anger (*wayyōsep ʾap-yhwh laḥărôt*) incite David to partake in actions later defined to be grave sin (*ḥāṭāʾtî mĕʾōd*; 2 Sam 24:10, 17) and for which David is then punished by Yahweh? The punishment comes via Yahweh's pestilence (*deber*; 2 Sam 24:15; cf. Hab 3:5) with a death toll of seventy thousand! Moreover, Yahweh is then said to have "repented of [further] 'evil'" (*yinnāḥem yhwh ʾel-hārāʿâ*), as he stayed the hand of the *malʾak*-Yahweh that was poised to destroy Jerusalem (2 Sam 24:16). The passage is fascinating for its allusion to Yahweh using multiple (and overlapping) agents of destruction: *ʾap-yhwh*, *deber*, and *malʾak*-Yahweh. The independent actions of the anger of Yahweh and the *malʾak*-Yahweh are especially visible.

In McCarter's (2008a: 91) words, "This apparently contradictory scenario makes sense only if we understand that Yahweh's anger is now a fully hypostasized independent entity who acts independently of Yahweh himself." What is especially conclusive is how 2 Samuel 24:1 was understood in later biblical tradition (1 Chr 21:1). Again, McCarter: "It is especially noteworthy that the Chronicler replaces *ʾap-yhwh*, 'the anger of Yahweh,' with *śāṭān*, 'Satan,' a substitution which, though it resolves the conflict by imposing on the text the dualistic theology of the Persian Period, nevertheless shows that the Chronicler understood the independence and potentially hostile status of Yahweh's anger in the original." The use of the anger of Yahweh here is not unlike the lying spirit (*rûaḥ šeqer*) in 1 Kings 22:22.

Returning to the use of divine fire, it would be tempting to assert a similar usage. Fire and anger are used as parallel concepts to a great degree. As Yahweh's anger could be construed as independent of Yahweh, so too could fire. The examples include the fiery being in Genesis 3:24, "burning" seraphim in Isaiah 6:1–7, the *mal'ak*-Yahweh's ascent in flames (Judges 13:20), and fiery flames as "ministers" (Ps 104:4), known especially for going before Yahweh as if part of a divine entourage (Ps 97:3; Isa 29:5–6; Deut 33:2; Ps 78:49–50). Yet in the end we are forced to conclude that we lack any clear-cut tradition for the use of Yahweh's fire as a fully hypostasized independent entity (which could act out of accord with Yahweh's will) as we have with anger in 1 Samuel 24. The most we could confidently assert from our texts at hand would be to adapt McCarter's vocabulary— that the Hebrew Bible attests to fire as a "quasi-independent" entity.

Deuteronomic/Deuteronomistic Views of Divine Fire

The presence of divine fire in the book of Deuteronomy as well as the Deuteronomistic History has been referenced on several occasions. An archaic tradition describes fire as being a part of Yahweh's entourage in Deuteronomy 33:2 (admittedly a difficult text). Yet another tradition knows of some version of the burning bush episode (Yahweh is "He who dwells in the bush" [*šōknî sĕneh*]; Deut 33:16), while yet others describe mountain theophanies "ablaze with fire" (*bōʿēr bāʾēš*; Deut 4:11; 9:15). The author of the introduction to Deuteronomy (known as Moses' first discourse) is aware of the "pillar of fire by night" (*ʿammûd ʾēš laylâ*) tradition, yet references it in his version without any hint of the pillar (*bāʾēš laylâ*; Deut 1:33), perhaps due to a visceral condemnation of pillars of another kind (i.e., the *masseboth*; cf. Deut 7:5; 12:3; 16:22). As for the Deuteronomistic History, we have seen the *mal'ak*-Yahweh go from a cloaked human to ascendant flames (Judg 13:2–23) in the Samson narrative, a story that echoes the Gideon narrative's *mal'ak*-Yahweh. In Judges 6:19–24 we read yet again of the *mal'ak*-Yahweh (once cloaked?; cf. 6:22), together with a consuming fire into which the *mal'ak*-Yahweh seems to disappear (6:21). Gideon, like Samson's parents, has a potentially lethal encounter, having met the divine "face-to-face" (*pānîm ʾel-pānîm*), only to be granted a dispensation of divine favor that allows him to go on living (6:22–23).

Many of the other occurrences of fire in these literary corpora are unremarkable. There are the expected (and numerous) references to Yahweh sending fire to destroy enemy cities, military hardware (especially chariots), and foodstuffs. The divine images of other (especially foreign) deities are burned by fire (Deut 7:5, 25; 12:3; 2 Kgs 19:18), as are other objects of any cult deemed illegitimate (Deut 9:21; 2 Kgs 23:11). That Yahweh consumes his rivals via fire fits well with the depiction of Yahweh as "a devouring fire, a jealous God" (*ʾēš ʾōkĕlâ hûʾ ʾēl qannāʾ*; Deut 4:24; cf. 9:3).[166]

What is striking in the book of Deuteronomy is the repeated notion that Yahweh revealed his presence via his voice (*qôl*)—that he spoke (*yĕdabbēr*) out of *the midst of fire* (*mittôk hāʾēš*) (Deut 4:12, 15, 33, 36; 5:4, 19, 21, 23; 9:10; 10:4).[167] The theophanies described in Deuteronomy are similar to those of J/non-P (Gen 15:17; Exod 19:18) as well as those of P (Exod 24:17) in that fire is a dominant element. At the same time, Deuteronomy's vocabulary is quite distinct. For this tradition, the entire mountain is engulfed, "burning with fire to the heart of the heavens" (*hāhār bōʿēr bāʾēš ʿad-lēb haššāmayim*; Deut 4:11; 9:15). We have seen how *qôl* was used simultaneously to depict both Yahweh's "thunder" as a storm god and his anthropomorphic "voice" (Ps 18:8–15 [Eng 18:7–14]; Isa 30:27–30). Yet whereas Psalm 18 emphasizes Yahweh's *qôl* as "thunder" encompassed by natural phenomena (earthquakes, smoke, fire, coals, clouds, hailstones) and cosmic warfare (arrows//lightning), Deuteronomy emphasizes Yahweh's *qôl* as "voice" together with forms of communication: "the sound of words" (*qôl dĕbārîm*), speaking (*yĕdabbēr yhwh*), hearing (*šāmaʿ*), and writing (*kĕtubîm bĕʾeṣbaʿ ʾĕlōhîm*) (Deut 4:12, 15, 33, 36; 5:4, 19–23; 9:10; 10:4; 18:16). This repeated emphasis should not be missed. Here *qôl* is the voice of Yahweh more than it is his thunder, and yet *qôl* retains its preternatural force in that it still emerges "out of the midst of fire" (*mittôk hāʾēš*), evoking the non-P burning bush tradition (Exod 3:1–6).[168] Should there be any doubt about the *qôl* being preternaturally awesome, one need only notice that hearing "the divine voice out of fire" is believed to be as lethal as any of the God sightings.

> [Moses speaking:] Did any people ever hear the voice of a god speaking out of the midst of a fire, as you have heard, *and still live* [*wayyeḥî*]? (Deut 4:33)

> Yahweh spoke with you[169] face-to-face at the mountain, out of the midst of the fire. I stood between Yahweh and you at that time, to declare Yahweh's word to you; *for you were afraid because of the fire* [*kî yĕrēʾtem mippĕnê hāʾēš*], and you did not ascend the mountain. . . .
> These are the words Yahweh spoke to your whole assembly at the mountain out of the midst of fire, the cloud, and the thick darkness, with a mighty voice [*qôl gādôl*]. . . . When you heard the voice out of the darkness, while the mountain was burning with fire . . . you said, "Incredibly, Yahweh our God has just shown us his glory and greatness [*kĕbōdô wĕʾet-godlô*], and we have heard his voice out of the midst of the fire; *we have this day seen God speak with someone and the person still live* [*rāʾînû kî-yĕdabbēr ʾĕlōhîm ʾet-hāʾādām wāḥāy*]. So now, why should we die [*lāmmâ nāmût*]? For this great fire [*hāʾēš haggĕdōlâ*] will consume us; *if we hear the voice of Yahweh our God any longer, we shall die* [*ʾim-yōsĕpîm ʾănaḥnû lišmōaʿ ʾet-qôl yhwh ʾĕlōhênû ʿôd wāmātnû*]. For who of all flesh has ever heard the voice of the living God speaking out of the midst of fire, as we have, and still lived [*kî mî kol-bāśār ʾăšer šāmaʿ qôl ʾĕlōhîm ḥayyîm mĕdabbēr mittôk-hāʾēš kāmōnû wayyeḥî*]? (Deut 5:4–5, 19–23 [Eng 22–26])

Hendel (1997: 220–224) has drawn attention to the leitmotif of lethal God sightings in biblical tradition, a concept that "is attested across biblical sources" (cf. Exod 33:20; 19:21). According to Hendel (1997: 221–222), "The belief that one cannot see God and live is best understood as a motif of Israelite folklore, rooted in popular conceptions concerning purity and danger. That which is holy is also dangerous, and that which is most holy is most dangerous. . . . The Godsightings in the Bible that do not result in the viewer's death are the exceptions that prove the rule." We have already remarked on two narratives where the fiery *malʾak*-Yahweh (called "extremely terrifying" [*nôrāʾ mĕʾōd*] in Judg 13:6) occasions viewers (Gideon, Manoah and his wife) to fear for their lives because they have seen God. Isaiah feels "destroyed" (*nidmêtî*) from his viewing of the flaming *śĕrāpîm* that attended Yahweh's theophany (Isa 6:5). The real-life danger and destruction associated with fire (hence the expression "devouring fire," *ʾēš ʾōkelet*) made it a most apt symbol to express the danger (i.e., Otto's *tremendum*) of seeing divinity.

With a fascinating twist, Deuteronomy 4–5 reformulates the leitmotif of lethal God *sightings* into a leitmotif of lethal God *hearings*.[170] Themes of hearing and seeing the divine (via voice and fire) are interwoven throughout these passages.[171] In Deuteronomy 4:36, Yahweh causes his voice to be *heard* (*hišmîʿăkā ʾet-qōlô*) and his fire to be *seen* (*herʾăkā ʾet-ʾiššô*). When the leaders of the people *hear* Yahweh's fiery voice (*kĕšomʿăkem ʾet-haqqôl*) in Deuteronomy 5:20–21 (Eng 5:23–24), they conclude that Yahweh has *shown* them (*herʾānû*) his glorious presence. The mixed metaphor is even made explicit: "We have *heard* his voice [*ʾet-qōlô šāmaʿnû*] out of the midst of the fire; we have *seen* God speak" [*rāʾînû kî-yĕdabbēr ʾĕlōhîm*].[172] Later in the storyline we read of a recapitulation of the theme: "Let me not *hear* again the voice [*lišmōaʿ ʾet-qôl*] of Yahweh my God, or *see* this great fire [*hāʾēš haggĕdōlâ hazzōʾt lōʾ-ʾerʾeh*] any more, lest I die" (Deut 18:16).

It is as if the divine speech acquires a lethal *tremendum* when mediated through fire. (Again, the episode of Yahweh appearing and speaking "in the fiery flames of the burning bush" [*bĕlabat-ʾēš mittôk hassĕneh . . . bōʿēr bāʾēš*] in Exod 3:1–6 is paradigmatic.) Clearly it is the divine fire that is the lethal component, for the Hebrew Bible records multiple instances of God speaking directly with humans that did not result in fatalities. Moreover, as we are reminded from the specific vocabulary of Deuteronomy 5:23 (Eng 5:26), the frightened humans (who are made of "flesh" [*bāśār*]) lived in a world where "flesh" (*bāśār*) (of animals) was regularly burned with fire in cultic and non-cultic settings.

Lastly, note the telling use of the Hebrew root *gdl* in Deuteronomy 5:19, 21 (Eng 5:22, 24) and 18:16 to blend divine presence, voice, and fire. Yahweh's "majestic Presence" (JPS) is described by the nouns "*glory*" and "*greatness*" (*kĕbōdô wĕʿet godlô*). The adjective is used to describe Yahweh's *great* voice (*qôl gādôl*) as well as his "*great* fire" (*hā'ēš haggĕdōlâ*). Blending these verses together, one could render: Yahweh's radiant majesty is made manifest in dangerously awesome fire out of which he speaks with majestic voice.

Divine Fire and the Aniconic Tradition
Before we leave this material, it is important to note how Deuteronomy 4–5 has played a key role in how scholars have reconstructed the biblical prohibitions of images, especially "programmatic aniconism in its uncompromising form" (Mettinger 1997: 175).[173] Deuteronomy 5:8 specifically rules: "You shall not make for yourself a sculptured image [*pesel*], any likeness [*kol-tĕmûnâ*] of what is in the heavens above, or on the earth below, or in the waters below the earth" (cf. Exod 20:4). Following key studies by Frank-Lothar Hossfeld (1982: 21–31), Christoph Dohmen (1985: 236–277), and Timo Veijola (1996: 258–260), many scholars view this as a late phenomenon.

In addition to dating the Deuteronomic aniconic tradition, scholars also parse the precise way in which divine presence is articulated focusing on the following key verses:

> Then you came near and stood at the foot of the mountain. The mountain burned with fire to the heart of heaven, dark with densest clouds. Then Yahweh spoke to you out of the midst of the fire; you heard the sound of words [*qôl dĕbārîm*], but saw no [concrete] form [*tĕmûnâ*]; there was only a voice (*qôl*). . . .
> Be most careful, for your own sake—since you saw no [concrete] form [*kol-tĕmûnâ*] on the day when Yahweh spoke to you at Horeb out of the midst of the fire—not to act corruptly by making for yourselves a sculptured image in any likeness whatever [*pesel tĕmûnat kol-sāmel*], the likeness [*tabnît*] of male or female. (Deut 4:11–12, 15–16)

These passages articulate a clear linkage. Given their experience of the blazing mountainous theophany with its lack of "form" (*tĕmûnâ*), the people should refrain from making any concrete images of the divine. Because the voice was said to come from the heavens (Deut 4:36), it was easy for some scholars to argue that these passages advocated the transcendence of Yahweh, who was thought to reside in heaven alone. That Yahweh's "name" took up residence in the Jerusalem Temple seemed to forge an ironclad argument for the invisibility of Yahweh. Thus Moshe Weinfeld wrote:

> The commandments were heard from out of the midst of the fire that was upon the mount, but they were uttered by the Deity from heaven. Deuteronomy has, furthermore, taken care to shift the centre of gravity of the theophany from the visual to the aural plane. . . . The book of Deuteronomy . . . cannot conceive

of the possibility of seeing the Divinity. The Israelites saw *only* "his great fire" which symbolizes his essence and qualities. . . . God himself remains in his heavenly abode. (Weinfeld 1972b: 207–208; emphasis mine)

Two decades later, Weinfeld would reiterate:

According to Deuteronomy, there was nothing to see: God revealed himself by sounds of words *only*. This served for the author as the basis of the prohibition of physical representation of the Deity. . . . [T]he revelation at Sinai was achieved without the appearance of the divine person, or the use of any image. (Weinfeld 1991: 204–205; emphasis mine)

Weinfeld was followed by Stephen Geller (1996: 39), who speaks of "the exclusively auditory rather than visual nature of the central event of revelation,"[174] as well as by Mettinger:

The Deuteronomistic theology is programmatically abstract: during the Sinai theophany, Israel perceived no form (*tĕmûnâ*); she only heard the voice of her God (Deut 4:12, 15). The Deuteronomistic preoccupation with God's voice and words represents an auditive, non-visual theme. (Mettinger 1982b: 46).

A ready challenge came from Ian Wilson's (1995: 89–97) study of divine presence in Deuteronomy, where he noted how these scholars have overstated the evidence. According to Wilson (1995: 97), "Deuteronomy . . . envisage[s] the localization as well as the transcendence of YHWH." Visible phenomena are clearly referred to in the mention of "fire," "darkness," "cloud," and "gloom" (Deut 4:11, 5:20 [Eng 5:23]; Wilson 1995: 92–93). For Wilson, Deuteronomy makes no affirmation that it is impossible to see Yahweh. "That the danger of hearing YHWH's voice is presented as a major emphasis . . . is certainly true . . . [yet] in addition to emphasizing the danger associated with the voice (an aural phenomenon), [Deuteronomy] three times mentions that associated with the fire (a visual one)" (Wilson 1995: 95–96). Said otherwise, when Deuteronomy 4:12, 15 states that the people saw no form, it means that they saw no *concrete* form or *physical* form, for fire is ethereal.

Our analysis agrees. Weinfeld's misstep was to argue that "God revealed himself by sounds of words *only*"—missing the dominant motif of the voice emerging "from the midst of fire." Mettinger is correct when he writes of "the Deuteronomistic preoccupation with God's voice and words," yet such preoccupation is not at the expense of fire. Indeed, as we have argued, it is the divine fire (through which the voice is mediated) that constitutes the *tremendum*. The numinous, heat-producing, and destructive nature of divine fire is what rendered the voice lethal. Such a tradition is not novel. The non-Deuteronomic Exodus

20:15–16 (Eng 20:18–19) has the people begging Moses to speak to them after experiencing terrifying (yîrĕʾû[175] hāʿām wayyānuʿû) fiery phenomena (thunder, lighting, smoke [qôlōt, lapîdim, hāhār ʿāšēn]): "You speak to us ... but let not God speak to us, lest we die" (ʾal-yĕdabbēr ʿimmānû ʾĕlōhîm pen-nāmût).

The earliest poets knew too well that "the voice of Yahweh splits off flames of fire" (qôl-yhwh ḥōṣēb lahăbôt ʾēš).[176] Wilson (1995: 65–66) sums up well: "There is therefore a strong case for understanding YHWH's speaking 'out of the midst of fire' in terms of his own Presence within that fire." Weinfeld's note that "the Israelites saw *only* 'his great fire' " is clearly missing the forest for the trees. Deuteronomy 9:3 provides a fitting ending for our analysis. The verse is often translated "Know then this day that Yahweh your God (he is the one who goes before you) [hûʾ-hāʿōbēr lĕpānêkā]—a devouring fire is he [ʾēš ʾōkĕlâ hûʾ]." The emphasis of the Hebrew (fronting the first "he" [hûʾ] but not the second, preferring ʾēš ʾōkĕlâ) begs for a more powerful rendering: "Know then this day that it is Yahweh your God who goes before you and he is none other than a devouring fire."

The Impossibility of Crafting the Essence of Fire

Finally, understanding the essence of fire might help unpack the passages about the people not producing a sculpted image (pesel tĕmûnat) or likeness (tabnît) of anything rivaling Yahweh (Deut 4:11–12, 15–16). To these passages we should add Deuteronomy 4:23–24:

> Take heed to yourselves ... lest you make a sculpted image in the form of anything which the Yahweh your God has forbidden you. Because Yahweh your God is a devouring fire, a jealous God [ʾēš ʾōkĕlâ hûʾ ʾēl qannāʾ].

The motif of divine jealousy is dominant. Yahweh will tolerate no rivals. Yet if we strip away the Deuteronomistic (monotheistic) overlay, one wonders whether those who prized the use of fire as an apt symbol for divinity advocated aniconism for the obvious reason: ethereal fire *cannot* be sculpted without losing its essence.[177] Once concretized, fire cannot burn with intense heat, nor give off incandescent light, nor instill the feeling of the numinous through flickering flames. A stone or metal image of fire can be held in the hand. *Tremendum*, they might have thought, cannot be so contained.

Divine Radiance

The Use of Radiance to Depict the Presence of Yahweh

As with numinous fire, the concept of gods being present via radiance is a prevailing and enduring theme throughout the ancient Near East and in every chronological period. Thus while certain authors made the radiance of Yahweh a focal point (see especially the Priestly material), it would be a mistake to think that they coined an original idea. Rather, as with numinous fire, the concept of gods being radiant was forged with the very idea of divinity. Ornan (2011: 259; cf. Winter 1994) suggests that the shimmering of precious metals that were used as overlays on divine images correlates with textual notions of divine radiance.

What do we mean by "radiance"? In short, we refer to that which the authors of the Hebrew Bible tried to convey through words such as *hôd, hādār, kābôd,* and *nōgah,* among others (cf. de Vries 2016: 61–70). No single English word is capable of the wide range of meanings associated with these Hebrew concepts, which include glory, majesty, brilliance, splendor, dignity, strength, and sovereignty.[178] Even a brief glance at modern translations of these four Hebrew words will reveal a variety of renderings. Our use of the word "radiance" as a catchall term is heuristic and pragmatic. Different authors used these words variously, yet their semantic overlap is considerable.[179] Consider, for example, how the exuberant psalmist can write of "the glorious splendor of the majesty" of Yahweh (*hădar kĕbôd hôdekā*; Ps 145:5).

The Antiquity of Divine Radiance in Ancient Israelite Religion

The antiquity of divine radiance in Israelite religion can be seen from several ancient (or archaizing) poems preserved in the Hebrew Bible. Examples include Habakkuk 3:2–5, Deuteronomy 33:2, and Psalm 29 (cf. Ps 104:1–4). In addition, we have *kābôd* traditions in prose that are distinct from and predate the "Glory of Yahweh" (*kābôd yhwh*) traditions of the P source and the book of Ezekiel. These earlier prose traditions include material in Exodus 33:17–23, a reference from early Shilonite cult involving the Ark palladium, and a text from the eighth-century BCE prophet Isaiah.

Divine Radiance in Early Poetry

Though Habakkuk 3 (as we find it preserved) was the work of "postexilic editors . . . caught up in the apocalyptic fervor of their era," Theodore Hiebert (1986: 1) has argued that it was truly archaic in origin. Devoting an entire monograph to the poem, he concluded that "the original text, linguistic features, literary form, historical allusions, and religious motifs all suggest that this poem was composed in the premonarchic era as a recitation of the victory of the divine warrior over cosmic and earthly enemies." Francis Andersen (2001: 260) concurred: "It bears all the marks—or most of it does—of being an ancient poem. Very ancient indeed, perhaps it is one of the oldest in the entire Hebrew Bible." An equally likely alternative is that our author is looking back with an antiquarian interest to the lore of the distant past (Hab 3:2), as many other authors were wont to do (e.g., Ps 44:2 [Eng 44:1]; 74:12–17; 77:12 [Eng 77:11]; 143:5; Isa 51:9–10; Deut 4:32–34; 32:7; see Chapter Eight, pp. 442–448). Thus to flavor his narrative he could be archaizing (cf. Andersen 2001: 329).

> O Yahweh, I heard of your fame,
> I was frightened [*yārē'tî*], Yahweh, by your deeds . . .
>
> Eloah came from Teman,
> Qadosh [the Holy One] from Mt. Paran.
>
> His glory [*hôdô*] covered the heavens,
> His splendor [*tĕhillātô*]¹⁸⁰ filled the earth
> [His] radiance [*nōgah*] was like light [*'ôr*].
>
> He had horns/rays [coming out] from his hand
> There he cloaked [?] his power
>
> Before him went Pestilence [*dāber*],
> Plague [*rešep*] marched at his feet . . .
>
> Sun and moon stood exalted,
> At the brilliance [*'ôr*] of your flying arrows,
> At the radiance [*nōgah*] of your lightning-like spear. (Hab 3:2a, 3–5, 11)

We will treat the use of this poem to depict the divine warrior elsewhere (see Chapter Eight, pp. 451–452). Suffice it here to note how the march of the divine warrior from Teman parallels other archaic passages that have Yahweh marching from the same general region near Edom, Seir, and Midian (Judg 5:4–5; Deut 33:2; Ps 68:8–9, 18–19 [Eng 68:7–8, 17–18]). Of special note is the mention of Yahweh of Teman in the late ninth- or early eighth-century BCE inscriptions found at Kuntillet ʿAjrud, which is in the northeast Sinai Desert (see Chapter Six, pp. 239–240, 279–282).

The radiance conveyed here by four overlapping terms (*hôd*, *tĕhillâ*, *nōgah*, *'ôr*) is that of Yahweh, as he is depicted as a divine warrior going to battle. The war poem in Exodus 15:11 describes Yahweh as "terrible of radiance" (*nôrā' tĕhillōt*). In 2 Kings 6:18 Yahweh strikes the Aramean army with "a blinding light" (*sanwērîm*).¹⁸¹ While at first glance one recognizes sun imagery behind such terms, it soon becomes clear that such language can be used of a god who controls nature and is going to battle.¹⁸² In Habakkuk 3, note especially the presence of *deber* and *rešep* (known elsewhere as deities) serving as a military entourage. The following verses (Hab 3:8–15) turn cosmic, with Yahweh's anger (*'ap*) battling rivers (*nĕhārîm*) and sea (*yām*), a narrative with strong echoes of combating the mythological Sea//River.¹⁸³ Yahweh mounts his chariot and rides to battle with bow and arrows in hand.

Note the similar use of sun imagery in a battle context in Deuteronomy 33:2 (already noted due to its use of divine fire):

> Yahweh came from Sinai
> He shone [*zāraḥ*] from Seir...¹⁸⁴
> He beamed forth [*hôpîaʻ*] from Mt. Paran.
>
> With him¹⁸⁵ were myriads of holy ones [*ribĕbōt qōdeš*],
> At/From his right fire flies forth [*ēš dāt*].¹⁸⁶

Yet another picture of Yahweh as a radiant (*kābôd*) warrior who was thought to manifest his presence via storm theophanies is found in Psalm 29. The notion that this passage is archaic and makes strong allusions to (or, some would say, is even dependent upon) Canaanite mythology has been universally adopted following the groundbreaking work of Harold Louis Ginsberg in 1936.¹⁸⁷

> Ascribe to Yahweh, O divine beings [*bĕnê ʾēlîm*],
> Ascribe to Yahweh glory and strength [*kābôd wāʻōz*],
> Ascribe to Yahweh the glory [due] his name [*kĕbôd šĕmô*];
> Bow down to Yahweh in the splendor of the sanctuary [*hadrat-qōdeš*].¹⁸⁸
>
> The voice of Yahweh is over the waters;
> the god of glory [*ʾēl-hakkābôd*] thunders,
> Yahweh [thunders] over many waters.
>
> The voice of Yahweh—with power [*kōaḥ*],
> The voice of Yahweh—with splendor [*hādār*],
> The voice of Yahweh shatters the cedars...
>
> The voice of Yahweh splits off flames of fire [*qôl-yhwh ḥōṣēb lahăbôt ʾēš*],¹⁸⁹
> The voice of Yahweh makes writhe the steppe,
> Yahweh makes writhe the steppe of Qadesh...
>
> In his temple, all say "Glory!" [*kābôd*]
>
> Yahweh sat enthroned at the Deluge,
> Yahweh sat enthroned as eternal king!

This poem repeatedly emphasizes the voice/thunder (*qôl*) of Yahweh (Ps 29:3–5, 7–9) as well as his *kābôd* (Ps 29:1, 2, 3, 9).¹⁹⁰ Yahweh is "the god of glory" (*'ēl-hakkābôd*), whose radiance is such that his sanctuary acquires splendor (*hadrat-qōdeš*).[191] Yahweh is to be ascribed glory by both divine beings and humans. As a direct result of his glory, power, and splendor (as made manifest via a stormy and fiery theophany), the people proclaim "Glory!" (*kābôd*) in the temple. One cannot help but think of another ancient poem where "Yahweh of Armies" (*yhwh ṣĕbā'ôt*), "mighty in battle" (*gibbôr milḥāmâ*), was repeatedly celebrated as the "King of Glory" (*melek hakkābôd*; Ps 24:7–10).[192] Yet another theophany of Yahweh as storm god and king is Psalm 97 (translated on p. 348). After describing various meteorological phenomena (clouds, thick darkness, fire, lightning), the psalmist proclaims: "All peoples see his glory [*kābôd*]" (Ps 97:6). As Mettinger (1982: 119) writes, "The word *kābôd* [in Ps 97:6] seems to be used as a summary description of the theophany . . . that is, as a comprehensive term for the royal apparel of God, which is composed of cloud, fire, and lightning."

Lastly, we need to mention Psalm 104, whose date is uncertain, with advocates for both early and late settings. The exact date need not concern us here, nor should we become preoccupied with the degree to which the poem was modeled on (or influenced by) the Great Hymn to Aten, Enuma Elish, or even the Ugaritic Baal Cycle.[193] What is of note is how once again a poet thought of Yahweh as majestically radiant ("wrapped in light") and described him a storm god riding on the clouds with an entourage of wind and fire.

> O Yahweh, my God, you are very great!
> You clothed yourself with glory and majesty [*hôd wĕhādār lābāštā*],
> You are he who wraps light as [your] robe [*'ōṭeh-'ôr kaśśalmâ*];
>
> You are he who stretches out the heavens like a tent cloth,
> Who fashions his rafters out of the waters;
>
> He who makes the clouds his chariot [*haśśām-'ābîm rĕkûbô*],
> Rides on the wings of the wind [*hamĕhallēk 'al-kanpê-rûaḥ*];
>
> He who makes the winds his messengers [*'ōśeh mal'ākāyw rûḥôt*],
> fiery flames his ministers [*mĕšārtāyw 'ēš lōhēṭ*]. (Ps 104:1–4)

Exodus 33:17–23: Moses' Request to See the Divine *Kābôd*

At the outset, this fascinating story has Moses assuming that he (as a unique leader shown divine "favor") could actually see the *kābôd* of Yahweh.[194] With respect and boldness he requests to have Yahweh "allow him to see" (*har'ēnî*) the divine presence. Yet one of the purposes of this tale in its present form is to have God reply with multiple responses that we would frame as: "Not so fast. You know not what you ask. It's more complicated than you think. It's not for everyone."

> And Yahweh said to Moses, "This very thing that you have asked, I will do because you have found favor in my sight, and I know you by name." [Moses] said, "Allow me to see your *kābôd*" [*har'ēnî nā' 'et-kĕbōdekā*].
>
> And [Yahweh] said, "I will make all my goodness [*kol-ṭûbî*] pass before you, and I will proclaim the name 'Yahweh' before you [*wĕqārā'tî bĕšēm yhwh lĕpānêkā*]; and I will be gracious to whom I will be gracious, and I will show mercy on whom I will show mercy."
>
> "But," [Yahweh] said, "you cannot see my face [*lō' tûkal lir'ōt 'et-pānāy*]; for no mortal can see me and live" [*kî lō'-yir'anî hā'ādām wāḥāy*].
>
> And Yahweh said, "Here is a place near me. Take your stand on the rock [*ṣûr*]; and, as my glory [*kĕbōdî*] passes by, I will put you in a crevice of the rock, and I will shield you with my hand [*kappî*] until I have passed by. Then I will remove my hand [*kappî*], and you shall see my back ['*āḥōrāy*]; but my face [*pānay*] must not be seen."

As will become clear, the core of this pericope has none of P's key earmarks and certainly comes from what Cross (1973: 193) termed "archaic lore." According to Cross (1973: 166), "Exodus 33:17–23 is Yahwistic in its present form, and it is very likely that the tradition is older."[195] Brevard Childs (1974: 595–597) too recognized "an earlier tradition" "lying behind the present form of the story." Childs astutely noted several reworkings of the original story where there are multiple shifts in focus, including how "the revelation of God [comes to be] in terms of his attributes rather than his appearance." More recent scholarship (e.g., Billings 2004) also underscores the reworking of early tradents.[196]

At its core is Moses' request to have an unmediated view of divine radiance, which is denied because seeing the divine is lethal. As Childs notes, such a request is parallel to Moses' appeal to know the essence of Yahweh's Name in Exodus 3:14.[197] As Moses was indeed allowed to know the name Yahweh, so too "a partial concession is made and for this reason the story was undoubtedly treasured in a cycle which was related to Moses's special office" (Childs: 1974: 595–596). Of particular note is what seems to be yet another use of "transcendent anthropomorphism," where the full (and dangerous) nature of divine "radiance" (*kābôd*) and "essence" (*pānîm*) is not seen but rather is shielded via Yahweh's "hand" (*kap*), resulting in Moses seeing only Yahweh's "back" ('*āḥōr*). That God uses a part of himself (his hand) to shield Moses from him constitutes a "strange paradox"—unless here we have a remnant of a hypostatic (i.e., independently acting) *kābôd* similar to the hypostatic anger ('*ap*) in 2 Samuel 24 (see pp. 351–353).[198]

Divine *Kābôd* in Pre-Priestly Cultic Settings

In arguing that "the concept of the [divine] *kābôd* was [not] an invention of the Jerusalem priesthood [found in the so-called P source]," Victor Hurowitz (2007: 98–99) looks to the cultic settings of the Elide priesthood at Shiloh and "the *kābôd*'s entry into the Temple of Solomon. . . in the (pre-Priestly) description of dedicating the Temple in 1 Kgs 8:10–11." To these two references we could also add the mention of *kābôd* in the commissioning of Isaiah that is portrayed as taking place in the Jerusalem Temple.

The Absent Deity: 'Î-kābôd in 1 Samuel 4:19–22

Key traditions about the temple in Shiloh that antedated Solomon's in Jerusalem come down to us via the so-called Ark Narrative (1 Sam 2:12–17, 22–25; 4:1–7:1).[199] Within the storyline of war with the Philistines, we find the following birth narrative:

> Now [Eli's] daughter-in-law, the wife of Phinehas, was pregnant and ready to give birth.[200] When she heard the report that the Ark of God [*'ărôn hā'ĕlōhîm*] was captured, and that her father-in-law and her husband were dead, her labor suddenly began, and she crouched down and gave birth. As she lay dying, the women attending her said, "Do not be afraid, for you have borne a son." But she did not respond or pay attention. She named the child Ichabod [*'î-kābôd*], saying, "The glory was exiled from Israel!" [*gālâ kābôd miyyiśrā'ēl*] because the Ark of God [*'ărôn hā'ĕlōhîm*] had been captured and because of [the death of] her father-in-law and her husband.[201] And she said, "The glory was exiled from Israel [*gālâ kābôd miyyiśrā'ēl*] when the Ark of God [*'ărôn hā'ĕlōhîm*] was captured." (1 Sam 4:19–22)

The details are few but focused. The woman went into premature labor when she learned that the Ark of God was captured by the Philistines and that her husband and father-in-law (the famous Shilohnite priest Eli) were dead. The author of this brief episode highlights the capture of the Ark, twice fronting its taking before referencing the death of the woman's relatives (1 Sam 4:19, 21). The shorter (preferred) reading of why the child was so named (i.e., verse 22, as opposed to the expansionist verse 21) has no mention of her relatives' deaths. The woman's lack of response to her attendants is as if to say that "faced with the loss of the Ark she can have no thought of herself" (McCarter 1980a: 115). Indeed, even her own tragic death from the complications of childbirth (cf. Gen 35:17–18) is of little importance for the narrator's Ark-centric focus.

Previously the author of our passage noted how the Philistines were terrified (*wayyīr'û happĕlištîm*) because they interpreted the Ark as "God" (or "gods"; *'ĕlōhîm*) coming into their enemy's camp (1 Sam 4:7–8).[202] They exclaimed: "Woe to us! Who can deliver us from the power of this mighty God [or "these mighty gods"; *hā'ĕlōhîm hā'addîrîm hā'ēlleh*]? He is the same God [or "these are the same gods"] who struck the Egyptians with every kind of scourge and pestilence."[203]

In 1 Samuel 4:21-22, the *kābôd* functions in the same way as *'ĕlōhîm* did in 1 Samuel 4:7-8: it represents the very (here radiant) presence and power of the deity—not unlike the radiant *melammu* of Aššur, whose unseen presence in battle frightened enemies (see p. 339, n. 127). From the woman's perspective, the god (whom she knew as Yahweh) who once moved into the Israelite camp is now exiled and residing in the Philistine camp. The name Ichabod (*'î-kābôd*) is the central reason for the telling (and preservation) of this birth narrative. As noted by McCarter (1980a: 116), *'î-kābôd* "means, 'Where is (the) Glory?' or 'Alas (for the) Glory!' [and] belongs to a distinctive group of names referring to lamentation for an absent deity." As McCarter goes on to note, the clearest example of this is the name Jezebel (*'î-zebel*), which means "Where is the Prince [i.e., the Phoenician Ba'l-Haddu]?" Here the Ugaritic text KTU 1.6.4.4-5 is most instructive. After Ba'lu descends into the gullet of the god Death (Motu) and is mourned as dead by the gods 'Ilu and 'Anatu, we read (in a dream sequence of 'Ilu's) of the lament:

> *'iy 'al'iyn b'l*   Where is Mighty Ba'lu?
> <u>*'iy zbl b'l 'arṣ*</u>   Where is the Prince, Lord of the Earth?

Such a thesis is supported further when the Ark Narrative is situated against the ancient Near Eastern practice of capturing divine images in battle and exiling them.[204] In other words, this birth narrative gives further evidence that the word *kābôd* was used to express the very presence (and, for the Elide priesthood, lack of presence) of the deity Yahweh.[205]

Divine Kābôd in 1 Kings 8:10-11

1 Kings 8:10-11 presents a challenge to interpreters, and not because of the words and their meaning, for they are clear enough. During the dedication of Solomon's temple, the Ark is carried "into the inner sanctuary of the Temple, into the most holy place" (*'el-děbîr habbayit 'el-qōdeš haqqŏdāšîm*) by the priests (1 Kgs 8:6). We then read:

> When the priests emerged from the sanctuary, a cloud ['*ānān*] filled [*mālē'*] the temple of Yahweh so that the priests were not able to stand to minister because of the cloud ['*ānān*]; for the *kābôd* of Yahweh filled [*mālē'*] the temple of Yahweh. (1 Kgs 8:10-11)

Overall, 1 Kings 8 is filled with key Deuteronomistic teachings, from its erection of the central sanctuary in Jerusalem to its strong emphasis on the so-called Name Theology, in which divine presence is localized via Yahweh's *šēm* (1 Kgs 8:16, 17, 19, 20, 29, 33, 35, 42–44, 48). With this in mind, the vocabulary of 1 Kings 8:10–11 seems at first glance strikingly out of place. A comparison with Priestly vocabulary (e.g., the mention of the *ʿānān* and the *kābôd* Yahweh *filling* sacred space in Exodus 40:34–35) has led many scholars to see the hand of a Priestly editor at work.[206] Thus Gary Knoppers' (1995a: 230; 2000: 372) summary represents the situation well: "Virtually all scholars recognize the presence of both a preexilic source and some priestly editing in 1 Kgs 8:1–13."

Without minimizing the substantial source-critical puzzle before us, a more fruitful avenue of exploration is to see how 1 Kings 8:10–11 functions rhetorically for the Deuteronomist. Here Knoppers (1995a: 240; 2000: 382) has written insightfully: "The transfer of the ark to the temple appears not as a revolution but as the culmination of one era and the beginning of another. . . . The consecration of a central sanctuary . . . becomes the point of a new departure in Israelite history. The temple, not the ark, is now the central, unifying cultic institution in Israelite life. The temple thus encompasses and supersedes the previous cultic symbol." In like manner, one could assert that the Deuteronomist's new emphasis on divine presence via God's name (*šēm*) encompasses and supersedes the previous radiant model of divine presence known from archaic lore far older than P (see the earlier discussion of Hab 3:2–5; Deut 33:2; Ps 29; Exod 33:17–23; 1 Sam 4:19–22).

While the use of older *kābôd* language may indeed fit the Deuteronomist's rhetorical purpose, we should expect him to say precious little about how "radiance" depicts divine presence. Previously the Deuteronomistic History spoke of Yahweh bestowing *kābôd* on Solomon as an incomparable royal prerogative (1 Kgs 3:13). In 1 Kings 8:1–12 we hear of the Ark and its divine glory for the last time with its transfer to Jerusalem. Though the language of 1 Kings 8:12 is not specific (i.e., mentioning the sun [so LXX] and not *kābôd*), perhaps one could speculate and say that for the Deuteronomist, divine "radiance" should reside in the heavens, with the temple encased in darkness (*ʿărāpel*). Perhaps the Deuteronomistic tradition had a fear of the physical Ark being captured once again (even though the Philistine story ended with the Ark being victorious), and thus it turned to a different type of aniconic representation of divine presence. But we are getting ahead of ourselves. The P source has much more to say about the radiant presence (*kābôd*) of Yahweh.

Divine Kābôd in Isaiah 6:1–5

The theme of "glory" can be seen throughout the book of Isaiah, and the remarks here cannot begin to trace the development of *kābôd* from its use by the eighth-century BCE prophet Isaiah ben Amoz to its use in post-exilic eschatology (cf. Williamson 1999). Instead, we will focus on one key Isaianic passage that can give us insight into how the prophet envisioned divine presence in the Jerusalem Temple.

The description of Isaiah's commissioning in Isaiah 6:1–5 is firmly fixed in the eighth century BCE. Williamson (2007: 123) notes how it "is recognized to be Isaianic by even the most rigorous of minimalists." Wildberger (1991: 256) boldly asserts that "Isaiah 6 bears all the marks of authenticity; it is a report about a genuine experience and must have been composed or dictated by Isaiah himself." Because Isaiah 6 serves as a prelude to 7:1–8:15, most scholars date it around the time of the Syro-Ephraimite war (734–733 BCE) and the second western campaign of the Neo-Assyrian king Tiglath-Pileser III.

> In the year of King Uzziah's death, I saw the Lord sitting on a throne, high and exalted; and the edges of his garment filled the temple. Above him were attendant seraphim; each had six wings: with two he would cover his face, and with two he would cover his feet, and with two he would fly. One would call to the other: "Holy, holy, holy is Yahweh of Hosts; the whole earth is full of his glory [*kābôd*]."
>
> The doorposts of the threshold shook [*wayyānuʻû*] at the voice [*qôl*] of the one who called, while the House kept filling with smoke [*yimmālēʾ ʿāšān*]. Then I cried, "Woe is me! I am lost; for I am a man of unclean lips, and I dwell among a people of unclean lips; Yet my own eyes have seen the King, Yahweh of Hosts!" (Isa 6:1–5)

Various themes found in this passage have been mentioned in the texts discussed previously, and later we will read of Ezekiel's version of winged creatures attending Yahweh's *kābôd*. The danger implied in the prophet's seeing Yahweh (Isa 6:5) resonates with the lethal God sightings we have already noted. In Exodus 40:35 and 1 Kings 8:11 we saw how the *kābôd* Yahweh filled (*mālēʾ*) the tabernacle (*miškān*) and the Jerusalem Temple (*bêt yhwh*), respectively. Yet here Isaiah has smoke filling the temple (*habbayit yimmālēʾ ʿāšān*), while the *kābôd* fills the entire earth (*mĕlōʾ kol-hāʾāreṣ kĕbôdô*). The vocabulary of such praise sounds liturgical, and Hugh Williamson (2007: 133–134), following Friedhelm Hartenstein, is right to point to the nearly identical vocabulary in Numbers 14:21 and Psalm 72:19 (*wĕyimmālēʾ kĕbôdô ʾet-kol hāʾāreṣ*), not to mention "the recasting of the same formula as an eschatological wish in Hab 2:14" (cf. Isa 11:9). Williamson concludes that the use of such identical language "indicates that it had a wider currency in ancient Israel" and likely had "deep roots in the cult tradition." More loosely, one could compare Isaiah 6:4's quaking of the thresholds from the sound (*qôl*) of the fiery seraphim to Psalm 29's thunder and fire (esp. *qôl-yhwh ḥōṣēb laḥăbôt ʾēš* in Ps 29:7), where *kābôd* is ascribed to Yahweh, the god of glory (*ʾēl-hakkābôd*), by gods (*běnê ʾēlîm*) and humans alike.

Yet more on target is Wildberger (1991: 268), who claims that "there is no mistaking the fact that the thought world of Psalm 24 is in the background as Isaiah formulates the description of how he experienced his call." Psalm 24 is also liturgical.[207] Its call for purity (*něqî kappayim ûbar-lēbāb*) in the sanctuary (*měqôm qodšô*; Ps 24:3–4) resonates with Isaiah's desire to have his unclean lips (*ṭěmē-śěpātayim*) purified as he too stands on ground made holy by Yahweh (*qādôš qādôš qādôš*).[208] The royal focus of Psalm 24, repeatedly envisioning the entry of Yahweh as "the king of glory" (*melek hakkābôd*), resonates with Isaiah's seeing Yahweh as King (*melek*). Both texts refer to Yahweh as "Yahweh of Armies" (*yhwh ṣěbāʾôt*). Finally, Psalm 24:1's mention of Yahweh's sovereignty over "the earth and its fullness" (*la-yhwh hāʾāreṣ ûmělôʾâ*) echoes Isaiah's sentiment that "the whole earth is full of Yahweh's *kābôd*" (*mělōʾ kol-hāʾāreṣ kěbôdô*).

Before we leave Isaiah 6, we need to note a possible allusion to the Mesopotamian notion of *melammu*. Many scholars have argued that Isaiah was well versed in the "official rhetoric" of Assyrian kings.[209] In Isaiah 8:7 (also coming from the days of the Syro-Ephraimite war in 734–733 BCE) we read of how Yahweh will bring "the King of Assyria and all his glory" (*melek ʾaššûr wěʾet-kol-kěbôdô*) against the Syrian king Rezin and the Israelite king Pekah. Williamson has astutely suggested that with this phrase Isaiah may be making a wordplay on the well-known Assyrian military theology of *melammu*.[210] In this line of thinking, the Assyrian king is assured of victory because he wields the "the awe of the radiance [*pulḫu melamme*] of Aššur" against any foe.[211] (Indeed, the ideological narratives presented in text and iconography edit out any notion of Assyrian casualties in battle.)[212] Yet more than wordplay is going on. Again in Isaiah 10:5–19, the king of Assyria (even with Aššur's *melammu*) is moved by Yahweh like a chess piece to his ultimate demise. Glory ("the Light of Israel will be fire") is fighting glory (cf. esp. 10:16–19 and the occurrence of *kābôd* in 10:16, 18). Moreover, by using Isaiah 6:3 as an introduction to this material, Isaiah underscores that Yahweh's worldwide *kābôd* overpowers even that of Aššur.

In conclusion, it is clear that Isaiah 6:1–5, an eighth-century BCE text, joins 1 Samuel 4:21–22 and 1 Kings 8:10–11 in describing the presence of Yahweh via his *kābôd* in a cultic setting prior to P's description. According to Isaiah 6:3, the divine *kābôd* certainly filled every recess of the temple and beyond. Yet there is no mention of cloud (*ʿānān*) coverings nor divine "abiding" (*šākan*) in either a tent of meeting (*ʾōhel môʿēd*) or a tabernacle (*miškān*). For these images we now turn to P.

The *Kābôd* Yahweh in P

The "Glory of Yahweh" (*kābôd yhwh*) in the Priestly source as well as in the book of the prophet Ezekiel is one of the most notable phrases designating divine presence in the Hebrew Bible. As a result, the secondary literature on the topic is overwhelming and will not be treated here in any detail.[213] The literary context within which we find P's "Glory of Yahweh" material is extremely complex and has challenged interpreters from the medieval period to the modern era. Source-critical scholars might be on the same page with regard to how all of these texts are from P, yet they are not of one accord with how P has blended sacred space traditions of tent (*'ōhel mô'ēd*), tabernacle (*miškan*), and Jerusalem Temple.[214]

Yet we should not miss the forest for the trees. What should be underscored is that there are two distinct groups of material. One of these deals with crisis events during the wandering experiences (especially the "murmuring" traditions), while the other deals with Sinai and the cult (see Mettinger 1982b: 80ff., following Rendtorff 1963). Moreover, with regard to the latter, P's four primary passages about the *kābôd* Yahweh (Exod 24:15–18; 29:43–46; 40:34–38; Lev 9:1–24) reveal a well-defined narrative arc.

P's Narrative Arc: The Appearance of the Kābôd *Yahweh*
At the outset of the story arc we find the *kābôd* Yahweh enveloped in a cloud as it is "dwelling" (*yiškōn*) "like a devouring/consuming fire" (*kĕ'ēš 'ōkelet*) on the top of Mt. Sinai (Exod 24:16–17). Moses is privileged to ascend the mountain and experience divine communication (*wayyiqrā' 'el-mōšeh*). Moses presumably sees the divine fire (as did the people of Israel) and is even allowed to enter the cloud (24:17–18). By the time we get to the end of Exodus 29, the mountaintop abode has been exchanged for the tent of meeting (*'ōhel mô'ēd*), where God promises to meet and speak to the people (*'iwwā'ēd . . . lĕdabēr*; Exod 29:42). Proper cultic actions are laid out previously in the chapter, yet ultimately it will be the *kābôd* Yahweh that serves to sanctify both space and personnel (29:43–44). God's promise to "dwell" (*wĕšākantî*) with his people is characterized as being the very reason for their liberation from Egypt (*lĕšoknî bĕtôkām*; 29:45–46). Arriving at the end of the book of Exodus, we find tent and tabernacle fused ("the tabernacle of the tent of meeting" [*miškan 'ōhel mô'ēd*]; 40:2), fulfilling an earlier desire by Yahweh to have the people make a "dwelling" (*miškan*) in which the deity could "dwell" (*šākantî*; 25:8). After Moses finishes the work on the new tabernacle, we read of a recapitulation and updating of the earlier theophany. Now the cloud covers the tent of meeting (*'ōhel mô'ēd*), while the *kābôd* Yahweh fills the newly completed tabernacle (*miškan*; 40:34). This time Moses is unable to enter the clouded tent because it houses the divine presence.

The final episode of the narrative arc is found in Leviticus 9, where we read of the commencement of the high priesthood of Aaron, who is assisted by his two sons in rendering proper cult within sacred space. This inauguration fulfills as it recapitulates the earlier promise of Yahweh to sanctify his chosen religious officiants (Exod 29:44). Moses, as preeminent orchestrator of events, directs

Aaron and his sons in their duties with the promise to the people that "today Yahweh will appear to you" (*yhwh* nir'â 'ălêkem). Of special note is how the promise is repeated with the language "the *Glory of Yahweh* will appear to you" (*wĕyērā' 'ălêkem kĕbôd yhwh*), underscoring the identity of the two (Lev 9:4, 6).

After Aaron and his sons carry out their sacred duties (especially blood manipulation) on behalf of the people, Aaron joins Moses in entering the tent of meeting, for what purpose we know not. Upon their exit, the *kābôd* Yahweh appears to all the people (*wayyērā' kĕbôd-yhwh 'el-kol-hā'ām*; Lev 9:23). The *tremendum* of divine fire (which we remember from the very start of the story arc as the "*consuming* fire" [*kĕ'ēš 'ōkelet*] on Mt. Sinai) is then made manifest as it *consumes* (*tō'kal*) the offerings on the altar. Jacob Milgrom (1991: 574) has underscored the relevance of this material:

> The importance of the theophany in the newly consecrated Tabernacle cannot be exaggerated. It renders the Tabernacle the equivalent of Mount Sinai. . . . P, in effect, regards the theophany at the Tabernacle as more important than JE's theophany at Sinai.[215] The equivalence of the Tabernacle to Sinai is an essential, indeed indispensable, axiom of P. The Tabernacle, in effect, becomes a portable Sinai, an assurance of the permanent presence of the deity in Israel's midst.

It is little wonder then to read of the appropriate response by the people—to cry out in joy (and/or awe?) and to fall on their faces, a response to divine fire attested elsewhere (cf. Judg 13:20; 1 Kgs 18:38–39; Ezek 1:28; 2 Chr 7:3).

From Fascinans *to* Tremendum: *Nadab, Abihu, and Lethal Fire*
Milgrom is correct. With the appearance of the *kābôd* Yahweh via fire in Leviticus 9:23–24 we have reached the apex. Yet it seems that another summit now comes into view, and in a most curious way.

Leviticus 9 is not the end of our narrative arc. It is preparatory for Leviticus 10:1–3. Three times in Leviticus 9 we read of the appearance of Yahweh/*kābôd* Yahweh (Lev 9:4, 6, 23) that culminates in the divine "consuming" fire. (As we will see, Lev 10:2–3 also makes Yahweh's *kābôd* manifest in "consuming" fire.) Moses' declaration that "today" Yahweh (or *kābôd* Yahweh) "will appear to you [pl.]" is directed to the people, but only as they bring their offerings, which are then presented to Yahweh by the three priests (Aaron and his two sons, Nadab and Abihu). These three are, after all, the priesthood that Yahweh had promised to sanctify in Exodus 29:44.

The reader's every inclination at this stage is to affirm the legitimacy of Nadab and Abihu's priesthood. Indeed, archaic lore (i.e., the JE epic material in Exod 24:9–11) tells the story of how Nadab and Abihu were among the chosen few allowed to see the God of Israel in radiant appearance (a privilege elsewhere given only to the blessed elite).²¹⁶ Not only did they behold God, but they also ate and drank (with him) (*wayyeḥĕzû ʾet-hāʾĕlōhîm wayyōʾkĕlû wayyištû*).

But then we are shocked to read:

> Now Aaron's sons, Nadab and Abihu, each took his firepan, put fire in it, and laid incense on it; and they offered foreign/illicit fire [*ʾēš zārâ*] before Yahweh, such as he had not commanded them. Then fire came forth from the presence of Yahweh and consumed [*tōʾkal*] them. Thus they died before [due to?] Yahweh. Then Moses said to Aaron, "This is what Yahweh meant when he said: 'Through those near to me [i.e., the priests], I will manifest holiness [*ʾeqqādēš*]; Before all the people I will manifest *kābôd* [*ʾekkābēd*].'" And Aaron was silent. (Lev 10:1–3)

Once again Yahweh's "*consuming* fire" (*kĕʾēš ʾōkelet*) is operative, yet here *consuming* (*tōʾkal*) priests rather than offerings—and in some way Yahweh's action is related to making manifest his *kābôd*. For years speculation has abounded as to the precise reason for Nadab and Abihu's death. The text describes the two as offering "foreign fire" (*ʾēš zārâ*) that was unauthorized (*ʾăšer lōʾ ṣiwwāh ʾōtām*).²¹⁷ Suffice it to say that here we have a popular story at odds with the archaic lore of Exodus 24:9–11. Nadab and Abihu here are lessons of divine danger, not blessed guests at a divine meal.

The meaning of P's expression *ʾekkābēd bĕ-* ("I will manifest *kābôd* through X") is clear, for P uses it three other times in Exodus 14: in verses 4 and 17–18 (cf. too Ezek 28:22). In these passages, Yahweh manifests his *kābôd* (i.e., his awesome presence, power, and majesty) through achieving victory "over Pharaoh, over all his force, over his chariotry, and over his horsemen" (*ʾikkābĕdâ bĕparʿōh ûbĕkol-ḥêlô bĕrikbô ûbĕpārāšāyw*). In addition, we have the immediate context where our passage parallels Lev 9:24a. In Andreas Ruwe's (2003: 72) analysis, we have here "a decidedly twofold or two-phase manifestation of the *kābôd* Yahweh," for "both appearances of the godly fire parallel each other since both cases are phrased identically (*wattēṣēʾ ʾēš millipnê yhwh wattōʾkal*; Lev 9:24a//Lev 10:2)."

In Leviticus 10:3, Moses, the grand orchestrator and interpreter, defines for Aaron how this episode was meant to be understood: Yahweh via the lethality of his divine fire makes his *kābôd* manifest through the deaths of Nadab and Abihu, much as he manifests his holiness through priests (i.e., "those near to him"). Priests, through their separate status and their cultic actions, exhibit the distinction between the sacred and the profane. In other words, Yahweh shows how he is sacred (i.e., separate or "other") through the nature and actions of the priests (whom he himself has sanctified for such office; Exod 29:44). Accordingly, through the deaths of Nadab and Abihu (themselves priests but here violating their sacred office) Yahweh also manifests his sacred *kābôd*-ness—that is, his awesome presence, power, and majesty. The visible presence used to exhibit such *tremendum* is that of fire, a divine image with the longest and most enduring of legacies.

Sommer (2009: 120) is right on target when he adopts Otto's vocabulary to describe Leviticus 10:1–3:

> The manifestation [of the *kābôd* Yahweh] takes the form of incineration. This verse points toward the chaotic side of the holy. The erection of the tabernacle is an attempt at domesticating what the theorist of religion Rudolph Otto called the *tremendum*, the overwhelming, dangerous, and repelling aspect of the divine.... [P]recisely at the moment in which the domestication of the *kabod* climaxes and specifically among those who have direct access to that divine presence, it becomes brutally clear that holiness cannot be contained.

The lethal nature of Yahweh's *kābôd* (here made "brutally clear") underlies the various passages in P's narrative arc that we have already explored. Again and again P focuses on the presence of the cloud (*ʿānān*), for it is the cloud that is able to shield against the lethal presence of deity. When the deaths of Nadab and Abihu are briefly revisited in the preface of the Yom Kippur ritual (Lev 16:1–2), they serve as a warning for their father, Aaron, who must carry out his duties precisely "lest he die" (*yāmût*).[218]

The second group of *kābôd* Yahweh traditions (those associated with crisis events and the "murmuring" motif during the wandering experience) also reveal a lethal divine presence. In Numbers 14, the people's murmuring and desire to return to Egypt are portrayed as rebellion (*timĕrōdû*; 14:9) and as despising Yahweh (*yĕnaʾăṣunî*; 14:11). In response, when the *kābôd* Yahweh appears to all the people at the tent of meeting, Yahweh says he "will strike the people with pestilence and disinherit them" (*ʾakkennû baddeber wĕʾôrišennû*; 14:12). Moses then intercedes, referring to Yahweh's presence in cloud and fire and following this with an appeal against killing (*hēmatâ*) and slaughtering (*yišḥāṭēm*) the people (14:14–16).

By far the most famous story in this group of *kābôd* Yahweh passages is the rebellion led by Korah found in Numbers 16:1–35; 17:1–15 [= Eng 16:1–50].[219] After the stage is set, the *kābôd* Yahweh again appears at the tent of meeting, with Yahweh giving notice that he is about to "annihilate [Korah and his followers] in an instant" (*ʾakalleh ʾōtām kĕrāgaʿ*; Num 16:19–21). The subsequent destruction entails "the earth opening up its mouth and swallowing them" together with "fire emerging from Yahweh" (*ʾēš yāṣĕʾâ mēʾēt yhwh*) that consumed (*watōʾkal*) 250 men offering incense (Num 16:32, 35). Yahweh is a "devouring fire" indeed! Remarkably, after such a climax, the story continues. The motif of murmuring immediately returns; this time the complaining is about the killing just witnessed.

Again the *kābôd* Yahweh appears at the tent of meeting, with Yahweh again threatening "to annihilate the rebels in an instant" (Num 17:7-10 [= Eng 16:42-45). Moses instructs Aaron to make atonement for the people, "for wrath [*qeṣep*] has gone forth from Yahweh, the plague has begun" (cf. the earlier discussion on divine anger). Aaron does as directed, standing "between the dead and the living" until the plague stops, but only after the deaths of 14,700 additional people.

The *Kābôd* Yahweh in Ezekiel

Although associated with P by many scholars, and with the Zion-Sabaoth theology by others (esp. Mettinger 1982b: 97-115), Ezekiel's dramatic description of the *kābôd* Yahweh as preternatural, intense radiance is like no other portrayal.[220] The expression "*kĕbôd* Yahweh" appears ten times in the book (1:28; 3:12, 23; 10:4 [twice], 18; 11:23; 43:4-5; 44:4), with a similar expression, *kĕbôd ʾĕlōhê yiśrāʾēl*, occurring five times (Ezek 8:4; 9:3; 10:19; 11:22; 43:2). The most riveting description of the *kābôd* Yahweh is found in the opening scene. In Daniel Block's (1997: 108) words, "Everything about the vision [in Ezek 1] is in the superlative mode." The attention-grabbing start of what Ezekiel experiences (Ezek 1:4) sets the stage for the fantastic cherubim creatures and chariot throne that follow (Ezek 1:5-25), culminating in Ezekiel seeing the very presence (*kābôd*) of deity (Ezek 1:26-28).

> Suddenly I saw a stormy wind blowing in from the north [made up of] a tremendous cloud [*ʿānān gādôl*], fire flashing back and forth [*ʾēš mitlaqqaḥat*], and surrounded by radiance [*nōgah*]. Out of it—out of the fire—appeared something that looked like white-hot light [*ḥašmal*].[221] (Ezek 1:4)

While one's first impulse might be to envision storm theophanies, based on the mention of wind and cloud (and there is certainly some of that here and in what follows), the dominant motif is one of fiery radiance, conveyed by the words *ʾēš*, *nōgah*, and *ḥašmal*. The emphasis on brilliant (even metallic), fiery radiance continues in the description of the four living creatures (*ḥayyôt*, later termed *kĕrubîm*) and the chariot throne vision that follows, not to mention the climactic appearance of Yahweh via his *kābôd*. A startling number of words are used. Mention is made of "burnished bronze" (*nĕḥōšet qālāl*; 1:7), "burning coals of fire" (*gaḥălê-ʾēš bōʿărôt*; 1:13), "torches" (*lappidîm*; 1:13), "radiant fire" (*nōgah lāʾēš*; 1:13), "lightning issued from fire" (*min-hāʾēš yōṣēʾ bārāq*; 1:13), "darting sparks [?]" (*rāṣôʾ wāšôb kĕmarʾēh habbāzāq*; 1:14), "gleaming of chrysolite" (*kĕʿên taršîš*; 1:16), "terrifyingly radiant" (*gōbah wĕyirʾâ*; 1:18);[222] "awe-inspiring gleam of crystal" (*kĕʿên haqqeraḥ hannôrāʾ*; 1:22), "sapphire" (*sappîr*; 1:26), "white-hot light" (*ʿên ḥašmal*; 1:27), "fire" (*ʾēš*; 1:27 [twice]), "radiance" (*nōgah*; 1:27, 28), "rainbow" (*qešet*; 1:28), and "glory" (*kābôd*; 1:28).

Even words that do not at first glance seem to evoke images of radiance contribute to the overwhelming image. Christoph Uehlinger and Susanne Müller Trufaut (2001: 159–160) analyzed *galgal* (Ezek 10:2, 6, 13; traditionally translated simply as "wheelwork") based on Pierre Grelot's 1998 study and additional Mesopotamian iconography. They conclude that "*galgal* may refer to some cosmic halo, a system of brilliance and lightning related to celestial bodies ... [T]he whole system of moving circles [the four wheels in Ezek 10:12–13] ... i.e., the overall system of stars and planets moving according to principles of spatial and temporal circularity ... is viewed as a mysterious source of fire, lightning and shining brilliance."

The additional *kābôd* passages add even more data to this already impressive accumulation. The figure (man?)[223] in Ezekiel 8:2 has "the appearance of fire" (*kĕmarʾēh-ʾēš*), with fire below his loins and "brightness, like white-hot light," above (*zōhar kĕʿên haḥašmalâ*). In chapter 10, the court is full of "the radiance of the glory of Yahweh" (*nōgah kĕbôd yhwh*; 10:4), and "burning coals" (*gaḥălê-ʾēš*) are taken from the "wheelwork" (*galgal*). Near the end of the book, as a result of the return of the *kābôd* Yahweh, "the earth shone with his glory" (*hāʾāreṣ hēʾîrâ mikkĕbōdô*; 43:2). In short, Aster's (2006: 407–428) conclusion that "in the book of Ezekiel ... *kebod YHWH* is consistently a radiant phenomenon" with distinct parallels to the Mesopotamian concept of *melammu* is well grounded.

Understanding Ezekiel's preoccupation with depicting Yahweh's theophany with such multifaceted radiant imagery helps us interpret the climactic scene in Ezekiel 1:26–28.

> Above the firmament over [the *kĕrubîm*'s] heads there was the likeness [*dĕmût*] of a throne, in appearance like [*kĕmarʾēh*] sapphire; and seated above the likeness [*dĕmût*] of the throne was a likeness [*dĕmût*] similar to the appearance [*kĕmarʾēh*] of a human being [*ʾādām*]. And upward from what had the appearance of his loins [*kĕmarʾēh motnāyw*] I saw as it were white-hot light [*kĕʿên ḥašmal*], like the appearance of fire [*kĕmarʾēh-ʾēš*] enclosed round about; and downward from what had the appearance of his loins [*kĕmarʾēh motnāyw*] I saw as it were the appearance of fire [*kĕmarʾēh-ʾēš*], and there was radiance [*nōgah*] round about him. Like the appearance of the rainbow [*kĕmarʾēh haqqešet*] that is in the cloud on a rainy day, such was the appearance of the radiance [*marʾēh hannōgah*] round about. Such was the appearance [*marʾeh*] of the likeness [*dĕmût*] of the Glory [*kābôd*] of Yahweh. When I saw [the *kābôd* Yahweh], I fell upon my face, and I heard the voice of one speaking.

Because of the prophet's use of the words "human being" (*ʾādām*) and "loins" (*motnayîm*), it is common to read comments about how Ezekiel's portrayal

THE ICONOGRAPHY OF DIVINITY: YAHWEH 375

of divinity is "thoroughly" and "extraordinarily anthropomorphic [in] nature" (Sommer 2009: 7, 227 n. 83) or "blatantly anthropomorphic" (Hurowitz 2007: 99). Weinfeld (1972b: 201) writes that the "most singular feature [of Ezekiel's theophany] is the anthropomorphic imagery." Israel Knohl (1995: 129 n. 16) juxtaposes Ezekiel over against P, whose "description of the Presence (*kbwd*) of God . . . lacks all human dimension." Years ago Julian Morgenstern (1914: 45) was of a similar opinion: "We find P [in contrast to Ezekiel] no longer picturing the *kᵉbhod* Jahwe in human form." Such comments are true, but only to a degree. Based on several of the passages we have already dealt with, I would frame and nuance the discussion quite differently.

Clearly, P does not use human terms (*'ādām*, *'îš* [?], *motnayim*, *yād*) to describe Yahweh (and his *kābôd*), as does Ezekiel (1:26–27; 8:2–3). In light of the prevalent and consistent anthropomorphic language used of Yahweh throughout the Hebrew Bible (see pp. 288–290), P's reticence is conspicuous and remarkable.[224] Ezekiel's use of anthropomorphic language for the divine then is *not* extraordinary, but rather is following the norm—unless one would not expect such from the hands of Ezekiel the priest (Ezek 1:3).

Three Avenues to Unpack Ezekiel's Vision
Yet clearly Ezekiel's vision of the divine has no mere mortal in mind despite his use of *'ādām* and *motnayim*. Human bodies are not made of fire and radiant brilliance; neither can they fly on the wings of cherubim. What then are we to make of Ezekiel's use of human imagery? Three avenues of research prove helpful in unpacking Ezekiel's specific usage of anthropomorphic language: (1) the relevance of Mesopotamian iconography, (2) the Hebrew Bible's long-standing tradition of "fiery transcendent anthropomorphisms," and (3) the distinct rhetoric of circumvention used in Ezekiel 1:26–28.

Given Ezekiel's setting in Mesopotamia, one would have thought that the region's rich iconographic traditions would have been an obvious resource for commentators when it came to unpacking the images found in Ezekiel 1.[225] Yet only recently has this been attempted, and in certain circles such comparative study is still minimized.[226] As noted by several scholars, the depiction of the storm god Aššur with radiant *melammu* and fire from the time of the ninth-century BCE king Tukulti-Ninurta II (Figure 7.23) provides an apt analogy for the visual symbols found in Ezekiel 1:26–28.[227] The winged god is anthropomorphic from the waist up, with taut bow in hand. Most importantly, he is encircled with flames together with wavy lines depicting a radiance of some kind. There is little wonder that scholars have described this as perhaps our best example of *melammu* (a radiant supernatural force) being depicted in art. Though Ezekiel the priest/prophet is no worshipper of Aššur (indeed, cf. his harsh words against non-Yahwistic forms of religion throughout the book), he certainly could have

376 THE ORIGIN AND CHARACTER OF GOD

Figure 7.23 A depiction of the Mesopotamian storm god Aššur with radiant *melammu* and fire from the time of the ninth-century BCE King Tukulti-Ninurta II.
From Hugo Gressman, *Altorientalische Texte und Bilder zum Alten Testament* (Berlin: de Gruyter, 1927), tafel CXXXIII, 333, "Assur in den Regenwolken."

adapted Mesopotamian artistic motifs for his literary portrayal of the *kābôd* Yahweh. Needless to say, Ezekiel no more thought of Yahweh as a mere man than did Aššur's artists envision their majestic deity as being a simple mortal. Radiant deities—though anthropomorphic at a glance—can manifest their power and majesty by flying through the air engulfed in fire.

The tradition of Yahweh appearing along with and/or via fiery human form is of long standing, what I have referred to (adapting Hendel's vocabulary) as "fiery transcendent anthropomorphisms." Ezekiel's depiction of Yahweh with human terms along with fiery and radiant imagery should be understood within this enduring tradition. As early as Psalm 18 (//2 Sam 22), we read of a terror-inspiring theophany with smoke arising from Yahweh's *nostrils* and devouring fire blazing from his *mouth*. His *voice* as thunder rends the heavens. (See p. 346.) As did Aššur, Yahweh let loose his arrows as he discharged his lighting (*yišlaḥ ḥiṣṣāyw// bĕrāqîm*; Ps 18:15 [Eng 18:14]; 2 Sam 22:15). Yahweh is drawn with the most human of terms (nostrils, mouth, voice, [arms] drawing a bow), yet at the same time the psalmist uses multiple fiery images (fire, coals, brilliance, hailstones, lightning) to sketch a radiant (*nōgah*) god who transcends the human plane. As with Aššur, Yahweh was airborne, riding on the wings of the wind (*yāʿōp/yēdeʾ*[228]

'al-kanpê-rûaḥ), and like Ezekiel's depiction (but unlike Aššur), Yahweh was mounted on a cherub (yirkab 'al-kĕrûb; Ps 18:11 [Eng 18:10]).[229]

A similar mixture of the anthropomorphic with the fiery appears in Isaiah 30:27-33 (see pp. 346, 387).[230] With literary flair, the poet directs his words against Aššur. The Assyrians, who knew the terror of Aššur's *melammu* fighting on their behalf, are now to be stricken by Yahweh's terror, bringing about Aššur's demise (yēḥat 'aššûr; Isa 30:31). Once again Yahweh's portrait is drawn to appear human, with mention of his nostrils, lips, tongue, breath, voice, and arm ('appô, śĕpātāyw, lĕšônô, rûḥô, qôlô, zĕrô'ô, nišmat yhwh), yet at the same time coupled with burning (bō'ēr), devouring fire ('ēš 'ōkālet), thunder (qôl), and flames of fire (lahab 'ēš 'ōkēlâ). Yahweh is human-like and yet far beyond human in terms of his fiery manifestation.

Also appropriate for the background to Ezekiel 1:26-28 are the stories of divine presence within the *mal'ak*-Yahweh traditions, especially the one we find in Judges 13:2-23. As noted on pp. 349-350, Yahweh (via the *mal'ak*-Yahweh) appears repeatedly as a "human" ('îš; Judg 13:6, 8, 10-11) in this story, but clues abound as to its preternatural essence. This "human" entity is described by Manoah's wife as being "extremely terrifying" (nôrā' mĕ'ōd) in appearance— one who knows the future and promises the (miraculous?) birth of a dedicated (Nazirite) child who turns out to be none other than the super-strong Samson. The "human" of Judges 13:18 is shrouded in divine mystery, for he does not reveal his name, which he describes as "wonderful" (*pil'î), an adjective whose related nouns are used almost exclusively to describe God's mighty acts (Conrad 2001: 540-545). Eventually the divine/preternatural nature of this "human" is revealed as he ascends in fire from the altar. Thus once again we have a figure who manifests humanity yet whose fiery essence provides the climax of the story. In this instance, the human-divine figure causes Manoah and his wife to wonder why they were not killed, for when they encountered this human-figure-turned-fire, they "had actually seen God" (môt nāmût kî 'ĕlōhîm rā'înû).

Lastly, we must remind ourselves again of how Moses, because of his special favor, was allowed to see "human" body parts of Yahweh: his back ('āḥôr) and hand (kap) (Exod 33:17-23). In contrast to the passages we have already examined, there is no explicit mention of fire in this passage, yet the divine body language does take place in the context of Yahweh showing Moses a part of his *kābôd*. The radiance associated with *kābôd*, as we have demonstrated, can be described with fire, clouds, storms, brilliance, light, and so on, so it is hard to unpack the precise way in which Yahweh would have "passed by" Moses—although seemingly it was airborne. (In J's account in Exodus 34:6, Yahweh's "passing by" happens after he comes down in a cloud.) The potential lethality of the encounter (Exod 33:20) and Yahweh's shielding of Moses from this danger could designate that fire was a part of the *kābôd* theophany, as fire is the most frequent lethal divine agent used elsewhere. Again, this passage, like the three previous, exhibits a tradition of Yahweh appearing as part "human" and yet so much more. The author of Exodus 33:17–23, especially with his warning in Exodus 33:20, would assert that any notion of reducing Yahweh down to the human level (even with his accommodating vocabulary of ʾāḥôr and kap) would fall far short of encapsulating the *tremendum* of divinity.

To judge from these four narratives (Ps 18//2 Sam 22; Isa 30; Judg 13; and Exod 33), we must conclude that such stories were well known. When Ezekiel described Yahweh as being a "human" and yet so much more than human, it must have sounded fantastic indeed to his audience. Yahweh's "humanness" was absorbed in fire (kĕmarʾēh-ʾēš) from his loins both upward and downward, together with encircling radiance (nōgah)—not to mention the ḥašmal substance. The language must have sounded surreal, yet such a depiction was not out of character from what they had previously heard about Yahweh's "fiery transcendent anthropomorphisms."

A third avenue of unpacking Ezekiel 1:26–28 is to study its specific rhetoric of circumvention. Ezekiel desires to express his claim that he actually witnessed the very presence (kābôd) of Yahweh at the river Chebar. Ezekiel is not claiming that he saw Yahweh manifesting his "glory" via deeds in human history. Rather, Ezekiel is claiming (using the language of theophany and kābôd) that he has joined the select few who have actually seen the very presence of the divine. Most remarkably, Ezekiel does *not* state (as others have in the past) that his experience was potentially lethal and that he was blessed to live to tell the story. This is key for our interpretation.

As noted on pp. 289–290, close attention to the rhetoric of Ezekiel 1:26–28 reveals that the author went out of his way to use three terms of circumvention (marʾeh, dĕmût, ʿên) to avoid explicitly describing the presence of deity. That these three "buffer terms" (Greenberg 1983: 53) occur fourteen times in just three verses is intentional. Through their use the author is able to sketch, by analogy, the "human" form of Yahweh that is at the same time beyond human in its majesty and otherness. Ezekiel "signifies unwillingness to commit oneself to the substantial identity of the seen with the compared" (Greenberg 1983: 53). This is especially true when he approaches words for "human" before which he uses double qualifiers. Ezekiel 1:26 reads: "Seated above the likeness [dĕmût] of a throne was a likeness [dĕmût] similar to the appearance [kĕmarʾeh] of a human being [ʾādām]." Similarly, Ezekiel 8:2 has "I looked and there was a likeness [dĕmût] similar to the appearance [kĕmarʾeh] of a man [ʾîš]."[231] The prophet concludes his vision with a triple qualification. Rather than saying that he "saw God face-to-face," Ezekiel uses exceptional restraint: "Such was the appearance [marʾeh] of the likeness [dĕmût] of the Glory [kābôd] of Yahweh."

It bears repeating that Ezekiel is doing just what we would expect from a Judean priest: differentiating the Most Sacred from the profane. There is no doubt that

Ezekiel's (sacred) "man" of radiant fire should be differentiated from an ordinary (profane) human being of flesh and bone. Yet Ezekiel does not cry out in his profane state "Woe is me!" as does Isaiah in his encounter with the Most Holy (Isa 6:5). Nor does Ezekiel mediate the theophany by cloaking "extremely terrifying" (*nôrā' mě'ōd*), "wondrous" (*pil'î*), and fiery divinity via a human-looking *mal'āk* figure (Judges 13). Ezekiel chooses here not to emphasize (as does P) a cloud covering that shields onlookers against lethal danger (but cf. Ezek 10:4) nor how (as does JE/non-P) the very hand of God protects the prophet from Yahweh's *kābôd* (Exod 33:22). Rather, Ezekiel uses the concealment and shielding of language. By using his buffer terms and comparisons by analogy, he keeps the (lethal) divine at a safe distance. One explicit term that is here (and missing or implied in the other lethal divine sighting passages) is the medium of revelation being "visions" (*mar'ôt 'ĕlōhîm*; Ezek 1:1; 8:3). Perhaps this too added an extra layer of protection.

In conclusion, it is shortsighted to reduce this grandest of the *kābôd* theophanies, as do scholars who use language similar to Weinfeld's (1992: 201) to say that the "most singular feature [of Ezekiel's theophany] is the anthropomorphic imagery." Rather, the radiant, fiery picture Ezekiel paints of the *kābôd* Yahweh is one of *fascinans* and *tremendum*.

Divine "Name"

The Use of the Divine "Name" (*Šēm*) to Depict the Presence of Yahweh

So far we have depicted how various authors of the Hebrew Bible have used the concepts of fire and radiance (with emphasis on *kābôd*) to describe the presence of divinity. Such abstract concepts do not lend themselves to iconographic portrayal (though, as we saw with the *melammu* of Aššur, attempts were made). A wide variety of writers of the Hebrew Bible went beyond physical objects to craft divinity through ethereal images and exquisite words specifically chosen to describe that which fascinates and frightens. This vocabulary includes *'ēš, 'ēš 'ōkelet, bě'ôr 'ēš, bělabbat-'ēš, lappîd 'ēš, gaḥălê-'ēš, śěrāpîm, mal'ak-Yahweh, 'ap, qôl mittôk hā'ēš, kābôd, pānîm, nōgah, hôd, hādār, paḥad, gě'ôn, nôrā' mě'ōd, pil'î*, and *kěrubîm*. Note that even this lengthy list does not include the many images associated with Yahweh's storm theophanies, not to mention a host of meteorological and astronomical terms as well as Ezekiel's gleaming gems and shining metals.

A radical departure from these streams of tradition is found in what has come to be called the Name Theology, associated with the book of Deuteronomy and the Deuteronomistic History. The discussion focuses on terminology that has Yahweh saying that he will reside in sacred space *through the presence of his name* (*šēm*). The formulaic phrase that has received the most attention states that the privileged sanctuary is marked as "the place where Yahweh, your God, will choose to cause his name to dwell" (*hammāqôm 'ăšer-yibḥar yhwh 'ĕlōhêkem bô lĕšakkēn šĕmô šām*; Deut 12:11; 14:23; 16:2, 6, 11; 26:2; cf. Jer 7:12; Ezra 6:12; Neh 1:9). Related phrases include (1) the place where Yahweh chooses "to put his name there" (*hammāqôm 'ăšer-yibḥar yhwh lāśûm 'et-šĕmô šām*; e.g., Deut 12:5); (2) the place in which Yahweh's Name will "be there" (*'el-hammāqôm 'ăšer yihyeh šĕmî šām*; e.g., 1 Kgs 8:29); (3) "building a house for the Name of Yahweh" (*libnôt bayit lĕšēm yhwh*; e.g., 1 Kgs 5:19 [Eng 5:5]); and (4) "calling the Name over the place" (*kî-šimkā niqrā' 'al-habbayit*; e.g., 1 Kgs 8:43).[232]

Where Yahweh's Name dwells constitutes sacred space. Indeed, according to this tradition, it is the *only* legitimate sacred space, a central site where cult should take place. Accordingly, it is the place where burnt offerings, sacrifices, tithes, contributions, votive offerings, free will offerings, and the firstlings of herds and flocks were to be brought to Yahweh (Deut 12:5–6, 11, 13–14; 26:2–4). In addition, this chosen place was intended to be festive, a place where households were "to eat before Yahweh" (*'ăkaltem-šām lipnê yhwh*) and "celebrate" (*ûśĕmaḥtem*) their blessings (Deut 12:7, 12, 18). The question at hand is whether the name (*šēm*) of Yahweh represents divine presence, and if so, how.

Four Key Tenets of Traditional Name Theology
As traditionally understood by scholars, the Name Theology embraced the following four tenets:

1. It was occasioned by the cognitive dissonance that resulted from the national tragedies of 597 and 586 BCE.
2. Its abstract notions were reactionary in nature, arguing against former expressions of worship (i.e., JE/non-P) that were thought to be too immanent and too anthropomorphic, or against the Zion-Sabaoth traditions.
3. It had Jerusalem solely in mind as the chosen place.
4. While the Name of Yahweh resides in the Jerusalem Temple, Yahweh's true self abides (transcendently) in heaven alone.

Tenets give the impression of uniform and widespread solidarity. Richter (2002: 9) even comments on the "profound impact that this interpretive paradigm has had on the field of biblical studies." Yet numerous critiques have modified this traditional portrayal in significant ways. Already in 1969 S. Dean McBride would write that "the shape of the biblical [Name Theology] tradition ... is more disparate than has generally been recognized." The subsequent decades of scholarship have proven that the topic is even more complicated.[233] Yet for the sake of argument, the discussion that follows will be structured around these four convictions.

The First Tenet
The ancient Near East (including ancient Israel) was filled to the brim with notions of how deities were embodied by their names and lived in their temples. Whatever the understandings of these concepts were throughout ancient Israel's past, leading scholars understand the occasion for articulating the Name Theology to be the national catastrophes of 597 and 586 BCE. According to Mettinger (1982b: 60–61), "The events of 597 [where the Babylonians 'penetrated into the House itself'] fueled the development of the notion of the Name in the Temple." He elaborates: "The fully developed Name theology first appears after the devastation of the Temple [in 586 BCE]. Accordingly, the Name theology may be regarded as a device for resolving the cognitive dissonance which arose when the established tenets of the Zion-Sabaoth theology [Yahweh of Hosts enthroned upon the cherubim] were confronted with harsh reality." Elsewhere, Mettinger (1998: 1) argues that these "historical events provoked an existential crisis of national scope."

Granted, Mettinger's (1982b: 60) reconstruction (which is chosen here as just one representative of traditional Name Theology scholars) is based on his preference "to date the first edition of the D-work to the time of the Exile." Those scholars (including the present writer) who would point to earlier editions of the Deuteronomistic History (especially during the reign of Josiah) would see this presupposition as a substantial flaw. Mettinger (1982b: 56), for all his emphasis on the events of 597 and 586 BCE, is nonetheless wise to underscore that "the Name theology that we have found in the D-Work ... in all likelihood ... had ancient roots." Here he has in mind similar phraseology in the Amarna letters (EA 287.60–61; 288.5–7) as well as pre-Deuteronomistic passages including J/non-P theophanies (e.g., Exod 34:5–6; cf. Ps 29:2), *malʾāk* traditions (Exod 23:20–21), the "old altar law" of Exodus 20:24, and *kābôd* traditions in JE/non-P (Exod 33:19).[234] Such conclusions resonate with other assessments such as McBride's (1969: 51) that the "Name Theology must have been rooted in the early traditions of Israel." Exodus 20:24, with its reference to making offerings *"in every place"* (*bĕkol-hammāqôm*) where Yahweh causes his name to be remembered (*ʾăšer ʾazkîr ʾet-šĕmî*), is especially fascinating, for it lacks any notion of the centralization of worship, a hallmark of Deuteronomistic teachings. More recently, Naʾaman (2011b: 310) uses the mention of "the Name of El" (*šm ʾl*) in the ninth-/eighth-century BCE Kuntillet ʿAjrud plaster inscription 4.2 to argue that "the roots of biblical name theology may be sought in the Kingdom of Israel of the eighth century, if not earlier."

The Second Tenet
Whatever the historical occasion (if ever such could be demonstrated), the second traditional tenet of understanding Name Theology asserts that it is reactionary

along theological lines. Here Gerhard von Rad (one of the most influential of the Name Theology architects) is the perfect spokesman.[235] Von Rad (1953: 37–44; 1966a: 103–124) was of the opinion that northern Ark versus southern tent traditions could help unpack the D and P positions, respectively, on divine presence, including the former's Name Theology and the latter's *kābôd* theology. Suffice it here to say that von Rad's reconstruction was "open to serious question" (McBride 1969: 30). Yet von Rad's influence was long-lasting when he asserted that "the Deuteronomic theologumenon of the name of Jahweh clearly holds a polemic[al] element, or, to put it better, is a theological corrective... replacing the old crude idea of Jahweh's presence" (von Rad 1953: 38–39). Von Rad (1962: 184) wrote elsewhere that Deuteronomy is "obviously attacking the older and more popular idea of Jahweh's immediate presence at the place of worship."

Yet when it comes to immanence and anthropomorphism used of Yahweh, the Hebrew Bible is replete with examples. Such notions are not found in just early material, and they are hardly "crude." Thus other analysts would see the Name Theology as a corrective directed in another direction. Mettinger (1982b: 60) argues forcefully that the Name Theology "functions polemically against the Zion-Sabaoth traditions." Given the events of 597 and 586 BCE, it was much easier to avoid speaking of a powerful Yahweh sitting enthroned in a violated and/or destroyed Jerusalem Temple. Instead, for Mettinger (1998: 8), "emphasis shifted to God's transcendence," where Yahweh was "relocated to the heavens above." But what is at issue here is the nature of Yahweh's presence and whether his locale was only in the heavens (see the upcoming discussion of the fourth tenet).

The Third Tenet
The single sanctuary that is "chosen" to house Yahweh's Name has almost universally been seen to be Jerusalem, with prominent advocates being Martin Noth, Josef Schreiner, R. E. Clements, and S. Dean McBride.[236] This is not to say that other northern locales (e.g., Shechem, Bethel) have not been advocated in the past and especially by those who emphasize the northern origins of Deuteronomy's Ur-tradition.[237] Key to settling on Jerusalem has been McBride's (1969: 46, 198–204) study of the use of the verb *bḥr* ("to choose") and how it was employed to express the divine election of both the Davidic lineage and Zion. When *bḥr* is used in the Name Theology formula, "it is never explicitly associated with a sanctuary other than the Jerusalem Temple" (McBride 1969: 198).

At the same time, McBride (1969: 197) argues that "there is no substantial reason to suppose that the Name Theology [per se] had a Jerusalem provenance." Here once again, one is forced to consider the data mentioned in our discussion of the first tenet, especially Exodus 20:24. Thus McBride (1969: 209) concludes that the final formula ("the place where Yahweh, your God, will choose to cause his name to dwell") presents us with "a synthetic construction" where the Name

Theology "in origin had nothing whatsoever to do with a singular or a centralized Yahwistic cultus" yet came to embody "the election terminology of Jerusalem."

Before we leave this section, it is important to mention the use of the Name Theology as it is applied to Shiloh in Jeremiah 7:12. In his famous "temple oracles" (Lundbom 1999: 458), the prophet warns those who hold fast to the inviolability of Jerusalem to consider their past history. "Just go to my place that was in Shiloh, where I made my name dwell at first [*mĕqômî ʾăšer bĕšîlô ʾăšer šikkantî šĕmî šām bāriʾšônâ*] and see what I did to it because of the wickedness of my people Israel." As noted by McBride (1969: 47), this is "the only biblical passage which explicitly associates Name Theology with a shrine other than the one in Jerusalem." This passage has been dismissed as secondary, the result of the close connection between the authors and editors of the Deuteronomistic material and the book of Jeremiah, and/or the rhetoric of the prophet making an "ironic comparison, not engaging in tradition historical speculation."[238] Yet we should not dismiss this material, especially when it is taken along with other venerable passages that use Yahweh's Name to designate his presence. The rhetoric of Jeremiah's "carefully wrought discourse" against the Jerusalem Temple (the "named" house of Yahweh [7:14]) would lose all its effectual power were there no solid tradition of Yahweh's Name once residing at Shiloh.[239] In addition, Jeremiah's connection to Anathoth (Jer 1:1) would have made it likely (according to Lundbom 1999: 468) that he would "have learned about Shiloh's destruction firsthand," for "Shiloh's traditions were doubtless preserved in Anathoth, which lay only a short distance to the south and which carried on the Shiloh priestly line through Abiathar (1 Kgs 2:26–27)." In the end it is preferable to side with Mettinger (1982b: 132) when he concludes that Jer 7:12 (together with 2 Sam 6:2 and the name Samuel) yields "evidence that God's Name was the object of special veneration, and . . . may have played an important role in Shiloh, where the Ark for a time made its home."

Lastly, Sandra Richter (2002) has presented a dramatic challenge to traditional Name Theology (see the next section). If Richter's analysis holds true, then one should consider how Richter (2007) also argues that the earliest locale for the placing of Yahweh's Name may have been at Mt. Ebal. Following an observation first made by A. C. Welch in 1924, Richter (2007: 350 n. 23) notes "the incongruity of a book supposedly focused on the centralization of worship in *Jerusalem* portraying Moses [in Deut 27:1–8] commanding the Israelites to perform sacrifice and worship at *Mt. Ebal*" (emphasis Richter's). Probing further, Richter asks a most insightful question: "Who would try to legitimize a cult site at Ebal?"

The Fourth Tenet
The fourth tenet of Name Theology scholarship is by far the most controversial and the one subject to the most revision in the days since the Name Theology

paradigm was first crafted. We will consider four views with regard to how the placing of the Name functioned to designate divine presence: (1) that the Name is only a symbol or marker of divine presence that functions to direct attention toward Yahweh's true and only abode, the heavenly realm; (2) that in a mysterious way, the Name functioned as a marker of the practical presence of Yahweh, who was also thought to be (simultaneously) in the heavens; (3) that the Name functioned in a hypostatic way (or semi-hypostatic way) to represent Yahweh; and (4) Richter's bold claim that placing Yahweh's Name marked his ownership and hegemony thus undermining all the tenets of traditional Name Theology.

Option 1. A dominant understanding of the Name Theology for many scholars is grounded in the mention of Yahweh's lack of "form" (*těmûnâ*) in Deuteronomy 4:11–12, 15–16 (studied on pp. 356–358) mixed with the repeated emphasis in 1 Kings 8 that Yahweh hears prayers from his location in heaven (1 Kgs 8:22, 30, 32, 34, 36, 39, 43, 45, 49, [54]). Indeed, four of these references (1 Kgs 8:30, 39, 43, 49) *explicitly* call heaven Yahweh's "dwelling place" (*měqôm/měkôn šibtěkā*). As if to make the matter even clearer, 1 Kings 8:27 asks rhetorically:

> But will God really dwell on earth? Even heaven and the highest heavens cannot contain you; how much less this house that I have built!

From this aggregate of data, scholars conclude that such texts "emphasize that God dwells in heaven and nowhere else" (Sommer 2009: 62). According to Clements (1965b: 91), the Deuteronomistic Historian "fully and firmly rejected" "all who believed that Yahweh dwelt on Mount Zion in his temple . . . Yahweh is not a God who can be said to dwell anywhere on earth, but his only abode is in heaven." To again use Mettinger's (1998: 8) language, "emphasis shifted to God's transcendence" where Yahweh was "relocated to the heavens above."

As a result, and with Solomon's prayer in 1 Kings 8:23–53 serving as the definitive statement, "no longer does the temple symbolize the land to provide a link between the natural and supernatural words. . . . Instead it is a house of prayer" (Clements 1965b: 91). Similarly, Mettinger (1998: 6) writes: "God dwells in heaven [alone] and the temple becomes a house of prayer."

Yet such a view seems strained and overly restrictive. We have already noted (pp. 357–358) the insightful critique of Wilson (1995: 97) that Deuteronomy envisions "the localization as well as the transcendence of YHWH." While there is no concrete "form" (as in a divine statue of precious metal), there is nonetheless the localization of deity on earth through fire and other ethereal images. Deuteronomy 4:36 explicitly refers to the presence of Yahweh both in heaven and on earth via "his great fire" that the people are indeed allowed to see (*wěʿal-hāʾāreṣ herʾăkā ʾet-ʾiššô haggědôlâ*).[240] We need also to remember the older traditions that inform what we have in Deuteronomy, such as laws of warfare and notions of Yahweh going before the people in battle (e.g., Deut 1:30; 20:4; 31:6 and 23:15 [Eng 23:14]).[241] Here Yahweh is described as "the one who marches with you to fight for you against your enemies" (*yhwh ʾĕlōhêkem hahōlēk ʿimmākem lĕhillāḥēm lākem ʿim-ʾōyĕbêkem*) and as "the one who walks in the midst of your camp" (*yhwh ʾĕlōhêkā mithallēk bĕqereb maḥănekā*).[242]

Moreover, past interpretations of 1 Kings 8 have been unduly narrow and overly privileged.[243] Those verses mentioning Yahweh's presence in heaven have been emphasized, while those that specifically mention the localized presence of divinity (e.g., the Ark in 1 Kgs 8:5–9 and the *kābôd* in 1 Kgs 8:10–11) have been minimized or ignored. Of particular note are the cultic observances that coincide with the localized presence. Specific mention is made of the sacrifice of sheep and oxen in great (even exaggerated) quantities by Solomon and all Israel both at the beginning (8:5) and end of the chapter (8:62). In 1 Kings 8:62 these sacrifices are done "before Yahweh."[244] In short, if 1 Kings 8 is treated as a whole, then—as with Deuteronomy 12 (cf. 12:5–6, 11, 13–14; 26:2–4)—the place where Yahweh's Name dwells constitutes sacred space, and as such was a place of cultic activity. It would make little sense in the context of ancient Near Eastern temple economies to have such cultic activity if the Jerusalem Temple was envisioned as only a "forwarding station" for prayer.

The only way in which we could imagine 1 Kings 8 as not localizing Yahweh both on earth and in heaven would be if we separated Solomon's prayer and its Name Theology from its present context and dated them to the exilic period, when the Temple is destroyed. Yet Knoppers (2000; 1995a) has argued decisively that there is "substantial literary evidence" for the unity of 1 Kings 8, which functions much better in a late pre-exilic context ("the time in which the Deuteronomist likely wrote his work") to legitimize the Jerusalem Temple.[245] Knoppers (2000: 370) argues: "Rather than indicating a devaluation or demythologization of the Temple, the Solomonic blessings, invocations, and petitions expand the Temple's role in Israelite life."[246]

Thus in our opinion, this option is the weakest of the positions (so too Hundley 2009: 551). It is preferable to consider the way in which the Name of Yahweh functioned to mark the real presence of Yahweh on earth (along with his presence in heaven). Options 2 and 3 address just such a notion.

Option 2. This option, according to Hundley (2009: 553), argues that "the presence of YHWH's name in the temple expresses God's practical yet ineffable presence.... [T]he name does not ensure physical presence [but] it does ensure practical presence." Emphasizing the covenantal context of the various name formulae, Hundley adds that "the Deuteronomist's use of the name attaches YHWH to the temple so that his power, character, actions and reputation are intimately connected with it and the people who worship in it."

The Deuteronomistic Name tradition could indeed be reacting (in accord with the second tenet) against the conceptual matrix of Zion-Sabaoth traditions and yet not necessarily because of the "catastrophe of exile" (in contrast to the first tenet). According to Mettinger (1982b: 24–28), the Zion-Sabaoth tradition emphasized two key aspects: Yahweh Sabaoth is depicted as king (e.g., Ps 24:7–10), and Yahweh is invisibly enthroned on the cherubim in the Jerusalem Temple (Ps 46:5–8 [Eng 46:4–7]; Ps 76:3 [Eng 76:2]; Jer 8:19). This results in a dual conception of divinity. This portrayal of Yahweh, according to Mettinger (1982b: 25), "is simultaneously both aniconic (i.e., without icon) and anthropomorphic . . . No divine image reposes on the cherubim throne [and yet] God reigns there invisibly like a king in his palace."

The Deuteronomistic Name Theology could be emphasizing the second aspect (Yahweh's presence in the Jerusalem Temple) yet without the anthropomorphic problem that is inherent with the notion of a king sitting on throne. While the Name Theology might be termed "mysterious" (Hundley 2009: 552–554), it is not overly so. By choosing Yahweh's Name to depict his essence and active, abiding presence, the Deuteronomistic tradition is simply choosing one abstract expression over other abstract ideas (e.g., invisibility, *kābôd* radiance). If 1 Kings 8 with its frequent Name Theology (1 Kgs 8:16–20, 29, 41–44, 48) is a unified whole, then the Deuteronomist is even more adept as he sews his new (and supersessionist) religious ideas into the folds of older Ark (1 Kgs 8:5–9) and *kābôd* (1 Kgs 8:10–11) traditions. Once again, Knoppers (2000: 393; 1995a: 251) comments: "Even as [the Deuteronomist's] dedication of the temple inaugurates a new era in Israel's history, it begins and ends with cultic institutions of the Sinaitic era."

Option 3. The third option is a nuanced variant of the second option. It too underscores that Yahweh was present in a very real way in the Jerusalem Temple via the presence of his name. What it adds to the discussion is how divine names can function hypostatically.

McBride (1969) articulated the most nuanced and best-researched defense of this position, which he grounded in the study of the Hebrew Bible's ancient Near Eastern context.[247] The tendency in the ancient Near East to personify and then deify temples and related cultic objects is well known. McCarter (1987: 147–148) points to the deity Bethel as one of the best examples.[248] McBride (1969: 130) stresses that there was also "a tendency to personify in greater and lesser degree the epithets, functions, attributes and qualities of high gods." In turn, "the various facets of a god . . . were themselves often portrayed as semi-independent deities." In other words, we are dealing with the hypostasization of a deity. The noun "hypostasis" is well known from Greek authors (cf. Liddell and Scott 1996: s.v. "hypostasis"), philosophy, and Christian theology to designate the essential nature, essence, or underlying reality of a substance.

McBride defined it as follows:

> Specifically, by "hypostasis" is meant a quality, epithet, attribute, manifestation or the like of a deity which through a process of personification and differentiation has become distinct (if not fully independent) divine being in its own right. (McBride 1969: 5)

This is not the place to discuss the various types of hypostatic representations of deities.[249] Suffice it here to note that *names* of deities were used hypostatically, with the best Northwest Semitic examples being ʿAthtartu-*Name*-of-Baʿlu from Ugarit, "the *Name* of El" (*šm ʾl*) at Kuntillet ʿAjrud, the deity ʾăšîmāʾ mentioned in 2 Kings 17:30 (cf. Cogan 1999), and *Eshem*-Bethel from Elephantine (cf. McCarter 1987: 147).[250] In addition, there are a large number of Northwest Semitic examples where the noun "name" functions as the theophoric element in onomastica.

Such Northwest Semitic examples are relevant for setting the backdrop of Deuteronomistic Name Theology. Other biblical texts fill in additional background. The best example of a hypostatic use of "the Name of Yahweh" in the Hebrew Bible is found in Isaiah 30:27–33:

> The Name of Yahweh [*šēm-yhwh*] comes from afar,
> In blazing wrath . . .
> His tongue like a devouring fire,
> His breath like a raging torrent . . .
> In raging wrath,
> In a devouring blaze of fire,
> In tempest, and rainstorm, and hailstones.
> Truly, at the thunder of Yahweh
> Assyria will be seized with terror,
> As [Yahweh] smites with [his] staff. (Isa 30:27–28a, 30b–31)

In many ways, the process of hypostasization is most understandable when one considers the many instances where the Name of Yahweh is used in parallel to Yahweh. To cite just one such passage, consider Psalm 20:

> May Yahweh answer you in the day of trouble!
> May the Name of the God of Jacob protect you! . . .
>
> May we shout for joy over your victory,
> arrayed by [military] standards in the Name of our God! . . .
>
> They [call] on chariots, they [call] on horses;
> but we invoke the Name of Yahweh our God: . . .

"O Yahweh, grant victory!"
May the King answer us in the day of our invocation. (Ps 20:2, 6, 8, 10 [= Eng 20:1, 5, 7, 9])

Applying the phenomenon of hypostasization to the Name Theology results in the following nuanced understanding. The "personified" Name of Yahweh (due to its semi-independent nature) can "dwell" in the Jerusalem Temple, while at the same time Yahweh can reside in heaven. Because it is distinct (and semi-independent), the Name can reside in the temple apart from Yahweh in heaven, and yet because it still captures the "essential nature" or "essence" of Yahweh, its use avoids any charge of bifurcation of Yahweh. Or, using the words from option 2, the Name of Yahweh can in a real hypostatic way represent the *practical presence* of the deity, who can simultaneously reside in heaven.

Note that by personifying an abstract concept such as a "name," the Deuteronomistic tradition can once again avoid the anthropomorphism of the deity that characterized the Yahweh Sabaoth traditions. The notion of a "name dwelling" is qualitatively different from the picture of a king sitting on a throne. Moreover, because the Name is associated with the divine warrior and Ark traditions, the Deuteronomists are again able to weave their new portrayal into the fabric of ancient Israel's past lore.

To see this, one needs to consider how divine names were thought to contain "effectual power" that could be accessed in the here and now if properly invoked (Lewis 2011). For the present discussion, notice how the divine name Yahweh is particularly associated with the use of the Ark as a war palladium. In 2 Samuel 6:1–2 we find the following description that includes a performative utterance:

> David assembled all the elite troops of Israel—thirty thousands—and [he] and the entire army that was with him went to Baalah to bring up from there the Holy Ark over which the [following] name was invoked [*'ăšer-niqrā' šēm*]:
> The Name: "Yahweh of Armies, He Who Is Seated upon the Cherubim"
> [*šēm: yhwh ṣĕbā'ôt yōšēb hakkĕrubîm*]251

Consider also how the divine name functions in "ritual warfare," as articulated in the "Song of the Ark" found in Numbers 10:35–36. The following words were pronounced when the Ark set out to battle and then returned from battle:

> Arise,252 O Yahweh,
> May your enemies be scattered;
> May your adversaries flee before you . . .
> Return, O Yahweh, [with] the myriads
> [El with] the thousands of Israel.253

If we wed these Ark traditions with Jeremiah 7:12's mention of Shiloh being the first place where Yahweh "made his Name dwell," then perhaps one could posit that military contexts formed part of the backdrop of the developing Name Theology. Consider here the popular story of David battling Goliath:

> Then David said to the Philistine, "You come against me with sword, spear and scimitar; but I come against you with the Name of Yahweh of Armies [*běšēm yhwh ṣěbā'ôt*], the God of the ranks of Israel, whom you have defied." (1 Sam 17:45)

In many respects, 1 Samuel 17:45 is like the Name Theology (and contrary to the Yahweh Sabaoth traditions) in how it avoids anthropomorphic details about Yahweh going to battle. It is not Yahweh of Armies (*yhwh ṣěbā'ôt*) who goes to battle like "a man of war" (*'îš milḥāmâ*) (so Exod 15:3), but rather "the *Name* of Yahweh of Armies" that achieves victory (and without sword and spear, according to 1 Sam 17:47).[254] In an analogous way, just as the divine warrior was thought to return to and reside in his temple after victory, so the Name Theology has the Name of Yahweh residing in his chosen sanctuary.[255]

We might also add here a fragment of epic tradition. According to McBride (1969: 208), in Exodus 23:20–22 (classically assigned to the E literary strand) "we find Yahweh's 'name' functioning as a semi-hypostasis, embodied in the figure of the divine *mal'āk*." In this passage, Yahweh says:

> "I am sending [my] *mal'āk* before you, to guard you on the way and to bring you to the place that I have prepared. Give heed to him and listen to his voice. Do not rebel against him, for he will not pardon your offenses; *for my name is in him* [*kî šěmî běqirbô*]. But if you listen attentively to his voice and do all that I say, then I will be an enemy to your enemies and an adversary to your adversaries."

This passage should be paired with Exodus 33:2–3, which again shows how the semi-independent *mal'āk* serves as a barrier against lethal divinity:

> "I will send [my] *mal'āk* before you, and I will drive out the Canaanites, the Amorites, the Hittites, the Perizzites, the Hivites, and the Jebusites. [Go up to] a land flowing with milk and honey; but I will not go up in your midst [*běqirběkā*], lest I consume you [*pen-'ăkelkā*] on the way, for you are a stiff-necked people."

As we saw elsewhere with Yahweh being portrayed with the language of "consuming fire" (*'ēš 'ōkelet*), here Yahweh's lethality is "consuming" (*'ăkelkā*). As we saw earlier (especially in Judges 13), here the *mal'āk* figure is used once again to depict divine presence in a way that shields people from the danger of a direct encounter with divinity.

In summary, we should ask how the "hypostatic theory" ties in with the Name Theology's additional emphasis on Yahweh residing in heaven. It would seem that while Yahweh dwells in heaven, from which he answers prayers (1 Kgs 8: [22], 30, 32, 34, 36, 39, 43, 45, 49, [54]), on earth his hypostatic name (representing lethal power in battle and otherwise) resides in the temple with the Ark, the war palladium. Deuteronomistic Name Theology rejects the throne image and its anthropomorphism but embraces an aniconic name that *nonetheless contains effective power* and especially in the contexts of battles that are fought on earth, not heaven.[256]

Option 4. The final view with regard to how the placing of the Name functioned to designate divine presence is that of Richter. Richter's study on Name Theology is so impressive that even her critics call it "a high-profile contribution" that "stands head and shoulders above much that is being published in the discipline of Hebrew Bible" (Mettinger 2003: 753). As with the third option, Richter grounds her new insights by situating the Name Theology phraseology within the context of the ancient Near East, in particular cognate expressions in Akkadian.

After examining Akkadian cognate expressions for the Hebrew *lĕšakkēn šĕmô šām* and *lāśûm šĕmô šām,* Richter concludes that the idiom and usage are so close that the two Hebrew phrases must be, respectively, a loan adaptation and a calque of the Akkadian. The basic meaning of the Akkadian *šuma šakānu,* occurring especially on royal monumental inscriptions, is "to place one's inscription upon a monument in order to claim that monument as one's own and to commemorate one's great deeds" (Richter 2002: 183, 204). Extended meanings of placing one's name include claiming territory and acquiring fame. Of special note, argues Richter (2002: 203), is the presence of such idiomatic expressions in the first-millennium Levantine monumental tradition, with particular attention being assigned to the ninth-century BCE inscription from Tell Fakhariyah. This text is particularly noteworthy because it is a rare bilingual example that can show Akkadian and Old Aramaic counterparts.[257]

Thus, according to Richter (2002: 205, 217), the Deuteronomist tradition is "not generating a new idiom" but rather adopting Akkadian vocabulary "to emphasize the sovereignty and fame of YHWH by right of conquest. As had the great kings and heroes of Mesopotamian history and legend, YHWH states that he has 'placed his name' in the Promised Land. The king has captured this new territory; he has claimed it as his own."

According to Richter, then, the simple transitive meaning of the Hebrew *lĕšakkēn šĕmô šām* ("to place his name there") is to be preferred over the D factitive translation ("to cause his name to dwell"). As a result, there is no Deuteronomistic Name Theology with the divine name dwelling in the temple

THE ICONOGRAPHY OF DIVINITY: YAHWEH   391

to represent Yahweh's presence. According to Richter (2002: 216), the scholarly construction of a Name Theology "simply cannot be defended." "The deuteronomic idiom used in Deuteronomy and the D[euteronomistic] H[istory], outside of a Kings 8 and 2 Kgs 23:27 ... [has] nothing to do with a reinterpretation of the mode of divine presence at the cult site."

For all of Richter's many insights, significant problems remain. The biggest drawback of Richter's study is its lack of any discussion of how cultic observance was understood by the Deuteronomist under her scenario.[258] If there is no representation of the deity (even an aniconic symbol or the "practical presence" of a hypostatic name) residing in the Jerusalem Temple, then how does cult take place? Where does one bring offerings "before Yahweh"? Why would the Deuteronomistic tradition concentrate so much effort on centralizing worship to a sacred locale if no cult could take place because there was no deity present to receive it? Would the space absent a deity still be sacred enough for the purpose of sacrifice and pilgrimage? (How often was pilgrimage made and offerings brought to monumental stelae in the ancient Near East commemorating a deity's ownership and hegemony?)

Moreover, John van Seters (2003a) has astutely noted how the idiom of "building a house for the name of Yahweh" (*libnôt bayit lĕšēm yhwh*) "was created by [the Deuteronomist] as the equivalent of *lĕšakkēn šĕmô šām,* and yet it is not directly dependent upon any foreign usage and cannot be explained by Richter's metaphorical use." Richter (2002: 71) did address one such passage (2 Sam 7:13) in her monograph and nicely noted (based on 2 Sam 7:26) how such a house could be built to increase the reputation of Yahweh, a notion that would coincide with her revised understanding. Yet where her analysis breaks down is with a passage such as 1 Kings 3:2 (on which she fails to comment): "The people were sacrificing the high places because no house had yet been built for the name of Yahweh." Here it is clear that the temple that was built for the Name was thought to be a place of sacrifice, not just commemoration.

Richter's theory then would fall under the same critique as that leveled at option 1, where the temple was reduced to a place of prayer only. Indeed, Richter would have an even harder time responding, for she does not hold to an exilic date for the Deuteronomist, as does Mettinger (Richter 2002: 5–7). Hurowitz has challenged Richter on precisely these grounds:

> Without Name Theology, the Temple on earth will be rendered completely void of divine presence, serving at most as a forwarding station for prayer and periscope into the true divine essence above. Is it reasonable to assume that even reformers such as the Deuteronomists could deviate so far from the ancient Near Eastern norm as to devoid the highly esteemed place of worship of all vestiges of its original essence as a house of God? (Hurowitz 2004–2005)

Conclusion: The Use of the Divine "Name" (*Šēm*) to Depict the Presence of Yahweh

As was hinted at the outset, little remains of the four traditional tenets that made up the systematic Name Theology of past generations. The revised Name Theology presented here affirms the following: (1) Name Theology adherents were working within long-standing traditions that were in place well before the events of 597 and 586 BCE. In addition, we side with those scholars who argue for pre-exilic editions of the Deuteronomistic History that included Name Theology. (2) Name Theology was indeed reactionary in that it did not choose the rich vocabulary of "radiance" to describe divine presence (yet cf. 1 Kgs 8:10–11). For that matter, it even avoids completely any reference to divine fire (cf. Deut 4:36)![259] Nor was it comfortable with the anthropomorphism of divinity implied by Yahweh marching forth to battle, walking in the camp, or sitting as a king on a throne. At the same time, as represented by 1 Kings 8 (if 1 Kgs 8:5, 10–11 are not secondary), it is preferable to envision the Name Theology as representing a parallel stream of tradition that incorporated, rejected, and supplemented the particulars of alternative modes of divine presence. (3) While Jerusalem eventually comes to be understood as the chosen place where Yahweh has his name dwell, references to different, earlier understandings are noteworthy. These included various locales where Yahweh's presence would be manifest via his name (Exod 20:24) and especially the use of Name Theology with regard to Shiloh (Jer 7:12). (4) As to the way in which Yahweh was present through his name in the Jerusalem Temple, the preference here is to reject both options (1 and 4) that reduced the temple to a mere house of prayer. The phenomenon of temples being understood as houses where deities reside is ubiquitous throughout the entire ancient Near East, of which ancient Israel was a part. The temple economies associated with such an understanding and the core nature of sacred space as a place of sacrifice and pilgrimage demand the presence of divinity. The most likely avenue to unpack Name Theology is to understand the effective power of divine names and the way in which they could function hypostatically as the practical presence of the deity.

Sacred Emptiness and Archaeological Correlates

If seeing is believing, then not seeing may be even more so. Where our eyes can no longer penetrate, or can barely distinguish the outlines of things, sight gives way to insight. (Mack 2007: 208)[260]

Modern worshippers (especially in Judaism, Christianity, and Islam) are so accustomed to worshipping an invisible God that little thought is given to how revolutionary the idea was in its original ancient Near Eastern context. Elsewhere throughout the ancient Near East, images of the deity (or deities) were the focal point of religious ritual performance. The greatest of care was taken in the production of such images, including the selection of the artisans, the precious materials used, the place of manufacture, and the manner by which the images were "quickened," "birthed," and/or consecrated for ritual use. Elaborate attention was given to how images of the divine then functioned in the cult.

In this context, to come across the sacred emptiness of the Jerusalem Temple is striking. As we have noted, many abstract ideas (some complementary and some exclusionary) vied for attention as to how best to conceptualize a deity who did not take up residence through an anthropomorphic divine image made of precious metal or even a standing stone as in the Arad temple. The Yahweh-Sabaoth traditions perceived Yahweh to be invisibly enthroned on cherubim, and the Name Theology articulated a cultically available presence that was nonetheless unseen. Other Judean theologians argued not for invisibility but for the ethereal images of radiance and fire that they thought better captured the *fascinans* and *tremendum* of Yahweh.

It is nearly impossible to suggest archaeological correlates for such abstract expressions, and there is no possibility of exploring the material culture of the Jerusalem Temple. (Yet scholars [e.g., Monson (2006), Dever (2006)] have tried to correlate the literary description of the Jerusalem Temple in the Hebrew Bible with what we know of other Iron Age temples in the Levant that are attested in the archaeological record.) Many have addressed sacred space from both archaeological and literary perspectives. Thus our discussion here will remain brief.

The impact of the Iron Age Ayn Dara temple in neighboring Syria needs to be weighed in any discussion of sacred emptiness in the Levant. See the discussion and pictures on pp. 340–343 (Figures 7.21–7.22). The abstract artisans here depicted a transcendent, enormous unseen deity who was nonetheless immanent, as evidenced by the footprints he/she left behind (cf. Ezek 43:7; Ps 77:20 [Eng 77:19]). Studies in materiality help us to understand the power of such art in sacred space to reinforce (repeatedly over time) its message of both transcendence and immanence to any person with access to the temple.

Such an artistic rendering provides a strong corrective to any who would suggest that the religious ideas of the Iron Age Levant were narrow, small-minded, or conceptually primitive. Some scholars who advocate that there must have been an anthropomorphic image of Yahweh in the Jerusalem Temple flirt with such notions, downplaying any historical reality behind the various aniconic/abstract streams of tradition. A priori, there should not be any barrier to assuming that Judean sculptors (especially those employing Phoenician artisans) were capable of similar abstract representation. In other words, the representation of an invisible yet colossal deity in the Iron Age Ayn Dara temple makes the portrayal of a larger-than-life Yahweh invisibly seated on a cherubim throne roughly 17 ft. (5.2 m) high (Figure 7.24) worth considering as a historical reality and not

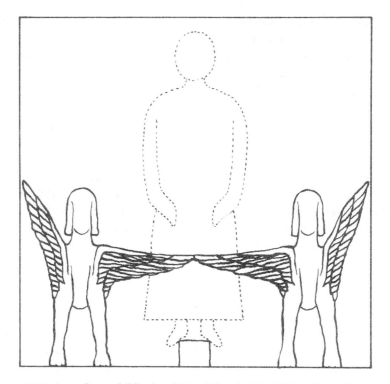

Figure 7.24 According to biblical tradition, Yahweh is invisibly enthroned on two large cherubim in Solomon's Temple.
Image from T. N. D. Mettinger, *In Search of God*, © Fortress Press. Reproduced by permission.

the mere musings of literary religion. Bloch-Smith (1994: 21), who also notes the relevance of the Ayn Dara temple, writes: "A god of cosmic size is omnipotent, omnipresent, and reigns for eternity. The immense cherubim throne in the [Jerusalem] Temple *děbîr*, 10 cubits high and 10 cubits wide (ca. 5.3 by 5.3 m), attests to the Israelites' vision of their god as superhuman in size."[261]

Pragmatic Focal Points: Ark and Cherubim
In our discussion regarding the lack of an anthropomorphic image of Yahweh in the Jerusalem Temple, we noted two astute questions raised by Niehr: how would Yahweh have been perceived as being vitally present in the Jerusalem Temple, and how would actual temple ritual have worked without a divine image? We have sketched the various ways in which abstract traditions envisioned Yahweh's presence. What remains is Niehr's second query, the actual practice of ritual. In other words, most sacred spaces have a focal point of some kind riveting the actions (and eyes) of participants to what is most important. Even aniconic traditions

have such focal points. Modern examples include the *qibla* pointer or *mihrab* niche in a mosque that indicates the direction of the Kaaba in Mecca and hence the direction Muslims should face when praying. In the center of most Jewish synagogues one finds an elevated platform known as the *bimah* that directs one's eyes to the reading of the Torah. In Roman Catholic churches the raised altar is the focal point, as it is the place where reside the bread and wine that undergo the process of transubstantiation.

According to the Yahweh-Sabaoth traditions, the focal points for the Jerusalem Temple were the Ark and the cherubim.[262] These metonymic representations were sanctioned, with no hint of polemic ever being recorded against their legitimacy.[263] As noted by Cross (1998: 91), "the portable Ark with its cherubim became the 'centerpiece' usurping the place of the divine image of Canaanite temples." Na'aman (1999a: 410–411; 2006a: 329) comments in similar fashion and notes the role of the Ark as an attention-focusing device:

> Like the divine image in other ancient Near Eastern civilizations, the ark was a focal point of the divine presence. It was carried into battle in accordance with the idea that God marches in front of His people, just as standards of gods were taken to battle by other Near Eastern nations. . . . The great sanctity attached to the ark in biblical historiography and the psalms was because it was the most sacred object of YHWH that was taken out of the temple and shown in public. Although the Cherubim throne was located inside the Holy of Holies and was seen only by a few priests of high rank, the ark was taken out for festivals and wars and was seen by the people.

Knoppers (2004: 591–592) notes the "tremendous reverence for the Ark" as well as "the association between the Ark and Yhwh's presence that led the Israelites to bring the Ark into battle. . . thinking that the ancient palladium's power would ensure victory . . . [T]he Ark is associated with lethal power." Traditions about the Ark as Yahweh's effective presence in war are attested in the early cult at Shiloh (1 Sam 4:3–4). We have already noted (pp. 364–365) how the Hebrew Bible portrays the terror of the Philistines, who interpreted the Ark as "God" (or "gods," *'ĕlōhîm*) coming into the camp (1 Sam 4:7–8). As to its association with divine lethality, one need only read the tragic story of the well-intentioned Uzzah in 2 Samuel 6:6–7 (//1 Chr 13:9–10).[264]

As for cultic contexts, Mettinger (1982b: 19) remarks how the Ark "no doubt possessed a numinous aura." Hillers (1968: 48) has noted that "there seems to be a general agreement that the ark was carried in recurring cultic processions, into Jerusalem and into the temple."[265] One of the key building blocks for establishing this consensus was Sigmund Mowinckel's hypothesis about the enthronement festival of Yahweh that has since undergone harsh criticism.[266] Nevertheless, it is clear that one need not embrace Mowinckel's enthronement hypothesis to see how the Ark was used in procession as a focal point that directed attention to Yahweh's presence. This is especially evident in Numbers 10:35-36, Psalm 132, 2 Samuel 6, and Psalm 24 (cf. too Ps 47:6 [Eng 47:5]; 68:1).

The oldest Ark tradition seems to be preserved in the ritual warfare of Numbers 10:35-36, the "Song of the Ark" (see translation on p. 388). It is clear that the Ark stands for Yahweh (either as a pedestal for the invisible deity or as a representational emblem of the deity). It is addressed as such as it proceeds forth to battle and returns. With similar language Psalm 132:8 proclaims:

> Advance O Yahweh to/from[267] your resting place,
> You and your powerful Ark.

Cross (1973: 94) views these words as an "allusion to the processional of the Ark when Yahweh first took up his abode on Zion." It is not a coincidence that these words are quoted in later tradition by the Chronicler as he describes Solomon's prayer to Yahweh as he enters into the temple (2 Chr 6:41). Hans-Joachim Kraus (1989: 481) concurs: "Psalm 132 is clearly dominated by the entry of Yahweh and the election of the sanctuary." We are reminded here of "entry rituals" elsewhere in the ancient Near East where divine images were carried in procession into royal palaces and sanctuaries (see Chapter Five, pp. 136-138). Such actions were often carried out as a part of the royal cult.

When the Ark was initially brought to Jerusalem (2 Samuel 6), David danced and sacrificed before it. Such actions were repeatedly described as being done "before Yahweh" (2 Sam 6:5, 14, 16-17, 21). While Psalm 24 makes no explicit mention of the Ark, scholars universally view its liturgy of divine entry into the temple ("Who is this King of Glory?" [*melek hakkābôd*]) as involving the Ark.[268] Cross views Psalm 24:7-10 as "a tenth-century B.C. liturgical fragment," an "antiphonal liturgy . . . (that) had its origin in the procession of the Ark to the sanctuary at its founding, celebrated annually in the cult of Solomon and perhaps even of David."[269] Kraus (1988: 312, 316) agrees that Psalm 24 ("that reflects events of the time of David") "involves a cultic antiphonal song, a liturgical ceremonial, which doubtlessly is connected with an entrance of the holy ark to the temple in Jerusalem."

Thus, in addition to being a focal point of divine presence in battle and cultic contexts, the Ark also played a symbolic role of divine presence for royal legitimation. Baruch Halpern (2001: 334-335) has noted the prestige that accords to Solomon in 1 Kings 8 as he invites Yahweh (via the Ark) to a sacrificial "banquet" at the consecration of the Jerusalem Temple (1 Kgs 8:5, 62-64). This is analogous, says Halpern, to how Aššurnasirpal II received prestige when he invited his state god Aššur and "the gods of all the land" (presumably via their cult statues) to his elaborate sacrificial banquet when he consecrated his palace at Nimrud (ancient Kalhu/Calah).[270] "The purpose" of both banquets, complete with large numbers inflating the amount of sacrifices, was "to invite the presence of the chief god into the king's monumental construction."

While documenting the actual Ark may be the fascination of Hollywood productions and sensationalized documentaries about its presence in Ethiopia, readers will find no coverage of it in any respectable archaeological reference work. This doesn't mean that scholars have kept silent about describing parallel phenomena of similar-sized chests and carrying poles, with examples from Egypt being mentioned most often (e.g., Kitchen 1993: 125*; cf. Zobel 1974: 367–368; Seow 1992: 388).

The importance of the cherubim is reflected in Zevit's (2001: 316) comment that the cherub was "the icon most closely associated with YHWH." The majesty of these creatures has caused scholars to refer to them by terminology other than "cherubim" (e.g., Propp [2006: 386] prefers "griffin") lest readers conjure images of cute, plump winged toddlers from the canvas of Raphael's *Sistine Madonna* or his *The Vision of Ezekiel*. The Hebrew Bible attests to varying conceptions of these mysterious, hybrid winged beings (cf. Wood 2008). Yet despite different portrayals, it is safe to say that wherever cherubim appear, attention is focused. We have remarked on the attention-grabbing start of Ezekiel's vision, with its fantastic cherubim creatures (Ezek 1:5–25), which leads to seeing the very presence (*kābôd*) of deity (Ezek 1:26–28).

The J (or non-P) literary source found in Genesis 3:24 describes how Yahweh stationed the cherubim along with "the flame of the ever-whirling sword" (on which see p. 349) to guard (*lišmōr*) the way to the tree of life. This is one of the few explicit references to the guarding function of the cherubim, a striking absence when one considers the frequent mention of winged composite beasts (so-called *Mischwesen*) that acted as guardians in the ancient Near East (cf. the *aladlammu* discussion that follows).[271] The P source has an altogether different understanding that associates paired cherubim with the tabernacle (Exod 25:18–22; 37:7–9). Here they are made of hammered (?) gold and are of the same approximate size as the Ark of the Testimony (*'ărōn hā'ēdut*) on top of which they were fixed (i.e., 2.5 cubits [about 42 in. (106 cm)] long, 1.5 cubits [25 in. (63 cm)] wide, and 1.5 cubits [25 in. (63 cm)] high [cf. Exod 25:10; 37:1]). What they lack in size, they make up in symbolism. According to this P material, the cherubim are intimately tied to the "atonement dais" or "mercy seat" (i.e., the *kappōret*, "cover") atop the Ark, where Yahweh promises "to meet" (*wĕnô'adtî*) with the priestly representative (Exod 25:22). Hence the tabernacle (*miškān*) is called the "Tent of Meeting" (*'ōhel mô'ēd*). There is a curious reference in Exodus 25:20 (cf. 1 Kgs 8:7) to the cherubim functioning "to shelter" or "to shield" "over the *kappōret* cover" with their wings (*sōkĕkîm hĕkanpêhem 'al-hakkappōret*). Perhaps this is elliptical for shielding (the priest) from the danger of divine lethality as the two parties met at the *kappōret*.

The most imposing examples of cherubim are the paired colossal beasts in the Jerusalem Temple. According to 1 Kings 6:19–28, they were majestic in beauty (gold overlay) and sheer size, and were located (like P's cherubim) in the innermost sanctuary (*děbîr, bětôk habbayit happěnîmî*; 1 Kgs 6:23, 27; *běbêt-qōdeš haqqŏdāšîm*; 2 Chr 3:8–10). Each was 10 cubits (approx. 15–17 ft. [4.6–5.2 m]) high, and their combined wingspan was 20 cubits (approx. 30–34 ft. [9.2–10.4 m]). In terms of the dimensions of the innermost shrine, their wings reached from one wall to the other (1 Kgs 6:20, 23–27; 2 Chr 3:8–13).

In presentations large (1 Kgs 6) and small (Exod 25, 37), the cherubim are unmistakable focal points. Their importance is reinforced further by their replication on the furnishings of the sanctuary, including repetitive cherubim scenes on fabric (Exod 26:1, 31; 36:8, 35; 2 Chr 3:14), on carvings (1 Kgs 6:29, 32, 35; Ezek 41:18–20; 2 Chr 3:7), and on metalwork (1 Kgs 7:29, 36). (Figure 7.25 represents a cherub/sphinx carved in ivory from ninth-century BCE Hazor.) Granted, the

Figure 7.25 A cherub/sphinx carved on an ivory plaque from ninth-century BCE Hazor.
Courtesy of the Selz Foundation Hazor Excavations in Memory of Yigael Yadin.

number of viewers of the cherubim in the inner sanctum was severely restricted; only elite priests could see them, thanks to the gradations of holiness found in the Temple complex, where the holier the space, the more restricted the access.

The sheer size of the cherubim in 1 Kings 6 evoked divine wonder similar to how viewers (ancient and modern) were/are awed at first glimpse of a hybrid Neo-Assyrian *aladlammu* (a human-headed winged bull) that can stand 16 ft. (4.9 m) high. (Well-known examples are at the Louvre [Figure 7.26], the British Museum, the Oriental Institute Museum, and the Metropolitan Museum of Art.)[272] Zevit (2001: 317) also notes these sculptures (sometimes referred to as *lamassu* figures), pointing out how their precise form and function (especially their guardian and apotropaic uses) keep them distinct from cherubim. Alice Wood (2008: 155) argues the contrary position. It is worth noting that cherubim do have guarding functions (Gen 3:24). The physical arrangement of the two colossal cherubim in 1 Kings 6:23–28 may have served symbolically to guard Yahweh's throne. Notice too should be made of how the consensus regarding the

Figure 7.26 A hybrid Neo-Assyrian human-headed, winged bull called *aladlammu* or *lamassu*.

Marie-Lan Nguyen, taken at the Louvre. https://commons.wikimedia.org/wiki/File:Human_headed_winged_bull_Louvre_AO19859.jpg.

etymology of Hebrew *kĕrubîm* points to a relationship with the Akkadian cognate *kāribu* ("one who gives adoration"), a term used of the Neo-Assyrian monumental guardian sculptures.[273] Be that as it may, our point here is that the existence of extant *aladlammu* (*lamassu*) sculptures can serve heuristically to help us imagine the wonder of seeing the monumental cherubim that have not been preserved for us.[274] Both would have created a sense of respect, fear, mystery, and wonder because of their size and their mixed (i.e., unearthly) form. We have already noted the connection between large size and divinity (see pp. 393–394). As for physical form, Meyers (1992b: 900) has remarked how the appearance of the cherubim "made them apt symbols for divine presence, since deities moved where humans could not and were something other than either animals or humans."

Yet the wonder does not stop here. While the cherubim of the tabernacle and Temple are stationary, others are in motion, as one could have surmised from their wings. (Ezek 1:15–21 adds omnidirectional wheels.)[275] Poetic lore describes Yahweh as a storm god riding on the clouds, similar to Ugaritic Ba'lu (cf. Ps 68:5 [Eng 68:4]), with the following imagery:

> [Yahweh] bent the heavens and came down,
> A storm cloud under his feet.
> He rode [*yirkab*] a cherub and flew,
> He soared on the wings of the wind.[276] (Ps 18:10–11//2 Sam 22:10–11)

For a poetic focal point, note how the movement of the cherubim in Ezekiel's vision fixes and holds the prophet's attention, as does the thunderous sound of their wings, which is likened to "the voice of El Shadday when he speaks" (Ezek 1:4–26; 10:1–5).

As for a functional focal point, according to Numbers 7:89 the voice of Yahweh was thought to speak "from between the two cherubim." When King Hezekiah receives the disturbing communiqué from the *rab-šāqēh*, he goes up to the temple of Yahweh to pray. He spreads out the letter "before Yahweh," whom he then addresses as "O Yahweh [of Armies], God of Israel, who is enthroned [above] the cherubim" (*yhwh [ṣĕbā'ôt] 'ĕlōhê yiśrā'ēl yōšēb hakkĕrubîm*; 2 Kgs 19:15; Isa 37:16). The Psalmist begs entry into the sanctuary, where Yahweh and his mighty Ark reside, in order to bow down in worship at the divine footstool (*ništaḥăweh lahădōm raglāyw*; Ps 132:7–8).

Such phrases denoting Yahweh's enthronement point to how some traditions envisioned the cherubim as representing a throne, a prominent focal point in almost every royal setting. Following Mettinger, we have noted (p. 386) how the Zion-Sabaoth tradition depicts Yahweh Sabaoth as king (e.g., Ps 24:7–10) and as invisibly enthroned on the cherubim in the Jerusalem Temple (Ps 46:5–8 [Eng 46:4–7]; 76:3 [Eng 76:2]; Jer 8:19). The fullest articulation of the divine name

Yahweh Sebaoth is "Yahweh of Armies who sits [enthroned on/between] the cherubim" (*yhwh ṣĕbā'ōt yōšēb hakkĕrubîm*; 1 Sam 4:4; 2 Sam 6:2; 2 Kgs 19:15; Isa 37:16; cf. Ps 80:2 [Eng 80:1]; 99:1). Most scholars, such as McCarter (1980a: 103–104), note the use of cherubim as an essential part of Canaanite royal iconography. McCarter concludes: "Yahweh is conceived of as a seated monarch flanked by a pair of sphinx-like creatures." That the Ark (located underneath the cherubim) was thought by some to designate Yahweh's footstool (1 Chr 28:2; cf. Ps 99:5; 132:7–8; Lam 2:1) also supports the notion of a cherubim throne. Lastly, though Ezekiel places most of his emphasis on divine radiance (*kābôd*), he nonetheless mentions that he saw "the likeness of a *throne*" (*dĕmût kissē'* on which Yahweh's fiery person sat (Ezek 1:26; 10:1).

Deities sitting on thrones placed on the top of majestic animals (including *Mischwesen*) are known elsewhere, such as in the portrayal of Ishtar/Mullissu in Figure 7.27, Figure 7.28, and Figure 8.2.[277] If such data were not enough, several

Figure 7.27 The deity Mulissu/Ishtar seated on a star-lined throne placed atop a *Mischwesen* creature.

Adrien de Longpérier, *Choix de monuments antiques pour servir à l'histoire de l'art en Orient et en Occident; Texte explicative Musée du Louvre* (Paris: L. Guérin, 1868–1874), planche bronzes babyloniens I no. 4.

Figure 7.28 Maltai rock relief depicting the deity Mulissu/Ishtar, whose throne is placed atop a majestic animal.

V. Place, *Ninive et l'Assyrie*, vol. 3 (Paris: Imprimerie impériale, 1867), pl. 45.

scholars have shown how iconography can help us envision precisely the imagery of a royal cherubim throne where the king is physically seated on cherubim.[278] Consider the two examples shown in Figure 7.29 and Figure 7.30, which depict the tenth-century BCE Phoenician king Ahiram of Byblos as he is depicted on his sarcophagus and an unknown ruler who is portrayed enthroned on an ivory plaque from Late Bronze Age II Megiddo.[279] From Iron Age IIA Hazor we have a scarab of an anthropomorphic figure on a cherubim throne (Figure 7.31; Keel 2012a: 568–570; Ben-Tor 2016: 164, fig. 117). For an unprovenanced example of

Figure 7.29 The tenth-century BCE Phoenician king Ahiram enthroned on a cherub/sphinx throne as depicted on his sarcophagus.
Courtesy Theodore J. Lewis.

Figure 7.30 An unknown ruler seated on a cherub/sphinx throne from an ivory plaque from Late Bronze Age II Megiddo.
Kim Walton, taken at the Israel Museum.

Figure 7.31 A scarab from Iron Age IIA Hazor depicting an anthropomorphic figure on a cherub throne.
Courtesy of the Selz Foundation Hazor Excavations in Memory of Yigael Yadin

Figure 7.32 An unprovenanced example of a ruler on a winged and wheeled throne as depicted on a silver drachma from the Persian period.
Wikimedia Commons. https://commons.wikimedia.org/wiki/File:YHD_coins.jpg.

a ruler on a winged and wheeled throne from the Persian period, see Figure 7.32. Edelman (1996b: 190, 225, fig. 2) suggests that this figure (on a silver drachma) may even depict Yahweh (as does Niehr [1997: 81]).[280]

At the same time, there are traditions that avoided placing Yahweh on a throne because it would suggest anthropomorphic qualities of the deity. An example of this tendency in material culture may be illustrated by a late ninth-/early eighth-century fragmentary seal impression on a bulla from the city of David. As described by Keel (2012b: 331–332, fig. 95) and Ornan (2019), here we have the depiction of an empty throne together with two winged discs, well-known symbols associated elsewhere with divinity (Ornan 2005b). Keel (2012b: 332) suggests that the image "may represent the divine symbol in the Debir (dĕbîr) of the Jerusalem temple in the 9th cent. B.C.E." Ornan (2019: 207) cautions that the bulla "was found outside of the Temple precinct" and thus does "not necessarily, then, reflect the complete actual cultic paraphernalia kept within the Jerusalem shrine." Nonetheless, she too argues that "the throne is to be considered as the seat of Yahweh." The ancient artisans are here "alluding to Yahweh, who is not presented through his (conceived) anthropomorphic image" (Ornan 2019: 206–207).

For examples of this tendency in literature, we noted in particular the Deuteronomistic Name Theology's rejection of throne imagery, with special notice of how it is *the Name* of Yahweh that goes forth to battle (1 Sam 17:45; cf. Isa 30:27–30) rather than a striding warrior with mace in hand (see pp. 387, 389). Propp (2006: 519) has pointed out how "striking" it is that "when 1 Kgs 6:23–28; 8:7; 1 Chr 28:18; 2 Chr 3:10–13; 5:7–8 describe the Griffins [i.e., the cherubim], the term *kissē*' 'throne' never appears." Propp goes on to note the Deuteronomist's "ambivalence toward monarchy and its trappings (Deut 17:14–20; 1 Sam 8)," which denies Yahweh "some of the accoutrements of royalty." Yet because the Deuteronomistic History is such a complexly woven document, it begs further nuancing.[281] DtrH does indeed incorporate notions of Yahweh on a throne, such as in Micaiah's vision in 1 Kings 22 (cf. Isa 6:1; Ezek 1:26). Here the prophet sees "Yahweh sitting on a throne [*yhwh yōšēb 'al-kisʾô*] and all the host of heaven standing on his right hand and on his left hand" (1 Kgs 22:19). It seems more apt to argue that it is adherents of the Name Theology in particular who have a problem placing Yahweh on a royal throne. Propp (2006: 390) also argues (contra Haran 1959: 35; 1978: 251–254) that the description of the cherubim in "Exodus 25 does not describe a throne. There is no seat, no armrests, no footstool." If Propp is correct, then this would fit nicely with P's similar desire to avoid anthropomorphizing the deity.

Pragmatic Focal Points: Fire and Glory

Fire is such a dominant image for expressing divine presence that our treatment (see pp. 344–358) has but scratched the surface. Additional references are ubiquitous. For example, we read of the prophet Isaiah being purified of his sin by divine fire from the altar (Isa 6:5–7; cf. Mal 3:2–3). Elsewhere in a judgment context, it is said that Yahweh, "the Light of Israel," will become a fire, the Holy One a flame (wĕhāyâ ʾôr-yiśrāʾēl lĕʾēš ûqĕdôšô lĕlehābâ; Isa 10:17). The prophet Zechariah describes an unheard-of defense strategy where Jerusalem will be unwalled—for Yahweh "will be a wall of fire encircling her" (waʾănî ʾehyeh-lâ ḥômat ʾēš sābîb; Zech 2:9 [Eng 2:5]). As Carol Meyers and Eric Meyers (1987: 157) have observed, "The metaphorical depiction of Yahweh as a 'wall of fire' transfers the security and autonomy implied by a wall to the presence of Yahweh."

Yet even the most beautiful metaphors are less satisfying for pragmatists who desire a focal point for worship. There is no need to articulate the obvious way in which real fire (combining *fascinans* and *tremendum*) would have served as an attention-focusing device. The texts we have documented are filled with references to people turning aside to see the fire of a theophany or trembling in fear of a consuming fire that they interpreted as lethal divine presence.

As far as a practical presence within sacred space, one need only think of the various lamps within the tabernacle and the Jerusalem Temple (1 Kgs 7:49), some of which seem to have been lit perpetually (Exod 27:20–21).[282] The large golden lampstand (Exod 25:31–40; 37:17–24) associated with the tabernacle (yet not Solomon's Temple; cf. Meyers 1979) occasions Propp (2006: 512) to write of how "light betokens Yahweh's presence and his favor . . . The idea of a light shining within the otherwise obscure outer chamber is a perfect symbol for 'Yahweh, my lamp . . . who illumines my dark' (2 Sam 22:29; cf. Ps 18:29)." This may very well be true; yet one cannot ignore that having fire in the dark recesses of the sanctuary could be purely functional in nature. Perhaps a better symbol for divinity is the kindling of fires for sacrifices. Such ritual performance would remind adherents of how Yahweh from ages past appeared in fiery theophanies. The presence of holy priests wearing sacred garments (cf. Lev 6:2–6 [Eng 6:9–13]) while they manipulated fire would have underscored differences between the sacred and the profane, with fire a symbol of the former. Of particular note are the ʿōlâ, or "burnt offerings" (which "go up" to Yahweh). These offerings were completely burned and hence of no benefit for humans.[283] Their theocentric nature focused attention on the deity rather than on priests or donors who might have looked to obtain a share of the meat.

Yet there seems to be even more going on conceptually with the ʿōlâ offering. According to Exodus 29:41–45, the "*continual* burnt offering by fire to Yahweh" (ʾiššeh leyhwh ʿōlat *tāmîd*) was linked to Yahweh's promise to dwell among the people of Israel as their God (wĕšākantî bĕtôk bĕnê yiśrāʾēl wĕhāyîtî lāhem lēʾlōhîm). Another P passage unpacks this further. As with Exodus 29, Leviticus 6 emphasizes that there should be an "*ever-burning* fire" (ʾēš *tāmîd*) on the altar (Lev 6:2, 5–6 [Eng Lev 6:9, 12–13]). Richard Friedman (2001: 329–330), who notes the emphatic writing regarding "an ever-burning fire" (*'ēš tāmîd*) "that will not go out" (*lō' tikbeh*) [Lev 6:6 [Eng 6:12]), underscores how this unquenchable fire is "reminiscent of the account in Exodus of Moses' encounter with YHWH at a bush that burns without being consumed" (*hasseneh bō'ēr bā'ēš wĕhasseneh 'ênennû 'ukkāl*; Exod 3:2). Furthermore, Milgrom (1991: 389) points out the importance of Leviticus 9:24, where "the sacrifices [specifically the *'ōlâ* and the *ḥălābîm*] offered up at the inauguration of the public cult were consumed miraculously by a divine fire, and it is *this* fire which is not allowed to die out." (One could compare Judg 13:16–20, where the preternatural *mal'ak*-Yahweh miraculously ascends in the fire of the *'ōlâ* offering.) If Friedman and Milgrom are correct, then the perpetual fire symbolizes (and acts as an attention-focusing device for) the ongoing presence of Yahweh within sacred space.[284] Moreover, especially for the P tradition, which strongly avoids anthropomorphizing Yahweh, fire can represent God in an awe-inspiring and numinous way without any of the limitations of human imagery. After all, the symbolism of a royal throne for Yahweh resonates only if one views kingship as a favorable institution, and such was certainly not always the case for how the priesthood saw Israelite and Judean kings.

Articulating how an abstract concept such as "radiance" (*kābôd*) might have a physical counterpoint that served as a focal point for ritual seems nearly impossible. This is certainly the case for Ezekiel's mystical vision. Yet repeatedly, radiant (*kābôd*) imagery is linked to the Ark (e.g., 1 Sam 4:19–22; 1 Kgs 8:6, 11; Ps 24:7–10) and the cherubim (e.g., Isa 6:1–5; cf. Ezek 9:3; 10:4, 18; 11:22; Sir 49:8; Heb 9:5) as well as to fire (e.g., Exod 24:17; Lev 9:23–24; Deut 5:21 [Eng 5:24]; Isa 10:16; 2 Chr 7:1, 3; Zech 2:5). Thus the presence of these three tangible symbols within sacred space could also have conveyed divine radiance. That the inner sanctum of the Jerusalem Temple was covered in gold may have also created a visual spectacle in which viewers felt that they were seeing the gleaming chambers where a radiant Yahweh must reside—even though they didn't see him.[285]

Pragmatic Focal Points: Name and Invisibility

Yahweh taking up his residence via his hypostatic Name is such an abstract expression of divine presence that it is hard to imagine how it would have served as a focal point—unless the name Yahweh was carved in a central location in a way that conveyed his habitation. Here we can only speculate. Studies in materiality reveal that a person's inscribed name on a stela can represent his personhood and presence such that the name can even become a recipient of cult.[286] Our best example here is the eighth-century BCE Katumuwa inscription that explicitly mentions the post-mortem essence (*nbš*) of the deceased who is named on the stela inhabiting the stone itself and receiving regular offerings. See pp. 333–334, where it is suggested that such inhabiting can be used analogously to explore divinity inhabiting betyls ("houses of God").

As for materiality and divinity, Alice Mandell and Jeremy Smoak (2016: 241–242) stress "the importance of the repeated references to the divine name Yahweh in the [tomb] inscriptions" at Khirbet Beit Lei. Emphasizing "the importance of the placement of the divine name into the ritual space," they argue that "the authority of the inscriptions . . . materially link the divine name [Yahweh] with the physical space of the tomb."[287] Can such materiality perspectives inform our understanding of Deuteronomic/Deuteronomistic Name Theology? In some ways, this brings us back to Richter's insight that the placing of a name can mark ownership and hegemony. While this is true, it does not go far enough. As we have argued, the D factitive translation of the idiom *lĕšakkēn šĕmô šām* ("to cause his name *to dwell*") requires the name *to inhabit* the space—and (because the space is sacred) in such a way that it can be a recipient of cult.

The Name that was thought to be Yahweh's practical presence is intimately tied up with the presence of the Ark. The Temple as the *place* (*māqôm*) of Yahweh's Name is also "the *place* of the Ark" (*māqôm lāʾārôn*; 1 Kgs 8:16–21). Thus the Ark itself could represent a focal point for those who advocated Name Theology. Some scholars who discuss the presence of the Ark in Deuteronomistic Name Theology demote it to a mere receptacle for the two tablets of stone that make up the Decalogue (1 Kgs 8:9). According to Mettinger (1982b: 50), "The Ark also doubled as a storage chest . . . the old numinous role of the Ark as the footstool of the present God gives way to the more prosaic job of storing the tablets of the Law (Deut 10:1–5; 1 Kgs 8:9, 21)." Yet close attention to the wording in 1 Kings 8:9, 21 shows that the author is emphasizing not just the two tablets but also the context in which "Yahweh made a covenant . . . when he brought them out of the land of Egypt." The part of the Decalogue that emphasizes this liberating role is at the very beginning, where the divine name is prominent: "*I am Yahweh, your God, who brought you out of the land of Egypt*" (Exod 20:2; Deut 5:6). Van Seters (2003a: 872) drives the logic home: "The idiom (*lĕšakkēn šĕmô šām*) and its Dtr modifications refer to the building of a house for the ark in which are the two tablets of the Decalogue *on which is inscribed the name of the deity*. All of the usages [of the idiom] fit this understanding of the written name of the deity deposited in the Temple" (emphasis mine).

In short, perhaps the answer to our probing for a pragmatic focal point is remarkably simple: Yahweh's Name was literally inscribed somewhere in the Jerusalem Temple (likely on the Ark itself or on its enclosed sacred texts, as Van Seters suggests). Materially, within such sacred space, Yahweh's Name represented his personhood and presence such that it could be a recipient of cult.

Invisibility as a focal point works only if gifted artisans such as the sculptors at Ayn Dara can create a sense of the deity being in residence without actually being there. Once again we marvel at Ayn Dara's enormous footprints that represent an invisible deity through concrete representation. Biblical traditions leave us with only metaphorical descriptions of how the temple is "the place of Yahweh's throne and the soles of his feet" (*měqôm kapôt raglay*; Ezek 43:7). In light of *kābôd* theology, Isaiah 60:13 intriguingly describes Yahweh's sanctuary as where the divinity "makes the place of his feet *glorious*" (*měqôm miqdāšî ûměqôm raglay 'ăkabbēd*). Contrarily, the Psalmist (Ps 77:20 [Eng 77:19]) strips away even the metaphor when he asserts that Yahweh's trek through the sea left unseen footprints (*wěʻiqqěbôtêkā lōʾ nōdāʻû*)!

As for the Jerusalem Temple, the most we can assert from our literary references is that its artisans with their large cherubim throne were attempting something similar to Ayn Dara's sacred emptiness.[288] By building such a huge edifice (upon which no mere human could ever sit) they awakened believers' imaginations, leading them to conclude that only a supersized, superhuman being (i.e., only a god like Yahweh) could ever fill such a seat. Without having archaeological remains of the Jerusalem Temple, we can proceed no further in unpacking such literary references with material culture.[289] Though the notion of Yahweh being invisible is linked most strongly to the Jerusalem Temple and antecedent Ark traditions (especially at the sanctuary in Shiloh), scholars have sought to document "empty space aniconism" elsewhere in ancient Israel, notably at Kuntillet ʿAjrud and Tell Taanach. Yet each of these examples, to which we now turn, is problematic.

The Archaeology of Empty-Space Aniconism?

The inscriptions from Kuntillet ʿAjrud that mention "Yahweh and his asherah" have already been discussed (see pp. 236–240), as has the iconography of its standing figures (see pp. 325–330). Two basic conclusions emerged from a close examination of this material: (1) the exclusive use of masculine singular verbs underscored Yahweh as the primary/sole agent of blessing despite the mention of "his asherah," and (2) if the standing figures on Pithos A are linked to the god Bes and thus used apotropaically, then they are unlikely to represent Yahweh.

Conclusions about Pithos A at Kuntillet ʿAjrud (its inscriptions and iconography) have impacted how Pithos B is to be viewed, particularly its "procession" scene of worshippers with upraised hands (Figure 7.33). This is especially so in a thesis by Schmidt (2002; 2016: 68–70, 89–90), who argues that shared artistic techniques reveal an essential unity between the two central scenes of Pithos A (see Figure 7.15 on p. 325) and Pithos B. According to Schmidt, the layouts of both the scenes and the inscriptions of the two pithoi mirror each other. With this in mind, Schmidt (2002: 114) claims:

> Pithos B contains the artistic rendering of what has been referred to as *empty space aniconism*. . . . The parallels shared by these two scenes [i.e., those of Pithos A and Pithos B] . . . strongly suggest that the empty space in the pithos

Figure 7.33 A scene of worshippers with upraised hands on Pithos B from Kuntillet ʿAjrud.

Courtesy of the Israel Exploration Society, Jerusalem.

B scene is demarcated as sacred space where the divine presence was visually *imagined* by the viewer. The divine images most readily called to mind would be those immediately accessible on the pithos A scene.

In other words, because of "the deliberate omission of the two Bes-like figures" in the scene on Pithos B, "it is very likely that [its] inscription 'writ in the sky' presupposes the *empty space aniconic* presence of two deities [i.e., Yahweh and Asherah]" (Schmidt 2002: 121, his emphasis).

The hurdles that would have to be overcome to embrace such an argument are high. While the tradition of empty space aniconism is firmly in place in the Jerusalem Temple, it is only understood to be functional (philosophically and pragmatically) there within the frameworks of Ark, *kābôd*, and Name Theologies. How easy would it be to transfer such abstract understandings to a hill site overlooking Wadi Quraiya without the symbolic architecture of the golden inner sanctum of the Jerusalem Temple with its resident Ark (containing

Yahweh's Name) and majestic cherubim? Moreover, we have no mention of the goddess Asherah being portrayed through empty space aniconism. As we have seen (p. 327), Ornan argues against the theory that Kuntillet ʿAjrud's iconography represents coherently integrated scenes. Lastly, doubts about whether Yahweh is even represented on Pithos A would undermine any notion of his invisible presence on Pithos B.

While Schmidt's theory has won few followers, the same cannot be said about a popular proposal by Taylor that an invisible Yahweh is represented on the Taanach cult stand discovered in 1968 (hereafter "the 1968 Taanach cult stand" to distinguish it from the one found at the same site in 1902). Tell Taanach is located on the southwest side of the Jezreel plain southeast of Megiddo. In biblical tradition Taanach is known as being a place where Deborah and Barak fought the Canaanites (Judg 5:19) as well as being one of Solomon's administrative districts (1 Kgs 4:12). The 1968 Taanach cult stand (Figure 7.34) has been discussed with

Figure 7.34 A much discussed and debated cult stand from Taanach (discovered in 1968).
Courtesy Gary Lee Todd WorldHistoryPics.com. https://www.flickr.com/photos/101561334@N08/42312681665/in/album-72157698086736974.

reference to the sphinx motif that appears in register three (see pp. 315–317) as well as the identity of the quadruped in register one (see pp. 323–325). (The registers are counted from the top down.)

Taylor (1993: 30; 1994) has suggested that the empty space in tier three of the 1968 Taanach cult stand "is an iconographic representation of Yahweh of Hosts, the unseen God who resides among the cherubim, the earliest 'representation' of Yahweh known in the archaeological record." Taylor's argument is based on symmetry, specifically the idea that tiers two and four correspond to the goddess Asherah while tiers one and three reflect the god Yahweh.[290] Suffice it here to note that Taylor, with good reason, assumes that the goddess is represented by the naked female between the lions on tier four and by the symbolic tree between the two ibexes on tier two (and yet cf. this motif on the *male* deity from Hazor depicted in Figure 5.37). Taylor then argues that Yahweh, as a solar deity, is represented by the winged sun disk on tier one, noting the mention of horses being dedicated to the sun at the entrance to the temple of Yahweh in 2 Kings 23:11. With this foundation in place, Taylor (1993: 33) presents the following logic: "Since the same deity (Asherah) is represented on alternate tiers two and four, one naturally expects the pattern of alternation to continue through the representation of the same deity (Yahweh) on the other pair of alternate tiers, one and three" (cf. Figure 7.35). Tier three has two cherubim creatures, and Taylor can then easily suggest that the empty space between them represents "Yahweh Sebaoth who sits [invisibly between] the Cherubim" (*yhwh ṣĕbāʾôt yōšēb hakkĕrubîm*).

Though popular, Taylor's ingenious thesis is not without its critics. Those scholars who argue that the quadruped on tier one is bovine rather than equine would take away the key linkage to 2 Kings 23:11. Even if the animal is equine, Keel and Uehlinger (1998: 157–160) argue that the horses are more likely to be associated with Anat-Astarte (cf. Cornelius 2004: 40–45, 117–123), the cherubim with guardians, and the solar disk with the heavens. Smith (2014a: 208) adds another complication in seeing the naked goddess in register four as ʿAštart, not Asherah.

Yet the biggest hurdle for Taylor's argument would seem to be how almost every cult stand has fenestrations (i.e., stylistic openings). Thus it is extremely hard to argue against the notion that the fenestration on tier three may be merely conventional, serving artistic and perhaps functional purposes.[291] Consider the number of additional fenestrations on the sides of the 1968 Taanach cult stand (Figure 7.36) and especially the two rectangular fenestrations on its undecorated back (Figure 7.37). These are hardly symbolic of divinity, as they would be out of view.[292] The 1902 Taanach cult stand (Figure 7.38) with its many parallels (e.g., lion, sphinx, and flanking ibex motifs) also has three clearly demarcated fenestrations. Zevit (2001: 323), who adopts Taylor's thesis in part, admits that

Figure 7.35 The top and third registers of one of the cult stands from Taanach (discovered in 1968) depicting an animal (equine? bovine?) under a winged sun disk in the former and an empty space between two cherubim in the latter.
Kim Walton, taken at the Israel Museum.

Figure 7.36 The side of the cult stand from Taanach (discovered in 1968) showing multiple fenestrations around the bodies of the lions and the cherubim.
Kim Walton, taken at the Israel Museum.

Figure 7.37 The back of the cult stand from Taanach (discovered in 1968) showing two rectangle fenestrations on its otherwise undecorated back.
From R. Hestrin, "The Cult Stand from Ta'anach and Its Religious Background," in *Phoenicia and the East Mediterranean in the First Millennium B.C.*, edited by E. Lipinski (Leuven: Uitgeverij Peeters, 1987), 64, fig. 3. Used by permission.

THE ICONOGRAPHY OF DIVINITY: YAHWEH   415

Figure 7.38 Another cult stand from Taanach (discovered in 1902) with multiple fenestrations.

Courtesy Ziony Zevit, *The Religions of Ancient Israel: A Synthesis of Parallactic Approaches* (London: Continuum, 2001), 318, fig. 4.8.

Taylor's "argument from silence would allow for the implicit presence of three or four deities here," a very tough sell. The more cult stands that are brought into the discussion, the more unlikely is the thesis that the fenestration on tier three of the 1968 Taanach cult stand is an attempt to represent empty space aniconism. Consider the following sampling from Tell Revov (Figure 7.39), Ai (Figure 7.40), Beth Shean (Figure 7.41), and Megiddo (Figure 7.42), to which many more could be added. Indeed, it would be rare *not* to have fenestrations.

One could also bring in here the same critique used against Schmidt's thesis. The types of empty space aniconism that were used for Yahweh were embedded in complex and abstract systems of thought that were inseparable from the Jerusalem Temple. While cult stands can represent model shrines, to ask the 1968 Taanach cult stand to bear the weight of the complex symbol set of the Jerusalem Temple (at least the symbol set of the Ark, *kābôd*, and Name theologies) would be a stretch. As noted by Mettinger, who is hesitant to adopt Taylor's thesis, the empty space could reflect a temple entrance (so Hestrin as well as Keel and Uehlinger) or a place where an object of some sort was set (so Weippert).[293] Or, again, it could be merely stylistic.

Figure 7.39 An Iron Age II cult stand with fenestrations from Tell Revov.
Kim Walton, taken at the Israel Museum.

Figure 7.40 A cult stand with fenestrations from Ai.
Courtesy Gary Lee Todd WorldHistoryPics.com. https://www.flickr.com/photos/101561334@N08/
43217373371/in/album-72157698086736974.

Figure 7.41 A cult stand with fenestrations from Beth Shean.
Courtesy Gary Lee Todd WorldHistoryPics.com. https://www.flickr.com/photos/101561334@N08/42498529894/in/album-72157698086736974.

Figure 7.42 A cult stand with fenestration from Megiddo.
Courtesy of the Oriental Institute of the University of Chicago.

Conclusion

Any attempt to describe the iconography of the god Yahweh will necessarily be unwieldy given the long span of time during which Yahwism is attested, the numerous geographic locales of cultic activity, and the nature of our source material (textual and archaeological). This chapter has attempted to provide a sketch to orient the reader to a much wider debate. Section I treated anthropomorphic and theriomorphic traditions, while Section II dealt with aniconic and abstract representations.

The Iconography of Yahweh: Anthropomorphic Traditions

Anthropomorphism is a necessity for depicting the divine. Humans (ancient and modern) naturally default to what they know of themselves and their world to find vocabulary to describe divinity. Thus to find anthropomorphic language used of Yahweh should not come as any surprise, surely not to any reader of the Hebrew Bible. Page after page of the biblical text attests to how Yahweh was described through human imagery, although within certain limits—for example, there is no description of Yahweh's genitalia, no representation of sordid activity, nor any portrayal of a death scene with a lifeless body. Yahweh is ever "the living God" (*'ēl ḥay*; cf. *ḥay yhwh*).[294] At the same time, to understand how certain traditions (e.g., the Priestly Source, the Zion Sabaoth traditions, *kābôd* theology, Deuteronomistic Name Theology) struggled with and even fully rejected portraying Yahweh anthropomorphically is key to understanding formative tradents within ancient Israelite religion, tradents that impact how God is often portrayed in later Judaism, Christianity, and even Islam.[295]

These two polar portrayals (one using anthropomorphisms lavishly, the other finding such usage uncomfortable or even anathema) are both text-based. Here the nature of the Hebrew Bible presents substantive challenges. Does the overall picture of Yahweh drawn in the Hebrew Bible adequately present the viewpoints of the general population that lived in ancient Israel for hundreds of years? Or is this picture narrow, expressing only the views of certain elite groups whose writings have been preserved? Might others in society have begged to differ? To achieve a fuller picture of how Yahweh was represented physically in ancient Israel, the literary portrayal of Yahweh in the Hebrew Bible must be juxtaposed with the archaeological record. Moreover, the ancient Near Eastern context within which Israel was a part must be brought to bear. The pervasive practice of representing deities physically (and especially through anthropomorphic statuary) sets the bar extremely high should one try to prove that a culture such as ancient Israel traveled a different path.

Looking to material culture to document divine images is not as easy as one might assume. What are the essential characteristics that any object would need to have to be marked for divinity? The ideal criteria (presented in Chapter Five, p. 142) would include accompanying inscriptional identification, precious metals, a secure cultic find spot (sacred architecture together with an assemblage of cultic objects), and markers of divinity such as horns, hairdo, insignia, or a symbolic animal. With these criteria satisfied, one would then have to determine what specific markers would designate the deity Yahweh as opposed to other Levantine male deities (e.g., Athtar, Baal, Baal Hammon, Bethel, Chemosh, Dagan, El, Elyon, Eshmun, Gad, Hadad, Horon, Melqart, Milcom, Molek, Mot, Qadosh, Qaus, Reshep, Shamash, Yahweh, Yam, and Yarikh).

Over the years, scholars have nominated four candidates for possible anthropomorphic representations of Yahweh in material culture. These include a bronze seated figurine from Hazor (Figure 5.6), a stick figure from Gezer (Figures 5.7, 5.8), a terra-cotta vessel published in 1993 by Jeremias (Figure 7.6), and a geometric pair from Jerusalem (Figure 7.7). None of these comes close to being a representation of Yahweh. The striking fact is that we have a notable absence of male divine figures from Iron Age Israel and Judah. Multiple reasons were explored to explain this lack, from economic arguments (bronze images were made but melted for reuse) to sacred burials. Given the presence of female divine images in the archaeological record, one cannot rely solely on these arguments. It seems reasonable then to posit that ideological reasons also contributed to the lack of any Yahweh images. Yet any prohibition against making an image of Yahweh, such as the biblical *Bilderverbot*, surely resulted from people doing just that (cf. Dohmen 1987). Thus while the total absence of any definitive anthropomorphic image of Yahweh found in clear Iron Age context remains striking, it would nonetheless not be surprising if one did turn up in a future excavation.

The Iconography of Yahweh: Theriomorphic Traditions

The theriomorphic representation of Yahweh (i.e., Yahweh being represented via animal form) is another matter, and one that has been debated at length. As with anthropomorphic language used of divinity, any reader of ancient Near Eastern literature will hardly be surprised to see a god being described with animal imagery, especially remembering that we are dealing with agrarian cultures. According to the biblical text, the Jerusalem Temple complex was filled with animal decorations such as the bulls that adorned the Molten Sea and the wheeled cultic stands. As for archaeology, the two cult stands from Tell Taanach come readily to mind with their multiple lions, cherubim, and paired ibexes.

The three clearest literary candidates of theriomorphic imagery used of Yahweh all have to do with bulls. (There are no clear examples of lion epithets used of Yahweh.) One is the epithet "the Mighty One of Jacob," used formerly of El and later applied to Yahweh. Likewise, the second example takes the tradition of El bringing Israel out of Egypt "like the horns of wild ox" and applies it to Yahweh. The third and most famous literary reference is Jeroboam's making of bull images that cannot be separated from the literary traditions of Aaron doing likewise. To judge from the eighth-century BCE prophet Hosea, a tradition about "the bull of Samaria" (if he had Jeroboam's in mind) was known for more than a hundred years. The prevailing opinion among scholars is that Jeroboam was a master strategist who engaged in a type of competitive aniconic theology against the cult of the Jerusalem Temple. Whereas the latter chose to enthrone Yahweh invisibly upon cherubim, Jeroboam, so the theory goes, set Yahweh upon a bull image that served as a pedestal. The prevalent iconography of storm deities riding upon bulls (cf. Chapter Five, Figures 5.23–5.28) adds considerable weight to this theory. In contrast to the critiques leveled against using Figure 7.33 (Kuntillet ʿAjrud) and Figures 7.34–7.37 (the 1968 Taanach cult stand) to represent Yahweh invisibly, the substantial sacred complex at Tel Dan could have been a place where Jeroboam replicated symbol sets analogous to those of the Jerusalem Temple to underscore an aniconic Yahweh upon his bull. A different option would be that Jeroboam was not depicting any type of empty space aniconism but rather simply setting up divine bull images of Yahweh (or, less likely, of some other deity such as El or Baal).

Turning to the archaeological record, we discussed three serious candidates that have been suggested to depict Yahweh theriomorphically. Two of the three possibilities (the quadruped on the top register of the 1968 Taanach cult stand and the tallest standing figure at Kuntillet ʿAjrud on Pithos A) are the subject of intense debate. A strong case could be made that these two artifacts are the most-discussed physical items when it comes to unpacking ancient Israelite religion. The reason for such intense interest is precisely what the present chapter addresses: the iconography of divinity. The 1968 Taanach cult stand (Figures 7.34-7.37) immediately piques the interest of historians of religion with its artistic motifs of winged sun disk, sphinxes, lions, and caprids flanking a tree. That this stand has a close counterpart (Figure 7.38, discovered much earlier, in 1902) from the same site is quite remarkable. The winged disk conjures images of solar religion. Though this disk more properly designates the divine emblem in the top register, discussion has concentrated on identifying the species of the quadruped underneath and to what degree it represents (or is associated with) Yahweh. Even drawing on the expert opinion of zoologists, scholars have not come to a consensus as to whether the animal is a horse or a bull. Some scholars advocating the former link the animal to Yahweh through an explicit reference to horses being located at the entrance to the temple of Yahweh (2 Kings 23:11), while others prefer either the goddess Aštart or Anat. Those who see the animal as a bull have their choice of Baal or Yahweh (with literary examples lending support). The youth of the animal (be it a horse or a bull) led us to question its suitability for symbolizing Yahweh if we are correct in applying Fleming's (1999a) research on how senior/creator deities (and thus Yahweh) are not portrayed as offsprings. If Yahweh is represented on this cult stand, it is more likely to be the sun disk that portrays his divinity, with the animal serving as the beast upon which he is mounted.

While there is no consensus on the species of the standing figures at Kuntillet 'Ajrud (bovine or leonine), there is a consensus that we are dealing with either Bes images or Bes-like images. The historical development of Bes reveals his leonine heritage, and thus the scales are tipped decidedly in this direction—unless the Kuntillet 'Ajrud artist decided to break with convention. Be that as it may, two important factors help us resolve whether we do have Yahweh portrayed here via theriomorphic form. Each of these factors turns out to be negative. The first is the lingering doubt about whether the inscription mentioning "Yahweh and his asherah" should serve as a diagnostic key if the inscription predated the drawings, as seems likely. Without the inscription, would anyone have labeled the standing figures as being Yahweh and his consort? Second, Bes images have a widely seen (both chronologically and geographically) apotropaic function. Though hundreds of amulets in the shape of deities have been found in ancient Israel, there is no evidence of any of them being linked to an apotropaic power of Yahweh. Thus it is more reasonable to view the two standing figures at Kuntillet 'Ajrud as Bes or Bes-like images serving a protective function for the site and with no clear association with Yahweh.

What this leaves us with is one clear candidate for an example of Yahweh being represented theriomorphically: the exquisite bronze bull figure from the Bull Site (Figure 5.70). The features and craftsmanship of this figurine were discussed in Chapter Five (pp. 200, 202). Though its final identification remains uncertain due to the lack of any accompanying inscription or other indicator of divine identity, its workmanship is superb. Most interpreters speak of its ritual function. The deities most often mentioned (because of their bull symbolism elsewhere) are El, Baal, and Yahweh.

The Iconography of Yahweh: Aniconic Traditions

Section II of this chapter dealt with the question of how Yahweh might have been represented by those who preferred aniconic and abstract portrayals. We followed the lead of Mettinger in defining different types of aniconism. Material aniconism has the deity represented by standing stones rather than anthropomorphic or theriomorphic statues. Another type involves sacred emptiness, with traditions that favor the use of abstract images to portray the deity. At the same time, these traditions include pragmatic attention-focusing devices to rivet eyes and actions on the sacred during cultic activity.

The rich array of relevant standing stones for ancient Israelite religion was treated in detail on pp. 169–196 and 333–336. One cannot miss the dramatic way in which such monoliths focused attention on what ancient architects deemed central within sacred space. Precisely what (or whom) such stones signified is a matter of debate, yet their religious character is hard to miss. The occurrence of a single stone in six of our sacred spaces (Shechem, the Bull Site, Hazor Area B, Hazor Area A, Arad, and Khirbet Ataruz) led us to conclude that they most likely marked a type of monolatrous worship. Regrettably, without any inscriptional evidence it is impossible to determine the identity of the deity associated with such standing stones. Literary traditions underscore El's associations with such *masseboth* (see pp. 169–196). The present chapter reveals that Yahweh too had such associations (see pp. 333–336). Many of our examples must be inferred from pejorative texts that critiqued or outlawed such activity. Yet one remarkable passage includes a positive reference to "a *massebah* to Yahweh" alongside "an altar to Yahweh" (Isa 19:18–22).

The Iconography of Yahweh: Abstract Traditions

Abstract portrayals of divinity are attested throughout the ancient Near East, and thus it is not surprising that we find similar representations in the religion of ancient Israel, which, despite its particulars, was fully a part of this world. Following the lead of scholars such as van der Toorn, Jacobsen, and Sommer, we utilized the vocabulary of Rudolph Otto to describe how abstract representations were far better suited to convey both the *fascinans* and the *tremendum* of divinity. In other words, a variety of authors of the Hebrew Bible used abstract pictures to describe how Yahweh was irresistibly fascinating and awesome (the allure of the ultimately Sacred) as well as frighteningly dangerous if not lethal.

The various authors employing these abstract descriptions (e.g., Zion-Sabaoth traditions, Ark ideology, *kābôd* theologies, Deuteronomic/Deuteronomistic Name Theologies) had decidedly distinct ideas about how Yahweh should be represented. That the Hebrew Bible is bound today as a single volume should not obscure the fact that within its pages are philosophically distinct systems of abstract thought as to how best to represent Yahweh. Yet despite their differences, in the aggregate these views are unified in one respect: they constitute a long-standing and substantial turn away from the dominant ancient Near Eastern tradition of having an anthropomorphic (or theriomorphic) divine image as the focal point of ritual activity.

The analysis in this chapter has surveyed four abstract ways (via fire, "radiance," name, and invisibility) in which Yahweh was portrayed in the Hebrew Bible. Fire, with its numinous and ethereal qualities, was repeatedly chosen by a wide variety of authors of the Hebrew Bible as a way to describe the self-revelation of Yahweh on earth. For such poets, fire was not just a natural phenomenon (producing intense heat and giving off incandescent light) over which they cooked their food or by which they set enemy camps to ruin. Nor was it only an agent used by Yahweh against his adversaries. Rather, the essence of fire contained enough mystery that (when combined with the right preternatural setting) it was thought to manifest the Almighty. Thus we read of a burning bush that is divinely set ablaze, so that the plant (i.e., the fuel source) is (contrary to experience) not consumed. Elsewhere, the fire of Yahweh falls from heaven in dramatic fashion to answer Elijah's "proof of divinity" contest. Fire appears on mountaintop theophanies, and as a flaming torch to represent a divine covenant partner. A curious twist is that some of these fiery theophanies combined fire with anthropomorphic imagery, such that Yahweh's mouth breathed fire and his nostrils snorted smoke. This larger-than-life cosmic motif was termed "fiery transcendent anthropomorphism" (building on Hendel's terminology).

A parallel phenomenon personified fire to the degree that it could march at the vanguard of Yahweh's battle forces or serve as a guardian at the Garden of Eden. A mysterious "messenger" of Yahweh (or Yahweh himself?) turns out to be no mere mortal when his "extremely terrifying" "human" appearance turns into flames rising from the altar. Such stories make one question whether fire was ever used hypostatically (as was Yahweh's anger) and especially as an independent agent. Yet from our extant data, the most we can say is that at times fire was understood to be a "quasi-independent" entity.

Lastly, this section explored the lethality of divine fire, a leitmotif in the book of Deuteronomy. Previous analysis of divine representation in this book was excessively narrow, as it emphasized that Yahweh manifested his presence "by words *only*." The vital importance of God speaking should not be minimized. Nonetheless, the voice of Yahweh was lethal (similar to lethal God sightings) precisely because it spoke "out of the midst of fire."

The second abstract representation of divinity was broadly defined as "radiance," with the Hebrew *kābôd* serving as a catchall term for the sake of discussion. Yet the lexical stock (e.g., *hôd, hādār, kābôd* and *nōgah*) for such notions revealed a rich heritage that cannot be tightly confined. Theologies of divine "radiance" are normally thought to be the exclusive domain of the Priestly Source together with Ezekiel's particular nuancing. Yet the discussion noted how concepts of divine "radiance" were attested throughout the ancient Near East (e.g., Akkadian *melammu*) and were known in the oldest lore from ancient Israel. Moreover, the concept of a divine *kābôd* within pre-Priestly cultic settings was well known and thus hardly the invention of the Jerusalem priesthood. In addition, the ways in which the divine *kābôd* intersected with fire and Ark traditions exhibited the interweaving of various streams of tradition.

When we examined P's *kābôd* theology for divine presence, we were treated to the work of a literary architect. P, often the presenter of consummate structure, described the appearance and development of *kābôd* as divine presence through an intentional narrative arc (from Exodus 29 to Leviticus 9). The *kābôd* Yahweh that at first dwelt on Mt. Sinai enveloped in a cloud ("like a consuming fire") found its eventual resting place in a newly constructed tabernacle with newly ordained priestly officiants (Aaron and his two sons, Nadab and Abihu). The "consuming" fire of the *kābôd* manifested its physical presence by "consuming" the offerings on the newly constructed altar. Such an apex, as Milgrom pointed out, rendered the tabernacle the functional equivalent to the theophany on Mt. Sinai. Yet it was argued that P's intent was to continue his narrative arc through Leviticus 10:1–3 in order to demonstrate how Yahweh's *kābôd* also contained what Otto termed the *tremendum*. The accessible Yahweh (via the tabernacle cult) was nonetheless still the God of holy danger. This lethal "consuming" side of the divine *kābôd* was made manifest through the deaths of Nadab and Abihu. P also underscored the lethal nature of the divine *kābôd* through his telling of the rebellion of the sons of Korah, their subsequent destruction, and the aftermath of the plague that followed.

Ezekiel's portrayal of divine radiance is like no other in the Hebrew Bible. Though he too focused his attention on the word *kābôd*, it was shown how his theophanic narrative was filled with multifaceted radiant imagery. In contrast to P, who avoided anthropomorphic language, Ezekiel did indeed use human vocabulary for the divine. Yet it was argued that it is a mistake to conclude that Ezekiel was "thoroughly" anthropomorphic, for his human language is in reality not very human at all. His divine "man" is a man of fire and flies on the wings of the cherubim. Thus his "human" *kābôd* Yahweh is, in the end, so much more than human. He is a preternatural "human," not unlike the "human" messenger who ascends in fire in Judges 13. To characterize Ezekiel's *kābôd* as only "anthropomorphic" would be to miss the obvious thrust of his radiance-filled narrative. Not to be missed in unpacking Ezekiel's vision is the strong influence of Mesopotamian iconography, the enduring biblical tradition of "fiery transcendent anthropomorphisms," and the prophet's unique rhetoric of circumvention.

The third way in which biblical authors tapped into abstract ideas to depict Yahweh was through the Deuteronomic/Deuteronomistic Name Theology. Though the Name Theology is known for its four primary tenets, it was demonstrated that today there are few scholars who affirm them without qualification. At the heart of the Name Theology is an anti-anthropomorphic ideology that has Yahweh residing in heaven while at the same time manifesting his presence in the Jerusalem Temple through his Name. Rather than seeing the Temple as a mere forwarding station for prayer, our analysis sided with those scholars who argue that the Name was indeed a practical presence. To understand this, we looked again (building especially on the work of McBride) at how an attribute of a deity can function hypostatically (or semi-hypostatically). Certain biblical passages (especially Isa 30:27–33) remove all doubt about how Yahweh's Name is portrayed as a semi-independent entity that is at the same time fully representative of the deity. In short, the Name of Yahweh captures his "essential nature," yet in a way that avoids the human limitations of other traditions (such as those of Zion Sabaoth ideology) that place Yahweh on a throne. In addition, the Name contains effectual power, and especially so in military contexts. This notion ties the Deuteronomistic Name Theology into older traditions of ritual and mythic warfare.

Pragmatic Focal Points and Archaeological Correlates

Now we turn to a conceptual question raised at the outset of this chapter. If the abstract traditions in Israel did indeed part ways with the broad ancient Near Eastern practice of erecting anthropomorphic statues in the inner sanctum, then how did cult in the Jerusalem Temple actually work? In other words, what focal points were used within ritual contexts to direct attention to what was deemed most worthwhile in sacred space? What do our texts tell us, and are there any archaeological correlates that coincide with these literary traditions?

Methodologically, the sacred emptiness of the Iron Age temple at Ayn Dara, Syria, was offered as a corrective to misperceptions and prejudices of the past that relegated the artistic visions and capabilities of Levantine sculptors to backwater status. In our discussion that followed, the Ark and the cherubim (large and small) were described as the preferred "attention-focusing devices" in the Jerusalem Temple. No archaeological correlates exist for the Ark. The large cherubim are analogous to the huge human-headed winged bulls (*aladlammu* or *lamassu*) so prevalent throughout the Neo-Assyrian empire. On a smaller scale, we noted several examples of Levantine rulers sitting "enthroned between the cherubim"—that is, sitting on their thrones, which were constructed with two side panels decorated with carvings of sphinxes.

Though ethereal and numinous in nature, the practical presence of real fire within the temple certainly served to focus attention on divinity. This is especially so with regard to the holy nature of sacrificial fire and, in particular, the "continual" fire of burnt offerings (*'iššeh leyhwh 'ōlat tāmîd*). There is good reason to associate such perpetual fire with the perceived ongoing presence of Yahweh within sacred space. To judge from our narrative descriptions, physical counterpoints helping to convey the "radiant" presence of Yahweh may have been found in the Ark, the cherubim, and fire. In other words, the literary descriptions of Yahweh's *kābôd* were woven together with these three physical images that were located within sacred space.

The notion of Yahweh residing in the Jerusalem Temple via his Name or via his invisible essence on a throne is even more abstract. Yet it was suggested that even here there may have been pragmatic focal points. Once again the Ark could have functioned in such a role, in that it contained (according to the Deuteronomistic traditions) the two tablets of the Decalogue on which Yahweh's sacred Name was inscribed. We are at a loss when it comes to understanding the portrayal of divine invisibility apart from the literary descriptions of the huge size of the empty cherubim throne. The large Ayn Dara footprints (representing a deity of enormous size, though invisible) may serve as an analogy to what was behind the portrayal of the majestic guardian beasts on which an invisible Yahweh was imagined to sit. There is a slim possibility that an invisible Yahweh was portrayed on the Taanach cult stand discovered in 1968. Yet stylistic reasons for the empty space on tier three of this stand are just as likely, so we cannot support this suggestion with any confidence.

A Final Note

It is only proper as we conclude this chapter to note how the various parties responsible for the final representations of divinity that are found in the Hebrew Bible chose to weave together the various colored strands into the tapestry we have before us. When traditions were at odds with each other (e.g., anthropomorphic notions vs. anti-anthropomorphic notions), both were included as authors tried to describe the "God of Being" who was *yahwēh*.[296] (How does a sculptor craft "being"?) I would note that such multifaceted (conflicting and complementary) portrayals of divinity as we have documented in this chapter continued to be handed down both within subsequent Judaism and within nascent Christianity. Perhaps then we should use the various streams of tradition within the Hebrew Bible as windows into the history of perennial intellectual thought. Sommer (2009: 97) advocates something similar when he writes forcefully that scholars of the Hebrew Bible have been guilty of "historicist reductionism" by failing to "understand a religious text as manifesting religious intuitions that are essentially timeless."[297]

8
The Characterization of the Deity Yahweh
Part One: Yahweh as Warrior and Family God

Introduction

As noted at the beginning of Chapter Six, the writers and editors of what has come down to us in the Hebrew Bible presented a view of the deity Yahweh fully in line with the El traditions they inherited. One need look no further than the Priestly Tradition's assertion that Yahweh was indeed a later manifestation of the god El Shadday (Exod 6:2–3). The Bible does not record factional El and Yahweh parties at odds with each other. We read of no narratives where El officiants wrestle the control of cult away from Yahwistic priests or vice versa. The onomastic record's "equating names" reveal that El and Yahweh could be thought of as one.[1] At the same time, it is patently clear that historical, sociological, and cultural changes led to portraying Yahweh in ways that would transform Israelite El religion. What follows articulates some of these dramatic changes.

Though the traditions that have come down to us in the Hebrew Bible have wedded El and Yahweh traditions, in Chapter Four we posited (with cautions about the precarious nature of the enterprise) that our extant El traditions lacked certain characteristics that were associated with Yahweh. These included the following:

- Israelite El is not portrayed as a combat deity who slays cosmic creatures the likes of Leviathan and Yam, nor an agrarian deity who battles the forces of Death (Mot).
- Israelite El is not portrayed as a storm deity who uses the voice of lightning to manifest his nature.[2]
- Apart from Habakkuk 3:3, Israelite El's origin is rarely said to have been from the lands south/southeast of the Dead Sea (Seir, Teman, Paran, Midian), although some traditions localize him in the vicinity (e.g., El-Roi at Beer Lahai Roi "between Qadesh and Bered," El at Kuntillet ʿAjrud).
- Israelite El is not portrayed as a national deity whose worship is entwined with the support of a royal hierarchy.
- The narratives about El do not exhibit the intolerance that comes to characterize later Yahwism.

Thus it makes sense to start with these characteristics in our investigation of how Yahweh was portrayed. Mark Smith (2001b: 146; 2017: 42–43) suggests that "the original profile of Yahweh may be permanently lost." When we then consider the mere 5 percent of the data that we have (cf. the Propp Principle on pp. 66–67), we face considerable uncertainty. Yet at least we can sketch certain diagnostic features that have a higher probability of being on the right track.

Yahweh was portrayed in many different ways. Given space restraints, our treatment must be selective. The three chapters that follow will look at five of the primary ways in which the ancients characterized Yahweh. This chapter will juxtapose Yahweh as divine warrior with Yahweh the compassionate god of family religion. Chapter Nine will examine Yahweh as king and as judge. Chapter Ten will consider Yahweh as the holy one. Though these five portrayals do not come close to exhausting Yahwistic divinity, they do provide cultural, historical, social, and ritual windows into the various military-mythic, familial, royal, legal, and cultic understandings of Yahweh.

Section I: Yahweh as Divine Warrior

Setting the Stage

The Ancient Near Eastern Culture of Warrior Gods

When compared to El, Yahweh is strikingly militaristic. We need not posit a specific historical setting (e.g., an exodus from Egyptian slavery) or sociological setting (e.g., the collapse of the Late Bronze Age) to underscore how the ancients *at all times* felt the need to believe in a warrior deity who could protect their livelihood. Such a belief was a constant throughout the ancient Near East geographically and chronologically. Texts and iconography reveal that divine warriors were present in every pantheon from ancient Mesopotamia (Tishpak, Ninurta, Marduk, Aššur, Ishkur/Adad/Hadad, Inanna/Ishtar) to Egypt (Amun-Re, Seth, Baal, Reshep), from Anatolia (Teshub, the sun goddess of Arinna) to Syria (Ba'lu, Hadad, Rashpu, 'Anatu, 'Athtartu), from Phoenicia (Baal, Reshep, Astarte) to Israel and Judah (Yahweh, Baal, Reshep), from Moab (Chemosh) to Edom (Qos) and beyond. Universally, people thought that their warrior god fought the battles that kept them safe (unless of course they felt that they had fallen out of divine favor).[3]

It was not only the Israelites who embraced the notion of a god who went before his people fighting on their behalf. Yahweh says to King Jehoshaphat and his people: "Fear not! Be not dismayed at this great multitude. For the battle is not yours but God's" (2 Chr 20:15). So too the gods of the nations were viewed as fighting for their people. Even at the well-fortified Late Bronze Age city of Ugarit we come across a prayer whose stated purpose is clear: "Whenever a strong one attacks your gate, a warrior your walls . . ." (*k gr ʿz tǵrkm qrd ḥmytkm*). The solution is similarly transparent: "You shall lift your eyes to Baʿlu" (*ʿnkm lbʿl tšʾun*) and petition him (with a vow of offerings) to "drive the strong one from our gate, the warrior from our walls" (*y bʿlm hm tdy ʿz l tǵrn y qrd [l] ḥmytny*; KTU 1.119.26ʹ–29ʹ).[4] We have already noted how Assyrian kings were assured of victory because they wielded "the awe of the radiance [*pulḫu melamme*] of the god Aššur" against any foe.[5]

Consider the amount of information we can glean about divine warrior mentality from even a single text. In a mid-ninth-century BCE Moabite display text King Mesha recounts his battles with Israel under the Omrides (KAI 181; see Figure 6.4). In it he gives clear witness to his understanding of divine warfare. In first-person discourse he speaks of his god Chemosh, who "saved me from all the [enemy] kings and caused me to gloat over all my enemies" (*ky hšʿny mkl hmlkn wky hrʾny bkl śnʾy*; Mesha stela, line 4). Granted, there were dark days when the Israelite king Omri had the upper hand, yet Mesha's theology understood that this too revealed the sovereignty of Chemosh, who allowed such oppression because he was "angry with his land" (*ky [y]ʾnp kmš bʾ[r]ṣh*; line 5). When the king went to war, it was under divine command. Twice we read of the king receiving a personal imperative to "go and seize" (*wyʾmr ly kmš lk ʾḥz*; line 14) or to "go down and fight" the enemy ([*wy*]*ʾmr ly kmš rd hltḥm*; line 32). When King Mesha was victorious, he would relate that it was his god "who drove out [the enemy king] before me" (*wygrš kmš m*[*pny*]; line 19). It was Chemosh who "restored" (*wyšb*; line 9, cf. line 33) cities held in foreign hands back to his people. It is thus not surprising to read King Mesha say that the towns he captured ultimately "belonged to Chemosh and Moab" (*hqr ryt lkmš*; line 12),[6] or that he was devoting (*hḥrmth*; line 17) the war booty to his god using the same technical vocabulary (*ḥrm*) as that which designates booty in biblical holy war (*ḥērem*).[7] Of special note is how the enemy's cultic paraphernalia was "dragged before Chemosh" (*wʾsḥb . . . lpny kmš*; lines 12–13, 18).[8]

In short, the presence of divine warriors is ubiquitous in the ancient Near East—the very ancient Near East that included Israel and Judah, whose holy war traditions have come down to us in the Hebrew Bible and are echoed in Iron Age epigraphic sources.[9]

Yahweh as Divine Warrior

In contrast to most modern sensibilities, in Iron Age Israel going to war was considered *holy* activity.[10] Troops "*consecrated* themselves for war" (*qaddĕšû ʿālêhā milḥāmâ*; Jer 6:4). In ancient Israelite religion, it was the god Yahweh (and not the god El) who repeatedly led troops into battle. Yahweh was assigned several battle related titles: "Yahweh is a man of war" (*yhwh ʾîš milḥāmâ*; Exod 15:3;

cf. Isa 42:13), "Yahweh, mighty in battle" (*yhwh gibbôr milḥāmâ*; Ps 24:8), and "Yahweh of Armies" (*yhwh ṣĕbāʾôt*; e.g., Ps 24:10).[11] The battle cry of Yahweh marching to battle is heard in Numbers 10:35:

> Arise, O Yahweh, may your enemies be scattered;
> May your adversaries flee before you.[12]

Moses proclaimed that "Yahweh will fight for you!" (*yhwh yillāḥēm lākem*), and the deity's heroic actions in war were gathered into collections such as "the Scroll of the Wars of Yahweh" (*sēper milḥămōt yhwh*; Num 21:14). While this specific collection has not been preserved, it is likely that it would have contained epic poems similar to what we find in Exodus 15:1–18, 21; Numbers 10:35–36; Deuteronomy 33:2; Judges 5:3–5; Psalm 29; Psalm 68; and Habakkuk 3:3–15. The concept of Yahweh as divine warrior also played a significant role in Judean royal cult, as we will see.

Divine Warriors on a Cosmic Scale

The holiness (*qdš*) of divine war (i.e., that which made it "other," operating on a plane beyond human reality) was grounded in cosmic warfare of old. Holy war was birthed in the world of the gods, echoing from the legendary past. Bards told tales set in remote antiquity[13] of how a super-endowed deity was able to vanquish gods and other preternatural beasts (especially unearthly composite figures, or *Mischwesen*) on a cosmic scale.[14] Myths of divine heroism quickened human imagination. Warrior gods were larger than life; they possessed such battle prowess that they were able to succeed against insurmountable odds and supernatural foes. Humans were captivated by such alluring tales, while understandably terrified by the window that such stories gave them into the awesome power a god could harness (see Otto's *fascinans* and *tremendum*). Little wonder they responded with proper cult and desperate supplication.[15]

The Ancient Near Eastern Backdrop of Cosmic Warfare

The character of Yahweh as a divine warrior fighting on a cosmic scale is best understood within its ancient Near Eastern setting. Divine combat myths (known in German as *Chaoskampf* traditions) have a long pedigree and are well attested in a wide variety of texts.[16] Mesopotamian iconography provides a rich documentation of mythological scenes such as the visual narrative found in Figure 8.1, where a divine warrior (Ninurta? Adad?) is fighting a *Mischwesen* monster (Asakku? Anzu?). This ninth-century BCE monumental stone relief from the main entrance to the Neo-Assyrian king Aššurnasirpal II's temple to the god Ninurta at Kalhu (modern Nimrud) depicts a warrior god (notice his horned

Figure 8.1 A divine warrior fighting a *Mischwesen* monster from Aššurnasirpal II's temple to the god Ninurta at Kalhu (modern Nimrud).
Courtesy Vles1. https://commons.wikimedia.org/wiki/File:Chaos_Monster_and_Sun_God.png.

crown) wielding stylized lightning bolts in each hand with sword and scimitar at the ready. A similar depiction is found in Figure 8.2, yet with a bow and arrow as the weapon of choice. His foe, a beast with leonine and bird features, aggressively bares his claws and fangs, though the stance of the two figures reveals that it is the god (also winged) who is in rapid pursuit.[17]

Using mythology even older than the famous tale of Enuma Elish, Mesopotamian bards told tales of the warrior god Tishpak, the chief god of Eshnunna (Tell Asmar) and prototype of the more well-known Marduk. At the outset of our best-preserved text celebrating Tishpak as a divine warrior (CT 13.33–34) we hear of distraught cities crying out in distress, seemingly (though the text is broken) because of the presence of a monstrous dragon creature whose dimensions are of true mythic proportions:[18]

> Fifty "miles" is his length,
> One "mile" [his width],
>
> Six cubits his mouth,
> Twelve cubits [his ...];
> Twelve cubits is the circumference of [his] ea[rs];

Figure 8.2 A divine warrior fighting a *Mischwesen* monster from a Neo-Assyrian cylinder seal.
Courtesy the Trustees of the British Museum.

> At sixty cubits he [can snatch] birds;[19]
> In water nine cubits deep he drags [ ];
> He raises his tail, he [sweeps the sky]. (CT 13.33–34:8–13)

In a scene reminiscent of divine combat myths elsewhere, the pantheon despairs at the mere description of the opposing beast.[20] The gods fearfully ask who will slay the dragon and deliver the land, offering kingship to such a victor.

> All the gods of heaven [were afraid(?)].
> In heaven the gods bowed down before [Sin],
> And [they gra]sped Sin's [robe] by its hem:
>
> "Who will go and [slay] the raging dragon,
> [And] deliver the wide land [ ]
> And exercise kingship [ ]?" (CT 13.33–34:14–19)

A divine spokesman charges the hero Tishpak with the challenge, repeating the words of the cowering gods.

> "Go, Tishpak, sl[ay] the raging dragon,
> And deliver the wide land [ ],
> And exercise kingship [ ]."[21] (CT 13.33–34:20–22)

Tishpak at first refuses to fight the dragon, evidently claiming that he is not familiar with his adversary's features, capabilities, or modus operandi. The text then breaks off, before what is perhaps another description of the monster's actions. After presumably being instructed in the art of warfare by a deity, Tishpak engages in a cosmic battle with the dragon. The battle scene involves the storm language of stirred-up clouds, lightning, a violent tempest, and the "cylinder seal of his life/throat," which Thorkild Jacobsen took to represent thunder.[22] The dragon's size is such that when he is slain his blood flows for three years and three months, day and night.

> He [Tishpak] burst open the clouds [and made] a violent storm,
> The seal of his life/throat [ ] before him,
> He shot [at him] and [slew] the raging dragon.
>
> For three years [and] three months, day and [night]
> The blood of the raging dragon flowed [ ]. (CT 13.33–34: Reverse 5–9)

Preternatural Dragons

Of special note is the description of the dragon in the story. I have noted elsewhere how "many battle stories, divine and human, ancient and modern, use a standard technique: *the greater the foe, the greater the victory*. Combat myths go to great lengths to build up the strength of the negative protagonist so that greater glory can then be accorded to he who is able to vanquish such a warrior" (Lewis 2008b: 92). Such is especially true of mythic battles, where the imagination of poets can run free. In the text cited at the end of the previous section the dragon is no ordinary serpent, as seen by his designation as a ^{MUŠ}[*bašmu*], a term used for mythological creatures (e.g., one of Tiamat's warriors), even the constellation Hydra. He exhibits animal characteristics (ears, tail, catching birds) in addition to specifically serpentine characteristics (fifty "miles" long, travels through water). A parallel fragment from KAR 6[23] describes another *bašmu* dragon with huge eyes whose feet[24] take strides twenty "miles" long. He devours fish, birds, wild asses, and even humans. Yet the most astonishing aspect of the dragon that Tishpak battles is his description in our text as a "raging" (cf. Akk *labābu*) composite creature with serpentine and leonine characteristics (cf. the use of the word *labbu*, "lion"). Various iconographic depictions of *Mischwesen* help us better understand the fantastic portrait that the Tishpak myth was trying to sketch. While I make no claims of one-to-one correspondence between the following figures and our text, consider the iconography of composite beasts that blend leonine and serpentine features (Figures 8.3, 8.4, 8.5, 8.6), seven-headed dragons (Figures 8.7, 8.8), and a seven-headed serpent (Figure 8.9).[25] The seven-headed dragon is especially associated with Ninurta, who hung such a beast as a hunting trophy on his chariot and whose mace "has seven heads like a serpent wreaking carnage" (cf. Figure 8.10).[26]

Figure 8.3 Fantastic creatures with lion heads and serpentine necks from an Uruk cylinder seal impression.
After Henri Frankfort, *Cylinder Seals* (London: Macmillan and Co., 1939), plate IVd. Drawing by Theodore J. Lewis.

Figure 8.4 Composite beasts with leonine and serpentine features (Uruk).
Photo from William Hayes Ward, *Cylinders and Other Oriental Seals in the Library of J. Pierpont Morgan* (New York, 1909), plate XX, #137.

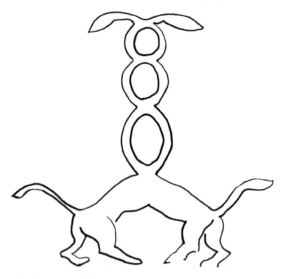

Figure 8.5 Composite beasts with leonine and serpentine features (Uruk).
After Henri Frankfort, *Cylinder Seals* (London: Macmillan and Co., 1939), pl. Ivf. Drawing by Theodore J. Lewis.

Figure 8.6 Composite beasts with griffin heads, bull bodies, and serpentine necks (Late Uruk–Incipient Jemdet Nasr).
© RMN-Grand Palais/Art Resource, NY.

Figure 8.7 An engraved shell plaque depicting a god battling a seven-headed monster.
Zev Radovan/Bible Land Pictures.

Figure 8.8 A warrior deity piercing a seven-headed dragon from Tell Asmar.
Courtesy of the Oriental Institute of the University of Chicago.

Figure 8.9 An unknown individual holding two heads that he cut off from a seven-headed serpent (Early Dynastic III, Tell Asmar).
Courtesy of the Oriental Institute of the University of Chicago.

THE CHARACTERIZATION OF THE DEITY YAHWEH 437

Figure 8.10 A mace head depicting a seven-headed serpent (Early Dynastic). Courtesy of the Oriental Institute of the University of Chicago.

Enuma Elish: The Exaltation of Marduk Through Cosmic Warfare

The well-known Babylonian creation story Enuma Elish[27] likewise describes the warrior god Marduk[28] engaged in a battle of mythic proportions with Tiamat (the personified primeval Sea)[29] and her brood of monstrous *Mischwesen*. In contrast to the Tishpak myth (or at least what we have preserved of it), Enuma Elish goes to great lengths to celebrate the awesome nature of both participants.

Once again, the features of the antagonist are articulated to evoke fear and dramatic suspense. A refrain (repeated four times to heighten the drama) describes Tiamat and her fantastic army:

> Tiamat has convened an assembly, furious with rage . . .
>
> Angry, scheming, never lying down night and day,
> Making warfare, rumbling, raging,
> Convening in assembly, that they might start hostilities.
>
> Mother Hubur, who can form anything,
> Added countless invincible weapons,
> Gave birth to monster serpents,

> Pointed of fang, with merciless incisors [?],
> She filled their bodies with venom for blood,
>
> Fierce dragons she clad with glories,
> Causing them to bear aura like gods, [saying]
>
> "Whoever sees them shall collapse from weakness!
> Wherever their bodies make onslaught
> They shall not turn back!"
>
> She deployed serpents, dragons, and hairy hero-men,
> Lion monsters, lion men, scorpion men,
> Mighty demons, fish men, bull men,
> Bearing unsparing arms, fearing no battle.[30]

The divine warrior Marduk is more than equal to the challenge. Unlike Tishpak, Marduk shows no hesitation to go to battle, as we would expect from his description at the outset of the story:

> Marduk suckled at the breasts of goddesses,
> The attendant who raised him endowed him well with glories.
>
> His body was splendid, fiery his glance,
> He was a hero at birth, he was a mighty one from the beginning! ...
>
> His members were fashioned with cunning beyond comprehension,
> Impossible to conceive, too difficult to visualize:
>
> Fourfold his vision, fourfold his hearing,
> When he moved his lips a fire broke out.
>
> Formidable his fourfold perception,
> And his eyes, in like number, saw in every direction.
>
> He was the tallest of the gods, surpassing in form,
> His limbs enormous, he was surpassing at birth ...
>
> He wore [on his body] the aura [*labiš melammē*] of ten gods ...
> Fifty glories were heaped upon him.[31]

The gods endowed Marduk with "unopposable weaponry" and then charged him to "go, cut off the life of Tiamat." Having "filled/covered his body in fiery flames" (*nablu muštaḥmiṭu zumrušu umtalli*), the champion went forth with bow and arrow, mace and thunderbolts, and a net with which to enmesh Tiamat. Deploying the Four Winds and raising the Deluge, "his great weapon," Marduk mounted his chariot and set his face toward the raging Tiamat, making sure to have a magic spell at the ready.

For all the buildup of protagonist and antagonist, the battle proper is remarkably brief, with fast-paced action:

> Tiamat and Marduk, sage of the gods, drew close for battle,
> They locked in single combat, joining for the fray.
>
> The Lord spread out his net, encircled her,
> The ill wind he had held behind him he released in her face.
>
> Tiamat opened her mouth to swallow,
> He thrust in the ill wind so she could not close her lips.
>
> The raging winds bloated her belly,
> Her insides were stopped up, she gaped her mouth wide.
>
> He shot off the arrow, it broke open her belly,
> It cut to her innards, it pierced the heart.
>
> He subdued her and snuffed out her life,
> He flung down her carcass, he took his stand upon it.[32]

As for Tiamat's army, "they trembled, terrified, they ran in all directions." And thus the victory was won and with it the crowning of Marduk (prearranged in an agreement) as sovereign over all the gods. Indeed, though Enuma Elish is frequently referred to as the Babylonian tale of creation, it is more fittingly "the exaltation of Marduk."[33]

Ugarit: The Exaltation of Baʻlu and ʻAnatu Through Cosmic Warfare

Turning to the Levant, we find similar *Chaoskampf* mythologies used to elevate the prominence of deities and their cult.[34] As noted in Chapter Six, p. 266, we have a clear reference to Adad, the Lord of Aleppo, wielding weapons in his defeat of Tiamat. That Adad let King Zimri-Lim use these very weapons underscores the political and social dimensions of such mythology. It should be emphasized that we are not arguing for a meta-narrative in which every ancient Near Eastern culture adopted a singular story about cosmic warfare and the elevation of its gods. Each culture wove its stories in culturally specific ways. One need only look at how the artisans in the citadel of Aleppo chose to picture their storm god, the Lord of Aleppo—not in battle with a *Mischwesen* monster but rather riding on a chariot being pulled by a bull (Figure 5.29).

As has been widely acknowledged, the Ugaritic Baʻlu myth (commonly referred to as the Baal Cycle) "had a long prehistory among the Amorite peoples," utilizing "poetic conventions . . . surely descended from the old Amorite poetic traditions" (Pardee 1997c: 241; cf. Durand 1993; Bordreuil and Pardee 1993). As a composition, it is extraordinary. Representing "one of the classics of ancient literature" (Smith 1994b: xxii), it "constitutes, by its length and relative completeness, the most important literary work preserved from those produced by the West Semitic peoples in the second millennium BCE" (Pardee 1997c: 241). The Baʻlu myth contains two stories of divine combat, the first against the deity Yammu (the personified Sea), the second against the god Motu (personified Death). Only the first will be considered here. As with Tiamat in Enuma Elish, the Sea described in the Baʻlu myth is no mere body of water. Rather, Yammu/Sea is a cosmic foe whose allomorph is a multiple-headed dragon creature (who presumably lives in the Sea) named both Litanu and Tunnanu.

A quartet of gods is associated with bringing about the defeat of Yammu. Baʻlu certainly takes center stage in the epic tale named after him. Yet unlike Enuma Elish's effusive description of Marduk from the outset of its tale (see pp. 438–439), here there is no lengthy buildup celebrating Baʻlu's battle prowess. In stark contrast, in the Baʻlu myth, ʾIlu, the patriarch of the pantheon, is more than willing to hand Baʻlu over, declaring: "Baʻlu is your slave O Yammu / Baʻlu is your slave O River / The Son of Dagan your captive" (KTU 1.2.1.36–37).

Thus it is that Baʻlu must rise to the occasion. He is assisted by the artisan god Kotharu-wa-Hasisu, who crafts two weapons that he renders effective through incantations.[35] Dramatic suspense is added when the first weapon (with the name Driver) proves ineffective. Champions like Yammu are not so easily defeated.

> The [first] weapon dances in Baʻlu's hand,
> Like a raptor in his fingers.
>
> It strikes Prince Sea on the shoulders,
> Judge River on the chest.
>
> [But] Sea is strong, he does not collapse.
> His joints do not buckle.
> His body does not slump.[36] (KTU 1.2.4.15–18)

A reengagement with Ba'lu wielding a second mace by the name of Expeller proves victorious:

> The [second] weapon dances in Ba'lu's hand,
> Like a raptor in his fingers.
>
> It strikes Prince Sea on the head,
> Judge River between the eyes.
>
> Sea collapses,
> He falls to the ground.
> His joints buckle,
> His body slumps.[37]
>
> Ba'lu grabs Yammu and sets about dismembering [him],
> He sets about finishing Judge River off.[38] (KTU 1.2.4.23–27)

The goddess 'Athtartu now comes to Ba'lu's side and, similar to when Kotharu-wa-Hasisu used incantations to render the weapons effective, she hexes Yammu to assist in the defeat.[39]

> By Name, 'Athtartu hexes [Yammu] [with the following words]:
> "Scatter/dry up [Yammu], O Mighty [Ba'lu],
> Scatter/dry up [Yammu], O Rider of the Clouds."
> "Indeed, Prince [Yammu] is our captive,
> Ruler Naharu is our captive." (KTU 1.2.4.28–30)

'Athtartu's proclamation of Yammu being taken captive is a splendid poetic reversal of the earlier prospects for Ba'lu when 'Ilu agreed to his captivity (KTU 1.2.1.36–37; Smith 1994b: 357). At this crucial juncture our text breaks off! Enough is preserved that we are certain that Ba'lu is finally victorious in scattering Yammu (*ybṯnn 'al'iyn b'l*), resulting in the proclamation that

> Yammu is surely dead!
> [Ba'lu reigns!]
> Indeed, he rules! (KTU 1.2.4.34–35)

'Anatu, the third deity who assists Ba'lu, is the most riveting of deities; at Ugarit, her lore was unmatched for its vivid intensity. Her battle exploits include cutting off the heads and hands of her enemies, affixing them to her back and waist, and then plunging back into the bloody gore because her lust for battle remains unsated (KTU 1.3.2.5–20; 1.13.5–6). When news arrives that an enemy has risen against her brother Baʻlu, she brags of her battle prowess with the following claim:

> Surely I have smitten Yammu [Sea], the Beloved of ʾIlu
> Surely I finished off Naharu [River], the Great God,
> Surely I bound Tunnanu [the dragon] and destroyed him.
>
> I have smitten the Twisting Serpent [bṯn ʻqltn],
> The Powerful One with seven heads. (KTU 1.3.3.38–42)[40]

These words placed on ʻAnatu's lips closely echo a description later in the story where the god Motu (Death) speaks of Baʻlu:

> When you smote Litanu [ltn], the Fleeing Serpent [bṯn brḥ],
> When you finished off the Twisting Serpent [bṯn ʻqltn],
> The Powerful One with seven heads . . . (KTU 1.5.1.1–3)[41]

Another Ugaritic text (KTU 1.83) rehearses a goddess's victory over the Yammu/Tunnanu dragon creature, yet it is not explicit with regard to the identity of the goddess. The author could have either ʻAnatu or ʻAthtartu in mind as he writes:

> She sets a muzzle on Tunnanu
> She binds him on the heights of Lebanon [with the following words]:
> "Parched, may you be dried up/scattered, O Yammu,
> with tumultuous terror, O Naharu,
> May you not see, lo, may you be scorched/churned." (KTU 1.83.8–14)[42]

In summary, the northwestern Levant, like its Mesopotamian neighbors to the east, had its own rich traditions of warrior gods (male and female) fighting cosmic battles against a personified Sea and a mythological seven-headed dragon creature. The pervasiveness of this motif both chronologically and geographically should not be missed. Such ubiquity sets the context for Iron Age Israel, where we would expect a similar scenario.

Yahweh as Divine Warrior on a Cosmic Scale

The mythopoeic and mythopoetic traditions that made up the lore of Israelite religion over hundreds of years used the power of cosmic warfare to exalt Yahweh. Like its neighbors, ancient Israel found such stories to be captivating for articulating the prowess of their god. Such literary genres proved to be the perfect vehicles to articulate the alluring nature of Yahweh and to command the respect, fear, and reverence that he was due (cf. again Otto's categories of *fascinans* and *tremendum*).

Within Israelite religion we find the same pervasiveness of our motif both chronologically and geographically. The earliest and latest of traditions, northern and southern—they all employ the vehicle of Yahweh as a warrior fighting (1) on a cosmic scale (the likes of Yam, Leviathan, Rahab, the Tannin-dragon, and Mot), and (2) on the historical plane (fighting synergistically with Israelite troops and fighting alone). Each of these will be addressed in turn.

Ever since Hermann Gunkel's 1895 *Schöpfung und Chaos in Urzeit und Endzeit*, scholars have discussed the so-called *Chaoskampf* traditions found within the pages of the Hebrew Bible.[43] The discovery of the Ugaritic texts (starting in 1929) added even more fuel to the exploration of such mythpoeic traditions in ancient Israel. Though dragon-slaying is a widespread and aged motif in the ancient Near East and certainly a part of the oldest biblical lore, as we will see, the most explicit biblical narratives regarding dragon-slaying like that practiced by Marduk, Baʿlu, and ʿAnatu come from later texts. Psalm 74 likely emerged during the early exilic period, with its references to the thorough destruction of the Jerusalem Temple (Ps 74:3, 7).[44] Yet our poet fixes his gaze on the ancient past, a time in remote antiquity when Yahweh as a "king of old" (*melek miqqedem*) provided deliverance. The reference to Yahweh as king in conjunction with the cosmic warfare that follows is not a coincidence. As noted by John Day (1985: 19), Psalm 74 together with Ps 93 and Ps 29 "explicitly associate the *Chaoskampf* with Yahweh's kingship, just as the Ugaritic Baal myth connects Baal's victory over Yam with his enthronement and Enuma Elish links Marduk's kingship with his overcoming of Tiamat."[45]

Psalm 74 is the most explicit biblical text when it comes to describing the multiple-headed dragon that Yahweh vanquishes:

> O Yahweh,[46] my king from of old,
> The one who enacts deliverance throughout the land;
> It was you [*'attâ*] who divided Sea [*yām*] by your might,
> You who smashed the heads of the dragons [*rāʾšê tannînîm*] in the waters;
> It was you [*'attâ*] who crushed the heads of Leviathan [*rāʾšê liwyātān*],
> You who left him as food for the denizens of the desert;
> It was you [*'attâ*] who cleaved open spring and torrent,
> It was you [*'attâ*] who dried up the ever-flowing rivers [*nahărôt ʾêtān*].
> The day is yours, the night too;
> It was you [*'attâ*] who ordained moon and sun,
> It was you [*'attâ*] who fixed all the bounds of the earth;
> Summer and winter—it was you [*'attâ*] who formed them. (Ps 74:12–17)

The stylistic repetition of ʾattâ ("It was *you* [O Yahweh] who...") seven times is a dramatic literary vehicle. With it our poet reminds Yahweh of his powerful past juxtaposed against his inactivity in the present. His plea is for a god who is renowned for defeating the most powerful of preternatural enemies to act against human adversaries who are "wild beasts" (ḥayyat; Ps 74:19) in their own right. Our poet does not explicitly enumerate the heads of the preternatural dragon creature as seven, yet the motif is so dominant in text and iconography that surely he had seven in mind.[47] Note how the four Hebrew terms for the dragon and the water in which he resides (yām, nahărôt, tannin, liwyātān) are direct cognates with those we find at Late Bronze Age Ugarit (ym, nhr, tnn, ltn). Thus Day's (1985: 4) argument that "the immediate background of the Old Testament allusions to the sea monster is not Babylonian but Canaanite" is well founded.[48] The linkage of the combat myth to creation (Ps 74:16–17) also resonates with what we know of comparable ancient Near Eastern traditions. Note too how the combat material of Psalm 74:12–17 is linked to the destruction of the Jerusalem Temple earlier in the psalm (74:1–11). Combat myths in the comparative material resulted in the construction of a temple in honor of Marduk and Baʿlu. Marvin Tate (building on the work of Lelièvre and Day) notes that "it would be inappropriate for a divine king to allow his house, a house which was rightfully his because of his victories over the Sea, and the sea-monsters, to be so ill-treated."[49]

Another exilic text that reminisces about ancient times is found in Isaiah 51:9–10. As with Psalm 74, the context is a communal lament whereby the current inactivity of Yahweh results in an urgent plea for him to rouse himself into action as he did in "the days of old" (yĕmê qedem//dōrôt ʿôlāmîm).

> Awake, awake, clothe yourself with strength,
> O arm of Yahweh!
> Awake, as in days of old,
> As in the distant past!
>
> Was it not you who hewed Rahab in pieces,[50]
> who pierced the Dragon [tannîn]?
> Was it not you who dried up the Sea [yām],
> the waters of the great deep [tĕhôm rabbâ]?
> Who made the depths of the sea
> a way for the redeemed to traverse?
>
> So those ransomed by Yahweh will return,
> and come to Zion with joyful shouting;
> crowned with everlasting joy;

> they will obtain joy and gladness,
> while sorrow and sighing will flee away.[51] (Isa 51:9–11)

Our poet recalls the former ages, by which he means the exodus from Egypt. Using this backdrop, he envisions a new exodus, this time from Babylon to Jerusalem (cf. *yĕmê-ʿôlām* in Isa 63:11–12).[52] He combines the various words for the cosmic Sea (*yām* and *tĕhôm*, the latter cognate with Akkadian Tiamat) and the dragon (*tannîn*) with yet another word, Rahab (*rahab*), a double entendre that can designate a dragon as well as Egypt as the traditional enemy.[53] The verbs for the actions directed against the dragon—hewing (*maḥṣebet*), smiting (*mōḥeṣet* according to the variant in 1QIsa^a), and piercing (*mĕḥôlelet*)—describe a battle scene equal to that depicted in the iconography discussed earlier (hewing in Figures 8.7 and 8.9, piercing in Figure 8.8).

Turning our focus to wisdom literature, more specifically to the book of Job, we see how authors of other genres also utilized the widespread *Chaoskampf* motif. Indeed, the author of the book of Job has a remarkably large number of references to Yahweh as a divine warrior on a cosmic scale. This might come as a surprise to readers who have thought of wisdom literature as void of traditional deliverance themes (e.g., the exodus) and/or salvation motifs that are found in non-wisdom books.[54]

While this absence of traditional motifs may be true of the Book of Proverbs and Qohelet, it is certainly not true when it comes to the book of Job's concentration on the divine combat myth (Job 3:8; 7:12; 9:8, 13; 26:12–13; 40:9–41:26 [Eng 40:9–41:34]; cf. 38:8–11).[55] Day (2000: 100) notes two reasons for this: (1) the connection of *Chaoskampf* myths to the theme of creation (see Ps 74:16–17) and (2) how the author of the book of Job "clearly saw a parallel between Job's argument with God and the conflict between the dragon/sea and God." In particular, Day points to Job 7:12, where the suffering Job laments: "Am I Sea [*yām*] or the Dragon [*tannîn*], that you station a siege guard against me?"[56] Regardless of why such traditions resonate for our Joban author, the motif of Yahweh as cosmic warrior is pervasive:

> By his power, [Yahweh] quelled the Sea [*yām*],
> By his skill, he smote Rahab [*rāhab*].
> By his wind, the heavens . . . ,
> His hand pierced the Fleeing Serpent [*nāḥāš bārîaḥ*].[57] (Job 26:12–13)[58]

Of the other Joban passages, the author's prefatory remarks to the Behemoth/Leviathan pericope in Job 40:9–41:26 (Eng 40:9–41:34) are most telling. In a passage without precedent, Yahweh surprisingly challenges Job to be a god—to clothe himself with divine radiance (*hôd wĕhādār tilbāš*; 40:10), to unleash his wrath (*'ap*), and to achieve victory such that Yahweh himself would praise him (*wĕgam-'ănî 'ôdekā*; 40:14)![59] The lengthy description that follows accentuates that the human Job simply cannot do what Yahweh can in subjugating and defeating Behemoth and Leviathan. The point is clear: preternatural *Mischwesen*—especially a fire-breathing dragon (41:10–13 [Eng 41:18–21]) like Leviathan—are of such a cosmic nature that only a god can bring about their defeat. To refine the point further, even divine beings (*'ēlîm*) cower in fear (41:17 [Eng 41:25]) before such an invincible dragon, who knows not fear and can stir up the abyss (41:22–24 [Eng 41:30–32]). Yahweh alone can rule him (41:25–26 [Eng 41:33–34]).[60]

Lastly in this brief overview, consider the way in which the *Chaoskampf* motif appears in apocalyptic (and proto-apocalyptic) literature. Here Isaiah 27:1 is our parade example:

> On that day Yahweh will punish—
> With his harsh, great and strong sword—
> Leviathan [*liwyātān*], the Fleeing Serpent [*nāḥāš bāriaḥ*],
> Leviathan, the Twisting Serpent [*nāḥāš 'ăqallātôn*];
> He will kill the Dragon [*tannîn*] that is in the Sea [*yām*].[61] (Isa 27:1)

The five different references for the preternatural beast(s) in this verse resonate with those found in earlier biblical texts and the much older alphabetic cuneiform texts from Late Bronze Age Ugarit—with even the Twisting Serpent (*nāḥāš 'ăqallātôn*) making an appearance (cf. *bṯn 'qltn* in KTU 1.3.3.38–42 and KTU 1.5.1.1–3). Here they function eschatologically. The slayings of Sea and the dragon function not to establish the rule of Yahweh as the divine warrior among competing gods (Marduk, Ba'lu, 'Anatu), not to rouse Yahweh to action in light of his perceived inactivity, and not to juxtapose the greatness of divine omnipotence against the smallness of Joban pronouncements. In Isaiah 27:1 the divine battle lies in the distant future (*bayyôm hahû'*), not the distant past (*yĕmê qedem// dōrôt 'ôlāmîm*). Yet this final battle in the eschaton recapitulates the cosmogonic victory of primeval times, even at the creation of the world (the so-called *Urzeit wird Endzeit* motif). Thus Joseph Blenkinsopp writes that "the scribe has in mind the final overcoming of evil as a metahistorical and metaphysical force." What is noteworthy is what Blenkinsopp has called the "durability" of these ancient *Chaoskampf* motifs—here in a proto-apocalyptic text and later still in Jewish and Christian apocalyptic literature.[62]

Searching for Archaic Lore in Israelite Religion

The texts discussed here (the majority of them late) demonstrate the enduring theme of Yahweh engaged in cosmic warfare, a theme that was employed across a variety of literary genres and one that was central to Judean identity formation. If one of these Judean authors was asked to describe how he came to know such lore, he would not have pulled a *written* copy of Enuma Elish or the Ba'lu Cycle from an archive, though cuneiform texts are attested in the land of Canaan/Israel from the Middle Bronze Age to the Iron Age.[63] He likely would have pointed to lore from "the days of old" (*yĕmê qedem*//*dōrôt ʿôlāmîm*) handed down *orally* across the generations:[64]

> Remember the days of old [*yĕmôt ʿôlām*],
> Consider the years of generations long ago [*šĕnôt dôr-wādôr*];
> Ask your father [*ʾābîkā*], he will tell you;
> your elders [*zĕqēnêkā*], they will inform you. (Deut 32:7)

Yet other exhortations to remember "bygone days" (*yāmîm riʾšōnîm*) date the memory of effective divine warfare to the days of creation (*min-hayyôm ʾăšer bārāʾ ʾĕlōhîm ʾādām ʿal-hāʾāreṣ*; Deut 4:32–34; cf. the disputation speech in Isa 40:21–24).

Wisdom traditions, like what we find in the book of Job, held that the understandings of one's ancestors that accrued over time were qualitatively different from those that could be acquired in a single, transitory life. Such collective knowledge had a didactic authority that was able to instruct the present ephemeral generation, those who are "but of yesterday."[65]

> Indeed, inquire of bygone generations [*lĕdōr rîšôn*],
> Ascertain the insights of their fathers [*ʾăbôtām*];
>
> For we are but of yesterday and know nothing,
> Our days on earth are but a shadow.
>
> Will they not teach you and tell you,
> Utter words out of their understanding? (Job 8:8–10)

Such aged lore regularly focused on God's actions, whether with regard to theodicy (in Job's case) or (for the author of Psalm 44) God's military victories:

> We have heard with our own ears, O Yahweh,[66]
> Our fathers [*ăbôtênû*] have told us
>
> Of the [military] deeds you executed back in their days,
> in the days of old [*bîmê qedem*]. (Ps 44:2 [Eng 44:1])

In turn, such oral traditions were to be passed on to future generations with, according to another psalmist, song being a primary medium:[67]

> Give thanks to Yahweh! Invoke him by name!
> Proclaim his deeds among the peoples.
> Sing to him, make music to him!
> Tell of all his wondrous acts. (Ps 105:1–2)

Yet in emphasizing orality and performance, one should not forget written narratives and how they too would have served cultural and educational purposes. Accounts of Yahweh's warfare were collected in written form (*sēper milḥămōt yhwh*; Num 21:14), probably early. No longer do scholars envision a linear evolution in which an exclusively oral society becomes exclusively literate. In Robert Miller's (2011: 121) words, "Oral and written literatures were simultaneously part of ancient Israel for the entire time of the Hebrew Bible's composition.... There was an interplay of oral and written composition and performance throughout Israel's history." David Carr (2007: 41; 2011: 36) also emphasizes "ongoing oral-written education" as a much better model for understanding the transmission process. The textual data that we have at our disposal are "the distillate of a transmission-historical process, shaped to varying extents by the exigencies of memory and performance." Dobbs-Allsopp (2015: 110) also emphasizes that we are dealing with "a textuality forged at the interface with orality... [T]he traditional techniques and tropes of orality remain critical to the production and successful reception of poetry.... [B]iblical poems, even once written down, are decidedly more oral and aural than not."

As for precise dating, a historian is at a loss when it comes to tracing mythic lore handed down from ages past. By definition, such stories are of a timeless, unknown origin. The oldest remnants of *Chaoskampf* tales in the Hebrew Bible can be found embedded in passages like Psalm 29, Exodus 15, Psalms 29, 68, 89, 93, and the archaic (or archaizing) Habakkuk 3.[68] It is likely that literature such as Psalm 29 used the power and imagery of such traditions intentionally as part of anti-Baal propaganda (Pardee 2005: 158) that likely dated very early.

The Divine Battle at the Sea and with Sea

The preservation of certain memories over others is telling. With respect to Yahweh's actions as a divine warrior, no event captured the ancient Israelite imagination as much as the exodus from Egypt and Yahweh's victory at the sea over Pharaoh's armies. The lengthiest poetic account is found in Exodus 15:1–18, an archaically flavored passage that is often considered one of the grandest poems in the entire Hebrew Bible.[69]

While our epic poet focuses on Yahweh as "a man of war" who marches out to do battle with Pharaoh at the sea, he nonetheless embraces the divine warrior on a familial level. Our lyric poet exalts Yahweh both as his personal god (*zeh 'ēlî*) and as his ancestral god (*'ĕlōhê 'ābî*) who acts redemptively on behalf of his clan (*'am*) (Exod 15:2, 13, 16).[70] Divine care is expressed as "loving" (*ḥesed*), together with the imagery of a shepherd guiding his flock to pasture (*nēhaltā...'el-nawēh*) (Exod 15:13).

As for the cosmic battle, it is recast such that the battle is no longer *with* a preternatural Sea but *at the* sea. It is still cosmic in that a god is fighting with such *tremendum* (cf. *ne'dārî, 'addîrîm, ne'dār, nôrā'*) that humans and gods alike respond with fear (Exod 15:6, 10–11). In particular, the expression "terrible of radiance," *nôrā' tĕhillōt*, reminds one of the terrifying *melammu* of the Neo-Assyrian god Aššur in battle.[71]

Let me sing/Sing to Yahweh,	(1) *'āšîrâ/šîrû*[72] *leyhwh*
For he is highly exalted;	*kî-gā'ōh gā'â*
Horse and charioteer	*sûs wĕrōkĕbô*[73]
He cast into the sea.	*rāmâ bayyām*
Yah[weh] is my might and stronghold,	(2) *'ozzî wĕzimrāt yâ*
May he be my salvation.	*yĕhî-lî lîšû'â*[74]
This is my god whom I exalt,	*zeh 'ēlî wĕ'anwēhû*
The god of my father whom I glorify.	*'ĕlōhê 'ābî wa'ărōmĕmenhû*
Yahweh is a man of war,	(3) *yhwh 'îš milḥāmâ*
Yahweh is his name	*yhwh šĕmô*
The chariots of Pharaoh and his army	(4) *markĕbōt par'ōh wĕḥêlô*
He has cast into the sea.	*yārâ bayyām*
His choice troops	*ûmibḥar šālišāyw*
Were drowned in the Sea of Reeds.[75]	*ṭubbĕ'û bĕyam-sûp*
The abyss covered them,	(5) *tĕhōmōt yĕkasĕyumû*
They sank into the depths like stone.	*yārĕdû bimĕṣôlōt kĕmô-'āben*
Your right hand, Yahweh,	(6) *yĕmînkā yhwh*
terrible in strength;	*ne'dārî bakkōaḥ*
Your right hand, Yahweh,	*yĕmînkā yhwh*
Shattered the enemy.	*tir'aṣ 'ôyēb*

With your massive cresting[76]	(7) *ûběrōb gě'ônkā*
You crushed your foes	*tahărōs qāmêkā*
You sent forth your fury	*těšallaḥ ḥărōnĕkā*
It consumed them like straw.[77]	*yō'kĕlēmô kaqqaš*
At the blast of your nostrils	(8) *ûběrûaḥ 'appêkā*
Waters were laid bare;[78]	*ne'ermû mayim*
Sheets of water stood like a wall,[79]	*niṣṣĕbû kĕmô-nēd nōzĕlîm*
The abyss congealed in the heart of the sea...	*qāpĕ'û tĕhōmōt bĕleb-yām...*
You blew with your breath,	(10) *nāšaptā běrûḥăkā*
Sea covered them.	*kissāmô yām*
They sank like a lead weight	*ṣālălû ka'ôperet*
In dreadful waters.	*běmayim 'addîrîm*
Who is like you among the gods, Yahweh?	(11) *mî-kāmōkâ bā'ēlim yhwh*
Who is like you, feared in holiness?	*mî kāmōkâ ne'dār baqqōdeš*[80]
Terrible of radiance,[81] worker of wonder.	*nôrā' tĕhillōt 'ōśēh pele'*
You extended your right hand,	(12) *nāṭîtā yĕmînĕkā*
The underworld swallowed them.[82]	*tiblā'ēmô 'āreṣ*
	(Exod 15:1–12)

Just because the battle is no longer *with* Sea but rather *at the* sea does not mean that we are dealing with just any battle or with just any body of water. Yahweh is described as a striding warrior with upraised right hand (Exod 15:6, 12; cf. Figures 7.1, 7.2, 7.3). Archery imagery is likely behind the verb *rāmâ* in Exodus 15:1 (cf. esp. Hab 3:9, 11). Multiple watery forces (the sea, the abyss, the depths, cresting waves, the dreadful waters), wind (personified as divine breath), and even the underworld serve as the military agents by which Yahweh crushes his foe (Exod 15:7). In addition, the divine arsenal includes Yahweh's anger (*ḥărōn*, *'ap*; Exod 15:7–8) and perhaps even the divine name.[83]

Psalm 77:17–21 (Eng 77:16–20), like Isaiah 51:9–11, is another late snippet of a once larger poem that recalls God's "wonders of old" (*miqqedem pil'ekā*). Such wonders are exemplified foremost by "the [military] actions of Yah[weh]" (*ma'allê-yā*) at the sea (Ps 77:12 [Eng 77:11]). There is no doubt that the poet is referencing the exodus saga, as he mentions Yahweh guiding his people "together with the agency of Moses and Aaron" (Ps 77:21 [Eng 77:20]).

The battle at the sea is poetically depicted through four watery terms: *mayim*, *tĕhōmôt*, *yām*, and *mayim rabbîm*. Yahweh's arsenal (clouds, rain, thunder, lightning, whirlwind) is befitting a storm god. Yahweh marches through the sea (*bayyām*) of Exodus fame, yet the gravitas of this historic march is heightened through the anthropomorphization of the sea. The Waters see Yahweh's battle march and are terrified.

> When the Waters saw you, O Yahweh,   rāʾûkā mayim yhwh[84]
> When the Waters saw you, they were afraid!   rāʾûkā mayim yāḥîlû
> Even the Abyss trembled! . . .   ʾap yirgĕzû tĕhōmôt
>
> Your march [O Yahweh] was through the sea,   bayyām darkekā
> Your path through the mighty waters,   ûšĕbîlĕkā[85] bĕmayim rabbîm
> Your footprints were unmarked![86]   wĕʿiqqĕbôtêkā lōʾ nōdāʿû
>   (Ps 77:17, 20 [Eng 77:16, 19])

Similarly, Psalm 114:3, 5 has Sea "looking" (elliptically at Yahweh as a divine warrior marching to battle [cf. 114:7]) and fleeing in fear. One could compare this description to the flight of Tiamat's army after they encounter the mighty Marduk. When we add all such passages together (Exod 15:11, Ps 77:17 [Eng 77:16], Ps 89:8–9 [Eng 89:7–8], and Ps 114:3, 5), it is clear that it is not just humans who were thought to experience *tremendum* when faced with the lethal presence of Yahweh in battle dress.[87]

Yet another anthropomorphized battle is described in the archaic/archaizing Habakkuk 3.[88] According to Habakkuk 3:2, the author had heard of Yahweh's military actions in the distant past and found such knowledge quite frightening (yārēʾtî yhwh pāʿālĕkā). Habakkuk 3:8–15 (a structural unit based on its repetitive water vocabulary) portrays Yahweh as a charioteer armed for battle with bow and arrows as well as a spear (3:8–9, 11). We enter the story midstream. One can only guess at the plotline that led our poet to cry out:

> Were you angry with the rivers [nĕhārîm], O Yahweh,
> Was your wrath against the rivers [nĕhārîm],
> Did you rage against the sea [bayyām],
>
> When you drove your steeds,
> Your victorious chariots?
>
> You laid bare your bow,
> . . . [your] shafts . . .[89]
>
> Torrents of water [zerem mayim] swept by,
> The abyss [tĕhôm] gave forth its voice . . .
>
> At the brilliance of your flying arrows,
> At the radiance of your lightning-like spear . . .
>
> You smote the head of the wicked one[90]
> slashing, head to foot.

> With his own spear you pierced [*nāqabtā*] [his] head,⁹¹
> When his warriors stormed out to scatter us . . .
>
> You trampled the sea [*bayyām*] with your horses,
> You parched the many waters [*mayim rabbîm*].⁹² (Hab 3:8–11, 13b–15)

Francis Andersen (2001: 316) notes "the fusion of the mythological and the historical," with "the historical focus on the crossing of the Reed Sea." The hostile "nations" mentioned within the poem (3:12–14, 16) are for Andersen (2001: 334) "universal, potentially eschatological," whereas for Day (1985: 105) they point toward the Babylonians. Where Andersen (2001: 317) sees "only an echo" of the original mythological tale behind Habakkuk 3:8, Theodore Hiebert (1986: 6–7, 23) asserts that the formulaic pair *yām//nāhār-m* (which he renders as singular, following Albright) constitutes "the waters of chaos, Yahweh's cosmic foe . . . an enduring reflection of the ancient name of the dragon of chaos." Indeed, for Hiebert (1986: 108), "the enemy is a cosmic one. It is the ancient dragon of chaos, River//Sea." Nonetheless, Hiebert too agrees that we have a "blending of the cosmic and historical realms," and the "cosmic battle is recited to celebrate God's victory in earthly wars."

Finally we come to the prose account of the victory at the sea in Exodus 13:21–14:22, a composite text of several sources (JE/non-P and P plus additions) that often serves as a classic example of how independent accounts were woven together.⁹³ The conflated text emphasizes Moses' agency to a greater degree than any of the other exodus accounts previously mentioned. In the battle scenes, it is his "outstretched *hand* over the sea" (Exod 14:16, 21, 26–27) that is emphasized rather than Yahweh's right hand (cf. the threefold use of *yāmîn* in Exod 15:6, 12).⁹⁴ The people put their faith in Moses as well as in Yahweh (14:31). Similarly, the account here devotes a surprising amount of attention to describing Pharaoh's military might, especially his "choice" chariotry (14:7, 9, 17–18, 23, 25–26, 28), with no description of Yahweh as a charioteer with weapons at the ready (cf. Hab 3:8–11, 15). Nonetheless, these two highlighted humans reinforce the consistent theme of Yahweh as the divine warrior par excellence. The emphasis on Pharaoh's military prowess illustrates once again the notion that the greater the foe, the greater the victor; the greater the odds, the greater the victory (cf. p. 433). Though Moses' outstretched "hand" (*yād*) is highlighted throughout the battle scenes, it is clearly Yahweh's empowerment that renders it effective. The concluding line makes this explicit: "Israel saw 'the great hand' [*hayyād haggĕdōlâ*] that Yahweh wielded against the Egyptians" (14:31).⁹⁵ Yahweh is the one who provides deliverance (√*yš'*; 14:13, 30); Yahweh is the one who does the actual fighting (√*lḥm*; 14:14, 25)—"panicking" (14:24) the Egyptian army and "shaking them out" (14:27) into the sea.⁹⁶ It is Yahweh who drives back the sea, drying it up and cleaving its waters using the agency of a mighty wind (14:21) that only a god can control.

Not to be missed are other signs of divine activity, such as the "messenger of God" figure (*malʾak hāʾĕlōhîm*) portrayed in Exodus 14:19a as Yahweh's military leader protecting the front and rear flanks of the army (cf. Isa 52:12). With nearly identical language (suggesting a conflation of two variants), Exodus 14:19b describes a flanking "cloud pillar" (*ʿammûd heʿānān*) that is coupled earlier in the account with the "fire pillar" (*ʿammûd ʾēš*; Exod 13:21). The use of fire as symbol of divine presence (and of a destructive nature) was discussed in Chapter Seven, pp. 344–358. Most commentators view the two pillars as a single apparition designating divine presence.[97] While this famous pillar has been used to guide the way for Israel to travel (Exod 13:21), here is it militaristic. Indeed, it is the locale from which Yahweh "looks down" (*yašqēp*) on the Egyptian army just prior to bringing about their panic (Exod 14:24).

Apart from a brief reference to impairing chariot wheels, our text does not flesh out the precise mode of Yahweh's fighting or the means by which he brought about the Egyptians' terror. Yet it should be underscored that "fear" is a bracketing motif in the narrative. Due to the Egyptians' pursuit, the people of Israel are in "great fear" (*wayyîrʾû mĕʾōd*; 14:10) at the outset of the story and cry out (in fear) to Moses. Moses tells them to "fear not" (*ʾal-tîrāʾû*; 14:13), only to then cry out (in fear) himself to Yahweh.[98] After Yahweh terrifies (*yāhom*; Exod 14:24) the Egyptians, they flee (in fear), but are vanquished nonetheless. As a result of Yahweh's awe-inspiring deliverance, the people then rightly direct their fear toward Yahweh (*wayyîrʾû hāʿām ʾet-yhwh*; 14:31), in whom they put their faith.

As for the divine mechanism, the associations here between a God on high and fire remind one of traditions elsewhere of a militant Yahweh flying through the sky (Deut 33:2), even "bowing the heavens and descending" as he routs his enemies (Ps 18:8–11, 13–15 [Eng 18:7–10, 12–14]//2 Sam 22:8–11, 13–15). The notion of a Yahwistic theophany causing terror (*yāhom*; Exod 14:24) among enemy troops is also found in Ps 18:15//2 Sam 22:15, where a thundering Yahweh lets loose his arrows/lightning as he terrifies (*yĕhummēm/yāhom*) his foes (so too Ps 144:5–6).[99]

Yahweh as Cosmic Warrior and Royal Legitimization

When we contextualize Yahwistic *Chaoskampf* traditions within their broader ancient Near Eastern setting, it is logical to posit that the description of Yahweh's cosmic warfare was tied to concepts of royal supremacy from the outset. It is thus not surprising that the cosmic poem in Exodus 15 ends with Yahweh reigning eternally (15:18).[100] Nor is it surprising that such mythology was appropriated for legitimizing Judean royalty.[101]

As we have noted, the primary motif running through the *Chaoskampf* traditions about Tishpak in Eshnunna, Marduk in Babylon, and Baʻlu at Ugarit was divine supremacy, and such preeminence was articulated via the language of royalty.[102] Moreover, in the telling of such myths of divine exaltation—with the Marduk story being our best example—it was the other gods of the pantheon who assign royal supremacy to the victor of the cosmic battle. This widespread motif surely forms a backdrop to Psalm 29, where we read of "divine beings" (*bĕnê ʾēlîm*) according Yahweh the divine apparel of radiance and strength (*kābôd wāʿōz*) because of his victory over the chaotic waters (*mayim rabbîm, mabbûl*) over which he sits enthroned as eternal king (*wayyēšeb yhwh melek lĕʿōlām*).[103] Psalm 97 echoes similar notions in having "all gods bow down before Yahweh" (97:7), a storm god who reigns as king (*yhwh mālāk*; 97:1) and whose "royal apparel . . . is composed of cloud, fire and lightning" (Mettinger 1982: 119; cf. Ps 97:2–6).

We have already noted how the biblical text that is most explicit in its language of a multiple-headed dragon addresses Yahweh as a king whose cosmic victories were fought in the distant past (*melek miqqedem*; Ps 74:12). Archaic passages such as Psalm 29 and Exodus 15 underscore this age-old tradition, as do Psalm 89 and Psalm 93. Frank Moore Cross (1973: 135) grouped Psalm 89:6–19 (Eng 89:5–18) and Psalm 93:1–4 together as examples of psalms coming from the early royal cult ("probably of the tenth century B.C.") whose "language is purely mythic, with no reference to the historical event at the Reed Sea remembered in Israelite tradition."

In contrast to Psalm 29—whose echoes of mythopoeic tradition resound with a time when the gods "gave" (*hābû*) Yahweh the divine trappings of radiance and strength (*kābôd wāʿōz*)—the poet of Psalm 93 asserts (using a reflexive *hitʾazzār* in 93:1) that Yahweh clothed himself with grandeur and strength (*gēʾût/ʿōz*). Of particular note is the verb used for "robing/clothing" (*lābēš*), whose Akkadian cognate (*labiš*) is also used of the gods being "clothed" with divine traits such as *melammu* radiance and *puluḫtu* awe.[104]

Yahweh is king,	*yhwh mālāk*
Robed in grandeur;	*gēʾût lābēš*
Yahweh has robed himself,	*lābēš yhwh*
Girded himself with strength.	*ʿōz hitʾazzār*
The world is established;	*ʾap-tikkôn tēbēl*
it cannot be shaken.	*bal-timmôṭ*
Your throne is established from of old;	*nākôn kisʾăkā mēʾāz*
since the distant past You have existed.	*mēʿôlām ʾāttâ*
[Back then] the rivers had lifted up, O Yahweh,	*nāśĕʾû nĕhārôt yhwh*

the rivers had lifted up their thunder,	nāśĕʾû nĕhārôt qôlām
the rivers had lifted up their roaring.	yiśĕʾû[105] nĕhārôt dokyām
Mightier than the thunder of the chaotic waters,	miqqōlôt mayim rabbîm
Mightier than the breakers of the sea	ʾaddîrîm mišbĕrê-yām
Was/is Yahweh, mighty on high.	ʾaddîr bammārôm yhwh.

(Ps 93:1–4)

Through use of the root *kwn*, the poet of Psalm 93 weds the establishment and permanence of Yahweh's throne to the establishment and permanence of the world itself. As for the two expressions (*mēʾāz*//*mēʿôlām*) designating remote antiquity in Psalm 93:2, Hans-Joachim Kraus (1989: 234) poses the probing question: "What [actually] happened in primeval time?" Kraus (building on the work of Gunkel) finds his answer in the following verse, which depicts "the waters of chaos revolt[ing] against their creator God" and where "conceptions of the myth concerning the battle against dragons and chaos come through." Once again we find multiple terms for the chaotic waters (*nĕhārôt, mayim rabbîm, yām*) that resonate with the *Chaoskampf* texts noted earlier, both at Ugarit and elsewhere in the Hebrew Bible.

Psalm 89 is one of the most complex poems in the Psalter. It may provide a clue that divine cosmic warfare appeared early in the history of ancient Israel, as it is linked to the legitimization of David and his dynasty to follow. Scholars are divided as to whether Psalm 89:6–19 (Eng 89:5–18) constitutes an archaic hymn (some even dating it to the tenth century BCE) reused by a later poet or a composition that is integral to a unified lament.[106] In its final form and functioning as a whole, Psalm 89 constitutes a late lament occasioned by the military weakness and failure of a reigning (unnamed) Davidic king. The poet makes the accusation that Yahweh is culpable for not sustaining the king in battle and bringing down his throne (89:41–45 [Eng 88:40–44])—charges predicated on steadfast promises that Yahweh had sworn to David and his lineage in the distant past (*hāriʾšōnîm*; 89:20–38, 50 [Eng 89:19–37, 49]). As a result, the royal "servant" and "anointed" of Yahweh has become the object of scorn (89:51–52 [Eng 89:50–51]).[107]

As part of his rhetoric, the poet starts by extolling Yahweh as a militant god (*yhwh ʾĕlōhê ṣĕbāʾôt*), known for his incomparable power (*mî-kāmôkā ḥăsîn yâ*), who is greatly feared (*naʿărāṣ rabbâ*//*nôrāʾ*) in the divine assembly (Ps 89:6–9 [Eng 89:5–8]).[108] As proof, the poet articulates Yahweh's cosmic victory:

The heavens praise your wonders, O Yahweh,
Your faithfulness too in the assembly of holy beings,

For who in the skies can equal Yahweh,
Can compare with Yahweh among the divine beings?

A god greatly dreaded in the council of holy beings,[109]
Held in awe by all around him?

O Yahweh, god of armies,
Who is mighty like you, O Yah?

It is *you* [*'attâ*] who rules the raging of the sea/Sea [*yām*],[110]
When its waves surge, it is *you* [*'attâ*] who calm them.
It was *you* [*'attâ*] who crushed Rahab as a carcass,[111]
With your powerful arm you scattered your enemies.

The heavens are yours, the earth too;
The world and all it holds—[112]
It was *you* [*'attâ*] who established them.

North and south—[113]
It was *you* [*'attâ*] who created them,
Tabor and Hermon joyfully shout in your name.

Yours is an arm endowed with might,
Your hand is strong;
your right hand raised high.

Righteousness and justice are the foundation of your throne,
Loyalty and fidelity go before you . . .

Indeed! Yahweh is our shield,   or: Our shield belongs to Yahweh,
The Holy One of Israel our King!   or: Our king to the Holy One of Israel.[114]
                                         (Ps 89:6–19 [Eng 89:5–18])

The section that follows, Psalm 89:20–38 (Eng 89:19–37), builds on the opening of the poem in representing one of the Hebrew Bible's strongest articulations of Judean royal ideology. The psalmist has Yahweh (speaking in first-person discourse) proclaim that he took a covenant oath to secure an enduring dynasty for David, his chosen servant (Ps 89:4–5 [Eng 89:3–4]//89:29–30, 35–38 [Eng 89:28–29, 34–37]). As Psalm 93 wedded the establishment and permanence of Yahweh's throne to the establishment and permanance of the world itself, so here the permanence of David's throne is as firm as the sun and moon.

David is described with grand terms: a warrior (*gibbôr*) upon whom Yahweh has conferred strength, a chosen hero from the army (*bāḥûr mēʿām*) whom Yahweh has exalted. He is a divine servant whom Yahweh has consecrated for battle (89:20–21 [Eng 89:19–20]). He is unstoppable in war for one undeniable reason: Yahweh's empowerment.

> Of old,[115] you spoke in a [prophetic] vision,
> to your faithful one [David] you said:[116]
>
> "I [Yahweh] have conferred power [*ʿēzer*][117] on a warrior,
> I have exalted a chosen [warrior] from the army.
>
> I have found David my servant,
> With my holy oil I have consecrated him [for battle],[118]
>
> My hand will be permanently with him,
> Yes, my arm will strengthen him.
>
> No enemy will attack him,
> No wicked one will violate him;[119]
>
> I will crush his foes before him,
> I will strike down those who hate him.
>
> My faithfulness and steadfast fidelity will be with him,
> By my name[120] will his horn be exalted." (Ps 89:20–25 [Eng 89:19–24])

A bold military climax then sounds in Psalm 89:26 (Eng 89:25):

| I [Yahweh] will set his hand on Sea, | *wĕśamtî bayyām yādô* |
| His right hand on River. | *bannĕhārôt yĕmînô* |

Though the tradition coming down to us in the MT has demoted the preternatural, chaotic waters to natural entities (*the sea*//*the rivers*), it is clear that the original lore would have made no sense if one envisioned David's military power being exercised against mere bodies of water. The scene is not one of military troops traversing watery locations in an ancient counterpart to Washington crossing the Delaware. The climax of Yahweh's empowerment of David is that the deity allows him victory over the cosmic sea, *a battle only gods can fight*. It may not be a coincidence that Yahweh also exalts David's horn (*qeren*), a common symbol of divinity. Granted, David is not being deified (discussed later). The poet clearly prefers the notion of the king being the adopted firstborn son of God (*běkôr*; Ps 89:28 [Eng 89:27]; cf. Ps 2:7; 2 Sam 7:14). Nonetheless, David as king is extra-human in that he is given the status of "most high" with respect to earthly kings (*ʿelyôn lěmalkê-ʾāreṣ*) in Psalm 89:28 (Eng 89:27), a datum certainly not lost on those who knew the traditions that celebrated Yahweh ʿElyon as the "great king over all the earth" (*melek gādôl ʿal-kol-hāʾāreṣ*; Ps 47:3 [Eng 47:2]).[121] Compare too Psalm 21:6 (Eng 21:5), where Yahweh endows the king with divine radiance (*kābôd, hôd, hādār*).[122]

Once again, an ancient Near Eastern perspective can help us understand the way in which David is being divinely empowered for cosmic warfare. The outset of this pericope claims that Yahweh's elevation of David was revealed via prophetic intermediation (*ḥāzôn*; Ps 89:20 [Eng 89:19]); this resonates with other biblical accounts (e.g., 2 Sam 7:4–17; 23:1–7). Thanks to cognate material (especially Mari and Neo-Assyrian texts), we learn of the ubiquitous presence of prophetic intermediation for legitimating monarchs.[123] For example, the military success of the Neo-Assyrian king Esarhaddon was ensured by the gods, who constantly sent oracles promising that they would annihilate his foes.[124] Earlier still is the prophetic revelation to the Mari king Zimri-Lim where Adad of Aleppo asserted (via the *apilu* Abiya) that thanks to his weapons the king would never meet his equal:

> I [Adad] restored you [Zimri-Lim] to the th[rone of your father's house], and the weapons with which I fought Sea I handed you [*kakkī ša itti têmtim amtahṣu addinakkum*]. I anointed you with the oil of my luminosity, nobody will offer resistance to you.[125]

Just as this prophetic text from Mari references *Chaoskampf* traditions to underscore Zimri-Lim's prowess in battle, so Psalm 89:26 (Eng 89:25) echoes similar legitimization for David.[126] The notion of mortals being divinely empowered is nothing new, as we have seen with Moses' outstretched hand being Yahweh's incorporeal hand in action and with Moses' rod being at the same time the deity's rod.[127] Ezekiel 30:24–25 will even have Nebuchadnezzar wielding Yahweh's sword, and Isaiah 10:5 will turn Assyria into the rod itself. Yet the reference to battling Sea//River in Psalm 89:26 (Eng 89:25) neatly ties the legitimization of Davidic royal ideology to the *Chaoskampf* traditions mentioned earlier in the poem (Ps 89:6–19 [Eng 89:5–18]; cf. esp. Dumortier 1972). Compare too the poem in 2 Samuel 22:35//Psalm 18:35 that has David praising Yahweh for training his hands for war (*mělammēd yāday lammilḥāmâ*) such that he is skilled at archery.

Before leaving the connection between *Chaoskampf* traditions and Judean royal ideology, we need to revisit Psalm 24. In the discussion in Chapter Seven, p. 396, it was noted that this poem is likely a liturgy of divine entry into the temple via the Ark. Because the ritual was located in Jerusalem and celebrated divine kingship, it is likely that it was associated with the royal cult. Cross (1973: 91–99) has gone further to suggest that Psalm 24:7–10 is a liturgical fragment that reenacts Yahweh's *Chaoskampf* victory, which culminated in the warrior god's enthronement "in his newly built (cosmic) temple," in a way similar to what we find in the Ugaritic Ba'lu myth and Enuma Elish.

Lift up your heads, O gates	śĕ'û šĕ'ārîm rā'šêkem
Lift yourselves up, O ancient doors!	hinnāśĕ'û pitḥê 'ôlām
The King of Radiance enters!	yābô' melek hakkābôd
Who is this Radiant King?	mî zeh melek hakkābôd
Yahweh mighty and valiant!	yhwh 'izzûz wĕgibbôr
Yahweh valiant in war!	yhwh gibbôr milḥāmâ
Lift up your heads, O gates	śĕ'û šĕ'ārîm rā'šêkem
Lift yourselves up, O ancient doors!	śĕ'û [hinnāśĕ'û?] pitḥê 'ôlām
The King of Radiance enters!	yābô' melek hakkābôd
Who is this Radiant King?	mî hû' zeh melek hakkābôd
Yahweh of Armies	yhwh ṣĕbā'ôt
He is the Radiant King!	hû' melek hakkābôd
	(Ps 24:7–10)

Of special note is the commandment given to the personified temple gates to lift their heads, an "odd" and "bizarre" metaphor according to Cross (1973: 97–99). Cross suggests that what we have here is a demythologized command that was once addressed to the divine council as they hailed the return of their warrior king from battle. In support Cross notes the nearly identical wording found in the Ugaritic Ba'lu myth. There the gods of the divine assembly were panicked at the advent of chaotic Yammu, and they bowed their heads on their knees in fear (KTU 1.2.1.20–24).[128] Ba'lu the warrior (and eventual victor over Yammu) rebuked them for so doing and commanded them: "Lift up your heads, O gods!" (š'u 'ilm r'aštkm; KTU 1.2.1.27).[129]

If Cross is correct, we would have another remnant of mythopoeic Canaanite lore residing here in mythopoetic dress. The artistry of the author is not to be missed. Even as our poet reduces the gods to animate objects (cf. Deut 7:12–13; 28:4, 18, 51), he at the same time exalts Yahweh's "radiance" (*kābôd*), an attribute that our divine king achieved through war (*gibbôr milḥāmâ*).[130] To judge from the similar *kābôd* terminology in Psalm 29 (itself filled with Canaanite mythic combat and concluding with divine kingship), the war our poet has in mind was certainly cosmic.[131] Lastly, if the entry ritual of Psalm 24:7–10 did indeed form a part of the royal cult, then we have yet another example of the prestige of the divine king's *Chaoskampf* mythology rubbing off on the human king. (See Chapter Nine on Yahweh as king.)

Yahweh Swallows up Death Forever (Isaiah 25:8)
As we have demonstrated, biblical authors used Canaanite *Chaoskampf* traditions in various ways. Yet there was one biblical poet who stands out for providing a unique twist. This author of the so-called Isaianic Apocalypse (Isa 24–27) is very conversant with *Chaoskampf* traditions. We have already looked at his artistry in describing Yahweh's eschatological victory over the creature who churns the sea (Isa 27:1; see p. 446).

To set the backdrop, one needs to look briefly at a negative protagonist we have glossed over in our survey of chaotic waters and the seven-headed dragons that lived therein. At Late Bronze Age Ugarit, the Baʿlu myth's final episode climaxed with the god Motu (Death) swallowing Baʿlu and with him the forces of nature. Sterility reigned until Baʿlu achieved final victory (together with a dissection of Motu by the goddess ʿAnatu). The depiction of the monster Motu has him wielding two scepters that befit the god of death:

In one hand a scepter of bereavement,	bdh ḥṭ ṯkl
In the other hand a scepter of widowhood.	bdh ḥṭ ʾulmn
	(KTU 1.23.8–9)[132]

As death comes to all, so Motu's appetite is insatiable; he ravenously eats with both his hands (*bkl<ʾa>t ydy ʾilḥm*; KTU 1.5.1.19–20).

When Baʿlu sends messengers to Motu he instructs them about the danger of getting to close to Motu "lest he put you in his mouth like a lamb, crush you like a kid in his jaws" (KTU 1.4.8.17–20). Later in the story we find a description of Baʿlu's descent into the very throat of Death, whose voracious appetite is described in graphic detail:

[One lip to the e]arth [underworld?],	[špt lʾa]rṣ špt lšmm
one lip to heaven,	
[Motu] [stretches out his] tongue to the stars.	[yʾark l]šn lkbkbm
Baʿlu enters his innards,	yʿrb bʿl bkbdh
He descends into his mouth . . .	bph yrd . . .
	(KTU 1.5.2.2–4)[133]

In the Hebrew Bible it is hard to deny the presence of a personified Death, *māwet/ mōt* (cf. Lewis 1992b). The vocabulary used to describe ravenous Death's (and Sheol's) insatiable appetite in Habakkuk 2:5, Job 18:13–14, and Isaiah 5:4 is remarkably reminiscent of Motu's greedy appetite in KTU 1.5.1.19–20; 1.5.2.2–4.[134] In light of the descriptions of Mot's (and Sheol's) voracious hunger, which include imagery of swallowing victims whole, it is quite significant to find Yahweh swallowing Death/Mot (*billaʿ hammāwet*) in Isaiah 25:8.[135] Our gifted poet turns the mythological tables with the turn of a phrase: he who swallows now becomes swallowed. Lastly, this once-and-for-all victory (*billaʿ hammāwet lāneṣaḥ*) provides a discernible contrast with the recurrent conflict that we read in the agrarian Baʿlu myth.

Using a theoretical approach, one could again employ Rudolph Otto's categories of *fascinans* and *tremendum* to describe the human fascination with and overwhelming fear of death, especially personified and/or mythologized Death.[136] Even the mighty god Baʿlu is afraid of Motu (KTU 1.5.2.6–7). In contrast, even though biblical poets describe Death as "the King of Terrors" (*melek ballāhôt*; Job 18:14), Yahweh never stands in fear of him.[137]

Yahweh as Divine Warrior in Non-Cosmic Battles

The Hebrew Bible gives ample evidence of Yahweh being perceived as a divine warrior not only wresting victory from chaotic and cosmic forces but also triumphing in the human arena. Explicitly or implicitly (but mostly explicitly), Yahweh is the empowering force behind almost every military victory mentioned in the Bible—from Abraham's battle against the four eastern kings (Gen 14:19–20) to Zechariah's apocalyptic war "on that [future] day" when "Yahweh will go forth and fight against nations as when he fights on a day of battle" (Zech 14:1–21). When we read accounts of humans in battle without any mention of Yahweh, typically the humans suffer defeat (e.g., 1 Sam 31:1–13; 2 Sam 1:17–27; contrast 2 Sam 5:17–25). For biblical authors, the Sennacheribs of the world—even with their myriads of troops—are no match for Yahweh (Isa 37:36//2 Kgs 19:35).

There is no need to rehearse the self-evident ways in which Yahweh is portrayed as a divine warrior affecting human battles. Yet it should be noted that these military stories are nuanced in two different ways. Some streams of tradition have Yahweh commanding, authorizing, and empowering human efforts in war, even giving tactical orders. Other streams of tradition stress the efficacy of Yahweh alone. These traditions emphasize divine power to the exclusion of human efforts. Human agency is not needed nor desired. The necessity of human military endeavors is to be replaced by a trust in Yahweh alone as the warrior who will bring victory. These differing streams of tradition are age-old, as shown by two of our earliest texts. Exodus 15 demonstrates how "the victory was total—and totally Yahweh's.... Israel contributed nothing then or later."[138] In contrast, the Israelite combatants in Judges 5:2, 9 "offered themselves willingly" to fight, coming "to the assistance of Yahweh among [his] mighty warriors."[139] The Deuteronomist twice proclaims how David fights Yahweh's battles (1 Sam 18:17; 25:28).

The Synergism of Human and Divine War (Ḥērem Warfare)

The streams of tradition that describe Yahweh as a warrior deity who commands military endeavors by his followers is best known through the various texts describing *ḥērem* warfare, often described as "holy war."[140] *Ḥērem* warfare is cultic warfare in that it has to do with the utter destruction of an enemy at the behest of a deity to whom all booty is consecrated (or "devoted"). The cultic character of war is demonstrated throughout the Hebrew Bible. I will restrict my treatment, for the most part, to military narratives or codes in the book of Deuteronomy and the Deuteronomistic History.[141]

That *ḥērem* warfare was thought to constitute sacral activity is supported by the broader Near Eastern context.[142] At Late Bronze Age Ugarit, *ḥrm* warfare is associated with the goddess 'Anatu (KTU 1.13.3–7), the most capable of warriors, whose other battles include *Chaoskampf* traditions as well as extreme bloodletting (KTU 1.3.2.3–41).[143] It is not a happenstance that the warrior judge Shamgar is called "son of Anat" (either a patronymic or an honorific military title)[144] in Judges 3:31 and 5:6, nor that 'Anat's name is also found on three inscribed bronze arrowheads.[145] Closer chronologically and geographically is the ninth-century BCE Mesha stela (see Figure 6.4). Here, as with the biblical material, *ḥērem* warfare is undertaken at the behest of the deity, in this case Chemosh. The utter destruction is described in words that dovetail with biblical *ḥērem* traditions (only here the Moabite king has the Israelite locale of Nebo in his crosshairs):

> Chemosh said to me: "Go! Seize Nebo against Israel." [So] I went at night and fought against it from the break of dawn until midd[ay]. I s[ei]zed it and killed all [of it]: 7,000 [men, bo]ys, women, [girl]s, and female slaves, because I had devoted it [hḥrmth] to Ashtar-Chemosh. I took the [ve]ssels of Yahweh, and I drag[ged] them [as booty] before Chemosh. (Mesha Inscription lines 14–18)[146]

In 2007, Lauren Monroe reanalyzed the Sabaean text RES 3945 and argued for its relevance to biblical *ḥērem* warfare. This text mentions the devoting the city of Nashan to the *ḥrm* by burning (cf. lines 7, 16), as a consecration for the national Sabaean moon god Almaqah. Another early Sabaean text, DAI Ṣirwāḥ 2005-50, also describes the complete *ḥrm* destruction of multiple cities by fire.[147]

From the biblical data (which are buttressed by extra-biblical support) we see how these wars were thought to be sacred activities. Yahweh the divine warrior is fully involved in working synergistically with Israelite troops who have "boots on the ground" at every stage. The commander of Yahweh's army (śar-ṣĕbā'-yhwh) arrives with drawn sword prior to the famous battle at Jericho (Josh 5:13-15). Yahweh then gives tactical (and ritual) orders to Joshua and his army, an army that includes seven priests (kōhănîm) who appear repeatedly in the narrative as central actors (Josh 6:4, 6, 8, 9, 12, 13, 16). Indeed, the priests bear Israel's paramount weapon, the Ark of Yahweh, and it is their horn blast that is tied to bringing down the city walls (cf. Num 10:9; 2 Chr 13:14-15). The ritualistic seven days of the battle culminating in a sevenfold circuit (Josh 6:15) can represent "the sacred time of a military campaign undertaken by divine command" (Fleming 1999b: 213; Klingbeil 2007: 168-169). Yahweh is present in battle from beginning to end, either explicitly (through mention of the commander and the Ark)[148] or implicitly (the miraculous power that fells the city walls). Joshua proclaims to the army prior to their victory shout that "Yahweh has given you the city" (Josh 6:16). After the walls come crumbling down through no physical effort, the human army, working synergistically with Yahweh, takes the city and then engages in carrying out the ḥērem (Josh 6:20-21). As for the booty of precious metals, it is "consecrated to Yahweh" (qōdeš hû' layhwh) and taken into "the treasury of the sanctuary of Yahweh" ('ôṣar bêt-yhwh; Josh 6:24; cf. 6:19; 2 Sam 8:11).[149] Similar accounts of exclusive reservation and consecration of booty occur in other ḥērem texts, including the so-called private ḥērem mentioned in Leviticus 27:28-29:

> But of all that anyone owns, be it a person or animal or field of his holding, everything that a person declares as ḥērem for Yahweh [ḥērem 'ăšer yaḥărim 'îš layhwh], it cannot be sold or redeemed; every ḥērem is totally consecrated [lit. "holy of holies"] to Yahweh [qōdeš-qodāšîm hû' layhwh].[150]

The cultic character of Yahwistic wars can be fleshed out further. When we look to material culture, the fortress temple at Arad is our best-preserved example of a Yahwistic sanctuary serving the needs of the military, especially between the ninth and eighth centuries BCE.[151] In addition to the inner sanctum with its standing stones (see Chapter Five, pp. 183-187), we also have two nearby incense stands, a sacrificial altar made of unhewn fieldstones (cf. Exod 20:22 [Eng 20:25]; Deut 27:5-6), various votive objects, and two bowls with inscriptions referring either to a priesthood (reading q-k, an abbreviation for q[ōdeš] k[ōhănîm], "holy objects of priests") or to their sacred character (reading q-š, an abbreviation for qdš, "holy").[152]

As for additional textual material, ancient Near Eastern prophetic texts as well as many biblical accounts (e.g., 1 Sam 30:7–8, Judg 6:36–40; 7:13; 18:5; 20:9; 20:27–28; 1 Kgs 22:5ff.) give evidence of how divination and oracles (priestly and prophetic) were sought to determine whether one should go to battle in the first place.[153] Priests are described as presenting an exhortation of divine assistance at the outset of the campaign (Deut 20:1–4), and elsewhere troops are charged to "consecrate themselves for war" (*hitqaddāšû*, Josh 3:5; *qaddĕšû ʿālêhā milḥāmâ*, Jer 6:4; cf. Joel 4:9 [Eng 3:9]). Weapons were rubbed with oil for functionality but perhaps also for cultic anointing (2 Sam 1:21; Isa 21:5; cf. 1 Sam 21:6, 10 [Eng 21:5. 9]).[154] The military encampment itself was required to adhere to purity laws precisely because "Yahweh your God walks about in your camp" (*kî yhwh ʾĕlōhêkā mithallēk bĕqereb maḥănekā*), a reference to Yahweh being embedded with the troops as they march to battle (Deut 20:4; 23:15 [Eng 23:14]). Thus the camp must be holy (*qādôš*) lest God see any indecency and turn away (Deut 23:15 [Eng 23:14]). Additional codes of conduct require leaving the camp after nocturnal emissions and some degree of sexual abstinence during times of war (Deut 23:11–12; 1 Sam 21:6 [Eng 21:5], 2 Sam 11:11), and in certain cases abstaining from tonsure rituals (Judg 5:2; cf. Judg 13–16).[155] Lastly, though accounts are rare, after battles military hardware could be placed in sanctuaries for commemoration and/or veneration (1 Sam 21:10 [Eng 21:9]; 1 Sam 31:10).

Not to be forgotten are the stories of warrior judges who were thought to be "clothed" (*lābēš*; Judg 6:34) with the vitalizing force (*rûaḥ*) of Yahweh. For Samson, the *rûaḥ* of Yahweh "rushed upon" (√*ṣlḥ*) him in such a way as to empower him with extraordinary strength (Judg 14:6, 19; 15:14). A "rushing spirit" will also grip Saul, then later leave him and descend upon David (1 Sam 10:6, 10; 11:6; 16:13–14).[156] Given the cultic nature of holy war, it comes as no surprise to read stories of war in conjunction with the building of cult places (Josh 8:30–31; Mesha Inscription, line 3; RES 3945, line 16)[157] or of war combined with intercessory prayer, fasting, and sacrifice (e.g., Judg 20:26; 1 Sam 7:5–11; 13:9, 12).

Minimizing Human Involvement: The Ideology of the Underdog

Judean writers would be the first to assure us that the victories resulting from these synergistic battles were achieved by Yahweh. Throughout our stories, the divine empowerment of human troops is described explicitly and implicitly. Yet other streams of tradition wanted to erase all doubt about the efficacy of Yahweh and his direct action by either minimizing human involvement or erasing it altogether. And once again, such ideology is attested from our earliest texts (e.g., Exod 15) to our latest texts (e.g., Zech 4:6), especially including (proto-)apocalyptic literature (Ezek 38–39; Zech 14:1–5; Dan 7:13–14).

The most famous story that describes the limiting of human troops in order to emphasize divine victory comes again from the Deuteronomistic History.

The tale found in Judges 7 is famous for twice reducing the number of Gideon's military forces (from 32,000 to 10,000, and then to 300) that were to face the already overwhelming 135,000 Midianite troops (Judg 8:10). The reason given is explicit: "lest Israel claim for themselves the glory [*yitpā'ēr*] due to [Yahweh]" by asserting that they achieved military victory through their own machinations (Judg 7:2). With the odds set outlandishly against them (450 to 1), only Yahweh could receive the glory. A similar notion is found elsewhere in the Deuteronomistic History when we read of Jonathan instructing his armor bearer that "nothing can hinder Yahweh from a military conquest, by many *or by few*" (*mĕ'āṭ*; 1 Sam 14:6). To prove the point, the narrative has the two lonely underdogs defeat ten times as many Philistine solders.[158] The panic (*ḥărādâ*) that results throughout the Philistine garrison—together with the earth quaking—is divinely caused (*ḥerĕdat 'ĕlōhîm*; 1 Sam 14:15). P. Kyle McCarter (1980a: 239) notes how such a tradition lived on in the history of the Maccabees, where we "read almost like a midrash" the following comment: "And Judas [Maccabaeus] said: 'It is easy for many to be overpowered by a few; nor is it different before Heaven to save by many or by few! For not on the size of the army does victory in battle depend: rather it is from Heaven that strength comes!'" (1 Macc 3:18–19).

As for Yahweh supporting the lone underdog, no story was more popular than that of courageous David with his sling going up against the heavily armed giant Goliath.

> Then David said to the Philistine, "You come against me with sword, spear and scimitar; but I come against you with the Name of Yahweh of Armies,[159] the God of the ranks of Israel, whom you have defied. This day Yahweh will deliver you into my hand . . . that all the earth may know that there is a god in Israel, and that this whole assembly may know that it is not by sword or spear that Yahweh gives victory! For the battle is Yahweh's and he will hand you over to us." (1 Sam 17:45–47)

McCarter (1980a: 297) notes the symbolism of the story—how "David, small, apparently defenseless, with none of the bearing or equipment of a trained soldier," is "the perfect personification of the tiny nation of Judah." David, of course, strikes down the mighty Goliath and cuts off his head (1 Sam 17:46, 50–51).[160] Nonetheless, Millard Lind (1980: 106), writing from a pacifist tradition, argues that David's speech here "states well the theology of Israelite warfare . . . Although Israel fought, Yahweh did not save with, by, or through Israel's sword or spear." Such notions are echoed in Psalm 44:4 (Eng 44:3) and in the divine speech to Zerubbabel: "Not by might, nor by power, but by my Spirit, says the Yahweh of Armies" (Zech 4:6). The enduring legacy of such teaching, providing hope for the marginalized as it warns against relying on humans alone, can be illustrated by the choice of Zechariah 4:6 for the Haftarah for the First Shabbat of Hanukkah.

Here the rabbis were intentional about minimizing the role of Maccabean military activism in deference to divine deliverance.[161]

Yahweh Alone in Battle

For yet other true believers, it was not enough to say that underdog Israel—with Yahweh's divine assistance—came through the toughest of battles despite overwhelming odds. Instead they emphasized traditions such as those we find in Exodus 14:14 (Yahweh fighting at the Reed Sea) or 2 Chronicles 20:15–17 (Yahweh speaking to King Jehoshaphat) that underscore that Yahweh's people need only sit still (√ḥrš) and watch as Yahweh fights on their behalf.

> Fear not, and be not dismayed at this great multitude; for the battle is not yours but God's [kî lōʾ lākem hammilḥāmâ kî lēʾlōhîm]. . . . You will not need to fight in this battle [lōʾ lākem lĕhillāḥēm]; take your position, stand still, and see the victory of the Yahweh on your behalf, O Judah and Jerusalem. (2 Chr 20:15–17)

Nissinen (2008: 185, 189) has shown how similar notions can be found in the Neo-Assyrian inscriptions of Esarhaddon and Aššurbanipal, where the goddess Ishtar admonishes the kings to trust in her ability to fight wars on their behalf: "Do not trust in humans! Lift up your eyes and focus on me! I am Ishtar of Arbela."[162]

2 Kings 6:15–23 records a poignant story in which the prophet Elisha tells his fearful attendant that he need not be afraid of the overwhelming Aramean army surrounding the city, as Yahweh has so many invisible (preternatural) troops lining the hills that the numbers are actually in their favor (2 Kgs 6:16). That the lowly servant ultimately "sees" the heavenly host whereas the powerful enemy is subdued through being "blinded" is a literary gem.

The prophet Isaiah consistently argued that Judah should not join international coalitions that trust in military hardware rather than divine providence (e.g., Isa 7; 19–20; 30:1–7; 31:1–3). The ruling Judean monarchs both accepted and rejected such advice. During the Syro-Ephraimite war (ca. 733 BCE), King Ahaz did not join the anti-Assyrian coalition, aligning himself instead with Tiglath-Pileser III rather than embracing Isaiah's theocentric idealism. And initially King Hezekiah kept a policy of compliance with Assyria. For example, in 714 BCE he did not join the revolt by the Philistines (under King Azuri of Ashdod) and the Egyptians (under the Cushite Shabaka), perhaps because of Isaiah's advice (Isa 20:6). Yet Hezekiah, the realist, did join an anti-Assyrian alliance after the death of Sargon II in 705 BCE. By so doing he brought upon Judah the wrath and visitation of King Sennacherib, whose punishing western campaign in the Levant in 701 BCE is well known, especially from the archaeological remains of the destruction of Lachish and its portrayal in iconography. Hezekiah's humiliating acquiescence is known from biblical and Assyrian sources, as is the substantial amount of tribute he was forced to pay.[163]

We will never know what actually happened in 701 BCE when, according to biblical tradition, Sennacherib turned away from Judah.[164] Scholars have suggested that his retreat was the result of a plague or a disease among his troops, and/or the security preparations of Hezekiah. The biblical portrayal of the defeat of Sennacherib's armies (in 2 Kgs 19:32–38 and Isa 37:33–38) has Yahweh proclaim that *he* "will defend Jerusalem to save it" and that Sennacherib would not shoot a single arrow. The defeat itself is described as a miraculous killing of Assyrian troops via the *mal'ak*-Yahweh. As Nahum Sarna (1999: 50) aptly notes, "By definition, miracles are outside the historians' ken."

The Zion Traditions: The Inviolability of Zion/Jerusalem
Scholars have looked to these events of 701 BCE as a backdrop to what they have termed "the inviolability of Jerusalem," the notion that Jerusalem is unassailable by even the mightiest army thanks to divine presence and protection. Micah, a strong critic, provides us with the poetic sound bite that encapsulates such thinking:

| Is not Yahweh in our midst; | *hălô' yhwh běqirbēnû* |
| Disaster will not overtake us. | *lō'-tābô' 'ālênû rā'â* |

Such an ideology is found in certain Zion hymns (e.g., Ps 46, 48, 76) and various Isaianic traditions (Isa 10:27b–34; 14:24–27, 32; 17:12–14; 28:16; 29:1–7; 30:27–33; 31:1–8; 33:17–24).[165] Other voices strongly dissent (Mic 3:12; Jer 26:17–19; Isa 1:21–26; 5:14; 10:5–11). The Judean traditions that fostered the notion of Jerusalem's inviolability blended notions of Yahweh alone fighting on behalf of his people with the unique status of Zion/Jerusalem as "the city of God" (Ps 46:5; 48:2, 9; 76:3 [Eng 46:4; 48:1, 8; 76:2]). Zion was the city of Yahweh of Armies, the city of the great king (Ps 48:3, 9 [Eng 48:2, 8]). It was his beautiful, holy mountain (Ps 48:2–3 [Eng 48:1–2]); it was "the joy of all the earth" (Ps 48:3 [Eng 48:2]) that Yahweh loved (Ps 78:68). Zion was Yahweh's holy dwelling place (Ps 46:5; 76:3 [Eng 46:4; 76:2]). It was the abode that Yahweh himself founded securely, stone by stone (*'eben 'eben*), such that it was "exceedingly firm" (*mûsād mûssād*; Isa 14:32; 28:16).

Nonetheless, the threat (real and perceived) posed by "the nations" was a considerable one, especially during the Neo-Assyrian empire and in subsequent days leading to the Babylonian destruction of Jerusalem. The threat lived on into later apocalyptic thought, when multiple authors recast preexisting hymns about the inviolability of Jerusalem. The poet of Isaiah 17:12–13a (who yields no clear historical indicators)[166] describes the palpable threat as follows:

> Ah, the roar of many peoples
> Who roar as does the sea,
> The raging of nations who rage
> As the raging of mighty waters—
> Nations raging like many waters rage!

Yet the Zion traditions were more than equal to the challenge, asserting that Yahweh was in the midst of Jerusalem (Ps 46:6, 8, 12 [Eng 46:5, 7, 11]) as her helper (Ps 46:2, 6 [Eng 46:1, 5]), her refuge (Ps 46:2, 8, 12; 48:4 [Eng 46:1, 7, 11; 48:3]), and her strength (Ps 46:2 [Eng 46:1]). At one point Isaiah 31:4–5 declares that Yahweh of Armies will descend to wage war upon Mt. Zion, hovering like a bird to shield, deliver, protect, and rescue Jerusalem (cf. Deut 32:11). Yet another image has Yahweh possessing a fire and oven in Zion (Isa 31:9). While this imagery could echo the notion of Yahweh taking up residence in Jerusalem, Hans Wildberger (2002: 228) rightly notes the consuming nature of divine fire (see Chapter Seven, pp. 353, 369–371, 424).

As for the battle proper, the Zion traditions have Yahweh acting alone. Any mention of human initiative is disparaged as non-belief (Isa 31:1–2; cf. 30:15–16). When there is mention of a sword, the poet accentuates that it was not wielded by a human (Isa 31:8). The Isaianic Zion traditions make use of several visual images, from Yahweh as a logger felling trees (Isa 10:33–34; cf. 37:24) to Yahweh as a lion fighting on Mt. Zion (Isa 31:4).[167] Chief among the portraits is Yahweh as storm god who comes with thunder, earthquakes, whirlwinds, tempests, downpours, hailstones, and raging torrents combined with blazing wrath and devouring fire (Isa 29:6; 30:27–33; cf. 17:12–13).[168] Yahweh forcibly disarms the nations (Ps 46:10; 76:4–7 [Eng 46:9; 76:3–6]) and puts a stop to wars throughout the earth (Ps 46:10 [Eng 46:9]; cf. Isa 2:4; 11:6–9).[169]

Due to the "very present" (*nimṣā' mĕ'ōd*) divine assistance, Judah is to fear not, to simply relax (*harpû*) in the knowledge of Yahweh's military prowess (Ps 46:2–3, 11 [Eng 46:1–2, 10]).[170] Isaiah 30:15 has Yahweh admonishing his people with counterintuitive words:

> By returning [to Yahweh] and quietness will you be delivered,
> in quietness and trust [in Yahweh] lies your strength.[171]

Appropriately, when "terrifying" Yahweh rises to execute judgment and girds himself with fury, the land is "quieted" with fright (Ps 76:8–11 [Eng 76:7–10]).

The once aggressive nations are now panic-stricken and take flight (Ps 48:6–7 [Eng 48:5–6]; Isa 17:13). At Yahweh's blast (*gaʿărâ*), even the most stouthearted soldiers lie stunned (together with their horses) as if in a sleepy stupor, unable to even use (lit. "find") their hands (Ps 76:6–7 [Eng 76:5–6]).[172]

It is little wonder then that such potent rhetoric led to the notion that Zion "shall not be moved" (Ps 46:6 [Eng 46:5]), especially when reinforced by the historical realities of Sennacherib's departure from what had looked like the sure defeat of Jerusalem. Psalm 48:9 [Eng 48:8]) says as much: "The likes of what we heard we have now witnessed in the city of Yahweh of Armies, in the city of our god. Yahweh has established [will establish] it forever!"[173] The psalmist goes on to urge the reader to engage in an empirical tallying to prove his case by walking around Zion and counting its many towers, ramparts, and citadels (Ps 48:13–14 [Eng 48:12–13]; cf. 48:4 [Eng 48:3]) that had not fallen to the enemy (e.g., Sennacherib) despite overwhelming odds. The psalmist's faith-based conclusion lived on (again using Micah's encapsulation):

Is not Yahweh in our midst,	*hălōʾ yhwh bĕqirbēnû*
Disaster will not overtake us.	*lōʾ-tābôʾ ʿālênû rāʿâ*

Obviously, the "inviolability of Jerusalem" ideology came crashing to the ground with the destruction of the Jerusalem Temple in 586 BCE. At that time, prophets like Ezekiel presented a theodicy to depict Yahweh's willful departure ahead of the destruction together with a narrative of how a polluted temple could no longer house its protective holy deity. Yet it should be noted that even prior to the destruction of Jerusalem, there were already voices articulating that the election of Zion was no guarantee of security if the people of God were unfaithful in seeking holiness and justice (e.g., Isa 1:16–20; Mic 3:9–12; Jer 7:1–15; 26:4–6).

Lastly, just because Yahweh battles the nations by himself in the Zion traditions, with no hint of a human Davidide wielding Yahweh's power (contrast Ps 89:26 [Eng 89:25]), it does not mean that such hymns had no relation to royal power. Miller (2010: 228–229) argues that Zion's symbolic connection to Yahweh's kingship (Ps 48:3 [Eng 48:2]; 84:4 [Eng 84:3]) "consequently raises human kingship to symbolic dimensions." The symbolic universes of the Zion traditions "establish power and order to keep chaos at bay" in such a way as to "support the established political and cultic hierarchies as immutable institutions" (Miller 2010: 230–233).

Apocalyptic Battles

Where the notion of "divine providence alone in battle" finds its fullest expression is in (proto-)apocalyptic thought. Here there is no synergistic fighting whereby Yahweh empowers his human troops on the ground. In these texts, marginalized and oppressed peoples place no hope in an earthly fighting force. Poets yearn for divine intervention where Yahweh alone "rends the heavens and comes down" such that "mountains quake at His presence" (Isa 64:1). It is Yahweh alone who can shake the earth, darken the sun, and turn the moon to blood with the advent of his "greatly terrifying day" (*yôm-yhwh nôrā' mě'ōd/yôm yhwh haggādôl wěhannôrā'*; Joel 2:10–11; 3:3–4 [Eng 2:30–31]).

The apocalyptic narrative in Ezekiel 38–39 is filled with military hardware, but only belonging to the enemies against whom Yahweh fights. There is detailed mention of the enemy's military strategies (Ezek 38:11–13) as well as their armies, horses, horsemen, armor, and wide variety of weapons (Ezek 38:4, 15; 39:3). Indeed, their weapons are so numerous that upon their defeat they will serve as Israel's fuel source for seven years (Ezek 39:9–10)! In stark contrast, the only mention of Israel has the people dwelling quietly and securely without the need for walls, bars, and gates (*haššōqěṭîm yōšěbê lābeṭaḥ*; 38:8, 11, 14; cf. Zech 2:4–5). Not a single word is needed to depict Israel's military hardware or even their defense system because this is solely Yahweh's war. Yahweh's arsenal includes his wrath, sword (terror?), torrential rains, hailstones, fire, and brimstone (38:18, 21–22).[174] With the language of a hand-to-hand combatant, Yahweh declares about Gog: "I will strike your bow from your left hand//I will make your arrows drop out of your right hand" (Ezek 39:3). Such chaotic battles against the nations, cast into the eschatological future, are well known (e.g., Jer 25:31; Isa 66:15–16) and provided fertile ground for recapitulating the age-old *Chaoskampf* scenes, as noted in the description of Isaiah 27:1 (see p. 446).

War and Peace

Let us end this short military survey with two polar views on divine warfare and its aftermath—one of bloodletting, the other of inspirational peacemaking. The former comes from two passages in Third Isaiah (Isa 59; 63:1–6) where the poet twice emphasizes the lack of human agency in fighting evil such that Yahweh's own arm must achieve military victory (Isa 59:16; 63:5).[175] In Blenkinsopp's (2003: 250) words, "The author has definitely abandoned the expectations placed on Cyrus in Isa 40–48." What we have here "marks a turning away from the historical arena . . . [coming] a step closer to embracing an apocalyptic world view."

The broader context describes people rushing to evil as they shed innocent blood (Isa 59:3, 7). "Justice is turned back//righteousness stands at a distance// for truth stumbles in the public square//uprightness finds no entry" (59:14). In response Yahweh the warrior directly intervenes by putting on his armor, which consists of righteousness as a coat of mail and triumph as a helmet. Yet he is also clothed in garments of *nāqām* (retribution/vengeance) and fury (*bigdê nāqām// mě'îl qin'â*; Isa 59:17).[176] In his return from battle, marching from Edom, Yahweh is radiant in attire (*hādûr bilĕbûšô*).[177] Shockingly, in one of the Hebrew Bible's most vivid portrayals, his garments are turned red, stained with blood (Isa 63:1-3; cf. Isa 34:2-10; Deut 32:41-42). This dramatic depiction has been compared to ʿAnatu's bloodletting frenzy or the obligation of blood revenge associated with tribal groups.[178] In a passage where overall "blood is the dominant motif" (Blenkinsopp 2003: 250), Yahweh declares:

> My own arm wrought me the victory,
> My fury—it upheld me.
>
> I trampled peoples in my anger,
> I made them drunk with my fury,
> I hurled their lifeblood to the ground.

Condemnation oracles such as what we find in Nahum 3:1-18 (against "the bloody city" of Nineveh) reveal that such raw, militant language against one's enemies stirred the hearts of the oppressed who suffered from heinous violence.[179] Using agrarian images, Micah 4:11-13 commands Daughter Zion to "arise and thresh" the nations whom Yahweh has gathered as sheaves. Pulverizing with her "iron horn and bronze hooves," she will present *ḥērem* booty to Yahweh. Joel 4:9-16 (Eng 3:9-16) is similarly militant, deploying troops to a war of such proportions that even agricultural implements (plow tips and pruning tools) will be beaten into swords and spears.[180] The result—the harvesting of the nations via a sickle during the Day of Yahweh—remains the same. Such prophetic speech does not stand alone. A wide variety of literary genres were employed to give voice to the emotions of the oppressed, including imprecations (e.g., Ps 137:7-9, Ps 79:10-12, Obad 11-16), curses (cf. 1 Sam 14:24), curse rituals (Deut 27:19), sympathetic magic (Jer 51:59-64), and execrations texts (cf. Jer 19:1-11; Amos 1:2-2:16).

A Different Type of Rhetoric: Swords into Plowshares

Lest we forget in examining the pervasive portrayals of Yahweh as divine warrior, ancient Israel had (and preserved) a plurality of voices. Remarkably, we even come across juxtaposed similes saying in a single breath that Yahweh is *both* "like a warrior" *and* "like a woman giving birth" (Isa 42:13-14). The portrayal of Yahweh as a compassionate family god will be explored shortly. Yet already within the prophetic speeches of Isaiah and Micah we come across a different type of rhetoric, that of disarmament. The power of this rhetoric (opposed to the rhetoric of power) has lived beyond the Iron Age to appear inscribed at the United Nations Headquarters in New York City and incarnated within the nearby bronze sculpture by Evgeniy Vuchetich.[181]

Rather than using agrarian images of threshing and harvesting one's foes, the famous "plowshares" passage presents the most idyllic of scenarios. That the nearly identical poem is found twice (Isa 2:2–4//Mic 4:1–3) attests to its popularity, as does the fact that a later author played off its themes (Joel 4:9–16 [Eng 3:9–16]).[182]

> In the latter days to come,
> The mount of Yahweh's temple shall be established
> above the mountains; it will tower above the hills.
>
> All the nations will stream to it,
> Many peoples shall go and say:
>
> "Come, let us go up to the mount of Yahweh,
> To the temple of the God of Jacob;
>
> That He may teach us of His ways,
> that we may walk in His paths."
>
> For instruction shall issue from Zion,
> Yahweh's word from Jerusalem.
>
> Thus [Yahweh] will judge [šāpaṭ] among the nations
> arbitrate [hôkîaḥ] for the many peoples;
>
> They shall beat their swords into plowshares,
> their spears into pruning hooks:
>
> Nation shall not take up sword against nation;
> They shall never learn of war any more.

As noted by John Willis (1997: 296), "Yahweh's ultimate concern here is the well-being of the nations." Contrast, for example, the treatment of the foreign nations in Micah 4:11–13, where they are gathered, threshed, and pulverized, to that in Isaiah 2:2–4, where (having made pilgrimage) the foreign nations are nurtured, being "taught the right way to live by God."[183] The utopian vision described here has the nations disarming themselves. Whereas elsewhere the nations were forcibly disarmed by Yahweh, here they voluntarily decide to turn their weapons into agrarian implements.[184] Disarmament brings about international peace, which in turn renders the study of military tactics needless.

Hugh Williamson (2006: 185) writes that this disarmament "is presented as the natural consequence of the nations seeking, receiving and acting upon God's instruction and arbitration." At the same time, it should be pointed out that even this passage continues to underscore Yahweh's prowess as a divine warrior, in that the biblical root *špṭ* (used of Yahweh "judging" the nations in Isa 2:4//Mic 4:3) often connotes military action.[185]

Section II: Yahweh the Compassionate and Family Religion

*Before I formed you in the womb I knew you,
and before you were born I consecrated you.*
—Jeremiah 1:5

Grandma, all the same, burned a candle on the anniversary of Mr. Lausch's death, threw a lump of dough on the coals when she was baking, as a kind of offering, had incantations over baby teeth and stunts against the evil eye. It was kitchen religion and had nothing to do with the giant God of the Creation who had turned back the waters and exploded Gomorrah, but it was on the side of religion at that.
—Bellow 1953: 10–11

Setting the Stage

As the previous section detailed, Yahweh's militaristic nature is strikingly different from the benevolent El traditions articulated in Chapter Four. Yet it would be a grave mistake to conclude that Yahweh was not a family deity but El was. It would skew our evidence to suggest that Yahweh was known solely for having sword in hand and being void of compassion—or that sociologically he was a state/national deity worshipped within hierarchical structures without any connection to the household religion of average Judeans. The exact opposite is true: Yahweh was viewed as the most intimate of deities. Thus the prophet Jeremiah could poetically describe Yahweh as forming him in his mother's womb. As we will demonstrate, yet other prophets will pick up on Yahweh's maternal nature, a tradition dating back to old El lore (cf. Deut 32:6, 18; Chapter Four, pp. 110–111). Research over the past decade has asserted that family religion was central to the religious expression of Iron Age Israel and Judah, and as important as the elite religion of king, priest, and prophet.[186] Avraham Faust (2019: 1) argues "that cultic activity in temples was the exception rather than the norm and that typical Israelite cult was practiced in the household and in other, non-temple settings."

Once again it is helpful to situate our discussion in the context of the ancient Near East, especially using Levantine traditions.[187] The Late Bronze Age religion at Ugarit can serve as a cultural backdrop, even with its differing sociological, political, and theological factors. Kings, high-ranking officials, elite merchants, and priests shared certain familial concerns with commoners. All alike petitioned the gods for personal health and prosperity; for safe births, fit children, and sturdy livestock; for snakebite remedies and sexual potency; for good weather, adequate water, and abundant crops. The overlap between elite and non-elite religious concerns was likely quite large. Yet elite religion was occupied more with obtaining, securing, and bequeathing power (e.g., the throne, the temple economy) via divine and human diplomacy than with the transitions of life (birth, marriage, death) that characterized the religion practiced in the common household.[188]

Viewing the Gods as Family at Late Bronze Age Ugarit

Language of the family (father, mother, husband, wife, son, daughter, brother, sister, in-law) permeates the Ugaritic pantheon at every turn. Baʻlu, for example, is described as the son of Dagan, the father to three daughters (Pidray, Tallay, and Arsay), and the brother of ʻAnatu if not also her husband.[189] Baʻlu invites his brothers//his kinsmen//the seventy sons of the mother goddess ʼAthiratu to a family feast in his house (built by permission of his father, ʼIlu, through the intervention of ʼAthiratu, ʼIlu's wife; KTU 1.4.6.38–59).

According to Mark Smith (2001b: 54–60), building on J. David Schloen's (2001) significant work on the patrimonial household:

> The notion of the family [in the Ugaritic pantheon provides] a cohesive vision of religious reality.... It is evident from the language of family relations that the model of the patriarchal household is central to the Ugaritic texts' presentation of divinity.... Equally fundamental to the family unit is the language of parentage.... The social metaphors for chief deities overwhelmingly reflected the patriarchal experience in households non-royal and royal alike.

Though family language is attested throughout the pantheon, a brief look at the two most prominent family deities (ʼIlu and ʼAthiratu) will serve to illustrate the point. As detailed in Chapters Four and Five, ʼIlu was portrayed in text and iconography with gray hair and beard, apt depictions for "the father of years" who was understood to be "father" to gods and humans alike. In a text celebrating his prowess, women cry out to him, "Father, father," "Mother, mother" (ʼad ʼad// ʼum ʼum; KTU 1.23.32–33).[190] In this same text, he impregnates women who cry out to him as "husband, husband" (mt mt) and bear him two children, the gods Šaḥru and Šalimu (see pp. 77–78).

ʼIlu is known for his benevolence (lṭpn ʼil d pʼid), especially regarding the granting of children. In response to a request from Baʻlu, ʼIlu blesses Danilu with a son in the tale of Aqhatu. In the story of Kirta, ʼIlu blesses the king (himself the

Figure 8.11 An ivory panel from LB Ugarit showing a winged goddess with bull's horns and a Hathor-style headdress surmounted by a disk. She is suckling two (royal?) individuals.

Photo from J. Gachet-Bizollon, "Le panneau de lit en ivoire de la cour III du palais royal d'Ougarit," *Syria* 78 (2001): 29, fig. 7, pl. 2/H. Reproduced by permission of Institut français du Proche-Orient and Mission archéologique de Ras Shamra–Ougarit.

"son of 'Ilu") with a wife and children (KTU 1.14.1.26ff; 1.15.2.12ff). The same story also tells of 'Ilu's beneficence in healing an ailing Kirta on the verge of death (KTU 1.16.5.10ff).[191] Time and time again Ilimilku, the famous scribe of this text, underscores that 'Ilu is the divine parent of the king.

The goddess 'Athiratu was referred to as the mother of seventy minor gods, who were characterized as her "sons" (šbʿm bn ʾaṯrt; KTU 1.4.6.46). She suckles newborn gods in KTU 1.23.24, 59, 61.[192] Iconography such as the ivory panel of a winged goddess suckling two (royal?) individuals (Figure 8.11) may lend support to her nurturing role, although this relief is uninscribed and thus it is unclear which goddess is represented. Because 'Athiratu is Queen *Mother*, she can be approached by royalty such as King Kirta, who makes a vow to offer her gifts of silver and gold in exchange for her assistance (along with father 'Ilu's aid earlier in the story) in obtaining Hurraya as his wife (KTU 1.14.4.34–43).[193] Elsewhere

'Athiratu, "the Great One" (*rbt*), is described as approachable as she goes about common domestic chores. Her activities are remarkable for their non-elite character. Every Ugaritic woman could fully relate to 'Athiratu's working with a spindle, washing laundry, and setting pots over fire and coals (KTU 1.4.2.2–11).[194] Thus, even though 'Athiratu's maternal nature is primarily focused on gods and royal children, non-elites would have felt a special affinity for her, much as Catholic parishioners hold Mary to be their mother even though her royal status is that of Theotokos.[195]

Onomastics, Blessings, Inviting the Gods into One's Home

Onomastic evidence gives us yet another window into how the gods were perceived. The theophoric elements attested in Ugaritic personal names are filled with familial and other intimate terms (e.g., "father," "mother," "ancestor," "brother," "lover," friend," "benevolent," etc.).[196] Letters, though formulaic in nature, nonetheless reveal petitioners looking to caring gods to guard the well-being of their loved ones, to grant them favor, and to satiate them with old age.[197] Consider too how the gods of one's family could be included in greeting formulas as the givers of blessings:

> Peace be upon you.
> May the gods of the land of Tibat
> and the gods of the lands of Ugarit,
> and *all the gods of our family* [*dingir-meš bīt ab[ini]*],
> keep you in good health,
> and give you favor
> and satiate you with old age
> before *the gods of [our] family* [*dingir-meš bīt ab[ini]*]—forever.[198]

On the literary level, the poignant story of Aqhatu (KTU 1.17–1.19) is filled with references to family religion. At the center of the story is a legendary patriarch named Danilu, known for defending the claims and needs of widows and orphans (KTU 1.17.5.4–8). Day after day Danilu presents food and drink offerings to the gods, motivated by his longing for a son. The god Ba'lu compassionately intercedes on the childless Danilu's behalf with the benevolent 'Ilu (*'il d p'id*), the father of humanity. 'Ilu grants his request, blessing Danilu and his wife with conception, recognized as a divine gift in this text and elsewhere at Ugarit (KTU 1.15.2.16–28; KTU 1.24.5–7) just as much as Judeans recognized it in their traditions (e.g., Genesis 16:11; Isaiah 7:14).

Divine visitation follows. The Kathiratu (goddesses of conception and wedlock) come to Danilu's house.[199] There he holds a six-day feast in their honor that includes the slaughtering of an ox (KTU 1.17.2.24–38). Note the simple fact that the feast is held in the home. No pilgrimage to a temple (with a specialized priesthood and cult) is necessary for family religion. The divine can be immanent in daily life and daily surroundings. Because the gods too have families who eat, drink, and sleep in houses (*bêtu*), it is proper for a petitioner to show them hospitality in his own house (*bêtu*). While the occasion (divinely inspired conception) is indeed special, the notion of having gods over for dinner is itself unremarkable; for family religion, it is understood. Indeed, later in the narrative we hear of a second feast in Danilu's home arranged for a visit by Kotharu-wa-Hasisu, the artisan deity. Whereas Danilu served the first feast, his wife, Danataya, is the central character in the second, preparing a lamb for Kotharu-wa-Hasisu. She "dines and wines the gods, serves and honors them" (KTU 1.17.5.21–31).[200]

Viewing Yahweh as Divine Parent

Yahwistic religion in Iron Age Israel and Judah resonates with the cultural world of its northern Late Bronze Age neighbors, as it too envisions Yahweh as a divine parent. As the male 'Ilu could be described as both "father and mother" (*'ad 'ad//'um 'um*; KTU 1.23.32–33) in his role as procreator, so too the male Yahweh is described with both fatherly and motherly aspects as a merism denoting his parentage. This is not to assert that all things are equal when it comes to divine parentage, for the constraints of Yahwistic religion are considerable. For example, while we have the expression "sons of God" well attested in the Hebrew Bible (e.g., Gen 6:2), nowhere in the Hebrew Bible is Yahweh called "the father of the gods." And even though Yahweh is intimately present in domestic space, no descriptions tell of his banqueting on a splendid household meal such as the ones Danilu and Danataya offered to the Kathiratu goddesses and Kotharu-wa-Hasisu.[201]

The notion that gods are parents of humans is tied to their role as creators. We already noted in Chapter Four, pp. 110–111, how the El tradition in Deuteronomy 32 combines fatherly creation with motherly birthing (Deut 32:6, 18). When describing Yahweh as a creator/potter, Isaiah 45:9–12 juxtaposes the images of a begetting father and a mother in labor (Isa 45:10). The author of the book of Job writes similarly of Yahweh when he puts the following words on his lips in the context of creation:

> Has the rain a father?
> or who begot the drops of dew?
>
> From whose womb came forth ice?
> Who gave birth to the frost of heaven? (Job 38:28–29)

In contrast to some commentators, the answer to the first of these four rhetorical questions is affirmative. Yahweh as parent and procreator is indeed the father of rain (cf. Job 5:10; 12:15; 26:8; 28:25–26; 36:27–28) and "breather" of ice (Job 37:10). He is at the same time the mother from whose womb creation emerges (as will be discussed later). Such figurative language is well within reason (cf. again Deut 32:6, 18), and Job 38 consistently emphasizes Yahweh's acts as creator.[202]

In addition to the context of creation, the language of the divine parent is expressed in contexts of caregivers of helpless children (and by extension caring for the oppressed). Such a core idea lived on in later traditions such as the Thanksgiving Hymns at Qumran:

> My father did not know me, my mother abandoned me unto you. For you are a father to all the [son]s of your truth. You rejoice over them as a [mother] who is compassionate [*mrḥmt*] with her nursing child, as a nurse ['*wmn*][203] you care for all your creatures in [your] bosom. (1QHodayot^a, xvii, 35–36)

As with Ugaritic 'Ilu, the language of god as father and mother should not be used to extrapolate an androgynous or hermaphrodite character for Yahweh, who, like 'Ilu, is a male deity. Cognate expressions from the ancient Near East can help clarify the use of such metaphors, as Jeffrey Tigay (1996: 307) and Erhard Gerstenberger (1996a: 5) have already argued. Hittite prayers and hymns to the male sun god (^{d}UTU) and to the male storm/vegetation god Telepinu refer to the god as the "father [and] mother to all the lands" as well as the "father [and] mother" of the orphaned, the bereaved, the oppressed, and the widowed.[204] Egyptian tomb inscriptions describing personal piety tell of how "God is a father and mother to him who takes him into his heart,"[205] and creation hymns call both male and female deities (especially Amun-Re and Neith) "father of fathers, mother of mothers."[206] A Neo-Assyrian hymn to the male moon god Sin includes an eightfold praise to "*Father* Nanna" that continues to also praise him as

> Womb that gives birth to everything,
> which dwells in a holy habitation with living creatures,
> Begetter, merciful in his disposing,
> who holds in his hand the life of the whole land . . .
> O progenitor of the land . . . O father begetter of gods and men . . .
> Father begetter, who looks favorably upon all living creatures . . .[207]

Such father and mother language was not restricted to male deities. The Neo-Assyrian king Esarhaddon receives the following oracles of encouragement from the goddess Ishtar:

> I am Ishtar of [Arbela] ...
> I am your great midwife;
> I am your excellent wet nurse.
>
> I am your father and mother.
> I raised you between my wings.[208]

Rulers adopted similar familial language in order to promote their benevolence to their subjects, whom they treated (so they said) as compassionately as a parent would his child. Thus the late ninth-century BCE Kulamuwa inscription found at Zincirli reads: "To some I was a father, and to some I was a mother, and to some I was a brother."[209] Rulers could be godlike in their parentage of their people. Thus the bilingual Phoenician-Hieroglyphic Luwian Karatepe inscription from the late eighth/early seventh century BCE has Azitawada proclaim that "Baal made me a father and a mother to the Danunians."[210] One could also examine birth narratives, which, as Hennie Marsman (2003: 16) has argued, were mostly told from the male perspective (the male to whom the child was born) with little or no notice of the mother actually giving birth. In short, the fact that male gods such 'Ilu, Yahweh, Shamash, Telepinu, and Sin were referred to as "father and mother" is a descriptor of their role as divine parent, not any assertion of androgyny. Where we do have anthropomorphic iconography attested (cf. 'Ilu, Shamash, Sin) these gods are male, never female.

Viewing Yahweh as Father

The fatherhood of male gods is so common in the ancient Near East that tracing the concept in each culture would be an overwhelming task. Similarly, the Fatherhood of God has become such a dominant motif in history (from Qumran, the New Testament, and rabbinic literature to the present), in philosophy and theology (from Philo, Origen, and Athanasius to the present), and in cultural criticism (especially feminist literature) that surveying its contours could also overwhelm the researcher.[211] Suffice it here to keep our focus narrowly on ancient Israel as viewed through the Hebrew Bible and onomastic evidence.

The Hebrew Bible's literary references to divine fatherhood concentrate on Israel as God's firstborn son and thus serves the larger purpose of legitimizing the election of Israel over all other nations (cf. Deut 32:8–9). Surprisingly, there are only eighteen explicit references to God as father in the literary texts.[212] Yet we know from onomastica that the concept was prevalent in ancient Israel. Where Jeaneane Fowler (1988) has used such names to articulate the general nature of how God was perceived, Rainer Albertz (1978: 49–77; Albertz and Schmitt 2012: 245) has concentrated on their sociological dimension, concluding that "the personal names of the Hebrew Bible do not reflect the Israelite religion in any general way; instead, they specifically attest the personal piety of Israelite and Judean families."

Personal Names Attesting to God as Divine Father
The following catalog of names emphasizes the ubiquitous way in which God was viewed as the divine father who assisted his worshippers in manifold ways.[213] In the Hebrew Bible we have the following personal names attested mostly of men but also of women: ʾAbiʾel, "[My divine] Father is El/god," ʾAbiʾasaph, "[My divine] Father has gathered," ʾAbibaʿal, "[My divine] Father is Baal/lord," ʾAbigayil, "[My divine] Father is [my] rejoicing," ʾAbidan, "[My divine] Father has judged," ʾAbihayil, "[My divine] Father is fear," ʾAbyadaʿ/ʾAbidaʿ, "[My divine] Father has acknowledged [me]," ʾAbiyah[u], "[My divine] Father is Yah[weh]," ʾAbihuʾ, "He is [my divine] Father," ʾAbihud, "[My divine] Father is glory," ʾAbiḥayil, "[My divine] Father is strength," ʾAbiṭub, "[My divine] Father is goodness," ʾAbiṭal, "[My divine] Father is dew," ʾAbimelek, "[My divine] Father is king," ʾAbinadab, "[My divine] Father has proved himself generous," ʾAbinoʿam, "[My divine] Father is kind," ʾEbyasaph, "The [divine] Father has added," ʾAbiʿezer, "[My divine] Father is help," ʾAbiram, "[My divine] Father is high, exalted," ʾAbishag, "[My divine] father is[?]," ʾAbishuʿa, "[My divine] Father is salvation," ʾAbishur, "[My divine] Father is a [protecting] wall," ʾAbshalom/ʾAbishalom, "[My divine] Father is salvation," ʾEbyatar, "The [divine] Father is rich, gives generously," ʾAbner, "The [divine] Father is light," ʾAbram/ʾAbraham, "The [divine] Father is exalted," ʾAḥʾab, "The [divine] brother is a [divine] Father," Yoʾab, "Yahweh is [divine] Father."

Several of these names are also found attested in the epigraphic record.[214] In addition, inscriptional sources add the following Hebrew divine father names to our repertoire: ʾAb, "[the one of the divine] Father," ʾAbiḥay, "[My divine] Father is alive," ʾAšʾab, "The [divine] Father has given," and Yehoʾab, "Yahweh is [divine] Father." Non-Hebrew divine father names attested epigraphically include ʾAbyaqi, "[My divine] Father is [my] protector [?]" (Aramaic), ʾAbishuri, "[My divine] Father is my [protecting] wall" (Aramaic), ʾAbiḥay, "[My divine] Father is alive" (Ammonite), ʾAbidišše ʿ "[My divine] Father has caused to thrive[?]" (Ammonite), and ʾAbišillem, "[My divine] Father has replaced" (Phoenician).[215]

El as Father and Yahweh as Father
As for the Hebrew Bible's literary references to divine fatherhood (particularly of Israel, God's firstborn son), it is clear that biblical traditions wove the notion of El as Father and Yahweh as Father into a single garment. We do not have at our disposal the mechanisms by which this weaving happened, yet the process was certainly facilitated by the ability of the word ʾl to designate the common noun "god." For example, the epithet ʾēl raḥûm, "a compassionate god," was used in

Deuteronomy 4:31 to describe Yahweh, who will not forget the covenant of the fathers. Yahweh was often described as being "a compassionate and gracious god [*'ēl raḥûm wĕḥannûn*], slow to anger, abounding in steadfast love and faithfulness" (Exod 34:6 and Ps 86:15; cf. Ps 103:8; 145:8; Jon 4:2; Neh 9:31).[216] Similarly, Yahweh is referred to as *'l ḥnn*, "God/El the compassionate," in the sixth-century BCE Khirbet Beit Lei inscription (Cross 1970: 302). Personal names showing how El/God and Yahweh were looked to for favor are well attested in the onomastic evidence in the Hebrew Bible and the epigraphic record (*ḥnn'l*, *'lḥnn*, *ḥnnyh*, and *yhwḥnn*).

Both El and Yahweh traditions used the language of fatherhood alongside God's creation of humankind. Previously we looked at the way in which these two motifs were combined in the El tradition in Deuteronomy 32:6b, and it bears repeating:

| Is not he your father, who created you | *hălô'-hû' 'ābîkā qāneka* |
| Who made you and brought you into existence? | *hû' 'āśĕkā wayĕkōnĕneka* |

Similar juxtapositions of divine fatherhood and creation can be found in Malachi 2:10 ("Have we not all one father? Has not one God created us?") as well as within the Isaianic traditions. Here we have several references to Yahweh as father and creator, with special emphasis on the way in which he fashioned Israel, his child, like a potter (√*yṣr*):

> O Yahweh, you are our Father;
> We are the clay, and you are our Potter;
> We are all the work of thy hand. (Isa 64:7 [Eng 64:8]; cf. Isa 43:1–7; 45:9–12)[217]

Yahweh as Caring Father

In addition to begetting his children, Yahweh is also described as rearing his children (Isa 1:2), caring for them, and nurturing them in the most compassionate of ways. Hosea 11 paints our fullest picture:[218]

> When Israel was a child, I loved him [*'ōhăbēhû*],
> Out of Egypt I called my son . . .
>
> I was the one who taught Ephraim to walk,
> taking them by the arms/up in my arms[219]
> . . . I healed them.

> I drew them with cords of human [kindness],
> with the bands of love ['ahăbâ],
> I was to them as one who eases the yoke on their jaws,
> I bent down to them that I might feed them.[220] (Hosea 11:1, 3–4)

The portrait here is of Yahweh as a tender, caring parent who loves Israel, his young child. Yahweh, the patient father (Yahweh as mother will be discussed later), teaches his youthful son to walk, either holding his hand as he takes his first precarious steps or taking him up in his arms. Yahweh the father heals his child's injuries, eases his suffering, and stoops to provide him nourishment. Such notions of fatherly care were also utilized by the psalmist, who wrote:

> As a father has compassion for his children,
> so Yahweh has compassion for those who fear him. (Psalm 103:13)

At the same time, the mention of Israel's deliverance from Egypt in Hosea 11:1 adds a layer of rescue to our familial portrait, especially when we remember that the language of Israel as Yahweh's firstborn son is used in the exodus narrative (Exod 4:22). A father will go to dramatic lengths to liberate his son from the yoke of oppression.

Yahweh, Father to the Fatherless

Yahweh's fatherly care is extended to those who are bereft of the security and the sense of belonging that families provide. Hosea 14:4b (Eng 14:3b) adds to the tender picture by affirming that in Yahweh orphans find compassion. Various hymns were sung to describe how Yahweh is "father of the fatherless" and "the helper of the fatherless" (Ps 10:14; 68:6 [Eng 68:5]). The orphan, along with the widow and the gēr (the non-Israelite resident or "client"),[221] typified the powerless in ancient Israel (Exod 22:21–24; Deut 10:18 etc.).[222] Prophets describe the abuse of these individuals by those in power (e.g., Jer 7:6; Isa 1:17, 10:2; Mal 3:5). Yahweh provides protection, justice, food, and clothing to these disadvantaged segments of society (e.g., Deut 10:18; Ps 68:6 [Eng 68:5]; cf. Ps 146:9; Prov 15:25; 23:10b–11). Such concern about the marginalized was a widespread motif used of father figures (especially deities and monarchs) throughout ancient Near Eastern literature.[223]

Rebellious Children

The filial duties of children toward their parents, especially those of sons toward their fathers, is well attested in the ancient Near East.[224] Note, for example, the duties of "the ideal son" that form a fourfold refrain in the Ugaritic Tale of Aqhatu.[225] A father was to be held in high esteem in Israelite culture. Analogously, Father Yahweh (known elsewhere for his *kābôd*)[226] was to be accorded the honor (√*kbd*) due one's parents (Exod 20:12; Deut 5:16) as well as the reverence (√*yr'*) in which one's father and mother were to be held (Lev 19:3).[227] Such an analogy allowed prophets to press the case against the disobedient behavior of Israel (Yahweh's firstborn son) using the language of the rebelliously defiant child (cf. Deut 21:18–21).

Isaiah 1:2–3 has Yahweh speaking of rearing his "sons" (i.e., Judahites) only to have them rebel against him. Williamson (2006: 33) aptly comments that the rebellion here "is clearly to be understood as rejection of parental authority with all that that entails of family breakdown, something of great social significance in a society where the family unit was the chief means of support, not least in old age."[228] The fuller context of the poignant passage from Hosea 11 is that of the child Israel running away from the nurturing and loving father Yahweh, not realizing that his father was the source of his healing (Hosea 11:2–3).[229] Jeremiah 32:33 portrays Israel as not listening to Yahweh's instruction (presumably in the role of a father; cf. Prov 3:12; 4:1) even though he constantly taught them.[230]

Jeremiah 3:19 presents yet another vignette: Yahweh as a father musing about how he would allot the fairest of his land to firstborn Israel such that his child's appreciative response would surely be to call out "My Father!" Alas, here too the Father is betrayed by the faithless child despite such a rich inheritance. As noted by Jack Lundbom (1999: 318–319), the author here seems to be playing off Deuteronomy 32:8–9 with its description of allotment and special inheritance (cf. too how the status of children is tied to election in Deut 14:1–2). Similarly, as recognized by William Holladay (1986: 104), Jeremiah 2:27 seems to be playing off Deuteronomy 32:6, 18. Those insightful verses described El/Yahweh as a father-creator and yet also a personified Rock who like a mother gave birth to her newborn Israel—only to be forgotten.[231] In Jeremiah 2:27 the wayward people call out to an illegitimate tree as their father and a false stone as the mother who gave them birth.[232]

Lastly, consider how Malachi 1:6 places the following on Yahweh's lips as he addresses the abuses of priests:

> "A son should honor [*yĕkabbēd*] his father, and a servant his lord. If then I am a father, where is the honor due me [*kĕbôdî*]? And if I am lord, where is the reverence due me [*môrā'î*]?" says Yahweh of Hosts to you, O priests who despise my name. (Mal 1:6)

Michael Fishbane (1985: 332–334) has written about how the prophet's diatribe in Malachi 1:6–2:9 "is *exegetical* in nature . . . [taking] the contents of the Priestly Blessing [Num 6:23–27]—delivered by the priests, and with its emphasis on blessing, the sanctity of the divine Name, and such benefactions as protection, favorable countenance, and peace—*and inverted them*" (emphasis Fishbane). Similarly, one could argue that the prophet exegetes the way in which *kābôd* can designate both honor and glory. The prophet has taken the command to honor one's human father, a command surely handed down by priests (cf. Exod 20:12), and inverted it to accuse priests of withholding the honor (*kābôd*) due their divine Father. Those to whom the *kĕbôd* Yahweh appeared as a priestly prerogative (Lev 9:4, 6) have withheld from Yahweh his due glory (*kābôd*).[233]

The Reproving of the Father

It comes as no surprise that the analogy of Yahweh as Father included fatherly correction and discipline ($\sqrt{ysr}$/*mûsār*). We read in Proverbs:

> For Yahweh reproves him whom he loves,
> as a father the son in whom he delights. (Prov 3:12; cf. Job 5:17; Ps 94:12)

Deuteronomy 8:5 expresses a similar sentiment with regard to the hardships of the desert wandering of Israel, who is metaphorically Yahweh's firstborn son: "Bear in mind that Yahweh your God disciplines you just as a man disciplines his son." At times Yahweh's discipline of Israel is expressed within the context of loving correction. At other times it is punitive, similar to the harshness of Deuteronomy's treatment of a defiant child (Deut 21:18–21).[234] This is especially so with regard to cultic sins and apostasy, for which no toleration is shown. Thus the Holiness Code has Yahweh respond with fury, personally chastising Israel sevenfold for their sins (Lev 26:27).

Prophets pressed the case that disobedient behavior by the wayward child necessarily led to disciplinary treatment, even the severe discipline of the exile (e.g., Hos 7:12–13; Jer 30:14; 32:31–35; Zeph 3:7). Hosea, through the telling of a symbolic family story, says that there are desperate times when a daughter no longer receives her father's compassion (*lō' ruḥāmâ*) and a son no longer belongs to his father's kin (*lō' 'ammî*; Hos 1:6, 8–9). Jeremiah symbolically contrasts the inhabitants of Jerusalem (i.e., Yahweh's children), who repeatedly reject their (fatherly) *mûsār* instruction (35:13, 14b,15b, 16b, 17b), with the Rechabite sons of Jonadab, "who obey their father's command" (35:14, 16a, 18–19). As a result, the destruction of Jerusalem looms in the former's future, in contrast to the secure position bequeathed to the latter (35:17–19). Ezekiel too elaborates on how Yahweh's children rebelled against the instruction of their Father (e.g., Ezek 20:18–21).

Should a challenge to Yahweh's manner of parenting ever be mounted (cf. Ezek 18:25, 29), Ezekiel and Second Isaiah were ready with their responses.[235] Telling his own story of three generations of father-son relationships, Ezekiel underscores how sons are responsible for the consequences of their own behavior (Ezek 18). Second Isaiah again uses the imagery of God fashioning Israel, his child, like a potter (√*yṣr*):[236]

> Woe to him who strives with his Maker,
> you who are but mere clay,[237]
>
> Should the clay say to its potter:[238]
> "What are you making?"
> or "Your work has no hands"?
>
> Woe to him who says to a father:
> "What are you begetting?"
> or to a woman:
> "What are you bearing?"
>
> Thus says Yahweh,
> the Holy One of Israel, and his Maker:
>
> "Will you question me on the destiny of my children,[239]
> or instruct me concerning the work of my hands?
>
> It was I who made the earth,
> and created humans upon it;
> It was I—my hands that stretched out the heavens,
> and I commanded all their host." (Isa 45:9–12)

To the picture of Father Yahweh disciplining Israel as firstborn son we should also add the notion of Yahweh treating Jerusalem as his "daughter." The feminine grammatical gender was applied to cities, and Jerusalem was personified through a variety of female images.[240] The expression "Daughter Zion" (*bat-ṣiyyôn* is an appositional genitive) is used to personify Jerusalem with references to her destruction and eventual restoration (more detail to follow). The use of daughter language occurs in pejorative contexts, yet without the emphasis (in contrast to Israel as firstborn son) on being a disobedient child in need of a father's discipline (yet cf. Jer 31:22; Deut 31:19–20). Instead the emphasis is on the vulnerability of Zion as a captive daughter—the way in

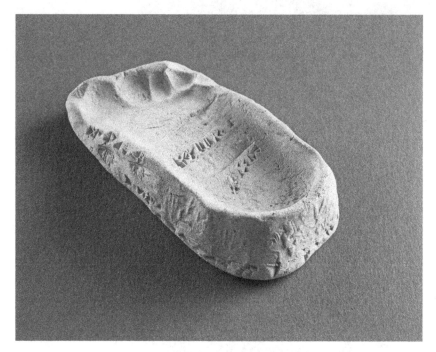

Figure 8.12 A terra-cotta imprint of the foot of a child sold into slavery together with his inscribed name. From Late Bronze Age Temple M1 at Emar.
© Philippe Maillard/akg-images.

which she is besieged and violated by foreign soldiers, her suffering even at Yahweh's hands, and her bitter mourning (e.g., Isa 1:7–8; Mic 4:10; Jer 4:31; 6:1–7, 22–26; Lam 1:10, 15; 2:4, 8, 13, 15, 18).[241]

Fatherly Redemption

Throughout the Hebrew Bible, however and wherever the children of God end up in distress, Yahweh, their father, acts as deliverer. A paradigm passage is found in Exodus 4:22–23, where Yahweh proclaims his fatherly relationship to Israel ("Israel is my firstborn son") to Pharaoh, followed by the command "Let my son go." The severity of his demand is underscored by a Father-to-father threat: "Should you refuse to let my firstborn son go, I will kill your firstborn son." The language of deliverance is often that of "redemption" ($\sqrt{g'l}$). With the choice of this specific $g'l$ vocabulary, the emphasis is once again on familial solidarity.[242] Clans (and ideally the nearest male relative) bore the responsibility to rescue (i.e., "redeem" or "buy back") a family member who, out of economic despair, had sold himself into indentured slavery (cf. Lev 25:39–55; Neh 5:8). Indentured slavery, a last resort to ensure survival for those who lost all their possessions, was known throughout the ancient

Near East, and the children of debtors could be enslaved by the parents' creditors (e.g., 2 Kgs 4:1; cf. Chirichigno 1993). A poignant illustrated example comes from Emar, where parents were forced to sell their children into slavery to satisfy a debt. We know of this transaction thanks to the discovery of the actual imprints (in terra cotta) of the feet of children whose names are inscribed (see Figure 8.12). Three of four children are named: Baʿla-bia, a two-year-old girl, and her twin brothers, Baʿal-belu and Ishmaʿ-Dagan, each one year old. The parents (Zadamma and his wife, Kuʾe) themselves pressed each foot in the clay.[243]

The notion of Yahweh protecting helpless children became proverbial, especially so for orphans, whose property was at risk because they lacked a protecting kinsman who could advocate for their legal rights. To their aid comes Yahweh as a "mighty kinsman redeemer" ($gō\bar{}ēl\ ḥāzāq$) who contends on their behalf (Prov 23:10b–11; cf. Deut 10:18; Ps 68:6).[244] The literature found in Isaiah 40–55 is particularly fond of applying the metaphor of God as (kinsman) redeemer ($gō\bar{}ēl$).[245] In a tender passage Yahweh the creator/father/redeemer speaks:

> But now—thus says Yahweh,
> He who created you, O Jacob,
> He who formed you, O Israel:
>
> "Fear not, for I have redeemed you [$gĕ\bar{}altîkā$];
> I have called you by name, you belong to me.
>
> When you go through water, I will be with you;
> and through rivers, they shall not sweep you away;
>
> When you walk through fire you shall not be burned,
> and a flame shall not scorch you.
>
> For I, Yahweh, am your God,
> the Holy One of Israel, your savior.[246]
>
> I give Egypt as your ransom [$kōper$],
> Ethiopia and Seba in exchange for you.
>
> Because you are precious in my eyes,
> honored, and I love you,
>
> I give men in return for you,
> peoples in exchange for your life.

> Fear not, for I am with you;
> I will bring your offspring from the east,
> and from the west I will gather you;
>
> I will say to the north, 'Give [them] up,'
> and to the south, 'Do not withhold [them]';
>
> 'Bring my sons [*bānay*] [back here] from far away,
> and my daughters [*běnôtay*] from the end of the earth,
>
> All who are called by my name,
> whom I created for my glory,
> whom I formed and made.'" (Isa 43:1–7)

Yahweh, the one who brought Israel into existence in the first place, acts to redeem Israel as would the nearest male relative, who acts with a sense of personal ownership (*lî-ʾattâ*, Isa 43:1) to keep the bonds of family intact. Those whom Yahweh redeems are called sons and daughters, those who bear his name (cf. the special emphasis on *qrʾ běšem* in Isa 43:1, 7). Yahweh will pay an extravagant cost to redeem his precious children, whom he loves.[247] Indeed, he pays the monetary equivalent of entire countries, especially Egypt with its vast resources, as a ransom (Isa 43:3b). Yahweh's geographic reach spans the compass; no land is beyond this father's reach when it comes to bringing home his sons and daughters who are called by his name (Isa 43:5–7).[248] Later Isaianic traditions will pair the fatherhood of Yahweh with his redemptive nature as traditions they inherited from past ages:

> You, O Yahweh, are our *Father* [*ʾābînû*],
> From of old, your name is "Our *Redeemer*" [*gōʾălēnû*]. (Isa 63:16)

When we now revisit the "Daughter Zion" material, we see a dramatic contrast in expression. Whereas the pejorative "Daughter Zion" texts highlighted captive Jerusalem's vulnerability, suffering, and eventual destruction with sober, harsh, and bitter language, the redemptive and restorative passages are ebullient in their proclamations to Daughter Zion to rise and sing with joy. Such poems are found in Deutero- and Trito-Isaiah along with Zechariah and Zephaniah. Captive Daughter Zion is to shake herself free of dust and loosen the fetters from her neck, awakening as a holy city, clothed in royal splendor (Isa 52:1–2). Daughter Zion is to sing, shout, rejoice, and exult with all her heart (Zeph 3:14). The catalyst for her joy is the triumphant king, Yahweh, who has secured her salvation (Zech 9:9; Isa 62:11) and promises to reside in her midst (Zech 2:10).

Viewing Yahweh as Mother

As demonstrated, Yahweh is distinctly male, whether dressed as a warrior or as a father. Yet certain biblical authors considered exclusively male categories to be too limiting for how they wanted to describe the full nature of divinity. Could the warrior imagery of a deity fighting on behalf of his people, or even the picture of a benevolent father figure, express the strength and compassion they knew of motherhood? Israelite believers living out the realities of family religion within day-to-day affairs (especially the transitions of life such as birth, marriage, and death) would find it unimaginable to think that their family god was not motherly. This is a personal god, after all, who can draw so intimately close as to wipe away tears from one's face (Isa 25:8).

In addition, for those who understood Yahwistic belief to funnel the multiplicity of divinity into the singular, logically that one divine entity (even if he was male) had to encompass the motherhood of the goddesses. Did not "the rhetoric of sexuality" found in Genesis 1:27 use the vehicle of "male and female" to express humankind in its fullness? Though transcending human sexuality, did not Yahweh birth all things female as well as male? "Though the Bible overwhelmingly favors male metaphors for deity," were not "societal roles and relationships" of females (a pregnant woman, a mother, a midwife) together with those of males (father, husband, king, warrior) used as metaphors to point toward a fuller understanding of the character of God?[249]

The family religion associated with El traditions (which comes down to us woven within Yahweh traditions) used figurative language to describe God as a father who sired his human children (Deut 32:6) as well as a mother who writhed with labor pains in giving them birth (√*ḥwl*; Deut 32:18; cf. Ps 2:7).[250] Poems such as Genesis 49:25, written in Israel's earliest history and faithfully preserved for hundreds of years, sang of how El Shadday was "the God of the father" who at the same time provided "the blessings of breasts and womb." The prophet Jeremiah said that God knew him (and consecrated him for his mission) even prior to his creation in and emergence from the womb (Jer 1:5; 20:18).[251] Ancestral stories tell of Yahweh opening and closing wombs (Gen 18:9–15; 21:1–7; 20:1–18; 25:19–28; 29:31–35; 30:1–8, 22–24; Judg 13; 1 Sam 1:1–20; 2 Kgs 4:8–17).[252] The author of Psalm 139:13–15 speaks of Yahweh "weaving" (*tĕsukkēnî, ruqqamtî*; cf. Job 10:11; Prov 8:23) him in his mother's womb in the most wondrous of ways (*nôrāʾôt niplêtî*).[253] Yet another psalmist (desperately ill at the time of writing) chose in his petition for divine favor to describe how Yahweh was present at the moment of birth and ever thereafter:

> Indeed, you issued me from the womb,[254]
> Made me secure at my mother's breast;
>
> Upon you was I cast right from the womb,
> Ever since emerging from my mother's womb, you have been my God. (Ps 22:10–11 [Eng 22:9–10]; cf. Ps 71:6)

The notion that Yahweh was like a mother to Israel was well enough known that the author of Numbers 11:12 could place the following on the frustrated Moses's lips:

> Did I conceive [*hārîtî*] all this people? Did I give them birth [*yĕlidtîhû*], that you should say to me, "Carry them in your bosom, as a nurse carries the sucking child [*hā'ōmēn 'et-hayyōnēq*], to the land that you have promised on oath to their fathers?"

With this penchant for the dramatic, Moses implicitly says that it is Yahweh who is responsible for conceiving and bearing child Israel and thus it is Yahweh who should serve as wet nurse, not him. The masculine term *'ōmēn* is nonsensical if applied literally to a male as a wet nurse, and thus translators regularly render it as "attendant" or "guardian." We do indeed have passages where a male *'ōmēn* served as a caretaker of children (cf. 2 Kgs 10:1, 5; Isa 49:23; Est 2:7). Yet the context here clearly implies that Yahweh conceived and gave birth (rather than siring) and the word used for the infant child is "suckling" (*yōnēq*). Due to the constrains of grammatical gender, the author does not use the female term for wet nurse (*'ōmenet*) to remove all doubt, yet the implications that Yahweh, though male, is like a mother nourishing a newborn are obvious.[255]

The heaviest concentration of explicit motherly language used of Yahweh is found in Second (and Third) Isaiah. Mayer Gruber (1983) argues that these Isaianic traditions are intentional with their choice of explicit maternal language for Yahweh. "The anonymous author," writes Gruber (1983: 358), was intentionally counterbalancing "the insensitivity of his predecessors such as Jeremiah and Ezekiel who had intimated that in the religion of Israel maleness is a positive value with which divinity chooses to identity itself while femaleness is a negative value with which divinity refuses to identify itself." John Schmitt (1985: 558) argues against Second Isaiah being "the first to come up with this [maternal] imagery as an independent, creative insight," given the pervasive notion of Zion as mother.

For Schmitt (1985: 563), "Second Isaiah had a deep sense of the motherhood of Zion ... [that] inspired the prophet to make motherhood as an aspect of God."

Isaiah 42:13–16 astutely juxtaposes Yahweh as male and female with an unexpected pairing of similes: Yahweh is described as both a man of war active in battle and as a woman in the throes of labor.

> Yahweh marches forth like a warrior [*kaggibbôr*],
> like a man of war [*kĕʾîš milḥāmôt*] he excites his zeal;[256]
>
> He raises the battle cry, he shouts aloud,
> He manhandles his enemies.
>
>> "I have held my peace far too long,
>> I have kept still, exercising restraint;
>>
>> But now I cry out like a woman giving birth [*kayyôlēdâ*],
>> Breathlessly panting.[257]
>>
>> I will scorch mountains and hills,
>> All their verdant plants I will wither ...
>>
>> And I will lead the blind along unknown roads,
>> along paths they have never encountered, I will guide them.
>>
>> turning the darkness before them to light,
>> leveling the rough ground to even paths.
>>
>> These are the promises I will keep,
>> I will not abandon them." (Isa 42:13–16)

The backdrop of this "new song" (Isa 42:10) is the perceived inactivity of the deity. As we saw in several of the war poems, divine inaction led to pleas for Yahweh's arm to rouse itself to battle (*ʿûrî ʿûrî*) as in the distant past, when Yahweh vanquished cosmic enemies (Isa 51:9–10; cf. Ps 74:12–17). Here there is no need for such pleas; Yahweh rouses himself with zeal (*yāʿîr qinʾâ*). Yahweh inwardly reflects on his delay, framing the inactivity as intentional restraint. Yet the period of gestation is over and the warrior's intense battle cry is echoed by the cry of a woman in the travails of childbirth.[258] The pent-up warrior of zeal can no more hold back than can a woman whose labor is at its peak. Yahweh is "both parturient-like and warrior-like" at the same time (Bergmann 2010: 53). The effectual results are similarly twofold, a warrior's destruction of his enemies paired with the enlightening guidance of one who takes those who dwell in darkness by the hand to lead them along safe paths (cf. Isa 42:6–7).

Isaiah 49:14–15 and Isaiah 66:13 use the imagery of a mother's intimate compassion for her infant child to describe Yahweh's compassion. Expressed within the context of Zion's bereavement and her feelings of desertion, Yahweh's first-person rhetorical question is remarkable for its poignancy:

> Zion says:
> "Yahweh has forsaken me,
> my Lord has forgotten me."
>
> "Can a woman forget her baby,
> or show no compassion for the child of her womb?
> Granted, women may forget,
> Yet I never could forget you." (Isa 49:14–15)
>
> "As a mother comforts her son,
> so I will comfort you;
> you shall find comfort in Jerusalem." (Isa 66:13)

Elsewhere authors used paternal love to express such compassionate thoughts (e.g., Ps 103:13). The notion of Yahweh as "a compassionate and gracious god" (*'ēl raḥûm wĕḥannûn*) is pervasive and likely dates back to the earliest formations of El religion. Thus Gruber (1983: 352 n. 4) is correct in critiquing Phyllis Trible that the words for "compassion" (√*rḥm*) need not imply a "uterine metaphor" or "uterine perspective" based on the cognate *reḥem* "womb."[259] Moreover, the language of desertion in Isaiah 49:14 suggests an accusation against an absentee husband (cf. Isa 50:1; Blenkinsopp 2002: 310; Baltzer 2001: 321–322). And yet these Isaianic traditions highlight the qualitative difference of a mother's compassion for her newborn. In addition to the explicit association of this maternal imagery with Yahweh, the author goes on to add in Isaiah 49:15b that Yahweh's love is even more enduring. As a psalmist notes, there are tragic instances where parents do indeed forsake their children, yet never Yahweh (Ps 27:10). On this matter, Hosea would agree—Yahweh's love is of an altogether higher level, for he is, after all, not a mere human. He is *'ēl raḥûm*.

> How can I give you up, O Ephraim?
> How can I surrender you, O Israel? . . .
>
> My heart twists within me,
> my compassion is overwhelming.

> I will not act on my wrath,
> I will not turn to destroy Ephraim;
> for I am God, not human [*kî 'ēl 'ānōkî wĕlō'-'îš*]
> the Holy One in your midst,
> I will not come in fury. (Hos 11:8–9)[260]

Other Aspects of Yahweh as a Family Deity

There are many additional areas of family religion involving Yahweh, yet a comprehensive examination lies outside the scope of the present volume. Thankfully, the field has seen an ever-increasing amount of research done in this area.[261] Of these, the work by Rainer Albertz and Rüdiger Schmitt (2012) needs to be highlighted as particularly helpful. In addition to a fresh examination of material culture, the volume contains a synthetic look at what can be gleaned about the familial character of the god Yahweh from personal names. Albertz and Schmitt structure their analysis using two main categories: "the religious significance of childbirth" and "family beliefs related to experiences of crisis."

Personal names attesting to Yahweh's connection to childbirth are itemized by Albertz and Schmitt (2012: 269–297) under the following subcategories: (1) the distress of infertility ('Asapyahu, "Yahweh has taken away [the stigma of childlessness]"); (2) prayers and vows (Šubnayahu, "Do come back, O Yahweh"; 'Ananyahu, "Yahweh has responded to me"); (3) birth oracles ('Amaryahu, "Yahweh has spoken"); (4) conception and pregnancy (Petaḥyah, "Yahweh has opened [the womb]"); (5) the religious dimension of pregnancy (Sebakyahu, "Yahweh has woven [the child in the womb]"); (6) the religious dimension of confinement during pregnancy (Daltayahu, "You, Yahweh, have drawn out [my child]"); (7) divine support for the newborn (Ḥawwiyahu, "Yahweh has brought [the child] to life"); (8) acceptance, naming, and circumcision of the child (Mattanyahu, "Gift of Yahweh"; Malyahu, "Yahweh has circumcised [the child]"); and (9) infant mortality and substitute names (Neḥemyahu, "Yahweh has comforted"; Šellemyahu, "Yahweh has replaced").

Personal names attesting to Yahweh's familial connection to the crises of everyday life are itemized by Albertz and Schmitt (2012: 298–336) under the following subcategories: (10) divine attention in names of thanksgiving (Šemaʿyahu, "Yahweh has heard"); (11) divine salvation in names of thanksgiving (Yešaʿyahu, "Yahweh has saved"); (12) divine assistance in names of thanksgiving ('Azaryahu, "Yahweh has helped [me]"); (13) divine protection in names of thanksgiving (Šemaryahu, "Yahweh has protected [me]"); (14) divine attention in names of confession (Ḥanniyahu, "Yahweh is my mercy"); (15) divine salvation in names of confession (Yehošuaʿ, "Yahweh is [my] salvation"); (16) divine assistance in names of confession (Ḥizqiyahu, "My strength is Yahweh"; ʿImmadiyahu, "Yahweh is with me"); (17) divine protection in names of confession (Yehoʿaz, "Yahweh is [my] strong protection"); (18) trust in God in names of confession (Mibṭaḥyahu, "My trust is Yahweh"); and (19) names of praise (ʿAliyahu, "Yahweh is exalted").[262]

In conclusion, it is clear that Yahweh was perceived to be a family deity in every way. Yahweh is indeed fatherly. Yahweh is indeed motherly. Yet as with the material we find in the Hebrew Bible, which rarely includes explicitly maternal language for God (e.g., Second and Third Isaiah), our onomastic data also reveal that Yahwists only rarely chose *explicitly* to refer to God as mother. In contrast to the numerous ʾAbi-X ("My divine father is X") and X-ʾab ("X is a divine Father") names detailed on p. 480, we have only a single clear example using ʾem, "mother," as a theophoric element: ʾAḥiʾem, "[My divine] brother is like a mother [to me]."[263] Yet one must factor in the incomplete nature of our dataset. Just as the majority of the authors of the Hebrew Bible are male, so too the majority of the personal names that are attested are masculine. Carol Meyers (1998: 251–252) has astutely noted how 1,315 of the Hebrew Bible's 1,426 personal names are male: "The enormous gap between the number of women's and men's names signals the male-centered concerns of biblical literature."

The overall impression that familial religion leaves is that El/Yahweh was personal and accessible. This dual emphasis is remarkable in the contrast it provides to certain forms of elite religion that asserted the lethality of Yahweh, a god who could only be approached by select religious officiants who had undertaken specific ritual precautions. The gradations of holiness (with restricted access) that come to define priestly sacred space are at odds with the personal deity who meets families in their homes. And yet, lest we draw this distinction too severely, we need to keep in mind that the boundaries between elite and non-elite religion were porous. As noted at the outset of our discussion, all—be they king, priest, prophet, or commoner—petitioned Yahweh, a caring parent, for their personal health and prosperity.

9
The Characterization of the Deity Yahweh
Part Two: Yahweh as King and Yahweh as Judge

> *Neither Hammurapi nor Darius, nor a Sassanid king nor Constantine relied on prayer alone to establish their kingships; but ... from the authority and power of the god they sought to legitimize. The gods stand behind those who exercise worldly power.*
>
> —Walter Burkert (1996: 95)

Section I: Yahweh as King

Introduction

Tryggve Mettinger (1988: 92) suggests that the metaphor of Yahweh as king may well be at the very center of the Hebrew Bible's understanding of God. Yet it is difficult for modern readers to set aside our notions about kingship to look at ancient Israelite kingship afresh. How and why have we drawn the pictures we hold in our minds? Does the literary presentation of monarchs hold sway (Malory's Arthur, Shakespeare's Richard III, Tolkien's Aragorn), or do we think of a debatable top-ten list from the pages of history (Suleiman I of the Ottoman Empire, James I of England, John III of Poland-Lithuania, Meiji of Japan, Gustav II Adolf of Sweden, Augustus of Rome, Cyrus of Persia, Frederick II of Prussia, Victoria of the United Kingdom, Louis XIV of France)?[1] Do we think only of noble monarchs, or do we call to mind the world's cruelest despots to underscore the abuse of royal power? Is Lord Acton right that "great men are almost always bad men"?

Even if we are intentionally self-aware of the picture we have drawn, this does not necessarily keep us from projecting modern notions onto the Iron Age monarchs. Some comfort can be found in the realization that the ancients kept their own lists and assessments—from the Sumerian King List to the Deuteronomistic criteria for the good and bad kings of Israel and Judah—and had their own predilections. All such reminders are important for the topic at hand, Yahweh as king. For ancients and moderns alike use what they know of the human institution of kingship to conceptualize what it means for Yahweh to be the monarch par excellence. In addition, aged lore across the entire ancient Near East told of how gods became kings, often through a tale of a warrior god who rose to preeminent kingship through cosmic battle. Such fantastic stories quickened the imagination of Yahwists as they explored the royal status and sovereignty of Yahweh in ways that went far beyond human kingship. Even "incomparable" kings such as Hezekiah and Josiah (2 Kgs 18:5; 23:25) could not slay a seven-headed dragon or bring about the creation of the world by royal decree.

A Brief Overview of Royal Cult in the Ancient Near East

The Religious Lives of Kings and Their Putative Divinity

The religious lives of ancient Near Eastern kings need to be stressed at the outset of our discussion. A modern interpreter who thinks that there is a clean separation between church and state could easily project the same on the ancient world. Yet nothing could be further from the truth. Egypt presents the parade example of the king's close association with divinity and thus his role as the primary religious officiant who provides access to the gods. According to Thomas Schneider (2004: 323), "Upon his accession to the throne the king became 'a human in the role of a god,' the successor on earth of the god Horus 'upon the throne of (the god) Geb.'" As for the performance of cult, John Baines (1998: 27–28) remarks how "the king's entire life was ritualized" such that ideologically he is portrayed in temple relief "as the sole officiant interacting with the gods . . . Only the king was depicted performing the temple cult." Donald Redford (2013: 28) writes of Akhenaten: "The active role adopted by the king . . . is absolutely unique and excludes all others: he is the 'High-Priest' of the Disc. . . . And in his capacity as sole celebrant, the king is the very image of the radiant Disc." Certainly the priesthood would have been delegated to carry out the day-to-day management of the cult; yet ideologically "the king was the chief ritualist and therefore responsible for the maintenance of the cult in temples," with the building of temples constituting "one of his most important duties" (Frandsen 2008: 47–48).[2]

In noting how the Sumerian King List tells of kingship being sent down from heaven, Jacob Klein (2006: 115) underscores how "the Neo-Sumerian and early Babylonian kings wanted their subjects to believe that kingship had been a divinely ordained institution from time immemorial."[3] According to Klein (2006: 126–127), literary *topoi* of royal legitimation "endowed [Neo-Sumerian kings] with superhuman qualities, such as perfect wisdom, immense physical power, [and] heavenly beauty"; they were described as "ideal rulers [and] righteous shepherds of their people, who uphold social and religious order in their land." Chief among their responsibilities was "the proper maintenance of the cult." Nicholas Postgate (1995: 398) concurs: "The kings included their care for the temples among their principal titles, this remaining integral to their moral claim to the right to rule."

Writing on Assyrian kingship, Peter Machinist (2006: 156, 186) unpacks the role of the king as *šangû*. "It makes sense," he argues, "to translate *šangû* as 'priest' and *šangûtu* as 'priesthood,' and to say that one of the roles of the Assyrian king is as chief priest of his realm." In such a role "the king [is] the primary nexus between heaven and earth: the lynchpin that allows the two realms to communicate with and sustain each other." Other Assyriologists agree. Jerrold Cooper (2008: 261) writes: "The vast majority of Mesopotamian sovereigns [were content] to be mediators between their subjects and the gods. . . . [K]ingship in Mesopotamia was always sacred." Piotr Michalowski (2008: 34) concurs: "All kings are sacred and mediate between sacred and profane." So does Irene Winter (2008: 86): "The sacral aspects of kingship . . . were what was foregrounded in the Neo-Assyrian period, no less than in earlier phases."

The royal cult in Ḫatti portrays the king "as the steward of the divine" and "as chief priest of the main deities," presiding over the state-sponsored cult (Gilan 2011: 280; see Beckman 1989: 101). Harry Hoffner (2006: 132, 138) demonstrates the importance of the king's religious duties by noting how his "presence at major religious festivals took precedence even over his duties as a battlefield commander." Hoffner illustrates this with the example of King Muršili II leaving the battlefield to travel back to Ḫattuša to partake in a religious ritual. Gary Beckman (1995: 532) also writes of how the king's religious obligations, "which underlay the entire system of thought supporting the monarchy," were more important than his administrative, judicial, diplomatic, and even military duties. The king's central religious role appears at every turn: donning priestly dress, offering prayers, presiding over the worship, undertaking activities during the festivals (breaking bread, pouring libations, washing of hands, making hand gestures, drinking, assuming body postures), building and maintaining sacred spaces.[4] Of special note are two calendrical/agricultural festivals (each lasting up to forty days) during which the king and his entourage visit cult centers throughout the empire.[5]

Turning to ancient Syria, we see how the Ugaritic mythological text about King Kirta tells of the god 'Ilu's patronage of the king as he faces three personal issues that impact the stability of the realm's political, social, and sacral order: the problem of succession, the monarch's personal health, and challenges to the king's rule.[6] At the heart of the royal cult at Ugarit is the divine benevolence toward the king. Simon Parker (1977: 173–174) sees this epic tale as intentionally underscoring "the virtues of 'Ilu as the incomparable savior" of the king. Such literary praise of benevolent divinity finds cultic expression in the Ugaritic ritual texts that attest to the king's participation in offering cult.[7] Paolo Merlo and Paolo

Xella (1999: 296) write that the king "was by far the principal officiant [and] often the main celebrant within a liturgy." Dennis Pardee (2002a: 239) notes the scholarly dilemma when it comes to reconstructing the full picture of Ugaritic religion: the ritual texts focus so much on the king as the central cultic actor that they are virtually silent when it comes to describing the other officiants who actually performed the cult.

KTU 1.119, a ritual calendar describing cultic activities in a specific month of the year, can serve to illustrate the primacy of the Ugaritic king in ritual. In this text the king must undergo a purifying rite of washing (*yrtḥṣ mlk brr*), and when he is finished with his cultic obligations he returns to a profane state (√*ḥll*). Such actions in the biblical sphere are associated with the priesthood (e.g., Lev 16:4, 23–24) rather than with the cultic actions of kings.[8] In KTU 1.119, the offering of sacrifice is the central activity in the ritual and the king is specifically described as sacrificing in the temple of the god 'Ilu (*ydbḥ mlk bt 'il*). Another monthly rite known to us from two texts (KTU 1.41, 1.87) also describes the king washing himself and being in a clean/pure state when engaging in cultic acts and in a profane state when free from his cultic obligations. As for his specific cultic acts, in addition to sacrifice (at one point on a roof), the king also pours libations (√*ntk*) and makes recitations while in a state of purity (*mlk brr rgm yṯtb*).[9] Elsewhere we have descriptions of so-called entry rituals where the king (and other members of the royal family) would take part in processions of divine images (cf. KTU 1.43; 1.112). Finally, in KTU 1.40, the king (specifically Niqmaddu) and queen are at the center of a national sacrificial ritual (although not officiating) that some have called an "atonement" ritual, similar in some respects to the Israelite *yôm kippûr*. That we have this ritual attested in multiple copies and at various find spots attests to its importance.[10] Various foreigners, along with the citizenry of Ugarit—differentiated as male participants (*bn 'ugrt*) and female participants (*bt 'ugrt*)—are described as taking part in a rite of expiation for personal and cultic offenses. According to Pardee (2002a: 78), "The rite may have been to promote communion, both between the social groups named in the text and between humans and deities honored ('Ilu and his family)." The royal concerns lying behind this text (for the citizenry at large and for diplomatic relations) match the ideology presented in the story of King Kirta (KTU 1.16.6.45–50; cf. KTU 1.17.5.4–8; KTU 1.23; Lewis forthcoming a). It too underscores that the king's role (religious and otherwise) included championing the case of the non-elite (the widowed, the poor, the oppressed, the orphaned, the non-resident).

The King's Role in Cultic Activities in Pre-Exilic Israel: A Sampling
Apart from Psalm 110:4 with its idyllic mention of the priest-king Melchizedek (discussed later), kings in ancient Israel and Judah (at least according to our biblical data) were not called "priests" (*kōhănîm*).[11] And apart from a single

monarch (King Ahaz, who is discussed later), they did not engage in the distinctive priestly activity of blood manipulation.[12] Nonetheless, kings were religious officiants involved in the performance of the cult as well as the primary sponsors who built and maintained altars, sanctuaries, and temples. In Ziony Zevit's (2001: 452) words, "Biblical and extra-biblical sources indicate that royal involvement with cultic affairs was the rule rather than the exception."[13] Jacob Milgrom (1991: 557) concurs: "The king had the right to officiate in the cult and indeed exercised it."

Saul, the very first king, is described as making "burnt" offerings (*'ōlôt*) as well as the so-called peace offerings (*šĕlāmîm*) (1 Sam 13:9–14).[14] In what seems to be an independent and earlier tradition (there is no mention of any censure), 1 Samuel 14:31–35 portrays Saul as being particularly concerned about whether the people had sinned against Yahweh by eating meat with blood (cf. Deut 12:16; Lev 19:26). Saul goes on to supervise the animal slaughter so that it is done properly at an altar he built to Yahweh. Notably, no priests are mentioned in the narrative. That the text mentions that this was "the first time Saul built an altar to Yahweh" (1 Sam 14:35) implies that he built additional altars, yet our extant texts are incomplete and give us no further details.

In Psalm 89:21 (Eng 89:20) David is divinely anointed as king, with Yahweh using "holy/consecrating oil" (*bĕšemen qodšî mĕšaḥtîv*; cf. 1 Sam 16:13; 2 Sam 12:7). Elsewhere we have similar royal anointing (1 Sam 10:1; 2 Kgs 9:3, 6) where the manner (pouring on head) and ritual substance (*šemen hammišḥâ*) remind us of the anointing and consecration of the high priest.[15] David's cultic activities are concentrated in the narrative about bringing the Ark of Yahweh to Jerusalem. During this transport David is described as sacrificing an ox and a fatling (2 Sam 6:13), engaging in ritual dancing (2 Sam 6:16), and making *'ōlôt* and *šĕlāmîm* offerings "before [the Ark of] Yahweh" (2 Sam 6:17).[16] During two other episodes David uses priestly divinatory means (the ephod and presumably the Urim and Thummim) to determine Yahweh's will (1 Sam 23:6–12; 30:7–8; cf. 1 Sam 23:1–5). Though a straightforward reading could suggest that David himself manipulated the sacred lots, it seems more likely that the text is elliptical and that he used them via the agency of the priest Abiathar.[17]

As for sacred space, David pitches a tent for the Ark (2 Sam 6:17) and later builds an altar on which he again makes *'ōlôt* and *šĕlāmîm* offerings (2 Sam 24:18–25; 1 Chr 21:15–30). Not to be missed in this latter account is the way in which Davidic traditions place him at the center of a remarkable transformation of mundane space. According to the Chronicler's tradition (1 Chr 21:15–1 Chr 22:1; 2 Chr 3:1), David's decision to build an altar and sacrifice on Ornan's threshing floor (Aravnah's in the Deuteronomistic tradition)—in faithful response to an angelic command—ultimately led to this ordinary agrarian space being transformed into sacred space of the highest order: the Jerusalem

Temple. In order to understand this episode, many factors need to be considered, including the historicity of the Chronicler's tradition in view of the Deuteronomistic History's silence on the matter. Such a foundation story (if historical) underscores considerable royal influence in Jerusalem's religious affairs from the outset, or (if not historical) it highlights the need to assert a royal origin for the Temple to bolster the Davidides' power and influence during a time when they must have been weakened. What is again noticeable in the royal cult described here is the lack of priestly involvement. This absence is more dramatic than the non-mention of priests in the Saul narrative noted earlier. For (if this account is historical), priests would have to assert their influence in a major way to redefine this mundane, openly accessible, agrarian space into restricted sacred space with gradations of holiness under their sole purview. One can only imagine the ways in which royal and priestly interests negotiated the repurposing of a threshing floor into the ultimate symbol of divine presence and power.[18] What needs to be emphasized in the present discussion is the way in which this foundation story of what was to become the religious *axis mundi* attached itself to King David. Similar workings (machinations?) are involved in the Chronicler's portrayal, which celebrates David's primacy in organizing the acquisition of building materials and craftsmen for the Jerusalem Temple (1 Chr 22:2–5, 14–16; 29:2–5), his organization of (and cultic instructions to) the Levites (1 Chr 23), his orchestration of the music to be used in the Temple (1 Chr 25:1; 2 Chr 7:6), and his drawing of the architectural plans with detailed specifications of various cultic paraphernalia (1 Chr 28:11–19).

Not to be outdone, the royal cult associated with King Solomon is privileged to an even greater degree in biblical tradition. Such an elevated role required a nuanced articulation vis-à-vis the religious traditions of King David. The solution was, of course, to emphasize Solomon as David's religious heir apparent, divinely chosen to be *the* Temple builder in his place (2 Sam 7:11–16; 1 Kgs 5:5; cf. Ps 132:11–18). The Chronicler makes a special point of having David proclaim that it was indeed his intention to build the Jerusalem Temple but that God had resolved to have Solomon as the builder because of the blood David had shed in the past (1 Chr 22:7–8; 28:2–3; cf. 1 Kgs 5:17 [Eng 5:3]).[19]

Prior to the building of the Jerusalem Temple, Solomon's cultic activities include sacrificing and burning incense at high places, with his sacrifice of 1,000 ʿōlôt offerings at the "great high place" of Gibeon being singled out (1 Kgs 3:2–4).[20] After his legitimizing dream revelation at Gibeon, Solomon returned to Jerusalem, where he made ʿōlôt and šĕlāmîm offerings before the Ark (1 Kgs 3:15).[21] Solomon's building of the Temple receives extensive treatment in both the DtrH and Chr traditions. The detailed narratives go far beyond David's providing of the building materials. Solomon gathers building materials as well, yet his construction narrative is fleshed out to a much greater degree by including technical descriptions, specific architectural features, and the articulation of a workforce made up of general laborers and those with specialized skills (1 Kgs 5:15–8:13 [Eng 5:1–8:13]; 2 Chr 1:18–6:11 [Eng 2:1–6:11]). Though these laborers accomplished the actual work, the authors are keen on using third-person *singular* verbs to describe over and over again how it was *Solomon* who built the Temple.[22] Notice in particular how Solomon is given credit for building the innermost shrine (*dĕbîr*), the Holy of Holies (*qōdeš haqqŏdāšîm*), in which the Ark of Yahweh was housed and guarded by two huge cherubim (1 Kgs 6:16–36; 2 Chr 3:8–13). Gold abounds in every aspect of his crafting. Thus we read of Solomon's proclamation at the dedication ceremony: "I [O Yahweh] have built you an exalted house" (1 Kgs 8:13//2 Chr 6:2).[23]

Royal cultic activities formed a central part of the temple's dedication ceremony, with Solomon engaging in two sacrificial episodes. In the first his sacrifices of oxen and sheep are beyond number (1 Kgs 8:5//2 Chr 5:6), while in the second they are exaggerated to be 22,000 oxen and 120,000 sheep as *šĕlāmîm* offerings as well as *ʿōlôt*, grain, and fat offerings (1 Kgs 8:62–64//2 Chr 7:5–7).[24] This is not to imply that Solomon absorbed all priestly prerogatives, for priests alone are privileged to bear the Ark into the Holy of Holies (1 Kgs 8:3–11//2 Chr 5:4–7).[25]

Subsequent traditions speak of Solomon's (regular?) cultic activity of making *ʿōlôt* and *šĕlāmîm* offerings three times a year (1 Kgs 9:25; cf. 2 Chr 8:12–13). Most scholars view *wĕheʿĕlâ* in 1 Kgs 9:25 as a frequentative ("Solomon used to...") and combine it with the Chronicler's understanding (2 Chr 8:13) to argue that Solomon officiated at the three great pilgrimage feasts of Unleavened Bread, Weeks, and Sukkot (cf. Exod 23:14–27; Deut 16:1–17).[26] The Chronicler adds that like his father, David, Solomon also appointed priests and Levites to their service (2 Chr 8:14). DtrH inserts disparaging comments about Solomon engaging in syncretistic worship linked to the religion of various foreign women to whom he was married. DtrH specifically highlights his building of sacred space (the notable "high places") for two of these deities (the Moabite Chemosh and the Ammonite Molek), yet adds that the cultic activities per se were enacted by the wives, not Solomon (1 Kgs 11:7–8).

All in all, the Judean royal cult of Solomon (building on the foundation of David) was remarkable in its reimagining of religion: at the end of his reign, the nature of Yahweh was infused with royal imagery. Ancient Israelites certainly knew of kingship before they had their own monarch; Yahweh was thought to be king in their earliest poems. Yet with the erection of the Solomonic Temple, Yahweh now sat enthroned as king in his royal abode in the heart of Jerusalem. Yahweh the king, at the center of a hierarchical royal and priestly administration, has traveled some distance from the family god who shepherded his people in the most intimate of ways.

Many other kings (Israelite and Judean) were very involved with religion and cultic matters—from Bethel being called "the king's [i.e., Jeroboam II's] sanctuary" and "a temple of the kingdom" (*miqdaš-melek hû' ûbêt mamlākâ hû'*; Amos 7:13) to the reforming kings who constructed and deconstructed cultic apparatuses.[27] Royal cult also saw queens and queen mothers as cultic actors, with our best examples being Jezebel and her sponsoring of Baal and Asherah worship (1 Kgs 18:19), Athaliah and her patronage of Baal (2 Kgs 11), and Maacah and her erection of an *asherah* image, likely in the Jerusalem Temple (Ackerman 1998a: 142–146).[28]

Two royal actors need to be singled out for special comment. The first is the Israelite king Jeroboam I (ca. 930–908 BCE), whose religious activities are described by Zevit (2006: 192) as "the *locus classicus*" of royal cultic participation. Like Solomon, Jeroboam I is a builder of sacred space, with his sanctuaries at Bethel and Dan that served as pilgrimage centers. At these sanctuaries, he makes and installs divine bull images of either El or Yahweh (see Chapter Five, pp. 198–200, and Chapter Seven, pp. 318–320). In addition, he installs non-Levitical priests, reforms the cultic calendar, and sacrifices to his bull images at the altar (1 Kgs 12:28–33).[29] Remarkably, Jeroboam I also asserts his prerogative to offer incense (1 Kgs 13:1), an activity elsewhere reserved for priests.[30]

The extensive royal cult of the Judean king Ahaz (735–727 BCE) is unmatched by any biblical king, Israelite or Judean. The DtrH narrative of his cultic activities is found in 2 Kings 16:3–4, 10–16. At the outset, DtrH uses its stereotypical vocabulary to list Ahaz's "abominable" acts of child sacrifice as well as his cultic activities "on the high places, hills and under every green tree."[31] What is unique is the description that follows, which tells of the king's travels to Damascus, where he sees an altar that captivates his attention. He then sends a model and pattern of the altar to Uriah the priest, who builds a replica in Jerusalem. Upon its completion, King Ahaz engages in the cultic acts of making his own burnt (*'ōlâ*), grain (*minḥâ*), and drink (*nesek*) offerings.[32] He also brings about considerable innovations in the Jerusalem cult, including the dismantling of established cultic paraphernalia (2 Kgs 16:14–18). Yet what is most surprising and unparalleled within royal cult is his taking on a distinctly priestly role: "King Ahaz scattered the blood of his *šĕlāmîm* offering against the altar" (2 Kgs 16:13).[33] Nowhere else does a king manipulate blood in such a fashion. Elsewhere such activity is solely the prerogative of priests. Zevit (2006: 195) argues that "the historian's point in describing Ahaz's selective officiating at the altar ... was to illustrate its peculiarity.... It was the exception; not the rule."

It is also noteworthy to read that King Ahaz then commands the priest Uriah to engage in various sacrificial offerings, including blood manipulation, and the priest complies with his every demand (2 Kgs 16:15–16). Such a statement helps to confirm Deborah Rooke's reconstruction of the royal-priestly dynamic when it came to the actual performance of cult. According to Rooke (1998: 195), it was

> *normally* the job of the senior priest to function *in loco regis* and carry out what were technically delegated royal duties on a daily basis ... it seems reasonable to conclude that the king would have had the right, if not the duty, to perform quite a number of ritual observances, but that his responsibilities were largely delegated to the senior priest. (My emphasis)

And yet, *pace* Rooke's insights, certain episodes in Judean history (e.g., the Jehoida-Jehoash narratives [2 Kgs 11–12; 2 Chr 24], the Uzziah/Azariah confrontation and its aftermath [2 Chr 26:17–18]) give evidence of when the situation was not "normal" and of where there were priestly efforts to limit the cultic (and political) role of the king.[34] The Deuteronomic Law of the King (Deut 17:14–20) similarly attempts to restrict royal power, including in the cultic sphere.[35] Moreover, in later periods, one would see dramatically different perspectives, ranging from Ezekiel's limiting royal power with his vision of a diarchical reign—with its demotion of the *melek* to a *nāśî'* figure (cf. Levenson 1976)—to the mysterious disappearance of the Davidide Zerubbabel in the book of Zechariah that resulted in a priestly consolidation of power (Lewis 2005b).

To conclude, we return to Zevit (2006: 194), who provides a convenient summary of the role of pre-exilic (and especially early) Israelite and Judean kings in cult:

> Biblical texts suffice to indicate that the kings of Israel from the tenth century and of Judah from the middle of the ninth century acted like their more powerful royal counterparts and contemporaries in cultic affairs, politics and construction.

At the same time, there are clear priestly prerogatives (e.g., bearing the Ark of Yahweh, entering the Holy of Holies, wearing sacral vestments, ritual washings, handling cultic pollution, blood manipulation, offering incense) that over the course of time—especially with the development of the priestly culture reflected in the P and H material—distinguished priestly cult from its royal counterpart.[36] In view of the royal use of the cognate term for "priest" (*khn*) in neighboring Phoenicia, one could assume that the Judean priesthood exerted strong influence in keeping the term *kōhēn* for themselves.[37]

The Question of Divine Kingship
Having briefly looked at the functional nature of the early royal cult, it is time to look at the ideological nature of kingship, especially Judean kingship within

its ancient Near Eastern setting.[38] Regrettably, the history of past scholarship on the sacrality of kingship has often been mingled with speculations about divine kingship. This was especially true of the myth-and-ritual approach (see Chapter Two, pp. 27–29) and biblical scholars such as Sigmund Mowinckel, who argued that the Judean king was a "*divine* being... a powerful, superhuman being... He is a god" (Mowinckel 1956: 62, emphasis his). More recent assessments have eschewed the "patternist" approach whereby the notion of the king as god has been assumed from the outset and replicated throughout the entire ancient Near East. Granted, Egypt presents a special case with its articulations of the king's divinity. Yet even here we need to nuance the extent to which all kings at all times were regarded as divine/semi-divine, for there is clear evidence of what Alexandra von Lieven (2010: 2) calls a "historical evolution of deification."[39] Moreover, though it would be unwise to minimize the power of royal ideology, the fact that non-royal elites were also deified (including certain women) reveals that it is not kingship alone that marked one for deification. As for the nature of deification per se, Marie-Ange Bonhême (2001: 403) cautions that "the divinity of kings ... derived from the gods and is therefore not original." Using Ramses II as an example, she adds: "On the one hand, the efficacy expected of the king is comparable to that of Re, the luminous god who repels the enemies of Egypt into the shadows; the king and Re collaborate in the magical protection of the lands of Nubia. On the other hand, the king, who is not the god, is the sign of the efficacy of the god's power, which requires royal intermediation to be actualized."

The character of Mesopotamian kingship has played a central role in formulating past reconstructions of divine kingship in Judah.[40] Current understandings of the topic are considerably different from those of past generations. In contrast to adherents of Frazer's grand, sweeping paradigm, we now read much more nuanced assessments such as that of Michalowski, who discusses the divine kingship of particular individuals (Naram-Sin of Akkade and Shulgi, the second king of the Ur III Dynasty) while weighing the vicissitudes of their historical context. In contrast to the grandiose claims of the Frazerian past, Michalowski (2008: 39, 41–42) concludes that divine kingship had a relatively "short shelf life." Moreover, it had "nothing to do with any autonomous symbolic system" but was rather "but one component in a complex fabric of economic, structural, and ideological reformations that took place in a concrete historical context." Cooper (2008: 261) concurs that kingship was "rarely divine" and that its divinity was "a historically contingent phenomenon," as does Winter (2008: 87), who stresses "the political parameters of the explicit ascription of divine status to rulers when it does occur."[41]

Divine Vocabulary Used of Kings: The "Infusing of Divinity"
At the same time, we need to be careful not to be so reductionist that we fail to appreciate the sacral and mediating roles of the king where he could be viewed as

"the primary nexus between heaven and earth." Illustrious vocabulary was used to depict how the king could partake of the divine. Consider the Middle Assyrian king Tukulti-Ninurta I (1243–1207 BCE), whose legacy lived on into the Neo-Assyrian period. As noted by Machinist (2006: 170, 184, 186), Tukulti-Ninurta I was the "favorite" and "beloved" of the gods, divinely birthed and nurtured, even adorned with divine radiance. Of particular note is the way in which the king represented the god as his "image" (*ṣalmu*), reflecting the deity's "capacity and character." Machinist concludes: "It is difficult to deny that these [attributes] look to some kind of divine status for the king." Winter (2008: 88) offers yet another way to conceptualize the topic: "Mesopotamian kingship was consistently treated as if *infused by the divine*, 'sacral kingship' being the constant in which all rulers participated. As such, kingship itself was always 'divine' " (my emphasis).

The Infusing of Divinity and Judean Kingship

Machinist's emphasis on how divinely chosen and endowed kings can be garnished with illustrious (divine-like) depictions and Winter's terminology of "infused sacral divinity" are both helpful when applied to the debate over divine kingship in Judean royal ideology. Such analyses strike a middle ground, not advocating that Judean kings were thought to be deities in their own right while not devaluing or minimizing the divine support of the Judean king or his central role as a cultic actor. Contrary to the assertions of the myth-and-ritual school, there is no explicit evidence that any Judean king ever underwent a process of deification, nor is there any ritual data that would indicate that he became the recipient of cult. We have prophetic polemics against foreign monarchs who portray themselves as gods (Isa 14:12–15 against the king of Babylon; Ezek 28:2–10 against the prince of Tyre; cf. Dan 3). That we have no record of such polemics being written against Judean kings is telling, for prophetic critiques certainly would have been penned had any Judean monarch made a bold claim to divinity.[42]

Nonetheless, Judean ideology articulated how Yahweh's chosen king was endowed with divine traits, traits needed to rule as God's steward. The Davidic king is portrayed as the firstborn son of Yahweh. It was Yahweh who gave him birth and Yahweh who relates to him as a father to a son (Ps 2:7; 89:28 [Eng 89:27]; 2 Sam 7:14; Isa 9:5).[43] Yahweh extends his divine *ḥesed* (a word whose semantic range includes loyalty, faithfulness, goodness, and graciousness) to his anointed king (2 Sam 7:15; Ps 18:51 [Eng 18:50]//2 Sam 22:51; Ps 21:8 [Eng 21:7]; 2 Chr 1:8; Prov 20:28). The illustrious lore of David and Solomon is particularly interesting. As previously noted, David's kingship is superlative in that like Yahweh he fights the cosmic Sea and is granted the status of "*most high*" with respect to earthly kings (*'elyôn lĕmalkê-'āreṣ*; Ps 89:20–28 [Eng 89:19–27]).[44] In 1 Kings 3:13 (//2 Chr 1:12) Solomon is granted incomparable "radiance" (*kābôd*) by

Yahweh, who is elsewhere described as "the King of Radiance" (*melek hakkābôd*; Ps 24:7–10; see p. 459). Incomparable "majestic strength" (*hôd*) is bestowed upon Solomon (1 Chr 29:25) by Yahweh, who is also characterized by *hôd* (Ps 8:2; 148:13). Eventually Solomon is referred to as "beloved" (*'āhûb*) of God, the only king to receive such a designation (Neh 13:26).

Psalm 21:4–8 (Eng 21:3–7) provides us with a nice summary. After noting how the king enjoys divine protection and divine access (Ps 21:2–3 [Eng 21:1-2]), the psalmist praises God and king with the following words:

> You [God] have proffered him [the king] blessings of good things,
> have set upon his head a crown of fine gold.
>
> He asked You for life; You granted it—
> length of days, lasting forever [*'ōrek yāmîm 'ôlām wā'ed*].
>
> Great is his radiance [*kābôd*] through Your victory;
> You have endowed him with splendor and majesty [*hôd wĕhādār*].
>
> You bestow on him blessings forever,
> you gladden him with the joy of Your very presence.[45]
>
> Indeed, the king trusts in Yahweh,
> Due to the *ḥesed* of the Most High
> he will not be shaken.

According to Judean royal ideology, along with a golden crown, God also blessed (infused) his chosen monarch with God's very presence, as well as the deity's victory, goodness, *ḥesed*, and ongoing blessings. In short, the character of Yahweh's king was portrayed as reflecting that of his divine benefactor: majestically radiant, trustworthy, unshakable, and with a lengthy reign.

As Psalm 21:7 (Eng 21:6) describes the intimate presence (*pānîm*) of Yahweh being with the king, so the Isaianic ideal has the very spirit (*rûaḥ*) of Yahweh "resting" on the king to "gird" him with the following divine qualities: wisdom (*ḥokmâ*), understanding (*bînâ*), counsel (*'ēṣâ*), might (*gĕbûrâ*), knowledge (*da'at*), justice (*mišpāṭ*), righteousness (*ṣedeq/ṣĕdāqâ*), equity (*mîšôr*), and faithfulness (*'ĕmûnâ*) (Isa 11:2–5). The idyllic Davidide of Isaiah 9:5–6 (Eng 9:6–7) is similarly described, as he bears the illustrious/divine names that point simultaneously to the character of Yahweh and the divine traits of his chosen king. These traits of Yahweh and his Davidide emphasize a superb warrior (*'ēl gibbôr*; cf. Isa 10:21) whose rule nonetheless promotes never-ending well-being (*śar-šālôm*); a King/king known for unfathomable counsel (*pele' yô'ēṣ*; cf. Isa 28:29);

and an enduring fatherhood (*ʾăbî ʿad*) that, as we have seen, was the hallmark of a benevolent ruler.

Psalm 45, used excessively by the myth-and-ritual school, should be situated in the context of such illustrious vocabulary.[46] Once again we meet a king described with superlatives: most handsome of men, graceful of speech, eternally blessed, a majestically radiant warrior (i.e., with *hôd* and *hādār*) who victoriously rides to defend what is true and right (45:3–5 [Eng 45:2–4]). The Hebrew Bible is fully at home within its broader world, for such glorious descriptions of the perfect king are, in the words of Hans-Joachim Kraus, "painted with every imaginable Near Eastern color." Grandiose language is needed for the "king [who] represents the royal presence of God on earth" (Kraus 1988: 457). The king sits on the very throne of God, as explicitly stated in 1 Chronicles 29:23 about (once again) the illustrious Solomon: "So Solomon sat on the throne of Yahweh as king [*kissēʾ yhwh lĕmelek*]." Thus there can be no other way to understand Psalm 45:7 (Eng 45:6) ("Your throne, O God, endures forever" or, better, "Your divine throne endures forever") than as referring to an illustrious king "infused" with divinity as he sits on God's eternal throne.

To summarize: the Judean king is *not* God, he is *not* deified, and he never receives cult. At the same time, ideologically, he is so gifted, so infused with divine qualities, that his rule can exhibit godly equity (*mîšōr*) and righteousness (*ṣedeq*) (Ps 45:7–8 [Eng 45:6–7]) and, idyllically, well-being (*šālôm*), justice (*mišpāṭ*), and righteousness (*ṣĕdāqâ*) in the fullest sense of the terms (Isa 9:5–6 [Eng 9:6–7]; 11:1–9).[47] To complete the picture we should add Psalm 110, which highlights the cultic role of the king that was described earlier. This psalm too uses illustrious language: we read of the king being granted a seat at God's right hand (Ps 110:1), followed by a divine proclamation that he will be invested with the priest-king mantel (*kōhēn lĕʿôlām*) once held by the legendary Melchizedek (Ps 110:4; Gen 14:18).[48] Prophetic voices endorse the king's esteemed cultic office as well. Consider Jeremiah 30:21's use of distinctly priestly vocabulary to describe how God grants his noble ruler (*ʾadîrô*//*mōšĕlô*) the ability to draw near (*qrb*) to approach the divine— "for who would otherwise dare approach me?" (*kî mî hûʾ-zeh ʿārab ʾet-libbô lāgešet ʾēlay*).[49]

Yahweh as Sovereign

The preceding excursus on Judean kingship, functional and ideological, sets the stage for considering how Judeans envisioned Yahweh as king. If kingship (variously understood) was the dominant political, judicial, military, and religious institution throughout the ancient Near East, then it goes without saying that kingship was chosen as the obvious metaphor to describe the sovereignty of the gods. In every Near Eastern culture, it is common to read of gods reigning as kings and of a particular god ascending to preeminent kingship. In light of such a constant, it is odd to read scholars who assert that the notion of Yahwistic kingship arose only with advent of monarchies in ancient Israel and Judah. For example, Horst Dietrich Preuss (1995: 153) writes: "From the period prior to the formation of the state, there appears to be no instance of YHWH's kingship."

Here it would be helpful to revisit the linguistic and religious cultural continuum articulated in Chapter Six, pp. 256–269. The breadth of the linguistic attestations of the root *mlk* as it is applied to human and divine royalty (as masculine and feminine nouns, as verbal nouns, in various verbal stems, and in abstract expressions of "kingship" and "kingdom") is staggering, as it includes Akkadian, Amarna Canaanite, Amorite, Arabic, Aramaic (in all its dialects), Eblaite, Ethiopic, Hebrew (biblical and epigraphic), Mandaic, Moabite, Old South Arabic, Phoenician, Punic, Syriac, and Ugaritic, not to mention Greek transcriptions of *malk-* and *melk-*. In addition to attestations in wide-ranging literary genres (royal hymns and inscriptions mentioning God as king being the most prominent), one needs to add attestations of *mlk* as a theophoric element in personal names (e.g., *malkiyyāhû*, "my king is Yah[weh]").

Thus it makes most sense from an ancient Near Eastern perspective to assume that the metaphor of god as king was readily adapted as early as any believer chose Yahweh as his preeminent deity. One need not require state formation to conceptualize one's favored deity as a monarch and a preeminent one at that. Mesopotamian lore has kingship handed down from the heavens in pre-dynastic, antediluvian times, and in Egypt "there were kings ... from prehistory, before the state had come into being" (Baines 1998: 16). Ugaritic ideology (see KTU 1.23) promotes the idea that god and king from time immemorial are responsible for the blessings of agriculture (Lewis forthcoming a). Thus John Gibson (1994: 104), in studying the kingship of Yahweh against its broader Canaanite background, rightly concludes:

> If we read the evidence honestly and fairly, there seems to me to be no reason why ... Yahweh could not have been thought of from the start as something of a creator deity, as a god who had power over the forces of nature, as superior to other gods and therefore *entitled to be called King over the gods*. ... *The germs of all these leading facets of Israel's faith ... did not suddenly emerge only after the establishment of the monarchy*. (My emphasis)

Gibson's claim is buttressed with our earliest attested texts where Yahweh is referenced as king. The climax of the Song of the Sea proclaims: "Yahweh will reign [*yimlōk*] forever and ever" (Exod 15:18). Deuteronomy 33:5 has Yahweh tribally as king in Yeshurun; Psalm 29:10 has Yahweh cosmically enthroned as king (*wayyēšeb yhwh melek*) over the flood; the Balaam Oracles proclaim the battle cry of the king Yahweh (*tĕrûʿat melek*; Num 23:21b); and Psalm 68:25 (Eng 68:24) sings of the procession of "god and king" (*ʾēlî malkî*) into Yahweh's sanctuary.[50] Such archaic passages are what the psalmist has in mind when he proclaims that Yahweh is his king "from of old" (*miqqedem*; Ps 74:12).

The Superlative Quality of Yahweh's Kingship
Describing divine kingship can easily exhaust our supply of superlatives. It is no wonder that the word *ʾĕlōhîm* in Hebrew could be used grammatically to mark the superlative degree (Joüon and Muraoka 1991: §141n; Waltke and O'Connor 1990: 268). Yahweh was understood to be "king of kings and lord of lords," though this exact expression is not to be found in the Hebrew Bible (it comes rather from the apocalyptic battle scene in Rev 19:16).[51] Prophets have Yahweh himself proclaim in unmistakable clarity: "I am a great King" (*melek gādôl ʾānî*; Mal 1:14; cf. Isa 44:6; Jer 46:18) and poets extol that his kingship is eternal (*yhwh melek ʿôlām wāʿed*; Ps 10:16; Lam 5:19).

Superlative expressions of Yahweh's sovereignty stretch beyond legendary human kings (*mĕlākîm gĕdōlîm*//*mĕlākîm ʾadîrîm*; Ps 136:17–20) to include his reign over all the nations and their gods. This is particularly fleshed out in late literature. Deuteronomic traditions have Yahweh as absolute sovereign, the "god of gods and lord of lords, the great god, mighty and awesome" (Deut 10:17), who theologically has no rivals (Deut 4:35, 39; 6:4; 32:39; cf. Isa 44:6). The author of Psalm 136 uses similar language, adding that Yahweh *alone* performs great wonders, especially those of creation (Ps 136:2–4). Other psalmists praise Yahweh as "the king of all the earth," the enthroned, holy sovereign who "reigns over the nations" (Ps 47:7–9 [Eng 47:6–8]). Yahweh is "the great god, the great king above all gods [*melek gādôl ʿal-kol-ʾĕlōhîm*]" (Ps 95:3). Within the sociological and psychological contours of apocalyptic thought, divine sovereignty enjoys full expression. Yahweh is "truly the God of gods, the Lord of kings" (Dan 2:47).

Obviously, to assert that Yahweh is the king of kings or, better, the (divine) king of (divine) kings, implies that other divine monarchs were also worshipped in ancient Israel. This is clearly the case with the Queen of Heaven (*mĕleket haššāmayim*), likely ʿAshtart, mentioned in Jeremiah 7:16–20; 44:15–30. This deity, who had both royal and household cults, is treated in detail in the Conclusion. According to the Deuteornomistic Historian (1 Kgs 11:5, 33; cf. OG to 1 Kgs 11:7; 2 Kgs 23:13), the Ammonite god Milkom was worshipped by King Solomon. The Judean monarch even built a sanctuary to Milkom east of Jerusalem that Josiah then defiled. As for the putative god Molek (so often associated with child sacrifice), the most recent research makes it most unlikely that there ever was such a Judean deity (see Dewrell 2017: 4–36).

Yahweh's Kingship: Cosmic Warfare, Jerusalem Enthronement, and Zion Theology

To repeat, if kingship (in its various parameters) was the dominant institution throughout the ancient Near East including the southern Levant, then diachronically we can assume that the notion of Yahweh as king was a constant throughout Israelite and Judean cultures, though our extant texts provide us with a very incomplete record. We agree with Mettinger (1988: 92) that understanding Yahweh as king is at the very core of how many authors of the Hebrew Bible conceptualized Yahweh. The episodes of Yahweh's kingship that have withstood the ravages of time include the following highlights.

As discussed in Chapter Eight, pp. 453–460, the language of cosmic warfare marked Yahwistic kingly warrior cults from our earliest texts onward. Because such language used royal imagery, it was appropriated to legitimate Davidic/Judean kingship. To reiterate briefly, the vehicle of *royal* military might was frequently employed to flesh out Yahweh's *Chaoskampf* victories. Or, put differently, stories of preternatural *Chaoskampf* victories carried such cultural weight that they were the obvious choice to sing of how such a skillful, divine warrior should be accorded preeminent, *royal* status. It is Yahweh *as king* who fights on a cosmic scale (Exod 15:18; Ps 24:8, 10; Ps 29:10; Ps 74:12–15; Ps 89:6–19 [Eng 89:5–18]; Ps 93:1–4; Ps 97:1–5), and Yahweh's incomparable victory is the justification for worshipping him *as king* in his sanctuary that was built for just such a purpose (Ps 24:7–10).

As noted in Chapter Seven (pp. 366–368), Isaiah 6 paints a detailed portrait of Yahweh as king sitting on his throne in the Jerusalem Temple:[52]

> In the year of King Uzziah's death, I saw the Lord sitting on a throne, high and exalted; and the edges of his garment filled the temple [*wāʾerʾeh ʾet-ʾădōnāy yōšēb ʿal-kissēʾ rām wěniśśāʾ wěšûlāyw mělēʾîm ʾet-hahêkāl*]. Above him were attendant seraphim...
>
> Then I cried, "Woe is me! . . . my own eyes have seen the King, Yahweh of Hosts!" (Isaiah 6:1–2a, 5)

Our description in Chapter Seven concentrated on the radiant presence of Yahweh, described via winged creatures attending Yahweh's *kābôd*, and the danger for Isaiah, the prophet, when he "saw" the divine, a danger known from other passages that articulate the lethality of seeing God. We noted too the accompanying language of shaking thresholds and a smoke-filled temple, language that resonates with various cultic traditions. To these powerful images, we would now add the additional force of Yahweh as king, including his royal attire and lordly stature. What is of particular note is the size of the royal paraphernalia, which indicates that Yahweh is being portrayed as a supersized king. As noted by Jonas Greenfield (1985) and Mark Smith (1988), notions of deities sitting on superhuman-sized thrones were used at Ugarit (KTU 1.4.6.56–57; 1.6.1.56–65; 1.101.1–10) and in the description of God's enormous (10 cubits high by 10 cubits wide) cherub throne in the Jerusalem Temple (1 Kgs 6:23–28).[53] Elizabeth Bloch-Smith (1994: 20–25) emphasizes that this enormous throne is complemented by the immense basin known as "the Molten Sea," both of which served symbolic purposes: "Great size signified importance, sovereignty, and, ultimately, divinity. . . . [T]he enormous size symbolized the spatial and temporal magnitude of the deity." Bloch-Smith also emphasizes (as does Hugh Williamson [2005b: 125]) how the artists at Ayn Dara used extraordinarily large footprints to imagine a superhuman-sized God.[54] The imagery behind all of these large-scale portrayals, argue Greenfield, Smith, and Williamson, informs the royal vision in Isaiah 6 with Yahweh seated on a high and exalted throne (*yōšēb ʿal-kissēʾ rām wĕniśśāʾ*). Williamson (2005b: 124, 129–130) further adds how the enormous size of Yahweh's throne is also implied "if merely the edge of the Lord's garment [*šûlāyw*, traditionally translated 'train'] fills the sanctuary." In short, a supersized throne is yet another indicator of the superlative nature of Yahweh's kingship. Other signs are the various divine council traditions that elevate Yahweh's lofty throne to the heavens: "I saw Yahweh sitting on His throne, and all the host of heaven standing by, on His right hand and on His left" (1 Kgs 22:19//2 Chr 18:18; Ezek 1:26; 10:1; Dan 7:9; cf. Job 1:6; 2:1).[55]

A look back at the Zion traditions (see Chapter Eight, pp. 467–469) underscores how the notion of Yahweh as king was appropriated to underscore the inviolability of Jerusalem. The various Zion traditions, for all their similarities, nonetheless employ a wide array of visual images to depict Yahweh actively protecting his city. Yahweh is a helper and a refuge, a hovering bird, a burning fire, a logger felling trees, a lion, and a storm god. Within this literary variety is a dominant motif: Yahweh as capable, strong warrior who willingly chooses to defend his city. As the texts mentioned earlier indicate, Yahweh's military might is often couched in the language of a kingly warrior. Thus it is that we read that Mt. Zion is unassailable precisely because it is "the city of the great king" (*qiryat melek rāb*) and thus under his protection (Ps 48:3 [Eng 48:2]).[56] Yahweh has chosen Zion as his habitation and that of his Davidic king (Ps 132).

The Cultic Enactment of Yahweh's Kingship

The enactment of Yahweh's kingship in cult is a complicated topic. The field of biblical studies has experienced a long debate about the proper interpretation of a handful of psalms (maximally including Ps 47, 93, 95–99) whose theme is

Yahweh's kingship. These poets proclaim that God is worthy of praise as king. As warrior king, he sits enthroned robed in a majesty (*gē'ût lābēš*) and girded with a strength (*'ōz hit'azzār* Ps 93:1) that befits his victory over the nations and his sovereignty over the world (Ps 47:3, 7–9 [Eng 47:2, 6–8]; 93:1; 96:10). Such victories include hoary cosmic victories that allow the psalmist to write that his throne was "established from of old" (*nākôn kis'ăkā mē'āz*; Ps 93:2). Such victories were also harbingers for a warrior king coming in the future as righteous judge to adjudicate the world with equity (Ps 98:9).

If Yahweh is to be praised for being a "great king above all gods" (95:3), how did these poets think that this praise should be enacted in cultic ritual? How should his glory be best "proclaimed among the nations" (Ps 96:3)? Certainly such a cultic proclamation should come with loud and joyful shouts, the music of harps, and the trumpeting of horns (Ps 98:5–6). Beyond this we cannot be certain about any accompanying ritual, although several scholars (e.g., Day 1985: 18–21; Kraus 1989: 232–233, 236) are on solid footing when they suggest that (at least during certain times) Yahweh's kingship was central to *sukkôt* celebrations. This suggestion is based on a clear reference in Zechariah 14:16–17:

> All who survive of those nations that came up against Jerusalem shall go up from year to year *to worship the King*, Yahweh of Armies [*lĕhištaḥăwōt lĕmelek yhwh ṣĕbā'ôt*], and to observe the Feast of Booths [*ḥag hassukkôt*]. Any of the families of the earth that do not come up *to worship the King*, Yahweh of Armies [*lĕhištaḥăwōt lĕmelek yhwh ṣĕbā'ôt*], shall receive no rain.

On a much shakier footing is the suggestion of other scholars that these kingship psalms point to a coronation ritual that enacts as it celebrates that "Yahweh has become king." In other words, the proclamation is thought to be one of investiture. This suggestion is most closely connected to the work of Mowinckel and his followers, who interpret a phrase that occurs four times in these psalms (*yhwh mālāk*) as referring to Yahweh *becoming* king (Ps 93:1; 96:10; 97:1; 99:1). Thus these psalms are often referred to as "enthronement psalms."

Marc Brettler's (1989: 125–158) aptly titled book *God Is King* contains a detailed and perceptive analysis of this material, underscoring the methodological hurdles facing the historian who attempts to reconstruct ancient Israelite coronation rites, be they human or divine. Should these hurdles be overcome, the strongest case for Yahweh becoming king in a coronation ritual would be based on Psalm 93. A majestically robed Yahweh is indeed enthroned, and one can imagine his worshippers celebrating his kingship as they call to mind his victory over the chaotic waters (Ps 93:1–4; see pp. 454–455). In this sense, Yahweh has indeed *become* king (i.e., exercised his sovereignty) over those whom he vanquished. And yet our poet at the same time proclaims of Yahweh: "Your throne is established *from of old*" (Ps 93:2). For Brettler (1989: 146, 157, 167), this "counter-image" "implies that he has always been king." Contrary to Mowinckel's thesis, Yahweh "always 'was' and never 'became' king." Brettler (1989: 147–151, 167) also draws attention to the "significant anomaly" of non-Israelite nations being called upon to proclaim Yahweh's kingship in the so-called enthronement psalms. Sociologically, it is hard to imagine such a scenario being enacted in pre-exilic Judean cult. Brettler's alternative (seeing these motifs as eschatological visions of God as "judge of all nations" being projected into the present) makes much better sense. Moreover, if Psalm 93 is indeed our strongest evidence for a coronation ceremony, then it would seem relevant to underscore that it is Yahweh who robes himself with grandeur and strength dating back to the days of creation (see pp. 454–455).

Section II: Yahweh as Judge

A Royal Framework for Divine Justice

The traditions of divine warfare, Jerusalem enthronement, and Zion theology were perfect vehicles though which Judean royal ideology could construct and reinforce the very nature of power and by so doing promote the interests (and vital necessity) not just of God but also of king and state. Yet such royal power would not be sustainable (certainly from the perspective of the governed) unless it wielded judicial power. Consider the model portrayal of Absalom in his coup d'état (2 Sam 15:1–6). It was not enough to have the reality and the spectacle of military grandeur with horses, chariot, and an entourage (cf. 1 Sam 8:11; 1 Kgs 1:5). A proper king had to be seen as an accessible and responsive judge (*šōpēṭ*) at the city gate, a site chosen for a wide array of royal appearances (2 Sam 18:1–5; 19:9; 1 Kgs 22:10; 2 Chr 32:6; May 2014: 91–94).[57] A legitimate king is one to whom the populace looks to govern (*špṭ*) the nation successfully (1 Sam 8:5, 20).

Throughout the ancient Near East (and beyond), the ideology of the king as the embodiment of justice is grounded in a cultural understanding that earthly kings were to mirror the judicious behavior of the gods. Theologically, it was the gods who bestowed discernment upon earthly kings and then entrusted them with the duty to be righteous and wise judges, legitimizing their legal authority. In Mesopotamia, as noted by Mario Liverani (1995: 2360), "the quality of the king as righteous judge . . . finds expression in specific kinds of texts, namely the law codes whose aim is to demonstrate, through a lengthy list of practical examples, how correctly the kingdom was run under the king who authored the code." The Laws of Hammurabi were engraved on a basalt stela 7 feet (2.1 m) tall where the king stands before an enthroned Shamash, the god of justice (Figure 9.1).[58] The

Figure 9.1 King Hammurabi standing before an enthroned Shamash, the god of justice, on the stela bearing his laws.
Courtesy Mbzt. https://commons.wikimedia.org/wiki/File:F0182_Louvre_Code_Hammourabi_Bas-relief_Sb8_rwk.jpg.

message of the iconography could not be clearer: the god of justice and the king of justice work in tandem. Martha Roth (1995: 17) underscores how "the gods, and especially Marduk, Hammurabi's patron deity of Babylon, and Shamash, the god of justice, entrusted the king with the administration and equitable application of the principles of 'truth and justice' (*kittum u mīšarum*)" so that he, in the words of the law code's prologue, would "provide just ways and appropriate behavior for the people of the land" (prologue, vv. 16–19). The contours of justice are fleshed out in detail in the code's epilogue, with its focus on god and king (or, one could argue, king and god, for it is hard to miss Hammurabi's ego):

> In order that the mighty not wrong the weak, to provide just ways for the waif and the widow, I have inscribed my precious pronouncements upon my stela and set it up before the statue of me, the king of justice [*šar mišārim*], in the city of Babylon, the city which the gods Anu and Enlil have elevated, within the

Esagil, the temple whose foundations are fixed as are heaven and earth, in order to render the judgments of the land, to give the verdicts of the land, and to provide just ways for the wronged. (xlvii 59–78)

Let any wronged man who has a lawsuit come before the statue of me, the king of justice [*šar mīšārim*], and let him have my inscribed stela read aloud to him, thus may he hear my precious pronouncements and let my stela reveal the lawsuit for him; may he examine his case, may he calm his [troubled] heart [*libbašu linappišma*], [and may he praise me], saying: "Hammurabi, the lord, who is like a father and begetter to his people [*ša kīma abim wālidim ana nišī ibaššû*], submitted himself to the command of the god Marduk, his lord, and achieved victory for the god Marduk everywhere. He gladdens the heart of the god Marduk, his lord, and he secured the eternal well-being of the people and provided just ways for the land." May he say thus, and may he pray for me with his whole heart before the gods, Marduk, and Zarpanitu, my lady. (xlviii 3–47; Roth 1995: 17–18)

Juridical vocabulary understandably fills this narrative, yet the way in which it is framed is equally important.[59] We read of the king's justice not only in formal legal contexts (e.g., as he settles disputes and renders lawsuit verdicts). In addition, we hear of him especially as the protector and vindicator of the disadvantaged of society who have been wronged and are in need of legal safeguards. The language of the king as a father giving birth to his people (and as one who sets people's minds at ease) resonates with the familial portrayal of divinity. Procuring justice for the land secures "the eternal well-being of the people" and in so doing gladdens the very heart of Marduk. Once again, king and god work in tandem in their love for justice.

Ideologically, such is the case for every ancient Near Eastern monarch who seeks to be viewed as the representative of the gods in carrying out justice (cf. Weinfeld 1995b: 45–74). At Mari in the eighteenth century BCE, King Zimri-Lim was given the following charges by the god Adad:

When a wronged man or wo[man] cries out to you, be there and judge their case. This only I have demanded from you. (A. 1121 + A. 2731 lines 53–55)

Now hear a single word of mine: If anyone cries out to [you] for judgment, saying "I have been wr[ong]ed," be there to decide his case; an[swer him fai]rly. [Th]is is what I de[sire] from you. (A. 1968 lines 6′–11′)[60]

The Hittite king Arnuwanda I (ca. 1390s–1370s BCE) provided instructions that his "governor of the post, the magistrate [and] the elders shall judge law cases properly, and they shall resolve [them]" (CTH 261.I §37′; cf. §38).[61] His specific judicial instructions include the following admonitions:

Let no one accept a bribe. He shall not make a superior case inferior; he shall not make the inferior superior. You shall do what is just! ... and for whomever a law case is [pending], judge it for him/her and resolve [it for] him/her. If there is a law case [pending] for a male or a female servant or a woman without kin,[62] then decide it for them and resolve [it for] them. (CTH 261.I §39′, §40′)

Egypt too preserves the delegation of judicial authority with instructions written in a way that has God foremost in mind (cf. also Moses' judiciary, discussed later). Rekhmire was the royal vizier during the latter days of Thutmose III (ca. 1490–1436 BCE). The pharaoh installed him in office with the following charge:

Do not judge [?] [unfairly (?)], for God abhors partiality.... Regard him whom you know like him whom you do not know, him who is near you like him who is far [from you]; as for the magistrate who acts thus, he will be successful in his place.... See, the [real] worth of a magistrate is that he does justice.... And as for the office in which you judge, there is a spacious room in it full of [the records (?) of all (past)] judgments. As for him who shall do justice before all men, he is the vizier.... Do not do your [own will] in matters whereof the law is known.[63]

Rekhmire describes how the pharaoh "gave me a court of justice under my authority" because "[My Majesty] knows the decisions are many and there is no end to them, and the judgment of cases never flags." Rekhmire's autobiography describes how he was faithful to the judicial ideal:

I judged [poor and] and rich alike. I rescued the weak from the strong.... I defended the husbandless widow. I established the son and heir on the seat of his father. I gave [bread to the hungry], water to the thirsty, meat and ointment and clothes to him who had nothing ... I judged great matter[s?].... [I caused] both parties to go forth at peace. I did not per[vert justice] for reward. I was not deaf to the empty-handed, nay more, I never accepted anyone's bribe.[64]

The judicial ideal at Late Bronze Age Ugarit is seen from the challenge of the rebellious son Yassubu (cf. biblical Absalom), who demands that his father, King Kirta, step down from kingship, asserting that he has failed to carry out the essential duties of adjudicating the legal cases of widows and the oppressed, and casting out those who prey upon the poor (*ltdn dn 'almnt/lttpt tpt qṣr npš/ ltdy tšm 'l dl*; KTU 1.16.VI.44–48). Sharing the same notion of justice, another legend (the tale of Aqhatu) speaks of the admirable Danilu, who was known for providing justice for the widow and the orphan (*ydn dn 'almnt/ytpt tpt y[tm]*; KTU 1.17.V.7–8; cf. 1.19.I.23–25). A remarkable royal ritual text (mentioning king and queen) describes public confessions and various sacrifices culminating in a rare (and highly valued) donkey sacrifice.[65] On a national scale, the ritual's aim was to promote "justice" (*mšr*) for those in various sociopolitical groups, including the non-native residents (*gr*) living within the walls of Ugarit. Nothing in any of these texts explicitly says that the justice being sought out is that birthed of the gods, yet such an understanding is clearly implicit. King Kirta is "the son of 'Ilu," after all, and the symbiotic relation of god and king for the good of society is attested elsewhere, especially in KTU 1.23 (cf. Lewis forthcoming a). The "donkey sacrifices of justice" ('*r mšr*) in KTU 1.40 are offered to 'Ilu (and his divine family) with the dire hope and confidence that 'Ilu will indeed grant their request to restore and reestablish the well-ordered state of justice that he required.

Judean Royal Judicial Ideology

Biblical tradition espouses similar judicial ideology about Judean monarchs. The idyllic Davidide in Isaiah 11:2–4 will judge the poor and meek judiciously (*ṣedeq//mîšôr*) due to his piety, with the spirit of Yahweh's wisdom and counsel resting upon him (cf. Isa 9:6 [Eng 9:7]; Jer 23:5). Similar to the prayer on behalf of King Hammurabi (LH xlviii 41–47), the royal Psalm 72 prays:

> O Yahweh,[66] endow the king with your justice,
> The king's son with your righteousness
>
> That he may judge your people rightly,
> your poor justly.
>
> May he [righteously] judge the common poor,
> provide deliverance to the needy,
> and crush those who oppress [them]. (Ps 72:1–2, 4; cf. 72:12–14)

As Hammurabi's divinely elevated city of Babylon is ordained as the seat of justice and its temple as the seat of cult (LH xlvii 59–78), so too a psalmist proclaims that Jerusalem with its temple is a divinely ordained city where the thrones of the Davidic house are established as "thrones of justice" (*šāmmâ yāšĕbû kisʾôt lĕmišpāṭ kisʾôt lĕbêt dāwîd*; Ps 122:3–5).

Four Judean "Kings of Justice"

Four individuals (David, Solomon, Josiah, and Jehoshaphat) are portrayed in biblical tradition as ideal "kings of justice," to borrow the Akkadian phrase.[67] David is certainly the most surprising on this list, given his abuse of power. The Court History is frank with the unsavory details of his reign. Baruch Halpern (2001: xv, 73–103) labels him a "serial killer" with a "homicidal policy," and

Robert Wilson (1983: 243) describes his judicial behavior as "often arbitrary," with David "unwilling to apply the law evenhandedly." A later section will deal with David's criminality regarding the Bathsheba-Uriah episode and his missteps as judge. For now, consider the positive judicial traditions of David that endured along with tales of his dark side.

The Tekoite wise woman who brings a pretend legal case (prompted by Joab) before David flatters him by describing his judicial discernment as "like an angel/ messenger of God" (kĕmal'ak hā'ĕlōhîm kēn 'ădōnî hammelek lišmōa' haṭṭôb wĕhārā'; 2 Sam 14:17). Indeed, David is discerning enough to see her fictitious case for the ruse that it is (2 Sam 14:1–20).[68] Though those who suffered under his reign would beg to differ, David is said by the Deuteronomist to have exercised justice and equity (mišpāṭ ûṣĕdāqâ) for all his people (2 Sam 8:15). David is also presented as an ideal, just monarch in Psalm 89, where equity and justice (ṣedeq ûmišpāṭ) form the very foundation of his throne (Ps 89:15 [Eng 89:14]). A similar notion is found in Jeremiah 22:3, which presents an appeal for justice (including advocating for the widowed, the fatherless, and the non-Israelite resident or gēr) to the royal house "who sit on the throne of David." Divine justice also influences David's political behavior. Consider the legal language contained in the portrait of David sparing Saul's life in 1 Samuel 24. Rather than taking matters into his own hands by killing Saul, David defers to Yahweh as the ultimate judge (dayyān) who will plead his case (yārēb 'et-rîbî), arbitrate between him and Saul (yišpōṭ bênî ûbênekā), avenge David (nĕqāmanî; cf. Deut 32:35), and ultimately provide him with vindication over Saul (wĕyišpĕṭēnî miyyādekā) (1 Sam 24:13, 16 [Eng 24:12, 15]). When one combines all these legal stories, it is understandable that David's name is mentioned in passages that hope for a future idyllic "king of justice" (Isa 9:6 [Eng 9:7]; 11:2–4; 16:5; Jer 23:5).

Notwithstanding this picture of David's judicial prowess, Solomon's justice is of a much greater magnitude. Just as Solomon is portrayed as exceeding his predecessor when it comes to royal cult (see pp. 500–501), so too he is depicted as outshining David with regard to royal justice. Mettinger (1976: 238–246) speaks of Solomon being "charismatically" granted God's own judicial wisdom (cf. Ps 45:5, 7–8 [Eng 45:4, 6–7]; 72:1–4; Prov 16:10–15). Keith Whitelam (1979: 166, 219) even calls him "*the Just King par excellence*." Such impressions are certainly understandable; yet they ignore Solomon's breaking of cultic law (e.g., 1 Kgs 11:1–13), the machinations whereby he secured the throne (1 Kgs 1–2), and episodes of his self-aggrandizement—such that the Deuteronomic "Law of the King" (Deut 17:14–17) has him in mind as a lawbreaker.[69] On that note, according to the Deuteronomic restrictions on the monarchy, Solomon should not have had judicial authority to begin with (cf. Levinson 1997: 140–141).

The positive impressions of Solomon's justice come especially from the literary artistry that tells of his dream request of God (1 Kgs 3:3–15) and the memorable story of his adjudicating between two women each claiming to be the mother of the same child (1 Kgs 3:16–28). Solomon's dream request at Gibeon is sandwiched between mentions of his proficiency in cultic sacrifice at Gibeon and Jerusalem (1 Kgs 3:4, 15; cf. 2 Chr 1:3–6, 13).[70] Laying aside any thought of long life or wealth, the Deuteronomist instead has Solomon asking God for the ability to govern with justice: "Give your servant an understanding mind to provide justice [*lišpōṭ*] for your people, able to discern between good and evil" (1 Kgs 3:9). For verification, the narrative of the two women with conflicting testimonies immediately follows, and with it Solomon's perceptiveness and ability (via his shocking remedy by sword) to bring about a perfectly just decision. Little wonder then that Solomon's fame as one who possessed "the wisdom of God to render justice" (*ḥokmat ʾĕlōhîm bĕqirbô laʿăśôt mišpāṭ*; 1 Kgs 3:28) spread widely, to the Queen of Sheba in distant lands (1 Kgs 10:9; 2 Chr 9:8), and throughout subsequent history, even to the present as an archetype.[71]

King Josiah is the favorite of the Deuteronomist (i.e., Dtr1), in whose work he, like Solomon (1 Kgs 3:12) and Hezekiah (2 Kgs 18:5), receives incomparable status. Yet his incomparability lies in his religious reforms (2 Kgs 23:25), not in Solomon's wisdom and justice nor in Hezekiah's unparalleled trust (Knoppers 1992a: 413). For traditions about Josiah's idyllic justice, we turn not to a Deuteronomistic portrayal but to Jeremiah 22, which contrasts his just actions with the injustice of his son and successor Jehoiakim. The outset of this chapter articulates the divine expectations that those who sit on the throne of David will promote justice:

> Thus says Yahweh: "Act with justice and righteousness [*mišpāṭ ûṣĕdāqâ*]. Deliver from the defrauder anyone who has been robbed. Do no wrong or violence to the *gēr* [non-Israelite resident], the orphan, and the widow, or shed innocent blood in this place." (Jer 22:3)

Rhetorically, these expectations are highlighted prior to the prophet bringing indictments against Jehoiakim for how he ruled without righteousness and without justice (*bĕlōʾ-ṣedeq; bĕlōʾ mišpāṭ*; Jer 22:13). The sharp critique of Jehoiakim's injustice is poetic in its contrast with his father's behavior:

> Are you more of a king
> because you compete in cedar?
>
> As for your father [King Josiah],
> Did he not eat and drink
> and execute justice and equity?
> Then it went well with him.

> He advocated justice for the poor and needy;
> Then all was well.
> Is not this to know me?
> declares Yahweh.
>
> But your eyes and mind
> are only on your dishonest gain,
> on shedding the blood of the innocent,
> on practicing oppression and violence. (Jer 22:15-17)

It is not clear whether the reference to Josiah eating and drinking in Jer 22:15 is meant to underscore his enjoyment of life (Lundbom 2004: 138), his contentment with the simple necessities of life in contrast to Jehoiakim's extravagant building projects (cf. JPS footnote), or (as translated here) a metaphor for his appetite for justice (see Holladay 1986: 596). The justice that made Josiah an admirable king is characterized by the ancient Near Eastern royal ideal of caring for the disadvantaged. As expected, the prophet grounds such activity in the divine. Josiah's judicial concern for the poor and needy stems from and exhibits his knowing of Yahweh (Jer 22:16).

The narratives about King Jehoshaphat's judiciary (2 Chr 17:7-9; 19:4b-11) are complicated, with a lengthy history of scholarship. The king's very name ("Yah[weh] judges") almost begs scholars to advocate for the historicity of his ninth-century BCE judiciary (Albright 1950a) or, due to etiological suspicions, to argue for the total lack thereof (Wellhausen 1965: 191).[72] Jehoshaphat's judiciary has also been retrojected into pentateuchal narratives, especially the judicial structures of Moses in Exodus 18:13-27 and Deut 1:9-18; 16:18-20; 17:8-13. Yet clearly Gary Knoppers' (1994: 62, 79-80) sober assessment should prevail: the Chronicler, as a monarchist, reformulates earlier traditions to fit his own ideological concerns—namely, to "consistently ascribe," in contrast to Deuteronomic restrictions, a "pivotal role . . . to the king in governing Israel."[73] The Chronicler's royal ideal is as juridical as it is cultic, military, and political. "The Chronicler's king cares about military security and juridical reform and is equally adept at achieving both" (Knoppers 1994: 80). At the same time that Jehoshaphat's judiciary centralizes power in the crown, it also balances the competing interests of cult personnel (with priests and Levites) and traditional clan magistrates (with "heads of the fathers") (2 Chr 17.8; 19:8; Andersen and Freedman 2000: 350-351).

Yet as much as he reformulates his received traditions, there is one constant that the Chronicler does not change: the notion of Yahweh as supreme judge whose perfect justice must be emulated by those he designates to judicial office:

> Jehoshaphat said to the judges [he appointed], "Be intentional about what you are doing—for it is not on behalf of human beings that you render justice, but on

behalf of [none other than] Yahweh. He is with you in rendering justice. Now, let the dread of Yahweh be upon you; adjudicate with care. For with Yahweh our God, there is no injustice, favoritism, or bribe-taking." (2 Chr 19:6–7)

The Chronicler does not mention the disadvantaged triad of orphan, widow, and *gēr* so common elsewhere, preferring instead to concentrate on the serious nature of a human judge's position. Jehoshaphat's admonition is two-sided, severe yet supportive. It underscores Yahweh as the perfect judge in whom there is no injustice (cf. Deut 10:17–18; 16:19; 32:4) and for whom earthly judges act as proxy. Here, as noted by Knoppers (1994: 77), the king's exhortation echoes that of Moses, that justice is ultimately of God, with no need for earthly judges to fear human backlash (Deut 1:17). Wielding such responsibility, they are to carry out justice with guarded care (*šimrû ʿăśû*) and dread (*paḥad*), knowing that God, the unerring ultimate magistrate, will in turn be judging their judgments. At the same time, earthly judges can take heart in knowing that the supreme judge is indeed with them in the act of rendering justice.

Non-Royal Frameworks for Divine Justice

With kingship being such a dominant social and political institution, it made sense to look here first—and at the ideal of the just king—in order to view the Hebrew Bible's theology of God as judge. Consider the personal name Malkîṣedeq, "My [divine] king is [my] justice." The thematic catchphrase "There was no king in the land, everyone did as he pleased" in the book of Judges (Judg 17:6; 21:25; cf. 18:1; 19:1) also implies the need for a royal administration to bring about a just society. And yet, as Brettler (1989: 113) astutely observes, "the role of judging was never confined to the royal sphere, and most texts connecting judgment to God do not mention his kingship." As such, "we may not assume that all texts which use juridical terminology of God are a projection of *royal* justice on to him." Looking elsewhere bears this out.

Family Religion and Divine Justice on the Personal Level

As family and household religion (Chapter Eight, pp. 473–494) gave us a needed complement to the royal warrior cult (Chapter Eight, pp. 428–472), so too a look outside the notion of royal justice will prove instructive. Sources that open a window into the legal realities of the individual, of the household unit, and of small towns as opposed to the complex societies and elite hierarchies that produced urban law are few but telling. Moreover, if family religion emphasizes God as a "father to the fatherless," then it will complement the royal ideal that provides protection for the orphan. Familial language is used to proclaim that Yahweh is "father of orphans and the one who provides justice [*dayyān*] for widows" (Ps 68:6 [Eng 68:5]).

Rainer Albertz studied personal names found in the epigraphic record as a window into personal piety. Albertz documented two subgroups that either look to divine protection in providing justice[74] or employ judicial imagery in acts of confession.[75] Such imagery need not require a juridical setting with enemies as legal adversaries.[76] And yet, even if the language of Yahweh as judge is used metaphorically, it nonetheless testifies to a pervasive desire for divine justice in all walks of life. The names in Albertz's study include the following: ʾElyārîb, "El has contended/adjudicated [on my behalf]"; Yišpōṭ, "[God] has rendered justice [on my behalf]"; Šěpaṭyāhû, "Yahweh has rendered justice [on my behalf]"; Šāpāṭ, "[God] has rendered justice [on my behalf]"; Šipṭān, "Our legal assistance is of God"; Ṣādōq, "God" was/is just"; Yěhôṣādāq, "Yahweh was/is just"; Ṣidqīyāhu, "My justice is Yahweh"; Yědīnyāhû, "Yahweh has judged [in my favor]"; and Yôʿēd, "Yahweh is [my] legal witness."

The personal expression of trust and confidence in God as an active and caring judge that underlies these personal names is also found in individual laments in a number of psalms. Examples of acts of confession employing judicial language are found in Psalm 140 and, blending in royal language, Psalm 9:

> I know[77] that Yahweh will enact justice [*yaʿăśeh dîn*] for the poor,
> execute justice [*mišpaṭ*] for the needy. (Ps 140:13 [Eng 140:12])

> For you have executed a just verdict on my behalf [*mišpaṭî wĕdînî*];
> Enthroned as righteous judge [*šôpēṭ ṣedeq*] . . .
> [Yahweh] has established his throne for justice [*mišpāṭ*],
> It is He who judges [*yišpōṭ*] the world with righteousness,
> Judges [*yādîn*] the people with equity.
> Yahweh is a haven for the oppressed,
> A haven in times of trouble. (Ps 9:5, 8b–10 [Eng 9:4, 7b–9])

Such confidence and trust underlie the petitions of Psalms 7, 26, 43, 54 and Lamentations 3, which cry out with a similar voice:[78]

> Yahweh ordains justice [*mišpāṭ*] . . .
> Yahweh judges [*yādîn*] the peoples,
> Execute justice on my behalf [*šopṭēnî*], O Yahweh,
> According to the rightness and integrity that is in me. (Ps 7:7b, 9 [Eng 7:6b, 8)])

> Execute justice on my behalf [*šopṭēnî*], O Yahweh,
> for I have walked in my integrity,
> I have trusted in Yahweh without wavering. (Ps 26:1)

Execute justice on my behalf [*šopṭēnî*],
According to your rightness, O Yahweh, my God.
Do not let them [the accusers] rejoice over me. (Ps 35:24)

Execute justice on my behalf [*šopṭēnî*], O Yahweh,[79]
Defend my legal case [*rîbâ rîbî*] from the [accusations of] the ungodly,
From those who are deceitful and unjust deliver me! (Ps 43:1)

O Yahweh,[80] deliver me by your name,
Adjudicate for me [*tĕdînēnî*] by your might. (Ps 54:3 [Eng 54:1])

You have seen the wrong done to me, O Yahweh;
Render my cause with justice [*šopṭâ mišpāṭî*]! (Lam 3:59)

Additional Judicial Locations

Sociologically, the various traditions that have come down to us in the Hebrew Bible contain additional judicial locations beyond the royal sphere and expressions of personal piety. The degree to which the literary presentations of such social settings reflect historical realia continues to be debated and will not be taken up here in great detail. Yet the durability of these traditions underscores in additional ways how the notion of God as judge was a constant that permeated all social levels. However society was structured (or imagined to be structured for literary presentation), the ideal of God as an active, fair, and caring judge was a core belief. This certainly does not mean that issues of theodicy never arose, for indeed they did, and were articulated with poignant artistry (discussed later).

Wilson (1983) has courageously attempted to say what can be said of "Israel's judicial system in the preexilic period," with attention given to both premonarchic and monarchic judiciaries, although with minimal exploration of competing judiciary "origin myths" having to do with Moses (discussed later). Repeatedly and honestly acknowledging how little we really know of ancient Israel's judiciary in the pre-monarchic period, Wilson sketches viable scenarios from the gleanings of a handful of texts (Gen 31, 38; Josh 7; Judg 19–21), juxtaposed with anthropological theory on kinship groups.[81] With little help from the archaeological or epigraphic record, any historical reconstruction is obviously tentative.

Working with uncertainties at every turn, Wilson nonetheless is able to posit how legal proceedings may have worked within kinship-based social structures. For example, the judicial authority of the paterfamilias would have been significant within the household and extended family. This is reflected in patriarchal narratives in Genesis 31 and Genesis 38, in contrast to later legal codes that imagine no such scenario (Num 5:11–31; Deut 21:18–21; 22:13–21;

Wilson 1983: 233). Legal proceedings among different kinship groups would have necessitated a role for town elders (*zĕqēnîm*; references provided later) and were perhaps, if Ruth 4:1–12 is any guide, located at city gates (cf. Josh 20:4).[82] And yet—as nuanced by Raymond Westbrook and Bruce Wells (2009: 37), who add Genesis 16:1–6 into the mix—the patriarch Abram is portrayed as a co-litigant alongside Sarai rather than a family head with ultimate judicial power. Likewise in Genesis 38, Judah's legal rights are those of a litigant, not, contrary to Wilson (1983: 233), those derived from being a paterfamilias judge. As for the legal maneuverings of Genesis 31, a tribunal of kinsmen (*'aḥîm*, brothers), not elders, from both families are proposed as judges (Gen 31:32, 37), only in the end to give primacy to divine judgment (Gen 31:49–54), a topic to be taken up later. Further complicating the pre-monarchic picture are the various social levels within lineage systems where "judicial proceedings might have taken place at any level" and with varying degrees of success (Wilson 1983: 232–233, 237–239).

Moreover, a brief mention of Deborah as judge reveals that such an office need not always be exclusively male.[83] According to Judges 4:4–5, when Deborah was serving in a judicial capacity (*šōpĕtâ*), "the Israelites came up to her for a legal decision/justice [*lammišpāṭ*]." Regrettably, as Jack Sasson (2014: 256) remarks, we have no information "to explain how or under what circumstances Deborah assumed her role as judge," and yet "the narrator is so keen about placing Deborah among the judges that a special parenthetical clause addresses how and where she conducted her business." Later Sasson speculates that perhaps we have a "sly comment" by the narrator, who wants to address "God's capacity to empower other than those at palaces and temples."

Carol Meyers (1988: 154–157; cf. Knight 2011: 72–73) complements what we see in Deborah with anthropological and archaeological models that look at the ways in which women were involved in legal matters within the household unit. Early Israelite society was agrarian, and the household unit constituted the "basic level of social organization." The "ongoing dynamics" of the pre-state agrarian household included "socialization, education, and even religious observance and jural (judicial-legal) action." "There can be no doubt," Meyers (1988: 149) continues, "that women play a unique and critical role in the socializing process, broadly conceived." Of particular interest is the way in which laws regarding parental authority include men *and women* (Exod 21:15; cf. Exod 20:12; Deut 5:16).[84] Meyers (1988: 157) is quick to provide nuance that we are not talking about women having absolute jurisdiction within the household unit. Yet women's economic roles in the pre-monarchic economy were substantial, to such an extent that women had "considerable informal power and at least some legal authority."[85]

The Origin and Organization of Early Israelite Judiciaries

Sketching the history of Israelite judiciaries becomes even more complicated when one tries to factor in the various and distinctly different "origin myths" (Levinson 2008: 58–68; 2005: 89–100) that describe a highly organized judicial authority with Moses at the center. The Hebrew Bible preserves two accounts (Exod 18:13–26; Deut 1:9–18), perhaps three if one counts Numbers 11:16–25. Exodus 18 was addressed earlier for the key role that it has played in questions about the origin of Yahwism, the identity of Moses' father-in-law, and the Midianite hypothesis (cf. Chapter Six, pp. 271–276). As we saw, Jethro, the priest of Midian, becomes a Yahwist, either as a result of Moses' testimony about Yahweh liberating his people from Egyptian slavery (the position taken here) or prior to Moses' encounter with the deity (implying that Jethro, as a priest, played a vital role in teaching Moses about Yahwism). In either scenario, Jethro proclaims his faith in Yahweh with exuberant praise and the offering of cult (Exod 18:9–12). Joining Moses and Jethro at the sacrificial feast was Aaron—not only as Moses' brother but also in anticipation of his eventual consecration as high priest—and, remarkably, all the elders of Israel (*kōl ziqnê yiśrā'ēl*).

We read that immediately following the feast Moses was seated (some would say enthroned) in his judicial role (*wayyēšeb mōšeh lišpōṭ*).[86] His judgment is in such demand that people are willing to stand in wait from morning to evening. Moses describes the logistics of his role to his father-in-law as follows:

> The people come to me to [have me] inquire of God. When they have a legal matter, it comes before me and I adjudicate [*šāpaṭtî*] between one person and another, and I make known to them the statutes of God, that is, his very laws. (Exod 18:15b–16)

Here Moses, a well-versed judge, acts as a surrogate for God when it comes to legal matters. In addition to his role adjudicating cases, Moses also acts as an instructor of divine law. Such a dual role is acknowledged and restated by Jethro in Exodus 18:19b–20 with more detail: (1) Moses alone represents the people before God as he presents their legal cases before God's very presence, and (2) Moses is also the people's law professor who will clarify (*hizhartâ*) statutes and laws, applying them to all of life (lit. "how to walk and what to do").

The forward-thinking Jethro, realizing that Moses is taxed by such a heavy workload, proposes a division of judicial labor that will keep Moses from wearing himself out. Honest, competent men of godly character are to be chosen from the entire populace (*mikkōl-hāʿām*) to adjudicate the easier cases. With organizational (some would say military) precision, they are to serve as "officers" (*śārîm*) and "heads" (*rāʾšîm*) of variously sized divisions (thousands, hundreds, fifties, tens) (Exod 18:21-22, 25-26).⁸⁷ Moses precisely follows Jethro's orders in implementing this new judiciary. Noticeably absent is any mention of (or emphasis on) the aforementioned elders (Exod 18:12). This omission is particularly noticeable when juxtaposed with a variety of traditions that accord judiciary roles to elders (cf. Ruth 4:1-12; Deut 19:12; 21:1-9, 18-20; 22:15-18; 25:7-9; Josh 20:4; 1 Kgs 21:8; Isa 3:14; Jer 26:17; see too Num 11:16-25).

The origin of the Mosaic judiciary in Deuteronomy 1:9-18 (with parallel instructions in Deut 16:18-20 to follow) is prefaced with a remark about how Moses "undertook to expound" (*hôʾîl bēʾēr*) Yahweh's law (Deut 1:5).⁸⁸ The immediate focus is twofold: on the need to depart for the land sworn to the patriarchs and their descendants, and on the urgency of an expanded judiciary because of the growth of the population, which now numbers "as the stars of the heavens." The difficulty that accompanies such a population expansion is the heavy burden placed on Moses alone to adjudicate lawsuits (Deut 1:12). Thus Moses proposes that people choose wise, discerning, and experienced men from their tribes that he then appoints as judicial "heads" (*rāʾšîm*). Having done so, Moses installs their "tribal heads" (*rāʾšê šibṭêkem*) to function as "officials" (*śārîm*) over the variously sized divisions (Deut 1:15). Perhaps to clarify, their functions are described as those of tribal *šōṭĕrîm* (Deut 1:15); the term's Akkadian cognate, *šaṭāru*, points toward those skilled at actually writing legal documents (cf. CAD Š II, 231-234). Though *šōṭĕrîm* elsewhere can designate nondescript officials, scribes with Levitical connections, or even military officials (cf. HALOT 1441; Weinfeld 1977: 83-86), the judicial character of these *šōṭĕrîm* is made explicit in Deuteronomy 16:18.⁸⁹

As installed "judges" (*šōpĕṭîm*; Deut 1:16), they are ethically charged by Moses to adjudicate justly (*šĕpaṭtem ṣedeq*; cf. Deut 16:18-20). They are to render decisions without partiality, providing justice for natives and non-native residents (*gēr*) alike, with all social rungs (*kaqqāṭōn kaggādōl*) receiving equal treatment (Deut 1:17; cf. 10:17; Isa 11:3). The most difficult cases are reserved for Moses, who remains the supreme earthly judge.⁹⁰ Yet the judicial ideology and the premise upon which judicial ethics are grounded are the same: principled judges must not bow to human intimidation, "for justice is of God" (*kî hammišpāṭ lēʾlōhîm hûʾ*; Deut 1:16-17).

When juxtaposed with the account in Exodus 18, the absence of Jethro is striking. It is not merely that his role in forming the judiciary is minimized in favor of that of Moses. Rather, in the words of Bernard Levinson (2008: 66; 2005: 97), he "has been completely 'air-brushed' out of the retold, now sanitized, narrative as if to remove even the possibility of the Israelite system of justice having any foreign derivation. Jethro lives on only as spectral, textual trace, assimilated into the character of Moses, who now gives Israelite voice to the Midianite original plan."⁹¹ Rather than Jethro emphasizing Moses' role as the surrogate for God who clarifies and applies divine law to all of life, the focus here is on Moses' voice with its ethical charge of equal treatment under the law (*kaqqāṭōn kaggādōl*), for justice is of God.

A third tradition about the distribution of Moses' authority among seventy elders is found in Numbers 11:16-25. This shared governance tradition has been discussed as yet another narrative about the origins of the judiciary (e.g., Westbrook and Wells 2009: 37-38), and it very well might be. Yet with the present state of our text, it is hard to press the case, though there are tantalizing details. As the text is currently formulated, the shared governance being described is absent of any explicit reference to a judiciary. There is no mention of lawsuits being brought before Moses, God's judicial surrogate, nor is there any ethical charge to subordinate judges to be just in their legal renderings. Instead we have here an account situated within a literary complex that addresses the distribution of Moses' prophetic (not judicial) authority among seventy elders (Num 11:10-25), with addenda addressing the specific situation of Eldad and Medad (11:26-30) and that of Miriam and Aaron (12:1-16).

The broader literary complex includes yet another tradition about Moses' Midianite father-in-law, here called Hobab, as a reluctant wilderness guide who has to be urged to become involved (Num 10:29-32). Moses is once again the overburdened solitary leader of a huge populace, here concerned with providing enough meat to eat (Num 11:4-15). The subordinate leaders are elders (*zěqēnîm*), seventy in number, who are chosen not because of their godly and just reputations (though they may have been so regarded) but because they are known to be elders and *šōṭěrîm* officials (Num 11:16). No information is given about selecting them because they are impartial or competent in seeking justice for the disadvantaged.

Obviously, there are enough differences in this tradition to deny its status as a judiciary origin tale with sound justification. And yet it remains tantalizing to speculate that underneath the present formulation we may have a variant judiciary tradition about Moses and his father-in-law that eradicates the role of Hobab, much as Deuteronomy 1:9-18 airbrushes Jethro out of significance.[92] The notion of elders as judicial figures resonates with Wilson's anthropological reconstruction and with the numerous texts that, as we have seen, explicitly mention elders as judges. The selection of the *šōṭěrîm* officials alongside the elders in Numbers 11:16 is intriguing, especially if the term designates someone skilled in legal documentation, as suggested earlier with regard to Deut 1:15 with support from Deut 16:18-20. There, the *šōṭěrîm* officials along with the judges are clearly adjudicating cases. It may be telling that elders (*zěqēnîm*), *šōṭěrîm* officials, and judges (*šōpěṭîm*) form a triad in Joshua 8:33—and with the addition of "heads" (*rāʾšîm*) a quadriad in Joshua 23:2, 24:1. In such a light, one again wonders about the presence of elders in Exodus 18:12 and what the motive was for them not being mentioned among the competent men (*'anšê-ḥayil*) who make up the judiciary in Exodus 18:21, 25. Lastly, as hinted at by Baruch Levine (1993: 338, 342), who sees a common *Sitz-im-Leben* for Numbers 11–12 and Exodus 18, the selection of prophetic leaders in Numbers 11:16–25 may not be an obstacle for speculating about a judiciary. Exodus 18:15b notes that when the people have a legal dispute they come to Moses "to inquire of God" (*lidrōš 'ĕlōhîm*). Oracular inquiry was evidently one of the ways by which Moses obtained judicial knowledge from Yahweh. Thus the gap between judicial leaders and chosen prophetic leaders may not be as large as a modern person might envision.

The Overarching Belief in Yahweh as Absolute Judge

Clearly, the sketch given here has only scratched the surface in regard to the many ways in which justice was rendered and judiciaries were perceived throughout ancient Israel. A more detailed examination would require a consideration of the ways in which priests were sometimes also involved in adjudicating cases (e.g., Num 27:21; Deut 17:8–12; 19:15–19; 21:5; 2 Chr 19:8; cf. Josh 8:33; Jer 26:11, 16; Ezek 44:24; Mic 3:11), how trials could be brought before the congregation (*'ēdâ*) at large (e.g., Num 35:12, 24; Josh 20:6; cf. Ps 1:5), and how kings could sometimes function as the final court of appeal (e.g., 2 Sam 14:4–11).[93]

Yet what is patently evident from this sketch is that at every turn God is portrayed as the judge par excellence, the source of law, the ideal practitioner of justice, and the one to whom those who have suffered injustice may appeal. A return look at the wide-ranging texts discussed earlier will illustrate the point. In Genesis 31, though an earthly tribunal made up of kinsmen of both Laban and Jacob (*'aḥay wĕ'aḥêkā*) is to arbitrate between the two litigants (*yôkîḥû bên šĕnênû*; Gen 31:37), Yahweh is called upon to be an ever-present sentry watching between the two parties (*yiṣep yhwh bênî ûbênekā*) "when they are absent [lit. 'hidden'] from each other," that is, when one mistrusts what the other is up to (Gen 31:49). Each litigant is to act justly toward the other party in realization that Yahweh is a "witness" between them (*'ēd bênî ûbênekā*), not in the sense of a witness testifying on behalf of the defense or prosecution but as a divine witness who superintends the ongoing process and to whom they swear allegiance (Gen 31:50; cf. 1 Sam 12:5–6; 20:12).[94] To bind them to their commitments, a formal oath is taken by each party together with a sacrificial ritual. Each party states that the judging per se (√*špṭ*) will be carried out by the god of one's ancestor, with Jacob swearing by "the Fear of his father Isaac" (*paḥad 'ābîw yiṣḥāq*; Gen 31:53–54).

Deuteronomy 21:1–9 presents a case of homicide with no evidence and in open country where questions of jurisdiction need to be resolved. Once it is determined that they shoulder the responsibility, the elders of the nearest city grasp their liability for the crime.[95] A complicated ritual ensues that involves the killing of a heifer by breaking its neck. The elders wash their hands over the heifer while testifying that they did not commit the murder nor were they witnesses to the murder (Deut 21:6–7; cf. Ps 26:6). Though it is not stated outright, the elders implicitly assert that no one in their city is criminally responsible, either as an accessory to the murder or complicit in some other way (e.g., harboring the fugitive). Overseeing these legal disclaimers are the priests who are chosen to be God's judicial representatives to settle such a dispute involving assault (*kol-rîb wĕkol-nāgaʿ*; Deut 21:5). Yet no mention is made of their verdict. Instead the narrative centers on the Ultimate Judge, the only one who can truly decide such a case with so many unknowns. After their ritual actions, the elders beseech God for absolution (*kappēr*) of the blood guilt (lit. "innocent blood," *dām nāqî*), absolution that only God can provide. Such a purge (*bʿr*) of blood guilt is "exercising what is just [*yāšār*] in the estimation of Yahweh" (Deut 21:9)—a favorite Deuteronomic expression (cf. 6:18; 12:25, 28; 13:19 [Eng 13:18]) for Yahweh as the giver of law and its absolute judge.

Returning to royal justice, time and again we read that the Judean monarch's judicial ability is ordained of God (Ps 72:1–4, 12–14), and his renderings are authoritative only insofar as they reflect the justice of the Ultimate Magistrate, who is the author of law. David's judicial discernment is that of "an angel/messenger of God" (2 Sam 14:17). Solomon possesses "the very wisdom of God to render justice" (1 Kgs 3:28). It is not a coincidence that Josiah's "knowing" of God exhibits itself in acts of justice for the poor that reflect those of the Absolute Judge (Jer 22:16). Likewise, Jehoshaphat's admonition to his judiciary to be righteous judges is in imitation of "Yahweh in whom there is no injustice, favoritism or bribe-taking" (2 Chr 19:6–7). His magistrates are to fear Yahweh, for they exercise their roles "not for humans but as His surrogates." Indeed, Yahweh's very presence is with them in the act of adjudicating justly (2 Chr 19:6, 9). The poetic proclamation found in Isaiah 33:22 typifies royal justice:

Yahweh is our judge,	*yhwh šōpĕṭēnû*
Yahweh is he who inscribes our [laws],[96]	*yhwh mĕḥōqĕqēnû*
Yahweh is our king,	*yhwh malkēnû*
He will deliver us.	*hûʾ yôšîʿēnû*

Sources such as personal names and individual laments give windows into the voices of those least likely to have power (royal or otherwise) and often those oppressed by such power. What they share is a confidence that Yahweh is indeed the ultimate judge (e.g., Ps 9:5, 8b–10 [Eng 9:4, 7b–9]; Ps 140:13 [Eng 140:12]), and one who will come to the address their plight (e.g., Ps 26:1; 35:24; 43:1; 54:3 [Eng

54:1]; Lam 3:59); sometimes both beliefs are expressed in the same prayer (e.g., Ps 7:7b, 9 [Eng 7:6b, 8]). Independent of circumstances (pre- or post-vindication), the sentiment is the same: Yahweh is a judge unlike any earthly judge. Whereas human judges—even idealized judges—fail, Yahweh's justice is constant (Amos 5:24 would say "ever flowing"), ever true, and ever fair. Whereas human judges, even those with the best intentions, fall short, there is a divine judge who never overlooks those downtrodden by injustice, one who never fails to see and rectify the injustice of their dire circumstances. Such personal piety sees in Yahweh the "Father of orphans and the one who provides justice for widows" (Ps 68:6 [Eng 68:5]).

Divine Justice Cast into the Future

Triumphal visions announce the advent of a teacher par excellence who in the future will teach justice as he arbitrates disputes, resulting in an unheard-of period of disarmament where "nation shall not lift up sword against nation, neither shall they learn war any more." The idyllic "swords into plowshares" passage, preserved near verbatim in two prophetic traditions (Isa 2:2–4//Mic 4:1–3), was addressed earlier for its irenic vision (see Chapter Eight, pp. 471–473). There it was pointed out that Yahweh's "judging among the nations" (šāpaṭ bên haggôyim Isa 2:4; cf. šāpaṭ bên ʿammîm rabbîm in Mic 4:3) can connote military action, as the root špṭ is indeed used in battle contexts, most notably in the book of Judges (e.g., Judg 2:16).[97] Blending with Yahweh the ultimate warrior whose might brings about a disarmed surrender is Yahweh the ultimate teacher-judge.[98] The disarmament of the nations is predicated on Yahweh's "judging" via the teaching of his law (tôrâ) and practice (děrākāyw//ʾōrḥōtāyw) as well as arbitration on an international scale (wěhôkîaḥ lěʿammîm rabbîm; Isa 2:4; cf. wěhôkîaḥ lěgôyim ʿăṣumîm ʿad-rāḥôq; Mic 4:3).

The Isaianic traditions also contain the most expressive hopes for a Davidide who excels all others in upholding justice. According to Isaiah 9:6 (Eng 9:7), the authority of this just king will be realized by Yahweh's zeal (qinʾâ). With such divine dispensation, justice will be enduring (mēʿattâ wěʿad-ʿôlām).

> [His] authority will be expansive
> peace without end,
> over David's throne and his kingdom—
> to establish it, to sanction it
> with justice and with equity
> from this time forth and ever more.
> The zeal of Yahweh of hosts will accomplish this.

Isaiah 11:2–5 adds that it is Yahweh's spirit (with its qualities of wisdom and reverence) that will allow this Davidide to judge without partiality, as does Yahweh (cf. Deut 1:17; 10:17). By so doing, he will achieve the hoped-for ideal of providing true justice for the poor.

> A shoot will grow from Jesse's stump,
> a branch will sprout from his roots.
>
> The [very] spirit of Yahweh will rest on him,
> a spirit of wisdom and understanding,
> a spirit of counsel and strength,
> a spirit of knowledge and the fear of Yahweh.
> His delight will be in the fear of Yahweh.
>
> He will not adjudicate based on appearance,
> or arbitrate based on hearsay,
> rather he will righteously judge the poor,
> and arbitrate with equity for the earth's downcast . . .
>
> Righteous justice will be the belt around his waist,
> Faithful renderings the belt around his loins. (Isa 11:1–5)

Such hopes were echoed elsewhere, as in Jeremiah 23:5:

> Yes, days are coming—oracle of Yahweh—
> when I will raise up for David a righteous Shoot.
> He will reign as king and he will succeed [*hiśkîl*],
> He will execute justice and equity in the land.

The use of the root *śkl* to designate "success" in a Davidic passage such as this is noteworthy. Royal success is often thought of in military terms, especially when we turn to a passage such as 1 Samuel 18, which uses the root *śkl* four times to celebrate success on the battlefield (1 Sam 18:5, 14, 15, 30). Yet Tova Forti and David Glatt-Gilad (2015) posit that even in such a militaristic context we see divine patronage at work in molding the ideal king. Looking at the use of *śkl* in sapiential literature, they argue that David's overall "success" as a *maśkîl* is based on him being "a God-fearing individual, who possesses insight and sensitivity to pursue a path consistent with God's ethical standards" (2015: 5–6). More specifically, it could be said that sapiential literature (Ps 32:8; 41:1; 119:99; Prov 1:3) and Deuteronomistic traditions (Josh 1:7; 1 Kgs 2:3; cf. Deut 29:9) converge in articulating that to have success (*śkl*) one must adhere to divine law and execute justice.

Proverbs 1:2–3 nicely summarizes the way in which the book of Proverbs should serve as a manual for judicious behavior:

> For use in learning wisdom and discipline,
> for understanding words of understanding,
> for acquiring the discipline of insight [*haśkēl*]:
> righteousness, justice, and rectitude [*ṣedeq ûmišpāṭ ûmêšārîm*].

Jeremiah 23:5 is fully in line with these ethics. A successful future king will necessarily be a just king, as was Josiah (cf. Jer 22:16). Such hopes recapitulate an earlier statement found in the book (Jer 9:22–23 [Eng 22:23–24]; cf. 8:8). When humans boast of their accomplishments, they should privilege knowing Yahweh, and, by so doing, imitate His just actions.

> Thus said Yahweh: "Let not the wise boast of their wisdom, let not the strong boast of their strength, let not let the wealthy boast in their wealth; but let those who boast boast in this: that they understand and know me [*haśkēl wěyādōaʿ ʾōtî*], for I Yahweh act with steadfast love, justice, and righteousness in the earth, for in these things I delight." Oracle of Yahweh. (Jer 9:22–23 [Eng 22:23–24])

Divine Justice and Apocalyptic Literature

The historical and sociological vicissitudes that contributed to proto-apocalyptic and apocalyptic themes are gnarled and difficult to unravel. Instead of the idyllic "swords into plowshares" future of "all the nations" coming peacefully to Jerusalem to have Yahweh instruct them in *tôrâ* (Isa 2:2–4//Mic 4:1–3), we read of eschatological battles with "all the nations" violently plundering Jerusalem and raping its women (e.g., Zech 14:1–2). In place of the idyllic spirt-filled Davidide governing the future with justice, we have the mysterious disappearance of the hoped-for Davidide Zerubbabel, and thus the loss of Yahweh's signet ring (*ḥôtām*) endowed with divine authority and power (Hag 2:23).[99] In the midst of tragic turns of history that led to apocalyptic despair, biblical writers were nonetheless resolute in proclaiming a sovereign judge who would bring about a judicial reckoning to right all wrongs. As for the violent nations, the prophet Joel asserts that Yahweh will "in those days and at that time" bring them to the symbolically named Valley of Jehoshaphat (lit. "Yah[weh] judges"), where the deity will execute judgment against them (*nišpaṭṭî ʿimmām*; *ʾēšēb lišpōṭ*; Joel 4:2, 12 [Eng 3:2, 12]). "On that day" when the legendary enemy Gog and his horde come against Israel, they will meet the all-powerful Storm God bringing his tempestuous fury, pestilence, and bloodshed as he executes judgment upon them (*nišpaṭṭî ʾittô*; Ezek 38:18–23).

As for the disadvantaged poor who suffer legal injustice the most, here too stands Yahweh with redress. Joseph Blenkinsopp (2000: 409) opines that the following Isaianic words represent "the restorationist eschatological view . . . at the great turning point of history":[100]

> On that day the deaf will hear the words of a scroll,
> The eyes of the blind will see
> Freed of their gloom and darkness;
> The downtrodden will rejoice in Yahweh once again,
> the poorest of all will exult in the Holy One of Israel.
> For the ruthless will be no more,
> the scoffer will come to an end,
> all those who watch to do evil will be cut off—
>> those who criminalize a person with a [just] case,
>> who entrap the arbiter in the gate,
>> who nullify the one in the right. (Isa 29:18–21; cf. Amos 5:7, 10–12)[101]

The notion of God as eschatological judge is found in the most famous of apocalyptic writings in the Hebrew Bible, which is set "in mythic space" (Collins 1993: 303).[102] In this passage we hear of a fiery scene of judgment:

> As I was envisioning
> Thrones were set in place,
> And the Ancient of Days sat [enthroned].
>
> His garment was like white snow,
> The hair of his head like pure wool;
>
> His throne was fiery flames,
> Its wheels were burning fire.
>
> A river of fire flows,
> streams forth from his presence.
>
> Thousands upon thousands serve him,
> Myriads upon myriads attend him.
>
> The court was seated [*dînāʾ yĕtib*],
> the records [of judgments] were opened. (Dan 7:9–10; cf. 7:21–22; 12:1–3)

Daniel's symbolic throne vision weaves together a wide array of inherited *Chaoskampf* traditions that also appear in extra-biblical apocalypses such as 1 Enoch. Unpacking these is beyond the scope of the present work. What is relevant is the judicial execution that John Collins (1993: 291) argues is "a distinctively Jewish adaptation of the myth." The notion of a court of law being seated (lit. "judgment sat") in Daniel 7:10 together with the mention of plural thrones in the previous verse suggest to some that we might have the divine council rendering judgment (cf. the "thrones for judgment" in Ps 122:5).[103] Note too the mention of judicial records (*siprîn*), which have antecedents in the traditions underlying Psalm 56:9 (Eng 56:8), Isaiah 65:6, and Malachi 3:16, and even more so in 1 Enoch 81; 89:70; 90:20; 103:2 and Jubilees 5:12–19; 16:9. For our purposes, these late texts contribute to notions of a final judgment day (cf. already the "Day of Yahweh" in Amos 5:18) and once again envision a royal figure as Supreme Judge.

Counter-Discourses: Questioning the Ideal of the Just (Human) Judge

To this point we have been describing both the divine Ideal Judge and Just King and the earthly versions. Obviously, positing ideal justice that is grounded in the divine and executed by God's earthly designate does not make it so. Human nature guarantees that ideal justice will always remain theoretical, even if Plato's wise philosopher-king were magistrate.[104] Abstract notions of perfect justice cannot ensure legal redress. Injustice was (and is) an ever-present reality for countless humans. Tragically, injustice is regularly committed by the very people who, by the nature of their office, are charged with living up to the ideal. We need to admit that an ideal portrayal may very well "present a man who never did exist, a ruler altogether too good to be true" (Halpern 2001: xvi). We need to acknowledge the injustice that goes unaddressed, such as biblical slavery—especially, argues Wilda Gafney (2017: 72), "the sexual use of female slaves for the personal, individual gratification of slave-holding males and perpetual production of subsequent generations of slaves though forced pregnancy."

Prosecuting the Abuse of Justice

In biblical tradition, prophets took center stage in prosecuting the case against the abuse of justice by all who misused power, be they king, judge, elder, priest, prophet, or fellow citizen. Indeed, the oppositional voice speaking divine truth to unjust power has become a lasting appeal of the prophets. Nathan, Yahweh's emissary (2 Sam 12:1), boldly rebukes the king whom he otherwise supports and for whom he had declared the promise of an enduring dynasty (2 Sam 7:11b–16). The king in question is, surprisingly (or not), the "just king" David.[105] The involved tale of David having sex with (raping?) another man's wife (Uriah's wife, Bathsheba), her becoming pregnant, the cover-up of the adultery, and the subsequent murder by proxy of Uriah are well known (2 Sam 11). Nathan's story of the poor man's lamb (2 Sam 12:1–15), which he will use to rebuke David for his criminal activity, begins with Nathan presenting a legal case before the king in his role as judge.[106] In what P. Kyle McCarter (1984: 304–305) calls a "juridical parable" (cf. 2 Sam 14:4–11; 1 Kgs 20:39–40), Nathan humanizes the fate of the poor when abused by power with such artistry that "David the royal judge" ends up "condemn[ing] David the rich oppressor."[107]

Elijah is the voice of God's harsh sentence upon Ahab and Jezebel of the ninth century BCE for the orchestrated charade (with fabricated witnesses and charges, plus a tampered jury) that led to the judicial murder of Naboth (1 Kgs 21:1–24). The narrative marks this episode as an abuse of royal power by noting how Jezebel uses the royal seal to coerce her co-conspirators (1 Kgs 21:8).[108] In the eighth century BCE, we find Amos's indictment against those who turn justice into wormwood and poison (Amos 5:7; 6:12b) and trample the poor (Amos 2:6–8). Its prosecutorial zeal is biting:

They hate the arbiter at the gate,
they abhor the one who speaks for the innocent. [109]

Therefore, because you trample on the poor,
extract levies of grain from them,

the houses of hewn stone you built,
you shall not reside in them;
the desirable vineyards you planted,
you shall not quaff their wine.

For I know the huge number of your violations,
The countless throng of your sins—

you who afflict the upright
who take a bribe,
who thrust aside the needy at the gate. (Amos 5:10–12)

Francis Andersen and David Noel Freedman (1989: 502) are certainly correct in seeing in this passage corrupt magistrates who are taking bribes from "wealthy exploiters who are under indictment." The poor are "doubly helpless" in that they are victims of economic oppression who also fail to receive a fair trial. Though God is not explicitly mentioned here as a judge who carries out a sentence, he is clearly the indignant voice behind the "knowing I" in Amos 5:12, the one for whom Amos is speaking, and the effectual power behind the curse.[110]

For all his fame as the prophet advocating Yahwistic justice and its constancy (Amos 5:24), Amos is not alone in protesting the subversion of justice, as seen especially in the eighth-century BCE prophets Isaiah and Micah. In the Isaianic traditions (which originate in the eighth century BCE and continue into the postexilic period) we see once again the coupling of the widow and the orphan as particularly vulnerable to economic injustice at the hands of a corrupt legal system.[111]

> Cease to do evil,
> Learn to do good,
> Seek out justice,
> Rescue the oppressed,
> Judge on behalf of the orphan,
> Adjudicate on behalf of the widow . . .
>
> How the faithful city
> has become a whore!
> Once full of justice,
> equity lodged in her—
> but now murderers! . . .
>
> Your princes are rebels,
> partnered with thieves.
> They all love bribes,
> pursuing gifts.
> They provide no justice for the orphan,
> the widow's lawsuit never comes before them.
>
> Therefore—oracle of the Sovereign, Yahweh of hosts,
> The Mighty One of Israel,
> I will assuage my wrath on my enemies,
> Avenge myself on my foes. (Isa 1:16b–17, 21, 23–24)
>
> Woe to those who draft wicked decrees,
> who write oppressive statutes,
> to turn away the needy from justice
> to rob the poor of my people of justice,
> that widows may be your spoil,
> that they may plunder orphans! (Isa 10:1–2)

Though Jerusalem is said to have once been known for its justice (cf. the judicial characterizations of David and Solomon presented earlier), there is no longer any hint of a "just king" living up to judicial ideals. Rather, the lament (*'êkâ*; Isa 1:21) turned indictment charges royal judicial figures (*śārîm*) with conspiring with thieves in taking bribes, with the consequence that those already most economically deprived are stripped of legal redress.[112] The second passage accuses drafters of manipulating legal statutes to disadvantage the destitute in ways that amount (literally and figuratively) to robbing and plundering. Blenkinsopp (2000: 186, 212–213) sees royal scribes (with particular focus on the eighth century BCE) writing legislation aimed at sequestering the property of widows. In a patrilineal society, widows would not regularly have had rights of inheritance when it comes to ancestral land (*naḥălâ*; cf. Lewis 1991: 609–612).

Looking elsewhere in the eighth century BCE, we see yet more concerns about bribery corrupting the legal system. Isaiah 5:23 mentions judges acquitting the guilty in exchange for a bribe and thereby depriving the innocent of justice. An extended judgment oracle addressing a similar situation is found in Micah 3:9–12:

Listen up, you magistrates [*rā'šîm*] of the House of Jacob
and you adjudicators [*qĕṣînîm*] of the House of Israel,

who detest justice
and pervert all that is upright,[113]

He who builds Zion with bloodshed
and Jerusalem with injustice.

Its magistrates provide a legal ruling for a bribe,
its priests teach for a price,
its prophets divine for money;

Yet they lean upon Yahweh retorting
"Is not Yahweh within our midst?
Disaster cannot come against us."

Therefore, on account of you
Zion will be plowed like a field;
Jerusalem will become a heap of rubble,
and the temple mount like forested high places. (Mic 3:9–12)

The parallel terms used for the rulers in 3:1, 9 (*rā'šîm, qĕṣînîm*) can be used for leaders in general, both civil and military. Here their positions are clearly judicial.[114] Micah 3 begins with a bold challenge: "Should you not know justice?" This is followed by visual depictions reminiscent of Neo-Assyrian atrocities of war (Mic 3:2–3; cf. Lewis 2008b: 88). Caustic declarations conclude that these magistrates detest justice, "twisting" straight justness (*yĕšārâ*) into a perversion (paralleling the roots *tʿb* and *ʿqš*). Their bribery scheme includes the collusion of priests and prophets, who, as we have seen, can also be involved in rendering legal decisions.

Judgment oracles such as this one imply a judge and a prosecutor. Yahweh is the judge par excellence who demands justice in his courtroom and carries out sentences against violators. In the present case, the Divine Judge judges corrupt judges who assumed that Yahweh was in their pocket (Mic 3:11b). Micah the prophet is the voice of Yahweh's prosecutor, divinely empowered for the task at hand:

Dynamically, I am filled with power,
with the [very] spirit of Yahweh,
with [His] justice and might,
to declare to Jacob his violations
and to Israel his sin. (Mic 3:8)

The emphasis here is on power rightly used for the cause of justice. Whereas the magistrates abused their power (resulting in "bloody" injustice caused by bribery), Micah speaks the voice of the divine, as powerful as it is just. Bruce Waltke (2007: 174), following Hans Walter Wolff, aptly quotes Pascal: "Justice without power is powerless. Power without justice is tyrannical. . . . Justice and power must therefore be connected so that what is just is also powerful and what is powerful is also just" (*Pensées*, §298).

These early prophets of Israel (Nathan, Elijah, Amos, Isaiah, Micah) were part of a broad sociological trend that saw central and peripheral intermediaries alike (cf. Wilson 1980) speaking out against the injustice of those who abused their positions of power. Courageously advocating for justice was their perennial task; this prophetic legacy was carried on in the decades that followed (e.g., Jer 5:28; 7:5; Ezek 18:30; 21:30; 24:14; 34:17; 36:19; Zeph 3:3).

Judgment Oracles and Covenant Lawsuits

Judgment oracles abound throughout the Hebrew Bible's prophetic corpus. The enduring heritage of speaking divine truth to power often concentrates on the breaking of cultic law, and this makes absolute sense when "laws were considered stipulations of the covenant between Israel and God" (Frymer-Kensky 2003: 991). Yahweh was seen to be the one who promulgated law, especially through Moses, and legally held his people accountable. Many scholars (e.g., G. E. Mendenhall, H. B. Huffmon) set such metaphors against the backdrop of international treaty diplomacy, wherein a suzerain sets out stipulations that a vassal must obey. Other scholars (e.g., F. C. Fensham, C. Westermann) imagine civil courts to be the proper setting envisioned, perhaps at the city gate,[115] while yet others (e.g., R. Hentschke, E. Würthwein) see the lawsuit as being liturgical in nature and litigated within temple ceremonies.[116]

Judgment oracles have been studied and nuanced over the years by genre critics, with two overlapping categories being particularly relevant for the current discussion: trial speeches (*Gerichtsreden*) and judicial speeches.[117] Though structures vary, constituent parts can include (1) a messenger formula, where the prophet speaks for the deity ("Thus says Yahweh") or a divine proclamation/summons ("Hear the message that Yahweh has spoken"), (2) an indictment of charges, and (3) a sentence of judgment.[118] Thus it is that we read of Yahweh proceeding to court: "Accuse me, let us go to trial together; litigate [your legal case] that you may be proved right" (Isa 43:26).[119]

The Juridical Situation Known as *Rîb*

A specific theme highlighting Yahweh taking his people to court is the *rîb*, often referred to as a "covenant/prophetic lawsuit." Writing on the topic in general, Pietro Bovati (1994: 29–30) defines *rîb* as a "juridical controversy" "that takes place between two parties on questions of law." In order for the case to proceed, "it is necessary that they [the two parties] refer to a body of norms that regulate the rights and duties of each," for "the progress of a dispute is substantiated by juridical arguments and requires a solution in conformity with the law."[120] Micah 6:1–8 is the parade example, for it gives voice to both litigants, Yahweh and Israel (cf. Isa 1:2; Jer 2:4–14; Ps 50; Deut 32). I have added my interpretive headings and explanations. The poet, for whatever reason (dramatic effect? vividness?), does not identify the various speakers, and thus the headings are deduced from the context.

The Charge to Listen This is an address by an unidentified speaker (seemingly Micah as an official of the court, or perhaps an offstage narrator) charging an unidentified group of people (addressed with a second person masculine plural verb; seemingly the accused Israel) to listen to the forthcoming legal case.[121]

Hear [*šimʿû-nāʾ*] what Yahweh says.

The Charge to Present An unidentified speaker (Yahweh or perhaps an offstage narrator) charges an unidentified male person (addressed with second person masculine singular imperatives; seemingly Micah) to present the legal case.[122]

> Arise [*qûm*], plead the legal case [*rîb*] before the mountains,
> let the hills hear your voice.

Opening Remarks An unidentified speaker (likely Micah as an officer of the court speaking on Yahweh's behalf) gives opening remarks.

> Hear, O mountains, Yahweh's legal case [*rîb*],
> O enduring foundations of the earth;
> for Yahweh has a legal case [*rîb*] against his people,
> he will litigate with Israel.

The Plaintiff Speaks to the Accused Here Yahweh, as the plaintiff, is speaking to the accused, Israel.

> My people! What have I done against you?
> How have I wearied you?
> Testify against me!
>
> Indeed, I brought you up from the land of Egypt,
> from the very house of slavery I redeemed you;
> I sent before you
> Moses, Aaron, and Miriam.
>
> My people! Remember what he schemed,
> that is, King Balaq of Moab,
> [Remember] how he answered him,
> that is, Balaam son of Beʿor.
> [Remember all that happened] from Shittim to Gilgal,
> that you may know Yahweh's just acts [*ṣidqôt yhwh*].

The People's Retort Here the people present their defense strategy.

> With what should I come before Yahweh,
> [with what] should I bow down before God on high?
>
> Should I come before him with burnt offerings?
> With calves a year old?

> Would Yahweh be pleased with thousands of rams?
> With myriads of rivers of oil?
> Should I give my firstborn [as an offering] for my transgression?
> The fruit of my body [as an offering] for my own sin?

Resolution The resolution is offered by an unidentified speaker.

> He has told you, O human, what is good,
> what Yahweh requires of you:
> but to execute justice [*mišpāṭ*], to love acting justly [*ḥesed*],
> and to walk intentionally with your God. (Mic 6:1–8)

It is obvious why Micah 6:1–8 has received accolades, especially with its final words that eloquently summarize divine expectations for ethical living. Yet there is far more here than that summary, grand as it is. Though litigious in nature, Yahweh acts as a plaintiff who speaks personally with his own people (*'ammî*), not as a draconian judge who has depersonalized the accused. His appeal is based on their history together, a history marked by his benevolent actions of rescue, even from slavery, and his presence via earthly representatives (Moses, Aaron, Miriam, Balaam). Here those scholars who note the typical historical prologue of suzerainty treaties are right on the mark (e.g., Huffmon 1959: 294). As a suzerain tells of his benevolent deeds, he underscores his faithfulness to the treaty along with reminders that the vassal must be similarly faithful to the agreed-upon terms of the treaty. Thus Yahweh, in a legal setting, asserts that his consistent actions over their entire history together are just (cf. how *ṣĕdāqâ* often parallels *mišpāṭ*). And such just actions (*ṣidqôt yhwh*) provide the evidence for his people to know his just nature (Mic 6.5).

The defense strategy by the accused is brilliant, though in the end it fails.[123] Yahweh challenges his people to "testify against" him (*'ănēh bî*; Mic 6:3b), and this is precisely what they do. Their retort quickly shifts the imagery of a personal god speaking to his people to that of a God on high to whom they must bow in deference (Mic 6:6). The language is not that of intimate knowing, but rather "coming before" (√*qdm* in the D stem) a superior. Using ascending hyperbole, they assert that they do not know the requirements by which they are being measured, those that would "please" (*rṣh*) an overly demanding superior such as Yahweh. In fact, they assert—using rhetoric that would do a lawyer proud—the requirements border on the absurd. Reparations in the amount of a thousand rams (if they were to be had) would bankrupt any single individual apart from wealthy Solomon (1 Kgs 3:4; 8:5, 62–64). One cannot imagine the nonsensical offering of a river of oil for one's sins, and yet that may be what Yahweh does indeed require—or perhaps even a myriad of such rivers.

Strikingly, the third payment due is within actual reach, shockingly so. Does Yahweh indeed demand the sacrifice of one's eldest son (Mic 6:7b)? There is precedent, they might add, in that the Covenant Code states forthrightly, "The firstborn of your sons you will give to me" (*běkôr bānêkā titten-lî*; Exod 22:28b [Eng 22:29b]). In the traditions that Ezekiel inherits, Yahweh himself admits that he is responsible for "defiling" his people by giving them "bad laws and statutes by which they could not live" (*'ănî nātattî lāhem ḥuqqîm lō' ṭôbîm ûmišpāṭîm lō' yiḥyû bāhem wā'ăṭammē' 'ôtām*; Ezek 20:25–26). What were these bad laws and the motive behind them? They were none other than the law of child sacrifice (*wā'ăṭammē' 'ôtām . . . běha'ăbîr kol-peṭer rāḥam*), with the motive being that his people might "know" Yahweh (Ezek 20:26; cf. Mic 6:5). Historical reflection cuts both ways. Yahweh's law requiring child sacrifice was—by his own admission, the people assert—"defiling" and "not good," so how could they have kept such a law? But it was a divinely given law, after all; is child sacrifice what he really wants? The plaintiff's conflicting requirements have led to their paralysis of action. The defense rests.[124]

The legal case (*rîb*) is resolved in Micah 6:8. Once again the speaker is unidentified, though interpreters often see the prophet Micah having the last word. The voice is authoritative. The ruling implicitly reveals that the defense, despite its rhetoric, did not prove its case against Yahweh. The resolution concludes that Yahweh's requirements are indeed good (i.e., just), and he has articulated them in the past (*higgîd*).[125] Perhaps this look to the past is why the case is presented before the aged mountains and foundations of the earth (Mic 6:2a), who were witnesses to Yahweh penning the law in remote antiquity—perhaps a reference to Mt. Sinai (cf. Exod 24.12; 31.18; 32:16) or even to the time of creation (cf. Sarna 1991: 206).

Given the synonymous parallelism of Micah 6:8a, it would be fair to conclude (contrary to Ezek 20:25, discussed later) that the resolution asserts that what Yahweh requires is good, and—vice versa—that what is good is what Yahweh requires. And it is clear from what follows that Yahweh's requirements are defined by justice, as one would expect from the constant emphasis we have seen on how "justice is of God" (*kî hammišpāṭ lē'lōhîm hû'*), for he is the one who "does" justice (*'ōśeh mišpāṭ*). Numerous passages concur in equating "goodness" with justice (e.g., Amos 5:15; Jer 22:15; Job 34:4; Prov 2:9; Neh 9:13). The three descriptors that follow are a hendiatris used to flesh out these requirements. To execute justice is to love the concept of *ḥesed*, and both are the result of intentionally living a life (lit. "walking") in communion with a just God. Though our text is not explicit in this regard, Waltke (2007: 393) nicely points out how *ḥesed* often occurs in situations where the stronger party meets the needs of the weaker party. This type of *ḥesed* relationship would match the concept of ideal justice that above all looks out for the disadvantaged. Though the last requirement is traditionally translated as having to do with humility, the hapax *ṣnʿ* followed by *ʿim-ʾĕlōhêkā* seems to have more to do with living prudently, circumspectly, and intentionally in full view of Yahweh's just character.

Summation: Counter-Discourses Questioning the Ideal of the Just (Human) Judge

Overall, the many biblical traditions that happen to have come down to us (edited and reinterpreted along the way) are fully aware of the ideal of what true justice should look like. When it comes to practitioners, only four kings are promoted as "kings of justice," and two of the four (David and Solomon) have blemishes preserved alongside their accolades. The bulk of what has been preserved through the weathering of time and at the hands of editors and scribes is realistic rather than idealistic: injustice occurs at every turn, especially when looking at power dynamics. The abuse of justice is well documented in the pages of the Hebrew Bible, with special attention given to economic injustice and the failures of corrupt magistrates to provide relief. Bribery and partiality within the court system are of special concern. Moreover, with laws being perceived as stipulations of a divine suzerain, all laws are thereby religious law. Thus civil injustice and cultic injustice are equally serious offenses against a godly judge.

Four ancient responses rise to the surface: (1) When it comes to the abuse of justice, prophetic traditions were firm in their belief that the power of rhetoric (together with occasional sign-acts) could be effectually wielded to chastise corrupt kings and magistrates. Those who were oppressed by powerful rulers and a court system rife with bribery needed a voice. They found it in courageous prophets speaking divine truth to power. (2) The constant failure of humans to live up to the judicial ideal is paralleled by the dominant motif that God remains the ideal judge. Though this belief is ubiquitous, questions of theodicy surfaced as well, as we will see. (3) God is appealed to as the rescuer of those who suffer injustice and the restorer of justice. Personal names and heartfelt laments bid Yahweh to rescue them from the hand of their judicial oppressors. In the face of rampant injustice, voices proclaim that Yahweh will restore faithful judges for a future Zion "redeemed by justice" (Isa 1:26–27). (4) In addition to prophetic chastisement, there are clear signs of strategies limiting the judicial power of the king. Here the Deuteronomic voice is striking, especially when juxtaposed with that of the Deuteronomistic History.[126] The Deuteronomic position is clear when it comes to a judge living up to the royal ideal advocated throughout the ancient Near East: the ideal judge is Yahweh and Yahweh alone.

> For Yahweh, your god, He is God of gods and Lord of lords. [He is] the Great God, mighty and awesome, who [as judge] shows no partiality, nor does he ever take bribes. He [and not an earthly king] is the one who executes justice ['ōśeh mišpāṭ] for the orphan and the widow. He is the one who loves the gēr [non-native resident], providing him with food and clothing. (Deut 10:17–18)

Pragmatically, this requires earthly representatives who serve as God's judiciary. It is quite remarkable, especially in an ancient Near Eastern context, that the Deuteronomic strategic plan has no mention of the king playing any judicial role. None of the two (three?) origin stories about human judiciaries hints at any role for the king. In the immediate context of the stories in Exodus 18 and Deuteronomy 1:9–18, this makes perfect sense, for the setting is the present-day distribution of Moses' judicial authority. The advent of the monarchy is unknown to the actors. Yet the forward-looking perspective of Deuteronomy 16–18 (written and/or edited from subsequent history and projected backward) is a different matter. Its authorial voice gives instructions about the four institutional offices needed to govern society: the judge (Deut 16:18–20), the monarch (Deut 17:14–20), the priest (Deut 18:1–8), and the prophet (Deut 18:9–22). The king's absence in the future judiciary is astonishing, especially in an ancient Near Eastern context where royal judicial power is well attested.

> You shall appoint for yourself judges and šōṭĕrîm officials [note: not kings] at all your [city] gates that Yahweh your God is giving you for your tribes, and they shall adjudicate [the cases of] the people with righteous justice. You must not distort justice; you must not show partiality; and you must not accept bribes, because a bribe blinds the eyes of the wise and subverts cases of righteous judgment. Righteous justice, and only righteous justice, you shall pursue, so that you may live and occupy the land that Yahweh your God is giving you. (Deut 16:18–20)

Sandwiched between this appointment of a judiciary (Deut 16:18–20) and the declaration about the king's role (Deut 17:14–20), we find two sections dealing with hypothetical legal cases. The first deals with the violation of cultic law based on hearsay, and the second with difficult legal cases of homicide, civil legislation, and personal injury. When they are taken together, we see that care is taken to describe the accused (17:2), the nature of the crimes (17:2–3, 8), research into the crime (17:4), the location of litigation (17:5, 8), the acting judges (17:9, 12), the role of witnesses in providing evidence (17:6–7), the sentences (17:5, 9, 12), and instructions about carrying out the sentence (17:10–11). Here too is the glaring absence of any judicial role for the monarch. This is surely intentional. The function of the king with respect to the law is addressed in the next few verses (Deut

17:18–19): it is one of copying and constantly reading the law. The king's behavior is molded by the keeping of God's laws. The aim is to keep the king's heart "from being exalted above his brethren" (*lĕbiltî rûm-lĕbābô mēʾeḥāyw*). The king's royal power does not elevate him to the position of a supreme judge above the law; rather, because he is subject to the law, he must not turn aside from it, either to the right or to the left (Deut 17:20).

Such a drastic realignment of societal roles must stem from writers who wanted to limit the judicial power of the king because of abuses in the legal arena. Whereas prophets responded to royal abuse with rhetorical chastisement in the name of Yahweh, the absolute judge, the Deuteronomic tradition attempted to strip the king of any judicial office. That these passages are set in a time prior to entering the land allows Deuteronomic advocates to challenge any reigning king's judicial misdeeds with an appeal to remote antiquity, when Yahweh demanded that the king have no judicial role to begin with. Such a challenge hit a nerve. Quoting Levinson (2001: 533–534) once again:

> So radical was it in its own time that, shortly after its promulgation, it was effectively abrogated, as the Deuteronomistic Historian, while purporting to implement the norms of Deuteronomy, restored to the king precisely those powers denied him by Deuteronomy.

Counter-Discourses: Questioning the Ideal of the Just (Divine) Judge

We have solid evidence from the Hebrew Bible that questions of theodicy existed alongside the dominant and ubiquitous motif of God as a never-failing, absolute judge. One can imagine passionate, intricate, sometimes tempestuous debates raging in antiquity as they do in modernity. Probing how "the Torah and subsequent texts provide occasion and rationale for slaveholding," Gafney (2017: 73) poignantly asks: "Is the God of Abraham, Isaac, and Jacob truly the God of Hagar, Sarah, Keturah, Rebekah, Leah, Rachel, Bilhah, and Zilpah? . . . [N]o issue forces this question [of theodicy] more than the biblical sanction of the sexual subordination of women in and through chattel slavery."

One could say that Yahweh brought such questioning upon himself. As we have seen in Micah 6:3b, Yahweh challenges his people to "testify against" him (*ʿănēh bî*). According to Ezekiel 20:25, he admits to being a judge who gave bad statutes and judgments! In Isaiah 1:17–18a, right after challenging his people to live up to the judicial ideal ("to cease evil, to learn goodness, to seek out justice, to rescue the oppressed, to judge on behalf of the orphan, to adjudicate on behalf of the widow"), Yahweh beckons "Come, let us argue it out" (lĕkû-nāʾ wĕniwwākĕḥâ).[127] Elsewhere Isaianic tradition has God proclaim: "Accuse me, let us go to trial together; litigate [your legal case] that you may be proved right" (Isa 43:26). And accuse they did—from Genesis' "Shall not the judge of the entire earth execute justice?" (hăšōpēṭ kol-hāʾāreṣ lōʾ yaʿăśeh mišpāṭ; Gen 18:25) to Malachi's "Where is the God of justice?" (ʾayyēh ʾĕlōhê hammišpāṭ; Mal 2:17). Jeremiah considers taking God to court over why the wicked prosper and the treacherous live at ease (Jer 12:1). Unyielding Job boldly demands an indictment written by the God he calls his legal adversary (rîb; Job 31:35).

Wisdom Literature: Setting the Stage for Theodicy

Nowhere in the Hebrew Bible is theodicy addressed at greater length than in its wisdom literature, specifically in the books of Qoheleth and Job. Yet to frame the discussion properly, it needs to be stressed that wisdom literature across the entire ancient Near East affirms the connection between the gods and justice. So-called perceptive hymns from Mesopotamia celebrate how Shamash carries out justice and oversees how it is practiced on earth:

> You dismiss [to the underworld] the rogue...
> You bring up from the underworld river him entangled in a lawsuit...
> What you say in a just verdict, Shamash...
> Your manifest utterance may not be changed...
>
> You give the unscrupulous judge experience in fetters.
> Him who accepts a present [bribe] and lets justice miscarry
> you make bear his punishment.
> As for him who declines a present [bribe]
> [and] takes the part of the weak,
> It is pleasing to Shamash, and he will prolong his life.[128]

Precepts warning rulers about what will happen if they miscarry justice threaten the intervention of a wide array of gods who are at the ready to send their retribution:

> If a king does not heed the justice of his land, Ea, king of destinies, will alter his destiny.... If he improperly convicts a citizen... Shamash, judge of heaven and earth, will set up foreign justice in his land.... If citizens... are brought to him for judgment, but he accepts a present [bribe] and improperly convicts them, Enlil, lord of the lands, will bring a foreign army against him.... If he hears a lawsuit... but treats it frivolously, Marduk, lord of heaven and earth, will set his foes upon him, and will give his property and wealth to his enemy.... If the

adviser or chief officer ... obtains bribes ... at the command of Ea, king of the Apsû, the adviser and chief officer will die by the sword.[129]

In Egypt, the Instructions of Amenemope look to the god Thoth as judge, and rightly so, for elsewhere he is referred to as "the Vizier of Re," the wise judge and mediator of disputants (*wep rehwy*).[130] The sixth chapter of the Instructions speaks against the one who is greedy for land and encroaches upon the boundaries of a widow by unjust means (e.g., by false oaths), with the warning that "he will be caught by the might of the Moon"—that is, the judge Thoth in his lunar manifestation. Similarly, the second chapter of the Instructions notes how the Moon (Thoth) will declare the crime of the lawbreaker.[131]

Proverbial Understandings of Divine Justice
The wisdom literature of the Hebrew Bible likewise includes these positive affirmations of God as the absolute, fair judge who also oversees human affairs. The summation in Proverbs 5:21 is so succinct that Michael V. Fox (2000: 204) suggests that it "may have existed as [an] independent proverb" prior to its current context:

> For a man's ways are before Yahweh
> and He assesses [*mĕpallēs*] all his paths.[132] (Prov 5:21)

This "broad principle," according to Fox, "remind[s] the audience that God is omniscient and guarantees justice." Elsewhere, Wisdom (*ḥokmâ*), divinely created in primeval days (Prov 8:22–31), declares with her personified voice that she is the source of just laws and their royal implementation:[133]

> By me kings reign,
> Governors inscribe just laws,
> By me rulers rule,
> So too nobles, all the just judges. (Prov 8:15–16)

Other proverbs provide precepts and instructions for just behavior (especially for monarchs) with affirmations of positive divine retribution:

> An [honest] balance and scales of justice are Yahweh's
> All the weights of the purse are his work;

> Wicked actions are abominations for kings
> For the throne is established by righteousness/justice.

> Kings favor just lips,
> They love he who speaks of just matters. (Prov 16:11–13)
>
> A wise king winnows the wicked,
> Rolls the threshing wheel over them . . .
>
> *Ḥesed* justness and truth preserve the king,
> and his throne is upheld by *ḥesed* justness. (Prov 20:26, 28)
>
> By justice a king provides stability to the land,
> but one who makes heavy exactions destroys it. . . .
>
> A king who judges the poor with equity,
> his throne will be established forever. . . .
>
> Many make petitions of a ruler,
> But it is from Yahweh that one obtains justice. (Prov 29:4, 14, 26)

Similar instructional wisdom is found in Psalm 37. Writing with a voice of time-tested confidence, the elderly sage reviews his life experience prior to giving his advice. Unlike the psalmist who called out to God to rescue him because he felt forsaken (*ʾēlî ʾēlî lāmâ ʿăzabtānî*; Ps 22:2 [Eng 22:1]), the conviction of the sage is presented with absolute certainty:

> I was once young, and now am old,
> and never have I see a righteous person forsaken [*neʿĕzāb*]
> nor his child begging bread . . .
>
> Turn aside from evil and do good;
> so you shall abide forever.
>
> For Yahweh loves justice,
> he forsakes not [*lōʾ-yaʿăzōb*] his faithful ones . . .
>
> The mouth of the righteous utters wisdom,
> His tongue speaks justice.
> The law of his God is in his heart,
> His steps do not waver.
>
> The wicked watches for the righteous,
> And seeks to kill him.

> Yahweh will not abandon him [*lōʾ-yaʿazbennû*] to his power
> Nor let him be condemned when he is brought to trial. (Ps 37:25–28, 30–33)

Qoheleth's Theodicy

Such positive affirmations of divine justice are what one expects from the book of Proverbs and a wisdom psalm such as Psalm 37. Yet they are also foundational to Qoheleth, who, unlike the sage of Psalm 37, blends his belief in a God of justice with notions of theodicy. The premise upon which the challenge is made is that God is indeed just, but, maddeningly, one finds evidence that points to the contrary.

Three times the book of Qoheleth explicitly affirms God's role as judge, with the book concluding, in its epilogue, on this singular note:[134]

> I said to myself, God will judge the righteous and the wicked.
> For there is a time for every matter and for all that is accomplished. (Qoh 3:17)

> Rejoice, O youth, while you are young,
> Let your heart cheer you in your youthful days;
> Follow the inclinations of your heart,
> The desires of your eyes;
> And/but know that for all these things
> God will bring you into judgment.[135] (Qoh 11:9)

> For God will bring every deed into judgment,
> Including every secret deed, whether good or evil. (Qoh 12:14)

Against this understanding of God's judicial nature Qoheleth highlights his observations of unjust retribution. The verse prior to the first affirmation states the inequity he sees:

> Moreover, I saw [the following reality] under the sun:
> In the place of justice, there is wickedness,
> In the place of equity, there is wickedness. (Qoh 3:16)

He elaborates on the topic elsewhere:

> I have seen it all living in my own days of absurdity [*bîmê heblî*]:
> There are righteous people who perish in their righteousness,
> And there are wicked people who prolong their life by acting evil. (Qoh 7:15)
> There is an absurdity [*hebel*] that takes place on earth:
> There are righteous people who are accorded the deeds of the wicked,

And there are wicked people who are accorded the deeds of the righteous.
I said that this too is absurd [*hābel*]. (Qoh 8:14)

What one makes of Qoheleth the speaker and Qoheleth the book depends on larger questions about the frame narrative, how the epilogue mediates Qoheleth's words to the reader (Fox 1989: 316–329), and whether there are one or two epilogists.[136] Suffice it here to say that Qoheleth is an existentialist philosopher who, unlike atheist existentialists such as Sartre, situates his questions of theodicy within a framework of theism. He is a realist who acknowledges that despite his belief in a God who adjudicates, the absurd is a reality in human experience, and one that confronts anyone holding a simplistic view of retribution. Similar questions of retribution are represented elsewhere, as in the prophetic disputation speech found in Malachi 3:13–15. Speaking to the post-exilic community in Jerusalem who are questioning the profit of serving God, the prophet responds: "Once again, you will see the difference between a righteous person and a wicked one, between one who serves God and one who does not" (Mal 3:18).[137] Qoheleth's understanding of the "absurd" (*hebel*) does not allow him such certainty.[138]

Qoheleth's rhetorical style with regard to theodicy is powerful, but in an understated way that is not disputational. Qoheleth does not directly challenge God with a straightforward question, like Genesis' "Shall not the judge of the entire earth execute justice?" (*hăšōpēṭ kol-hā'āreṣ lō' ya'ăśeh mišpāṭ*; Gen 18:25) or Malachi's "Where is the God of justice?" (*'ayyēh 'ĕlōhê hammišpāṭ*; Mal 2:17). For Qoheleth, it is poignant enough to juxtapose the notion of a just God with his real-life observation of unjust retribution. As Fox (1989: 9–28; 1999: 1–26) has insightfully pointed out, his style is one of juxtaposing contradictions (i.e., antinomies), thereby making his audience feel unsettled when there is no easy reconciliation.

This is not to say that Qoheleth lacks bite. His observational style includes this peppery passage:

Consider God's handiwork:
Indeed, who can straighten what He has twisted [*'iwwĕtô*]?
In the day of prosperity, enjoy!
In the day of adversity, ponder this:
God has made the one as well as the other,
So mortals may not find out anything after them. (Qoh 7:13–14)

Regarding God's "twisting," note Amos' use of the root *'wt* to describe the economic oppression of the poor and needy by those who "practice twisted/crooked behavior by falsifying balances" (*lĕ'awwēt mō'znê mirmâ*) as they weigh out grain and wheat (Amos 8:4–6).[139] Psalm 146:9 presents the poetic justice one desires for Amos's miscreants. God comes to the aid of the disadvantaged (once again using the three social categories of the judicial ideal) by contorting the wicked:

> Yahweh guards/watches over non-native residents [gēr],
> He upholds the orphan and the widow,
> But he twists [yĕʿawwēt] the way of the wicked.

The book of Job explicitly applies the root ʿwt to the cause of justice. Bildad's rhetorical questions that challenge Job's blustery words (Job 8:2) affirm God as a just judge who certainly does not distort or pervert matters of justice:

> Does God twist [yĕʿawwēt] justice?
> Does Shadday twist [yĕʿawwēt] the right?[140] (Job 8:3)

Elihu uses declarative pronouncements to assert the same:

> Far be it from God to do evil,
> [Far be it] from Shadday to do wrong.
>
> Rather, he repays a person according to his deeds,
> Has the results of one's own conduct befall him.
>
> Surely God would not do evil,
> Nor Shadday twist [lōʾ yĕʿawwēt] justice. (Job 34:10–12)

Job, as we will shortly see, does think that God can twist justice, at least when it comes to God "twisting him about" (ʿiwwĕtānî; Job 19:6). Yet whereas Job will come to level legal charges directly at God, Qoheleth presents his theodicy with a philosophical and existential statement of the state of affairs as they are. Qoheleth is resigned that the situation is what is it. He had previously affirmed that what is crooked cannot be made straight (Qoh 1:15), and nothing has changed his mind on this. Like Job, he observes that humans are not able to litigate (lōʾ-yûkal lādîn; 6:10) with one who is stronger (cf. Job 9:4–5; 14:20). Given such a reality, Qoheleth does not press the case directly. In contrast, Job does not let this disparity keep him from filing his legal complaint with passionate zeal.

Job and Divine Justice

The book of Job is remarkable in how it wrestles with theodicy altogether differently than anything else we have seen in the Hebrew Bible. Here we have a human being who imagines entering into formal litigation with God and then, after fully acknowledging the insurmountable odds, proceeds to file an actual legal case. Though there is debate over whether the book as a whole should be seen as a legal drama,[141] all scholars agree that legal rhetoric and judicial metaphors fill the book.[142] Yair Hoffman's tally reveals that "judicial terminology is used no less than 150 times" in the book.[143] For Edward Greenstein (1996: 242), "The poetic speeches of Job are laced with legal rhetoric and shaped to express the hero's mounting desire to meet his God in a court of law." Sylvia Scholnick (1982: 521) asserts that "the meaning of divine justice" "is central to an understanding of the book of Job." Norman Habel (1985: 54) comments that "legal metaphor is a major literary device" that is "integral to the structure and coherence of the book of Job."

That Job the protagonist raises questions of theodicy is verified from the very lips of the divine, who retorts in Job 40:8:

Will you really break my justice?[144]	ha'ap tāpēr mišpāṭî
Make me out to be wicked so you may be just?	taršî'ēnî lĕma'an tiṣdāq

As further proof, one need look no further than Job 9:22, where Job does indeed deny God's justice, using equally strong language:

> It's all the same. That's why I say:
> Blameless [tām]. Wicked [rāšāʾ]. It is He who destroys [mĕkalleh] them both.

What occasioned the use of such harsh language? The author of the book sets off Job's response by having his friend Bildad confidently assert that God certainly does not "twist" justice (see 8:3) and thus

> it's patently obvious:
> God does not reject the blameless [tām].
> Nor does He take the hand of the wicked [mĕrēʿîm]. (Job 8:20)

Eliphaz had rhetorically asked a similar question, though using verbs of destruction:

> Think now, who indeed being innocent ever perished?
> Where have the righteous ever been destroyed? (Job 4:7)

However, Job knows from the death of his children and his physical suffering that Bildad's confidence misses the mark. We readers know this too, aware that Job is described as blameless (tām) by none other than Yahweh in the prologue (1:8; 2:3). As for Eliphaz's apology, Job has a ready counterexample. In Job 9:22 he uses an active verb of destruction (mĕkalleh) with God as subject, to drive the point home. Thus we find Job starting to ponder the likelihood that he would succeed were he to file a legal case against God. In his imagination he thinks through the eventualities and finds little hope for redress.

Job's Imaginary Lawsuit
Job presents his legal dilemma beginning in chapter 9 with what C. L. Seow (2013: 541) calls "a cluster of terms" (twelve different words, with repetitions occurring a total of twenty-three times) "at home in court law." Job first assesses his odds of success in Job 9:2 and finds them overwhelmingly stacked against him—either because God would never deign to appear at the bar to answer a human (cf. 9:16; 33:13) or because humans are in no position to answer the Almighty (cf. 9:14–15, 32).[145] Adding to such hopeless odds, Job admits that God is so much wiser and stronger that resistance is futile (9:4b)—not to mention that God seems to have a destructive nature and a propensity toward anger (9:5–8, 13). And yet Job does resist, further bemoaning his imaginary lawsuit. Though he believes that he is in the right (Job 9:15, 21), Job does not think God would give him the hearing he desires (9:16), and God would likely use his might, as he has in the past, to crush him further (9:17–18).[146] Backed into a legal corner, Job, though innocent (9:15, 20–21), can only imagine a situation in which he has to (falsely) plead guilty and then plead for mercy (*'etḥannān*) from, of all people, his opponent-at-law (*měšōpěṭî*)—that is, from God (9:15).[147] Yet even then God would twist his words against him (*yaʿqěšēnî*; 9:20). Questioning himself at this stage and loathing his life (9:21), he asks his friends bluntly:

> The earth is given into the hand of the wicked.
> He [God] covers the faces of its judges.
> If it is not He, then who is it?[148] (Job 9:24)

In a direct contradiction to the belief that the righteous possess the land (e.g., Ps 37:9; Prov 2:21–22; 10:30), Job asserts the very opposite. Rather than God being the quintessential impartial judge who alone carries out the judicial ideal, Job claims that God is in fact behind a cover-up of justice. The climax of Job's brutal indictment challenges Bildad and Eliphaz to produce an alternative malefactor. If not God, then who is it? Hence we have Job's statement of theodicy that God unjustly destroys the blameless along with the wicked (9:22).

One would think that with such hopeless odds Job would simply give in and drop his imagined legal case, and this is precisely what he ponders next. Yet should he do so because his days are fleeting? Or should he attempt to scrub himself clean, even though he would still stand accused as wicked (*'ānōkî 'eršāʿ*), with God ready to douse him with filth (9:25–31)?[149] The dire conclusion cannot be avoided: God is not a mortal with whom one could proceed to court (9:32). The only way to imagine such a scenario would be to have an arbiter (*môkîaḥ*) who could adjudicate between them (9:33). Yet with God being God and no arbiter having higher authority, this could never happen in reality. It resides solely in the realm of "if only."[150]

Job Files His Legal Complaint
As Job's suffering continues and the seemingly endless debates with his friends plod on, Job's intention to file a futile lawsuit changes, and with it comes an even more intense bravado. In chapter 16, we find some of the harshest language in the book. Job lashes out at Yahweh, describing him as his enemy (*ṣar*) coming at him like a wild animal, gnashing his teeth as his wrath "rips [him] open" (16:9).[151] God grabs him by the scruff of the neck and bashes him about (16:12). Switching metaphors, Job tells of Yahweh the divine warrior (*gibbôr*) setting him up as an archery target, slashing him open without mercy (16:12–14). In Seow's (2013: 736) words, "This is a God aiming to kill." In the midst of the divine assault, Job once again asserts his innocence together with a certainty that a heavenly witness exists who can vouch for him (*hinnēh-baššāmayim ʿēdî wĕśāhădî bammĕrômîm*; 16:17b, 19). The identity of this witness is not made clear. Is it God in his mercy and love rather than God in his wrath? The imagined arbiter of Job 9:33? An angelic intercessor? Job's case for vindication personified?

From a forensic standpoint, the soliloquy in Job 29–31 is a rhetorical high point. Using Mesopotamian parallels describing trial appeals when pre-trial arbitration has proven unsuccessful, Michael Dick has argued that these chapters are "pivotal both for the structure and for the theme of the Book of Job."[152] Seow (2013: 61) too sees this section as "critical to the book's design." According to Dick, here we have Job as a defendant swearing an oath of innocence (though laden with wisdom influence) that legally compels his opponent-at-law, God, to appear in court. Such a legal maneuver skillfully answers the dilemma we saw earlier (in Job 9), where the odds against putting God in the dock were insurmountable. The unimaginable filing of a legal case becomes a reality in chapters 29–31. Seow (2013: 59–61, 68–69) argues that these chapters are the culmination of the judicial language running throughout the book, yet only here, "for the first time in the book," does the author employ a formal legal genre. Where Dick saw "a defendant's plea," Seow sees Job as a plaintiff.[153] For support, Seow turns to the epigraphic record and F. W. Dobbs-Allsopp's (1994) study of the genre of the Meṣad Ḥashavyahu ostracon.[154] For Seow, Job is a plaintiff filing a signed judicial complaint that, like the Meṣad Ḥashavyahu inscription, accuses a superior of abusing his power (Job 30:19–23). Like the plaintiff in the inscription, Job too files a declaration of his innocence. Yet unlike the plaintiff in the inscription, Job does not have human companions who will vouch for him, and so he must turn to the heavenly witness mentioned previously.[155] Even more significant for the legal case at hand is that, whereas the litigant in the inscription can appeal to a higher official for redress, Job has no uninterested third-party authority to whom to appeal.

Whether defendant or plaintiff, Job's defiant summons is a dramatic climax:

Oh that I had someone to hear [šōmēʿa] me!
Here is my mark!
Shadday—let him answer me!
Oh that my adversary-at-law [ʾîš rîbî] would write out an indictment!
   (Job 31:35)

As with the heavenly witness in Job 16:19, determining the identity of the "hearer" (šōmēʿa) that Job had in mind is guesswork. Is he imagining a third-party magistrate who would be impartial regarding his case (cf. 9:33)? Or does he want a hearing from the Almighty, as is implied by the request for a divine indictment that immediately follows? The latter scenario would align with Job's earlier request to be weighed in just scales by a God who sees all (Job 31:4, 6; cf. too Judg 11:10 on God as a šōmēʿa between two parties).

The Divine Speeches and Theophany

Dramatically, Job gets his wish. If the Elihu speeches (Job 32–37) are secondary (a near consensus among scholars), then the divine speeches immediately follow Job's bold request. Without the Elihu material, Fox (1981: 56) remarks, "neither Job nor the reader has a chance to catch his breath." Once again forensic language is employed. Scholnick (1987: 187) writes: "There can be no doubt that chs. 38–41 were intended by the poet to be understood as the testimony of the divine defendant in the lawsuit brought by the plaintiff from Uz." The first imperative out of God's mouth ("Gird up your loins") denotes a rigorous struggle ahead, with military and perhaps legal connotations.[156] In Job 40:2, Yahweh explicitly asks: "Will he who legally contends with Shadday correct [me]? Will he who chides God answer that?"[157]

The standard reading of the divine speeches suggests that their tone is harsh, sarcastic, adversarial, and humiliating, perhaps even bragging and bullying. David Clines (2011: 1097) concludes:

God tells Job without qualification that he regards him as his opponent and enemy who will need courage and strength—not a just [legal] cause—to be able to confront him. God . . . makes no secret that the legal dispute will only be ... a trial of strength.... Job had better understand that summoning God to trial will not lead to a calm, rational, orderly legal process. God takes Job's summons personally, and he intends to fight ... he intends to get his revenge.

In contrast, Fox (1981: 58–60) argues that the rhetorical technique of piling up questions regarding matters known to questioner and auditor alike is intended to "set up a special intimacy of communication" based on shared knowledge. This particular form of rhetoric, suggests Fox, is not sarcastic and humiliating but rather "a stern gentleness" where "God demands humility, not humiliation." "With compassion and gentleness" God "remind[s] Job of the limitations of human wisdom."

Whatever the tone, God highlights that Job had indeed called his justice into question (cf. Job 9:24). His stern question to Job bears repeating:

Will you really break my justice?	ha'ap tāpēr mišpāṭî
Make me out to be wicked so you may be just?	taršîʿēnî lĕmaʿan tiṣdāq
	(Job 40:8)

Scholnick (1982; 1987: 194) and Dick (2006: 268) argue that the use of the word *mišpāṭ* here is key to solving the meaning of the divine speeches. They illustrate how Hebrew and Ugaritic (cf. too Akkadian) use the root *špṭ/ṭpṭ* to designate both forensic rulings appropriate to a court of law and executive rulings of a king amounting to "dominion" and "kingship." Job the litigant argues the forensic side of "justice" (*mišpāṭ*) without appreciating the way in which *mišpāṭ* includes, for Yahweh the King, his right to manage the cosmos in the way that he sees fit, for only he has title to it. Using 1 Samuel 8:11 as an example, Scholnick (1982: 522–523) describes how the executive "justice" (*mišpāṭ*) of a king allows him to take away children and servants as well as to appropriate property, similar to what happens to Job in the prologue. Thus when it comes to Job's legal claim, God's actions are within his jurisdiction as king. According to Scholnick, "God is acting as Ruler to test His subject, not as Judge to punish him for wrongdoing." In response, Job retracts his legal claim.[158]

Greenstein adds yet another piece to the forensic puzzle of the divine speeches. Taking his cue from the definition of a legal witness (*ʿēd*) in Leviticus 5:1 as one who has "seen" or who "knows" of something relevant (cf. David as witness in 1 Sam 24:8–22), Greenstein (1996: 245) highlights the same vocabulary found on Job's lips in Job 13:1–2. Job validates his standing as a formal witness whose eye has seen and whose ear has heard and understood justiciable evidence. Immediately following this, he proclaims his desire to argue a legal case with God (*wĕhôkēaḥ ʾel-ʾēl*; 13:3; cf. 23:4–5). In contrast to Scholnick, Greenstein (1996: 251–253) has God adopting his own legal maneuver "to throw Job's case out of court for cause." Directly challenging Job's standing as an informed witness, God repeatedly assaults Job's "knowledge," "harping on the verb 'to know.'" Thus for Greenstein (1996: 250), "Yhwh does not answer any charges." He does not have to submit to litigation because Job has already acknowledged that his incompetence in testifying (Job 42:3) excludes him from bearing witness. Greenstein concludes that "in disqualifying Job's status as witness, Yhwh implies no quarrel with the content of Job's charges."

There are many ways of viewing the book of Job apart from a judicial focus. However one understands the divine speeches and how they respond or do not respond to Job's litigation and assertions of injustice, our theodicean poet settles his case with Job being satisfied. The divine theophany has the effect of bringing Job to a place of resolution. His final words just prior to his repentance in dust and ashes concentrate on the experiential:

> I had heard of you by the hearing of the ear,
> But now my eye sees you. (Job 42:5)

The legal rhetoric of the book of Job is powerful and unique. Nowhere else do we read of a human filing a legal case that puts God in the dock. Yet even the most skilled verbal rhetoric falls short of a personal encounter. Job "had heard" of Yahweh—his co-litigant, his adversary at law, and his judge—as he pressed forward with the particulars of his legal case. Yet once in court, he undergoes a more rigorous cross-examination than he could have imagined— one that leaves him acknowledging "things too wonderful for me, that which I did not know" (Job 42:3). Contrary to Job's expectations (voiced in Job 9), God did deign to appear at the bar to answer a human (cf. 9:16; 33:13). Yet in line with Job's expectations, humans are indeed in no position to answer the Almighty (cf. 9:14–15, 32). As the theophany reaffirmed, God is indeed so much wiser and stronger (9:4). Yet, poignantly, God allowed Job "to see" the ethereal divine, an encounter accorded only to a precious few (Jacob, Moses, Gideon, Manoah, Isaiah).[159] Though priestly teaching would assert that one does not "see" God and live to tell about it (Exod 33:20), Job in fact does. He gets his wish (Job 19:26–27). The powerful "adversary" whom Job had fully expected "to destroy the blameless along with the wicked" (Job 9:22) here does not. Rather, the Almighty powerfully humbles him, occasioning Job's repentance (Job 42:6b). Then, according to the epilogue (and with no mention of any arbitrated courtroom settlement), God doubly restores Job's possessions (Job 42:10–17).

God as Law Writer and Lawgiver, and the Unique Role Assigned to Moses

We come at last to what may come to mind first when one thinks of God as judge: he is the ultimate author of all law and the giver of law to Moses, who acts as his delegated intermediary. God is indeed presented as the primary (sole?) promulgator of law in ancient Israel.[160] Yet for the historian of religion, this theological truism needs to be set within its historical, sociological, and literary contexts.

The ancient Near Eastern legal historian Raymond Westbrook (2003: 1) states succinctly: "Law has existed as long as organized human society." A priori, all societies, large and small, have laws and lawgivers. The origins of Near Eastern law are hard to trace, with "virtually no mention in the surviving documents" (Wells 2005: 184), yet shared ancient Near Eastern scribal legal codes, royal decrees (ṣimdat šarrim), and societal customs had to have played significant roles.[161] The attested categories of law are staggering in number and variety: laws regarding personal status (e.g., citizenship, class, gender, age, slavery), family law (e.g., marriage, dissolution of marriage, children, adoption), property (e.g., tenure, inheritance, transfer, female inheritance), contracts (e.g., findings, terms, social consequence), crime and delict (e.g., punishment, offenses against the gods, offenses against the king, homicide, adultery, rape, perjury, slander, theft), and international law (e.g., treaties, customary law).[162]

The Need for Royal Legislation

Given the societal necessity and complexity of law, it is surprising to read uncritical, non-nuanced, and reductionist summations that assert, for example, that "Israel's kings never give law" (Watts 1998: 417). Even the great Roland de Vaux's (1961: 150–151) summation is overly circumspect. In comparing ancient Israelite law with Mesopotamia's production of law codes, de Vaux writes:

> In Israel, granted the religious nature of the law, and its connection with Covenant, nothing of the sort was possible, and in fact the historical books never allude to any legislative power of the king. . . . The king had of course an extensive administrative authority; he organized his kingdom, appointed his officials and made decrees, but he did not enact law. It is remarkable that the two "laws of the king" (1 S 8:11–18; Dt 17:14–20) make no allusion to any power of the king to lay down laws. . . . [T]he king is nowhere mentioned in the Deuteronomic Code. . . . [T]he king could add nothing to the authority of a law to which he himself was subject (Dt 17:19; 1 K 8:58; 2 K 23:3). . . . On the other hand, the king was a judge, and held judicial power.

It is hard to imagine how ancient society would function without a head of state being involved in the promulgation of laws. To imagine the legalities of a working monarchy, one need only look at the extensive collections of legal transactions from the royal court of Nineveh.[163] Granted, the Neo-Assyrian Empire at its height is a poor comparison for the much smaller Judean monarchies. Yet though the scale would not be as large in the Judean kingdoms, the intricacies of the purchase and loan documents from Nineveh are informative, for they reveal the obvious need for law when it comes to the realities of economic agreements. Moreover, de Vaux's own words belie his conclusion when he speaks of kings making decrees, administering their kingdoms, and holding judicial power. One need not wait until the Persian period (cf. Est 1:19; 8:8; Ezra 6:1–12; 7:12–26; Elephantine Papyri) to imagine kings issuing legal edicts that were a necessity for the governing of society.

Though royal legislation is poorly documented because of the way the Hebrew Bible is edited (further discussion to follow), we nonetheless read of Samuel writing a legislative document about royal rights/regulations (*mišpaṭ hammělukâ*) that he "laid before Yahweh" (*wayyannaḥ lipnê yhwh*), presumably in a sanctuary (1 Sam 10:25; cf. McCarter 1980a: 193–194). We hear of Saul issuing a decree that necromancy should be outlawed (1 Sam 28:9–10). Prior to being king, David makes "a statute and ordinance" for Israel that continues to exist at the time DtrH is writing (*wayěśimehā lěḥōq ûlěmišpāṭ lěyiśrāʾēl ʿad hayyôm hazzeh*; 1 Sam 30:25).[164] Once David becomes king, his rendering of a legal verdict in the Tekoite woman's (fictional) case is seen as his own "angelic" act, and Solomon's dealing with the two female litigants is presented as ideological proof that he is divinely endowed (as discussed earlier). Whitelam extrapolates (1979: 215–216): "There is no explicit reference to the promulgation of law in either of these cases, but the ideological implications of the internalization of divine wisdom in judicial affairs certainly suggest that the king was believed to possess the potential to create law." Elsewhere we read of King Omri issuing statutes (Mic 6:16). Both Hezekiah and Josiah, in enacting God's ordinances, certainly had to issue decrees for carrying out the specifics of their religious reforms, as would Manasseh in his counter-reform. King Zedekiah, according to Jeremiah 34:8–10, decrees the manumission of all slaves (*liqrōʾ děrôr*).[165] To govern is to legislate.

The judicial ideal holds that kings emulate divine justice. It became proverbial to speak of rulers "inscribing just decrees" (*rôzěnîm yěḥōqěqû ṣedeq*; Prov 8:15). Judean royal seals and bullae attest to administrative involvement in economic matters, some of which had to involve legal decrees and legal redress regarding property. As for the abuse of justice, Isaiah 10:1–2 likely has kings in mind when it expresses woe because of "those who inscribe wicked decrees and write oppressive statutes" (cf. Ps 94:20).[166] In short, political and sociological considerations require human lawmakers; with the monarchy constituting a (or the) dominant institution of power, kings were certainly involved in promulgating legislation.[167]

The Absence of Royal Legislation in the Hebrew Bible

Given this reality, how then should one account for the absence of texts in the Hebrew Bible documenting royal legislation? As noted earlier, we have detailed descriptions of the thousands of offerings that King Solomon rendered, yet nary a word about the myriad of written legal statutes that this "just king par excellence" must have issued. On display are King Jehoshaphat's noble admonitions that a godly judiciary is without favoritism or bribe-taking, not his utilitarian edicts regulating the functioning of society.

Three overlapping answers are readily apparent, the first redactional, the second theological, and the third political/sociological. The first is that the editing of what comes to be the Hebrew Bible was a selective process with certain content outside the interests of its redactors. I have written elsewhere of how texts describing the day-to-day family religion of non-elite actors were outside the scope of editors who were part of the priestly management and portrayal of cult (Lewis 2012: 109–110, 113). Similarly, royal promulgations and regulations (cf. Akk *ṣimdat šarrim*) as well as the royal supervision of economic legal transactions (cf. again the records from Neo-Assyrian Nineveh) were simply not considered to be germane—for whatever reason—by those editors (e.g., priestly, prophetic, poetic, Deuteronomistic, Chronistic, wisdom-related) who were involved in forming what we now know to be the Hebrew Bible. Their interests simply lie elsewhere. Their portrayals were decidedly literary, often exhortatory, rarely utilitarian.[168] We have precious few remnants of the legal transactions of the working monarchies of ancient Israel and Judah no matter the time period.

The second is that theological interests were dominant. Yahweh is *the* giver of law. "Justice is of God" (*hammišpāṭ lēʾlōhîm hûʾ*; Deut 1:16–17). It is God's prerogative to legislate, with humans (from king to commoner) being assigned the role of faithfully carrying out his "statutes" (*ḥuqqîm*), "instructions" (*tôrōt*), and "ordinances" (*mišpāṭîm*). Humans are admonished to "be careful to observe" (√*šmr laʿăśôt*) divine legislation. Whether one turns to God handing down the law on Mt. Sinai or to poetic formulations, Yahweh, not the human king, is the royal legislator par excellence. Consider again the rhyming poetry of Isaiah 33:22:

Yahweh is our judge,	*yhwh šōpĕṭēnû*
Yahweh is he who inscribes our [laws],	*yhwh mĕḥōqĕqēnû*
Yahweh is our king,	*yhwh malkēnû*
He will deliver us.	*hûʾ yôšîʿēnû*

If Yahweh is the one and only just king and impartial judge, then necessarily only Yahweh can establish ideal laws. When we juxtapose the dominance of this theological motif with the sociological need for and reality of a human monarch legislating, it only makes sense to understand Yahweh as the sole creator of perfect law as a type of legal fiction, as does Whitelam (1979: 209–210). Legal fictions (here viewed positively, not pejoratively) are necessary whenever theory and practice are at odds (cf. rabbinic law).[169] The conflicts of theory and practice are threefold. (1) The first conflict results from how a law mediated solely by Moses can be conveyed once he has died. Though theoretically Moses alone is God's legislator, we immediately hear of Joshua filling his role once he has died (Josh 8:32; 24:26). In the remarkable Mt. Ebal traditions, the people inscribe law (Deut 27:3). In the future, Jeremiah envisions Yahweh bypassing human mediators altogether to write his law on people's hearts himself (Jer 31:33; cf. Ezek 36:27). (2) The second conflict results from the Deuteronomic notion that divine law is unalterable (Deut 4:1–2; 13:1 [Eng 12:32]; cf. Josh 1:7; 23:6; Qoh 3:14).[170] Whitelam suggests that historians who accept such statements of immutability at face value (and thus conclude that kings did not legislate) are boxed in when "pentateuchal laws [become] obviously inadequate to deal with all eventualities in a dynamic and expanding ... society as that created by the inauguration of the monarchy and the subsequent expansion of the Davidic kingdom." (3) Another conflict of theory and practice arises from the abuse of justice by those charged with rendering impartial justice. The theological way to deal with those "who inscribe wicked decrees and write oppressive statutes" (Ps 94:20) is to strip them of any legislative authority. The functionality of the legal fiction that Yahweh is the sole giver of impartial law is readily understandable.

The third explanation of the lack of texts in the Hebrew Bible documenting royal legislation is sociological and political. Here we turn yet again to priestly and prophetic voices chastising the monarchy, and to Deuteronomic restrictions on royal power. These constituencies aimed at restricting the power of the monarchy to help avoid abuse of justice as well as abuse of cult. Though in practice kings could not be kept from legislating, these ideological voices attempt to restrict the king's role in the cult, in the judiciary, and in providing legislation. The Deuteronomic view has been called "more utopian than pragmatic" (Levinson 2001: 533). Be that as it may, the passion to deny the king such powers of office and to direct him instead to meditating on his own copy of divine law in order to live a godly life and to avoid self-exaltation is undeniable (Deut 17:18–20).

The Unique Role of Moses as God's Delegated Mediator of Law
The various traditions that have been preserved in the Hebrew Bible speak with one voice: the prophet/scribe Moses, not any royal figure, is the face of God's delegated legislator. Some would suggest that Moses's legal role is indeed that

of a royal figure, one that is patterned after Yahweh as the just king. Yet James Watts (1998: 416–417), who acknowledges aspects of idyllic royalty that align with Moses, concludes that overall the portrayal of Moses is contrasted with royalty. Jean-Louis Ska (2009: 215) is more forceful in concluding: "Moses is not a king and there is nothing of the oriental monarch about him."

We have already looked at the various "origin myths" of Mosaic judiciaries. As these traditions wrestle with the distribution of judicial authority, they at the same time heighten the prestige of Moses. In Exodus 18:13–26, Moses's judicial role is described as a divine conduit, for people come to him "to inquire of God" (*lidrōš 'ĕlōhîm*). The expression here is certainly elliptical—that is, the people come to Moses to (have him) inquire (on their behalf) of God—yet also tantalizing in the impression it leaves that Moses is divine-like. If this ellipsis is intentional, one is reminded of two expressions elsewhere in Exodus (4:16; 7:1) where Moses is portrayed as a god.[171] As God's legislator, Moses is positioned to make known (*hôdîaʿ*) and to clarify (*hizhîr*) divine statutes and laws (Exod 18:16, 20). The other judiciary origin tradition (Deut 1:9–18) also mentions how Moses undertook "to expound" (or perhaps "to promulgate") Yahweh's law and ends with him handling the most difficult cases (Deut 1:5, 17).[172] Whether Numbers 11:16–25 is related to this material has already been discussed. What is clear is that the Numbers 11–12 complex also heightens Moses' prestige, and clearly along prophetic lines. There is no other individual like Moses, says the authoritative voice of God, one to whom he "speaks face-to-face" (*peh 'el-peh 'ădabber-bô*). Moses sees the very "form" (*mar'eh/tĕmûnâ*) of God and is entrusted with his entire estate (*bĕkol-bêtî ne'ĕmān hû'*; Num 12:7–8). Speaking against God's servant Moses should occasion "fear," for God's wrath is at the ready (Num 12:8b–9). The unique intimacy that Moses shares with the divine is also on display in Exodus 33:11, where God is said to have spoken with Moses "face-to-face, as one speaks to his friend" (*pānîm 'el-pānîm ka'ăšer yĕdabbēr 'îš 'el-rēʿēhû*).[173] Deuteronomy 34:10 echoes that sentiment: "Never again did there arise a prophet in Israel like Moses, whom Yahweh knew face-to-face" (*'ăšer yĕdāʿô yhwh pānîm 'el-pānîm*).

The prophetic role of Moses is underscored in all of these traditions, from the language chosen in the judiciary tradition to depict Moses inquiring of God (*lidrōš 'ĕlōhîm*) to the explicit use of the word "prophet" (*nābî'*) in Numbers 11:29, 12:6, and Deuteronomy 34:10. Yet assigning Moses the unqualified title "prophet" undercuts the way Numbers 12:6–8 privileges Moses's prophetic office, calling it one of a kind. Other prophets, it is said, receive divine communication mediated through dreams and visions (Num 12:6). Such mediation is implied in two of the key terms for "seers" (*ḥōzeh, rō'eh*) used throughout the Hebrew Bible's prophetic corpus. In contrast, Moses' prophetic office is one mediated by direct auditory communication with the divine. Visions and dreams require interpretation, unlike direct speech from God. Here the auditory clearly trumps the visual.[174] And yet Moses receives direct visual communication too, as he sees God's "form" directly rather than in the mediated dream-like visions of lesser prophets. Levine (1993: 338, 341) speaks of Moses as being "the sole person with oracular access to God ... There is nothing intervening between God and Moses in the transmission of God's voice." For Levine, phenomenologically, the Tent of Meeting in Exodus 33:7–11 is "an oraculum." Were one to blend in the tradition of Numbers 12:8, one would conclude that even this oraculum is like no other, for Moses sees as well as hears the divine. Adding in the even later tradition of Deuteronomy 34:10 provides a "knowing" intimacy that is unparalleled.[175]

Given such tradents about the auditory, visual, and "knowing" closeness that Moses shares with the divine, it is not surprising to read of the conflation of "the law of Yahweh" (Exod 13:9; 2 Kgs 10:31; Isa 5:24; 30:9; Jer 8:8; Amos 2:4; Ps 1:2; 19:8 [Eng 19:7]; 119:1; Ezr 7:10; Neh 9:3; 1 Chr 16:14; 22:12; 2 Chr 12:1; 17:9; 31:3–4; 34:14; 35:26) and "the law of Moses" (Josh 8:31–32; 23:6; 1 Kgs 2:3; 2 Kgs 14:6; 23:25; Mal 3:22 [Eng 4:4]; Ezr 3:2; 7:6; Neh 8:1; 2 Chr 23:18; 30:16; Dan 9:11, 13; cf. 2 Chr 25:4). The conversance, fellowship, and familiarity of God and his chosen mediator allow divine law to be constituted by a human being. Thus though the law is written by God (Exod 24:12; 34:1; Deut 5:22; 10:2, 4; Isa 33:22), even with his very finger (Exod 31:18; Deut 9:10), it can be mediated through Moses' penmanship, especially when it is God who commands him to write (Exod 17:14; 24:4; 34:27–28; Num 33:2; Deut 31:9; 31:22, 24). Leviticus 26:46 summarizes the way that this arrangement was thought of from a theological perspective: "These are the statutes and ordinances and laws that Yahweh gave/established [nātan] between himself and Israel on Mt. Sinai through the agency of Moses" (běyad-mōšeh; cf. Lev 10:11; Num 36:13; 2 Chr 33:8; 34:14; Neh 9:14). God (and God only) is the "establisher" and "giver" of law, yet he does so through Moses' agency.[176]

It is anyone's guess as to how such a theocentric and "Moses-centric" philosophy/theology of law actually worked on a day-to-day level, in which various constituencies (Yahwist and non-Yahwist) were necessarily involved in legislating all the legal affairs of working tribes and monarchies, with a variety of locations (e.g., urban centers or agrarian villages). We must return again to ponder the many and varied social locations where judicial affairs (broadly construed) were decided. Certainly these many constituencies (e.g., elders, kinsmen, family and tribal "heads" [rāʾšîm], kings, judges, śārîm officals, šōṭĕrîm officials, priests, local officials, competent men [ʾanšê-ḥayil], household actors including women) would need to negotiate how laws were promulgated and enforced. All legislative matters would have been subject to the dynamics of who possessed power, influence, and resources, and to what degree.[177]

Conclusion

The texts surveyed here are partial indicators of the many ways in which juridical topics were engaged and framed in ancient Israel. It is impossible to recover the full breadth of legal affairs of any society that existed for hundreds of years, even with the best of records. It is that much more challenging to piece together the legal affairs of ancient Israel using the Hebrew Bible as our primary source. We have meager data for the legal historian—certainly not the day-to-day utilitarian records of working judiciaries (cf. Démare-Lafont et al. forthcoming). This is not to imply that the minutiae of law were not seriously engaged, for what we have preserved reveals that they were, and on a wide variety of topics (cf. Frymer-Kensky 2003). And, as just noted, our extant texts do mention a wide variety of social actors with stakes in legal affairs.

What is privileged in the edited sources that have come down to us is ideological, counter-ideological, and theological in nature. We read of a judicial ideal that resonates with broader ancient Near Eastern ideals: that the most disadvantaged in society (typified especially by widows and orphans, and in ancient Israel also by the *gēr*) deserve special judicial protection. Time and again Yahweh is proclaimed with confidence and faith to be the quintessential just judge. Theologically, Yahweh is the author of law that he enacts through the prophet/scribe Moses.

As ideal judge, Yahweh is the object of individual prayers for judicial redress and corporate prayers that the king may be endowed with divine justice in order to protect those in need (Ps 72:1–14). Ideologically, four Judean monarchs are portrayed as trying on the mantle of the "just king," with David and Solomon, especially David, requiring serious editorial alterations for a proper fit. When it comes to the monarchy overall, the record preserved counters ideological pretensions. There are ample reports of the abuse of justice by those in power, especially royal power. According to the critics (especially prophetic voices), the ideal of an earthly "king of justice" remained distant, with little redress for actual judicial suffering apart from divine intervention. At times of severest oppression and loss of earthly hope, judicial redress was so very distant that it could only be imagined in an apocalyptic future. Here too Yahweh was the source of judicial rescue, raising up an idyllic offshoot of David who would at last execute justice in the land (Jer 23:5).

Just as prophetic voices (and Deuteronomic utopian restrictions) did not shrink from pressing their case against royal injustice, so too voices raising the question of theodicy did not fail to file their grievances against the perceived injustice of a divine monarch. Their wrestlings took various forms, from Qoheleth living with his contradictions to the experiential voice in Job 42:5–6. Whether or not these voices proved satisfying for their ancient (or modern) audiences, in the end they present an optimistic theodicy in line with Leibniz's definition of the concept of *théodicée*—that is, a vindication of the justice of God and his actions in light of reality.[178]

Two additional perspectives need to be presented prior to wrapping up this abridged look at Yahweh as judge. These final words, from psalmists and the author of the book of Jonah, probe the extent of God's judicial authority and his mercy.

A Psalmist's Look at the Vast Extent of God's Judicial Authority

The various traditions we have examined profess Yahweh as the absolute judge of all human legal affairs. As displayed in the prophetic "judgment oracles against the nations," Yahweh's exclusive judicial authority is global in nature, judging foreign (non-Yahwistic) peoples even without their acknowledgment of his legal prerogative. Yet, according to an exceptional psalmist, one should not stop with the earthly plane. If Yahweh is indeed absolute judge, then his legal authority must transcend human society. It must extend to the realm of the gods. Psalm 82 is one of the most visionary poems in the entire Hebrew Bible, as it applies Yahweh's judicial authority to the wrongdoings of the gods.[179] Yahweh places the gods in the dock in the divine assembly (cf. Ps 29:1–2; 89:6–9 [Eng 89:5–8]; Job 1:6, 2:1, 15:8; 1 Kgs 22:19–22; Isa 6:1–8; Jer 23:18, 22; Zech 3; Dan 7:10).[180]

Setting the Judicial Stage

Elohim [i.e., Yahweh] takes his stand in the council of El,	'ĕlōhîm niṣṣāb baʿădat-'ēl
In the midst of the gods he renders judgment.	bĕqereb 'ĕlōhîm yišpōṭ

Accusation of Injustice

How long will you judge unjustly?	'ad-mātay tišpĕṭû-'āwel
[How long] will you show favoritism to the wicked?	ûpĕnê rĕšāʿîm tiśśĕ'û
[Rather] render justice to the poor and the orphan	šipṭû-dal wĕyātôm
Adjudicate on behalf of the poor and destitute.	'ānî wārāš haṣdîqû
Rescue the poor and needy	pallĕṭû-dal wĕ'ebyôn
From the power of the wicked—save [them]!	miyyad rĕšāʿîm haṣṣîlû

Summary Statement

They neither know nor understand,	lō' yādĕʿû wĕlō' yābînû
They walk around in darkness	baḥăšēkâ yithallākû
All the foundations of the earth totter.	yimmôṭû kol-môsĕdê 'āreṣ

Decree of Sentence

I say:	'ănî-'āmartî
"You are gods	'ĕlōhîm 'attem
Even sons of Elyon, all of you.	ûbĕnê ʿelyôn kullĕkem
But now, like humans you shall die,	'ākēn kĕ'ādām tĕmûtûn
Like one of the officials, you shall fall."	ûkĕ'aḥad haśśārîm tippōlû

Divine Charge/Plea

"Rise up, O Elohim [i.e., Yahweh],	qûmâ 'ĕlōhîm šopṭâ
judge the earth!	hā'āreṣ
For You inherit all nations!"	kî-'attâ tinḥal
	bĕkol-haggôyim

Psalm 82 is filled with a plethora of legal vocabulary, with four occurrences of the verb *špṭ* (to initiate a judicial proceeding, to adjudicate, to render judgment) together with additional vocabulary common to juridical texts (e.g., *haṣdîq, pallĕṭû* [cf. Ps 43:1]).[181] However one imagines the divine scenario, the judicial setting is unmistakable. Of the assorted topics that scholars have addressed over the years, the primary crux of Psalm 82 is the identity of *'ĕlōhîm* in verses 1, 6 and 8. Ample rehearsals of the various theories elsewhere allow me simply to note that I align myself with those scholars who interpret all four instances of the word *'ĕlōhîm* as referring to divinity. Beyond this, one's understanding of transmission and cultural history necessarily determines how one then parses the divinity of these four references to *'ĕlōhîm* vis-à-vis the two additional references to divinity, the mention of El in Psalm 82:1 and Elyon in Psalm 82:6. Or, in other words, how the ancients understood Psalm 82 (as well as how we moderns understand it) is determined by where the author, audience, and interpreter stand on the mythopoeic-mythopoetic continuum.

An Imagined Mythopoeic Scenario for Psalm 82
Mythopoeically, one can imagine (as one drinks deep of comparative mythologies, especially 'Ilu's divine council at Ugarit) a robust vision of a subordinate

deity, Yahweh (= ʾĕlōhîm in Ps 82:1a), who takes his stand in the divine council presided over by the senior deity, El (baʿădat-ʾēl; Ps 82:1a). El, whose epithet "God Most High" (Elyon) is referenced in 82:6, would be seen as sovereign over his divine council.[182] Thus it would be El, surrounded by his divine council (ʾĕlōhîm), who would be rendering judgment (yišpōṭ) in Ps 82:1b.

The purpose of Yahweh's stance at El's court of law would be to bring a legal accusation of injustice (Ps 82:2–4). Surprisingly, his accusation is directed at the very gods gathered for the occasion. His appeal is to a tribunal of one, El alone in his sovereign role as head of the divine council. Yahweh's accusation references the judicial ideal, how the gods were charged with rendering (safeguarding) impartial justice to the disadvantaged of society. Yahweh's accusation is framed as part lament ("How long?"), part admonishment ("Render justice!"). With no indicator of there being a break in who is speaking, it seems that Yahweh is the one who concludes with a summary statement (addressed to El the judge) that the gods are found wanting. In their darkened understanding, they do not understand the nature of impartial justice and its advocacy for the needy. As a direct result of their failure, injustice flourishes such that the very foundations of the earth cannot help but totter (82:5).

El's voice is then privileged as he addresses his children (who bear his epithet), recognizing their divine status (Ps 82:6a). The guilty verdict on the first-degree charge of allowing injustice to flourish occasions the severe sentence of mortality (Ps 82:6b). The gods are stripped of their divinity, a fitting sentence for those who have not behaved as gods should (Ps 82:7). El then turns to charge Yahweh as their replacement (Ps 82:8). Humans need a judge on high. Not only does Yahweh win his legal case, but El grants him the inheritance of being the judge of humanity, for whom he has already expressed his advocacy.

An Imagined Mythopoetic Scenario for Psalm 82

Mythopoetically—though rich with mythic imagery, even mythic vibrancy—our psalm is Yahweh-centric, for he is the god (= ʾĕlōhîm in Ps 82:1a) whose "Most High" epithet (Elyon) is referenced in 82:6. As numerous biblical tradents attest, Yahweh and Yahweh alone is absolute judge, the author of law, the impartial judge who never wavers in executing the judicial ideal. There is no higher and no other preternatural judicial authority, and this psalm tells of how such a scenario came about. Being subordinate to none, Yahweh takes up his role in his divine council, the name of which comes from one of Yahweh's own ancient names, El (baʿădat-ʾēl; Ps 82:1a). Yahweh presides over his El council made up of subordinate deities (perhaps with ʾĕlōhîm mythopoetically reduced to angels; cf. LXX), whom he then judges (yišpōṭ; Ps 82:1b).

Yahweh's accusation of injustice among the gods remains the same as in the mythopoeic scenario. Yet the accusation in the mythopoetic scenario is delivered by Yahweh as judge, not Yahweh in a subordinate, prosecutorial role. The appeal to the judicial ideal, the framing as lament and admonishment, the gods' ineptitude and lack of knowledge, and the ramifications for a tottering earth filled with injustice remain the same (Ps 82:2–5). Yahweh's voice, the sole operative voice in this scenario, sentences the gods (his subordinate children) to a mortal life based on the severity of their inaction and miscarriage of justice (Ps 82:6–7).

The final verse is then not a charge from a senior god (El) to a lesser god (Yahweh). Rather, for the psalmist, Yahweh is El of old, the divine magistrate, to whom the psalmist pleads to act in executing godly judicial sovereignty over the earth, indeed over all the nations (Ps 82:8).

The Masoretic Understanding of Psalm 82
It is impossible to know how the story behind this psalm was understood as it was told and retold—written, copied, and recopied over the years in the history of ancient Judah by various hands. That these same tellers, writers, editors, copiers, and interpreters handed down traditions such as those found in Deuteronomy 32:6b–9 and Psalm 29 suggests the existence of a variety of views lying along the mythopoeic-mythopoetic continuum. As we saw in Chapter Four (pp. 91–92), we have preserved one tradition of Deuteronomy 32 where (El-)Elyon establishes national boundaries by assigning land and people to various divine beings (4QDeut^j's *běnê 'ělōhîm*; cf. LXX)—with Yahweh acquiring Israel. Yet another transmission of the same text tells of an alternative tradition where it is (Yahweh-)Elyon making these same decisions corresponding to the numbers of the sons of Israel (MT's *běnê yiśrā'ēl*). No mention of any gods remains in this mythopoetic variant. Later traditions will tell the story yet differently, with references to Jacob's family descending to Egypt (cf. Tigay 1996: 514–515). As for Psalm 29:1, we seem to have all the evidence we need to reconstruct a transition from the mythopoeic (the gods give Yahweh radiance and strength) to the mythopoetic (David asks subordinate preternatural beings [angels] to assign Yahweh radiance and strength).[183]

What understanding do we have in the Masoretic Text of Psalm 82? While remnants of mythopoeic traditions seem to seep through the letters, the Masoretic tradition stands fully in line with those acknowledging one deity only as absolute judge. It leans heavily toward the mythopoetic and then some.[184] Thus' my translation, which places Yahweh's name in brackets glossing the word *'ělōhîm*. As I noted at the outset of the present chapter and at the beginning of Chapter Six, the traditions preserved in the Hebrew Bible fold El traditions into those of Yahweh. For the Masoretes, there is no polemic that sets El and Yahweh at odds. There is no hierarchy that reduces Yahweh to a subordinate in El's divine council. This is not to say that there were not considerable differences of opinion with regard to the nature of the ʾĕlōhîm whom Yahweh judges in Psalm 82:2–7. The identity of these ʾĕlōhîm also depended on the interpreter and lay somewhere on a continuum from the divine to the preternaturally angelic.

Not to be missed in such reconstructions by historians of religion is how our exceptional psalmist reconceptualized the nature of Yahweh's judicial authority: it is so very vast that it extends even to the realms of the divine council.

Divine Mercy: Psalm 103 as Representational

We end with divine mercy. For what is a judge if he cannot grant mercy? An unrelenting judge who sees all can forever find legal fault. Just ask Job. The eloquence of Psalm 103, with its economy of words and heartfelt poetry ("the most soaring lyric in the Psalter," says Jacobson [2014a: 769]), can stand as representative (cf. Exod 34:9; Mic 7:18–20; Ps 78:38–39; Neh 9:29–31; Dan 9:9–10).[185] Yahweh, the hymn proclaims, is to be praised from one's very depth of being (*nepeš; běkol qěrābîm*), mindful of the "benefits" that Yahweh has accomplished on one's behalf (*gěmûlāyw*). They are articulated as follows:

> [Yahweh is] the one who forgives all your offenses,
> who heals all your diseases.
>
> Who redeems your life from the Pit,
> Who crowns you with steadfast love and mercy [*ḥesed wěraḥămîm*] . . .
>
> Yahweh is he who executes just rulings [*ʿōśēh ṣědāqôt*],
> [Enacts] ordinances [*mišpāṭîm*] for all who are oppressed.
>
> He made his ways known to Moses,
> His deeds to the children of Israel.
>
> Yahweh is merciful and gracious [*raḥûm wěḥannûn*],
> Slow to anger, abounding in steadfast love [*rab-ḥāsed*].
>
> He does not always legally contend [*yārîb*],[186]
> Nor does he harbor a grievance forever.[187]
>
> He does not deal with us according to our sins,
> Nor does he requite us according to our offenses.
>
> For as the heavens are high above the earth,
> So great is his steadfast love [*ḥesed*] toward those who fear him.

> As distant as the east is from the west [lit. "the rising from the setting" (of the sun)],
> So far has he distanced our transgressions from us.
>
> As a father has compassion on his children,
> So Yahweh has compassion for those who fear him.
>
> For He knows how we are formed;
> He is mindful that we are but dust. (Ps 103:3–4, 6–14)

A few lines later in the psalm, Yahweh is celebrated as king with a heavenly throne and a universal kingdom (Ps 103:19, 22b). Thus we end our study of Yahweh as judge as we began (see pp. 513–521), by reflecting on how the ancients commonly looked to a royal framework for justice. Yet, remarkably, our psalmist does not concentrate on a royal metaphor or even a royal ideal when he talks of Yahweh's mercy. The only mention of a crown is that of Yahweh's mercy gracing the head of those he redeems (*měʻaṭṭěrēkî ḥesed wěraḥămîm*; Ps 103:4). Instead of a royal judge, our psalmist turns to the image of Yahweh as a father who is compassionate toward his children, a creator-father, one who knows the fragile nature of human "formation" (Ps 103:13–14; cf. Ps 136:13–16). The parental metaphors of Yahweh as a caring father that we looked at earlier (see Chapter Eight, pp. 479–482) come flooding back, yet here with judicial overtones. We are again reminded that Yahweh is "father of orphans and the one who provides justice [*dayyān*] for widows" (Ps 68:6 [Eng 68:5]). Moreover, Yahweh's mercy is extended to all the children of Israel who revere him.

The vast extent of Yahweh's mercy is emphasized here as much as the vast extent of his justice was emphasized in Psalm 82. In Psalm 103 Yahweh's patient mercy abounds in magnitude (*raḥûm wěḥannûn yhwh/ʾerek ʾappayim wěrab-ḥāsed*; Ps 103:8). The height of the heavens marks the expanse of his love. The distance from east to west marks the gulf that this merciful judge puts between his people and the offenses that prove their guilt (Ps 103:11–12). The questions of justiciable offense and guilt here are not in doubt. They are acknowledged, but only to illustrate how the magistrate of mercy lays them aside (Ps 103:10). For the psalmist, such mercy exists alongside justice. Yahweh is still proclaimed as executing just rulings and ordinances—with Moses highlighted once again (Ps 103:6–7a). The notion that God does not always (or forever) legally contend (*yārîb*) implies that he can indeed file his *rîb* lawsuits, as we saw earlier, using Micah 6:1–8 as a prime example. Yet when merciful, Yahweh sets aside his legal rights.

Mercy in the Extreme: The Story of Jonah and the Ninevites

It is a sad state of affairs when the intent of a serious author is distorted so completely as to obliterate any trace of his original purpose for writing. I am thinking, of course, of the reception history of the book of Jonah. Most non-specialists can readily tell the story of a whale (that never existed) without any hint of the serious topic at hand. To give the book of Jonah its due, it should be treated as "a conceptual treatise on the essence of justice," aligned more with the books of Job and Qoheleth than with the prophetic twelve with which it is grouped (Levine 2002: 172).[188] More specifically, the book explores the limits of mercy rather than the execution of retributive justice, for the repentant Ninevites at no point provide any restitution to those whom they were guilty of victimizing.

Why Nineveh?

Understanding the role of Nineveh provides the interpretive key to the book of Jonah. The book begins with God's first words charging Jonah to "arise, go to Nineveh" (Jon 1:2) and ends with God's last words admonishing Jonah for failing to understand his mercy to Nineveh (Jon 4:11). Scholars often situate the book of Jonah in the post-exilic period, referencing especially its concern about foreigners (sailors and Ninevites) against the backdrop of xenophobia on display in passages such as Ezra 9–10 and Nehemiah 13:23–25 (cf. Isa 56:1–8).[189] This is very sensible, although the Neo-Assyrian city of Nineveh was so well known and so paradigmatic that it would have resonated for any first-millennium BCE audience. As Sasson (1990: 70) notes, "Nineveh's reputation as a center of savage power is reason enough for Jonah to have made out of it a paradigm for utter wickedness reprieved by utter mercy." Sadly, Sasson's correct analysis here is in the minority, with few interpreters probing the depth of this reputation for a key to the meaning of the book.

At the outset, the author of the book highlights "wickedness" (*rāʿâ*) as the primary descriptor of Nineveh, apart from its "greatness," and it is the wickedness that prompts God to act (Jon 1:2). Once Jonah is redirected on his mission, the message he conveys to the great city is solely that of a definitive judgment oracle (Jon 3:4). The Ninevites' wickedness (Jon 3:8, 10) is implicitly the underlying reason for Jonah's consternation. The book of Jonah is not alone in its characterization of Nineveh as paradigmatically wicked. Nahum's "oracle concerning Nineveh" (*maśśāʾ nînĕwēh*) gives clear evidence of the hatred felt by certain Yahwists/Judeans toward the Assyrians. The imprecatory language looks forward to divine judgment against "the bloody city" (*ʿîr dāmîm*; Nah 3:1) whose "unrelenting evil" (*rāʿâ tāmîd*) has allowed no escape (Nah 3:19). Isaiah 37:11 has the *rab šāqēh* of Sennacherib brag to Hezekiah that the Assyrians have a well-known reputation for annihilating their enemies (√*ḥrm*). Sennacherib himself, according to the Chronicler, speaks of the "utter destruction" (√*ḥrm*)

Figure 9.2 Assyrian depictions of violence done by Aššurbanipal's troops to his Elamite enemies.

Drawings from Austen Layard's 1882 *Nineveh and Babylon: A Narrative of a Second Expedition to Assyria During the Years 1849, 1850, & 1851.*

wreaked by Neo-Assyrian armies (2 Chr 32:14). To these biblical references, we can add a substantial amount of Neo-Assyrian war propaganda in text and iconography that attests to atrocities that included beheadings, flaying, impaling, bodily mutilations, and maiming. In contrast to the biblical narratives, these heinous portrayals are not caricatures drawn by their detractors but a part of official Assyrian record-keeping. Consider Figure 9.2. In the upper register two naked men are being staked to the ground with their legs spread apart. Two Assyrian executioners bending over them with knives flay them (alive, according to Layard).¹⁹⁰ To their right a soldier carries away a decapitated head. Below one finds a bound prisoner of war whose head is held by the beard by one soldier and with tongs by another as he is being decapitated. On the lowest register of this scene, a bound prisoner of war is held to the ground as an Assyrian soldier tears out his tongue. Layard writes about an adjacent scene not visible here: "The bleeding heads of the slain were tied round the necks of the living who seemed reserved for still more barbarous tortures."¹⁹¹

Paralleling the pictorial evidence are inscriptions from Neo-Assyrian kings (e.g., Aššurnasirpal II, Shalmaneser III, Tiglath-Pileser III, Sennacherib, Esarhaddon, Aššurbanipal) who brag of their victories at war, including acts of torture. Granted, the texts we are dealing with are stereotypical. Consider the following two representative examples from Aššurnasirpal II (883–859 BCE) and Sennacherib (704–681 BCE), respectively.¹⁹²

> I burnt 3,000 captives from them. . . . I captured alive [PN] their city ruler. I made a pile of their corpses. I burnt their adolescent boys (and) girls. I flayed [PN] their city ruler (and) draped his skin over the wall of the city [GN]. . . . I felled 50 of their fighting-men with the sword, burnt 200 captives from them. . . . I burnt many captives from them. I captured many troops alive: from some I cut off their arms (and) hands; from others I cut off their noses, ears, (and) extremities. I gouged out the eyes of many troops. I made one pile of the living (and) one of heads. I hung their heads on trees around the city. I burnt their adolescent boys [and] girls.¹⁹³

> I cut their throats like lambs, I cut off their precious lives (as one cuts) a string. Like the many waters of a storm, I made (the contents of) their gullets and entrails run down upon the wide earth. . . . (Their) testicles I cut off, and tore out their privates like the seeds of cucumbers.¹⁹⁴

Jonah's Justified Position

In short, Jonah's refusal to extend mercy to the Assyrians is well justified. He is not being narcissistic or petty, as some have proposed. The *primary* concern of the book of Jonah is not what scholars often suggest (e.g., unfulfilled prophecy, to show the possibility of repenting, to encourage repentance among Judeans, to encourage missionary activity to gentiles, to condemn xenophobia). Rather, the main question it poses is one of theodicy: What is the extent of mercy? Can mercy be extended to an extreme such that it would apply even to the most heinous of actions—with Neo-Assyrian "wickedness" (*rāʿâ*) as the evidence submitted for trial? If we can be anachronistic, the question posed is the ancient equivalent of war crimes trials, where to extend mercy to those who committed atrocities does an injustice to their victims. Jonah is angry (Jon 4:1) and has "a right to be angry" (cf. 4:4). Consider Yahweh's question in Jonah 4:4. If the C stem of the root *yṭb* in Jonah 4:4 (*hahêṭēb ḥārâ lāk*) refers to a judicial right ("Do you have a right to be angry?"; cf. Jer 7:5–6), the answer to Yahweh's question is "Yes!"[195] The Ninevites may have repented of their actions, yet they have provided no restitution to the victims (and how could they?) that a court could deem an appropriate punishment.

Jonah is incensed at the very idea of extending mercy to such perpetrators of wickedness. From a judicial standpoint, he is delighted to proclaim a fitting punishment ("in 40 days Nineveh will be overthrown"; 3:4) as an act of divine retributive justice. For Jonah, the atrocities of the Ninevites are of such severity that they do not allow him, like Abraham in Genesis 18:22–33, to negotiate to spare the "great" city if a few righteous people can be found.

Mercy

Ultimately the book of Jonah is about mercy. Mercy, by definition, is judicially unfair. Yet it is a judge's prerogative to grant mercy, even mercy that overrides retributive justice. Yahweh's final words are "And should I not have compassion on Nineveh?" (Jon 4:11a). This is the question of the book. When extreme "wickedness" is in play, is there a limit to the extension of God's mercy? The book of Jonah, in contrast to Qoheleth 12:13–14 and Job 42:5–6, does not resolve the matter neatly, with Jonah replying positively to Yahweh's final question. We do not hear Jonah's answer. This is intentional.

Yahweh's position is clear. As absolute judge, he has the prerogative to grant mercy, and he does indeed grant mercy—for which all who are desperately guilty and in need of (judicially unfair) mercy give thanks (Ps 25:11; 51:3–7 [Eng 51:1–5]). It is clear that the intent the author of the book of Jonah is to underscore that such acts are acts of severe mercy that must be taken with ultimate seriousness.

10

The Characterization of the Deity Yahweh

Part Three: Yahweh as the Holy One

Introduction

"*God is holy.* Herein we touch on that which constitutes the deepest and innermost nature of the God of the Old Testament." In his comprehensive *Holiness in Israel,* John G. Gammie (2005: 3) chose this quote by the prolific historian, theologian, and archaeologist Ernst Sellin to underscore the centrality of divine holiness.[1] And yet Gammie (2005: 72–74) bemoans the lack of attention devoted to this topic in recent decades by historians of Israelite religion, as divine holiness "has been preempted by other biblical motifs" such as God the divine warrior and God the divine suzerain. Gammie's observation that "the holiness of God . . . seldom became the object of particular or focused inquiry" is especially astute now that we have far more cognate data than was available to Sellin in the 1930s. The widespread concept of holiness (*qdš*) in multiple Northwest Semitic cultures from the Late Bronze Age forward demands a closer look by historians of Israelite religion, and not just those interested in priestly understandings of ritual and cultic holiness.[2]

Setting the Stage: Northwest Semitic Holy Gods

While endeavoring "to answer the fundamental question of what a deity was considered to be" in the ancient Near East (and especially in the Ugaritic texts and the Hebrew Bible), Mark Smith (2001b: 83) came up with a short list of key traits that includes holiness. Smith (2001b: 93) writes: "Deities were generally marked for holiness as can be inferred from the general designation of deities as 'holy ones.'" Sacred places "are marked and demarcated for holiness, and divinity is perceived to partake fully of holiness." The Ugaritic deity ʾIlu is called "the Holy One" (*qdš*), as is the dual-named deity Qudšu-wa-ʾAmrur, who personally attends the goddess ʾAthiratu.[3] Baʿlu may be referred to as "the Holy One against River," yet the text is quite broken (*bʿl qdš-m bnhr*; KTU 1.179.17 = RS 92.2016.17).[4] A Syro-Anatolian goddess known as "the Holy One" (*qdšt*, conventionally rendered as Qedeshet) had a substantial presence in New Kingdom

Egypt. Her linguistic and iconographic cognate (*qdš*, conventionally rendered as Qudshu) is well attested in the Northern and Southern Levant of the Late Bronze Age. Both holy goddesses are regularly depicted with a lion.[5] At Iron Age Arslan Tash, the deity Hawron/Horon (*ḥwrn*) is referred to as "the lord of holiness" (*bʻl q[d]š*).[6] In fifth-century BCE Phoenicia, ʻAštart is called "holy queen" (*mlkt qdšt*).[7] ʼEshmun bears the epithet "holy prince" (*šr qdš*).[8] In ancient Israelite religion, we read of "the Holy One" (*qādôš*) coming from Mt. Paran, parallel to Eloah coming from Teman (Hab 3:3). A reference to a Holy Warrior likely occurs in a late ninth-/early eighth-century BCE inscription from Kuntillet ʻAjrud (discussed later).

At Late Bronze Age Ugarit the plurality of the gods can be referred to as "the sons of the Holy One" (*bn qdš*).[9] A reference in the fourteenth-century BCE Amarna texts to the gods of Byblos being holy (DINGIR^{meš} ^{uru}*gubla qadišū*; EA 137.31–32; see Rainey 1996a: 2:291; 2015: 698–699) resonates with the tenth-century BCE Phoenician Yaḥimilk inscription that refers to "the assembly of the holy gods of Byblos" (*mpḥrt ʼl gbl qdšm*; KAI 4, lines 4–5, 7; cf. KAI 14.9, 22). A seventh-century BCE incantation plaque from Arslan Tash mentions "the assembly of all the Holy Ones" (*dr kl qdšn*) alongside "all the sons of the gods" (*kl bn ʼlm*; KAI 27.11–12). This shared cultural understanding of divine beings being holy is also found in Israelite psalmody (Ps 89:6, 8 [Eng 89:5, 7]; see text immediately following) and in ancient lore proclaiming that "myriads of holy ones" (*ribĕbōt qōdeš*) form Yahweh's military retinue (Deut 33:2).[10] Such understandings about "holy ones" are enduring as attested by much later usage (cf. Zech 14:5; Job 5:1; 15:15; Dan 8:13). Aramaic literary traditions concur (e.g., *qaddîš/qaddîšîn* in Daniel 4:5–6, 10, 14–15, 20 [Eng 4:8–9, 13, 17–18, 23]; 5:11; 7:18, 21–22, 25, 27 and *qdšn* in Ahiqar, TAD 3, C1.1.79).

As for sacred space, Ugaritic ʼIlu is worshipped in the holy sanctuary of ʼIlu (*qdš ʼil*; KTU 1.119.6), as is Baʻlu in his holy residence (*qdš bʻl*; KTU 119.33ʼ). Psalm 46 speaks of (El/Yahweh) Elyon's holiness with respect to his dwelling (*qĕdōš miškĕnê ʻelyôn*; Ps 46:5 [Eng 46:4]),[11] as does Psalm 24:3 of Yahweh's holy mountain (*har yhwh*//*mĕqôm qodšô*). Other biblical traditions describe how Yahweh brought his people to his "holy encampment" (*nĕwēh qodeš*) and his holy sanctuary (*miqdāš*) (Exod 15:13, 17). Psalm 68:6 (Eng 68:5) will locate Yahweh's familial and judicial actions in his holy dwelling (*bimeʻôn qodšô*).

Epigraphically, the use of *qdš* to designate cultic objects is attested as early as the eighth century BCE and perhaps the late ninth century BCE (more later on the reading *qšdš* at Kuntillet ʻAjrud). The full writing of *qdš* is attested at Hazor (on the rim and exterior of a late eighth-century BCE bowl [stratum V]), at Beersheva (on a late eighth-century BCE krater), at Arad (on a body sherd), and at Philistine Tel Miqne (on four seventh-century BCE storage jars).[12] In biblical traditions, one of the earliest material consecrations appears in the account of

Micah's mother "solemnly consecrating (*haqdēš hiqdaštî*) silver for Yahweh" that in turn will be made into cultic objects (Judg 17:3).[13]

The Centrality of Yahweh's Holiness

The attributes of Yahweh regularly overlap, and thus it should come as no surprise that the Divine Warrior, Father, King, and Judge we looked at earlier was also understood to be the Holy One. A small sampling of biblical passages will suffice to illustrate the point. *Yahweh of Armies* is exalted by *justice*, "the *Holy* God who shows himself *holy*" (*hāʾēl haqqādôš niqdāš*) by his *righteousness* (Isa 5:16). Yahweh is "*Father* of orphans and *judge-advocate* of widows, the God who [resides] in his *holy* habitation" (*bimĕʿôn qodšô*; Ps 68:6 [Eng 68:5]). Yahweh, *the Mighty King*, lover of *justice*, is extolled: "*Holy* is He" (*qādôš hûʾ*; Ps 99:4–5; cf. Isa 43:15). Yahweh (the *Judge*) proclaims that when he executes his *judgments*, he is manifesting his *holiness* (*baʿăśôtî bah šĕpāṭîm wĕniqdaštî bah*; Ezek 28:22). Returning again to Gammie's critique, the motif of Yahweh as holy should not take a backseat to any of his other attributes. Divine holiness was central to how Yahweh was understood and portrayed, from our earliest to our latest texts.

Yahweh as Holy: Non-Cultic Understandings

The fullest articulation of divine holiness in the Hebrew Bible is found in the cultic traditions about purity (moral, ethical, and social) that have come down to us in the P and H tradents (discussed later). This is especially true for H, as is reflected in its very name, the *Holiness* Code. We cannot help but be influenced by these formative witnesses. Yet we run the risk of being mono-focused (and anachronistic) in understanding the diachronic development of the concept of holiness if we privilege these perspectives. It is important first to look at traditions outside of P and H, and especially those that seem to be earlier. Many of these traditions are surprisingly non-cultic in nature (hence our subheading). Yet even here we have a dire need for cultically managing holiness, as we will see in the various Ark traditions.

Holiness as Awesome Power

The notion of Yahweh being holy is found in our earliest biblical traditions. As noted previously, among the many tales we have about the divine warrior marching from the south/southeast, the poet of Habakkuk 3:2–3 chose to accentuate "the Holy One" (*qādôš*) coming from Mt. Paran, who causes him fright (*yārēʾtî*).¹⁴ Though the parallel line refers to Eloah, overall biblical lore (including elsewhere in Habakkuk 3:2, 8, 18, 19) consistently looks to Yahweh as the Divine Warrior on the march. Deuteronomy 33:2 presents a fiery Yahweh coming from Seir with "holy ones" accompanying him as combatants (see Lewis 2013b).

Yahweh's Holiness: Exodus 15, Psalm 68, and Psalm 89

Three additional texts that preserve early lore mentioning divine holiness (Exodus 15, Psalm 68, Psalm 89) are most instructive. Exodus 15, one of our very oldest texts, is a parade example of how the Hebrew Bible preserves divine warrior traditions about Yahweh, and has been treated as such in other chapters.¹⁵ And yet, illustrating Gammie's critique, the many historians of religion who have pored over Yahweh's militancy have rarely, if ever, explored the fact that Exodus 15 also mentions holiness three times. Yahweh, proclaims the poet, is "feared in holiness" (*neʾdār baqqōdeš*; Exod 15:11), a god who creates holy space (*něwēh qodeš; miqdāš*) to which he guides his people (Exod 15:13, 17).

Yah[weh] is my might and stronghold,	*ʿozzî wězimrāt yâ*
May he be my salvation . . .	*yěhî-lî lîšûʿâ* . . .
Your right hand, Yahweh,	*yěmînkā yhwh*
terrible in strength;	*neʾdārî bakkōaḥ*
Your right hand, Yahweh,	*yěmînkā yhwh*
Shattered the enemy . . .	*tirʿaṣ ʾôyēb* . . .
You sent forth your fury . . .	*těšallaḥ ḥărōněkā* . . .
Who is like you among the gods, Yahweh?	*mî-kāmōkâ bāʾēlim yhw*
Who is like you, *feared in holiness*?	*mî kāmōkâ <u>neʾdār baqqōdeš</u>*
Terrible of radiance, worker of wonder.	*nôrāʾ těhillōt ʿōśēh peleʾ*
You stretched out your right hand,	*nāṭîtā yěmîněkā*
The underworld swallowed them.	*tiblāʿēmô ʾāreṣ*
You faithfully led	*nāḥîtā běḥasděkā*
the people whom you redeemed,	*ʿam-zû gāʾāltā*
You guided in your might	*nēhaltā běʿozzěkā*
to your *holy encampment*.	*ʾel-<u>něwēh qodšekā</u>*

The peoples heard, they shudder,	šāmĕʿû ʿammîm yirgāzûn
Horror seized the inhabitants of Philistia.	ḥîl ʾāḥaz yōšĕbê pĕlāšet
They were dismayed	ʾāz nibhălû
the clans of Edom,	ʾallûpê ʾĕdôm
the rams of Moab	ʾêlê môʾāb
seized by terror,	yōʾḥăzēmô rāʿad
melted—all Canaan's inhabitants.	nāmōgû kōl yōšĕbê kĕnāʿan
You fell on them	tippōl ʿălêhem
[with] terror and dread,	ʾêmātâ wāpaḥad
By your great power	bigdōl zĕrôʿăkā
they were still as stone.	yiddĕmû kāʾāben
While your people passed over, Yahweh,	ʿad-yaʿăbōr ʿammĕkā yhwh
While your people whom you created passed over,	ʿad-yaʿăbōr ʿam-zû qānîtā
You brought them, you planted them	tĕbiʾēmô wĕtiṭṭāʿēmô
in the mount of your heritage.	bĕhar naḥălātĕkā
The dais of your throne	mākôn lĕšibtĕkā
which you made, Yahweh.	pāʿaltā yhwh
The *holy sanctuary*, Yahweh	*miqdāš* ʾădōnāy
which your hands created.	kônĕnû yādêkā
May Yahweh reign/Yahweh, he will reign	yhwh yimlōk
forever and ever.	lĕʿōlām wāʿed

(Exod 15:2, 6, 7b, 11–18)

The date, structure, and genre of Psalm 68 are notoriously difficult.[16] The psalm has been dated extremely early by some based on Ugaritic parallels (cf. Albright's date of the thirteenth through tenth centuries BCE) and extremely late by others based on apocalyptic themes (e.g., Gerstenberger and Cook). Where some scholars argue that the psalm is made up of short independent strands (cf. Albright's thirty incipits), other scholars (e.g., Tate, Fokkelman) find themes and structures pointing toward a coherent whole. Suggestions for the psalm's genre include cantata, hymn, prayer, procession liturgy, and victory song.

Even those who date the psalm late acknowledge early elements that have been redacted (e.g., the reference to Mt. Bashan in Ps 68:16–17 [Eng 68:15–16] as God's dwelling woven into later Zion traditions). Portions of Psalm 68 are regularly placed within the corpus of archaic Hebrew poetry. Of note is the extremely close wording of Psalm 68:8–11 (Eng 68:7–10) and the archaic Judges 5:4–5 (cf. Deut 33:2–3).[17] As with Exodus 15, this poem celebrates the military side of Yahweh—here as a charioteer and storm god on the march—while repeatedly mentioning the holiness of his residences.

May Yahweh arise,	yāqûm yhwh*
may his enemies be scattered;	yāpûṣû ʾôyĕbāyw
may his foes flee before him.	wĕyānûsû mĕśanʾāyw mippānāyw

As smoke is blown away	kĕhinnādēp[18] ʿāšān tindōp
So may you [Yahweh] blow them away;	
As wax melts before the fire,	kĕhimmēs dônag mippĕnê-ʾēš
So may the wicked perish before Yahweh.	yōʾbĕdû rĕšāʿîm mippĕnê yhwh* . . .

Sing to Yahweh, sing praise to his name,	šîrû la-yhwh* zammĕrû šĕmô
Extol him who rides through desert lands	sōllû lārōkēb bāʿărābôt
[alt: who rides on the clouds]	[alt: ʿărāpôt][19]
—his name is Yah[weh]—	bĕ-yah[20] šĕmô
and rejoice before him.	wĕʿilzû lĕpānāyw

| Father to orphans, Defender of widows, | ʾăbî yĕtômîm wĕdayyan ʾalmānôt |
| is Yahweh in his *holy dwelling*. | yhwh* <u>bimĕʿôn qodšô</u> |

Yahweh restores the lonely to their homes,	yhwh* môšîb yĕḥîdîm baytâ
he brings forth prisoners . . .[21]	môṣîʾ ʾăsîrîm bakkôšārôt . . .
O Yahweh, when you marched before your people,	yhwh* bĕṣēʾtĕkā lipnê ʿammekā
when you marched through the wilderness,	bĕṣaʿdĕkā bîšîmôn

the earth quaked,	ʾereṣ rāʿāšâ
yea, the heavens rained,	ʾap-šāmayim nāṭĕpû
before Yahweh, the One of Sinai,[22]	mippĕnê yhwh* zeh sînay
before Yahweh, the God of Israel . . .	mippĕnê yhwh* ʾĕlōhê yiśrāʾēl . . .

| Yahweh's chariotry [numbers] in myriads | rekeb yhwh* ribbōtayim |
| Thousands upon thousands; | ʾalpê šinʾān[23] |

Yahweh comes from Sinai into his *holy sanctuary* . . .	*yhwh bāʾ missînay baqqōdeš* . . .[24]
Blessed be Yahweh Day by day he supports us, El,[26] our deliverance.	*bārûk yhwh*[25] *yôm yôm yaʿămos-lānû* *hāʾēl yĕšûʿātēnû*
El is for us, a God of deliverance, Yahweh [provides] escape from death . . .	*hāʾēl lānû ʾēl lĕmôšāʾôt* *wĕla-yhwh*[27] *lammāwet tôṣāʾôt* . . .
They see your processions, O Yahweh the processions of my God, my King into the *holy sanctuary* . . .	*rāʾû hălîkôtêkā yhwh** *hălîkôt ʾēlî malkî baqqōdeš* . . .
Summon your power, O Yahweh; [show us] your strength, O Yahweh as you have done before.	*ṣiwwāh yhwh* ʿuzzekā*[28] *ʿûzzâ yhwh** *zû pāʿaltā lānû*
From your temple above Jerusalem, Where kings bring you tribute.	*mēhêkālekā ʿal-yĕrûšālā(y)im* *lĕkā yôbîlû mĕlākîm šāy*
O kingdoms of the earth, sing to Yahweh, sing praise to Yahweh,	*mamlĕkôt hāʾāreṣ šîrû la-yhwh** *zammĕrû yhwh*[29]
to Him who rides the ancient skies above, who thunders with his powerful voice.	*lārōkēb bišmê šĕmê-qedem* *hēn yittēn bĕqôlô qôl ʿōz*
Proclaim the power of Yahweh, whose majesty is over Israel, whose power is in the skies.	*tĕnû ʿōz la-yhwh* *ʿal-yiśrāʾēl gaʾăwātô* *wĕʿuzzô bašĕḥāqîm*
You are awesome, O Yahweh, [as you march] from your *holy places*; El of Israel— He gives power and strength to his people.	*nôrāʾ yhwh* mimmiqdāšêkā* *ʾēl yiśrāʾēl* *hûʾ nōtēn ʿōz wĕtaʿăṣumôt lāʿām*
Praise be to Yahweh!	*bārûk yhwh**

(Ps 68:2–3, 5–9, 18, 20–21, 25, 29–30, 33–36
[Eng 68:1–2, 4–8, 17, 19–20, 24, 28–29, 32–35])

Similarly, Psalm 89, part of which is archaic in origin,[30] professes:

The heavens praise your wonders, O Yahweh,	wĕyôdû šāmayim pil'ăkā yhwh
Your faithfulness too in the assembly of *holy beings*	'ap-'ĕmûnātĕkā biqĕhal *qĕdōšîm*
For who in the skies can equal Yahweh,	kî mî baššaḥaq ya'ărōk lĕyhwh
Can compare with Yahweh among the divine beings?	yidmeh lĕyhwh bibĕnê 'ēlîm
El, the greatly dreaded in the council of *holy beings*,	'ēl na'ărāṣ bĕsôd-*qĕdōšîm*
Held in awe by all around him? . . .	rabbâ wĕnôrā' 'al-kol-sĕbîbāyw
Indeed! Yahweh is our shield,	kî lĕyhwh māginnēnû
The Holy One of Israel our King!	wĕliqdôš yiśrā'ēl malkēnû

(Psalm 89:6–8, 19 [Eng 89:5–7, 18])

All three of these passages—with their language of Yahweh being "feared in holiness" (ne'dār baqqōdeš), "greatly dreaded in the council of holy beings" ('ēl na'ărāṣ bĕsôd-qĕdōšîm),[31] and "held in awe" (nôrā')—affirm *that to say that Yahweh is holy is to say that he is dynamically and terrifyingly powerful.* The poet of Exodus 15 uses a startling number of different words to depict how Yahweh's holy power and fury ('oz, zimrâ, kōaḥ, yāmîn, ḥārōn, qōdeš, zĕrô'a) is of such magnitude that it occasions fear, terror, and dread (ne'dār [twice], nôrā', rgz, ḥîl, bhl, rā'ad, mwg, 'êmātâ, paḥad). The end of Psalm 68 repeats the word 'oz/'uz, "power," six times (Ps 68:29, 34–36 [Eng 68:28, 33–35])—together with the synonym ta'ăṣumôt—to describe "awesome" (nôrā') warrior Yahweh, here portrayed as a thundering storm god. As the awe-inspiring terror of a holy Yahweh (nôrā'//ne'dār) inspires the poet of Exodus 15 to describe him as an incomparable "worker of surpassing/extraordinary wonder" ('ōśēh pele'; Exod 15:11), so too the author of Psalm 89 speaks of "terrifying awe" (nôrā'//na'ărāṣ), with the heavens praising Yahweh's incomparable "wonders" (pele'; Ps 89:6, 8 [Eng 89:5, 7]).

In all of these passages, holiness, rather than being about cultic purity (i.e., cleanness void of moral, social, and/or ritual pollution), equals a type of incomparable power known only to the realm of the gods. Considering the broader cultural context, it should occasion no surprise that 'Ilu the Holy One is iconographically and textually represented as Bull 'Ilu (ṯr 'il), nor that Yahweh the

Holy One has both bull and lion associations, nor that the goddess Qudshu's (Qedeshet's) symbolic animal is that of a powerful lion. When the Phoenician king Eshmunazor contemplates potential violators of his tomb, he invokes "the holy gods" (*'lnm hqdšm*) "to deliver them up and to cut them and their seed off forever" (KAI 14.21–22). *Holy gods are powerful gods.* Theirs is a lethal power appropriately and respectfully feared and dreaded. In Exodus 15 and Psalm 89, Yahweh's power is superlative, incomparably superior even among the gods (*'ēlîm*; Exod 15:11//*běnê 'ēlîm*; Ps 89:7 [Eng 89:6]) who, being called *qědōšîm* (Ps 89:8 [Eng 89:7]), have their own holy power. Understanding that holy gods are powerful gods is foundational for understanding ancient Israel's portrayal of war as a *holy* enterprise. Note how troops "*consecrated* themselves for war" (*qaddĕšû 'ālêhā milḥāmâ*; Jer 6:4; cf. Deut 23:15 [Eng 23:14]). In other words, soldiers used cultic rites "to make themselves holy/powerful/godlike" as they prepared for battle.[32]

Excursus: A Holy Warrior at Kuntillet ʿAjrud?

The celebrated late ninth-/early eighth-century BCE inscriptions from Kuntillet ʿAjrud (Ḥorvat Teman) ground our understanding of Israelite religion with datable epigraphic data from a southeastern site. (See Chapter Six, pp. 236–241, 281–282; Chapter Seven, pp. 325–330.) The plaster fragment documented in Figure 10.1, Figure 10.2, and Figure 10.3 (= Meshel 2012: inscription 4.2) (hereafter KA 4.2) stands out as truly remarkable. It represents a militaristic wilderness theophany couched within what has been called "the oldest known Hebrew poem" outside of the Hebrew Bible.[33] I have treated this inscription at length elsewhere—including its language (Hebrew, not Phoenician), script, and contested readings—and thus my discussion here will remain brief (see Lewis 2020).

KA 4.2 clearly belongs with those texts that describe a divine warrior whose advent causes the travail of nature. That we have a militaristic context is clear from the double mention of the word *mlḥ[mh]*; that we have nature dramatically responding is certain from the mention of the earth quaking (*rʿš*), a verb used in similar contexts to describe Yahweh's march from the southeast (Judg 5:4; Ps 68:9 [Eng 68:8]; cf. too 2 Sam 22:8//Ps 18:8 [Eng 18:7]; Isa 29:6). In addition to these two motifs, the text may refer to the notion of "God dawning" (*wbzrḥ 'l*), a motif that is paralleled in the archaic poetry of Deuteronomy 33:2, where Yahweh comes from Sinai and "dawns" from Seir (*yhwh missînay bā'*//*zāraḥ miśśē'îr*).[34] The concept of mountains melting and peaks being crushed (*wymsn hrm wydkn pbnm*) resonates with biblical traditions about Yahweh as a storm god on the march (e.g., Ps 97:5; Mic 1:4; cf. Ps 68:3 [Eng 68:2]; Hab 3:6).

Figure 10.1 The ninth-/early eighth-century BCE Kuntillet ʿAjrud Plaster Inscription 4.2 that describes a militaristic wilderness theophany.
Courtesy of the Israel Exploration Society, Jerusalem.

Figure 10.2 Kuntillet ʿAjrud Plaster Inscription 4.2, including a smaller fragment that may mention [Ya]hwe[h].
Courtesy of the Israel Exploration Society, Jerusalem.

THE CHARACTERIZATION OF THE DEITY YAHWEH   585

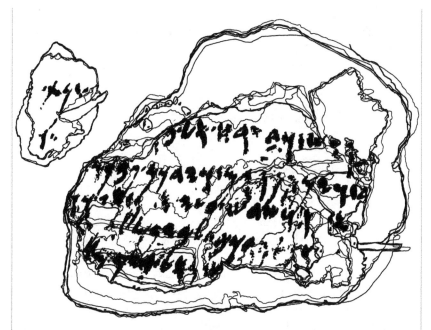

Figure 10.3 A composite drawing of Kuntillet ʿAjrud Inscription 4.2 layering the information of six different photographs.
Courtesy Theodore J. Lewis; Drawings by Marina Escolano-Poveda.

Kuntillet ʿAjrud, Plaster Fragment 4.2
(1) ... šnt* ... [35]
(2) ... brʿš.wbzrḥ. [or wbyrḥ] ʾl b[ʿš] [y]hw[h]* ...
(3) ... r.wymsn. hrm. wydkn. pbnm
(4) ... [ ]ʾrṣ.qšdš.ʿl°y.ʾt°n°/m°. ḥz.kr/s[
　　Or: ... [m/b]ʾrṣ.qšdš.ʿl°y.ʾt°n°/m°. ḥz.kr/s
(5) ... ° kn lºbrk. bʿl. bym. mlḥ[mh] ...
(6) ... [lhl]l šm ʾl. bym. mlḥ[mh] ...

... second time/years* ...
... with/during the earthquake, when El shines forth [or buffets?] [with fire?]; [Ya]hwe[h]* ...
... The mountains melt, the hills are crushed ...
... earth. The Holy One at/against the ever-flowing waters.[36] He gazes like ...
　　Or: [From/In] the land of Qadesh at the ever-flowing stream he looked upon [with favor]
... ?? to bless the [war-]lord [El? Yahweh?] on a day of war ...
... [to prai]se the Name of El on a day of wa[r] ...

What is striking for our present concerns is how El at Ḥorvat Teman seems, at first glance, to be portrayed as "the Holy One" (q[š!]dš),[37] a direct parallel to what we read in Habakkuk 3:3 about Eloah//the Holy One (qādôš) coming from Teman//Mt. Paran.

> Eloah came from Teman, ĕlôah mittêmān yābô'
> Qadosh [the Holy One] from Mt. Paran... qādôš mēhar-pā'rān...

The Identity of the Holy Warrior at Kuntillet ʿAjrud

Assuming the reconstructed reading of qdš can be sustained (as no other plausible solution has arisen for the enigmatic qšdš), the obvious question pertains to the identity of the Holy One (unless we are dealing with a GN Qadesh).[38] The overall context of the main fragment would seem to mention two distinct Canaanite gods (El in line 2 and Baal in line 5)—unless the words 'l and b'l are the regular nouns "god" and "lord"—to which one can add the presence of El via his (hypostatic?) Name (šm 'l) mentioned in line 6. According to the editors of the final report, KA 4.2 also includes a second smaller fragment mentioning [Ya]hwe[h] ([y]hw[h]; Figure 10.2).[39] We are left with two options. Either the mention of El and Baal in our text refers to independent Canaanite deities worshipped at Kuntillet ʿAjrud or these two terms are indicators of the syncretistic nature of worship at Kuntillet ʿAjrud, where overall a single deity, Yahweh, was prominent. The script of KA 4.2 is Phoenician (cf. too inscriptions 4.1–4.5 in Meshel 2012), which could make one favor El or Baal.[40] Yet the language of KA 4.2 is Hebrew (Aḥituv, Eshel, and Meshel 2012: 105, 123–127; McCarter 2000a:173; Lewis 2020), which could make one favor El, Yahweh, or Baal.

Elsewhere the plaster inscriptions attest to a single male deity only. KA 4.1.1 twice refers to "Yahweh of Teman/the south" ([y]hwh tymn; yhwh hty[mn]). If one broadens the scope to include all of the inscriptions at Kuntillet ʿAjrud—those incised in stone (KA 1.1–1.4) and in pottery (KA 2.1–2.9), and those written with ink on pottery (KA 3.1–3.16)—a fuller divine profile emerges. *As for male divinity, apart from KA 4.2, only Yahweh occurs, both as an independent proper name as well as a theophoric element in personal names.*[41] If we situate KA 4.2's mention of 'l, šm 'l, and b'l within this profile, a striking observation is apparent: apart from KA 4.2, neither El nor Baʿal is attested anywhere else with independent divine names.[42] As for onomastica, Baal never occurs as a theophoric element. This seems striking. For his part, El does occur in a single instance ('lyw), yet it likely represents what Rainer Albertz calls an "equating name" meaning "El is Yahweh."[43]

What then are we to make of the divine profile in KA 4.2 when it is situated within the other textual references at the site? Without any other attestation of

Baal (either in KA inscription 4.4.1 or in the onomastica), it is preferable—due to synonymous parallelism—to see *b'l* in line 6 as a reference to El as (war-) lord. At this juncture, two options remain: either KA 4.2 is an El-centric text that represents an additional, more pluralistic viewpoint at the site alongside Yahwism, or KA 4.2, like all other inscriptions at the site, refers to Yahweh as god (*'l*) and lord (*b'l*).

If our text reads [Ya]hwe[h] in line 2, we have a game-changer for defining the divine profile of KA 4.2. Rather than leaning toward a pluralistic option (i.e., KA 4.2 as an El-centric text in contrast to the Yahwism documented elsewhere at the site), it seems best to see KA 4.2 as incorporating Yahweh in a way that complements the Yahwism elsewhere at the site. If our text is poetic, and if the placement of the smaller fragment is correct, then [Ya]hwe[h] in the B line may form a poetic couplet with El in the A line, as suggested by Shmuel Aḥituv and Esther Eshel.[44]

The presence of a deity known as "the Holy One" at Kuntillet 'Ajrud is possible only if we posit a scribal mistake. At first glance, reconstructing this deity here based on the sole foundation of textual criticism seems overly speculative. Yet there is substantial and widespread evidence documenting Yahweh as "the Holy One" (*qdš*) elsewhere—in similar contexts of military theophanies, in similar blended El-Yahweh traditions, in similar blended northern-southern traditions, and during similar chronological periods (eighth century BCE) (see Lewis 2020). Thus, with the usual cautions, one can assert that there is a better-than-average likelihood that Yahweh was portrayed as "the Holy One" (*qdš*) in KA 4.2's militaristic wilderness theophany.

Rudolph Otto Once Again

Expressions of holy power (*'oz, zimrâ, kōaḥ, yāmîn, ḥārōn, qōdeš, zĕrô'a*) and fear (*ne'dār, nôrā', rgz, ḥîl, bhl, rā'ad, mwg, 'ēmātâ, paḥad*) remind us of Rudolph Otto's theoretical approach to holiness, which we looked at earlier (Chapter Seven, pp. 337–339, 372. Otto's notions of the holy-numinous as containing both *fascinans* (the irresistibly appealing and alluring) and *tremendum* (the overwhelming and even lethal) provided useful ways of thinking about how certain portions of the Hebrew Bible (especially P, Ezekiel, and Deuteronomy) used the abstractions of fire and *kābôd*-radiance to depict divinity.[45] Otto's dual notions are on full display in Exodus 15, Psalm 68, and Psalm 89. These authors find Yahweh so irresistibly attractive that they cannot help but break out in praise. At the same time, the inherent danger of encountering such an awesomely powerful deity is underscored. Yahweh's enemies perish, melting as wax before fire (Ps 68:2–3 [Eng 68:1–2]), and fire is indeed the most dominant symbol of Yahweh (see Chapter Seven, pp. 344–358). The earth itself quakes at his march, with only his chosen escaping death (Ps 68:9, 21 [Eng 68:8, 20]). If other gods and subordinate preternatural beings—that is, the *qĕdōšîm* who have their own *tremendum*—are in dread of Yahweh, "the Holy One" (*qādôš*),[46] how much more so the human realms (Exod 15:14–15 mentions Philistia, Edom, Moab, and Canaan), including his own people?

Divine Holiness Turned Benevolent

Remarkably, then, the gods may—should they benevolently so choose—exercise their holy power on behalf of their chosen people. Thus Bull 'Ilu's dual epithet is simultaneously "the Gracious One and the powerfully Holy One" (*ltpn wqdš*), that is, a god of incomparable power who nonetheless is gracious toward his people.[47] Similarly, Yahweh is simultaneously "feared in holiness" (*neʾdār baqqōdeš*) as he faithfully leads (*nhh*), guides (*nhl*), and redeems (*gʾl*) his people—even bringing them to his "holy encampment" (*nĕwēh qodeš*; Exod 15:13), that is, the holy sanctuary (*miqdāš*) he has established to interact with his people (Exod 15:17; cf. Ps 78:54). Yahweh, "the Holy One of [his people] Israel," is viewed as "a greatly dreaded deity" (*ʾēl naʿărāṣ*) who at the same time is a protective shield (*māgēn*) for his people (Ps 89:8, 19 [Eng 89:7, 18]). Consider especially the remarkable language used in Psalm 68. Yahweh is the thundering Divine Warrior par excellence who brings death to his enemies as surely as wax melts in fire. Yet, exults our poet, he is also Father to the fatherless and Judicial Defender of widows, and is accessible at his holy dwelling (*bimĕʿôn qodšô*; Ps 68:6 [Eng 68:5]). Though elsewhere we hear of the tradition that humans "may not see God and live" (Exod 33:20), here the people whom God "daily supports" and "delivers" (Ps 68:20–21 [Eng 68:19–20]) are invited to "see" Yahweh as he makes procession into his holy sanctuary (*baqqōdeš*). (The Ark as the visible symbol of Yahweh will be discussed later.)

Two aspects should be summarized as we look toward the continuing biblical tradition. First, the early-attested incomparable and superlative nature of holy power will eventually form the backdrop for the theology of God alone as holy and God as unapproachable (discussed later). Second, the ancient traditions about the gracious and benevolent exercise of holy power toward humanity will form the backdrop for God's invitation for his people—in *imitatio Dei*, imitation of the divine—to join him in "being holy as he is holy" (discussed later).

The Song of Hannah: Yahweh the Incomparably Powerful Holy One Acting on Behalf of the Disadvantaged

A similar early tradition lies behind the Song of Hannah (1 Sam 2:1–10).[48] With beautiful poetic artistry, this thanksgiving song celebrates how Yahweh is a holy and knowing God who reverses fortunes, especially on behalf of the disadvantaged (the weak, the hungry, the barren, the poor, and the needy; 1 Sam 2:4–8). Such divine care for the underprivileged echoes what we saw with Yahweh as the ideal judge, and here too the poet praises him as magistrate of the ends of the earth (*yhwh yādîn ʾapsê ʾāreṣ*; 1 Sam 2:10).

Similar to the incomparable praises we saw in Exodus 15:11 (*mî-kāmōkâ . . . mî-kāmōkâ . . .*) and Psalm 89:7–9 [Eng 89:6–8] (*kî mî . . . mî-kāmōkâ . . .*), twice the composer of the Song of Hannah praises Yahweh's holy nature as he proclaims his incomparability: "There is no Holy One like Yahweh" (*ʾên qādôš ka-yhwh*) . . . "Who is holy like Yahweh?" (*mî qādôš ka-yhwh*) (1 Sam 2:2, 10).[49] This remarkable poem, which seems to have been a model for the Magnificat (Luke 1:46–55), deserves to be read in full.[50]

| My heart exults in Yahweh; | *ʿālaṣ libbî ba-yhwh* |
| My horn is exalted in my God. | *rāmâ qarnî ba-ʾĕlōhāy*[51] |

| My mouth is enlarged over my enemies;[52] | *rāḥab pî ʿal-ʾôyĕbay* |
| I rejoice in your victory. | *śāmaḥtî ba-yēšûʿāteka* |

| *There is no Holy One like Yahweh*; | *ʾên-qādôš ka-yhwh* |
| There is no Rock like our God. | *ʾên ṣûr ka-ʾĕlōhênû*[53] |

| Do not multiply haughtiness; | *ʾal-tarbû gĕbōhâ*[54] |
| Let not arrogance come from your mouths.[55] | *yēṣēʾ ʿātāq mippîkem* |

For[56] Yahweh is a God of knowledge,[57]	*kî ʾēl dēʿôt yhwh*
A God who weighs deeds.[58]	*ʾēl tōkēn ʿălilôt*
The bow of the mighty is broken;	*qešet gibbōrîm ḥattâ*[59]
But the weak gird on strength.	*wĕnikšālîm ʾāzĕrû ḥāyil*

| The well-fed hire themselves out for food; | *śĕbēʿîm balleḥem niśkārû* |
| But the hungry do not [hire themselves out] anymore. | *ûrĕʿēbîm ḥādēllû ʿōd*[60] |

| The barren woman bears seven; | *ʿăqārâ yālĕdâ šibʿâ* |
| But she who has many children[61] languishes. | *wĕrabbat bānîm ʾumlālâ* |

| Yahweh brings death and makes alive; | *yhwh mēmît ûmĕḥayyeh* |
| He brings down to Sheol and raises up. | *môrîd šĕʾōl wayyāʿal*[62] |

| Yahweh makes poor and makes rich; | *yhwh môrîš ûmaʿăšîr* |
| He brings low, he also exalts. | *mašpîl ʾap-mĕrômēm* |

He raises the poor from the dirt;	mēqîm mēʿāpār dāl
From the ash heap he exalts the needy;	mēʾašpōt yārîm ʾebyôn[63]
To make them sit with the nobility of the people,	lĕhôšîb ʿim-nĕdîbê ʿam[64]
He has them inherit a throne of honor.	wĕkissēʾ kābôd yanḥilēm
For the pillars of the earth are Yahweh's;[65]	kî layhwh mĕṣuqê ʾereṣ
He has set the world upon them.	wayyāšet ʿălêhem tēbēl
The feet of his faithful ones he guards;	raglê[66] ḥăsîdāyw yišmōr
But the wicked are silenced in darkness.	ûrĕšāʿîm baḥōšek yiddāmmû[67]
For it is not by might that one prevails.[68]	kî-lōʾ bĕkōaḥ yigbar-ʾîš
As for Yahweh, his adversaries are shattered,	yhwh yēḥattû mĕrîbāyw
Who is holy like Yahweh?	*mî qādôš ka-yhwh*[69]
The Exalted One[70] thunders in the heavens;	ʿēlî baššāmayim yarʿēm
Yahweh judges the ends of the earth.	yhwh yādîn ʾapsê-ʾāreṣ
May he give strength to his king;	yitten-ʿōz lĕmalkô
May he exalt[71] the horn of his anointed.	yārēm qeren mĕšîḥô

(1 Sam 2:1–10)

The Song of Hannah goes beyond Exodus 15 and Psalm 89 in exploring how a god of incomparable, even thundering (*yarʿēm*; 1 Sam 2:10) power is accessible. The poet here does not emphasize dreaded holiness as does Exodus 15, though in his portrayal holy Yahweh is indeed powerful, as he shatters his adversaries (1 Sam 2:10), breaks weapons of the mighty (1 Sam 2:4), and silences the wicked (1 Sam 2:9) as he achieves his victory (*yēšûʿâ*; 1 Sam 2:1). In his depiction of the many reversals of fortune, it is fascinating how the author—like the poet of Psalm 68:6–7 (Eng 68:5–6)—portrays Yahweh as the compassionate god of family religion (see Chapter Eight). At the end of the poem, we read of Yahweh judging (*yhwh yādîn*), which echoes Yahweh as the one who judicially defends widows (*dayyan ʾalmānôt*) in Psalm 68:6 (Eng 68:5). Once again we have overlapping divine traits. The author saw nothing incoherent about Yahweh being a thundering, judging god of holy power (1 Sam 2:10) while at the same time one who is intimately concerned with so-called life-cycle events (childbirth, death) and issues of poverty and deprivation (1 Sam 2:4–8). He also freely blends traditions of Yahweh as a god of the royal cult (1 Sam 2:10; cf. Chapter Nine) and Yahweh as creator (1 Sam 2:8).

Two Prophetic Voices from the Eighth Century BCE

"Yahweh You Shall Regard as Holy": Isaiah 8:11–15

Two eighth-century BCE prophetic passages, one from Isaiah, the other from Hosea, add to our understanding of holiness in the early period. Isaiah 8:11–15 is, according to Hans Wildberger (1991: 356), "without question . . . authentic" to the eighth-century BCE Isaiah ben Amos, coming from the time of the Syro-Ephraimite War (734–733 BCE). Yahweh addresses the prophet with a warning that is also directly targeted to his associates (who are distinguished from "this people" in Isa 8:11), for the verbs that follow in Isaiah 8:12–13 are in the plural (*tōʾmĕrûn, tîrʾû, taʿărîṣû, taqdîšû*). There is a debate over the referent for the political conspiracy (*qešer*) in verse 12: does it refer to an internal group within Jerusalem (desiring to place a Tabelite on the throne; cf. Isa 7:6) (e.g., Wildberger 1991: 358) or to the external threat of King Rezin of Damascus and King Pekah of Samaria (e.g., Blenkinsopp 2000: 242)? Since the *qešer* is an object of fear (Isa 8:12b), the military might of the two kingdoms would be a more fitting referent. That the prophet consistently advocates that Judah should trust in God rather than trusting in military alliances also argues for the latter. Compare especially the admonishment in Isaiah 30:15; 31:1 (discussed later) that Judah should put its trust in the Holy One of Israel rather than in Egypt's military machine. Regardless of the specific referent, the meaning of the passage is the same: someone far more dreaded than mere humans is on the scene.

> For thus Yahweh spoke to me, with his hand strong upon me, admonishing me not to walk in the way of this people:
>
> | | |
> |---|---|
> | "Do not call conspiracy | *lōʾ-tōʾmĕrûn qešer* |
> | whatever this people calls conspiracy, | *lĕkōl ʾăšer-yōʾmar* |
> | | *hāʿām hazzeh qāšer* |
> | | |
> | Do not fear what they fear, | *wĕʾet-môrāʾô lōʾ-tîrʾû* |
> | nor be in dread. | *wĕlōʾ taʿărîṣû* |
> | | |
> | Rather, Yahweh of Armies, | *ʾet-yhwh ṣĕbāʾôt* |
> | *Him you shall regard as holy;* | *ʾōtô taqdîšû* |
> | He should be the one you fear, | *wĕhûʾ môraʾăkem* |
> | He should be the one you dread. | *wĕhûʾ maʿăriṣkem* |

He will be a holy place,	wĕhāyâ lĕmiqdāš
a smiting stone,	ûlĕʾeben negep
a rock of stumbling	ûlĕṣûr mikšôl
for both houses of Israel;	lišĕnê bāttê yiśrāʾēl
a trap and a snare	lĕpaḥ ûlĕmôqēš
for the inhabitants of Jerusalem.	lĕyôšēb yĕrûšālā(y)im
Many among them shall stumble;	wĕkāšĕlû bām rabbîm
they shall fall and be broken;	wĕnāpĕlû wĕnišbārû
they shall be ensnared and taken captive."	wĕnôqĕšû wĕnilkādû.

(Isa 8:11–15)

Rather than fearing and being in dread of any human entity, says the prophet, Yahweh admonishes his followers to reevaluate that which is truly worthy of fear and dread—namely, Yahweh in his warrior dress (*yhwh ṣĕbāʾôt*). With a dramatic syntax that highlights Yahweh four times in a single verse (fronting *ʾet-yhwh, ʾōtô, wĕhû', wĕhûʾ* in verse 13), our prophet underscores the powerful holiness of Yahweh as the rationale for holding him in dread and fear. In other words, as we have seen, in recognition of Yahweh's holiness (*ʾōtô taqdîšû*), properly understood as awesome power, people should shudder in fear at the prospect of such power being wielded against them.

The reference to Yahweh being a "sanctuary" (*miqdāš*) in Isaiah 8:14 has proven to be a major stumbling block for interpreters, many of whom think that it "makes no sense in the context" (Blenkinsopp 2000: 241) or that it cannot be parallel to the following two references to a smiting stone and a rock of stumbling (Wildberger 1991: 355), not to mention the subsequent trap and snare (Isa 8:14).[72] Such understandings are predicated on a narrow definition of *miqdāš* as a benign sacred place where one interacts with a deity via cultic rituals that mediate the sacred and the profane. More appropriately, a *miqdāš* is the place where the deity manifests his holy presence; if holiness is to be equated with incomparably awesome power, then a deity's residence (*miqdāš*) is the most dangerous of places. One need look no further than the notion that the high priest Aaron could potentially die in the Holy of Holies (Exod 28:35). Consider too the deaths of Aaron's sons Nadab and Abihu due to Yahweh's holy wrath (Lev 10:1–3; discussed later). The fear that the Israelites express in Numbers 17:27–28 (Eng 17:12–13) is perfectly understandable: "Surely we are about to perish—we are all lost; we are all lost! Every person who approaches the Tabernacle dies! Will we ever cease perishing?"[73]

In our view, the mention here of Yahweh being a *miqdāš* is ideally appropriate, especially when considering the traditions in Exodus 15 and Psalm 68. The masterly poet of Exodus 15 went out of his way to accentuate Yahweh's terrifyingly powerful holiness even as the deity simultaneously redeems his people, whom he benevolently brings to his "holy encampment" (*něwēh qodeš*) and his holy sanctuary (*miqdāš*) (Exod 15:13, 17). In Psalm 68:6 (Eng 68:5), Yahweh's *holy* dwelling (*bimĕʿôn qodšô*) is the locale of his gracious familial and judicial actions. So too in Psalm 89 and 1 Samuel 2, where the incomparably holy and powerful Yahweh nonetheless makes himself accessible to his people, even attending to the needs of the disadvantaged. In contrast to these redemptive passages, Isaiah 8:11–15 is a harsh warning set against the backdrop of the Syro-Ephraimite war with Judah. Where Yahweh's *miqdāš* in Exodus 15 is a mountainous place of holy refuge (Jerusalem) where he "planted" his people (Exod 15:17),[74] in Isaiah's warning Yahweh's *miqdāš* is smiting, stumbling, entrapping, and ensnaring the inhabitants of Jerusalem (Isa 8:14–15). Where the Song of Hannah celebrated Yahweh as the Holy One and Rock providing victory over enemies (1 Sam 2:1–2), Isaiah turns the picture of Yahweh's holiness and rock-like nature into the cause of Jerusalem's downfall.

Yahweh as the Holy One in Hosea 11:9
Scholars take radically different approaches to interpreting the mention of Yahweh as the Holy One in Hosea 11:9. Does Yahweh's holiness express itself with destructive power or with accessible benevolence? This passage is also firmly situated in the eighth century BCE, with Hans Walter Wolff (1974: 197) dating it to the first half of the reign of Shalmaneser V, around 727 BCE. The two representative translations listed here are diametrically opposed with regard to Hosea's intentions. The first translation (option A), by far the consensus view, resounds with the prophet's (or editor's) voice of compassion, an inspired perspective in a book dominated by judgment oracles. The second translation (option B) is consistent with the book's overall theme of judgment against the northern kingdom.

Option A

How can I give you up, Ephraim?
How can I hand you over, O Israel?

How can I make you like Admah?
How can I treat you like Zeboiim?

My heart recoils within me;
My compassion grows warm and tender.

I will not execute my fierce anger;
I will not again destroy Ephraim;

for I am God and no mortal,
the Holy One in your midst,
and I will not come in wrath. (NRSV)

Option B

How can I give you up, Ephraim?
How can I relinquish you, Israel?

How can I make you like Admah?
How can I deal with you like Zeboiim?

My mind is turning over inside me.
My emotions are agitated all together.

I will certainly act out my burning anger.
I will certainly come back to destroy Ephraim.

For I am a god and not a human.
I, the Holy One, will certainly come into the midst of your city.

(Andersen and Freedman 1980: 574–575)

James Luther Mays (1969: 157) articulates the theology underlying the translation of option A: "Responding to the desire of his heart and poignancy of his compassion Yahweh declares three times that his wrath shall not have the final word about Israel's destiny . . . wrath cannot be the final decree. Yahweh will not turn from his election of 'my son' and destroy the Ephraim created by his saving acts." Other passages in the book (Hos 1:7; 2:1–2, 16–25; 6:1–3; 14:5–8 [Eng 1:7, 10–11; 2:14–23; 6:1–3; 14:4–7]) suggest that Hosea 11:1–6 is yet further evidence of how the author and/or editor weave(s) oracles of restoration with oracles of judgment. In contrast, the rationale underlying the translation of option B (which interprets the three occurrences of *lʾ* not as negative but rather as asseverative) is best voiced by Francis Andersen and David Noel Freedman (1980: 589–591): Hosea 11:9 is "registering the renewed determination of Yahweh to carry out his threatened judgments, in spite of the claims of the sentiment expressed in v 8 . . . The historical events evince wrath against Israel, not mercy for it; so all the later prophets interpreted the fate of the northern kingdom." Further supporting the translation of option B is the simple observation that the judgment and destruction of Israel/Ephraim is the most repeated theme within the book. Deciding between these two views is extremely difficult, for both have merits.[75] One simply cannot deny the judgment oracles against Israel in the book, and yet to strip the book of its divine compassion is to rob it of the profound appeal that contributed to the preservation and ultimately the canonization of the book. There is the possibility that both options may have existed throughout the text's long transmission history, with the final editors choosing option A over option B. Regardless, each translation looks to Yahweh as the Holy One in Hosea 11:9, *the* operative force behind his terrifying, destructive power (option B) or his radical benevolence toward his people (option A).

Yahweh's Holy Ark

As we saw in Chapter Seven (pp. 364–366, 388–389, 394–397), the Ark served as a pragmatic focal point metonymically representing Yahweh. The Ark marked Yahweh's presence on the battlefield, in ritual warfare, and in processions, especially those associated with the Jerusalem Temple. As such, it was treated as a sacred object. In Nadav Na'aman's (1999a: 410–411; 2006a: 329) understanding, the Ark was "the most sacred object of YHWH" to which "great sanctity [was] attached" in that it was accessible to the public, in contrast to "the Cherubim throne that was located inside the Holy of Holies and was seen by a few priests of high rank." Yet it would be a mistake to use such accessibility to minimize the fact that the Ark was also a holy object. According to 1 Kings 8:6 (//2 Chr 5:7), in Jerusalem the "place" where the Ark resides when not in procession is none other than "the inner sanctuary of the Temple, in the most holy place [*měqômô ʾel-děbîr habbayit ʾel-qōdeš haqqŏdāšîm*], underneath the wings of the cherubim."

Yet what does it mean for the Ark to be holy? Was it an object of veneration or religious respect in the sense that it was an attention-focusing device that substituted for a divine image? Or was it thought to be a vehicle that was capable of exhibiting divine power? Or did it have a mediating role whereby divine (lethal) power could reside among humans?

The Ark and Lethal Holiness: The Cultic Management of a War Palladium

Clearly, the pre-Jerusalem traditions about the portable Ark's presence on the battlefield are all about how the Ark was perceived as divinely powerful. After a Philistine defeat, the elders of Israel bring the Ark from Shiloh "so that it/he [Yahweh] may come among us and save us from the power of our enemies" (1 Sam 4:3). The portrait of the Philistine reaction is painted with fear, as they twice cry out in terror (*ʾôy lānû*) knowing that they are about to do battle with divinity, with one mighty enough to have smitten the Egyptians with every sort of scourge and pestilence (1 Sam 4:6–8).[76] With legendary flair, the Ark dismembers the image of the Philistine god Dagon (1 Sam 5:1–4). The Ark is the source of "incredible panic" (*mĕhûmâ gĕdôlâ mĕʾōd*) to the Philistines, who are afflicted with divinely caused plagues (1 Sam 5:9). The Ekronites conclude that the divinely empowered Ark is lethal as their panic grows "deathly" (*mĕhûmat-māwet*; 1 Sam 5:10–11). The variant reading found in 4QSam[a] underscores that the "deathly panic" is at the same time "the panic of [caused by] Yahweh" (*mhwmy yhwh*).

When the Ark eventually arrives at Beth-Shemesh, the Judean inhabitants rejoice and offer sacrifices (1 Sam 6:13–14). Levites emerge on the scene for the proper handling of the Ark (1 Sam 6:15; cf. 1 Sam 7:1),[77] and additional sacrifices are offered by the citizens of the city (1 Sam 6:14–15). Curiously, seventy of the Beth-Shemeshites are subsequently killed either for not having a sanctioned priest to handle the Ark or for mishandling the sacred object themselves.[78] What follows is instructive for our purposes. After mourning the deaths of so many (called "Yahweh's great slaughter"), the surviving Beth-Shemeshites exclaim: "Who is able to stand before Yahweh, *this Holy God*?" (1 Sam 6:20). The phrasing here ("to stand before") is a double entendre in that it can refer to the ability of a designated religious officiant—using the proper ritual precautions—to attend a lethal deity (cf. Jud 20:28; Ezek 44:15; 1 Sam 7:1), while also referring to the inability to withstand such divine power (cf. Exod 9:11). In either case, the holiness of Yahweh marks overwhelming power.

A similar tradition mentioning the lethality of divine holiness associated with the Ark is found in 2 Samuel 6:1–11 (//1 Chr 13). There are many questions swirling around the death of Uzzah, who seems to have good intentions when he puts forth his hand to stabilize a falling Ark after the oxen stumble. David's response to the killing of Uzzah is, in equal measure, anger toward and fear of Yahweh (2 Sam 6:8–9//1 Chr 13:11–12). The divine anger that strikes Uzzah dead is said to have "burst forth with an outburst" (*pāraṣ yhwh pereṣ*), employing a verb used elsewhere for divine lethality unleashed against those who would approach the Unapproachable without proper consecration (see Exod 19:22, 24, discussed later). The stated rationale for the (hypostatic?) Anger of Yahweh killing Uzzah is "because he reached out his hand to the Ark" (2 Sam 6:7//1 Chr 13:10),[79] yet this only begins to answer our questions; one can appreciate David's consternation. Once again, we find scholars probing the question of whether Uzzah's death was due to cultic violation and/or not having the proper priestly status (cf. 1 Chr 15:13). Matters become even more confused when other Ark traditions are added into the mix. 1 Kings 2:26 says that the priest Abiathar carried (*nśʾ*) the ark before David, and most scholars see this as a reference to 2 Samuel 6 (cf. 1 Chr 13:2–3; 15:11–15). The priestly and Levitical divisions of labor with regard to handling the Ark are found in Numbers 4. (A more thorough treatment of P's and H's understanding of holiness is on pp. 615–643.) Baruch Levine (1993: 175) summarizes:

> According to Numbers 4:4–12 both priests and Levites were involved in attending to the Ark, but the division of labor is consistent: the Aaronide priests prepared the Ark for transport, because only they were permitted to handle it before it was wrapped and its poles had been inserted. Actually, only priests were permitted to enter the Shrine in order to remove the Ark (Num 4:17–20). But it is the nonpriestly Kohathites [Kohathite Levites] who transport the Ark, not the priests.[80]

Yahweh's instructions given in Numbers 4:15–20 with regard to the Kohathite clan of Levites is again instructive for our purposes:

> When Aaron and his sons have finished wrapping [the sacred objects within] the Holy [Shrine] [*haqqōdeš*] and all the vessels of the Holy [Shrine] [*haqqōdeš*] at the departure of the encampment, only then shall the Kohathites come and transport [*nśʾ*] them, so that they do not come in contact with the Holy [Shrine] [*haqqōdeš*] lest they die. . . . Do not allow the tribal clans of Kohathites to be cut off from the [rest of the] Levites. This is how you should manage them so that they may remain alive and not die whenever they approach the Holy of Holies [*qōdeš haqqŏdāšîm*]: Aaron and his sons shall enter and assign each of them to his duties and to his porterage. But let not [the Kohathites] go inside and view the Holy [Shrine] [*haqqōdeš*] even for a moment, lest they die. (Lev 4:15–20)

The tradition here could not be clearer, as it resonates with the other Ark traditions: divine holiness is lethal. Only the proper personnel (for Numbers 4, the Aaronid priests; cf. 1 Chr 15:2–15) are able to attend to the Holy. Yet even they would die without divinely sanctioned ritual precautions (discussed later). Even Aaron, the high priest, is warned about the risk of dying when he comes before the Ark (Lev 16:2).

Accessing Holy Yahweh via the Ark

As Yahweh is holy, so he is powerful and even lethal. Likewise, as the Ark is holy (or, better, associated with and representing Yahweh's holiness), so it is powerful and even lethal. In this light, what is most remarkable about the Ark (prior to its residence in the Jerusalem Temple) is its portability and accessibility. Whereas humans "cannot see Yahweh and live" (Exod 33:20), they are indeed able via processions to experience the Ark, a cultic object representing Yahweh's power and presence in their midst outside of the Holy of Holies.[81]

Such divine accessibility can only occur at divine invitation. As we saw in the various texts treated earlier (especially Exod 15:13, 17), Yahweh makes it possible for his people to commune safely with him in holy space (*miqdāš*), what logically should be the most dangerous of places. The priestly traditions such as those found in Leviticus 4 and elsewhere underscore that this can only be accomplished (whether within the *miqdāš* or in accessing the Ark) through a select number of personnel who have undergone consecration (√*qdš*) together with sanctioned ritual precautions.

Accessibility is articulated in yet another priestly Ark tradition (Exod 25:8–22; cf. Exod 37:1–9; Deut 31:24–29). After detailed instructions about the fashioning of the Ark, we read of Yahweh's overture:

> Speak to the people of Israel. . . . They shall make for me a holy sanctuary [*miqdāš*] so that I may dwell in their midst. . . . They shall make an Ark. . . . You [Moses using artisans] shall make a *kappōret* of pure gold . . . and you shall make two cherubim of gold . . . on the ends of the *kappōret*. . . . Place the *kappōret* on top of the Ark, and inside the Ark you shall set the Testimony [*'ēdut*] that I will give you. There I will meet with you [Moses] [*wěnôʿadtî lěkā šām*], and I will speak you [*wědibbartî 'ittěkā*] from above the *kappōret*—from between the two cherubim that are on top of the Ark of the Testimony—all that I will command you concerning the Israelite people. (Exod 25:2, 8, 10, 17–18, 21–22)

For P (H?)[82] here, the explicit purpose of Yahweh's holy *miqdāš* is to make it possible for God "to dwell" (or "to tent")[83] (*škn*) among his people (Exod 25:8). The Ark with its *kappōret* and *'ēdut* Testimony is the locale of divine presence and communication ("*There* [*šām*] I will meet with you"; Exod 25:22). Rather than the Ark occasioning fear of death, here we have an invitation by the Almighty to treat the Ark as a locale where (a medium by which?) he will meet with Moses in order to provide instruction for his people. In explaining the "complex amalgamation of traditions" that we find in P's articulation that the Tabernacle can be both locative and locomotive, Benjamin Sommer (2001: 57–59) appeals once again to the theoretical models of Jonathan Z. Smith and Rudolph Otto:[84]

> The opposition embodied in the priestly tabernacle results from the tension between two religious impulses, neither of which is confined to a particular period, place, or culture. One impulse emphasizes the Ottonian *fascinans*, which produces a desire to approach the divine and hence that God is locatable . . . the other impulse is rooted in *mysterium* and *tremendum* . . . hence the divine can never be confidently located by humans. Examples of these impulses can be found throughout the history of religions, often in a single tradition.

The Ark and the all-important *kappōret* highlight the tension while at the same time resolving it.[85] Though these two objects are divinely holy and thus potentially lethal (Otto's *tremendum*), remarkably much about them involves human accessibility—their construction by consecrated artisans (divinely chosen, empowered, and instructed; Exod 35:30–36:1), their handling by Aaron and Aaronid priests, their transportation by Kohathite Levites, their viewing by the people at large (cf. Ps 68:25 [Eng 68:24]), their role as a meeting place with Moses, their providing instruction (via *'ēdut* Testimony) to the people.

The Holy One of Israel in Isaianic Traditions

Interestingly, portrayals of Yahweh as the Holy One of Israel (*qĕdôš yiśrā'ēl*) are found most often in Isaianic traditions. In the Hebrew Bible, the full phrase *yhwh qĕdôš yiśrā'ēl* occurs only in Isaiah 10:20, 30:15, and 45:11. According to the thorough studies of H. G. M. Williamson (2001; 2006: 43–46), the phrase "the Holy One of Israel" (*qĕdôš yiśrā'ēl*) occurs some twenty-five times in the Isaianic corpus, with similar vocabulary (e.g., "his/your Holy One," "the Holy One of Jacob") growing the number of occurrences to twenty-nine. Though the divine title occurs throughout the book of Isaiah (with some scholars seeing it as a unifying theme), Williamson (2001: 38; 2006: 44) argues that "Deutero-Isaiah is in reality the writer to have made most intensive use of the title," which was then rarely employed in Third Isaiah (2001: 24–27). Deutero-Isaiah's rationale for choosing the title was (once again) not in reference to cultic purity or ethical holiness, but rather a reference to the saving acts of Yahweh executed on behalf of his people. The "Holy One of Israel" is Israel's savior (*môšîa'*; Isa 43:3; cf. Isa 30:15). Echoing ancient praise (cf. √*g'l* and √*qdš* in Exod 15:13), six times Deutero-Isaiah prefaces Yahweh's title "Holy One of Israel" with the appellation "Redeemer" (*gō'ēl*), emphasizing his helping (*'āzar*), teaching (*limmēd*), guiding (*hidrîk*), and choosing (*bāḥar*) of Israel (Isa 41:14; 43:14; 47:4; 48:17; 49:7; 54:5).

As for First Isaiah, where Wildberger (1991: 24) finds seven authentic passages (Isa 1:4; 5:19, 24; 30:11, 12, 15; 31:1), Williamson (2001: 27–31) reduces the number to only four by omitting Isaiah 1:4 and 5:24 as redactional and by being agnostic with regard to the date of Isaiah 5:19. Only those passages associated with Sennacherib's invasion in 701 BCE are authentic to the eighth-century prophet.[86] As a result, where others see Yahweh's epithet "the Holy One of Israel" as central to Isaiah's understanding of the divine (compare especially Isa 6:3), Williamson (2001: 31, 35, 37) sees it as a "relatively obscure title." Applying the Propp Principle (see pp. 66–67, 283–284), one could easily take issue with such a quantity argument. It assumes that our extant texts constitute a full dataset representative of the prophet's religious culture. More likely, what has been preserved allows us only a glance, so we should be careful not to draw overarching conclusions from such an incomplete dataset. Be that as it may, the Sennacherib passages that are certainly authentic reveal that "the Holy One of Israel" was thought to be a God who intervened militarily. Isaiah 31:1 aptly summarizes the prophet's advocacy of relying on Yahweh as a divine warrior rather than trusting political alliances:

> Woe to those who go down to Egypt for help,
> Who rely on horses—
> They trust in chariots due to their vast number,
> In horsemen due to their incredible strength,
> But do not look to the Holy One of Israel
> Nor search out Yahweh.

At risk of being redundant, once again we note that holiness here has to do with divine power rather than cultic, ritual, social, or ethical holiness. In Isaianic traditions, early and late, to say that Yahweh is the Holy One of Israel is to say that Yahweh is the military deliverer and redeemer of his people and nation.

Possible Origins of the Title "the Holy One of Israel"

There is a good deal of speculation with regard to the earlier traditions that might have informed the Isaianic understanding of Yahweh as "the Holy One of Israel." Claus Westermann (1969: 75) is representative of those who think that the title in Isaiah 6 "derives from Isaiah in the eighth century... to express the truth... that God's numinous holiness is holiness turned toward Israel." Gammie (1989: 74–76) looks to the expression "the Holy One in your midst" in Hosea 11:9 as "probably the source of inspiration" behind Isaiah's coining of the title for Yahweh. Referring to the "Holy One of Israel" in Psalm 71:22 (cf. Ps 78:41; 89:19), Joseph Blenkinsopp (2000: 183) suggests that the title "probably derives from the liturgy of the Jerusalem temple and, further back, from the war prophecy of Israel's beginnings in association with the ark." Similarly, Wildberger (1991: 24–26) focuses on the Jerusalem cult, noting that it is "not by chance" that the prophet Isaiah encounters "the Holy God" (*hāʾēl haqqādôš*) who is "holy-holy-holy" (*qādôš qādôš qādôš*) "right in Jerusalem" (Isa 5:16; 6:3).

Using the Title "the Holy One of Israel" to Speculate About Early Israelite Religion

Yet due to the rarity of the title in the psalter and hence its "narrow" use, Wildberger (1991: 24) probes earlier source material. He adamantly argues: "It is most certain that reference was made to God as the Holy One in Jerusalem even before the Israelite era." For Wildberger, an unspecified "Holy One" (cf. Isa 5:16) was made specific as "the Holy One *of Israel*" on analogy with "the Mighty One of Jacob" (Gen 49:24; Isa 49:26; 60:16; Ps 132:2, 5), "the Mighty One of Israel" (Isa 1:24), and "the Holy One of Jacob . . . the God of Israel" (Isa 29:23). In a lengthy reconstruction, Wildberger, like Blenkinsopp, looks to psalmody and Ark traditions to conclude:

> Based on Psalm 132, it is quite likely that the name *'byr y'qb* (Mighty One of Jacob) came to Jerusalem in connection with the ark and its traditions, so that *qdwš yśr'l* (Holy One of Israel) provides us with an instructive example to show the way in which Jerusalem traditions and old Israelite traditions were synthesized, as can be seen in the way these traditions developed in the city where the temple was located. . . . The parallel expression *'byr y'qb* (Mighty One of Jacob) gives one reason to believe that Yahweh is called "Holy One of Israel" insofar as he turns toward Israel, leads and protects the people. . . . [T]he Holy One of Israel is the God of the covenant who is viewed as the kind father who has raised his people.

In his own lengthy study of the topic, Williamson (2006: 45; 2001: 27–35) concludes that the eighth-century BCE prophet "Isaiah had certainly used" the title "the Holy One of Israel" "on occasion," yet "he did not himself . . . coin the phrase." Williamson agrees with Wildberger that the understanding of the God of Jerusalem as Holy dates to pre-Israelite cult. Building on the work of Werner Schmidt and comparative material about Ugaritic 'Ilu as holy (see the opening of the present chapter), Williamson paints the background to Yahweh as holy by referring to "the holy dwelling of (El-) Elyon" in Psalm 46:5 (Eng 46:4).[87] He suggests the following scenario:

> There need be little doubt that the ascription of holiness to Yahweh . . . was . . . probably predicated of El Elyon in the pre-Israelite Jerusalem cult . . . whence it would have been transferred to Yahweh sometime after Jerusalem became part of Israel.

Williamson here echoes the conclusion of Werner Schmidt (1983: 154): "So the Jerusalem city god (El) Elyon seems to have been worshipped as holy, and Yahweh has succeeded him in this." Evidence of the blending of El and Yahweh traditions with respect to holiness are found in Psalm 68:36 (Eng 68:35),[88] which proclaims: "You are awesome, O Yahweh, [as you march] from your *holy places*, El of Israel [*nôrā' yhwh* mimmiqdāšêkā 'ēl yiśrā'ēl*]."[89] The use of the plural here (*miqdāšêkā*) to designate the deity's sacred locales may preserve an early tradition that is in line with the many different sanctuaries associated with El (cf. the description of El Berith at Shechem, El Bethel at Bethel, El Elyon at (Jeru-)salem, El Olam at Beersheba, El of Peniel, and El Roi at Beer Lahay Roi).[90] Clearly, the reference to these plural sanctuaries (and Mt. Bashan in Ps 68:16 [Eng 68:15]) is prior to the elevation of Jerusalem to its sole place of prominence.

Schmidt and Williamson's emphasis on antecedent El-Elyon worship as a prelude to Yahweh worship at Jerusalem is also supported by the presence of the god El-Elyon at (Jeru-)salem (Gen 14:18–22). See too the way in which Deuteronomy 32:6b–9 has (El)-Elyon allocating deities to peoples, an allocation that results in Yahweh acquiring Israel (see Chapter Four, pp. 91–92). As for the absorption of the El-Elyon traditions into Yahwism, in addition to Psalm 68, numerous other psalms either have Yahweh and Elyon as parallel terms (Ps 9:3; Ps 18:14 [Eng 18:13] = 2 Sam 22:14; Ps 21:8; Ps 87:5–6; 91:9; 92:2 [Eng 92:1]; 107:1, 11) or simply apply the epithet of "the Most High" to Yahweh, that is, Yahweh Elyon (Ps 7:18 [Eng 7:17]; Ps 47:3 (47:2); Ps 97:9).[91] Finally, consider again how the way in which one understands Psalm 82 (mythopoeically or mythopoetically) is directly relevant to one's understanding of El-Elyon and Yahweh. (See Chapter Nine, pp. 565–569.)

El, "The Mighty One of Jacob/Israel"//Yahweh, "The Holy One of Israel"

The notion of Yahweh as powerfully holy, which we emphasized earlier, would make the Schmidt-Wildberger-Williamson proposal even more attractive (cf. too Blenkinsopp). On formal grounds these scholars have equated El, "the *Mighty One* of Jacob/Israel," with Yahweh, "the *Holy One* of Israel." There is abundant evidence to support the thesis that holy gods are powerful gods. Thus in addition to their formal similarities, these two divine titles mirror each other ideologically. Isaiah 10:17–21 says as much in speaking of how the Holy One of Israel becomes a fiery destroyer (playing off "the light of Israel") such that the remnant of Jacob will lean on "Yahweh, the Holy One of Israel" as they return to mighty El (*'ēl gibbôr*).

Both titles ("the Mighty One of Jacob/Israel" and "the Holy One of Israel") also affirm the double sense of divine power that is awesomely militant against God's enemies (including lethality against improper cult) while protectively powerful (and benevolently gracious) toward God's people. If we are correct that El traditions were more at home within family religion in contrast to the cosmic militancy of certain Yahweh traditions (i.e., *Chaoskampf* traditions), then we can speculate a bit further.

The traditions about El as "the Mighty One of Jacob" such as we find in Genesis 49:24–25 emphasize that El is a father who provides "the blessings of breasts and womb." Traditions preserved in Deuteronomy 32:6b, 18 affirm El as father and creator, coloring that portrait with birthing imagery. (On these two passages, see Chapter Four, pp. 106, 110–111) Is it just a coincidence that Hosea's mention of Yahweh as "the Holy One in your midst" (Hos 11:9) is set within a familial context? Several Isaianic traditions also locate "the Holy One of Israel" within familial contexts. Isaiah 1:2–3 describes the rebelliousness of Yahweh's "sons" (i.e., Judahites) whom "he reared and brought up," together with the vocabulary of forsaking Yahweh, the Holy One of Israel. Second Isaiah depicts Yahweh, "the Holy One of Israel and his maker," challenging those who question him (using parental language) about the destiny of his children (Isaiah 45:9–12). Using positive imagery, Yahweh, the Holy One of Israel, who formed and created Jacob/Israel, gives extravagant ransom for his sons and daughters, whom he loves, for they are precious in his eyes (Isa 43:1–7). Of special note is Second Isaiah's frequent choice of the appellation "[kinsman] Redeemer" (*gō'ēl*) to describe the Holy One of Israel (Isa 41:14; 43:14; 47:4; 48:17; 49:7; 54:5). As we saw in Chapter Eight, the traditions of El as Father were fully wed with those of Yahweh as Father. Thus sociologically, perhaps it was the locus of family religion that facilitated the wedding of a mighty El protecting his clans with the more cosmically militant and holy-powerful Yahweh traditions.[92]

Summation of Non-Cultic Understandings: To Be Holy Is to Be Powerful

Setting aside the Ark traditions for the moment, what is particularly noteworthy in the streams of non-P traditions discussed to this point is the lack of what comes to define holiness in Priestly, Deuteronomic/Deuteronomistic, and Chronistic traditions (discussed later). There is no hint here of the concept of cultic purity, wherein the ritually holy is "that which is withdrawn from common use." There is no implication here that holiness stands in contrast to pollution occasioned by moral and ritual violations. There are no admonitions to social and ethical holiness, no mention of sacerdotal privilege. The worshipers in Exodus 15, Psalm 68, Psalm 89, and 1 Samuel 2 (cf. too Kuntillet ʿAjrud inscription 4.2) acknowledge Yahweh's awesome power (with the fear of lethal holiness in Exod 15 and Ps 89), yet they do not then proceed to engage in a series of ritual precautions in order to approach the Unapproachable. They do indeed risk boldly as they approach the powerful, dreadful Yahweh in worship, praising him for his past victories on their behalf (especially at the sea and against Sea in Exod 15) as well as his ongoing protection (the "shield" metaphor in Ps 89) and daily support (Ps 68:20 [Eng 68:19]). With confident audacity (and again without undertaking any ritual precautions), the royal ideology underlying Psalm 89 dares to proclaim that the *Holy* King of Israel will marshal his awesome power in support of the earthly king David.[93] A familial perspective is found in Psalm 68. The holy space of Yahweh, the charioteer and sovereign to whom kings bring tribute, is not associated with an elite priestly class, but rather is the locale where he is a father to orphans and a judicial advocate for widows (Ps 68:6 [Eng 68:5]). The Song of Hannah is even more remarkable, with Yahweh the Holy One reversing the fortunes of the disadvantaged, the weak, the hungry, the barren, and the poor. Turning to Yahweh's epithet as "the Holy One of Israel," we see that numerous Isaianic references fit well within these streams of tradition. Their repeated focus is on Yahweh's mighty deliverance of his people as savior and redeemer, not on the management of divine lethality through ritual holiness.

The Ark Narratives as a Cultic Corrective

Having emphasized holiness as divine power, it would be a grave mistake for one to use these data to assert that there was no cultic perspective within these streams of tradition, or that ritual holiness came only with the advent of the P and H traditions. Here adding the Ark traditions proves to be corrective. One cannot read the Ark narratives without being impressed by the power of the Ark as it symbolizes divine might on the battlefield and elsewhere. The Ark was perceived as Yahweh's holy vehicle occasioning "deathly panic" to the Ekronites, dismemberment to Dagon's divine image, and actual death to seventy of the Beth-Shemeshites and the well-intentioned Uzzah. Somewhere in the transmission of the tradition, Levites appear on the scene in 1 Samuel 6:13–15 to handle the Ark (though with the people sacrificing).[94] Though not appearing in the narrative in 2 Samuel 6:1–11, "priests and Levites" join David in transporting the Ark in the reformulation of the tradition in 1 Chr 13:2–3 (cf. 1 Chr 15:11–15; 1 Kgs 2:26). Somewhere in recounting these two tales, the focus has turned to the reason for the deaths of Yahwistic Judahites. (Philistine deaths occasioned no such probing.) Scholars plausibly reconstruct the possible reasons to be either cultic violation and/or the lack of a sanctioned priest to handle the Ark. The difference of P's emphasis on the cultic management of the holy Ark is clearly seen when one juxtaposes the accounts in 1 Samuel 6:13–15 and 2 Samuel 6:1–11 (// 1 Chr 13) with the detailed instructions of Numbers 4. There we see the precision of P, who takes special care to describe how the Aaronid priests are charged with attending the Holy Ark per se, with the Kohathite Levites being assigned the responsibility of its transportation. For P, the sanctioned privilege of physically handling the Ark itself (e.g., the wrapping of the naked Ark for travel) is the sole purview of the Aaronid priests, in contrast to the Kohathite Levites, whose contact is with a wrapped Ark—and even then using the poles attached to it.

This leads us now to turn to a fuller examination of the various cultic understandings of holiness. Yet as we do, we need to keep in mind that the notion of dread induced by the power of the holy/divine is an enduring concept, even when ritualized holiness becomes more of a focal point. In calling to mind Yahweh's victory in "the days of old" (i.e., his victory over Sea), a late psalmist proclaims that the (personified) Cosmic Waters and the Abyss were afraid (*yāḥîlû*) and trembled with fear (*yirgĕzû*) when they saw Yahweh on the march, for his way is holy and powerful (*ʾĕlōhîm baqqōdeš darkekā mî-ʾēl gādôl kēʾlōhîm*) (Ps 77:14, 17 [Eng 77:13, 16]). Another psalmist channels such fear of the holy into the language of worship:

> Prostrate yourself to Yahweh majestic in holiness [*bĕhadrat-qōdeš*],
> Tremble [*ḥîlû*] before him, all the earth! (Ps 96:9)

Yahweh as Holy: Systematic Cultic Frameworks, or the Cultic "Management" of Holiness

Having laid a foundation of holy power and lethality, we now turn to where the Hebrew Bible places much of its emphasis. For lack of a better term, let us call this the cultic "system" or "management" of holiness, although such functional vocabulary should not be used to minimize the deep passion involved in this pursuit of and thirst for the holy. If God is both lethally holy and at the same time one who invites his people to commune with him at his holy residence (*miqdāš*), how then should one approach? Remarkably, God also invites his people—in *imitatio Dei*—to join him in "being holy as he is holy" (Lev 11:44–45; cf. 19:2; 20:7; 21:8). Pragmatically, how does one achieve such holiness?

To explore such notions, we turn to Jacob Milgrom, the sage of our time who spent most of his career studying concepts of holiness in the Hebrew Bible. Milgrom summarizes:

> *Holy* is . . . "that which is unapproachable except through divinely imposed restrictions" or "that which is withdrawn from common use." . . . Holiness [in the Bible] is not innate [i.e., not in nature, as with animism]. The source of holiness is assigned to God alone. Holiness is God's quintessential nature, distinguishing God from all beings (1 Sam 2:2). It acts as the agency of God's will. If certain things are termed holy—such as land (Canaan), person (priest), place (sanctuary), or time (festival day)—they are so by virtue of divine dispensation. . . . The holy things of the Bible can cause death to the unwary and the impure who approach them without regard for the regulations that govern their

usage. Indeed, though biblical *qadosh* attains new dimensions, it never loses the sense of withdrawal and the separation. (Milgrom 2007: 850; 2000: 1711–1712)

If we posit that the definition of God as holy is "he who is quintessentially unapproachable"—especially since an encounter with the divine could prove lethal—it then says a great deal that the ancients felt the allure of the divine as so irresistibly enticing that they found ways to approach him despite the risk. Or, to borrow the words of William Propp (2006: 686), "the whole purpose of biblical worship, and ancient worship in general, is to bring the human and divine into *safe* contact." The process by which they made such an approach has everything to do with the many parameters of "holiness" (√*qdš*). These variables include the management of sacred space and sacred time as well as the sociological factors involved in the selection of proper religious officiants and the theological tenets used to construct efficacious ritual precautions.

Early Attestations of Cultic Holiness

Though notions of holiness as having to do with cultic purity are best known in the Hebrew Bible from later priestly traditions, it would be erroneous to think that cultic holiness is a late idea. One need only consider a reflective comment found in one of the Rib-Adda letters written in Amarna Canaanite to the Egyptian pharaoh in the mid-fourteenth century BCE. In EA 137, the king of Byblos describes why he is personally unable to travel to Egypt: "I am old and there is a serious illness in my body. The king, my lord, knows that the gods of Gubla [Byblos] are holy [*qadišū*], and [my] ailments are severe, for I com<mit>ted my sins against the gods [*ù ḫīṭī ep<šā>ti ana ilāni*]." Rib-Adda here confesses that his commission of sins against the Phoenician gods is the cause of his illness; because he offended the holy nature of the gods, they are punishing him.[95] Non-priestly biblical traditions concur, as we have seen in the passages regarding the Ark where a holy God meted out his punishment upon the offending Beth-Shemeshites and Uzzah.

In ancient Syria, cultic holiness is well attested at Late Bronze Age Ugarit and Emar. From the former we have a fascinating text (KTU 1.119) that includes a royal sacrificial ritual along with a votive prayer to the god Baʿlu. The first part of the text mentions many ritual elements, including cultic actors (divine recipients of cult, the king as the primary officiant who sacrifices, *mḫllm*-purifiers), numerous references to sacred time and sacred space (*bt* temples to both ʾIlu and Baʿlu, a *ʿd* room of Baʿlu, a *qdš* sanctuary of ʾIlu, and a *bt* house of the *ṯāʿiyu* priest), ritual washing and purifying (of the king), ritual states of sacralization/desacralization (*ḥl*, again of the king), a wide array of offerings (ram, cow, ewe, lamb, city dove, *ṭaʾû*, bull, fire, *šnpt*, neck, donkey, birds, liver, burnt), and the use of oil (specifically *šmn šlm*, "the oil of well-being") and libations. The text concludes with a votive prayer that contains three explicit references to cultic holiness (*qdš*).

O Baʿlu	*y bʿlm*
If you drive the strong one from our gate,	*hm tdy ʿz ṯġrny*
The warrior from our walls,	*qrd [l] ḥmytny*
A bull, O Baʿlu, we shall present [to you] as a holy offering	*ʾibr y bʿl nšqdš*
A vow, O Baʿlu, we shall fulfill.	*mdr bʿl nmlʾu*
[A fir]stborn, O Baʿlu, we shall present [to you] as a holy offering	*[b]kr bʿl nš[q]dš*
A *ḥtp* offering, O Baʿlu, we shall fulfill.	*ḥtp bʿl nmlʾu*
A banquet, O Baʿlu, we shall offer [to you].	*ʿšrt bʿl n[ʿ]šr*
To the sanctuary, O Baʿlu, we shall ascend,	*qdš bʿl nʿl*
That path, O Baʿlu, we shall tread.	*ntbt b[ʿl] ntlk*

(KTU 119.28′–34a′)[96]

One of the lines refers to the place where people make ascent to offer cult to the deity Baʿlu—namely, at his "holy place" (*qdš bʿl*).[97] The description of worshippers making an ascent (*nʿl*) fits the topography of the Baʿlu Temple located on the Acropolis at the highest elevation of Tell Ras Shamra (Yon 2006: 106–110). Such language resonates with Psalm 24:3–4, which speaks of virtuous worshippers making an ascent to Yahweh's holy place (*yaʿăleh . . . mĕqôm qodšô*).[98] As Mark Smith (2001b: 93–94) articulates well, at Ugarit sacred spaces "are marked and demarcated for holiness." "Deities' sanctuaries . . . partake of holiness" due to the divine presence that "imparts holiness to those places." It is not only biblical tradition that defines a once-profane place as holy due to divine residence (Exod 3:5; 19:10–25; Josh 5:15). The two other references to holiness (KTU 1.119.30′–31′) reveal, fittingly, how people vow to offer holy cult (*nšqdš*) to a powerful deity in response to divine aid. English translations of *nšqdš* can prove murky (e.g., "we shall sanctify/dedicate/consecrate") with their lack of specificity. The Ugaritic verb *nšqdš* in the Š stem (/*našaqdišu*/ or /*nušaqdišu*/) is here doubly causative (with direct object and implied indirect object): "We will cause animals [here bulls and firstborn males] to be holy offerings by the process of presenting them to a deity [here Baʿlu]."

A similar situation occurs in several of Emar's festivals that mention a variety of rituals occurring "on the day of sanctification" (*ina ūmi qaddusi*) or elliptically "in the [day of] sanctification" (*ina qaddusi*).⁹⁹ The text dealing with the installation of the high priestess mentions two such rituals occurring during the first two days of the festival—and with bread and beer as ritual substances! Daniel Fleming (1992a:10–11, 49, 51) translates the relevant passages as follows:

> During the shaving sanctification (*ina qaddusi ša gallubi*), they will sanctify (*uqaddasū*) all the gods of Emar with bread (and) beer. (Emar 369.6)

> On the day of the sanctification of the installation (*ina qaddusi ša malluki*), they will sanc[tify] (*[uqa]ddasū*) all the gods of Emar [with bread (and) beer]. (Emar 369.22)

In describing what he means with his translation of "to sanctify" (based on an older English use of the term), Fleming (1992: 49 n. 4) writes that here "the Emar verb *qaddusu* appears to mean 'to treat as holy, or sacred,' not 'to consecrate or purify.' Gods do not need to be made pure." Elsewhere, Fleming (1992: 162) elaborates that while humans can be indeed consecrated (e.g., cleansed and purified) for divine use, "one does not 'consecrate' gods because they are already sacred. Emar's *qaddusu* appears to mean 'to treat as sacred' by means of concrete offerings. This special 'sanctification' offering apparently makes the festival holy by giving cult to the gods as holy."

The Process of Consecration in Exodus 19:10–25

A relatively early Israelite tradition is found in Exodus 19:10–25. Source-critically, those who see it as mostly a unit lean toward J (or a mixture of J and E), with others seeing an earlier tradition that has then undergone Priestly and/or Deuteronomistic redaction.¹⁰⁰ Attention is often focused on the theophany that depicts Yahweh's fiery and thundering presence on a Mt. Sinai wrapped in smoke (Exod 19:18–19) along with the special privileging of Moses. Others use the mention of a covenant (*běrît*) in Exodus 19:5 and the subsequent Decalogue to frame the entire narrative that follows (e.g., Beyerlin 1965: 145–151). Yet if we approach this material through the lens of holiness another picture emerges. The focus of this passage then becomes how people and priests alike need to be "consecrated" (Exod 19:10, 14, 22) in order to avert death at the hands of the deity. Both parties must be "made holy" (*qdš* in D and tD stems) in order to survive interacting with the holy divine.

Ritual performance facilitates approaching the Unapproachable—at least to a degree.¹⁰¹ Via the theophany on Mt. Sinai, Yahweh allows himself to be partly seen and heard by all the people (*lĕ'ênê kol-hā'ām*; Exod 19:11). Exodus 19:17 explicitly mentions how Moses brought the people out of the camp "to encounter God" (or "toward God") (*liqra't hā'ĕlōhîm*), and Exodus 19:22 describes priests who "approach Yahweh" (*hakkōhănîm hanniggāšîm 'el-yhwh*). Yet each group can do so only once they have been "consecrated." The consecration process is occasioned by divine instruction to Moses, Yahweh's emissary turned officiant, whose presence is repeatedly emphasized, together with mention of Aaron, whose access is also privileged over priests and people (Exod 19:24).

The ritual performance contains six elements: (1) sacred time involving a three-day enactment, (2) the washing of clothes (Exod 19:10, 14), (3) abstinence from sex (Exod 19:15), (4) the delimiting of sacred space (Exod 19:12, 21, 23), (5) ritual warnings about divine lethality (Exod 19:12–13, 21–24), and (6) the entering into sacred space (with visuals and sound) that is marked by gradations of holiness in that the people remain at the base of the mountain while Moses (and later Aaron) ascends to its summit to encounter Yahweh up close.

> Yahweh said to Moses: "Go to the people and consecrate them [*qiddaštām*] today and tomorrow. Have them wash their clothes and prepare for the third day, because on the third day Yahweh will come down upon Mt. Sinai in the sight of all the people [*lĕ'ênê kol-hā'ām*]. You shall set boundary limits [*wĕhigbaltā*] for the people all around, saying, 'Beware not to go up the mountain or to touch the edge of it. Whoever touches the mountain shall be put to death.' (No hand should touch him. Rather he should be either stoned or shot [with arrows]; whether animal or human being, he shall not live.) When the ram's horn [*yōbēl*] sounds a long blast, they may go up on the mountain."
>
> So Moses came down from the mountain to the people. He consecrated [*wayĕqaddēš*] the people, and they washed their clothes. He said to the people, "Prepare for the third day; do not approach ['*al-tiggĕšû*] a woman."
>
> On the third day, as morning dawned, there was thunder and lightning, as well as a dense cloud on the mountain, and an extremely loud blast of a *šōpār* horn, so loud that all the people who were in the camp trembled [with fear] [*yeḥĕrad*]. Moses led the people out of the camp to meet God [*liqra't hā'ĕlōhîm*]. They took their places at the base of the mountain.
>
> Now Mt. Sinai was all in smoke, because Yahweh had descended upon it in fire; the smoke rose like the smoke of a kiln, while the whole mountain trembled violently [*yeḥĕrad . . . mĕ'ōd*]. As the blast [*qôl*] of the *šōpār* horn grew louder and louder, Moses would speak and God would answer him in thunder [*qôl*]. When Yahweh descended upon Mt. Sinai, to the top of the mountain, Yahweh summoned Moses to the top of the mountain, and Moses went up

Yahweh then said to Moses: "Go down and warn the people not to break through to Yahweh to gaze [*yehersû 'el-yhwh lir'ôt*], lest many of them perish. In addition, the priests who approach [*hakkōhănîm hanniggāšîm*] Yahweh must consecrate themselves [*yitqaddāšû*] lest Yahweh break out [*yiprōṣ*] against them."

But Moses said to Yahweh: "The people are not permitted to come up to Mt. Sinai; for you yourself warned us, saying, 'Set boundary limits around the mountain and keep it holy'" [*hagbēl 'et-hāhār wĕqiddaštô*].

So Yahweh said to him: "Go down, and come up bringing Aaron with you; but do not let either the priests or the people break through to come up to Yahweh [*'al-yehersû la'ălōt 'el-yhwh*], lest He break out against [*yiprōṣ*] them." So Moses went down to the people and told them. (Exodus 19:10–25)

Sacred Time, Purity and Pollution

The first three elements (dealing with sacred time, purity, and pollution) are surprising for their lack of detail when compared to priestly treatments of such rituals elsewhere. Propp (2006: 687) calls the rites here "rudimentary." One can safely conclude that any Priestly redaction of this narrative about an outdoor ritual is minimal.[102]

As historians of religion studying cultic calendars throughout the ancient Near East have long noted, time is as important a category as space, and it too can be sacred or profane.[103] The setting of our narrative (the theophany at Mt. Sinai) is a one-time event, and thus its minimal temporal regulations are understandable in contrast to the attention given elsewhere to repeated cultic times of day, week, month, and year, especially within priestly circles (e.g., Lev 23). The setting is also non-agrarian and non-sacrificial and thus separate from regulations of cultic time linked to agricultural seasons and animal sacrifice (e.g., Exod 13:6–7; 23:10–19; 34:18–26; Lev 9:1–14; Num 28–29; Deut 161–17; Ezek 45:18–25; cf. the tenth-century BCE Gezer Calendar).[104]

Though the ritual here has minimal regulations of sacred time, such time is nonetheless a focal point. To carry out the consecration process Moses must act immediately and for two consecutive days (*hayyôm ûmāḥār*; Exod 19:10). The third day, when divinity appears, is the climactic event, for which the people must ritually prepare themselves (*wĕhāyû/hĕyû nĕkōnîm layyôm haššĕlîšî*; Exod 19:11, 15). The advent is marked with powerful visuals (lightning, dense cloud, fire, smoke) and auditory blasts (thunder, loud soundings of the *šōpār* horn), both of which have the desired effect of producing violent trembling (√*ḥrd*) for people and mountain alike (Exod 19:16, 18).[105] The third day is also the day when Moses leads the people (in a ritual procession?) "to meet God" at the sacred space allotted to their status. Finally, the third day also contains the elevation of Moses to his uniquely privileged position, marked by an even louder demarcating blast of sacred sound (*qôl haššôpār hôlēk wĕḥāzēq mĕ'ōd*; Exod 19:19).

The instructions about the washing of clothes (*kibbĕsû śimlōtām*; Exod 19:10, 14) and sexual abstinence (Exod 19:15) have to do with rites of purity and pollution (cf. Frymer-Kensky 1983). In contrast to priestly literature, which goes into much greater detail, the particulars here are scant and have no stated rationale. Compare the simple reference to the washing of clothes in the present text with the fastidious details found in Leviticus and Numbers that concern the different types of garment soiling (by blood from a sin offering, semen, unclean animal, scapegoat, leprosy, female bleeding, corpse, battle, etc.). As for the span of time for this consecration ritual, the two days of washing here pale in comparison to the involved seven-day ritual washing (and rewashing) of garments and bodies in the priestly material.[106] Though the rationale is not stated, Nicole Ruane (2007: 69) suggests that "the laundering defines the cultically privileged group . . . , changes the status of those who have gone from common people to chosen people," and "help[s] to forge the ritual community." Turning to sexual abstinence, here too we find the briefest of references, which pales in comparison to the wide variety of priestly legislation on sex that Tikva Frymer-Kensky sums up simply: "Emissions from the genitalia were considered polluting agents."[107]

Delimiting Sacred Space and Divine Lethality

In contrast to the briefness of the remarks having to do with sacred time, purity, and pollution, the narrative expends considerable energy on the delimitation of sacred space and on deathly warnings should one violate defined borders. Even more odd is how a text that at first glance wants to convey how the people encountered God via a theophany spends most of its time keeping them at a good distance. As we will see, there is a strong ideological reason for this.

Two different expressions are used for delimiting the sacred space for the people. One uses a denominative verb from the noun *gĕbûl*, "border," to mark the actual physical space, followed by the modifier "all around" (*sābîb*) to underscore its completeness (Exod 19:12, 23). The sacred space allotted to the people is later said to be located at the base of the mountain (*bĕtaḥtît hāhār*; Exod 19:17), a great distance from its summit (*rō'š hāhār*), where Yahweh has descended (Exod 19:20). The second expression involves the enforcement of this limit, where the people are not allowed "to break through" (*hrs*) the border to ascend the mountain (Exod 19:21, 23).[108]

The potential offense of crossing this limit is "to gaze upon Yahweh" (*'el-yhwh lir'ôt*). The stated rationale for delimiting space on the mount is "to keep it holy" (*wĕqiddaštô*) or, more accurately, to guard the lethal power of divine holiness from "breaking out" (*prṣ*) against the people lest a great number of them die (wĕnāpal mimmennû rāb; Exod 19:21-22, 24). These two concepts go hand in hand. Seeing the holy powerful divine is lethal (Exod 33:20). The author of Psalm 78:54, using synonymous parallelism, equates Mt. Sinai with Yahweh's "holy border" (gĕbûl qodšô; cf. Arb jabal "mountain"). Crossing a divinely set border into holy space—that is, a place where one might see or encounter the Holy One in all his power—is lethal. The verb used here for Yahweh, "breaking out" (prṣ) with deadly effect, is the same verb used of Yahweh killing Uzzah in 2 Samuel 6:8 for his cultic violation with the Ark (previously discussed).

Gradations: Social/Cultic Status and Physical Space

The divine-human interaction on the holy mountain is marked by gradations that correlate elevated social and cultic status with elevated physical space. The people who have undergone consecrating rites are described as going up the mountain to meet God (yaʿălû bāhār . . . liqraʾt hāʾĕlōhîm). In reality they only ascend to the base of the mountain (taḥtît hāhār; Exod 19:13, 17). Socially and cultically above the people are the priests, who also undergo consecration rites (Exod 19:22). While they are assigned the privilege of "approaching Yahweh," curiously in the present text they too are grouped with the people at large who must stay in delimited space lest they "break through to come up to Yahweh" (ʾal-yehersû laʿălōt ʾel-yhwh; Exod 19:24). From what we see regarding the privileged status of Moses and Aaron in the present text (and elsewhere as in Exodus 24), we would have expected the priests to have occupied space elevated from the people. While this may indeed have been the case, no explicit mention occurs in our narrative. As the text stands, the priests' higher social and cultic status is not correlated with physical elevation.[109]

The higher rungs of social and cultic status that correlate with the elevated physical space on the holy mountain are reserved for Aaron and especially Moses. The same divine command that forbids priests "coming up" (ʿălōt) to Yahweh—by grouping them with the non-ascending people—bids Moses to come up (ʿălîtā ʾattâ) and then groups Aaron with him (Exod 19:24). Here physical elevation alone marks Aaron's premier status (pregnantly priestly); other traditions will use elaborate rituals of washing, vestments, anointing oil, sacrificial blood, and food consumption to mark his consecration (lĕqaddĕšô) and ordination (yĕmallēʾ ʾet-yad) (e.g., Exod 29:4-5; Lev 8:7-9, 12, 23, 30-33). Remarkably, though Exodus 19 regulates the priesthood (their consecration, physical space, and approach), in this Sinai narrative Aaron is never called a priest.[110]

The Unique Status of Moses in Exodus 19

At every turn, the ritual performance of Exodus 19:10-25 accords Moses the highest possible human status. As it is currently framed, Moses is already on the mountain abiding in Yahweh's presence and receiving divine directives. Tellingly,

Moses simply and repeatedly "goes up to God" (*ʿālâ ʾel-hāʾĕlōhîm*) without any mention of the need to be consecrated (Exod 19:3, 20, 24). Moses does not engage in any rites of purification or sacerdotal investiture. Instead Yahweh directly summons him to the summit (*wayyiqrāʾ yhwh lĕmōšeh ʾel-rōʾš hāhār;* Exod 19:20). Moses freely crosses delimited space without any worry of divine holiness "breaking out" (*prṣ*) against him and causing his death. Moses never has to "break through" (*hrs*) any border barrier as he comes up to Yahweh.

The summit of the mountain, the most restricted (and thus privileged) gradation of sacred space, is reserved for Yahweh and Moses alone. Granted, Aaron does ascend the mountain with Moses, as he does elsewhere (cf. Exod 19:24; 24:1, 9), yet there is no mention of him being on the summit, where Moses alone approaches Yahweh (cf. Exod 24:2). In the tradition found in Exodus 19, there is no explicit mention of Moses "seeing" Yahweh, nor any mention of dining (contrast Exod 24:9–11). Instead, the emphasis here is on an auditory experience with the divine similar to the traditions about Moses' unique prophetic role (cf. Chapter Nine, pp. 562–563). There are indeed powerful theophanic visuals of fire, smoke, and lightning, yet the "voice of thunder" (*qôl*) metaphorically acts as Yahweh's mode of conversation with Moses (Exod 19:19). Sociologically, Moses is Yahweh's designated mediator. He acts as Yahweh's emissary in communicating the deity's instructions and warnings. Simultaneously, as Yahweh's chosen officiant, he carries out the consecration rituals of the people, leads them (in procession) to the mountain, and sets their sacred boundary limit.

Ideological Holiness

To review, the Mt. Sinai narrative in Exodus 19:10–25 is rudimentary when it comes to ritual details, emphasizes the consecration (*qdš*) of people and priest set against a backdrop of divine lethality,[111] and prescribes gradations of sacred space that correlate with social and cultic status.

As the narrative continues in Exodus 20:15 (Eng 20:18), the people are physically terrified (*wayyirāʾ/wayyirʾû* [cf. LXX] *hāʿām wayyānuʿû*) upon seeing and hearing Yahweh's impressive theophany with its thunder, lightning, smoke, and blast of the *šōpār* horn. In contrast to having sacred space delimited for them (Exod 19:12, 23), here they are portrayed as willingly choosing "to stand at a distance far away" (*wayyaʿamdû mērāḥōq;* Exod 20:15, 18 [Eng 20:18, 21]). They remain at a distance even after Moses tries to assure them that they need not be afraid. They also urge Moses to be their intermediary with God lest the direct hearing of the divine result in their death (Exod 20:16 [Eng 20:19]).

Such a response reminds us of Catherine Bell's (1997: 75) comments on "the emergent quality of ritual" whereby "prestige has accrued to some but not others" with a self-reflective component "that enables the community to stand back and reflect upon their actions and identity." In the literary (and ideological) presentation of the ritual and its aftermath before us, prestige has accrued to Moses, who has unique (safe) access to Yahweh, and the people happily accede to such prestige out of a fear of divine lethality. The *qdš* consecration rituals of purity and pollution do indeed allow Israelites a partial approach to the Unapproachable Yahweh, even as non-Israelites have no such access. Yet their approach is partial (at the base of the mountain), reflecting the limitations of their social and cultic standing. Upon reflection, they acknowledge Moses' unique ability to draw near to God and to receive his instructions, which they pledge to obey (Exod 20:16–18 [Eng 20:19–21]; cf. Exod 24:2–3).

Returning to Moses, Milgrom states: "Moses himself acts as priest—indeed, as Israel's first priest, the one who not only established Israel's cult, but also officiated alone during the first week of its existence."[112] Moses, as Holy Yahweh's representative, is instructed "to make the people holy" (*qiddaštām*) in Exodus 19:10 through the two-day purity and pollution rituals. Moses likely oversaw the consecration of the priests in Exodus 19:22 as well. Yet, as astutely underscored by Freedman (quoted in Milgrom 1991: 557), "it is most significant that no one consecrates or invests Moses. His authority comes directly from God and is not mediated as is the power of both priests and kings." As noted earlier, whereas in our text both people and priest undergo *qdš* consecration rituals, the verb *qdš* is never used of Moses.[113] In fact, *nowhere* in the entire Hebrew Bible is the root *qdš* used of Moses apart from a single (and telling) remark in Isaiah 63:11. Though this text is very late, it preserves a tradition worth noting here for its extraordinary language of God putting his holy spirit within Moses (*haśśām běqirbô ʾet-rûaḥ qodšô*):

But they [the people of Israel] rebelled and grieved his holy spirit.	*wěhēmmâ mārû wěʿiṣṣěbû ʾet-rûaḥ qodšô*
So he became their enemy, he himself fought against them.	*wayyēhāpēk lāhem lěʾôyēb hûʾ nilḥam-bām*
Then he [God? the people?] remembered the days of old: Moses. His people.	*wayyizkōr yěmê-ʿôlām mōšeh ʿammô*[114]
"Where is he who brought them up from the Sea? With the shepherd of his flock?'	*ʾayyēh hammaʿălēm miyyām ʾēt rōʿeh ṣōʾnô*[115]
"Where is he who put within him his holy spirit?	*ʾayyēh haśśām běqirbô ʾet-rûaḥ qodšô*

> Who made his glorious arm
> proceed at the right hand of Moses?"

> *môlîk lîmîn mōšeh*
> *zĕrôaʿ tipʾartô*

(Isaiah 63:10–12a)

The historical reminiscence of this hymnic poetry laments how God fought against his own people who grieved "his holy spirit" (*rûaḥ qodšô*; Isa 63:10). Then, through a series of rhetorical questions, Israel asks if Yahweh is as powerful in the present as he was in the glorious past. Memories of the Exodus come to mind, specifically the memories of a victorious warrior who delivered his people with Moses playing a privileged role. Moses is highlighted four times in a verse and a half. The name of Moses is the very first item remembered, either by God or by the people as he/they reminisce (Isa 63:11).[116] The victory at the sea (and over Sea) immediately follows, with Yahweh using Moses as the shepherd of his flock.[117] Yahweh manifests his military power by having "his glorious Arm" proceed at the right hand of Moses. Additionally, and above all these accolades, Yahweh proclaims that he placed "his holy Spirit" within Moses (*haśśām bĕqirbô ʾet-rûaḥ qodšô*). Such a personal and direct investiture of divine essence and power (and with it prestige and authority) is unparalleled.

Holy Personnel in the Priestly Traditions

Priestly authors would certainly agree with the confessions of faith we have looked at earlier, those proclaiming that "there is no Holy One like Yahweh" (*ʾên-qādôš ka-yhwh*; 1 Sam 2:2) and that Yahweh is "he who should be regarded as holy" (*ʾōtô taqdîšû*; Isa 8:13). In worshipful response they too would acknowledge that Yahweh is the incomparable one who should be "feared in holiness" (*mî kāmōkâ neʾdār baqqōdeš*; Exod 15:11) and that devotees should prostrate themselves before "Yahweh majestic in holiness" (*bĕhadrat-qōdeš*; Ps 96:9). Yet in addition, they would advance notions about how a holy Yahweh should be revered in decisively different ways. Rhetorically, consider the difference between the third-person confessions *about Yahweh's holiness* and the dramatic first-person declaration *by God himself* found in Leviticus 11:44–45:

> I am Yahweh ... I am holy

> *ʾănî yhwh ... qādôš ʾānî*

Such a proclamation resonates with the authority and supremacy we saw earlier in the divine speech contained in Hosea's prophetic oracles:

> For I am God, not human,
> the Holy One in your midst.
>
> *kî 'ēl 'ānōkî wĕlō'-'îš*
> *bĕqirbĕkā qādôš*
>
> (Hosea 11:9)

Yahweh's incomparable holy essence is the theological foundation that undergirds all the pragmatics of managing holiness in space and time. Conceptually, it simultaneously emphasizes the divine/human divide as it begs the selection of proper personnel and the enactment of ritual to bridge the divide.[118] Of course, the priestly writers knew that saying that a human (priest or people) should be holy (consecrated) is categorically different from saying that God is holy. God is essentially holy; he can be no other. The essence of humans, in contrast, is not. If human essence were holy, there would be little need for intricate consecration rituals and rhetorical admonishments to ritual, moral, and ethical holiness. Yet despite this qualitative difference, as we will see, priestly traditions—with ultimate seriousness—showcase in varying ways how priests (for P and H) and also the community at large (for H) can be holy (i.e., to be godly, godlike). This partaking of the divine (though in an imitative sense only) is quite remarkable.[119]

The Complicated Nature of Holiness in Priestly Traditions

The Hebrew Bible preserves an array of priestly viewpoints of holiness, many of them similar, others quite divergent from one another. Differences in theology depend on the eye of the beholder. For Milgrom (1992: 454), "when it comes to theology, P and H mostly form a single continuum; H articulates and develops what is incipient and even latent, in P." For Robert Kugler (1997: 26), "Leviticus is a book at war within itself theologically . . . the two parts of Leviticus represent distinct theological and ideological perspectives." Unraveling priestly viewpoints on holiness that have been woven together over years of transmission and redactional activity is a daunting if not impossible task. Only a sketch will be given here.

The Management of Holiness: Holy Personnel

The rudimentary Mt. Sinai narrative in Exodus 19:10–25 depicted four gradations regarding personnel coming into Yahweh's holy presence, five demarcations if one wanted to add in the mention of animals in Exodus 19:13. Moses is ranked alone as preeminent, with Aaron ranked second, as indicated by his ascending the mountain along with Moses. Third in order would be the priests (*hakkōhănîm*), who are described as "approaching" Yahweh, though in the narrative their space is delimited. Lowest in rank are the people at large, who remain at the base of the mountain. The last two groups are explicitly described as undergoing consecration rituals. Moses consecrated (*qiddēš*) the people and could likely have overseen the consecration of priests, though the reflexive verb used (*yitqaddāšû*) puts emphasis on their agency in consecrating themselves.

The priestly traditions found in P and H essentially agree on these four gradations of holy personnel (Moses followed by Aaron followed by the sacerdotal officiants [priests/Levites] and then the people), though they differ considerably in how they nuance the last two groups, and in the spirit with which they approach sanctification. These matters will be discussed in detail shortly. For now, Jacob Milgrom and Israel Knohl present a helpful overview. In summarizing his views of how "P and H sharply diverge on many theological fundamentals," especially "in their contrasting conceptions of holiness," Milgrom (1991: 48) notes: "Holiness of persons is restricted in P to priests and Nazirites; H extends it to all Israel." Unpacking the latter, Milgrom describes how H, "though it concedes that only priests are innately holy (Lev 21:7), repeatedly calls on Israel to strive for holiness." Moreover, for H, "sanctification is an ongoing process for priests as well as for all Israelites," both of whom "bear a holiness that expands or contracts in proportion to their adherence to God's commandments." Knohl (1995: 180–181) writes in a similar fashion. For P (Knohl's PT or Priestly Torah), "only the priests, Aaron and his descendants, are sanctified for eternity," whereas H "expands the realm of holiness" such that it "applies to the entire community of Israel." Using H's connection of honoring one's parents with holiness, Knohl adds: "One may clearly not restrict holiness to the Temple and the priests."

The Supremacy of Moses in Priestly Tradition: Moses as Priest?

According to non-P (J?) tradition, during his very first and unexpected encounter with the fiery divine, the shepherd Moses is able to stand on holy ground (*'admat-qōdeš*) without having undergone any type of priestly *qdš* investiture ritual (Exod 3:5)—but with the admonishment to remove his sandals (cf. Josh 5:15). Later in the story, other non-P (E?) traditions have Moses demanding that Pharaoh allow Israel to leave Egypt due to the necessity of sacrificing to Yahweh (Exod 3:18; 5:3, 8, 17; 8:8, 25–29; 10:25). Later still, as we just saw, in the mountain theophany in Exodus 19, Moses is depicted as God's intimate conversation partner (Exod 19:19, 23) who serves as an emissary for the divine, communicating his instructions and mediating his lethal power on behalf of the people. Cultically, Moses serves as Yahweh's chosen officiant, who carries out consecration rituals. Moses himself holds such stature that he never undergoes any type of consecration ritual in order to approach divinity, in contrast to all other humans. In yet another non-P (E?) tradition in Numbers 12:8, Moses is Yahweh's servant, with whom Yahweh "speaks face-to-face" (*peh ʾel-peh ʾădabber-bô*; cf. Exod 33:11) and to whom he makes himself known in prophetic visions. Additionally, Moses is one of the select few who are able to see Yahweh at least partially (*těmunat yhwh yabbîṭ*) and live to tell about it (cf. Chapter Seven, pp. 296–297, 354–355). In all of these traditions, no "holy" status is assigned to God's special servant. As we have seen, the only place where holiness comes explicitly into the picture is in a late Isaianic portrayal where the shepherd Moses possesses Yahweh's holy spirit (*rûaḥ qodšô*; Isa 63:11). To this we now add Ps 99:6's reference to Moses as priest alongside Aaron (*mōšeh wěʾahărōn běkōhănāyw*). Yet this is the only reference of its kind in the entire Hebrew Bible, and one that is often discounted as not referring to *kěhunnâ* priesthood in its technical sense.[120]

What about in P and H? The supremacy of Moses is seen throughout this material, with scholars referring to him as "the exalted inaugurator of the cult" (Gorman 1990: 141) or "the appointed mediator between the deity and the community" (Rooke 2000: 16). For Propp (2006: 531), "Moses stands apart as a once-in-history phenomenon." Yet there is no certainty as to his sacerdotal status. Acknowledging how "P is uneasy about Moses' priestly role," Milgrom (1991: 555–558)—writing on Leviticus 8—nonetheless asserts that "Moses himself acts as priest—indeed, as Israel's first priest, the one who not only established Israel's cult, but also officiated alone during the first week of its existence." Not only did Moses "officiate at the priestly consecration," "he even received in part the priestly prebends from the sacrifices (Lev 8:29b)." Building on the well-documented role of the king as the central cultic actor in the ancient Near East (including ancient Judah and Israel), Milgrom (1991: 557) asserts that Moses' cultic leadership (dedicating the Tabernacle and investing the priests) is kinglike. And it is thus "Moses' regal role [that] entitles him to act as a priest."[121] Others frame matters quite differently, with Aelred Cody (1969: 49) concluding that "Moses does not appear in any way that clearly makes him a priest. . . . [T]he truly ancient traditions on Moses preserved for us do not offer any evidence of an aetiological attempt to trace the origins of priesthood to a Moses." Levine (1989: 49) also remarks that "it would be incorrect . . . to regard Moses as a priest." Erhard Gerstenberger (1996b: 112) takes a middle path. In Exodus 29, "Moses is the officiating priest," but in P "the role of priestly forefather is most certainly not to be ascribed to Moses."

What stands out among Moses' sacerdotal associations is not primarily his acts of consecrating others or receiving priestly prebends, though each of these carries some weight. Logically, one must be holy to sanctify others, and according to P's worldview, prebends constitute "holy" food (Exod 29:33–34). Rather, there are three marks of distinction that are striking: (1) Moses' unique approach to the Unapproachable One (typically, the closer to the Holy One, the more holy the officiant); (2) Moses' role as Yahweh's emissary, mediating lethal divinity and divine precepts to humans, and (3) Moses' manipulation of blood (Exod 24:4–8; 29:12, 16, 20–21; Lev 8:15, 19, 23–24, 30). The last of these is quite noticeable, for elsewhere it is consistently a privilege accorded only to priests (e.g., Lev 1:5, 11; 3:2, 8, 13; 4:25, 30, 34; 7:2; 8:15; 9:9; Ezek 43:18–20; 2 Chr 29:22, 24; 30:16).[122] Ziony Zevit (2004: 200) sums up well: "So far as P was concerned, all such blood manipulation fell in the province of *kohanim*."

In light of P's and H's interest in sacerdotal affairs (discussed later), we must take seriously the fact P and H never have Moses undergo any consecration ritual, nor do they ever refer to Moses as a priest (*kōhēn*). A tempting solution would be to see the suppression of a Mosaic priesthood due to P's and H's pro-Aaronid stance. Much has been made of the existence of a Mushite priesthood (based in Shiloh and Nob) rivaling that of the Aaronids (based in Bethel), building especially on the work of Frank Moore Cross and using as evidence such passages as Exodus 32, Deuteronomy 33:8–11, and Judges 17–18 (discussed again later).[123] Yet the omission of *qdš* language and priestly (*kōhēn*) vocabulary for Moses occurs throughout the entire Hebrew Bible (apart from Ps 99:6), not just in a handful of polemical texts. Something else must account for the universal omission of holy, priestly terminology for Moses.

Some suggest a sociological and/or rhetorical answer without appealing to any type of polemic. Moses' stature is secure. It is the Aaronids that need legitimation. Milgrom (1991: 557, together with Freedman) notes how Moses' "authority comes directly from God and is not mediated." As such, "his capacity as priest" can be "intentionally bypasse[d] . . . in order to confer divine sanction upon Aaron and his sons." Deborah Rooke (2000: 16) similarly comments that Moses is viewed as a "pre-existing authority figure who never loses his authority even when Aaron has been inducted as high priest." Frank Gorman (1990: 141–149), building on the work of Victor Turner, provides a more satisfying anthropological answer. Moses' role as Yahweh's representative who inaugurates the cult is singular. His position is unlike any other, his horned visage godly (Exod 34:29). "His role . . . goes well beyond that of 'mediator,'" and is thus a liminal one that straddles the divine and the human. As such, "he stands outside of and transcends the normally operating cultic structures."

The High Priest Aaron and His Priestly Sons: The Ritual Act of Clothing

P's treatment of Aaron is elaborate, as can be seen in many passages (e.g., Exod 28–29; 39:1–31; 40:12–15; Lev 1–8, 16; Num 3). It is easy to understand why. Aaron stands for (personifies) every Aaronid high priest who occupies this most elevated cultic position of prestige and power, including the high priest(s) at the time(s) of P's writing and editing. The Priestly writer(s) is (are) writing of himself (themselves). For P, nothing could be more serious than regulating who should be allowed to approach the Unapproachable and to what degree. Using genealogical descent as a mechanism of legitimation, P has Aaron as *the* ancestor of "priesthood" (*kĕhunnâ*; Num 3:10; cf. Exod 40:15; Lev 16:32). This supreme Aaronid office is a divine "gift" (*mattānâ*; Num 18:7). It is to be "guarded" against the "outsider" making approach, with death in the offering for such violation (*hazzār haqqārēb yûmāt*; Num 3:10; Num 18:7).[124]

Several priestly consecration (*qdš*) rituals have to do with the body (e.g., movement, posture, washing, clothing, anointing). Over the past three decades, social scientists, anthropologists, philosophers, and scholars of gender have trained us to look for the ways in which the treatment of the body, especially in ritual, constructs and reinforces social realities and hierarchies.[125] Of the priestly consecration rituals, two (clothing and anointing)[126] are highlighted as marking Aaron (and symbolically every high priest) as preeminent—elevated far above ordinary priests, though lower in rank than Moses. P's description of the ritual performance of clothing Aaron in one-of-a-kind garments is explicit with regard to its function. Yahweh clearly states his rationale: "You shall make holy vestments for Aaron—for glorious radiance [*lĕkābôd ûlĕtip'āret*] . . . to consecrate him for his priestly service to me [*lĕqaddĕšô lĕkahănô-lî*]" (Exod 28:2–3; cf. Lev 8:30). The reference to Yahweh's radiant *kābôd*, a key feature of P's theology of divine presence, is hard to miss.[127] Writing on the ideology of ritual performance, Gorman (1990: 118) astutely puts emphasis here on "*the act of clothing*" and how it "serves as a marker of Aaron's passage to his new status." Visually, Aaron's "holy vestments" (*bigdê-qōdeš*) "give tangible evidence of his changed position in society and serve as a symbol of his unique status." In short, the ritual clothing of Aaron is an act of investiture that formally bestows and confirms the authority due his rank.

As for the holy garments per se, every one of them marks the privileged position of the high priest in expense and in function.[128] That the expenditure of resources (materials and workmanship) correlates with rank is on full display with the four outer garments worn only by the high priest, in contrast to the undergarments worn by all priests.[129] These four include the holy *ṣîṣ nēzer* diadem (Exod 28:36–38; 39:30–31; Lev 8:9), the *ḥōšen* breastpiece (Exod 28:15–30; 39:8–21; Lev 8:8; Num 27:21), the ephod (Exod 28:6–12; 39:2–7; Lev 8:7), and the robe (Exod 28:31–35; 39:22–26; Lev 8:7). The materials used include pure gold (*zāhāb ṭāhôr*), gold, hammered gold leaf, twelve engraved precious stones (for the *ḥōšen*), two engraved onyx stones, gold bells, pomegranates (jewelry?), and richly embroidered and colored wool and linen. As astutely noted by Menahem Haran (1985: 210), "in quality, materials, and workmanship" the high priest's garments "are correlated with the inner curtains of the tabernacle and the golden vessels within it," whereas regular priestly garments "are correlated with the hangings and curtains of the court."

The functions associated with Aaron's vestments also mark his elevated authority and status. It is when Aaron performs the rites that are his sole prerogative that he dons "the garments of gold and linen-wool mixture which he alone may wear" (Haran 1985: 211). The pure gold *ṣîṣ nēzer-haqqōdeš* diadem on which is engraved "Holy to Yahweh" (*qōdeš lyhwh*) is ever present (*tāmîd*) on Aaron's forehead as he carries out his elite mediation role on behalf of the people.[130] Propp (2006: 448) goes so far as to suggest that this engraving marks Aaron as "Yahweh's major domo," who possesses "the greatest sanctity to which a mere human can attain." The function of the high priest's ephod with its "breastpiece of judgment" (*ḥōšen mišpāṭ*; Exod 28:15, 29) is equally elite. The breastpiece contains the divinatory Urim and Thummim, which, according to P, only the high priest may employ when he enters into "the holy [sanctuary]" (*haqqōdeš*; Exod 28:29–30; but cf. Num 27:21).[131] As for the robe with its gold bells, it too is worn only by the high priest as he enters into the most holy recesses of the temple. Here again the rationale given ("so that he may not die") underscores his unique privilege to approach holy divinity, lethal though it may be.[132]

Along with the social markings of status, power, and privilege that clothing provides, for P there is a vital theological tenet. This is seen in the all-important Day of Atonement/Purgation (*yôm kippûr*), which focuses considerable attention on the ritual acts of washing and clothing (Lev 16:4)—and the act of disrobing (Lev 16:23)—to mark the entry into and out of "the Holy" (*haqqōdeš*). According to Leviticus 16:2, "the Holy" is a reference to physical space (the inner shrine with its veiled Ark and its *kappōret*) and to the place of clouded theophany with its potential lethality. The clothes that Aaron wears to enter "the Holy" are appropriately designated "holy vestments" (*bigdê-qōdeš*). His tunic is a "holy linen tunic" (*kĕtōnet-bad qōdeš*). The vestments are made of linen (Lev 16:4) to mark his subservience before God, in contrast to the previously mentioned ornate golden vestments that mark his elevated status before humans. Milgrom (1991: 1016), following Talmudic tradition, notes how angels are mentioned wearing linen in their "ministration on high" (cf. Ezek 9:2–3, 11; 10:2; Dan 10:5), and thus Aaron's garb is fitting, for "entry into the adytum is equivalent to admission to the heavenly council."

Yet even in a passage that marks Aaron's subservience before Yahweh, there remain markers of his elevated authority and status vis-à-vis other humans. Leviticus 16:26–28 describes those who assist with the scapegoat ritual (cf. the *'îš 'ittî* in Lev 16:21)[133] and the burning of the bull and goat *ḥaṭṭā't* offerings. Only the laundering (*kbs*) of the clothing of these individuals is mentioned (Lev 16:26, 28), unlike Aaron's ritual clothing and disrobing. For these minor figures, the handling of their clothing is purificatory only (note too their ritual washings). Though they too necessarily had to put on and take off their clothing, there is no mention of the ritual act of clothing (and disrobing) to mark investiture and divestiture, as there is with Aaron, who alone is granted the privilege of temporarily entering "the Holy" as he approaches the Unapproachable.

Finally, underscoring the ritual act of clothing, the appendix found in Leviticus 16:29–34 distills P's instructions about the Day of Atonement/Purgation rituals "for all time" (*wěhāyětâ lākem lěḥuqqat ʿôlām*) in order to promote the authority and status of the current ruling priesthood. To summarize: the high priest (who has been anointed and ordained to his hereditary office [*lěkahēn taḥat ʾābîw*]) "shall put on the linen vestments, the holy vestments" in order to effect purgation (Lev 16:32).

The High Priest Aaron and His Priestly Sons: The Ritual Act of Anointing

This brings us to the way in which the ritual act of anointing (*mšḥ*) served to consecrate (cf. Gorman 1990: 118–121). Cornelis Houtman (1992; 2000: 574–587) has articulated the way in which "holy anointing oil" (*šemen mišḥat-qōdeš*) and a specialized mixture of incense with spices that makes it pure and "most holy" (*qěṭōret . . . qōdeš qodāšîm*) are sensory markers of sacred space (see Exod 30:22–38; 37:29).[134] Such sacred oil and pure incense are reserved for Yahweh alone, to mark his "special fragrance," which "becomes an expression of his personality" (1992: 462, 465; 2000: 575). Every space and every object associated with Yahweh's presence (Tent of Meeting, Ark of the Covenant, incense altar, altar of offerings, table, lampstand, utensils, basin) must be "consecrated" with divine aroma (Exod 30:26–29). Once consecrated—and thus being made "most holy" (*wěqiddaštā ʾōtām wěhāyû qōdeš qodāšîm*)—these objects possess holy contagion for anyone who handles them (Exod 29:37; 30:29).[135] Thus officiants too must be consecrated with holy oil (Exod 30:30). The exquisite quality of these fragrances and their restricted use mark elevated status for those whom Yahweh allows to enter his "atmospheric curtain" by "imparting" his fragrance to them (Houtman 1992: 463–464; 2000: 575). The seriousness of these holy fragrances being used for Yahweh alone is emphasized in Exodus 30:32–33, 38, where any individual who uses them for ordinary cosmetics is cut off from the people.

The P traditions provide three windows into priestly anointing, found in Exodus 29, Leviticus 8–9, and Exodus 40.[136] The beginning of Exodus 29 is similar to Exodus 28:1 in that it starts with Yahweh's ritual instructions to Moses about what he is to do to Aaron and his sons to consecrate them for priestly service (*lěqaddēš ʾōtām lěkahēn lî*; Exod 29:1). As Exodus 29 begins, so it ends, with

Yahweh's proclamation: "I will consecrate Aaron and his sons to serve me as priests" (*'et 'ahărōn wĕ'et-bānāyw 'ăqaddēš lĕkahēn lî*; Exod 29:44). The content of the chapter reveals how anointing is a core aspect of the consecration process (see items 3 and 6 in the following list), and yet it is not done in isolation. Rather, it is part of a complex system of rituals and instructions that include the following fourteen components:

1. The securing and transporting of sacrificial animals and unleavened foods (29:1b–3)
2. The ritual transport, washing, and garbing of Aaron and his sons (29:1–6, 8–9a)
3. The special anointing ritual for Aaron (29:7)
4. The particulars of the bull sacrifice (e.g., location, blood manipulation; 29:10–14), including the effectual priestly transference of sins via hand-laying (29:10)[137]
5. The particulars of the first ram sacrifice (e.g., blood manipulation, dismemberment, complete burning; 29:15–18), including the effectual priestly transference of sins (29:15)
6. The particulars of the second *millu'îm* ("filling" → "ordination"?) ram sacrifice (e.g., blood manipulation; 29:19–21), including the effectual priestly transference of sins (29:19) and a special anointing of the priests and their garments with oil *and blood* from the altar (29:21)
7. Additional *millu'îm* ram rituals, which together with unleavened bread constitute priestly *tĕnûpâ* offerings, which then become a fire offering (29:22–25)
8. Additional *tĕnûpâ* instructions with regard to priestly portions (29:26–28)
9. The use of Aaron's holy garments and succession (29:29–30)
10. The priests' privileged eating of the "holy" *millu'îm* ram and unleavened bread, which functions as an atoning (*kuppar*)[138] means of ordination and consecration (*lĕmallē' 'et-yādām lĕqaddēš 'ōtām*) (29:31–34)
11. A summary statement mentioning a seven-day ordination ritual and the atonement function of the bull sin offering (*ḥaṭṭā't . . . 'al-hakkippurîm* 29:35–36a)
12. Instructions for carrying out a sin offering to effect atonement for the altar, whose resulting holiness is contagious (29:36b–37)
13. Additional instructions regarding the perpetual nature of the altar offerings (29:38–42a)
14. Yahweh's promise to meet with and speak to his people as he dwells among them at the Tent of Meeting; the "consecrated" Tent of Meeting and altar with its "consecrated" priests (29:44) will ultimately be sanctified by the very presence of Yahweh's *kābôd* (*wĕniqdaš bikĕbōdî*; 29:43)[139]

Where Exodus 29 is instructional in nature, the narrative in Leviticus 8–9 articulates the process. Moses faithfully carries out Yahweh's designs for the consecration and ordination of Aaron and his sons. Detailed mention is made of Moses securing the relevant parties (priests and people) and ritual ingredients (oil, sacrificial animals, and unleavened bread) at a sacred location (the entrance of the Tent of Meeting) (Lev 8:1–4). Moses' ritual washing of the priests (Lev 8:6; cf. Exod 29.4) and ritual garbing of Aaron are described with step-by-step precision. The latter recounts each particular vestment (tunic, sash, robe, ephod, decorated band, breastpiece, Urim and Thummim, headdress, gold frontlet) and each particular mode of dressing (putting on, fastening/girding, clothing, tying, setting), including an exclusive use of a denominative verb (*ʾpd*) formed from the word *ʾēpōd* (Lev 8:7–9; cf. Exod 29:5–6).

The anointing procedure begins with Moses anointing the Tabernacle (*miškān*) and its paraphernalia as an act of consecration (Lev 8:10–11), a feature found elsewhere in P (Exod 40:9; Num 7:1) but not in Exodus 29.[140] Leviticus 8:11 also mentions anointing the altar, as does Exodus 29:36 (cf. Exod 40:10), yet the former does so seven times.[141] Turning to Aaron, we find the same elite practice of pouring oil on his head that was described in Exodus 29:7, though the Leviticus narrative explicitly underscores how this too was *an act of consecration* (*wayyiṣōq miššemen hammišḥâ ʿal rōʾš ʾahărōn . . . lĕqaddĕšô*; Lev 8:12; cf. Lev 21:10; Ps 133:2). Though the narrative is arranged differently than in Exodus 29, Leviticus 8:30 also mentions the surprising anointing of the priests and their garments with oil *and blood* from the altar (cf. Exod 29:21). Blood from the *milluʾîm* ram is also used in both narratives to mark the right ears, thumbs, and big toes of Aaron and his sons (Lev 8:23–24; Exod 29:20) and to land on the altar (Lev 8:19, 24; Exod 29:16, 20).[142] In addition, Leviticus 8 includes the priestly transference of sins via hand-laying (cf. Lev 8:14, 18, 22; cf. Exod 29:10, 15, 19) as well as the atonement (*kpr*) function of various ritual actions (Lev 8:15, 34; 9:7; cf. Exod 29:33, 36–37).[143]

The subtle differences between Exodus 29:31–37 and Leviticus 8:31–35 are fascinating. Each of these sections deals with the priestly eating of a portion of the "ordination" (*milluʾîm*) ram. Distinctively, Exodus 29 emphasizes the "holy" nature of the food to be eaten (29:33–34), giving the rationale that this is "the food by which atonement is made in order to ordain and consecrate" the Aaronid priests (*wĕʾākĕlû ʾōtām ʾăšer kuppar bāhem lĕmallēʾ ʾet-yādām lĕqaddēš ʾōtām*; Exod 29:33). A telling exclusionary command then appears: "an 'outsider' [*zār*] shall not eat [of the food] for it is holy." It is curious that Leviticus 8 is silent on this matter, especially in light of the severe concern about "the outsider" (*hazzār*) making priestly approach (with resulting death penalty) found elsewhere in P (Num 3:10; Num 18:7).[144]

Exodus 29:36–37 also emphasizes a seven-day consecration ritual for the altar involving sacrificial atonement and anointing (cf. Ezek 43:18–27). As a result, the altar is "most holy" and a vehicle of holy contagion. Though Leviticus 8:11 echoes the anointing and consecrating of the altar that we find in Exodus 29:36—and with an added sevenfold emphasis—the rest of Leviticus 8 does not include an explicit seven-day altar ritual.[145] Instead, Leviticus 8:33–35 preserves an explicit seven-day segregation for the priests that is totally lacking in Exodus 29:35, which mentions only a generic seven-day ordination. The Leviticus perspective here makes much of this segregation process, both how it takes a full seven days and nights for the atonement/ordination process to be completed and how violation of the stated procedure will result in the priests' death (Lev 8:35). Milgrom (1991: 538, 568–569) and Lester Grabbe (2003: 213 n. 12) understand this as following the classic presentation of a rite of passage whereby the person transitioning from one stage to another finds himself in a potentially dangerous liminal state that requires ritual precautions.[146] One might think that the end of the segregation on the eighth day would ensure safety (cf. Lev 9), yet—as vividly demonstrated in Leviticus 10:1–3—when one approaches the divine with its holy power, lethality can strike whenever there is a failure to carry out the requisite ritual performance.[147]

Anointing: Ritual Manner Designating Rank—Pouring Versus Sprinkling
The manner in which the anointing ritual is performed demarcates social and cultic status. Aaron alone as high priest is anointed (*mšḥ*) in his person with the *pouring* (*yṣq*) of anointing oil (*šemen hammišḥâ*) on his head (Lev 8:12; Exod 29:7). Leviticus 8:12 is explicit in describing this bodily rite as consecratory (*qdš*). Elsewhere in the Hebrew Bible, the pouring of oil on the head as an anointing ritual is elite, used only of Yahweh marking royalty (Saul as *nāgîd* in 1 Sam 10:1; Jehu as *melek* in 2 Kgs 9:3, 6).[148] The elite pouring rite used to elevate Aaron contrasts with a sprinkling (*nzh*) ritual used to mark lesser priests (also using anointing oil) as they are garbed in priestly vestments (Exod 29:21; Lev 8:30). This sprinkling ritual is also viewed as consecratory (*qdš*; Exod 29:21b; Lev 8:30b). To make certain that this sprinkling ritual is not seen in any way as privileging these lesser priests above Aaron, both passages point out that Aaron as priest is also accorded this rite.

As orderly as this hierarchy seems, other traditions add texture and perhaps hints of conflict. One tradition underscores the importance of the high priest by referring to "*the* anointed priest" (singular) (*hakkōhēn hammāšîaḥ*; Lev 4:3, 5; cf. Exod 29:7; 40:13; Lev 6:13, 15 [Eng 6:20, 22]; 8:12; 16; 21:10), whereas another underscores the importance of distributed authority by referring to "the anointed priests" (plural) (*hakkōhănîm hammĕšuḥîm*; Num 3:3; Exod 30:30; Lev

7:36; 10:7).[149] The former tradition emphasizes how the high priest "is greater than his brothers" (*hakkōhēn haggādôl mēʾeḥāyw*). The latter tradition stresses the legitimation of Aaron's sons and succession (cf. Exod 40:13–15). They are anointed to be Yahweh's priests "as was *their father* (Aaron),"and such anointing serves to mark "a perpetual priesthood for their future generations" (*likěhunnat ʿôlām lědōrōtām*; Exod 40:15; cf. Lev 16:32; Num 3:10).

While these two perspectives can be harmonized, Levine (1993: 155) prefers to see "two discrete traditions or viewpoints" that present "alternative view[s] of the Israelite priesthood," when it comes to "the status of the high priest." See too Fleming's (1998: 408–409, 412, 414) suggestion of "independent origins for the two anointing rites," "truly separate cultic offices," and "two separate priestly heritages." Both Levine and Fleming are responding to the foundational work of Martin Noth (1984: 237–240), to which we now turn.

The Demise of Martin Noth's Royal Interpretation

As already noted, the manner of Aaron's priestly anointing (pouring oil on the head) resonates with royal anointing. Privileging the latter, Noth (1984: 237–240) developed an influential reconstruction that asserted that priestly anointing was not a phenomenon of the pre-exilic period.[150] Rather, for Noth and many who followed him, anointing was an "institution of kingship [and] from there it was passed on to the post-exilic high priest" due to his "special *royal* status" (emphasis mine). For Noth, "the act of anointing did not originally belong to the office of priest ... anointing enters the Old Testament tradition with the monarchy." For comparative support for his royal scenario, Noth (1984: 239) looked to the Syro-Hittite realm. Subsequent comparative study has revealed the narrowness of Noth's perspective. As Fleming has shown, "anointing was an essential part of everyday life in the ancient Near East" and involved a wide variety of social actors and social transactions (e.g., kings, priests, prophets, brides, merchants, parties conducting property obligations).[151] Anointing functioned in a variety of ways, from marking social bonding to a change in social status.

As for priestly anointing, the Syro-Hittite realm to which Noth appealed now undermines his royal argument. Milgrom (1991: 519, 554), following Harry Hoffner, has pointed out that both Hittite priests and kings were anointed, with the former even being referred to as "the anointed" (*tazzelli* = Sum $GUDU_4$ = Akk *pašišu*). From Late Bronze Age Syria, the relevant texts come from Emar, an outpost city on the southeastern edge of the Hittite empire.[152] One of the city's most important indigenous rituals involved a two-day anointing of the high priestess of the storm god at Emar (NIN.DINGIR ^{d}IM) as part of a fuller nine-day installation rite that has references to "days of sanctification."[153] Mention is made of the recipients of cult (the gods of Emar), the lead officiant and his payment (the diviner, shekels of silver), additional personnel, the ritual substance (fragrant oil), its place of procurement (temple of the goddess ᵈNIN.KUR and palace), method, location (at the gate of the storm god), timing (daily markers, evening), and associated rituals (lot casting, animal sacrifice of oxen and sheep, offerings of breadstuffs and liquid [esp. wine], shaving ceremony). Of note for our present discussion is that anointing the priestess involves pouring oil on her head. Thus, as Fleming (1998: 401–402) notes, "the ancient Near Eastern evidence does not sustain a late evolution from the preexilic anointing of kings to the postexilic use of the rite for priests." In addition, the priestess undergoes anointing on two different occasions (cf. Aaron) and as a part of a much larger complex of rituals that includes sacrifice.[154] Thus what we read in Exodus 29 and Leviticus 8—while constituting P's literary portrayal of priestly consecration—is nonetheless woven out of a historical conceptual fabric. While there are elements that are "idealized" or "utopian" (cf. Grabbe 2003: 215–224), Fleming's (1998: 412) nuanced wording provides a nice balance: "These should not be regarded as ritual texts in the sense of having full correspondence to actual practice . . . but they are the work of professionals familiar with both ritual and its recording."

Anointing: Ritual Substance—Oil and Blood

Prior to leaving these texts on priestly anointing, we must revisit the two references to the anointing of the priests and their garments with oil and blood from the altar (Lev 8:30; Exod 29:21). Until recently, the unlikely mixture of these two substances was unknown outside of our Hebrew texts. Anointing with oil is common, yet the use of blood typically points to an altogether different ritual event (sacrifice) with altogether different ritual functions. E. E. Evans-Pritchard has tabulated fourteen possible motivations underlying sacrifice ("communion, gift, apotropaic rite, bargain, exchange, ransom, elimination, expulsion, purification, expiation, propitiation, substitution, abnegation, homage"), none of them involving anointing.[155]

As first pointed out by Fleming (1998), here too Late Bronze Age Emar provides our closest comparative data with its highly important *zukru* festival. The *zukru* festival is fascinating in that we have variant traditions ranging from a short annual rite focused on a single day to an elaborate seven-day festival planned a full year in advance.[156] The former has no human actors and minor mention of organized offerings by "the city," while the latter is as expansive as it is expensive, with offerings for all the gods of the city (about ninety in number) and with the palace and king picking up the majority of the cost. One cannot miss how the festival underscores royal patronage and benevolence. Yet, curiously, the king has no active role in the ritual, contrary to expectations (for kings are the primary religious officiants in the ancient Near East). What is important for our present concern is an anointing ritual that occurs in both short and long versions. Surprisingly, it involves the use of oil and blood (Ì^{meš} ÚŠ^{meš}) rubbed on standing stones (*sikkānu*) that seem to function as divine images.[157] As Fleming (1998: 410) notes, of all the many anointing rituals attested in the ancient Near East, the distinctive mixture of oil and blood occurs only in Emar's *zukru* festival and the anointing of the priests and their vestments in Exodus 29:21 and Leviticus 8:30.

While it would be tempting to draw direct parallels between the Emar texts and the biblical texts due to the ritual nature of both corpora (cf. Hess 2007b: 112–123), proper comparative methodology—where differences are highlighted along with similarities—suggests that we proceed with caution. While Emar does have the anointing of a priestly figure similar to Exodus 29 and Leviticus 8 (and with the same manner of pouring oil on the head), Emar's officiant is a priestess rather than a priest. While Emar does attest indigenous West Semitic ritual practices (no such rites are attested in Mesopotamia), they are set against a historical backdrop of thirteenth-century BCE Hittite hegemony that is a world apart from P's historical context. While some of the installation rituals at Emar resonate with Exodus 29 and Leviticus 8 (e.g., priestly anointing with oil, sacrifice), there are just as many rites that diverge (e.g., lot casting, wine offerings, shaving ceremony). And while the *zukru* festival at Emar does attest both oil and blood being used as anointing substances, they are rubbed onto standing stones as opposed to the biblical sprinkling on priests and their garments. Functionally, Fleming (2000: 83) argues that the *zukru* anointing is not a rite of "consecrat[ing] the stones as new cult objects, since it is repeated at the end of the festival as well as during the sixth year." While Yitzhaq Feder (2011: 121) does allow for the Emar anointing "to endow the object with a level of sanctity," he, like Fleming, notes how the repetitive nature of the rite points away from consecration and toward "the preparation for the passage of Dagan between the stones." Patrick Michel (2013: 192) concurs: "The unction cannot then be considered as a consecration rite."

If not for consecration, then what was the purpose of the anointing of the standing stones in the *zukru* festival? Fleming (1998: 410; 2000: 86–87) understands the ritual as "a form of cultic care" whereby "the stones [representing the collected gods] are anointed in preparation for the moment of meeting" the god Dagan as he (via his divine image) proceeds from the city to their rural locale. Upon arrival, Dagan "passes between them to receive their homage," and, as a result, "the cults of two domains salute and establish a basis for continuity." For Fleming (2000: 97), this is "the ritual center of the *zukru*, the reason for [Dagan, the pantheon head] leaving the city for a shrine of upright stones." Michel's (2013: 196) reconstruction is similar: "The *Zukrum* should primarily be the moment when [the anthropomorphic statue of] Dagan meets his own [aniconic] stone, in front of all the deities." Clearly, for our purposes, the similarities of Emar's anointing of standing stones with oil and blood are outweighed by the manifold differences with P's use of the two substances for his priestly consecration ritual.

The Ritual Act of Anointing: Consecratory Expiation
We are still left with trying to ascertain the full meaning of the anointing of the priests and their garments with oil and blood in Exodus 29:21 and Leviticus 8:30. Both texts are clear that this ritual action results in officiants and vestments being made holy (*qdš*). As noted earlier, the anointing with oil is common (cf. Exod 30:22–30). It is the additional anointing with blood that is remarkable.

When both passages mention the blood, they point back to the altar: "You shall take [Then Moses took] some of *the blood that is on the altar*" (Exod 29:21a; Lev 8:30). Thus here is where we need to look. Leviticus 8:10–11 and Exodus 40:9–10 explicitly mention the anointing of the altar with "anointing oil" (*šemen hammišḥâ*), and Exodus 29:36 implicitly says the same. As for blood, the altar undergoes a cleansing rite ($\sqrt{ḥṭ'}$) by means of the sin (*ḥaṭṭā't*) sacrifice and as part of a complex process of purgation/expiation (*kpr*) and consecration (*qdš*) (Lev 8:15; Exod 29:36; cf. Feder 2011: 49–50, 99–105). When this altar blood is then used for priestly anointing, it must carry with it a related effectual power. As for the mechanism by which blood can have both expiatory and consecratory power, Milgrom (1991: 533–534) appeals to the principle of holy contagion as expressed in Exodus 29:37b: "As soon as the blood impinges upon the altar it partakes of its holiness and is then able to impart holiness to others." "The sacrificial blood is sanctified; only consecrated blood can consecrate."[158]

Holy Personnel: Restriction and Expansion (P and H)

Up to this point, we have been concentrating our discussion on the ways that P conceptualizes holy personnel. For P, priesthood (*kĕhunnâ*) is an elite Aaronid office. Consecrated Aaron—being marked with uniquely "radiant" vestments (Exod 28:2–3) and an exclusive anointing ritual—is the "father figure," and only his loins produce legitimate priestly descendants. Time and again we read in P of "Aaron and his sons" (Exod 27:21; 29:4, 9–10, 15, 19, 28, 32, 35, 44; 30:19, 30; 39:27; 40:12, 31; Lev 2:3, 10; 6:9, 16, 20; 7:31; 8:2, 6, 14, 18, 22, 31, 36; 9:1; 24:9; Num 3:9, 10, 38, 48, 51; 4:5, 15, 19, 27; 8:19). For P, the Aaronid priesthood is an exclusive "gift" (*mattānâ*) directly given by Yahweh (Num 18:7). Moreover, its legitimacy should never be challenged, for Yahweh proclaimed their priesthood to be "a perpetual ordinance" that is valid "for all generations to come" (*kĕhunnâ lĕḥuqqat 'ôlām/likĕhunnat 'ôlām lĕdōrōtām*; Exod 29:9; 40:15; cf. Exod 27:21; Num 25:13). As we have documented, P uses every aspect of the ritual ingredients and ritual performance to construct and reinforce the status, power, and privilege of the consecrated Aaronid priesthood. (On ritual space, see discussion later.) In particular, William Gilders (2004: 103–104) emphasizes the way in which the manipulation of blood during the ordination rituals serves to index the Aaronids as holy. As a result, they possess "an existential relationship" with the altar, which they alone are privileged to access.

Expansive Holiness in the Holiness Source (H)

H conceptualizes the situation quite differently.[159] Knohl (1995: 180–186) looks to Leviticus 19 to articulate H's "striking expression" of inclusive holiness. H's succinct rhetoric with its plural imperative in Leviticus 19:2 (cf. Lev 11:1–2a, 44–45; 20:1, 7–8; 20:26; Num 15:40) could not be more powerful.[160] Yahweh instructs Moses:

> Speak to the entire congregation of the people of Israel and say to them: "Be holy, for I, Yahweh your God, am holy" [*qĕdōšîm tihyû kî qādôš 'ănî yhwh 'ĕlōhêkem*]. (Lev 19:2)

When juxtaposed against P's restrictive Aaronid holiness, this expansive view of sanctity is indeed striking. Leviticus 19 then provides a comprehensive list of instructions that are to be followed by the collective community (all the verbs are plural) to achieve holiness. The remarkable contrast with P's cult-oriented holiness could not be more noticeable. Leviticus 19's "laws of holiness" includes a wide variety of social, cultic, judicial, economic, and moral topics: revering one's parents, Sabbath observance, idolatry, acceptable *šĕlāmîm* sacrifices, reaping with the marginalized in mind, theft, lying, false swearing, fraud, concern for the deaf and blind, just legal renderings, slander, interpersonal relationships and neighborly love, improper mixtures, sexual relations, moratorium on harvesting fruit, diet, divination, tonsure rites, bloodletting, tattooing, prostitution, reverence of the sanctuary, false intermediaries, the elderly, the non-Israelite resident, and business ethics (Lev 19:3–36).

Fifteen times in this single chapter—more occurrences here than anywhere else in the entire Hebrew Bible—we find divine self-declarations ("I am Yahweh" or "I am Yahweh, your God") interlaced with the commands to undertake a life of holiness. This interlacing identifies Yahweh's personhood with his commands, which are expressions of his holy character. His relational identifier ("*your* God") binds Yahweh with the community, which is to carry out the laws of holiness as they relate one to another. Thus Leviticus 19, verse by verse, unpacks its opening and closing *imitatio Dei* admonitions: "Be holy, for I, Yahweh your God, am holy" (Lev 19:2); "Keep all my statutes and all my ordinances and observe them; I am Yahweh" (Lev 19:37). Leviticus 19 is framed by two additional chapters (Lev 18, 20) where H also has the holiness of the entire community in view. Twice more Yahweh explicitly instructs his people to consecrate themselves to living a holy life due to their relationship with (and imitation of) him and his holiness (Lev 20:7, 26). As much as the people themselves do so, symbiotically it is Yahweh himself who carries out the process of sanctification (*'ănî yhwh měqaddiškem*; Lev 20:7-8; cf. 21:8). Additionally, these two chapters address ethnic identity, especially by using the C stem of √*bdl* to relate the people's "distinguished/separated" practices (above all with regard to diet) to how Yahweh "distinguished/separated" them from their neighbors. Yahweh did so, says H, in order that they might be marked as his possession (Lev 20:24b-26; cf. Lev 10:10; 11:47).

Though H in Leviticus 19:30 does indeed promote reverence for the sanctuary (*miqdāšî tîrā'û*), when it comes to the place where holiness is to be practiced, here too H is expansive. Holiness is to be carried out wherever the people live their lives. The same can be said of sacred time. Rather than it being solely tied to a cultic calendar, for H the people are to practice holiness continuously.

The Priesthood in H

H's expansive holiness does not mean that he disregards the elevated role of the Aaronid priesthood and its vital role in mediating holiness within sacred space and time. H devotes two detailed chapters (Lev 21-22) to priestly regulations. H proclaims how the high priest who holds Aaron's office "is greater than his brothers" (*hakkōhēn haggādôl mē'eḥāyw*). He is marked by the pouring rite of anointing and by unique vestments (Lev 21:10, 12). His level of sanctity must be the highest possible, so extreme measures are in force with regard to his hair, garments, marriage, and defilement (Lev 21:10-15). For example, he is not even allowed to leave the sanctuary for his own parents' funeral lest he return with the impurity arising from corpse contamination (Lev 21:11-12).

Though the Aaronid priests are included in the comprehensive "laws of holiness" that apply to the community at large and all aspects of social engagement, they are marked with an additional level of sanctity. They are the focus of increased regulations with regard to defilement, tonsure, and marriage. H's rationale for their elevated level of sanctity is given in Leviticus 21:1-8:

> Yahweh said to Moses: Speak to the priests, the sons of Aaron, and say to them: [Defilement ordinances and tonsure regulations specific to priests.] They shall be holy to their God [*qědōšîm yihyû lē'lōhêhem*], and not profane the name of their God; for they offer Yahweh's offerings by fire,[161] the food of their God; therefore they shall be holy [*wěhāyû qōdeš*]. [Increased marriage regulations.] For they are holy to their God [*kî-qādōš hû' lē'lōhāyw*], and you shall treat them

as holy [wĕqiddaštô], since they offer the food of your God; they shall be holy to you, for I Yahweh, I who sanctify you [plural], am holy [qādōš yihyeh-lāk kî qādôš 'ănî yhwh mĕqaddiškem]. (Lev 21:1–8)

As Knohl (1995: 192) observes, this "highest grade of holiness," "in which Israelites [at large] and Levites may not participate," is that which "emanat[es] from the cult." The specific cultic act is mentioned twice: approaching Yahweh on behalf of the people to offer their sacrifices via fire. Elsewhere H unpacks what is terse here. The priests are charged with incinerating the offerings, producing the smoke that is a "pleasing aroma" (rêyaḥ nîḥōaḥ) to Yahweh (Num 28:2).[162] The logic is clear: the Aaronid priests have to adhere to additional regulations to increase their level of sanctity if they are to approach the Holy One with proper cult. Significantly, they then do so using fire as the means by which the offerings are made acceptable to Yahweh. Christian Eberhart (2011: 28) speaks of this as "a process of transforming the material offering into a new, ethereal essence during the burning rite." In sum, holy priests using fire are allowed entry to Yahweh, the Holy One, who manifests his presence and power most often via fire (see Chapter Seven, pp. 344–358).

Additional priestly regulations (having to do with priestly blemishes) are then pronounced in Leviticus 21:16–23, again raising the restrictive bar higher for Aaronids who make approach (qrb; ngš) to make offerings to Yahweh. Concerns about priestly provisions, simply called "holy [foods]" (qodāšîm), are addressed in detail with regard to restrictive states of impurity (Lev 22:1–9).[163] As with blemishes, H understands the economics of the situation, for such "holy [foods]" were the chief means of the priests' sustenance. Priests with blemishes or those in states of impurity are allowed (for the latter after purificatory washings and waiting until the evening) to eat of the "holy [provisions]" (Lev 21:12; 22:6–7). Economics are also in view with regard to priestly families (and slaves acquired into priestly households), as the possibility of their eating the holy food under certain conditions is then pronounced (Lev 22:10–16). The notion of a priest's holy status extending to his family reminds us of the bonds of family religion (see Chapter Eight).

P's Expansive Holiness: Temporary Nazirite Vows for Women and Men

H's expansive notion of a broadly defined holiness for the entire community does indeed stand in stark contrast to P's narrow concentration on the cultic holiness of the Aaronid priesthood. Yet P's restrictive focus should not be taken to mean that P has no mechanism for non-priests who desire a higher level of sanctity. For P, non-priests, both men *and women*, are able to achieve a level of holy distinction by becoming Nazirites.

Limited data make any reconstruction of the Nazirites provisional.[164] Several passages suggest that the institution has an old pedigree, and the early nature of the Nazirites is quite different from P's formulation. Their storied history includes tribal references to Joseph as well as the episodes about Samson and Samuel. In two parallel poetic blessings, Joseph is said to be "the *nāzîr* of his brothers" (Gen 49:26; Deut 33:16). There is no indication of what secures his status as the *nāzîr*. Curiously missing is any votive language that typifies Nazirite narratives elsewhere. Joseph's status is an elevated one, judging from the related noun *nezer*, "crown," and how the blessing comes upon his head (cf. the anointing of elite personnel on their head). Some scholars have suggested a "consecrated" status, though there is no indication of any cultic role for Joseph.[165] Such a portrayal would make sense only if broadly construed (e.g., how God used Joseph to bring about his will in Gen 50:20; thus de Hoop 1999: 217). For a clearer cultic use of the root *nzr* elsewhere, compare the devotees who "became *nāzîr* of Baal" (*yinnāzĕrû labbōšet*) at Baal-Peor as portrayed in Hosea 9:10.[166]

We have more distinct information regarding Samson and Samuel as Nazirites. In each case we read of a mother dedicating her son to be a lifelong Nazirite prior to his birth. (Note again the primacy of family religion and with women in primary roles.) Samson's mother's dedication is described as the result of a preternatural visitor (the fiery *mal'ak*-Yahweh) who instructs her to do so.[167] The mention of Samson being "a *nāzîr* of God" is explicitly described in Judges 13:5, 7 and 16:17. Judges 13:7 underscores the lifelong commitment (*min-habbeṭen 'ad-yôm môtô*). Samuel's mother's dedication is expressed as a vow (*neder*) should Yahweh bless her with a long-desired son (1 Sam 1:11, 22).[168] In its fullest formulation (see discussion of P later), a vow to be a Nazirite involves a threefold abstinence: (1) refraining from cutting one's hair, (2) avoiding intoxicants (probably even all products of viticulture; cf. Judg 13:14; Amos 2:11–12; Num 6:4) and unclean food, and (3) avoiding any contact with a corpse. Only the first applies to Samson; curiously and significantly, it is his mother who is the observant devotee abstaining from products of viticulture and impure food (Judg 13:4, 7, 14; cf. Levine 1993: 230). In Samuel's case, the uncut hair provision is clear, as with Samson, while the intoxicant stipulation depends on one's textual criticism.[169] Neither the Samson tradition nor the Samuel tradition mentions corpse contamination.

In Numbers 6, P's reformulation of whatever Nazirite traditions he inherited is distinct and transformative. P clearly states that this is a consecrated (though temporary) vocation (Num 6:5, 8). Mayer (1998: 307) argues that the verb *nzr* refers to consecration and thus P's *nāzîr* can be translated "consecrated one." The Septuagint translator(s) of Numbers 6:1–21 would certainly agree, for "as a rule, we find a derivative of *hagi*- . . . or *hagn*-" to render these terms. In Numbers 6:6–12, P adds a third abstinence condition for Nazirites (a strict avoidance of corpse contamination) that is found nowhere else. As many have noted, this prohibition closely tracks that of the high priest (cf. Num 6:6–8 with H's Lev 21:11–12). Note especially how each passage mentions close family members and how "the *nēzer* consecration of God" is on their respective heads, though the high priest alone is marked by anointing oil (*nēzer ʾĕlōhāyw ʿal-rōʾšô*; Num 6:8; *nēzer šemen mišḥat ʾĕlōhāyw ʿālāyw*; Lev 21:12). Lastly, it is not a coincidence that the "holy diadem" placed on the high priest's head and engraved "Holy to Yahweh" is called a *nēzer haqqōdeš* (Exod 29:6; 39:30; Lev 8:9).

So, what is P up to with his portrayal of the Nazirites' vow and their regulations? It seems that P is anticipating what H fleshes out on a broader societal scale. Though the Aaronid priesthood is preeminently and restrictively holy with its offering of cult, allowances must be provided for people at large who desire higher levels of sanctity and want to be recognized for such. Of special note is how the office of the Nazirite is open to *women* who have no other cultic role in P's scheme (*ʾîš ʾô-ʾiššâ kî yapliʾ lindōr neder nāzîr lĕhazzîr lĕ-yhwh*; Num 6:1).

P's mechanism to satisfy this desire is to provide for an elevated, holy office that is publicly recognized. Social awareness comes from the practitioners making a public vow and their subsequent adherence to the three abstinences noted earlier. The nature of a vow (*neder*) and the difficulty of the threefold abstinence (along with legislation for their violation; Num 6:9–12) adds to the solemnity of the vocation. Public recognition is especially facilitated by what we read in Numbers 6:13–21 that describes rituals at the end of a Nazirite's period of observance. Here again we see how ritual practice constructs and reinforces social realities and hierarchies. The Nazirites are ceremonially brought in procession to sacred space (Num 6:13). Their provisions of multiple offerings (three unblemished rams, various foodstuffs, wine, oil) underscore their economic and social standing along with their piety (Num 6:14–15). The acceptance of these offerings by the deity, to borrow the rite's technical vocabulary, facilitates a wholesome "well-being" (*šĕlāmîm*) between Yahweh and the Nazirite (Num 6:16–17). A solemn handling of the body follows, with two deconsecrating tonsure rites: the shaving and burning of the Nazirite's hair, both of which occur within sacred space (the entrance of the Tent of Meeting and the altar; Num 6:18).

Yet as much as P provides this esteemed avenue toward holiness for people at large, he at the same time exercises control over the vocation so as not to yield the authoritative status of the Aaronids. Importantly, P restricts the Nazirite institution to a temporary position, in direct contrast to the lifelong Nazirite. The position is also framed as being an internal, individual path toward holiness, without any governance of (or power over) another's affairs. In contrast to Samuel, the child Nazirite who grows up to engage in a variety of cultic roles (e.g., sacrificing, royal anointing; 1 Sam 9:13; 10:1, 8), P's Nazirite has no authority. P's Nazirite does not mediate the affairs of others;

his/her vocation is an individual one. Most significantly, although P's Nazirite can undertake a personal vow (Num 6:2), his/her position is under the authority of the Aaronid priests. They are the ones who enforce the legislation for a Nazirite's violation of observance (Num 6:9–12). Repeatedly the *kōhēn* is described as the one who offers cult on the Nazirite's behalf (Num 6:10–11, 16–17, 19–20). In short, the stature of the Nazirite's temporary state of inner holiness is quantitatively and qualitatively inferior to that of the perpetual priesthood of the Aaronid priests (*likĕhunnat 'ôlām lĕdōrōtām*; Exod 40:15). Writing on hierarchy in biblical representations of cult, Saul Olyan (2000: 61) sums up the situation well:

> If anything, the contrast between Nazirite holiness and that of priest and high priest only serves to reinforce and underscore the difference between the priestly class and all others in the Priestly schema, including Nazirites. The very presence of the Nazirite is a reminder that even the elite among non-priests, those willing to embrace restrictive lifestyle modifications, have no enduring claim to holiness as do priests.

Though P strongly privileges the power and prestige of the Aaronid priests, it would be unbalanced to allow this to be the last word on Nazirite holiness. Milgrom (1990: 357) squarely sets out two parameters for gauging the social dynamic between priests and Nazirites: "How did the priesthood regard the Nazirite institutions: with favor, as an opportunity for the layman to achieve holiness, or with disfavor, as an unproductive, wasteful form of life?" Using H's broad understanding of societal holiness as his benchmark (particularly Lev 19), Milgrom argues for the latter:

> Israel indeed can aspire to holiness ... but not in the way of the Nazirite. Rather, Israel achieves holiness by adhering to a series of moral and ritual rules that impinge on the total life of the individual, affecting as much the relationship with his fellow as with his God ... The Nazirite, on the other hand, owes no service either to his God or to his people. His priestlike abstentions may satisfy his inner emotional need but they are of benefit to no one else. Only a behavioral transformation, especially as it alleviates the plight of the underprivileged in society, is the true gauge of holiness.

Such harsh wording toward the Nazirite is striking for anyone who values the contemplative and ascetic traditions that are found in most, if not all, religions. As P must have understood, society must allow a mechanism for inward seekers who choose a contemplative path, and it must do so in a way that is supportive rather than demeaning. Thus whereas Milgrom chooses the latter of his two parameters, it is more likely that both were in play as the social dynamic was lived out by people of different persuasions and prejudices (especially against women Nazirites). As for P, he explicitly writes that "all the days of the Nazirite's observance are *holy to Yahweh*" (Num 6:5, 8)—and P never uses the term *qādôš* lightly. Moreover, P uses very specific language in Numbers 6:1 to introduce the topic. Numbers 6:1 is typically translated something like: "If anyone, man or woman, *explicitly utters a* [or *makes a special*] Nazirite vow, to set himself apart for Yahweh." As noted as early as Ibn Ezra (whom Milgrom [1990: 44] acknowledges), the verb *pl'*, used here to modify the making of a vow (*yapli' lindōr neder*), is used elsewhere of God's "wondrous" deeds (cf. the related nouns *pele'* and *niplā'ōt*).[170] Thus in Numbers 6:1, P is framing the nature of the Nazirite vow as remarkably positive. As for Milgrom's critique about the civil good, an inward path can result in benefits for the community at large if the ascetic is socially minded (e.g., Thomas Merton, Gandhi).[171] For some inward seekers, their thirst for justice and engagement with the marginalized flows out of their asceticism.

The Holiness of Levites

The complicated history of the Levites and the question of their consecration is too tangled to be unraveled.[172] The braided threads that end up in the Hebrew Bible attest to several traditions, early and late, that point to inter-priestly conflict. It seems that the Levites were regularly faced with negotiating priestly power and position with Aaronid and Zadokite priests, and more often than not they came out on the losing end. As for our present concerns, Olyan (2000: 35) writes perceptively: "Among the ranks of the cultic elite, distinctions of status . . . are often expressed through the idiom of holiness."

As we have demonstrated, P's and H's views of priestly power and status privilege the Aaronids. Thus it comes as no surprise to find traditions minimizing the stature of the Levites. While the services of the Levites are highly valued, they are hierarchically subordinate to those of the Aaronid priesthood. Yet prior to turning to this material, we should first look at alternative traditions that hint at a different scenario, one in which the Levites had a more prominent position. What tangles our understanding of all of these traditions is the genealogy revealing that Aaron is himself a Levite (Exod 4:14; 6:16–25), and in particular the geneaology of the house of Kohath and the family of Amram (Num 26:58–59). Thus the texts that seem to give clear evidence of an internecine Aaronid-Levite conflict can be reframed as legitimating the Aaronids, who are, after all, Levites.[173]

The Prestigious Levite of Judges 17–18

One of the earliest traditions about the prestige of a Levite is found in Judges 17–18, where a mobile Levite comes to be installed as a priest (*kōhēn*).[174] Rather than being connected to the organized sacred space we come to associate with priestly activity (Tabernacle, Tent of Meeting, Ark, Temple), here the locus of cultic activity is a family shrine (*bêt ʾĕlōhîm*) with a divine image and related cultic paraphernalia (Judg 17:3–5; 18:14, 17–18, 20, 24, 30–31). At the start of the narrative, the shrine's priest (*kōhēn*) is one of the sons of its owner, a man named Micah (Judg 17:5; cf. 2 Sam 8:18). In accord with family religion, when Micah secures the services of the Levite, he uses familial language: "Be to me a father and a priest [*hĕyēh-lî lěʾāb ûlěkōhēn*]."[175] Unlike P's priestly ordination language (cf. Exod 28:41; 29:29, 33), when Micah installs (*millēʾ yād*) the Levite into his priestly vocation, there is no mention of any anointing (*mšḥ*) or consecration (*qdš*) rite. The Levite is "in the house of Micah," becoming to him "like one of his sons" (Judg 17:10–12). The prestige of securing the services of a Levite is clear throughout the story of Micah's familial shrine as well as in the subsequent narrative where the Danites steal the priest and the cultic paraphernalia for larger tribal service (Judg 18). Functionally, the Levite's duties as *kōhēn* are mentioned only as oracular (Judg 18:5–6), not sacrificial.[176]

Levite Prominence in Exodus 32:25–29 and Deuteronomy 33:8–11

Another tradition highlighting the prominence of the Levites is found in Exodus 32.[177] In the famous golden calf episode, Aaron comes off poorly. In Houtman's (2000: 614–615, 628) description, he is a "bumbling" "failure as leader"—"the incompetent leader; lacking in moxie to stand up to the wishes of the people," who "tries to make the best of it by resorting to syncretism." (As discussed later, Deut 9:20 has an angered Yahweh seeking to kill Aaron for his offense.) This is hardly P's consecrated leader who wears "radiant" vestments and undergoes an exclusive anointing ritual, the one who is allowed to make approach on behalf of the people to minister to Yahweh. In contrast, coming to Moses' side in Exodus 32 are the stalwart Levites, who, at Yahweh's command, strap on the sword to kill large numbers of apostates even if they are sons, brothers, friends, or neighbors (Exod 32:27, 29). According to Exodus 32:29, these actions at such a great cost are etiological, as Moses proclaims how "this day" the Levites have ordained themselves for service to Yahweh (*milʾû yedkem hayyôm lě-yhwh*).[178]

> Deuteronomy 33:8–11 includes similar notions:[179]
> Of Levi he said:
> Give to Levi your Thummim,[180]

Your Urim to your faithful man,
Whom you tested at Massah,
Whom you tried at the waters of Meribah;

[Levi] who says of his father and mother,
"I have no regard for them."
His own brothers, he did not acknowledge.
His own sons, he did not know.

For they [alone] obey your command,
They [alone] guard your covenant.

They [shall] teach your ordinances to Jacob,
Your law to Israel.
They [will] set incense for you to smell,
A whole offering on your altar.

Bless, O Yahweh, his might,
Be pleased with the work of his hands.

Smite his foes [on] the loins,[181]
His enemies, so they rise no more.

This fascinating passage speaks of Levi, the ancestral collective term standing for the Levites as a group, as is soon made clear with the use of plural verbs (*šāměrû, yinṣōrû, yôrû, yāśîmû*; Deut 33:9–10). The poem contains hints of what may be a military context in asking Yahweh to bless Levi's might as he smites his foes (Deut 33:11). The reference to Levi having no regard for one's relatives (Deut 33:9a) might resonate with the Levites' purge of similar groups making up the golden calf apostates (Exod 32:27, 29).[182] Deuteronomy 33:9b's mention of the Levites (alone?) obeying Yahweh's word would nicely parallel their obedience to Yahweh's command in Exodus 32:26–29. Some scholars even make a connection between the trials at Massah and Meribah and the springs where the ashes of the golden calf are dissolved (e.g., Propp 2006: 568), though the explicit reference is clearly to Moses bringing water from the rock for the quarrelling Israelites (Exod 17:1–7; Num 20:2–13).[183]

Whether or not such connections between Deuteronomy 33:8–11 and Exodus 32:26–29 amount to anything, it is clear that the former, like the latter, elevates the Levites. Moreover, Deuteronomy 33:8–11 is far more expansive, as it fleshes out three priestly roles for the Levites: (1) the handling of the Thummim and Urim, (2) the teaching of ordinances and law, and (3) the offering of cult to Yahweh himself. The first of these functions is quite remarkable on several accounts. Its atypical word order is attested only here (as opposed to the common order of Urim and Thummim). What this tells us is hard to say, but at the least it suggests a non-standardized (non-Aaronid? non-P?) phrasing. These oracular devices, used to determine the divine will, remind us of the oracular function of the Levite in Judges 18:5–6, especially with the mention of a cultic ephod in the story (Judg 17:5; 18:14, 17–18, 20). Deuteronomy 33:8's assigning of the Thummim and Urim to the Levites (who passed the Massah/Meribah trials) contrasts with P's usage, where these divinatory objects are used only by the Aaronid high priest and most often when he enters into "the holy [sanctuary]" (*haqqōdeš*) (Exod 28:29–30). Only in Deuteronomy 33:8 are the Thummim and Urim marked as Yahweh's very own possession, which he bestows upon the Levites, who are labeled as his loyal followers (*ḥăsîdekā*). The second function, the teaching (*yrh*) of Yahweh's ordinances, fits with what we see elsewhere in Deuteronomy for the duties of the Levitical priests (e.g., Deut 17.10–11; 24:8), yet it is also used by P for the Aaronids (Lev 10:11), and it too resonates with the Thummim and Urim being housed, according to P, in the "breastpiece of judgment" (*ḥōšen mišpāṭ*; Exod 28:15, 29).[184] The third function, the offering of incense and cult at the altar, is striking if juxtaposed with P's restrictions on the cultic duties of Levites. For P, the Aaronids, not the Levites, have charge over the altar (Num 18:7). For P, a death penalty is assigned to the Levite approaching the altar (Num 18:3, 7). For P, as we will soon see, the same penalty is assigned to non-Aaronid Levites offering incense to Yahweh (Num 16:35; 17:5 [Eng 16:40]).

The Levites' Rebellion in Numbers 16: Their Punishment and Work Profile in P

The most explicit narrative describing the priestly conflict between a certain group of Levites and the Aaronid priesthood is found in Numbers 16.[185] Led by Korah, a Kohathite Levite (like Moses and Aaron), the rebels present a very focused charge:

> They assembled against Moses and against Aaron, and charged them, "You have gone too far! The community in its entirety is holy [*kullām qĕdōšîm*], and Yahweh is among them. So why then do you exalt yourselves above Yahweh's congregation?" (Num 16:3)

While the charge is initially against both Moses and Aaron (Num 16:2–3), as the narrative continues it becomes clear that Aaron is the primary focus of the rebels' animosity (Num 16:11). Olyan's (2000: 35) perceptive remark needs to be quoted again: "Among the ranks of the cultic elite, distinctions of status ... are often *expressed through the idiom of holiness*" (emphasis mine). The redacted narrative, coming from the hands of P (but cf. Knohl 1995: 83, 105, 187), dramatically affirms the holiness of the Aaronids who are divinely chosen to control the priesthood. The Aaronids, or, more specifically, the Kohathite-Amram branch of the Levites, is promoted over the Kohathite-Izhar Levites led by Korah. The rebels' notion of the entire community being holy (Num 16:3) is quite fascinating, for it aligns precisely with H's expansive view of holiness, in contrast to P's restrictive approach (Knohl 1995: 81).

The mechanism used to resolve the complaint is a ritual contest. Quoting the very charge back at Korah and his followers ("You Levites have gone too far!"), Moses proposes the following ordeal:

> In the morning Yahweh will make known who belongs to Him, and who is holy [*'et-'ăšer-lô wĕ'et-haqqādôš*], and He will grant [him] approach to Himself; the one whom He chooses He will grant approach to Himself.
>
> Do the following: take firepans, Korah and all his company. Tomorrow put fiery coals in them, and lay incense over them before Yahweh. Then the man whom Yahweh chooses, he shall be the holy one [*hû' haqqādôš*]. You Levites have gone too far! (Num 16:5–7; cf. 16:16–17)

Once again we see how ritual practice (or, more accurately, the literary portrayal of ritual practice) is used ideologically to construct and reinforce power, prestige, influence, and status (Bell 1997). The ritual contest (the offering of incense) is appropriate to what is at stake: priestly status and control. For, as the narrative will go on to teach, only Aaronid priests are allowed to offer incense (Num 17:5 [Eng 16:40]). Even the Aaronids must carry out the rite properly or else they too face death, as is demonstrated by the demise of Aaron's own two sons, Nadab and Abihu (Lev 10:1–2; cf. 2 Chr 26:16–20).[186]

Moses' pre-contest diatribe against Korah continues:

> Listen up, you Levites! Is it of so little importance to you that the God of Israel has distinguished [*hibdîl*] you from the community of Israel, to allow you to approach him in order to perform the duties of Yahweh's Tabernacle, and to stand before the community to serve them?
>
> He has allowed you to approach [him], and all your Levite kinsmen with you. Yet you seek the priesthood [*kĕhunnâ*] as well! In reality, you and all your company have banded together against Yahweh! As for Aaron, what is he that you should rail against him? (Num 16:8–11)

With just a few sentences, Moses demarcates P's views on the cultic privileges of the Levites juxtaposed with their cultic restrictions (elsewhere, see Num 1:50–53;

3:5–10; 4; 8:14–22; 18:1–7). Both have to do with gradations of holiness and rank. Hierarchically, the Levites are higher in status than the people but lower than the Aaronid priests. Theirs is a remarkable entitlement: they are qualified to approach the Unapproachable One (*lĕhaqrîb 'etkem 'ēlāyw*; Num 16:9). Yet their so-called access to the divine is immediately defined and constrained. In reality, they do not make a literal approach to serve Yahweh cultically, but rather serve in an operational role that facilitates the functioning of the community and the management of sacred space.[187] For P, Levitical service is to stand before (i.e., to attend to) the community (*la'ămōd lipnê hā'ēdâ lĕšārĕtām*), not before Yahweh (Num 16:9). Only the Aaronids have claim to the priesthood that allows access to "the Holy."

As one could predict from this P tradition, the situation does not go well for the rebelling Korah and his Levites seeking the office of priesthood. Moses reframes their rebellion against Aaron as one of banding together against Yahweh (Num 16:11). When they engage in the exclusive priestly rite of offering incense (Num 16:18), Yahweh responds directly via his powerful fiery *kābôd* presence, threatening destruction (Num 16:19–21).[188] Despite (or as a result of) Moses and Aaron's intercession on behalf of the entire community, the episode ends with Yahweh's consuming fire killing (only) the 250 men who had illegitimately offered incense (Num 16:35). P concludes with the destruction of Korah and his band of Levites—visibly marked through the repurposing of their scorched firepans as bronze plating for the altar—serving as a "warning sign" (*'ôt*) and "reminder" (*zikkārôn*) that a similar fate awaits any "outsider" who seeks Aaronid priestly prerogatives (Num 17:1–5). As we have seen elsewhere in P, the Aaronids lay claim to "a perpetual priesthood for future generations" (*likĕhunnat 'ôlām lĕdōrōtām*; Exod 40:15; cf. Lev 16:32; Num 3:10) that is a result of "a perpetual ordinance" (*kĕhunnâ lĕḥuqqat 'ôlām*; Exod 29:9; cf. Exod 27:21; Num 25:13). Nothing legitimizes one's hold on an office more than recounting the dramatic story of God killing one's challengers.[189]

The Cultic Privileges of the Levites According to P

A final word on P's attitude toward the cultic privileges of the Levites is in order.[190] Though the non-Amram branches of the Levites are restricted from attaining the highest priestly status that would allow them to handle *sancta* (Num 18:2–5), it would be unbalanced to leave the impression that their service was not highly esteemed by P. An imbalance is often found in opinions that reduce their service to "menial tasks" (e.g., Soggin 1993: 434). Rather, as Olyan (2000: 29) underscores, the Levites "occupy a privileged position," as indicated by the way in which Yahweh "distinguishes" (*hibdîl*) them from the people as he brings them near himself (C stem of √*qrb*), two idioms used elsewhere to describe priestly status.

The degree to which we appreciate the vital importance of sacred space is the degree to which we esteem the portrayal of the Levites managing the Tabernacle complex. The Levites construct, disassemble, and transport the Tabernacle along with its equipment (Num 1:50–51; cf. 1 Sam 6:15).[191] They risk death as they transport the potentially lethal Ark (Lev 4:15, 18–20). Overall, their "guarding" (*mišmeret*) and "work" (*'ăbōdâ*) within sacred space are in service of the people at large and especially the Aaronid priests, whom they "assist" (*šēret*; Num 3:5–10). The Levites, according to P, are "unreservedly given" (*nětûnim nětûnim*) to service the Aaronid priests (Num 3:9; cf. 8:19).

Yet more importantly, P also underscores (using Yahweh's voice) that the Levites are "unreservedly given" (*nětûnim nětûnim*) to Yahweh as well (Num 8:16; cf. 18:6). Thus it is that the Levites undergo their own special initiatory ritual, though one of "purification" (√*ṭhr*) and "dedication" (√*ntn*), not priestly "consecration" (√*qdš*), for as Milgrom has astutely pointed out, "nowhere in P is the root *qdš* used in connection with the Levites."[192] This public rite for the Levites includes the laundering of clothes, the shaving of the body, and a sprinkling of water (Num 8:7), followed by bull sacrifice and meal offerings (Num 8:7–10). The first of these rituals is of a markedly lesser rank than what is done for priestly investiture, where we find garbing with special vestments and anointing with blood and oil.[193] Yet the procedures for the Levites are significant nonetheless. For what follows next is theologically remarkable. In addition to the actual bull sacrifice, the narrative goes on to describe how the Levites themselves constitute a symbolic offering to God. This is expressed in two different ways. First, P describes the Levites as figurative *těnûpâ* offerings that Aaron presents to Yahweh (Num 8:11, 13, 15, 21). This so-called elevation offering is combined with the Israelites' laying on of hands (Num 8:11) to set apart the Levites as representing Israel's symbolic sacrifice. The Levites are given over to become "Yahweh's possession" (*wěhāyû lî halěwiyyim*; Num 3:12, 45; 8:13–14, 16). The second symbol is even more dramatic. According to P (likely reformulating Exodus 13), Yahweh has claim to the firstborn (of humans and animals) and deems the Levites worthy of being a substitute.[194] P repeatedly describes the Levites' substantive role in providing a redemptive replacement:

> For [the Levites] are unreservedly given to me from among the Israelites; I have taken them for myself, in place of all that open the womb, the firstborn of all the Israelites. For all the firstborn among the Israelites are mine, both human and animal. On the day that I struck down all the firstborn in the land of Egypt, I consecrated them for myself. I have thus taken the Levites in place of all the firstborn among the Israelites. (Num 8:16–17; cf. Num 3:12–13, 40–42, 45; Num 18:15–17)

It is quite fascinating to read in Numbers 3:13 and Numbers 8:17 how the Levites function as substitutes for Yahweh's "consecrated" firstborn when they themselves never have consecrated status.[195] Yet they do become Yahweh's possession. Just as God acquired Israel's firstborn in the days of the Egyptian Exodus through redemption (Exod 13:15), so too Yahweh now acquires the Levites as he personally takes (*lqḥ*) them for himself (Num 3:12, 42, 45; 8:16, 18).

In summary, the importance of the cultic privileges of the Levites should not be minimized. They are qualified to approach (operationally) the Unapproachable One (*lĕhaqrîb ʾetkem ʾēlāyw*; Num 16:9). Their Tabernacle service, undertaken at great personal risk, and their representation as symbolic offerings set them apart from and above the people. Thus the various traditions we find woven in P are mixed. They harshly restrict the functions of non-Amram Levites (e.g., Num 16–17) while at the same time praising the Levites for their management of sacred space. The entire cultic system simply could not operate without the significant service of the Levites. Theirs is an elevated position, just not as highly elevated as the priesthood. While their cultic service is esteemed, it is not as highly esteemed as the cultic manipulation of blood, which remains the sole prerogative of the priesthood (cf. Lev 1–7). Whereas others might rightly associate Levitical service with holy endeavors on behalf of God and people, P restricts the term "holy" solely to the priests. Thus for P, holiness is not about personal piety and service. We assume that most Levites were pious and most giving of their time and energy in the service of godly religion. For P, holiness is about status, rank, and power—all of which God possesses supremely (see the first part of this chapter). Correspondingly, for P, those who approach a holy God must have the highest possible human rank, status, and power. Only the Aaronid priests are deemed holy, and that by an act of divine consecration.

Holiness and Holy Personnel in the Book of Ezekiel

The Book of Ezekiel plays a key role in scholarly reconstructions of the priestly writings (be they P and/or H), and this is equally true with respect to priestly understandings of holiness as regards cultic service, sacred space, and sacred personnel.[196] Much of what one reads about holiness in the book of Ezekiel resonates with what we have already articulated. Yet Ezekiel's systematic approach is distinctive enough to have Gammie (1989: 45) label him the "theologian of the Holiness of God." Daniel Block (1997: 47–48) writes with similar admiration:

> Although Ezekiel avoids the title "Holy One of Israel" (*qĕdôš yiśrāʾēl*),[197] so common in Isaiah, the attribute of Yahweh's holiness is high in his mind. From

the form and radiance of the inaugural vision to the concentric gradations of holiness built into the design of the temple in the final vision (chs. 40–43), everything about Yahweh's character and actions proclaims "Holy! Holy! Holy!"

Ezekiel's interest in all matters cultic is certainly related to his own priestly vocation (Ezek 1:3). When it comes to cultic holiness, Ezekiel articulates the textbook definition fully in line with Leviticus 10:10. Yahweh is the sanctifying agent (D stem of *qdš*) of the people (Ezek 20:12; 37:28) and of time (Ezek 20:20). God requires a distinction to be made between the sacred and the profane (*hibdîl bên-qōdeš lĕḥōl*), between clean and unclean (*bên-haṭṭāmēʾ lĕṭāhôr*; Ezek 22:26). Sacred time—that is, the Sabbath (Ezek 22:8)—and sacred space should also be distinguished (Ezek 42:20). Because former priests (*kōhănîm*) did "violence" in this regard (Ezek 22:26; cf. Zeph 3:4b), Ezekiel's restored (Zadokite) priesthood of the future will rectify the situation (Ezek 44:23–24).[198] Priestly notions of holy vestments (42:14; 44:19), holy offerings (42:13; 44:13), holy paraphernalia (44:13), holy space (41:21, 23; 42:13–14; 44:19, 27; 45:1–7; 46:19; 48:10, 12, 14, 18, 20–21)—including the "Holy of Holies" (41:4) and Jerusalem as Yahweh's "holy mountain"[199] (Ezekiel 20:40; 40:2; 43:12)—holy time (Ezek 20:12; 22:8), and holy contagion[200] (44:19; 46:20) appear throughout the book.

Ezekiel, more than anyone else, describes Yahweh's concern about damage done to his "holy name" by his people through their profaning acts of illicit cult (Ezek 20:39; 36:20–22; 39:7, 26; 43:7–8; cf. 13:19; 22:26; 39:25).[201] As part of his theodicy, Ezekiel presents these desecrating acts as causal agents resulting in the destruction of Yahweh's Temple in Jerusalem and the exile of Yahweh's people. Both of these resulted in yet another desecration of Yahweh's reputation, for it was easy to conclude that Yahweh was too weak or too unwilling to protect his own people (cf. Isa 59:1) or that he had decided to forsake them (cf. Ezek 8:8; 9:9). Thus we read Ezekiel's response:

> When they came to the nations to which they came, they desecrated my holy name, in that it was said of them, "These are Yahweh's people, and yet they had to go out of his land."[202] But I was moved to save my holy name that the house of Israel had desecrated among the nations to which they came.
>
> Therefore say to the house of Israel: Thus said Lord Yahweh: It is not for your sake, O house of Israel, that I am about to act, but for the sake of my holy name, which you desecrated among the nations to which you came. I will sanctify my great name [*wĕqiddaštî ʾet-šĕmî haggādôl*] that has been desecrated among the nations, which you desecrated among them; and the nations shall know that I am Yahweh, says the Lord Yahweh, when I assert my holiness [*bĕhiqqādĕšî*] through you in their sight. (Ezek 36:20–23)

Implied in the nations' slanderous assertion in Ezekiel 36:20 is that gods are tied to their land, over which they exercise sovereign control.²⁰³ Thus any violence done to the people of a land implicates the god of that land.

As demonstrated through the many traditions documented at the beginning of this chapter (see pp. 577–605), *to say that Yahweh is holy is to say that he is dynamically powerful.* Repeatedly Yahweh promotes his superlative reputation as a holy/powerful God through delivering his people from their oppressors.²⁰⁴ Thus the corollary pertaining to the events of 597 and 586 BCE is obvious: Yahweh's failure to protect Jerusalem (and the very Temple that constituted his "house")— combined with some of his people being killed and others turned into deported refugees—can only mean that Yahweh is not holy, not powerful. Yahweh's response to such a misperception is twofold: first, he himself sanctifies (i.e., declares as holy/powerful) his name, which has always remained "great" (*wĕqiddaštî ʾet-šĕmî haggādôl*) despite mischaracterizations (Ezek 36:23a). Borrowing from Ezekiel 38:23, one could say that Yahweh's assertion of his holiness is the assertion of his greatness and vice versa (*wĕhitgaddiltî wĕhitqaddištî*).

Second, Yahweh will again use his actions on behalf of his people (this time with the coming restoration) to assert his holy power (*bĕhiqqādĕšî*) for all to see (Ezek 36:23b). The future restoration entails Yahweh settling his people back in their own land (again, as an act of his holy display, *wĕniqdaštî bām*; Ezek 28:25). Using priestly vocabulary, Yahweh declares that he will accept his people themselves as a "pleasing aroma" (Ezek 20:41).²⁰⁵ Climactically, Yahweh will again take up his holy dwelling (using both priestly terms *miškān* and *miqdāš*) with his people as he did in the past (Ezek 37:26–27). This too is verbally described as an act of Yahweh's sanctifying power (*ʾănî yhwh mĕqaddēš*; Ezek 37:28; cf. 39:27).²⁰⁶

Ezekiel's Zadokite Priests and Their Cultic Service

Whereas P contrasted an elite, consecrated Aaronid priesthood (coming from the Kohathite-Amram branch of the Levites) with a second-tier non-consecrated class of (non-Amram) Levites as temple operatives, Ezekiel titles his elite leaders "the Levitical priests, the sons of Zadok" (*hakkōhănîm halĕwiyyim bĕnê ṣādôq*; 44:15). Zadok has a storied history as one of David's two chief priests along with Abiathar (2 Sam 8:17; 15:24–29, 35–36; 1 Kgs 1:7–8) and then as Solomon's favored high priest over Abiathar (1 Kgs 1:22–39; 2:26–27, 35)—though, surprisingly, neither P nor H has any mention of him. As we will see, the Deuteronomistic tradition had foretold (via an anonymous "man of God" prophecy) the coming of the faithful priest (*kōhēn neʾĕmān*) Zadok and his "faithful [priestly] house" (*bayit neʾĕmān*) in the days of Samuel and the corrupt Shilonite priesthood (1 Sam 2:35).

As for cultic service, Ezekiel's Zadokite priests, like P's Aaronid priests, are hierarchically elevated over other lesser-ranked Levites. Whereas the Zadokites minister to Yahweh directly, the other Levites again play an operational role. The Zadokite priests are accorded the privilege of "drawing near to Yahweh to minister to Him" (*haqqĕrēbîm ʾel yhwh lĕšārĕtô*; Ezek 40:46; 43:19; 44:15; 45:4). They are allowed to enter holy space, but only in holy linen garments (Ezek 42:14; 44:17–19) and having adhered to precise regulations with regard to hair cutting, drinking wine, marriage, and contact with the dead (Ezek 44:20–27).[207] Unpacked, their cultic duties involve having charge over the sanctuary (44:1; cf. 40:45–46)[208] and the altar (40:46). Everything about the altar—its design and measurements, placement, purification, and consecration—receives special attention (Ezek 43:13–27), culminating in a seven-day sacrificial ritual and once again the all-important rites of blood manipulation and *kpr* purgation (43:18–21, 26). Having undergone this installation procedure, the altar is able to fulfill its function as a place where Yahweh (via Zadokite priestly sacrifice) will again accept his people (*wĕrāṣîʾtî ʾetkem*; Ezek 43:27).

The Zadokite priests' "ministering" is accomplished by "attending to [lit. standing before] Yahweh" as they present offerings that are symbolically seen as Yahweh's "food" at his table (44:15–16). Most remarkably, Ezekiel's envisioning of Zadokite priestly service makes no explicit mention of the role of a high priest. Ezekiel has no parallel to P's unique clothing of the high priest with "holy vestments" (*bigdê-qōdeš*), from the ephod with its *ḥōšen* breastpiece to the *ṣîṣ nēzer* diadem. There are no consecratory rituals that pour "holy anointing oil" (*šemen mišḥat-qōdeš*) on his head, nor expiation rites that anoint his body and garments with oil and blood. There are no cultic rituals described that require a high priest's unique service, as in the Day of Purgation (*yôm kippûr*) rites in Leviticus 16. What are we to make of such omissions by Ezekielian writers who pay such close attention to a wide variety of other cultic minutiae? How loud does the silence speak? Frustratingly, any conclusions drawn from these omissions (regarding a possible democratized hierocracy or the negation of the position of high priest) are necessarily speculative.[209]

The Restrictions on the Levites in Ezekiel 40–48

Where the Zadokites (i.e., "the Levitical priests, the sons of Zadok") are described positively with language of what they can do cultically, the non-Zadokite Levites are described with pejorative language of what they cannot do: "The Levites ... shall not come near to me, to serve me as priest; and they shall not come near any of my holy areas or the most holy offerings" (Ezek 44:13). The reason given is that they formerly "went far away" from Yahweh by "going astray after their idols" (Ezek 44:10, 12; 48:11; cf. 8:14; 14:11). The precise historical infraction that the author has in mind is unknown,[210] yet "their abominable transgressions" (*tôʿăbôtām*) result in the Levites "bearing their punishment" and "their shame" (*wĕnāśĕʾû ʿăwōnām . . . wĕnāśĕʾû kĕlimmātām*; Ezek 44:10, 12b, 13). Such harsh language reflects an intersacerdotal polemic similar to those we listed earlier.[211] That the Levites are restricted from accessing not just Yahweh but also "holy areas" and "the most holy offerings" (Ezek 44:13) leads us to note yet again the truism of Olyan (2000: 35): "Among the ranks of the cultic elite, distinctions of status . . . are often expressed through the idiom of holiness." And once again, we need to balance this harsh language by juxtaposing the restrictions on the Levites with the cultic (operational) privileges that they still retain (Ezek 44:11, 14). Block (1998: 629) prefers to talk about "two sides of the same coin," where the Levites' responsibility for their infractions is balanced with "the renewed privilege [of] the Levites [being] reinstalled as guarantors of the sanctuary of the temple."

Holiness and Holy Personnel in Deuteronomy

The book of Deuteronomy presents both a challenge and a singular opportunity for understanding divine holiness. The challenge comes from the absence of the word "holy" (*qādôš*) ever being used of God in the book.[212] The opportunity, summed up by Gammie (1989: 106), is that here we find "one of the most complex and impressive theologies of holiness." Complicating and enlivening the discussion further are the ways in which Deuteronomic traditions contrast with Deuteronomistic views of holiness.

The book of Deuteronomy occasionally mentions cultic holiness using explicit *qdš* language. We read of the command to keep the Sabbath day holy (*šāmôr . . . lĕqaddĕšô*) by abstaining from work (Deut 5:12), and to consecrate firstborn males of herd and flock to Yahweh (*taqdîš lĕyhwh*; Deut 15:19). Holy offerings (*qodāšîm*) are aligned with votive gifts (*nĕdārîm*) as obligations to be presented at Yahweh's chosen central sanctuary (Deut 12:26). Deuteronomy 23:17 speaks out against illicit cultic behavior by "holy" officiants, female and male (*qĕdēšâ/qādēš*).[213] None of these commands is particularly surprising. Yet then we read instructions about the military camp being holy that are indeed quite remarkable.

> Because Yahweh your God walks about [*mithallēk*] within your camp—to deliver you and to hand over your enemies to you—so your camp must be holy [*qādôš*], so that he may not see among you anything indecent and turn away from you. (Deut 23:15 [Eng 23:14])

The context is purity of bodily functions for engaging in holy war, as seen in the opening verse of this section, which refers to being encamped against one's enemies (Deut 23:10 [Eng 23:9]; cf. Deut 20:1; 21:10). As Jeffrey Tigay (1996: 213) has noted, the regulations regarding the sanctity of the military camp are "even stricter" than those pertaining to the residential encampment even with its sanctuary. The rationale is that "God is directly present in the military camp." Tigay (1996) and Moshe Weinfeld (1992: 209) underscore how Yahweh's presence is not mediated through a representational object (i.e., the Ark), as happens elsewhere (e.g., 1 Sam 4:6–7). Tigay (1996: 386 n. 47) rightly labels the present tradition "pre-Deuteronomic," for its anthropomorphic Yahweh walking about (*mithallēk*) in the military camp (cf. too Yahweh on the march in Deut 20:4) is very much at odds with the Deuteronomic conception of Yahweh's "dwelling place" (*mĕqôm/mĕkôn šibtĕkā*) being localized in heaven with his fiery voice manifesting his earthly presence (cf. Deut 4:36; 1 Kgs 8:30, 39, 43, 49).[214] Where Deuteronomy 26:15 pleads with Yahweh to "look down from his holy abode that is heaven" (*hašqîpâ mimmě'ôn qodšĕkā min-haššāmayim*), the tradition here has a holy Yahweh physically embedded with his troops at a military camp that must be made holy by carrying out purity regulations.[215]

What we have here is a fascinating tradition that preserves (1) the notion of holiness being militarily powerful, which we saw at the outset of this chapter, (2) the framing of purity regulations to ensure holiness quite apart from priestly cult and priestly personnel (e.g., P and H), and (3) unmediated holiness via Yahweh's actual presence quite apart from Ark or sanctuary. Once again we are reminded of the cultic nature of war. Cosmically, a holy, powerful Yahweh marches to battle with a military entourage that includes "myriads of holy ones" (*ribĕbōt qōdeš*; Deut 33:2–3).[216] Earthly troops "*consecrated* themselves for war" (*qaddĕšû 'ālêhā milḥāmâ*; Jer 6:4). See too the dispensation of "holy bread" to David and his soldiers in 1 Sam 21:1–7 (Eng 21:1–6) (discussed later).

Deuteronomy's Chosen Holy People

Similar to H's understanding of an expansive holiness incorporating the community at large (and in contrast to P's restrictive priestly holiness), Deuteronomy views the people of Israel as holy. Deuteronomy frames its particular understanding through a theology of election. Repeatedly we read:

> For you are a holy people ['*am qādôš*] to Yahweh your god; Yahweh your god chose you [*bāḥar*] from among all the peoples on earth to be his treasured people. (Deut 7:6; 14:2, 21; 26:18–19; 28:9; cf. Deut 4:20; 9:29; 27:9; 29:11–12 [Eng 29:12–13])

Jack Lundbom (2013: 336) describes election as a "bedrock concept" in the Hebrew Bible, with examples ranging from Abraham's call (Gen 12:1-3) and Amos's Israel (Amos 3:2) to Jeremiah's prophetic office (Jer 1:5) and Second Isaiah's Servant Songs (Isa 41:8-9; 42:1; 43:10, 20; 44:1-2; 45:4; 49:7), where the "election of Israel becomes a full-blown concept." The examples from Deuteronomy underscore how Israel was chosen from the surrounding nations, and this fits well with the notion of "holiness" (*qdš*) as that which is set apart. Yet rather than a priestly notion of being set apart for cultic use, Deuteronomy prefers to speak of Israel as Yahweh's "treasured" (*sĕgullâ*) people, which results in them being his "possession" or "hereditary property" (*naḥălâ*; cf. Deut 32:8-9). According to Deuteronomy 7:8, Yahweh's motivation is one of love (*kî mēʾahăbat yhwh ʾetkem*) and loyalty to the oath he made with Israel's ancestors. The mention of divine fidelity toward the "fathers" (*ʾābôt*) reminds us of the familial aspects of Israelite religion, documented in Chapter Eight, where Yahweh, the Divine Father, is portrayed as the caring parent. Yet as we saw there, Yahweh the father can at the same time be Yahweh the warrior. Similarly in Deuteronomy, a powerful Yahweh elected Israel as his people by delivering them militarily from Egyptian oppression. Via his mighty hand (*bĕyād ḥăzāqâ*), outstretched arm (*bizĕrōʿăkā hannĕṭûyâ*), and mighty power (*bĕkōḥăkā haggādōl*), Yahweh redeems his people from the "iron smelter" that is slavery in order to constitute them as his holy people (Deut 4:20; 7:8; 9:26, 29).[217]

Yet the love language used here is even more profound. As shown most lucidly by William Moran (1963),[218] the rhetoric of "love language" together with familial language (e.g., "father," "son," "brother") was used throughout the ancient Near East to describe the sociopolitical bonds of treaties. Thus it is not a coincidence that Deuteronomy 29:9-14 (Eng 29:10-15) situates Yahweh's establishment of Israel as his people in the context of entering into a covenant relationship. The stipulations and mutual obligations of treaties are also woven throughout the Deuteronomic texts that have Israel becoming Yahweh's holy people.[219]

Deuteronomy's Levitical Priests

We have already reviewed Deuteronomy 33:8-11 (pp. 637-639), one of the early passages where the Levites enjoyed a much more prominent role than what is preserved in the P and H traditions. In Deuteronomy 33:8-11 we saw that Levites, described as Yahweh's loyal followers (*ḥăsîdekā*), handled the Thummim and Urim and even offered cult to Yahweh. These cultic privileges were directly opposed to P's regulations restricting such activities to the Aaronid priests.

Yahweh's Desire to Kill Aaron in Deuteronomy 9:20

Deuteronomy 9:20 preserves another tradition that certainly did not sit well with Aaronid proponents. In striking contrast to the verses mentioned earlier that have Yahweh choosing and delivering Israel to be a "holy people" (ʿam qādôš), Deuteronomy 9:6–24 has only invective for the people's behavior. Ever since the Exodus, they have been a stubborn, "stiff-necked people" (ʿam-qĕšēh-ʿōrep) provoking Yahweh's wrath (Deut 9:6–7, 13–14). Their rebellious (√mrh) nature led to Yahweh becoming so angry that he was ready to destroy them (Deut 9:8; cf. 9:24). Echoing what we find in Exodus 32:7–14 (discussed earlier), the people's making of a golden calf is the last straw. Yahweh initially rebuffs any intercession by Moses: "Leave me alone, that I may destroy them and blot out their name from under heaven.[220] And I will make of you a new nation mightier and greater than they" (Deut 9:14). Moses intercedes nonetheless— even though he is afraid of Yahweh's fierce wrath[221]—and Yahweh hears his intercession (Deut 9:19). As the narrative continues, we see that the intercessory vocabulary used by Moses relies on the very words used elsewhere for Israel as Yahweh's "holy people." Moses makes his appeal to Yahweh based on the people being his "heritage" (naḥălâ), the descendants of the patriarchal fathers, whom he redeemed by his great power and outstretched arm (Deut 9:26–27, 29; cf. 7:8).

The narrative then turns to Aaron and his role in the golden calf incident. Again Yahweh is so very angry with Aaron that he is ready to destroy him (bĕʾahărōn hitʾannap yhwh mĕʾōd lĕhašmîdô). And again destruction is averted due to Moses' intercession (Deut 9:20). Clearly, those handing down these traditions are not enamored with P's holy Aaron as the illustrious father of the holy Aaronid priesthood. The subsequent mention of Aaron's death and burial is terse (Deut 10:6). There is no fanfare for the original high priest of ancient Israel. There is no hint here of P elsewhere assigning Aaron (and every subsequent high priest) elevated authority and status and consecrating him with radiant garments and unique anointing rituals. Strikingly, when juxtaposed with P's pervasive and positive treatment, Aaron is mentioned in Deuteronomy only three times: in the story here about Yahweh's desire to kill Aaron (Deut 9:20), when Aaron and Moses break faith with Yahweh at Meribath-qadesh (Deut 32:51), and in the curt death and burial announcements (Deut 10:6; 32:50).[222]

Deuteronomy's Sacerdotal Vocabulary

The status of priests and Levites elsewhere in Deuteronomy is complicated. The combined terminology is twofold: (1) "the Levite priests" or "the priests, the

Levites" (*hakkōhănîm halĕwiyyīm*; Deut 17:9, 18; 18:1; 24:8; 27:9) and (2) "the priests, the sons of Levi" (*hakkōhănîm bĕnê lēwî*; Deut 21:5; 31:9), although one also comes across (3) just "priest/priests" (*kōhēn, hakkōhănîm*; Deut 18:3; 19:17), (4) just "Levite/Levites" (*lēwî, hallēwî, halĕwiyyīm*; Deut 10:9; 12:12, 18–19; 14:27, 29; 16:11, 14; 18:6–7; 26:11–13; 27:12, 14; 31:25; 33:8), and (5) "tribe of Levi" (*šēbeṭ lēwî/šēbeṭ hallēwî*; Deut 10:8; 18:1). The history of priesthood in Deuteronomy (including cultic and juridical roles) is too gnarled to be addressed here, though not for the lack of scholarship specifically devoted to the topic. Suffice it to say that many scholars believe that Deuteronomy teaches that all Levites are potential priests (cf. Deut 18:1–8), although others argue that Deuteronomy can be aligned closer to P's understanding in restricting their religious prerogatives.[223] Yet others argue that economics (esp. the tithe) are the key to seeing how Deuteronomic cult centralization (ultimately under royal authority) undermined the Levites' support and power.[224] Still others (Na'aman 2008) see Deuteronomy's Levites as a marginal, landless social group providing cultic service who are in need of welfare from Judahite landowners. Their neediness is especially evident in their being grouped with sojourners, orphans, widows, and the poor (Deut 14:29; 16:11, 14; 26:11–12).[225]

For our present interest in holiness, it is quite remarkable, especially when juxtaposed with P, that the words for priest/priests (*kōhēn, kōhănîm*)—not to mention Levite/Levites (*lēwî, lĕwiyyīm*)—are never modified by the adjective "holy" (*qādôš*) in the entire book of Deuteronomy.[226] For Deuteronomy, as we have already documented, it is the people who are holy (*'am qādôš*). They are accorded this standing not through consecration and anointing rituals nor through their own merit (cf. Deut 7:7), but rather by Yahweh's election. Yet because they have been chosen as a holy people, ritual requirements and purity codes do indeed apply, as do a full range of covenant obligations amply documented throughout the entire book (e.g., Deut 27:9–10). Thus in its own particular way (and without explicitly calling Yahweh the Holy One), the book of Deuteronomy returns the focus to Yahweh as the sole agent of chosen holiness.

Deuteronomistic Conceptions of Divine Holiness and Holy Personnel

In the opening portion of the present chapter we looked at how DtrH incorporated traditions about Yahweh being powerfully holy. The Song of Hannah proclaims how Yahweh is incomparably victorious—especially in fighting on behalf of the unfortunate—such that the poet's rhetorical question "Who is holy like Yahweh?" finds its own answer in the doxology "There is no Holy One like Yahweh" (1 Sam 2:2, 10; see pp. 588–591). We have also explored Yahweh's holy Ark as a war palladium whose death toll causes the Beth-Shemites to cry out, "Who is able to stand before Yahweh, this Holy God?" (1 Sam 6:20). The Deuteronomistic historians are fully aware of the need for Levites and cultic precautions when handling the lethally holy Ark, as famously recounted in the killing of Uzzah (2 Sam 6:1–11//1 Chr 13; see p. 596). Lastly, given our study of the Isaianic "Holy One of Israel" (see pp. 599–603), it comes as no surprise that the single reference to this epithet for Yahweh in DtrH is found on the lips of Isaiah ben Amoṣ (2 Kgs 19:22; Williamson 2001: 32).

"You Cannot Serve a Holy Yahweh!" (Joshua 24:19)

As for divine holiness elsewhere in DtrH,[227] Joshua's response to the Israelites during the covenant renewal at Shechem in Joshua 24 has been called "perhaps the most shocking statement in the OT [Hebrew Bible]" (Butler 1983: 274). Following a lengthy recitation of divine benevolence dating from patriarchal times to the then present, Joshua challenges the people to worship Yahweh, and memorably proclaims how he and his household will worship/serve Yahweh (*'ānōkî ûbêtî na'ăbōd 'et-yhwh*; Josh 24:15b). The people echo Joshua as they too reiterate Yahweh's historic benevolence and as they proclaim: "We too will worship/serve Yahweh, for he is our God" (*gam-'ănaḥnû na'ăbōd 'et-yhwh kî-hû' 'ĕlōhênû*; Josh 24:18b).[228] Having secured the desired profession of faith, Joshua's next response is indeed shocking:

> But Joshua said to the people, "You cannot serve Yahweh, for he is a holy God [*kî-'ĕlōhîm qĕdōšîm hû'*]. He is a jealous God [*'ēl-qannō' hû'*]. He will not forgive your transgressions or your sins. If you forsake Yahweh and serve foreign gods, then he will turn and do you harm, and consume you [*wĕhēra' lākem wĕkillâ 'etkem*], after having done you good." And the people said to Joshua, "No, we will serve Yahweh!" (Joshua 24:19–21)

The ways in which scholars respond to this passage reveal their interests. Trent Butler (1983: 274) has documented how those specializing in redaction history (e.g., Noth, Möhlenbrink, Schmitt) look to either the fall of the northern or, more often, the southern kingdom as the occasion where an earlier tradition would have been edited to show God's displeasure and lack of forgiveness. Theologians (e.g., Preuss, von Rad, Eichrodt) use the combining here of Yahweh as "holy" and "zealous/jealous" as an opportunity to describe the intensity and uncompromising exclusivity of Yahweh worship, for he "desire[s] for Israel to share his divine status with no one."[229] Butler (1983: 274–275) argues that defining the service of Yahweh "based on the nature of God himself" (i.e., the "total devotion" of "His holy purity and jealous love") necessarily results in expectations that are "too high" and cannot be fulfilled.

While these reflections are true of a fully monotheistic theology, the present monolatrous context points toward Joshua using drastic vocabulary rhetorically to bring about the desired result of a more passionate commitment by the people. And such an ardent resolve is exactly what transpires (Josh 24:21–24). Sociologically, such a resolve is precisely what the context requires, as it structures relational obligations (socially and theologically) of the assembled tribes together with their elders, heads, judges, and (judicial?) officers (Josh 24:1).[230]

Priestly Personnel in the Deuteronomistic History

In contrast to Deuteronomy's limitation of royal power and influence over the cult,[231] DtrH preserves many traditions about the primary roles that monarchs played in the cult, from sacrificing to temple and altar construction (see Chapter Nine, pp. 498–503). Yet in ancient Israel, unlike in ancient Phoenicia, we have no explicit reference to a king being called a "priest" (*kōhēn*).[232] Even the extensive cultic acts of King Ahaz, which include blood manipulation (elsewhere the sole prerogative of priests), do not lead to him being referred to as a *kōhēn*.

It is often said that DtrH "has no particular interest in priestly concerns" (Nelson 1991: 143). This is only partly true if one is referring to intricate cultic vocabulary and rites. J. G. McConville's (1999: 86) assessment is more on the mark: "Dtr has an intrinsic interest in priesthood." It is significant that DtrH mentions many priests and priestly groups as well as sacerdotal land (e.g., the Levitical cities in Josh 21).[233] As discussed in the voluminous literature on the topic,[234] scholars have used DtrH to try to reconstruct the history of the following priestly groups: Aaronids, Levites, Mushites, the priests of Nob, Shilohnites, Zadokites, and groups known variously as "priests of the second order" (*kōhănê hammišneh*; 2 Kgs 23:4), "the priests of the high places" (2 Kgs 23:20), and the *kĕmārîm* priests (2 Kgs 23:5).[235]

Scholars have also focused their energies on the extensive list of individual priests mentioned in DtrH. The explicit tally includes Abiathar (1 Sam 22:20–23; 23:6; 1 Kgs 2:26–27), Ahijah (1 Sam 14:3), Ahimaaz (2 Sam 15:36), Ahimelek (1 Sam 21:1; 22:11–19), Azariah, son of Zadok (1 Kgs 4:2), Eleazar (Josh 14:1; 21:1; 24:33), Eli (1 Sam 1:9), Eli's sons Hophni and Phineas (1 Sam 1:3), Hilkiah (2 Kgs 22:4; 23:4), Ira the Jairite (2 Sam 20:26), Jehoida (2 Kgs 11–12), Phinehas (Judg 20:28), Seraiah (2 Kgs 25:18), Uriah (2 Kgs 16:10–16), Zabud, son of Nathan (1 Kgs 4:5), Zadok (1 Sam 2:35–36; 2 Sam 8:17; 15:24–29, 35; 19:11; 1 Kgs 1:7, 22–39; 2:26–27, 35), and Zephaniah (2 Kgs 25:18).[236] Even David's sons are called priests (2 Sam 8:18).[237]

The Deuteronomistic History's Holiness and Holy Priests

As for holiness, one certainly assumes that many of the priests mentioned in DtrH were viewed as holy by their followers. Pragmatically, one would also guess that many of them underwent some type of a marking ritual, be it a consecration or installation rite. Yet DtrH chooses to preserve precious little in this regard. It is not that DtrH avoids the subject of holiness. In addition to telling of a holy and lethal Yahweh (discussed earlier), DtrH describes sacred space as holy due to divine presence. The preternatural commander of Yahweh's army (*śar-ṣĕbā' yhwh*) demands that Joshua remove his sandals, "for the place where you stand is holy" (*kî hammāqôm 'ăšer 'attâ 'ōmēd 'ālāyw qōdeš hû'*; Josh 5:15).[238] The narrative about the building of the Temple is replete with mentions of its inner recesses constituting "the most holy place" (*qōdeš haqqŏdāšîm*; 1 Kgs 6:16; 7:50; 8:6; cf. 1 Kgs 8:8, 10). Sacred space is "consecrated" (*qiddaš/hiqdîš*) by monarch and deity (1 Kgs 8:64; 9:3, 7), as are solemn assemblies (*qaddĕšû 'ăṣārâ*)—even if for the Canaanite god Baal (2 Kgs 10:20). Prophets such as Elisha can be termed "a holy man of God" (*'îš 'ĕlōhîm qādôš*; 2 Kgs 4:9). People at large are admonished to sanctify themselves when traveling with the potentially lethal Ark (Josh 3:5),[239] when eradicating the contamination brought about through Achan's sin (Josh 7:13), and when preparing to sacrifice (1 Sam 16:5). Certain precious metals, votive gifts, and other cultic paraphernalia are designated as "holy to Yahweh" (*qōdeš hû' lĕ-yhwh*; Josh 6:19; 1 Kgs 8:4; 15:15; 2 Kgs 12:4, 18) and consecrated as such (Judg 17:3; 2 Sam 8:11; 2 Kgs 12:18).[240] As for bodily purity codes, though DtrH shares little with P's or H's intricate understandings, it nonetheless is aware of purifying states of holiness, as evidenced by Bathsheba's removal of menstrual impurity (*mitqaddešet miṭṭum 'ātâ*; 2 Sam 11:4).[241]

Yet when it comes to using the explicit language of holiness with respect to priests, DtrH's references are few and far between. There are only one or two references to the consecration of priests. 1 Samuel 7:1 refers to the consecration of Eleazar, the son of Abinadab, to have charge of the Ark of Yahweh (*wĕ' et-'el'āzār bĕnô qiddĕšû lišmōr 'et-'ărôn yhwh*). Admittedly, Eleazar is never explicitly termed a priest or even a Levite, and it is the people of Kiriath-jearim, not a sacerdotal official, who carry out his act of consecration.[242] The second reference is that of Jeroboam's double infraction of selecting non-Levite priests and installing them for service at illicit high places (1 Kgs 12:31; 13:33; discussed further later).

Holy (Priestly) Food, Holy Bodies, and Holy War (1 Samuel 21:1–7 [Eng 21:1–6])

DtrH contains a story about priests and holiness in a war context in 1 Samuel 21:1–7 (Eng 21:1–6; cf. Deut 23:10–15 [Eng 23:9–14]). Here David requests food for his soldiers from the Nobite priest Ahimelek, who has charge over "the holy bread" (*leḥem qōdeš*), which is also defined here as "the Bread of Presence" (*leḥem happānîm*; 1 Sam 21:5, 7 [Eng 21:4, 6]). In P's tradition, the *leḥem happānîm* is "most holy" (*qōdeš qŏdāšîm*) and only to be consumed by Aaronid priests within sacred space (Lev 24:5–9).[243] In contrast, though DtrH's portrayal also emphasizes priestly prerogative, an exception can be made for non-priests. Ahimelek's dispensation is presented not in response to possible starvation (cf. David's plea), but rather on the level of sanctity required for holy war. In Deuteronomy 23:10–15 [Eng 23:9–14], we saw how Yahweh's embedded presence in the military camp required holiness with regard to bodily functions, including nocturnal emissions. In 1 Samuel 21, sexual abstinence is described as being required for holy war, with David assuring the priest that his soldiers' "vessels" (used euphemistically for genitalia) have been kept "holy" (1 Sam 21:6 [Eng 21:5]). A similar taboo seems to inform the story of the soldier Uriah, who refuses to have sexual relations with his wife, Bathsheba, while home on furlough (2 Sam 11:8–13).[244]

Holy Priestly Prerogatives

Another link between priests and holiness in DtrH is found in the Solomon-centric Temple dedication in 1 Kings 8. The traditions privileging King Solomon's royal cult, both in DtrH and in Chronicles, have been surveyed in Chapter Nine (pp. 500–501). Though Solomon's illustrious cultic activities prior to construction of the Temple are fleshed out in detail (e.g., his sacrifice of a thousand ʿōlôt offerings at the "great high place" of Gibeon in 1 Kgs 3:2–4), his construction and dedication of the Temple in God's chosen city of Jerusalem takes center stage. Royal cult, with the king as the primary religious officiant, is on full display with Solomon's dual sacrificial activities at the Temple's dedication (cf. esp. Knoppers 1995, 2000). Solomon's amplified sacrifice is described at first as being far too large to tally (1 Kgs 8:5//2 Chr 5:6) and then with extraordinarily large numbers (22,000 oxen and 120,000 sheep as *šĕlāmîm* offerings, as well as ʿōlôt, grain, and fat offerings; 1 Kgs 8:62–64//2 Chr 7:5–7). In view of this portrayal of a Solomon-centric cult, a respect for certain priestly prerogatives stands out.

The Ark plays a central role in the Temple's dedication. As noted earlier, DtrH uses third-person *singular* verbs to give Solomon credit for building the innermost shrine (*dĕbîr*), the Holy of Holies (*qōdeš haqqŏdāšîm*), in which the Ark of Yahweh was housed (1 Kgs 6:16–36; cf. 2 Chr 3:8–13). Like David, Solomon and the people sacrifice before the Ark (2 Sam 6:17–18; 1 Kgs 8:5).[245] Yet when it comes to handling the Ark, the focus—either by authorial design and/or through redactional skill—is squarely on priestly prerogative (1 Kgs 8:3–11).[246] In this brief unit, priests (*kōhănîm*) are mentioned five times, once combined with the Levites (*hakkōhănîm wĕhalĕwiyyim*; 1 Kgs 8:4). It is they who are explicitly described as transporting the Ark, the Tent of Meeting, and holy cultic paraphernalia (8:3–4). It is priests alone who bring the Ark to the inner sanctum (*dĕbîr*), the most holy place (*qōdeš haqqŏdāšîm*), where it will then reside underneath the massive wings of the impressive *Mischwesen* known as cherubim (1 Kgs 8:6–7).[247] While their visit is temporary, the priests alone are privileged to enter "the Holy [place]" (*haqqōdeš*; 1 Kgs 8:10). Lastly, once again the ancient notion of divine lethality is referred to (though only implicitly) as preventing the priests from remaining within sacred space once Yahweh arrives (1 Kgs 8:11). Yet that they risked such danger to be so close to divinity is in itself a badge of prestige.

The Lack of Priestly Consecration in the Deuteronomistic History

Even though DtrH underscores the central role of the monarch in the cult, it nonetheless acknowledges certain priestly prerogatives having to do with holiness. Thus we are forced to ask why DtrH preserves no positive references to priestly consecration apart from a brief nod to Eleazar (1 Sam 7:1), noted previously. During the lengthy historical timeline covered by DtrH, there were certainly many and varied rituals to mark religious officiants who were deemed holy. As we saw from Emar, in the Levant legitimizing priestly sanctification and installation rituals date as early as the Late Bronze Age. And, as we have already seen, P goes out of his way to detail the elaborate and gradient clothing and anointing rituals required to secure priestly prestige, rank, and power. In contrast, DtrH describes no such involved rituals. When it does cross into this area (only twice), we find DtrH employing two different rhetorical strategies, the first to destroy a dynasty (Jeroboam's), the second to wed the dynasties of his favored king (David) and priest (Zadok).

Richard Nelson (1991: 144–147) observes how DtrH uses priests "as redactional tools to drive home ideological truths." A case in point is how DtrH scorns those priests it deems illegitimate, especially Jeroboam's non-Levites (1 Kgs 12:31; 13:33). DtrH is upset not only with Jeroboam's selection of non-Levites to serve illicit high places but also with Jeroboam's lack of discrimination with regard to the institution of priesthood itself. As king, says DtrH, he installed "anyone who wanted be a priest" from the "entire population" (*wayya'aś miqṣôt hā'ām kōhănê bāmôt heḥāpēṣ yĕmallē' 'et-yādô wîhî kōhănê bāmôt*; 1 Kgs 13:33; cf. 1 Kgs 12:31; 2 Kgs 17:32). The contrast between this statement and other priestly traditions that take special care to produce genealogies to legitimize sacerdotal heritage could not be starker.[248] For our purposes, note how DtrH uses an illicit priestly installation ritual as a rhetorical strategy to undermine Jeroboam's reign. According to 1 Kings 13:33-34, it is the key evidence to demonstrate how King Jeroboam's refusal "to turn from his evil way" led to the destruction of his dynasty.[249]

On the positive side, consider DtrH's favored priest, Zadok, whose obscure origin has occasioned a cottage industry of scholarly publications.[250] The complex "man of God" pericope in 1 Samuel 2:27-36 uses prophecy (not a consecration rite) to legitimate Zadok and his priestly house. Set during the days of Eli and the fall of the Shilonite priesthood, Yahweh proclaims through his prophet:

> I will raise up for myself a *faithful* priest [*kōhēn ne'ĕmān*] who shall act in accordance with my nature and [divine] will; and I will build him a *faithful* [priestly] house [*bayit ne'ĕmān*]. He shall go in and out before my anointed one [i.e., the king] forever. (1 Samuel 2:35)

Yahweh, according to Deuteronomy 7:9, is a "faithful God" (*hā'ēl hanne'ĕmān*) who maintains covenant loyalty with his adherents. He seeks faithful servants such as the "faithful prophet" Samuel (*ne'ĕmān šĕmû'ēl lĕnābî' lĕyhwh*; 1 Sam 3:20).[251] Yet for DtrH, Yahweh's design for history culminates in his "faithful" king David, whose dynasty is foretold not once but twice. During the Nabal incident, Abigail proclaims to David: "Yahweh will surely make my lord a faithful house" (*bayit ne'ĕmān*; 1 Sam 25:28). Later Nathan, speaking with Yahweh's voice, famously predicts: "Your house and your kingdom shall be made faithful forever [*wĕne'ĕman bêtĕkā ûmamlaktĕkā 'ad-'ôlām*]; before me your throne shall be established forever" (2 Sam 7:16). P. Kyle McCarter (1980a: 93) summarizes DtrH's wedding of David and Zadok: "The Books of Samuel and Kings display a relentless march of history toward not only David, the chosen king, but also Jerusalem, the chosen city, and along with the latter, Zadok of Jerusalem, the chosen priest."[252] For our purposes, it is clear that DtrH chooses the rhetoric of a "faithful priesthood" to legitimate Zadok in contrast to any cultic consecration or installation ritual that would be favored by P.

Holiness and Holy Personnel in Chronicles

One could make a strong argument for Chronicles studies being one of the most vibrant subfields within biblical scholarship in recent times.[253] Readers should consult the voluminous secondary literature to see whether scholars think that the Chronistic presentations align with the realia of the monarchic period, or whether they think Chronicles retrojects practices from the present into the past, or whether they view its portrayal as mostly imaginative (or some combination of all three). Some of the most exciting scholarship sets Chronicles against the backdrop of research on rewritten biblical texts. And yet, as astutely demonstrated by Gary Knoppers (2004: 129–134), Chronicles defies categorization. It is indeed a decidedly new work whose literary accomplishment needs to be understood on its own merits.

Chronicles and Yahweh's Holiness

Once readers understand the centrality of the Temple and sacerdotal affairs in Chronicles, it comes as no surprise to learn that statistically Chronicles contains the second-highest concentration of the Hebrew root *qdš* in the entire Hebrew Bible, bettered only by the book of Leviticus. The number of times that the root is found in Chronicles as compared to DtrH is dramatically different.[254] Both traditions are poetic in their praise of Yahweh as holy, yet with distinct vocabulary. DtrH incorporates the incomparability statements ("There is no Holy One like Yahweh"; "Who is holy like Yahweh?") from the Song of Hannah (1 Sam 2:2, 10) and the epithet "Yahweh, the Holy One of Israel" (2 Kgs 19:22) from the Isaianic tradition. For its part, Chronicles incorporates hymnody praising Yahweh as "radiantly holy" (*hadrat-qōdeš*; 1 Chr 16:29; 2 Chr 20:21) that echoes Psalm 29:2 and Psalm 96:9. As demonstrated in Chapter Seven, *hādār* is one of many words that have been used to describe Yahweh as radiantly majestic and powerful (corresponding to Otto's *fascinans* and *tremendum*). When combined with *qōdeš*, yet another term designating divine power, the result is dramatic, as showcased in the battle narrative we find in 2 Chronicles 20.[255]

Prior to the battle, Jehoshaphat's prayerful lament for divine assistance acknowledges Yahweh's incomparable power and might (*kōaḥ ûgĕbûrâ*) such that none is able to withstand his rule (2 Chr 20:6). Israel's history has been one characterized by Yahweh exercising his might on their behalf. Acknowledging their current powerlessness against their foes, the good king focuses the nation's *eyes* on Yahweh (2 Chr 20:12). An Asaphite Levite, appropriately named Jahaziel, "God *sees*," enters the scene. He prophetically proclaims Yahweh's encouragement: "Fear not, and be not dismayed at this great multitude; for the battle is not yours but God's" (*kî lōʾ lākem hammilḥāmâ kî lēʾlōhîm*; 2 Chr 20:15). The people need not fight. As with the battle at the sea (and with Sea), they need only be still and *see* how Yahweh achieves victory (2 Chr 20:17; cf. Exod 14:13–14). The battle is engaged the next day, with Levite singers proceeding in front of the army praising "a radiantly holy/powerful" (*hadrat-qōdeš*) Yahweh, who does indeed achieve a resounding victory by having the enemies destroy one another.[256]

Elsewhere when Chronicles speaks of Yahweh's holiness it does so by referring to his consecration (*hiqdîš*) of the Jerusalem Temple, a sanctuary (*miqdāš*) where he has chosen to have his name dwell forever (2 Chr 7:16, 20; cf. 1 Kgs 9:3, 7; 2 Chr 30:8). The parallels here with DtrH are not surprising, nor are the plethora of references to Yahweh having Solomon (and not David) build a house for his Name.[257] Yet in three occurrences Chronicles alone borrows from known psalms to emphasize how Yahweh's name is "holy." In 1 Chronicles 16:10, it is again the Asaphite Levites who sing praises to Yahweh's holy Name (*hithalĕlû bĕšēm qodšô*; cf. Ps 105:3). And 1 Chronicles 16:35 borrows from Psalm 106:47 to plead with Yahweh to provide rescue from the nations so that thanksgiving can be offered to his holy name (*lĕhōdôt lĕšēm qodšekā*). Lastly, having provided for the building of the Temple, David offers a prayer of thanksgiving that puts human provisions in proper theological perspective. Everything required for building a house for Yahweh's holy Name (*libnôt-lĕkā bayit lĕšēm qodšekā*) ultimately comes from Yahweh: "For all things come from you, and of your own we have given you . . . all this abundance . . . comes from your hand and is all your own" (1 Chr 29:14, 16). Throughout the ancient Near East, there is a theological notion (theological fiction?) that only the divine can beget the truly divine. This was best articulated in the fashioning of divine images, where, to paraphrase the words of Esarhaddon, "only a god can make a god."[258] Implicitly the Chronicler's devout prayer asserts something similar, as does the underlying ideology of consecration rituals. Though humans indeed build the physical "holy space" (*miqdāš*) for Yahweh's Name (1 Chr 22:19; 2 Chr 20:8), the language of piety can say that only a holy Yahweh can provide for the building of a sanctuary (*miqdāš*) that could house his holy Name (*šēm qodšô*).

Holy Personnel in Chronicles

These brief references to Levites singing the praises of a holy Yahweh are indicative of what we see of holy personnel throughout Chronicles. The history of the status and privileges of Levites is gnarled, as we have seen. The Hebrew Bible preserves voices that are at odds with each other and reflect seemingly constant negotiations over sacerdotal power and position. The language used to designate privilege is that of holiness (Olyan 2000: 35). A short review is in order.

On the restrictive side, we've seen how P never speaks of the Levites as "holy." They never undergo a "consecration" ritual. Only the Aaronids (who, to be clear, are of the Kohathite-Amram branch of the Levites) hold the position of priest (*kōhēn*), and for P, only priests are holy. Only priests are consecrated. As P powerfully affirms in the dramatic tale of Korah's rebellion in Numbers 16, any attempt by non-Aaronid Levites to assert that holiness is to be found outside of the priesthood is anathema to Yahweh, so much so that it occasions a death sentence. For P, Yahweh strictly differentiates that it is only the Aaronid priest "who belongs to Him and who is holy" (*'et-'ăšer-lô wĕ'et-haqqādôš*; Num 16:5). The Aaronid priests alone are able to offer cultic service to divinity. As for the work profile of the non-Aaronid Levites, theirs is an operational function serving (*šēret*) the priests within sacred space. Their sacerdotal status is indeed quite elevated from that of the non-sacerdotal people at large, and they constitute symbolic offerings to Yahweh. Nonetheless, their rank falls far short of priestly holiness.[259]

Summarizing what we have seen, Ezekiel 40–48 (with its own particular vocabulary) is similarly restrictive when it comes to Levites and their holy status. The priests who are once again privileged in status and in function are referred to as "the Levitical priests, the sons of Zadok." In contrast to these Zadokites, the Levites are once again of lesser status and function. They are not privileged to come near to a holy Yahweh as priest, nor are they allowed access to holy space or holy offerings (Ezek 44:13). As in P, the Levites are never referred to as "holy."

On the expansive side, we saw how H conceptualized holiness quite differently. The Aaronid priesthood retains status and cultic privilege, and it is marked (via additional regulations) with the highest possible degrees of sanctity. Precise descriptions of the status of Levites depend on how widely one chooses to define H's corpus.[260] What is clear is that the Levites are never marked for consecrated service. And yet for H, the entire congregation of the people of Israel can achieve holiness ("Be holy, for I, Yahweh your God, am holy"; *qĕdōšîm tihyû kî qādôš 'ănî yhwh 'ĕlōhêkem*; Lev 19:2). In contrast to P's cult-centered holiness, H's vision of holiness is comprehensive, covering a wide array of cultic, economic, judicial, moral, and social parameters. To be fair, as noted earlier, P does hold out a dispensation for Nazirites to be "holy to Yahweh" (Num 6:5, 8) on a temporary basis (and as governed by priestly authority).

As we have seen, in Deuteronomy 33:8–11 Levi is granted wide cultic privileges, and many scholars feel that Deuteronomy advocates that all Levites are potential priests, especially with its term "Levitical priests" (*hakkōhănîm halĕwiyyim*; Deut 18:1–8). Yet rather than modifying "priest" or "Levite" with the adjective "holy," Deuteronomy also speaks of an expansive holiness. Yahweh has chosen Israel from among all the peoples on the earth to be his holy people (Deut 7:6; 14:2, 21; 26:18–19; 28:9). Interestingly, Deuteronomy's distinctive language of "a holy people to Yahweh" (*'am qādôš lĕyhwh*) is never found in DtrH. People are indeed admonished to sanctify themselves on various occasions (Josh 3:5; 7:13; 1 Sam 16:5), yet in DtrH they are not assigned this lofty title of election. As for religious officiants, DtrH does explicitly associate priests (and Levites) with holiness (1 Sam 7:1; 21:1–7 [Eng 21:1–6]), and especially so with regard to transporting the Ark to the most holy place (*qōdeš haqqŏdāšîm*), which the priests alone are privileged to enter (1 Kgs 8:3–11). And yet, despite their sacerdotal status, DtrH has little interest in preserving any detailed consecration rituals that would mark their rank. Instead, when it does want to privilege a priest, DtrH uses its own distinctive and prophetic vocabulary of Yahweh establishing an enduring "faithful house" (*bayit neʾĕmān*) to wed Zadokite priesthood with Davidic monarchy.

Nowhere in Chronicles do we find the language of an enduring "faithful house" (*bayit neʾĕmān*) associated with priest or monarch.[261] Such a contrast with DtrH is striking. What we do find is once again the use of the word "holy" to legitimate priestly power and influence. Though Chronicles presents distinct functions for priests and Levites (e.g., only priests manipulate blood; 2 Chr 29:22, 24; 30:16), distinct allotments (e.g., 2 Chr 35:8–9), and distinct sacred space (2 Chr 29:15–16), both are explicitly referred to as holy. The Chronicles account of the priest Jehoida's power in bringing the child king Joash to the throne (and death to Athaliah) reformulates 1 Kings 11 with a sacerdotal emphasis that has priests and Levites (not the Carites and the royal "outrunners") serving as the Temple guard. The rationale is explicit: "Let no one enter the Temple of Yahweh except the priests and serving Levites [*hakkōhănîm wĕhamĕšārĕtîm halĕwiyyim*]; they may enter, for they are holy [*hēmmâ yābōʾû kî-qōdeš hēmmâ*]" (2 Chr 23:6; cf. 2 Chr 30:15; 31:16; 35:5).

The expanded narrative in Chronicles about Josiah's Passover mentions the cultic duties of priests and Levites, with the latter explicitly called holy (2 Chr 35:3). Sara Japhet (1993: 1047) notes how the notion of being "holy to Yahweh" is widely used in H (for priests; Lev 21:7–8) and P (for Nazirites; Num 6:5, 8) and even for the people at large in H (Lev 19:2) and Deuteronomy (Deut 7:6; 14:2, 21; 26:18–19; 28:9). Yet for the Levites per se, only here in 2 Chronicles 35:3 (together with 2 Chr 23:6) are they individually marked for holiness. A possible reason may be found in the verse itself, which notes that a key function of the Levites (transporting Yahweh's mobile Ark) has now come to an end with the Ark finding a permanent home in the Jerusalem Temple (2 Chr 35:3; cf. 1 Chr 23:25–32). Thus their expanded duties—while not elevated to that of the priests—are legitimized by having "holy" status and the priestly authority to teach law (cf. 2 Chr 15:3). Note especially the innovative intermediary role they play between priest and people in conveying sacrificial blood (2 Chr 30:16).[262]

Consecrated Priests in Chronicles: The Case of King Uzziah's Cultic Overreach (2 Chr 26:16–21)

As for priestly consecration rituals, while DtrH chose to preserve only a single occasion with regard to Eleazar having charge over the Ark (1 Sam 7:1), Chronicles cannot speak often enough about the centrality of consecration and sanctification (discussed later). Yet to be clear, the consecratory vocabulary in Chronicles never speaks of any formal priestly investiture, though the sacerdotal language (e.g., *qdš* in D, tD, and C stems) is similar, and elsewhere even identical (e.g., *millēʾ yad lĕyhwh*; 1 Chr 29:5; 2 Chr 29:31). There is no mention of any type of complex clothing and anointing rituals involving oil and blood similar to what we find in P as it promotes the enduring nature of the "consecrated" Aaronid priesthood (cf. pp. 619–629).

The clearest example of Chronicles' use of consecration to mark position and privilege is found in the conflict between priests and royalty in 2 Chronicles 26:16–21. King Uzziah is the Chronicler's parade case to prove the proverb that "pride goes before destruction" (cf. Prov 16:18; 18:12). Where DtrH is minimalist about how Yahweh smote the good king with a *ṣāraʿat* skin disease[263] that lasted until the day he died (2 Kgs 15:5), the Chronicler is expansive. DtrH is completely silent with regard to what occasioned Yahweh's smiting of a king who reigned for fifty-two years, typically a sign of divine favor. In contrast, the Chronicler is quite vocal about the king's violation of priestly prerogatives. After achieving great strength (agriculturally[264] and especially militarily) through Yahweh's blessings, the king "grew proud to [his own] destruction" (*gābah libbô ʿad-lĕhašḥît*; 2 Chr 26:16). Pridefully, "he wronged Yahweh" (*wayyimʿal bĕyhwh*) by entering into Yahweh's temple to offer incense on the incense altar. Despite the widespread tradition of pre-exilic monarchs enjoying cultic privilege (see Chapter Nine, pp. 498–503), here the king is strongly rebuked by priest and deity. Nowhere else do we read of such a confrontation (but cf. 1 Kgs 13:1–10):

> The priest Azariah went in after him, with eighty priests of Yahweh who were men of valor. They withstood King Uzziah, and said to him, "It is not for you, Uzziah, to burn incense to Yahweh, but [only] for the priests, the descendants of Aaron, who are consecrated to burn incense [*hamĕquddāšîm lĕhaqṭîr*]. Get out of the sanctuary [*hammiqdāš*]! For you have done wrong [*māʿaltā*]! It is not for you to have radiance [*kābôd*] from the god Yahweh. (2 Chr 26:17–18)

Rhetorically, the language of holiness is used to invalidate the king's cultic overreach. For only Aaronid priests who have been made holy through a consecration ritual (*hamĕquddāšîm*) are able to offer incense to Yahweh within the holy space (*hammiqdāš*). The ritual offering of incense, as we saw earlier, demarcates priestly privilege in P, with the death penalty for non-Aaronid violators (Num 16:35; 17:5 [Eng 16:40]). Earlier the Chronicler underscored this Aaronid prerogative by appealing to Mosaic legislation (1 Chr 6:34 [Eng 1 Chr 6:49]; cf. 1 Chr 23:13). Equally fascinating is the Chronicler's assertion that the non-consecrated King Uzziah does not possess Yahweh's *kābôd*. This too shows an awareness of the consecrated priestly service of the Aaronids being one of mediating Yahweh's "radiance," as we saw in P (Exod 28:2–3; 29:43–44; cf. Lev 10:1–3).

The drama of the Uzziah episode continues as the king angrily protests against the priestly rebuke, taking up the censer to offer incense only to have Yahweh smite him with the ṣāraʿat skin disease at that precise moment. King and priests alike, understanding the polluting nature of his new affliction, rush to leave holy space. To his dying day, the defiled king is excluded from the Temple (2 Chr 26:19–20).[265] As we saw earlier with the putting down of the rebellion of Korah and his band of Levites who strove for priestly prerogatives, nothing legitimizes one's hold on an office more than recounting a dramatic story of God miraculously taking one's side. Yet in Chronicles we are presented not with P's internecine Aaronid-Levite conflict but rather with a struggle between priestly and royal cultic control. The Chronicler's literary portrayal astutely uses consecration language to legitimize Aaronid cultic prerogatives as it applies a lifelong polluting ṣāraʿat affliction to delegitimize those of royalty.

Cultic Consecration: Priests and Levites

As for other consecration rituals, Chronicles follows the many other sacerdotal traditions we have seen elsewhere, with its mention of priests and Levites needing to sanctify themselves in order to handle the Ark of Yahweh (1 Chr 15:12, 14; cf. 2 Chr 5:4–11). Becoming ritually holy was also necessary whenever they dealt with sacred space (2 Chr 5:11; 23:6; 29:5, 19) and especially with regard to making sacrifices or engaging in other cultic acts such as offering incense or carrying out purificatory rituals (2 Chr 26:18; 29:5, 15, 19, 31–34; 30:3, 15, 17, 24; 35:6). Among these many texts there are two fascinating but opaque remarks noting particular acts of sacerdotal consecration.

As a part of Hezekiah's cleansing and rededication of the Temple described in 2 Chronicles 29, both priests and Levites sanctify themselves. Priests play a central role in sacrifice and blood manipulation (2 Chr 29:20–24) and are complemented by the Chronicler's prominent Levite musicians, whose worship accompanies the sacrifice (2 Chr 29:25–30).[266] When the consecrated assembly subsequently brings their sacrifices in overwhelming numbers (seventy bulls, a hundred rams, a hundred lambs), the Chronicler notes the lack of enough priests to skin them and the need for additional priests to undergo consecration rituals to help out. In the meantime, the Levites assist the priests, with the Chronicler marking a comparison: "Now the Levites were more conscientious than the priests in sanctifying themselves" (kî halĕwiyyim yišrê lēbāb lĕhitqaddēš mēhakkōhănîm; 2 Chr 29:32–34). Later the Chronicler gives us a more positive portrayal of sanctification when he remarks how "they [seemingly the priests and the Levites][267] were enrolled with all their little children, their wives, their sons, and their daughters, the whole multitude; for they kept themselves most holy in their [respective] positions of trust" (*kî be'ĕmûnātām yitqaddĕšû-qōdeš*; 2 Chr 31:18).[268]

The brief remark about the Levites being more conscientious (*yišrê lēbāb*) with respect to making themselves holy has occasioned a great deal of speculation with regard to how Chronicles views the relationship between priests and Levites. Those who consider the Chronicler's overarching purpose to be advocating for an *elevated* role for the Levites see here a proof text.[269] The Levites "were more upright in heart" (so RSV), and this can only mean that they were superior in cult and piety to wayward priests, who must have been compromised in their service during King Ahaz's reign.[270] Thus in comparison with the various traditions articulating the status of the Levites noted earlier, for these scholars the Chronicler aligns more with the book of Deuteronomy (cf. its vocabulary of "Levitical priests," *hakkōhănîm halĕwiyyim*) in advocating for priestly prerogatives for the Levites. Buttressing such a reconstruction is the status of officiating "holiness" that the Chronicler assigns to Levites (2 Chr 23:6; 35:3), an unimaginable concept for P and Ezekiel (and likely H).

Complicating such a reconstruction are the distinct prerogatives that Chronicles assigns to priests over against Levites. 2 Chronicles 23:6 does indeed note that both priest and Levite are able "to enter the temple of Yahweh" due to their holy status. Yet as for the specific parameters of sacred space, 2 Chronicles 29:16 describes how the priests entered "the *inner part* of the temple of Yahweh" (*pĕnîmâ bêt-yhwh*)—also referred to as the "Holy of Holies" (*qōdeš haqqŏdāšîm*; 1 Chr 6:34)—whereas the Levites are located in "the *court* of the temple of Yahweh" (*ḥăṣar bêt yhwh*; 2 Chr 29:16). Hierarchically, as we saw with the confrontation involving King Uzziah's cultic overreach, Aaron and his sons are additionally "consecrated to burn incense" within the sanctuary (*hamĕquddāšîm lĕhaqṭîr*; 2 Chr 26:18). Whether the Levites were granted the prerogative of offering incense is complicated by conflicting evidence, but many scholars do not think that the Chronicler assigns them this right.[271] Chronicles twice describes in full the cultic actions of the Aaronids, underscoring this cultic prerogative, and it also mentions the making of atonement:

> Aaron and his sons were making offerings [*maqṭîrîm*] on the altar of burnt offering and on the incense altar for every work of the Holy of Holies [*qōdeš haqqŏdāšîm*] to atone for Israel according to all that Moses the servant of God had commanded. (1 Chr 6:34 [Eng 1 Chr 6:49])

> Aaron was set apart in order to consecrate the most holy objects [*lĕhaqdîšô qōdeš qodāšîm*], he and his sons forever, to make offerings [*lĕhaqṭîr*] before Yahweh, to serve him and to pronounce blessings in his name forever. (1 Chr 23:13)

Most importantly, as in every other tradition, only priests are described as having the privilege to manipulate blood (2 Chr 29:22, 24; 30:16).[272] The Chronicler is clear that the Levites' association with blood is that of conveying it to the priests (2 Chr 30:16). Thus it seems wise to side with Knoppers' (1999; 2003b; 2004: 613–618; 820–826) reconstruction of the Chronistic data that argues for a complementary relationship between priests and Levites. Priests are marked for holiness and have elevated prerogatives. The Chronicler goes out of his way to celebrate the exemplary priest Jehoida.[273] Yet notably (and quite remarkably given the lack in other traditions), Levites are also marked for holiness (2 Chr 23:6; 2 Chr 35:3). In addition, Yahweh has chosen (*bḥr*) the Levites (2 Chr 29:11), and such a term of election "is one of the clearest indications of the esteem in which the Levites are held" (Knoppers 2004: 613).

Holy Personnel (Mostly) Missing from the Record: Holy Prophets

Biblical texts explicitly referring to additional religious specialists thought to be holy (or to be able to mediate divine holiness) are fragmentary, revealing once again that the data that we have to work with are meager. Cases in point are the few scattered references to prophets explicitly called holy.[274] The call narrative in Jeremiah 1:5 has Yahweh consecrating (*hiqdaštîkā*) Jeremiah for prophetic service while he was still in his mother's womb. Later, as an adult, Jeremiah reflects on the ways in which he has been overwhelmed by the "immense power" of Yahweh's holy and fiery words (*dibrê qodšô, dĕbārî kā'ēš*; Jer 23:9, 29; cf. 20:9; Lundbom 2004: 182). Yet Jeremiah is exceptional. For the most part, attestations of "holy" prophets are missing from the biblical record even though the relationship between prophets and priests is well attested, with Ezekiel held up as the classic example.[275] Moreover, while Ezekiel's *kōhēn* priesthood is clearly mentioned (Ezek 1:3), other sacerdotal activities of prophets are not so marked. As Zevit (2004: 202) notes with respect to the famous Mt. Carmel incident, "Both Elijah and the prophets [of Baal] construct altars, slaughter and dress sacrifices, and pray. The ritual involving sacrifice appears to have been sacerdotal, yet none of the protagonists is identified as a priest." Nor is such cultic activity referred to as holy.

"A Holy Man of God" (2 Kgs 4:9)

Outside of Jeremiah, we have one truly exceptional reference to explicit prophetic holiness, yet scholars have situated the discussion within literary and anthropological (rather than sacerdotal) frameworks. The mention is found in the story of Elisha and the Shunemite woman in 2 Kings 4. At the outset of the story, even before the prophet manifests his divine power in resurrecting her dead son, the woman is confident that the roving prophet "is a holy man of God" ('îš 'ĕlōhîm qādôš hû'; 2 Kgs 4:9). What is said here of Elisha could be said too of Elijah, though there is no explicit reference to the latter's holy powers. The traditions of these two prophets are so much alike that scholars group them together and, tellingly, categorize them under the genre of hagiography. Such legendary material, writes Blenkinsopp (1996: 59), "comes to us from that remote time in the past" and exhibits "an impression of enormous and dangerous spiritual power and energy."

The list of Elijah's divine, miraculously powerful activities is lengthy; Elisha's is even more so. Elijah is fed by ravens or angels (1 Kgs 17:1–7; 19:5–8), controls the weather (1 Kgs 18:41–45), multiplies the food of a widow (1 Kgs 17:8–16), raises her dead son to life (1 Kgs 17:17–24), miraculously defeats the prophets of Baal on Mt. Carmel using divine fire (1 Kgs 18:20–40), runs a semi-marathon at incredible speeds (1 Kgs 18:46), experiences a Moses-like theophany on Mt. Horeb (1 Kgs 19:9–12), brings destructive fire down from the heavens (2 Kgs 1:9–16), and at the end of his life is carried up to heaven in a whirlwind with a chariot of fire and horses of fire (2 Kgs 2:11–12). Elisha, the Hebrew Bible's miracle worker par excellence, multiplies jars of oil (2 Kgs 4:1–7), raises the Shunemite woman's dead son to life (2 Kgs 4:8–37), makes inedible (poisonous?) food edible (2 Kgs 4:38–41), cleans a water supply with salt (2 Kgs 2:19–22), provides abundant water for a military campaign (2 Kgs 3:9–20), multiplies food (2 Kgs 4:42–44), cures the skin disease of Naaman (2 Kgs 5) and brings it upon the deceptive Gehazi (2 Kgs 5:26–27), makes a sunken iron axe head float (2 Kgs 6:1–7), and knows the words that a distant king speaks in his private bedroom (2 Kgs 6:12). After Elisha's death, even his bones have miraculous powers of revivification (2 Kgs 13:20–21). As for tapping into divinely destructive power, where Elijah twice used deadly fire, Elisha uses a divinely empowered curse to kill forty-two mockers (2 Kgs 2:23–25) and a divine strike of blindness (together with subsequent hospitality!) to bring enemy troops into submission (2 Kgs 6:18–23).

Three scholars have nuanced how it is that both Elijah and Elisha constitute "holy men of God" even though only Elisha is explicitly called such (2 Kgs 4:9).[276] Alexander Rofé (1988:16) brings attention to the genre of these types of popular stories where the miraculous (even lethal) performance of the prophet "is a logical consequence of the conception of the Holy displayed in these tales—the Divine as an awesome, mighty power." Citing Rudolph Otto, Rofé affirms that the presence of the holy man of God "brings blessing . . . however, it constitutes a danger too." Preferring Clifford Geertz's theoretical model, Thomas Overholt

(1996: 24–68) argues that social anthropology holds the key to understanding Elijah and Elisha as "men of power," especially in how their feats of the miraculous resonate with the actions of shamanic holy men across the world. David Petersen (2002: 6, 228), who calls Elisha "a preternaturally *powerful* person," defines such people (Elijah too) as those who "possess the *power of the holy* and hence are dangerous, *powerful*, and due appropriate respect." "The holy man," he continues, "personifies the deity in the midst of the profane world . . . Such *powers* belong to the world of the sacred" (my emphasis). In this respect we again see what we uncovered earlier in the present chapter: to be holy is to be powerful. Elijah's and Elisha's representation and/or mediation of divine holiness necessarily results in power-laden, even lethal activity. The essence of this type of holiness is not that of cultic sanctification or sacerdotal rank. It is not about consecration rituals of clothing and anointing, or the need to demarcate the sacred and the profane, or who is accorded what cultic privilege. And we see again within Otto's theoretical framework that the two sides of holiness are at every turn, from the benevolence of providing a widow with the means of sustenance (2 Kgs 4:1–7) to the lethal results of not respecting the danger of divine power (2 Kgs 2:23–25).

Holy Personnel: Women as Holy Functionaries

Women functioned as religious specialists in a variety of capacities, though they were termed "holy" only in the case of P's female Nazirite (see pp. 632–636) and in the case of the often misunderstood *qĕdēšâ* (plural *qĕdēšôt*). As Susan Ackerman (2008a, 2013, 2016) astutely points out, whereas state-sponsored religion (for example at Jerusalem, Bethel, and Dan) restricted women's cultic agency,[277] women found fewer constraints in regional sanctuaries and especially in household shrines. Hannah's performative rituals at Shiloh, which include prayer, the making of a vow, the provision of offerings, and perhaps sacrificial slaughter (1 Sam 1:21–28), are illustrative.[278] It is Hannah's prayer that gives us one of our earliest declarations of Yahweh's incomparable holiness (*'ên qādôš ka-yhwh, mî qādôš ka-yhwh*; see pp. 588–591). Other women who participated in a variety of religious acts include those serving (*ṣōbĕ'ōt*) at the entrance of the Tent of Meeting (Exod 38:8; 1 Sam 2:22),[279] those participating in the Queen of Heaven cult (Jer 7:16–20; 44:15–19, 25), Zipporah's activites connected with blood and circumcision/expiation (Exod 4:24–26),[280] Micah's mother acting as patron in commissioning a divine image in a household shrine (Judges 17:1–4),[281] Ma'acah making an image of Asherah (1 Kgs 15:13), Solomon's foreign wives offering incense and sacrificing to their gods (1 Kgs 11:8), female prophetic intermediaries (Miriam, Deborah, Huldah, the unnamed prophetess in Isa 8:3,

Noadiah, the daughters who prophesy in Ezek 13:17–23), female necromancers (Lev 20:27; 1 Sam 28; Isa 57:3), the women mourning for Tammuz (Ezek 8:14), and so on.

In many other cultures some of these ritual specialists would be referred to as holy personnel. Yet as we have seen, the presentation of "holiness" in the Hebrew Bible is overwhelmingly ideological and androcentric. This can also be seen in how women are never referred to as "priests" (*kōhenet; kōhănôt*), and the same can be said with regard to their Late Bronze Age Ugaritic neighbors to the north. As Ackerman (2013: 165) notes, "It is difficult to identify within either the Ugaritic or Hebrew Bible corpora a woman, or women, who might be said to fulfill a priestly role or assume priestly obligations." What makes such restrictions stand out are the prominent roles of priestesses elsewhere in the ancient Near East. One calls to mind the focus on the high priestess of the storm god and the *maš'artu* priestess at Late Bronze Age Emar as well as the prominent role of 'Ummî'aštart, the fifth-century BCE Phoenican "priestess of 'Aštart" (*khnt 'štrt*).[282]

Cultic Prostitution?

The Hebrew Bible preserves a handful of references to "consecrated women" (*qĕdēšâ/qĕdēšôt*; Gen 38:21–22; Deut 23:18 [Eng 23:17]; Hos 4:14), whose function may or may not be parallel to that of "consecrated men" (*qādēš/qĕdēšim*; Deut 23:18 [Eng 23:17]; 1 Kgs 14:24; 22:47 [Eng 22:46]; 1 Kgs 15:12 [Eng 15:11]; 2 Kgs 23:7). These terms have had a tortured history of interpretation.[283] None of these passages refers to Aaronid priests, Levites, or Nazirites (female or male) who are considered holy or consecrated in other traditions. These four specific terms (*qĕdēšâ/qĕdēšôt, qādēš/qĕdēšim*) never occur in the sacerdotal discussions found in P, H, Ezekiel or Chronicles.[284]

Due to a mere three instances where *qĕdēšâ/qĕdēšôt* occurs in contexts mentioning *zōnâ/zōnôt*, "prostitute(s)," or *znh*, "to play the harlot; to whore" (Gen 38:15, 21–22, 24; Deut 23:18–19 [Eng 23:17–18]; Hos 14:4), all four terms have frequently been used to argue for a Judean practice of cultic prostitution, female and male. English editions of the Bible regularly translate these terms as "female/male cultic prostitutes." Karel van der Toorn (1989: 201–202) notes how this practice is typically defined as "sympathetic magic," where the sexual encounter is intended "to heighten the chances of human offspring, the increase of the flocks, and an abundant harvest." Van der Toorn's assessment is curt: "Sacred prostitution understood in this sense never existed in ancient Israel."[285] Writing on the male terminology (*qādēš/qĕdēšim*), Phyllis Bird (1997b: 37) concurs: "A class of 'male cult prostitutes' in ancient Israel . . . is questionable on literary, linguistic, and sociological grounds." Kristel Nyberg (2008: 319) summarizes that "the conclusion that widespread cultic prostitution existed in ancient Israel is outdated," with Jessie DeGrado (2018) stating that it's time to put the myth of the sacred prostitute to bed.

The majority of scholars who have synthesized the meager data that we possess have concluded that these "consecrated" individuals were cultic functionaries who were considered illegitimate by the Deuteronomistic Historian(s). The pejorative language of harlotry and promiscuity was used to disparage their actions, which were deemed illicit. The beginning of the book of Hosea with Gomer, the "wife of harlotry" (*'ēšet zĕnûnîm*), is a prime example of metaphorically equating Israel's worship of other deities with marital infidelity.[286] There are attempts to label these practitioners as "Canaanite," though even here one cannot support any notion of sacred prostitution from the references to *qdš*-functionaries in the Ugaritic texts.[287] Others have looked to the Mesopotamian sphere for parallels. Here Mayer Gruber's (1986: 146) summary is apt: "The Akkadian *qadištu* . . . was a wetnurse, a midwife, a functionary (primarily a cultic singer) in the cult of Adad, occasionally an archivist, and in late times even a sorceress, but by no means a prostitute, cultic or otherwise" (cf. Westenholz 1989: 250–260).

Nonetheless, due to the clear juxtaposition of *qĕdēšâ/qĕdēšôt* and prostitution in three texts (Deut 23:18; Gen 38:21–22; Hosea 4:14), the issue remains unresolved for many interpreters. DeGrado (2018: 23) notes how the translation of "cultic prostitute" remains appealing precisely due to its explanatory power for all three of these texts. She summarizes two conflicting approaches to handling these texts. One view is to see the *qĕdēšâ* as a priestess who was not a prostitute but polemically portrayed as such (e.g., Westenholz). The alternative view is to see the *qĕdēšâ* as a prostitute (in line with post-biblical Hebrew usage) and not at all a cultic functionary (e.g., Gruber).

Problematically, neither view is satisfactory for interpreting all three texts. In response, DeGrado shows how scholars have mistakenly reduced a multivalent *qĕdēšâ* to an all-encompassing definition without concern for diachronic and geographic variation. DeGrado (2018: 30, 32) argues that *qĕdēšâ* originally marked a cultic functionary (with no emphasis on sexual rites) and thus, socially, a single woman working outside of the male-dominated household. Later, "through a process of generalization and pejoration, the Hebrew word shifted from designating priestesses to single women more generally, with the implication of uncontrolled sexuality." The diachronic evolution of the word was one of "shifting from describing a priestess to a working woman and, by the rabbinic period, a prostitute."[288]

In short, in contrast to many Bible translations, there is a clear consensus among scholars that there is little support for cultic prostitution being practiced in ancient Israel, especially as it is defined as a type of sympathetic magic. What we do have are clear references to certain women in ancient Israel being referred to as "consecrated functionaries" (qĕdēšâ/qĕdēšôt). Regrettably, we do not have sufficient data to be able to say much more—other than that their practices ran counter to those who preserved their history. It is also telling that the sources that used holiness (qdš) as an ideological category of power, prestige, influence, and status (especially P) give no hint that there were indeed qĕdēšâ/qĕdēšôt and qādēš/qĕdēšim in ancient Israel.

Conclusion

This chapter began by quoting Ernst Sellin's remark about the centrality of divine holiness in the Hebrew Bible—how holiness was thought to "constitute the deepest and innermost nature" of God. Such a strong assertion was then situated within the broader Northwest Semitic context to underscore the widespread notion that holiness is one of the primary markers of divinity. When exploring this divine trait in the Hebrew Bible, one cannot help but notice how often holiness was contextualized within the fabric of society. For some it meant the thunder of God working on their behalf, with the incomparably powerful Holy One reversing the fortunes of the disadvantaged (1 Sam 2:1–10) or emboldening a monarch (Ps 89:19 [Eng 89:18]). Poets embodied Yahweh's power, saying that he bares "his holy arm" (zĕrôaʿ qodšô) to achieve military victory for Jerusalem (Isa 52:10; Ps 98:1). Others envisioned divine power in categories of cultic lethality, rehearsing well-known tales of victims such as Nadab, Abihu, and Uzzah. How could humans approach the Unapproachable when immediate death came to those lacking ritual safeguards? For others (especially P and Ezekiel), holiness had to do with social privilege, restricted sacerdotal status, and the management of cult. God chose a select few to be his holy representatives and provided detailed regulations to administer what was deemed sacred (space, time, personnel, offerings, cultic paraphernalia, etc.). For yet others (especially H), holiness was inclusive, as it placed demands on society at large to aspire to God's character, virtues, and desires regarding a wide variety of social, cultic, judicial, economic, and moral topics. In short, to be holy is to embody the principle of *imitatio Dei*—"to be holy as he is holy" (Lev 11:44–45; cf. 19:2; 20:7; 21:8). Any understanding of Yahweh as holy must shun reductionism and incorporate all of the aforementioned voices, the theological as well as the sociological.[289]

To conclude, we need briefly to comment on three additional aspects of holiness. The first has to do with a handful of texts that have Yahweh proclaiming that he will manifest his holiness. The second involves the broad topic of sacred space. The third brings in voices from wisdom literature.

"Yahweh Shows Himself to Be Holy"

Linguistically, the reflexive use of the N and tD stems of *qdš* with God being the subject reminds us that Yahweh was thought to show himself to be holy. Overwhelmingly these expressions revert to the notion of Yahweh's power that we saw at the outset of this chapter. Due to the prevalence of Yahweh, "the Holy One of Israel," in the Isaianic tradition (see pp. 599–603), we are not surprised to read that the prophet exults "the Holy God *who shows himself holy*" (*hāʾēl haqqādôš niqdāš*) against the haughty through his justice and righteousness (Isa 5:15–16).[290] Yet, curiously, most of the reflexive usages occur in material (P and Ezekiel) where one would assume the notion of divine holiness would be tied to the management of cult rather than divine power. Ezekiel repeatedly has Yahweh manifesting his holiness to Israel and especially to the nations by his powerful acts of redeeming Israel from their lands and returning them to Judah (Ezek 20:42; 28:25–26; 36:23; 39:25–27).[291] Yahweh's destruction of Sidon (Ezek 28:22–23) and Gog (Ezek 38:16, 23) are also described as examples of the self-manifestation of Yahweh's holy (military) power. P's account of Yahweh's revelation of his holy power takes us back to the deaths of Nadab and Abihu. The specific vocabulary is illuminating. Yahweh's destructive fire occasions Moses to remark: "This is what Yahweh meant when he said: 'Through those near to me [i.e., the priests)], I will manifest holiness [*ʾeqqādēš*]; before all the people I will manifest *kābôd* [*ʾekkābēd*].'" As discussed in Chapter Seven (pp. 358–379), Yahweh's *kābôd* represents his radiant presence, power, and majesty (cf. Exod 14:4, 17–18). Thus, as in Ezekiel 28:22, these two expressions are parallel. Yahweh's destructive power is a manifestation of his holiness and his radiance.

Holy (Sacred) Space

Theologically, it is Yahweh who sanctifies (*qiddaš/hiqdîš*) space. Functionally, religious officiants carry out the process through ritual. Existentially, as poets and psalmists frequently proclaim, Yahweh's presence was thought to make any space or location holy, as seen in a wide array of sacred vocabulary: "sanctuary" (*miqdāš*), "the holy [place]" (*haqqōdeš*), "the holy place" (*māqôm haqqōdeš*), "holy encampment" (*nĕwēh qodeš*), "holy dwelling" (*mĕʿôn qodšô*), "holy mountain" (*har haqqōdeš/har qodšî*), "holy border" (*gĕbûl qodšô*), "holy heaven" (*šĕmê qodšô*), "holy height" (*mĕrôm qodšô*), "holy ground" (*ʾadmat-qōdeš*), "holy throne" (*kissēʾ qodšô*), "holy temple" (*hêkal qodšô*), "holy inner sanctum" (*dĕbîr qodšekā*), and "the most holy place" (*qōdeš haqqŏdāšîm*). P would note that the place where Yahweh appears must be sanctified due to his theophanic "radiance" (*wĕnôʿadtî šāmmâ . . . wĕniqdaš bikĕbōdî*; Exod 29:43). Deuteronomistic Name Theology would argue that Yahweh himself consecrated sacred space to make it a proper residence for the lodging of his Name (e.g., 1 Kgs 9:3). Other voices focus on reverence: if Yahweh (or his preternatural representative) resides in space, one had better remove one's sandals (*kî hammāqôm ʾăšer ʾattâ ʿōmēd ʿālāyw ʾadmat-qōdeš /qōdeš hûʾ*; Exod 3:5; Josh 5:15).

In recent years, a plethora of research has been devoted to sacred space with regard to the Hebrew Bible's presentation and beyond. Theoretical studies abound, from those using a naive understanding (like the classic yet now dated formulation by Mircea Eliade) to those sensitive to the social dynamics of contested space based especially on the spatial theories of Henri Lefebvre, Edward W. Soja, and Jonathan Z. Smith. Obviously, a comprehensive overview of holy (sacred) space is beyond the parameters of the present study. In addition to (1) the multiple literary locations of divine residence (from the Garden of Eden to the Jerusalem Temple to cosmic and sacred mountains),[292] (2) gradations of holiness as they relate to spatial configurations,[293] and (3) the various contours of spatial theory (e.g., Lefebvre's trifold spatial practice, representation of space, and spaces of representation),[294] a comprehensive survey would also have to include (4) a contextualizing of sacred space within Israel's perceptions of space per se (Faust 2010, 2017, 2019) and (5) the rich documentation from the archaeological record.[295] For the last of these, a look at Zevit's (2001) impressive analysis reveals the daunting nature of the task, especially when one considers the many and varied forms of sacred architecture, with an ever-increasing number of examples coming from each new season of excavations. Building on Colin Renfrew's (1985) criteria for correlating material culture with patterned religious behavior (i.e., "the archaeology of cult"), Zevit (2001: 123–124) perceptively formulates a taxonomy of ten different types of sacred space: cult place, cult room, cult corner, cult cave, cult complex, cult center, temple, temple complex, shrines, and cult site.

The Last Word: Wisdom Literature

Having written much, we now leave the last word on Yahweh's holiness to the wisdom tradition (Qoh 12:12–13). The notion of Yahwistic holiness within the wisdom tradition has not been treated at any length, for the root *qdš* rarely appears in Proverbs, Qoheleth, Job, and the wisdom psalms.[296] Sages certainly taught disciples about Yahweh as a holy god and the need for humans to engage in holy activity (cf. Gammie 1989: 125–149, 150–172). The prologue to the Book of Job lifts up the pious and priestly Job as a prime example of someone who sanctified his children (*yĕqaddĕšēm*) by sacrificing burnt offerings just in case they had sinned (Job 1:5). The dialogue presents Job, the sufferer of unrelenting pain, proclaiming that he "has not suppressed the words of the Holy

One" (lōʾ kiḥadtî ʾimrê qādôš; Job 6:10). The meaning is difficult, as it is not clear if the "words" in question are *by* God or *about* God. Is Job saying that he has not held back from articulating holy Yahweh's precepts either in general or with regard to his situation? Or is Job saying, as translated by NJPS, that he has not suppressed his words of complaint against the Holy One? The latter would be a statement of challenge, whereas the former would be a profession of piety.[297] Later in the book, as Job's words grow vehement, the author certainly pushes the envelope in questioning divine justice (see Chapter Nine, pp. 551–557), yet he never questions the holiness of Yahweh. For the edginess of wisdom literature challenging the social status quo, we must turn to the single occurrence of the root *qdš* in Qoheleth. In a setting of sacred space (měqôm qādôš), the author strikes out against the absurdly positive treatment of the wicked in contrast to that of the righteous.[298]

Proverbially, we are left with the following advice, which Michael Fox (2000: 112) calls "the apex of *ḥokmah*, the highest degree of wisdom and Torah":

The fear of Yahweh is the beginning of wisdom,	těḥillat ḥokmâ
	yirʾat yhwh
The knowledge of the Holy One is understanding.	wědaʿat qědōšîm bînâ

(Proverbs 9:10)

Though *qědōšîm* in this verse could refer to holy principles or God's holy attendants, Fox (2009: 855) is certainly correct that here it is used in synonymous parallelism to refer to Yahweh as the Holy One. The plural *qědōšîm* being used of the singular Yahweh poses no difficulties, with linguists categorizing it as a "plural of majesty/excellence," "an intensive plural of rank," an "honorific" plural, or a plural of abstraction.[299] The "fear of Yahweh" reminds us of the *tremendum* documented at the outset of this chapter, where divine presence and holy power occasion fear.[300] Yet where the fear of the divine in Exodus 20:15–18 (Eng 20:18–21) kept people at a distance, here in Proverbs it is invitational, beckoning them to live a godly life. The "knowledge of the Holy One" reminds us of the many detailed regulations of cultic, moral, and ethical holiness documented in the second half of this chapter. For as Fox (2000: 112) astutely observes, "knowledge of God, in Proverbs as elsewhere in the Bible is never mere cognition of facts . . . [it] requires commitment as well . . . [and] this commitment must be realized in action."

Conclusion

The distillate described in the opening chapter sketched a process whereby the flavor of Israelite religion could be tasted through a selective sampling. A distillate provides more depth than an introductory work and is thus appropriate for a reference volume to which a reader can turn for primary and secondary research materials. What is sacrificed is breadth of coverage, for indeed, a comprehensive analysis is unattainable in a single volume (see again the many topics mentioned in Chapter One). And yet the synthetic samplings offered in the preceding chapters are robust enough to present some of the core complexities of ancient Israelite religion.

Selectively, we have chosen the following seven "tastings" as representative of the whole: (1) the literary and cultural portrayals of El, the deity who appears in the name of the eponymous ancestor Isra*el* and whose worship is often family based; (2) the ways in which El was represented via comparative iconography and via standing stones attested archaeologically, both of which complement our literary portrayals; (3) a historical analysis of the origin of Yahweh via the Hebrew Bible's foundation stories and the epigraphic record; (4) an iconographic and literary analysis of the degrees to which Yahweh was represented anthropomorphically, theriomorphically, and via abstract expressions; (5) the ways in which Yahweh was characterized as a mythic warrior as well as a divine parent at home in family religion; (6) the characterization of Yahweh as king within the setting of royal cult and as judge against a backdrop of Israelite judiciaries; and (7) an exploration of the holiness of Yahweh, with particular focus on sacerdotal hierarchies. Of these seven parameters, the last three intentionally use divinity as a lens by which to explore the practice of cult sociologically (e.g., family religion, royal cult, priestly cult, prophetic perspectives, reflective traditions) together with a variety of cultic actors, ideologies, and religious understandings.

Using divinity as an organizing principle runs a certain risk. Obviously, Israelite divinity and religious culture were more holistic and pluralistic than what is presented here. Out of necessity, many divine traits that readers might consider essential have been treated minimally in the foregoing pages. Certainly a strong case could be made for in-depth coverage of Yahweh as creator, Yahweh as an agrarian deity, Yahweh as a transcendent god, Yahweh as an eternal god, Yahweh as lord, Yahweh as storm god, Yahweh as "the living God," Yahweh as a solar deity, Yahweh as a forgiving and merciful god, Yahweh as shepherd, Yahweh as a rock of stability, Yahweh as healer, Yahweh as one strengthening the weak, Yahweh as a jealous god, Yahweh as a source of wisdom, Yahweh as teacher, Yahweh as a patient god, Yahweh as divine lover, and so on. The list of divine features is unending. How the ancients might have privileged a certain attribute or wedded various traits will be addressed shortly. Yet first we need to revisit Israelite divinity broadly construed.

Israelite Divinity Broadly Construed

As for pluralism, the astute reader has certainly noticed glaring omissions in our treatment. In our opening chapter we sketched what it would take to describe the various "structures of divinity," to borrow a phrase from Mark Smith (2001b: 25). In contrast to the wide panorama of divinity in ancient Israel, the scope of the present volume concentrates on male divinity and singular divinity (i.e., El and Yahweh). Minimal treatment is given to female divinity, the plurality of divinity, hypostatic representations of divinity, and the many expressions of the preternatural both angelic and demonic.
Why?

Let me be clear: The omission of this material should not be read as a slight to female divinity or to polytheism or to the fascinating world of the preternatural, all of which are subjects I have explored elsewhere. The exact opposite is true. These weighty topics are of such substance for understanding ancient Israel and its cultural world that they deserve full-length treatments in their own right.

Excursus: ʿAštart as an Illustrative Case

Consider, for example, what it would take to analyze just one of the many relevant goddesses from ancient Israel: ʿAštart, better known through her Greek name, Astarte.[1] To do the goddess justice, one must start by overturning decades of misinterpretations that have either minimized her nature to the point of boredom or eroticized her to the point of orgy. For the former, consider the evaluation of André Caquot and Maurice Sznycer (1980: 15) that "at Ugarit . . . Athtart was a very colourless deity. She was really no more than a pale reflection of Anath. . . . [T]his inevitably makes one ask whether 'Athtart' was really no more than a name for 'goddess,' with no special mythical significance at all."[2] For the latter we have William Foxwell Albright's (1968a: 185–186) conclusion that "Astarte was best known as the patroness of sexual reproduction." Elsewhere he writes: "At its worst . . . the erotic aspect of their [i.e., Anath and Astarte's] cult must have sunk to extremely sordid depths of social degradation" (Albright 2006: 76–77; cf. R. Schmitt 2013: 213 n. 1). Turning to the archaeological record has frequently confused matters, with any naked female being labeled "Astarte" and with her temples said to be scattered everywhere. Elizabeth Bloch-Smith's (2014: 167) critique succinctly summarizes: "Studies of Astarte suffer from a lack of methodological rigor."

After clearing away past debris, one could start afresh by initially treating the data from the Hebrew Bible, where we run immediately into questions of orthography, vocalization, and etymology (not unlike the challenges faced with regard to the meaning of the name Yahweh in Chapter Six).[3] The goddess is well known from other Levantine sources, appearing as ʿAštart (ʿštrt) in Phoenician, as ʿAthtartu (ʿṯtrt)/ ^{d}Ištar at Ugarit (respectively in the Ugaritic/Akkadian texts), and as ^{d}Ištar (^{d}INANNA/^{d}Iš$_8$-tár) at Emar. In the Hebrew Bible we have, confusingly, ʿštrt vocalized both as a singular (ʿaštōret) and as a plural (ʿaštārôt) and with the Greek renderings as Astartē. Just as an original Yahweh was "revocalized" by the Masoretes by using the vowels of ʾădōnay, so too the original vocalization of the goddess (seemingly ʿaštart) was revocalized to ʿaštōret by using the vowels of the pejorative bōšet, "shame." (A similar recasting elsewhere turned baʿal names into bōšet names.) Once again, we have to clear away a later pejorative patina just to begin our work.

The Biblical Portrayal of ʿAštart

As noted in most studies, despite the widespread prominence of ʿAthtartu/ ʿAštart/Astarte in the Northern and Southern Levant as well as in Egypt and the expanded Phoenician colonies (cf. Bonnet 1996; Cornelius 2004; Christian and Schmitt 2013a; Sugimoto 2014; Wilson-Wright 2016), ʿštrt appears a mere three times in the Hebrew Bible as a singular goddess and six times to mark the divine plurality (but cf. 1 Sam 31:10, discussed later). An additional eight occurrences of the plural form (ʿaštārôt) mark toponyms, with four other instances marking a specific idiom (ʿštrt ṣōʾnekā, "the fecundity of your flock") in the book of Deuteronomy (Deut 7:13; 28:4, 18, 51). Such a meager dataset underscores the limitations facing the historian of Israelite religion. Moreover, redaction and ideological criticism come into play as once again we face a pejorative framing of the goddess long before the Masoretes touched the text. The three explicit DtrH references to the goddess associate her with the Sidonians (1 Kgs 11:5, 33; 2 Kgs 23:13) and the cult of Solomon's wayward years. Yet another likely reference can be found in 1 Samuel 31:10, where she is associated with the Philistines.[4] In 2 Kings 23:13, the cult of ʿAštart is labeled as "abominable" (šiqquṣ), an anathema that Josiah's reform eradicated. DtrH's evaluations of the plural form (ʿaštārôt) are equally negative, often associating these female divinities with illicit Baal worship.

Reading between the lines, we find undeniable indications that ʿAštart was worshipped as a vibrant goddess in some segments of ancient Israelite society, though our data allow us to say next to nothing about how widespread her cult was (but see the discussion later). Two lines of evidence may provide windows into the nature of her cult, or at least help us to form hypotheses that can then be tested. The idiom mentioned earlier (ʿštrt ṣōʾnekā) seems to be a "demythologizing" of ʿAštart, recasting her divinity to address agrarian concerns.[5] The Deuteronomic author recharacterizes not just one but three known Canaanite deities (ʿAštart, Shagar, Dagan) in order to promote Yahweh as the sole benefactor of agriculture and livestock.[6] Just as our author turns a personalized ʿAštart (actually ʿAštarts, plural)[7] into a common noun, "the *fecundity* of your flock" (ʿštrt ṣōʾnekā), so too Dagan becomes "your *grain*" (děgānĕkā) and Shagar becomes "the *increase* of your cattle" (šĕgar-ʾălāpêkā). In context, these three demythologized phrases sit easily beside similar phrases—"the fruit of your womb" (pĕrî-biṭnĕkā), "the fruit of your ground" (pĕrî-ʾadmātekā), "your wine and oil" (tîrōšĕkā wĕyiṣhārekā)—as ways in which Yahweh will love (ʾhb), bless (brk), and multiply (rbh) his people (Deut 7:13). The following verse summarizes the blessings: Yahweh's people (male and female) and their livestock will not be barren (lōʾ-yihyeh bĕkā ʿāqār waʿăqārâ ûbibhemtekā). Thus one could hypothesize that the ʿAštart cult that is being appropriated to serve Yahwism had agrarian concerns that included fecund humans and animals.

A second line of potential evidence is the "Queen of Heaven" (*malkat haššāmayim) material known from Jeremiah 7:16–20; 44:15–30. The secondary literature on the identity of this queenly goddess is too vast to survey here.[8] A reigning theory (see Day 2000: 148–150) asserts that the Queen of Heaven should be identified as ʿAštart (or a syncretism of West Semitic ʿAštart and East Semitic Ishtar). The nature of the Queen of Heaven cult is multifaceted. The MT's vocalization again presents a deliberate disparagment that refers to *mĕleket haššāmayim* ("the work of heavens") rather than *malkat haššāmayim ("the Queen of Heaven"). According to Jeremiah 7:18, the cult seems to have a component of family religion, with mention of women (mothers?), fathers, and children as ritual actors and with cult being on a local/domestic scale. Susan Ackerman (2008a: 143) thus refers to "the household-based cult of the Queen of Heaven." Jeremiah 44:17 likewise refers to an ancestral connection (ʾābōt), yet also mentions royal cult (see the mention of kings [mĕlākîm] and royal officials [śārîm] as ritual actors). Such elite cultic actors would be hierarchically fitting for the worship of a divine queen. If the punishment in Jeremiah 7:20 is related to the nature of the cult, then again the focus is on agriculture (ʿēṣ haśśādeh; pĕrî hāʾădāmâ) and livestock (bĕhēmâ). In Jeremiah 44:17–18, the Judean cult (which involved vows, offerings, and libations) was said to address concerns over famine and war. The latter resonates with 1 Samuel 31:10, where DtrH's presentation of the Philistine ʿAštart includes a trophy of war (Saul's armor) being placed in her temple.

Using the data from these Queen of Heaven texts, one could hypothesize that the Judean ʿAštart cult was sociologically diverse (familial and royal cults) and addressed general concerns of prosperity, but especially food production and safety from war.

ʿAthtartu/ʿAštart/Astarte in Syria (Emar and Ugarit), Egypt, and Phoenicia

These meager data about the presence of ʿAštart in ancient Israel address biblical religion only—that is, the literary (re-)presentation of ʿAštart cult as found in a narrow slice of biblical tradition. These thin threads hardly provide the materials needed to weave a robust picture of the goddess. Any hypotheses about the deity's nature would have to be situated within ancient Israel's broader cultural world. Questions of cultural contact with other ʿAštart traditions would have to be fully explored via cognate literatures, iconography, and archaeology, and yet with cautions against making generalizations. Just as Chapters Four and Five situated Israelite El worship within the context of broader cognate material (especially ʾIlu at Late Bronze Age Ugarit), even a preliminary study of Israelite ʿAštart would have to be situated (1) within Late Bronze Age Syrian traditions from Ugarit and Emar, (2) within Egyptian traditions, especially in the New Kingdom, and (3) within later first-millennium BCE Phoenician sources. A full analysis would require incorporating the extensive Neo-Assyrian Ishtar cults (cf. Ornan 2001, 2006; Allen 2015: 141–199). What follows is a preliminary sketch.

Aštartu at Emar

Thankfully, ʿAthtartu/ʿAštart/Astarte studies are undergoing a renaissance, with scholars working in many of these areas.[9] Yet, as these many studies point out, the various ways in which the goddess was perceived transhistorically and transculturally makes any study of cultural contact and appropriation extremely complicated. There are certainly points of similarity, especially with regard to the warrior nature of the goddess, a feature that is only briefly noted in the biblical portrayal (of the Queen of Heaven). At Emar, where the goddess is a major recipient of cult taking place at a dedicated temple, we repeatedly read of "Aštartu of Battle (*ša taḫāzi*)" (Fleming 1992a: 98–99, 211, 229; Smith 2014a: 187, 196; 2014b: 44–45, 56). A key ritual (Emar 370) describes the installation of the goddess's priestess (called the *maš'artu*), whose cultic function, according to Fleming (1992a: 211, 229), involved "battle-preparation and military success." Aštartu "alone dominates [the] festival in her role as war goddess."[10] In contrast to what we saw in the biblical texts, in this Emar Aštartu ritual, "there is no sign of rural/agricultural interests."

Astarte in Egypt

Egypt likewise features the warrior aspect of the goddess, especially in the Eighteenth and Nineteenth Dynasties, starting with Amenhotep II (ca. 1427–1400 BCE).[11] As Thomas Schneider (2003: 160–161) has astutely pointed out in commenting on religious ideology, "the appropriation of horse and chariot led to the borrowing of Astarte as a goddess who protected royal horses and chariot." Even the core ideology of royalty was open to cultural appropriation, as shown in the Astarte papyrus—"dated to a precise day in the 5th regnal year of Amenophis II [that] is to be connected with the inauguration of the Astarte sanctuary in Perunefer in Amenophis' II 5th year." Here we have an Egyptian version of the Canaanite myth of Baal versus Sea reconfigured such that "the Canaanite Baal was promoted to be a god of the Egyptian kingship by Amenophis II!" As for Astarte, she is referred here as "the furious and raging goddess" (*ntrt qndt nšny*). Elsewhere the Egyptian iconographic record is replete with Astarte as a war goddess in a menacing posture with weaponry (spear, shield, mace, blade mace, bow and arrow, battle axe) as well as on horseback (Figure C.1) (Cornelius 2004: 81–83, 85–86, 93–94; Hoffmeier and Kitchen 2007: 127–136; Tazawa 2009: 83–95; 2014: 106–109; R. Schmitt 2013: 222–224). In short, the cultural appropriation of West Semitic Astarte as a war goddess into Egypt was historically contingent (cf. Wilson-Wright 2016: 27–70). And once again, as we saw with Emar Aštartu, there is no emphasis on Egyptian Astarte as an agrarian deity.

ʿAthtartu at Ugarit

Late Bronze Age Ugarit presents its own particular formation of the goddess ʿAthtartu, who was known to have had a temple, perhaps even within the royal complex (KTU 4.219.2).[12] Surprisingly, in light of what we have just seen with the materials from Emar and Egypt (and the mention of war in Jer 44:17–18; 1 Sam 31:10), there is no explicit reference to ʿAthtartu at Ugarit as a warrior deity fighting on behalf of a monarch. There is no mention of the

Figure C.1 Astarte as an Egyptian war goddess on horseback.
Courtesy James K. Hoffmeier.

goddess's battle prowess legitimizing royalty, though we do know of her presence in royal cult (discussed later). This is not to say that the goddess lacks an aggressive, even combative nature; clearly she has one, as seen in five (possibly six) mythological texts (KTU 1.180 [RIH 98/02]; KTU 1.2.1.40; KTU 1.16.6.54–57; KTU 1.2.1.7–8; KTU 1.2.4.28–30; KTU 1.83).

1. In KTU 1.180 (RIH 98/02), ʿAthtartu is described as a "mighty panther" (*nmr ḫtrt ʿttrt*) as well as a "lioness" (*lbʾi*). Two verbs refer to her "pouncing" (*trqṣ*) and "conquering" (*tkšd*). Militarily, we have mention of her "quiver and bow" (*ʿutpt wqš[t]*). The tantalizing remains of this still-to-be-published text strongly suggest that ʿAthtartu is associated with divine combat myths (see Lewis 2011: 225–227; Wilson-Wright 2016: 130–133).[13] See especially KTU 1.83 (discussed later).
2. KTU 1.2.1.40 is only a snippet of material, yet it seems to refer to ʿAthtartu joining ʿAnatu (a warrior goddess) in restraining the god Baʿlu by seizing his hands, which were holding smiting weapons.

3 and 4. Two almost verbatim passages (from the tale of King Kirta and the Baʻlu Cycle) document the use of the goddess's name in a curse: "May ʻAthtartu-Name-of-Baʻlu smash [*tbr*] your skull" (KTU 1.16.6.54–57; KTU 1.2.1.7–8; cf. KAI 24, line 15; KAI 14, line 18 [discussed later]). As a fixed formula, one can extrapolate that the goddess's ferocity and destructive nature were widely known.

5. Regarding KTU 1.2.4.28–30, I have argued elsewhere (Lewis 2011; cf. Wilson-Wright 2015: 337; 2016: 128–129, 135) that it makes little sense for ʻAthtartu to "rebuke/admonish" (*gʻr*) her brother Baʻlu in the very midst of his battle against Yammu; rather, she is joining him in warfare by hexing Yammu with a "blasting" (*gʻr*) incantation.[14] Just as Kotharu-wa-Hasisu used incantatory language to render Baʻlu's weapons effective, so ʻAthtartu joins Baʻlu's efforts with an effective curse against Yammu. As a result, she can rightly proclaim: "Yammu is *our* captive."

6. KTU 1.83 refers to an unnamed goddess battling Yammu//Naharu//the Tunnanu dragon. It is very plausible, especially in light of KTU 1.180 and KTU 1.2.4.28–30, that ʻAthtartu is the goddess in question (see Lewis 2011: 217–218).

Another portrayal of ʻAthtartu at Ugarit, privileged by Smith (2014a: 188–194; 2014b: 45–53), has to do with her hunting capabilities (cf. Wilson-Wright 2016: 135–138). In a detailed study of KTU 1.92 on which the bulk of the thesis depends (see too KTU 1.114.23–24, 26'–28'), Smith (2014a: 194; 2014b: 45, 53) argues that "the profile for the goddess" is "as huntress in Ugaritic literary traditions."[15] In KTU 1.92 the goddess is explicitly described as "ʻAthtartu the huntress" (*ʻttrt ṣwd*[*t*]), and in the beginning of the text she hunts with her spear in the steppe land (*mdbr*).

A third portrayal of the goddess at Ugarit reveals an agrarian nature. This is most clearly seen in a bilingual (Ugaritic-Hurrian) ritual text whose title is "The Sacrifice of ʻAthtartu, Gathering at the Threshing Floor" (*dbḥ ʻttrt qrʼat bgrn*// *dbḥ ʼatḥlm tʼutkd*; KTU 1.116.1–3).[16] That agrarian threshing floors can serve as cultic spaces, even for sacrifices, is well known, primarily due to the Chronistic tradition about David erecting an altar and sacrificing on Ornan's threshing floor (1 Chr 21:15–1 Chr 22:1; 2 Chr 3:1).[17] The manifestation of the goddess as ʻAthtartu of the Field/Steppe Land (*ʻttrt šd*) also underscores her agrarian nature. Deities were certainly multifaceted, and thus such a title need not minimize the goddess's connection to royalty and urban space (discussed later) or to the hunt.

To say that the goddess ʻAthtartu is tied to fields and steppe lands (*ʻttrt šd*) is to say that she plays a significant role in food production and the textile industry (on which see the later discussion). The word *šd* can designate cultivated lands as well as steppe lands. For the former, we have a plethora of texts in various genres documenting the symbolism of cultivated fields (šd) as well as the produce and transactions associated with their maintenance, which was so central to the economy.[18] As for steppe lands (šd and mdbr), here archaeological studies (e.g., van Zeist and Bakker-Heeres 1985; Akkermans and Schwartz 2003) and studies of ancient diet (e.g., Altmann 2013) prove instructive. Archaeobotanical research reveals the complex nature of steppe lands. Though lacking in rainfall, seasonal "shrub steppe" and "dry" vegetation led to the predominance of sheep and goat pastoralism, supplemented by hunting activity.[19]

For the connection to royal cult, note how two of the texts that mention ʿAthtartu of the Field/Steppe Land (and a third that mentions ʿAthtartu-ḫurri)[20] are so-called entry rituals, involving the procession of the divine image of the goddess into the royal palace (bt mlk; KTU 1.43.1; KTU 1.91.10; 1.148.18–22). KTU 1.43 mentions (the cult statues of) ʿAthtartu-ḫurri and the Gatharuma "entering" (ʿrb) the royal palace, followed by offerings and a banquet. The king has a prominent role in the procession, welcoming the gods and walking seven times (in a sevenfold circuit?) after their statues.[21] KTU 1.91 refers to ʿAthtartu of the Field/Steppe Land and (two?) Rashap (statues) entering the royal palace in conjunction with royal sacrifices. In KTU 1.148.18–22, after ʿAthtartu of the Field/Steppe Land enters the royal palace, numerous offerings are presented.

Though these urban rituals take place in royal space (bt mlk), this certainly does not minimize the agrarian nature of ʿAthtartu of the Field/Steppe Land.[22] Indeed, ideologically, agricultural sustenance per se is due to the blessings of the gods and the administration of king and state (Lewis forthcoming a). Moreover, entry rituals typically involved the procession of the deity's divine image from one temple to another, and there are indications that the home sanctuary of ʿAthtartu of the Field/Steppe Land may have been located in a rural area.[23] Here KTU 1.48 and KTU 1.148 (cf. KTU 4.182.55, 58) are particularly informative. KTU 1.48 seems to mention two non-royal human actors (mzy bn [PN] and slḫʾu) and a gittu farm complex together with familial language (tpḥ = špḥ). We learn from texts such as KTU 1.79 and 1.80 that a gittu is a rural agricultural community often under control of the king.[24] Moreover, such gittus can contain "houses/local sanctuaries" (bt) where the cult took place.[25] Thus Wilson-Wright rightly underscores the connection between ʿAthtartu of the Field/Steppe Land and the "agricultural setting" of KTU 1.48.[26]

A dedicated section of the royal entry ritual in KTU 1.148.18–22 describes the actual cult associated with ʿAthtartu of the Field/Steppe Land (ʿṯtrt šd). It is telling that these offerings have to do with livestock (sheep), agriculture (oil), and other produce (balsam, honey) from rural areas that resonate with the goddess's name (šd). Four different types of garments are mentioned, along with three hundred units of wool (šʿrt). An economic text detailing divine offerings twice mentions ʿAthtartu of the Field/Steppe Land (KTU

4.182.55, 58).²⁷ As with KTU 1.148.18–22, it likewise mentions a wide variety of garments, with special emphasis on wool, both in quantity (seven hundred units) and type (esp. 'iqn'u, lapis [blue] wool) along with linen (pṯt, flax) garments. Weaving (mḫṣ) is also mentioned here in conjunction with the goddess. When we situate such data with what we know about the importance of the textile industry for the overall economy of Ugarit including its religious economy, we come away even more impressed with the vitality and importance of the cult surrounding ʿAthtartu of the Field/Steppe Land.²⁸

Lastly, though Ugaritic iconography is notoriously difficult to analyze (see Lewis 2005a), the portrayal of a so-called Mistress of Animals from Minet el Beida (Figure C.2) that has been attributed to ʿAnatu, Qudshu, and even ʾAthiratu may in fact be that of ʿAthtartu of the Field/Steppe Land.²⁹ Note in particular the presence of the motifs of both cultivated land (stalks of grain) and steppe land (goat) pastoralism.³⁰ Realizing how ʿAthtartu is also associated with the finest of textiles, one wonders if the elegant female with the long, expertly braided dress (Figure C.3) from the royal precinct of Ras Shamra's

Figure C.2 A lid of an ivory box from Late Bronze Age Ugarit (Minet el-Beida) depicting the "mistress of animals."
Reproduced by permission of Mission archéologique de Ras Shamra–Ougarit.

Figure C.3 An elite female wearing a long, expertly braided dress from the royal precinct of Ras Shamra's Hurrian Temple.
Reproduced by permission of Mission archéologique de Ras Shamra–Ougarit.

Hurrian Temple might also be a rendering of our goddess (also known as ʿAthtartu-*ḫurri*).[31]

ʿAštart in Phoenicia and Its Extended World

With the DtrH's references to ʿAštart, the goddess of the Sidonians (1 Kgs 11:5, 33; 2 Kgs 23:13), our expectations run high for finding the best comparanda in Phoenician sources. Here we are not disappointed when it comes to the prevalence of ʿAštart worship in time and space. Claude Doumet-Serhal (2017: 26–27) notes the presence of a model ʿAštart shrine (with a head of a lion, her symbolic animal) in the imposing temple at Sidon built around 1500 BCE. Using both archaeology and epigraphy, Bloch-Smith (2014) summarizes: "The earliest Phoenician temples for Astarte worship appear in 10th century BCE Trye/Sidon followed by 9th century BCE Kition-Kathari. Phoenician Astarte's worship peaks in the 5–4th centuries and dwindles through the 3rd and 2nd centuries BCE."

Yet our rich dataset is less than forthcoming when it comes to the specific nature of Phoenician ʿAštart. A seventh-century BCE treaty between the Neo-Assyrian king Esarhaddon and King Baal of Tyre depicts the warrior nature of the goddess that we have repeatedly seen elsewhere. Esarhaddon invokes the following curse should the treaty be violated: "May ʿAštartu [^{d}as-tar-tú] break your bow in the thick of battle and have you crouch at the feet of your enemy" (SAA 02 005, line r.e.18; Parpola and Watanabe 1988: 27). Yet elsewhere we have little Phoenician evidence for the militant side of ʿAštart.[32]

Instead we find substantial evidence of ʿAštart as a patron deity to whom a wide range of cult was offered at temples and smaller shrines throughout Phoenicia's extended reach on the mainland (esp. Tyre and Sidon) and overseas sites.[33] As Bloch-Smith (2014: 169–176) demonstrates, two texts from Kition (eastern Cyprus) are extremely informative with regard to the ritual performance surrounding ʿAštart. What we have preserved of the older of the two texts (the Kition Bowl from ca. the eighth century BCE) involves a tonsure rite and a prayer ritual devoted to ʿAštart, together with (seemingly) the offering of sheep, lambs, and the individual's hair.[34] That the rite may be familial is suggested by the mention of a lamb being offered for the family of the individual (ʾyt bt PN šʾ).[35] The second text, from the fifth century BCE, is remarkable for documenting the expenditures related to the cultic personnel associated with ʿAštart's temple.[36] Here the goddess is called "holy queen" (mlkt qdšt; KAI 37, A 7, 10), and the functionaries include a chief scribe (rb sprm), bakers (ʾpm), cultic barbers (glbm pʾl ʾl mlʾkt), female musicians playing frame drums (ʿlmt; see Ackerman 2013: 177–178), guards(?) (prkm, ʾadmm), sacrificers (zbḥm), sculptors/engravers (ḥršm), singers (šrm), temple builders (bnm ʾš bn ʾyt bt), water masters (bʿl mym), and non-specified servants/officiants (nʿrm, prmn, npš bt). The number of these individuals allows us to imagine the scope of the festival, while their varied functions allow us to imagine the temple ritual's diverse activities and perhaps the ways in which they were gendered.[37]

As for the mainland, three exceptional texts (KAI 13, 14, 15) provide us windows into the royal cult associated with ʿAštart from sixth-/fifth-century BCE Sidon.[38] As at Kition, the royal and elevated nature of the goddess is emphasized with her epithets. She is "the great one" (rbt) and "the queen" (hmlkt) who is "enthroned in the mighty heavens" (yšb!n ʾyt ʿštrt šmm ʾdrm) (KAI 14, lines 15–16). She also bears the epithet "Name of Baal" (ʿštrt šm bʿl; KAI 14, line 18), which underscores her close relationship to the mighty storm god (cf. KTU 1.16.6.54–57; 1.2.1.7–8; Lewis 2011). Iconographically, we have the inscribing of the "great ʿAštart" (rbt ʿštrt) on a small votive throne flanked by winged cherubs found just south of Tyre (KAI 17; Davila and Zuckerman 1993; Bonnet 1996: planche V).

The Sidonian royalty in question are (in chronological order): King Eshmunazor I (KAI 13, 14), King Tabnit (KAI 13, 14), the co-regent Queen

ʾUmmîʿaštart (or ʾImmîʿaštart) (KAI 14), King Eshmunazor II (KAI 14), and King Bodʿaštart (KAI 15–16; CIS I, 4). What little we know of Eshmunazor I comes from inscriptions written by his descendants. His son Tabnit, when listing his own lineage on his sarcophagus (Figure C.4), identifies his father as a "priest of ʿAštart" (*khn ʿštrt*) prior to adding his father's royal title, "King of the Sidonians" (*mlk ṣdnm*)—and Tabnit notes that he too bore both titles, again listing his sacerdotal office before his royal capacity (KAI 13, lines 1–2). One assumes the office was that of chief priest and was hereditary. We learn elsewhere (KAI 14, line 15) that Tabnit had a high-ranking "priestess of ʿAštart" (*khnt ʿštrt*) for a sister (appropriately named ʾUmmîʿaštart, "My [divine] mother is ʿAštart"), whose office was also perhaps hereditary.[39] These (brother and sister) officiants marry and produce an heir, Eshmunazor II, who, curiously, is not called a priest despite his triple blessing of having both parents as well as his grandfather as priests. Yet Eshmunazor II does build multiple temples, along with his mother, two of which were explicitly for the goddess ʿAštart in her differing manifestations (KAI 14, lines 16, 18). Yet another descendent who is named after the goddess, Bodʿaštart (grandson of Eshmunazor I and nephew of Tabnit and ʾUmmîʿaštart), also builds monumental architecture that he dedicates "to his [go]ddess ʿAštart" (*l[ʾ]ly lʾštrt*; CIS I, 4; Bonnet 1996: 33–34; Zamora 2007; Peckham 2014: 379).

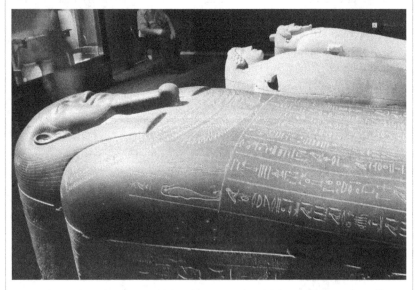

Figure C.4 The sarcophagus of the Phoenician king Tabnit, who was also a "priest of ʿAštart."

Courtesy Homonihilis. https://commons.wikimedia.org/wiki/File:Safrcophagi_in_the_Istanbul_Archaeological_Museum.JPG.

ʾUmmîʿaštart, the priestess of ʿAštart, deserves special comment. As most scholars have recognized, a close reading of KAI 14 reveals that her role in the cult was equal to (or likely more prominent than) that of her son, Eshmunazor II. Moreover, in Brian Peckham's (2014: 378) words, "as co-regent, she could slip in a word or two on her son's coffin" to emphasize her achievements. In KTU 1.14, lines 15–18, speaking in the first-person plural, our female co-regent describes how "surely it was *we* [together]" who engaged in temple building, including the two temples to "*our* Lady" Queen ʿAštart (*ʾštrt rbtn hmlkt...ʾm bnn ... wyšrn... wʾnḥnʾš bnn ... wʾnḥnʾš bnn*). Stunningly, she also highlights her sacerdotal role as she erases those of her father and husband. Whereas KAI 13 twice mentions the prominent sacerdotal role of both Eshmunazor I and Tabnit as "priests of ʿAštart," neither king is accorded the title in KAI 14. Instead, the only mention of such activity is that of ʾUmmîʿaštart, "the priestess of ʿAštart" (*khnt ʿštrt*; KAI 14, line 15). Both male figures receive their royal epithets (*mlk ṣdnm*; KAI 14, line 14), with nary a mention of their sacerdotal titles.[40] Such a striking "editing" (if that is indeed what we have here) is not without warrant. For, according to Ackerman's (2013: 171) study of our inscription in its broader context, "there is something in particular about the Astarte cult that facilitates women's priestly engagement," and especially "*aristocratic* women's priestly engagement." Ackerman (2013: 171–172, 175–178) is quick to add an anthropological perspective, noting that women did not engage in blood sacrifice. Nonetheless, it occasions no surprise that "Queen" (*mlkt*) ʿAštart should have a queenly priestess in ʾUmmîʿaštart.

Reassessing the Biblical Portrayal of ʿAštart in Context

Having contextualized the worlds of ʿAthtartu/ʿAštart/Astarte worship, we now return to the biblical portrayal. What first stands out is the paucity of the evidence, with a mere three (probably four) occurrences of the singular ʿAštart in the Hebrew Bible. It should come as no surprise that writers and editors favoring Yahweh would omit positive narratives about the goddess. Yet as polemics go, if the goddess was ubiquitous, one might expect a slew of apologetic defenses to show that the goddess is ineffectual, similar to what we find in the counter-response to the charge in Jeremiah 44:18 (discussed later). Thus it is quite understandable to assume that ʿAštart worship was on the decline. Smith (2014b: 82; cf. 2014a: 323) writes of "a general trend toward the demise of ʿAštart's cult," with the goddess being "largely a coastal phenomenon in this period [Iron II] while she seems to be fading in Israel and further inland." In what follows we will try to nuance this situation with an eye toward showing how the goddess was worshipped more than one might think, and how her legacy remained influential even among her detractors.

Historical Musings

As noted earlier, the Hebrew Bible's three explicit DtrH references to the goddess associate her with the Sidonians of Solomon's time (1 Kgs 11:5, 33) and with Josiah's eradication of a Sidonian ʿAštart sanctuary east of Jerusalem in the seventh century BCE (2 Kgs 23:13). Whatever historians do with the historical Solomon and the so-called tenth-century question, they still need to posit a historical time period, occasion (trade and diplomacy facilitated through syncretistic religion?), and ideology that would resonate with a cultural memory of a Solomonic royal cult that provided a sanctuary for "ʿAštart of the Sidonians." As noted earlier, Bloch-Smith has documented the enduring traditions of ʿAštart worship at Sidon. Though our clearest evidence of a royal cult of Sidonian ʿAštart worship comes from the Eshmunazor dynasty (in the sixth/fifth centuries BCE), we also have an eighth-century BCE inscription on a krater from Sidon mentioning the goddess and her priesthood (kh<n>t ʿštrt).[41] As for iconography, both the model shrine with a head of a lion from the mid-second-millennium BCE temple at Sidon and another mid-eighth-century BCE krater "decorated with the tree of life and flanked by goats" (Doumet-Serhal 2017: 29) may depict ʿAštart. All of these texts and iconography underscore the long duration of ʿAštart's cult, which elsewhere (in Northern Syria and Egypt) had a substantial Late Bronze Age pedigree. As for the realia of Sidonian ʿAštart worship in the tenth century BCE in Jerusalem, we cannot say yet the cultural continuum of ʿAštart worship is beyond doubt.

King Josiah's seventh-century BCE interactions with Sidonian ʿAštart (2 Kgs 23:13) are tantalizing in light of widespread ʿAštart worship, amply attested from the eighth through the fourth centuries BCE for the Phoenician mainland cites and their extended colonies. Coming inland, note how a late seventh-century BCE Transjordanian Ammonite seal inscription that refers to an individual making a vow to "ʿAsht[art] in Sidon" (ʿšt<rt> bṣdn) shows how the goddess' fame was known beyond the coastal areas.[42] As noted earlier, the seventh-century BCE Neo-Assyrian king Esarhaddon refers to a militant ʿAštartu in his treaty with nearby Tyre. These data certainly cannot prove the existence of an actual temple for the goddess located east of Jerusalem, yet the prominence of Phoenician ʿAštart elsewhere (even in inland northern Israel in the sixth century BCE)[43] cautions us not to reject the idea. When we then factor in the Queen of Heaven cult mentioned in Jeremiah 44:17–18, the notion becomes more appealing, especially if the Queen of Heaven cult is indeed devoted to ʿAštart (a near consensus). Here in the sixth century BCE we have mention of an older royal (ʿAštart) cult of more than one generation (note the plural *mĕlākîm*) that was (forcibly?) stopped. It is hard not to conclude, as many have, that reference is being made to the seventh-century BCE cult practices of Manasseh and Amon followed by the centralizing restrictions of Josiah.[44]

Jack Lundbom (2004: 163) suggests that "Manasseh's long and peaceful reign" was nostalgically in mind when the people referenced the bounty and peaceful prosperity that they attributed to the Queen of Heaven (Jer 44:17b).

Lastly (or better firstly), consider the ever-growing iconographic documentation for the goddess's presence in the southern Levant. In light of Ugarit ʿAthtartu being called a lioness (lbʾi) in the recently published KTU 1.180 (RIH 98/02), Smith (2014a: 208) suggests that the goddess holding the ears of two lions on the tenth century BCE Taanach cult stand may in fact be ʿAštart.[45] Consider too ʿAštart/Ishtar on a tenth-/ninth-century BCE bronze plaque from Tel Dan, on several eighth-/seventh-century BCE seals from Israel (Shechem, Tel Dor, Nahal Issachar, Beth-Shean), and on a seventh-century BCE silver pendant from Tel Miqne-Ekron (cf. the reference to Philistine ʿAštart in 1 Sam 31:10). As discussed by Tallay Ornan (2001, 2006), we often have a blending of Assyrian, Syrian, and Phoenician Ishtar/ʿAštart iconography together with local inspirations that she terms "a process of visual syncretism" (2006: 303). In view of this visual narrative, perhaps we should call the DtrH's portrayal of Solomon's blending of the foreign and the local in 1 Kings 11 a process of literary syncretism.

The Biblical Portrayal of ʿAštart's Features: The Queen of Heaven

As noted at the outset of our discussion, the description of the worship of the Queen of Heaven in Jeremiah 7:18; 44:17–18 is portrayed as *both* a royal cult and a household-based cult (to use Ackerman's phrase). Treating the former first, we have seen ample evidence that elsewhere the goddess ʿAthtartu/ʿAštart/Astarte is regularly tied to monarchic concerns, religiously and ideologically (in Egypt, Ugarit, Emar, and Phoenicia). As we saw in Chapter Nine, monarchs are regularly involved in cult, often as the primary ritual actor.[46] This is especially the case for Late Bronze Age Ugarit, with the king's role (sacrificial and otherwise) in "entry rituals" that involved the divine image of ʿAthtartu proceeding into the royal palace. Yet the trophy for outstanding royal ʿAštart cult goes to the five Sidonian rulers of the Eshmunazor dynasty, who built multiple sanctuaries to the goddess (and who date slightly later than Jeremiah). Three of these individuals (two kings and one queen as co-regent) used their epithets of priest (khn) and priestess (khnt) of ʿAštart to highlight how their sacerdotal service to the goddess comes before all else. In summation, it is safe to say that the royal nature of the Queen of Heaven cult (of ʿAštart) portrayed in Jeremiah 44:17–18 reads perfectly naturally. After all, she is a queen.

According to the adherents of the Queen of Heaven, the goddess was effectual with regard to war ("the sword") and famine (baḥereb ubārāʿāb; Jer 44:18).

As demonstrated earlier, the warrior and aggressive side of the goddess is a constant in the Northern Levant (Emar and Ugarit) and Egypt as well as in the estimation of the Neo-Assyrian king Esarhaddon—and yet with surprisingly little mention in Phoenician sources. Should one rightly blend in the warrior traditions of Neo-Assyrian Ishtar (cf. the hybrid iconography noted earlier), it is easy to understand how worshippers of the Queen of Heaven felt that she was a goddess of military prowess who wielded the sword on their behalf.

With regard to providing food, we see the imbalance of portrayals shifted again, with little emphasis of Emar Aštartu and Egyptian Astarte as agrarian deities in contrast to a substantial agrarian emphasis for Ugaritic ʿAthtartu. (The familial ʿAštart cult at Kition deserves honorable mention.) As previously noted, the Ugaritic goddess ʿAthtartu in one manifestation is associated with sacrifices at an agrarian threshing floor, while in another she is distinctly tied to food production (as reflected in her epithet ʿAthtartu of the Field/Steppe Land), and in yet another with providing game (as ʿAthtartu the huntress). As the goddess associated with cultivated lands and steppe lands, she was the patron of the major sources of food production (agriculture, sheep and goat pastoralism, and hunting activity).

As we saw in Chapter Eight, there are porous boundaries between elite and non-elite religion when it comes to family/household religion. Thus the depiction of the Queen of Heaven cult as involving family religion alongside royal cult causes no concern. In a series of treatments,[47] Susan Ackerman (2008: 143) has stressed how "women played a particularly significant role" "in this household-based cult."[48] Ackerman (1989: 113–116) notes especially the role of food production and ʿAštart religion. (Note the phrase "we had plenty of food" in Jer 44:17.) She unpacks the mention of *kawwānîm* cakes in Jeremiah 7:18, 44:19, with its Akkadian cognate (*kamānu* cake) being used in Ishtar cults, and a similar mention of baked goods (*ḥlt*) mentioned in the temple expenditures of the Kition ʿAštart cult (see earlier discussion of KAI 37, A 10; so too Peckham 1968: 314). Carol Meyers (2003a: 430–432, 435–436; 1988: 146–148; 2010) provides additional support through her ethnographic and socioeconomic analysis of women's prominent role in food production, emphasizing a more heterarchical (rather than hierarchical) model for understanding the agrarian nature of Iron Age settlements.

In addition, Meyers' (2003a: 432–436; 1988: 147–148; 2013a: 133) research underscores a similar prominent role for women in textile production. Once again, Ackerman (2008) astutely fleshes out the religious implications, concluding that goddesses were the likely patrons of the textile industry. Based on a single reference from the Baal Cycle that describes ʾAthiratu holding a *plk* spindle (KTU 1.4.2.3–4), Ackerman (2008: 8–9) concludes that the Ugaritic goddess "had a special association with spinning and weaving." She then uses this and other evidence (e.g., the Taanach cult stand, fabrics from Kuntillet ʿAjrud, loom weights from Tel Miqne-Ekron) to extrapolate that Asherah was "the goddess of spinning and weaving in the Late Bronze Age and Iron Age West Semitic world" (2008: 29). While there is much to appreciate here, the conclusions are overly reductionist. Different genres yield different information.[49] Ackerman's reliance on the Ugaritic mythological texts to reconstruct (a literary portrayal of) cult needs to be balanced with the Ugaritic ritual texts and economic texts that give us windows into which deities actually received cult and of what type and in what quantity. As has been demonstrated, the cultic and economic realia of ʿAthtartu of the Field/Steppe Land (*ʿṯtrt šd*) involved various types of wool (*šʿrt*) of substantial quantity, linen (*pṯt*, flax) and weaving (*mḫṣ*), not to mention an impressive number of garments of varying types.

The Biblical Portrayal of ʿAštart's Features: The Deuteronomic Appropriation

Deuteronomy's ideological portrayal of non-Yahwistic divinity is similar to and yet quite different from what we see in the Deuteronomistic History.[50] Consider again the language used by the latter to portray Josiah's polemic:

> The king defiled the high places that were east of Jerusalem . . . which King Solomon of Israel had built for ʿAštart, the detestation [*šiqquṣ*] of the Sidonians, for Chemosh the detestation [*šiqquṣ*] of Moab, and for Milcom the abomination [*tôʿēbâ*] of the Ammonites. (2 Kgs 23:13; cf. 1 Kgs 11:5, 7)

Here DtrH's rhetorical approach is to use a language of contempt (*šiqquṣ, tôʿēbâ*) to delegitimize non-Yahwistic divinity. The book of Deuteronomy does likewise, yet then adds an altogether different (theological/philosophical) rhetorical strategy.

Commenting on ʿAštart, Judith Hadley (2007: 163) astutely observes: "Although the Deuteronomistic History has treated the goddess negatively and in a polemical way, it is still possible to discern the presence of a deity in the references." In contrast, writes Hadley (2007: 157), though "the author of Deuteronomy recognizes that other deities do in fact exist"—compare expressions like "the gods of the nations" (*ʾĕlōhê haggôyîm*; Deut 29:17 [Eng 29:18])—he "avoids mentioning deities (other than Yahweh) by name, preferring instead the designation 'other gods' (*ʾĕlōhîm ʾăḥērîm*) . . . or 'foreign' or 'strange gods' (*ʾĕlōhê nēkar*)."[51] Though this omission looks minor on the surface, it constitutes an intentional rhetorical strategy that turns even more cunning.

According to the pragmatic author of Deuteronomy 29:17 (Eng 29:18), worshipping deities other than Yahweh was a viable option both for individual worship and for corporate allegiance (i.e., for "a man or a woman, or a family or a tribe"; *ʾîš ʾô-ʾiššâ ʾô mišpāḥâ ʾô-šēbeṭ*). Such socially widespread cults were not just those of an errant Solomon gone bad; they resonate with the broad-based Queen of Heaven cult. Our Deuteronomic author considers the threat to be invasive, referring to devotees of "the gods of the nations" as constituting "a root sprouting poisonous and bitter growth" (*šōreš pōreh rōʾš wĕlaʿănâ*).

Deuteronomy's strategy is threefold. Similar to the DtrH, the author of the Deuteronomic polemic first reduces the gods to profane objects (wood, stone, silver, gold) of human construction.[52] Then he vilifies them with the language of "detestation" (*šiqqûṣ*), "abomination" (*tôʿēbâ*), and "filth" (*gillul*), similar to the rhetoric of the DtrH.[53] If used of a person, one would call such harsh rhetoric "dehumanizing." Used of deities, it is a rhetoric of "depersonalizing," a divesting of worth and individuality.

Deuteronomy's third and most cunning stroke is to strip away the deities' personal names and by so doing strip away their essence—once again turning the sacred into the profane. As mentioned at the outset of our discussion, in four instances Deuteronomy turns a personalized ʿAštart into a common noun, "the *fecundity* of your flock" (*ʿštrt ṣōʾnekā*; Deut 7:13; 28:4, 18, 51). A personalized Dagan becomes "your *grain*" (*dĕgānĕkā*), and a personalized Shagar becomes "the *increase* of your cattle" (*šĕgar-ʾălāpêkā*). The author is treating the personal names of these foreign deities as if they were nonexistent. One wonders if our author is committing the very verbal assault against these deities that he forbids being used of Yahweh: "You shall not mention [lit. raise (to one's lips)] the name of Yahweh, your God to [i.e., as if it were] nothing [*laššāwʾ*]" (Deut 5:11; cf. Exod 20:7).[54] Elsewhere Deuteronomy sharply labels any non-Yahwistic deity (idol) as "that which is no God" (*lōʾ ʾēl*; Deut 32:21) because, logically, "there is no other god" besides Yahweh (*ʾên ʾĕlōhîm ʿimmādî*; Deut 32:39)

I have argued elsewhere that the blasphemous language of "piercing [√*nqb*] God's name" in Leviticus 24:11, 16 is telling in that it was referencing a type of linguistic deicide where one would blot out the name of a deity and thereby his essence (see Lewis 2017). In effect, this is exactly what the book of Deuteronomy is doing with the goddess ʿAštart.

For humans, names are integral to one's sense of self and family, and central to identity formation as people navigate their place in society. How we use and treat the names of others is equally telling about social perception and negotiation. Due to such significance, the obliteration of one's name is a profound act. Only extreme situations occasion individuals to employ the severe rhetoric of blotting out (*mḥh*), cutting off (*krt*), or destroying (*ʾbd, šmd*) a person's or a people's name—and with it their identity, essence, and memory (for examples, see Lewis 2017). The seriousness of causing injury to one's name through performative speech (perceived to be powerful and efficacious) is evidenced by capital punishment being assigned to the cursing of God and king (Exod 22;27 [Eng 22:28]; 1 Sam 3:13–14; 1 Kgs 21:10, 13; Isa 8:21–22).

In every biblical episode cautioning against impious blasphemy, the referent is Yahweh and only Yahweh. In contrast, other (foreign) gods are fair game for attack in biblical polemics. Indeed, Deuteronomy 12:3 commands the physical destruction of divine images representing illicit gods such that their names are metaphorically destroyed (*wĕʾibbadtem ʾet-šĕmām*). With literary dexterity, this is precisely what is happening when Deuteronomy depersonalizes ʿAštart, Dagan, and Shagar (Deut 7:13; 28:4, 18, 51), turning the once sacred into the profane. There is no performative speech here.[55] It is an act of literary deicide.[56]

Such an astute rhetorical strategy sets the stage for Deuteronomy's cultural appropriation. As we have seen, ʿAštart is well attested as a goddess of food production and the textile industry. Compare especially Ugaritic ʿAthtartu as a goddess of agriculture, sheep and goat pastoralism, and hunting activity as well as Jeremiah's Queen of Heaven, who is efficacious in providing "plenty of food" to eliminate famine. Realizing ʿAštart's appeal for his audience, our Deuteronomic author appropriates the goddess's patronage of sheep and goats for Yahweh. Through an adroit etymological sleight of hand, he coins the expression *štrt ṣōʾn* to refer to the fecundity of sheep and goats. What was once a divine epithet of ovine husbandry (ʿAštart of Flocks) becomes a profane reference to ovine fertility ("the fecundity of flocks"). Deuteronomy's newly created idiom depicts an earthly blessing of Yahweh that fits perfectly with his other gifts of children, cattle fecundity (considered by some a blessing of Shagar), grain (considered by some a blessing of Dagan), wine, and oil—all constituting ways in which Yahweh (and not ʿAštart, Dagan, or Shagar) will love (*ʾhb*), bless (*brk*) and multiply (*rbh*) his people (Deut 7:13).[57]

Summary of Excursus on ʿAštart in Ancient Israelite Religion

This excursus has been devoted to articulating in brief what it would take to analyze just one of the many relevant goddesses from ancient Israel: ʿAštart. Our initial demonstration of findings included the following:

- On its own, the Hebrew Bible presents meager data to analyze the question. The texts at our disposal are pejorative literary presentations of ʿAštart and an unnamed goddess (the Queen of Heaven) who may indeed be ʿAštart.

- Acquiring extra data from archaeology is a desideratum for such a study. An ever-growing iconographic corpus reveals visually syncretistic portrayals of the goddess blending Assyrian, Syrian, and Phoenician features together with local inspirations.
- Analyzing extra data from the surrounding cultural world is a desideratum, with significant material coming from the Northern Levant (Late Bronze Age Emar and Ugarit), Egypt (especially Eighteenth- and Nineteenth-Dynasty New Kingdom), and the first-millennium BCE Phoenician mainland (especially sixth-/fifth-century BCE Sidon) as well as its extended colonies (especially eighth- and fifth-century BCE Kition). A full analysis would require incorporating the extensive Neo-Assyrian Ishtar cults.
- Representations of the goddess in cognate cultures reveal that a given culture can have a multifaceted portrait of the goddess (e.g., the three distinct portrayals of Ugaritic ʿAthtartu). Conceptual designs must be flexible to allow for multiple manifestations of the goddess.
- Representations of the different natures of the goddess should caution against any generalization of the goddess and against reductionism. (Compare here the past sins of reducing ʿAštart to a "fertility goddess.") There is no single "essence" of the goddess that can be generalized transhistorically and transculturally.
- Nonetheless, there are some features of the goddess that regularly appear such that they seem to be dominant characteristics, though they are historically and geographically contingent (i.e., they are not universal). These include a military/aggressive nature (Emar, Egypt, Ugarit); a connection with agriculture as well as steppe land pastoralism of sheep and goats (Ugarit); a patronage of hunting, also in the steppe land (Ugarit); and a vibrant association with royal cult (Ugarit, Egypt, Phoenicia).

If we use cognate Near Eastern cultures (assuming a broadly construed cultural continuum, as described in Chapter Six) together with the iconographic record of hybrid Ishtar/ʿAštart images in ancient Israel, we can give tentative answers to the hypotheses stated at the outset.

- ʿAštart was worshipped as a vibrant goddess in some segments of ancient Israelite society, though our data allow us to say very little about historical particulars and the extent of her cult. The widespread attestation of tenth- through seventh-century BCE Ishtar/ʿAštart iconography in Israel (and at seventh-century BCE Tel Miqne-Ekron), together with a royal ʿAštart cult in neighboring first-millennium BCE Phoenicia, form a historical backdrop for the literary presentation of a royal ʿAštart cult associated with

DtrH's Solomon and Josiah, and the kings (Manasseh and Amon?) mentioned in Jeremiah's Queen of Heaven ('Aštart) cult.
- The hypothesis that a Judean Queen of Heaven ('Aštart) cult could be sociologically diverse (involving familial and royal cults) aligns with what we know of the porous boundaries between elite and non-elite religion elsewhere. The Ugaritic cult of 'Athtartu of the Field/Steppe Land provides a nice analogue. In particular, the goddess's association with food production and the textile industry that intersected the rural and the royal (together with ethnographic studies of women as key administrators) resonates with the central role of women in the Queen of Heaven ('Aštart) cult.
- The hypothesis that a Judean 'Aštart cult had agrarian concerns that included fecund humans and animals as well as agricultural bounty finds an analogue with (again) the Ugaritic cult surrounding 'Athtartu of the Field/Steppe Land.
- The hypothesis that a Judean Queen of Heaven ('Aštart) cult looked to a deity who had such military prowess that she could provide safety in times of war resonates with similar widespread notions in Emar, Egypt, and Ugarit.
- Other aspects of the goddess (e.g., associations with apotropaic magic [Ugarit, Egypt] and *Chaoskampf* traditions [Ugarit]) find little if any footprint in our extant data from ancient Israel.[58]

In summation, once one frames the research project to encapsulate a full study of the many details only sketched in this excursus, it is clear that the Israelite goddess 'Aštart deserves her own full-length treatment. Conceptually, one would need also to address the goddess's association with other goddesses (cf. Cornelius 2004; Smith 2014a: 200–201; 2014b: 64–65, 74–77; Tazawa 2009: 163–165; 2014) and whether the data point to a unified or a divided portrait (see Wilson-Wright 2016: 8–11). Several volumes have attempted more comprehensive and comparative analyses (e.g., Bonnet 1996; Christian and Schmitt 2013a; Sugimoto 2014; Wilson-Wright 2016), though still with limited coverage.

A similar assessment applies to the thirty-some Iron Age Levantine deities mentioned in the Introduction (Chapter One, p. 2), each of which deserves a full-scale treatment that provides windows into the practice of Israelite religion. The same can be said for the study of the plurality of divinity and other preternatural beings. Acknowledging the scope of such necessary and yet daunting research, the present volume is restricted to providing coverage of only El and Yahweh traditions. It is hoped that many other historians of Israelite religion will continue to fill this gap.

There are splendid models that provide an *overview* of this material, such as Zevit's (2001: 513, 583–585) look at "non-Yahwistic cults (and cultic phenomena and complex rituals) celebrated by Israelites" in his magisterial study of the multiplicity of ancient Israelite religions; Smith's many studies (esp. 2001b, 2002a, 2008, 2014a, 2016) that situate Israelite and Judean Yahwism in its broader cultural context; Day's (2000) juxtaposing of Yahweh over against the gods and goddesses of Canaan; and the look at religious diversity in the volume edited by Stavrakopoulou and Barton (2010). Yet the need for comprehensive volumes dedicated to each and every Canaanite deity remains.

Yahweh Traditions: Data-Rich (and Yet Limited)

Our decision to concentrate on El worship and even more so on the deity Yahweh and the observance of his cult is data-driven and pragmatic. The parameters of Israelite religion for which we have the richest data are Yahweh-centric. And because Yahweh is unattested outside of ancient Israel—apart from the tantalizing though minimal Shasu texts and the "shepherd of Yah" reference (see Chapter Six, pp. 229–233)—there is little comparative work to do. Unlike what we just observed with ʿAštart, there is no need to explore questions of cultural contact and appropriation. Though the challenges of studying the religious expressions surrounding Yahweh are extensive, because Yahweh was an indigenous deity they are not nearly as complicated as they could be. (The same cannot be said of El religion.)

Our data-driven analysis has also concentrated on the bulk of the evidence that is Judean. Though these materials represent dominant traditions, they are only a partial look at the breadth of the religion experienced within ancient Israel. Such a Judean-centric portrayal needs to be complemented, data permitting, by comprehensive studies of local Yahweh cults elsewhere. Again, we have splendid glances at this material, such as that of P. Kyle McCarter (1987) and that of Jeremy Hutton (2010b), who look to Mesopotamian and Ugaritic analogues. Yet regrettably, even with what we find at Kuntillet ʿAjrud (see Chapter Six), this area of study remains in its infancy (and will for the foreseeable future) due to the lack of textual and archaeological resources. We do not have, for example, a dataset that would compare to the one we have for the local cults of Hittite Anatolia of the Late Empire period (esp. the thirteenth-century BCE reigns of Ḫattušili III and Tutḫaliya IV). There we find numerous religious texts regarding the interaction between the central royal administration and the cults of provincial villages. In particular, we have "cult inventories" that provide an unparalleled look at the actual practices of local religion. In Michele Cammarosano's (2018: 1) words, the cult inventories "offer an all-around report on the state of local shrines, cult images, festivals, and cult offerings" that provide a window into the "composition of local panthea, materiality of cult images and iconography of the gods, religious beliefs at different levels of the society, local festivals, theory and practice of the offering system, agricultural calendar, cult administration and record-keeping."[59] We have nothing of this sort to reconstruct the local cults of Yahweh worship.

Conceptualizing Yahweh: Wedding and Privileging

A significant percentage of the world's population conceptualizes religion through a theistic lens, especially those inheriting Abrahamic traditions. How we (like the ancients) conceptualize our deity is a twofold process of wedding certain divine traits and privileging (consciously and subconsciously) those of our liking. Thus what we (like the ancients) think of God has very much to do with ourselves as we express our sociological and psychological needs and desires. Do we (did they) think of God as a righteous king to whom one may appeal for justice or as a tender mother drying one's tears? Or do we (did they) think of an intimidating force whose love has ceased, whose promises go unfulfilled, who has forgotten to be gracious, whose anger has stifled his compassion (Ps 77:8–10 [Eng 77:7–9])? In short, is God near or far off (haʾĕlōhê miqqārōb . . . ʾĕlōhê mērāḥōq; Jer 23:23)?

How did the ancients (elite and non-elite, individually and corporately) wed divine traits when it came to Yahweh? Did intellectuals weave many threads into a seamless garment, as would a modern systematic theologian? Did ritual specialists petition God on behalf of the corporate body with a litany of divine epithets? Were private prayers similar, or did a situational need have a supplicant favoring a single divine attribute aligned with her plight? How often did people juxtapose opposing metaphors to describe God as both a warrior and a mother in the travails of labor (Isa 42:13–14)?

We have little way of knowing. If we cannot know the inner psyche of modern Jews or Christians as to how they daily integrate the many attributes of God, how much less possible is that with the ancients? Occasionally well-known corporate prayers such as the Jewish mourner's Kaddish or the Christian's Lord's Prayer provide some insight, yet private prayer remains private.[60]

Certainly the many passages treated in this volume reveal particularistic desires to view Yahweh primarily as divine warrior, as king, as judge, as holy, or as a parent relating to Israel, his child—or as a silent deity whose inactivity occasions cries of despair and theodicean dissent. Other authors luxuriated in wedding divine traits, often in doxologies. A Chronistic post-exilic tradition says of David:

> Then David blessed Yahweh in the presence of all the assembly; David said: "Blessed are you, O Yahweh, the God of our ancestor Israel, forever and ever. Yours, O Yahweh, are the greatness, the power, the glory, the victory, and the majesty; for all that is in the heavens and on the earth is yours; yours is the kingdom, O Yahweh, and you are exalted as head above all. Riches and honor come from you, and you rule over all. In your hand are power and might; and it is in your hand to make great and to give strength to all. And now, our God, we give thanks to you and praise your glorious Name . . . All things come from you. . . . O Yahweh, our God, all of this abundance for building a house for your Holy Name comes from your hand . . . [M]y God, you search the heart, and take pleasure in righteousness/justice. . . . O Yahweh, the God of Abraham, Isaac, and Israel, our ancestors . . . direct the hearts [of your people] toward you. (1 Chr 29:1–18; cf. 1 Chr 16:7–36)

Here in a single utterance we have interlaced attributes of Yahweh, the God of Israel. He is both a personal deity ("my God," *ʾĕlōhay*) and a corporate deity ("our God," *ʾĕlōhênû*), defined first as a god of their ancestors (*ʾābînû*), a god of family religion. (See Chapter Eight, pp. 473–494.) Our author reaches into the distant past, tracing the affirmation of his god to a time-honored, multigenerational heritage (*yhwh ʾĕlōhê ʾabrāhām yiṣḥāq wĕyiśrāʾēl ʾăbōtênû*). He looks back especially to the eponymous ancestor, the patriarch Isra__el__ (*yhwh ʾĕlōhê yiśrā_ʾēl_ ʾābînû*), whose name confesses how El strives on his behalf. A proclamation about Yahweh's eternal nature immediately follows (*mēʿôlām wĕʿad-ʿôlām*), reminding us of aged El Olam and Yahweh El Olam traditions. (See Chapter Four, pp. 97–99.)

Yet this god of the family did not remain provincial with the advent of state formation. Thus here he is also proclaimed to be an absolute monarch who rules over all (*wĕʾattâ môšēl bakōl*). Royal epithets are used to celebrate his military prowess with words of power (*gĕbûrâ*), might (*kōaḥ*), victory (*nēṣaḥ*), and majesty (*hôd*). (See Chapters Eight, pp. 453–460, and Nine, pp. 495–513.) As absolute judge he tests his peoples' hearts, taking pleasure in justice (*mêšārîm tirṣeh*). (See Chapter Nine, pp. 513–574.)

Probing, our poet urges further reflection: human analogies are inadequate to describe Yahweh fully. He is more than even the most illustrious father, king, and judge. His essence must be described with abstract superlatives of "greatness" (*gĕdullâ*), "radiance" (*tipʾeret*), and "holiness" (*qōdeš*). (See Chapters Seven, pp. 358–379, and Ten, pp. 575–606.) Mysteriously, Yahweh's essence can be encapsulated in his hypostatic Name, which is equally radiant and holy (*šēm tipʾartekā; šēm qodšekā*). (See Chapter Seven, pp. 379–392.)

Finally, what list of attributes would be complete without the mention of a deity's creative powers and sovereignty over heaven and earth (*kî-kōl baššāmayim ûbāʾāreṣ lĕkā*)? Remarkably, for our poet, all of Yahweh's attributes—from Creator and Father to King, Judge, and Holy Other—serve his benevolent nature. God extends his radiant richness to his people (*hāʿōšer wĕhakkābôd millĕpānêkā*), granting them the blessings of "all things" (*kî-mimmĕkā hakōl*). He impartially magnifies and strengthens all (*bĕyādĕkā lĕgaddēl ûlĕḥazzēq lakōl*). Such benevolence reminds us again of the oldest of Israelite lore, of Yahweh/El the Compassionate (*ʾēl rahûm*). (See Chapter Eight, pp. 477–482.)

This multi-layered confession defies a reductionist approach to conceptualizing divinity. Though a particular attribute of God can be emphasized to meet a particular need (sociologically or psychologically), the overall witness of ancient Israel's religious expression is that God cannot be reduced to a single attribute, a single explanation. God's traits do not exist in isolation from one another. They are holistic and integrated. They are simultaneous expressions of a God who is both near and far (Jer 23:23; Lundbom 2004: 201).

Concluding Remarks

The use of doxologies as concluding remarks is known from the Psalter (Ps 41:14 [Eng 41:13]; 72:19; 89:53 [Eng 89:52]; 106:48; Wilson 1985: 182–186) and the performance of cult. Thus I am certain that the ancients would agree that it is only fitting to conclude a book about God and his people, even a scholarly tome, with a benediction:

bārûk-yhwh ʾĕlōhê yiśrāʾēl
min-hāʿôlām wĕʿad hāʿôlām
wĕʾāmar kol-hāʿām ʾāmēn

Blessed be Yahweh, the God of Israel,
from everlasting to everlasting.
And let all the people say, "Amen."
(Ps 106:48)

Notes

Chapter 1

1. Compare Yahweh of Jerusalem/Zion vis-à-vis Yahweh of Samaria vis-à-vis Yahweh of Teman vis-à-vis Yahweh in Hebron. Similar multiplications could be tabulated for El and even more so for Baal in his various manifestations. See McCarter 1987: 139–143; Hutton 2010b; and more broadly Sommer 2009.
2. Asherah has received the lion's share of analysis due to her appearance in the Ugaritic texts (as ʾAthiratu) as well as in inscriptions from Kuntillet ʿAjrud and Khirbet el Qom. The secondary bibliography is overwhelming. Influential treatments include Maier 1987; Olyan 1988; Dietrich and Loretz 1992; Wiggins 1993; Frevel 1995; Kletter 1996; Binger 1997; Keel and Uehlinger 1998: 177–281; Hadley 2000; Day 2000: 42–67; Smith 2002a: 108–147; Cornelius 2004; Dever 2005; Albertz and Schmitt 2012: 62–65; Darby 2014: 34–46; Römer 2015: 160–172; and Schmidt 2016. See additional literature in Chapter 2, note 87. For the presence of "Yahweh and Asherah" in the iconographic record, including Kuntillet ʿAjrud, see Chapter Seven, pp. 325–330.
3. See the preliminary study of ʿAštart in the Conclusion, pp. 675–696.
4. Throughout this volume the use of the term "cult" designates the performance of religion and is not value-laden (cf. Latin *cultus*, "care, worship"; Lang 1993: 475–477).
5. See Chapter Ten for bibliography addressing these topics (e.g., works by Gilders, Klawans, Milgrom, and Feder).
6. See Fox 2000: 28–43 on the various words for wisdom and for folly used in the book of Proverbs.
7. See Greenstein 2016 and Holm 2013.
8. The choice to restrict the present treatment to El and Yahweh with minimal coverage of female divinity, other Southern Levantine male gods, and the plurality of divinity is pragmatic out of respect for what such an endeavor would entail. These topics deserve full-scale treatments. See additional comments in the Conclusion, pp. 675–696.

Chapter 2

1. Greenspahn (1987: 245) documents how "many of the methods and concerns most typical of contemporary scholarship can be found already among medieval Jews." The late Moshe Held was fond of challenging students with the assertion that the best insights of modern biblical and Talmudic scholars were already to be found in the medievals.
2. On Herder, see Iggers 1968; Willi 1971; and Knight 1973: 58–60.

3. See Oden's (1987: 4ff.) remarks about the need for a sociological study of biblical scholarship. In particular, he notes the Christian institutional settings of the majority of influential German scholars of the nineteenth century.
4. It is common to find scholars choosing the 1787 inaugural address of Johann Gabler (1753–1826) as the initial reference point for articulating Germanic scholarship, especially as it relates to Old Testament theology. Cf. Hayes and Prussner 1985: 2–5; Albertz 1994: 3; and Preuss 1995: 1–2. Compare the title of Gabler's address: "On the Proper Distinction Between Biblical and Dogmatic Theology and the Specific Objectives of Each." Albertz (1994: 3) has noted that Gabler's program "in no way led to a really historical account of biblical religion . . . which began to become an independent area of study in the subsequent period." In addition, many Christian and Jewish scholars prior to Gabler had wrestled with similar methods. Hayes and Prussner (1985: 4–34) point to the Protestant reformers and Spinoza as predecessors as well as C. Haymann, S. Schmidt, and J. Cocceius.

    Were the present work a complete history of scholarship, one would have to include discussions of many other predecessors, such as Richard Simon (1638–1712) and Jean Astruc (1684–1766). Readers are directed to many of the works on the history of scholarship, including Knight 1973; Clements 1976; Zimmerli 1979b; Miller 1985; Hayes and Prussner 1985; Oden 1987: 1–39; Preuss 1995: 1–19; and Dozeman 2017.
5. For more on de Wette, see Reventlow 2010: 231–245. For more on the "discovered scroll" in the ancient Near East and its legitimation of Josiah's cult reform, see Na'aman 2011a.
6. At the same time, it should be noted that there were more than a few disagreements between these two scholars, with de Wette being quite critical of Vatke's approach and partly responsible, along with Hengstenberg, for Vatke's lack of receiving *ordinarius* professorial stature (cf. Hayes and Prussner 1985: 101; Albertz 1994: 5).
7. On Vatke, see Perlitt 1965.
8. Vatke's works lost their voice primarily due to his Hegelian overlay. Indeed, Graf came to his conclusions not through Vatke but through building on de Wette and his teacher Eduard Reuss (see Wellhausen 1965: 3–4; Morgan and Barton 1988: 79). One of the first scholars to execute the Grafian theory of Israelite history was A. Kuenen (1828–1891) of Leiden. See Dirksen and van der Kooij 1993.
9. See Berman 2014b: 39, who asserts that Graf's study of the legal collections of P and D as statutory codes (as opposed to common law) earns him the title of "the father of the modern study of biblical law."
10. Wellhausen (1965: 368) remarks later in his book: "I always go back to the centralisation of the cultus, and deduce from it the particular divergences. My whole position is contained in my first chapter."
11. In particular, see Miller's (1983: 63) and Oden's (1987: 21) comments on Wellhausen's value judgments. As for Bultmann, his comments are eerie to read in light of charges of anti-Judaism. For a history of the issue, see De Valerio (1994).
12. I owe this quote to Oden (1987: 24).
13. Geller has perceptively pointed out Wellhausen's methodological failures. Due in part to "a paucity of external, archaeological evidence for biblical and ancient Near

Eastern history, Wellhausen . . . created an essentially literary theory" (1985: 42). See too Knight's (1973: 68) comments on Wellhausen's failure to grasp the "traditio-historical possibility."

14. Cf. Blenkinsopp 1983: 29, who notes how Ewald ended up in one of Bismarck's prisons, not to mention being removed from his teaching post at Göttingen.

15. I am indebted to Wilson (1980: 3) for this assessment of Ewald. Wilson also remarks that for Bernhard Duhm, another one of Ewald's students and a close friend of Wellhausen, the prophets "raised the level of Israelite religion to new moral and ethical heights." Blenkinsopp (1983: 28) concurs, commenting that for Duhm "the ethical idealism of the prophets represents the essence of true religion." Blenkinsopp states his "suspicion that the ghost of Hegel is hovering nearby."

16. For evaluations of Robertson Smith's life and legacy, see Bediako 1997; Johnstone 1995; Hendel 1989; and Beidelman 1975.

17. On Wellhausen's admiration of Robertson Smith's *Lectures on the Religion of the Semites*, see Smend 1995: 239. Of course, I am not stating that the field of sociology per se started with Robertson Smith. See Rogerson 1985.

18. Cited by Oden (1987: 24), to whom I am indebted.

19. Day 1995: 28–29; Oden 1987: 25–26. Elsewhere Robertson Smith (1972: 14) writes: "In many respects the religion of heathen Arabia . . . displays an extremely primitive type, corresponding to the primitive and unchanging character of nomadic life." Robertson Smith (1972: 49) also described "the character of the Semitic genius"—"deficient in plastic power and in the faculty of sustained and orderly effort"—as being the reason the Semites were never able to develop a mythological epic poetry like the Greeks.

See too the famous monograph of Said (1991) that charged Robertson Smith with being guilty of "Orientalism," a prejudice of European superiority that denigrates the Eastern as primitive and thereby inferior (with the ultimate goal of domination in a Foucauldian sense). See the rejoinder by Skinner in Johnstone 1995: 376–382.

Another scholar who, like Wellhausen and Robertson Smith, championed the primitive nature of ancient Hebraic religion was Smend (1893), who wrote one of the earliest full treatments using the new Graf-Wellhausen paradigm.

20. Cf. Robertson Smith's more popular works *The Old Testament in the Jewish Church* and *The Prophets of Israel*, which attempted to mediate the critical scholarship of his day, including Wellhausen, with a general Christian audience. See the various articles in Johnstone 1995 dealing with Robertson Smith's relations to the Free Church in Scotland and biblical scholars at large.

21. For further information on Gunkel and the history of the *religionsgeschichtliche Schule*, see Klatt 1969; Kraus 1969: 341–367; Gressman 1914; Rogerson 1974: 57–65; Oden 1987: 29–39; Hayes and Prussner 1985: 128–136; and Scurlock and Beal 2013.

22. This not to say, as some have asserted, that Wellhausen and Robertson Smith were ignorant of Assyriology. Manuscripts of the second and third parts of Robertson Smith's Burnett lectures (published by John Day) reveal his acquaintance with the newly emerging field of Mesopotamian studies (in particular the creation myth Enuma Elish) prior to Gunkel's famous treatment (Day 1995: 29). It should be noted

that Gunkel had no formal training in Assyriology and relied on the expertise of the Assyriologist H. Zimmern.

For additional analysis of Gunkel and the *Chaoskampf* traditions, see Chapter Eight, pp. 443–461.

23. For further reading on the interface of Wellhausen and Gunkel, see McKane 1979: 225–228 and O'Neill 1995.
24. See Larsen 1995 (with bibliography). See also Finkelstein 1958; Huffmon 1987; Johanning 1988; and Lehmann 1994.
25. For an annotated bibliography of some of the Assyriological material that was already in print at this time, see Carena 1989: 21–45.
26. See Cecil's (1989–1996) biography of Wilhelm II.
27. It should be noted, however, that Gunkel objected to the way in which Delitzsch denigrated biblical tradition, which Gunkel tried to elevate through his comparative approach. See Oden 1987: 32–33.
28. All three lectures were combined and published as *Babel and Bible: Three Lecture on the Significance of Assyriological Research for Religion, Embodying the Most Important Criticisms and the Author's Replies* (Chicago: Open Court, 1906). Several contemporary reactions to the first two lectures (including those of Wilhelm II, Harnack, Halevy, and Cornill) and Delitzsch's replies are included in this work. For further analysis of anti-Semitic tendencies in these lectures and Delitzsch's subsequent work *Die grosse Täuschung*, see Larsen 1995: 103–106.
29. See Carena 1989: 96–111.
30. I owe each of these quotes to Oden 1987: 32.
31. See Carena's (1989: 102–110) description of "non-supporters of Panbabylonism."
32. See Landsberger 1976 and Hess 1994: 8–11.
33. Pals 2015: 108–109. Harrison (1969: 50) argues that explaining "all phenomena in terms of one relatively uncomplicated single feature, process, or principle" was "the basic defect of the nineteenth-century *Zeitgeist*."

Along with Durkheim, one should also mention M. Weber's *Sociology of Religion* (itself a part of his larger *Economy and Society*). In contrast to Durkheim, Weber's system still left room for animated spirits and deities, although it was so economically oriented ("the most elementary forms of behavior motivated by religious or magical factors are oriented to *this* world") that it proved too empirical for the worldview of theologians. See the bibliographies in the following critiques: Samuelsson 1964; Kimbrough 1972; Schäfer-Lichtenberger 1991; Pals 2015: 143–184.

Finally, from Scandinavia, see the anthropological/phenomenological work of J. Pedersen, whose four-volume work *Israel, Its Life and Culture* appeared first in 1926.
34. Childs 1970b: 14–31. On the various societal issues at this time in America, see Noll 1992: 364–436; Marsden 1994; and Larson 1997.
35. The presentation here is only a sketch. For broader contextualization, see Ackerman 1991 and Bell 1997: 3–22.
36. In addition to the major works written and edited by Hooke (1933, 1935, 1938, 1958, 1963), see Rogerson 1974: 66–84. On Mowinckel, see the bibliography assembled by Kvale and Rian (1988) as well as the other articles in this issue of the *Scandinavian*

Journal of the Old Testament, which is devoted to Mowinckel's scholarship; cf. too Kapelrud 1967; Ap-Thomas 1966; and Gnuse and Knight 1992.

37. A thirteenth volume was added as a supplement in 1936, and an abridged single volume by which *The Golden Bough* became popular with a much wider audience first appeared in 1922.
38. On divine kingship, see note 40 and Chapter Nine, pp. 503–507.
39. See Brandon 1958: 261–291; Fontenrose 1966; Kirk 1970: 8–31; Rogerson 1974; Talmon 1978b; and Smith 1994c.
40. See the bibliography in Rogerson 1974: 81–84 as well as van der Toorn 1991b; Black 1981; and Hecker 1974: 1–23. Note too Lambert's (1965: 295) succinct comment: "Too much has been made of the recitation of *Enūma Eliš* in the New Year rites." Michalowski (2008: 33, 41–42) writes of how the study of divine kingship in Mesopotamia is still haunted by the "lingering ghosts, James Frazer and Edward Evans-Prichard." In contrast to the "highly overrated" and "highly overstated" views of "Frazer and his successors," Michalowski (2008: 33–34, 41–42) argues that any notion of divine kingship had a "short shelf life" and was due to historically specific phenomena. We are better off emphasizing how "all kings are sacred and mediate between sacred and profane, but not all kings are gods." See additional discussion in Chapter Nine, pp. 503–507.
41. Additional assessments of Frazer's impact and the critique of his theory can be found in Ackerman 2002 and Smith 1978: 208–239.
42. See Ringgren 1966, 1972, 1977. For an appreciation, see Frerichs 1987. See too Albertz 1994: 9.
43. For the history of the excavations at Ras Shamra, see the frequent publications in *Syria, Ugaritica,* and *RSO* (*Ras Shamra Ougarit*) as well as the summary in Yon 2006. See too the entries on C. Schaeffer and C. Virolleaud in Meyers 1997: 4:496–497, 5:304) as well as the many publications by the Mission archéologique syro-française de Ras Shamra: https://www.mission-ougarit.fr.
44. For further details, see Chapter Six, pp. 259–264.
45. Early works (in chronological order) include those of Virolleaud, Albright, Montgomery, Jack, Nielsen, Schaeffer, Dussaud, Ginsberg, Pedersen, Eissfeldt, de Langhe, Gordon, Obermann, Cassuto, Gaster, Kapelrud, van Selms, Pope, G. R. Driver, Gray, Caquot and Jacob. For bibliographic details of these early works, see Dietrich 1973 and Dietrich and Loretz 1996.
46. See Chapter Six, pp. 256–264, for a more properly nuanced description of the Canaanite religious continuum between Late Bronze Age Ugarit and Iron Age Israel.
47. See Childs 1970b: 47–49; Miller 1985: 202–203; and Albright 1940, 1957. See also the entries on these three scholars with bibliographies in Meyers 1997: 1:61–62, 2:344, 3:205.
48. Albright's influence was felt through more than a thousand publications, through three decades of teaching at the Johns Hopkins University (1929–1958), through thirty-eight years as the editor of the *Bulletin of the American School of Oriental Research* (1930–1968), and through twelve years of service as the director of the American School of Oriental Research in Jerusalem (1920–1929, 1933–1936). This

archaeological institute, founded in 1900, constitutes the oldest American research center for ancient Near Eastern studies in the Middle East. In 1970 it was renamed the W. F. Albright Institute of Archaeological Research (AIAR). Lastly, it should also be underscored that Albright, together with his student and later colleague Samuel Iwry, were two of the earliest scholars to authenticate the Dead Sea Scrolls. For two of the many overviews of Albright's contributions, see Machinist 1996 and Lewis 2006b, which include further bibliography.

49. As noted by Beaulieu (2002: 12), "Between 1912, when his first contribution appeared in a scholarly journal, and 1926, he [Albright] published some thirty-five articles on Mesopotamian religion, literature, chronology, philology, and history, roughly one third of his total output."

50. In this brief survey of scholarship on ancient Israelite religion we are certainly slighting giants who have made monumental contributions. Such was Harold Louis Ginsberg's (1903–1990) role in early Ugaritic studies. For an appropriate appreciation (including the highest praise from Albright), see Smith 2001a: 25–26, 45 n. 104.

51. For Albright's work on Ugaritic at the Johns Hopkins University, prewar and postwar, see Smith 2001a: 24–25, 67–73. See too Smith's (2002b) retrospective summary of Albright's work in Ugaritic studies as it impacted Israelite religion.

52. Alongside Albright's commanding presence we find other giants, especially among Israeli archaeologists (e.g., B. Mazar, Y. Yadin, Y. Aharoni). Key to Albright's method was the study of typology (be it for scripts, pottery, or architecture). According to Frank Moore Cross (1989: 17), who inherited and perfected Albright's command of epigraphy and paleography, "Albright was a master of the typological sciences."

53. Cf., e.g., Albright's (2006: 176) comment that "only through archaeological research can biblical history become a scientific discipline, since history can in general become scientific only by the consistent application of archaeology or other equally rigorous methodology."

Albright would also use the "science" of archaeology to combat what he saw as the ahistorical approach of many of the German critics listed earlier. For Albright (2006: 3), one cannot understand history via internal literary analysis alone. In his words, "history . . . is a complex web of interacting patterns." Moreover, "the evolution of historical patterns is highly complex and variable; it may move on any direction and it cannot be explained by any deterministic theory." Albright argued that Wellhausen's brand of source criticism employed without archaeological control would result in an ahistorical and skewed portrait. According to Albright, the "organismic nature of history makes unilinear 'historicism' unsuitable as a clue to the complexities of the history of religion. For this reason, Wellhausen's Hegelian method was utterly unsuited to become the master key with which scholars might enter the sanctuary of Israelite religion and acquire a satisfying understanding of it."

In contrast, Albright (2006: 176) boldly asserted that "there can be no doubt that archaeology has confirmed the substantial historicity of Old Testament tradition." Because of such comments, Albright is sometimes unfairly dismissed as being narrow, unduly influenced by his theological conservatism. A close reading reveals that Albright was a critical scholar. On Albright's brand of conservatism (presenting the Bible "in terms of the history of ideas") and how he was equally frustrated by "radicals who challenged the whole historical premise of biblical religion" as well as by "ultra-conservatives who made it an article of faith, thus allowing no possibility of fruitful discussion," see Freedman 1989: 35–38. Albright (2006: 177) asserted that "neither radicalism nor ultra-conservatism receives any support from the discoveries and the deductions of the archaeologist."

Though he was very critical of the Wellhausian *theoretical* paradigm, Albright was no textual fundamentalist. In Albright's (2006: 3) opinion, one could not deny that Wellhausen's source criticism was "a useful tool for historical research." Albright was critical of "those scholars who reject the Documentary Hypothesis *in toto*." "There can be no doubt," Albright (1968a: 30) would write elsewhere, "that nineteenth-century scholarship was correct in recognizing different blocks of material in the Pentateuch." See also Albright's (1957: 249–254) discussion of "the Documentary Sources" in his *From Stone Age to Christianity. Monotheism and the Historical Process*. Anyone who has worked through Albright's articles on what he determined to be the oldest poetic corpus in the Hebrew Bible is well aware of the way he would speculatively repoint, realign, or even rewrite the Masoretic Text of the Hebrew Bible. See, for example, Albright 1944: 207–233; 1950b: 1–18; 1950–1951: 1–39; 1959: 339–346.

54. It is easy to see the battle lines drawn between Albright's method, which analyzed ancient Near Eastern sources in the service of highlighting Israel and its Bible, and the *Eigenbegrifflichkeit* methodology of Benno Landsberger, which asserted that the ancient Near East was no mere handmaid to biblical studies and must be studied and appreciated on its own. See Landsberger's 1926 *Die Eigenbegrifflichkeit der babylonischen Welt*, later published in English in 1976 as *The Conceptual Autonomy of the Babylonian World*.

55. Regrettably, Albright also played a key role in demonizing Canaanite religion, as he underscored the supremacy of biblical religion. See Chapter Six, pp. 259–260.

56. In a positive tribute, Greenberg (1964: 77–89) calls Kaufmann the "foremost Jewish biblicist of our time." See similar assessments by Levenson (1987: 290–291) and Sommer (2009: 2). Contrast the views of Dever (1990: 51), who labels Kaufmann as an "Israeli scholar of conservative bent" with presuppositions "almost identical to those of some Protestant fundamentalists." Geller (1985: 45) calls him a "semi-fundamentalist." Morgan and Barton (1988) fail to have an entry for Kaufmann! Sommer (2009: 260–261 n. 5) notes Albertz's "stunning" failure to mention Kaufmann, "the most important historian of Israelite religion in the twentieth century." For more on Kaufmann, consider the work of Jindo, Sommer, and Staubli (2017: xi), who assert: "No other figure, not even Martin Buber, has had such a profound influence on the work of Jewish scholars of the Bible."

57. Kaufmann 1956, 1972. See also his article on the Bible and mythological polytheism (1951).

58. Perhaps this is due to the inaccessibility of his works, which are written in Hebrew, yet an abridged translation of his history has been available since 1960. While well recognized as a biblical scholar, Kaufmann writes more with the heart of a philosopher than that of a theologian. His prior training and work in philosophy is evident

throughout his work. Greenberg (1964: 77) notes that Kaufmann's Berne dissertation was a philosophic "treatise on the sufficient reason" (*Eine Abhandlung über den Zurreichenden Grund*). The label "Jewish apologist" is often attributed to Kaufmann, yet he prefaces his work by stating that "it is not undertaken in an apologetic spirit." Indeed, Kaufmann's embrace of critical scholarship offended Orthodox Judaism and brought him much religious and political reproach. Neither was Kaufmann a defender of biblical literalness, as he is sometimes made out to be. Whereas Kaufmann, unlike classical critics, did embrace the biblical claims for early monotheism, he nevertheless considered the prophetic and historiographic claims of polytheism as mere hyperbole, to be taken with a grain of salt. Kaufmann's later works (e.g., his view of the conquest/settlement, commentaries on Joshua/Judges) were more idiosyncratic and did not meet with a great deal of acceptance. Once again, for a greater appreciation, see Jindo, Sommer, and Staubli 2017.

59. Kaufmann 1951: 193. See too Tigay's (1996: 433–436) excursus on Moses and monotheism.

60. Moshe Greenberg (1964: 87), Kaufmann's translator, admits that Kaufmann himself qualified his categorical statements: "The qualification . . . usually makes its appearance sooner or later."

61. Smith (2014a: 36, 40) evaluates Cross as producing "the best scholarship of his generation" on early Israel while also describing his theorizing about epic as "a questionable scaffolding."

62. Cross 1973: viii; 1983b: 13–19; 1998; 2009. In a summary of critiques of Cross' use of epic, Smith (2014a: 38–40) notes "the problem of scale; epic is generally considered a poem of considerable length, and there simply is no such epic poem attested in the Hebrew Bible . . . Cross seems to be saying that this early war poetry [Exod 15; Judg 5] is not so much epic as lyric, which at most draws on known epic elements."

63. Albright's (1968a: 185) wording echoes Kaufmann's sentiments: "It may be confidently stated that there is no true mythology anywhere in the Hebrew Bible. What we have consists of vestiges—what may be called the 'débris' of past religious culture." In Albright's assessment, these vestiges, though great in number, were "minor." As far as the attenuation of myth in the Bible, Albright (1968a: 193) argued that "Israelite thought was indeed influenced by Canaanite mythological patterns . . . [but] such Canaanite patterns were depotentized and demythologized rapidly, so that by the end of Old Testament times official Yahwist religion had been demythologized to a rather extreme degree."

64. Kirk 1970; Rogerson 1974; Doty 1986; Puhvel 1987; Oden 1992; Batto 1992: 4–12; Smith 1994c; Ballentine 2015. See especially Ballentine's (2015: 1–21) chapter "Theorizing Myth in Ancient West Asian Studies." For a study of mythology in Mesopotamian literature and art as well as that of Anatolian cultures, see the entry "Mythologie" by Heimpel, Green, Beckman, and van Loon in Edzard et al. 1997: 537–589.

65. See Oden 1992: 946; Batto 1992: 6.

66. Ballentine (2015) builds on the theoretical work of Jonathan Z. Smith, Bruce Lincoln, and Russell T. McCutcheon.

67. Note the astute critique of Rogerson (1974: 173), who noted how scholars have often been more preoccupied with finding an all-purpose definition of "myth" than with understanding the cultures we face. Catherine Bell (2007: 283), writing on the search for the perfect definition of ritual, comments: "No field ever moves forward because a good number of people agree on the definition of some central concept that then allows them to get down to work."
68. I owe this quote to Smith (1994c: 305).
69. See, for example, the works of Gressmann (1909) and Pritchard (1969a, 1969b).
70. For the numerous volumes in the Orbis Biblicus et Orientalis series, see https://www.zora.uzh.ch/view/subjects/OBO.html. On using seals for reconstructing ancient Israelite religion, see Avigad 1987.
71. Keel and Uehlinger 1992; Caubet 1995; Green 1995; Hornung 1995; Cornelius 1999; Wyatt 1999b: 580–583; de Hulster, Strawn, and Bonfiglio 2015.

    Yet not all signs are promising. Contrast Keel and Uehlinger's (1992) extensive treatment with the entry on "Iconography and the Bible" in the *New Interpreter's Dictionary of the Bible* (Sakenfeld et al. 2008: 5–7). The latter's extremely brief treatment (a single page!) deals mostly with early Christian art (with a small nod to the Dura Europos synagogue). The Hebrew Bible and ancient Israel is left out entirely!

    On the positive side, the field of ancient Near Eastern iconographic studies is maturing, as seen in new works (e.g., Gansell and Shafer 2020) that ask us to reexamine the canon of our material.
72. See the many contributors to the forthcoming *Iconography of Deities and Demons in the Ancient Near East*, http://www.religionswissenschaft.uzh.ch/idd. See too the Bibel+Orient Datenbank Online: http://www.bible-orient-museum.ch/bodo.
73. For a brief description of subsequent literature from the 1980s to the present—admittedly written by the chief critic of the revisionist approach—see Dever 2017: 19–24, 34–36, 45–58.
74. For revisionist historians of this generation applying their method to Israelite religion, see Lemche 1991b: 97–115; Thompson 1995; and Edelman 1995. See the reviews of Edelman by Smith (1996) and Emerton (1997).
75. See the following for a representative sample: T. Thompson 1974, 1992, 1995, 1999; Van Seters 1975, 1983, 1992, 1994; Lemche 1985, 1991a, 1991b, 1993, 1996a; Ahlström 1986, 1991, 1993; Whitelam 1986, 1996; Coote and Whitelam 1987; Garbini 1988; Coote 1990; Davies 1992, 1995; and Gelinas 1995. The controversial nature of these scholars' work spilled over into the pages of more popular works on Bible and archaeology. See Davies 1994; Halpern 1995; Hackett 1997; Shanks 1997a, 1997b; Na'aman 1997.
76. The literature cannot be detailed here due to its volume. It certainly demonstrates how the revisionist historians struck a sensitive nerve. See Knoppers 1997 (with bibliography). For archaeologists' critiques, see Dever 1995, 1996a, 1996b; Bloch-Smith 1997. Minimalist historians got the attention of the epigraphic community when they challenged the presence of King David's mention in the Tell Dan inscription and, even more so, when they challenged the eighth-century BCE dating of the Siloam inscription. For bibliography on the Tell Dan inscription, see Knoppers 1997: 37–40.

For the Siloam inscription, see the who's who of leading epigraphists (F. M. Cross, A. Lemaire, P. K. McCarter, J. A. Hackett, A. Yardeni, E. Eshel, and A. Hurvitz) assembled to denounce what was labeled pseudo-scholarship. And see Hackett 1997 and Hendel 1996.

Finally, cf. the critiques of Na'aman (1994a) and Rainey (1996b) against Lemche's (1991a) handling of the biblical historiographers' understanding of Canaan and the Canaanites.

77. There is no adequate intellectual history of biblical/Syro-Palestinian archaeology, especially with regard to the contributions of Israeli archaeologists (e.g. Y. Aharoni, R. Amiran, M. Avi-Yonah, N. Avigad, G. Barkay, S. Bechar, D. Ben-Ami, A. Biran, A. Ben-Tor, T. Dothan, A. Faust, I. Finkelstein, Y. Garfinkel, S. Gitin, Z. Herzog, D. Ilan, O. Lipschits, A. Maeir, A. Mazar, B. Mazar, E. Mazar, Z. Meshel, E. Netzer, R. Reich, E. Shukron, E. Stern, D. Ussishkin, Y. Yadin, A. Zertal, S. Zuckerman). See, provisionally, Silberman 1982; Moorey 1992; Dever 1985, 2017; and Davis 2004; see also King's (1983) history of the American Schools of Oriental Research.

78. For more recent studies, see Faust 2012 and Schloen 2016. See too how the title *Exploring the Longue Durée* was used for the 2009 Festschrift for L. E. Stager (Schloen 2009).

79. For early works of this emerging trend, see Binford 1962, 1989; Bintliff 1991; Renfrew and Bahn 1991; Hodder 1985, 1992a, 1992b; Shanks and Tilley 1987; and Tilley 1993.

80. See Hodder 1989, 1992a, 1992b; Preucel 1991.

81. It is beyond the scope of the present volume to address ongoing debates about the use of archaeology for matters of state formation and Israel's ethnogenesis, yet works such as Faust 2006 exhibit a markedly different anthropological approach. Readers are directed to specialists working with this material. See, for example, the 2007 issue of *Near Eastern Archaeology* that features a forum discussing the opposing views of Finkelstein and Faust, and the updated discussion in Dever 2017.

82. See Holladay 1987, 1995.

83. See Dever 1987, 1991, 1994, 2005, 2017; general references to religion in the Iron Age in Weippert 1988 and Mazar 1990; and the methodological treatise in Ahlström 1991. For a sampling of works that have integrated archaeology and textual analysis with respect to religious studies, see Stager's studies of Judges 5 and the family (1985a, 1988) as well as the Midianite hypothesis (1998: 142–149); Bloch-Smith's work on burial practices (1992a, 1992b), temples (1994), and standing stones (2005, 2006, 2015); Hadley's (1994, 2000) use of the Kuntillet 'Ajrud excavations; Mettinger's (1995) detailed study of standing stones; the Fribourg school's (see discussion in this chapter) use of iconography, especially as it applies to divine images (Keel and Uehlinger 1998; Uehlinger 1997); McCarter's use of epigraphic data (1987); Tigay's (1986) use of onomastic evidence; Meyers' (1988, 2002, 2003a, 2005) use of archaeology for unpacking the religious life of women; Lewis' (1998, 2005a) study of divine images and beliefs about the dead (2002); and the most impressive work in recent years, Zevit's (2001) "parallactic" study of ancient Israelite religions.

84. Gottwald 1993; Eilberg-Schwartz 1990: 1–28; Herion 1986; Rogerson 1985; Rodd 1981.

85. Cf. Bird 1987. Bird notes how this is particularly important methodologically for understanding the religious roles of women.
86. Regrettably, the final report of the excavations at Kuntillet ʿAjrud did not appear until thirty-seven years after the initial excavations. See Meshel 2012.
87. In addition to the literature cited in Chapter 1, note 2, see the following treatments of this material: Ackerman 1993, 1998a; Bird 1987, 1991; Collins 2005: 99–129; Frymer-Kensky 1992; Hestrin 1987; Meyers 1988, 2002, 2005; and Winter 1983. For an updated treatment written after the publication of the final report, see Schmidt 2016. For more recent studies of the divine profile at Kuntillet ʿAjrud that incorporate the new readings of plaster inscription 4.2, see LeMon and Strawn 2013 and Lewis 2020. And see Chapter Ten, pp. 583–587.
88. For Albertz's discussion of "internal religious pluralism," see Chapter Three, p. 50.
89. Cf. the review in Lewis 2014b.
90. Linafelt (1999: 503) tabulates that "147 out of 198 essays bear her initials."
91. See too Trible's (1984) study of "texts of terror."
92. For surveys, see J. Collins 2005: 75–98; Scholz 2013–2017; and Ackerman 2016. Three decades ago, Meyers (1988: 6) wrote that "hardly a week goes by without the appearance of a new publication dealing with 'women and religion.'" With the advent of electronic publication, the pace has quickened even more, such that Ackerman (2016) refers to the "exponential" increase of feminist Hebrew Bible scholarship. Ackerman notes the continuing publication (2011–) of the twenty-one-volume *The Bible and Women: An Encyclopaedia of Exegesis and Cultural History*.
93. Meyers (2002: 278) notes how "some studies, eager to claim biblical authority for women's present-day aspirations, are highly positive if not apologetic," while other studies are "highly critical assessments, indignant at what is perceived as male domination and female subordination and thereby asserting that the Bible represents irretrievably misogynist views."
94. For probing discussions with additional bibliography, see Marsman 2003: 1–31 and Fuchs 2008.
95. Bach (1993: 198–199) argues that feminist literary studies have a limited future.
96. See note 87 in this chapter as well as Meyers 1983, 1988, 1991; Bird 1987, 1991, 1997a; Hackett 1989; Frymer-Kensky 1981, 1989, 1992; Westenholz 1990; and Henshaw 1994.
97. See Meyers 1988, 2002, 2003a, 2005, 2010, 2013a; Meyers and Meyers 1987, 1993. For more extensive appreciation of Meyers' work and legacy, see Ackerman, Carter, and Nakhai 2015.
98. A huge stumbling block, writes Meyers (2003a: 434), is our "present-mindedness," whereby contemporary middle-class Western values are overlaid on premodern societies: "This is most salient in the tacit appraisal of what is masculine as inherently powerful and/or prestigious, with women's activities considered supportive and secondary, thereby being trivialized and marginalized." Due to "the removal of significant economic processes from the household as part of the industrial revolution," "women's unpaid tasks came to be seen as simply housekeeping chores, the economic

Chapter 3

1. For a lucid example exploring the Hebrew Bible's philosophical ideas, see Davies 2011. Contrast Zevit's (2001: 79) argument that "as a matter of research strategy" one should "avoid emphasizing sources that are most prone to theological interpretation." Sources that make "normative types of statements," argues Zevit, may be addressed, but "only within a history of ideas (and not a theological) discourse."

   For an insightful debate regarding the historical reading of the Bible vis-à-vis a philosophical reading, see Levenson 2017; Diamond 2017.

2. Though it is healthy to interrogate our categories (cf. Nongbri 2013), I still find the term "religion" to be a useful analytical category, as do scholars in many other disciplines (anthropology, sociology, history, folklore, and religious studies). As the pages that follow will make clear, I agree with Nongbri's main assertion that there was not a separation of the "religious" from the "secular" in antiquity.

   Should the reader find it imperative to have a succinct working definition of "religion," here are two offered by current historians of Israelite religion:

   > Israelite religions are the varied, symbolic expression of and appropriate response to the deities and powers that groups or communities deliberately affirmed as being of unrestricted value to them within their worldview. (Zevit 2001: 15)

   > The service and worship of the divine or supernatural through a system of attitudes, beliefs, and practices. (Hess 2007b: 15)

   Zevit (2001: 15–16) includes a list of "pithy definitions" of religion from Durkheim to Tylor. As the current work is also devoted to study of divinity, those seeking a framework for defining the divine can find no better introduction than that by Smith (2001b).

3. Cf. Zevit's (2001: 690) conclusion (entitled "Reductio") to his volume on Israelite religions, where he writes: "The multiplicity of Israelite religions . . . can all be explained reductively as bio-psychological expressions of citizenship in a cosmos perceived of as disharmonious."

4. For an introduction to the way in which Eliade was able to assert such a statement while (contra Durkheim) holding to the irreducible nature of religious phenomena, see John Clifford Holt's introduction to the 1996 edition of Eliade's *Patterns in Comparative Religion*.

5. Bellow 1953: 17. I owe this quote to Andrew R. Davis.

6. In order to find genuine Israelite traditions, Fleming sets up criteria to determine the basic sense of Israel's nature and to highlight its political features. According to Fleming (2012: 20), the political assumptions of historical Israel and historical Judah are "strikingly different" to such a degree that they can be used as valid diagnostic criteria. Fleming (2012: 24–27) proposes that "biblical content originating in Israel

can be distinguished from the dominant content from Judah" by (1) contrasting political assumptions (e.g., Israel was known for its relative decentralization), (2) geography, and (3) the absence of Judah-oriented themes (e.g., the palace-Temple linkage in Jerusalem, whereas "royal capitals are never identified with Israel's principal sacred centers" (p. 26). Despite Fleming's thorough treatment, the examples of Bethel (Amos 7:13) and Samaria (1 Kgs 16:29–34; 2 Kgs 10:18–27) remain problematic.

7. To solve the mechanism question, Fleming (2012: 310) posits an Israelite refugee population constituting an "exile" community in Jerusalem that was "involved in creating a body of [genuine] Israelite written tradition." To support this position, he relies on Sanders' (2009: 130–133) theory of craft scribes working independently of the royal (Judean) court. For possible settings for maintaining the continuity of Israelite tradition, Fleming (2012: 310–312) points to communal religious festivals (e.g., 1 Sam 1) and, even more intriguing, the mustering of military troops that could occasion contacts between people across greater distances. As for dating, Fleming (2012: 47–49, 308) comes to the very reasonable conclusion that 720 BCE may reflect a significant moment in consolidation and preservation of ideas about what Israel had been. If he is correct, this would go a long way toward addressing the very knotty problem that he notes on p. 319: "How long would the survivors of the Israelite kingdom retain a coherent sense of its political character as distinct from that of Judah?" Fleming (2012: 320) is quite correct that "memory would tend to drift with the assumptions of newer political circumstances."

8. Simple illustrations can be found in the large number of epigraphic articles included in *Ancient Israelite Religion: Essays in Honor of Frank Moore Cross* (Miller, Hanson, and McBride 1987) and the large amount of epigraphy (including line drawings) in Zevit's *The Religions of Ancient Israel* (2001). For a history of Northwest Semitic epigraphy overall, see Lemaire 2014.

9. For a sampling of the epigraphic literature on forgeries, see Naveh 1982; Cross 2003a; Rollston and Vaughn 2005; and Rollston 2003, 2004, 2006, 2013a, 2014, 2015b.

10. The pioneering works of Tallqvist (1906, 1966) and Stamm (1939) also deserve special mention.

11. See Sanders 2014, 2015; Aḥituv, Eshel, and Meshel 2012: 128–133; Albertz and Schmitt 2012: 245–386; Rechenmacher 2012, 1997; Hutton 2010a: 153–156; Hess 2007a; 2007b: 269–274; Smith 2002a: 4–5, 35; 2001b: 139, 141; Zevit 2001: 586–609, 631–635, 648–652, 687; Day 2000: 226–228; Callaway 1999; van der Toorn 1996a; 1996b: 225–231; Zadok 1988; Fowler 1988; Tigay 1986, 1987; Albertz 1978: 49–77; Cross 1973: 60–71.

12. For ancient Near Eastern historians, onomastic study is combined with lexicography that involves the classification of a wide range of topics (including building installations, cult functionaries, deity lists, flora, fauna, lexical lists, medicine, sacred objects, etc.) that could be used in scribal curricula. See Civil 1995. For contextualizing the production of the Hebrew Bible within the scribal culture of the ancient Near East, see van der Toorn 2007.

13. For an optimistic attempt at correlating the epigraphic and biblical material, see Mykytiuk 2004, 2009.

14. On forgeries in the epigraphic record, see note 9. On the unprovenanced nature of many of the seals and seal impressions that we work with, see Vaughn and Dobler 2006 and Bordreuil 2014. Of the sixteen hundred West Semitic inscribed seals that he studied, Bordreuil (2014: 138) estimates that he can be certain of the genuineness of only about 10 percent!
15. Such features can be very important for determining meaning, with, for example, a long *ā* in *qātil* marking an active participle (**sāpir-* → *sōpēr*, "scribe") as opposed to a *qatil* adjective (**daqin-* → *zāqēn*, "old"), or a doubled letter such as the middle letter in a **qattal* pattern representing a noun of occupation (e.g., **dayyan-* → *dayyān*, "judge").
16. For an introduction to the onomastic evidence from Ugarit, see the overview in Hess 1999, which includes a full bibliography. Note in particular the works by D. Pardee, D. Sivan, F. Gröndahl, W. H. van Soldt, and W. G. E. Watson.
17. Pardee (1988b: 141) humorously asks if those who named their child Resheph in 1 Chr 7:25 might have meant "Sparky" without any awareness of the deity Ršp.
18. Cf. again Pardee 1988b, which compares Hebrew, Phoenician-Punic, Ugaritic, and Eblaite onomastica. See too Sanders 2014, 2015, which broaden Albertz's approach to include royal material. For Sanders (2014: 220, 224; cf. 2015: 81), "large-scale patterns in naming provide one way of mediating between royal, regional and state level religion." He hypothesizes: "Judahite and perhaps also Israelite rulers made the unconventional move to select as their dynastic god one already strongly associated with the people they intended to rule," i.e., the "dynastic god Yahweh [who was] also a dominant family god."
19. "Verbal sentence names," summarizes Zadok (1997: 93), are "the most important type of names in Akkadian."
20. Erisman's (2013: 552) description of "the fractured state of the discipline" is ironic in light of Carr's influential 1996 volume, entitled *Reading the Fractures of Genesis*.
21. Sparks (2002) has collected the works up until 2002, and thus they will not be mentioned here. Subsequent works include Dozeman 2017; Gertz et al. 2016; Van Seters 2013; Baden 2012, 2009; Carr 2011, 1996; Dozeman, Römer, and Schmid 2011; Dozeman, Schmid, and Schwartz 2011; Hutton 2009; Ska 2009, 2006; Levinson 2008; Knoppers and Levinson 2007; Römer 2007; Stackert 2007; Dozeman and Schmid 2006; Friedman 2005; Nicholson 2003; Gertz, Schmid, and Witte 2002.
22. Already decades ago, Pardee (1988b: 123 n. 15) would speak of "the present cloud over source criticism."
23. The first two sources were traditionally thought to present corresponding legal codes, with the Covenant Code aligned with the E source in response to J's Ritual Decalogue. Categorizing biblical law collections as legal "codes" has been challenged (Levinson 2008: 31), as has the assumption that biblical law is statutory in nature (codifed) in contrast to common law (Berman 2014b, 2016).

    Should one desire to probe further, the Samaritan Pentateuch on Exodus 23:19 includes an expansion stating that when one engages in this activity as an act of sacrifice, he is forgetting and enraging the God of Jacob (*ky ʿśh zʾt kzbḥ škḥ wʾbrh hyʾ lʾlhy yʿqb*).

24. See Propp's (2006: 285–286) summary and Ratner and Zuckerman's (1986) epigraphic analysis, which poured cold water on the enthusiasm for using KTU 1.23 as a "Canaanite" parallel.
25. For a comparative analysis, past scholarship often accused all Canaanites of engaging in widespread child sacrifice, due to biblical polemics (e.g., Lev 18:21; Deut 12:31; 2 Kgs 3:27; 21:6; 23:10) and later expansions by classical and patristic writers who excoriated tophet cult sites. Today scholars are more circumspect, acknowledging that, at least for the Ugaritians, such a notion cannot be supported from the extant ritual texts. There may be a reference to sacrificing a "firstborn" ([b]kr) to Baal in KTU 1.119.31′, yet it is in all likelihood the sacrifice of a firstborn animal. This is not to say that there was no child sacrifice in the Levant, perhaps even in Syria. Cf. the actions of the Sepharvites mentioned in 2 Kgs 17:31, whom some scholars place in late eighth-century BCE Syria. Yet our best evidence comes from Phoenician religion, notably among the Carthaginians. Even here, scholars disagree over whether ritual infanticide was an exceptional and localized custom used in extreme circumstances or a regular practice. See Gras, Rouillard, and Teixidor 1991; Schwartz et al. 2012; Xella et al. 2013; Quinn 2018: 91–112. More generally, see Porter and Schwartz 2012.
26. A case in point is Dozeman's (2017) otherwise excellent introduction, *The Pentateuch: Introducing the Torah*. Though Dozeman is fully aware of the many scholars who still work within a four-source framework (see pp. 179–199), his volume often presents the data in a P/non-P format that flattens out the data (yet cf. pp. 265–266). Should the introductory reader want to explore basic issues (e.g., whether there is such a source as what is traditionally labeled "J" or "E"), she has no way of seeing such data through the use of non-P terminology.
27. As will be apparent throughout the volume (e.g., Chapter Six, note 210; Chapter Eight, note 68), I agree with Hebraists and Semitists (e.g., Cohen, Fassberg, Garr, Gianto, Hornkohl, Hurvitz, Joosten, Kofoed, Medill, Miller-Naudé, Polak, Rendsburg, Schniedewind, Sommer, Zevit) and most Hebrew grammarians (e.g., Blau 2010: 7–9; Mandell 2013; Pat-El and Wilson-Wright 2013; Hornkohl 2013) who argue that historical linguistics can be used to study biblical Hebrew diachronically (e.g., the stages of Archaic Biblical Hebrew [ABH], Standard Biblical Hebrew [SBH], and Late Biblical Hebrew [LBH]). The challenges by Young, Rezetko, and Ehrensvärd (2008) and Vern (2011) represent a minor position. See Sommer 2011: 104 n. 53 for a bibliography, to which one should add the various articles in Miller-Naudé and Zevit 2012 as well as Joosten 2012, Mandell 2013, Pat-El and Wilson-Wright 2013, Hornkohl 2013, and Garr and Fassberg 2016.
28. Personal communication.
29. On sacred space, see Chapter Ten, pp. 671–672.
30. ANET = Ancient Near Eastern Texts Relating to the Old Testament (Pritchard 1969a). LAPO = Littératures anciennes du Proche-Orient (https://www.orient-mediterranee.com/spip.php?rubrique794&lang=fr). TUAT = Texte aus der Umwelt des Alten Testaments (https://www.degruyter.com/view/serial/533938). LAS = The Literature of Ancient Sumer (2006) by Jeremy Black, Graham Cunningham, Eleanor Robson, and Gábor Zólyomi. CDLI = Cuneiform Digital Library Initiative (https://cdli.ucla.edu). CCP = Cuneiform Commentaries Project (https://ccp.yale.edu).

ETCSL = The Electronic Text Corpus of Sumerian Literature (http://etcsl.orinst.ox.ac.uk). Oracc = The Open Richly Annotated Cuneiform Corpus (http://oracc.museum.upenn.edu).

31. Occasionally we are presented with tight historical and geographical parameters that allow a narrow analysis. Cases in point would be the study of Deuteronomy set against the backdrop of treaty language and the study of the book of Ezekiel in its narrow Neo-Babylonian context.

Ever since Esarhaddon's Succession Treaty (EST) was first published by Wiseman in 1958, but even more so with Lauinger's Tayinat publication in 2012, scholars have debated whether EST can serve as a literary model for Deuteronomy (esp. chapters 13 and 28), either for emulation or for subversion. For studies on Deuteronomy and the Neo-Assyrian *adê* tradition, see the writings of Levinson, Steymans, Pakkala, and Crouch in Lauinger 2019.

The comparative study of the book of Ezekiel within its narrow sixth-century BCE Neo-Babylonian context has benefited from ever-increasing data about the lives of Judeans in exile (e.g., Pearce and Wunsch 2014). For a summary of comparative data with respect to vocabulary, literary motifs, and iconography, see Liebermann 2019.

Chapter 4

1. Consider too the theoretical difficulties presented by Hoffmann (1994: 103–104).
2. For female divinity, see the Conclusion, pp. 675–696.
3. See Chapter Three on the relevance of theophoric elements in personal names for reconstructing religious belief. For an older bibliography and discussion of the name Israel and its etymology, see Zobel 1990. The earliest reference to Israel as a historical entity is found in the well-known Merneptah stela of ca. 1207 BCE. See Kitchen 1982: 12–19; Hasel 1994, with additional bibliography. Krebernik (1996: 248, item 46) suggests that *Iš-ra-il* at Ebla "most probably corresponds to biblical *Yiśrā'ēl*." Cf. Sanders 2015: 74–75. If such an etymological correspondence is valid, it points to Israel as an El name with an ancient pedigree. Cf. too *yšril* at Ugarit (KTU 4.623.3). Diachronically, one must underscore that the name Israel as designating a political entity evolves considerably from the late thirteenth century BCE through the fifth century BCE. See especially Monroe and Fleming's (2019) description of an early "Little Israel" in contrast to a "Greater Israel" of the ninth century BCE.
4. Pope (1955: 16) underscores what he calls "the futility of the endeavor" with the following comment: "Much ink has been expended on the problem of the etymology of *ilu/'el* with no sure results except the emphasis of uncertainty."
5. For a discussion of which came first, see Pope 1955: 1–6.
6. Cross 1973: 13–14; 1974a: 243–244. Contrast Cross's view (1973: 14) that the use of *'Il* as a proper name "belongs to Proto-Semitic as well as its use as a generic appellative" with that of Herrmann (1999: 275), who asserts that "in Ancient Mesopotamia *ilu* is attested as an appellative for deities, though a deity *Il* is not attested." Cross relies on Gelb (1961: 6), who writes: "We may note the very common use of the element

Il in the Akkadian theophorous names, which seems to indicate that the god *Il* (= later Semitic *'El*) was the chief divinity of the Mesopotamian Semites in the Pre-Sargonic period." Cf. too Edzard 1976. In contrast, Di Vito's (1993: 242) study of third-millennium personal names concludes that "the element *il* in the onomastic evidence . . . does not represent a DN Il, but a writing of the common noun *ilum*, probably a 'Kish'-type logogram."

For the Amorite material, see Huffmon 1965: 162–165; Gelb 1980: 58; Layton 1996: 610. The Amorite name Ḥinni-El ("O the grace of El") also occurs in an OB administrative text from Hazor (Horowitz and Shaffer 1992: 28). It should be noted that the Amorite material played a significant role in the work of some mid-twentieth-century scholars associated with the Albright school. Their "Amorite hypothesis" associated such West Semitic names with the migrations of the patriarchs in the Ur III period. See de Vaux 1978: 58–64 and the opposition by Thompson (1974), van Seters (1975), Westermann (1985: 61–62), and Grabbe (2017: 50–52, 57–60).

7. An example of how acute this ambiguity can be is the Foundation Inscription of Yaḫdunlim, King of Mari, which contains the phrase *ištu ūm ṣât alam Mari*[ki] *DINGIR inbû* (I.34–35). While some scholars translate it as "Since time immemorial when the god [most likely Dagan] built Mari," others make West Semitic El the "founder" of this major city and see evidence of a "Canaanism." See Malamat 1992: 213 n. 12.
8. For convenience, see the entry *ilu* by Moran in CAD I/J (1960: 91–103).
9. It is not even certain that Ildayyi is a Semitic name. So says Moran (1992: 261, 382), but cf. Na'aman 1988: 188 n. 41. Even if Ildayyi is an El worshipper, he still adopts the protocol of calling the Egyptian pharaoh his king, lord, and god (EA 175). Note how Rainey (2015) reconstructs the name as Ilu-Dayyān[i].
10. Unless he thought that the deity Milku was his god, another way to render his name.
11. See the semantic categories relating to deities in Hess 1993: 191–194.
12. For discussion of this material, see Hamilton 1995: 178–179; Ahlström 1993: 230; Zobel 1990: 189; Aḥituv 1984: 200; Freedman 1963; and Yeivin 1959. The location of Yaqub-ilu is unknown, though Ahlström suggests a Transjordanian site in the vicinity of Gadara. In addition to the Egyptian material, Hamilton (1995: 179) notes how the name Yaqub-ilu also occurs in Mesopotamian texts (in the Chagar Bazar inscriptions, and at Qattuna, Kish, and Tell Ḥarmal). The full name Jacob-el is unknown in the Hebrew Bible, but compare Freedman 1963, which argues for its occurrence in Deut 33:28.
13. In 1975 Rainey read *'d ḏ 'lm* for the second title. Dijkstra read *zu šiba(ti)*, "the Grey-haired One," and *n[g]d.p'lm*, "the overseer of the workers." See Rainey 1975: 115 and Dijkstra 1997: 92–93; 1987; 1983: 35–36, 38 fig. 2). P. K. McCarter (personal communication, November 2003) writes:

> The photograph that led Cross to propose his reading of Sinai 358 was contaminated with red dust that obscured the second sign of the right-hand column, which is in fact the fish, not the shepherd's crook. Thus the reading is *'alep-dalet-edh-'ayin-lamed-mem*. . . . The inscription is too short to offer a decipherment, especially since it's uncertain that there were not more letters preceding and/or succeeding this sequence. There's at least a decent chance that the word

ʿalam-, "perpetuity," appears, but the ʿayin-lamed-mem sequence could belong to other words, too.

Hamilton's detailed volume *The Origins of the West Semitic Alphabet in Egyptian Scripts* also reads ʾdḏʿlm (2006: 357–358).

14. To help grant the Ugaritic data their own independence (especially when in the past they have been used as mere handmaids to Biblical studies), I use the name ʾIlu for the Ugaritic deity and the name El for the Israelite deity. Yet all quotations of other scholars' work (most of which refer to Ugaritic El) will remain verbatim. In the same manner, I use Baʿlu for Baal, ʾAṯiratu for Asherah, ʿAnatu for Anat, and so on.

15. A detailed analysis of using the Ugaritic material to illustrate the Canaanite cultural continuum of the Levant can be found in Chapter Six, pp. 259–264.

16. The meaning of these terms is debatable. See Naccache 1996; Smith 1994b: 225–234; Mullen 1980: 281–283; Cross 1973: 36–39; Lipiński 1971a; and Pope 1955: 95–96 for discussions of the various locales of ʾIlu's abode (including the meeting place of two cosmic oceans, the underground streams of ʾIlu's mountain, the headwaters of the netherworld, Mt. Lebanon, etc.), as well as the relevance of this material for the location of the divine council. Smith also documents attempts by Pope and Keel to document ʾIlu's/El's abode through iconography (on which see Chapter Five).

17. For the language of family applied to Ugaritic conceptions of the divine, see Korpel 1990: 232–264; Smith 2001b: 54–80; Lewis 2008a; Watson 2013; and Chapter Eight (pp. 473–477), which also treats divine parentage (god as father and mother).

For older literature on family relations at Ugarit, see Selms 1954 and Rainey 1965, the latter being based on his more extensive 1962 Brandeis dissertation, "The Social Stratification of Ugarit." Cf. too the Hebrew rendition (Rainey 1967).

According to Pardee and Bordreuil (1992: 709), KTU 1.65 describes the "household of El" in hierarchical fashion: "El, the sons of El, the circle of the sons of El, the assembly of the sons of El, Thukamuna-wa-Shunama, El and Athirat." Cf. too Smith 2001b: 43–44. KTU 1.65.4 reads *trmn wšnm*, which is a mistake for *tkmn w šnm*. See similarly in KTU 1.40.

18. KTU 1.3.5.8; 1.4.4.24; 1.5.6.2; 1.6.1.36; etc. I prefer this traditional understanding of ʾab šnm over Pardee's suggestion that šnm refers to a deity (thus ʾIlu is the "father of Shunama") based on KTU 1.114, which describes the double deity Ṯukamuna-wa-Šunama playing the role of a son bringing ʾIlu home when he is drunk (cf. the refrain in KTU 1.17.1.31–32, which is repeated three more times). Cf. Ṯukamuna-wa-Šunama in the "household of ʾIlu" in KTU 1.65 and 1.40. See Pardee 1997c: 245; 1988b. This view was previously advocated by Gordon and Lipiński. See Margalit 1983: 90–91 for bibliography and a less likely suggestion that ʾab šnm refers to ʾIlu as "the father of the exalted ones" based on an Arabic cognate (cf. Pope 1955: 33).

Cross (1973: 16; 1974a: 245) and L'Heureux (1979: 169–171) considered *rpu mlk ʿlm* in KTU 1.108.1 to be referring to ʾIlu as "the Hale One, King Everlasting" (see too the works of J. Blau, J. C. Greenfield, and J. Day), yet the identity of *rpu* is far from certain, with other scholars suggesting Baʿlu, Milku/Maliku, and a deity in its own right, Rapiu. See Rouillard 1999 for bibliography, especially the works of Pardee

(1988a: 85–90) and van der Toorn (1991a: 55–60). Finally, cf. KTU 1.10.3.6-7, which may refer to ʾIlu as eternal (ʿl[m?]), but the text is broken.

19. See the epithets qny (KTU 1.10.3.5) and bny bnwt, "creator of creatures" (KTU 1.4.2.11; 1.4.3.32; 1.6.3.5; 1.17.1.24), and the phrase ʾil mlk dyknnh, "king El who installed/created(?) him" (KTU 1.3.5.35-36; 1.4.4.48; cf. 1.10.3.6-7). Contra Kraus (1986: 29), ʾIlu is *not* called qn ʾrṣ at Ugarit. Compare the discussions of Pope (1955: 50–54; 1987: 220, 222), Cross (1973: 15), de Moor (1980: 173–176; 182–183), Clifford (1994: 117–133), Herrmann (1999), and Lewis (2013a: 191–194; 2014a). See also the Hittite Elkunirsha myth described later.

See too Deuteronomy 32, which Greenfield (1987b: 554) has described as containing antecedent literary traditions about El.

20. Pope 1955: 49–50; 1987: 221. I have taken the liberty of updating Pope's 1955 quote with his remarks from his 1987 article. The latter successfully counters the more excessive claims of de Moor (1980).

21. The biblical references for this famous motif are Genesis 2:7 and Job 10:9; 33:6, with Job 33:6 (qoraṣtî) using the same cognate verb as in KTU 1.16.5.29 (yqrṣ) and as in the Akkadian phraseology of "pinching off" or "nipping" of the clay (karāṣu + ṭiddu/ṭīdu) to make humans. For the numerous Akkadian texts, as well as how ʾIlu (like Enki) also uses magic to create the exorcist Shaʿtiqatu, see Lewis 2013a, 2014a.

22. For the full text plus an introduction to the critical questions surrounding its interpretation, see Pardee 1997e: 274–283; Lewis 1997: 205–214; forthcoming a; and especially Smith 2006. I argue (in Lewis forthcoming a) that ideologically KTU 1.23 is ʾIlu-centric, and the picture it paints of him together with his wives contains images (male *and female*) that construct and reinforce the power and prestige of Ugaritic royalty. The very nature of agricultural sustenance comes from ʾIlu, the Guardian of the sown land (nǵr mdrʿ). See pp. 103–104. The use of royal imagery for ʾIlu throughout KTU 1.23 promotes the interests (and vital necessity) of god, king, and state.

23. The meaning of the root mnn (repeatedly used in KTU 1.23.37, 40 44, 47) is quite difficult. The parallel line refers to ʾIlu lowering his "scepter," designating a king's act of invitation (cf. Esth 4:11; 5:2). Using a blatant double entendre, I see in the paired line a reference to ʾIlu being equally "generous" (mnn) and inviting with the "staff in his hand." For support, cf. Arabic √mnn, "to be generous," the use of maninnu in Akkadian to designate exchange gifts that promoted good relations between kings, and the Hebrew (mān, mann-) and Aramaic (mannāʾ) words for manna, showcasing divine benevolence. Thus, contrary to Smith's suggestion (2006: 85), I am not following Cross's line of interpretation. For a full explanation, see Lewis forthcoming b.

24. On ʾIlu as *deus otiosus*, see Pope 1979 and Casadio 1987; on the use of KTU 1.23 for the *deus otiosus* theory, see Lewis 1997: 206; forthcoming a. Nor does KTU 1.1.5 refer to the castration of ʾIlu, as argued by Pope and Oldenburg. See Smith 1994b: 129–130.

25. KTU 1.23 gives agency to the two women as to whether they see ʾIlu as a virile husband or as a father figure. ʾIlu is decidedly masculine in this text. There is no warrant for using KTU 1.23.32-33 to suggest an androgynous character for ʾIlu. See Chapter Eight, pp. 478–479.

26. See Smith 1994b: 128, which notes other occurrences as well as the PN *tr*, possibly a hypocoristicon for *'iltr*, "El is bull."
27. See the broader study by Thomas (2019) that equates the god Gad (whose name indicates that he determines fate and fortune) with El.
28. See note 31.
29. Pardee (1997c: 245 n. 28), who notes the Arabic cognates of both terms, states that the Arabic denotes "aspects of the heart as an organ and seat of various abstract concepts (mind, spirit, courage . . .)." He thus concludes: "Without usages closer to Ug. it is impossible to know whether it there denoted primarily courage or generosity (cf. 'big-hearted'), or some other notion."
30. KTU 1.16.1.11, 21–22; 1.2.1.21; 1.2.3.20. It is preferable to see *qdš* as a title of 'Ilu ("the Holy One") rather than as a noun ("holiness") referring to Qudshu, a putative title of the goddess 'Athiratu in all these passages (so too Pardee 1997c: 246, 248; 1997a: 339). It would be more likely to have a feminine form (*qdšt*) if the goddess was meant (cf. Wyatt 1999c: 100). Those arguing for the presence of Qudshu include Albright (1968a: 121, 146), Cross (1973: 33–35), and some of Cross' students—Mullen (1980: 119), Maier (1986: 27–28, 42–44, 81–96), and Olyan (1987b: 163 n. 15; 1988: 2, 40), as well as Gibson (1978: 156), Day (1986: 388–389, 399), and Margalit (1990: 291–292). For a thorough argument against this position, see Wiggins 1991: 386–389. Note especially KTU 1.14.4.34, where the syntax and poetic structure require that King Kirta is arriving "at the *sanctuary* of 'Asherah of Tyre" (so too Pardee 1997a: 336; Coogan and Smith 2012: 78). This is not to deny the presence of Qudshu/Qedeshet in Egypt (see Chapter Ten, pp. 575–576). Yet the Egyptian material should not be privileged in reconstructing the Ugaritic pantheon.

    For a full discussion of what it means for a deity to be "holy"—especially with respect to Yahweh—see Chapter Ten.
31. The name of the exorcist is Sha'tiqatu, and she is a significant character in the story, for (working at 'Ilu's behest) she cures the mortally ill king when none of the gods is either willing or able to do so. Indeed, through her physical handling of the king's body as well as through her actions as an expeller of illness (*ydt mrṣ gršt zbln*), she removes the illness and causes Death to take flight. Her victory is then celebrated ("Death is crushed! As Sha'tiqatu is powerful!") with vocabulary that echoes Ba'lu's victory over the god Motu. For an analysis of the narrative (in KTU 1.16.5.10–1.16.6.14) and the identity and function of Sha'tiqatu, see Lewis 2013a, 2014a.

    For 'Ilu's connection to healing elsewhere, see too the presence of his name at the head of twelve deities invoked in a therapeutic text dealing with snakebite (KTU 1.100). Yet in this text 'Ilu does not provide the necessary remedy (incantation), which comes from another deity, Horanu, more skilled in such matters. Horanu was the last of the twelve deities to be addressed, and thus the rhetoric shows the tale to be etiological, as noted by Levine. Levine also argues that because Horanu is so successful in exercising spells here and elsewhere, he receives a "promotion" in another snakebite text (KTU 1.107.38'), where he is paired alongside 'Ilu. See Levine and de Tarragon 1988: 506.

32. See Lewis 1989: 80–94; 2008a: 74–76; Smith 1994b: 140–144; Pardee 1996; McLaughlin 1991, 2001; McGeough 2003; and Greer 2007. Though the institution is variously spelled (Lewis 1989: 81–82), scholarly convention defaults to using the Hebrew term *marzeaḥ*.
33. According to Pardee (1997b: 303), the Ugaritic *marziḥu* may be associated with the so-called Temple aux Rhytons discovered at Ugarit. A small stone statue of what seems to be ʾIlu was also discovered here; see Figure 5.20. It should be noted that, in addition to ʾIlu, other deities were seen as patrons of various *marzeaḥ* organizations (Lewis 1989: 84; Smith 1994b: 142). On ʾIlu's presence at vintage rites, see Levine and de Tarragon 1993: 105. On ʾIlu's involvement in other cultic rituals, see KTU 1.23, 1.40, 1.65; Lewis forthcoming a.
34. As pointed out by Pardee (1997b: 304 n. 13), the double deity here fulfills one of the duties of the good son mentioned in KTU 1.17.1.31–32; 1.17.2.5–6, 19–20, namely, to assist one's father when he has too much to drink.
35. "Earth" here designates the underworld.
36. Schloen 1993b. A very sensible analysis of the conflict theory can be found in Smith 1994b: 87–114.
37. Classified as such (list [gods]) by KTU in each of these entries. Cf. Pardee 2000: 291–319, 520–531, 659–660; 2002a: 11–24.
38. See, for example, the imbedded lists in the snake incantations KTU 1.100 and 1.107. Cf. de Moor 1970, which collects and analyzes most of the relevant material. As for the offering lists, Pope (1955: 85) writes: "The lists of offerings to El in the ritual texts do not show him to have had a markedly preferred status as compared with the other gods." Now see the statistics in Pardee 2002a: 222.
39. Much has been made of this text in the past. As a corrective to Eissfeldt's overenthusiasm (making ʾIlu here the "god of gods," who contains the "essence" of all the gods), see Pope 1955: 85–91. See also note 17.
40. On the royal ideology of KTU 1.23, see note 22.
41. Herrmann 1999: 279. ʾIlu even lives in a palace (*hkl*), to which he invites the shades for a banquet in KTU 1.20–22 and the gods in general for a *marzeaḥ* feast in KTU 1.114. Seow (1989: 34–37) sees similar motifs in the El cult at Shiloh.
42. Cf. Mullen 1980: 84, stating that ʾIlu is "the only god given the title *malku*, 'king.'"
43. Smith 1994b: 95–96. Cf. Mullen 1980: 84–85; Casadio 1987; Handy 1994.
44. Cf. Miller 1967; 1973: 48–62; Cross 1973: 40; 1974a: 251; Freedman 1976: 66 = 1980: 87; Seow 1989: 18–19; Toews 1993: 60–61; Vaughn 1993. Cf. Pardee 1997c: 263 n. 192. To this material should be added Kuntillet ʿAjrud plaster inscription 4.2, which describes a militaristic wilderness theophany mentioning "when El shines forth . . . the name of El on the day of wa[r]." See Chapter Ten, pp. 583–587, and Lewis 2020. Cf. too the etymology of "Israel," which is often taken to mean "El reigns supreme" or "El contends" (see note 3).
45. See Hoffner 1965; 1990: 69–70; Handy 1994: 34–37; Beckman 1997; and Singer 2007. For an additional Anatolian reference to El, see Yakubovich 2010: 385: "The content of the Iron Age Luwian inscription TÜNP 1 leaves no doubt that its author saw El as a part of his own cultural universe, not an exotic foreign deity." See note 50.

46. The rendering of the sibilant as š is not as bothersome as it might seem (cf. Seow's mention of "certain phonological problems" [1989: 20 n. 52]) because there is only one *s* in Hittite. Only š signs are used.
47. For photograph and line drawing, see Aḥituv 2005: 30–31; 2008: 40–42.
48. See the Elyon discussion; cf. too the PN Elqanah, for which see Seow 1989: 19–22.
49. For voices of dissent, cf. Della Vida 1944: 1 and Vawter 1980; 1986. For biblical passages arguing for *qnh* referring to creation, cf. Gen 4:1; Deut 32:6; Ps 139:13; Prov 8:22. See the detailed discussion in Fox 2000: 279–280, to which can now be added the opening line of the Katumuwa inscription from Zincirli that is inscribed on a stela bearing Katumuwa's likeness: "I am Katumuwa, the servant of Panamuwa, who made for myself [*qnt ly*] [this] stele during my lifetime." One could argue that as an elite figure, Katumuwa certainly did not fashion the stela himself. He commissioned the stela to be made by a craftsman. Pardee (2009: 59) notes the use of *qn* as fashioning a concrete object in KAI 25, and suggests that the sense of the Zincirli text is that Katumuwa "personally oversaw the production of" the stela. Yet Hogue (2019: 200) has shown that *qnt ly* is likely a calque of a Luwian phrase, and "the pronoun ['I'] "emphasizes the speaker's activity." Using theories on monumentality (see Osborne 2014), Hogue concludes: "As the key ritual participant in monumentalization, the monumenter [Katumuwa] claimed the sole prerogative in all the monumenting acts. He is thus the monument's creator, installer, and inaugurator."
50. See the discussions that follow, which include the mention of El in the Hadad inscription (KAI 214), the Panamuwa inscription (KAI 215), the Kulamuwa inscription (KAI 24, if either Baal-Hamon and/or Rakib-El refers to El), one of the Sefire inscriptions (KAI 222), the Deir ʿAlla texts, and the plaster inscription 4.2 found at Kuntillet ʿAjrud, not to mention the widespread attestation of the title "El, the creator of the earth" from places such as Karatepe (KAI 26), Palmyra (KAI 244), and even Jerusalem (restored). Tyrian El may be reflected in Ezek 28 (see Pope 1955: 98–99; Zimmerli 1983: 77–78; Loretz 1989; Greenberg 1997: 573; Smith 2002a: 63). El also occurs in a host of Iron Age anthroponyms and toponyms as early as the twelfth century BCE. (See *ʾyʾl*, "Where is El?," in the Qubūr el-Walaydah inscription [Cross 1980: 2–3; Smith 2002a: 28].) See Tigay 1986: 12, 83–85; Fowler 1988; de Moor 1997: 10–40; and especially the exhaustive treatment of personal names in Albertz and Schmitt 2012.

El may also be present in disguise if deities such as Baal Hamon and Baal Shamem refer to him, as some scholars argue (e.g., Cross 1973: 10, 26–28, 35–36; Olyan 1988: 12, 52–53; Oden 1977; cf. Niehr 1990). Yet these equations have not been demonstrated conclusively. On Cross and Olyan's Baal Hamon thesis, see Lipiński 1983: 309; Day 1989: 37–40; and Smith 1994a: 209–211. On Oden's Baal Shamem thesis, see Olyan 1988: 62–64; Niehr 1990; and Chase 1994: 113–114, 134, 172–173, 183, 225; Chase's work provides a complete treatment of Baal Shamem in the epigraphic material.

This is not to say that El figures are never associated with the heavens. See Smith 2001b: 61–66; 1994a: 212–214 on the astral background of El's family at Ugarit and

Yakubovich's (2010) analysis of the phrase "above the sky belongs to El" in a mid-eighth-century BCE Luwian land contract (TÜNP 1) from Gaziantep.
51. For treatments of divinity in Aramean religion, see Lipiński 2000: 599–636; Niehr 2013, 2014a; and, briefly, Chapter Six, pp. 264–268.
52. There is some debate about the presence of El in Ammonite onomastica, and Aufrecht (1999: 159) admits that he is working with "meager and ambiguous evidence." He makes his case by contrasting the 150 occurrences of ʾl with the 9 occurrences of *mlkm*, by comparing the presence of El at Deir ʿAlla, by seeing the Atef-crowned Ammonite statuary as representative of El, and by referencing similar analogues within the biblical record of Yahweh and El traditions. There is obviously the possibility that ʾl could be a generic term for deity (see Hess 2007a: 304). For further discussion, see Tigay 1987: 171, 187 n. 66; Aufrecht 1989: 356–376; 1999; Zevit 2001: 651 n. 75; Albertz and Schmitt 2012: 340–342, 354–355, 510 (table 5.10).
53. Yet contrast the study of forty-seven Iron Age I arrowheads by Hess (2007c: 116–117), which has only a single example (ʾlbʿl = El is [my] lord") that could be interpreted differently (i.e., "Baal is [my] god"). Granted, these arrowheads do not come from controlled excavations and thus their relevance is diminished.
54. It will be argued in Chapter Eight that Yahweh, in addition to connections with royal religion, is also intimately associated with family religion, having absorbed El traditions. Albertz and Schmitt (2012: 357) also note how Yahweh could be "divested of military and political characteristics that had been so important for the state religion. Yahweh thus became a typical family god." They posit that "the process through which the national god YHWH became the most prominent family god in Israel and Judah" took place after the eighth century BCE (2012: 55).
55. E.g., Cross 1973: 13–75; 1974a; Levine 1985; Seow 1989: 9–78; Wyatt 1992; Smith 1994a: 206–214; Day 1994: 35–40; Kottsieper 1997; Albertz and Schmitt 2012.
56. Many of these articles are collected together in Freedman 1980. In this volume, note in particular those articles originally published as Freedman 1975, 1976, 1977, and 1979. For Freedman's later contribution on using early poetry to reconstruct Israelite religion, see Freedman 1987.
57. Cross's work concentrates on epigraphy, which provides a historical framework for dating ancient biblical poetry. See a partial bibliography of Cross's works through the mid-1980s in Miller, Hanson, and McBride 1987 and some of his collected epigraphic papers in Cross 2003b. The earlier studies that provided the foundation for their future work are Cross and Freedman 1952, 1972, and 1975.
58. See Chapter Three, p. 715, note 27.
59. See Smith 2012; 2014a: 211–266 for his subsequent discussions of "old poetry" especially with respect to Judges 5.
60. It seems likely that only one deity would have played the role of treaty partner and patron in a single locality, and thus we must choose between El Berith and Baal Berith as the Shechemite deity of Judg 8–9. That El Berith should be given preference is supported by (1) the Israelite tradition of Gen 33:20 ("El, the god of Israel"), (2) the occurrence of the title *il brt* in a Hurrian hymn to El found at Ugarit (RS 24.278; KTU 1.128.14–15; but cf. Dijkstra 1993), (3) Cross's argument that the role of divine

covenant partner is an extension of the role of a deity as a divine kinsman (typically an El figure; see Lewis 1996a: 415 n. 79), and (4) the possible El typology of certain bronze figurines associated with Tell Balâṭah.

61. This phrase is often translated "blessed be Abram *by* El Elyon," with the *l-* designating the agent of the passive verb. On the expression *brk l-* designating a verbal blessing directed *to* a deity, see Pardee 1976: 221–223.

62. L'Heureux (1979: 46) and Seow (1989: 52 n. 146) argue that the *waw* in *'l w'lyn* may be a *waw explicativum*: "El, that is, [the] Elyon."

63. See Levine 1985: 336: "Indeed the Sheol oracle of Isaiah 14 is El literature."

64. The common translation "the Upper Beth Horon" could just as easily be translated "the temple of Horon Elyon," but cf. 1 Chr 7:24, which mentions the upper and lower (*hattaḥtôn we'et hā'elyôn*) Beth Horon. 2 Chr 8:5 also has the article prior to the adjective: *bêt ḥôrôn hā'elyôn*. Despite the mention of what may be the temple of Beth Horon in one of the Tell Qasile ostraca, Horon is never attested as the head of a pantheon and thus worthy of the Elyon ("the Most High") attribute.

65. Compare compelling parallel passages such as the modified Ps 68:8–9 (Eng 68:7–8) with the exact wording in the unmodified Judg 5:4–5. The Elohistic Psalter is the subject of renewed study, with varying hypotheses to account for the data. See Wilson 1985: 196–197; Millard 1994: 169–188; 1998: 75–110; Rösel 1999; Joffe 2001, 2002; Zevit 2001: 674–678; Hossfeld and Zenger 2003; 2005: 4–5; Süssenbach 2005; Burnett 2006; and Ben-Dov 2011. For a synthesis of the history of scholarship with bibliography, see Hossfeld and Zenger 2003: 35–40; Süssenbach 2005; and Burnett 2006. For a defense of Delitzsch's view that the use of *'ĕlōhîm* is compositional rather than redactional, see Wardlaw 2015 and the critique by Kselman (2016), who underscores how the double usages of *'ĕlōhîm* (e.g., Ps 43:4; 45:8; 51:19) are better solved by redactional theories.

See too the single and only use of *mālak 'ĕlōhîm* in Ps 47:9 (Eng 47:8), which if read as *mālak yhwh* then joins the four other uses of *yhwh mālak* in the so-called enthronement psalms as well as elsewhere. See discussion in Chapter Nine, pp. 511–513.

66. That is, if the editor of the Elohistic Psalter has replaced an original Yahweh with *'ĕlōhîm* (discussed later).

67. Reading the root as *ḥlh*, "to be sick" (cf. the versions), as opposed to MT, which mistakenly inserts a dagesh, resulting in the root *ḥll*, "to pierce."

68. Freedman (1980: 89) has correctly argued that Num 24:16 represents the original form of the couplet, whereas 24:4 is "a defective, and erroneously revised, version of the former."

69. Levine 1985; 1991: 58, 72; 1993: 48, 63. See p. 116.

70. A fuller discussion of the Deir 'Alla texts (especially questions of dialect) can be found in Chapter Six, pp. 268–269.

71. See the reconstructions by Hamilton (in Hackett reference), Hackett (1980: 25, 27, 29, 33), and Puech (1985: 356), followed by Greenfield (1987a: 77 n. 35), which incorporate Fragments V (e) and XV (c). Contrast Lemaire's (1985: 318) reading: *w[ymllw.'lw] h kml[y]' 'l*, "and they spoke to him according to these words." See too Van der Kooij

1991: 247. Weippert (1991: 154–155) retains El but not the visions in his *[wy'mrw l]h kmš' 'l*, "[And they spoke to] him according to the utterance of El."

See too Hackett's (1987: 134) comments that "the interpretation of *'l* as El in I,2, and II,6, is not at all certain." Levine (1985: 328) argues that El plays a prominent role at Deir 'Alla and that "the Iron Age temple at Deir 'Alla was an El temple."

72. For an exhaustive treatment of Deut 32 as a whole, see Sanders 1996. Among the many studies of Deut 32:8–9, see Smith 2008: 195–212; Machinist 2011: 225–230, 238, 240; and Schmidt 2016: 163–186.

73. Following Tigay (1996: 302, 402 n. 38) and others in seeing *knn* as referring to creation (cf. Ps 119:73). On *qnh* and *knn,* see notes 19 and 49.

74. Reading *běnê 'ělōhîm* with 4QDeut^j (cf. LXX) as opposed to MT's *běnê yiśrā'ēl*. See Duncan 1995: 90, Plate XXIII for the Qumran reading. See Tigay 1996: 546 n. 2 and Himbaza 2002 for the history of previous analyses, including the incorrect reconstruction "the sons of El" (cf. BHS). See Tigay 1996: 514–515 for the rationale that led later scribes to replace the original *běnê 'ělōhîm* with *běnê yiśrā'ēl*. For a similar tendency to omit *'ělōhîm* from Deut 32:43a, see 4QDeut^q and Tigay 1996: 516–518.

Though speculative, Joosten's (2007) appealing suggestion that the original text read "the sons of Bull El" (*běnê šōr 'ēl*) would better account graphically for the reading of *běnê yiśrā'ēl* that we find in the MT. For additional support, Joosten mentions Tur-Sinai's "inspired emendation" that *kî mî šōr 'ēl* ("For, who is Bull El") was the original text behind the MT *kî miyyiśrā'ēl* ("for from Israel") in Hos 8:6. As Joosten (2007: 552–552) admits, the epithet "Bull El" never appears in the Hebrew Bible, the phrase "the sons of Bull El" never appears in the Ugaritic texts, and the reading that he reconstructs never appears in any textual witness.

75. One must choose between a stative and a fientive use ("being"/"becoming") of the verb "to be" in this verse. The former is reflected in the RSV and JPS translations: "the LORD's portion is his people." The latter, which seems to be original, can be seen in Tigay 1996: 303.

76. Cf. Collins 1993: 374, which notes how similar notions are found in the Rabshakeh taunt in 2 Kgs 18:35 = Isa 36:20 and in Dan 10:13.

77. See Albertz 1994: 271 n. 69, which notes how Ugaritic deities also have cities that are described as "lands of inheritance" (*'arṣ nḥlt*), presumably assigned by the deity 'Ilu.

78. For a detailed look at Ps 82, see Chapter Nine, pp. 565–569.

79. Cf. the assertion in Ps 82:7 that the gods will die like mortals (*kě'ādām těmûtûn*) with the question of Kirta's son in KTU 1.16.1.22: "Do gods die?" (*'u 'ilm tmtn*).

Yahweh Elyon is especially associated with nationalistic tendencies. Because Yahweh is Elyon, he is then able to establish Israel as Elyon over all the nations of the earth (cf. Deut 26:19; 28:1).

80. Seow (1989: 50–52) has previously collected some of this material and applied it to the cult at Shiloh.

81. Or, following Kraus (1988: 167–168), one could omit Yahweh here on prosodic grounds and translate "I will sing the name of Elyon."

82. Cf. Freedman 1980: 13, which notes the parallel with 1 Sam 2:10. On the textual history of the Song of Hannah, see Lewis 1994.

83. It is likely that *šimkā* is a later addition occasioned by Ps 83:17b (Eng 83:16b).
84. The text is difficult and commentators typically change one of the suffixes to harmonize the parallelism of the passage (yet cf. JPS). See Eissfeldt 1966a.
85. It is possible that Yahweh was originally omitted here.
86. It is likely that Job 7:8 alludes to this passage. See Seow 2013: 504–505.
87. Cf. Koenen 1988.
88. On the setting of the story and the history of scholarship on Gen 16 (including traditional source criticism, which ascribes the bulk of the narrative to J), see Westermann 1985: 234–237. On a womanist interpretation that highlights the forced nature of Hagar's impregnation and the sexual abuse and exploitation of so many enslaved women, see Gafney 2017: 33–45, 72–82. Gafney (2017: 41), building on the work of Renita Weems and Delores Williams, notes how Hagar "is on the underside of all the power curves in operation at that time ... she is female, foreign, enslaved."
89. Cf. Num 24:16: "he who hears [*šōmēa'*] the words of El ['*imrê 'ēl*]." Cf. too the frequent personal names *yšm"l* and '*lšm*' in Israelite onomastica (Tigay 1986: 84–85).
90. Wyatt 1996: 236; cf. Loretz 1976. Elsewhere Wyatt (1994: 145) argues that Gen 16 and KTU 1.23 represent "two versions of a common myth," but this is far from clear.
91. Both Loretz (1976: 453 n. 1) and Hamilton (1990: 454) point to 1 Sam 1:20 ("She called his name Samu*el* for she said, "I have asked him of *Yahweh*"") for a parallel to the MT of Gen 16:11 ("you shall call his name Ishma*el* because *Yahweh* has heard of your distress") because they both contain an "X plus El name being explained with a phrase using the tetragrammaton." Yet the analogy of 1 Sam 1:20 is complicated by the incongruence between "Samuel" (*šĕmû'ēl*) and the verb "to ask" (*š'l*). Many scholars have wondered whether the name Saul (*šā'ûl*), which is based on the same root, rather than Samuel, might have been involved in the original wordplay (cf. 1 Sam 1:20, 27–28; cf. also McCarter 1980: 62–63; Mandell 1996).
92. Note the wordplay in Gen 16:7, where the "God of *seeing*" meets Hagar at "the *spring* ['*ayin*, which can also mean 'eye'] on the way to Shur." Cf. Gen 21:19; contra Van Seter's (1975: 199) comment that the well "functions only as a meeting place in the desert." Cf. Noth 1981: 107–109.
93. On the expression '*el ḥay*, "the living God" (Boling [1982: 164], following Freedman, translates Josh 3:10 as "El the living"), its relation to the discussion of dying and rising gods, and its denotation of a deity who intervenes in personal and national affairs, see Mettinger 1988: 82–91.
94. While still problematic, more likely translations include JPS's "Have I not [reading *hălō'* for *hălōm*?] gone on seeing after He saw me?" and Hamilton's (1990: 455–457) "Have I really seen the back [reading '*aḥărê* as a substantive] of him who sees me?" (following Lindblom) or "Have I really looked upon [*rā'â 'aḥărê*] the one who sees me?"
95. The most comprehensive treatments of the word '*ōlām*, including cognate material, are still to be found in the works of Jenni (1952, 1953, 1984).
96. See note 13. A great many scholars have relied on this material, including Dahood (1968a: 215–216), Sarna (1989: 150), Hamilton (1995: 94), and Tigay (1996: 334).

97. Cf. Heider 1985: 118–123; Pardee 1988a: 85–90, 2002a: 192-195, 204 n. 6; Cooper 1987; and van der Toorn 1991a: 57–59.
98. For the content and dialect of the Arslan Tash incantations, see Chapter Six, p. 268. For discussions of their authenticity, see Teixidor 1983; Amiet 1983; Dijk 1992; Lewis 1996a: 408–410; Pardee 1998; and Cross and Saley 2003: 269. Bibliographic details can be found in Cross and Saley 2003: 269 nn. 49, 51.
99. On the phrase *mlk ʿlm*, see further Cooper 1987.
100. Cf. the Egyptian terminology for "Lord of Eternity" (*nb nḥḥ, ḥḳ3 ḏ.t*) as documented by Cooper (1987: 2-3). Cooper (1987: 7) astutely observes that "the substantive *ʿlm* never entirely loses its connections with death and the netherworld." Though the dead continue to exist in the afterworld and could even be referred to as *ʾĕlōhîm*, they do not have the type of immortality that would be described as *ḥay lĕʿōlām* (Gen 3:22). Perhaps they are best described as the *mēt lĕʿōlām*, "eternal dead" (cf. *mētê ʿōlām* in Ps 143:3//Lam 3:6 and *ʿam ʿôlām* in Ezek 26:20 describing those who "descend to the Pit" and "dwell in the netherworld among the primeval ruins"; cf. too *rpʾim qdmym* in KTU 1.161.8). They exist, in Qoheleth's words, in an "eternal home" (*bêt ʿôlām*; cf. Qoh 12:5; *byt ʿlmn* at Deir ʿAlla, and *bʿlm* in the Ahiram inscription). See further DNWSI s.v. *byt2* (vol. I, p. 160); Negev 1971: 50–51.

Because of the many nuances and applications of the word *ʿôlām*, one need not restrict its use, thereby suggesting that the epithet is "especially fit for solar deities" and that "El-olam should be seen in the context of the 'solarization' of the system of religious symbols" (see de Pury 1999b: 290).

101. See too the title *šarru ᵈšamaš dārītum*, "the king, the Eternal Sun," used to describe Pharaoh in the Amarna letters (EA 155: 6, 47; reconstructed in EA 146: 6-7; cf. EA 149: 24ff.), as already pointed out by Jenni (1953: 7 n. 1), Gevirtz (1961: 143 n. 5), Cross (1962a: 237), and Cooper (1987: 3). It should be noted that an individual named *nmry* (Nimmuriya = Amenophis III?) is also called *mlk ʿlm* in this same text (KTU 2.42.9).
102. Cf. Pury 1999b: 290, which suggests that *ʾlt ʿlm* at Arslan Tash designates "the goddess, the everlasting," but it would seem better to see a reference to a covenant here (Cross and Saley 1970; Zevit 1977; Lewis 1996a).
103. Such a usage may occur in the toponym Beth ʿOlam, which occurs among the Hebrew place names in Shishak I's (945–924 BCE) topographical list from Karnak (*btʿrm*, #36; Aḥituv 1984: 77). Many have taken *ʿrm* here as a reference to the deity (Cross 1962a: 236; Wyatt: 1994: 142), though the expression *bêt ʿôlām* in Qoh 12:5 and its cognate at Deir ʿAlla (see note 100) makes one wonder if the toponym here is a reference to a necropolis. In any event, one should not be tempted, as is Wyatt (1994: 142), to identify the location of Beth ʿOlam (or possibly even Beth ʿAruma; cf. Kitchen 1986: 436 n. 66) with Beersheba based on the biblical narrative. As shown by Kitchen, this part of the list of toponyms spans the area from Megiddo south to Socoh in the eastern Sharon.
104. Compare the same dilemma with "the last words of David" found in 2 Sam 23:5. Freedman (1980: 95–96; 1976: 73–74) has argued that the designation *bĕrît ʿôlām* is late and thus this earlier poem should be rendered as "Utterly secure is my

dynasty with El [*ʾēl*], for the Eternal has executed a covenant in my behalf" (*kî bĕrît ʿôlām śām lî*).
105. See Cross's (1973: 48 n. 18) remark that "had he found fewer instances his case would appear stronger." Yet Cross (1962a: 234 n. 31) was of the opinion that Dahood was "no doubt correct" in regard to his reconstruction of Psalm 75:10.
106. One would expect the verb *ngd* to govern an accusative, as in Ps 9:12 (Eng 9:11), where we have the same paired verbs: "Sing to Yahweh [*zammĕrû lyhwh*] who dwells in Zion//Tell his deeds [*haggîdû . . . ʿălîlôtāyw*] among the peoples."
107. Dahood 1964: 397. For the Piel form of *gdl*, used of magnifying God, see Ps 69:31 (Eng 69:30) (with accusative suffix) and Ps 34:4 (Eng 34:3) (with *lĕ-*).
108. Contrast Dahood 1968a: 186, 191 with Kraus 1989: 83.
109. Cross and Freedman 1948: 209 n. 85; 1975: 102–103, 120–121; Cross 1962a: 236; 1973: 48, 157; Freedman 1976: 92; 1980: 114; Van den Branden 1990: 36; Tigay 1996: 334. On the dating of Deut 33, see Smith 2002a: 54 n. 102.
110. The translation here follows most scholars who view MT's *kāʾēl* ("like the god of") as a secondary pious correction for an original *kĕʾēl* ("like El"). Wyatt (1978: 103), followed by van der Toorn (1996b: 258), argues that "the article has been added in an attempt to destroy the titular use of the term here, altering its sense from 'El' to 'the god (of) . . . '" Alternatively, one could read a haplography ("there is no god like El, O Jeshurun / like the god of Jeshurun," *ʾên <ʾēl> kĕʾēl*), following Cassuto (1926: 249–250; 1973: 102, 120) and Cross and Freedman (1948: 209; 1975: 102, 120).
111. Alternatively, Cross and Freedman (1947) redivide MT's *bʿzrk* to read "Who rides the heavens mightily [*bʿz*], who rides [*rk<b>*] gloriously the clouds." On the deity Rakib-El in the Zincirli inscriptions, see note 156.
112. Numerous proposals have been offered for this *crux interpretum* (see literature in note 109), yet it remains unsolved.
113. Cross (1962a: 236; 1973: 48 n. 18) notes that one could retain the word "arm" here as a hypostasis of divine power. Cf. the "arm of Yahweh" (*zĕrôaʿ yhwh*) in Isa 51:9ff. and the common expression *zĕrôaʿ nĕṭûyâ*, referring to Yahweh's arm as an instrument of deliverance and judgment.
114. See Lundbom 2013: 937–938 and note 156.
115. Studies on the Jacob narratives are almost beyond counting. For a taste of more recent works, see Dozeman 2017: 251–267; Chapman 2016: 173–183, 206–209; and Carr 1996: 256–271, 298–300, 340.
116. Elsewhere Bethel is hypostasized and itself becomes an object of worship. Hypostasization, which was evidently common in the ancient Near East, involves the personification of objects or ideas associated with the divine, be they sanctuaries, cult objects, attributes, or abstract features. It can be taken to such an extent that the resultant hypostasis functions as a surrogate for the deity. See the discussion in Chapter Seven.

A divine Bethel is attested in the treaty between Baal, king of Tyre, and Esarhaddon; in the succession treaty of Esarhaddon; in the Demotic Papyrus Amherst 63 (in Aramaic); in the Aramaic texts from fifth-century BCE Elephantine;

and in a host of Greek material. In the Hebrew Bible, compare Jer 48:13, where Bethel appears to designate a deity (parallel to Chemosh). On the mushrooming literature on Bethel, see the following works and their more complete attestations and bibliographies: Hyatt 1939; Porten 1969; Vleeming and Wesselius 1984; van der Toorn 1986, 1992a, 2019; McCarter 1987: 147; Na'aman 1987; Mettinger 1995: 35, 130–132; Röllig 1999b; Ribichini 1999; Blenkinsopp 2003; and Knauf 2006.

117. See note 110. Cf. Joosten 2007: 549, 551.

118. Na'aman (1987: 14) suggests that Beth Aven (*'āwen*), "House of Wickedness/Idolatry," which occurs seven times in the Bible (notably in Hos 4:15; 5:8; and 10:5), may have been a wordplay on Beth Aben (*'āben*), "House of the Stone Pillar," which was the original name for Bethel (cf. Amos 5:5).

119. On the use of *masseboth* as divine symbols, see Mettinger 1995; Lewis 1998; and the iconographic discussion in Chapters Five and Seven.

120. In the past, dreams were thought to typify the E source, but in today's source criticism this is called into question (Westermann 1985: 453).

121. The same wordplay on Shadday and *day* (meaning "enough," referring to God's limiting the spreading of heaven and earth) is found in Gen Rab (V8 on Gen 1:11; XLVI 3 on Gen 17:1). Another wordplay on Shadday from Gen Rab refers to suffering "enough" (XCII 1 on Gen 43:14). The passage that did contribute to the notion of God's self-sufficiency is Gen Rab XLVI 3 (on Gen 17:1). It is stated here that it should be "enough" for Abraham that God is his god and patron. While this does not refer explicitly to God speaking of his own self-sufficiency or omnipotence, it could be understood in this sense (cf. Rashi on Gen 17:1). Biblical Hebrew does not use *day* ("sufficiency") in relation to God's nature. The origin for this notion may have come from Aquila and Symmachus, who translate Shadday with the Greek word *hikanos*, "sufficient, able." See further Bertram 1958, 1959.

122. Albright 1935; Weippert 1961a; 1984; Cross 1962a: 244–250; 1973: 52–60; Bailey 1968; Koch 1976; Wifall 1980; Knauf 1985; 1999; Mendenhall 1987: 354; Mettinger 1988: 69–72; Albertz 1994: 31; Caquot 1995; Day 2000: 32–34; Niehr and Steins 2004.

123. See Clifford 1972: 35–57; 158–160. Cf. *harĕrê 'el* in Ps 36:7 (Eng 36:6). In Ps 80:11 (Eng 80:10) mountains are paralleled with the "cedars of El" (*'arzê 'ēl*), the latter eventually denoting the superlative "mightiest cedars" (Waltke and O'Connor 1990: §14.5b #17). Cross (1973: 56–57) acknowledges that El Shadday would be "an appropriate epithet" for Canaanite (Ugaritic) 'Ilu but ultimately concludes that "there is [not] sufficient evidence to establish such a thesis." He opts for seeing El Shadday as "an epithet of Amorite 'El in his role as divine warrior, identified by the Fathers with Canaanite 'El." For more on mountains and their use in marking sacred space, see Talmon 1978a.

124. Num 1:6; 2:12; 7:36, 41; 10:19. *ṣûrî-šadday* forms an exact parallel to *ṣûrî-'ēl*, "El is my Rock" (Num 3:35; cf. the PN *'elî-ṣûr*, son of *šĕdê[*šadday]-'ûr*, "Shadday is a Light"). From numerous poems we learn that *ṣûr*, "rock," refers to the deity not as a mountain dweller but as a protector and redeemer.

125. For *'il šd(y)*, see KTU 1.108.12. For the ways in which 'Athtartu was tied to fields and steppe lands (*'ṯtrt šd*) as well as food production and the textile industry, see the Conclusion, pp. 681–683.
126. Depending on how one translates KTU 1.23.13, the text could explicitly make the connection between 'Athiratu's field and that of 'Ilu. This would involve analyzing *šd 'ilm* as *šadû 'ili-ma*, "the field of 'Ilu" ('Ilu + enclitic *m*). Cf. Smith 2006: 51, which notes that "the pairing of El and Athirat wa-Rahmay makes excellent sense." Alternatively, one can just as easily see this as "the field of the gods," *šadû 'ilīma*.
127. Cross (1973: 58) is correct when he adds that Shadday may have received these traits due to his assimilation to Yahweh.
128. See note 44.
129. For further discussion of the *šdyn* at Deir 'Alla, see McCarter 1980b: 57; Weippert and Weippert 1982: 88–92; Weippert 1991: 170; and Smith 2002a: 58. Hackett (1980: 88–89; 1987: 133–134) and Stavrakopoulou (2004: 261–272) suggest that the Shaddayin may also be connected to child sacrifice at Deir 'Alla, but see the critique of Dewrell (2017: 59–64).
130. The use of *'eben*, "stone," to designate the deity in the Hebrew Bible is unexpected and occurs only here. The term is also absent as a theophoric element in personal names. In contrast, compare the personal name 'Ilu-'Abnu, "'Ilu is a rock," attested at Ugarit (KTU 4.226.3). See Lipiński's (2000: 602–604) description of Amorite cults of betyls.

    In our passage, one would expect the frequent *ṣûr* to designate the deity as a "rock" (see Korpel 1999a, 1999b). Due to the strangeness of this usage, a *lectio difficilior* argument (followed here) would retain the title as an ancient variant that fell out of use. Cf. Sarna 1989: 344, which notes the Jacob traditions that involve setting up a stone as a *maṣṣēbâ* at Bethel (Gen 28:12, 22; 35:14). A less likely alternative is to emend *'eben* to *bĕnê*, "*sons of* Israel." See Cross and Freedman 1975: 75, 90–91.
131. Many scholars (e.g., Vawter 1955: 12; Cross and Freedman 1975: 75, 91; Cross 1973: 9 n. 23; Freedman 1976: 86; O'Connor 1980: 177; Westerman 1986: 219–220; Mettinger 1988: 50) restore *'ēl šadday* for MT's *'ēt šadday*. The letters *l* and *t* are not at all similar through all periods, so a graphic confusion is unlikely. Early poetic texts are known for their lack of prosaic particles, and thus it seems that the original text of Gen 49:25 lacked *'ēt* entirely. It seems to have been introduced as a prosaizing addition at a later time in the transmission process. After this insertion, the variant tradition arose (Sam, Gk, Syr) of substituting *'ēl* for *'ēt* to make an original *šadday* conform to the *'ēl šadday* usage elsewhere (especially in patriarchal worship; cf. Gen 17:1; 28:3; 35:11; 43:14; 48:3; Ex 6:3) and to form a more synonymous pair with *'ēl 'ăbîkā*. (The alternative explanation does not make text-critical sense. Assuming that the text originally read *'ēl šadday*, and acknowledging that *l* and *t* are hard to confuse graphically, what would motivate a scribe to change *'ēl šadday* to *'ēt šadday*?)
132. If scholars are correct that the etymology of the name Shadday has to do with breasts, there is a nice symmetry between *šadday yĕbārĕkekā* (49:25a) and *birkōt*

šādayīm (49:25c). Some scholars suggest that the phrase "breasts and womb" is a divine epithet of Asherah, who is paralleled to El in this passage as his consort. See Vawter 1955: 12–17; Cross 1973: 56 n. 44; Freedman 1976: 87; 1987: 324–325; O'Connor 1980: 178; Smith 2002a: 48–52; and Lutzky 1998: 24–25. Asherah may be associated with "breasts and womb," but this phrase does not constitute an epithet. Asherah is nowhere (at Ugarit or elsewhere) called "Breasts and Womb" (or, more properly, "She of the Breasts and Womb"). Lutzky (1998) goes so far as to see Shadday itself as an epithet for a goddess, although this is very speculative.

133. See the discussion by Levine (1993: 136–137), whose analysis is followed here for the most part.
134. The origin of the "god of the fathers" traditions most likely combined *both* El traditions (as in Gen 49:25, where the parallel term "Shadday" argues for translating "El" and not "god") and ancestor worship (see van der Toorn's work on *ilib* [1993; 1996b: 155–169]).
135. See also Freedman 1976, 1977. Contrast de Hoop 1999: 62, which argues that "the early date of Genesis 49 is no longer taken for granted." For additional treatments of Genesis 49, see Vawter 1955; Cross and Freedman 1975: 69–93; O'Connor 1980: 169–178; Westermann 1986: 215–244; Sarna 1989: 331–346; de Hoop 1999; and Smith 2002a: 48–52; 2014a: 43. Freedman (1987: 321) underscores the difficulty of this poem when he writes that "we are laboring here largely in the dark, and the prospects are relatively unpromising." On the Oracles of Balaam, see Albright 1944; Freedman 1987: 331–334; 1976: 88–90; O'Connor 1980: 185–193; Milgrom 1990: 467–476; and Levine 1993: 73–74.
136. See Albertz 1994: 252 n. 33 and 34 and his critique of Köckert.
137. See the excursus on Num 1:5–15 by Kellermann (1970: 155–159) followed by Knauf (1999: 751).
138. Those unaware of P's periodization of history (crafted around three eternal covenants, each with a specific deity and sign) should consult Anderson 1986: 463–464 for an introductory treatment.
139. The literature on the Amurru is immense. For overviews situated with the biblical material, see Westermann 1985: 61–66 and Grabbe 2017: 50–52.
140. Mettinger 1988: 71, building on the work of Bailey (1968) and Ouellette (1969).
141. See note 6.
142. Cf. also the possible mention of "El the creator/establisher of Saphon" (*'ir3 k3n'i d3p3n* = *'l qny ṣpn*?) at Sheik Sa'd in the Transjordan in the so-called Job stone of Ramses II. Also Giveon 1965: 197–200; de Moor 1997: 148–149; and Cornelius 1994: 145.
143. See Smith 1994b: 122–123; 232–233; 286–287, which includes a discussion of references to Jebel el Aqra in the ancient Near East, a bibliography debating whether the Saphon of Isa 14:3 and Ps 48:3 should be equated with Mt. Saphon of Uqaritic fame, and a discussion of the Yahwistic appropriation of El and Baal motifs. See too the works of Roberts cited by Smith.
144. For an attempt at correlating a relative chronology for divine names and titles with ancient poetry, see Freedman 1976.

145. In contrast to Albertz (1994: 30), who says that some of the El deities (El Elyon, El-Bethel, and El-Olam) "can be understood as a local manifestation of the great god *of heaven*, El" (emphasis mine).
146. As noted (p. 77), KTU 1.23 does describe 'Ilu fathering two astral deities, Dawn and Dusk.
147. See Trible 1978: 62–64. Trible rightly notes that those translations that render "the God who *fathered* you" (e.g., JB) are "inadmissible" (1978: 70 n. 9). As noted too by Tigay (1996: 307), *yālad* "is used far more often for giving birth than fathering," and the Polel of *ḥwl* "refers literally to the mother's labor pains."

On family religion and divine parentage, as well as God (and kings) as mother and father, see Chapter Eight, pp. 473–494.
148. Cf. the similar wording of Canaanite religion, but portrayed negatively and with a reversal of gender in Jer 2:27 that is playing off Deut 32:18: "Who say to a tree, 'you are my father'; [Who say] to a stone: 'You gave me birth'" (['ōmĕrîm] lā'eben 'at yĕlidtinî). Cf. Holladay 1986: 103–104.
149. Van der Toorn 1996b: 206–265, esp. 255. For further treatments of cults of the dead from both archaeological and textual perspectives, see Bloch-Smith 1992a, 1992b and Lewis 1989, 2002 and their bibliographies.
150. See further Lewis 2002: 173 on the characteristic P phraseology of the dead being "gathered to his kin," *wayyē'āsēp 'el 'ammāyw* (Gen 25:8, 17; 35:29; 49:29, 33; Num 20:24, 26; 27:13; 31:2; Deut 32:50) and the Deuteronomist's "lying with one's ancestors," *šākab 'im 'ăbôtāyw*.
151. For bibliography on the name Yaqub-ilu, see note 12.
152. See Gen 49:25 and Ps 77:10 (Eng 77:9); Chapman 2016: 113–116; and Chapter Eight, p. 492. Compare *Yĕraḥmĕ'ēl* ("May El/the god have compassion") and the gentilic *yĕraḥmĕ'ēlî* ("the Yerahmeelites"). For the use of personal names using El and Yahweh with √*ḥnn*, "to have compassion," see Chapter Eight, p. 481.
153. Ps 77:14 (Eng 77:13). As noted, in its present form this verse refers to Yahweh, with the following *'ĕlōhîm* being the result of the editor of the Elohistic Psalter.
154. See note 3.
155. On the *'ăbîr/'abbîr* problem, see later discussion. For literature on El as warrior, see note 44.
156. See Deut 33:26, which (if we are correct that MT's *kā'ēl* is a secondary pious correction for an original *kĕ'ēl*) seems to describe El "riding through the heavens" (*rōkēb šāmayîm*) followed by a description of an ancient divine figure that may be a reflex of El Olam (as has been discussed). Cross (1973: 157 n. 52) argues that Deut 33:26 juxtaposes El epithets with those of Baal. Compare Elyon's connection to thunder in Ps 18:14 (Eng 18:13) = 2 Sam 22:14, but it is clear in this verse that Elyon refers to Yahweh, not El.

For the notion of a divine cloud rider, compare Ugaritic *rkb 'rpt* (referring to Ba'lu frequently), Israelite *rōkēb bā'ărābôt* (referring to Yahweh in Ps 68:5 [Eng 68:4]; cf. Ps 104:3), and the divine name Rakib-El, which occurs regularly in the inscriptions from Zincirli (cf. the Hadad inscription [KAI 214.2–3, 11, 18] and the Panamuwa inscription [KAI 215.22]). In the Panamuwa (KAI 215.22) and Kulamuwa (KAI 24.15–16) inscriptions, Rakib-El is referred to as the dynastic god (*b'l byt, b'l bt*).

See Greenfield 1987: 69. Cross (1973: 10 n. 32) argues for an identification with the lunar god Yarih.
157. Num 23:22; 24:8; cf. 23:8. See the conclusion of this chapter for a discussion of those who see El as the original god of the exodus tradition.
158. I do not agree with the view suggested by de Pury (1999b: 290) that "'patriarch' religion is the form of national religion—another form of Yahwism—that was prevalent among the tribal elites of Israel down to the monarchic period . . . in Northern Israel where the Jacob legend functioned as a national legend of origin of its own."

On the other hand, I do not mean to deny that royal images may have been used of El's cult at Shiloh, as nicely articulated in Seow 1989.
159. On the ways in which royal wives (divine and human) were used ideologically in KTU 1.23, see Lewis forthcoming a.
160. On the divine assembly, see Chapter Nine, p. 565.
161. The question of Phoenician/Punic El's association with human sacrifice is tied up to how one identifies Molek and Baal Hamon and the veracity of source material such as Philo of Byblos (discussed previously). See, for example, Cross 1973: 10, 26–28, 35–36; Olyan 1988: 12, 52–53; and Ackerman 1992: 157–159. These topics will be treated later. It should be noted that Ugaritic 'Ilu was *not* associated with human sacrifice even though Ugarit had cults dedicated to deceased ancestors. The same can be said for Israelite El.

Gen 22 (the Aqedah) is sometimes used to draw the connection between patriarchal religion and human sacrifice, with some scholars arguing that the practice was widely accepted (e.g., Levenson 1993). First, for the present discussion, it should be noted that El does not occur in the narrative. As for the putative ubiquity of human sacrifice, compare Hendel 1995: 15, which argues that the rhetoric of Genesis 22 must be taken in the opposite direction: "If the sacrifice of the first-born son was commonly accepted in Israel, then where is Abraham's greatness? He would be no greater than any other child-sacrificer. . . . The greatness of Abraham argues that he be willing to do what ordinary men are incapable of doing. . . . If the sacrifice of the first-born were an ordinary act, then Abraham would be an ordinary man." For a comprehensive analysis of child sacrifice in ancient Israel and a reassessment of the Molek material, see Dewrell 2017.
162. We do not know the exact location of Beer Lahai Roi nor its two adjacent cities mentioned in Gen 16:14. Biblical tradition places them in the southern wilderness "on the way to Shur" (Gen 16:7), so perhaps Qadesh refers to Qadesh-Barnea in northeast Sinai. Bered occurs only in Gen 16:14. See again Num 23:22. There is no clear evidence that "El Elyon is a southern form of El," as suggested by Wyatt (1992: 85). On the presence of El at Kuntillet ʿAjrud, see Lewis 2020.
163. In Exod 34:14 and elsewhere $\bar{\,}\bar{e}l\ qann\bar{a}$ is used of Yahweh. See the study by Guinn-Villareal (2018), who argues against seeing the term $qin\,\hat{a}$ as solely one of emotion in light of its clear use in sociolegal contexts.
164. See, for example, the deities mentioned in the inscriptions found in note 50.
165. The closest we come in Gen 49:25, but see note 132.
166. See pp. 80–81, 104–105. See too the discussion of Ps 68 in Chapter Ten, p. 581 and note 26.

167. See note 44.
168. Mettinger is by no means alone in such musings. See Wyatt 1992 and Smith 1994a: 207–208. More recently, Smith (2001b: 147) builds on the work of Seow to underscore Moses's connection to an El cult, especially at Shiloh.
169. Cf. too Evans 1995: 203–205, esp. 202, building on the work of Mettinger and Toews as well as that of Coats (1987: 4–7) on Ps 22:22b (Eng 22:21b) to suggest that "there are reasons to believe that a calf or bull image was used in Yahweh worship prior to the time of Jeroboam I."
170. Andersen (2001: 292) comments well: "The language of Habakkuk 3 is so shrouded in mythological imagery that historical statements are hard to nail down in it. But its historical memories are closer to the Exodus than to any other known event. It does not describe the conquest of Canaan."
171. On Habakkuk 3 as well as the remarkable parallels with Kuntillet ʿAjrud plaster inscription 4.2, see Chapter Six, pp. 280–281; Chapter Seven, pp. 359–360; Chapter Eight, pp. 451–452; Chapter Ten, pp. 583–587; and Lewis 2020.
172. Compare Ps 29; Exod 15:1–5; Isa 27:1; 51:9–11; Ps 18:7–16 (Eng 18:6–15); Ps 74:12–14 (reading *yhwh* rather than MT's *ĕlōhîm*, which reflects the editing of the Elohistic Psalter); Ps 89:9–11 (Eng 89:8–10); Ps 104:1–9. But compare Job 6:4, 9; 7:12; 9:13; and 40:9, 19.

For a detailed discussion of the way in which cosmic combat myths were used in the ancient Near East and especially assigned to Yahweh in biblical tradition (rather than to El), see Chapter Eight, pp. 428–461.

Chapter 5

1. Contrast the frequent literary representations of divinity. See Chapter Seven.
2. Though not treated in any detail here, the study of semiotics is very important for understanding the biblical notion of legitimate versus illegitimate images. See Halbertal and Margalit 1992; Evans 1995. Such scholars use Charles Sanders Peirce's semiotics to describe the nature of representation of the divine. In short, biblical tradition forbids similarity-based representations of God, but it allows metonymic representations.
3. Parts of what follows appeared originally in Lewis 2005a. I thank Andrew G. Vaughn and the American Schools of Oriental Research for their permission to reuse the material here.
4. Keel and Uehlinger 1998: 11. See note 190 on Pakkala's (2008) attempt to understand Jeroboam's bull images without any reference to iconography.
5. The bibliography on Asherah is overwhelmingly large. For an overview, see Hadley 2000.
6. For more information on the IDD and online prepublication of many entries, see http://www.religionswissenschaft.uzh.ch/idd.
7. For example, Caquot and Sznycer's *Ugaritic Religion* (1980), which appears in the Groningen Iconography of Religions series, has little analysis of iconography.

8. Yon 1997: 158–159 and KTU 6.62. On the presence of Reshef in New Kingdom Egypt, see Tazawa 2009.
9. For a sample of dragons and *Mischwesen* monsters elsewhere in the ancient Near East, see Chapter Eight. The lack of certain artifacts is due to both the lack of (and poverty of) production in Iron Age Israel and the nature of the archaeological enterprise. These questions are explored in detail in Chapter Seven, which wrestles with the question of what accounts for the absence of male divine figures in the Iron Age archaeological record.
10. See note 141.
11. For older collections of the Judean pillar figurines, see Kletter 1996 and Gilbert-Peretz 1996. The most thorough study is Darby 2014. See too the conclusion by Albertz and Schmitt (2012: 64–65) that the Judean pillar-figurines functioned as "multipurposed ritual objects," not representations of goddesses.
12. See Lewis 1998: 45–46 and bibliography therein.
13. Yon 1997: 156. Cf. KTU 1.14.2.6–26; KTU 1.119.13–16: "A flame-sacrifice [*'urm*] and a presentation sacrifice [*šnpt*] the king must offer [at] the temple of 'Ilu: a *npš* for 'I[lu?], a *npš* for Ba'lu[. . .] and a donkey ('*r*) for [. . .]." See Pardee 1997d: 284.
14. Yon 1997: 156; 2006: 146–147. See the additional description of this mug on pp. 144–146.
15. Dever 1984; 1990: 144–148.
16. A full critique of Dever's position can be found in Hadley 1994: 245–249; 2000: 144–152.
17. Dever 1983: 583. See detailed discussion of this figurine on pp. 157–159.
18. Specifically, this small item (Field II, Area 3, Locus 3192) was found "in destruction debris of Str. 6B on a 6B surface" (Dever 1974: 67). Locus 3187 (stratum 6B), which has been dated to the tenth-ninth century BCE, contains "some later intrusive elements from Trenches 3044 and 3113" (Dever 1974: 126). Trench 3113 contains mostly seventh-/sixth-century BCE material (Dever 1974: 123). Trench 3044 contains considerable Iron II/Persian material and even Hellenistic material of the third/second centuries BCE (Dever 1974: 120). Thus if either of these trenches is responsible for the chalk altar in question, its dating to the tenth century BCE would be unfounded. (My thanks to Sy Gitin [personal communication] for raising these questions.)
19. Pardee (2002a: 224) notes from his study of the ritual texts that "the prestige [of El] is enough . . . to discount attempts to make of him a *deus otiose* in Ugaritic religion." See Pardee 2000: 900, 963.
20. The astute reader will recognize how the biblical material is woven through this general look at the ancient Near Eastern view of divine images. This is intentional in order to help combat the misperception lying behind references such as "the Bible/ Ancient Israel *and* the Ancient Near East," as if the former were not a part of the latter.
21. Oppenheim 1964: 183. Winter (1992: 36 n. 1) offered her treatment of royal images as a "foundation for such an undertaking."
22. For Mesopotamia, see Walker and Dick 1999, 2001; Berlejung 1997; and Hurowitz 2006. For Egypt, see Ritner 1997a and Lorton 1999.
23. I am indebted to Ben-Tor (2006: 3) for the New Kingdom reference, which may be found in Lichtheim 1976: 198. The fuller text (known as "The Destruction of

Mankind") reads: "Re, the self-created . . . Mankind plotted against him, while his majesty had grown old, his bones being silver, his flesh gold, his hair true lapis lazuli." The Inanna reference is found in her descent into the underworld (lines 43–46). Here I am indebted to Hurowitz (2006: 6–7), who is in turn dependent on Buccellati and Gaebelein. Hurowitz's treatment discusses *mēsu* wood at length.

24. Hurowitz 2006. Did the use of such a base material as clay designate a lesser deity (e.g., the clay figurines of the minister god Ninshubur) or even the lack of divinity (cf. protective clay figures such as the "creatures of the Abzu")?
25. Arnaud 1991: 143–44; text 87. See too Avalos 1995b: 623.
26. Because this material is fairly straightforward, I have omitted the figurines that were produced in my original presentation. For this documentation, see Lewis 2005a: figs. 4.2, 4.3, 4.7, 4.18, 4.19, 4.20, 4.21.
27. Once again, I have omitted the specific figurines. See the documentation in my original presentation: Lewis 2005a: figs. 4.1, 4.6, 4.22, 4.23, 4.24, 4.25, 4.26, 4.27.
28. A type of inventory list is found in Exod 35:5–9. RSV's translation reads: "gold, silver, and bronze; blue and purple and scarlet stuff and fine twined linen; goats' hair, tanned rams' skins, and goatskins; acacia wood, oil for the light, spices for the anointing oil and for the fragrant incense, and onyx stones and stones for setting." Yet this list has to do with the ephod and breastpiece, not a divine image per se.
29. Clay images are mentioned in the Apocrypha (Bel and the Dragon, verse 7; Wisdom of Solomon 15:6–17). I am indebted to Hurowitz for these references.
30. On the use of clay to make humans, and especially the expression "the pinching off" or "nipping" of clay," see Lewis 2014a: 3–8, 24, 27.
31. See Walker and Dick 1999: 66, 116–117 for a discussion of the debate between Borger and Landsberger regarding the translation of *(w)alādu*.
32. Walker and Dick 1999; 2001, with summary in 1999: 114–116. See also Ashur 418 (= Ebeling 1931: §27, 108–114), which differs from other "mouth washing" texts in that it uses diagrams to illustrate the actual placement of the cultic apparatus (e.g., reed mats, *paṭiru*-altars, bricks, and curtains).
33. Cf. Sanmartín 1995; Vita 1999: 486–490.
34. Walker and Dick 1999: 62. Cf. KTU 1.43.8, which mentions Kothar in one of the Ugaritic "entry" texts.
35. Num 21:8–9; Exod 32:1–4, 8, 20, 23–24; Judg 8:24–27. In the Numbers passage, Moses is actually commanded by the deity to fashion the bronze serpent.
36. Its huge size (60 cubits [approx. 90 ft.] high, 6 cubits [approx. 9 ft.] wide) reminds one of monumental architecture in Egypt and Mesopotamia, and the 3-ft.-long footprints at Ayn Dara in Syria (on which see Chapter Seven). Known from texts only, we have Baʻlu's large throne (KTU 1.6.1.56–65) and Yahweh's cherub throne (10 cubits by 10 cubits). Later parallels more fitting to the date of the book of Daniel are also known; see Collins 1993: 162, 180. On the size of Yahweh's throne in the Solomonic temple and ancient Near Eastern parallels, see Bloch-Smith 1994: 25. As Bloch-Smith notes, "A god of cosmic size is omnipotent, omnipresent, and reigns for eternity."
37. In contrast, note that the large statue in Dan 2:31–36 represents the course of history rather than a deity.

38. See the so-called Verse Account of Nabonidus, translated by Oppenheim (1969: 313), as noted by Collins (1993: 180–181).
39. I owe this reference to Beckman 2011: 101. The installation of a newly constructed divine image is described as follows: "They smear the golden divine image, the wall [of the temple], and all of the implements of the new [deity] with blood so that the [new] deity and the temple will be pure" (*KUB* 29.4 IV 38–40 [*CTH* 481]).
40. Yet compare the description of God vivifying the human clay in Gen 2:7.
41. All of this bears little resemblance to the Mesopotamian *mīs pî* ritual. Scholars often cite how this "ceremony of dedication of the image . . . can be illustrated from Babylonian and Assyrian inscriptions" (Porteous 1965: 57). At best, this may be a type of cultural memory of Mesopotamian dedication ceremonies. Cf. "mnemohistory" as articulated by scholars such as Assmann (1997).
42. Elsewhere this pillar is described as receiving anointing (Gen 31:13) and libations (Gen 35:14). Yet is it clear that the *massebah* in these narratives is commemorative in nature. In anthropological terms, it marks sacred space where an adherent witnesses a theophany. The *massebah* marks "the place where he spoke with him" (Gen 35:14). The place in question is Bethel (Gen 35:7, 15), where sacred vows were made (Gen 31:13). "Bethel" is a complicated word in that it later becomes a hypostasis for deity.
43. See Walker and Dick 2001.
44. Avishur 2000: 193.
45. Younger 1998: 19, 36–40; 2000a: 150.
46. See Virolleaud 1957: xxxi–xxxii, 137–142; texts #106 (RS 15.115), #107 (RS 15.82).
47. Pardee 2002a: 226, 109 n. 98. The goddess ʿAthartu is particularly associated with textiles. See the Conclusion, pp. 681–683.
48. Whether this garment was intended to clothe the image is not stated. Line 22 is broken. See del Olmo Lete 1999: 260, 286 n. 96, 308–309 for the idea that such passages do refer to the "ritual attire of the gods."
49. 2 Sam 12:30. See McCarter 1984: 311–13 for the textual criticism on this passage. Cf. the mention of the ephod in connection with Micah's image in Judg 17–18. Cf. Andersen and Freedman's (1980: 242) comments on Hos 2:10, a passage that finds a close parallel in Ezek 16. It is plausible that the author of Ezek 16 used the imagery of dressing a cult image in his description of Yahweh dressing Jerusalem.
50. Andersen and Freedman (1980: 631–32) argue that the (majestic) plural "calves" refers to the singular image of Baal as a young bull.
51. It is often said that "Tushratta of Mitanni twice sent the statue of Ishtar of Nineveh to Egypt to help heal the pharaoh" (Bienkowski 2000: 200). See too Wilhelm 1995: 1251: "On . . . hearing of an illness of the pharaoh [Amenhotep], Tushratta sent him the statue of the famous goddess Shawushka of Nineveh, as his father Shuttarna had already done before him."

In contrast, Moran (1992: 61–62) argues that the statue was not sent to heal the aging king. "This explanation rests purely on analogy and finds no support in this letter. . . . More likely, it seems, is a connection with the solemnities associated with the marriage of Tushratta's daughter." The text (EA 23:13–17) says simply: "Thus Shaushka, of Nineveh, mistress of all lands: 'I wish to go to Egypt, a country that I love, and then return.' Now I [Tushratta] herewith send her and she is on her way."

52. Foster 1993: 382, 385. For a discussion of the "theology of travel," see Meier 2007: 193–194.
53. Note how del Olmo Lete (1999: 283 n. 86) says that "we have no idea precisely why they [the statues of the gods] were carried around in Ugarit."
54. Pardee 2000: 214–264; 2002a: 69–72; del Olmo Lete 1999: 285–291.
55. Merlo and Xella (1999: 294–95) note how this ritual, "which is focused completely on the procession of divine statues," has "the role carried out by the king and his family . . . completely in the foreground."
56. Pardee 2000: 489–519; 2002a: 214–216; del Olmo Lete 1999: 257; Merlo and Xella 1999: 295.
57. Pardee 2000: 779–806; 2002a: 44–49; del Olmo Lete 1999: 132.
58. Pardee 2000: 630–642; 2002a: 36–38; del Olmo Lete 1999: 140, 245.
59. Aziru, son of Abdi-Ashirta, to Tutu (an Egyptian official): "Here are my gods and my messenger . . . thus you are to be put under oath to my gods."
60. See Hallo 1983: 14–15, which notes that Deutero-Isaiah has Nabonidus in mind.
61. Some scholars think the cultic images known as *teraphim* were healing in nature. Yet not one of the fifteen occurrences of the word in the Hebrew Bible notes this function. See Lewis 1999: 848.
62. Keel and Uehlinger 1998: 219–222. See too the discussion of Bes with regard to the Kuntillet ʿAjrud drawings in Chapter Seven, pp. 325–330.
63. In KTU 1.23.23–24, 59, 61, the gracious gods "suck the teats of ʾAthiratu's breasts." There is also a reference in KTU 1.15.2.26–28 to two goddesses serving as wet nurses to Yassib, King Kirta's son. Yet the broken nature of the text has resulted in various readings. Traditionally scholars read ʾAthiratu in the first line and reconstructed [Anatu] in the parallel line. Based on new photographic evidence, Greenstein (1997: 25, 45 n. 66) read the first line as ʿAthtartu (Astarte). Pardee presented a new tablet join at the 2008 meetings of the American Oriental Society that has us now read the first line as *nrt*, "the Luminary," a reference to the goddess Shapshu. See Pardee 2012a: 184–185, 194–195. For Anat's putative role as wet nurse, see Walls 1992: 152–154.
64. Whether the winged goddess depicted here is Anat cannot be determined with certainty. See Ward 1969 and Walls 1992: 153–154.
65. On the function and identity of Shaʿtiqatu, see Lewis 2013a, 2014a.
66. Perhaps a marriage gift due to the use of the word *mhr*. See del Olmo Lete 1999: 369; Parker 1997: 223 n. 10.
67. In addition to figurines, Levine and Tarragon (1988) note the serpents on the Ain Samia goblet. See Avalos 1995a: 342 n. 161 for bibliography. For snake figurines and the *namburbi* rituals, see Avalos 1995a: 342ff.
68. See Avalos 1995a: 337–349 on this passage and the temple as a therapeutic locus. Avalos (1995a: 347) notes that the Nehushtan "was regarded as a deity itself."
69. Beckman 2006: 219–221. For the capture of foreign gods as war booty in Hittite literature, see Schwemer 2008b.
70. See Younger 2000b: 294; see further Cogan's (1974: 22–41) discussion of "Assyrian spoliation of divine images."

71. For additional images of the looting of divine statues, see Ornan 2005a: 259–260, figs. 117–120.
72. Recognized already by Cogan (1974: 116–117). Naaman, in his attempt to continue to worship Yahweh in his homeland, Syria, takes with him two loads of Israelite earth (2 Kgs 6:17). Seemingly there was no opportunity to secure an image of (the aniconic?) Yahweh.
73. Cogan 1974: 22–41. The Bavian Rock inscription of Sennacherib describes the capture and destruction of Babylon: "My men took the [images of the] gods who dwell there and smashed them. . . . Adad and Shala, the gods of Ekallate, which Marduk-nadin-ahhe, king of Babylon had taken and carried off to Babylon during the reign of Tiglath-pileser [I], king of Assyria, I brought out of Babylon and returned them to their place in Ekallate." See Cogan 2000a. See too the enigmatic Papyrus Amherst 63 (the so-called Aramaic Text in Demotic Script), which describes the trampling and smashing of the divine statue (XIII.9–17). See Steiner's (1997a: 319) translation as well as those of van der Toorn (2018a: 11, 69–70, 177–185; column XIV.9–17) and Holm (forthcoming).
74. On the precise language used in Moses' destruction of the young bull, see Knoppers 1995b: 102 n. 28, building on the work of Loewenstamm and Begg.
75. Note Cogan 1974: 116, showing how David did not do this in 2 Sam 12:30.
76. One judge acts similarly. Gideon tears down the altar of Baal (no mention of his image) and cuts down the *asherah* (Judg 6:25–32).
77. Cogan (1974: 116) writes: "2 Sam 5:21 reports that after successfully routing the Philistines at Baal Perazim, David and his men carried off the idols left behind by the retreating Philistines." Cogan is certainly correct that the plain sense of the passage indicates that "David actually despoiled the Philistine images." The Chronicler has David burning the images (1 Chr 14:12).
78. For the textual criticism on this passage, see McCarter 1984: 311–313.
79. See Chapter Seven, p. 788, note 32 on using the language of "desacralizing" to describe such treatment of divine figurines.
80. As has been noted, clay can certainly be used for divine images. Solid examples would include the terra-cotta goddess seated on a throne from Emar, the nude female on the bottom register of the Taanach cult stand, and the horned goddess from Horvat Qitmit. For pictures, see Lewis 2005a: figs. 4.1, 4.21, and 4.27.

    The notion that the investment of resources can correlate with prestige is certainly true (and thus the norm is to find divine figures made of precious metals), yet one must factor in how poorer individuals would have accessed divine images. They certainly would have used more affordable media such as clay or wood. Yet using such materials to demarcate between the sacred and the profane is much more difficult precisely because they are so abundant in everyday use.
81. Though horns regularly mark divinity, we must be careful not to insist on their essentiality. Compare, for example, the exquisitely made bronze figure from Hazor documented in Figure 5.36 that is lacking horns but clearly divine.
82. Regrettably, we have precious few examples of inscriptions with images in the Levant such as the Old Aramaic Hadad inscription (KAI 214, line 14; cf. lines 1, 16), where

King Panamuwa I has the words "a statue for this Hadad" carved on a large (approx. 13 ft. [4 m] high) horned statue of the god Hadad. (I thank Adam Bean for reminding me of this.) See too how most scholars affirm that the letters ʾlt (written left to right!) on the Late Bronze Age Lachish ewer do indeed designate the goddess Elat, as represented by a sacred tree drawn immediately beneath (see the summary provided in Hadley 2000: 156–161). In contrast, scholars are very divided about whether the inscription "Yahweh and his asherah" should be equated with the drawings of the two standing figures on the Kuntillet ʿAjrud Pithos A (see Figure 7.15). That the crown of the left standing figure goes straight through the inscription (at the very point of two names nonetheless) argues strongly for two different hands, and thus raises the bar quite high against any linkage between the iconography and the inscription. Moreover, the distinct Bes-like character of the two standing figures makes any such equation almost impossible. See the full discussion of this important material in Chapter Seven, pp. 325–330.

83. Cf. Negbi 1976: 46–57 and Moorey and Fleming 1984: 70. The treatment here, concentrating on examples from Late Bronze Age Ugarit, is necessarily brief. For an earlier Middle Bronze Age example of a seated El figure (flanked by offering table, worshipper, and priest) on a serpentine cylinder seal coming from a burial cave near Ras ʿAli in Naḥal Zippori, see Brandl 2014: 7–9. Brandl dates this seal to the sixteenth century BCE and argues that it is a product of " 'Greater Canaan,' perhaps a workshop in Ugarit."

84. See the studies of bronze figurines mentioned in note 113.

85. Cf. also Nebgi (1976: #1441), an Egyptianizing figurine that also comes from Ugarit. In contrast to our figurines, this one does not have a beard. Cf. a similar beardless figurine from Byblos (Negbi 1976: #1443) and the beardless figurines in Figures 5.35, 5.36, 5.38, 5.39, 5.41, and 5.42—but note the beard on Figure 5.40 from Megiddo.

86. See Lewis 2008a. Analysis of the South City Trench and insights into domestic architecture and how this part of the city was planned can be found in RSO I (Callot 1983) and RSO X (Callot 1994). For an easily accessible description of the South City Trench, see Yon 2006: 91–97. The elite nature of some of these homes can be seen in Block X, House B, the so-called House of Literary Tablets (Callot 1994: 53–61). These Ugaritic and Akkadian texts included portions of the Gilgamesh Epic and wisdom literature.

Of course, one could emphasize that this part of the city contained a metallurgical workshop. Indeed, an earlier designation had labeled this area "the House of the Bronze Smith." Yet according to Yon (2006: 96), "this interpretation . . . lacks sufficient basis." See further Callot 1994: 186–188.

87. This bronze statuette with gold foil covering is Museum No. Damascus S3573 (RS 23.394). Its find spot: South City Trench, block XIII, Locus 38, topographic point 2755. See Callot 1994: 187, 224, 414 fig. 393, Yon 2006: 133. Its dimensions: height: 5.3 in. (13.5 cm); width: 2 in. (5 cm); depth: 3.5 in. (9 cm). Early treatments of this figurine include Caquot and Sznycer 1980: 23, plate VIII, and Negbi 1976: 171, #1442.

88. This stela, found in the eighth campaign in 1936, is currently housed in the Aleppo Museum (A 4622 = RS 8.295). The most complete treatment is that of Yon (1991: 305–307, 336 fig. 16). In addition to Yon's bibliography, see Wyatt 1983.

89. This mug was found on the South Acropolis in 1961 and is now in the Damascus Museum (no. 6881 = RS 24.440). For a brief summary of the numerous religious objects (especially divinatory) in the House of the Magician-Priest, see Yon 2006: 100.
90. On Yon's interpretation, see p. 123 and notes 13 and 14. For the ritual texts, see Pardee 2000, 2002a. The literature on royal cult is vast. See, for example, Tarragon 1980: 79–129; Merlo and Xella 1999: 296–300; and Lewis forthcoming a. Even the sacrifice of a foreign king is mentioned in KTU 2.40.14–17. See Clemens 2001: 223–233.
91. On the meaning of *prln* as "diviner" corresponding to Akkadian *bārû*, see van Soldt 1989: 367–368 and the bibliography in Clemens 2001: 876–877. On ʾAttānu-purulini, see further Lipiński 1988: 131–133.
92. For the history of scholarship on the term *ḥrṣn*, now taken by most scholars to be a personal name, see Lipiński 1988: 126–131 and Clemens 2001: 489–491.
93. See Lipiński 1988: 133–137.
94. Excavations took place between 1978 and 1982. See Yon 1996.
95. This stela, found in 1988, is currently housed in the Latakia Museum (RS 88.70). See Yon and Gachet 1989; Yon 1991, 1993, 2006: 130–131.
96. But Pope (1955: 36) has ʾIlu twiddling his fingers.
97. See Keel 1997: 47–49; 1986: 309; Keel and Schroer 2015: 35–36, fig. 19; and Amiet 1960. For further analysis of this seal, see the bibliography of works by Parrot, Amiet, and Vanel listed in Green 2003: 160 n. 20.
98. Amiet (1960: 220) even connects the deity with the pointed lance with Ugarit's *Baal au foudre* stela, and Keel connects the two stars with "the stars of El" in Isaiah 14:13. Smith (1994b: 226) gives tentative approval to Keel's theory. Hess (2007b: 83, 86) also sees the depiction here as "an aged El-type deity enthroned on a mountain," and "if it is indeed El in his abode, then perhaps Baal is the one who pierces that waters (Yamm, 'Sea')."
99. See Pritchard 1969: 160; §464; Keel and Uehlinger 1998; and Day 1992.
100. See Miller 1970; Dohmen 1987: 147–153; Schroer 1987: 81–104; Evans 1995: 201–205.
101. Figure 5.22 can be found in Collins 2005: 41, fig. 2.12. This image and its function were previously noticed by Olyan (1988: 31). Collins (2005: 40), in commenting on Tudhaliya IV's restoration of divine images, notes that "the majority of replacements is toward theriomorphic forms—specifically, storm gods are given images in the form of bulls."
102. See Cornelius 1994: §2.2.2.3; §4.3; 2004.
103. This list is by no means complete. For a catalogue of Neo-Assyrian and Neo-Babylonian seals in the British Museum with the "god on a bull" motif, see Collon 2001: 141–147; §276–284. For a more recent catalogue of storm god figures riding bulls, see Bunnens 2006. For additional examples of bull riders beyond what we have presented here, see Bunnens 2006, fig. 33 (from Emar), fig. 34 (from Emar), fig. 57 (from Karaçay Köy), fig. 71 (from Ankara Museum), fig. 117 (from Tasliköy), fig. 119 (from Tilhalit), fig. 120 (from Gölpinar), fig. 121 (in Aleppo Museum), and

fig. 122 (from Arslan Tash). For examples of goddesses on bulls, see Chapter Seven, note 62.

As for storm gods with chariots, cf. the mention of Baal hitching his chariot (*bʻl ʼsr mrkbty*) in Arslan Tash Incantation II, lines 1–2.

104. ANEP §534; cf. too the two kilted deities that stand on two *aladlammu* creatures (i.e., human-headed winged bulls) in an eighth-century BCE Neo-Assyrian cylinder seal. See Collon 2001: 142–143, §277; Danrey 2004: 137–138, fig. 10.
105. The find spot of this bronze is the same as Figure 5.16, i.e., South City Trench, Block XIII, Locus 38, topographic point 2755. See Callot 1994: 187, 224, 414 fig. 393; Yon 2006: 133. See earlier Caquot and Sznycer 1980: 22–23.
106. Caquot and Sznycer 1980: 22.
107. Cf. KTU 1.12.2.53–55, where Baʻlu falls *like* a bull (*npl bʻl km ṯr*).
108. See Caquot and Sznycer 1980: plates IX, X; Cornelius 1994: 165. There is also the possibility of foreign imports. On bull cults and weather deities in the Anatolian and Mesopotamian spheres, see Haas 1994: 315–338.
109. If Cornelius is correct, this would argue against A. Mazar's critique (1982: 32) of Schaeffer's view. Mazar had argued that the bull figurine could represent Baal due to the striding figurine also found in South City Trench, Block XIII, Locus 38, topographic point 2755.
110. It should be mentioned that Beck (1989: 337) entertained the idea that the bull rider from Hazor Temple H Str 1B (Figure 5.27) may have been El. Yet it is more likely that here we have a storm deity with lunar traits, as we have at Bethsaida. So Bernett and Keel 1998: 37 as well as Ornan 2001: 17–18.

Many more bulls are attested elsewhere, although, according to Mazar (1982: 29), "only a few bronze bull figures are known from the Levant." See the various references in Moorey 1971 and Mazar 1982: 29–31.
111. Stager (2008: 579) suggests that the Ashkelon figurine depicts "a male calf about a year old."
112. Stager (2008: 579–580) argues for Baʻal Ṣaphon.
113. Cf. Collon 1972; Negbi 1976, 1989; Muhly 1980; Seeden 1980, 1982; Moorey and Fleming 1984; Keel and Uehlinger 1998; Cornelius 1994; Uehlinger 1997.
114. Dever 1983: 574 (emphasis mine).
115. On the question of proto-Israelites at Hazor, see Ben-Tor 1998; 2016: 113–126; Dever 1995; 2017: 95–96, 157–158.
116. Ahlström 1970–1971; 1975.
117. Keel 1973: 325–336; Hallo 1983: 1–2. More recently, see Ben-Ami 2006: 127 and Zuckerman 2011: 390.
118. Dever 1983: 583 as well as personal communication; Negbi 1989: 360; Ben-Ami 2006: 127; Zuckerman 2011: 390.
119. Later biblical tradition records the face, eyes, nose, ears, mouth, and tongue of the deity, but no cheeks, chin, or beard. See Korpel 1990: 100–108.
120. Ornan 2011: 278–279 uses the "uniquely large" size of this image and its exquisite manufacture to argue that it is a "cult statue" of the deity (i.e., an object that was the focus of veneration and the recipient of cult) and not a votive offering to the deity.

121. Ornan (2011: 255–258) argues that the highly unusual portrayal of the right arm may be due to the manufacturing process "to promote the flow of metal into the mold," especially in view of the statue being cast in one piece.

    Ornan (2011: 273) suggests that the lack of a beard may be diagnostic for identifying this figurine as Baal rather than El. Yet caution must be exercised in making any particular feature an essential aspect of a divine profile (see note 81)—especially when one considers how the same god can be perceived differently over space and time. If Ornan is correct, then one should also reclassify the various beardless enthroned figures in this chapter as other than El (e.g., Fig. 5.35, 5.38, 5.39, 5.41, 5.42). See Ornan 2011: 273, where she acknowledges that, taking the seated posture with its "more eminent and dignified pose" into consideration, "the identification of Levantine enthroned metal figures as El seems plausible."

122. For another example of male (bull) imagery juxtaposed with an ibex, see the remnants of a storage jar found at Khirbet Ataruz that was decorated with seven bulls and one ibex (Figure 5.72). Regrettably, its broken state doesn't reveal any information about the presence of a sacred tree.

123. For pictures of each of these, see Cornelius and Niehr 2004: 30, abb. 45; 46, abb. 71.

124. In addition to Lewis forthcoming a, see Chapter Four, pp. 103–104, with the application of this material for El-Shadday. Note too the Middle Bronze Age cylinder seal from Ras ʿAli in Naḥal Zippori that portrays a quadruped animal standing on a table (altar?) before a seated deity, likely El. See note 83.

    While it is speculative, note how Keel and Uehlinger associate El as "Lord of the Animals" with a hunting scene on a seal from Beth Shean. See pp. 166–170.

125. Figure 5.38 was tentatively identified as Baal or Reseph by Ben-Tor and Rubiato (1999: 36). Hazor's wealth of divine figures also includes a yet-to-be-published large (4 ft. [1.2 m]) basalt statue found in the courtyard of Area A close to the palace entrance. In a preliminary note, Ben-Tor described this figurine (= reg. no. A/15227) as "the largest Bronze Age statue of a deity to have been found in the country to date." The notion that we have a Canaanite deity here is due to an emblem depicting a circle filled with rays and a crescent. See Ben-Tor 1995: 285, fig. 2; 2006: 6, no. 10.

    It is clear that not all of the Hazor anthropomorphic bronze figurines were divine, as seen in the depiction of an enthroned ruler/dignitary from Locus 7420 (reg. no. A/44949). See Ben-Tor 2016: 110, fig. 74.1, and Ornan 2011: 254 n. 3 with additional bibliography.

126. See Horowitz, Oshima, and Sanders 2006: 65–87.

127. For the various deities attested in personal names, see note 163.

128. In addition to this bronze, a cult stand from twelfth-century BCE Megiddo has a robed, seated male figure on each of its four sides. Another male stands opposite. See Dayagi-Mendels 1986: 154–155, §74: "The lack of details and the crude execution make it difficult to detect any divine attributes, and therefore it is impossible to determine whether these scenes represent a deity worshipped by an adorant or a ruler receiving homage."

129. The bronze, first published by Hansen (1957), was acquired in Jerusalem from N. Ohan in 1906 by D. G. Lyon. From the records of purchase, it would seem that

Ohan kept quite detailed accounts of the proveniences. Acquisitions from antiquities dealers are notoriously suspicious, especially those said to come from well-publicized excavations. In this case the identification might be a little more believable because the first excavations at Tell Balâtah, under the direction of E. Sellin, did not begin until 1913. The lack of archaeological context should be underscored and any conclusions, even cautiously drawn, must be held in check. Compare Negbi's (1976: 48) uncritical reference to this figure as "the Shechem figurine" and "the figurine from Shechem."
130. Negbi 1976: 49, 57; Hansen 1957: 15.
131. Grant and Wright 1939: 154.
132. Personal communication.
133. Negbi (1976: 48) notes parallels with New Kingdom representations of Osiris but concludes that the Beth Shean figurine's appearance "bears closer resemblance to the Canaanite god Mekal."
134. Contrast the observations by Keel and Uehlinger (1998: 58) that "it is too facile a solution to identify all enthroned gods as El and all striding gods as Baal" with the detailed study of the markers for the gods Baal and Reshef by Cornelius (1994).
135. See Lewis 1996a. Textual analysis underscores the preeminence of the deity El-Berith at pre-Israelite Shechem, but the lack of secure context for the Harvard Semitic bronze prevents us from going any further. The deity does hold a cup in his right hand, which reminds one of 'Ilu's excessive drinking in the Ugaritic text KTU 1.114 (see Chapter Four). Yet drinking is certainly not restricted to 'Ilu at Ugarit (cf. Baʿlu in KTU 1.3.1.10–11) and elsewhere (cf. Judg 9:13).
136. While Keel and Uehlinger (1998: 312 n. 30) date this seal to the end of the eighth century BCE or early seventh century BCE, the uncertainty of both its location and its date needs to be underscored.
137. Without textual support, we have no way of knowing or confirming whether the cultic symbol here functioned "to mediate the blessing" of a god.
138. I have replaced Keel and Uehlinger's vocabulary of "deity" here so as not to prejudice the conclusion from the outset.
139. See also the critique by Hartenstein (1995: 82–84). Uehlinger's (1997: 142) later comments conclude that this seal "cannot be regarded as decisive evidence," yet it remains "suggestive" and gives "some welcome support."
140. The early use of *byt ʾlhy* (*bātay ʾilāhayyaʾ*) to refer to stelae—but note with the plural, "the houses of the gods"—occurs in the eighth-century BCE Old Aramaic treaty text from Sefire (Sefire II C [= KAI 223], lines 2–3, 7, 9–10). On the use of the term "betyl" in classical literature, see Fitzmyer 1995: 131–132 and Mettinger 1995: 35 n. 102.
141. When discussing this material, scholars use the conventional terms *massebah* (singular) and *masseboth* (plural) without the diacritics of the Hebrew terms *maṣṣēbâ* and *maṣṣēbôt*.

Avner (1984, 1993, 1996, 2018; Avner et al. 2016) has shown that the use of standing stones dates back as early as the eleventh millennium BCE and is well attested in desert areas of the Southern Levant from the sixth to the third millennia, especially in the Southern Negev. The number of desert cult sites with standing stones is staggering. Avner (2018: 29) notes more than 450! See especially Avner's probing of what might be inferred from context (standing stones in open-air sanctuaries vs. standing stones incorporated into tombs) and the properties of the stones themselves. These include orientation (more likely to the east than to the west), shape (with broad stones perhaps indicating female and narrow stones perhaps indicating male), and numbers (most often singular, pairs, and triads, but also groups of five, seven, and nine).

See too Graesser 1969, 1972; Mettinger 1995: 33–34, 168–174; Zevit 2001: 256–259; and LaRocca-Pitts 2001. Standing stones were equated with deities elsewhere in the ancient Near East, as seen in the *sikkānu* standing stones at Late Bronze Age Emar. See note 156 and Chapter Ten, pp. 627–628. As Michel (2013) observes, such stones could be used of all the gods, male and female.

142. For example, the ten large standing stones at MB Gezer, according to Dever (2014: 53), were "large-scale *public* monuments" that "functioned to commemorate a covenant-renewal ceremony... among 10 towns or tribes in the vicinity."

143. Even this could be elliptical, where the "pillar of Baal" could refer to a pillar dedicated to Baal in thanks for his beneficence or to mark his theophany without necessarily denoting the actual cultic symbol of Baal, but this is improbable. The Covenant Code is ambiguous when it states, "You shall not bow down to their gods [i.e., those of the prior inhabitants of the land], nor serve them ... but you shall utterly overthrow them and break their [i.e., the inhabitants' or the gods'?] *masseboth* in pieces" (Exod. 23:24). The most natural reading would suggest the inhabitants' *masseboth* and not the *masseboth* of the deities. Lev 26:1 is less explicit. It prohibits "bowing down" to an *'eben maśkît* (on which cf. Hurowitz 1999) in connection with not erecting a *massebah*.

There are other passages in which *masseboth* are dedicated to foreign gods but not explicitly called symbols of the deities. Jer 43:13 mentions the *maṣṣĕbôt bêt šemeš*, "the stone pillars of the Sun temple."

144. For splendid examples of standing stones in grave complexes, see the rich collection of material from Avner's many studies of Southern Negev sites from the sixth through third millennia (see note 141) as well as the Wadi Fidan 40 cemetery in the Faynan region in southern Jordan that Levy connects with the Sashu nomads. (On the latter, see Chapter Six, pp. 229–232.) In addition to standing stones in circular mortuary monuments, note especially the presence of "highly abstract anthropomorphic standing stones with stylized nose and ear features." See Levy 2005: 471–473; 2009a: 258; Levy, Adams, and Shafiq 1999.

145. Yet if one wanted to adopt a minimalist perspective, even here they could have been seen as markers of sacred space where one came into contact with the deity/deities (similar to Jacob's use of a *massebah* in Gen 28:18–22).

146. A preliminary report of the 2013 excavations at Tel Rechesh in the Tabor River Reserve in northern Israel documented "a Canaanite *massebah*-like stone or stele of basalt that was in secondary use." See Hasegawa and Paz 2015, fig. 7.

147. Here Stager (1999, 2003) is challenging earlier interpretations such as those of G. E. Wright, the American excavator of Shechem, who had placed Temple 1 in the

Middle Bronze Age IIC period (1650–1550 BCE). See too Campbell 2002: 169–185 and G. R. H. Wright 2002: 97–104.

148. Stager 1999: 233. For detailed discussions and pictures of these two stele, see Wright 1965: 82–83, 87, 93, 99, figs. 36–37, and Graesser 1969: 180–181. Graesser writes: "As cultic stones they marked the area as sacred and also served as boundary stones, indicating the limits of the special sacredness of the temple.... [They] formed the focal point for ritual enacted at the entrance to the temple. The duality of the stones was probably not intended to indicate a pair of deities. It seems rather to stem from a feeling for symmetry, and perhaps from imitation of the use of pairs of other objects before entryways, such as guardian winged beasts, pillars, etc."

149. Stager (1999: 233; 2003: 33) notes how writing on plaster is documented by the eighth-/seventh-century BCE Trans-Jordanian Deir ʿAlla texts (which may have even been written on a stela rather than walls, as usually assumed), as does Richter (2007: 359–360), who also points out the plaster inscriptions from the eighth-century BCE inscriptions at Kuntillet ʿAjrud (see Chapter Six, pp. 268–269; Chapter Ten, pp. 583–585).

150. Yet note how the author of Deut 27 consciously does *not* use the vocabulary of *masseboth* to designate his plastered stones (*ʾăbānîm*); this fits with Deut 16:22, which outlaws the setting up of a *massebah*, "which Yahweh your God hates." Likewise, the verb for erecting the stones is the hiphil of *qwm* (Deut 27:2, *hăqēmōtā*; 27:4, *tāqîmû*), not *nṣb*, which also would be associated with the *masseboth*.

151. Similar to Deut 27 (see note 150), again note how the vocabulary in Josh 24:26–27 uses *ʾeben* rather than *maṣṣēbāh* and the verb *qwm* rather than *nṣb*.

152. The MT's notion of a tree being "erected" (*muṣṣāb* = Hophal ptc) makes little sense. As our translation indicates, we follow those who associate *muṣṣāb* with *maṣṣēbāh*. See the suggestion by LaRocca-Pitts (2001: 58) that the author's slight change in vocabulary could "serve to free the author to paint [the Abimelek] episode negatively while at the same time reduce the possibility that any of the negative taint which characterizes Judg 9:6 might rub off of this story onto the traditions of Joshua 24 and its stone of 'witness.'" For a discussion of the textual debate as well as the interplay between Josh 24 and Judg 9 and including the archaeological material, see Campbell 1983.

153. See Chapter Four, notes 124 and 130. There is no need to change the text from *ʾeben yiśrāʾēl* to *bĕnê yiśrāʾēl*, "the sons of Israel," as do Cross and Freedman (1975: 53, 62). To the charge that *ʾeben* "is nowhere else used as a divine name or in association with God" (Sarna 1989: 344), see 1 Sam 7:12. Sarna is more on track when he suggests that "'Stone of Israel' may have been a very ancient title ... derived from the traditions about Jacob setting up a stone pillar at Bethel."

154. Mazar (1982: 36, 39, fig. 11) tentatively suggests that the "undefined bronze object" ("a folded piece of flat bronze sheet containing a fragment of a bronze handle") may be "a bronze mirror of Egyptian type." As for the cult vessel ("a fragment of a large ceramic cult object"), Mazar (1982: 36, 39 fig. 10) suggests that it "could be either an incense burner ... or a 'model shrine.'"

155. Alternatively, though his material is *much* earlier, Avner argues that the many examples of broad stones from the Southern Negev are indicators of female divinity. See note 141.
156. Intriguingly, Jacob names the location of this sacred stone site Bethel, a name that will later come to be used hypostatically as a surrogate for the deity. See Chapter Four, note 116.

    As for the lack of foodstuffs associated with sacred stones, one could also compare (though admittedly far afield) Avner's desert sites and the use of *sikkānu* stelae at Emar. Fleming (1992a: 78) has written about the role of *sikkānu* stelae in the Emar *zukru* ritual "with special connection to the gods." "A *sikkānu* of ᵈNIN.URTA makes an appearance at the beginning of the *zukru* festival, and the gate of the *sikkānu*'s ... is perhaps the central sacred site of the whole feast. This gate is where the gods are brought out from the city, and a chariot bearing statues of the gods is driven 'between the stelae' (*bērat sikkānāti*) at several points in the ritual. They are anointed with oil and blood at least twice." See too Fleming 1992a: 17, 52 [= lines 34–35]; Dietrich, Loretz, and Mayer 1989: 134; Sommer 2009: 49–50; and Michel 2013.
157. Ben-Ami (2006: 42, 45) argues that the stones here "are found in a clear cultic context." Of special note are three female figurines (one of silver, two of bronze) that must be factored into our analyses. For pictures, see Ben-Ami 2006: 40–41 and Ben-Tor 2016: 53 fig. 29. Yet Ben-Ami also notes that the large number of standing stones ("more than 30 clustered together") "can hardly fit any of the artistic descriptions of gods in Near Eastern iconography." Thus he concludes that these "were probably designed to commemorate some high-ranking individuals who were part of the government bureaucracy ... The *masseboth* were not meant for the eyes of the worshippers, but for those of the *deity*, and they served here as a constant reminder in front of the latter" (my emphasis; note Ben-Ami's use of the singular "deity").
158. Zuckerman (2011: 391–393) documents a wide variety of "ruin cults" elsewhere. Borrowing vocabulary from Sara Morris' descriptions of Troy, Zuckerman refers to these as "value-laden" sites that should be considered "landscapes of memory."
159. It has been suggested that Shelley's poem was inspired by news that the British Museum had acquired the broken top half of Ramses II's impressive statue from Thebes.
160. In addition to Ben-Tor 1996; 2016: 177, 181 fig. 131; Ben-Tor and Yadin 1989: 80–81, brief discussions can be found in Gilmour 1995: 23–34; Ilan 1999: 154–156; Zevit 2001: 202–205; Ben-Ami 2006: 125–127; and Zuckerman 2011.
161. One stand came from room 3283, while the adjacent rooms 3275 and 3307 each contained two cult stands.
162. Contrast Gilmour 1995: 23–34, yet note that Gilmour penned his treatment prior to the 1996 restoration project.
163. See Horowitz, Oshima, and Sanders 2006: 74–77, which updates some of the readings in the earlier yet more comprehensive preliminary edition found in Horowitz and Shaffer 1992: 21–33. See too Ben-Tor 2016: 70–71. As noted by Horowitz and Shaffer, the tablet, written in cursive Old Babylonian, contains the theophoric elements El, Addu/Hadad, and the moon god Erah. Of these, Addu/

Hadad predominates (Horowitz and Shaffer 1992: 22), and Ben-Tor (2016: 71) suggests that he was the main god of the city. In contrast, assuming that Hadad and Erah were associated with the Area H and Area C temples, respectively, Bonfil (1997: 101, followed by Hesse [2008: 163]) suggested that the LB Northern Temple of Area A was dedicated to the god El. Granted, our evidence is minimal and thus all such associations are speculative.

As for personal names, despite the genre of the text, one cannot be absolutely certain that the people involved are locals. Distinguishing Amorite names from straightforward Akkadian names is difficult. Even enticing names such as Ishpuṭ-Addu that exhibit a West Semitic vocalization (i.e., *yašpuṭ; cf. Mari išpiṭ; ARM 14.48) nonetheless are written with Ish-, not Yash-. (I am indebted to personal conversations with Herb Huffmon.)

By emphasizing West Semitic/Canaanite deities for the Area B standing stone, we are not implying that East Semitic/Mesopotamian deities were never worshipped, for indeed we have the mention of Ishtar and Nergal written on an earlier Middle/Late Bronze Age fragment of a liver model found at Hazor (see Horowitz, Oshima, and Sanders 2006: 66–68).

By reducing our candidates to El and Addu, we are not suggesting that Canaanite goddesses were unknown. Horowitz, Oshima, and Sanders (2006: 66–68) note the possibility of the goddess Anat in two personal names (Bin-Hanuta, Sum-Hanuta) in a court record from Hazor. Yet the presence of the male statuette would eliminate a goddess as candidate for the standing stone. Moreover, standing stones are predominantly male in orientation.

164. For summary descriptions of the Iron IIB temple, the *masseboth*, the two incense altars (with burnt organic remains), the altar, and the Judean pillar figurines at Arad, see Bloch-Smith 2015: 101–106; Herzog 2013: 38–41; and Darby 2014: 257 n. 220. On the different ways of interpreting the two inscribed bowls from stratum X, see Chapter Ten, note 12.

165. See the following bibliography: Aharoni 1967; 1968; 1982: 229–234; Herzog et al. 1984; Herzog, Aharoni, and Rainey 1987; Herzog 1987, 1997a, 1997b, 2001, 2002, 2006, 2010, 2013; Ussishkin 1988; Manor and Herion 1992; Mettinger 1995: 143–149; Na'aman 1999a: 405–408; 2006a: 324–327; Zevit 2001: 156–171; Singer-Avitz 2002; Uehlinger 2006; Bloch-Smith 2005: 32–33; 2006: 76–77; 2015: 101–106, 112–115. Bloch-Smith (2015: 105) concludes: "Dates for either the temple's construction or its demise cannot be conclusively ascertained. The most persuasive evidence is the Str. X ceramics, dated to the late ninth and eighth centuries."

166. Herzog 2006: 221; 2010: 174–175; 2013: 40. Herzog goes on to comment: "A second stele, often misinterpreted as simultaneously used, was in fact inserted into the back wall of the niche." See Herzog 2010 for assigning this phase to stratum IX (not X or XI).

167. See Graesser's comments in note 148 with regard to the Shechem temple.

168. For bibliography on Area T stratum III (ninth century BCE) and stratum II (eighth century BCE) as well as a synthetic analysis, see Davis 2013.

169. The Israelite gates in Areas A and AB are documented in Biran, Ilan, and Greenberg 1996: plan 2.
170. Cf. too note 156 on the use of the cultic use of *sikkānu* stelae at Emar's gate complex.
171. Biran 1994: 239–241; Laughlin 2007: 12. For part of the debate, especially as it interacts with the gate shrine at Bethsaida, see Blomquist 1999: 63–64.
172. As noted by Ji and Bates (2014: 48–49), Ataroth (*ʿăṭārōt*) is mentioned in the Hebrew Bible as being rebuilt by the Gadites (Num 32:34) and in the Mesha inscription (KAI 181, lines 10–13), which describes "the men of Gad who had dwelt at Ataroth from of old" (*wʾš gd yšb bʾrṣ ʿṭrt mʿlm*). The same text includes a remark about how Omri, the ninth-century BCE ruler of the northern kingdom of Israel, had built Ataroth for himself (*wybn lh mlk yśrʾl ʾt ʿṭrt*), and how subsequently the Moabite king Mesha conquered the city, destroyed its inhabitants, and repopulated it (*wʾlthm bqr wʾḥzh wʾhrg ʾt kl hʿm*). Mention is made of resacralizing the town in the name of the Moabite deity Chemosh. Putting this description together with the material remains, Ji and Bates (2014: 49) conclude that the "new population continued to reuse part of the temple that had been originally built by Omri."
173. Preliminary publications indicate that another single standing stone (4.3 ft. [1.3 m] high) was found in the Western Courtyard near the "Western High Place." See Ji 2012: 210, 212. Ji (2012: 212–213) comments on the widespread distribution of standing stones in the vicinity dating back to the Chalcolithic and Early Bronze Age I periods and with prominent examples in the Late Bronze Age II and Iron Age periods—thus demonstrating that the two standing stones at Ataruz "were not isolated examples but represented a long and widespread tradition of monolith cults in the central Jordan."
174. Note the following comment by de Vaux (1961: 285–286):

> As an object of cult, it [i.e., the *massebah*] recalled a manifestation of a god, and was the sign of the divine presence.... It was a short step from this reasoning to accepting the stone itself as a representation of the divinity, and there was no need for the stone to be hewn into the form of a statue: even in its crude, natural shape, it was a symbol of the divinity.

175. Contrast the lunar symbol on a small Late Bronze Age stela in Hazor Area C. On the bull cult at Khirbet Ataruz, see pp. 202–205. As for Arad, Bloch-Smith (2015: 112) notes the presence of Baal worship in biblical literature and suggests that "perhaps the [Arad standing-] stone stood for Baal rather than Yhwh." The three Arad inscriptions that invoke Yahweh (#16, #18, #21) come from the late seventh/early sixth centuries BCE. Thus Bloch-Smith writes: "Accordingly, the large limestone massebah in the (late ninth- to) early eighth-century Arad temple niche arguably made manifest either Baal or Yhwh." Complicating such an analysis are the exclusively Yahwistic personal names that come from the eighth-century BCE Arad inscriptions found in strata X–VIII. These include inscriptions #67, #68 (stratum X); #60 (stratum IX); #40, 41, 49, 51, 56 (stratum VIII). On the exclusive use of Yahweh and not Baal names at Arad, see Tigay 1986: 47–63, appendix A. For the epigraphic dating of this material, see Parker 2013: 217 and fig. 34. Cf. too the restored name [Yahu]ah in Arad #79 that comes from stratum XI (ninth century BCE).

176. If Thomas (2019) is correct that the god Gad is to be equated with El, then references to the cult offered at the standing stone at Ataroth by early Gadites could have been to El (see note 172).
177. In contrast, an example of multiple gods being attested both in literature and in physical reliefs can be seen in the Hittite pantheon known especially for its "1,000 gods." See Beckman 1989 and the numerous deities depicted in the reliefs from Yazılıkaya.
178. See Cooke 1903: 295; §133, line 1.
179. See Porten and Yardeni 1986: 68–75 = TAD 1.A4.7.8–12 // 1.A4.8.7–11.
180. I write "near-fixed" due to the following minor variations:

Hadad Inscription line 2	Hadad Inscription lines 2–3	Hadad Inscription line 11	Hadad Inscription line 18
Hadad	Hadad	Hadad	Hadad
El	El	El	El
Rashap	Rakib-El	Rakib-El	Rakib-El
Rakib-El	Shamash	Shamash	Shamash
Shamash	Rashap	ʾArqu-Rashap	[Rashap]

181. It should be pointed out that the rulers of Sam'al (Zincirli) were not of one accord politically with the rulers of Aram-Damascus, whom we read as having contact with Tel Dan. Note how Panamuwa II died when fighting on the side of Tiglath-Pileser III in his battle *against* Damascus in 732 BCE. See further Lewis 2019.
182. Biran 1998: 45–46. It should be noted that cults of betyls are common throughout Aramean religion (see Lipiński 2000: 599–604).
183. On Ariel, see Feigin 1920; Albright 1920; Godbey 1924; Petzold 1969; Zimmerli 1983: 424–427; Block 1998: 600; Wildberger 2002: 71–72; and Strawn 2005: 69–74. While it seems clear that we are dealing with various etymologies for the various forms of Ariel (not just "the lion of El"/"El is a lion"), Albright's (2006: 151) suggestion that *harʾēl* in Ezekiel 43:15 is "a slight popular etymology of the A[kk]adian loan-word" *arallû* is brought into question by Zimmerli (1983: 426–427). Other suggested etymologies can be found in the various lexica (e.g., HALOT, vol. 1, p. 87).
184. Strawn (2005: 90–92) notes the connection of many seals to Egyptian Amun but suggests (following Keel and Uehlinger) that "the cult of Amun may nevertheless have influenced the cults of Canaanite El and/or Yahweh." On the use of leonine imagery in Iron Age II royal seals, see Strawn 2005: 101–105. Note in particular his discussion of the famous "Shemaʿ, the servant of Jeroboam" jasper seal from the 1904 excavations at Megiddo and whether it refers to Jeroboam I or Jeroboam II. McCarter (1996: 145) argues that "its archaic Hebrew script fits neatly into the reign of Jeroboam II."
185. At Arad we have a small bronze lion statuette "found beside the sacrificial altar" (Herzog, Aharoni, and Rainey 1987: 30, 32). The large basalt lion orthostat from the temple of Area H at Hazor is well known (Yadin 1961: plate CXX; 1972: plate

XVIIIa; Beck 1989: 327–328) and its twin was found in the summer of 1997 (Ben-Tor 2016: 108, fig. 72). A small lion orthostat was found in secondary use in the "Stelae Temple" of Area C buried under a stela (Yadin 1958: plates XXIX–XXX; 1972: 72, plate XVIIIb; fig. 17). All three are associated with entrance gates, with the two large lions functioning as guardians.

One of the most amazing discoveries was that of an actual lion skull at ancient Jaffa. The debates about the dating of the strata (Late Bronze Age II or Iron Age I) as well as whether the context was cultic (a "lion temple"?) keep us from drawing definitive conclusions about whether this skull should be associated with a particular deity. See Kaplan and Ritter-Kaplan 1993: 658, with photograph of skull on p. 656; Dessel 1997: 206; and Strawn 2005: 93–94 with further bibliography.

Cf. too the lion statue and lion-headed libation tray from Tell Beit Mirsim that may come from the Iron Age rather than the Late Bronze Age. See Amiran 1976 and Chapter Seven, p. 315. For a critique of Amiran, see Holladay 1987: 293–294 n. 125.

For an exhaustive collection of the various lions found in the archaeological record, see Strawn's (2005: 77–128) splendid catalogue.

186. See Chapter Seven, pp. 315–317. Preliminary reports note "a lion-like animal" on terra-cotta cult stand/model from Iron Age II Ataruz. See Ji 2012: 213; taf. 47B.
187. See Strawn 2005: 100.
188. Strawn (2005: 252–268) hypothesizes that Yahweh absorbed leonine aspects primarily from the goddesses Ishtar and Sekhmet.
189. See Müller 2004: 243–247 and HALOT 1996: 1163–1164. The latter concludes that "in the OT *rĕ'ēm* is *bos primigenius*, but in MHeb. and the Targum it is *Oryx leucoryx*." Though their etymologies are inexact, for the former cf. Akk *rīmu*, "wild bull," and for the latter cf. Arb *ri'm*, "white antelope."
190. Moreover, interacting with the hundreds of years of commentary would require a monograph of its own. Thus readers interested in the various intricacies of exegesis (from textual to source to form to tradition criticism) and the priority of one account over another (Jeroboam's versus Moses') can find treatments in the standard commentaries and other secondary literature such as Kennedy 1901: 340–343; Aberbach and Smolar 1967; Sasson 1968; Halpern 1976; Bailey 1971; Hahn 1981; Moberly 1983: 161–171; Dohmen 1987: 147–153; Schroer 1987: 81–104; Curtis 1990; Janzen 1990; White 1990; Wyatt 1992; Frankel 1994; Amit 2000: 99–129; Burnett 2001: 79–105; Berlejung 2009; Römer 2017; and Davis 2019. In particular, see Knoppers 1995b, an insightful article that also includes a nice overview of various source-critical issues.

The present approach tries to understand the literary traditions in the context of the ancient Near East and its richly documented bull iconography. At the outset of this chapter we noted the pitfall of textual scholars who fail to consider the contribution of the field of iconography. An example for the subject at hand is Pakkala's 2008 article, which is purely literary. Because Pakkala does not interact with the religious use of bull iconography throughout the ancient Near East and especially within the Late Bronze and Iron Age Levant, it is little wonder that the article reduces any reference to Jeroboam's bull images to "a late literary construct" not integral to the original text. See too Zevit's (2001: 451 n. 25) remarks against other scholars (e.g., van Seters, Hoffman, Davies) who consider most if not all of the Jeroboam episode "a contrived literary artifice bereft of historical value."

This is not to say that 1 Kgs 12:25–33 is lacking in rhetoric. Using parallels of two Sam'alian kings of the eighth century BCE (Panamuwa and Bar Rakib), Davis (2019) argues that the royal rhetoric we have here is that of renovating a cult place rather than founding one. As such, Davis posits, the presentation in 1 Kgs 12:25, 28–29, 32a—which references Jeroboam I's El worship for ideological continuity—is that of the eighth-century BCE reigns of Joash and/or Jeroboam II, who use it as a historical precedent. I thank Davis for sharing his research with me prior to publication.

191. Those advocating that Jeroboam's cult was devoted to Yahweh rather than El, as the present thesis holds, would present as an obvious critique that Aaron proclaims a "feast to Yahweh" (*ḥag lyhwh*) immediately after fashioning the young bull and building an altar before it (Exod 32:5).

In reply, the El hypothesis would underscore that mention of the "feast to Yahweh" is an addition by the P source, the "function" of which, writes Bailey (1971: 99), "is to 'rehabilitate' Aaron from his heinous apostasy." Bailey (1971: 99 n. 12) continues: "P's attempt to exonerate Aaron is visible in [Exod 32:] 21–24, 5b, the switch to the plural in the verbs of 4 and 6, and the contradictory verb 'made' in 35. It might be remembered that Aaron plays a minor role in J, is mentioned but twice in D (where God wants to kill him for making the calf [Deut 9:20], and when he dies [10:6]), but suddenly assumes total authoritative control of the priesthood in P, necessitating desperate attempts to excuse his behavior in Exod. 32."

192. Cross 1973: 75. Cross writes: "It is wholly implausible that an insecure usurper, in the attempt to secure his throne and to woo his subjects[,] would flout fierce Yahwists by installing a foreign or novel god in his national shrine." Kaufman (1972: 270) also argues that "the story does not link the calves with any foreign deity." Scholars typically point out the silence of any reference to Jeroboam's cult being devoted to Baal by passionate critics of Baal worship such as Elijah, Elisha, and Amos. Of particular note is Jehu, who destroys Baal worship with a vengeance (2 Kgs 10:18–28) and yet does not include Jeroboam's two bull images in his purge (2 Kgs 10:29). For a detailed elaboration of Kaufmann and Cross' thesis, see Toews 1993: 42ff.

An obvious complication is found in 1 Kgs 14:9, where the prophet Ahijah accuses Jeroboam of making "other gods, molten images, provoking Yahweh to anger" (cf. 2 Kgs 17:7–23, esp. vv. 16, 21–23). This datum is either skipped over as a later, southern viewpoint (e.g., Kaufman 1972: 270) or used to invalidate the entire consensus view (cf. Bailey 1971, advocating for the deity Sin). A similar judgment would have to be made for Exod 32:20. As Knoppers (1995b: 102) has pointed out, in the redacted text as we have it, Moses is portrayed "deliberate[ly]" as treating the bull image "as taboo . . . as a foreign cult symbol."

Another strong southern polemic against Jeroboam's cultic measures can be found placed on the lips of the Judean king Abijah in 2 Chr 13:4–12. In particular, Abijah proclaims that Yahweh gave kingship to the Davidides (2 Chr 13:5) and that Jeroboam cannot prevail against "the Kingdom of Yahweh in the hands of the Davidides" in the coming battle by relying on "the golden bulls [*'eglê zāhāb*] that

Jeroboam made for you for gods [*'ĕlōhîm*]" (2 Chr 13:8). The Chronicler considers the bulls to be "no gods" (*lō' 'ĕlōhîm*, 2 Chr 13:9), as did Hosea (*lō' 'ĕlōhîm hû'*, 8:6), on which see Chapter Seven, pp. 320–321. Finally, see Josiah's desecration of Bethel as part of his cultic reforms in 2 Kgs 23:15–20. Specific mention is made of Jeroboam's "altar at Bethel" and "high place" (2 Kgs 23:15), but the bulls go unmentioned.

193. Wellhausen (1957: 283) already noted in his 1878 prolegomena that "Jeroboam did nothing more than Solomon had done before him; only he had firmer ground under his feet than Solomon, Bethel and Dan being old sanctuaries, which Jerusalem was not." Propp (2006: 551) goes further in pointing out that "as far as we can tell, Jeroboam was more monolatrous than Solomon (cf. 1 Kgs 11:1–10)." On Jeroboam's archaizing use of El worship, see Cross 1973: 198–199; Toews 1993; and Chalmers 2008: 26–52, 127–133.

Burnett (2001: 80–105) adds yet another take on Jeroboam's archaizing by suggesting that by using the "*'ĕlōhîm* formula" he was "appropriating a well established cult formula."

194. For an alternative theory, see Berlejung 2009 and Römer 2017; both argue that the activities attributed to Jeroboam I in 1 Kgs 12 are from the time of Jeroboam II.

195. It should be underscored that the consensus of scholars takes Exod 32 to be a reflection of and attack against Jeroboam's cultic activities. For a clear demarcation between historical and literary issues, see Knoppers 1995b: 93–94: "From a historical vantage point, Jeroboam's calves may explain Aaron's calf; but from a literary vantage point, Aaron's calf predates Jeroboam's calves."

As for the Deuteronomist describing Jeroboam's rituals as dyotheistic, see again Knoppers 1995b: 101: "This is not misunderstanding, but invective."

196. Cf. *'ēgel massēkâ* in Exod 32:4, 8; Deut 9:16; *šĕnê 'eglê zāhāb* in 1 Kgs 12:28; *'ēgel* in Exod 32:19, 20, 24, 35; Deut 9:21; *'ăgālîm* in 1 Kgs 12:32; *massēkâ* in Deut 9:12. For the variant readings in the LXX and suggestions about understanding the textual history of the MT vis-à-vis the LXX, see Propp 2006: 542.

197. Noth 1962: 248, followed in part by Propp (2006: 550), who notes a similar disparaging use of "heifer" in Hos 10:5.

198. Cassuto (1967: 412) specifically asserts that *'ēgel* "is not a pejorative term for an ox, as many surmised. It denotes a young ox, an ox in the full vigour of its youth." Cassuto cites various references for the use of *'ēgel* and its female counterpart to designate mature aurochs. Propp (2006: 550) too has an extensive analysis, to which I am indebted. Note Propp's analogy to the similar imprecision and confusion with the Hebrew term *na'ar*, which can refer to youths and young adult males.

As for these two passages, note Ps 106:19–20, where *'ēgel//šôr* specifically refers to the Horeb incident, and Ps 29:6, where *'ēgel//rĕ'ēm* likely does too, especially if the author is referring to God "pulverizing" (LXX leads one to posit the Hebrew Vorlage *yādiqqēm*) like he did with the bull at Sinai rather than "causing to dance" (MT's *yarkîdēm*). See further Loewenstamm's (1992: 280–291) section "The Historical Background to the Septuagint Translation of Psalm 29:5–6" in his *From Babylon to Canaan*.

199. Of these two options, I would lean toward the former due to the more pervasive view of El as a non-warrior deity (see Chapter Four). Yet the iconography of a

mounted figure (typically used of striding storm and warrior gods) would lend further support to the notion that El was the original deity who led Israel out of Egypt.
200. See Yadin 1961: plate CCCXLI 1–4; Negbi 1989: 350–351.
201. See Ben-Tor 1996: 264–266, fig. 3; 2016: 105, 109, fig. 73.3.
202. Mazar 1982; 1983; Dever 1994: 110–111; 1990: 129–131.
203. Mazar 1982: 27, 32. Similarly, Dever (1994: 110; cf. 2017: 159–160, 178) stated that this is a "reasonably certain Israelite cult installation of the period of the Judges." For a summation of the Einun pottery debate between Finkelstein and Mazar and its relevance for dating the Bull Site, see Finkelstein 1998; Mazar 1999; and Zevit 2001: 178 n. 95.
204. Coogan 1987b. See too Mazar's response to Coogan (1988: 45).
205. Ahlström (1990: 80) has remarked: "If, however, the settlers came from the north, then Yahweh would be ruled out."
206. Though not functioning as a divine image in a cultic niche, one must underscore the appearance of a plethora of bovines on numerous cult stands as well as zoomorphic vessels likely used for cultic libations from the Philistine repository pit at Yavneh dated between 850 and 750 BCE. See Kletter, Ziffer, and Zwickel 2010, 2015 and the analyses of the bull iconography by Ziffer (2010: 69–73) and Horwitz (2015: 152–153). According to Horwitz (2015: 152–153), the bovine figures are domestic cattle, either short-horned *Bos indicus* (zebu) or long-horned *Bos taurus*, but not wild aurochs (*Bos primigenius*). She also "raises the possibility that zebu cows and not bulls are portrayed on the Yavneh cult stands."
207. Cf. too a terra-cotta cult stand (or model shrine) also found in the Main Sanctuary Room that depicts two male figures, one of which "holds the horn of either a bull or a calf with its left hand" (Ji 2012: 213; Tafel 47 A–C). A cylindrical stone incense altar was also discovered with what seems to be a late ninth-century Moabite inscription. Though this is extremely provisional, Rollston, the epigrapher in charge of its publication, suggests that one word could be read as *prn*, "which could, of course, refer to a category of offering, 'bull' or the like." See http://www.rollstonepigraphy.com/?p=631. Rollston also notes how the reading could be *grn*, "sojourners," an attractive suggestion in light of its presence in the Mesha stela. Now see Bean, Rollston, McCarter and Wimmer (2019: 7, 10–11).
208. Bourke (2012: 165 n. 2) comments that the Ugaritic texts imply this notion. Yet as seen from the discussion of the iconography of ʾIlu, this is not the case.
209. Farther afield, compare the clay figurines from the precinct of the Temple of Apollo at Kourion that depict religious personnel wearing bull masks. See Karageorghis 1976: 105, plate 82.
210. Ji (2012: 212) comments that "bull and calf were tied to the principal god of Baal or El," yet he mistakenly writes that "the Ugarit materials often call El and Baal 'the bull' in order to signify their strength and fertility." At Ugarit it is ʾIlu (not Baʿlu) who is consistently called *ṯôru*, "the bull" (KTU 1.1.4.12; 1.2.1.16; 1.3.4.54; 1.3.5.10, 35; 1.4.1.4, 1.4.2.10, 1.4.4.47, etc.). See Chapter Four, p. 78. Granted, iconography shows Baʿlu with small horns, and in our narrative evidence Baʿlu is mentioned along with horns in two broken texts (KTU 1.3.4.25–27; KTU 1.101.6), has a

bull-calf//ox (*'ibr*//*r'um*) born to him (KTU 1.10.3.35–36), slaughters bulls (*ṯrm*) for a divine banquet (KTU 1.4.6.40–43), and even "falls down like a bull" (*npl b'l km ṯr*) (KTU 1.12.2.54). In one ritual text a bull (*ṯr*) is put in fire for Ba'lu (KTU 1.48.8–9). Yet it is 'Ilu alone who was accorded the epithet "the Bull" (*tôru*).

211. In the Mesha inscription, see the mentions of Chemosh (esp. lines 11–12, mentioning Ataroth), Ashtar of Chemosh (line 17), Baal (cf. Baal-meon in line 9 and the mention of Omride influence, esp. lines 10–11), and Yahweh (lines 17–18). See Chapter Six, pp. 235, 251.

For Athtar elsewhere, see Smith 2001b: 65, which suggests that at Ugarit Athtar is a "full-fledged son of El" with astral associations. See further Smith 2014a: 168–169; 2001b: 62, 65, 136–137; 1995.

Chapter 6

1. For *'lyw* and *'lyhw,* see Dobbs-Allsopp et al. 2005: 130–131, 287, 297–298. See especially §BLei 6 and §KAjr 21 (= Aḥituv, Eshel, and Meshel 2012: 100–101). For *yhw'l* and *yw'l,* see Renz and Röllig 2003: 237; §10.25 (= CWSS 205: 523; Lachish) and Renz and Röllig 2003: 244; §10.46 (= CWSS 107:186; unprovenanced).

    Methodologically, in addition to discounting the unprovenanced *yw'l* (yet cf. *yô'ēl,* "Joel," in the Hebrew Bible), one needs to keep in mind that *'l* can be a generic designation such that the meaning of the names can be "The god is Yah[weh]" or "Yah[weh] is my god" as easily as "El is Yah[weh] or "Yah[weh] is El." Yet see Albertz's (in Albertz and Schmitt 2012: 348–350, 576–581) discussion of the phenomenon he calls "equating names." Contrast Rechenmacher 1997: 11–24. Zevit (2001: 687) and Finet (1993: 20) suggest that there are similar equations already in Amorite anthroponyms with explicit comparative names (*yahwi-ki-addu,* "Yahweh is like Addu"; *yahwi-ki-an,* "Yahweh is like El") alongside implicit equating names (*yawi-addu, yawi-dagan*). Yet Zevit is quick to caution against using the Amorite data to fill the gap leading up to the presence of Yahweh in the late tenth century BCE: "They would actually be vacuous verbal bridges between the unknown and the already-hypothesized uncertain."

    Literarily, it should be noted that the phenomenon of a single deity bearing two names in the same narrative (often synonymously parallel) is well attested in the ancient Near East. The parallel of Baal and Hadad for the storm/warrior god at Ugarit comes easily to mind, as does the double-named craft deity Kotharu wa Hasisu.

2. The two paradigmatic texts used by historians who try to tease out an earlier dualism from the texts that have come down to us would be Deut 32:8–9 (on which see Chapter Four, pp. 91–92; cf. Smith 2001b: 143) and Ps 82 (see Chapter Nine and the thesis of Frankel 2010). See too Hab 3:2–3.

3. On Yahweh as divine warrior, see Chapter Eight. On Yahweh as king and judge, see Chapter Nine. On the priesthood attending Yahweh, see Chapter Ten.

4. Reading *yhwh* rather than MT's *'ĕlōhîm,* which reflects the editing of the Elohistic Psalter. See Chapter Four, p. 724, note 65.

5. The older studies by Tigay (1986: 15; 1987: 194) tabulated a distribution of 94.1 percent Yahwistic names and 5.9 percent non-Yahwistic names occurring in the full inscriptional record (onomastic and non-onomastic evidence). Sanders (2015: 77) notes that if Tigay had included provenanced El names, the percentage would shift to "80% Yahwistic and 20% other (including El and other gods)." Elsewhere Tigay (1987: 161–162) writes of the percentage of the epigraphic onomasticon of pre-exilic Israelites being 47.6 percent Yahwistic (351 out of 738 individuals). Fowler's (1988: 366–367) subsequent study of Hebrew Bible names tallied 36 percent Yahwistic names during the United Monarchy (71 out of 197 names) and 74.3 percent during the Divided Monarchy (194 out of 261 names). Cf. Albertz and Schmitt 2012: 340 n. 209. Zevit (2001: 608 n. 95), using Zadok's (1988) dataset of 2,202 Israelite names, "guesstimate[s] that the percentage of Israelites with non-Yahwistic theophoric names would not exceed 20 per cent." Hess' (2007a: 310) updated discussion "certainly supports Zevit's estimate." Hess then adds that the percentage at Samaria "is fewer than 12 percent and this drops to between zero and 2 percent in late pre-exilic Judah." Albertz (Albertz and Schmitt 2012: 341, 508) figures 67.6 percent of the Hebrew onomasticon (1,978 names) to contain references to Yahweh.

   As to what can be precisely concluded from the onomastic material, see the methodological remarks in Chapter Three, pp. 56–60. Few of our tallies are pristine, with most not controlling for unprovenanced material. See Albertz and Schmitt 2012: 249, 260–262 and the critique in Sanders 2014: 222. A notable exception is Golub (2014, 2017), who restricts her analysis to names coming from controlled excavations. Golub's (2014: 638) analysis of 799 names from sixty-six sites argues for "the very limited use of god names other than Yahweh and [that] supports Tigay's conclusions." Yet her conclusions are more nuanced, noting how "*yhw* is the dominant theophoric element only in the later centuries" where "in the earlier centuries, *yw* was the most common element." Golub's (2017: 29) analysis of 625 names from a distinct subset of forty Iron Age II Judean sites reveals that "the extremely limited use of divine names other than YHWH or El (1%), the absence of *b'l*, a remarkably high use of *yhw* (74%), and a very limited use of *yh* are unique to Judah."

   Methodologically, see Chapter Eight (p. 494) on Carol Meyers' remarks about how women's names (and thus the deities they worshipped) are severely underrepresented. See Meyers 1998: 251–252.
6. Similarly, compare how the etymology of divine names plays an overly important role in Jacobsen's (1976) reconstruction of Mesopotamian religion.
7. In contrast to Albertz (1994: 50–51, following Rose [1978: 34]), who states that "it is relatively improbable that Israel was still aware of the meaning of the name Yahweh."
8. In ancient Israel, the name of Yahweh was revered. It was also used daily. Such reverence and utility can be difficult for different segments of our modern culture to comprehend. How can those in our society who curse and cuss with the name of God appreciate the reverence that the ancient Hebrews showed for God's sacred name? The problem of blasphemy is rarely a subject of our postmodern discourse. Even pious theists reduce the divine name to the casual. At the other end of the spectrum, how can those members of the post-rabbinic Jewish community who find the mere mentioning of God's name in speech or writing to be a violation of the Fourth Commandment appreciate that the name Yahweh was used on a daily basis in Iron Age Israel?

Consider too the care with which the divine name is treated once it is written. Even academicians bow to the *genizah* tradition, which forbids the destruction of ritual objects containing the name of God. For example, the late great Semitist M. H. Goshen-Gottstein (1979: 145)—in an article on the Aleppo Codex in a scholarly journal—appended the following personal request for his readers: "This article contains some reproductions from the Aleppo Codex for your convenience. In accordance with religious custom, as explained in Maimonides' Code, biblical texts—even though only reproductions—should not be discarded in such a way that the divine name might be profaned. Kindly make sure that you keep this issue in a specially safe place."

Biblical texts and onomastica alike show that the ancients did not write "G-d" or some substitute (*adonay, ha-shem, adoshem,* etc.) to avoid using the name of the god whom they worshipped. The "hedge around the Torah" of the Pirqe Avot had yet to be built. The Master of the Universe was called by his name, Yahweh. Once again, the gap between the Iron Age and ours is apparent. Yet maybe the gap is not so great after all. Societies by nature are pluralistic in their religion expressions. Iron Age Israel was not monolithic. It contained both those who penned laws against blasphemers (Lev 24:16) and, by inference, those to whom such laws were directed. On the severity of blasphemy, see Lewis 2017.

9. For a discussion of the *yawi-/yahwi-* forms in the Amorite onomastica and what seems to be the Akkadian equivalent, *ibašši-ilum* ("the god exists"), see Huffmon 1965: 70–73, 160, 191–192; Cross 1973: 62–64; de Vaux 1978: 342–343; Freedman and O'Connor 1986: 511–513; Hess 1991: 187; van der Toorn 1995: 244; and Kitz 2019.

The Amorite material and Greek transcriptions argue against Tropper's (2001) reconstruction (based on Neo-Babylonian personal names) that vocalizes the name of the deity as *Yahwa, a nominal lexeme of the *qatl*-pattern with the final *-h* of *yhwh* functioning as a *matres lectionis* to mark the case ending *a*.

10. Maas (1910: 329) finds the earliest reference to Jehovah in Raymund Martin's "Pugio fidei" of circa 1270 CE.

11. A similar practice occurs when *yhwh* and *'ădōnay* occur together. If the former were pointed following the usual practice, a redundancy would result (*'ădōnay 'ădōnay*). The Masoretes solved this problem by taking the vowels from Elohim ("God") and placing them on *yhwh*.

12. A splendid overview of the tetragrammaton can be found in Suriano 2013.

13. I am indebted here to de Vaux (1970: 56–57; 1978: 343–344), whose work in tracking down and debunking this material has saved many hours for us all. See also McCarthy 1978: 313.

14. For a slightly sympathetic appreciation of this etymology and a small bibliography of adherents, see de Vaux 1978: 344–345. Yet de Vaux ultimately sets it aside as unlikely.

15. Contrast Tropper 2001, who sees a nominal *qatl-* form based on vocalizations of Neo-Babylonian personal names that contain the theophoric element *ia-a-ma* that Tropper reads as *ia-a-wa$_6$* (/yaw/). See note 9.

16. So Andersen and Freedman 1980: 143, 198–199. Cf. too Mettinger 1988: 34–36; Mettinger, following Schoneveld, suggests that Ehyeh may simply be God's name declaration in Exod 3:14. This analysis (rendering God's reply as "Ehyeh! Because

I am") is strained due to the necessity of treating *'ăšer* as a relative conjunction with a casual sense. While this usage is not unattested (cf. Joüon and Muraoka 1991: §170 e), it is rare and one would expect *kî*.

17. The examples usually put forth to document a tautology expressing uncertainty or imprecision are Exod 4:13; 16:23; 1 Sam 23:13; 2 Sam 15:20; 2 Kgs 8:1; and Ezek 12:25; 36:20. See the discussions in de Vaux 1978: 351–352 and Mettinger 1988: 34–35. De Vaux argues that such paronomastic expressions can also indicate "totality or intensity" (cf. Exod 33:19; Ezek 12:25; 36:20).
18. Some of the earliest biblical scholars arguing for this view based on their studies of Hebrew syntax included Knobel (1857) and Reuss (1879). For more recent treatments, see Schild 1954; Lindblom 1964; de Vaux 1978: 353–355; and McCarthy 1978: 316–318.
19. See also the grammatical problems raised by Albrektson (1968) and addressed by McCarthy (1978: 316–317).
20. See note 9. This material was already noted by von Soden (1965: 177–187). Hyatt (1967: 373) suggests that the "existence" being described is "the confidence that the deity is actively present in the birth of the child, or . . . that the deity may be actively present in the continuing life of the child."
21. Old Babylonian Version, OB VA + BM ("Meissner Fragment") iii, 3–5. See George 2003: 278–279 and Moran 1995: 2329.
22. George's (2003: 192ff.) sigla for this Old Babylonian Yale tablet is OB III and the relevant section is column iv, lines 140–143 (= Gilg Y. IV, 5–8). Tigay (1982: 164) also notes the Sumerian version's remark that "a man, (even) the tallest, cannot reach heaven; A man, (even) the widest, cannot cover the earth" (GLL A, 28–29).
23. Dead gods, like dead humans, can even have ghosts (Moran 1970: 54). On the death of gods and deicide, see Machinist 2011 and Lewis 2017. The Phoenician Pyrgi inscription (KAI 277, lines 8–9) even describes the burial of the deity or a divine image (*bym qbr 'lm*)—unless Knoppers is correct that this refers to an ancestral figure. See Knoppers 1992b; Smith 2001b: 118–119; and Peckham 2014: 162–163.
24. For more on the creation of humans, especially via "pinching off" or "nipping" of clay (*kāraṣu + ṭiddu/ṭīdu*; cf. *mēḥomer qoraṣtî* in Job 33:6), see Lewis 2014a: 4–8.
25. Cf. the discussion of Yahweh-El-Olam in Chapter Four, pp. 97–99. See Gen 21:33; Isa 40:28; Jer 40:10.
26. See too Mettinger 2001, which reassesses the dying and god motif in response to J. Z. Smith and Mark S. Smith.
27. Granted, according to traditional source criticism, we are dealing with two different sources, with Exod 3:12, 14 assigned to E and Exod 4:12, 15 to J. The juxtaposition then would be attributed to the redactor of these two sources.
28. The prefixal *ya-* is also attested in Classical Arabic and Amorite personal names from Mari (cf. Huffmon 1965: 63ff.), yet this evidence is inconclusive because there is no evidence in these languages of the Barth-Ginsberg correlation (where **yaqtal* became *yiqtal*). On traces of an *i-* preradical in early Arabic, see Testen 1994: 431 n. 10. See Barth's (1894: 4–6) original formulation, Ginsberg's (1939: 318–322) and Gordon's

(1965: 71) application to Ugaritic, and Rainey's (1978; 1996a: 2:1–16) handling of the Amarna material. For a discussion of the Barth-Ginsberg correlation in the context of the I-*w* verbal class, see Testen 1994: 430–431 and especially Kitz 2019.
29. See note 9.
30. This view did not originate with Albright, who is following the lead of his teacher Paul Haupt. See Albright 1924: 375, which notes that treating Yahweh as a causative was suggested by Le Clerc (Clericus) in 1700.
31. There are other instances of finite verbs used as theonyms, although they are infrequent. See the discussion in Cross 1973: 67 and van der Toorn 1999b: 913–914.
32. In Albright's early writings (prior to the publication of the Amorite onomastica) he argued that these could be traced "unmistakably to Egyptian models of thought and expression." See Albright 1924: 377–378.
33. Contrast Albright's (1924: 376–377) more drastic emendation *'ahyeh 'ăšer yihyeh*, "I cause to be what comes into existence," which he then rendered in the third person as *yahyeh* (older *yahweh*) *'ăšer yihyeh*, "He causes to be what comes into existence." Once again Albright was taking his lead from Haupt.
34. Granted, the non-causative G stem of the root is used in P's creation account, serving, in Bernhardt's (1978: 378) words, "to express a theory of the process of creation that sees God's commanding word as the critical mark of his creative activity and accordingly interprets the earlier account of what God did by means of an account of what God said."
35. I do not feel the weight of Albertz's (1994: 259 n. 45) criticism that "the minimal significance that creation initially had in the religion of Israel tells against [the Cross-Freedman explanation]." It is inadvisable to assume that the minimal texts that are preserved in the biblical record constitute the full view of the ancient Israelites on a given subject. See Chapter Three, p. 66.
36. Wellhausen 1897: 25. For more recent advocates, see Knauf 1984: 469; 1988: 43–48 and van der Toorn 1999b: 915–916. Additional bibliography can be found in de Vaux 1978: 345 n. 111. Other scholars, such as Goitein (1956), have used Arabic cognates meaning "to love" to reconstruct Yahweh's origin as a god of passion.
37. I am not denying that the verb *hw'* with the meaning "to fall" may be attested once in Job 37:6 (cf. the nominal forms *hawwāh*, "destruction," and *hôwāh*, "disaster"; Pope 1965: 280; de Vaux 1978: 345). For the fullest analysis, see Dhorme's commentary (1967: 561–562).
38. Job 37:5–6 would be the type of passage that could have played on Yahweh as the god who thunders with his voice/lightning and causes snow to fall (*hw'*). But neither here (the text reads El) nor elsewhere—even with rain as the object—do we read of Yahweh acting as a storm god in conjunction with the verb *hwh* in the sense of its Arabic cognate.
39. Propp (1999: 276) astutely notes that whereas the occurrence of the name Yochebed ("Yo [= Yahweh] is Glory" or "Yo is glorified") presents no problem for the pre-Mosaic Yahwistic redactor in Exod 6:20, it is indeed very curious to find it in P (in Num 26:59). He further notes how elsewhere P likely changed the name of Joshua to Hoshea in Num 13:8–16.

40. See, for example, Keil 1986: 467–468 as well as the works by Cassuto, Kikawada, Quinn, and Radday mentioned in Pike 1990: 34.
41. The connection between P and the book of Ezekiel is well known. Cf. Ezekiel 37:26, where Ezekiel also uses the phrase bĕrît 'ôlām for his united kingdoms (//bĕrît šālôm) and he too has an 'ôt sign in the same verse. Perhaps then in 37:26 we should not be so quick to repoint MT's 'ôtām to 'ittām even with the LXX evidence (met' autōn).
42. Pike (1990: 71 n. 30) does note that this could be due to "the phenomenon of 'culture lag,' seen even in onomastics."
43. Westermann 1984: 340. Sandmel (1961: 27) traces this interpretation to Dillmann. See too early rabbinic exegesis, which analyzed hûḥal in Gen 4:26 to be from ḥll, "to profane, pollute" (cf. Targum Onkelos, Pseudo-Jonathan, Rashi, etc.) and saw here a reference to idolatry. The LXX translators (cf. Philo) seem to have read yḥl, "He hoped to call on the name of the Lord God." See Sandmel 1961 for the history of exegesis on Genesis 4:26.
44. Retrospective writing and editing, and the anachronisms that can result, are replete in the Bible. (As but one example among many, consider 1 Kgs 1:38, where Jeroboam is promised a lengthy dynasty *as long as* David's when, according to the storyline, only one king, Solomon, has ruled to date.) The presence of anachronisms is a natural feature of any literature that undergoes a long editorial process. This is especially true of literature that holds communal value and is thus preserved and updated over time. Scriptures fall into this category until a time of fixation occurs, a process that develops long before formal canonization.
45. Compare the reverse situation with the Elohistic Psalter, where Elohim seems to have been systematically substituted for Yahweh. See Chapter Four, p. 724, note 65.
46. See "The Politics of Ebla" (*Biblical Archaeology Review* 4 [1978]: 2–6), written by the pseudonymous "Adam Mikaya."
47. Pettinato 1976: 48; 1980: 203–205.
48. Scholars studying onomastica often refer to hypocoristic (or, rarely, caritative) suffixes or label a personal name as a hypocorism. By this they mean the addition of a suffix such as -*y* in the English names Bobby (for Bob), Scotty (for Scott), Danny (for Dan[iel]), etc. Such an ending can serve several purposes, including acting as a term of endearment, a diminutive, a euphemism, or a nickname. Other hypocoristica, rather than bearing a suffix, are apocopated forms, where the original consisted of a longer form (Ted for Theodore) or one with two or more elements. For a discussion of abbreviations in the Hebrew onomasticon, see Fowler 1988: 149–169.
49. The three interpretations are conveniently summarized with bibliography in Muntingh 1988: 168–169. See too Müller 1980: 83; 1981: 306–307; Lambert 1988: 140–141; Biggs 1992: 265; and van der Toorn 1999b: 910–911.
50. For bibliography and history of scholarship, see Gray 1953 and Rowley 1950: 148 nn. 4 and 5. Gordon (1965: 410 §1084) called Virolleaud's observation a "pioneer insight" that "has been brushed aside too hastily."
51. Contrast de Moor's more recent work (1990: 113–118; 1995b: 220–223) with his previous position (1971: 119; 1987: 25 n. 116).

52. De Moor 1990: 136–151. A fuller account can be found in de Moor 1997: 214–227. For further literature and critique, see Yon 1992: 119–120 and Malamat 1997: 24–25. Adrom and Müller (2017: 109) harshly refer to de Moor's thesis as one that takes us "purely into the realm of imagination."
53. For the relevant six place names, see Adrom and Müller 2017; Schneider 2007: 114; and Giveon 1971: nos. 6a and 16a. The Amenhotep III text is a geographical list from the temple of Amon at Soleb in Nubia (Sudan). Ramses II's list (which comes from Amara-West in Nubia) was copied from it. See note 59.

The literature on the Shasu is vast due to their relevance for discussions of the emergence of Israel with competing theories, especially with regard to pastoral and sedentarizing nomadism and agrarianism. For a sampling, see Giveon 1964, 1971; Weippert 1971: 106 n. 14; 1974a; 1974b; Lorton 1971–1972 (review of Giveon); Ward 1972; 1992; Hermann 1981: 76–77; 1973: 24–31; de Vaux 1978: 334; Astour 1979; Yurco 1978, 1986, 1990, 1991, 1997; Gottwald 1979; Aḥituv 1984: 121–122; Stager 1985b; Redford 1986: 199–200; 1992: 269–280; Ahlström 1986: 59–60; Mazar 1981: 7; Weinfeld 1987: 304, 312 n. 8; Coote and Whitelam 1987: 106–109; Axelsson 1987; Finkelstein 1988; de Moor 1990: 111–112; Coote 1990: 75–85; Rainey 1991; Rainey and Notley 2006: 92–96, 103, 111–112; Kitchen 1992; Hopkins 1993; MacDonald 1994; Edelman 1995: 8–9; Hasel 2003; Faust 2006: 170–187; Grabbe 2017: 53–55, 123–130; Dever 2017: 102, 200–207, 249–253; Adrom and Müller 2017; Smith 2017: 23–29; and Fleming forthcoming.
54. See Seti I's battle reliefs, portrayed on the northern outer wall of the Hypostyle Hall, and Merneptah's battle reliefs, depicted on the western face of the enclosure wall of the Cour du Cachetter. See Rainey and Notley 2006: 92–96, 103; 2001a; Hasel 2003: 28–31; and Yurco 1990: 33–35.
55. The parallels with Gen 12:10 and 42:2ff have been pointed out by Na'aman (1994b: 244–245). Compare Redford 1987: 141–142 and Kitchen 1992: 27.
56. Na'aman (1992) argues similarly. Weinfeld (1987: 310) also refers to the excavations at Timna (19 mi. [30 km] north of the Gulf of Aqabah) with its Midianite sanctuary and copper snake.
57. Edelman 1995: 8 n. 34 contains additional bibliography on theories regarding the location of Seir.
58. Cross 1973: 62, following Helck. Albright (1968a: 171) previously vocalized it as *Y(a)hw(e?)*, and Weippert (1971: 106 n. 14) vocalized Jah(u)wi'. Aḥituv, Eshel, and Meshel (2012: 129) give the following phonetic options: *ya/i/u-h-wa/i/u*.
59. I still view the *š3sw s'rr* material here to be relevant. Yet readers are directed to a forthcoming probing study by Daniel Fleming that argues that our oldest evidence associated with Amenhotep III was reinterpreted in light of the later Ramses II material with its connection to Seir and the southern wilderness. In short, Fleming argues that we should reconstruct the early history of Yhw3 without Seir. For Fleming, the Egytian Shasu Yhw3 is almost certainly a people and one that predated Israel. I thank him for sharing his perceptive analysis with me prior to publication.
60. Redford 1992: 272 n. 67, 273 n. 72. Weinfeld (1987: 312 n. 8) is also unduly harsh when he calls Weippert and Astour's objections "hypercritical and far-fetched." For a

review of the data, see Adrom and Müller 2017: 111; their conclusion is that "scholarship has not advanced much further" than in the days of Astour, with many of the same questions remaining unresolved.

61. ANET 262, Kitchen 1992: 27. Cf. EA 288 (so Edelman 1995: 9).
62. One of Schneider's onomastic specialties is the study of Asiatic personal names in New Kingdom sources. See esp. Schneider 1992.
63. See Zivie-Coche 2011; Tazawa 2009; Cornelius 1994, 2004; Redford 1992: 125–237. See too the discussion of Egyptian Astarte in the Conclusion, p. 679.
64. Credit for disproving the older reading "Azriyau of Yaudi" (known to many as Azriyau the Judean and equated with Azariah/Uzziah of Judah) and all that goes with it (namely, that the Judean king Azariah was strong enough to lead a massive anti-Assyrian coalition of north Syrian states against Tiglath-pileser) goes to Na'aman (1974). In addition to Dalley, see the treatments by Tadmor (1961); Gray (1965: 181–182); Pitard (1987: 181 n. 90); Cogan and Tadmor (1988: 165–166); Pike (1990: 40), and especially Kuan (1995: 149–150), who has a full history of scholarship of the "Azriyau episode."
65. Cogan and Tadmor 1988: 166; van der Toorn 1992a: 90.
66. By this I do not mean to imply that the proto-Israelites were made up *primarily* of nomads. See Dever's critiques and the other literature, especially that of Faust, in note 53.
67. For example, Rollston 2015a; 2013b: 377–382; Levin 2014; and Garfinkel et al. 2015: 230. Cf. Tigay 1986: 68–69. Whether Qeiyafa has a Judean (cf. Garfinkel 2017) or north Israelite affiliation (cf. Fantalkin and Finkelstein 2017) does not settle the debate about the identity of *bʻl*. Yet as noted by Golub (2017: 29 n. 15), the Qeiyafa PN constitutes "the first occurrence of the element *bʻl* in a name found in a Judaean site." Cf. the sole occurrence of *bʻl* at Kuntillet ʻAjrud in the plaster text KA 4.2 and similar debates about its referent. See Chapter Ten, pp. 583–587 and Lewis 2020.
68. Sanders (2009: 114) notes how it is also "the first known alphabetic inscription to address an audience in the first-person voice of the king."
69. See line 18 of the inscription as well as our discussion in note 125. Rather than reconstructing ʼ[*t k*]*ly yhwh*, "vessels of Yahweh" (cf. Isa 52:11), some scholars suggest ʼ[*rʼ*]*ly yhwh*, "Ariels of Yahweh," or ʼ[*y*]*ly yhwh*, "rams/strong men of Yahweh." See Jackson and Dearman 1989: 94 n. 5. Lemaire (1994: 33), who is preparing the *editio princeps* of the Mesha stela once planned but never realized by Clermont-Ganneau in the late nineteenth century, translates "the *altar-hearths* of YHWH," seemingly reading ʼ[*rʼ*]*ly*. Some scholars (e.g., McCarter 1996: 91) also reconstruct a missing [Yahweh] in line 8, yielding "<Yahweh> resided there [*wyšb bh*] there during his [Omri's] days ... but Chemosh resided there [*wyšbh*] in my days." Other scholars (e.g., Lemaire 1994: 33; Jackson 1989: 97) translate *wyšbh* as from *šwb*, "to return," and come up with "He [i.e., Omri] lived there during his days ... ; but Chemosh *restored* it in my days." See Jackson 1989: 110 for discussion and bibliography.
70. For more on the use of divine *ḥrm*-warfare in the Mesha stela and elsewhere (e.g., KTU 1.13.3–7; the Sabaean texts RES 3945 and DAI Ṣirwāḥ 2005-50), see Chapter

Eight, pp. 462–463. On the use of the Mesha inscription as a historical source, see Emerton's (2002) judicious critique of T. L. Thomson.

71. Bordreuil, Israel, and Pardee 1996, 1998. See also the translation in Pardee 2002d: 86 and Dobbs-Allsopp et al. 2005: 567–573.
72. Shanks 1997c: 31–32; Eph'al and Naveh 1998; Rollston 1998: 8–9; 2003: 146, 158–173; Zevit 2001: 364; Lindenberger 2003: 109, 112.
73. For the final report on Kuntillet ʿAjrud, see Meshel 2012. Previously, see Meshel 1992; 1993: 1458–1464; Beck 1982: 3–86, plates 1–16; Hadley 1987: 213f; 2000: 106–155; Davies 1991: 78–82; Renz and Röllig 1995: 47–64; McCarter 1996: 105–110; 2000: 171–173; Gogel 1998: 413–415; Keel and Uehlinger 1998: 210–248; Zevit 2001: 370–404; Mastin 2004, 2005, 2009; Dobbs-Allsopp et al. 2005: 277–298; and especially Aḥituv 1992: 152–162; 2005; 2008. Aḥituv's later views are replicated in the final report.

For analyses (with many additional bibliographies) since the publication of the final report, see Lewis 2020; Schniedewind 2017, 2014; Ornan 2016; Schmidt 2016; Puech 2014; Blum 2013; Lemaire 2013; and Parker 2013: 109–116, 263–278.

For a discussion of the Bes-like figures from Kuntillet ʿAjrud Pithos A and whether they represent Yahweh and Asherah, see Chapter Seven, pp. 325–330.
74. For the paleographic dating of the inscriptions to the late ninth and early eighth centuries BCE, see Meshel 2012: 73–142, esp. 73–75, and Parker 2013: 263–278, esp. 265 n. 1235 with bibliography. Schniedewind (2017: 138) uses the distinctly different letters *h* and *t* from plaster inscriptions 4.1, 4.2, and 4.3 to argue that we have at least three different scribal hands. The pottery assemblage found at the site has been dated to the late ninth and early eighth centuries BCE (Ayalon 2012: 205–274; 1995: 198) and is in line with the range of dates yielded by the carbon-14 data (Carmi and Segal 2012: 61–63; 1996). See Schniedewind 2017: 142–144 for the argument that the carbon-14 data allow for his suggested earlier phase.
75. Meshel 1993: 1463–1464; 1997: 312; Hadley 1993. For the final report of the phases of architecture, written by Zeʾev Meshel and Avner Goren, see Meshel 2012: 11–59.
76. Zevit 2001: 374, 378–381. But see too Mastin 2004: 329–330.
77. Yet see the strong critiques by Zevit (2001: 374–375, n. 47), Schmidt (2002: 96, 98–99), and Naʾaman and Lissovsky 2008: 187–190.
78. There is no way of proving or disproving Naʾaman and Lissovsky's (2008: 190) "daring hypothesis." It is quite speculative to suggest that "Kuntillet ʿAjrud was probably dedicated to the goddess [Asherah]" and constructed by "a (possibly Israelite) king . . . for the sancta and treasures of the goddess Asherata" (Naʾaman and Lissovsky 2008: 200–201). There is no indication that Asherah was the preferred deity at this site, especially with the mention of the gods El and Baal/baal, and even more so with the multiple references to only Yahweh as the god granting blessings (discussed later).
79. For a full list of the onomastic record, see Aḥituv, Eshel, and Meshel 2012: 128–129. As for male divinity, apart from KA 4.2 (on which see Chapter Ten, pp. 583–587, and Lewis 2020), only Yahweh occurs both as an independent proper name and as a theophoric element in personal names. The full DN *yhwh* occurs five times (in KA 3.1; 3.6; 3.9; 4.1.1 [twice]), with the shortened DN *yhw* occurring two times (in KA 1.2; 3.9).

Of some twenty-six personal names, thirteen contain theophoric elements, of which 100 percent are Yahwistic: ʾlyw, ʾmryw, ḥlyw, ywʿsh, yw[], ʿbdyw, ʿbd[yw] ʿzyw, rʾy[w], šknyw, smʿyw, smʾy[w], šmryw. Granted, four of these thirteen are reconstructed (yw[], ʿbd[yw], rʾy[w], šmʾy[w]), yet such reconstructions are likely. If they are not included, the 100 percent statistic remains the same.

80. Meshel 2012: 76–77 = Dobbs-Allsopp et al. 2005: §KAjr 9. Dobbs-Allsopp et al. 2005: 277–278 includes a cross-reference to the text numbers in the earlier editions by Meshel, Davis, and Renz.

The personal name ʿObadyaw with its -yw theophoric element is distinctly northern, in contrast to the southern -yhw. The divine name yhw here is unusual. We would expect the form yhwh that is well attested in the other inscriptions from Kuntillet ʿAjrud, although yhw does also appear in Pithos B (mentioned later). It is possible that we have a scribal error where the engraver left off the final -h (Lemaire 1984; McCarter 1996: 110) or defective writing (Dobbs-Allsopp et al. 2005: 284). See too Zevit 2001: 381, 399. Bibliography can be found in Dobbs-Allsopp et al. 2005: 284.

For the idiom "blessed be X of DN" (brk hʾ lyhw), see Dobbs-Allsopp et al. 2005: 284, citing several parallels from the Hebrew Bible (Ruth 2:20; Judg 17:2; 1 Sam 15:13, etc.).

81. Meshel 2012: 87–91, figs. 5.26, 5.27, 5.28 = Dobbs-Allsopp et al. 2005: §KAjr 18. Some scholars (e.g., Weinfeld [1980: 284], Meshel [1992: 107], and McCarter [2000:a 171 n. 1]) reconstruct ʾšyw hmlk so that the unknown speaker would refer to ʾAshyaw (= biblical Yawʾash/Joash), the king of Israel, whose reign (ca. 802–787 BCE) would fit nicely with the date of the Kuntillet ʿAjrud inscriptions. On the transposition of theophoric and verbal elements, see McCarter 2000a: 171 n. 1.

82. On the syntax of the expression "DN of GN" (which is rare according to biblical Hebrew grammar), see McCarter 1987: 139–143 and the expanded discussion in Smith 2016: 71–98.

83. For El and Baal, see their mention in one of the texts written on plaster (see details on KA 4.2 in note 79). Meshel (2012: 133) leans toward viewing these terms as indicators of the syncretistic worship of Yahweh. For a full discussion, see Lewis 2020.

84. Lemaire (1984: 133) suggests that the author was a northern Israelite. For an elaboration of this thesis, see Mastin 2004: 330–331.

85. Meshel 2012: 92–103, figs 5.36–5.46. Cf. Dobbs-Allsopp et al. 2005: 293–298, KAjr 19–21. The inscription described in the present text (Figure 6.7) is Meshel's inscription 3.6.

86. Meshel 2012: 95–97. See too Meshel 1978 and various commentators: e.g., Weinfeld 1984: 125; Chase 1982: 63; Davies 1991: 81, §8.021; Aḥituv 1992: 157–158; 2008: 320–321; Renz and Röllig 1995: 62; Zevit 2001: 394; Dobbs-Allsopp et al. 2005: 293, §KAjr 19.

Curiously, Pithos B also contains four incomplete abcedaries, partially overlapping the main inscription (Meshel 2012: 102–103; inscriptions 3.11–3.14). The precise function of these abcedaries in unknown. Zevit (2001: 398), following Naveh, suggests "that they might be a form of a charm." He concludes that "the Ajrud inscriptions may provide the earliest examples of the alphabet in magic use." In contrast, Schiedewind (2014: 277–280, 284–285) argues that they give evidence of a scribal curriculum.

87. Meshel 2012: 127–128; Schniedewind 2014: 290; Smoak 2015: 63. Cf. Naveh 1979: 28–29, which deals only with the root *brk*. See Lindenberger 2003: 9 on the absence of Kuntillet ʿAjrud's fuller elaborate greeting formula found elsewhere in Hebrew letters. Contrast a similar sentiment yet with distinctly different vocabulary in Ugaritic's *yšlm lk ʾilm [lšlm] tǵrk tšlmk*, "May it be well with you. May the gods protect you and keep you well." For attestations, see Loewenstamm 1969: 52 nn. 5, 6, to which now add RS 92.2005 and RS 92.2010. See Bordreuil and Pardee 2001: 371–379 and Pardee 2002b: 112.
88. The presence of third-person masculine singular verbs and hence only one blessing agent (Yahweh) has been pointed out previously (e.g., Tigay 1987: 190; Emerton 1999: 320), although frequently overlooked in subsequent (and especially popular) publications. The final report from Kuntillet ʿAjrud does indeed stress the masculine singular verbs, underscoring that this is "no trivial matter," as it has implications for the nature of the word *ʾšrth*, which "seems to refer to a sacred object rather than the goddess Asherah" (Meshel 2012: 132).
89. Naʾaman and Lissovsky 2008: 200–201, emphasis mine. Though Naʾaman and Lissovsky view the Kuntillet ʿAjrud complex as being built "for the sancta and treasures of the goddess Asherata" (on which see note 78 and Schniedewind 2014: 273–274), here they tone down her role, asserting that the goddess "may have acted as a divine intercessor between individuals and YHWH."
90. Cf. too Keel and Uehlinger's (1998: 237) conclusion underscoring the subordinate nature of the *asherah*: "Neither the iconography nor the texts [at Kuntillet ʿAjrud] force us to interpret the relationship between 'Yahweh . . . and his *asherah*' in Iron Age IIB in the sense of a (sexually-determined) relationship of two forces that are paired and thus compel us to assume that the *asherah* has the status of a partner. 'Yahweh's *asherah*' does not have equal rank with Yahweh but is rather a *mediating entity* that brings *his* blessing and is conceived in the mind in the shape of a stylized tree that was thus subordinate to Yahweh."
91. Meshel 2012: 98–100, inscription 3.9.
92. Note the presence of the article here (*htmn*, "the Teman"), which could easily designate "the Southland." See the grammatical parallels in the Hebrew Bible listed in Zevit 2001: 399. See too McCarter 2000a: 172 n. 1 on the northern (Israelite) form *tmn* in contrast to the southern (Judahite) *tymn*, which also occurs at Kuntillet ʿAjrud in one of the plaster texts (described later). For a sampling of some of the further analysis of the phrase "Yahweh of Teman," see Emerton 1982: 9–13; McCarter 1987: 139–143; Hadley 2000: 127–129; Zevit 2001: 395–396; Mastin 2004: 332; and Lewis 2020.
93. For this exact idiom, cf. Ps 20:5. The divine name *yhw* here, rather than the full *yhwh* that appears in this same inscription, also occurs in the stone basin. See note 80.

Just prior to this is a reference to a person (*ʾš ḥnn*) acting benevolently that has previously been read as a reference to Yahweh being a compassionate god (*ʾl ḥnn*) (McCarter 2000a: 172 n. 3, followed by Dobbs-Allsopp et al. 2005: 296). While we do have *yhwh* (and *yh*) being referred to as *ʾl ḥnn* at Khirbet Beit Lei (see note 111), the reading here (*ʾš ḥnn* and not *ʾl ḥnn*) seems clear (Meshel 2012: 98–100; Parker 2013: 270–271).

94. See inscriptions 4.1–4.6 in Meshel 2012: 105–121 as well as the treatments by Mastin (2009); Parker (2013: 109–116); Blum (2013); Lemaire (2013); Puech (2014); and Lewis (2020).
95. This text survives in a very broken state. My translation here reflects the readings on the photograph (*[y']rk.ymm . wyśbʿw/hyṭb.yhwh.[]y*) from Meshel 2012: 106, fig. 5.50b; see also Renz and Röllig 1995: 58. Similarly, see McCarter 2000a: 172; Gogel 1998: 413, §K. Ajrud 7; and Davies 1991: 80, §8.015. Other renderings (e.g., Dobbs-Allsopp et al. 2005: 285, §KAjr 14; Zevit 2001: 373; Meshel 1993: 1462; Aḥituv 1992: 158–159) include an extra middle line that has references to Yahweh and Asherah (*l[y]hwh []tmn wl[]ʿšrt*) based on other fragments. The blessings mentioned in this prayer are echoed with strikingly similar vocabulary in Deut 4:40, 5:16, and 22:7 as rewards for obedient living (cf. Deut 5:26, 12:25).
96. The two plural verbs in this text (*wyśbʿw, [wy]tnw*) refer to humans, not deities.
97. Aḥituv 2014: 36–37.
98. See Cross 1983, which dates the seal to the first half of the eighth century BCE. See too Avigad and Sass 1997: 25–26, 59, 466, and Avigad 1987: 197–198.
99. For the precise location of Khirbet el-Qom, see Dever's detailed map of Iron Age sites in the central Judean hills (1969–1970: 141, fig. I).
100. There has been some confusion in reporting where the inscription was found. Holladay (1992: 98) remarks that it came from Tomb I, while Dever (1997: 391) says that it came from Tomb III. Personal communication with Dever confirms that it was from Tomb II, as originally stated in Dever 1969–1970: 146.
101. Those scholars who have argued for an apotropaic function include Schroer (1983), Keel and Uehlinger (1998: 237), Puech (1992: 128), Hadley (2000: 103–104), Zevit (2001: 368–369), Lewis (2012: 109–112), Schmidt (2016: 149–162), Mandell and Smoak (2016: 242; 2017a: 190, 192), and Suriano (2018: 117). Note too the so-called ghost letters (i.e., the doubling and tripling of letters) in line 3, which have made this line extremely difficult to interpret. Zevit (2001: 362) notes how such letters "are found in much later incantations."

    Mandell and Smoak's (2017a) study also emphasizes the tomb as an interactive physical space that included non-linguistic modes of communication. Visual aesthetics (including the skeleton, architecture, and funerary objects as well as the darkness of the tomb itself) and olfactory sensations would have communicated through a "physical syntax."
102. Notable studies include Lemaire 1977; Naveh 1979; Miller 1981; Mittman 1981; Dever 1984; Zevit 1984; Hadley 1987; 1994: 242–245; Shea 1990; Hess 1991: 23–26; Renz and Röllig 1995: 199–211; Keel and Uehlinger 1998: 237–240; McCarter 2000d: 179; Dobbs-Allsopp et al. 2005: 408–414; Aḥituv 2008: 220–224; Smoak 2015: 54–55; Schmidt 2016: 144–162; Mandell and Smoak 2017a; and Suriano 2018: 112–117.
103. Zevit (2001: 360 n. 10) argues that the correct reading is *brkt*, "I blessed."
104. Personal communication, Daniel Fleming.
105. See conveniently Dobbs-Allsopp et al. 2005: 405–419, 575–578 and Aḥituv 2008: 226–230. For the *editio princeps*, see Naveh 2001: 194–207. See too Lemaire 2006: 231–238.

106. Mettinger (1988: 125, 152) notes that divine name Yahweh Sebaoth occurs 284 times in the Hebrew Bible, mostly (88 percent) in the prophets, and often in connection with the Jerusalem Temple.
107. The various dates assigned to these inscriptions range from the eighth to the sixth century BCE. Lemaire favors an eighth-century BCE date, while Zevit (2001: 420) follows Naveh in dating them ca. 700 BCE. Suriano (2018: 79, 122) dates them to the seventh century BCE, while Cross (1970) and McCarter (2000b: 180) date the texts to the beginning of the sixth century BCE. For bibliography, see Mandell and Smoak 2016: 194 n. 9, 211–213.

    See Zevit 2001: 405–438 for a detailed study of the epigraphy of these inscriptions. See too Niditch 2015: 92–99 and Mandell and Smoak 2016 for analyses of the overall materiality of the funerary complex, and Suriano 2018: 78–80, 117–123 for an analysis of the inscriptions in the context of the care for the dead at Khirbet Beit Lei. Mandell and Smoak make a strong case against the "refugee hypothesis," which argued that the inscriptions were written by later refugees and thus unrelated to the burials. Instead, Mandell and Smoak (2016: 244) argue that "the inscriptions and drawings were an integral element in the construction and design of the tomb."
108. This is a representative sampling. For further bibliography including the analyses of Miller and Mittmann, see Renz and Röllig 1995: 242–251 and Dobbs-Allsopp et al. 2005: 125–132.
109. Cf. Zevit's (2001: 429–430) reading, which does not reconstruct the missing *y* of Yahweh: *hwš' hwh*, "Save. Destruction."
110. Our texts are admittedly difficult to read. Cf. the following representative sampling of interpretations:

    Naveh 1963: 84–86:
    Yahve [is] the God of the whole earth [*yhwh 'lhy kl h'rṣ*]; the mountains of Judah belong to him, to the God of Jerusalem [*hry yhd lw l'lhy yršlm*]. / The [Mount of] Moriah Thou hast favoured, the dwelling of Yah, Yahveh [*hmwryh 'th ḥnnt nwh yh yhwh*].

    Cross 1970: 300–302:
    I am Yahweh thy God [*['ʾ]ny yhw 'lhyk*]: I will accept the cities of Judah and will redeem Jerusalem [*'rṣh 'ry yhdh wg'lty yršlm*]. / Absolve [us] O merciful God! Absolve [us] O Yahweh [*nqh yh 'l ḥnn nqh yh yhwh*].

    Lemaire 1976: 558–560, followed by Suriano 2018: 120:
    YHWH is the God of all the earth [*yhwh 'lhy kl h'rṣ*]; the mountains of Judah belong to the God of Jerusalem [*hry yhwdh l'lhy yršlm*]. Intervene, merciful YHWH; absolve Yh-YHWH [*pqd yhwh ḥnn nqh yh yhwh*].

    McCarter 2000b: 179–180:
    Yahweh is the god of the whole earth [*yhwh 'lhy kl h'rṣ*]. The highlands of Judah belong to the god of Jerusalem [*hry yhdh l'lhy yršlm*]. Intervene, O compassionate god! Absolve, O Yahweh [*pqd yh 'l ḥnn nqh yh yhwh*].

    Zevit 2001: 417–427:
    YWHW, my god, exposed/laid bare his land]*yhwh 'lhy glh 'rṣh*]. A terror he led for his own sake to Jerusalem [*'rṣ yhd lw 'l yršlm*]. / The source smote

the hand. Absolve [from culpability] the hand, YHWH [*hmqr yd hyh nqh yh yhwh*].

Note how a single letter in the first line is the difference between whether we have a confessional statement that Yahweh is the God of "the entire earth" (*kl h'rṣ*) (Naveh, Lemaire, McCarter) or, in Zevit's words, "the first extra-biblical documentation reflecting the notion that the god of Israel used other nations" to "expose [the nakedness]" of his land (*glh 'rṣh*). That the biblical idiom for the latter typically (always?) has the word *'erwāh* following the verb *glh* (i.e., "to expose the nakedness") makes one lean toward the former confessional interpretation.

111. Cross and McCarter read *'l ḥnn*, whereas Lemaire reads *yhwh ḥnn*. Both Cross and McCarter prefer to see the double use of *yh* as a vocative particle rather than a short form for Yah(weh).
112. The bibliography for older treatments can be found in Dobbs-Allsopp et al. 2005: 150–151. For the most complete treatment, including a composite drawing based on new photographs and readings, see Zevit 2001: 351–359 as well as Aḥituv 2008: 236–239.
113. Zevit (2001: 356–357) presents two different interpretations for the curse mentioned in line 1 of the inscription pictured here, which reads *'rr 'šr ymḥḥ*. Either the curse is against a person who might deface an inscription or it is against the Assyrians.
114. Yet Aḥituv (2008: 237–239) reads *yhw*[] as the theophoric element of a personal name and [*h*]*mlk*, "[the] king." Thus for Aḥituv, Yahweh does not appear in this text.
115. Aharoni 1966. For a brief description of the Arad inscriptions and their contents, see Lemaire 1997: 176–177. For collections of the Arad texts, see Aharoni and Naveh 1981; Pardee 1982; Davies 1991: 11–38; Aḥituv 1992: 54–96; 2008: 92–153; Renz and Röllig 1995: 347–403; Dobbs-Allsopp et al. 2005: 5–108. For convenient translations of selected texts, see Pardee 2002e: 81–85 and Lindenberger 2003: 113–124.
116. For other uses of the expression *bêt-yhwh* referring to sanctuaries other than Jerusalem, cf. Josh 6:24 and 1 Sam 1:7.
117. The first announcement of the inscriptions appeared in Hebrew in *Cathedra* (Barkay 1989: 37–76), with the formal expanded *editio princeps* appearing in English in the journal *Tel Aviv* three years later (Barkay 1992: 139–192). In between Ada Yardeni (1991) published one of the first substantial studies of the text. In 2004, a team of epigraphers (Bruce Zuckerman, Marilyn Lundberg, and Andrew Vaughn) teamed up with Gabriel Barkay, the lead excavator of Ketef Hinnom, to produce "a substantial revision and rereading" on which the present treatment is based. See Barkay et al. 2004. See too Aḥituv's (2012) response to Na'aman and Berlejung's attempts to date the inscriptions in the Persian period. For more recent studies of the inscriptions within their broader funerary context, see Smoak 2015; Schmidt 2016: 123–144; and Suriano 2018: 88–90, 123–127. Suriano too views the seventh-century BCE date as secure.
118. On the elite nature of the tombs, see Dever 1999: 10*.

119. See Chapter Four, pp. 85–86, on the deity El Berit.
120. For the epigraphic analysis of KH II. 2–5, see Barkay et al. 2004: 41–71. For the use of the Ketef Hinnom inscriptions as incantations (and an analysis of the key verb *gʿr* and the Dead Sea Scroll material), see Lewis 2012.
121. On the apotropaic character of the Khirbet el-Qom inscription, see note 101. Compare too the frequent appearance of (Egyptian) amulets in Judean tombs of the Iron II period. See Bloch-Smith 1992a: 85–86; Keel and Uehlinger 1998: 350; Lewis 2012: 103–104; and Schmidt 2016: 124–128, 140–144.
122. Barkay et al. (2004: 68) also contrast the social context here with that lying behind Num 6: "The use of the confessional statement in Ketef Hinnom I, however, introduces a context associated with personal piety and family life—that of family tomb and burial of an individual. The blessing itself [i.e., Num 6:24–26], which is found in a cultic context in the MT, is thus shown by these inscriptions also to have been used in personal and family context." For more on incantations and family religion, see Lewis 2008a: 76–77; 2012.
123. For an introduction to the Lachish inscriptions and various studies concerning their language and content (including the *editio princeps* of texts #1–18 by Torczyner), see Pardee 1997f: 323–324. For collections of the Lachish texts, see Pardee 1982; Davies 1991: 1–10; Aḥituv 1992: 31–54; 2008: 56–91; Renz and Röllig 1995: 405–440; Dobbs-Allsopp et al. 2005: 299–347. For convenient translations of selected texts, see Pardee 2002f: 78–81 and Lindenberger 2003: 124–131.
124. See in particular Lachish letter #3, which has been called "The Letter of a Literate Soldier," and Schniedewind's (2013: 106–110) comments about illiteracy being socially stigmatized.
125. See the Ataroth material discussed in Chapter Five, note 172. Cross' treatment (which follows the reconstruction "[ve]ssels of Yahweh," [*k*]*ly yhwh*, in line 18) forms a part of his reformulation and updating of the Midianite hypothesis (on which see pp. 276–277). The other traditional reconstruction ("the a[ltar-hea]rths of Yahweh," [*rʾ*]*ly yhwh*) is based on the unbroken occurrence of *ʾrʾl* in line 12. See, for example, Rainey's analysis in Rainey 2001b and Rainey and Notley 2006: 203–204, 211–212. Rainey (in Rainey and Notley 2006: 204) understands Nebo as "an isolated Israelite place" from which "Mesha was able to confiscate more cult objects of YHWH." The altar hearth served as "an enemy cult object captured" [as . . .] war booty . . . presented to the conquering [deity] Chemosh" (Rainey 2001b: 304). Cf. lines 10–13, where Mesha acted similarly at Ataroth, what Rainey terms "an original YHWH shrine facing a shrine to Chemosh" (Rainey and Notley 2006: 204). Rainey reads line 12 as "its *Davidic* altar hearth" (*ʾrʾl dwdh*), yet the possessive suffix on a personal name would be highly unusual.

Another reconstruction that has found less of a following is that of Lipiński (1971b: 335; cf. Kang 1989: 80), who reads "the [ra]ms of Yahweh" (*ʾ[t. ʾl]y yhwh*). This too would likely be cultic in nature, referring to animals sacrificed. Lipiński refers to Isa 1:11 and Mic 6:6–7a, which mention ram offerings to Yahweh. According to Lipiński, who cites 2 Kgs 3:4, the "rams of Yahweh" here refer to Moabite tribute that "belonged most likely to the Israelite royal temple of Bethel."

Thus he remarks that "one cannot conclude from the Moabite inscription that Nebo possessed a sanctuary of Yahweh." In other words, "the rams of Yahweh" were rams taken from Nebo (Mesha line 17, "and I took *from there*," *w'qḥ mšm*, clearly marks Nebo as the antecedent) but used for cultic activity elsewhere.

126. Compare Zevit 2001: 687, which likewise concludes: "YHWH was worshipped in some parts of Israel by the tenth century and . . . his cult spread and was pan-Israelite by the end of that century."
127. For a detailed list of these texts and secondary literature, see McCarter 2008b: 48–49.
128. Cf. Cross 2003: 198–199, fig. 29.5, which mentions the "provisional" reading of *ywḥnn* ("Yah[weh] is gracious") on an Old Canaanite arrowhead. If the reading is correct, Cross (2003: 199) notes how it would constitute "the earliest extra-biblical occurrence" "of a Yahwistic name" and one with "orthography following early (North) Israelite practice." Yet note Cross' caution that "there is still need for a careful study." Cf. too Bordreuil's (1992: 208, fig. 2) decidedly different reading.
129. See McCarter 1996: 77–80; Cross 2003: 200–202, 333; and Hess 2007c: 116–120. If the reading *'l'b* is secure on an Old Canaanite inscription from Lachish (Cross 2003: 293–296), then we would have a southern reference to the divine term *'il'ib*, which frequently designates either the divine ancestor or the god worshipped by one's ancestor at Ugarit. For the distinction, see Lewis 2008a: 69–70; for relevant Ugaritic texts, see Lewis 2008a: 84 n. 50–51; 1989: 56–59.

The theophoric element *lb't*, "Lioness," occurs, yet it is uncertain whether the name designates Asherah, Anat, or Astarte (cf. Hess 2007: 119–120). Hess also lists additional possibilities, yet they are ambiguous: *mlk* = Milku? king?; *rp'* = Rapi'u? (DN) heals?

130. Tappy et al. (2006: 41) note how "the importance of having recovered the inscribed Tel Zayit stone from a secure archaeological context can hardly be overstated." Tappy (Tappy and McCarter 2008: 4), the director of excavations at Tel Zayit, also notes that the inscription was found "in a secondary (or perhaps even tertiary) archaeological context" and thus was written even "prior to its use in the construction of the 10th-century wall."
131. Carr 2008: 124–125. With respect to documenting the presence of Yahweh diachronically, we are speaking of "literacy" in narrow terms, as that which is the result of some type of scribal production. More recently, the broader discussion has become better nuanced, with scholars differentiating between different types of literacies, including functional literacy, semi-literacy, professional literacy, and especially multimodal features (e.g., visual aesthetics, spatial theory) that communicate extra-linguistically beyond the world of skilled scribes. For social linguistics and Northwest Semitic epigraphy, see Mandell and Smoak 2017a, 2017b.
132. The identification "nascent Old Hebrew script" is Rollston's description of McCarter's view. See pp. 234–235 on the possibility that the reading of *b'l* in the late eleventh-/early tenth-century BCE inscription from Khirbet Qeiyafa may refer to Yahweh.

133. According to Garr's (1985: 229–230) study of the dialect geography of Syria-Palestine, "Hebrew was a minor linguistic center within the Canaanite domain."
134. See Dearman 2006: 533 for a convenient but brief listing of the specific references to "the land," "cities," and "province" of Canaan in the Amarna letters via correspondence coming from Alashia, Babylon, Byblos, Egypt, and Tyre. References in Ugaritic to Canaan will be discussed later in this chapter. A reference to "the land of Canaan" also appears on the statue of Idrimi, the king of Alalakh, as a place where the king temporarily goes into exile.

    A more detailed assemblage (including translations) of these texts can be found in Lemche 1991a. The most exhaustive and authoritative linguistic treatment is found in the monumental four volumes of Rainey 1996a. See too Rainey's (2015) new edition of the entire corpus.
135. A well-written narrative about the origin of the Canaanites and the term "Canaan" can be found in Tubb 1998: 13–24.
136. The bulk of these inscriptions are collected in *Corpus Inscriptionum Semiticarum* (CIS), which was begun in 1867 with Ernest Renan serving as the initial editor and completed in 1962 by J. B. Chabot and J. G. Février. For a survey of the extant corpus, see Schmitz 2004: 545–547.
137. This is *not* to say that such myths about Melqart of Tyre or Adonis of Byblos cannot be reconstructed from piecemeal Phoenician references and a wide array of outside sources. For a detailed and well-balanced overview of the data, see Mettinger 2001.
138. Convenient translations of some of the major the Phoenician (and Phoenician-related) monumental inscriptions and mortuary inscriptions can be found in Hallo and Younger (2000). These include the following inscriptions (and the following explicit mention of deities [i.e., setting aside the use of theophoric elements in personal names]):

    Yahimilk—KAI 4 (assembly of holy gods, Baal Shamem, Baalat)
    Yehawmilk—KAI 10 (Baalat, all gods of By[blos])
    Kulamuwa inscription—KAI 24 (Baal Semed, Baal Hammon, Rakib-El)
    Azitawada/Karatepe—KAI 26 (Baal, Baal Shamem, El, Reshep, Shemesh, the gods)
    Ahiram—KAI 1 (none mentioned)
    Tabnit—KAI 13 ('Ashtart, Rephaim)
    Eshmunazor—KAI 14 ('Ashtart, 'Ashtart-Name-of-Baal, Baal, 'Eshmun, holy gods, gods of Sidon, Rephaim)
    Pyrgi—('Ashtart)

    A translation of the Punic "Marseilles" Sacrificial Tariff (KAI 69) mentioning the temple of Baal-Saphon can be found in Hallo and Younger 1997: 305–309, §1.98. The seventh-century BCE treaty between Esarhaddon and King Baal of Tyre (Parpola and Watanabe 1988: 24–27; ANET: 533–534) mentions the following West Semitic/Tyrian deities: Anat-baytel, Ashtart, Ba'l Shamem, Ba'l Malage, Ba'l Saphon, Baytel, Eshmun, and Melqart.
139. Though the origin of the god Bes is in Egypt, it would be unfair to omit him from this list due to his ubiquitous presence in the Levant. See Chapter Seven, pp. 325–330.

140. See Gras, Rouillard, and Teixidor 1991; Smith et al. 2011; Schwartz et al. 2012; and Xella et al. 2013. For biblicists interacting with the Phoenician material as they wrestle with the question of child sacrifice in ancient Israel, see Dewrell 2017.
141. The Elyon passage is 1.10.15–30; see Attridge and Oden 1981: 46–55.
142. See too Barr 1974 and Lipiński 1983.
143. For a vigorous defense of the translation "rulers of foreign lands" rather than "shepherds" or "tribal leaders," see Rainey and Notley 2006: 57–60.
144. For a general introduction to MB and more recent terminology, see Burke 2014. For Middle Bronze Age IIA, cf. Cohen 2002; for an overview of the flowering of Canaanite culture in Middle Bronze Age IIB-C, cf. Tubb 1998: 55–69. Our emphasis on Egyptian cultural interactions is not to minimize what Schniedewind (2013: 31–32) refers to as the "long shadow" that Mesopotamian cuneiform culture cast over Canaan, as evidenced by the numerous cuneiform texts found at the MB city of Hazor (see Horowitz, Oshima, and Sanders 2006).
145. Cf. Redford 1992: 98–122; Oren 1997; Ryholt 1997: 118–150; Bietak 2001, 2010, 2016. These questions remain a vibrant area of exploration, as can be seen through the Egyptological ERC Advanced Grant awarded to the Hyksos Enigma project under the direction of Manfred Bietak under the auspices of the Austrian Academy of Sciences, with its bioarchaeological research component under the direction of Holger Schutkowski under the auspices of Bournemouth University, UK. See http://thehyksosenigma.oeaw.ac.at/news.
146. For translations of the New Kingdom Legend of Astarte and the Tribute of the Sea, see Wilson 1969b: 17–18 and Ritner 1997b: 35–36 as well as more recent research (e.g., Ayali-Darshan 2010, 2015). Ritner (1997b: 35) writes: "While this legend has been shown to have an indigenous Egyptian setting, it is yet parallel to, and likely inspired by, the Ugaritic story of the Fight between Baal and the sea god Yam, whose Semitic name is also used for the threatening deity in the Egyptian tale." See Ayali-Darshan 2015 on variant textual traditions across the ancient Near East.

On the syncretistic Egyptian/Canaanite pantheon attested in Proto-Sinaitic inscriptions at Serabit el-Khadim, see Chapter Four, pp. 75–76.
147. See, for example, Chapter Five, note 83, which describes a Middle Bronze Age seal depicting a seated El figure on a cylinder seal coming from a burial cave near Ras ʿAli in Naḥal Zippori.
148. Past studies include McGovern 1985; Bloch-Smith 1992a; Keel and Uehlinger 1992, 1996, 1998; Keel 1997; Zevit 2001; and the most comprehensive study to date, Christian Herrmann's multiple volume *Ägyptische Amulette aus Palästina/Israel* (1994, 2002, 2006, 2016). Zevit (2001: 344), using Herrmann's database, synthesizes the situation well:

> Egyptian amulets found at Israelite Iron Age sites reveal a remarkably restricted repertoire of gods and icons: Isis and the infant Horus; Sekhmet or Bastet; Bes; Ptah; and the divine eye, Udjet. Although Egyptian in design, the popularity of these particular figures may be indicative about the Israelites who purchased them. . . . These figures in Israelite comprehension and interpretation comprise a type of insurance against various ills that could befall the living. Inasmuch as

such amulets were sometimes used as grave goods, they may have also figured in Israelite conceptions of postmortem reality.

As for the reverse situation, Steiner (1992) has analyzed a handful of brief Northwest Semitic incantations found (transcribed in hieratic syllabic script) in the fourteenth-century BCE Egyptian texts known as the London Medical Papyrus. Some of these texts may also be found in Steiner 1997b: 328–329. The texts are brief, often fragmentary, and written in a *Mischsprache* type of language (e.g., Phoenician and Aramaic linguistic features) that remains puzzling. Nonetheless, it is clear that incantations were offered to several Semitic deities (e.g., Eshmun, Astarte) who were thought to be healing gods.

When first published, Steiner labeled these fourteenth-century BCE texts "the earliest Semitic texts written in an Egyptian script." In 2011 Steiner made news on a similar front by deciphering similar Semitic texts written in Egyptian but dating far earlier, to the twenty-fourth century BCE. See Steiner 2011, which notes that these incantations were used to prevent snakes from approaching the king's mummy. In particular, suggests Steiner, we are dealing with Byblian snakes that only understand incantations that are spoken in a Canaanite dialect and that appeal to the efficacious power of Semitic deities!

149. This institution has been well documented by many researchers, including this author, with ongoing studies incorporating new epigraphic sources. See Lewis 2008a: 74–76; 1989: 83–84; McLaughlin 2001; Greer 2007; and Dvorjetski 2016, the last of which includes a splendid survey and more recent bibliography.

150. Remarkably, the *marzeaḥ* institution is attested for nearly two millennia throughout the Levant and with consistent features. In addition to its presence at Late Bronze Age Ugarit (in Akkadian and Ugaritic texts), it is also attested in biblical texts (Amos and Jeremiah), Phoenician texts from Carthage and Piraeus, Aramaic texts from Elephantine, Palmyra, and Nabatea, rabbinical references by both the Tannaim and Amoraim, and the mosaic map at Madeba (sixth century CE). Though not homogenous, consistent features include the *marzeaḥ* organizations being associated with a particular patron deity, and with drinking (especially religious in orientation) as a primary activity. *Marzeaḥ* groups are gendered masculine, with the leader of the association consistently being referred to as the "head" (*rb mrzḥ*) and members referred to as the "men of the *marzeaḥ*" (*mt mrzḥ*) or the "sons of the *marzeaḥ*" (*bny mrzḥ*). Their activities regularly take place in a "*marzeaḥ* house" (*bt mrzḥ*), and real estate holdings can include vineyards.

151. For a general overview of Ugaritic studies, see Smith 2001a.

152. Smith (2002b) singles out the subtitle to W. F. Albright's book *Yahweh and the Gods of Canaan: A Historical Analysis of Two Contrasting Faiths*. Elsewhere, Albright (1961: 438) spoke of

> the extremely low level of Canaanite religion, which inherited a relatively primitive mythology and had adopted some of the most demoralizing cultic practices then existing in the Near East ... The brutality of Canaanite mythology ... passes belief.

Smith also refers to the following representative quotes by Gray and Oldenburg:

> The Canaanite literature never reaches the moral plane of the Old Testament.... The moral limitation of Canaanite religion was probably due to its preoccupation with ritual related to the phases of the agricultural year. This religion was essentially magical and, as such, a-moral. (Gray 1965: 257)

> The more I studied pre-Israelite religion, the more I was amazed with its utter depravity and wickedness. Indeed, there was nothing in it to inspire the sublime faith of Yahweh. His coming is like the rising sun dispelling the darkness of Canaanite superstition. (Oldenburg 1969: xi)

153. See the perceptive critique by Hillers (1985).
154. With regard to Albright's pejorative view of Ugaritic religion, Lewis (2006b: xxxi) writes as follows:

> As for being a historian of religion, Albright's days were those of particularism. The spirit of pluralism was rarely the mood of his times. (Vatican II was years away.) Lacking was any appreciation of Israel's Canaanite heritage when it came to language and archaeology. We must remember that when Albright went about working on Israelite religion, finds such as those at Kuntillet ʿAjrud (including an inscription mentioning "Yahweh and his asherah") lay buried. As for his depiction of the "brutality of the Canaanites," Albright was reacting against texts that were new in his day. ʿAnatu's "thirst for blood" and "massacre of mankind" in KTU 1.3 prompted his pejorative evaluation. Beautiful prayers we now know from our vantage point had yet to be published (cf. for example, KTU 1.119 whose *editio princeps* did not appear until 1978, seven years after Albright died).

For accessible surveys of the epigraphy and archaeology of Ugarit see Bordreuil and Pardee 2009; Pardee 2012b; and Yon 2006; to which add Matoïan and Vita 2014 on economic matters.

155. Broadly speaking, Rainey's and Naʾaman's articles critique the work of Lemche (1991a), whose rejoinder can be found in Lemche 1996b, 1998.
156. For an example of each position, compare Tropper (1994; 2000: 3–5), who is in favor of calling Ugaritic a Canaanite language, with Sivan (2001: 2–3), who opposes it.

Those in favor point to the following: the large shared vocabulary stock; NC > CC; *aw > $ô$ and *ay > $ê$; plural and dual endings with -m (contrast Aramaic); *$ṣ$ and *$ḍ$ > $ṣ$ (cf. Hebrew; contrast Aramaic); the Barth-Ginsberg law (*$yaqtal$ > $yiqtal$).

Those in opposition point to the following: Ugaritic has a fuller consonantal system (closer to Arabic); the $ā$ > $ô$ "Canaanite" shift is *not* in Ugaritic; the use of Š prefix for the causative stem; the relative = d/dt and not $š/˘š/˘ăšer$; the use of special forms for genitive/accusative of third-person pronouns (*huwati/hiyati/humūti*); the shift of $ẓ$ > $ġ$ (*$ẓuru$; Hbw $ṣur$; Arb $ẓirru$; Ugr $ġuru$); $ḏ$ > d (*ʾ$uḏnu$; Arb ʾ$uḏnu$; Ugr ʾ$udnu$) rather than $ḏ$ > z (Hbw ʾ$ozen$); the lack of definite article.

157. Tropper's (1994) analysis of Ugaritic as Northern Canaanite (as opposed to the Southern Canaanite of the Amarna letters as well as later differentiations between coastal dialects (Phoenician and Punic) versus inland dialects (Hebrew, Moabite, Edomite, Ammonite) makes good sense. Compare Halayqa 2008: 468. For the

assertion that Ugaritic is a direct descendant from a Levantine "Amorite" dialect, see Bordreuil and Pardee 2009: 19; Pardee 1997g: 376; 1997h: 262; 2012b: 23–24.

158. By asserting this we do not mean to ignore a significant overlap with Aramean religion. Cf., for example, the five deities attested in two Aramaic texts from Sam'al (Zincirli): Hadad, El, Rashap, Rakib-El, and Shamash. See further Chapter Five, p. 750, note 180.

159. For translations and analyses of the deity lists, see Pardee 2000: 291–319, 364–385, 400–402, 520–531, 659–660, 779–806 for a fuller treatment and 2002a: 11–24 for a brief synthetic presentation. The specific texts are: KTU 1.47 (RS 1.017); KTU 1.118 (RS 24.264+); KTU 1.148 (RS 24.643:1–9); Ugaritic V #18 (RS 20.024); RS 1.74 (RS 6.138); KTU 1.148 reverse (RS 92.2004/RS 24.643); KTU 1.102 (RS 24.246); KTU 1.65 (RS 4.474).

160. According to Pardee (2002a: 222), 234 different deities are attested in our extant ritual texts, "178 of which are specifically indicated in the sacrificial rituals as recipients of offerings."

161. For a detailed history of pioneering scholars in Ugaritology, see Smith 2001a and the summation in Schniedewind 2013: 40–44.

162. At the same time, Parker (1989b: 4) is adamant that he does "not wish to claim any direct connection" between Ugaritic and Hebrew narratives nor "to imply anything about the date of origins of the latter."

163. Polak acknowledges his indebtedness in building on the work of Cassuto and Cross.

164. Smith (2002a: 23) concludes that the "incidence of highly specialized sacrificial terms suggests a common Canaanite heritage."

165. Cf. too Ugaritic *šurpu*, which, according to Pardee (2002a: 225), "probably designates the holocaust or burnt-offering" similar to the Hebrew '*ōlāh*. Smith (2002a: 23) also sees the two terms as semantically equivalent. Yet one of the four major categories of offerings at Ugarit, the *ṭa'û* (an expiation sacrifice?), has no Hebrew parallel. Another dissimilarity is the presence of garments to dress the cult statue that are attested in Ugarit offering lists but not those of the Hebrew Bible.

For detailed analysis, see Pardee 2000. Pardee has written the most authoritative study of the Ugaritic ritual texts. According to Pardee (2002a: 224), ninety-two different types of objects representing offerings are documented. Although many of the terms are too hard to decipher, at least nineteen of the objects that were frequently offered are easily recognizable. In addition to Pardee, see the detailed work of Clemens (2001).

166. In a different direction, Sanders (2009: 4, 75) boldly argues that Ugaritic was "the first known vernacular literature in world history" and that it and Hebrew "represent the first attempts by people in the ancient Near East to write their own, local spoken languages." Furthermore, these "two oldest known major West Semitic vernaculars share a model of participation" and "a model of political communication" (2009: 66, 75).

167. For the mention of Arameans in the genealogies of Genesis and elsewhere in the Hebrew Bible, see Berlejung 2016; Younger 2016: 94–107.

168. For linguistic matters, see Huehnergard 1995; Fales 2011; and Gzella 2015: 53–103. For sociopolitical matters, compare what Neo-Assyrians referred to as "Aram" with what is presented in Old Aramaic inscriptions with the portrayal by biblical authors. See Younger 2016: 36–107.
169. For resources that detail much of what we know about the Arameans, see Pitard 1987, 1997; Sader 1987, 2014; Layton 1988; Schwartz 1989; Kuhrt 1995: 393–401; Dion 1995; Lipiński 2000, 2006: 203–244; 2013; Akkermans and Schwartz 2003: 360–397; Van de Mieroop 2004: 192–193, 211–214; Niehr 2014b; Gzella 2015; Sergi, Oeming, and de Hulster 2016; Younger 2016; and Berlejung, Maeir, and Schüle 2017.
170. This theory is that of Beaulieu (2006: 189; 2005: 44–46), who calls this portrayal "an invention of Sennacherib, who probably intended it as a mythological projection of the Assyrian king in his role as upkeeper of the imperial order, assisted in his task by the Arameans, who had become by then the largest non-native contingent in the Assyrian army and administration."
171. Following is the full list of deities mentioned in the major Archaic Aramaic inscriptions, including deities that are clearly Mesopotamian, Phoenician, and even non-Semitic. A full tabulation of divinity would need to incorporate iconographic representation and here too we have hybrid material. Compare Syro-Hittite representations such as those in Gilibert 2011 and Younger 2019.

The list is gleaned from the following texts, including both Old Aramaic texts and Sam'alian Aramaic texts: Bar-Rakib I, II—KAI 216–217; Hadad Inscription—KAI 214; Hazael inscription from Samos—KAI 311; Kulamuwa scepter inscription—KAI 25; Katumuwa (Pardee 2009); Bar Hadad/Melqart Stela—KAI 201; Nerab I, II—KAI 225–226; Panamuwa—KAI 215; Sefire—KAI 222–224; Tel Dan—KAI 310; Tell Fakhariyah—KAI 309; Zakkur—KAI 202; Bukan—KAI 320; the Ördekburnu inscription (Lemaire and Sass 2013). For an accessible introduction to Old Aramaic inscriptions, see Layton 1988, though it is out of date, as it does not include the Tel Dan inscription, discovered in 1993 (with two additional fragments found in 1994); the Bukan inscription, (re-)published in 1998; the Katumuwa inscription, discovered in 2008; and the new edition of the Ördekburnu that was published in 2013. For a scholarly edition, see Fales and Grassi 2016. As for including the Kulamuwa scepter inscription in the corpus of Old Aramaic inscriptions, see Yun 2008: 239 n. 6. According to Gropp (1997: 128), the language of the Nerab inscriptions "is transitional between the Old Aramaic of the ninth and eighth centuries [BCE] and the Official Aramaic of the Persian period." Sokoloff (1999: 106) places the Bukan inscription (ca. 700 BCE) in the Old Aramaic corpus as well even though it comes "from an area so far east of the Aramean homeland."

The order (arranged according to the English alphabet) is artificial.

The gods, *'lhy/'lhn/'lhyn* (Hadad, Tell Fakhariyah, Zakkur)
The gods of the house of my father, *'lhy byt 'by* (Bar-Rakib II)
The gods of Arpad, *'lhy 'rpd* (Sefire)
The gods of KTK, *'lhy ktk* (Sefire)
The gods of Y'dy, *'lhy y'dy* (Panamuwa)

The gods of the land, 'lhy mt (Hadad)
Abyss, mṣlh (Sefire)
'Arqu-Rashap, 'rqršp (Hadad)
Baal of Heavens/Ba'l-Shamayn, b'l šmyn (Zakkur)
Day, ywm (Sefire)
Earth/[God]s of the Earth, 'rq; ['lh]y 'rq (Sefire, Zakkur)
'Elyan, 'lyn (Sefire)
Hadad, hdd (Hadad, Hazael from Samos, Katumuwa, Panamuwa, Tel Dan, Tell Fakhariyah, Bukan)
Hadad of Aleppo, [hddḥ]lb (Sefire)
Hadad of Sikkan, hddskn (Tell Fakhariyah)
Hadad of the Vineyards, hdd krmn (Katumuwa)
Ḥaldi, ḥldy (Bukan)
Heaven/Gods of the Heaven[s], šmy[n]; 'l[hy] šmy[n] (Zakkur)
Ilu/El, 'l (Hadad, Panamuwa, Sefire)
Ilu-Wer/El-wer, 'lwr (Zakkur)
'Inurta (=Ninurta), 'nrt (Sefire)
Ir, 'r (Sefire)
Kadiah (?), kd'h (Sefire)
Kubaba, kbb (Katumuwa, Ördekburnu)
Laṣ, lṣ (Sefire)
Marduk, mrdk (Sefire)
Melqart, mlqrt (Bar-Hadad/Melqart)
Nabu, nb' (Sefire)
Nergal, nrgl/nyrgl (Sefire, Tell Fakhariyah)
Nikkal, nkl (Nerab I, Nerab II, Sefire)
Nikkar, nkr (Sefire)
Night, lylh (Sefire)
Nur, nr (Sefire)
Nusk, nsk (Nerab I, Nerab II, Sefire)
Rakib-El, rkb'l (Bar-Rakib, Hadad, Kulamuwa scepter, Panamuwa, Ördekburnu)
Rashap, ršp (Hadad)
Shahar/Śahr, šhr = śhr (Nerab I, Nerab II, Zakkur)
Shala, sl (Tell Fakhariyah)
Shamash, šmš (Hadad, Katumuwa, Sefire)
Sibitti, sbt (Sefire)
Sin, s[n] (Sefire)
Springs, m'ynn (Sefire)
Tashmet, t[šmt] (Sefire)
Zarpanit, zrpnt (Sefire)

172. The majority of these Mesopotamian deities occur in the Sefire inscriptions as witnesses to the treaty (Face A, lines 8–10) with 'Inurta (= Ninurta) singled out in the curse section (Face A, line 38). This stereotypical use causes Greenfield (1987a: 67) wisely to conclude that "the very god list was not 'Aramean' and cannot be used for

the discussion of the Aramean pantheon." Cf. too Lipiński (2000: 599): "The use of certain divine names in Aramean environment or even in texts written in Aramaic, for instance in the curses of the Sefire treaties, does not reflect *per se* the Aramean pantheon." One interesting point should be mentioned. Nergal occurs in the curse section of the Aramaic of the Tell Fakhariyah bilingual inscription but *not* in the corresponding Akkadian text (Tell Fakh, line 23). Cf. Gropp and Lewis 1985: 54.

As for Melqart's presence in the Bar-Hadad inscription, Pitard (2000: 153 n. 4) notes how this well-known Phoenician deity does not appear in any other Aramaic inscription. Pitard concludes that "there was a substantial relationship between Bir-Hadad's kingdom and the Phoenican coast." As for the Anatolian goddess Kubaba in the Katumuwa inscription, Pardee (2009: 62) suggests that Katumuwa "may be proclaiming his pan-Luwian ties."

173. These paired deities are attested in the witness section of the Sefire inscriptions (Face A, lines 11–12). Fitzmyer (1967: 38) argues correctly that "a certain numinous character was attributed to these natural phenomena, and they were probably objects of worship." Indeed, in the Sefire inscription they function as paired witnesses in the same way as do well-known Mesopotamian deities. On the other hand, they are not attested elsewhere in the other Archaic Aramaic inscriptions as named, functioning deities.

174. Elyan may not be an independent deity here but rather part of a double name for a single deity El-Elyan (cf. the Hebrew Bible's El-Elyon). See Chapter Four, pp. 86–95.

175. See Chapter Eight, pp. 439–440. For a convenient text and translation, see Nissinen, Seow, and Ritner 2003: 21–22, and Nissinen et al. 2019: 21–23 with additional bibliography.

For an example of Aramean royal cult involving the god Hadad, cf. the Old Aramaic Tell Fakheriyeh inscription. In lines 16–17, Hadd-yith'i, the king/governor of Guzan, mentions how vessels (*ma'nayya'*) inscribed with the king's name reside in the Temple of Hadad. That these vessels are cultic in nature is obvious from the context. Cf. too the use of the word *ma'nayya'* to describe the vessels of the temple of Jerusalem (Ezra 5:14, 15; 6:5; 7:19; Dan 5:2, 3, 23).

Interestingly, the Tell Fakheriyeh inscription also refers to Hadad as "a compassionate god" (Arm *'ilāh raḥmān*, line 5; Akk *ilu rēmē'û*, line 6), an exact etymological cognate to El and Yahweh being referred to as *'ēl raḥûm*. See Chapter Eight, pp. 480–481.

176. This has already pointed out by Greenfield (1976), Lemaire (1998), and Sokoloff (1999). For a nicely nuanced interpretation of Hadad's presence here among the Mannaeans (perhaps identified with the Urartian weather god Teisheba), see Eph'al 1999.

177. KTU 1.4.6.38–40; 1.4.7.35–39; 1.5.1.22–23; 1.5.2.21–23; 1.5.4.7; 1.10.2.1–2, 4–5, 32–33; 1.10.3.7–8; 1.12.1.40–41; 1.12.2.53–55.

178. Cf. Pardee 2002a: 11–24. There are two brief references to Haddu in KTU 1.102.15, 28: *[y]gbhd*, "Haddu is generous," and *ydbhd*, "Haddu is magnanimous." Pardee (2002a: 20) suggests that both these are references to hypostases of Ba'lu. Del Olmo

Lete (1999: 74 n. 79) refers to the reading of *add* in KTU 1.65.9, but this reading is very uncertain. Pardee (2002a: 23) reads *[n]dd*. For the use of Adad/Addu in personal names, see Gröndahl 1967: 114–115, 132–133, 318.

179. While there is some overlap, the Canaanite god Baʿlu/Baal should be distinguished from "the lord of the heavens," who occurs as Baʿl-Šamêm in Phoenician dress and as Baʿl-Šamayn in Aramaic (i.e., the Old Aramaic Zakkur inscription and the late seventh century BCE Adon/Adun Papyrus from Saqqarah [= KAI 266]). For a detailed treatment of this god, see Niehr 2003 and Chase 1994.

180. Fitzmyer 1995: 61; Younger 2016: 536 n. 170. Matîʿʾēl (Mati-ilu) is known from the famous mid-eighth-century BCE Old Aramaic Sefire inscriptions that mention his treaty with Bar-Gaʾyah, the king of KTK, as well as from his treaty with Aššur-nerari V (see Parpola and Watanabe 1988: xxvii–xxviii, 8–13 [Text 2]). For the most complete study of the reign of Matîʿʾēl, see Younger 2016: 526–547.

181. One plaque, the larger of the two, contains drawings of a type of winged sphinx along with a wolf that seems to be devouring a child. On its reverse is the drawing of a striding warrior deity with axe in hand. The second, smaller plaque contains the drawing of a large-headed ogre with what again seems to be human legs sticking out of his devouring mouth.

That both of these plaques are clearly incantations (complete with holes for hanging perhaps on a wall or around one's neck) comes from their content as well as the explicit designation of *lḥšt*, "incantation," that begins each inscription. We read of female "stranglers" known as *ḥnqt* (cf. Ugarit *ʾiltm ḥnkṭm*). The explicit spell spoken against them reads: "The house I enter you must not enter" (*bt ʾbʾ bl tbʾn*). This finds an exact parallel in the spell within the Ugaritic incantation KTU 1.169.18 (*bt ʾubʾu ʾal tbʾi*). Many aspects of the Arslan Tash incantations are debated (e.g., who are the *ʿpt*, "flyers"?), with many scholars advocating that they were used against night demons of some sort.

The secondary literature on these plaques (which includes discussions about their authenticity) is vast (cf. Chapter Four, note 98). See du Mesnil du Buisson 1939; Gaster 1942, 1973; Cross and Saley 1970; Cross 1974b; Zevit 1977; Sperling 1982; Teixidor 1983; van Dijk 1992; Pardee 1998; Avishur 2000; Conklin 2003; Cross and Saley 2003; and Berlejung 2010.

182. Cf. Garr 1985: 229; Huehnergard 1995: 276–282; Pardee 1998: 39–40; McCarter 2000c: 222; DeGrado and Richey 2017: 124 n. 89.

183. I follow most scholars in reading Baal rather than "lord" in Arslan Tash II, line 1. Scholars are divided with regard to rendering *bʿl* in Arslan Tash I, line 14. Here too I prefer the Canaanite god Baal, although the text may simply refer to "the lord [of . . .]." Regrettably, the context cannot help us decide, for the continuing text on the lower edge of the plaque is broken. I lean toward Baal due to his presence in Arslan Tash II as well as the preceding word *bʿlt* in line 14. Hence I prefer to translate *bʿlt bʿl* as "by the oath of Baal."

184. Line 2 mentions *ssm bn pdrš*, which can be taken as the Hurrian deity Sasm (McCarter 2000c: 222) or as a personal name designating the individual for whom the incantation was rendered (Conklin 2003).

185. On Balaam being referred to as being from Aram (Num 23:7), see Schüle 2017: 79.
186. So too Pfeiffer 2017: 115 n. 1-2; 143-144, who includes additional bibliography by Levin, Köckert, and Müller. Though Leuenberger (2017, 2015) does not embrace a northern provenance of Yahweh, he too includes additional bibliography of those who do. For resources on the widespread northern traditions of storm gods, see Schwemer 2001; 2008a; 2008b and Green 2003.
187. Fleming (forthcoming) has recently produced the most thorough study of the origin of the Midianite Hypothesis. Fleming shows how Tiele's argument was Kenite, not Midianite, and how his emphasis on the "wider desert" (i.e., not on the southern desert) would be lost in later formulations. I am indebted to Fleming for sharing his research with me prior to publication.

    For additional bibliography, see van der Toorn 1996b: 281-286; Blenkinsopp 2008; Blum 2012: 52-63; Römer 2015: 51-70; Pfeiffer 2017: 132-136; and Berner 2017: 193-196. Rowley (1950: 149 n. 4) claims that Stade's and Budde's adoption of the theory "brought about its wide acceptance." Wyatt (2005: 86) argues against conflating two distinct aspects of the hypothesis. He thus argues for separate terminology that distinguishes between the Kenite hypothesis and the Midianite hypothesis.
188. Bibliography on the archaeology of Midian is immense. Key works can be found in the bibliographies of Knauf 1988: 15-25; Parr 1988, 1992; Schloen 1993a: 31 n. 50; Cross 1998: 64 nn. 40, 41; Sawyer and Clines 1983; Rothenberg 1998, 1999a, 1999b; Levy 2009a, 2009b; and Monroe 2012. Stager (1998: 174) notes that Parr's archaeological survey is responsible for "the revival and revision of the Midianite hypothesis."
189. Sarna (1989: 36) goes on to emphasize the lack of any mention of Cain's lifespan or death notice as well as that of his immediate descendants: "[Cain's] entire line passes into oblivion."
190. Cf. Propp's (1999: 176) speculations about why P would write such invectives against the Midianites, who (we assume) were no longer a historical threat during his time. See too Monroe's (2012) study of the story of Cozbi the Midianite. She argues that the story goes back to an earlier human scapegoat tradition based on Hittite parallels (2012: 212 n. 1). On the latter, see too Westbrook and Lewis 2008.
191. Other passages that include hostility toward the Midianites include Num 22:4, 7; Josh 13:21; Ps 83:10 [Eng 83:9].
192. For discussion of the origin of judiciaries involving Jethro and Hobab, see Chapter Nine, pp. 525-528.
193. On the antiquity of this passage, see note 210.
194. This laudatory phrase is paralleled to "in the days of Shamgar, son of Anat." Regrettably, the heroic tales of this individual are only scantily recounted in a single verse (Judg 3:31).
195. Using cognate evidence from Mari (i.e., the term *ḫibrum*), Malamat (1962: 145) views the name Heber as "an allusion to a tribal subdivision that had broken away from the parent tribe." He is followed by Soggin (1981: 83), Halpern (1983: 393), Schloen (1993a: 32), and Ackerman (1998a: 99).

196. Deborah is specifically called a prophetess (*'iššâ něbî'â*) in Judg 4:4. See Ackerman's (1998a: 27–109) articulation of the roles of both Deborah and Jael in these narratives. In particular, note her intriguing suggestion (building on the work of Mazar [1965]) that Jael may have been a cultic functionary (Ackerman 1998a: 92–102).
197. These passages have been used to demarcate classic J and E literary strands. For example, Propp (1999: 50) writes that "a . . . difference between J and E is that the former calls Moses' father-in-law 'Reuel,' while the latter uses 'Jethro.'" As will be discussed, Num 10:29 (usually thought to be J) adds a wrinkle to the mix.

 It should be noted that Albright (1963: 5–6) deemed it "wholly unnecessary" to assume "that there were different traditions about the name of the 'priest of Midian.'" Yet Albright's solution is to eliminate Reuel from consideration due to it being a clan name. He does so by reconstructing Exod 2:18 to read originally: "[Jethro, son of] Reuel, their father." In my opinion, it makes more sense to consider varying literary traditions conflated together than to posit a different text for which there is no support in any of the versions.
198. More recent source-critical analysis (especially of Exod 18) finds little consensus. For a history of approaches, see Houtman 1996: 396–402 and Jeon 2017: 289–291. For his part, Jeon advocates for "multiple phases of composition and redaction," with Exod 18:1–12 constituting an early pre-Priestly strand, part of which (Exod 18:8–11) was reworked, revealing a "close linguistic affinity with late Levitical texts." In contrast, Pfeiffer (2017: 133) suggests that Exod 18:1–12 "may be a post-priestly addition, later updated by Exod 18:13–27."
199. For others who also view Hobab as the brother-in-law of Moses, see Moore 1958: 33 and Rowley 1950: 152. This seems easier than those who would equate Hobab and Jethro with Reuel being their father. See, for example, Milgrom 1990: 78 and Halpern 1992: 20.
200. Gray 1971: 208. For a brief overview, see Römer 2015: 62–68.
201. For the logical force of *'attâ* (whereby it should here be translated "and *as a result* I now realize that Yahweh is greater than all gods"), see Waltke and O'Connor 1990: 667, §39.3.4f. On *'attâ* as *Wendepunkt*, see Brongers 1965: 291–292. See too Schniedewind forthcoming.
202. Rowley's (1950: 159–160) apology strains credulity. He asserts that Yochebed's non-Yahwistic Levite ancestors married Yahweh-worshipping Kenites in Palestine in the Amarna Age (hence the eventual handing down of her Yahwistic name), but by her time her family of Levites (who had migrated to Egypt due to "some disaster") knew nothing of Yahweh. "Thus the name Yahweh might be known among the Israelites in Egypt, even though Yahweh were [*sic*] not the God whom they worshipped."
203. Moreover, what is the connection between this Reuel tradition and the Edomite Reuel traditions tracing back to a son of the legendary "Esau, the father of the Edomites in the hill country of Seir" (Gen 36:9–13)? In Gen 36:3–4, Reu-*El* is the son of Esau's wife Basemath, the daughter of Ishma-*El*. The name Reuel also appears in Tell el-Kheleifah Ostracon 6043.1 (Knauf 1992: 693).
204. For a history of the tribe of Reuben's inglorious past, see Cross 1998: 54 and Knoppers 2003a: 395–400.

205. Cross' theory contains his reconstruction of the priestly polemics between Mushite/Levite and Aaronid/Zadokite lines as well as the source criticism of the Baal Peor episode, the locating of Mt. Sinai/Horeb in southern Edom or northern Midian, the presence of a Reubenite shrine beneath Mt. Nebo, the Deuteronomist's tradition about the "second giving of the law" in the valley of Reuben, Num 33 as a pilgrimage station, and the nature of "Midianite ware," as well as various caravan traditions (cf. Schloen 1993a) and settlement theories. Herr 1999, Herr and Clark 2001, and Petter 2014 build on and update Cross' work by exploring the possibility of early Israelite identities in Central Transjordan, especially at Tall al-ʿUmayri and Tall Madaba.

206. The demise of caravan trade is clearly represented by the Hebrew ḥādĕlû ʾŏrĕḥôt (Judg 5:6). As with most scholars, we read "caravans" (ʾŏrĕḥôt) rather than MT's "paths" (ʾŏrāḥôt), the latter representing a slight mispointing that was occasioned in the MT by attraction to the "circuitous paths" (ʾŏrāḥôt ʿăqalqallôt) immediately following.

As for ḥādĕlû, Schloen (1993: 23) relies on the study by Lewis (1985) to counter the works of Thomas, Calderone, and Chaney (among others) that the root ḥdl (i.e., a putative ḥdl-II) refers to "peasantry growing plump."

207. Schloen here follows Coogan (1978: 148) in reading midyān for the MT's enigmatic middîn for which no other suggestion has won wide acceptance.

208. For his part, Cross (1998: 67 n. 48) referenced Schloen (1993a) in the 1998 reformulation of his original 1988 theory. Stager's (1998: 142–149, 173–174) synthesis combines elements of both Schloen and Cross.

209. Van der Toorn (1996b: 285–286) cites the following: (1) how the genealogies in Genesis (regarding the Edomites) and 1 Chr 2:50–55 (regarding the Gibeonites) correspond; (2) the presence of Doeg the Edomite in Saul's royal court, and (3) Saul's sparing of the Kenites in 1 Sam 15:6.

210. Note in contrast how Fleming (forthcoming) takes an altogether different approach. Fleming finds the Midianite Hypothesis to be fatally flawed and argues that the earliest Egyptian Shasu Yhw3 (that of fourteenth-century BCE Amenhotep III) should be interpreted apart from a southern origin.

As for old poetic expressions, we agree with those who see archaic material in Judg 5 (e.g., Smith 2014a: 211–266; Leuenberger 2017: 173–177; Fleming forthcoming) as well as in Ps 68, Deut 33:2, and Hab 3 (though the last could be archaizing), as opposed to Pfeiffer (2017: 121–129; 2005), who sees their origination in the post-exilic period with redactional layers in the Hellenistic period in the second century BCE. Pfeiffer (2017: 125) does allow that "the kernel of the history of origin is an epic song from the 9th or 8th century BCE." See Chapter Three, note 27; Chapter Eight, note 68; and Keel's (2017: 66) critique. The ninth-century BCE (or early eighth-century BCE) Kuntillet ʿAjrud plaster text 4.2 is particularly relevant for anchoring these traditions in the early period. See Lewis 2020; 2013b; and Chapter Ten, pp. 583–587. See too Schniedewind 2017 for the argument that some of the material at Kuntillet ʿAjrud may go back to the tenth century BCE.

211. On rendering yhwh zeh sînay as "Yahweh, the one of Sinai," see note 229.

212. Along with most scholars, we read yhwh throughout due to the rather consistent practice of the editor of the Elohistic Psalter to use the substitute ʾĕlōhîm out of

deference to the sacred name Yahweh. Comparing Ps 68:8–9 (Eng 68:7–8) with the exact wording in the unmodified Judg 5:4–5 is especially convincing in this regard. See note 229 and Chapter Four, p. 724, note 65.

213. On rendering *yhwh zeh sînay* as "Yahweh, *the one of* Sinai," see note 229.
214. *šin'ān* is a *hapax legomenon* for which there is no easy solution. We follow those who see it as an "equivalent to repetition" related to *šnh* (cf. HALOT, p. 1596). We reconstruct *yhwh* rather than the MT's secondary *'ǎdōnāy*. In addition, we follow most scholars in reading *yhwh bā' missînay* (cf. *yhwh missînay bā'* in Deut 33:2) rather than MT's *bām sînay* (lit. "among them, Sinai"). Alternatively, Albright (1950–1951: 14, 25) and Cross (1973: 102) reconstruct "when they/he came from Sinai" (*běbō'ām/běbō'-m missînay*) and take *yhwh* with the previous verse. Indeed, such a reconstruction is much better metrically.

This verse goes on to mention Yahweh coming from Sinai to enter into the sanctuary (*baqqōdeš*), a later reference to the Jerusalem sanctuary, which is also mentioned with the same word (*qōdeš*) in Ps 68:25 [Eng 68:24]. Yet if we consider the full weight of Deut 33:2's *wě'ātā mēriběbōt qōdeš* ("with him [**ittô-m*] were myriads of holy ones"), then it is certainly possible, as Cross (1973: 102) has reconstructed, that originally *qōdeš* referred to the divine retinue known as "the Holy Ones" and only later (by attraction to Ps 68:25) came to be understood as his royal sanctuary in Jerusalem.
215. For a more detailed discussion of this passage, see Lewis 2013b.
216. We leave the two occurrences of MT's *lāmô* ("upon them") untranslated, for they likely reflect a later understanding of Yahweh shining upon Israel. Because of its lack of antecedent, *lāmô* is an ill fit for the original setting. The reading of *lānû* ("upon us") found in several of the versions and reconstructed by many commentators seems to be a secondary change trying to deal with a *lectio difficilior lāmô*. The emendation to *lě-'ammô* ("upon his people/army") is a creative solution, yet too conjectural.
217. Here we follow most scholars who read the preposition "with" plus enclitic *-m* (*'ittô-m*) based on the LXX, Targums, and Vulgate rather than the MT's pointing *'ātâ* ("he came"). The MT's vocalization seems secondary, the result of the influence of late Aramaic (cf. also *wayyētē'* in 33:21). The occasion for the mispointing of the MT is surely its lack of knowledge of how *-h* in early (tenth-century BCE) orthography can represent a third-person masculine singular suffix, a feature well attested from our epigraphic sources. See Cross and Freedman 1975: 72 n. 8. Yet if the MT stands, the meaning of the passage remains unchanged.
218. The enigmatic *ēš dāt* is discussed at length in Lewis 2013b and Chapter Seven, pp. 348–349.
219. On *těhillâ* as radiance, see Aster 2006: 183–186; 2012: 133–135.
220. We leave out here the problematic prose phrase *taḥat 'āwen rā'îtî* ("under iniquity, I saw"), for which there is no suitable solution.
221. Our passage contains the only occurrence of *kûšān*. We agree with Andersen (2001: 312) that "this is certainly the Cush associated with Midian (and Moses), not Ethiopia or any other place." Cf. too HALOT (p. 467), which defines it as an "Arabian nomadic tribe."

The root *rgz* can refer to quaking with fear (Hab 3:16; Isa 32:10ff; Joel 2:1) as well as the physical quaking of the earth (e.g., Ps 77:19 [Eng 77:18]; Joel 2:10). Here the poet has inanimate tents quaking at the appearance of the divine warrior Yahweh, a theophany that at the same time strikes terror in the hearts of those who dwell in those tents (cf. *yārē'tî* in Hab 3:2a).

222. Meshel 2012: 95–97; Inscription 3.6 = Dobbs-Allsopp et al. 2005: 293–295; §KAjr 19A = McCarter 2000a: 171–172; §2.47B.
223. Meshel 2012: 98–100; Inscription 3.9 = Dobbs-Allsopp et al. 2005: 295–296; §KAjr 20 = McCarter 2000a: 171–172; §2.47B.
224. Meshel 2012: 105–107; Inscription 4.1.1 = Dobbs-Allsopp et al. 2005: 285–286; §KAjr 14 = McCarter 2000a: 172; §2.47C.
225. The two words (*šnt*, [*y*]*hw*[*h*]) marked with an asterisk (*) come from the second smaller fragment. For a detailed analysis of the readings of this text and whether it refers to Yahweh as "the Holy One," see Lewis 2020 and Chapter Ten, pp. 583–587.
226. McCarter (1992: 124) translates this as a place name, Yeshimon.
227. Our interest here is the origin of the deity Yahweh, not a people group named Yahweh. For this topic, see Fleming's (forthcoming) study of the Yahw3 of Shasu land, an early Yahweh people (*'am yhwh*; cf. Judg 5:13) apart from Israel.
228. See Chapter Three, pp. 66–68.
229. The expression "Yahweh, the one of Sinai" (*yhwh zeh sînay*) that is found in Judg 5:5 also occurred in an earlier version of Ps 68:9 that currently reads *'ĕlōhîm zeh sînay* in the MT. This later (secondary) reading resulted from the activity of the unnamed editor who regularly (though not universally) replaced *yhwh* with *'ĕlōhîm* in the Elohistic Psalter (Ps 42–83). Cf. too Ps 68:8's *'ĕlōhîm bĕṣē'tĕkā* for Judg 5:4's *yhwh bĕṣē'tĕkā* and Ps 68:9's *'ĕlōhîm 'ĕlōhê yiśrā'ēl* for Judg 5:4's *yhwh 'ĕlōhê yiśrā'ēl*. The extremely close (often word-for-word) relation of Judg 5:4–5 and Ps 68:8–11 reveals a common tradition that according to text-critical principles certainly read *yhwh zeh sînay*.

In the phrase "Yahweh, *the one of* Sinai" (*yhwh zeh sînay*), *zeh* functions as a nominal demonstrative. Lipiński (1994: 52–53) has noted the same exact function in Aramaic, Akkadian, and Arabic. See too Waltke and O'Connor 1990: 337 nn. 23, 24. Of particular note is the ninth-century BCE Old Aramaic inscription from Tell Fakheriyeh that reads "Hadd-yith'i, the king of Guzan, and *the one of* Sikan and *the one of* Azran" (*hdys'y mlk gwzn wzy skn wzy 'zrn*). That there is no *zy* in the phrase "king of Guzan" (*mlk gwzn*) shows that the two following occurrences of *zy* do not mark the genitive but rather function as a nominal demonstrative.

The ancient lore surrounding Yahweh's presence at Sinai is also reflected in the wordplay behind Yahweh's epithet "He who dwells in the bush" (*šōknî sĕneh*) in Deut 33:16. See Chapter Seven, note 140.

230. That the *nĕḥaš nĕḥōšet* lore is early (exactly how early one cannot know) is seen by its legitimacy in Num 21:9 in contrast to its illegitimacy in later Deuteronomistic traditions (2 Kgs 18:4).
231. Note the incongruity of the Mt. Ebal tradition in Deut 27:1–8 vis-à-vis centralized worship in Jeruasaelm. As Richter (2007: 350) correctly asks: "Who would try to

legitimize a cult site at Ebal? . . . Certainly the Judeans would have no interest in legitimizing this northern site."

232. This quote is from Fleming (2012: 314), who goes on to note how military muster might prove more advantageous for groups coming together ("more so than religious festivals"), for they "would not require the wider participation at a single site and so could be observed more locally by smaller gatherings. Moreover, this kind of [militarily mustered] assembly would not have been confided to a single location. . . . In general, muster would depend on the geographical demands of the threat and need not be restricted to one place."

233. Rehearsing the plethora of research on ethnic identity is beyond the scope of the present treatment. See Sparks 1998; Faust 2006, 2014, 2015a, 2015b; Nestor 2010; Crouch 2012, 2014, 2015; Faust and Lev-Tov 2014; Dever 2017: 210–218, 324–330, 475–476, 505–508, 601–603; and Sergi 2019.

234. I am influenced here by the perceptive comments of McCarter (1992: 129–134), to whom I am indebted.

235. Crouch (2014: 2) argues that "the long seventh century BCE" (i.e., from the late eighth century to the early sixth century BCE) is a particularly acute time for Judean identity formation in response to the Neo-Assyrian empire. Cf. Dever 2017: 603–616. For the role of cult in identity formation in the Iron I and early Iron IIA periods, see Sergi 2019: 48–49.

236. For a later theological reflex, cf. Deuteronomy's emphasis on the divine choosing of the people, the Temple, and the Davidic dynasty and with such election the demands of exclusive worship (e.g., Deut 7:1–8). See Weinfeld 1991: 368 and Crouch 2014.

237. For the textual criticism on this passage, see Chapter Four, note 74.

238. For the translation of this verse, see Chapter Four, note 75.

239. By noting the well-known El and Baal traditions, we are not suggesting that one should dismiss the traditions of other Canaanite deities (Reshep, Athtar, Dagan). Cf. Smith 2001b: 146, which warns us not to overlook the features of Athtar in our preference for El and Baal traditions that might turn out to be "partially misleading" for sketching "Yahweh's original profile," especially if they represent secondary developments.

240. On the processes of "differentiation" together with those of "convergence," see Smith (2002: 189–190, 195–202).

Chapter 7

1. On the suggestion that divine genitalia may be mentioned in Isa 6:1 and Ezek 16:8–14, see the critique of Smith (2001b: 88–89, 246–247 n. 37).
2. There is no consensus as to the source of Exodus 33:7–11. Detailed discussions can be found in commentaries such as Childs 1974: 584–585, 590–593; Houtman 2000: 605–607, 685–686; Propp 2006: 149–153; and Dozeman 2017: 349–351, 355–357.

3. Though it must be used with caution, a convenient and exhaustive collection of data can be found in Korpel 1990: 88–522. Among the many studies of divine embodiment and divine anthropomorphism, see Knohl 1995; Hamori 2008; Sommer 2009; Wagner 2010, 2014; Middlemas 2014; and Knafl 2014. Knafl also includes a history of scholarship (2014: 6–12).
4. On the former translation, see Milgrom 1991: 162–163; for the latter translation, see HALOT 696. For a fuller discussion, see Eberhart 2002: 40–52, 361–381.
5. Knohl 1995: 128–137, 170–172; 1996: 20. Knohl (1995: 162–163) writes of P's "desire to shape a cultic system completely detached from anthropomorphic images of God . . . the cultic system of PT [the Priestly Torah] concentrates on the essential numinous dimension of God." Yet cf. Knafl's (2014: 44–67, 89–95, 149–154, 168–172, 178–182, 202–203, 235–244, 269–271) emphasis that P, while indirect, still uses human descriptors to depict God's actions and bodily idioms to articulate his emotions and mental activity.

Knohl includes a much fuller discussion of the use of *rêyaḥ nîḥōaḥ* in P and H. The phrase is also found in Ezek 20:41 with a similar meaning. Yet most often, in contrast, Ezekiel uses the phrase to refer to idolatrous worship (Ezek 6:13; 16:19; 20:28). As we have noted, J, with his characteristic use of anthropomorphisms, also refers to the notion of Yahweh smelling the pleasing odor of Noah's burnt offerings (Gen 8:21).
6. Knohl 1995: 129. P's extensive *kābôd* theology is described on pp. 368–373.
7. Contrast the people who, according to Deuteronomy 4:12, 15, do *not* see the *těmunāh* of Yahweh but rather only hear "the sound of words" (*qôl děbārîm*). See too Elijah, who only hears the voice (*qôl*) of Yahweh (1 Kgs 19:12–13), though his portrait is modeled after Moses (complete with a theophany on Mt. Sinai/Horeb).
8. Milgrom (1990: 96) follows Driver (1895: 67) in suggesting that *těmunāh* refers to "the intangible, yet quasi-sensual manifestation of the Godhead vouchsafed to Moses."

On seeing the divine *těmunāh*, cf. too Ps 17:15, where the psalmist presents a parallel between seeing God's face and being satisfied with his *těmunāh*.
9. Where modern scholars look to the LXX and Akkadian cognates (cf. HALOT, 362; Greenberg 1983: 43; Bodi 1991: 88–93) to unpack the meaning of *ḥašmal* in 1:4, 1:27, and 8:2, concluding that it is a precious metal or stone, medieval and other older Jewish commentators (e.g., Rashi, Metsudat David) perceived much more. They speculated that *ḥašmal* had to do with angels or the essence of fire or even divine Essence. Yet because the word can be analyzed as expressing silence (*ḥaš*) with regard to one's words (*millāh*), it was thought best by some to keep silent about any implications with regard to the corporeality of God. While Rashi wrote much on Ezek 1:4, on Ezek 1:27 he merely stated that "one is not permitted to reflect on this reading" (*l' ntn ršwt lhtbwnn bmqr' zh*). See note 221.
10. For an introduction to the vast literature on the abstract concepts of Memra, Yeqara, and Shekinta, see Grossfeld 1988: 19–20, 25–30.
11. On P's suppression of anthropomorphic language used of God, see again Knohl 1995: 128–137 and the nuanced treatment in Knafl 2014.
12. For a description of Nimrud Prism IV integrating the archaeological context, see Tappy 2001: 563–584.

13. According to Mettinger (2006: 278), Niehr's treatment is "unduly literal."
14. Schwartz's (2010) study on metaphorical and literal language in biblical interpretation (with particular attention to the question of whether God has a body in Exodus 33) underscores how the interpretive framework that we bring to the text is often determinative.
15. These two significant texts have been recognized previously by several scholars, including Tigay (1986: 35 n. 71); Becking (1997: 79); Naʾaman (1999a: 414; 2006a: 332), and Mettinger (2006: 280).
16. On the insertion of Isaiah 10:10–12 by a later hand, its historical setting, and its literary style ("certainly not typically 'deuteronomistic'"), see Wildberger 1991: 411–426, esp. 422–423.
17. Niehr's (1997: 74) rebuttal to all of this could be that we cannot take the biblical texts "at face value." As for his historical reconstruction, Niehr (1997: 91) assumes that Yahweh's cult statue was stripped of its gold (rendering it "no longer suitable for use in the cult") and then was lost.
18. To these one should also add Hagar's encounter with El-Roi. See Chapter Four, pp. 95–97. See too Job's remark that he saw Yahweh (Job 42:5; Chapter Nine, p. 557).
19. Though Uehlinger has now changed his position, it should be noted that Keel and Uehlinger had earlier written (1998: 407): "We do not believe that there was an actual Yahweh iconography in Israel and Judah." Whereas Uehlinger's position has changed, Keel's (e.g., 2001) has remained the same.
20. Though now dated, three standard treatments include Collon 1972; Negbi 1976; and Seeden 1980. See too the review of Negbi in Muhly 1980 as well as Seeden 1982 and Moorey and Fleming 1984. More recent studies and bibliographies can be found in Cornelius 1994; Green 2003: 154–165; and Schwemer 2008a: 31–36.
21. Dates follow the traditional chronology. If the lower chronology proves to be correct, these would have to be adjusted downward, yet the general thrust of our conclusions would remain basically the same.
22. Keel and Uehlinger (1998: 60) suggest that this figurine "might be a depiction of the weather god, but it might also portray Reshef or possibly even the pharaoh." Hansen (1957: 17) opts for Reshef as well.
23. The material that follows is quoted from my earlier study of this bronze (Lewis 1996a: 416–418), to which now add Campbell 2002: 201–203.
24. Campbell 2002: 203, fig. 197; 1965a: 24–25, fig. 9; 1965b: 18–22, esp. 20 and fig. 1; Horn 1965: 284–306, esp. 304 and pl. XVI, C; Campbell and Wright 1970: 126–133, esp. 130; Collon 1972: 116, no. 20, fig. 2; Negbi 1976: 32–33, 41, 165, #1363.
25. Campbell 1965a: 24.
26. Campbell, personal letter to the author dated June 18, 1994.
27. Keel and Uehlinger (1998: 133ff.) devoted a substantial portion of their exhaustive study on divine iconography to the "general decline of anthropomorphic representations of the gods." Because this broad definition included male and female deities—and in all media—Uehlinger felt compelled to write another exhaustive study heavily revising his position. Yet Uehlinger (1997: 111) still refers to "the fact that metal statuary production receded during the early Iron Age."

It is tantalizing to speculate about the nature of the cult image mentioned in Judges 17:3. Micah's mother consecrates silver to Yahweh in order to make a *pesel* and a *massēkâ*, perhaps a hendiadys for a single image. Obviously, this image (or these images) is used in Yahwistic cult. Regrettably, our Deuteronomistically edited texts do not reveal the nature of the image(s). Ackerman (2008a: 129–141, esp. 138), who provides us with the most thorough analysis of Judges 17–18 to date, imagines that we have here "a small figurine—possibly anthropomorphic, possibly theriomorphic—that was cast in bronze and then covered with silver overlay."

28. Possible examples of anthropomorphic male divine figures in terra-cotta include the figures published by Jeremias in 1993 and the geometric pair from Jerusalem published by Gilmour. These will be dealt with in detail later.

    One must also factor in what Uehlinger (1997: 152) refers to as one of the "the most embarrassing problems relating to our topic," though it does not relate directly to the divine: "We are still not in a position to correctly understand the significance of the horse-and rider figurines which represent by far the most frequently attested type of male figurines from Iron II Judah."

29. The biblical texts themselves describe Hezekiah's activities being overturned by Manasseh (2 Kgs 21:3, 7).

30. See McCarter's (1980a: 119) treatment of the textual criticism of 1 Sam 5:4. Based on the LXX (cf. Targ *gwpyh*), McCarter reconstructs *gww*, "his back," which is missing from the MT's "meaningless" rendering "only Dagon was left upon him." Note that LXX^L mentions the feet of the statue as well.

31. The size of the statue must have been considerable if the crown alone weighed a talent (approximately 75 lbs. [34 kg]). It has long been acknowledged that the LXX^{BMN}'s reading of *milkōm*, "Milkom," is preferable to the MT's *malkām*, "their king" (so McCarter 1984: 311–313). Not only is there no antecedent for MT's 3 m. pl. suffix "their," but the MT's pointing requires the unlikely scenario of a human king wearing such a heavy crown. As for David, similar logic suggests that he then wore the precious stone about his neck, not the heavy crown on his head (so McCarter 1984: 311–313).

32. In contrast to the interpretation of Aharoni and his team, Na'aman (1999a: 408; 2006a: 326) astutely points out that the actions undertaken at Arad suggest "devotion and care," which is "in marked contrast to the description of Hezekiah's cult reform (2 Kgs 18:4) which stresses the breaking and destroying of the altars and *masseboth*." I would prefer to talk about "desacralizing," which does not necessarily impute motives that are hard to verify. "Desacralizing" can be positive (burying an image to protect from desecration [so Na'aman 2006a: 325] out of respect for its holiness and even with an intent to reuse), negative (burying out of disdain with no attempt to reuse), or semi-neutral (burying but not destroying due to an image simply wearing out). Na'aman's positive motive of Arad's "covering over" = "devotion and care" would be wrong if applied to Jacob's act of burying rather than destroying the images of foreign gods. It is clear from the narrative that Jacob is in no way devoted to these gods, but at the same time is unable (for whatever reason) to destroy them.

    Herzog (2013: 40; 2002: 35) uses alternative vocabulary, speaking of "a deliberate act of cancellation" and "purposeful abolition" at Arad.

33. Stone images would be less likely to be reused.
34. Yet cf. the large anthropomorphic statue of the god Hadad discovered in Gerçin 4.3 mi (7 km) north of Zinjirli on which is written the Sam'alian Aramaic Hadad Inscription (KAI 214) that dates to the mid-eighth century BCE. Cf. Niehr 2014a: 184–185.
35. The seal's designation is B58, referring to Bordreuil 1986: 55. Sass's treatment is found in Sass 1993: 226–227, fig. 124; section E2; 233, fig. 143; 236–237; section F8.3; 250. Uehlinger's treatment is found in Uehlinger 1993: 261, 275–276, fig. 11. On the reading of the inscription, see Bordreuil 1986: 55; Puech 1989: 590; Avigad and Sass 1997: 103.
36. See too the literature noted in Chapter Three, notes 9 and 14, about epigraphic forgeries and the problem of unprovenanced onomastica.
37. On the dating of the handles, see Vaughn 1999: 81–110.
38. Zevit (2001: 388 n. 76) remarks that "both faces are unclear, so that their gender is uncertain."
39. Jeremias did make good use of Young and Young 1955, among other studies.
40. Keel and Uehlinger (1998: 60) recognize these as humans too, though not unrelated to the famous bronze from Megiddo Grave 4. Yet the bronze does not exhibit the distinct inverted triangle body, and the figures on the sherds (as they point out) are bearded and lacking the headdress.
41. For the most complete analysis of Judean pillar figures, see Darby 2014.
42. Here I am thinking of the tomb inscriptions at Khirbet Beit Lei and their materiality. For bibliography, see Chapter Six, note 107. Niditch (2015: 95–97) notes the drawing of an X in two of Naveh's line drawings. One line drawing is that of a "praying figure" with an X marked at the top of his head. See Naveh (1963: 78, fig. 5). The other is on a pair of drawings that portray a square with four quadrants and a dome shape in three quadrants, the fourth with the X. The word 'wrr, indicating "one who curses" (or "cursed" with anomalous orthography), is between the two shapes. See Naveh 1963: 82, fig. 10; 198. These two immediate contexts beg for a functional/performative meaning for the use of the two Xs, especially in view of their larger funerary context, along apotropaic lines (cf. Niditch 2015: 96–97; Mandell and Smoak 2016: 219–221, 223, 241–245). Yet what gives us pause in pressing this argument further is whether the Xs are truly present or whether these lines are simple hatchings. Zevit's (2001: 409, 428, figs. 5.12, 5.26) line drawings do *not* include them!
43. As for an explicit example of any theriomorphic usage, scholars such as van der Toorn (1997b: 239) have noted the presence of the Nehushtan snake in 2 Kgs 18:4 as "positive evidence in the Bible of the worship of theriomorphic images."
44. Caution is in order in sifting this material when we consider how, in the words of Ornan et al. (2012: 6*), "the lion is a timeless motif in the ancient Near East, whose various representations are loaded with multivalent meanings."
45. See Brandl 2012: 383–384.
46. Most scholars reconstruct '[r']ly yhwh, "the altar hearths of Yahweh," in Mesha lines 17–18 because of Ezek 43:15–16 and the mention of "the 'r'l of dwdh" in line 12. Yet the reconstruction [k]ly yhwh, "vessels of Yahweh," is also possible. See Chapter Six, note 125.

Given the explicit context of Ezek 43:13–27, understanding *'r'l* as an altar hearth is preferable to Ahlström's (1993: 580) suggestion that "the *'ar'el* most probably was a lion postament for a deity statue."

47. Amiran 1976. In addition to the lion-headed libation tray, Amiran studied a small lion statue that was found at the site.
48. Brief note should be made of the two small ivory crouching lions from Samaria (Dayagi-Mendels 1986: 169). Though past scholars could not help but connect the Samaria ivories with the "ivory house" that Ahab built (1 Kgs 22:39), recent scholarship underscores "a great deal of hermeneutical tension between the archaeological data and the story as told in the biblical texts" (Tappy 2001: 494). See the thorough and nuanced evaluation in Tappy 2001: 443–495.
49. So much has been written on the Taanach cult stands that they may rank second only to the Kuntillet 'Ajrud pithoi as the cultic items that have garnered the most comments. Splendid detailed overviews can be found in Beck 1994 and Zevit 2001: 318–325.

    For closer parallels to bronze wheeled lever stands (*měkōnôt*) of 1 Kgs 7:27–37, see the various parallels from thirteenth- through eleventh-century BCE Cyprus. See Curtis 1988: 279.
50. Compare the lions and sphinxes that adorn the exquisite ivory box from the ivory cache from Megiddo's stratum VIIA palace. See Shiloh 1993: 1014 and Dayagi-Mendels 1986: 149.
51. Note that this is all we can say at this point, and we make no claim that this necessitates associations with Yahweh. As for the cult stand discovered by Sellin, note the depiction of a male fighting a snake that Keel and Uehlinger see as Baal (1998: 155; but cf. Zevit 2001: 324).
52. Holladay (1987: 296) goes on to call this a "nonconforming cultus" due to features, such as the nude female goddess, that would have been out of step with the cult found in the Jerusalem Temple.
53. Though scholars commonly translate *mar'ôt 'ĕlōhîm* as "divine visions" (e.g., Zimmerli, Greenberg)—that is, visions inspired by God (Ezek 8:3, 40:2)—it seems better to take the phrase here literally. In other words, the prophet was allowed to actually see some aspect of the divine (Ezek 1:28). Cooke (1936: 5) notes that it was perceived this way as early as the Aramaic Targums. As a priest, Ezekiel is very circumspect about describing such encounters (see the numerous qualifiers in Ezek 1:26–28). Such "divine sightings" are known elsewhere (Hendel 1997: 220–223). See the detailed discussions of Ezekiel's circumspect language and the cherubim on pp. 373–379.
54. Is it significant that the bull face of 1:10 is replaced with a cherub's face in 10:14? Perhaps we have here a further example that some variants of the cherub-*Mischwesen* creature were indeed bull-headed (cf. Figure 5.31 = ANEP 534).
55. See Chapter Four, pp. 115–118.
56. This theory is found as early as Obbink 1929: 267–269. More recent discussions can be found in Hahn 1981: 267–365 and Toews 1993: 41–69.

57. See the literature in Chapter Five, note 190. Sasson's (1968) thesis stands out among the others. His intriguing argument is that the bulls were (1) a substitute for Moses, who at this point in the narrative had disappeared (cf. too Moses's horns in Exod 34:29–35), and (2) the symbol of an older Sin worship. See too Berlejung's (2009: 27–28, 33) suggestion that in the Deuteronomistic presentation in 1 Kgs 12, the absence of Yahweh indicates "godless sanctuaries." "The calves are arbitrary human artefacts, and certainly no[t] markers of any divine presence." Such a literary portrayal would certainly not match the realia of cult practiced in Area T at Tel Dan. See Davis 2013.
58. This line of thinking is predicated on a more uniform narrative rather than seeing Exod 32:5 as a later addition. See Chapter Five, note 191.
59. Mettinger 1979: 21. For an updated article with a full bibliography of the works of Mettinger and his critics, see Mettinger 2006. Mettinger (2006: 280) reaffirms his understanding of Jeroboam's bull images as "different but parallel" to the Jerusalem cherubim. So too Fritz 2003: 147.
60. Numerous scholars affirm likewise: DeVries 1985: 162–163; Fritz 2003: 147; Sweeney 2007: 177.
61. See Ornan 2006 for both the date and an iconographic analysis of this bronze plaque.
62. Though Ornan (2006: 302) states that "it is difficult to ascertain the gender of the divinity," she settles on it being female and most likely Ishtar. Though the bull is often the animal of choice for male deities (see Chapter Five, Figures 5.23–5.29 and note 103; Collon 2001: 141–147, §276–284; Ornan 2001; Bunnens 2006), goddesses riding on bulls are found much earlier in Syria and southeastern Anatolia. See Ornan 2006: 308; Williams-Forte 1983; and Bloch-Smith 1994: 28 n. 2, the last of whom builds on the work of Collon and Amiet.
63. See note 54 commenting on Ezek 10:14, where the bull face of Ezek 1:10 is replaced by a cherub face, perhaps showing another example of the "visual syncretism" of which Ornan writes (2001; 2006: 303).
64. Cf. Dick's (1999: 10–11) remarks on the earliest image polemics in the context of discussing the prophetic parodies. For linguistic anomalies within the Elijah-Elisha narratives, see Schniedewind and Sivan 1997; Schniedewind 2013: 89–90.
65. This passage should be read alongside other prophetic parodies against making divine images. See Dick 1999a.
66. Again, contrast should be made with the other Deuteronomistic passages (1 Kgs 14:9; 2 Kgs 17:7–23, esp. 16, 21–23) that do level a critique of worshipping other gods. See Chapter Five, pp. 198–200.
67. In Hosea 8:6, Tur-Sinai emends the MT's *kî miyyiśrā'ēl* ("For from Israel . . .") to read *kî mî šôr 'ēl* ("For, who is Bull El?"). For bibliography and the application of this verse to Deut 32:8, see Joosten 2007: 552 and Chapter Four, note 74.
68. Again, see the parallel traditions of condemnation in Chapter Five, pp. 198–200. For a later reference to the apostasy of sacrificing to the bull Baal, see Tobit 1:5.
69. Niehr is here following Weippert (1971). In addition to Weippert, this view is held by Gressmann (1913: 207–208), Kraus (1962: 176–177), Haran (1985: 29 n. 28), and van der Toorn (2002: 49).

70. Na'aman 2006a: 332. This article first appeared in Na'aman 1999a.
71. For a preliminary photograph and description of the seal that includes the portrayal of a goddess (not a god) without any bovine imagery, see Avigad and Sass 1997: #835.
72. The date is that of Cross (1962b: 15, n. 12). See Sass 1993: 199, 225, 227 fig. 118; Uehlinger 1993: 272 n. 56, 278 n. 70, 280; Avigad and Sass 1997: 158, §374. Regrettably this seal is unprovenanced. This figure is described as a bull by Sass (1993: 226) and by Keel and Uehlinger (1998: 194).
73. The language of Papyrus Amherst 63 is Aramaic, but its script is written in a simplified version of Egyptian Demotic. For introduction, text, and translation, see Steiner 1997a, 2017; van der Toorn 2018a; and Holm forthcoming.

    In a provisional publication, Steiner (1997: 310) even suggests that the prayer found in Papyrus Amherst 63, "if correctly deciphered . . . [,] is a descendant of one used in Jeroboam's temple in Bethel." Steiner's updated treatment (where he omits the bull reference) can be found in Steiner and Nims 2017.
74. The fixed name here may or may not be rendered alphabetically, and this has led to considerable debate. It is found only in the so-called Israelite hymns (cols. XII 11–XIII 17 = Steiner 1997a: 317–318; van der Toorn 2018a: 66, 166–168; Holm forthcoming). Where Steiner reads Horus, other scholars read Yahu/Yaho (Zauzich, Vleeming and Wesselius, van der Toorn, Holm) or El (Kottsieper). Zauzich (1985) confidently reads the name as Yhw, with the Demotic aleph representing Semitic *y*, the Demotic *ḫr* sign as *h*, and the last sign as a *w*, not a divine determinative. For a complete discussion, see Holm forthcoming, to which I am indebted.
75. McCarter 1987: 147, 154 n. 55; 1996: 107.
76. Extensive bibliographies can be found in Keel and Uehlinger 1998: 154–160, esp. 158; Hadley 2000: 169–179; King and Stager 2001: 341–344; Zevit 2001: 318–325; and Dever 2005: 219. Miller (2000: 43–45) is appropriately skeptical and noncommittal. Dever's (2017: 490) more recent treatment is also noncommittal with its use of "quadruped."
77. For the disk on the forehead of terra-cotta horses (including the one from Hazor that Yadin also related to the sun god and 2 Kgs 23:11), see Keel and Uehlinger 1998: 343, where it is characterized as a forehead ornament.
78. See the bibliographies by Keel and Uehlinger and by Hadley in note 76, to which add Sommer 2009: 156–159. Hadley notes how Glock's later writing seems to embrace Hestrin's bovine identification.
79. See the extensive analysis of these two goddesses and their emblematic horses in Cornelius 1994: 78ff.; 2004.
80. Contrast Smith's view with the common assertion that the bottom register represents the goddess Asherah (e.g., Ackerman 2008b: 21; Sommer 2009: 156).

    The collocation of anthropomorphic figures on a terra-cotta cult stand with both a bull and a lion appears at Khirbet Ataruz, though with a human male. See Ji 2012: 213; Tafel 47.
81. Curiously, Taylor (1994: 57) in the same article describes the horse's posture as a "prancing" one that "conveys a horse's strength, agility, and athletic prowess." At the same time, he contrasts the putative "calf's posture of playfulness."

82. A convenient collection of horse iconography (especially associated with goddesses) can be found in Cornelius 2004. For a summary of horses in biblical and other ancient Near Eastern textual sources, see Borowski 2007. Borowski notes the dominant *military* use of horses throughout the ancient Near East. As for the Hebrew Bible, "the horse functioned only as a military machine and not as a power source for agricultural or other daily tasks."
83. Fleming's research demonstrates how senior/creator deities (and thus Yahweh) are not portrayed as offsprings.
84. There is the association of Yahweh with donkey colts in the demilitarized passage in Zech 9:9–10, but this passage is a good example of the exception that proves the rule.
85. For an introduction to the finds at Kuntillet ʿAjrud, see Chapter Six, pp. 236–241.
86. E.g., Gilula 1979: 130–133; Fritz 1979: 49; Coogan 1987a: 119; McCarter 1987: 147, 155 n. 55; Koch 1988: 100; Margalit 1990: 275, 288–289; Niditch 1997: 21; Hess 2007b: 319.
87. According to this theory, the standing figure to the right is also bovine in nature and designates the goddess Asherah. Yet as far as I know, there are no explicit examples of Asherah being portrayed using bovine imagery. There are other goddesses such as Egyptian Hathor that have ubiquitous bovine associations, and it is possible that Asherah was portrayed in Hathor dress. We seem to have Ishtar riding a bull at Tel Dan (see Figure 7.12) and an unidentified goddess (Athtartu?) enthroned on a bull from Late Bronze Age Ugarit (cf. Ornan 2006: fig. 9 = Cornelius 2004: fig. 2.2), but as Ornan (2006: 303) notes, "the representation here of a bull being ridden by a goddess is, indeed, unusual." As for Asherah, we would more likely have her associated with lions (which some do indeed see behind the Bes figures represented here).
88. Beck's 2012 analysis, originally published in 1992, is presented in the final report. Additional scholars affirming that we have Bes or Bes-like figures here include Meshel (1979: 30; 1992: 107), Stolz (1980: 170), Dever (1984: 25), Lemaire (1984: 46), Olyan (1988: 29, 31), Mazar (1990: 448), Emerton (1999: 317), Day (2000: 50–51), Zevit (2001: 387–392), King and Stager (2001: 351), Schmidt (2002: 107–108; 2013; 2016), Meyers (2002: 287), Kitchen (2003: 415, 588 n. 95), Hess (2007b: 320), and Ornan (2016).
89. Wilson (1975: 100) even refers to Bes as the "patron of music and dancing." Cf. Beck 1982: 30; Olyan 1988: 31; and Schmidt 2016: 87. Given Bes's nature, it seems likely that the music and dance would be used apotropaically rather than for entertainment; so Pinch 1994: 84–86, whose fig. 43 represents Bes making music and dancing. See too Schmidt's (2016: 86–87) description of the apotropaic "visual potency embodied in the physical appearance of Bes as a dwarf," whom he describes as "an evil-averting dancing god."
90. Note the important correction to the Beck 1982 article in the final report (Meshel 2012: 165; figs 6.20a, 6.21a) that shows nothing between the legs in illustration T. What was previously drawn as a "loop" or "appendage" between the legs (and taken either as a phallus or the tail of a lion garment) was later revealed to be a black soot deposit. Schmidt (2016: 59) refers to this as "a groundbreaking, mind-blowing revision."

91. Zevit (2001: 388) notes too how the "narrow, elongated somatotype" of Bes found at Kuntillet ʿAjrud finds a close parallel in Herrmann 1994: 352, #391. Cf. too Malaise's (2001: 179) description of Bes as a "full-faced ... bandy-legged gnome with a grotesque *lionlike* face" (my emphasis).
92. Yet for three-dimensional works, see the bull-headed stela from Bethsaida discussed later.
93. Dick (1999a: 6), for example, says that such an interpretation is "thoroughly flawed" in that "it is methodologically unsound to require that pictures correspond to inscriptions" and that "the figures are clearly two portrayals of the Egyptian god Bes."
94. Schmidt's early work (1996: 96–105; 2002: 91–125, esp. 97–98, 108) suggested that scholars needlessly reject Yahweh out of hand once they see that we have Bes figures here. He instead argued that Kuntillet ʿAjrud represents *Mischwesen* forms with Yahweh, Asherah, and Bes combined compositely with overlapping artistic techniques. Schmidt (1996: 103; 2002: 108) then elaborated, suggesting that "the composite image might point to Yahweh's former status as a lesser numen, a monster whose imagery was preserved long after he rose to higher rank." Yet see Uehlinger's (1997: 142–146, esp. 144) detailed response and his conclusion that "[Schmidt's] main thesis cannot withstand closer scrutiny."
95. Cf. Romano 1980: 49–50.
96. Hadley 2000: 144, 153. For her part, Hadley (2000: 143) notes how several other scholars (e.g., Dever, Keel, and Uehlinger) had also suggested that the Bes figures at Kuntillet ʿAjrud served an apotropaic function.
97. Keel and Uehlinger (1998: 240) write similarly: "An identification of the two Bes images ... with 'Yahweh ... and his Asherah' is impossible."
98. Cf. Beck 1982 on the multiple (three?) artistic hands possibly at work and Zevit's (2001: 381–385) attempt to consider "all the information on each pithos horizontally." See too Ornan's (2016) comprehensive analysis as well as Schniedewind's (2017) argument for multiple scribal hands. See Chapter Six, note. 74.
99. See KA plaster inscription 4.2; Chapter Ten, pp. 583–587; Lewis 2020.
100. Note Uehlinger's (1997: 144) remark that "there is, as yet, no clear evidence for a local Bes iconography in Iron Age Israel or Judah, apart from the Kuntillet ʿAjrud drawings." At the same time, this should be balanced with Meyers' (2002: 287) observation that "the Bes amulets are not simply Egyptian imports; discovery of several molds at Palestinian sites attests to indigenous production."
101. Bernett and Keel (1998) present solid evidence that the artistic motif on the Bethsaida stela is not unique. Very close parallels are found on two stelae from the Hauran, in several figures on a bronze box of unknown provenance, and on a stela in the museum at Gaziantep (southeastern Turkey), also of unknown provenance. Of particular importance is the ever-present rosette that is clearly portrayed on the bronze box as a quartered wheel/disc. Bernett and Keel use numerous iconographic parallels to other quartered discs and "globes" as one of the building blocks to show that the Bethsaida stela was dedicated to the moon god. According to Bernett and Keel, the element "four" may be related to the four phases of the moon, and the four "beams" (i.e., the extremities taken by others to be animal or human limbs)

102. Arav, Freund, and Shroder 2000: 46.
103. One should also include Colbow 1997; Collon 1997; and Braun-Holzinger 1993.
104. With the plural "stelae," Ornan (2001: 2) includes three parallel stelae, two from Syria (Tell el-Ašʿari and ʿAwas) and one from Turkey (Gaziantepe).
105. Mettinger (1995: 14) notes Tacitus, *Historiae* V, 5, which reads: "The Jews conceive of one god only, and that with the mind alone: they regard as impious those who make from perishable materials representations of gods in man's image; that supreme and eternal being is to them incapable of representation and without end. Therefore they set up no statues in their cities, still less in their temples."
106. The Aramaic word *nabš* is often translated "soul or "spirit," with a long history of scholarship devoted to the specific nuances of the term in Aramaic and its cognate (*nepeš*) in Hebrew. Suriano (2014: 385, 403) speaks of *nbš* as "a ritually centered object that marks identity," "a concept of self in portmortem contexts" (2014: 387), and one's "postmortem selfhood" (2014: 388).
107. See Schloen and Fink 2009; Struble and Herrmann 2009; Pardee 2009; and the catalog in Herrmann and Schloen 2014.
108. It is clear that I am indebted here to Pardee (2009: 63), who writes: "The word *nbš* appears . . . to refer to the very essence of [the deceased person] KTMW, as he is represented on the stele, eating and drinking at a feast; it was obvious to all that the exterior manifestation could neither eat nor drink, but the *nbš within* the stele was considered capable of doing so, apparently in a way very similar to that in which deities ate and drank the offerings presented to them" (my emphasis).

    For an alternative analysis, see Hawkins 2015, making the argument that the phrase in question refers to the offering of a ram to the likeness (*nbš*) of Katumuwa portrayed *on* the stela.
109. As noted in Chapter Four, one should remain cognizant of how earlier El passages necessarily come down to us through later Yahwistic hands. Methodologically, this adds a layer of uncertainty about whether the few mentions of Yahweh in these passages (Gen 28:13, 16; 31:3, 49) indicate his connection to the *masseboth* in the narratives. Given such a high level of uncertainty, these few references are *not* factored into the present analysis.
110. The notion of Yahweh being a "jealous God" is complex and often analyzed with regard to emotions only and without studying the social-anthropological implications of the term. For a refreshing contrast, see Guinn-Villareal 2018. See too Chapter Ten, pp. 652–653.
111. Cf. too the "polemical distortion of a cultic confession" (so Olyan) in Jer 2:27, where reference is made to a stone (*ʾeben*) giving birth. Olyan's (1987a: 258) study of the passage concludes "that the stone pillar was a perfectly legitimate Jahwistic symbol in early Israel, and came to be opposed only in certain circles."

    There are many other traditions about God being a "rock" (*ṣûr*), as evidenced in literature (e.g., Deut 32:4, 15, 18, 31, 37; 2 Sam 22:3, 32 = Ps 18:3, 32 [Eng 18:2, 31];

Ps 19:15 [Eng 19:14]; 28:1; 31:3–4 [Eng 31:2–3]; 71:3; 94:22; 95:1; 144:1–2; Isa 26:4; 30:29; 44:8) and in personal names (Elizur, Zuriel, Zurishaddai, Pedahzur), several of which occur in the archaic/archaizing Num 1:5–15 with its emphasis on the deity El (see Chapter Four, pp. 106–107). Cf. too the theophany described in Exod 33:21–22 in which Yahweh's *kābôd* passes by Moses at a rock (*ṣûr*). For a more complete discussion, see Fabry 2003.

Viewing God as a rock is an obvious image when one considers the terrain of the writers of the Hebrew Bible. Rock imagery is used to convey motifs of God as stable and permanent, as a source of refuge, as a firm stronghold and as a protector. Such ubiquitous motifs remind us of the dangers of interpreting stone imagery too narrowly. The ancients certainly saw more in these meaningful and practical metaphors than only the numinous inhabiting of a stone in sacred space.

112. Other relevant passages would be Hos 3:4; 10:1–2; and Isa 6:13, yet these texts are complicated. Some scholars view the various items listed in Hos 3:4 as entirely acceptable, while other scholars (cf. Graesser 1969: 250–252) view the items as pairs alternating between licit and illicit practices. For further discussion, see LaRocca-Pitts 2001: 93–96. Isa 6:13 is extremely difficult, yet see Iwry 1957, following 1QIsa^a.
113. See the overview of this material in Wildberger 1997: 268–274.
114. We follow those scholars and the JPS translation that treat *wĕhāyâ* as a collective, with both the altar and the *massebah* as subjects ("*they* shall serve"). The singular translation ("and it shall be") of the RSV, NAB, NEB, and NIV is literal. Yet it is misleading because the antecedent in these English translations is "the pillar" (*massebah*), which, being feminine, cannot be the subject of the masculine verb *wĕhāyâ*.
115. Renfrew and Bahn 2000: 408–409.
116. In addition to the many examples in the present chapter, see too the widespread use of abstract symbols (and the concomitant rejection of anthropomorphism) from first-millennium Mesopotamia. This rich tradition is best documented by Ornan (2005a), who titles her volume *The Triumph of the Symbol*. See too Mettinger 1995: 39–48.
117. For additional discussion of Otto, see Chapter Ten, pp. 587–588, 598–599, and especially Gammie 2005: 5–8 and Rappaport 1999.
118. See Meyers 1992a: 359, noting that "although the God of Israel was viewed as transcendent," the temple served to meet "the need for the assurance of divine availability." Meyers speaks of "humanity's insecurity about the nearness of divine power and protection."
119. Niebuhr 1960: 120.
120. Hendel (1997: 224) has also remarked how "the theology of [biblical] programmatic aniconism is clearly comparable to the intellectual speculations of the Mesopotamian and Egyptian texts . . . a product of critical reflection on tradition."
121. Yet see the brief overview of holiness in the ancient Near East in Chapter Ten.
122. See, for example, McBride 1969; McCarter 1987; Lewis 2011: 208–209, 224–225.
123. Smith (2001b: 93–95), building on the work of van der Toorn (1985), provides a caution to Otto's and Jacobsen's emphasis on the numinous being "wholly

other.'" Smith underscores how "divine holiness and its associated numinous characteristics" (especially the luminosity of cultic cleanliness [cf. Akk *ellu*]) adhered "to material *realia* and the religious processes in shrines, including theophanies." Smith continues: "Because such (numinous) experience is mediated by human experience and language, it is not by definition entirely 'Wholly Other.'"

124. Aster 2006, 2012. Two important earlier studies of *melammu* on which Aster builds his treatment are those of Oppenheim (1943) and Cassin (1968). Aster (2006: 31–38) is more critical of the former and more affirming of the latter.

    Aster's study provides a good model that avoids homogenizing the primary data, which are spread out over such a long time period. Overall, Aster (2006: 29) underscores how the concept of *melammu* "is both a physical object and a metaphor for abstract concepts." Specifically, in the second millennium the concept of *melammu* "refers to something concrete and tangible" (cf. especially the *melammus* of Huwawa) that could sometimes be "*associated* with radiance." This changes dramatically in the Sargonid period, where "*melammu* can be used as simply another term *for* radiance" (2006: 39, 75).

125. Aster (2006: 79–88) nicely notes how *melammu* is a quality not just owned by gods and kings but also found on occasion among monsters, mythic animals, illnesses, demons, healthy people, weapons, and even walls and buildings (the last is appropriate for nuancing Jacobsen's quote).

126. To be sure, Neo-Assyrian artists seem to have tried to portray *melammu*. Aster (2006: 151–167; 2012: 101–121) documents the three best examples that are portrayals of the god Aššur as a winged sun disk (with taut bow in hand) surrounded by stylized flames (cf. ANEP §536 [= Figure 7.23]; Mendenhall 1973: 44–47, figs. 10–13). Cf. too our later discussion of Ezek 1:26–28. Yet such attempts at artistic representation should not detract from how the ancients viewed *melammu* as an unseen supernatural power.

127. Grayson 1991: 199, 208; 1996: 14, 15. According to Liverani, "the terrifying splendour (*melammu, puluḫtu, rašubbatu*) of the Assyrian king is such that the enemy even from afar is afraid (*adāru*; cf. *ḫattu, ḫurbašu*, etc.) and runs away." See Liverani 1979a: 311 and Aster 2006: 116–132.

    Compare Exod 23:27, where Yahweh promises to send his *'êmâ*, "terror," against his enemies, who will be thrown into confusion. Hugh Williamson (personal communication) notes how Isa 8:7ff. may be playing off of the Assyrian concept of *melammu*. In this passage, Yahweh of Hosts (*ṣĕbā'ôt* = armies), known ubiquitously elsewhere as the God of Glory (*kābôd*), represents a divine counter-splendor to Assyria, with its glory (*kĕbôdô*) and armies.

128. See Assmann 1983: 155, where he translates: "Der sich selbst baut mit seinen Armen, die Bildhauer kennen ihn nicht." See also Assmann 1992: 165–166 and Murnane and van Siclen 1993: 23 (Version K, line 9), 39. A collection of such "building" (*qd*) epithets can be found in Leitz 2002: 228–229. For an easily accessible publication of the boundary stelae, see Sandman 1938: 111. I owe my colleague Richard Jasnow a deep debt of thanks for his help with this material.

129. The understanding of this as a "concession to anthropomorphism" is found in several scholars' works. See, for example, Redford 1984: 173 and Mettinger 1995: 49.
130. See Bryan's (2000: 261–263) judicious comments evaluating Johnson's thesis that Amenhotep III (Akhenaten's father) was deified as the disembodied Aten.
131. Cornelius 1997: 29. Cf. too Schlögl's (2001: 157) similar comments: "The perception of [Aten] was not so much the sun disk, but rather the light radiating from the sun." As noted by Robins (2005: 4) and others, "undoubtedly the actual sun in the sky served as the cult image of the Aten, rendering superfluous any cult statues in his temples." Of special note is the architecture of the Aten temples, which were constructed to be open to the sky.
132. It is unclear to whom the temple was dedicated. Some scholars favor Ishtar. See Abou-Assaf 1990: 42–44; n.d.: 13–14; Bloch-Smith 1994: 23; Monson 2000: 27–28; contrast Monson 2006: 296. Stager (2000: 44) suggests the god Baal-Hadad.
133. On the superhuman size of deities, see Greenfield 1985; Smith 1988: 424–427; Bloch-Smith 1994: 21–25; and Chapter Eight, note 108. M. P. Maidman (personal communication) has reminded me of Herodotus' description (iv. 82) of "a footprint of Heracles by the river Tyras stamped on rock, like the mark of a man's foot, but two cubits in length." See Godley 1957: 284–285.
134. E.g., *ḥayyîm*, "life"; *dēʿîm, dēʿôt*, "knowledge"; *ʾônîm*, "strength"; *ʾĕmûnîm*, "faithfulness"; *mêšārîm*, "rectitude, uprightness"; *nĕgîdîm*, "nobility"; *maḥămaddîm*, "beauty"; *ʿădānîm, taʿănûgîm, šaʿăšuʿîm*, "pleasure"; *mamtaqqîm*, "sweetness"; *raḥămîm*, "compassion"; *bînôt, tĕbûnôt*, "intelligence"; *ḥămûdôt*, "excellence"; etc. Cf. GKC 1976: §124d, e; Joüon and Muraoka 1991: §136g–i (cf. §136d); Waltke and O'Connor 1990: §7.4.2, 7.4.3.
135. Readers should note that I am using the comparison between Akkadian *melammu* and Hebrew *kābôd, hôd*, and *hādār* heuristically and am well aware of Aster's cautions against equating the terms on a one-to-one basis. As Aster (2006: 513) concludes, the Hebrew words *hôd* and *hādār* "share some, but not all, of the range of meanings of Akkadian *melammu*." Each specific biblical text (including those using *kābôd*) must be studied to see to what degree they resonate with the conceptual world of the Akkadian scribes who used the term *melammu*.
136. For a thorough exposition of Isa 2:6–22, see Williamson 2006: 189–230, especially his text-critical comments on 2:18–19 as to whether it is the idols entering the caves! For the connection of this passage to Akkadian *melammu* and the various motifs found in Neo-Assyrian royal inscriptions, see Aster 2006: 295–326.
137. Every interpreter of the current generation working on Pentateuchal criticism has staked a claim to the nature and the extent of the Yahwist as it applies to Exodus 3:1–4:18. See the convenient collection of articles in Dozeman and Schmid 2006, especially the article on the commission of Moses by Dozeman. Cf. too Dozeman 2017: 298–313. Our assertion of the ubiquitous nature of fire stands regardless of how one parses these literary strands.
138. Specifically, it occurs via the *malʾak*-Yahweh (on which see pp. 349–350, 353).

139. These are Sarna's (1986: 39) words. Analogously, Moses is not consumed when he approaches the fire of Yahweh in Exod 24:17 even though it is specifically described as a "consuming fire" (*'ēš 'ōkelet*).
140. The rare form for "bush" (*sĕneh*) is used only in our two passages (Exod 3:2-4; Deut 33:16). In Deuteronomy 33:16 it is preferable to retain the difficult phrase *šōknî sĕneh* (*lectio difficilior*) complete with *ḥireq compaginis* (cf. Waltke and O'Connor 1990: §8.2e) rather than to repoint as Sinai, as do Cross and Freedman (1975: 78) and many others. Preserving *sĕneh* keeps intact how a rare word was chosen precisely for its ability to form a play of words on Sinai (*sînāy*). On the epithet "Yahweh, the one of Sinai" (*yhwh zeh sînay*), see Chapter Six, note 229.
141. I have added my adjective "fiery" to Hendel's (1997: 223) astute phrase "transcendent anthropomorphism." Note similar modes of thinking when Aten as light nonetheless extends rays that end in human hands.

    The phrase "poetry of high antiquity" I borrow from McCarter (1984: 473). Readers interested in the variants between Ps 18 and 2 Sam 22 (and the underlying original poem that gave rise to both) are directed to McCarter's detailed textual analysis. See too Cross and Freedman 1975: 82-106.
142. *Bārād* is usually translated as "hailstones." For *bārād* here referring to fiery and not icy hail, cf. Exod 9:23-24.
143. On the root *hwm* designating divine terror, see Chapter Eight, note. 99 (esp. Exod 23:27).
144. The Hebrew word *qôl* is particularly apt for expressing such "transcendent anthropomorphism" in that it can equally express the *voice* of Yahweh that speaks (and in Isa 30:27-28, 30 with even the mention of his tongue [*lĕšônô*], lips [*śĕpātāyw*], and breath [*rûḥô*]) as well as the roar of divine *thunder*.

    It should be underscored that the metaphor of storm gods "thundering" with "voice" is found throughout the ancient Near East and Greece. See the many examples collected by Weinfeld (1983: 121-124, 141-143). A key example from Late Bronze Age Amarna Akkadian has also been pointed out by Pardee (2005: 167): "who gives forth his voice in the heavens like Adad, and all the earth is frightened at his voice" (*ša iddin rigmašu ina šamê kīma Adad u targub gabbi māti ištu rigmišu*; EA 147:13-15).
145. As for the authorship and date of this section of Isaiah, see Blenkinsopp 2000: 423: "The debate about whether this pericope was composed by Isaiah or an anonymous prophet during Josiah's reign or a much later apocalyptic writer of the Hellenistic period remains, predictably, without a definite resolution." Blenkinsopp offers a representative sampling of bibliography advocating each of these positions.
146. The meaning and syntax of MT's *qōrē' larîb bā'ēš* ("calling to contend with fire") in Amos 7:4 is difficult. Hillers' (1964) emendation (first suggested by Krenkel in 1866) is elegant (no change in the consonantal text) yet not without its difficulties. See the critique by Andersen and Freedman (1989: 746-747), who nonetheless agree with Hillers in translating "showers of fire." So too Wolff's "a rain of fire" (1977: 292-293). On the expression "*to rain* fire upon," cf. Gen 19:24 and Ezek 38:22, as well as Hillers 1964: 223 n. 9.

147. See Miller's (1965) remarks on fire in the mythology of Canaan and Israel. Miller notes divine iconography where storm gods carry lightning bolts and how "fire" (*'išt*) is used for Yammu's messengers in KTU 1.2.1.32 and one of the (divine?) combatants defeated by Anatu in KTU 1.3.3.45. Yet overall the presence of fire as an independent deity in the Levant is rare. Cf. Smith and Pitard 2009: 261–264; Watson 1999a, 1999b; and Smith 1994b: 306–307.
148. For a detailed text-critical analysis of this passage, see Davis 2013: 135–136.
149. It is crucial to recognize the polemical nature of such passages when they are used to reconstruct the history of ancient Israelite religion. Contrast, for example, how the late Nahum Sarna (1986: 133–134) used 1 Kgs 19:11–12 to underscore "with crystal clarity" "the striking contrast between Near Eastern paganism and Israelite monotheism." As we have argued, it is more apt, especially in light of other theophanies in the Hebrew Bible, to understand 1 Kgs 19:11–12 as polemical in nature, voicing the concerns of one specific group whose views are better described as a developing "biblical religion" or "Deuteronomistic religion" rather than the overarching term "Israelite religion." The latter term must include the wide variety of religious expressions that took place in the land of Israel throughout its long and varied history.
150. For my dedicated study of Deut 33:2, see Lewis 2013b.
151. On the two occurrences of *lāmô* in the MT, see Lewis 2013b: 793 n. 3.
152. Here we follow most scholars who read the preposition "with" plus enclitic *-m* (*'ittô-m*) based on the LXX, Targums, and Vulgate rather than the MT's pointing *'ātâ* ("he came"). The MT's vocalization seems secondary, the result of the influence of late Aramaic (cf. also *wayyētē'* in 33:21). The occasion for the mispointing of the MT is surely its lack of knowledge of how *-h* in early (tenth century BCE) orthography can represent a third-person masculine singular suffix, a feature well attested from our epigraphic sources. See Cross and Freedman 1975: 72 n. 8; Mandell 2013. Yet if the MT stands, the meaning of the passage remains unchanged.
153. All scholars struggle with the difficulty of translating the hapax *ḥōbēb*. The best solution may be to leave the word untranslated or to understand it (as does Miller 1973: 80) as a reference to troops being consecrated for war.
154. Cf. JPS's "lightning flashing at them from His right," RSV's "with flaming fire at his right hand," and NAB's "at his right hand a fire blazed forth."
155. See too the sequel essay by Steiner and Leiman (2009) and the exposition in Lewis 2013b.
156. The notion of a sword being described as "fiery" is known from Rassam Cylinder A III 118–127. Here the god Sin assures Aššurbanipal that he will end the lives of his enemies "with a flaming sword, conflagration of fire, famine, and plague." (I am indebted to William Reed for this reference.) Cf. too the notion of Yahweh's sword being described with the language of lightning (*běraq ḥarbî*) in Deut 32:41 (cf. Ezek 21:15 [Eng 21:10]).
157. See note 147.

158. This remains true even if we are dealing with a folk etymology. For more on the etymology of the seraphim, see Wildberger 1991: 264; Mettinger 1999; and Williamson 2007: 130.
159. Cf. Exod 33:20, Judg 6:22–23, and Hendel's (1997: 220–222) comments on the leitmotif of lethal God sightings. This will be discussed at greater length later.
160. Alternatively, ʾĕlōhîm here could designate a preternatural being (cf. 1 Sam 28:13); so Burney (1970: 346). Yet the close parallel in Judge 6:22–23 argues for the presence of the divine.
161. Though Hag 1:13 (cf. Mal 1:1; 3:1) shows that the title malʾak yhwh can indeed be applied to prophets, the reason for the title not being applied to Elijah seems obvious. The Deuteronomistic Historian preserves a tradition of the malʾak yhwh appearing to Elijah (1 Kgs 19:5–8) and thus must keep his categories distinct.
162. The MT of 2 Kgs 2:11 has dual vehicles of conveyance, with its mention of Elijah being transported heavenward "by a whirlwind" (baseʿārâ haššāmāyim) as well as by the fiery horses and chariot. Fritz (2003: 235) suggests that the mention of the whirlwind is redactional (cf. the identical wording [baseʿārâ haššāmāyim] in 2:1 that may have served as the occasion for such an insertion). According to Fritz, the fiery chariot was the only divine vehicle of transmission in the original text of 2 Kgs 2:11.
163. The images are fluid. Note how the apocalyptic theophany in Isaiah 66:15 has "Yahweh coming in fire" (yhwh bāʾēš yābôʾ) "to render his anger with fury/heat" (lĕhāšîb bĕḥēmâ ʾappô)//"his rebuke with flames of fire" (gaʿărātô bĕlahăbê-ʾēš). Immediately following, fire is described as an instrument of judgment parallel to a sword (bāʾēš//bĕḥarbô; Isa 66:16).
164. Many other passages are tantalizing. For example, the archaic (or archaizing) poem in Habakkuk 3 describes Yahweh as a divine warrior going off to battle, with Pestilence (deber) and Plague (rešep) marching as his military entourage (Hab 3:5). We then read in Hab 3:8, 12:

    Against River/rivers did it burn [ḥārâ] O Yahweh?
    Was your anger [ʾap] against River/rivers?
    Was your fury [ʿebrâ] against Sea/sea? . . .

    With rage [zaʿam] you trampled earth,
    with anger [ʾap] you threshed nations.

    The decision whether to translate "River" or "rivers" for MT's nĕhārîm (as well as choosing "Sea" or "seas" for MT's yām) depends on whether one thinks that the original contained mythopoeic or mythopoetic language. The same would apply to translating deber and rešep in Hab 3:5.
165. My translation follows, for the most part, that of McCarter (2008a: 87).
166. Similarly, it might not be just a coincidence that the verb used of burning illegitimate divine images in Deut 7:5, 25; 12:3 (tiśrĕpûn bāʾēš) is the same vocabulary behind Yahweh's attendant seraphim (śĕrāpîm) in Isaiah's vision (Isa 6:6).
167. For detailed bibliography on source-critical and other relevant matters, see Weinfeld 1972b, 1991; Geller 1996: 30–61; and Wilson 1995: 12–13, 54–56. For the

genre of Deut 4 as an oxymoronic "literary sermon," see Brettler 2000. For Deut 4 being an example of inner-biblical exegesis, see note 172.

168. Yahweh "speaks" (*wayyōʾmer*) to Moses three times out of the burning bush, yet note that there is no explicit mention of Yahweh's voice (*qôl*) in the account in Exod 3:1–6.

169. Levinson (1997: 151–152) comments that the insertion of "with you" "represents an audacious denial of the facts." Levinson continues: "The authors' true appeal is to their own contemporaries in late-seventh-century Judah, and with them, perpetually to every subsequent generation of the text's readers."

170. Divine lethality is not restricted to seeing or hearing God. It is also found in passages having to do with cultic lethality. See for example, Nadab and Abihu's death as a result of offering strange fire (see pp. 370–372), the killing of Uzzah because of his lacking in ritual precautions (see Chapter Ten, pp. 596, 604), or even God's intent to kill Moses for lack of being circumcised (Exod 4:24–26). There is an understandable backdrop to theophanies when God assures the visitee to "be not afraid."

171. Geller (1996: 36–37), in commenting on Deut 4's "well structured" and "impressive" literary patterning, cites these two verbs as examples of "the remarkable use of leading words" that reflects "the author's attempt to tighten and strengthen the message." We agree. Yet then, surprisingly, Geller upon "closer examination" argues that such leading words are "like a magician's clever distractions . . . the tight structures . . . reflect slapdash joinery rather than skillful craftsmanship . . . more an indication of intellectual desperation than a device to highlight a well-reasoned argument." In the end, Geller's strong comments focus on the structure of Deut 4 as a whole and do not impact our assertion of the prominence of the leitmotif of lethal God-hearings.

172. The mixed metaphor of "seeing" (*rʾh*) a "voice" (*qôl*) may have been occasioned by Exod 20:15 (Eng 20:18), where the people "see thunder" (*rōʾîm ʾet-haqqôlōt*). See the perceptive comments by Carasik (1999), building on the work of Held. Carasik (1999: 264) goes on to argue that Deut 4 represents "a moment of inner-biblical, exegetical insight" where the author created a "spark" "by the striking together of two texts—the preexilic version of the theophany in Deut 5:1–5 and the Sinai tradition of Exod. 20:15."

173. See too Feder's (2013) analysis of Deut 4 and its polemical rhetoric vis-à-vis the politics of identity formation.

174. Geller (1996: 39–42) concentrates on Deut 4:36 to argue that "what has been 'heard from heaven' stands over and above what was 'seen on earth.' The former is the true core of revelation, the latter secondary and subsidiary." Yet a close reading of Deut 4:36 argues for a "both/and" rather than an "either/or" approach to how voice and fire are complementary. As elsewhere, Deut 4:36's emphasis on the voice emerging "from the midst of fire" (*mittôk hāʾēš*) is key. (Note how Deut 4:36c's "you heard his words from the midst of [visible] fire" [*dĕbārāyw šāmaʿtā mittôk hāʾēš*] is clipped from Geller's translation and analysis on p. 40.)

When Geller (1996: 42) does analyze the mention of fire in Deut 4, he does so in a highly reductionist way: "Deuteronomy 4 conceives of the fiery aspect of traditional manifestations of God in purely physical terms, totally demythologizing and devoid of actual theophanic content . . . no longer is the flame viewed as enveloping the body of God." Our research would argue for just the opposite. There is no indication in Deut 4 (or elsewhere in the Hebrew Bible) that fire (when used in passages where Yahweh is made manifest) is "devoid of actual theophanic content."

175. I here agree with Propp's (2006: 114–115) text-critical analysis.
176. Ps 29:7. Note how the *qôl-yahweh* in this psalm occurs repeatedly in parallel to Yahweh (Ps 29:3, 5, 7–8). Ps 29 will be addressed later.
177. Similarly, artisans would have struggled with crafting divine *rûaḥ*.
178. Some of this material intersects with the question of whether Yahweh was portrayed as a solar deity.
179. Should one desire to study these words with greater precision as well as their possible connection to Akkadian vocabulary (e.g., *melammu, puluḫtu*), Aster's (2006, 2012) studies provide a good place to start. See too various entries in *The Theological Dictionary of the Old Testament*, including Warmuth 1978a, 1978b on *hādār* and *hôd*; Weinfeld 1995a on *kābôd*; and Eising 1998: 186–187 on *nōgah*. See too Cogan 2001: 280, arguing based on Gen 49:6 that *kābôd* can mean "essence, being, presence."
180. On *tĕhillâ* as radiance, see Aster 2006: 183–186; 2012: 133–135; de Vries 2016: 64, 68. See Chapter Eight, pp. 449–450, and Chapter Ten, p. 578, on Exod 15:11, where we find Yahweh being "feared in holiness" (*neʾdār baqqōdeš*)//"terrible of radiance" (*nôrāʾ tĕhillōt*).
181. Cogan and Tadmor (1988: 74), following Speiser, note how *sanwērîm* is a loan word from Akkadian *šunwurum*.
182. Andersen (2001: 290) suggests that "the imagery of this epiphany is like the iconography of the rising sun god." Andersen goes on to describe the "streams of light [coming] from the arms and shoulders of UTU (Shamash)" in Mesopotamian glyptic art as well as "the storm god hurling thunderbolts." On the latter, cf. Roberts 1991: 134–135, following Eaton 1964: 148. All of these scholars are trying their best to unpack the difficult phrase *qarnayim miyyādô lô* (Hab 3:4) and determine whether reference is being made to horns (of deities and/or bulls) or sun rays. If the latter, then in light of the mention of "hands" (*yād*), one might also consider the Egyptian god Aten, whose rays end in human hands. See pp. 339–340 on the mysterious nature of Aten and how this may resonate with the mention of "concealment" (*ḥebyôn*) in Hab 3:4.
183. See note 164.
184. There is a good possibility that sun imagery is used in the context of a militaristic war theophany (with the same verb, *zrḥ*, as in Deut 33:2) in one of the plaster inscriptions from Kuntillet ʿAjrud. Yet the epigraphy here is difficult, with either *bzrḥ ʾl* ("when El shines forth") or *byrḥ ʾl* ("when El buffets?") being a possible reading. For analysis of the passage used here (Kuntillet ʿAjrud plaster inscription 4.2), see Lewis 2020; Chapter Six, p. 281; and Chapter Ten, pp. 583–587.
185. See note 152.
186. See pp. 348–349.

187. The literature on Ps 29 is immense, with a considerable amount of bibliography on its Canaanite background. In addition to the standard commentaries, important works include Ginsberg 1936; Margulis 1970; Craigie 1972; Cross 1973: 151–156; Avishur 1979: 247–274; 1989: 25–75, esp. 25–40; 1994: 39–110; Loretz 1984; Kloos 1986; Greenstein 1992; and Pardee 2005. Not to be outdone, Malamat 1998 addresses the Amorite background of Psalm 29. For a modern advocate of Ginsberg's view that Ps 29 was originally a Phoenician hymn to the Canaanite god Baal that was later applied to Yahweh, see Greenstein 1992: 49 n. 1. For representatives of those challenging Ginsberg, see Kloos 1986 and Craigie 1972. I would agree with the summation by Pardee (2005: 158): "This poem is not an old Phoenician poem that has been adapted to Hebrew, but . . . it was an original composition in Hebrew. . . a poem originally conceived in Hebrew as a piece of anti-Baal propaganda. . . . The function of so transparent a presentation of Yahweh in Baalistic imagery was to provide a repudiation of the need to offer a cult to Baal."
188. My translation follows Pardee 2005: 154, 166–167. On the subject of the second-person masculine plural imperative (*hābû* √*yhb*) that commands the divine beings (*bĕnê ʾēlîm*) to "give" Yahweh radiance and strength, see Chapter Eight, note 103.
189. On the crux *ḥōṣēb*, see Pardee 2005: 167–168.
190. On *qôl* representing both the thunder and the voice of storm gods, see note 144. Due to the expressions *ʿānān kābēd* (usually translated "dense cloud") in Exod 19:16 and *bārād kābēd* (usually translated "heavy hail") in Exod 9:18, Mettinger (1982: 118) wonders if the word *kābôd* itself here had connotations of a thundercloud. Cf. the earlier comments of Cross (1973: 153 n. 30)
191. Cf. Ps 96:6:

Glory and majesty are before him [*hôd-wĕhādār lĕpānāyw*],
Strength and splendor are in his temple [*ʿōz wĕtipʾeret bĕmiqdāšô*].

1 Chr 16:27 reformulates this to read similarly:

Glory and majesty are before him [*hôd-wĕhādār lĕpānāyw*],
Strength and joy are in his place [*ʿōz wĕḥedwâ bimqōmô*].

See too the mention of Yahweh's (reading *yhwh*; MT's *ʾĕlōhîm* being due to the Elohistic Psalter's editorial change) sanctuary being "awesome" (*nôrāʾ*) in Ps 68:36 [Eng 68:35]. Cf. the mention of *melammu* surrounding the Emeteursag temple in the Code of Hammurabi (*muštašḫir melemmē Emeteursag*; CH ii 60–62) as well as the Jacobsen quote on pp. 338–339.

Propp (2006: 689–690), building on Haran's (1978: 187–188) remarks about the Tabernacle possessing a "lethal aura," comments: "Due to the West's secular-scientific orientation, and Christianity's emphasis on deferred retribution in the Hereafter, nobody anymore finds worship terrifying."
192. On Yahweh as the "King of Glory/Radiance," see p. 459. This material is connected to the procession of the Ark. See the fuller discussion on pp. 395–397.
193. It is easy to find scholars advocating parallels between Ps 104 and these three classic texts. As is often the case, differences outweigh similarities and no line of

dependency should be posited. A more fruitful avenue for Ps 104:1–4 is Aster's (2006: 207–211) astute observation that mutual themes are found in Adad-nirari III's (810–783 BCE) description of the storm god Adad. The relevant text reads:

> The god Adad . . . the perfectly splendid hero [*qardu šarḫu gitmālu*] whose strength is mighty . . . who is bedecked with luminosity [*ša ḫitlupu namrirrī*], who rides the great storms [*rākib ūmī rabûti*] [and] is clothed with fierce brilliance [*ḫālip melammē ezzūti*], who lays low the evil, who bears the holy whip, who makes the lightning flash [*mušabriq birqa*], the great lord.

See Grayson 1996: 208 (= text A.0.104.6, lines 1–5).

194. This passage forms the backdrop for Schwartz's (2010) broader study on metaphorical and literal language in biblical interpretation and the determinative interpretive framework that we bring to the text.
195. Cross (1973: 166) reasons that the "undoubtedly pre-Deuteronomic," "ninth-century B.C." Elijah narrative (the incubation in the cave of the Mount of God) "must in some way be dependent on Exodus 33:17–23." For literature on the conclusions of other source critics, see Durham 1987: 450–451.
196. Specifically, Billings (2004) sees two units (33:12–13, 17 ["perhaps E"] and 33:18, 21–23 ["perhaps J or E"]), each with redactional activity (33:14–16 ["perhaps P"] and 33:19 ["perhaps P"]). For more recent analysis of the contours of the non-P version of the sanctuary situated within the larger literary design of Exod 24–40, see Dozeman 2017: 344–361. See too Van Seters' (2013: 99 n. 22) brief comment suggesting that our passage is a later parody "perhaps influenced by the account of Elijah at Horeb in 1 Kgs 19:9–13." Yet the distinct language of *kābôd* that we find here does not appear in 1 Kgs 19.
197. Childs (1974: 596) also notes the use of the tautological *idem per idem* syntax in Exod 33:19 that parallels the *idem per idem* syntax in Exod 3:14.
198. The language of "strange paradox" is from Childs 1974: 596. On the hypostatic use of *kābôd*, see note 249.
199. For a concise overview of the history of scholarship on the Ark Narrative, see McCarter 1980a: 23–26. One of the most important works is Miller and Roberts 1977.

   However one dates the final compilation, all scholars agree that the material describing the cult at Shiloh preserves fragments of early tradition. Seow (1989: 11–54) argues that the Shilohnite cult preserves an old form of worship centered around Yahweh as he was venerated as El Elyon and associated with the Ark. Smith (2001b: 147) also suggests that "the god of the putative figure Moses and the Levitical priesthood in Shiloh was El." According to Römer (2007: 93–94), this material "contains very few traces of Deuteronomistic language [and] probably preserves an older tradition," yet "the present arrangement of 1 Sam 1–6 already seems to reflect the destruction of the temple in Jerusalem." Key for Römer is 1 Sam 4:21, which he views as "a redactional comment" that is "very close to the description of the departure of the Glory from the temple in Ezek. 8–10." For Römer, this suggests "that the story of the loss of the ark foreshadows the later destruction of the Jerusalem temple."

Consider too how, according to Haran (1962a; 1985: 198–204), P's "shrine legend" is referencing not Jerusalem but rather Shiloh. Or, in his more nuanced wording, P has in mind "a pre-Jerusalem shrine [i.e., Shiloh] legend now extant only in its Jerusalem dress" (Haran 1962: 23; 1985: 202–204). See similarly Milgrom 1991: 29–34.

200. The reading *lālat* here is either a rare example of a contracted infinitive construct written phonetically (*lālatt < *lāladt) or a graphic mistake for an original *lāle<de>t* < *lāladt. See McCarter 1980a: 112.
201. The fuller MT is represented here, although text-critically the LXX's shorter reading is preferable. The MT seems to conflate variant readings.
202. The dual translations here represent the ambiguity of the Hebrew, which can represent (1) the Philistines as polytheists who assume the Israelites to be polytheists too or (2) the Philistines as recognizing that a single god of the Israelites (whom they currently face) was none other than the sole god responsible for their victory over the Egyptians. As the current (MT) form of the narrative has it, one would have to lean toward the second, because according to 1 Sam 4:6, the Philistines "learned that Yahweh had come to the camp." Yet as recognized by several scholars including Driver, Polzin, and Sommer, subtle nuances (with humor and irony) abound in the passage. See Sommer 2009: 243 n. 84, including bibliography.
203. Following McCarter's (1980a: 104) astute reading of "and with pestilence" (*ûběmô-deber*) (taking a clue from the presence of a conjunction in the LXX), as opposed to MT's "in the wilderness' (*bammidbār*).
204. See Chapter Five, p. 140; EA 134; 252; Judg 18:24; Jer 48:7; 2 Chr 25:14–16; see especially the astute comments of Miller and Roberts (1977: 9–17, 76–87). We cannot agree with the conclusion of Sommer (2009: 61, 104–105). Sommer has Phinehas' widow speaking "of the very presence of her nation's God" in naming her newborn son Ichabod (*î-kābôd*). Yet he concludes: "Regardless of her intentions, we ought to understand the verse to refer to Israel losing its honor, not to God going physically into exile."
205. Compare Ps 78:61, which, though not using the specific vocabulary of *kābôd*, mentions God allowing "his glory" (*tip'artô*)—an allusion to the Ark—to be delivered into the hands of the Philistines. Thus the Psalmist keeps a firm distinction between the deity and his radiance as manifested in the cult object.
206. It is hard to ignore the collocation in our text of *kābôd* and *'ānān* that characterizes P elsewhere (e.g., Exod 16:10; 24:16; 40:34–35; Num 16:42; cf. Ezek 1:28; 10:4). At the same time, a full comparison reveals differences. 1 Kgs 8:10–11 does not have P's characteristic cloud "covering" (*ksh*; Exod 24:16; 40:34; Num 16:42) and radiance "appearing" (N of *r'h*; Exod 16:10; Lev 9:6, 23; 14:10; 16:42; 20:6). Moses in Exod 40:35 is unable "to enter" (*lābô'*), whereas the priests in 1 Kgs 8:10–11 were unable "to stand to minister" (*la'ămōd lěšārēt*). P's notion of "the cloud abiding" (*šākan 'ālāyw he'ānān*; Exod 40:35) is absent in 1 Kgs 8:10–11, with Solomon's subsequent declaration referring to Yahweh's abiding in darkness (*yhwh 'āmar liškōn bā'ărāpel*;1 Kgs 8:12). (1 Kgs 8:12 is often thought to be an independent unit; e.g., Mulder 1998: 396.)

For representative literature on the text and redaction of 1 Kgs 8, see Friedman 1981: 48–60; Hurowitz 1992: 262–266; McKenzie 1986; Knoppers 1995: 239–240; Mulder 1998: 394–395.
207. See note 192.
208. The Isaianic expression "the Holy One of Israel" is dealt with in Chapter Ten, pp. 599–603.
209. See Lewis 2008b: 88. For bibliography, see Lewis 2008b: 98 n. 53, especially the articles by Machinist.
210. Personal communication. See too Williamson 1999: 186.
211. See p. 797 and note 127.
212. See Lewis 2008b.
213. Works of note include Morgenstern 1911, 1914; Stein 1939; von Rad 1953; Davies 1962; Rendtorff 1963; Cross 1973: 163–169, 322–325; Weinfeld 1995; Mettinger 1982b: 80–115, 116–123; Milgrom 1991; Propp 1999, 2006; Aster 2006, 2012; and Sommer 2009: 68–79.
214. To describe these texts as being from P is an oversimplification. The history of research on the book of Leviticus shows varying opinions about its literary character. Ruwe (2003) summarizes four primary approaches: (1) those who work within the *Grundschrifthypothese* securely in place since Wellhausen's *Composition des Hexateuch*, and try to describe which parts of Leviticus are a part of the *Priestergrundschrift* (P^g) and which parts are supplementary to it (P^s) (e.g., Elliger, Pola, Otto, Frevel); (2) those who describe the current state of the text as resulting from differing priestly schools with different concepts of cult (e.g., Knohl and Milgrom); (3) those who "explain the lack of text unity in Leviticus as a result of flowing tradition processes" (e.g., Rendtorff, Blum, Crüseman, Gerstenberger); and (4) those who look to find a unified overarching structure in Leviticus expressed through a variety of literary conventions (e.g., Douglas, Smith). See Ruwe 2003: 55–56 for bibliography.

As for P blending a variety of sacred space traditions, see Mettinger's (1982b: 81–83) helpful analogy of thinking about this along the lines of "a photographic double exposure" where we can see in P "both an ancient pre-monarchial Tent tradition" as well as "the Temple theology of the Jerusalem tradition."
215. Milgrom (1991: 574) correctly juxtaposes "all the people" seeing the *kābôd* Yahweh in P's account in Lev 9:23 with the JE tradition of the leaders "seeing the God of Israel" in Exod 24:9–11. Yet he unduly writes (based on Lev 9:4) that "it is not God's *kābôd* but he, himself, who will be seen by all of Israel." Rather, in comparing Lev 9:4 with Lev 9:6, it is clear that for our author, Yahweh and the *kābôd* Yahweh are one and the same.
216. Hendel (1997: 222), following Barr, writes: "Only the special ones of the past are able to survive the 'holiness and awfulness of his aspect which must bring death to men who see him.' Seeing God and surviving is a form of blessing, an indication of religious worth."
217. Watts (2013: 429–552) provides a splendid rhetorical analysis of Lev 8–10 that underscores the refrain of Yahweh's commands. "Thus the object lesson of Nadab

and Abihu emphasizes the importance of the priests carrying out temple rituals accurately" (2013: 525).

Though the adjective *zārâ*, "foreign/forbidden," modifies the fire (*'ēš zārâ*), its foreignness could be tied to the incense mentioned in the same context (specifically, *qĕtōret* = frankincense), which was indeed a foreign import coming from Sheba (cf. Isa 60:6; Jer 6:20). Levine (1989: 58–59; 1993: 155–156) astutely notes the *qĕtōret zārâ* in Exod 30:9. Hess (2007b: 113–114; 2002) speculates that Nadab and Abihu were "participating in a West Semitic ritual that involved honoring other [non-Yahwistic] deities" based on the mention of a torch in the Emar installation ritual of a high priestess.

218. On the basis of Lev 16:1–2, Levine (1989: 59) suggests that "the offense [of Nadab and Abihu] consisted of penetrating too far into the sanctuary." In Lev 16:1–2, "Aaron is warned not to repeat the offense of his two sons by proceeding beyond the curtain (*parokhet*) in the sanctuary on any occasion other than Yom Kippur—'lest he die.'"

219. This material is dealt with in greater detail in Chapter Ten, pp. 639–641.

220. On P and Ezekiel, see Strine 2014: 272, noting how they "possess a family resemblance, but they are not identical twins. They are unquestionably related, yet unmistakenly distinct." Strine focuses especially on their differing concepts of the *imago Dei*. P has all of humanity bearing the divine image, whereas Ezekiel has the prophet himself (subverting the Mesopotamian *mīs pî* ritual) as the unique representation of Yahweh.

221. My translation of the enigmatic *ḥašmal* (which appears only in Ezek 1:4, 27; 8:2) follows Greenberg's (1983: 43) comment that "the context indicates a bright substance, with a color like that of fire," and yet I realize that most scholars think it refers to a gleaming metal or precious stone of some sort (see note 9).

222. Here *gōbah* and *yir'â* seem to be a calque on the Akkadian *puluḫtu* and *melammu*. So Waldman (1984), followed by Aster (2006: 317, 413–414).

223. The MT reads "fire" (*'ēš*) here, and this could easily be a graphic mistake for "man" (*'îš*), as witnessed by the LXX's *andros*, and as necessitated by the mention of the figure's "loins" and "hand." The occasion for the mistake could easily have been the *'ēš* that immediately follows. And yet even if the figure is human-like (with "loins" and "hand"), the author is portraying a preternatural, fiery, radiant entity that is beyond human. Thus MT's *'ēš* could be intentional after all rather than a scribal slip. If this was the case, then the LXX reading could be a graphic mistake and/or by attraction to the *'ādām* of 1:26.

224. Yet see P's use of *rêyaḥ nîḥōaḥ lĕyhwh* in note 5. See also the nuanced treatment in Knafl 2014.

While Sommer's (2009) study *The Bodies of God* is brimming with insights, I do not find his use of "body" to describe the divine *kābôd* as helpful, even though *kābôd* elsewhere (Isa 17:4; Ps 16:9) could at times refer to a physical body (cf. Weinfeld 1995a: 25; Sommer 2009: 60). Sommer (2009: 2, 71) defines "body" as "something located in a particular place at a particular time, whatever its shape or substance." Thus P's *kābôd* can be a "body" in this sense even though it is immaterial. Light and fire can also be "bodies" even though they are ethereal, not solid objects. And yet defining the word "body" in this particular way faces an uphill battle in that English consistently and universally uses the noun "body" to describe physical structure and material substance. The word "body" is used of a corpse, the trunk of a tree, the hull of a ship, the fuselage of a plane, the population of the American people, planets, and stars. Physics and geometry employ the word in its sense of mass, as do references to collective groups (the student body). Lastly, even wine can be said to have good body and structure.

Sommer (2009: 71) is more astute when he writes (using "the anachronism of applying Newtonian terms") that "the [divine] *kābôd* is made of energy but not matter."

225. Of the many studies on the Mesopotamian background of the book of Ezekiel, see especially Garfinkel 1983; Bodi 1991; Vanderhooft 2014; Winitzer 2014; Nissinen 2015; Stökl 2015a, 2015b; and Liebermann 2019.

226. Cf. Keel 1977: 125–173; 1992: 372; Mettinger 1982: 103–106; Allen 1994: 27–37; Uehlinger and Trufaut 2001; Aster 2006: 156–158, 422–424; 2015; Lewis 2013b: 800–803. For the minimal use of Mesopotamian imagery, cf. de Vries 2016: 243.

227. As mentioned in note 126, this image was noted already by Mendenhall in 1973 in connection to *melammu*, yet he made no reference to the book of Ezekiel.

While Uehlinger and Trufaut (2001: 147) acknowledge the value of this image to depict the phenomenology of *melammu*, they are too critical of those scholars (e.g., Keel and Allen) who use this image to unpack the visual symbols associated with the historical Ezekiel because of its ninth-century BCE date. For a response, see Aster 2006: 424.

Mayer-Opificius (1984: 200) and Klingbeil (1999: 260–261) prefer to see the god Shamash being represented in Figure 7.23 rather than Aššur (thus Pongratz-Leisten 2011: 172).

228. *Yāʿōp/yēdeʾ* are variants, as recognized by Cross and Freedman (1975: 99). The conflation of these two variants in the MT led to the misplacing of the *ʾatnāḥ* after *yāʿōp*, taking it, as a result, with the first line and making it overly long poetically. The prosody along with the parallel in 2 Sam 22:11 (reading *ydʾ*; cf. McCarter 1984: 457) argues for *yāʿōp* and *yēdeʾ* being two variant verbs.

229. Cf. Block 1997: 103–104, stressing the "numerous lexical links" between Ps 18 and Ezek 1.

230. Destructive water imagery is also present in the mention of a "raging torrent" (*naḥal šôṭēp*) in Isa 30:28 and "torrential rain" (*nepeṣ wāzerem*) in Isa 30:30. Given its collocation with fiery imagery, one wonders too if there are allusions to radiance (cf. *kōbed, hôd* in 30:27, 30) in this passage.

231. Provisionally reading "man" (*ʾîš*) along with the LXX (so the majority of commentators), as opposed to MT's "fire" (*ʾēš*). See note 223.

232. For a convenient and complete listing of all the references for these various phrases, see Mettinger 1982b: 39–40.

233. On the history of scholarship on the Name Theology and a vast bibliography, see McBride 1969: 6–65; Mettinger 1982b: 41–46; Keller 1996; Richter 2002: 7–36; and

Hundley 2009. To illustrate the variety of views, note Mettinger's (2003: 755) objection to being described as "unconscious apostles of Wellhausen." Ultimately, the positions that scholars take with regard to the Name Theology are tied to their understanding of the complexities of the formation of the book of Deuteronomy and the Deuteronomistic History. Obviously, then, the present discussion can only sketch the Name Theology, with the danger of oversimplification. For a more nuanced and detailed discussion, readers should consult the literature mentioned in the first five works cited in this note.

234. For the Amarna material, Mettinger (1982b: 56–57) is building on the work of de Vaux and McBride; for the theophanies, he stands on the shoulders of Weiser, Zimmerli, and others (see Mettinger 1982b: 124–126 and for bibliography 125 n. 27).

235. Richter (2002: 26) says that it was von Rad "who transported . . . the fledgling Name Theology into the mainstream."

236. See McBride's (1969) discussion of Noth (pp. 41–43) and Schreiner (pp. 43–45) as well as his own take on the material (pp. 45–53). See also the view of Clements (1965a, 1965b).

237. See McBride's (1969) discussion of Alt (pp. 34–36), Dumermuth (pp. 36–40), and Newman (pp. 40–41).

238. See the representative bibliography in Holladay 1986: 240 n. 7. Holladay, on the contrary, argues that "a close look at the phrases of the passage makes it clear that these phrases are not specifically 'Deuteronomistic' but make up a carefully wrought discourse with distinctive diction having a close relation to the poetry of Jrm . . . there is some overlap in phraseology between this passage and Deuteronomistic material but not to a significant degree."

The phrase "ironic comparison" is McBride's (1969: 47).

239. See note 238.

240. See Wilson 1995: 68–73. Mettinger (1998: 9) is able to concede Wilson's point here by noting that his "position is that the original Deuteronomic code does not contain a Name theology." Mettinger then critiques Wilson for not dealing with the Deuteronomistic History's Name Theology. Yet in response to Mettinger (and affirming Wilson's view), see Hundley 2009: 538 n. 23.

241. For bibliography, see Wilson 1995: 24, 118.

242. Sommer (2009: 217–218 n. 40) calls Deut 23:15 "an exception to the Deuteronomic theology of God's abode in heaven alone." While such passages do seem to stem from archaic lore, one should not simply relegate them to the past as "vestiges" (so Sommer) that would have no resonance with the world of the authors of Deuteronomy, who valued them enough to incorporate them into their framework.

243. The privileged position of 1 Kgs 8 for reconstructing Name Theology has been challenged by Hundley (2009: 551), who argues that "the context and uniqueness of 1 Kings 8 mitigates its extreme language; one must be cautious in applying this text unilaterally since the stress on divine presence [only] in heaven appears nowhere else so forcefully." Compare especially the Name Theology in 2 Sam 7:13, where, as Hundley (2009: 540) notes, "there is no reference to divine presence in heaven."

On 1 Kgs 8 Hundley adds: "The chapter nowhere explicitly denies divine presence on earth," including the potent reference in 1 Kgs 8:27. This verse "states that both earthly *and heavenly* dwellings are ultimately unfit for YHWH" (emphasis Hundley's). As for the context, Hundley (2009: 552) remarks that the rhetoric is that of a petitioner (Solomon) currying favor with a suzerain (God).

244. A great deal of significance has been attached to activities being performed "before Yahweh" (*lipnê yhwh*). An extensive analysis of this phrase as it applies to Deut 12-26 may be found in Wilson 1995: 131-197. Wilson (1995: 204-205) concludes: "The majority of the sixteen instances of *lipnê yhwh* in Deut 12-26 should be understood in the literal sense and thus that they point to the localized Presence of the Deity at the 'chosen place.' . . . God is represented as being present on earth not only in the context of the Wilderness wanderings and Holy War but also in that of the cult, and at the very place at which the divine Name is known to be present."

As for the sacrifices mentioned in 1 Kgs 8:62, compare the tradition preserved in 2 Chr 7:1-3, where these actions are *preceded* by the (divine) fire coming down from heaven (*hāʾēš yārĕdâ mēhaššāmayim*) that consumes the burnt offerings and sacrifices. 2 Chr 7:1-3 also contains a description of the *kābôd* filling the temple (cf. 1 Kgs 8:10-11).

245. See Knoppers 2000: 389; 1995a: 247. Knoppers (2000: 375; 1995a: 233) also speaks of the Deuteronomist's "deliberate authorial strategy" in 1 Kgs 8 with "recurring actions and speeches [that] unify the proceedings."

246. Knoppers (2000: 389; 1995a: 247) astutely questions: "Why would an exilic writer extend and expand the function of a temple that had been destroyed? The deuteronomistic trope of the temple as a site for prayer promotes the temple's value rather than devalues it."

247. McBride (1969: 4) argued strongly that "the Deuteronomistic Name Theology . . . simply cannot be understood on the basis of the internal biblical evidence alone." Instead one must use "ancient Near Eastern traditions directly bearing on the conceptual, formal and theological context of Old Testament Name Theology." A substantial portion of McBride's (1969: 66-176) unpublished dissertation is devoted to the ancient Near Eastern context of the Deuteronomic Name Theology.

248. See Chapter Four, note 116.

249. Cf. McCarter 2008a—on which see pp. 351-353—as well as Simone 2015 and de Vries 2016: esp. 56-57, 82-84, 113, 117, 351, 362-364. De Vries argues that the *kābôd* of Yahweh was also understood hypostatically.

250. On the Ugaritic and Kuntillet ʿAjrud titles, see Lewis 2011. The fragmentary Kuntillet ʿAjrud plaster inscription 4.2 is treated in Chapter Ten, pp. 583-587, and Lewis 2020.

251. We follow to a degree the translation and textual analysis of McCarter (1984: 161-63), except we think that the double occurrence of the noun *šēm* in the MT should be retained as key to the interpretation. Hence one of the uses of *šēm* should *not* be omitted as a dittograph nor repointed as *šām*, "there."

252. As noted by Cross (1973: 95 n. 19), the verb *qwm* is used here "in the sense of 'attack' " (cf. too Judg 5:12; Ps 132:8; 74:22; 82:8). So too Levine (1993: 312, 318). Cf. JPS's translation of *qûmâ yhwh* (Num 10:35) calling upon Yahweh to "advance" to battle.

253. The very tentative reconstruction of verse 36 follows that of Cross (1973: 100), who admits to the "hopelessly corrupt" nature of our text but nonetheless reconstructs with poetic pairs based in part on Ps 68:18 and Deut 33:2-3. One difficulty with this reconstruction is that any military side of the god El is rarely emphasized. Alternatively, one could translate, following Levine (1993: 312, 319) in part, "Return O Yahweh, [with] the myriads of Israel's militias."

254. As for combining anthropomorphisms and the effectual divine name in battle, cf. Ps 89:22-25 (Eng 89:21-24), which contains the Name of Yahweh empowering David in battle together with Yahweh's hand//arm. See further Isa 41:25, Ps 118:10-11, and the discussion of Ps 89 in Chapter Eight, pp. 455-458. For the broader ancient Near Eastern context, see Lewis 2011.

255. Cf. Cross 1973: 93ff., 142, 148, 156.

256. See Lewis's (2011) discussion of how divine names functioned in the context of war.

257. Cf. Gropp and Lewis 1985: 46, lines 10-12, 16-17. Richter (2002: 209) writes: "The Tell Fakhariyeh text serves to explain the relationship between Deuteronomy's *lĕšakkēn šĕmô šām* and Dtr[1]'s *lāśûm šĕmô šām*. Whereas Deuteronomy's *lĕšakkēn šĕmô šām* is best explained as a b[iblical] H[ebrew] loan adaptation of Akk[adian] *šuma šakānu*, Dtr[1]'s *lāśûm šĕmô šām* is best explained as a b[iblical] H[ebrew] calque of the same Akk[adian] idiom."

258. There are particulars that present problems as well, yet for considerations of space they will not be reviewed. See the details mentioned in the various reviews of Richter's study, including Mettinger 2003; Van Seters 2003a; Hurowitz 2004-2005; and Hundley 2009.

259. The only place we have divine fire is in the non-Deuteronomistic Elijah narrative (1 Kgs 18:24-25, 38).

260. I am indebted to Alice Mandell for this quote.

261. Compare the description of Marduk in Enuma Elish, Tablet I, lines 99-100, as translated by Foster (1997: 392).

> He was the tallest of the gods, surpassing in form,
> His limbs enormous, he was surpassing at birth.

The passage goes on to underscore how Marduk was "clothed [*labiš*] with the *melammu*s of ten gods."

262. The historical role of the Ark, its portrayal in various literary strands (Deuteronomy, P, and Chronicles), Psalms, and narratives (the "Ark Narrative"), and its function in sacred space will be addressed in another venue. See the overviews in Haran 1959; Woudstra 1965; Fretheim 1968; Gutman 1971; Zobel 1974; Campbell 1975, 1979; Miller and Roberts 1977; McCarter 1980a: 23-26, 101, 107-109, 124-126; Ahlström 1984; Metzger 1985 (based on his 1969 *Habilitationsschrift*); Seow 1985, 1989, 1992; and Birch 2006. It should be kept in mind that there are many more allusions to

the Ark than might be immediately recognizable. Seow (1992: 387) astutely points out how "the Ark, which represented the real presence of the deity, may be known simply by the divine name," similar to how "divine images of Mesopotamia were not always called statues, they were regularly referred to as 'gods.'" For example, Seow points out the comment by Yahweh that he dwelled in a tent in 2 Sam 7:6. This is "clearly to be equated with the Ark being in the tent" mentioned in 2 Sam 7:2.

263. Jer 3:16–17 is written against people being nostalgic about the Ark, not against the Ark per se. At the same time, the author does envision the city of Jerusalem as replacing the Ark as the throne of Yahweh (3:17).

As for metonymic representation, see Evans 1995, building on the work of Halbertal and Margalit (1992), who in turn are building on the semiotics of C. S. Peirce.

264. On the Holiness of the Ark and its lethal power, see Chapter Ten, pp. 595–599.

265. Hillers goes on to argue strongly against using Ps 132 to anchor this consensus. He emphasizes how Ps 132 has significant parallels with dedicatory inscriptions. Thus, for Hillers (1968: 52), it is "unnecessary to assume that the psalm was associated with any regularly recurring festival." At the same time, he moderates his view: "It is not claimed here that reinterpretation of Psalm 132:8 *disproves* the notion that the ark was carrier in ritual procession during the monarchy. . . . But it does seem that this can no longer be regarded as proven."

266. For a sample of Mowinckel's theory, see his *The Psalms in Israel's Worship*, vol. 1 (1962: 174–177). Commenting on 2 Sam 6, 1 Kgs 8, and Ps 132, Kraus (1989: 477) writes that "not even a trace of an enthronement of God can be found in these texts." On Ps 132:8 Kraus (1989: 481) adds: "An enthronement of Yahweh is completely out of place."

267. For the translation "from" based on the Ugaritic, see Hillers 1968: 48–55, which is followed by Cross 1973: 95. Kraus (1989: 480–481) suggests that the cultic call in Ps 132:8 "probably represents not only a reflective allusion to the ark saying in Num 10:35f., but the incorporation of the old war call into the cultic ceremonial."

268. Cf. the discussion of Ps 24's relation to Isa 6 on pp. 367–368 and its connection to *Chaoskampf* traditions in Chapter Eight, pp. 458–460.

269. For Cross's full discussion, see 1973: 91–105. The quotes used here are from pages 91 and 93. Cf. Craigie 1983: 213–214.

270. For the text and translation, see Grayson 1991: 292–293.

271. On Mesopotamian *Mischwesen*, see Chapter Eight, note 14. As noted by Zevit (2001: 317), the guarding function was totally different between these two cultures. In Mesopotamia, the guarding was often apotropaic in nature (see Danrey 2004), whereas in Gen 3:24 the guarding is to keep humans away from the tree of life (and hence divine lethality?).

Other references to a possible guarding (or sheltering or shielding) function of the cherubim involve the root *skk* (cf. Exod 25:20; 1 Kgs 8:7; Ezek 28:14, 16; Ps 91:4, 11). See Propp's (2006: 390–391) discussion, especially how he notes the difference between the Psalmist's comfort for all who take shelter within the Tabernacle ("even in the Holy of Holies, even beneath the Griffins' very wings") and P's perspective, which would have thought of such as "anathema."

272. The monumental *aladlammu* (*lamassu*) sculpture at the Louvre and similar ones at the British Museum, the University of the Chicago's Oriental Institue, and the Baghdad Museum come from the Palace of Sargon II (721–705 BCE) in Dur-Sharrukin (Khorsabad), Assyria. The Metropolitan Museum of Art's sculpture comes from Kalhu (Nimrud) and dates to the reign of Aššurnasirpal II (883–859 BCE). According to Danrey (2004), more than one hundred such sculptures have survived, with approximately forty coming from Nineveh. The earliest example of an *aladlammu* (*lamassu*) sculpture comes from the reign of Tiglath-Pileser I (1114–1076 BCE). These prevalent sculptures are attested in Neo-Assyrian history for more than four hundred years, stopping after the reign of Aššurbanipal (668–627 BCE) only to resurface in the Persian Empire during the reigns of Cyrus II, Darius I, and Xerxes. For detailed discussions, see Danrey 2004 and Ritter forthcoming.

273. Hartenstein 2007: 158. The most detailed discussion of the etymology of Hebrew *kĕrubîm* is found in Wood 2008: 141–155, arguing against Dhorme's (1926) use of the Akkadian to demonstrate an intercessory role for the Cherubim. In contrast, Wood (2008: 154) argues that attention should be focused on the Akkadian *kurību*, "a representation of a protective genius with specific non-human features . . . [which] certainly accords with the biblical description of the cherubim."

274. Scholars have long noted how biblical writers had a significant amount of knowledge about Assyrian kings and their "official rhetoric" as conveyed through text and iconography. For bibliography, see Lewis 2008b: 88, 98 n. 53. Thus it is possible that the Jerusalem Temple artisans and the author of 1 Kgs 6 knew of the *aladlammu* (*lamassu*) sculptures as they crafted their cherubim of similar size.

275. The addition of wheels was a feature with wide ramifications, for it led to Ezekiel's cherubim throne being viewed as a chariot, though Ezekiel himself makes no such explicit reference. Cf. too the notion of Yahweh "riding/driving" (*yirkab*) the flying cherub in Ps 18:11//2 Sam 22:11 (cf. Ps 68:5 [Eng 68:4]; 104:3) The lone explicit reference to the cherubim constituting a chariot (*hammerkābâ hakkĕrubîm*) in the Hebrew Bible can be found in 1 Chr 28:18. Subsequent references are found in the Apocrypha, the Qumran texts, the Pseudepigrapha, and, of course, the well-known Merkabah mystical texts. For specific references in this material, see Knoppers 2004: 934.

276. Cf. Ps 104:3, which has Yahweh traversing (*mĕhallēk*) on the wings of the wind. The psalmist also personified the "winds" as Yahweh's messengers (Ps 104:4; cf. 1 Kgs 22:19–23).

The notion of Yahweh mounting a cherub (*yirkab ʿal-kĕrûb*) juxtaposed with clouds being *beneath his feet* (*taḥat raglāyw*) could bring to mind the numerous images of a storm god standing on top of a bull or a *Mischwesen* such as in Figure 5.30. One might then object to paralleling such a *standing* figure with Yahweh *seated* (*yhwh ṣĕbāʾôt yōšēb hakkĕrubîm*) on or between the cherubim elsewhere. Yet it is clear from iconography such as what we have with the procession of deities in Figure 5.13 (where the first deity stands atop beasts followed by a second deity enthroned on a lion) that standing and seated figures were viewed as parallel

phenomena. For a close-up of the standing and seated figures in our Figure 5.13, see Figure 7.28 and Parpola 1997: 20, fig. 26.
277. I thank John Walton for directing me to the figure of Mulissu seated on a *Mischwesen* in Figure 7.27. Figure 7.27 and Figure 7.28 can also be found in Parpola 1997: XLI, fig. 18; 20, fig. 26).
278. E.g., Keel 1977: 15–45; Mettinger 1982a: 113–115, figs. 1–2; 1988: 127–131; Metzger 1985: 259–274; Tafel 113, figs. 1181, 1183; Schroer 1987: 121–130; Keel and Uehlinger 1998: 168; Hartenstein 2007: 159–160, figs 1, 2.
279. Though it is only partially preserved, see too the sphinx/cherub throne of King Idrimi of Late Bronze Age Alalakh.
280. In this Edelman follows Meshorer 1982.
281. In addition, one needs to wrestle with the competing ideologies of kingship between Deuteronomy and DtrH. See Chapter Nine, note 13.
282. Propp (2006: 428–429) notes Josephus' remark about lamps burning night and day. But cf. too 1 Sam 3:3.
283. What I mean by this is that humans do not consume any part of the ʿōlâ, in contrast to the offerings such as the *zebaḥ* and the *šĕlāmîm*, "whose meat is eaten by its offerer" (Milgrom 1991: 204, 221). There is certainly the conjunctive aspect of sacrifice whereby the donor attains a closer proximity to the divine.
284. In addition to the phrase "ever-burning fire" (*ʾēš tāmîd*) representing the continual presence of Yahweh, it could very likely indicate the perpetual devotion of the Israelite people toward Yahweh (Levine 1989: 36). Either of these interpretations is a viable option. Perhaps the ancients had both in mind.
285. For an analysis of the numerous golden vessels that were said to fill the First Temple, see Hurowitz 1995. See the suggestion (p. 359) by Ornan and Winter that gold and silver overlay were used to create a radiant aesthetic for divine images.
286. The examples here are funerary in nature, with our best examples being the Samʾalian Aramaic Katumuwa and Panamuwa inscriptions. Cf. Suriano 2014: 388, 396; 2018: 169; Lewis 2019: 363–364. Granted, these examples are not a perfect analogy, as they also include an anthropomorphic representation of the deceased.
287. Given the tomb context, Mandell and Smoak (2016: 241–242) argue for an apotropaic function.
288. This is *not* to suggest that this was a conscious decision motivated by a Judean who visited the Iron Age site of Ayn Dara and brought back its notions of sacred emptiness on a large scale. At the same time, biblical tradition (2 Kgs 16:10–11) does in fact describe King Ahaz (735–727 BCE) traveling to Syria, where he sees an altar in Damascus that he then has replicated in Jerusalem!
289. The most relevant avenues of research for empty space aniconism (in addition to Ayn Dara) would be the empty cherubim thrones known from Phoenicia. These small thrones were likely votive offerings. See Gubel 1987: 37–75; Mettinger 1995: 100–106; 1997b: 198–199; 2006: 285–287; Keel and Uehlinger 1998: 168. Cf. also the late ninth-/early eighth-century fragmentary seal impression on a bulla from the city of David mentioned previously (Ornan 2019; Keel 2012 b), and the small (1 in. [2.6 cm] high by 0.7 in. [1.7 cm] wide) ivory cherubim throne from Megiddo. For the

illustration, see Keel 1977: 20, Abb. 6; Mettinger 1982: 22, fig. 3; Metzger 1985: 259–261; Tafel 113, fig. 1182; and Keel and Uehlinger 1998: 63, fig. 66b.

290. Taylor is clearly influenced by the pairing of Yahweh and Asherah at Kuntillet ʿAjrud, to which he refers frequently to bolster his argument.

291. Though it might be tempting to think of the openings being used to vent smoke, there is no indication of any fire or smoke on the cult stand (Hestrin 1987: 61). Thus Lapp (1969: 44) was correct not to adopt Sellin's vocabulary of the Taanach cult stand being a *Räucheraltar*, assuming that fire was kindled to burn incense.

292. A comprehensive analysis of the Taanach cult stands would also need to include the perspectives of materiality, miniaturization, and micro-architecture (personal communication, Alice Mandell).

293. See Mettinger 1995: 165, n. 131 for bibliography. Hestrin (1991: 58) has also commented on the space being "probably the entrance to the shrine."

294. For a discussion and distribution of the references to "the living God" in the Hebrew Bible, see Mettinger 1988: 82–91.

295. The word "tradent" is common among biblical scholars (especially within text-critical circles) yet rare elsewhere and thus not found in most English dictionaries. In short, it refers to people who engage in a process of examining traditions for one's own time, preserving them and handing them down to future generations of believers. In the words of Sanders (1998: 22), "All scribes, translators, commentators, midrashists and even preachers are tradents.... [A]ll tradents of Scripture have had two responsibilities—to the text and to their community, that is, to the community's past and to its present. A tradent inevitably brings the past into the present in contemporary terms."

296. On the meaning of the name Yahweh, see Chapter Six.

297. Sommer (2009: 97) goes on to note how such historical reductionism, which is "so common among modern biblical scholars ... [,] does a disservice both to the Bible and to historicism." Sommer unpacked what he meant here in a 2009 SBL panel discussion of his book *The Bodies of God and the World of Ancient Israel*:

> My readings are constantly diachronic, or at least not synchronic in that I am constantly attending to the layering of biblical texts and to the ways texts like the Pentateuch, which is after all an anthology and not a book, record a variety of ancient Israelite voices as they converse and argue with each other. But I reject certain sorts of diachronic reading—for example, readings that attempt to line all these voices up along a sequence, so that P must come either before D or after it. I regard most of these voices as being streams of tradition that coexisted for centuries; indeed, I attempt to show that the mindsets they reflect and articulate coexist even today within Judaism and within Christianity.

Chapter 8

1. See Chapter Six, note 1.
2. Yet cf. the mention of El in conjunction with mountains melting and a "day of war" in one of the plaster fragments from Kuntillet ʿAjrud. See Chapter Six, p. 281, Chapter Ten, pp. 583–587, and Lewis 2020.

3. For a broader discussion on theorizing violence, especially ritual violence within biblical traditions, see Olyan 2015.
4. The full text (KTU 1.119 = RS 24.266, for which see Pardee 2000: 661–685; 2002a: 149–150) involves a petition to see if Baʿlu will indeed act, followed by vows of several offerings and an ascent to the sanctuary. The conclusion then proclaims that Baʿlu will certainly hear the prayer and act to drive the enemy away.
5. See Chapter Seven, pp. 334, 339, and note 127.
6. On the enigmatic *hqr ryt* in line 12, see Zevit 2012.
7. On the biblical *ḥērem*, see pp. 462–463.
8. The cultic paraphernalia is designated as an "altar hearth" (*ʾrʾl*) in line 12. Some scholars reconstruct the same word in line 18 ("the a[ltar-hea]rths of Yahweh," *ʾ[rʾ]ly yhwh*), while others reconstruct "[ve]ssels of Yahweh," *[k]ly yhwh*. See Chapter Six, note 125.
9. For an overview, see Miller 1973; Lind 1980; Kang 1989; and Klingbeil 1999. These are just a handful of the many books on divine war in the ancient Near East as it relates to biblical tradition. Many of the warrior traditions blend with storm god traditions. Here see the study by Schwemer (2001) and his summaries (2007, 2008a). For the epigraphic material, cf. the explicit mention of Yahweh Sebaoth in one of the seventh-century BCE cave inscriptions published by Naveh (2001; see also Chapter Six, pp. 244–245, and Figure 6.11) and the mention of Baal and the Name of El "on the day of war" (*bym mlḥ[mh]*) in one of the plaster fragments found at Kuntillet ʿAjrud. See Chapter Six, p. 281, Chapter Ten, pp. 583–587, and Lewis 2020.
10. On the connection between holiness and power, see Chapter Ten.
11. See Chapter Six, note 106 for Mettinger's statistics on the usage of Yahweh Sebaoth.
12. See Chapter Seven, pp. 388 and 396.
13. Cf. Enuma Elish, Tablet I, lines 1–2; Ps 74:12; 93:2.
14. For a detailed visual catalogue of the hybrid forms known as *Mischwesen*, see Green 1994: 246–264. An abbreviated version of this catalog may be found in Black, Green, and Rickards 1992.
15. On Otto's vocabulary (used of late by scholars such as Jacobsen, van der Toorn, and Sommer), see Chapter Seven, p. 337, and Chapter Ten, p. 587.
16. Ever since Gunkel's *Schöpfung und Chaos* (1895), the language of *Chaoskampf* has been commonly used in the study of conflict myths. Ballentine (2015: 186–198) argues that we should change our nomenclature, as these stories are primarily ideological productions. We should best "leave 'chaos' out of it."
17. For additional images of divine warriors fighting a wide array of fantastic creatures, see Lewis 1996b.
18. The story here is abbreviated. For the full text, including the Akkadian as well as secondary literature, see Lewis 1996b.
19. Bottéro and Kramer (1989: 465) add "[de sa langue(?)]."
20. For Canaanite examples of this pattern, see Cross 1973: 93.
21. Wiggerman (1989: 119) notes that the "kingship that is offered here to the victor is certainly not that over the gods [as in Enuma Elish], but that over the nation he saves from peril."

22. Jacobsen 1932: 54. Wiggermann (1989: 125) argues that we should translate this as "your/his very own [seal]." Bottéro and Kramer (1989: 468) suggest "un usage possible de cette masse de pierre, plus ou moins lourde et qui pouvait constituer une arme de choc, comme on contait qu'avait été assassiné le fils du grand Sargon, Rîmuš... 'à coups de sceaux-cylindres, par ses officiers.'"
23. See the treatments by Bottéro and Kramer (1989: 466), Heidel (1951: 143), and Ebeling (1916: 106–108).
24. Šēpāšu is reconstructed by Ebeling (1916: 107); CAD, A/I, 325; and others.
25. Though it should be noted that Figures 8.8 and 8.9 do come from Tell Asmar (ancient Eshnunna), whose chief god was Tishpak.
26. See Cooper 1978: 64–65, 80–81; Lewis 1996b: 45. For the former text, see lines 55–63 in "Ninurta's Return to Nibru: A Šir-gida to Ninurta" (http://etcsl.orinst.ox.ac.uk/cgi-bin/etcsl.cgi?text=t.1.6.1#). For the latter, the Akkadian reads ša kima mušmaḫḫi seba qaqaadāšu nērta inarru. See CAD S, 204.
27. Because of space considerations, we are not treating the combat story of Anzu. For an introduction to this material, see Ballentine 2015: 23–30. For the reflex of these stories in Egyptian and Hurro-Hittite texts, see Ayali-Darshan 2010, 2015.
28. In the Assyrian telling of the story it is Aššur rather than Marduk who plays the role.
29. Tiamat (Akkadian tiāmtu, tâmtu) is cognate with Hebrew tĕhôm, "deep," and Ugaritic thmt (which occurs in the deity lists; cf. KTU 1.148.6, 41; KTU 1.118.18; RS 20.024.18; RS 92.2004.29). Cf. Huehnergard 1987: 184–185; Smith 1994b: 85–86, 160 n. 81; Pardee 2000: 660, 779–806; 2002a: 14–15, 18–19; and Alster 1999: 867–869.
30. The translation here is Foster's (1997: 392, 393, 395, 396).
31. The translation here is Foster's (1997: 392).
32. The translation here is Foster's (1997: 398).
33. According to Hallo and Younger (1997: 391), the exaltation of Marduk in Enuma Elish is similar "to the exaltation of Yahweh as celebrated... in the Song of the Sea (Exodus 15)."
34. Our heuristic turn to look at the Ugaritic material only highlights the selective nature of our study. To explore the many cultural interplays of the East-West Semitic Chaoskampf traditions, one would certainly have to examine Assyrian-Aramean mixtures, such as when Sennacherib has the gods Aššur and Amurru riding together in a chariot going to do battle with Tiamat. See further Beaulieu 2005: 44; 2006: 189.
35. KTU 1.2.4.11–23; cf. Lewis 2011: 213–214. See too the very end of the Ba'lu myth (KTU 1.6.6.51–53), which petitions Kotharu-wa-Hasisu to expel (*yadiy > yadî) Yammu, ʾArišu, and the Tunnanu-dragon—all of whom are mentioned in KTU 1.3.3.38–43, where ʿAnatu brings about their defeat.
36. The translation follows Pardee 1997c: 248, yet it should be mentioned that the verb here (ydlp) has to do with "leaking," a fitting (and humorous?) description of the collapsing of the Sea.
37. See previous note.
38. The translation here follows Pardee's (1997c: 249) interpretation that the battle is ongoing, as opposed to other translators' assumptions that the battle has ended (e.g., Gibson 1978: 44: "Baal dragged out Yam and laid him down, he made an end of judge

Nahar"). Cf. too Smith's (1994b: 351) comment that line 27 "marks the formal end of the battle section." Pardee's analysis seems more likely given the use of the durative (*yaqtulu*) form of the verb *ykly* (*yakalliyu*), as opposed to the preterite *ykl* (*yakallî*).

Greenstein (1982: 205) suggests an alternative interpretation where "Yammu has been captured, not destroyed, by Baʿlu" and hence is deserving of ʿAthtartu's shaming rebuke. The consensus among scholars sees the three verbs as parallel (and thus the clear destructive meaning of *ykly* helps determine the nuances of *yqṯ* and *yšt*). In contrast, Greenstein translates as follows, with *yqṯ* being used intransitively and *ykly* functioning as a subjunctive: "Baʿlu ensnares and places Yammu [in the snare], He would destroy Judge Naharu."

39. See Lewis 2011. In this article I argue that ʿAthtartu is hexing (*gʿr*) Yammu in KTU 1.2.4.28–39 as a part of Baʿlu's defeat of the monster (as opposed to the consensus of scholars, which has the goddess rebuking Baʿlu at the very apex of the battle). See too Wilson-Wright 2015: 337 n. 14. The specific content of her effective (performative, magical) words uses the power inherent in Baʿlu's name, thus leading to her epithet ʿAthtartu-'Name'-of-Baʿlu.

On the verb *bṯ* and whether it refers to scattering or drying up (or even shaming), see Lewis 2011: 216 n. 62.

40. The narrative continues with several other enemies mentioned. See the full narrative in KTU 1.3.3.38–47. On the translation of *šlyṭ* as "Powerful One" versus Pope's "Potentate," see Smith and Pitard 2009: 251. It needs to be noted, as Pardee (1997c: 252 n. 91) does, that our narrative "as extant does not contain an [actual] account of ʿAnatu's defeat of Yammu/Naharu." Pardee suggests that "one may surmise that ʿAnatu intervened after Baʿlu's battle with Yammu, and hence that this passage refers to a sequel to the narrative in CTA 2 iv, or that the mention of someone driving someone from a throne in CTA 1 iv was related to a defense by ʿAnatu of Baʿlu's rights." The final act of ʿAnatu's battle prowess is her celebrated victory over Motu (Death). See KTU 1.6.2.9–37.

41. KTU 1.82.1, 38 contains two broken texts that seem to refer to this episode as well:

(1) [... *yi*]*mḫaṣ baʿlu* [...]*y tunnana*
May Baʿlu c[ru]sh [], May he [] the dragon.
(38) [...]*tadruk barīḫa ʾarṣa*
May you [O Baʿlu] tread the fleeing [serpent] to the ground.

42. For the ways in which this passage can be translated and the arguments for the identity of the goddess being either ʿAnatu or ʿAthtartu, see Pitard 1998 and Lewis 2011: 217–218.

43. On Gunkel and the "history of religion" school of thought, see p. 24. For a translation of Gunkel's treatment, see Gunkel 2006. On the numerous treatments of *Chaoskampf* traditions in the Hebrew Bible, see the thorough review of the relevant texts in Day 1985 and the analysis of these myths as ideological productions in Ballentine 2015.

44. See Hossfeld and Zenger 2005: 243–244. Others argue for later in the exile (e.g., Kraus 1989: 97) and yet others for the time of the Maccabees (yet cf. the critique by Hossfeld and Zenger as well as by Day [1985: 22 n. 59]).

45. As to whether the *Sitz im Leben* of Ps 74 is that of the Feast of Tabernacles, see Day 1985: 19–21 and the literature cited therein.
46. Ps 74 is a part of the Elohistic Psalter (on which see p. 724 note 65, and p. 784 note 229). Thus we reconstruct Yahweh (the likely original reading) for the MT's *'ĕlōhîm*. Indeed, Yahweh is the Israelite god who fights cosmic battles.
47. Commenting on the sevenfold *'attâ*, Dahood (1968a: 205) creatively envisions our poet—with "subtle artistry"—echoing the seven heads of the dragon.
48. Determining the precise mechanisms for the transmission of northern Late Bronze Age traditions into the southern Iron Age Levant is beyond our reach. Yet the cultural continuum from the Middle Bronze Age onward is without doubt. See Chapter Six, pp. 256–264, 286.
49. See Tate 1990: 254. A complete analysis of this psalm is outside of our scope. On Ps 74:15 and the relation of the ever-flowing rivers (*nahărôt*) to verses 13–14, see Emerton 1966: 122–133.
50. Scholars note how 1QIsa[a] has *mōḥeṣet*, "smiting" (cf. Job 26:12), rather than MT's *maḥṣebet*, "hewing," and prefer the latter as *lectio difficilior*. Be that as it may, *mōḥeṣet* functioned as a variant reading.
51. See Blenkinsopp's (2002: 333) discussion of how the "eschatological restoration of Judah" as depicted in Isa 51:11 might be appended here from Isa 35:1–10.
52. Cross (1973: 144) notes that "the Song of the Arm of Yahweh in Isaiah 51 is a superb example of [a] new synthesis in which the old Exodus is described in terms of the Creation myth and in turn becomes the archetype of a new Exodus."
53. Rahab (*rahab*) is used elsewhere as a symbolic name for Egypt (Ps 87:4; Isa 30:7) as well as for the cosmic dragon that Yahweh smites (Ps 89:11; Job 9:13; 26:12; Sir 43:25). Ezekiel is especially fond of using the *tannîn*-dragon creature in his depictions of Egypt (Ezek 29:3–5; 32:2b–8). See Lewis 1996b.
54. Note, for example, Murphy's (1985: 1135) comment that one of the primary traits of wisdom literature is that "there is an absence of reference to the typical salvation beliefs, such as the patriarchal promises, the Exodus, the Sinai covenant, etc." For a nuanced exploration, see Janzen 1987.
55. On Job 38:8–11 and its relation to the other *Chaoskampf* passages in the book of Job (esp. Job 3), see Cornell 2012.
56. My translation here follows that of Janzen (1989). Cf. too Habel's (1985: 561) comments on Job 40:25–41:26 (Eng 41:1–34): "Leviathan, Yahweh's mythic adversary, is described in magnificent detail. But Yahweh's real adversary is Job."
57. To interpret Job 26:12–13 one must wrestle with substantive problems that cannot be solved with certainty. Yet some solutions seem likely. It seems likely that this passage forms a part of Bildad's speech and not Job's reply, as 26:1 implies. Such is the consensus of scholars. See, for example, Dhorme 1967: xlviii, 368; Pope 1965b: xx; Habel 1985: 366.

The verb *rāgaʻ* (26:12) is translated in one of three ways. The root occurs in the G transitive stem only here and in Isa 51:15 = Jer 31:35, where it refers to Yahweh as "the one who stirs up [*rōgaʻ*] the sea so its waves roar." On *rgʻ* as "stirring up," cf. NEB's translation of Job 26:12 and the LXX to Isaiah 51:5 (*ho tarassōn tēn thalassan*).

Dhorme (1967: 374) argues for the "dividing" of the sea (cf. NEB and Tg *gzr*). Finally, a case can be made for *rgʻ* designating the "quelling, stilling" of the sea. Cf. LXX *katepausev*; see, for example, RSV, NRSV, NJPS, Pope 1965b: 185; Habel 1985: 365; Day 1985: 38. As Pope points out, *Chaoskampf* myths universally describe the quelling of Sea, not the agitating of it, and such an understanding is fitting for Job 26:12.

The MT of 26:13 is straightforward ("By his wind the heavens are luminous/fair"), yet it hardly fits the context of 26:12–13, which has the motif of combat repeating in every other line. The varying treatments in the versions (see Dhorme 1967: 375) attest to the long-standing confusion regarding the verse in general and *šiprâ* in particular. Recovering the author's original understanding is impossible. Yet Pope's (1965: 185–186) remark about the Akkadian word used for the net (*sapāru*; Enuma Elish IV, 41) in which Tiamat is ensnared is tantalizing (and beyond coincidence for our *šiprâ*?). While Pope's redivision of the MT's *šāmayim* ("By his wind he put Sea [*śm ym*] in a bag") seems drastic, his speculative analysis may very well approximate the original.

Lastly, the mention of *nāḥāš bārîaḥ* in 26:13 recalls the Fleeing Serpent (*bṯn brḥ*) that Baʻlu was said to vanquish in KTU 1.5.1.1–3 and KTU 1.82.38.

58. For the entire passage (Job 26:7–13), Ayali-Darshan (2014) suggests that the verses should be read in inverted order. Ayali-Darshan (2014: 414–416) then draws attention to the creation of Mt. Ṣāpôn as God's abode both in Job 26:7 and in Ps 89:13 (Eng 89:12) following the combat. See the fuller study of Mt. Zaphon by Day (2000: 109–116). Linking such traditions with Ugaritic lore (the Baal Cycle's "erecting an abode for Baal on Mt. Zaphon"), Ayali-Darshan concludes that "the cosmogonic tradition recorded in Job 26 and Psalm 89 was common in Canaan prior to the establishment of the kingdoms of Judah and Israel."
59. See Chapter Seven, pp. 351–353 on divine wrath (*ʼap*).
60. The motif of Job 41:25–26 (Eng 41:33–34) is that of Leviathan as king; yet the subtext is that it is Yahweh as creator who rules his creature Leviathan. Indeed, "mighty" Leviathan is a mere toy for Yahweh's amusement (40:29 [Eng 41:5]; so too Ps 104:26).
61. Space constrains us from delving into the many questions that, to use Blenkinsopp's colorful imagery, have resulted in exegetes "worr[ying] over this brief verse like a dog with a bone." See Blenkinsopp 2000: 372 for an overview of the various issues. Among the many helpful treatments, see Day 1985: 141–178; 2000: 105–107; Oswalt 1986: 490–491; Anderson 1994: 3–15; and Wildberger 1997: 574–580.
62. See Blenkinsopp 2000: 372–373 and Collins 1987: 19–20, 79–80. Wildberger (1997: 579) has also noted how the survival of this dominant motif "was more intense and varied in the Jerusalem cult than one would be led to believe." See too Day 2000: 106, following Emerton; Day writes that "the Canaanite dragon conflict is the single most important contributor to the background of Daniel 7."

Another example of the durability of *Chaoskampf* motifs is how they show up in unexpected places, including even the genre of love poetry. See here Wilson-Wright's (2015) argument (building on Calvert Watkins' study of inherited formulae) that Song of Songs 8:6b–7a "utilizes language and imagery from the Northwest Semitic combat myth to identify love with YHWH as the victorious Divine warrior."
63. See Horowitz, Oshima, and Sanders 2006.

64. On the complexities of oral communications, see Finnegan 1977; Niditch 1996; Schniedewind 2000; 2004: 11–17, 118–121; Carr 2007: 39–56; 2011; Miller 2011; Smith 2014a: 285–294; Schmidt 2015; and Dobbs-Allsopp 2015.
65. For a study of the ways in which such appeals to ancient tradition functioned literarily, see Habel 1976. Brettler (1995: 137) remarks that the "emphasis on recalling and remembering the past, even if it is typically for 'theologically-didactic' reasons, makes the Israelite attitude toward the past unique within the ancient Near Eastern world."
66. Ps 44 is a part of the Elohistic Psalter, which was systematically edited to remove the original reading of Yahweh. See p. 724 note 65, p. 784 note 229. Thus in Ps 44:2 (Eng 44:1) we reconstruct *yhwh* for MT's *'ĕlōhîm*.
67. For more on singing as a medium to pass on cultural heritage in ancient Israel, see Schniedewind 2004: 52–56.
68. On whether Hab 3 is archaic or archaizing, see Chapter Seven, pp. 359–361.

    The fuller corpus that has typically been defined as "archaic Hebrew poetry" has varied from scholar to scholar and been said to include Gen 49:2–27; Exod 15:1–18; Num 23:7–10, 18–24; 24:3–9, 15–19; Deut 33:2–29; Judg 5:2–31; 1 Sam 2:1–10; 2 Sam 1:19–27; Ps 29, 68, 89 (in part), 93; and the archaic or archaizing Hab 3 (cf. Albertz 1994: 51; Bloch 2012: 147–148; Mandell 2013). Substantial critiques of the older paradigm (such as that of Cross and Freedman [1975, 1997]) by critics such as Young (2005), Young, Rezetko, and Ehrensvärd (2008), Rezetko and Young (2014), Pfeiffer (2005, 2017), and Vern (2011) have reset the debate. Nonetheless, even if some of the poems date later (e.g., into the ninth century BCE [Smith 2014a: 219–220; Bloch 2012]), they are still our earliest witnesses to these venerable traditions. For an overview of the debate, with bibliography, see Smith 2012; 2014a: 211–266. See too Chapter Three, note 27, and Chapter Six, note 210.
69. Older studies include Mowinckel 1952; Watts 1957; Muilenberg 1966; Childs 1970a; Cross and Freedman 1955, 1975, 1997; Robertson 1972; Cross 1973; Freedman 1980; Day 1985: 97–101; B. Russell 2007; and S. Russell 2009: 133–148. See especially Propp 1999: 481–485, 550–554; 2006: 723–734 and Houtman 1996: 221–295 with additional literature.

    As for reassessing the date of Exod 15, in contrast to the hyper-early dates of Albright, Cross, Freedman, and Robertson (i.e., the early thirteenth century BCE [Albright 1968a: 11] or the late twelfth/eleventh centuries BCE [Cross 1973: 124; Freedman 2000: 144]), those advocating an early date today would be thinking more of the tenth/ninth centuries BCE (cf. Bloch 2012: 147–148; Smith 2014a: 219–220). Others date Exod 15 much later, viewing seemingly archaic or archaizing features as instead being the result of "the poetic nature of the text" (Houtman 1996: 244). Utzschneider and Oswald (2015: 330) argue that "the Song of Moses assumes . . . the version rendered by the P Composition."
70. The personalized vocabulary of Exod 15:2 has exact parallels twice elsewhere in the Bible (see note 74), a sign of its liturgical character.

    The use of the verb *qānîtā* in Exod 15:16 reminds one of the use of the same root in Deut 32:6, a passage with clear familial vocabulary describing Israel as a creation of their divine *father*. On this passage, see Chapter Four, pp. 91–92, 110–111.

71. Cf. Chapter Seven, p. 797 and note 127.
72. For the variant "sing!," *šîrû*, cf. Exod 15:21.
73. Given the historical difficulty of cavalry for such an early text, Propp (1999: 463, 471, 510) translates "his driver" and Cross (1973: 127 n. 48, following P. Haupt) reads *rōkēb*, "chariotry." Cf. the unambiguous *markĕbōt*, "chariots," in Exod 15:4. This translation follows Propp's (1999: 510) analysis that "*rōkēb* can denote a charioteer as well as a mounted rider" and does not translate the third-person masculine singular suffix simply for poetic artistry in the English.
74. MT's narrative form *wa-yĕhî* seems to be a later prosaizing change. MT's *zimrāt* is difficult. Has the -*y* suffix dropped out by haplography? Yet cf. the identical text in Ps 118:14 and Isa 12:2 (where the fuller form, Yahweh, seems to have been inserted as a gloss on the short form *yâ*):

For Yah (Yahweh) is my might and stronghold,   *kî-ʿāzzî wĕzimrāt yâ yhwh*
May he be my salvation.   *yĕhî-lî lîšûʿâ*

Thus *zimrāt* is seemingly the archaic feminine singular form. See Smith's (2012: 201 n. 32) note in response to Ian Young.

Propp (1999: 463, 471–472, 511–513) has a lengthy discussion of *zimrāt* and translates "power/music," suggesting that "we should not be deaf to the pun with *zmr* 'sing'" (1999: 513). In contrast, my translation, "stronghold," follows McCarter (1984: 476, 480) in finding a parallel in 2 Sam 23:1 that refers to Yahweh as "the stronghold of Israel."

75. The literature on *yam-sûp* as the Red/Reed Sea (and especially its rendering in the various LXX traditions) is too large to detail here. The consensus of critical scholars is to translate "Sea of *Reeds*," based on the clear usage of the word *sûp* in other biblical passages (cf. Exod 2:3, 5; Isa 19:6; Jon 2:6) and the Egyptian loan word *ṯwf* (cf. Ward 1974; Hoffmeier 1996: 204–215).

An alternative translation would envision the Egyptians coming to their *end* (cf. Hebrew *sôp*) at a distant sea located at the mythic ends of the earth. Snaith (1965: 397) analyzes our text as follows: "With its references to the Deeps [*tĕhōmōt*] and the depths [*mĕṣôlōt*] we have passed into the realm of the great Creation-myth, that story of the fight against the monster of Chaos. . . . The word *tĕhōm* does not refer to the depth of any natural sea. This is the depths of the primeval ocean, of Tiamat the great sea monster. . . . [Y]*am-sûp* means that distant scarcely known sea away to the south, of which no man knew the boundary. It was the sea *at the end* of the land" (emphasis mine). Batto (1983: 35) concurs that such a sea "at the end of the earth . . . was fraught with connotations of primeval chaos . . . The Egyptians . . . are appropriately cast into the Sea to perish . . . submergence into the Sea of End/Extinction."

Such an interpretation of *yam-sûp* ("Sea of the End/the Extinction") is quite appealing for the *Chaoskampf* traditions being sketched here, regardless of whether Exod 15:4 represents ancient lore or a later scribe playing on the words *sûp* and *sôp*. Nonetheless, our oldest interpretive traditions do *not* construe the text along these lines. As pointed out by Sarna (1986: 29; 1991: 9), followed by Propp (1999: 154), the description of Moses being hidden in and rescued from the *watery reeds (sûp)* in Exod 2:3, 5 (a J/non-P story) foreshadows the deliverance at the *Sea of Reeds (yam-sûp)* in Exod 15:4. Thus my translation follows the consensus.

Yet I do so with some uneasiness. In addition to J/non-P (or a redactor) foreshadowing events as he played off of the older Exod 15:4 tradition, one should also consider the interpretive tradition that comes down to us through Targum Onkelos. The targumic translator renders Exod 15:4 as *yamāʾ dĕsûp* without any hint toward Exod 2:3, 5 where he renders "reeds" by the word *yaʿărāʾ*. If the targum translator wanted to underscore the foreshadowing we seem to see in J, he would have rendered *yamāʾ dĕyaʿărāʾ*, not *yamāʾ dĕsûp*.

Yet our targumic translator also complicates the Snaith/Batto theory. Though the word *sopāʾ* is very much a part of his vocabulary (cf. Gen 3;15; 49:9; Num 24:20; Deut 32:20, 41) as well as the plural *sĕyāpe*, "end(s), extremity" (cf. Exod 26:28; 36:33; Deut 4:32; 13:8; 33:17—though not with water), the targumic translator renders Exod 15:4 as *yamāʾ dĕsûp*, not *yamāʾ dĕsopāʾ*. Thus perhaps Propp's simple "Suph Sea" (1999: 463) is the wisest translation of all.

76. Here I follow my colleague P. Kyle McCarter (personal communication), who notes the water imagery ("cresting") behind *gĕʾônkā* here and the hint of such imagery in *gāʾōh gāʾâ* in Exod 15:1. For the use of the root *gʾh* with water welling up elsewhere, cf. Ezek 47:5; Ps 46:4. Propp (1999: 510), following Garber, notes that "Exod 15:1b–18 features many verbs connoting elevation and depression, rising and falling," and draws a connection with the Sea's waves.

77. On the hypostatic use of Yahweh's anger and fury, see Chapter Seven, pp. 351–353.

78. There are two primary ways to interpret the verb *ʿrm* in our passage (with the translation here preferring the second): (1) referring to the heaping up of the waters (a denominative verb from the Hebrew *ʿărēmâ*, "granaries, heaps" [cf. LXX, MHeb, Syr, Arb]) or (2) evoking the picture of the streambed stripped naked, similar to what we find in 2 Sam 22:16//Ps 18:16. In these two parallel passages, the "effective rebuke" (*gʿr*) of Yahweh blasts the sea back to expose dry land.

> The recesses of the sea [*yām*] were exposed,
> The foundations of the world laid bare;
>
> At the rebuke [*gaʿărat*] of Yahweh,
> At the blast of the breath of His nostrils. (2 Sam. 22:16; cf. Ps 18:16)

Similar language is found in Nah 1:4; Ps 106:9; and KTU 1.2.4.28. The correct nuance of the root *gʿr* plays a crucial role in interpretation (on which see Lewis 2011: 220–212 and note 39 in this chapter).

79. Scholars agree that *nōzĕlîm* refers to water descending (cf. Arb). Downpours of rain can be described as "sheets," and crests of waves can appear to be a "wall of water." The biblical tradition of standing walls of water is clear (cf. *ḥōmâ* in Exod 14:2 and *nēd* in Ps 78:13; Josh 3:13, 16). Yet one wonders if the language associated with this theophany once used storm language with *nēd* (similar to Akkadian *nīdu*) denoting thunderclouds. I owe this insight to P. Kyle McCarter (personal communication).

80. On God as dangerously holy, see Chapter Ten. Alternatively, due to the parallel line, *qōdeš* could be understood here as a collective (cf. Deut 33:2). Cf. OG, Syro-hexapla that read the plural. In this case, one would translate: "Who is like you, feared among the holy ones?"
81. On the translation of *těhillōt* as "radiance," see my translations of Hab 3:3 on pp. 280 and 360. See Aster 2006: 183–186, and see Propp 1999: 464, 528, where it is translated as "dreadful of glory."
82. While victory over the Egyptians is certainly the focus of Exod 15:1–12, Propp (1999: 531) speculates that Yahweh's "swallowing" in Exod 15:11 could refer to Yahweh vanquishing the gods of 15:10. While even Propp calls his own suggestion "fanciful," he nonetheless appropriately notes how Ps 82:7 describes Yahweh's demoting the gods to mortal beings. Propp's thesis could be strengthened by translating Exod 15:10 in the way we have here (i.e., that the gods are *in fear of* Yahweh [following Cross and Freedman 1955: 242]) and referencing Isa 25:8, where Yahweh does indeed swallow (*blʿ*) the notorious Mot (known at Ugarit as the swallower of Baʿlu). That Yahweh would be using the underworld (*ʾereṣ*) in Exod 15:12 to do his swallowing would thus be quite fitting.
83. Exod 15:3. On the use of divine anger and the divine name (and their employment as hypostatic entities), see Chapter Seven, pp. 351–353, 387–390. On the use of divine names as weapons, see Lewis 2011. See too Propp's (1999: 516) comments about Yahweh's name functioning as "a talismanic weapon."
84. Again reconstructing what was likely the original reading of the text (*yhwh*) that has been obscured by MT's secondary reading of *ʾĕlōhîm*. On the editing of the so-called Elohistic Psalter, see p. 724 note 65, p. 784 note 229.
85. Reading the singular along with the Qere as opposed to the Ketiv's plural.
86. In contrast, cf. the use of *visible* footprints at the temple of Ayn Dara to depict the deity's presence (Chapter Seven, pp. 340–343 [Figures 7.21–7.22]). In Ps 77:20 (Eng 77:21), Yahweh's mighty acts leave no trace, perhaps a sign of how water washes away footprints left in sand and/or a theological statement by the psalmist wrestling with the lack of "visible proofs" of Yahweh's activity in his present distress. Cf. Kraus's (1989: 116–117) remarks about the psalmist juxtaposing the *deus absconditus* motif with that of the *deus revelatus*.
87. Discussion follows shortly.
88. See Chapter Seven, pp. 280–281, 359–360. On the similarities and differences between Hab 3 and Ps 77, see Andersen 2001: 327–329.
89. The textual complexities of Hab 3:9b are well known and gave rise, according to Hiebert (1986: 26) and Andersen (2001: 321), to more than a hundred interpretations already by the mid-1850s. There is no point to sifting through them here. Readers are directed to Hiebert and Andersen for a synthesis of the competing proposals, none of which has gained wide acceptance.

The words for "shafts" (*maṭṭôt*) seems clear enough at first glance, but one would expect "arrows" (*ḥiṣṣîm*) to parallel "bow" (*qešet*) in Hab 3:9a. Yet compare our poet's artistry in Hab 3:11, where "the brilliance of [Yahweh's] flying *arrows*" (*ʾôr ḥiṣṣêkā yěhallēkû*) parallels "the radiance of [his] lightning-like *spear*" (*nōgah běraq ḥănîtekā*). On the use of divine "radiance," see Chapter Seven, pp. 358–379.

90. The text here is difficult. The translation here follows Andersen (2001: 337) in seeing MT's *mibbêt* as a later insertion, rather than following the interpretation of Hiebert (1986: 36–40) and others who (using Ugaritic parallels) see a metathesis (*bmt*) referring to the "back" of the enemy. That the text has suffered from textual confusion is also seen in LXX's understanding that Yahweh brings death (*thanatos* = Hebrew *māwet*) on the heads of the wicked. In the following line, *'ārôt* is equally difficult, and here too we follow Andersen's understanding (2001: 337–338).

91. The verb *nqb*, "to pierce," is used here and twice in Job 40:24–26 (Eng 40:24–41:2) in mythological combat myths. Remarkably, the same root and tradition seem to form a mythological subtext of deicide underlying blasphemy in Lev 24. See Lewis 2017.

92. Pointing MT's *ḥōmer* as a D infinitive absolute (*ḥammēr*) as a substitute for a finite verb (so Anderson 2001: 339). On the root *ḥmr*, designating "to be hot, parched, dried up," see the cognate evidence (Ugr, MHeb, Arm, Arb) and esp. KTU 1.83.13 (so Pitard 1998: 279 and Lewis 2011: 217–218) as well as the bitumen pits (*be'ĕrōt ḥēmār*) in Gen 14:10. For additional references to Yahweh drying up the sea, cf. Nah 1:4 and Ps 106:9.

   Note how *yām* and *mayim rabbîm* are parallel terms here and elsewhere (Ps 93:4). Smith (1997: 168 n. 67, following Caquot, Sznycer, and Herdner 1974: 167 n. h), notes how Yammu's epithet "the great god" (*'il rbm*) in KTU 1.3.3.39 could be "elliptical for *mym rbm*, 'mighty waters' referring to the cosmic waters." So too Smith and Pitard 2009: 247–248.

93. See Levin's (2009) use of "the miracle at the sea" as a textbook case on how to understand source criticism. Levin writes that "the amalgamation of such parallel accounts is exceptional in the highest degree. It probably took place only once in the whole history of the Old Testament literature" (2009: 42).

94. For the various ways in which Yahweh's stretched-out arm and hand are used (and with varying vocabulary), see Martens 2001 and Strawn 2009; the latter also includes iconographic parallels.

95. Isa 63:12, yet another passage looking back to the exodus as "the days of old" (*yĕmê-'ôlām*), has Yahweh causing "His own glorious arm" (*zĕrôa' tip'artô*) to march out to assist "the right hand of Moses" (*lîmîn mōšeh*) by cleaving the waters.

96. Exod 14:27 reads *wayĕna'ēr yhwh 'et-miṣrayim bĕtôk hayyām*. Cf. the use of the verb *n'r* in Job 38:13, where the imagery is that of God using the dawn to grab the corners of the earth as if it were a dirty rug in order to shake out the wicked.

97. Cf. for example Sarna's (1991: 70) description of "a diaphanous, luminescent mist visible both day and night."

98. For a study of the phrase "fear not" in both Hebrew (*'al tîrā'*) and Akkadian (*lā tapallaḫ*), see Nissinen 2003.

99. *Yĕḥummēm* is attested in Ps 18:15 and in the Ketiv of 2 Sam 22:15. The Qere of 2 Sam 22:15 reads *yāhom*. As already noted by Propp (1999: 499), "the root *hwm* connotes divinely sent fear," with a prime example being found in Exod 23:27, where Yahweh sends forth his "terror" (*'êmâ*) ahead of his people in order "to panic" (√*hwm*) the army of their enemies. See too Josh 10:10 (Yahweh terrifying the armies of the five Amorite kings), Judg 4:15 (Yahweh terrifying Sisera, his army, and chariots), 1 Sam 7:10 (Yahweh terrifying the Philistines with his thundering voice), and Ps 144:5–6 (Yahweh bowing the heavens and descending with lightning//arrows to terrify his foes).

Though our composite text uses the verb *kbd* (in the P sections of Exod 14:4, 17–18), it refrains from using the specific language of *kābôd* to designate Yahweh's awe-filled radiance (on which see Chapter Seven, pp. 358–379).

For unpacking the possible conceptual world via iconography, consider the armed Aššur with his terrifying *melammu* depicted in Figure 7.23 (cf. Lewis 2013b: 800–803). See too Mendenhall 1973: 45, 58, which, in addition to referring to the Aššur iconography, also notes how the Egyptian god Horus of Bedḥet/Edfu "'stormed against' the enemy in the form of the winged disk," according to the Ptolemaic Legend of the Winged Disk. On this text and possible antecedents, see Taylor 1993: 46 n. 1.

100. For additional discussion of Yahweh as king, see Chapter Nine. For a detailed study of how conflict myths were used as royal ideological productions, see Ballentine 2015.
101. Several scholars (e.g., Day 1985: 18–21; Kraus 1989: 232–233, 236) emphasize that one of the primary cultic settings of such royal legitimization may have been the Feast of Sukkot (cf. Zech 14:16).
102. See comments on Ps 74 on pp. 443–444 and in Day 1985: 19. On kingship being the primary theme of the Baʿlu myth, see Smith 1986: 322–229; 1997: 83–85.
103. See Chapter Seven, pp. 361–362 and note 187 for past treatments of Psalm 29 and the poem's emphasis on divine radiance.

Who is the subject of the second-person masculine plural imperative (*hābû* √*yhb*) that commands the divine beings (*bĕnê ʾēlîm*) to "give" Yahweh radiance and strength in Ps 29:1? In the full mythopoeic telling of a *Chaoskampf* tale, it would be the head of the pantheon instructing the gods to fulfill their solemn promise of according divine supremacy to the warrior god who was able to defeat the powers of chaos (e.g., Marduk defeating Tiamat). See Foster 1993: 386–397. Possible remnants of such thinking may be behind Deut 32:6b–9 (see Chapter Four, pp. 91–92) and Ps 82, where, interestingly, the setting is judicial rather than that of a *Chaoskampf* (see Chapter Nine, pp. 565–569). In Judean liturgy (cf. Ps 148:1–2), such a divine scenario would have been transformed into having a religious officiant crying out for the angels to praise Yahweh (*halĕlûhû kol-malʾākāyw*). Similarly, Ps 29 (with its *mizmôr lĕdāwid* heading) came to be interpreted as David calling out for the heavenly host to ascribe glory to Yahweh.

104. Cf. CAD M/2 10 s.v. *melammu* and CAD P 506 s.v. *puluḫtu*.
105. Kraus (1989: 231–232, 235) notes the change from suffixal (*nāśĕʾû*) to prefixal (*yiśĕʾû*) tense in verse 3c and argues that "the singer is striving to actualize the primeval event" for "the present time" because "destructive, rebellious forces [are] still at work." Thus he translates accordingly ("floods *have lifted* . . . floods *are lifting*"; cf. RSV, NRSV). Yet thanks to prosodic studies of Hebrew and Ugaritic verse, the combining of prefixal and suffixal forms is unremarkable and need not require such exegesis. Compare the translations of JPS and NEB, which do not mark the contrast (e.g., "the ocean sounds . . . the ocean sounds"). See especially studies on other poetic passages similar to Ps 93:4 that use the same verb alternating suffixal and prefixal forms (e.g., Ps 29:10; 38:12; Prov 11:7; Amos 7:4; cf. Held 1962; Waltke and O'Connor 1990: 496–498). The translation here understands *yiśĕʾû* as a *yaqtul*

preterite form that parallels the two *qatala* forms (*nāśĕʾû*) to designate the distant past where Yahweh once subdued chaotic waters. This does not deny the past/present dimension. Our poet would certainly affirm that just as Yahweh *was* mighty in the past epic battle, he *is* at the same time mighty in the present.

106. Those scholars seeing an archaic hymn embedded here would include Cross (1973: 45 n. 6; 1998: 14, 91) and Kraus (1989: 203), yet the perception of the disunity of the poem dates as early as B. Duhm in 1899 (see Clifford 1980: 35). Scholars preferring to see a poem that is unified (or is for the most part unified) would include Dumortier (1972), Clifford (1980), and Hossfeld and Zenger (2005: 402). Clifford (1980: 35 n. 2) and Hossfeld and Zenger (2005: 402 n. 3) provide additional bibliography on those advocating disunity (e.g., Gunkel, Sarna, Lipiński) and unity (Ward, Rösel, Volger, Emmendörffer, Arneth).

    On Ps 89's relation to the *Chaoskampf* traditions, see Day 1985: 25–28.

107. Reading (along with 24 Hebrew manuscripts, LXX minuscule manuscripts, the Syriac, and most commentators) the singular "your servant," *ʿabdekā*, for MT's plural "your servants," *ʿăbādêkā*, in Ps 89:51 (Eng 89:50) to agree with the singular "your anointed" *mĕšîḥekā* in Ps 89:52 (Eng 89:51).

108. Once again, note the concept of *tremendum* that Yahweh occasions, a *tremendum* felt by the gods as well as humans. On the divine assembly, see Chapter Nine, p. 565 and note 180

    Ps 89:8 (Eng 89:7) speaks of Yahweh as "a terrifying god" (*ʾēl naʿărāṣ*). See Jer 20:11, where Yahweh is described as a "terrifying warrior" (*gibbôr ʿārîṣ*). Cf. Isa 2:19, 21. The same root, √*rṣ*, is used to refer to Yahweh bringing "terror" to Jerusalem in the Khirbet Beit Lei inscription. For the difficult text and various translations, see Zevit 2001: 421–426.

    Cross (1973: 160 n. 65) compares *ʾēl naʿărāṣ* to the Ugaritic god ʿAthtar's epithet "ʿAthtar the Terrible" (*ʿttr ʿrẓ*) in KTU 1.6.1.54–63, a text dealing with a replacement king sitting on Baʿlu's empty throne. Smith (2014a: 169) notes that elsewhere ʿAthtar is referred to as a lion, and one can assume that Ugaritians knew tales of his terrifying presence that gave rise to his epithet. While KTU 1.6.1.54–63 mentions ʿAthtar's epithet five times, his role in the narrative is that of a small-statured foil who cannot measure up to Baʿlu. (On large size as symbolic of divinity, see Chapter Seven, pp. 317, 341, and note 133.) Thus with regard to the rejection of ʿAthtar as king, perhaps the story plays off his name to say (if one might borrow and negate the language of Ps 89:8) that, contrary to his famous epithet, ʿAthtar the Terrible did *not* have the physical stature to be greatly feared among the divine council.

109. On Yahweh as powerfully holy, see Chapter Ten.

110. The MT's understanding of the tradition it has received has "the sea" (*hayyām*), a common noun with a definite article, yet such poetry (especially with the mention of the dragon Rahab that immediately follows) is rich with mythic imagery. As we have noted, just because the battle is no longer *with* Sea (Yam) but rather *at the* sea does not mean that we are dealing with just any skirmish or with just any natural body of water. Cross (1973: 160) and others try to reconstruct what they imagine

to be the earlier tradition with Sea personified. Following this notion, Yahweh rules (enthroned) "on the back" of Sea, and it is "*his* waves" that must be calmed.

111. Though Day has the parallelism of Ps 89:11b on his side, the use of the preposition *k*- argues for *keḥālāl* in Ps 89:11a referring to Rahab itself being slain ("*as* a slain [carcass/corpse]"—so Cross 1973: 160; Kraus 1989: 198; Hossfeld and Zenger 2005: 399—rather than the manner by which Rahab was slain ("*with* a mortal blow"), as suggested by Day (1985: 25).

112. Retaining here the MT's *ûmĕlōʾâ*, yet this could be a later addition that was filled in based on the common idiom of "the universe and the fullness therein." Cross (1973: 160 n. 69) reconstructs it without *ûmĕlōʾâ*.

113. On whether Ps 89:13 (Eng 89:12) refers to Mt. Zaphon, see Day 2000: 111–112 and Ayali-Darshan 2014: 412–414. See also note 58.

114. In its earliest dress (written or oral), the last verse here (i.e., Ps 89:19 [Eng 89:18]) celebrated Yahweh as protector ("shield"), Holy One, and King. The first of the two translations here reflects this, understanding *l-yhwh* to contain an emphatic *l-* (Cross 1973: 161 n. 72; Clifford 1980: 43 n. 20; Waltke and O'Connor 1990: 211 n. 94). Alternatively, as the poem functioned as part of the later royal ideology, the *l-* in question was understood to be possessive. As reflected in the second translation, the bicola underscores David's (and the Davidides') special relationship to Yahweh.

115. In contrast to Clifford's (1980: 43–44) opinion, the translation of *ʾāz* as referring to Yahweh making promises to David "back then"/"of old" (so RSV) in Ps 89:20 (Eng 89:19) is indeed appropriate, especially when one considers how such a time reference echoes the mention of Yahweh's oath to David in the "distant past" (*hāriʾšōnîm*) later in the psalm (Ps 89:50 [Eng 89:49]). Cf. Judg 5:8, 11, where past skirmishes are recounted with mention of how "back then" (*ʾāz*) battles were fought at the gates.

116. Reading here the singular *ḥăsîdĕkā* with multiple Hebrew manuscripts (so too Kraus 1989: 200) for MT's *ḥăsîdêkā*. For the original poetic bicola we would also expect the non-narrative form (*tōʾmer*), which seems to have been prosaized (*wattōʾmer*).

117. Reading *ʿēzer* as designating "strength, power, might." So HALOT 811, JPS, NIV; *ʿezrōh* in Ezek 12:14 should be added to the references in HALOT. Cf. the Ugaritic cognate *ǵzr*; Ginsberg 1938: 210–211; Held 1965: 278–279 n. 31; Miller 1970b; Rainey 1973: 139–142; and Clifford 1980: 44 n. 22. However, as astutely demonstrated by Rainey, there is no need to differentiate between "strength" (*ʿzr* II) and "help" (*ʿzr* I).

Alternatively, many commentators read *nēzer*, "diadem," used also in Ps 89:40 (Eng 89:39), and have Yahweh crowning his warrior (Kraus 1989: 200; Hossfeld and Zenger 2005: 400–401; so too RSV, NRSV, NAB, NEB).

Kraus's (1989: 200) rationale for the alleged reading of *nēzer* rather than *ʿēzer* (that it is "very likely an error in hearing or writing") is hard to support phonologically and epigraphically. It is hard to confuse a pharyngeal with a nasal and at no stage do *nun*s and *ʿayin*s look similar in our inscriptional data. Thus we retain the MT's *ʿēzer*. Granted, the verb *šiwwîtî* is difficult, yet the meaning of "placing" or "conferring" seems solid from passages such as Ps 16:8 and Ps 21:6 (cf. HALOT 1438 s.v. *šwh* II). It is understandable that 4QPs89 (= 4Q236) uses the root *šyt*. See Flint 1997: 42–43.

118. As seen in numerous passages (e.g., Jer 6:4), war is holy activity (especially with a god as commander in chief), and thus one must be consecrated for battle. For a full discussion of war and holy power, see Chapter Ten.
119. It should be noted that the verb used here in Ps 89:23 (Eng 89:22) for a wicked enemy "violating" (yĕʿannennû, a D stem from ʿnh II) the king is the same verb that Yammu//Judge River uses when he threatens to "violate" (ʿnnh) Baʿlu (KTU 1.2.1.[18], 35). For a detailed description of the Ugaritic verb, see Smith 1994b: 266 n. 82, 291–292.
120. For the use of the divine name in battle context, see Chapter Seven, pp. 387–390, and Lewis 2011.
121. On the Yahweh ʿElyon traditions, see Chapter Four, pp. 90–95. There is a great deal of literature on the divine sonship of the king and his description as *Urmensch* (so Mettinger). For a summary with older bibliography, see Mettinger 1976: 259–275.
122. On the various terms for divine radiance, see page 359.
123. For a convenient collection, see Nissinen et al. 2003, 2019.
124. Text Nin A i 1–ii 11. For a convenient text and translation, see Nissinen et al. 2003: 137–142; 2019: 149–154 with additional bibliography.
125. Text A.1968. For a convenient text and translation that we follow here, see Nissinen et al. 2003: 21–22; 2019: 21–23 with additional bibliography.
126. It goes without saying that we are not asserting any notion of direct dependency between these two texts, especially when one considers the eighteenth-century BCE date of our Mari material.

    Note 1 Sam 21:10 (Eng 21:9), where David reuses the sword he had previously wielded to kill Goliath. The sword has since been in the keeping of the priest Ahimelech at the sanctuary at Nob along with the *ephod*, thus marking its cultic nature and/or its function as an object of veneration. See too Saul's armor being placed in the temple of Ashtarot (1 Sam 31:10). Smith (2014a: 303) notes the dedication of a shield in KTU 1.162.2 and an ax that may have served as an offering at Tell Qasile. (Smith's listing of KTU 123.2 is a typographical error.) See further Malamat 2002.
127. I am indebted here to Propp's (1999: 227–229) analysis "Rod of Moses or Rod of God?" See Propp's collection of references that support how "the storehouses of myth are well stocked with magical weapons properly belonging to supernaturals, but bestowed on worthy mortals."

    As David is here accorded some type of divine trappings, cf. too how Moses is called ʾĕlōhîm in Exodus 4:16, 7:1. See further Rendsburg 2006.
128. I agree with those scholars (e.g., Ginsberg, Cross, Caquot, Sznycer, Herdner, Gibson, Coogan, Pardee) who emphasize the cowering of the gods who sit in fear at the thought of Yammu's arrival (triggered by the unexpected arrival of Yammu's messengers, who bring with them his ominous decree). Such fear is supported by ʾIlu's compliance in handing Baʿlu over to Yammu as his slave. For a detailed discussion of the various options for explaining the physical posture of the divine assembly, see Smith 1994b: 297–300 with bibliography.
129. Cross (1973: 98–99) clarifies: "While the Ugaritic verse is preserved only in a passage anticipating Baʿl's going to do battle with Yamm (Sea), we can claim

confidently, in view of the repetitive style of the Ugaritic texts, that the shout was repeated, addressed to the council of gods, when Ba'l returned in victory to receive kingship."
130. Granted, in the ancient Near East temples could be deified and thus the object of cult. Moreover, now that we know much more about the existence of gate shrines (e.g., Tel Dan, Bethsaida), such *šĕʿārîm* vocabulary resonates with cultic prestige (cf. Blomquist 1999).
131. On Ps 29, see Chapter Seven, pp. 361–362, and note 103 in this chapter.
132. For fuller analyses of KTU 1.23.8–9, see Smith 2006: 40–43 and Lewis forthcoming a.
133. Following most scholars, the reconstruction of the first line here is based on the similar idiom of voracity that occurs in KTU 1.23.61–62. The verb *y'rk* is reconstructed following Cross (1973: 117 n. 18), who notes the idiom *taʾărîkû lāšôn* in Isa 57:4.

 The poet goes on to describe how Yahweh will wipe away tears from all faces, a picture that is picked up by New Testament writers (Rev 7:17; 21:4) who also portrayed God's victorious swallowing of Death (1 Cor 15:54–57).
134. Cf. also Isa 5:14; Prov 1:12; 27:20; 30:15b–16; Ps 141:7; Cross 1973: 117; Lewis 1989: 152–153; 1992b. On the netherworld Sheol and the ways in which it was personified, see Lewis 1992a.
135. For other swallowing imagery used of Yahweh, cf. Lam 2:5; Ps 21:10 (Eng 21:9); 55:10 (Eng 55:9); Isa 19:3.
136. For additional references to Otto, see Chapter Seven, p. 337, and Chapter Ten, p. 587.
137. The identity of the deadly "King of Terrors" in Job 18:14 has been debated, with the leading candidates being Mot and Nergal (see Rüterswörden 1999: 486–488). Not to be missed is the way in which the author of Job used this phrase with a double entendre, with Yahweh as the real terrifying force behind Job's afflictions (cf. Job 23:15–16 and Lewis 2012: 110–112).

 For a brief overview of the Hebrew Bible's portrayal of the universality of death and Yahweh's power over it, see Lewis 2007: 66–69; cf. 2002.
138. Freedman 1980: 217.
139. Following Miller (1973: 100); cf. Ps 103:20. Alternatively, *baggibôrîm* could be translated "*against* [the enemy] warriors." Those who were not willing to fight in Yahweh's battle were placed under a curse (Judg 5:23).
140. I borrow the terminology of "synergism" from Miller (1973: 156), who writes that "at the center of Israel's warfare was the unyielding conviction that victory was the result of a fusion of divine and human activity." In contrast, see Lind 1980: 72, 81, 171.
141. For a brief note on Priestly laws of warfare, see note 155.
142. For discussions of other possible ancient Near Eastern analogues, especially at Mari (though without explicit *ḥrm* vocabulary), see Malamat 1966; Stern 1991: 57–87; and Lemaire 1999. For a Hittite analogue (CTH 1, 4, 61 II, 264 and esp. CTH 423), see Taggar-Cohen 2015.
143. For ʿAnatu's *Chaoskampf* traditions, see pp. 441–442. For KTU 1.13, see Smith and Pitard 2009: 178–180. While we have mention of ʿAnatu's soldiers (KTU 1.13.7;

1.22.8-10), in contrast to the biblical, Moabite, and Sabaean material, we do not have any extant texts preserved that describe Ugaritians participating in ḥrm warfare at the behest of ʿAnatu. See Smith and Pitard 2009: 180 for the suggestion that our accounts here "on the mythic level" may hint at an earthly counterpart.

144. See Cross 2003b: 219; Day 2000: 133–135. Shupak (1989) wonders if Shamgar had ties to ʿapiru/ḫabiru mercenary soldiers from the times of Ramses III and IV, based on the mention of "ʿprw of the troops of An[at] . . . 800 men" in an inscription from Wadi Hammamat.

145. Those arrowheads with the name Anat include one from El Khadr, 2.5 mi. (4 km) southwest of Bethlehem and another from the Beqaʿ valley; a third is unprovenanced. Cross (2003b: 213–230, esp. 217–220 [orig. 1980]) dates the arrowhead from El Khadr to the eleventh century BCE; see also Milik 1956: 3–6 and Deutsch and Heltzer 1994: 15, no. 3. For a list of arrowheads from El Khadr and elsewhere, see Cross 2003b: 195–202 (orig. 1996). For a script chart, see Cross 2003b: 55, fig. 4.2 (orig. 1995). For dating, Naveh (2009: 105 [orig. 1987]) favors from the thirteenth to the middle of the eleventh century BCE, McCarter (2008b: 48) favors the eleventh century BCE, and Sass (2005: 34, 43–44) prefers the tenth/ninth centuries BCE.

146. See Chapter Six, p. 235 and esp. notes 69 and 125 there, for a description of alternative suggestions for our reading of "the [ve]ssels of Yahweh," [k]ly yhwh.

147. DAI Ṣirwāḥ 2005-50 commemorates the activities of King Yiṯʿamar Watar, son of Yakrubmalik. The relevant ḥrm material is found in lines 2 and 4 following the mention of the king's sacrificing to the god ʿAthtar in line 1. See dasi.cnr.it/index.php?id=30&prjId=1&corId=0&colId=0&navId=696268692&recId=9521&mark=09521%2C004%2C012. I owe this reference to Jason Weimar.

Monroe (2007: 331) argues that the Sabaean text RES 3945 referencing ḥrm activity "may with caution be dated to the beginning of the seventh century (BCE)." For her detailed discussion of the problems of dating this text, see Monroe 2007: 327–331. See too Monroe 2007: 341 for perceptive suggestions about how texts such as the Mesha stela, Josh 8, and RES 3945 "reflect an interest in narrativizing emergent . . . collective cultural identity." Sanders 2015: 68–70 also interacts with Sabaean inscription RES 3945 and several others in a broader discussion of pantheon reduction.

148. Cf. the physical presence of Mesopotamian deities in battle via their divine images (van der Toorn 2000: 85).

149. Reading along with the MT as *lectio difficilior* (so too Soggin 1972: 82, 88). *Bêt* is missing from the LXX in what seems to be a harmonization with Josh 6:19 (so too Cooke 1918: 50). Rather than seeing *bêt* as anachronistic and designating the Jerusalem Temple, it makes more sense to see it as referring to an earlier sanctuary (at Gilgal?). For the expression *bêt-yhwh* denoting sanctuaries other than the Jerusalem Temple, cf. 1 Sam 1:7 and Arad ostraca #18 line 9 (see Figure 6.14).

150. On the complexities of this passage (with its voluntary ḥērem proscribing, in contrast to ḥērem proscribing elsewhere that is imposed by the deity), see Brekelmans

1959: 59–66; Levine 1989: 198–199; Stern 1991: 128–135; Milgrom 2000: 2391–2396; and Zevit 2012: 237.

See too Num 21:2, where a vow with regard to *ḥērem* warfare is sworn predicated on divine assistance in battle. See further Stern 1991: 135–138.

151. Herzog et al. 1984; Aharoni 1993; Zwickel 1994: 266–275; Herzog 2001; Zevit 2001: 156–171, 298–300; Albertz and Schmitt 2012: 236–237; Bloch-Smith 2015. Compare too the military presence at Kuntillet ʿAjrud.

152. See Chapter Ten, note 12.

153. For the prophetic texts, see Nissinen et al. 2003; 2019; Nissinen 1998: 164–165; van der Toorn 2000: 84–86; Weippert 1972: 472–476.

154. I follow McCarter (1984: 71, 76) here in seeing the shield rather than Saul being anointed with oil in 2 Sam 1:21. On the oiling of shields, see Millard 1978: 90. See note 126 on the sword of Goliath being housed in sacred space.

155. On Judg 5:2, 13–16 and untrimmed hair for warrior Nazirites, see Smith 2014a: 223–224.

For the various differences between Deuteronomic/Deuteronomistic and Priestly laws of warfare, see Weinfeld 1992: 238–239, with its discussion of "changing conceptions" of warfare. For P's distinctive ritual markers, see in particular Num 31, where soldiers who have killed or come into contact with the slain (i.e., corpse contamination) are required to purify themselves (and their captives) (Num 31:19). In addition, upon returning from war they must purify their battle attire and launder their clothes (Num 31:20, 24). Metallic objects must be purified by fire and non-metallic objects by water (Num 31:21–23). Soldiers present booty to the priest Eleazar as "a *tĕrûmâ* offering to Yahweh" (31:29) and as a *qorban* offering "to make expiation before Yahweh" (31:50). The booty is then brought into the tent of meeting as a memorial before Yahweh (31:54). On the intricacies of Num 31, see Levine 2000: 445–474.

156. For analysis of the verb *ṣlḥ* in Hebrew, see Tawil 1976.

157. I am indebted to Monroe (2007: 323, 325, 331, 335–338) for highlighting this feature of *ḥērem* warfare.

158. For similar odds, cf. the early eighth-century BCE Old Aramaic Zakkur Inscription (KAI 202.4–5), where Baʿl-shmayn gives the king victory over either seventeen or sixteen kings (*š[bʿt]/š[tt] ʿšr mlkn*).

159. On divine names being used effectually in battle, see Chapter Seven, pp. 387–390, and Lewis 2011.

160. Yet note how the text makes a point of saying that David *had no sword of his own* and thus had to use Goliath's sword to cut off his head (1 Sam 17:50–51). Thus technically, the traditions articulating "not by a [Judean] sword" (i.e., passages such as 1 Sam 17:47; cf. Ps 44:3 [Eng 44:3]) remain intact.

As for David's victory here, see the variant tradition about Elhanan slaying Goliath in 2 Sam 21:19 and the inner biblical corrective in 1 Chr 20:5. See further McCarter 1984: 450 and Knoppers 2004: 736.

161. See Meyers and Meyers 1987: 244; Fishbane 2002: 225, 366–367.

162. For the Akkadian texts, see Parpola 1997: 6 (text #1.4, lines 27–30); Nissinen et al. 2003: 105; 2019: 115 (text #71, lines 27–30). See too Nissinen's 2003 study of the phrase "fear not" in its ancient Near Eastern context.
163. Cf. 2 Kgs 18:13–19:37; Isa 36:1–37:38; 2 Chr 32:1–22; Ben Sira 48:17–22. See Grayson and Novotny 2012: #4, lines 49–58 (Rassam Cylinder); #15 iv, lines 6–25, 1′–14′ (Cylinder C); #16 iii line 74 through iv line 37 (Cylinder D); #17 iii, lines 38–81 (King Prism, Heidel Prism); #18 iii, lines 15–31, #19 i′, lines 3′–14′, and #22 iii, lines 18–49 (Oriental Institute/Chicago Prism, "Taylor Prism"); #23 iii, lines 16–42 (Jerusalem Prism), #26 i, lines 12′–13′; #34, line 15. Cf. Mayer 2003: 168–200; Frahm 1997; Cogan 2000: 302–303.
164. The historical nature of these passages has long been debated. For an optimistic treatment and bibliography, see Gallagher 1999. Archaeologically, one can also turn to the Level III city at Tell ed-Duweir (= Tel Lachish). See Ussishkin 2004 and Uehlinger 2003: 221–305.

Of course, Sennacherib's annals (see note 163) make no mention of any such plague breaking out. Rather, Sennacherib emphasizes how Hezekiah was overwhelmed with "the awe of his radiance" (*pulḫu melamme*) (see Chapter Seven, p. 797 and note 127) and offered him massive amounts of tribute.
165. The corpus of the Zion Hymns varies depending on the scholar, as do dating (from pre-Israelite Jebusite traditions to David to the post exilic period), *Sitz im Leben*, and thematic elements. See Miller 2010; Vermeylen 2007; Willis 1997; Kraus 1988: 89–92; Roberts 1973a (republished in 2002); Wanke 1966; Hayes 1963; Rohland 1956.
166. See Wildberger 1997: 192–197.
167. On Yahweh as divine forester, see Watts 1985: 163–167. On lion imagery used of Yahweh, see Strawn 2005 and Chapter Seven, pp. 313–317.
168. See the description of "fiery transcendent anthropomorphism" in Chapter Seven, pp. 346, 375–378.
169. These two motifs will play a prominent role in the famous "plowshares" passages, as we will see. On the influence of the Zion Hymns on the plowshares passages, see Willis 1997.
170. Given the prevalent motif that instructs God's people that they need not fight with Yahweh as the sole champion, I follow those interpreters (e.g., Dahood 1965: 282; Craigie 1983: 345) who see *harpû* as an exhortation to Judeans under siege to relax, not a command for the enemy's armies to "desist!" In addition, such an interpretation makes more sense stylistically. It complements the exhortation for God's people to "come, behold the works of Yahweh" (*lĕkû-ḥăzû mipʿălôt yhwh*) in Ps 46:9 (Eng Ps 46:8). Such an admonition is less fitting if addressed to enemy troops.
171. See Wildberger 2002: 156–157 for a lengthy description of the various ways in which scholars have analyzed *bĕšûbâ* in Isa 30:15a, resulting in a variety of translations (e.g., JPS, "by stillness"; NAB, "by waiting"; NRSV/RSV, "in returning"; NEB, "come back"; NIV, "in repentance").
172. The noun *gaʿărâ* and the verb *gʿr* are used to describe Yahweh's effective power against chaos creatures and historical enemies. See Nah 1:4; 2 Sam 22:16; Ps 18:16;

106:9; Isa 66:15; and Job 26:11–13. See too Lewis 2011: 210–212 with bibliography on the many studies of this root.

173. Due to the Elohistic editor's revision (which replaced the tetragrammaton with the generic noun for god), we read *yhwh* as original here for the MT's *'ĕlōhîm* (so too Kraus 1988: 472).

Corresponding to the events of 701 BCE, the verb *yĕkônĕnehā* can be read in several ways, from a hope-filled volitive ("May Yahweh establish [Jerusalem] forever"—so JPS) to a certain durative ("Yahweh establishes/will establish [Jerusalem] forever"—so NAB) to a belief that one has already tasted the reality of the future in the very present ("Yahweh has established [Jerusalem] forever"—so Kraus 1988: 472). Those holding to the conviction that Jerusalem was indeed inviolable would likely have understood *yĕkônĕnehā* in the latter two ways.

174. Where the MT reads "sword" (*ḥereb*) in Ezek 38:21a, the LXX has "terror" (*phobon* ~ Hebrew *ḥărādâ*). While the MT is *lectio difficilior* (especially with the difficult "my mountains," *hāray*, preceding), the LXX seems to be original, with the MT arising from a graphic error and by attraction to *ḥereb* in Ezek 38:21b. This is not to say that Yahweh does not employ a sword, for indeed it is one of his primary weapons (Deut 32:40–42; Isa 27:1; 31:8; 34:5–6; 66:16; Jer 14:12; 25:31; 46:10; Ezek 14:21; 21; cf. Reed 2018).

175. Scholars have long noted how "Isaiah 63:1–6 exhibits such a great number of linguistic and thematic affinities with 59:15b–20 that there can be no question the two passages are in some way related" (Matthews 1995: 80). See also Steck 1991: 177–186; Blenkinsopp 2003: 196–197, 248–249.

176. On the obligation of blood vengeance and the way in which this influenced notions of Yahweh as avenger, see Lipiński 1999: 1–9. See too Christensen 2009: 219–224.

177. Along with most commentators, we read "marching" (*ṣōʿēd*) for MT's "stooping, cowering" (*ṣōʿeh*). Cf. Judg 5:4, which describes Yahweh marching to battle from Edom (*bĕṣaʿdĕkā miśśĕdēh 'ĕdôm*). On the significance of Edom, see Isa 34. See too Matthews 1995: 78 and Blenkensopp 2003: 249 for the suggestion that our poet is reworking earlier traditions of Yahweh marching forth from the area of Edom (cf. Deut 33:2; Judg 5:4; Hab 3:3; Kuntillet ʿAjrud; see Chapter Six, pp. 279–281).

178. For those comparing our passage to ʿAnatu's bloodletting in KTU 1.3.2.3–41, see Hanson 1984: 360; Smith and Pitard 2009: 153. For comparison with blood revenge, see Holmgren 1974.

179. Mihelič (1948: 199–200), writing in the aftermath of Nazi atrocities during World War II, remarks: "If the critics of Nahum had lived in the last decade and witnessed the brutality that had been visited upon the helpless people in the European and Asiatic concentration camps, they would rather have joined their voices with Nahum and his joy over the fall of the 'bloody city,' than have condemned his righteous indignation in the comfort and security of their ivory tower." For this quote, I am indebted to Christensen (2009: 219), who was in turn indebted to Spronk.

Such comments can help contextualize the rhetoric of war within the realia of war. At the same time, they can lead to the caricature of the Assyrian Empire as "a uniquely efficient and remorseless warmongering and bloodthirsty military machine, with quasi-Hitlerian connotations: an 'evil empire' of antiquity" against which Assyriologists have justifiably spoken (Fales 2008: 17). Fales (2008: 17) nicely articulates the many benefits of the Pax Assyriaca, while not ignoring that "it is indisputable that the Assyrians made widespread use of their military power for the purpose of uniting the different cultures of the Near East in a single political structure." What has led to an unbalanced view of Assyrian military prowess (including Nahum's portrayal) is iconographic and textual narratives of Assyrian treatment of captives (drawn by their own artisans and scribes, not caricatures drawn by their detractors), on which see Lewis 2008b.

Rebalancing our understandings of the rhetoric and reality of war narratives also requires us to address portrayals that would condemn the Assyrians with the intent of highlighting Judean superiority. As I noted previously (Lewis 2008b: 89), Judeans would not have had to look very far afield for their own traditions, which included mass killings of enemies (1 Sam 15:7; 2 Sam 8:2–6), beheadings (1 Sam 17:51; 2 Sam 4:7–8; 2 Kgs 10:7–14), corpse mutilation (1 Sam 18:27), and torture of prisoners of war including hanging (Josh 10:24–26), eye gouging (1 Sam 10:27 [4QSam^a]), and dismemberment of hands and feet (2 Sam 4:12; cf. 2 Sam 12:31).

180. Joel 4:9–16 (Eng 3:9–16) represents a reversal of the famous "plowshares" passage of Isa 2:2–4//Mic 4:1–4. In contrast to Micah's charge to Daughter Zion to do the threshing of the many nations (*gôyim rabbîm, 'ammîm rabbîm*; Mic 4:11–13), for Joel the speaker's (presumably Yahweh's) proclamation to "sanctify for battle" (*qaddĕšû milḥāmâ*) goes out to the nations (*gôyim*) (not Israel) asking them to do the harvesting of the nations (*gôyim*). For interpretation of the various speakers and audiences of Joel 4:9–16 (Eng 3:9–16), see Crenshaw 1995: 186–196 and Wolff 1977: 71–86.

181. Examples could be multiplied, such as Mexican artist Pedro Reyes with his "Palas por Pistolas" and "Disarm" art projects, the former producing 1,527 shovels from an equal number of guns to plant an equal number of trees, the latter producing musical instruments from weapons. For scholars trying to evaluate the plowshares passage within the realpolitik world of the Neo-Assyrian Empire and juxtaposed against its understanding in modern international relations vocabulary, see Cohen and Westbrook 2008.

182. For a synthesis of the "welter of conflicting opinions" on the date and authorship of this poem, see Williamson 2006: 173–179. For text-critical analysis, see Williamson 2006: 166–171; 2005a: 203–211.

183. I agree with Williamson (2006: 183–184) that the instruction here is broader rather than narrower (so Wildberger 1991: 91).

184. See Ps 46:7–10 and 76:3–4, 6–7, and, with additional details, Willis 1997: 305–306 and Williamson 2006: 176.

185. One immediately thinks of the judges in the book so named, whose primary activity was on the battlefield: "Then Yahweh raised up judges [*šōpĕṭîm*] who saved them out of the power of those who plundered them" (Judg 2:16). Most telling for our purposes are several psalms (including some of the Songs of Zion that are clearly

related to our passage [Willis 1997]) where *špṭ* has this sense (e.g., Ps 9:4–9; 76:4, 6–7, 9; 82:8; 96:8–13; cf. Ps 98:9). Lewis (2008b: 90–93) notes:

> If Isaiah has indeed been influenced by the Songs of Zion traditions, then [these] texts may be significant for interpreting our "swords into plowshares" passage. Elliptically, Isaiah could very well have meant that nations will melt down and recast their weapons into agricultural implements because Yahweh has first rendered them ineffective. Broken spears, swords, and bows are useless. Thus those weapons of metal might as well be melted down and reused.

186. The discipline of family religion (also known as household and domestic religion) has grown considerably over the past generation. In addition to the various articles in Bodel and Olyan 2008, see Albertz and Schmitt 2012; Yasur-Landau, Ebeling, and Mazow 2011; Gerstenberger 2002; van der Toorn 1996b; and Albertz 1978.
187. Some of the following material appeared earlier in Lewis 2008a. I am indebted to Andrew Davis for the Saul Bellow quote.
188. It is not my intention to minimize the importance of securing an heir for the kingdom at large. Certainly commoners would have been impacted by the stability or instability of the monarchy.
189. See Smith 2001b: 56–57 on the debate (e.g., by Day and Walls) on whether ʿAnatu is the spouse of Baʿlu. For a comprehensive look at terms related to the family in Ugaritic, see Watson (2013).
190. Deities and monarchs alike adopted the familial merism of "father and mother" in order to promote their parental benevolence. See the following discussion and Lewis forthcoming a.
191. See Lewis 2013a, 2014a.
192. ʾAthiratu may also suckle King Kirta's heir (KTU 1.15.2.26–28), yet the reading of this text is now debatable. In KTU 1.15.2.27, Greenstein (1997: 25, 45 n. 66) reads ʿAṯtartu rather than ʾAthiratu. Pardee (1997a: 337) has the latter. Yet upon further analysis, Pardee (2012a: 184–188) argues that the reading is *nrt*, "the Luminary" (i.e., Shapshu), not ʿṯtrt.
193. While we have no text that explicitly says so, it is possible that non-elites (having heard the famous story) may have dreamed that they too could be favored with ʾAthiratu's assistance in obtaining a spouse. We can conjecture that similar vows were enacted within family religion. Compare the betrothal of the gods Yarikh and Nikkal-Ib in KTU 1.24, a text that was then used in human wedding ceremonies to assure mortals of a divinely blessed union.
194. A balanced summary of the numerous interpretations of this passage can be found in Wiggins 1993: 44–48.
195. See the conclusion in Wiggins 1993: 71.
196. See Gröndahl 1967: esp. 80 and del Olmo Lete 1999: 338–340. For Ugaritic onomastics in general, see Pardee 1989–1990: 390–513; Hess 1999; and an ongoing series of articles entitled "Ugaritic Onomastics" by W. G. E. Watson in *Aula Orientalis* starting in 1990.
197. One can certainly hope that there was heartfelt belief behind the standardized words ʿAzzīʾiltu (the son of the famous ʾUrtēnu) used to write to his parents: "May

it be well with you. May the gods guard your well-being, may they keep you well." In the same text, he addresses his sister similarly: "May it be well with you. [May] the gods keep [you] well, may they guard you, may they [keep] you [wh]ole." This is the translation by Pardee (2002b: 112).

198. This letter (RS 20.178 = Ugaritica V, #55) is one of the Akkadian texts found in the private residences of Ugarit's upper classes. It was written by a high government official by the name of Rap'ānu to his sister. The translation here (but with my emphasis) is that of van der Toorn (1996b: 168), to whom I am indebted for bringing my attention to this passage.

199. For further on the Kathiratu (or Kotharatu), see Pardee 1999: 491–492.

200. For the many other references to family religion in this text, see Lewis 2008a. In particular, note the four refrains that articulate the duties of an ideal son (who in this narrative comes to be named Aqhatu). Special mention is made of the son's cultic duty of setting up a stela for Ilu-ibi, a term that refers to either his divine ancestor or his ancestor's god.

201. Yet compare passages such as Exod 24:9–11, where Moses, the covenant mediator, along with priestly representatives and elders, "beheld God and ate and drank" (Exod 24:11). Sacrifices were often referred to as Yahweh's "food" (*leḥem*). On this material and the much larger (and nuanced) question about divine eating in the biblical tradition, see Lewis 2006a: 344–346.

202. For a survey of opinions, see Vall 1995. The majority of scholars have no problem answering the first question ("Has the rain a father?") in the affirmative, yet "to speak . . . of ice issuing from his womb is quite another" (Vall 1995: 511). Vall goes on speak of "the utter incongruity of ice coming forth from a womb" and how "metaphors of sexual reproduction cannot do justice to God's creation of the hydrous forms." Yet the mother imagery used of the male Yahweh should allow us to set aside concerns about such figurative language, as should the ancient Near Eastern sources I have documented here (see esp. the Sin text discussed later) that show that a male creator deity's "womb" can "give birth" to everything.

203. The form used for nurse here (*'wmn*) is masculine, as in Num 11:21, another text filled with maternal metaphors. To underscore the feminine imagery, Mansoor (1961: 162) translates *k'wmn* "as a nursing-father," whereas Schuller and Newsom (2012: 57) translate it "like a foster-father."

Earlier in our Qumran text, we come across the feminine form (*'wmnt*) in the context of a wet nurse: "Truly, it is you who from (the time of) my father have known me, and from the womb [you have sanctified me, and from the belly of] my mother you have nurtured me, and from the breasts of the one who conceived me your compassion has been present for me, and in the bosom of my nurse [*'wmnty*] was your great [kindness]" (1QHodayot^a, xvii, 29b–31a). The translation here is that of Schuller and Newsom (2012: 54–55).

Cf. the expression here in line 35 (*'aby l' yd'ny*, "my [earthly] father did not acknowledge me") and line 29b (*ky 'th m'aby yd'tny*, "for you [God] have known me since [the time of] my father") with the Hebrew personal name 'Abyada', "[My divine] Father has acknowledged [me]."

204. Schwemer 2019, lines 15–16, 21, 27, 35; Singer 2002: 30–40; Goetze 1969: 396–397.
205. Assmann 2008: 80. Cf. too Wilson's (1969: 371) translation of Papyrus Chester Beatty IV: "Do (not) widows say: 'Our husband art thou,' and little ones: 'Our father and our mother'?"
206. Lieven 2014: 20, 23, 32.
207. Stephens 1969: 385–386.
208. See Parpola 1997, xxxvi–xl, 7 (text 1.6, lines 7′, 15′–18′), 18 (text 2.5, lines 26′–27′); Nissinen et al. 2003: 105 n. a; 116, line 26′; Nissinen et al. 2019: 115 n. a; 127, line 26′; Machinist 2006: 166–167.
209. *Lmy kt 'b wlmy kt 'm wlmy kt 'ḥ* (KAI 24, lines 10–11).
210. *P'ln b'l ldnnym l'ab wl'm* (KAI 26 A I, line 3). This is of course the Phoenician text, on which see Younger 1998; 2000a: 148–149. The Hieroglyphic Luwian reads: "Tarhunzas made me mother and father to Adanawa." See Payne 2012: 21–22, 39 and Yakubovich 2015: 41, 43.
211. Even a list of representative literature on these topics could be unending. A brief start: Tellenbach 1976; Tasker 2008: 109–127; 2004; Nunnally 1992; Marchel 1963; Jeremias 1966; Goshen-Gottstein 2001: 470–504; Widdicombe 2000: 519–536; Daly 1973; Halkes 1981: 103–112; Gerstenberger 1996a: 1–12.
212. So Tasker 2008: 123. These explicit references include Deut 32:6; 2 Sam 7:14; Isa 63:16 (twice); 64:8; Jer 3:4, 19; 31:9; Mal 1:6; 2:10; Ps 68:6 (Eng 68:5]; 89:27 [Eng 89:26]; 103:13; Prov 3:12; 1 Chr 17:13; 22:10; 28:6; 29:10.
213. As to the Abî- first element in compound personal names, Waltke and O'Connor (1990: 127, §8.2c) have noted how the *î* may designate the first person singular pronoun ("*My* [divine] Father is X") or may be a remnant of a case vowel ("The Father is X"). We follow Bauer and Leander (1922: 524, §65g) in preferring the former, which we have leveled through our translations; for the most part these follow those given in HALOT.
214. The divine father names of the Hebrew Bible that are also attested in the Hebrew epigraphic record include ʾAbibaʿal, ʾAbigayil, ʾAbinoʿam, ʾAbiʿezer, ʾAbishuʿa, ʾAḥʾab, and Yoʾab. Those that are attested in non-Hebrew epigraphic record include ʾAbibaʿal (Phoenician), ʾAbinadab (Ammonite), ʾAbiram (Aramaic, Moabite), and ʾAḥʾab (Aramaic). I am indebted here to the database in Albertz and Schmitt 2012: appendix B.
215. I am again indebted here to the database in Albertz and Schmitt 2012: appendix B.
216. On the Jewish tradition that develops the "Thirteen Attributes of God" from Exod 34:6–7, see Sarna 1991: 216.
217. The notion of Yahweh as a creator god working as a potter with clay is found elsewhere in biblical tradition (Gen 2:7; Job 10:9; 33:6), but without the father imagery we have here (yet cf. Ps 103:13–14).

For the creation of humans out of clay elsewhere in the ancient Near East, cf. the Egyptian god Khnum at work at his potter's wheel, the Sumerian myth of Enki and Ninmaḫ, its Akkadian counterpart in the myth of Atraḫasis, and the Neo-Babylonian text VAT 17019. For bibliography as well as the way in which such creation out of clay could include the magical arts, see Lewis 2013a.

218. For the present discussion I have left out the way in which Israel turned aside to Baal worship, a subject I will address shortly.
219. The MT reads "taking them by *his* arms [zĕrô'ōtāyw]." If the final *waw* here originally was a conjunction used at the beginning of the next line (i.e., a dittography), then the text would read "in *my* arms" (zĕrô'ōtāy; cf. LXX), a reading favored by most translations (e.g., JPS, RSV, NRSV, NEB, NAB) and commentators (e.g., W. R. Harper, H. W. Wolff, J. L. Mays).
220. The last two lines here are complicated and readers are directed to the various commentaries, where attempts are made to justify a wide range of alternative readings (e.g., reading 'ûl, "infant," for MT's 'ōl, "yoke"). We uncomfortably follow the majority of analysts who read lô (so LXX) for MT's lō'.
221. On gēr as "client," see Stager 1988: 229–232.
222. See Havice 1978 and Fensham 1962.
223. Cf. KTU 1.17.5.4–8; Havice 1978: 88–93, 149–156, 169–172, 253–256, 263–270. Havice (1978: 270) notes that "the concept of the duty to the underprivileged was so central to the ideal of kingship that it came to epitomize the ideal of rule." For additional discussion of Yahweh's role as an ideal judge providing protection to the disadvantaged, see Chapter Nine.
224. See Eissfeldt 1966: 39–47.
225. The four refrains articulating the duties of an ideal son (named Aqhatu) to be born to Danilu are found in (1) KTU 1.17.1.25–34 (in the context of Ba'lu's intercession on Danilu's behalf); (2) KTU 1.17.1.43–48 (when 'Ilu grants his request); (3) KTU 1.17.2.1–8 (when a messenger delivers the birth announcement to Danilu), and finally (4) KTU 1.17.2.12–23 (when Danilu rejoices in the good fortune bestowed upon him by the gods). See further Lewis 2008a: 68–70.
226. See Chapter Seven, pp. 358–379.
227. Cf. Exod 21:15, 17; Lev 20:9; Deut 21:18–21; 27:16. Fathers and mothers were also to be held in esteem for their wise instruction (Prov 1:8–9; 6:20–21; cf. 10:1; 15:20).
228. Given the differing vocabulary between the two passages, Williamson (2006: 34) is certainly correct that "it is most unlikely that we have a specific reference to the law of the rebellious son" in Deut 21:18–21.
229. Though the word "love" in Hosea 11:1–4 is familial, it should not be forgotten that in the ancient Near East the language of "love" is also used of loyalty in treaties (cf. especially the Amarna correspondence, such as EA 17:24–28; 53:40–44; 83:51; 114:59–69; 121:61–63; 123:23; 138:47). See especially Moran 1963: 77–87 and note 247 in this chapter. As noted by Stuart (1987: 178), the double entendre adds further texture to the accusation against the rebellious child.
230. Lundbom (2004: 517) notes how Israel's failure to take Yahweh's instruction is "a recurring theme in Jeremiah's preaching (2:30; 5:3; 7:28; 17:23; 32:33; 35:13)."
231. See Chapter Four, pp. 110–111.
232. Scholars speculate as to whether the tree here indicates a wooden *asherah* symbol, with the stone then representing a male divine symbol, and with the reversal of sexual imagery (the female as the father and the male as the mother) being consciously sarcastic. See Holladay 1986: 103–104; Lundbom 1999: 284–285.

233. On the Priestly *kābôd* theology, see Chapter Seven, pp. 368–373.
234. See Darr's (1994: 46–84) chapter "Child Imagery and the Rhetoric of Rebellion" in her study on familial language in the book of Isaiah. Darr (1994: 61) summarizes: "The texts . . . depict unrepentant Israel as the very personification of the odious son of Deut 21:18–21."
235. For modern objections to and defenses of Yahweh's parenting style, see the representative works Lasine 2002 and Copan 2006, respectively.
236. Granted, the context of Isa 45:9–12 is Yahweh speaking against those who were questioning the commissioning of the Persian king Cyrus as his anointed, not questioning his parenting of a wayward child. Yet obviously the rhetoric that here is being applied by extension to the political sphere had its origin in the context of family dynamics.
237. Literally, something that is but a (clay) sherd among (other) earthen sherds (*ḥereś ʾet-ḥarĕśê ʾădāmâ*).
238. The clay here stands for humans, themselves made out of clay (on which see note 217). The pottery imagery here suggests a clay figurine coming to life to speak out against its potter. Cf. the animated clay figure of Shatiqatu at Ugarit (who strives helpfully alongside ʾIlu, not against the deity, as we have here in our text; cf. Lewis 2013a, 2014b). That most clay figurines regularly had arms and hands while others were stylized without arms (cf. the Judean pillar figurines, on which see Kletter 1996; Darby 2014) makes the criticism in 45:9 "your work has no hands [*yādayim*]" very understandable. There is no need to translated *yādayim* as the "handles" on a pot (so NRSV).
239. The Hebrew of Isa 45:11a has the imperative form *šĕʾālûnî*, "Ask me!" Perhaps the original intention was one of Yahweh sarcastically challenging his detractors: "Ask me . . . Command me (why don't you?) . . ." I owe this insight to Andrew Davis (personal communication).
240. According to Day (1995: 283–284), in addition to "daughter" (*bat*) terminology, cities in the Hebrew Bible are portrayed with the following female images: *bĕtûlâ*, "adolescent"; *ʾēm*, "mother"; *ʾalmānâ*, "widow"; *rabbātî*, "mistress/powerful woman"; *zônâ*, "adulterous/promiscuous woman"; *śārātî*, "ruler"; and *šĕbiyyâ*, "captive." Cities also are personified as wife and ex-wife (e.g., Ezek 16:8; 23:37; Isa 50:1).

On the use of female imagery and the negative portrayal of women (especially the "harlotry" imagery), see Ackerman 1998b (on Isaiah), O'Connor 1998 (on Jeremiah and Lamentations), and Sanderson 1998 (on Micah) in Newsom and Ringe 1998.
241. Lyke (2009: 988) comments: "The use of the term 'daughter Zion' likely has some connection with the historical realities of ancient warfare, when women were most vulnerable to rape and defilement." See Liebermann's (2019: 331) contextualizing of the literary portrayal of the treatment of women with what is known from refugee studies.

On the mourning of Daughter Zion and the city lament genre, see Dobbs-Allsopp 1993: 75–90 and McCarter 1999: 941.
242. As Fensham (1971) and Propp (1999: 217) have noted, this is not to deny the way in which Yahweh delivered Israel as his "vassal son" (cf. 2 Kgs 16:7).

243. These terra-cotta feet come from Late Bronze Age Temple M1. A sales contract reveals that the purchaser of these slave children was none other than an elite religious officiant, a chief diviner and scribe by the name of Baʿal-malik. See Zaccagnini 1994; Durand 1990: 74–75.
244. See note 242.
245. See in particular Baltzer's (2001: 155–160; 1987) comments on our passage and on debt slavery in Second Isaiah with his emphasis on the "sociomorpheme" of Yahweh as master with property rights over Israel the servant. Additional bibliography on the use of √g'l in Deutero-Isaiah can be found in Baltzer 2001: 158 n. 88.
246. On Yahweh as holy within Isaianic traditions, see Chapter Ten, pp. 599–603.
247. Observe that here is the only place in the Hebrew Bible where God says so forthrightly (in the first person singular address) "I love you" (*'ăhabtîkā*).

    On "love" terminology, see note 229 (esp. the work of Moran) as well as Baltzer 2001: 160, which notes how the word "love" can designate a "bond of loyalty" within treaties while "at the same time it undoubtedly expresses God's whole personal bond with his people, which rests on his free election."
248. Jer 31:7-9 also turns to father imagery to describe Yahweh gathering home "Ephraim his firstborn" from "the farthest parts of the earth." For more on this passage (especially with its emphasis on the blind, the lame, the pregnant, and those in labor), see Lundbom 2004: 419–426.
249. As should be clear with my choice of vocabulary, I am indebted here to the work of Trible (1978: 15–23; quotations from page 22). On Gen 1:27 in the context of the Priestly account's emphasis on the blessing of fertility, see Bird 1997a: 123–154.
250. See Chapter Four, pp. 91–92, 110–111. That we have figurative language in Deut 32:6, 18 is clear both with the notion of a deity and a "rock" (*ṣûr*) giving birth to a physical human being.
251. The verb of creation here (*yṣr*) once again uses pottery imagery. See Lundbom 1999: 231 for a collection of individuals called at birth (e.g., Pharaoh Piankhi, Aššurbanipal, Moses, Samuel, John the Baptist). Lundbom notes how Jeremiah's pre-birth call "goes well beyond this"; he stands alone with such "an advance appointment," to be echoed only by the call of Paul (Gal 1:15).
252. Fuchs (1985: 136) critically points out the male-dominated ideological nature of these narratives, whose "patriarchal framework . . . prevents the mother-figure from becoming a full-fledged *human* role model, while its androcentric perspective confines her to a limited literary role, largely subordinated to the biblical male protagonists."
253. On the association of weaving with goddesses, see Ackerman 2008b, which highlights the goddess Asherah (cf. 2 Kgs 23:7). For further analysis of the role of women in textile production, cultic and otherwise, see Meyers 2003: 432–434 and Ackerman 2008b: 144, as well as the Conclusion, pp. 681–683, 690–691, 695.
254. The meaning of the word *gōḥî* (G Ptc of √*gyḥ* with 1 common singular suffix) is straightforward yet difficult to render in English. The poet is certainly being creative in choosing a root (*gyḥ*) that could conjure a play between the noun *gāḥôn*, "belly" (Gen 3:14; Lev 11:42), and *beṭen* (twice in Ps 22:10–11 [Eng 22:9–10]). *Gyḥ*

is used figuratively in Job 38:8–9 of the sea as a baby "bursting forth" from its womb (*bĕgîḥô mērēḥem*) and then being swaddled by God. Cornell (2012: 9) writes of "God exercising an unmistakable maternal role towards the Sea."

Though *gōḥî* in our passage is hard to translate, it seems to refer to God acting as midwife to deliver the baby at birth (God as "burster"?), especially in light of lines in the psalm that have God place the infant on his mother's breasts. Cf. Isa 66:19; Ps 71:6. Cf. too the following treatment of Yahweh acting in the place of mother and father (e.g., Ps 27:9ff.).

255. Cf. 1QHodayot^a, xvii, 35–36, and note 203 in this chapter.
256. 1QIsa^a's *yôdîaʿ* ("he makes known") for MT's more poetic *yārîaʿ* ("he arouses, excites") represents an *r*/*d* graphic confusion.
257. On the difficulties of this verse, see Darr 1987: 568–570; Blenkinsopp 2002: 214 n. h; and Bergmann 2010: 51–53.
258. Darr (1987: 564, 567) writes that both similes serve "to underscore Yahweh's power," as they "share both profound intensity and a markedly auditory quality." In contrast to L. L. Bronner and P. Trible, Darr (1987: 567–571) argues that "the poem emphasizes that which blasts forth from the throat of God, and not a new creation to which Yahweh will give birth in pain. . . . The 'natal verbs' which appear in Ps 90:2 and frequently within Isaiah are not employed in 42:16 to describe Yahweh's redemptive acts."
259. Cf. Trible 1978: 38–50, 64–67 and Chapter Six, note 175, which references the use of *ʾilāh raḥmān* in the Tell Fakheriyeh inscription, line 5.

Chapman (2016: 114) is a moderating voice who agrees with Gruber that "in the vast majority of occurrences, [the] noun [*reḥem*] is used without any apparent awareness of its semantic connection to a mother's womb" while affirming that "Trible is correct, however, to highlight select cases where poets and narrators seem to activate and consciously play with the womb-sourced aspect of the term." See Chapman's (2016: 113–116) fuller discussion of *reḥem* as contextualized with texts from Ugarit.
260. The translation here follows the consensus among scholars and reflects the final understanding of the MT. Yet compare Chapter Ten, pp. 593–595, for an alternative (earlier?) understanding with exactly the opposite meaning.
261. See for example, Albertz 1978; van der Toorn 1996b; Bodel and Olyan 2008; Yasur-Landau, Ebeling, and Mazow 2011; and Albertz and Schmitt 2012.
262. The personal names given here are representative. For a comprehensive analysis, see Albertz and Schmitt 2012: 245–386 and app. B1–B6, esp. tab. 5.1–5.16.
263. ʾAḥiʾem (the maternal equivalent of the better-attested ʾAḥʾab, "the [divine] brother is like a father [to me]") is attested on four seal impressions at Lachish. See Barkay and Vaughn 1996a: 38–41; figs. 11–13; 1996b: 71; §61–64. See too Renz and Röllig 2003: 395; §21.50 as well as Avigad and Sass 1997: 261 §706, who read *ʾḥʾmr̲*, "ʾAḥiʾamar" (my emphasis). For discussions of alternative ways of analyzing ʾAḥiʾem (and the biblical ʾAḥiʾam attested in 2 Sam 23:33 and 1 Chr 11:35), see Barkay and Vaughn 1996a: 41 and Albertz and Schmitt 2012: 353.

See too the PN *ʾlʾm* from a late eighth-/early seventh-century BCE scaraboid-shaped seal bearing a winged sun disk from Tel Rehov (Mazar and Ahituv 2011: 276–279).

Chapter 9

1. The list here is the product of taking the first such list that came up on a Google search (produced on August 11, 2010), http://listverse.com/2010/08/11/top-10-greatest-monarchs.
2. See Baines 1998 and Frandsen 2008 for fuller interactions with those who argue against a straightforward divinity of the Egyptian king (e.g., Hornung, Posener).
3. Sumerian King List, lines 1, 41. For the composite text, see http://etcsl.orinst.ox.ac.uk/section2/c211.htm. For translation, see http://etcsl.orinst.ox.ac.uk/section2/tr211.htm. See too the mention of kingship descending from heaven in the Flood Story, also known as the Eridu Genesis. For the composite text, see the Flood Story, segment B, lines 6ff. in http://etcsl.orinst.ox.ac.uk/section1/c174.htm. For translation, see the Flood Story, segment B, lines 6ff. in http://etcsl.orinst.ox.ac.uk/cgi-bin/etcsl.cgi?text=t.1.7.4# as well as Jacobsen 1997: 514.
4. For specifics of these ritual activities of the king, see Hoffner 2006: 136–144. See too Beckman 1995: 533, noting that "while the king might have been the center of attention in the ceremonies in which he participated, his role was largely passive while the recitations and more elaborate ritual actions were carried out by professional priests."
5. On the so-called festival of haste and the festival of the AN.DAḪ.ŠUM plant, see Gilan 2011: 282–283 with bibliography.
6. Our selective use of Ugarit is pragmatic and implies no slight to kingship elsewhere in ancient Syria. For the religious roles of Aramean kings, see Niehr 2014a: 127–203. Note the limited role of the king in ritual at Emar. See Fleming 1992b; Adamthwaite 2001: 188–189; Klingbeil 2007: 223; and Thames 2016. Phoenician royal cult is also left out in this sketch, but it is treated in the Conclusion, pp. 684–687.
7. For a convenient translation of the various Ugaritic ritual texts described here (i.e., KTU 1.40; 1.41; 1.43; 1.87; 1.119; 1.112), see Pardee 2002a. For a comprehensive technical analysis (including philological and epigraphic remarks), see Pardee 2000 with bibliography.
8. On sacral vestments (*bigdê-qōdeš*) and priestly washing, see Milgrom 1991: 1016–1018, 1046–1049.
9. Cf. similar descriptions of the legendary King Kirta washing himself, offering libations, and then sacrificing on a roof in KTU 1.14.2.9–27; 1.14.3.52–1.14.4.9. We have additional, although brief, evidence that the queen also engaged in sacrifice (KTU 4.149.14–15; cf. KTU 1.170.1).
10. The first text attesting to this ritual (KTU 1.40) was discovered in the 1929 campaign. At present the ritual is documented in six copies (two well-preserved texts, KTU 1.40 and 1.84, and four fragments, KTU 1.121, 1.122, 1.153, and 1.154). The texts come from a variety of find spots including the royal palace (KTU 1.84), the house of the High Priest on the acropolis (KTU 1.40), and the House of the Magician Priest, south acropolis (KTU 1.121, 1.122, 1.152, 1.154). This observation, together with differing scribal hands, allows Pardee (2002a: 78) to conclude that "the texts were not the product of a single school."

11. Curiously, David's sons are called *kōhănîm* in 2 Sam 8:18, a tradition that is not reflected in the version in 1 Chr 18:17 that reads *hāri'šōnîm lĕyad hammelek*, "the first [sons of David] at the king's side." For the complicated textual and interpretive issues, see Knoppers 2004: 706, 708–710.

    Cf. the use of *khn* for Phoenician kings Eshmunazor I and Tabnit, who served as "priests of 'Aštart" (*khn 'štrt*), as documented in the Tabnit inscription (KAI 13, lines 1–2). Cf. too the use of *khn* in the Batnoam inscription (KAI 11) to describe "King Azbaal, son of Paltibaal, the priest of the lady [*khn b'lt*]." Queen co-regent 'Ummî'aštart, the sister and wife of Tabnit, is described as "priestess of 'Aštart" (*khnt 'štrt*). See the Conclusion, pp. 685–687.

12. As for sacrificing, according to Lev 17 and Exod 20:21 (Eng 20:24), any person can make *'ōlôt* and *šĕlāmîm* offerings (specifically mentioning sheep, goat, and oxen), yet blood manipulation is highlighted as being the special prerogative of priests.

13. The brief sketch of royal cult provided here is, for the most part, gathered from material that has come down to us through the mediation of the Deuteronomistic Historian. DtrH is used here because it provides a pragmatic model for conceptualizing the role of the king in the cult that resonates with the broader Near East. Contrasting DtrH's views with those of Deuteronomy is illuminating, as the former is at odds with the latter's utopian vision that limits the monarch's power and influence over the cult. Knoppers (1993, 1996, 2001), McConville (1998), Levinson (2001), Dutcher-Walls (2002), and Garfein (2004), among others, have written insightfully on these competing ideologies of kingship. As Knoppers notes (2001: 394, 398), "Many of the very trappings that elevate the king above his compatriots in Mesopotamia, Egypt, and Canaanite societies are proscribed in Deuteronomy.... In the Sumerian King List, the monarchy is 'lowered from heaven,' but in Deuteronomy the advent of the monarchy is neither necessary nor inevitable." With regard to cult, Levinson (2001: 523, 533–534) summarizes:

    > Just as Deuteronomy's Law of the King (Deut. xvii 14–20) denies the king any role in justice, so does it deny him a role in the cultus.... There is no provision for the monarch actively to participate in the cultus, still less to supervise it or serve as royal patron of the Temple. The converse is also true. Deuteronomy's cultic laws envision no role whatsoever for the monarch.... Deuteronomy's blueprint was more utopian than pragmatic... there is no evidence for the implementation of the judicial-political-religious charters of Deut xvi 18–xviii 22. So radical was it in its own time that, shortly after its promulgation, it was effectively abrogated, as the Deuteronomistic Historian, while purporting to implement the norms of Deuteronomy, restored to the king precisely those powers denied him by Deuteronomy.

14. Note in 1 Sam 13:11–14 how the DtrH tradition censures Saul for this activity but no censure is mentioned when David and Solomon engage in the same acts. Saul's precise offense is not stated and has led to various theories. See Tsumura 2007: 347–348.

15. See Chapter Ten, pp. 624–629, and Mettinger 1976: 185–232.

16. On the religious-political nature of this dancing, see Seow 1989. Though the vocabulary is different, cf. too the ritualized dancing of the prophets of Baal in 1 Kgs 18:26.

17. On the priestly use of the ephod containing the Urim and Thummim as well as King David using Abiathar the priest for his divinatory consultation, see Chapter Ten, p. 621 and note 131.
18. When David burned the wood of the threshing sledges for fuel for his sacrifice, he symbolically depicted the end of the agrarian activity on the site in service of its new cultic function. Yet afterward the space remained open and accessible to all, and the pragmatic need for a place to thresh grain could potentially override such symbolism. Yet with Solomon and the building of the huge Temple edifice, the original agrarian purpose of the threshing floor was obliterated, and with it open access to the non-elite. When one adds in the priestly control of this sacred space (with gradations of holiness restricting innermost access to priests alone), a remarkable transformation has occurred. The degree to which royal cult and priestly cult worked together and/or at odds with each other remains to be clarified. Yet what is clear is how the royal cult of King Solomon redefined the practice of religion and with it the nature of Yahweh, who was now enthroned.

    Note how 2 Chr 3:1 makes the connection to Mt. Moriah of Gen 22:2 fame. (These are the only two places to mention Mt. Moriah in the entire Hebrew Bible.) By thus linking the erection of the Temple to the place of Abraham's animal sacrifice, Chr provides a rational for introducing priestly animal sacrifice at a locale that was originally a place solely for threshing grain. For additional explorations on the topic, see Waters 2015.
19. For the various interpretations of David's offense (cultic, ethical, bloodshed), see Knoppers 2004: 772–775.
20. It is hereby acknowledged that using DtrH as source material is notoriously difficult, especially with its theological privileging of the centralization of worship in Jerusalem. Thus Solomon's sacrificing at the Gibeonite high place is prefaced by the disparaging remark that though Solomon loved Yahweh and followed Davidic statutes, he nonetheless engaged in cultic activity at high places (1 Kgs 3:3–4). This pejorative remark, however, is couched in an apologetic context that notes that (obviously) people were engaging in such activity at that time because the Temple had yet to be built (1 Kgs 3:2). Nonetheless, it is surprising to then read DtrH's comments about Gibeon being (1) "the *great* high place," (2) a place where Solomon's cultic activity was extensive (i.e., 1,000 ʿōlôt offerings), and (3) the sacred space subsequently chosen by Yahweh to reveal his blessing to Solomon via a dream revelation. However these semi-positive "Gibeon high place" traditions came to be here, DtrH does sufficient damage control by immediately having Solomon travel to chosen Jerusalem to enact his first post-dream revelation sacrifice, and he does so before the legitimate cult object of Yahweh's Ark (1 Kgs 3:15).
21. This narrative legitimizing Solomon's reign contains "incomparability" language (1 Kgs 3:12–13) with respect to his wisdom, riches, and *kābôd*, yet not with respect to cult—certainly because of his cultic activities denounced by DtrH in 1 Kgs 11. DtrH's language of "incomparability" in cult is reserved for the Yahwistic religious reforms of kings Hezekiah (2 Kgs 18:5) and Josiah (2 Kgs 23:25). See further Knoppers 1992a.
22. Granted, Hiram of Tyre, a master builder, is also highlighted as one who executed Solomon's work and is responsible for the various furnishings of the temple (1 Kgs

7:13–47; 2 Chr 2:13–16; 4:11–18). He is not to be confused with Hiram, King of Tyre (ca. 969–930 BCE), who also helps David and Solomon with securing materials and workmen for various building projects including the Temple.

23. The specific vocabulary of an "exalted" (*zĕbul*) house built on Canaanite models with Phoenician assistance may not have been lost on those who had heard traditions about the Canaanite god known at Ugarit as *zabūlu* Baʿlu.

24. For ancient Mesopotamian parallels, see Hurowitz 1992.

25. On the division of labor with respect to the handling the Ark by Aaronid priests and Kohathite Levites (cf. Num 4; 1 Kgs 8), see Chapter Ten, pp. 596–597, 642.

26. See Gray (1970: 253–254); Cogan (2001: 304–305); and Fritz (2003: 114).

27. In contrast to the minimal treatment in DtrH, see especially the significant amount of coverage that the Chronicler assigns to Hezekiah as he portrays the monarch's cleansing and rededication of the temple, his involvement with the Passover festival, and his significant dealings with priests and Levites (2 Chr 29–31). As Williamson (1982: 350–351) observes, "The Chronicler has gone out of his way to present Hezekiah as a second Solomon." For further analysis of the so-called reforming kings, see Lowery 1991.

28. Sadly, DtrH has left us with little data (mostly of a pejorative nature) on queens and queen mothers as cultic officiants. See Ackerman 1998a: 138–162 for a treatment of what evidence we do have with regard to the religious roles of Maʿacah, Jezebel, Athaliah, and Michal.

    This sparse treatment stands in contrast to what we know of their counterparts elsewhere, such as in Hittite religion (on which see Ackerman 1998a: 138–139). Cf. too Ugarit, where we know more about the substantive and extensive economic power of queens and queen mothers and their political and diplomatic overtures than about their roles as cultic agents (cf. Thomas 2014). Yet KTU 4.149 (found in the eastern archive of the royal palace) mentions "the sacrifice of the queen/queen mother in the sown land" (*dbḥ mlkt bmdrʿ*). KTU 1.23 invokes the gracious gods to bring blessing (*šlm*) to the reigning king and queen mother/queen (see Lewis forthcoming a). For the Sidonian queen co-regent ʾUmmiʿaštart, who served as the priestess of ʿAštart (*khnt ʿštrt*), see the Conclusion, pp. 685–687.

29. See Chapter Ten, pp. 656–657, for DtrH's negative portrayal of Jeroboam's illicit priestly installation (1 Kgs 13:33–34).

30. The remark about Jeroboam I "standing by the altar [at Bethel] to offer incense" is a part of the famous "man of God" episode (prophesying the coming of Josiah) in 1 Kgs 13:1–10. This dramatic episode goes on to narrate the destruction of the altar and the "withering" (and subsequent healing) of Jeroboam's hand that he stretched out to seize the prophet.

    See Chapter Ten, pp. 661–663, for King Uzziah's cultic violation of offering incense in 2 Chr 26:16–20 that resulted in his lifelong affliction of *ṣāraʿat*, a skin disease. Curiously, Chr makes no mention of Jeroboam's offering of incense.

31. For DtrH's stereotypical vocabulary elsewhere, see 1 Kgs 3:3; 14:22–24; 15:14; 22:43; 2 Kgs 12:3; 15:4; 15:35. For a discussion of the meaning of "to pass through fire" and the nature of Ahaz's sacrifice, see Dewrell 2017: 129–145.

32. Two verses in our narrative (2 Kgs 16:13, 15) explicitly refer to offerings that are for the royal cult, in contrast to those for the people at large. The first verse marks this with four references to "*his* [i.e., the king's] offerings" (*'ōlātô, minḥātô, niskô, haššĕlāmîm 'ăšer-lô*), while the second verse (describing the activities of Uriah, the priest) contrasts *'ōlâ* and *minḥâ* offerings on behalf of the king (*'ōlat hammelek wĕ'et-minḥātô*) with those on behalf of the people (*'ōlat kol-'am hā'āreṣ ûminḥātām wĕniskêhem*).

33. What is additionally remarkable is the origin of this tradition and how it found its way into DtrH. As noted by Lowery (1991: 124), "The temple narrative appears to have a pre-exilic, non-deuteronomic origin.... If this narrative is from temple archives, then the people writing official temple archives during Ahaz's reign were not deuteronomists." Lowery also notes the lack of a priestly critique against Ahaz's actions and concludes that this is "unsurprising [and] exactly what should be expected from official archival material."

34. On King Uzziah's cultic overreach, see Chapter Ten, pp. 661–663.

35. See note 13.

36. The eating of the priestly "Bread of Presence" (*leḥem happānîm*; 1 Sam 21:5, 7 [Eng 21:4, 6]) by David and his men is less clear, though it is likely the exception that proves the rule. See Chapter Ten, pp. 654–655.

37. See note 11.

38. Ritual theorists (e.g., Clifford Gertz, Catherine Bell, Jonathan Z. Smith, Bruce Lincoln, David Kertzer) have articulated the many ways in which political rituals, theologies, and mythologies construct and reinforce the power of king and state.

39. Von Lieven (2010) provides a good introduction to the topic. See too her earlier study (2004). Older studies that help nuance the degree to which kings were deified include Posener 1960; Hornung 1967: 123–156; Habachi 1969; Wildung 1973: 549–565; Barta 1975; Bickel 2002: 63–90; and Bonhême 2001: 401–406. I am indebted to Karen (Maggie) Bryson for her assistance in understanding such a nuanced topic.

40. Scholars have paid less attention to Iron Age Northwest Semitic (e.g., Aramaic, Phoenician) royal inscriptions in this regard because they lack the same quality of illustrious vocabulary. Nonetheless, this epigraphic material clearly shows that kings viewed the gods as placing them on their thrones, standing beside them to protect their reign, granting them favor with their people, and going before them especially in battle contexts. Such notions of divine election and presence were common throughout royal inscriptions from the ancient Near East, and especially in royal apologies (cf. Knapp 2015).

At the same time, during periods of Neo-Assyrian domination, these kings were astute enough to provide deference to their eastern overlords, such as when Bar-Rakib proclaims that there were two lords responsible for his rule: "My lord Rakib-el and my lord Tiglath-Pileser caused me to reign on the throne of my father" (*hwšbny mr'y rkb'l wmr'y tgltplysr 'l krs' 'by*; KAI 216.5–7). Hamilton (1998: 229) suggests that this phrase is more than a mere "admission of hard political reality." "It may have been also a kind of religious statement about the empire... Tiglath-Pileser [III] is not a

god, but he is clearly much more than a man, and one can speak of him and a god in the same breath." I owe this quote to Greg Church.
41. See too the overview on the topic in Jones 2005.
42. This insight was noted by Day (1998: 82), to whom I am indebted.
43. Scholars have long fleshed out and debated the legal adoption language used in these passages as well as the divine coronation language that has informed such expressions. Similar material has been found in Ugaritic, Mesopotamian, and Egyptian sources. For a sampling, see Paul 1979–1980; Parker 1988; Roberts 1997 (reprinted in Roberts 2002); Levinson 2001: 511–514. On the reception history of 2 Sam 7:11–17, see Schniedewind 1999.
44. Cf. Ps 82:7–8 and Deut 32:6b–9 as well as the discussion of the ʿelyôn status of Yahweh in Chapter Four, pp. 90–95.
45. Delitzsch (1986: 299) comments: "Joy in connection with (ʾēt) the countenance of God, is joy in delightful and most intimate fellowship with Him."
46. See Mowinckel 1956: 62–69.
47. It is important to underscore that we are here speaking of the *ideological* nature of Judean kingship and its *idyllic* portrayals. Dissenting voices about the ills of Judean kingship (not to mention Israelite kingship) and the abuse of royal power abound, so even a sampling provides the necessary corrective (e.g., Deut 17:14–20; 1 Sam 8–12; 2 Sam 11:27b–12:14; 2 Sam 15:2–6; 2 Sam 24; 1 Kgs 11:1–11; 2 Kgs 21:1–16; Isa 1:23; Jer 22:17; 36:30–31; Hos 8:4; Amos 7:11; Mic 3:1–4, 9–12; Ezek 34:1–10).
48. Again, this material emphasizing royal cult with illustrious language should be placed in contrast to the radical, utopian view of Deuteronomy (esp. its Law of the King in Deut 17:14–20) that restricted the king's role in the cult. The Deuteronomic view (in contrast to DtrH's view) has the king sitting on "the throne of his kingdom" and focusing solely on the Deuteronomic Torah so "that his heart may not be lifted up above his brethren" (Deut 17:18–20). See especially the work of Levinson (see note 13) who notes how Deuteronomy denies granting the Davidic monarch the status of divine scion in favor of nationalizing royal ideology. Levinson (2001: 530–531) writes: "Yahweh . . . formally adopts Israel. The Deuteronomic election formula *nationalizes* the older royal adoption formula so as to establish a contractual relationship between deity and people." As for the illustrious Davidic language of Ps 89:28 (Eng 89:27), Levinson opines: "While rejecting this mythologization of the monarch, the authors of Deuteronomy appropriate that resonant language in promising *national* hegemony as the blessing of covenantal obedience (Deut 28:1b)" (my emphasis).
49. Lundbom (2004: 407–408) notes the avoidance of using the term *melek* (cf. Ezekiel's preference for *nāśîʾ* rather than *melek*) and the use of *miqqirbô* to note that the ruler should be a native Judahite and not a foreigner (cf. Deut 17:15).

As for the distinctive use of *hiqrabtîw*, cf. Num 16:5, 10, where the same verb is used of Yahweh bringing priests near to him (on which see Chapter Ten, pp. 639–643), and 2 Kgs 16:12, where Ahaz draws near to the altar to perform cult.

For the date and setting of Jer 30:21, Lundbom (2004: 404) thinks that "it is best to take the oracle as Jeremianic preaching to a Judahite audience just after the fall of

Jerusalem," to which is appended a covenant formula (30:22) "to address an enlarged audience of Israelite and Judahite exiles (30:4)." See too Holladay 1989: 155ff, esp. 179, for the cultic connotations.

50. For *tĕrûʿat melek* in Num 23:21 referring to the battle cry of the divine king, see Levine 2000a: 184. In Psalm 68:25, we are reconstructing *yhwh* for MT's *ʾĕlōhîm* due to the editing of the Elohistic Psalter (on which see p. 724 note 65, p. 784 note 229).

51. Cf. too the use of the phrase in 1 Tim 6:15 where we find the fullest expression: God is "the blessed and only sovereign, the King of kings and Lord of lords, who alone has immortality and who dwells in unapproachable light, whom no human has ever seen or can see." Cf. too 1 Enoch 9:4.

For historical examples closer to the time of the Hebrew Bible, Lundbom (2013: 392) draws attention to similar "king of kings" type phrases (*šar šarrāni, bēl bēle, šar bēlē, bēl šarrāni*) among Near Eastern kings, especially seventh-century BCE Neo-Assyrian kings such as Esarhaddon and Aššurbanipal. Lundbom also notes how the Hebrew Bible uses the phrase "king of kings" for foreign kings (Ezek 26:7; Ezra 7:12; Dan 2:37). It is telling that the phrase is never used of even the most illustrious Judean kings, including the three (Solomon, Hezekiah, Josiah) who are described as "incomparable." See note 21 and Knoppers 1992a.

52. As convincingly argued by Williamson (2007: 123–126), the details of the passage describe the Jerusalem Temple and not a heavenly palace.

53. In addition to Canaanite analogues, Greenfield (1985: 196) notes the language of large size used in Mesopotamian descriptions of Marduk (Enuma Elish i 92–93; 99–100; iv 1; vi 61–66). On the large cherubim, see Chapter Seven, pp. 398–400. Smith (1988: 425) notes how Ugaritic texts also use superhuman size to depict gods traveling.

54. On the large divine footprints at Ayn Dara, see Chapter Seven, pp. 340–343.

55. See note 180 on the language of the divine council.

56. Cf. Mic 4:7; Ps 84:4; Ps 146:10; Ps 149:2; Zech 9:9. As for the use of *melek rāb* in Ps 48, we prefer the analysis of Barré (1988: 559), which situates the epithet of Yahweh as "great king" in the context of ancient Near Eastern suzerains (esp. in Hatti, Mesopotamia, and Egypt; cf. Akk *šarru rabû*) over against Treves (1988: 46–47), who references Antiochus VII in 138 BCE.

57. Broadly speaking, in the ancient Near East, the city gate can be the site of a wide range of legal proceedings (May 2014: 95–104; J. W. Wright 2002; Wilson 1983: 234, 239; Köhler 1956: 149–175), including, in biblical tradition, royal litigation (2 Sam 15:2–4; Jer 26:10–11; cf. Jer 38:7). For the role of elders adjudicating at city gates, cf. Ruth 4:1–12 and Josh 20:1–6. For judges and *šōṭĕrîm* officials adjudicating at gates, see Deut 16:18. For a strong prophetic critique regarding injustice at the city gate, see Amos 5:10–12 and the discussion of it later.

58. See further Hurowitz 2005: 497–532. Hammurabi is singled out here as but one example of idealized royal justice under divine aegis. For a wider appreciation, see Paul 1970: 3–26; Havice 1978; Whitelam 1979: 17–37; and Boecker 1980: 53–65.

59. On the original scribal-academic context of law codes and the way in which they were used for royal propaganda, see note 161.

NOTES 851

60. The translations here are those of Nissinen, Seow, and Ritner (2003: 19–20, 22) and Nissinen et al. (2019: 20, 22), to whom I am indebted.
61. The translations of all the Hittite texts here are those of Miller (2013: 228–231), to whom I am indebted.
62. Miller (2013: 385 n. 440) notes how McMahon (1997: 224b) translates "widow," yet argues that the word here (*wannummiya*) "can refer to a woman without children or simply to an orphan."
63. The translation here is that of Faulkner (1955).
64. Davies 1943: 80–82. Davies notes that the translation here is that of Alan H. Gardiner. For a more recent treatment along with a fuller discussion of the judicial duties of the vizier, see James 1984: 51–99.
65. See note 10. Among the many treatments of the text, see Pardee 2002a: 77–83; 2000: 92–142, 446–456, 686–690, 807–810; Shedletsky and Levine 1999.
66. Reading Yahweh for MT's *'ĕlōhîm* due to this psalm being a part of the Elohistic Psalter (Pss 42–83), on which see p. 724 note 65, p. 784 note 229.
67. For an insightful examination of ideal kingship vis-à-vis actual kingship in ancient Israel, see Whitelam 1979. Our brief sketch of David, Solomon, Josiah, and Jehoshaphat is no substitute for the many insightful works on the ideology of the king as judicial authority. Among the plethora of studies, note the following: de Vaux 1961: 150–152; Macholz 1972: 157–182; Whitelam 1979: 39–69; Boecker 1980: 40–49; Brettler 1989: 109–113; Knoppers 1993–1994; Levinson 2001: 518–519.
68. On the nature of the woman's claim against her ancestral estate, see Lewis 1991. In 1 Sam 18 another root (*śkl*), known elsewhere for its association with wisdom (cf. Fox 2000: 59–60), is used four times to underscore David's military "success." See Forti and Glatt-Gilad 2015 and the later discussion in this chapter.
69. Note the contrast between the Deuteronomic viewpoint here and that of the Deuteronomist who, as Knoppers (1993: 86–87 n. 59, 125; 1996: 336–337) stresses, "does not contain any negative editorialization upon Solomon" in this regard. "The Deuteronomist hails, rather than berates, Solomon for such might and opulence" (1993: 125), for he sees "Solomon's opulence, power, and international trade . . . as signs of divine favor" (1996: 337). For additional references, see note 13.
70. Note, as Japhet (1993: 526–528) underscores, how the reformulation in 2 Chr 1 introduces the Tent of Meeting at Gibeon in place of "the great high place" (cf. 1 Kgs 3:4; 2 Chr 1:3).
71. On the genre and social function of 1 Kgs 3:16–28, see Lasine 1989: 61–86, esp. 72ff.
72. Though originally written in 1878, the pagination here is from the 1957 Meridian edition.

Scholarly opinion flows from Albright's (1950a: 61) claim that "nearly all critical historians of Israel since the time of Wellhausen" dismiss the historicity of Jehoshaphat's judiciary to Knopper's (1994: 59) appraisal forty-four years down the road that Albright's "substantially correct" historical assessment "dominates contemporary scholarly opinion." See too Japhet 1993: 770–774. Adding another decade and a half finds Levinson (building on the scrutiny of Rofé and Knoppers) asserting that

the Chronicler's "deliberate compilation" simply "cannot be used as a reliable historical source." See Levinson (2008: 62 n. 29) with bibliography.
73. For Deuteronomic restrictions on royal power (in cult, politics, and the judiciary) in contrast to DtrH, see note 13.
74. One can only speculate as to the imagined legal setting. Albertz (Albertz and Schmitt 2012: 303) admits that the unjust legal actions could apply to human as well as demonic adversaries.
75. See Albertz and Schmitt (2012: 303–304, 311–312, 544–545 [= Appendix B 1.2.2], 555 [= Appendix B 2.2.2]). A significant number of these names also appear in the Hebrew Bible. Cf. too the name ʾĂbîdān, "My [divine] Father has provided justice [on my behalf]," which is attested five times in the Hebrew Bible yet is not in Albertz's epigraphic corpus.

Albertz (2012: 545) also includes in his list the names Pĕlayāh and Pālāl, which he translates as, respectively, "YHWH has made a just decision" and "[DN] has given justice." While the root *pll* can refer to intercession and even arbitration (see HALOT 934), there is no certain way of knowing whether this was with regard to a legal case.
76. For a helpful excursus on the "enemies" in individual laments, including legal adversaries who have denied justice to the petitioner who may have taken asylum in the sanctuary (cf. Deut 17:8–13), see Kraus 1988: 95–99.
77. The Qere reading (*yādaʿtî*, "I know") expressing the personal confidence of the speaker is to be preferred over the Ketiv reading (*yādaʿtā*, "You know"), likely a secondary change to exhort others.
78. Compare too the description of God as an active judge complete with military metaphors that is woven into Ps 35 (see especially verses 1, 10b, 11a, 23–24), a psalm with notorious problems including that of genre.
79. Psalm 43 is a part of the Elohistic Psalter (on which see p. 724 note 65, p. 784 note 229). Thus we reconstruct Yahweh (the likely original reading) for the MT's ʾĕlōhîm.
80. Reading Yahweh for MT's ʾĕlōhîm due to this psalm being a part of the Elohistic Psalter (Ps 42–83).
81. Wilson's cautious, tentative, and theoretical reconstruction is to be contrasted with McKenzie's (1964) optimistic reconstruction that applies the judicial data from the entire Hebrew Bible onto an imagined lawsuit. Weinfeld (1977: 84–88) agrees with Wilson's tone: "As we do not have data sufficient to reconstruct the development, any attempt to draw a scheme of historical progression in this area is doomed to failure." Nonetheless, Weinfeld firmly concludes that "the basic judicial procedure described [in the Hebrew Bible] was common to all ancient Near Eastern peoples and is known to us at least from the middle of the second millennium B.C. onwards."

Finally, methodologically, the historian seeking to reconstruct that past has the near impossible task of trying to nuance the difference between the laws that actually functioned in ancient Israel at various locations and at various times and the presentation of law in various biblical literary genres. See the helpful discussions in this regard in Knight 2011, Meyers 1988: 154–157; 2013a; and Milstein 2018.
82. Here Wilson is building on the work of Köhler (1956). For a brief look at elders settling disputes, see de Vaux 1961: 152–153.

83. Yet note, as pointed out by Sasson (2014: 256), the feminine form of the verb (*šōpĕtâ*) occurs only here in the entire Hebrew Bible. For the interplay of presentations about Deborah in Judg 4 and 5, see Ackerman 1998a: 29–47.
84. Meyers (1988: 157) notes how the male *and female* parental authority presented in Exodus 21:15 (about a child who strikes his father *or his mother*) contrasts with the similar law in Hammurabi's law code (§195) that only concerns itself with a son striking his father. In contrast to Wilson, Meyers writes: "There is no concept of a household chief quite equivalent to the *paterfamilias* known from classical sources."
85. Compare the First Temple seal of ʾElihanaḥ bat Goel (*gʾl*), written in Old Hebrew script, from the late eighth/early seventh century BCE. This seal was discovered in IAA excavations at the City of David, in the Jerusalem Walls National Park. Although the seal has yet to be published, the IAA's press release from March 7, 2016, reads: "According to the excavation directors: 'the owner of the seal was exceptional compared to other women of the First Temple period: she had legal status which allowed her to conduct business and possess property.'" Note how ʾElihanaḥ's father's name (Goel, *gʾl*) reflects economic and judicial concerns. See pp. 486–488.
86. On the debate over depicting Moses as a king dispensing justice, see Watts 1998: 416–418; Levine 1993: 342–343; and Ska 2009: 214–216.
87. On *śārîm* as judicial officers, see note 112.
88. The verb used here (D stem of *bʾr* I) occurs only three times in the Hebrew Bible (Deut 1:5; 27:8; Hab 2:2) and is usually seen as referring to Moses expounding on the law, much as he makes known and clarifies the law in Exod 18:16, 20. Schaper (2007) argues that the verb refers to the "promulgation" of law, that is, the process of publishing legal texts and putting them in force using both oral and written elements.
89. Lundbom (2013: 521), following Weinfeld (1977: 83–86), wonders if the *šōṭĕrîm* were assistants to the judges, functioning like modern court clerks. The legal function of these tribal officials (*šōṭĕrîm lĕšibṭêkem*; Deut 1:15) makes more sense than von Rad's (1966b: 114) blanket statement that all *šōṭĕrîm* were royal "officials of the State . . . whose sphere . . . lay chiefly in the affairs of the army" and whose position, function and authority were "essentially different" from that of tribal elders. Here von Rad is unduly influenced by reading Jehoshaphat's judiciary into the narrative. For reasons to avoid such an approach, see Weinfeld 1977: 87–88 and especially Knoppers 1994, as discussed on p. 520.
90. Note similarly how the Hittite king Arnuwanda I admonishes a judge to adjudicate "for whomever a law case is [pending]" (CTH 261.I §40′) and "he shall not make a superior case inferior; he shall not make the inferior superior" (CTH 261.I §39′). Echoing the elevated position of Moses, Arnuwanda I underscores that if "the law case becomes [too] onerous, he shall have it brought before His Majesty" (CTH 261.I §38′). See Miller 2013: 228–231.
91. For Levinson (2008: 63–68; 2005: 93–100), another relevant factor for Deuteronomy's need to revise the text—an "indirect form of rewriting and rethinking history [that] was almost certainly intentional"—is to make certain, in contrast to Exodus 18, that

the formation of the judiciary occurs *after* the giving of the law on Mt. Sinai. Cf. Num 11:16–25 and Lundbom 2013: 171.
92. On the multiple traditions about Moses' father-in-law with the variant names Jethro, Jeter, Hobab, and Reuel, see Chapter Six, pp. 273–276.
93. For a full treatment of priestly adjudication, special consideration needs to be given to P's understanding of priests and the judicial realm. Knohl (1995: 155–156, esp. n. 131), following Haran (but see Haran 1983: 122), writes about "the link between the holiness of the priests and their consequent isolation from the people and separation from judicial activity." Knohl (1995: 180) then contrasts P with H, where "there exists an intimate connection between the inclusion of justice and morality in the realm of holiness and the summons to the entire community of Israel to lead sanctified lives." Yet to provide nuance to P's dynamic, one would have to account for P granting the high priest the sole charge of the "judicial breastplate" (*ḥōšen mišpāṭ*; Exod 28:15, 29) containing the Urim and Thummim, binary lot-casting devices that were used, one would assume, for judicial purposes. Here see Levinson's (1997: 111–116) corrective, describing in detail various legal proceedings that took place in cultic contexts and within sacred space.

In addition, see Leuchter's (2007) study of "the Levite in Your Gates" in the book of Deuteronomy (arguing for juridical Levites) and the strong critique by Na'aman (2008: 261–262 n. 580). Hutton (2009b: 230) argues (using parallels with the Ahansal tribe of Morocco) that "the distribution of the Levitical cities at the extremities of Israel ... might be correlated to the Levites' function as intertribal arbitrators distributing justice in the gates."
94. The seriousness that comes with the invocation of divine witnesses is well known from ancient Near Eastern treaty language. See McCarthy 1963: 141.
95. On community liability for crime, see Lundbom 2013: 592. For additional ancient Near Eastern material, see Tigay's (1996: 472–476) excursus "The Ceremony of the Broken-Necked Heifer." See too Tigay's insightful comments about how we may have here the elders' exculpatory oath, with the slaughter of the heifer dramatizing what would happen to them should they be false to their oath.
96. Given the discussion of royal justice here, I see no need to be reductionist in eliminating the judicial aspects in Isa 33:22 (i.e., *šōpēṭ, mĕḥōqēq*) in preference for the military. Some scholars (e.g., Wildberger 2002: 297, 305) appeal to Judg 5:14b to argue the latter, yet Sasson (2014: 278, 297) renders "magistrates" and "makers of laws and setters of decrees." Blenkinsopp (2000: 447), who notes the "deliberately traditional and archaic" nature of Yahweh's titulary, wisely concludes that Isa 33:22 has a combination of the military and the judicial as in the book of Judges.
97. See Chapter Eight, note 185.
98. Yahweh as teacher of justice (as embodied in his just "ways," "paths" "covenant" and "decrees") is well illustrated in Ps 25:8–10. See too Ps 94:10–12 and Ps 119. For a complete analysis with bibliography on past research, see Finsterbusch 2005, 2007 and Abernethy 2015.
99. On the mysterious disappearance of Zerubbabel, the various parties involved, and the reworking of biblical texts accordingly, see Lewis 2005b.

100. Wildberger (2002: 109–110) discusses "the basic eschatological sense of the passage [that] is connected with the Isaiah apocalypse," though falling short of apocalyptic in "its full form."
101. On the shared legal vocabulary between Isa 29:21 and Amos 5:7, 10–12, see Andersen and Freedman 1989: 498–490.
102. For the religio-historical background of Dan 7 and interpretative issues relating to the use of similar literature (e.g., Canaanite, Mesopotamian), see Collins 1993: 280–294.
103. Collins (1993: 301) concludes that the plural thrones are for the Ancient of Days and the "one like a son of man" (Dan 7:13), "although originally there was probably a more inclusive reference to the divine council."
104. For a look at Solomon as an ideal philosopher-king who turns into the very opposite, see Parker 1992.
105. In contrast to the picture of David as a superb judge exercising justice and equity for *all* his people (2 Sam 8:15; Ps 89:15 [Eng 89:14]), the Court History is not kind to him in this regard. In addition to his criminality with regard to the Bathsheba-Uriah episode, note Absalom's charge against David's failed judiciary in 2 Sam 15:3–4, David's silence as royal judge in punishing Amnon for the rape of Tamar, and his acquiescence regarding Absalom's murder of Amon and rebellion against the crown. Wilson (1983: 243) summarizes: "As a judge David was often arbitrary and unwilling to apply the law evenhandedly, particularly in cases involving his own family."
106. McCarter (1984: 294) astutely points out how LXX^L preserves an explicit description of Nathan asking David as royal judge to "pass judgment on this legal case for me" in 2 Sam 12:1. See McCarter's argument for preferring the LXX^L as the original reading, which he retroverts in Hebrew as *haggēd-nāʾ lî ʾet hammišpāṭ hazzeh*.
107. Yet another episode has the prophet Gad delivering God's sentence on David, though in the matter of the census, not a miscarriage of justice (*mišpāṭ*) per se (2 Sam 24 //1 Chr 21). David appeals to the Divine Judge known for his great mercy (*rabbîm raḥămāyw*), yet the sentence is carried out nonetheless in considerable degree—but then stayed (2 Sam 24:14–16, 25//1 Chr 21:13–15, 27).
108. Using analogous phenomena at Ugarit, Alalakh, and Nuzi, Andersen (1966) wonders if the seal in 1 Kgs 21:8 is not the king's personal seal but rather the dynastic/state seal, "which showed endorsement by the state as such." This leads him to posit that Jezebel is not sending letters to the elders and city officials, but rather forged legal documents to them in their capacity as a judiciary. These forged documents would have claimed that either Naboth was not the legal owner of the vineyard or that he had promised to sell the property to the king but later reneged. Such speculation is hard to prove, yet Andersen argues that some type of legal scenario is necessary to understand how Ahab is able subsequently to take possession of the property (1 Kgs 21:16).
109. The translation here interprets *môkîaḥ* as the arbiter. As pointed out by Andersen and Freedman (1989: 498), the term could alternatively refer to the plaintiff who brings the accusation. We do agree with Andersen and Freedman (1989: 502) that *tāmîm* refers to the innocent.

110. Amos 5 is a part of the "Book of Woes" (Amos 5–6), material that "constitute[s] an extensive inventory of the person and activities that are the target of . . . Yahweh's wrath." And yet at this stage in Amos's rhetoric, the focus, according to Andersen and Freedman (1989: 461), is on "warning rather than judgment."
111. Williamson (2006: 85, 98–99), for example, prefers an earlier date for the original setting of Isaiah 1:11–17, but nicely nuances for 1:16–17 "the post-exilic setting which has to be presupposed for this redactional assemblage." See too Williamson's introduction (2006: 10–11) interacting with and building on the works of David Carr and Marvin Sweeney.
112. On the śārîm being judicial officers (overlapping with šōpĕtîm) and royal in nature here and elsewhere in prophetic literature, see Weinfeld 1977: 67–71. Note how śārîm judiciary officials occur in the two "judiciary origin myths" discussed earlier (Exod 18:21, 25; Deut 1:15).

    See too the presence of a śr judicial official in the Meṣad Ḥashavyahu ostracon, lines 1, 12, where a plaintiff (a harvester) makes a petition for the śr to adjudicate in the matter of a stolen garment. For the text and bibliography, see Dobbs-Allsopp et al. 2005: 358–370 and KAI 200. For a convenient translation, see Pardee 2002c: 77–78. For two treatments specifically devoted to the legal nature of the text, see Westbrook 1988: 30–35, esp. 35 n. 128 for the view that this is a "plea of gzl" with regard to wrongly seized property (cf. the root gzl in our next text [Isa 10:2] that deals with robbing the poor of justice), and Dobbs-Allsopp 1994 for the view that it is an extrajudicial petition for justice (comparing the Tekoite woman going to King David in 2 Sam 14:16). For similarities with Job 29–31, see notes 154 and 155.
113. For poetic flow, I have translated (as has the LXX) the third plural prefixal yĕʿaqqēšû ("they twist/pervert") as if it is a participle.
114. Cf. the judicial rāʾšîm in Exod 18:25; Deut 1:13–17, and the exhortation to the qĕṣînîm to execute justice in Isa 1:10, 17. As noted by Waltke (2007: 146), following van der Ploeg (1950: 52), etymologically Hebrew qāṣîn is related to the Arabic root qaḍā (cf. Hebrew qṣh, "to cut, decide") that has to do with deciding judicially (cf. Arb qāḍin "judge"; qaḍāʾ, "judicial decision, judiciary, justice"; qaḍan, "court ruling"; qaḍīya, "litigation, legal case").
115. On city gates as places of judicial activity, see note 57.
116. For a review of the literature especially as it applies to Mic 6:1–8, see Andersen and Freedman 2000: 507–511.
117. The secondary literature is immense. For a survey, see March 1974, which contains a lengthy bibliography; see particularly the formative works of Koch (1964) and Westermann (1991). See too the retrospective essays critiquing and rehabilitating form criticism in general in Sweeney and Ben Zvi 2003.
118. For the present discussion of Yahweh as judge, I am consciously using the trial language of an "indictment" and "sentence." Cf. Westermann 1991: 70, 129–136, 199–204 and Tucker 1971: 65. Of course, many judgment oracles do not envision a trial setting, and Melugin (1974: 301 n. 4) is correct in arguing against applying trial terminology to the genre as a whole.

119. On the legal terminology used here, see Blenkinsopp 2002: 230 and Paul 2012: 222. The Hebrew imperative *hazkîrēnî* (lit. "cause me to remember") has been viewed as citing evidence against and/or presenting a summons to trial.
120. The amount of secondary literature on *rîb* is also immense. Seminal treatments, in addition to Gunkle's foundational work, include: Würthwein 1952; Gemser 1955; Huffmon 1959; Harvey 1962; Wright 1962; Limburg 1969; and Nielsen 1978. Challenges are found in De Roche 1983 and Daniels 1987. For an update on Wright's argument that Deut 32 is more of a hymn with an embedded *rîb*, see Thiessen 2004.
121. Alternatively, Wolff (1990: 172) sees here the hand of the final redactor issuing "a new summons to hear" to his readers, as he did in Micah 1:2. Similarly, Waltke (2007: 373) sees here a "unique introduction calling upon the book's audience to hear the book's last and final section."
122. An alternative is the prophet calling upon Yahweh to speak because, as Mic 6:2 explicitly states, it is Yahweh's legal case (*rîb yhwh*; cf. Andersen and Freedman 2000: 514). In my opinion (which agrees with Huffmon 1959: 287), because the speaker in verse 2 refers to Yahweh in the third person, this must be the prophet speaking in response to being charged to get up and plead (*qûm rîb*) the case (Micah 6:1b). As the spokesperson for Yahweh by whom he is commissioned, he has ownership of the case. Huffmon writes that he is "acting as lawyer for the plaintiff, Yahweh."
123. I disagree with Huffmon (1959: 287), who suggests that what we have here may be "a mocking defense put into the mouth of the defendant." Similarly, Waltke (2007: 389) also fails to look at the passage from a rhetorical perspective. Quoting Wolff, he suggests that the author wants "to caricature more and more the nonsense of all sorts of excessive sacrificial performances."
124. See Dewrell 2017 for a diachronic analysis of the inherited traditions regarding child sacrifice. For a summary, see p. 64.
125. We prefer this line of interpretation rather than Andersen and Freedman's (2000: 527) suggestion that the people are being "cross-examined with a barrage of double questions" about what is good and what Yahweh seeks of them. If anything, the people's judgment on matters has been found wanting, and even a rhetorical questioning of their views on goodness and divine requirements seems odd.
126. For scholars treating this topic in greater depth, see notes 13 and 48.
127. Roberts (1973b: 164) argues that the language here "properly means 'to dispute together in court.'" See Williamson 2006: 111–112 for a fuller discussion of the legal and familial use of the root *ykḥ* and whether the locus of the term is best derived from a wisdom setting or a judicial setting. There is certainly an overlap between reprimanding (even legal) discipline in the household unit and litigation in a metaphorical courtroom setting. As we have seen, the various social locations for adjudication included roles for fathers, mothers, elders, and tribal kinsman/"brothers." Thus there is no need to draw a strong dividing line between the two settings. With the mention of the judicial ideal in Isa 1:17, it is clear that Yahweh is beckoning his people to raise issues of theodicy.
128. For this translation and the original text, see Lambert 1960: 128–129, 132–133.

129. For this translation and the original text, see Lambert 1960: 112–115.
130. Jasnow and Zauzich 2014: 31–37. Jasnow and Zauzich's 2014 volume is a distillation of and supplement to their 2005 *editio princeps* on *The Ancient Egyptian Book of Thoth*. The wise Thoth was so well known that he could be referenced in Job 38:36 ("Who put wisdom in Thoth?") along with, seemingly, the Egyptian god Sobek ("Who gave Sobek understanding?"). See Lewis 2015.
131. For a translation of these passages in the Instructions of Amenemope, see Lichtheim 1976: 150–151 (reprinted in 1997: 116–117).
132. The verb used for Yahweh "assessing" human behavior ($\sqrt{pls}$) is used of "scales of justice" in Prov 16:11, Isa 40:12, and Ben Sira 42:4 parallel with *mōʾznayīm*. Fox (2009: 615) suggests that "just measures may also be a metaphor for the royal administration of justice generally" as well as affirming (following Radaq) "that God is a righteous judge, assessing human works by true measures." Egyptian funerary images of the human heart being weighed against the feather emblem Maat (*m3ʿt*, truth, order, cosmic balance) readily come to mind.
133. On the origins, literary developments, and social settings of personified wisdom, see Fox 2000: 331–345. On the personification interludes, see Fox 2000: 353–359. Fox (2009: 949–950) also argues that "Lady Wisdom speaks wisdom—her own, not God's. Nowhere does she 'bear' revelation." She is "the daughter-like ward of Yahweh" raised "to be wise, in order to make her intellectually and morally fit to teach others." Interacting with Zimmerli's views, Fox prefers to characterize the teaching of Proverbs as "anthropological" and "anthropocentric." At the same time, "Proverbs is infused with religious aspiration and feeling. It constantly, and at all stages, speaks of Yahweh, his oversight of justice, his care for humanity, his demands for righteousness, his loves, and his hates."
134. For the ways in which scholars have understood the nature of the epilogue (Qoh 12:9–14) and the epilogist, see Fox 1977; 1989: 311–348; 1999: 350–377; Seow 1997: 391–396; Krüger 2004: 207–215; Schoors 2013: 826–854.

    Schoors (2013: 854), quoting Ginsburg, notes how the Masoretes felt compelled to repeat verse 13 after verse 14 for the ultimate ending of the book such that the final word would not be "evil" (*rāʿ*), though they did so without adding pointing to mark the repetition as secondary.
135. Scholars are divided about whether the *waw* of *wĕdāʿ* is a conjunctive or an adversative. For various views and the implications for meaning, see Schoors 2013: 791–792.
136. See note 134.
137. For a discussion of Mal 3:13–21 (Eng 3:13–4:3) addressed to the post-exilic restoration community, see Hill 1998: 355–363.
138. On translating *hebel* as "absurd," see Fox 1989: 29–48; 1999: 27–49 and Schoors 2013: 40–47.
139. On God using scales of justice, see note 132.
140. Somewhat unusually, the MT, Syriac, and Symmachus have *yĕʿawwēt* in both lines, whereas the LXX, Vulgate, and Targum employ two different verbs. While the latter could certainly be a stylistic choice, it has prompted scholars (e.g., Dhorme [1967: 112–113] and seemingly Pope [1973: 64–65]) to posit a second verb with

a similar appearance and meaning (ʿwh, "to bend"). The verb ʿwh does occur in Qoh 7:7b in reference to bribes perverting the mind (cf. Prov 12:8), according to 4QQohᵃ, which reads wîʿawweh in contrast to MT's wîʾabbed.

141. Cf. Seow's (2013: 59–61) remarks challenging Richter, Scholnick, and Magdalene. See too the cautions expressed by Strauss (1999: 83–90).

142. Our treatment here is intended only to scratch the surface. The literature on the legal background of the book of Job is vast. Among the more notable works are the following: Gemser 1955: 120–137, esp. 134–135; Richter 1959; Roberts 1973: 159–165; Frye 1973; Scholnick 1975, 1982, 1987; Dick 1977, 1979, 1983, 2006; Habel 1985: 54–57; Zuckerman 1991: 104–117; Greenstein 1996: 241–258; Strauss 1999: 83–90; Hoffman 2007: 21–31; Magdalene 2007a; 2007b: 23–59; and Seow 2013: 59–61, 68–69.

143. In addition to Hoffman 2007: 22, see too Hoffman 1996: 222–263, 314–316, which has a chapter devoted to "On God's Justice in the Book of Job" as well as four appendices breaking down the statistical occurrence and distribution of ten key terms having to do with justice.

144. For the root *prr* in the C stem used for the "breaking" of God's law (*hēpērû tôrātekā*) and the "breaking" of his commandments (*miṣwātô hēpar; lĕhāpēr miṣwôtêkā*), see respectively Ps 119:126, Num 15:31, and Ezra 9:14.

145. The subject and object of the phrase "He/he would/could not answer him/Him once in a thousand times" (*lōʾ-yaʿănennû ʾaḥat minnî-ʾālep*) in Job 9:3b are not made explicit, and scholars have come down on both sides, some seeing God deigning not to answer Job and others having Job unable to answer God. Similarly, there is debate about the unidentified subject of the previous line ("If one wishes to contend with him"; *ʾim-yaḥpōṣ lārîb ʿimmô*), though here it is more common to find interpreters seeing Job contending with God (cf. Job 19:16a; 29–31; 33:13). Yet, alternatively, if God is the subject of 9:3a, then what Job imagines taking place is exactly what does take place in Job 38–41, where the barrage of God's unanswerable questions must certainly have seemed to Job to have numbered a thousand.

146. Following Dhorme (1967: 135) we prefer to translate the particle *ʾim* in Job 9:15, 20 with Job asserting his innocence even in this imagined lawsuit ("*though* I am in the right," "*though* I am just"), where the alternative translation "*even if* I were in the right"/"*even if* I am in the right" (e.g., Seow 2013: 539) leaves room for doubt.

147. *Mĕšōpĕṭî* is a rare Poʿel participle of a strong verb that seems to designate God as Job's opponent-at-law (cf. Zeph 3:15; Ps 109:31). Alternatively, some repoint the MT to read *lĕmišpāṭî* and translate it as "I must supplicate for justice/to my Judge." Yet the MT is clearly *lectio difficilior*.

148. For the syntax of *ʾim-lōʾ ʾēpô mî-hûʾ*, compare Job 24:25 (*wĕʾim-lōʾ ʾēpô mî*). There is a Masoretic *sebir* on this phrase that would suggest a transposition: *ʾim-lōʾ hûʾ mî ʾēpôʾ*, yet *sebirin* actually support the MT in noting that such changes are "suggested" wrongly. See Tov 1992: 64.

149. The noun here is *šaḥat*, designating the netherworld as a pit, yet both the Greek and the Vulgate see the imagery to be one of filth. This has prompted some (e.g.,

Dhorme 1967: 143) to revocalize the text as *bĕśuḥōt*, "in filth," in fitting with Job's reference to self-cleansing. Yet the netherworld could indeed be thought of as a filthy realm, so no such emendation is necessary.

150. The syntagm *lō' yēš* in Job 9:33 never occurs elsewhere in the Hebrew Bible. Multiple Hebrew, Greek, and Syriac manuscripts read *lû'*, with the graphic similarity being obvious. Cf. the expression *lû yēš* in Job 16:4. Thus most interpreters do see Job expressing a condition contrary to fact. Alternatively (if one can accept the one-of-a-kind syntax), Job, even in his imaginary lawsuit, could declare, as in the MT, that there simply is no arbiter between them (*lō' yēš-bênênû môkîaḥ*); so Dhorme 1967: 144.

151. For the use of animal imagery for predatory hostility, cf. Ps 7:2–3 (Eng 7:1–2); 17:9–12; 22:13–14 (Eng 22:12–13).

152. Dick 1983: 31. Dick has written extensively on these matters. See the bibliography in note 142.

153. Greenstein (1996: 247) argues that Job "understands himself to be the defendant in God's case, as well as the initiator of a countersuit against God."

154. The relevance of the Meṣad Ḥashavyahu inscription (KAI 200) for Job 31 was already noted by Dick (1979: 43–44) and Greenstein (1996: 247).

155. Lines 10–12a of the Meṣad Ḥashavyahu inscription read: *wkl 'ḥy y'nw ly . . . [kl] 'ḥy y'nw ly 'mn nqty m'[šm]*, "Now all my companions will vouch for me . . . my companions will vouch for me that truly I am innocent of any gu[ilt]." Sadly, Job's companions do the very opposite. For more on the inscription, see note 112.

156. Clines (2011: 1096–1097) documents how loin girding is used most frequently for physical fighting (e.g., 2 Sam 20:8; 1 Kgs 2:5; Isa 5:27), with the picture here being verbal combat and legal dispute "such as Job had envisaged in 13:22 and 14:15." Scholnick (1982: 527) notes "the forensic force" of the expression in Jer 1:16–17. In that context, God is uttering his judgments (*mišpāṭîm*) and has the prophet "gird up his loins" to deliver the divine message.

157. For the various ways in which the forms *hărōb, yissôr*, and *ya'ănennâ* have been treated, see Clines 2011: 1084–1085.

158. Scholnick (1982: 528–529), Habel (1985: 576, 582), and Dick (2006: 268) interpret Job 42:6 as Job retracting his legal case. While such a translation of the difficult *'em'as* is possible (cf. *'em'as mišpāṭ* in Job 31:13, as pointed out by Scholnick), it is more of a stretch for the following *niḥamtî*.

159. On the so-called lethal God sightings, see Hendel 1997 and Chapter Seven, pp. 296–297, 354–355. I disagree with Clines (2011: 1216), who asserts that "Job has not actually *seen* Yahweh (there is no language of visual perception), but only heard him speak." Such an opinion minimizes the cultural understanding of the *sĕ'ārâ* ("whirlwind") theophany (38:1; 40:6). Ezek 1:4 reveals that a mystical *sĕ'ārâ* theophany can indeed be "seen" (*wā'ēre'*). Zech 9:14 also describes a *sĕ'ārâ* experience by saying that Yahweh "was seen by them" (*wyhwh 'ălêhem yērä'eh*). As for the wording in Job 38:1; 40:6, it implies that Job saw the *sĕ'ārâ* from which emerged the divine voice. (Cf. William Blake's 1823 illustration that has Job and his wife looking upward to see an anthropomorphic Yahweh wrapped in a stormy garment. See Blake 1875: pl.

XIII.) It would go against an author's logic to have Yahweh manifest his appearance in a dramatically visual *sĕʿārâ* if no one sees it. Cf. too Job 19:26–27.

I also disagree with Clines (2011: 1216) that "the dénouement of the whole Book of Job" is either to "find it a deeply sad and cheerless outcome" or to "feel it rather a blessed release to recognize that there is no underlying principle of justice in the universe." Troubling also is Clines' (2011: 1218) pejorative description of Yahweh's words in chapters 38–41 as "a long and self-regarding speech," and Job "is not going to be impressed by attempts to bill it as a divine-human encounter that shakes the foundations of his universe." Job's words in Job 40:3–5; 42:1–6 imply otherwise.

160. For reception history, see Hayes' (2015) study of the nature of divine law in the Hebrew Bible in contrast to Greco-Roman conceptions of law as well as her articulation of the various discourses on divine law in Second Temple Judaism.
161. See Westbrook 2009: 3–20 (originally published in 1985: 247–265). The royal appropriation of scribal law codes is a large topic beyond the scope of the present treatment. Westbrook and Wells (2009: 130) summarize well:

> Scribes appear to have assembled all sorts of lists (omens, medical symptoms, etc.) and the law codes fall into this category. The Laws of Hammurabi, for instance, almost certainly had nothing to do with King Hammurabi originally. The provisions contained in the code were complied and/or composed by scribes. What the Laws of Hammurabi show us is that such lists of laws could be used for purposes other than those initially envisioned by scribes who authored them. In the case of the Laws of Hammurabi and others (e.g. Laws of Ur-Nammu, Laws of Lipit-Ishtar), the lists/codes became tools for royal propaganda. They were lifted out of their original, scribal-academic context and inserted into an entirely different context: the royal inscription. They were then framed by explicitly propagandistic prologues and epilogues to give them the look and feel of royal proclamation. The laws and rules of these codes were meant to illustrate how well the king, in whose name they were published, had established justice throughout his realm.

See too Berman 2016 for the debates concerning the nature of biblical law—whether it is statutory (i.e., "codified") with jurisprudence using it as a reference point or "customary" and/or "common law" (i.e., an inherently fluid compendia of legal and ethical norms). Levinson's understanding is discussed in note 170.
162. These categories are those of Westbrook (2003: 35–86).
163. See Kwasman and Parpola 1991 and Mattila 2002.
164. See Whitelam 1979: 213–214, countering those scholars (e.g., de Vaux) who would argue that this material is irrelevant for depicting royal legislative actions because David is not yet king. Davidic thrones are described as "thrones for [legislating?] judgment" in Psalm 122:5.
165. For a discussion of Zedekiah's manumission in the context of ancient Near Eastern release of slaves and the Law of the Jubilee, see Lundbom 2004: 558–561. Whitelam (1979: 216–217) argues that "this law is attributed to the king himself" and "unmistakably points to the conclusion that the Israelite king, in certain circumstances, was able to decree remissive acts in order to alleviate particular socio-economic difficulties."

166. The Hebrew reads: *hôy haḥōqĕqîm ḥiqĕqê-'āwen ûmĕkatĕbîm 'āmāl kittēbû*. Wildberger (1991: 213) sees this passage being written against royal officials, though it is not explicit. Blenkinsopp (2000: 212) also sees this as a critique of "royal officialdom" during the days of Ahaz, as they are "manipulating the legal system ... to facilitate sequestration of property and the enclosure of peasant holdings."

167. We are not alone in using sociological theory to argue this case. See the astute analysis of Whitelam (1979: 207–218), who is in turn building on the work of Weingreen (1976: 23), who argues "the *a priori* consideration that an expanding society must regulate the growing complexity of its affairs by legal means." Whitelam (1979: 217) posits "that the king was probably the greatest contributor to the developing system of law necessary in such a dynamic society as that of monarchic Israel."

168. Even the separate collections of laws that we do have (the Covenant Code, the Holiness Code, and the laws of Deuteronomy) are far more literary than has been appreciated (cf. Levinson 2008: 30–39; Milstein 2018).

169. Alternatively, one could use Levinson's (2008: 34) language of illusion. He writes: "Literary history—human authorship and revision of law, the obvious need for new laws to develop in response to ongoing social and economic change—is everywhere ostensibly denied by means of the attribution of law to God or Moses. Yet precisely the thoroughness of such attributions undermines the veil of redactional illusion. The very repeated denial of literary history succeeds in affirming it."

170. Levinson's insightful study (2003; cf. 1997, 2008) builds on Jonathan Z. Smith's notion of "exegetical ingenuity" and Michael Fishbane's study of inner-biblical exegesis. Levinson demonstrates how the fixation and textual sufficiency of a closed "canon" can engender innovative strategies of reformulation and reapplication (especially through the covert subversion of prior authoritative texts via "sleights of scribal hand"), especially in the area of law. "By means of exegesis, the textually finite canon becomes infinite in its application" (2003: 8). Such creative and "learned reworkings of authoritative texts" are well known from later Jewish tradition (2003: 42). See 4Q158, 4Q524, 11QT, and Crawford 2008. Levinson argues that such sophisticated revisionist work is already present in ancient Israel. Alternatively, see Berman 2016.

171. On these two passages, see Rendsburg 2006, a provocative article.

172. See note 88.

173. On Moses' request to have an unmediated view of God's "radiance" in Exod 33:17–23, see Chapter Seven, pp. 362–363.

174. Wilson (1980: esp. 156–166) argues that being a prophet modeled after Moses who directly hears God's voice (cf. Deut 18:15–21) will be a key determinant used by DtrH in legitimizing a prophet. Note how the notion of God raising up a series of prophets like Moses after he has died is yet another way of distributing Moses authority while at the same time heightening his prestige.

175. On the unique status of Moses approaching the unapproachable Yahweh in Exodus 19, see Chapter Ten, pp. 608–615.

176. Granted, we do read of Moses as "writer" ($\sqrt{ktb}$) and "giver" ($\sqrt{ntn}$) of law to priests and elders in Deut 31:9.

177. In addition, the functional understanding of law must always be integrated with the literary presentations of law over time. Here we again refer readers to the work of Levinson. See notes 168, 169, and 170.
178. The full title of Gottfried Leibniz's 1710 volume is *Essays of Theodicy on the Goodness of God, the Freedom of Man, and the Origin of Evil (Essais de Théodicée sur la bonté de Dieu, la liberté de l'homme et l'origine du mal)*.
179. Precisely because Psalm 82 is indeed so remarkable, it has engendered a staggering amount of research regarding its meaning, for the text itself presents few text-critical challenges. Suffice it here to note Smith 2008: 131–139; Machinist 2011; Trotter 2012; and White 2014: 24–33, which refer in part to the voluminous history of research. As the reader will see, I follow those who see this psalm as a part of the Elohistic Psalter, and thus I restore the name Yahweh, which has been replaced with ʾĕlōhîm by a later hand. In contrast, see the stimulating work of Machinist (2011), who argues that the psalm plays off the double meanings of ʾĕlōhîm (i.e., for the gods and the God of Israel). If he is correct, then there is no original psalm with Yahweh instead of ʾĕlōhîm.
180. The plurality of divine beings around Yahweh is sometimes gathered in assembly, as the passages here reveal. At Ugarit, cf. the expressions pḫr ʾilm, pḫr bn ʾilm, and pḫr mʿd (see Smith 2001b: 41 for references), with Ugaritic pḫr being cognate to the well-attested Akkadian term puḫru (cf. puḫur ilani). For the Phoenician counterparts, cf. KAI 4.4–5 (Yahimilk) and KAI 14.9 (Eshmunazor).

At other times such beings form a part of his military entourage (e.g., Deut 33:2; Ps 68:18 [Eng 68:17]; Hab 3:3–5). For the wealth of secondary literature on the divine council, see the bibliography in White 2014: 1–10. Among the significant works are Mullen 1980; Handy 1994; Smith 2001b: 41–66; Garr 2003; Lenzi 2008; and White 2014.
181. Note too how various terms for the disadvantaged, so well known from the judicial ideal texts, also show up in Psalm 82 (*dal, yātôm, ʾebyôn, ʿānî, rāš*), as do the terms for their oppressors and their injustice (*rĕšāʿîm, tišpĕṭû-ʿāwel, pānîm tiśʾû*). In light of such judicial vocabulary, one wonders what to make of the term *śārîm* in Ps 82:7. Why did the psalmist use a term for "rulers, princes" in the context of the gods being stripped of their mortality and dying like mortals? Perhaps it is relevant that the *śārîm* were also involved in judiciaries (Exod 18:21, 25; Deut 1:15; see note 112). The imagery for Psalm 82 might be that the failed divine judges will fall like (failed) human *śārîm* judges.
182. On the likely lack of an independent deity Elyon, see Chapter Four, pp. 87–88.
183. On Psalm 29, see Chapter Eight, p. 454 and note 103, and Chapter Seven, pp. 361–362. A good example of a mythopoetic interpretation is found in deClaissé-Walford, Jacobson, and Tanner 2014: 284, where Jacobson understands the *bĕnê ʾēlîm* of Psalm 29:1 as referring to "the Lord's heavenly court" who are "at once eternal but less than God." Following Goldingay, Jacobson sees the *bĕnê ʾēlîm* as created beings who are subordinate to Yahweh as well as "metaphysically different" from Yahweh.

The MT's heading (*mizmôr lĕdāwid*) situates the ascription (of glory to Yahweh) in the human sphere rather than the divine. Note too the LXX's secondary addition to the superscription (*exodiou skēnēs*, "at leaving the tent") that places the human ascription at the Feast of Tabernacles (as noted by Craigie [1983: 242] and many others).

184. See Smith's (2008: 131–139) insightful study situating Psalm 82 within the conceptual category of the "translatability" of divinity or, in other words, the cross-cultural recognition of deities. For Smith (2008: 139), Psalm 82 "calls for an end to translatability" even as it presupposes it.

185. The broader topic of God's mercy and forgiveness beyond the juridical that we highlight here (e.g., the prophetic oracles of salvation), is beyond our scope. See, for example, Westermann 1979: 58–64: "Somehow [God] always moderates the punishment ... compassion breaks through in spite of judgment."

186. Cf. Kraus 1989: 288, 292, underscoring the forensic understanding of *yārîb* by translating it as "He will not always go to court."

187. The verb *nṭr* here seems to be elliptical, with the fuller expression referring to God nursing his anger (cf. Amos 1:11; Jer 3:12). The synonymous parallelism here suggests that the meaning of the expression in Ps 103:9 is that God will not maintain a rightful legal grievance that would arouse his angry response. Cf. Kraus 1989: 288, 292; Jacobson 2014: 761, 765. Cf. Lev 19:18, which has Yahweh legislating against taking vengeance and maintaining a grievance (*lōʾ-tiṭṭōr*) and instead loving one's neighbor as oneself. Milgrom (2000: 1650–1652), following Shiffman, discusses the judicial contexts of this verse within the Qumran community, where it "was a cornerstone of the sect's legal system."

188. For the many issues associated with the book and various interpretations, see Clements 1975; Sasson 1990; Levine 2002; and Ben Zvi 2003.

189. The rigorist nature of this material and whether it expresses xenophobic exclusion and/or religious perfectionism is complex. See Sasson 1990: 26 and Blenkinsopp 2003: 129–143.

190. As reported in Barnett, Bleibtreu, and Turner 1998: 96.

191. Barnett, Bleibtreu, and Turner 1998: 96.

192. For a full range of texts and iconography, a discussion of the stereotypical language of Assyrian royal annals, and the intended audiences, see Lewis 2008b.

193. Grayson 1991: 201; 1976: 126–127.

194. Luckenbill 1926–1927: sec. 254.

195. It is not at all clear that Yahweh's question implies a judicial right, and there are other ways to translate *hahêṭēb* (e.g., Sasson 1990: 286–287). Yet if the book of Jonah is indeed about the parameters of justice, then it is noteworthy to find "the doing of good" as constituting acting justly. Jeremiah 7:5–6 reads: "For if you truly cause your ways to be good [*hêṭēb têṭîbû*] and your doings, if you truly act justly one with another, if you do not oppress the alien, the orphan, and the widow" (*kî ʾim-hêṭēb têṭîbû ʾet-darkêkem wěʾet-maʿalělêkem ʾim-ʿāśô taʿăśû mišpāṭ bên ʾîš ûbên rēʿēhû gēr yātôm wěʾalmānâ lōʾ taʿăšōqû*). Thus Jonah would be "doing good" (i.e., acting justly) to be angry about the miscarriage of justice where the wicked Ninevites are not punished as justice demands (cf. Jer 7:3; 18:11; 26:13; Ps 119:68). Cf. too the expression "to do good and right" as an expression of carrying out laws and

commandments (e.g., Deut 6:17–18a; Ps 25:8; 125:4: Neh 9:13; 2 Chr 14:2–4; 31: 20–21). Cf. too the collocation of "good" and justice elsewhere (Amos 5:15; Mic 6:8; Jer 22:15; Ps 112:5; 119:35; Prov 2:9; Neh 9:13).

Chapter 10

1. Sellin wrote this statement in 1936. For a summary of Sellin's career, see Hayes 1999: 453–454.
2. To keep our treatment from mushrooming, we have restricted the analysis to the Northwest Semitic material. Readers should compare treatments of holiness elsewhere in the ancient Near East, especially cognates in Akkadian. Summaries can be found in Levine 1987: 242–243; Wilson 1994; Müller 1997; and Kornfeld 2003.
3. 'Ilu's full title is "the Gracious and Holy One" (*ltpn wqdš*). See Chapter Four, p. 79 and especially note 30, for references and the debate over whether *qdš* constitutes the title of a goddess. Qudšu-wa-'Amrur, best known as 'Athiratu's attendant in the mythological texts (KTU 1.3.VI.11; 1.4.IV.2, 8, 13, 16), also appears in ritual texts (KTU 1.123.26'; cf. *qdš mlk* in KTU 1.123.20'). The meaning of the god's second name ('*amrr*) is unclear. For suggestions, see Smith and Pitard 2009: 377–378.

    Smith (2014a: 186; 2014b: 40) notes the word *qdšt* in KTU 1.81.17–19, which he translates "the Holy One" prior to two occurences of 'Athtartu.
4. In the same broken text, compare the expression "Who is like the Holy One?" (*my k qdš*). See KTU 1.179.14 (= RS 92.2016.14).
5. See Budin 2015; Tazawa 2014; 2009: 96–101, 104, 113, 121–124, 135–136, 163–168; Cornelius 2004: 45–58, 83–87, 94–101, 123–142, 193; and van Koppen and van der Toorn 1999: 416–417. Budin does a splendid job of showing the iconographic differences between Egyptian Qedešet and Levantine Qudšu. Notably, whereas the former holds snakes, the latter never does.
6. For the Arslan Tash texts, see Chapter Six, p. 268.
7. KAI 37, A lines 7, 10. See Conclusion, p. 685. I am not including in the list here the ambiguous reference to *qdš l'šrt* at seventh-century BCE Ekron (cf. Smith 2001b: 73). Whereas *l'šrt* was initially thought perhaps to be the goddess Asherat (cf. Gitin 2012: 226 n. 17; Zevit 2001: 402), Gitin and Aḥituv (2015: 223) now translate "dedicated to the sanctuary (the holy place)."
8. KAI 14 (Eshmunazor II), Line 17; KAI 15, 16 (Bod'aštart). The reading of *šr qdš* in these three inscriptions is preferable to reading *šd qdš*, "Holy spirit (?)" (e.g., Peckham 2014: 183). Cf. *śārê haqqōdeš* in 1 Chr 24:5; Isa 43:28.
9. For the Ugaritic citations mentioning *bn qdš*, see Smith 2001b: 93.
10. See Chapter Seven, p. 348, and Lewis 2013b: 793.
11. The MT is difficult (lit. "the holiness of the dwellings of Elyon" or "the Holy One [who dwells among?] the dwellings of Elyon"; cf. Kraus 1988: 459). The LXX has a verbal form ("the Most High *has sanctified* his dwelling"), leading some scholars (e.g., Kraus 1988: 458–459; Dahood 1965: 277, 280) to repoint MT's *qĕdōš* as *qiddēš*.

12. The bibliographic details for all these finds can be found in Rollston 2015b. For the Ekron material, see Gitin and Aḥituv 2015: 223. Some of this material is also found in Dobbs-Allsopp et al. 2005: 104, 119–120, 136, 190–191. From the later Second Temple period we have *qdwš* inscribed on a store jar from Masada as well as the letter *q* on a broken vessel, which has been viewed as an abbreviation for either *qrb* (*qorbān* offering) or *qdš* (holy). See Yadin and Naveh 1989, no. 459; Aḥituv, Eshel, and Meshel 2012: 83; and Rollston 2015b: 241 n. 18.

Also at Arad (stratum X) we have, according to Aharoni (1968: 20), two "shallow, burnished plates on each of which two identical signs were incised, the letter *qof* in ancient Hebrew script, perhaps an abbreviation of *qodesh* (*qdš* 'holy'), and a sign resembling the ancient *kaf*." Upon further reflection, Aharoni (1981: 118) interpreted these markings as abbreviations for a *qorbān* offering based on a remarkable note from the Mishnah that explicitly says that a vessel inscribed with a *q* stands for a *qorbān* offering (*Maʿaser Sheni* 4:10–11; noted also in Meshel 2012: 83). According to Rollston (2015b: 242), "this interpretation . . . seems strained." Two examples from Kuntillet ʿAjrud show that (at least at that site) the abbreviation for *qorbān* seems to have been *qr* (cf. Aḥituv, Eshel, and Meshel 2012: 82).

Staying with the *q-k* readings, Rainey favored two abbreviations, for *q*[*dš*], "holy," and *k*[*hnm*], "priests," that interestingly coincided with the mention of *qdš khnm*, "a holy object of priests," inscribed on the ivory pomegranate scepter. See Herzog et al. 1984: 32; Herzog 2013: 39. For translating *qdš khnm* as "a holy object of priests" rather than "set aside for priests" (so Herzog 2013: 39; Herzog et al. 1984: 32), see Zevit 2001: 161 n. 58.

Rollston (2015b), along with Cross, sees the ivory pomegranate inscription as a probable modern forgery produced by a forger who may even have known of Rainey's reading of the Arad bowl inscriptions. See also Rollston's (2015b: 243 n. 26) reservations about a bowl inscribed with *qdš* coming from the antiquities market that Barkay deems ancient.

In contrast to Rainey's *q-k* readings, Cross (1979) argued that epigraphically the two letters were *q-š*, an abbreviation for *qdš*, "holy," although this required redating stratum X to the seventh century BCE, a proposal flatly denied by the excavators (Herzog et al. 1984: 12, 32). And yet over the years scholars have lowered stratum X into the eighth century BCE (Herzog 2013: 38–39; Mazar and Netzer 1986; Aharoni and Rainey 1985: 73; Zimhoni 1985, Zevit 2001: 169–171; Rollston 2015b: 242 n. 19), with Ussishkin even dating the shrine to the seventh century BCE (Ussishkin 1988: 151, 155) in line with Cross' date.

In evaluating Cross' proposal, it should be noted that elsewhere there is no definitive example of abbreviating the word for holy (*qdš*) with the letters *q-š*. And yet the use of such an abbreviation would provide the perfect text-critical solution to how the scribe at Kuntillet ʿAjrud mistakenly wrote *qš*(!)*dš* rather than *qdš* in inscription 4.2, line 4. On this inscription, see the immediately following discussion.

13. Ackerman (2008a: 136–141) situates this episode within household religion.
14. See Chapter Seven, pp. 359–360, on whether Habakkuk 3 is archaic or archaizing.

15. For our fuller treatments of Exodus 15, including textual notes, see Chapter Eight, pp. 448–450, and Chapter Six, pp. 285–286.
16. In addition to the many commentaries available (see esp. Kraus 1989: 43–56; Tate 1990: 159–186; Gerstenberger 2001: 34–46; Hossfeld and Zenger 2005: 158–169), see Tournay 1942; Albright 1950–1951; Miller 1964; Lipiński 1967; Caquot 1970; Gray 1977; Fokkelman 1990; Cook 1992; Emerton 1993; Loretz 2002; Strawn 2002; Arnold and Strawn 2003; Charlesworth 2004.
17. That the Judges parallel (Judg 5:4–5) twice has Yahweh where Psalm 68:8–11 reads ʾĕlōhîm underscores how the latter secondarily came to replace the former so consistently in the Elohistic Psalter (on which see Chapter Four, p. 724, note 65). The explicit reference to the name Yah[weh] (*yah šĕmô*) in Psalm 68:5b (Eng 68:4b) strongly advocates for reading Yahweh (not ʾĕlōhîm) earlier in the same verse (*šîrû la-yhwh* zammĕrû šĕmô*). Thus throughout Psalm 68 we have replaced all references to ʾĕlōhîm with *yhwh**.
18. The form *hindōp* in the MT is quite irregular and many scholars (including GKC §51k) repoint it as a proper N infinitive *hinnādēp*. GKC suggests that the form *hindōp* in the MT is a mixture of N and G infinitives, whereas others consider the vocalization of *hindōp* to be a poetic sound change to match the following *tindōp* (which is also irregular in its lack of NC > CC).
19. The MT's *ʿărābôt* refers to Yahweh's march through the desert steppe, and this is consistent with other early texts (including the late ninth-/early eighth-century BCE Kuntillet ʿAjrud traditions) that contain topographical allusions to Yahweh coming from the south/southeast (cf. Chapter Six, pp. 279–281) as well as the Hebrew Bible's many "wilderness" (*midbār*) traditions. I have written elsewhere (Lewis forthcoming a) of how the reference to a "holy *mdbr*" in KTU 1.23.65 resonates with biblical traditions:

> The *midbār* . . . is often a sacred place of sacrifice and offerings (Exod 3:18; 5:1, 3; 8:27–28; Lev 7:38; Num 9:5; 1 Chr 21:29) and a place where theophanies (Exod 16:10; Ps 29:8) and divine oracles were thought to occur (Num 1:1; 3:14; 9:1).

Thus the MT's "who rides through desert lands" (*rōkēb bāʿărābôt*) makes perfect sense (cf. too *yĕšîmôn* in Ps 68:8 [Eng 68:7]). There is no text-critical reason to emend the text to "the Rider of the Clouds" (*rōkēb bāʿărāpôt*)—with a simple *b/p* bilabial interchange—as many scholars are wont to do to echo Ugaritic lore about Baʿlu being "the Rider of the Clouds" (*rākibu ʿurpati*). In addition, as already pointed out by Arnold and Strawn (2003: 429 n. 9), the Ugaritic expression occurs in a genitive relationship without the preposition *b*.

This is not to say that our poet did not consider Yahweh as a storm god who could ride the heavens, as seen explicitly in the expression "he who rides the ancient skies" (*rōkēb bišmê šĕmê-qedem*) later in the poem (Ps 68:34 [Eng 68:33]). Perhaps our poet is forming a wordplay. Thus, in deference to colleagues who feel strongly about reading *rōkēb bāʿărāpôt*, I have listed it as an alternative reading.

20. The preposition in *bĕ-yah* is admittedly difficult, yet the meaning of the phrase is clear nonetheless. For discussion and possible solutions, see Arnold and Strawn 2003: 429–431, where the preference is to see here a "*bêt* of identity" (cf. Exod 6:3).
21. Though this phrase underscores Yahweh's benevolence, the meaning of *kôšārôt*, and hence of the entire expression, is unclear. It is commonly rendered "in prosperity," "unscathed," or even "deftly" (Pardee 1999: 492). For two of the more intriguing suggestions, see Lipinksi 1971d for the suggestion of a connection to midwives (cf. the *ktrt* in Ugaritic) delivering "children emprisoned in their mother's womb," and Dietrich and Loretz 1967: 542 for the suggestion (using Akkadian cognates) that Yahweh delivered prisoners of war who had been put in (iron) fetters.
22. On the translation of *yhwh zeh sînay* as a nominal demonstrative, "Yahweh, the One of Sinai," see Chapter Six, note 229.
23. On the hapax *šin'ān*, see Chapter Six, note 214.
24. On the restoration of *yhwh* for MT's *'ădōnāy*, and the preference of a verb (*bā'*) in line with Deut 33:2 for MT's preposition (*bām*), see Chapter Six, note 214.
25. Again reconstructing an original *yhwh* for MT's secondary *'ădōnāy*.
26. We have retained the personal name of the god El here in verses 20–22 (Eng verses 19–20) and also in verse 36 (Eng verse 35) attempting to reflect how El traditions were seamlessly blended with Yahweh traditions. The use of the definite article with *hā'ēl* in verses 20–22 (but not verse 36!) could certainly advocate for translating "the god." Yet the regular use of the definite article to render individuals in Hebrew makes rendering proper divine name El here altogether legitimate. See Waltke and O'Connor 1990: §13.6a; 13.5.1.b–c and especially the critical analysis in Barr 1989.
27. Omitting *'ădōnāy* both because it very likely is a secondary gloss and also due to prosodic considerations.
28. Reading *yhwh* for the secondary *'ĕlōhîm* in MT (see note 17), to which the suffix as then added (thus *'ĕlōhêkā*) by attraction to the following *'uzzekā*.
29. Again reconstructing an original *yhwh* for MT's secondary *'ădōnāy*.
30. For our additional treatment of Psalm 89, including textual notes and discussions of dating, see Chapter Eight, pp. 455–458.
31. On *'ēl na'ărāṣ*, see Chapter Eight, note 108.
32. On Israelite holy war, better termed *ḥērem* warfare, see Chapter Eight, pp. 462–463.
33. Aḥituv 2014: 36–37.
34. The reading of *wbzrḥ 'l* has been the consensus of scholars, including Aḥituv, Eshel, and Meshel, who published the final report in 2012. Yet the reading of the first letter of *zrḥ* in Line 2 is not at all clear. Alternatively, the reading could be *byrḥ 'l* (so Blum 2013: 25, 28, 31; Puech 2014: 179 n. 41, 180). If this were the case, the text would seem to be referencing a storm god using wind as a weapon with a buffeting type of action. See Lewis 2020 for discussion.
35. The two words (*šnt*, [*y*]*hw*[*h*]) marked with an asterisk (*) come from the second smaller fragment. See note 39.
36. My reading here differs from that of the final report. For justification, see Lewis 2020. Aḥituv, Eshel, and Meshel (2012: 110, 112) reconstruct the second half of line 4 to read *q(š!)dš 'ly 'lm*, "the Holy One over the gods." Aḥituv, Eshel, and Meshel astutely

point out three aged biblical traditions where Yahweh is described as fearfully holy and preeminent over the gods (e.g., Exod 15:11; Ps 29:1–2; 89:7 [Eng 89:6]). Just as Exodus 15:11 and Psalm 89:6–8, 19 (Eng 89:5–7, 18) explicitly remark about how a Holy Yahweh is incomparable "among the gods" (*bāʾēlim/ bibĕnê ʾēlim*), so this plaster inscription could be making a similar profesion. Aḥituv, Eshel, and Meshel expand on this notion of divine supremacy one step further by assuming that the war context of KA 4.2 (note esp. *milḥāmâ* in both lines 5 and 6) may also refer "to the defeat of the gods by YHWH." Aḥituv, Eshel, and Meshel (2012: 133) refer to the defeat of the gods in Zeph 2:11. One could also add Psalm 82.

37. The reading of *qšdš* is certain, and this provides a wrinkle in seeing a clear reference here to a deity known as "the Holy One" that should be written simply *qdš*. For a detailed discussion of the epigraphy (and the mistaken suggestions of reading *wšrš*, *wšdš*, or *dšdš*), see Lewis 2020.

   Aḥituv, Eshel, and Meshel (2012: 112, 133) note how the text as written (*qšdš*) represents "a meaningless combination" of letters (so too Aḥituv 2008: 326). They argue that the first *š* is a scribal mistake: "The scribe skipped ahead to *š* before writing *d* and did not bother to erase the first *š* (or the erasure wore out over time)." As support, they note (2012: 135 n. 6) the mistake of duplicating a letter in Samaria Ostracon 37 where "the scribe did not bother to erase the erroneous letter." (Cf.ʾḥ *mʾḥd* in Ezek 18:10.) While such visual eye mistakes can indeed occur, another rationale may be that the scribe unconsciously started writing *q-š* as an abbreviation for *qdš*, such as attested in two offering dishes from Arad (see note 12). The use of such an abbreviation would provide the perfect text-critical solution to how the scribe of KA 4.2 could have mistakenly written an abbreviation for "holy" (*qš*) when he meant to write the full word (*qdš*)—which he then immediately corrected, resulting in the text as we have it: *qš(!)dš*. Interestingly—in view of the Phoenician script of the Kuntillet ʿAjrud plaster inscriptions—Cross (1979: 77 n. 9) notes how abbreviations using a first and last letter of a word "is not infrequent in Phoenician." If then the reading of *qdš* can be defended, Aḥituv and Eshel's suggestion that it refers to a deity, "the Holy One," makes perfect sense given the theophanic nature of our text.

38. See Lewis 2020 for a full discussion of reading Qadesh.
39. See Lewis 2020 on the likelihood that this fragment mentions Yahweh and on the dilemma of whether the small fragment should used to identify the Holy One in the larger fragment.
40. That kings of the northern kingdom of Israel would have scribes trained in the Phoenician script occasions no surprise due to pragmatic political and economic reasons (cf. the Samaria Ostraca from the reigns of Joash and Jeroboam II). Moreover, from the same time period (ca. 825 BCE) we have evidence of Phoenician being used elsewhere by royalty due to its status as a prestige language—namely, its use by the Luwian named King Kulamuwa at Samʾal (KAI 24).
41. The full DN *yhwh* occurs five time (in KA inscriptions 3.1, 3.6, 3.9, 4.1.1 [twice]), with the shortened DN *yhw* occurring two times (in KA inscriptions 1.2, 3.9). Of some twenty-six personal names, thirteen contain theophoric elements, of which

100 percent are Yahwistic: 'lyw, 'mryw, ḥlyw, yw'šh, yw[], 'bdyw, 'bd[yw] 'zyw, r'y[w], šknyw, smʿyw, smʿy[w], šmryw.

42. Several scholars have mistakenly reconstructed Baʿal in KA 4.4.1. See Aḥituv, Eshel, and Meshel 2012: 117; Puech 2014: 183–184; LeMon and Strawn 2013: 95. Yet as Lemaire (2013: 92–93) has astutely noted, what Aḥituv and Eshel read as a *b* (of *bʿl*) is *certainly* a *p*, with *pʿl* likely referring to "making" or "work" of some sort. What remains of the letter in question reveals an open head and longer curving tail, both characteristic of *p* as opposed to the closed head and bent tail of *b* (as seen three letters down). For additional discussion, see Lewis 2020.

43. Dobbs-Allsopp et al. (2005: 287) state succinctly: "YHWH is *ʾēl* at Kuntillet ʿAjrûd." Alternatively, 'lyw could mean "The god is Yahweh" or "Yahweh is [my] god," and these too would underscore the universal occurrence of Yahweh as the male deity at the site apart from *ʾl* and *bʿl* in KA 4.2. For Albertz's study of equating names, see p. 755, note 1.

44. Aḥituv, Eshel, and Meshel 2012: 133. See too LeMon and Strawn 2013: 90, 92–93, quoting Clines, for the suggestion that we may have here an example of "the parallelism of greater precision."

45. Heuristically, and following most scholars, we are being reductive in looking at only the two key ideas of *fascinans* and *tremendum* from Otto. Readers are directed to Gammie's work (2005: 5–8) for a much better articulation of Otto's five categories of the holy numinous, which include *tremendum, maiestas, energicum, mysterium*, and *fascinans*.

46. Though Psalm 89:6–8 (Eng 89:5–7) does not explicitly say so, it certainly implies that Yahweh, "the Holy One" (*qādôš*), is the God who presides over "the holy ones" (*qĕdōšîm*). Compare, for an analogy, how the god Rapiʾu at Ugarit is the head of the *rapiʾūma* (cf. KTU 1.108).

47. ʾIlu is especially gracious toward the human king, as best exemplified through the story of King Kirta and KTU 1.23 (see Lewis forthcoming a).

48. Freedman (1978: 56*–57*, n. 1) dates the passage to the tenth century BCE, and McCarter (1980a: 76) says "perhaps as early as the ninth or late tenth century." Most scholars consider the poem with its reversal of assorted fortunes to have had a former life independent of its present context. The mention of the barren woman giving birth in verse 5b made this thanksgiving song wonderfully appropriate for the reversal of Hannah's barren situation.

In addressing the complicated textual history of the song elsewhere (Lewis 1994), I have suggested that questions of dating need to be nuanced with respect to textual variance. For example, variant readings for verse two include earlier notions of monolatry ("there is no holy one like Yahweh [among the gods]") as well as later notions (glosses?) more in fitting with self-conscious monotheism ("there is no holy one besides you"). See note 49. For further discussion of the many variants, see Lewis (1994: 27–29).

49. The textual history of these two verses is quite involved, and readers are directed to the fuller discussions in Lewis (1994: 27–29, 41). In short, we conclude that there are two variant bicolons for verse two:

Variant A:

'ên qādôš ka-yhwh   There is no Holy One like Yahweh;
'ên ṣûr ka-'ēlōhênû   There is no Rock like our God.

Variant B:

'ên qādôš biltekā   There is no Holy One besides you;
'ên ṣaddîq ka-'ēlōhênû   There is no Righteous One like our God.

The reconstruction of "Who is holy like Yahweh?" (*mî qādôš ka-yhwh*) in 1 Sam 2:10 is based on *kurios hagios* in Codex Vaticanus (B) that serves as the basic text of the Larger Cambridge edition of the LXX and on *my q[dwš kyhwh]* in 4QSam^a. McCarter (1980a: 68–70) also advocates such a reconstruction.

50. I have kept my text-critical notes here to a minimum. My reconstructed text is based on an earlier study of the song's textual history (Lewis 1994), and readers interested in such matters are directed there for a fuller discussion. The explanatory footnotes that follow are abbreviations of their fuller counterparts in the 1994 article.

   In addition, the 1994 reconstruction provides a heuristic attempt to reconstruct the passage free from known later linguistic developments (e.g., segholation, the so-called tripthongization of diphthongs, *ḥateph* vowels used secondarily with laryngeals, and the "rule of shewa") and avoiding the use of prosaic particles (e.g., *'ăšer, 'et, kî*, the article *h*) that seem to be later additions to the text. For a defense of this admittedly uncertain procedure, see Lewis 1994: 19–21.

51. See Lewis 1994: 26 for the rationale of reading *'ĕlōhāy* that is found in B, OL, several Syr mss, Syr-Hex, Pal-Syr, and V as opposed to *yhwh*, which is attested in MT and 4QSam^a.

52. The meaning of this phrase has been taken to mean either (1) "swallowing enemies," used figuratively to stand for triumphing over one's enemies (so BDB, NAB, McCarter 1980a: 68), (2) gloating over or deriding one's enemies (so JPS, RSV), or (3) an expression of joy paralleling the end of the verse and forming a quatrain. For being wide (with joy), cf. Isa 60:5.

53. As for reading a bicolon as opposed to a tricolon (so MT), see Lewis 1994: 27–29. The various textual witnesses suggest that originally there were two variant bicolons (see note 49).

54. MT's *tarbû* and *tĕdabbĕrû* seem to be ancient variants, each followed by *gĕbōhâ*. For additional witnesses and discussion, see Lewis 1994: 29.

55. Most translators translate the singular "mouth" due to the singular Hebrew form *mippîkem*. The Hebrew is a collective. The subject is plural, as seen in the second-person masculine plural suffix as well as the second-person masculine plural verbs.

56. Or "indeed." One could argue that *kî* is a prosaizing addition, yet it is attested in all the witnesses.

57. Here *'ēl dĕ'ôt* may mean "an all-knowing God" (so NAB, JPS). Such is the nuance of the same epithet at Qumran. For further discussion, see Lewis 1994: 24 nn. 23, 30.

58. The various textual witnesses give evidence of both active and passive constructions. We read the active here along with LXX^B, Syr-Hex, and OL, yet alternatively one

could read the passive "by him deeds are weighed" (*lô nitkěnû ʿălilôt*) with MT (Qere) and Syr. See further Lewis 1994: 30–31.

59. Rather than repointing as *qāšōt* (a rare masculine byform of the feminine *qěšātōt*) to agree with the MT's *ḥattîm*, as some scholars argue (see Lewis 1994: 32 for bibliography), it seems preferable to reconstruct an original singular verb (*ḥattâ*) that was later changed to the plural by attraction to *gibbōrîm*.

60. This verse has a long history of interpretation with wide-ranging suggestions. The reconstruction here (which argues against the existence of a *ḥdl* II and repoints MT's *ʿad* as *ʿōd*) is based on Lewis 1985, summarized in Lewis 1994: 33–34.

61. Alternatively, "a mother of children" (see Lewis 1994: 35).

62. From a poetic standpoint, the preterite verb *wayyāʿal*, while *lectio difficilior*, hardly makes sense. Perhaps one should reconstruct *yaʿl<eh>* on graphic grounds (confusion with the *h*s in the following *yhwh* or the preceding *měḥayyeh*?).

63. On the close parallel with Psalm 113 and questions of borrowing and dating, see Lewis 1994: 36.

64. Reading *nědîbê ʿam* as opposed to MT's *nědîbîm* based on LXX^B and Syr-Hex as well as on Ps 113:8, which corresponds closely with our passage. Ps 113:8 exhibits two true variant readings, not merely expansionist readings. MT's reading may have been influenced by the preceding *ʿim*. For additional discussion, see Lewis 1994: 37.

65. G. J. Hamilton (personal communication) has suggested that we may have here the older verbal force of *hwh* in the Hiphil and an emphatic *l*. Thus one could conceivably translate "Indeed, he brought the pillars of the earth into being," which would be a much more powerful description of the creation going on in this verse. It would also form a nice parallel to 8f.

66. 4QSam^a has a variant reading: *drk ḥ[sydw]*, "the *way* of [his] fai[thful ones]" (cf. Prov 2:8).

67. The LXX and 4QSam^a (partially) attest to another couplet that appears to be a secondary addition. It reads:

| He grants the vow to the vower, | *nōtēn neder lannōdēr* |
| He blesses the years of the just one. | *wa-yěbārek šānôt ṣaddîq* |

Freedman proposes reading *šānôt ṣaddîq* as a double accusative ("he blesses the righteous with years, i.e., long life"), as opposed to a construct chain. See Lewis 1994: 37–40 for discussion and bibliography.

68. The reason that this verse does not form a consistent thought progression following 9cd is that originally it seems to have followed 9ab (see following textual note).

69. On the reconstruction of *mî qādôš ka-yhwh* (based on LXX^B and 4QSam^a [partially]), see note 49 and Lewis 1994: 27–29, 41.

70. Alternatively, "against them (the adversaries of vs. 10a) he thunders" (so MT's *ʿālāyw*). The reading of *ʿēlî*, "the Exalted One," has had many advocates dating back to Nyberg. For full discussion with bibliography, see Lewis 1994: 41–42.

71. This verb occurs previously in vv. 1b, 7b, and 8b. These four occurrences leave little doubt that √*rwm* is the theme verb of the poem.

72. There is a long history (dating at least back to Duhm) of scholars, being uncomfortable with *miqdāš* in the present passage, emending to read otherwise (e.g., *môqēš*, "snare," or *měqaššēr*, "conspirator"). The later emendation results in Yahweh, to borrow Wildberger's (1991: 354) chapter heading, becoming "the True Conspirator" (cf. too Blenkinsopp 2000: 241). Such a textual overreach (there is no support in the versions) is unwarranted. Even more unaccountable, the MT's dramatic and powerful expression "Him you shall regard as holy" (*'ōtô taqdîšû*)—what we consider key to the entire passage—is also emended without textual warrant to "with him you should conspire" (*'ittô taqšîrû*). If anything, it would be more likely that our poet is playing off these words (*qeser, qāšer, taqdîšû, miqdāš*).

    Oswalt (1986: 233) aptly critiques: "While God is sometimes seen as the ultimate source of tragedy and disaster (Isa 45:7), he is not depicted as doing so in a devious, conspiratorial manner."
73. Both Propp (2006: 689) and Haran (1978: 187–188) document the various references to "the lethal aura surrounding holiness."
74. On Yahweh's "plantation" in Exodus 15:17 and Jerusalem references, see Propp 1999: 569–571.
75. The translation of option B is both consistent with the dominant theme of the book of Hosea, and the immediate context where just prior to this passage Israel's fortresses are promised to be destroyed, its mothers and children violated, and its king utterly cut off (Hosea 10:14–15), with a sword raging against God's people who persist in turning away from him (Hosea 11:6–7). Immediately following our passage Yahweh is described as roaring like a lion (cf. Qudshu the lion) and Israel as deceitful and lying (Hosea 11:10, 12:1 [Eng 11:10, 12]). The reference in Hosea 11:9 to Yahweh as the Holy One coming in judgment "into the city" (*bě'îr*) reads quite naturally in option B's translation. (Contrast the emendation to *bā'ēr* ["burning"/"in wrath"] in option A.)

    The weakness of option B is its reading of three occurrences of an asseverative (emphatic) *l'* where in each instance the MT reads (mistakenly, according to option B) the negative *lō'*. The use of asseverative *l/l'* in biblical Hebrew is treated only briefly, if at all, in most grammars (cf. Waltke and O'Connor 1990: §11.2.10i; Joüon and Muraoka 1991: §164g). The most complete linguistic study is Huehnergard 1983, with older works including Whitley 1975 and Nötscher 1953. In addition to its use in Akkadian, Huehnergard (1983: 581–584) documents instances in the Amorite and Ugaritic data and, rarely, in biblical Hebrew. While not discounting the possibility that an original asseverative *l/l'* could have been read by the Masoretes as the negative *lō'* (1983: 590 n. 191), from Huehnergard's data we would expect a proclitic *l-* rather than an independent (non-proclitic) particle. This is not to say that option B is impossible, just that the best examples of an independent (non-proclitic) particle *l'* misinterpreted by the Masoretes as the negative *lō'* are the famously difficult Amos 7:14 and Job 9:33. For representative scholars advocating such interpretations of these two passages, see Richardson 1966 and Clines 1989: 220, 243.
76. I am following McCarter (1980a: 102, 104), who retroverts the LXX to read *běmōdeber* in preference over MT's *bammidbār*.

77. It is common to find scholars (e.g., Levine 1993: 174) viewing the presence of the Levites here as a later interpolation, and some support may be found from Josephus, who makes no reference to them in recounting this very episode (*Antiquities* VI.1). McCarter (1980a: 131, 136–137) puts forth the attractive suggestion that the lack of Levites (who are officially sanctioned to handle the Ark) in the original tale is the reason for the deaths of the Beth-Shemeshites in 1 Sam 6:19 (cf. 1 Chr 13:2–7; 15:2–15). Here too Josephus adds support in explicitly noting that the Beth-Shemeshites' lack of priestly status occasioned their deaths. For verse 19, McCarter suggests that the reading of *bny yknyhw*, "sons of Jeconiah," found in LXX^B may be a graphic corruption of an original *bny hkhnym*, "sons of the priests." Thus McCarter (1980: 128) translates: "But no members of the priesthood had joined the celebration with the men of Beth-Shemesh when they saw the ark of Yahweh, and so he [Yahweh] struck down seventy of the people." The immediate mention of Eleazar (likely a Levite) then being consecrated (*qiddĕšû*) to care for Yahweh's Ark in 1 Sam 7:1 also supports this scenario. (On Eleazar's consecration [as a priest?], see page 654 and note 242.)

    In contrast, Tsumura (2007: 219, 221) retains the MT as it is (i.e., without any notion of interpolation) by viewing 1 Sam 6:15 a reversal of "the temporal order" of the previous verse. In other words, for Tsumura, the purpose of verse 15 (which is chronologically earlier than verse 14) is to let us know that "on the one hand" the Levites are the ones who manipulated the Ark, while "on the other hand" the Beth-Shemeshites offered the sacrifices "probably by the hand of priests." While such a harmonization avoids suggesting that we have a later interpolation, it comes across as special pleading. Whether one prefers the approach of McCarter or Tsumura, it must be underscored that text-critically the phenomenon of interpolation is a historical reality.

    As for the death of the Beth-Shemeshites in 1 Sam 6:19, Tsumura (2007: 226) reasons that their offense was "looking into" the Ark (i.e., actually opening the Ark).

78. For representative views regarding the death of the Beth-Shemeshites, see note 77. In 1 Sam 6:19, the number of the people killed is listed as 70, followed by what seems to be a gloss of 50,000 (!), a number with no basis in historical reality for the number of inhabitants of Beth-Shemesh. Either this expression is meant to designate a subset of the people at large ("one fifth of the clan?"; cf. Tsumura 2007: 227) or its exaggeration is intended to underscore the lethality of the Ark.

79. 1 Chr 13:10 clearly states this rationale, while *ʿal-hašal* in 2 Sam 6:7 is murky. See the text-critical analysis by McCarter (1984: 165). See too McCarter's (2008a: 88) study of how the Anger of Yahweh can operate hypostatically.

80. Levine's final comment, based on Num 4.15, does not square with 1 Kgs 2:26, which says that the priest Abiathar carried the ark. For additional priestly transport, cf. 1 Sam 14:18; 1 Chr 13:2–3; 15:11–15.

81. Technically, the Ark itself was not "seen" (and certainly not to be touched), for according to a priestly tradition in Num 4:5–6, when they break camp to travel with the portable Ark, Aaron and his sons wrap the Ark with the three coverings, the *pārōket* curtain, (dolphin?-) skin, and blue cloth (cf. Haran 1978: 158, 178; Levine 1993: 166).

82. The tabernacle material in Exod 25–31, 35–40 is typically viewed as "the parade example of the Priestly Source" (thus Propp 2006: 365–366), yet for Exod 25:8, compare

Knohl's (1995: 63) observation that "the use of the word *miqdāš* as a synonym for the parallel word *miškān* is never found in PT [the Priestly Torah], but is common in HS [the Holiness School]."

83. On the debate about whether P's use of *škn* represents a technical term ("to tabernacle, to tent"—so Cross) or simply refers to divine residence ("to dwell"—so Mettinger), see Cross 1973: 299–300 and Mettinger 1982b: 90–97.
84. Sommer 2001: 41–63. For Sommer's use of Otto elsewhere, see Chapter Seven, p. 337.
85. See page 621, where the *kappōret* in Lev 16:2 marks the place of clouded theophany with its potential lethality on the Day of Atonement/Purgation.
86. See Williamson 2006: 46 and Williamson's response (2001: 30–31) to Loretz.
87. W. Schmidt 1962; cf. 1983: 152–156. Wildberger (1991: 24–25) also refers to Ugaritic 'Ilu as holy, building on the work of Procksch.
88. Cf. Ps 68:20–22 (Eng 68:19–20); Hab 3:3; Ps 89:8 (Eng 89:7); and Kuntillet ʿAjrud inscription 4.2.
89. Granted, our understanding is predicated on the reading of Yahweh rather than *'ĕlōhîm*. See note 17.
90. Due to the mention of El in this verse, we have privileged these El locations. Cf. Chapter Four, pp. 85–101. One could of course see the mention of plural sanctuaries as a reference to the various locales of Yahweh worship known both from biblical texts (e.g., Seir, Edom, Teman, Sinai, Shiloh, Hebron, Zion) and from the epigraphic data from Kuntillet ʿAjrud (e.g., Yahweh of Teman, Yahweh of Samaria). Cf. McCarter 1987; Hutton 2010b; Bean forthcoming.
91. For the methodological dilemma of using Yahweh-Elyon and El-Elyon traditions, see Chapter Four, pp. 90–95. If we add in places in the Elohisitic Psalter where it seems that *yhwh* originally stood in place of the MT's secondary *'ĕlōhîm*, then the following Yahweh//Elyon passages should be included: Ps 46:5; 57:3; 73:1, 11; 78:56; 83:19 (Eng 83:18).
92. Though much later than the pre-Israelite religion that Schmidt, Wildberger, and Williamson have in mind, Second Isaiah astutely gives voice to this odd pairing. Isa 42:13–16 juxtaposes contradictory similes: Yahweh the battling warrior cries out as a woman in the throes of labor (see Chapter Eight, p. 491).
93. On the Davidic aspects of Psalm 89, see Chapter Eight, pp. 455–458, Chapter Nine, p. 499.
94. See note 77 on whether the Levites are original or secondary to the original text.
95. On the use of *u* to introduce a causal clause, see Moran 1992: 220 n. 4. We follow Moran (1992: 218) and Rainey (1996a: 2: 291; 2015: 698–699) in seeing *qadišū* as referring to holiness, as opposed to CAD Q (p. 50), which tentatively suggests translating *qadišū* as "angry (?)" based solely on context. For contextualizing Rib-Adda's numerous letters to Pharaoh, see Liverani 1979a: 3–13.
96. For the text of KTU 1.119 (= RS 24.266) we are following Pardee 2000: 661–685, fig. 23; 2002: 50–56, 149–150, and readers are referred there for a full analysis including epigraphy and bibliography of older works. See too the detailed study by del Olmo Lete (1999: 292–306). The two primary areas where KTU has different readings are in line 28, where KTU has [*a*]*l*, not a partial *hm* (so Pardee 2002a: 150; 2000: 664), and line 31, where KTU has *dkr*, not [*b*]*kr*.

97. KTU 1.119.33′; cf. too the *qdš* sanctuary of ʾIlu in line 6.
98. See too the ascent language in Psalms 120–134, the "song of ascents" (*šîr hammaʿălôt*), and elsewhere in the Hebrew Bible (see Crow 1996).
99. The translation here follows Fleming's (1992a: 158–162) detailed treatment of the "day of sanctification" (*ūmi qaddušī*). See too Fleming's (1998: 404) later treatment, where he uses the language of "consecration." On Emar's Installation of the High Priestess, the *mašʾartu* installation, and *zukru* festivals, see pp. 626–629.
100. As a part of the Sinai complex, the material here is, in Ska's (2006: 213) assessment, "one of the most complicated passages in the entire Pentateuch." Blenkinsopp (1992: 183–197), who provides a nice overview of the sources of the entire Sinai narrative, notes that the opening sections in Exod 19 "provide a first hint of the difficulties inherent in source criticism" (1992: 187; cf. too Blum 1990: 45–99).

    For representativive source/redaction analysis of our passage and its subunits, see Beyerlin 1965: 1–11; Dozeman 1989: 87–106; and Propp 2006: 143–145, 150–154. For Exod 19:10–25, Beyerlin sees Exod 19:1–2a as a P framework with Exod 19:2b–25 "bear[ing] witness to an older tradition" that he identifies as a mixture of J and E. Dozeman sees significant priestly redaction (Exod 19:11b,12ab–13, 15b, 16aa, 18, 20–25). Propp (2006: 143) sees Exod 19:10–15 as a unit that is "probably J" with 19:16–24 being a mixture of J and E material. Baden (2009: 155–156, 270 n. 26) likewise has Exod 19:10–20 as a mixture of J and E. See too the work of Van Seters (2003b: 53), who sees Exod 19:12–13a, 20–25 as P interpolations. For responses to Van Seters, see Wright 2004 and Levinson 2008: 284–295.
101. For a summary of performance models and ritual theory, see Bell 1997: 61–89, esp. 72–76.
102. See notes 100, 105 and 106.
103. Though historians of religion and social scientists regularly note the importance of integrating sacred time and sacred space, Calaway (2010) argues that the study of time is often subordinated to the study of space. Propp (2006: 532) argues that time, like space, "can possess graduated Holiness."
104. For ritual time, see Gorman 1990. For the important period of "seven days," see Klingbeil 1997. For the festival calendar, see Wagenaar 2005.
105. The use of the *šōpār* horn here (blown by whom?) is notable for its contrast with P's/H's use of various priestly (*ḥăṣōṣĕrâ, tĕrûʿâ, šōpār*) horn blasts (Num 10:10; Lev 23:24; 25:9; Milgrom 2001: 2016–2018). On Lev 23, compare the argument between Milgrom (2001: 2056) and Knohl (1995: 8–52) on whether this material is H or P.

    The *šōpār* horn together with Moses' speaking with God (Exod 19:19) contrasts with the lack of Moses speaking to God in P (Knohl 1995: 137; 1996: 20) as well as P's so-called sanctuary of silence. Here see Milgrom 1991: 19, 60–61 and Knohl 1995: 148–149; 1996, both building on the work of Kaufmann; cf. Ps 65:2 (Eng 65:1).
106. An overview of this material from Leviticus and Numbers (with specific biblical references) can be found in André 1995: 40–41, to which I am indebted. The references include: Lev 6:20[27]; 8:7; 11:25, 28, 40; 13:6, 34, 54–56, 58; 14:8, 47; 15:5–8, 10–13, 17, 21, 27; 16:26, 28; 17:15–16; 19:10, 21; Numbers 8:7; 19:7–8, 10,

19, 21; 31:24. See too Ruane's (2007) more extensive treatment, which discusses the overlap of laundering and bathing.
107. Frymer-Kensky 1983: 401; cf. Plaskow 1990 and Propp 2006: 163. Compare too the narrative between David and Ahimelek, the chief priest of the sanctuary at Nob, in 1 Sam 21:2-7 (Eng 21:1-6), which mentions sexual abstinence as a rationale for David and his men being allowed to consume "the bread of holiness" (*leḥem qōdeš*).
108. Exod 19:12-13 is most curious. It contains the warning for the people not to ascend the mountain, as also mentioned in Exod 19:23. In addition, it includes a provision that they are not even to touch (*ngʿ*) the edge of the mountain. Should they (or even an animal) do so, they suffer a death penalty. Moreover, the carrying out of the death penalty must be done at a distance (by stoning or via arrows) to avoid physical touch (*ngʿ*) and to prevent the enforcers themselves from trespassing into the restricted sacred space. As Dozeman and Van Seters have pointed out (see note 100), this material certainly seems to be a later P interpolation. P is especially concerned with contagion that comes from touching (*ngʿ*) the unclean.
109. Building on the comments of the medieval Nachmanides (Ramban), both Milgrom (1991: 142-143; 1970: 44-46) and Sarna (1991: 105) argue that Mt. Sinai serves as the archetype for the Tabernacle and thus the latter can be used to reconstruct gaps in the former. Methodologically, Milgrom and Sarna are also representative of those who use the variant Mt. Sinai tradition in Exod 24 to reconstruct gaps in Exod 19. For summaries of the source-critical discussions of Exod 24, see Blenkinsopp (1992: 189-192) and Propp (2006: 147-148). Blenkinsopp calls Exod 24 "the passage most resistant to the usual source-critical procedures."

Thus for Milgrom and Sarna (and many other scholars; e.g., Propp 2006: 300-301), there are three gradations of holy space on Mt. Sinai—the summit of the mountain, the cloud-covered slopes of the mountain, and the foot of the mountain—correlating to the Tabernacle's tripartite division of inner shrine (or Holy of Holies), outer sanctum (or Holy Place), and courtyard. These in turn correlate with the gradations of social positioning of (1) Moses/the high priest, (2) priests and elders, and (3) the people.

Comparatively, it is understandable to accentuate the similarities of these two traditions, yet methodologically the differences should also be studied prior to any conflated understanding. For example, George (2009: 128-129) has argued that where the Mt. Sinai tradition uses *vertical* privileging to showcase rank (the higher the ascent on the mountain, the higher the social and cultic status), the "conceptual space" of the tabernacle determines hierarchy through *horizontal* privileging (the further westward into the Tabernacle, the higher the social and cultic status). Another difference is the treatment of elders. A generic mention of "the elders of the people" appears in Exod 19:7 (where Moses sets the commandments of Yahweh before them), yet they are totally lacking from the ritual narrative in Exodus 19:10-25. In contrast, in Exodus 24 "seventy elders" are much more of a focal point, making the ascent up the mountain (alongside Moses, Aaron, and Aaron's two sons), where they then have the privilege of "seeing" and banqueting with the God of Israel (Exod 24:9-11). Conflating the traditions in their reconstructions of the ritual narrative in

Exodus 19:10–25, Milgrom (1991: 142–143) and Sarna (1991: 105) include the elders as making a partial ascent up the mountain along with the priests. At the other end of the spectrum is George (2009: 127–129, fig 4.3), who has the social hierarchy divided into four quadrants but, due to his focus on the Tabernacle (and not Mt. Sinai), leaves the elders completely out of his social taxonomy. The elders makes no appearance in the two major Tabernacle passages (Exod 25–31; Exod 35–40), yet they do occur in Lev 9:1, which George (2009: 1–2 n. 2) views as "less central" to his argument.

110. The Sinai narrative in Exodus 24 is equally curious. Though Aaron is grouped with his two sons (Nadab and Abihu), none of the three is here called a priest. The priestly activity that does occur involves Moses' altar building and blood manipulation, and the ʿōlōt offerings and šĕlāmîm sacrifices carried out by "young men of the people of Israel" (naʿărê bĕnê yiśrāʾēl; Exod 24:4–8).

111. Contrast the notable lack of any mention of either qdš consecration or divine lethality in the Mt. Sinai ascent of Exod 24. Granted, prior to the ascent Moses builds an altar for sacrifice, but surprisingly, it is "young men of the people of Israel" (naʿărê bĕnê yiśrāʾēl), not consecrated priests, who carry out the sacrifice, the blood of which Moses then manipulates (Exod 24:4–8). Another surprising difference in this ascent tradition is the addition of Aaron's two sons (Nadab and Abihu) and seventy elders who together with Moses and Aaron are able "to see the God of Israel" and eat and drink (wayyirʾû ʾēt ʾĕlōhê yiśrāʾēl . . . wayyeḥĕzû ʾet-hāʾĕlōhîm wayyōʾkĕlû wayyištû; Exod 24:9–11).

112. Milgrom (1991: 557) is commenting on Leviticus 8 (on which see the many references that follow), yet his comments resonate with Exod 19:10–25. For additional discussion about whether Moses was considered a priest, see pp. 617–619.

113. Aaron likewise has no consecration ritual in Exod 19, yet in contrast to Moses, Aaron elsewhere undergoes considerable consecration and ordination rites.

114. Though the MT is easily understood, its cryptic nature has led to it being rewritten by the Syriac ("Moses *his servant*") and Vulgate ("Moses *and* his people"), and omitted by the LXX. The MT is *lectio difficilior*.

115. There are two variant readings attesting to either Moses alone as Yahweh's shepherd (rōʿeh ṣōʾnô; LXX, Tg, Syr, Hbw mss) or together with Aaron (rōʿê ṣōʾnô; MT). See Paul 2012: 574; Oswalt 1998: 602 n. 44; and Barthélemy 1986: 439–441. Due to the consistent emphasis placed on Moses alone in the present context, we prefer the former.

116. The subject of the singular verb *yizkōr* in Isa 63:11 has been taken to be God due to the previous verse or the people, in line with the following verses, where they are the clear speaker.

117. Whatever variant one chooses to read in Isa 63:11 (see note 115), Moses remains Yahweh's shepherd, either by himself or with Aaron at his side.

118. Milgrom (2007: 851) speaks of an "unbridgeable gap" between divine holiness and human attempts at holiness. In writing of P's picture of society, Rooke (2000: 14) underscores the divide between "God's holiness . . . [and] human sinfulness and unholiness . . . [that has] to be reconciled . . . if the cultic community is to be meaningful; reconciliation is achieved by stipulating 'degrees of holiness.'" It needs

to be noted that this is a concern not only of priestly writers and editors. Propp (2006: 151), in commenting on the redactor who combined J and E traditions about Sinai/Horeb, notes how "the cumulative picture is of a delicate and complicated process whereby Israel becomes covenantly bound to Yahweh, a gradual bridging of the nigh-unbridgeable gulf between the divine and the earthly."

119. To these priestly voices one must add Deuteronomy's notion of election of Israel as a holy people. See p. 648–649.
120. E.g., Levine 1989: 49; Milgrom 1991: 556. A case in point is Rooke's (2000) comprehensive look at priesthood in ancient Israel, which ignores Ps 99:6 altogether.
121. Reexamining the exact nature of the priestly prebends, Milgrom (1991: 558) qualifies that Moses, according to P, "was the interim priest only by necessity and divine dispensation."

The study by Gray (1971: 196), originally published in 1925, also emphasized how "the Mosaic priesthood . . . was according to P the priesthood of a week." Yet in contrast to Milgrom, Gray (1971: 210) envisions Moses as a priest "in early Hebrew tradition" due to embracing a version of the Midianite hypothesis. In Gray's words, one can detect "behind the narrative of Exodus 18 a tradition of a Midianite priest instructing Moses and initiating him into the priesthood." For a fuller discussion of the Midianite hypothesis, see Chapter Six, pp. 271–279.

122. The exception that proves the rule is the illicit example of King Ahaz (2 Kgs 16:13).
123. See Cross 1973: 195–215; Halpern 1976; and Leuchter 2012. Cf. van der Toorn 1996b: 302–306 and Hutton 2010a: 160–161.
124. No single word can translate Hebrew *zār*, which involves culturally and cultically laden dynamics of being "foreign," "inappropriate," and "forbidden." For P, note especially the reference to Aaron's sons Nadab and Abihu offering "foreign/illicit fire" (*'ēš zārâ*) in Lev 10:1–3, for which they die (on which see Chapter Seven, pp. 370–372). Blending in the traditions of Num 3:10 and Num 18:7, it is conspicuous that the "outsiders who die" are the very sons of the high priest!

For a lengthy analysis of the term *zār* and the formula "the encroacher shall be put to death" (*hazzār haqqārēb yummat*), see the classic treatment in Milgrom 1970: 5–59.

125. Bell (1992: 94–117), in her study of "the ritual body," summarizes the most influential voices that have promoted the "body" and the "socialized body" as cross-discipline, analytical categories. Bell includes Bourdieu, Comaroff, Douglas, Durkheim, Foucault, Gilbert, Gubar, Hertz, Lakoff, Mauss, Rappaport, Showalter, Smith, and Turner. See too the discussion of priestly consecration as rites of passage by Milgrom (1991: 538, 566–569), Klingbeil (1997: 510–513), and Grabbe (2003: 213) as they interact with the works of van Gennep and Turner. To Bell's list should be added the archaeological study of status, and especially mortuary data that correlates the expenditure of energy and resources in treating the dead body with the ranking of social status. Here see Wason 1994, building on Tainter 1977.

Turning to the clothing of the body, see Roach and Eicher 1965; Schwarz 1979; Cordwell and Schwarz 1979; Hansen 2004; and Batten 2010. Where the former are anthropological in nature, Batten includes literature pertaining to the ancient Near

East, including biblical texts. See too Matthews' (1995) study of the anthropology of clothing as marking changes in social status in the Joseph narrative, Prouser's (1996) depiction of the symbolic use of clothing in the David and Saul narratives, and several studies of the gendered use of garments in Genesis 37–39 by Bal (1987: 89–103), Furman (1989), and Huddlestun (2002).

126. This is not to overlook the mention of ritual washing with Moses himself washing the bodies of Aaron and his sons (Exod 29:4; 40:12; Lev 8:6). Yet our preserved sources minimize washing in contrast to clothing and anointing.

127. On *kābôd* in P, see Chapter Seven, pp. 368–373.

128. For a detailed description of priestly vestments, see Haran 1985: 165–174. For the function of these garments in ritual contexts, see Haran 1985: 210–215. My treatment of this material is very much indebted to Haran. See too the treatment of vestments and their symbolism in Rooke 2000: 16–20.

129. For an artistic rendering of the two contrasting vestments, see Propp 2006: 434 fig. 16. Batten (2010: 151) remarks: "If [the priests'] garments were made according to the biblical instructions, they must have been spectacular."

See too Golani's (2013: 74–75) comments about the cultic significance of jewelry set against a broader archaeological discussion of jewelry from the Iron Age II Levant.

130. Specifically, Aaron's role here is "to bear the people's transgression" so that they may find favor before Yahweh as they consecrate as their holy gifts (*yaqdîšû běnê yiśrāʾēl lěkol-mattěnōt qodšêhem*; Exod 28:38). For speculations about the precise meaning of this expression, see Propp 2006: 448–449.

131. In contrast to the usage in P, two narratives in 1 Sam suggest a royal involvement with using the Urim and Thummim and presumably outside of an inner sanctum. 1 Sam 23:6–12 is cryptic in that it mentions David using the ephod yet without any explicit mention of the Urim and Thummim. Yet the context is clear in noting two crucial factors: David summons Abiathar, the (high) priest who has custody of the ephod (and outside of a temple context), and binary questions are posed that Yahweh then answers. The logical interpretation is that David employed Abiathar as high priest to ask binary questions of Yahweh as he manipulated the Urim and Thummim objects. The same scenario is found in 1 Sam 30:7–8. Once again David asks questions of Yahweh through the agency of Abiathar, the (high) priest who possessed the ephod that seemingly contained the Urim and the Thummim divinatory objects. These two explicit mentions of David employing Abiathar suggest that a similar situation lies behind David inquiring of Yahweh in 1 Sam 23:1–5, which elliptically makes no mention of David's use of personnel or means (cf. too 2 Sam 2:1; 5:23–24).

In contrast, Saul uses the Urim (only) in 1 Sam 28:6 with no mention of any priestly involvement. Such usage could suggest a customary royal practice, or it could be DtrH's attempt to suggest that Saul is carrying out illicit cult similar to the illicit necromancy in the narrative.

In short, biblical monarchs were certainly involved as religious officiants (see Chapter Nine, pp. 498–503), yet from the meager data at hand, the prerogative of using the Urim and Thummim seems to have been that of the (high) priest alone, yet one that could be used outside of the sanctuary. This makes its occurrence in Deut 33:8 quite noteworthy. See pp. 637–639.

132. On the rationale for having bells and who hears them, see Propp 2006: 445–446.
133. My late colleague Raymond Westbrook and I have addressed the identity of the ʾîš ʿittî in Lev 16:21 (see Westbrook and Lewis 2008). The *hapax legomenon* is often translated as "a man in waiting" or "a man designated for the task," renderings that do little to advance a meaning that is appropriate to the context. Based on Hittite and Greek scapegoat rituals and on a reanalysis of the etymology of ʿittî, we argue that the ʾîš ʿittî refers to a criminal acting as "a buffer between the high priest and the sin-ridden scapegoat."
134. Cf. the perfumed/spiced oil (šmn rqḥ) used as cultic offerings at Ugarit (e.g., KTU 1.41.21, 1.148.21).
135. For additional examination of "sancta contagion/contamination," see Haran 1985: 175–177 and Milgrom 1991: 443–456; 1992.
136. The literary relationship of Lev 8 and Exod 29 has occasioned much discussion concerning which tradition is derivative from the other and how they both relate to Exod 40. These tangled discussions are beyond the scope of the treatment here. For entry into this debate with secondary sources, see Watts 2013: 443–448; Feder 2011: 43–53; Nihan 2007: 124–147; Klingbeil 2000: 231 n. 3; 1998: 56–96, 104–107; Fleming 1998: 408–413, esp. 411–412; and Milgrom 1991: 545–549. See too Levine's (1965: 310–314) demarcation of Lev 8 as a *descriptive* text versus Exod 29 as a *prescriptive* text.

To make matters even more complex, note too how Knohl (1995: 65–68, 104–105) assigns Exod 29:38–46 and Exod 40 to H.

137. See Lev 16:21; 24:14; Num 8:10–12. For summaries of the various ways to interpret the hand-laying ritual, see Wright 1986; Milgrom 1991: 151–153; Propp 2006: 457–458; and Gilders 2013: 16–17.
138. See Propp 2006: 466–467 on the "virtue" of translating a polysemous *kpr*.
139. Again we need to note that Knohl (1995: 65–68, 104–105) assigns Exod 29:38–46 to H.
140. Exod 29:36 briefly mentions the anointing of the altar. but not its paraphernalia. Milgrom (1991: 513–516, 545; followed by Feder 2011: 45–48) argues that Lev 8:10–11 is an interpolation from Exod 40:9–11. Thus he concludes: "Lev 8 in its final form is subsequent not only to Exod 29 but also to Exod 40." Grabbe (2003: 209) posits that what we have here is simply evidence of "the ancient writer's logic": "How can Aaron offer sacrifices as part of his consecration ceremony if the sacrificial system has not already been initiated?"
141. For the rationale of the sevenfold anointing, cf. Milgrom 1991: 515–517.
142. The blood daubing on the right ear, thumb, and big toe has been seen as either purificatory (so Milgrom 1991: 528–529) or as an indexical sign (so Gilders 2004: 78–82, 96–104). For a summary of these positions, see Feder 2011: 44–45, which sides with Gilders.

As for blood on the altar, Meshel (2013) has challenged the consensus that sees the act of blood manipulation to result in the blood landing *on the side walls* of the altar due to the Hebrew expression using *sābîb* (*zāraq* [*'et haddām*] . . . *'al-hammizbēaḥ sābîb*). Instead Meshel argues that the blood lands *on the perimeter of the upper surface* of the altar (cf. Ezek 43:18; Deut 12:27; 2 Kgs 16:12–13).

143. Milgrom (1991: 525) see the comprehensive atonement function of the altar in Lev 8:15b as divergent from the "limited . . . immediate function of the consecratory sacrifices" in Exodus 29:33, 36–37. See too Feder's (2011: 48–53) diachronic reconstruction.

144. See note 124. The narrative in Lev 8–10 does address the *zār* with respect to the Nadab and Abihu incident in Lev 10:1–3, on which see Chapter Seven, pp. 370–372.

145. Lev 8:15 also includes putting the bull's blood on the horns and base of the altar in echo of Exod 29:12, yet with the added remark that by such ritual Moses "consecrated it to make atonement for it" (*wayĕqaddĕšēhû lĕkappēr 'ālāyw*).

There is a debate about whether the rituals described in Lev 8 would have been repeated on every day of the week. Milgrom (1991: 538) advocates this position. In contrast, see Klingbeil 1997: 512, which provides additional bibliography.

146. Grabbe (2003: 213 n. 12) does not speculate on the nature of the danger. Milgrom (1991: 569), following Victor Turner, speculates that the nature of the peril may be "the anarchical, amorphous status of the consecrands," or, following Mary Douglas, that the danger lies in "the anomalous position of the consecrands . . . that defies classification." Elsewhere, Milgrom (1991: 538) is more confident in stating that the danger to the priests during this liminal stage of consecration has to do with being exposed to human sin and impurity—hence their confinement within holy space. In a related discussion on the pollution of the sanctuary by human contamination, Milgrom (1991: 261) refers to "malefic impurity."

Propp (2006: 530–531), while writing on Exodus 29 (which does not mention the possibility of death, as does Lev 8:35), nonetheless also explores this material as a dangerous rite of passage. For Propp, the "ordination" (*millu'îm*) ram—which he translates "the Filling Ram"—is the key, for it does indeed die and its "blood represents the priests' own blood." "The bloodied finger, toe and ear are *symbolically severed*, which in turn symbolizes the priests' death" (emphasis Propp). See further Propp's (2004) broader study of symbolic wounds.

147. See Chapter Seven, pp. 370–372.

148. See Chapter Nine, pp. 498–503, on the cultic role of kings in ancient Israel. Cf. too the anointing of David as king, though without explicit mention of a pouring ritual (1 Sam 16:13; 2 Sam 12:7). The anointing of David in Ps 89:21 (Eng 89:20) is particularly fascinating, with the ritual substance being referred to as "holy/consecrating oil" (*bĕšemen qodšî mĕšaḥtîv*). For a much fuller analysis of royal anointing, including ancient Near Eastern references, see Mettinger 1976: 185–232 and the older Kutsch 1963.

149. The distribution of priestly *cultic* authority resonates with the distribution of *judicial* authority, priestly and otherwise. See Chapter Nine, pp. 523–528, on the organization of early Israelite judiciaries.

150. For the enduring influence of Noth's construction on later scholarship, see Fleming 1998: 401 n. 1; Klingbeil 2007: 65; and Watts 2013: 448–449. Martin Noth's original German edition, *Gesammelte Studien zum Alten Testament*, was published in 1957.
151. Fleming 1998: 405–408; cf. 1992a: 178–179. See too Mettinger 1976: 185–232.
152. Fleming 1992b includes an overview of the festivals at Emar that represent "deeply rooted native Syrian traditions."
153. On the Emar "days of sanctification," see p. 608. The text describing the installation of the high priestess of the storm god is Emar 369, for which there is a burgeoning amount of research. See Arnaud 1986: 326–337; Dietrich 1989; and Fleming 1992a. For a convenient translation, see Fleming 1997a: 427–431. For correspondences with Lev 8, see Fleming 1998 and Klingbeil 1998.

　See Fleming 1992: 71–198 for a detailed description of divine and human personnel (pp. 71–105) as well as the itinerary (pp. 105–119), the provisions (pp. 120–157), specialized rites (pp. 157–173), and the progress of the priestess (pp. 173–198).

　A sister text, the *maš'artu* installation (Emar 370), describes the installation of a priestess for the goddess Aštartu of Battle (*ša taḫāzi*). In what is preserved there is no mention of an anointing ritual, though Arnaud (1986: 338, 341) reconstructs the beginning to refer to "the day of sanctification" ([i-na u$_4$-m]i qa-ad-du-ši), on which see p. 608. See Arnaud 1986: 338–346; Fleming 1992: 98–99, 209–211, 229; 1992b: 54, 58–59. For specific mentions of Aštartu of Battle at Emar, see Smith 2014a: 196; 2014b: 56–57.
154. The double anointing via the pouring of oil on the head of the high priestess is mentioned on day 1 and day 2 of the installation ritual. For the text, see Arnaud 1986: 326–327 and Fleming 1992: 10, 14, 49, 51. For discussion, see Fleming 1992: 174–179.
155. See Lewis 2006a: 343, where I provide bibliography and note my indebtedness to Milgrom for material from both Evans-Pritchard and Bourdillon. See too Gilders' (2004) comprehensive study of blood rituals in the Hebrew Bible. The debates between Gilders (2004, 2013) and Klawans (2006, 2011)—whose specifics are beyond the scope of the present treatment—have done the field a supreme service in forcing interpreters to think through whether blood was used symbolically and/or instrumentally.
156. For the primary texts of the *zukru* festival, see Emar 375 (for the shorter single-day rite) and Emar 373 (for the longer seven-day festival). See Arnaud 1986: 350–371 and Fleming 2000: 233–267. For a convenient translation of the expanded ritual, see Fleming 1997b: 431–436. See too the detailed study in Thames 2016.
157. For the specific texts dealing with oil and blood (Ì^{meš} [*damu*] and ÚŠ^{meš} [*šamnu*]) and equating the *sikkānu* standing stone with deities, see Fleming 1998: 410 n. 42 and Michel 2013: 189, 192. Cf. the discussion of Hebrew *maṣṣēbâ/maṣṣēbôt* in Chapter Five, pp. 169–196, and Chapter Seven, pp. 333–336.
158. Milgrom is followed by Gilders (2004: 103) and Feder (2011: 45). In addition, Feder's (2011) study underscores both the antiquity of blood rituals in indigenous West Semitic religion of the Late Bronze Age as well as their Hurrian/Hittite heritage (esp. the *zurki* "blood" rituals imported from Kizzuwatna). It it hard to ignore

such significant material, no matter how one constructs the dating and development of the Hebrew Bible's various priestly traditions. On the Kizzuwatna rituals and the use of blood in Hittite ritual, see respectively the foundational studies of Miller (2004) and Beckman (2011) as well as the review of Feder by Mouton (2014).

159. H, or the Holiness Source/School/Code, is typically said to be found in Lev 17–26 and earmarked by its repeated use of the root *qdš*. For possible additional texts, see the influential list in Knohl 1995: 104–106.

160. Knohl (1995: 69, 105, 192) sees Lev 11:44–45 and Num 15:40 also to be a part of the Holiness School.

161. I here follow those scholars who see an etymological connection between the *'iššeh*-offerings and the Hebrew word for fire (*'ēš*), as opposed to those (e.g., Hoftijzer 1967; Milgrom 1991: 161–162; Rentdorff 2004: 63) who see these as food offerings related to Ugaritic *'tt*. Thus *'iššeh* can refer to offerings that are incinerated. See Eberhart 2002: 40–52, 361–381 and Watts 2013: 209–211 for balanced discussions that include the readings of the versions.

162. See Chapter Seven, p. 288. For detailed summaries of the ambiguous phrase *rêyaḥ nîḥōaḥ*, see Milgrom 1991: 162–163 and Watts 2013: 211–214. Cf. too Knohl's (1995: 128–137, 170–172) nuancing of the ways that P and H differ in using this phrase. Where H is comfortable with anthropomorphic language, P tends to suppress it.

163. See earlier on Exod 29:33–34, which also describes the holy nature of priestly food. H (in Lev 21:10, 12), like P (in Exod 29:33), draws a harsh line prohibiting the "outsider" (*zār*) from eating the holy food of priests.

164. Our treatment is merely a sketch. See the fuller analyses of the Nazirites in Olyan 2000: 61; Knohl 1995: 160–162; Levine 1993: 229–235; Cartledge 1989; 1992: 18–23; Mayer 1998; Milgrom 1990: 355–358; and Diamond 1997.

165. For scholars using the language of consecration, see Lundbom 2013: 931; de Hoop 1999: 217; Mayer 1998: 307–308; Westermann 1986: 241; Speiser 1964: 370. In contrast, Gunkel (1997: 461) argues that "the old meaning of *nāzîr* [that he translates as 'Israel's champion'] is to be accepted here, and not the later, weakened 'consecrated, noble, prince' (Lam 4:7)." While the portrayal of Joseph presents no priestly role, it does describe him as an intermediary with regard to dream interpretation (Gen 37, 40–41) and *nḥš* divination through the use of a cup, perhaps suggesting leconomancy (Gen 44:5, 15).

166. The use of *bōšet*, "shameful," in Hos 9:10 is the common replacement of the name of the deity Baal with a derogatory slur. See Andersen and Freedman 1980: 541 for the speculation that the historical deity (the "*ba'al*," i.e., lord) worshipped at Baal-Peor may have been Yahweh of Midian.

167. On this figure, see Chapter Seven, pp. 349–350.

168. While the context of the MT clearly has to do with Samuel being a Nazirite, there is no explicit use of the term *nāzîr* either in 1 Sam 1:11 or in 1 Sam 1:22. Many translators (e.g., McCarter 1980a: 53–54, 56) restore *nāzîr* in 1 Sam 1:11 based on its use in 4QSam[a] and LXX and in 1 Sam 1:22 based on 4QSam[a] (but not LXX). Other translators (e.g., Tsumura 2007: 118, 125; Tsevat 1992) hold to the MT.

169. The MT of 1 Sam 1:11 mentions only the uncut hair provision, while the LXX and 4Qsam^a also include the intoxicants. Thus McCarter (1980a: 53–54) restores the viticulture stipulation as "probably original," while Tsumura (2007: 118) refrains. Samuel's mother being mistaken by Eli as being drunk precisely when she is making her vow (1 Sam 1:13–15) surely plays into a Nazirite scenario.
170. The verb *pl'*, used here in the C stem, occurs elsewhere in the D (Num 15:3, 8; Lev 22:21) and C stems (Lev 27:2) for those undertaking a vow. See Cartledge 1989: 413 n. 12.
171. My reference to modern figures is heuristic only. Cartledge (1989: 410) critiques those who simplistically equate conditional Nazirite vows with modern religious vows that are "unconditional expressions of personal piety and simple devotion to God." For Cartledge (1989: 417), Nazirite vows were conditional promises "held out in prospect of answered prayer." Nazirite abstinence should be understood "as future payment for present requests." From this Cartledge extrapolates without warrant that the motivations of all Nazirites vows were merely transactional: "the Nazirites were not expressing their [unselfish] devotion so much as they were paying their debts" (1989: 422). Such a broad conclusion is overly reductionist. We simply do not know what was in the heart of these individuals. Just because a vow is conditional does not imply anything one way or another about the sincerity of an individual's devotion. Cartledge (1989: 409) admits as much when he begins his study by acknowledging that "there is no indication of what motivation lies behind the taking of the vow."
172. For fuller discussions of the incredibly complex and voluminous research on priesthood and the Levites, see Wellhausen 1957: 121–167; Gray 1971: 179–270; Gunneweg 1965; Cody 1969; Cross 1973: 195–215; Levenson 1976: 129–158; Halpern 1976; Duke 1987, 1988; Nelson 1991, 1993; Rehm 1992; Levine 1993: 150–151, 273–290, 423–432; Albertz 1994: 57–59, 219–223, 427–436; Grabbe 1995: 41–65; 2003; 2004: 224–237; van der Toorn 1996b: 302–306; Dahmen 1996; Nurmela 1998; Blenkinsopp 1998; Knoppers 1999; 2003b; 2004: 820–826; Propp 1999: 231–232; 2006: 565–574; McConville 1999; Rooke 2000; Schaper 2000; Sweeney 2001; Péter-Contesse 2003; Liss 2006; Stackert 2007: 198–204; 2011; Leuchter 2007; 2012; Na'aman 2008; McBride 2009; Hutton 2011a, 2011b; Leuchter and Hutton 2011; Altmann 2011; Cook 2011; Watts 2013: 123–129; and Samuel 2014.

Na'aman (2008: 266 n. 67) writes that "the investigation of the origin of the Levites has been treading water for many years, and neither new data nor new ideas have been adduced in recent ties to move it forward." In addition, one's reconstruction of the history of the priesthood is tied to one's position on the nature of the various sources and their dating. Grabbe (2004: 227) is astute in his assessment: "Although scholars have tried [to date texts], there is usually a circularity in the process, with a position about the development of the priesthood being the starting point rather than the endpoint."

Lastly, note Watts' (2013: 129) appeal for sensitivity to rhetoric. Though Watts underscores that there were clear "rivalries and conflicts between priests and priestly families" not to mention "simmering Levite resentments," he advises that "interpreters should not confuse rhetorical creativity with the social divisions that put such rhetoric to use." Thus Watts (2013: 123) is of the opinion that the various priestly traditions "do not contradict each other."

173. Thus we find conclusions like Houtman's (2000: 620, 666), that "in the Pentateuch *in its extant form*, [Exod] 32:25–29 is evidently intended to legitimate the consecration of Aaron and his sons as priests" (emphasis mine). In contrast, see the treatment of Exod 32:25–29 that follows. See Houtman for various ways to unpack Aaron the Levite vis-à-vis the Levites.

174. Albertz (1994: 58) writes: "Judges 17–18 offers a quite credible picture of the Levites in the period before the state."

175. On Judg 17–18 and family/household religion, see especially Ackerman 2008a: 129–141. See too Chapter Eight.

176. On the oracular function of Levites, cf. too Exod 4:14–15, where Aaron "the Levite" is the one chosen to serve as an oracular conduit to convey the words that Yahweh speaks to Moses.

177. Source-critical discussions of Exod 32 have resulted, according to Houtman (2000: 617), in "a hodgepodge of conceptions" (cf. Propp 2006: 148–149). The verses that are relevant for the present discussion (Exod 32:26–29) are viewed as integral to the chapter by some scholars, while others see them coming from another hand (thus Houtman 2000: 618).

178. Admittedly, the pointing of *mil'û* (seemingly a G stem second-person masculine plural imperative) is difficult: "Be full with respect to your hand." If the Levites have brought about their ordination through their valor, we might expect a second-person masculine plural D Pf *millēʾtem* ("you have filled your hand") along with the LXX's and Vulgate's understanding (Houtman 2000: 668). The best solution may be to see this form as a mispointed third-person masculine plural D Pf (*mallĕʾû*) used impersonally ("they have filled your hand" → "your hand has been filled"). Thus Propp 2006: 563, following Rashbam and Luzzatto. On the other hand, perhaps for an important ordination procedure with Moses speaking (performatively?), the MT tradition may not have wanted to be blatant in assigning agency to the Levites.

179. Deut 33:8–11, the so-called Blessing of Moses, is seen by many scholars as an archaic poem independent of the book of Deuteronomy, perhaps composed as early as the tenth century BCE (Lundbom 2013: 916–917; cf. Lewis 2013b). Compare similarly the archaic Blessing of Jacob in Gen 49.

180. Reconstructing *hābû lĕlēwî* following 4QDeut[h], 4QTestim, and LXX and assuming a loss in the MT as a result of some type of haplography after *lĕlēwî ʾāmar* (so Cross 1973: 197). In addition, as Duncan (1995: 280) notes, one would certainly expect a verb in the opening phrase. For the Qumran material, see Duncan 1995: 273–290.

181. This is an attempt to translate the awkward syntax of the MT. An alternative solution would be to translate "the loins of his foes," reanalyzing MT's *motnayim* as *motnê-m(i)* with an enclitic *m* (so Cross and Freedman 1997: 67, 76 n. 33, following Albright).

182. In contrast, there is no mention of parents in Exod 32:27, 29 as in Deut 33:9. Interestingly, the place where we find a priestly figure distancing himself from his

father and mother is in the Aaronid high priest's purity sanctions with regard to corpse contamination in Num 21:11 (cf. too the Nazirite in Num 6:7).

183. Thus Cross (1973: 197–206) concentrates on Levi and Moses being in parallel here as evidence of a Mushite priesthood. See additional literature in note 123.
184. For priestly judicial activity, see Chapter Nine, p. 854 and note 93.
185. Num 16 is part of a larger complex that runs from Lev 16 through Lev 18, to which Milgrom (1990: 129) assigns the rubric "Encroachment on the Tabernacle." As long recognized, the material gathered here is a complex literary tapestry that weaves together various traditions (JE and P as well as H, according to Knohl) about rebellious behavior. On the redaction of this material, see Milgrom 1990: 414–423; Levine 1993: 410–417, 423–432; and Knohl 1995: 73–85, 105. What facilitates the editing of these independent traditions into a whole? In the words of Milgrom (1990: 129), it is "the archconspirator... the Levite Korah, who instigates or is associated with all four rebellious groups."
186. See Chapter Seven, pp. 370–372. On King Uzziah's cultic violation in 2 Chr 26:16–20, see pp. 661–663.
187. On the "work profile" (ʿăbōdâ) of the various Levites, see Milgrom 1990: 343–344. On the Kohathite Levite's porterage (only) of the Ark that keeps them from coming into lethal contact with "the Holy (Shrine)," see pp. 596–597 on Num 4.
188. On Yahweh's kābôd in P and elsewhere, see Chapter Seven, pp. 358–379.
189. The ongoing narrative includes yet another legitimation of Aaron's priesthood (and his tribe of Levi) over persistent challenges. Here the sign is a divine manipulation of nature. In yet another contest—involving a wordplay, with maṭṭeh designating staff and tribe—God miraculously causes Aaron's staff to sprout, blossom and even produce ripe almonds (Num 17:16–26 [Eng 17:1–11]).
190. According to Knohl (1995: 53–54, 105), the three relevant passages treated here (Num 3, 8, 18) should be assigned to H. For a discussion of scholars who consider H to be more expansive than the traditional Lev 17–26, see Stackert 2007: 12–18.
191. The various procedures of maintaining the Tabernacle complex are broken down by Levitical clan (Gershon, Kohath, Merari) in Num 3. We have already noted the strict division of labor when it comes to the non-priestly Kohathite Levites' role in transporting the Ark (in contrast to its priestly wrapping by the Aaronids within the Holy Shrine) (see note 187).
192. See Milgrom 1970: 29 n. 103; 1990: 64. See too note 195.
193. See pp. 619–629 and Levine 1993: 273–274.
194. For a study of the diversity of testimony on child sacrifice in the Hebrew Bible as well as a diachronic study of the various firstborn traditions (Exod 13:2, 13:11–13, 22:28b–29, 34:19–20; Lev 27:26–27; Num 3:11–13; 8; 18:13–18; Deut 15:19–23), see Dewrell 2017. Dewrell wisely differentiates the *mlk* sacrifices from firstborn sacrifices.
195. Milgrom (1990: 17–18) extrapolates from ancient Near Eastern comparative material as well as rabbinic teachings, that "the first-born originally held a priestly status." He posits this as a possible reason for "the deliberate avoidance by the priestly texts of the word *kadosh*, 'holy,' in regard to the Levites."

196. Cf. e.g., Rooke 2000: 104–119. Rooke (2000: 108 n. 7) also provides a nice summary of scholarly positions on how the cultic material in Ezek 40–48 relates to the book as a whole.
197. It should be noted that we do have a reference to *yhwh qādôš běyiśrāʾēl*, "Yahweh, the Holy One *in* Israel" (Ezek 39:7), which Block (1998: 464) mentions elsewhere.
198. Block (1997: 725) points out how Ezek 22:26 "represents the only text . . . that casts members of Ezekiel's own social class, the priesthood, in a negative light." Greenberg (1997: 462) notes how this material was "evidently borrowed from Zeph 3:4" (so too Block 1997: 724).
199. See Block 1997: 655–656 for a description of how the use of this phrase in Ezekiel is distinct from the mountain concept within Zion Theology.
200. On "sancta contagion/contamination," see note 135.
201. Outside of Ezekiel, Yahweh's concern about his holy name (*šēm qodšô*) being profaned occurs in H (Lev 18:21; 20:3, 21:6; 22:2, 32). For the ideological portrayal of illicit cult as part of identity formation, see Rom-Shiloni's (2011) analysis of how Ezekiel focused on polemically differentiating his exilic community from the Judeans who remained in Jerusalem. See too Liebermann 2019.
202. Translating Ezek 36:20 as simply "they have gone forth" rather than "they (had) to go forth," Greenberg (1997: 729) adds that Yahweh's name would also be desecrated by being associated with the "corrupt," "miscreant" exiles, for "the deportees of Jerusalem [constituted] exemplars of depravity."
203. That gods were thought to be tied to their land is illustrated in the story about the conversion of the Aramean military commander Naaman to Yahwism. In order to worship Yahweh properly when he returns to his home country, the Aramean must bring with him some of the land (two mule-loads) of Yahweh's domain (2 Kgs 5:17; cf. Ps 137:4).
204. For the use of divine names in warrior contexts, see Lewis 2011.
205. On the meaning and use of *rêyaḥ nîḥōaḥ*, see Chapter Seven, p. 288.
206. I borrow the phrase "sanctifying power" here from Block (1997: 420–421), who also regards Ezek 37:26–28 as the climax of Ezekiel's restoration and astutely points out the "striking resemblance" to the priestly vocabulary in Lev 26:1–13.
207. For the ways in which these regulations relate to what we find in Leviticus, see Block 1998: 640–644.
208. Where Ezekiel 44:15 mentions the Zadokite priests (*hakkōhănîm halĕwiyyim bĕnê ṣādôq*) having charge over the *miqdāš*, Ezekiel 40:45 mentions "priests" (*kōhănîm*) having charge over the Temple (*habbāyit*). There is a long-standing debate regarding the identity of the latter. Some scholars, with Wellhausen (1957: 121–151) at the helm (e.g., Levenson 1976: 129–151; Zimmerli 1983: 368, 458–459), think that Ezek 40:45 is an early stratum referring to the *priestly* status of non-Zadokite *Levites* who subsequently became demoted. Others (e.g., Duke 1988; Block 1998: 537–538, 583; Milgrom and Block 2012: 80–81, 141–148) regard both groups of priests in Ezek 40:45–46 as Zadokites.

209. See Rooke's (2000: 116-119) summary as well as the literature in note 172. However one understands the Ezekelian perspective, it is clear that it lost out to P's views as the position of the high priest was prominent in the Second Temple period.
210. Dating back to Wellhausen's time, the transgressions were associated with the high places that are referenced in Josiah's reform (2 Kgs 23). This has now been called into question (e.g., Duke 1988). For various options for the Levites' idolatrous "abominations," see Milgrom and Block 2012: 145-153. Milgrom and Block (2012: 145) draw attention to the thousands of Judean pillar figurines (JPFs), including "hordes in the very shadow of the Jerusalem temple," such that "Ezekiel fires his verbal missiles at the idolatry of his own time in Jerusalem and Judah, an idolatry practiced by the people and supported by their Levite advisors." For a comprehensive study of the JPFs, see Darby 2014, though she does not weigh in on the idolatry mentioned in Ezek 44.
211. Duke (1988) suggests a more nuanced analysis of Ezek 44:6-16, arguing that the Levites are being restored to their traditional role of guarding the sanctuary rather than being demoted and punished. For Duke, the punishment that is mentioned here is the Levites bearing the responsibility for the people's cultic encroachment. Milgrom and Block (2012: 150-153) argue similarly that "the Levites' punishment [is] for their failure to guard the sanctuary . . . not for their complicity in Israel's idol worship." While this position has key strengths (esp. how it echoes similar vocabulary in Num 18 and how the Levites are not demoted priests à la Wellhausen), its weakness is not dealing sufficiently with the explicit mention of "idols" (*gillûlîm*; Ezek 44:10, 12; 48:11; cf. 14:11) and the "shame" (*kĕlimmâ*) that they incur (Ezek 44:13).
212. And yet see the discussion of Deut 23:15 (Eng 23:14) that follows (about the camp needing to be holy due to Yahweh's presence) as well as Deut 32:51, where Yahweh says that Moses and Aaron "broke faith" with him (*mĕʿaltem bî*) in that they did not treat Yahweh as Holy (*lōʾ-qiddaštem ʾôtî*) among the Israelites at Meribath-qadesh.
213. For literature on these religious officiants and the question of cultic prostitution, see pp. 668-670. See too Gruber 1986; Westenholz 1989; van der Toorn 1989, 1992b; Goodfriend 1992; Henshaw 1994: 218-256; Bird 1997b; Assante 1998, 2003; Day 2004; Stark 2006; and Bird 2015.
214. See additional discussions in Weinfeld 1992: 190-209 and Chapter Seven, pp. 353-356.
215. Yadin (1962: 290-291) notes how the DSS War Scroll (1 QM, col. VII, lines 6-7) uses the nearly exact vocabulary of Deut 23:11 (Eng 23:10) to describe how "any man who is not pure with regard to his sexual organs" (*ʾyš ʾšr lwʾ yhyh ṭhwr mmqwrw*) shall not participate on the day of battle. Yet rather than Yahweh himself being encamped, the War Scroll mentions "holy angels together with their armies" (*mlʾky qwdš ʿm ṣbʾwtm yḥd*).
216. See Chapter Seven, pp. 348-349, and Lewis 2013b: 793.
217. See too Deut 33:2, which has Yahweh acting as divine warrior on behalf of his people, yet the holy ones in this older tradition seem to be members of his military

entourage, not the people of Israel. See note 216. The holy ones in Deut 33:3 could refer to the people of Israel, but this is not certain. See Tigay 1996: 321 for a summary of various viewpoints.
218. See too E. E. Fleming 2016, which extends Moran's insights to the political use of *ḥpṣ* and *nʾm* with respect to David and Jonathan.
219. Again, see Moran's insightful treatment. Moran (1963: 77–78) writes of how the love language in Deuteronomy "is commonly predicated of Israel in relation to Yahweh; indeed, it epitomizes the book's central preoccupation, namely, the observance of the Law . . . Love in Deuteronomy is a love that can be commanded . . . a love defined by and pledged in the covenant—a covenantal love." More recently, see the rich literature on the Neo-Assyrian *adê* tradition and Deuteronomy as a result of the publication of Esarhaddon's Succession Treaty (EST) by Lauinger (2012). Lauinger (2019) nicely reviews the various views of Crouch, Levinson, Pakkala, and Steymans on whether EST can serve as a literary model for Deuteronomy (esp. chapters 13 and 28), either for emulation or for subversion.
220. On the severity of blotting out one's name (identity deformation), see Lewis 2017.
221. For an exploration of divine wrath in biblical tradition and at Ugarit, including hypostatic representation, see McCarter 2008a and Chapter Seven, pp. 350–352.
222. Propp (2006: 573) sees Deut 10:6 and Deut 32:50–51 coming from other hands, thus leaving only Deut 9:20 as the sole "extremely pejorative" mention of Aaron in the entire book.
223. For literature on the history of the priesthood overall, see note 172. Focused studies on the Levites in Deuteronomy include Wright 1954; Emerton 1962; Abba 1977; Duke 1987; Dahmen 1996; Achenbach 1999; Sweeney 2001:137–169; Leuchter 2007; Naʾaman 2008; McBride 2009; Cook 2011; and Altmann 2011.

For a primary example of the gnarled complexities of reconstruction, see Dahmen's (1996) influential study that advocates multiple levels of redaction. See too the harsh critique by Naʾaman (2008: 260–261), who writes of "Dahmen's hypothesis [being] fraught with difficulty."
224. E.g., Sweeney 2001: 137–169. But contrast Leuchter 2007.
225. Naʾaman (2008: 274–277) goes further to suggest that the occasion for these Levites becoming associated with the landless poor and migrating to Jerusalem was the destruction of Levitical settlements (especially in the Shephelah) during Sennacherib's 701 BCE campaign in Judah.
226. The only use of the root *qdš* in conjunction with the Levites is found in Deut 26:12 where the Levites receive "the sacred portion" (*haqqodeš*) along with non-native residents, orphans, and widows.
227. Since the groundbreaking work of Martin Noth, it is common to find treatments of DtrH's understanding of the priesthood and holiness to include the book of Joshua. See, for example, Nelson 1991; Gammie 1989: 118–122; and Rooke 2000: 43–79. Thus structurally I have followed this scholarly tradition in placing the Joshua material here. Yet readers should be aware of trends in the study of the book of Joshua that treat it as an independent composition apart from DtrH. See especially Dozeman 2015: 18–32. Yet contrast Nihan 2012.

228. For the distribution of the root ʿbd in the MT of Joshua (and LXX renderings), and its use for worship and cultic service in the closing chapters, see Dozeman 2015: 403–404.
229. Preuss 1995: 240–241; von Rad 1962: 203–203–212; Eichrodt 1961: 209–210. Eichrodt (1961: 201 n. 1) builds upon Hänsel's coining of the term *Eiferheiligkeit* ("jealousy-holiness") to argue further that such a theology constitutes "the basic element in the whole OT idea of God." So too Butler (1983: 275), to whom I am indebted for this reference.
230. On judicial roles for the *šōṭěrîm*, see Chapter Nine, pp. 526–527. On the use of the phrase "jealous God" (*ʾēl-qannōʾ*), see Guinn-Villareal 2018 for an argument against reductionist translations that limit the root *qnʾ* and noun *qinʾâ* to the realm of emotions and thereby miss the social-anthropological implications of the term.
231. See Chapter Nine, notes 13 and 48.
232. For references to Phoenician kings being called *khn*, see Chapter Nine, note 11. Without any additional comment, 2 Sam 8:18 records briefly that David's sons were priests. On the prominent role of ʾUmmîʿaštart, the fifth-century BCE Phoenican "priestess of ʿAštart" (*khnt ʿštrt*), see note 282.
233. On the Levitical cities in Josh 21 and 1 Chr 6:39–66, see Knoppers 2003a: 430–450 and Hutton 2011a.
234. See note 172. See especially Nelson 1991 and McConville 1999.
235. See the mention of two *kmr* priests of the Aramean moon god Śahr in the Nerab inscriptions (KAI 225:1; KAI 226:1).
236. This list is certainly incomplete when it comes to the many individuals who served as priest over the hundreds of years in question. A glance at the fuller Levitical genealogies in 1 Chr 6:1–38 (that have their own ideologies) reveals a most complicated history. See Knoppers 2003a: 415–430.
237. See Chapter Nine, note 11.
238. Dozeman (2015: 329–330) argues that sacral status accrues to Jericho here not due to any association with a cultic sanctuary (contrast the holy mountain in Exod 3:1–5), but rather due to the city being "placed under the ban as a sacrifice to Yahweh ... The holy status of Jericho signals the divine claim on the city through execution of the ban." See too Dozeman's (2015: 329–330) remarks (following Savran 2005) about the composition of the theophany of Josh 5:13–15 as it relates to the similar wording of Moses removing his sandals on holy ground in Exod 3:5.
239. Divine lethality is implied in Josh 3:4–6, where the people must keep a substantial distance (about half a mile) away from the Ark as well as undergo a process of sanctification due to the "wonders" that Yahweh will do in their midst (*hitqaddāšû kî māḥār yaʿăśeh yhwh běqirběkem niplāʾōt*; Josh 3:5). Comparing similar language of a holy Yahweh working military wonders (*ʿōśēh peleʾ*) in Exod 15:11 (see pp. 578, 582), Dozeman (2015: 287) suggests that our author is drawing a comparison between the Ark crossing the Jordan and the Song of the Sea.
240. Special mention is given to David's holy treasures (2 Sam 8:11; 1 Kgs 7:51). Note, however, that such "holy" votive gifts, though set apart for the divine, could be

repurposed, as when Jehoash sends them off as booty to King Hazael of Aram (2 Kgs 12:18).
241. See further Wright 1995 and Philip 2006: 25–28. Wright astutely points out the literary use of purity and impurity throughout the David-Bathsheba-Uriah story in 2 Sam 11–12. With respect to constructing 2 Sam 11:4, I agree with McCarter (1984: 286) and Wright (1995: 218 n. 9) that the sense of the MT stands even if one omits (as one should) *miṭṭumʾātâ* following the *lectio brevior* reading of 4QSam^a.
242. The larger narrative of this complex story (which relates the death of Uzzah for mishandling the Ark) begs for Eleazar being (according to P's parameters in Numbers 4) at least a Kohathite Levite to transport the Ark if not an Aaronid priest to handle the Ark per se. See the reformulation of the tradition in 1 Chr 13:2–3; 15:11–15 that explicitly mentions priests and Levites, yet without any mention of Eleazar. For further discussion, see note 77. Edelman (1992) writes that "Eleazar is said to have been consecrated *as a priest* to have charge of the ark" (my emphasis) and that "it is likely that Abinadab [Eleazar's father] was himself a well-known priest."
243. For a more detailed discussion of P's *leḥem happānîm*, see Milgrom 2001: 2091–2101. Milgrom (2001: 2092, 2097) uses the 1 Sam 21 tradition (juxtaposed with comparative ancient Near Eastern material) to assert that 'there can be no doubt that the bread display was integral to Israelite worship from earliest times.'
244. On the literary use of purity and impurity throughout the David-Bathsheba-Uriah narrative, see Wright 1995.
245. On DtrH's articulation of a "solidarity between monarch and people" to promote the temple as a national place of worship, see Knoppers 1995a: 251–252 = 2000: 393–394.
246. For redactional issues, see Chapter Seven, pp. 365–366. On the central role of the priestly handling of the "highly cultic" Ark elsewhere in DtrH, see McConville 1999: 76–77, 80–82, 86. McConville writes: "This activity of the priests . . . not only marks the ark out as holy, but by the same token, shows that Dtr holds cultic matters and the priestly role in them to be very significant."
247. On DtrH's portrayal of the imposing Cherubim and their connection to an aniconic Yahweh, see Chapter Seven, pp. 398–405.
248. See Knoppers' (2003a: 245–265) most helpful overview of the various forms and functions of genealogies, as well as his study (2003b) of priestly genealogies.
249. A related example is DtrH's portrayal of Jehu's cunning "consecration" ceremony (*qaddĕšû ʿăṣārâ*), which brings about the death of the religious officiants of Baal in 2 Kgs 10:18–28.
250. See especially the overviews in Ramsey 1992; Rehm 1992: 305–307; and Rooke 2000: 63–72, as well as Rowley 1939; Cody 1969: 88–93; Cross 1973: 209–215; McCarter 1980a: 87–93; Olyan 1982; Nelson 1991: 136–141; McConville 1999; and Knoppers 2003a: 405–406, 414–415.
251. Compare Yahweh's servant Moses as the faithful one (*neʾĕmān*) in Num 12:7.
252. Note here that McCarter (1980a: 92) is referring to the Josianic Deuteronomist (Dtr1). See McConville's (1999: 87) study of the priesthood throughout DtrH and his conclusion: "For Dtr, priesthood is bigger than the Davidic synthesis of palace

and temple. When it falls into Babylonian exile, it is the end of a chapter in its story. But in Dtr's open-ended history, there is no obituary for priesthood as such."
253. For a lucid and comprehensive overview, see Knoppers 2003: 47–137.
254. For these statistics, I am indebted to Kornfeld (2003: 527), who in turn is indebted to Müller (1997: 1106–1107). Kornfeld writes: "[The root *qdš*] occurs 48 times in the Dtr History but then 120 times in the Chronicler's History, including 60 times in 2 Chronicles alone."
255. On the Chronicler's expanded coverage of Jehoshaphat in 2 Chr 17–21 in contrast to the minimal attention he receives in DtrH, see Williamson 1982: 277–303 and Japhet 1993: 742–803.
256. Our interpretation squares with that of Knoppers (2004: 638–639) in seeing *hadrat-qōdeš* as referring to Yahweh rather than the sanctuary or any type of holy apparel worn by worshippers. If one does see *qōdeš* as a reference to the sanctuary (see our comments on Ps 29:2 in Chapter Seven, pp. 361–362), the meaning would be essentially the same. For the sanctuary would only possess radiant holiness (*hadrat-qōdeš*) due to Yahweh taking up residence.
257. For discussion of the so-called Name Theology, see Chapter Seven, pp. 379–392.
258. See Chapter Five, p. 133, on the nuancing that could take place to acknowledge the obvious role of artisans while at the same time giving the gods their due.
259. It needs to be reiterated again that for P holiness is not about personal piety but rather about status, rank, and power.
260. Knohl (1995: 104–106) advocates for an expanded H. Yet even in this enlarged corpus, "the verb *bḥr* (elect) appears in HS [the Holiness School] only in connection with the sanctity of priests, the sons of Aaron . . . the verb *qdš* (sanctified) . . . never appears in the context of the Levites; its absence indicates that HS's intent was to stress the special sanctity of the priesthood" (Knohl 1995: 192).
261. The only reference to *ne'ĕmān*, "faithfulness," in adjacent material is found in Neh 9:8, which reaches back into patriarchal times to portray Yahweh as finding Abraham to have had a "faithful heart" (*māṣā'tā 'et-lĕbābô ne'ĕmān lĕpānêkā*).

As for royalty, the Chronicler's illustrious portrait of Hezekiah speaks of his being "the truthful/faithful one" (*hā'emet* < √'*mn*) before Yahweh (2 Chr 31:20; 32:1) but with no mention of an enduring "faithful house" (*bayit ne'ĕmān*). Japhet (1993: 972) notes how Hezekiah's trifold epithet of being "good and right and faithful before Yahweh" is found nowhere else.

As for sacerdotal officiants, Chronicles regularly speaks of them in "positions of trust" (*'ĕmûnâ*; 1 Chr 9:22, 26, 31; 2 Chr 31:15, 18). The priests and Levites in Jehoshaphat's judiciary are charged with adjudicating "faithfully" (*be'ĕmûnâ*; 2 Chr 19:9).
262. I borrow terminology here from Japhet (1993: 950), who speaks of the Levites' blood conveyance as the Chronicler's "innovation when compared with the sacrificial laws of Leviticus 1ff." Elsewhere Japhet (1993: 1047) writes of "underemployed" Levites who have lost "the raison d'etre of their existence as a clerical order." Underscoring their intermediary role further in Chronicles' portrayal of Josiah's most organized Passover, Japhet (1993: 1045) writes: "Except for the acts which are

exclusively priestly [the manipulation of blood], everything connected with the Passover sacrifice is now transferred to the Levites: slaughter, flaying, conveyance of the blood, removal of the fat parts, roasting of the Passover sacrifice, and its distribution according to fathers' houses."

263. For analysis of this skin disease, which is often referred to as leprosy, see Kitz 1994.

264. Note the fascinating and unique comment that Uzziah "was a lover of soil" (*kî-'ōhēb 'ădāmâ hāyâ*) in 2 Chr 26:10.

265. On the sociological and exclusionary use of a *ṣāra'at* diagnosis by priests, see Kitz 1994 and Garfein 2004: 53–54.

266. See Knoppers' (2004: 619–620) balanced conclusion about the Chronicler's portrayal of the prominent roles of cultic singers and musicians, roles that are absent from DtrH as well as P. Situating this material within its broader historical context, Knoppers notes how "musicians and singers were a constituent feature of temple worship" throughout the ancient Near East. Thus rather than Chronicles inventing fictional scenarios, "the complete absence of singers from the Pentateuch and from most of the Deuteronomistic work tells us more about the limitations of these sources than it does about the conditions of the Jerusalem Temple during the monarchy."

267. Williamson (1982: 377) and Japhet (1993: 972) are correct that those translations (e.g., RSV, NRSV) that explictly insert the subject being solely the priests go beyond the MT that leaves the subject unexpressed. Williamson is likely correct that both priests and Levites are being referenced.

268. For *'ĕmûnâ* designating a "position of trust" (so JPS) rather than faithfulness (so RSV, NRSV, NIV), see note 261.

269. For the voluminous research on the Levites, see note 172. For a summary of how scholars reconstruct the role of Levites and priests in Chronicles, see Knoppers 1999; 2003b; 2004: 820–826.

270. The obvious priestly infraction would be Uriah's carrying out various cultic actions under the direction of King Ahaz, notably replacing the Solomonic Yahwistic altar with a Damascus-inspired Aramean model (2 Kgs 16:10–16). Yet in contrast to DtrH, the Chronicler is silent with regard to the priest Uriah's involvement in Ahaz's apostasy. Instead 2 Chr 28:22–25 focuses solely on the king sacrificing to the gods of Damascus as well as dismantling the Jerusalem sanctuary, constructing multiple altars around Jerusalem, and erecting high places in every city of Judah to make offerings to other gods.

271. Chronicles strongly emphasizes the Aaronids' prerogative to offer incense (*lĕhaqṭîr*) within the sanctuary in three places (1 Chr 6:34 [Eng 6:49]; 1 Chr 23:13; 2 Chr 26:18) and the firm impression is that it is their sole prerogative, as in other traditions (e.g., P in Exod 30:7; Lev 2:2; 3:5; 7:31; 10:1; Num 4:16; 16:5–7, 16–18, 35; 17:5, 11–12 [Eng 16:40, 46–47]; cf. Zadok as a priest offering incense in 1 Sam 2:28). The sole complicating factor is found in 2 Chr 29:11, which refers to Yahweh choosing the Levites as his ministers offering incense (*lihyôt lô mĕšārĕtîm ûmaqṭirîm*). While the verb *hiqṭîr* can refer to making an offering go up in smoke (and thus not necessarily involving *qĕṭoret* incense; see Clements 2004), the immediate context refers

to the failure of former officiants to offer incense in Yahweh's sanctuary (*ûqĕṭōret lō' hiqṭîrû . . . baqqōdeš lē'lōhê yiśrā'ēl*; 2 Chr 29:7; cf. 2 Chr 28:24). Thus (*pace* Japhet 1993: 919) the offering of incense seems to be referred to in 2 Chr 29:11.

Yet scholars universally recognize the potential inconsistency, especially with 2 Chr 26:18. Thus Williamson (1982: 354) writes that the priests and Levites referred to in 2 Chr 29:4 must be in view throughout this section, despite the sole mention of the Levites in 2 Chr 29:5. He argues: "It would be unthinkable for the Chronicler, following his emphatic assertions in 26:16–21, to contemplate anyone else [other than priests] undertaking this duty." Japhet (1993: 919) argues similarly that this material is "addressed to the tribe of Levi as a whole" with the specific reference to *maqṭirîm* "directed at the priests among the 'Levites.'"

To return the discussion back in favor of the Levites offering incense, see Deut 33:8–11.

272. The sole exceptions that prove the rule are the cases of Moses in Exod 24:6–8 and King Ahaz in 2 Kgs 16:13. The Chronicler makes no mention of King Ahaz engaging in the cultic act.

273. Williamson (1982: 314, 322) calls Jehoida "the Chronicler's ideal priest." He is recorded as living to the age of 130 years. Due to his benevolence "for God and his house," the Chronicler has him "buried in the city of David among the kings" (2 Chr 24:15–16). Williamson writes about burial locations expressing personal assessment and concludes: "Clearly no greater honour is this respect was possible than that recorded here of Jehoida."

See too McConville's (1999: 82–87) advocacy of "the exceptional character of the reform of Jehoida" that goes unappreciated because "the emphasis in studies of DtrH has fallen too heavily on Josiah."

274. We have four references to the prophetic "consecration" of war activity (Mic 3:5; Jer 6:4; 22:7; Joel 4:9 [Eng 3:9]), which come as no surprise given solid biblical and extra-biblical evidence for the prophetic involvement in war. For the extra-biblical material, see the collection of prophetic texts from Mari and Neo-Assyria in Nissinen, Seow, and Ritner 2003 and Nissinen et al. 2019. On the cultic nature of war in biblical tradition, see Chapter Eight, pp. 463–464. On prophetic involvement with cult and cult places, see Nissinen 2013: 104–122.

275. On the history of the "prophet versus priest" antagonism hypothesis, see Zevit 2004. Ezekiel's dual priest/prophet identity construction is particularly fascinating in light of his refugee status where he finds himself unable to carry out the majority of his priestly duties due to the destruction of the Jerusalem Temple. These include the priest's ability to maintain his own purity as well as his role in sanctifying the community. See especially Ezekiel's objection to God's command to cook food over human dung due to its defiling nature (Ezek 4:14). For an insightful study of identity formation in the book of Ezekiel, examining the role of the body and bodily practices, see Liebermann (2019).

276. Petersen 2002: 6, 227–231; Overholt 1996: 24–68; Rofé 1988: 13–51.

277. Ackerman (2013: 175–178; 2016) writes about the ways in which an institutionalized and bureaucratized priesthood together with blood rituals and purity codes

(cf. Lev 12:1-8; 15:19-30) would have restricted the cultic agency of women. "The Leviticus purity laws would have significantly limited women's access to the Jerusalem temple during their reproductive years."

278. See Ackerman's (2016) discussion of the MT vs the LXX and DSS renderings of 1 Sam 1:25. In contrast to the MT, the latter two witnesses have Elkanah alone sacrificing (cf. 1 Sam 1:4).
279. Susan Ackerman (personal communication) sees the *ṣōbĕ'ōt*-women as guardian figures proving apotropaic protection within sacred space.
280. On this difficult "bridegroom of bloodshed" passage, see Propp 1999: 233-238. Ackerman (1998a: 92-102), building on the work of Benjamin Mazar, uses Zipporah's activites to suggest that Jael may also have been a cultic functionary.
281. See Ackerman 2008a: 136-141.
282. One the former, see pp. 626-629; on the latter, see the Conclusion, pp. 685-687. Ackerman (2013: 160-165) finds at least fourteen Phoenician inscriptions that document the presence of priestesses to which she adds numerous iconographic representations. Ackerman (2013: 175-178), building on Nancy Jay's theoretical work on blood sacrifice within patrilineal societies, suggests that the activities of Phoenician priestesses did not include blood sacrifice, which remained an exclusively male rite.
283. Chavalas (2014: 2-3) blames William Robertson Smith for uncritically promoting the idea of sacred prostitution among Semitic deities that was then popularized by Sir James Frazer's *Golden Bough* (cf. Assante 2003). See too Nyberg 2008 and DeGrado 2018: 25.
284. Dion (1981: 44, 47) remarks: "Whenever . . . *qādēš* turns up in Kings, the parallel place in Chronicles is sure to bypass it." He attributes this to the "deliberate suppression of particularly abhorrent memories." Dion (1981: 45, 47) also analyzes the various LXX manuscripts and concludes that the Greek translators are so "in the dark when confronted with the word *qādēš*" that the institution "was apparently little known among the Jews of the last two centuries B.C."
285. Van der Toorn (1989) does find cultic prostitution in a narrow sense, describing women who engaged in the practice as it was economically related to the temple. Specifically, women engaged in prostitution in order to pay off religious vows that they had made without their husband's approval. Cf. Nyberg 2008: 313.
286. Much of this has to do with pejoratively defining "the other." Westenholz (1989: 248) writes: "To the Hebrew author, the pagan priestess must be a harlot, and vice versa, the harlot must have been a pagan priestess."
287. In Ugaritic administrative texts, the *qdšm* are royal functionaries who are often listed next to *khnm*, "priests." A single ritual text (KTU 1.112.21) notes how a *qdš* can function as a singer. See Gruber 1986; Westenholz 1989: 249-250; Pardee 2002a: 239-240.
288. Thus for DeGrado (2018: 32-34), what we have in Hos 4:14 (that juxtaposes *zōnôt* and *qĕdēšôt*) contains a "double valence" that she translates: "For it is the men who go off with sluts, and with the *qdešot* functionaries they sacrifice."

289. Gammie (1989: 41–44) defends the need for biblical scholars and historians of religion to appreciate both theology and the social sciences.
290. In some respects, such a self-proclamation is equivalent to Yahweh's speaking of his mighty holiness in the first-person prophetic discourse (e.g., Isa 43:14–17).
291. Ezek 36:23 and 39:25–27 doubly emphasize holiness in adding that Yahweh's self-display of his redemptive holiness is tied to the sanctifying of his holy name. In one instance Ezekiel does mix in cultic vocabulary with his holy redemption. In Ezekiel 20:41, Yahweh's manifesting of his holy power (*niqdaštî*) is prefaced by a remark about accepting the people "as a pleasing/appeasing odor" (*rêyaḥ nîḥōaḥ*), on which see Chapter Seven, p. 288.
292. For an introductory survey, see Kang 2008. Other works addressing the biblical text include Cohn 1981; Bokser 1985; Gorman 1990; Levine 1997; Japhet 1998; Biran 1998; Zevit 2001; Gittlen 2002; Berquist and Camp 2007, 2008; George 2009; Davis 2013; and Flebbe 2016.
293. Noted works include Haran 1978; Gorman 1990; Jensen 1992; George 2009; and Calaway 2010.
294. There are far too many theoretical works to list here. A short list includes van der Leeuw 1938; Eliade 1949; Lefebvre 1974, 1991; Soja 1989, 1996; Smith 1978, 1987b, 1993; Gorman 1990; Scott and Simpson-Housley 1991; Branham 1993; Chidester 1994; Kunin 1998; Flanagan 1999; Knott 2005; Tweed 2006; Kort 2007; George 2007; Berquist and Camp 2008; and George 2009: 17–44. The last of these provides a nice overview of spatial theory.
295. For Israel's perceptions of space, see Faust's (2010) remarks about the *consistency* of "bounded landscapes" with boundary walls differentiating "inside" cultured space (with living human settlements) from the "outside" and nature (cultivated fields, grazing areas, burial sites). Faust (2010, 2017, 2019) also challenges the consensus of historians of Israelite religion regarding the prevalence of Israelite and Judan temples. Faust (2019: 1) argues "that cultic activity in temples was the exception rather than the norm and that typical Israelite cult was practiced in the household and in other, non-temple settings."

For additional archaeological studies, see Mierse 2012 and his bibliography. Special note should be made of those studies that attempt to wed theory, text and material culture. A good example is found in Davis' (2013) look at Tell Dan in its northern cultic context.
296. For statistics, see Kornfeld 2003: 527. On holiness in Sirach and the Wisdom of Solomon, see Gammie 1989: 153–172.
297. This verse is commonly translated as an expression of piety regarding Job not "denying" (cf. the meaning of the verb *kḥd* in Rabbinic Hebrew) God's precepts (thus RSV, NRSV, NIV). Some scholars go so far as deleting it as a pious gloss. Driver and Gray (1950: 61) refer to Job 23:11–12 and remark that Job is insisting that he has "not disowned or disregarded God's (moral commands)."

For Job 6:10 being a statement of challenge, Seow (2013: 460) writes: "Job, it seems, sees himself as a theological whistleblower. He dares to expose the hard truth, even if it is theologically dangerous to do so, and he takes comfort in that fact."

Habel (1985: 147) writes more forcefully: "From Job's vantage point the decisions of God relating to his life are ugly, unfair, and unholy. For these decisions to be designated the decrees of the "Holy One" is clearly satirical."

298. While the general "absurd" meaning of Qoh 8:10 is agreed upon and matches what we find in Qoh 8:14 soon to follow, regrettably the specific meaning of the passage is hard to determine. For example, Fox (1989: 249–251; 1999: 282–284), followed by Seow (1997: 284–286), argues that the absurdity has to do with a proper burial being given to the wicked (who are eulogized within sacred space and given a funeral procession to the gravesite) in contrast to neglecting ("forgetting" < MT's *yištakkĕḥû*) the corpses of the righteous (cf. Job 21:32–33). For comparison, Schoors (2013: 625) has the wicked being unjustly "praised" (reconstructing instead *yišta<u>bb</u>ĕḥû* < LXX) for their hypocritical devotion" within sacred space.

299. Blau 2010: 272; Fox 2009: 855; Burnett 2001: 21–24; Waltke and O'Connor 1990: 122–124; GKC §124 g–i. One could also reanalyze *qĕdōšîm* as a singular with enclitic *m* (*qādôš-m*).

300. For a broad study of fear in the ancient Near East (esp. the expression "fear not!"), see Nissinen 2003.

Conclusion

1. One could certainly choose Asherah, yet since the discovery of the Kuntillet ʿAjrud finds in the mid-1970s, she has not lacked for discussion, dominating the scholarly landscape. See Chapter One, note 2.
2. It is still common to find scholars (e.g., Schmitt 2013: 224) arguing that "LBA evidence paints a picture of [ʿAthtartu/ʿAštart as] a second-tier goddess with no prominent functions in mythology."
3. Debates over the etymology of the name ʿAthtartu/ʿAštart are as complicated as any of those regarding the name Yahweh. Brief treatments can be found in Anthonioz 2014: 125 and Smith 2014b: 33 n. 3. The fullest treatment is that of Wilson-Wright (2016: 16–25).
4. In this passage the Philistine "Temple of *ʿštrt*" (as a single building) is best understood as being devoted to the singular deity ʿaštart rather than to the Masoretes' plural *ʿštrwt/ʿaštārôt*. Cf. LXX, McCarter 1980a: 441; Smith 2002a: 127.
5. Hadley (1996: 132; 2007) favors calling this process "de-personalizing" or "de-deification." Smith (2014a: 323; 2014b: 79) uses the terminology "genericization." See too the earlier work by Delcor (1974: 14), who concludes that we have here "une manière de démythiser des croyances profondément enracinées dans l'âme des paysans israélites."
6. The present treatment covers only ʿAštart and not Dagan and Shagar, for which see Hadley's (1996, 2007) analysis. On these three deities occurring together in the Emar *zukru* festival, see note 10.

   Though it is less attested, Hadley (2007: 169–170) suggests that the reference to "new wine" (*tîrôš*) in Deut 7:13, 28:51 may designate a fourth Canaanite deity based on the Ugaritic presence of Tirāṯu in a deity list (KTU 102.9) and (partially reconstructed) in a ritual where he receives an ewe sacrifice (KTU 1.39.16). Pardee (2002a: 285) asserts that Tirāṯu is "certainly a wine-god."

7. With the singular referents *Dagan and *Shagar in Deut 7:13, it is likely that ʿštrt was originally pointed as singular (ʿaštart) and not the plural (ʿaštārōt) of the Masoretes' understanding. Similarly, see the "Temple of *ʿštrt" in 1 Sam 31:10 in note 4.

8. A full analysis of the goddess would necessarily have to evaluate the many treatments, including Weinfeld 1972a; Olyan 1988; Ackerman 1989, 1992, 1998a: 117; 2008a: 142–145; Houtman 1999; Ellis 2009; and Smith 2002a: 126–132; 2014b: 81–82.

9. See, for example, Christian and Schmitt 2013a; Sugimoto 2014; and Wilson-Wright 2016.

10. "Aštartu of Battle" also appears in the longer *zukru* festival, though with the variant "Aštartu of *the man* of Battle" (^{d}Iš$_8$-tár LÚ *ša taḫāzi*), referencing the goddess's support of soldiers (see Emar 373+, line 15). Though Aštartu is mentioned here, the four primary deities of the *zukru* are Dagan *bēl bukkari* ("Lord of the first yield [of animals?]," ^{d}NIN.URTA, Šaššabêttu, and Šaggar. (See Chapter Ten, note 153.) Note how the three reconstructed deities in the Deuteronomic idiom mentioned earlier (Aštart, Dagan and Šagar) are all attested here in the longer *zukru* festival.

11. New Kingdom Egypt appropriated six primary Syro-Palestinian deities. In addition to Astarte, we also find Anat, Baal, Hauron, Qedeshet, and Reshep. Standard works on these Levantine deities in Egypt include Helck 1966 and Stadelmann 1967, which now need to be updated with Zivie-Coche 1994, 2011; Cornelius 2004; Schneider 2003, 2006; Tazawa 2009, 2014; and Wilson-Wright 2016: 27–70.

For the prevalence of Astarte in the Eighteenth and Nineteenth Dynasties, see Tazawa 2009: 83, 113, table 11. For the various media documenting iconographic and epigraphic attestations of Egyptian Astarte, see Tazawa 2009: 83, 104, table 10. For the geographic breadth of Astarte worship, from northern to southern Egypt, see Tazawa 2009: 83, 109, map 5. For the complicated relationships of Egyptian Astarte with Anat, Qedeshet, and Hathor, see Tazawa 2009: 163–165; 2014: 111–123.

12. See Clemens 2001: 380–381. Cf. too the mention of a house/temple in KTU 1.116.8–10 that Pardee (2002a: 93) suggests "could be either the royal palace or the temple of ʿAṯtartu." Consider also how twice "ʿAṯtartu of the Steppe Land" is described as participating in a royal "entry ritual" that typically involved the procession from one temple to another (discussed later).

Cf. too the mention of a *kunaḫu* sanctuary in RS 17.22+, 17.87.21–23; Smith 2014a: 185–186; 2014b: 38–39; Wilson-Wright 2016: 113.

13. See the preliminary publications of RIH 98/02 (KTU 1.180) by Pardee (2007a) and Bordreuil, Hawley, and Pardee (2010).

14. For ʿAthtartu's other associations with incantatory texts, see KTU 1.100.20; KTU 1.107.39; KTU 1.179:18 (RS 92.2016); Smith 2014a: 186–187; 2014b: 40–41; and Wilson-Wright 2016: 67–68. Schmitt (2013: 221, 225) and Tazawa (2014: 110; cf. 2009: 94–95, docs. 44, 46; EA 23) comment on Egyptian Astarte's association with apotropaic magic. See too Mathys' (2008) analysis of ʿAštart's role in the so-called

Magische Qaudrate, four fragmentary Phoenician marble inscriptions of the fourth century BCE from the Phoenician sanctuary of Bostan esh-Sheikh near Sidon.
15. For a new edition of KTU 1.92, see Pardee 2008. Smith (2014a: 194–195; 2014b: 54) and Wilson-Wright (2016: 137–138) also document Aštartu's hunting capabilities at Emar.
16. Taʾutka (Šauška), the Hurrian equivalent of ʿAthtartu, appears throughout the text. Cf. EA 23, where a statue of the goddess Šauška/Ishtar (ᵈINANNA) of Nineveh is sent to Nimmureya (Amenhotep III), the king of Egypt, by Tushratta, the king of Mitanni.
17. See Chapter Nine, pp. 499–500. Waters (2015: 151–163) surveys other Ugaritic threshing floor passages that have a loose connection to sacred space (e.g., the presence of the *rapiʾuma* at threshing floors for ʾIlu's banquet in KTU 1.20–22), although none of these connections are as explicitly cultic as KTU 1.116.1.
18. Cf. DULAT 2003: 807–809; Heltzer 1976; 1978; 1999: 425–427, 446, 450–451; McGeough 2007.
19. Rollefson (2007: 102; cf. Akkermans and Schwartz 2003: 72–73) underscores the "surprising array of animals in hyperarid deserts" that could be hunted, yet "due to their low densities, they are generally not dependable food sources." Mythologically, KTU 1.23.68 describes how hunger forces "the gracious gods" to hunt for food in the steppe land (called both *šd* and *mdbr*).
20. On ʿAthtartu-*ḫurri*, see Wilson-Wright 2016: 115–120.
21. Cf. KTU 1.112.6–8, which mentions the king's sons and daughters going up seven times to the "*ḫmn* sanctuary," followed by the divine statues doing likewise.
22. Similarly, both Smith (2014a: 186–187; 2014b: 43–44, 76) and Wilson-Wright (2016: 108–120, esp. 114–116) emphasize ʿAthtartu of the Field /Steppe Land as "a divine guarantor of treaties and oaths." Here too, such a role need not deny the goddess's agrarian nature, as the commodities associated with ʿAthtartu of the Field/Steppe Land (esp. blue and red wool and linen textiles) played a major role in international tribute (e.g., KTU 3.1//RS 17.227, RS 17.382+, 380) and commerce (cf. Heltzer 1999: 439–447; McGeough 2007: 324–332).
23. Cf. Pardee 2000: 334–335; 2002a: 69–70; Smith 2014a: 185–186; 2014b: 39; Wilson-Wright 2016: 112–113.
24. KTU 1.79 and 1.80 were both found in the Royal Palace. For *gt* texts, see Heltzer 1999: 425–426 and McGeough 2007: 130, 376–377.
25. On family, household, and local religion at Ugarit, see Lewis 2008a and Chapter Eight, pp. 474–477. The "house/family sanctuary" in KTU 1.80.2 is that of an individual (ʿUbbinniyana), while the "house/local sanctuary" in KTU 1.79.8 involves a local assembly of some sort (*bt qbṣ*). Both texts describe a religious officiant by the name of Ṣitqānu. In one text he sacrifices (*dbḥ*) seemingly a kid (*gdy*) to the god Rashpu (1.79.8), while in the other text he slaughters (*tbḥ*) a ewe and a ram, yet without mention of any deity as recipient.
26. Wilson-Wright 2016: 112–113, following Pardee 2000: 334–335. Contrast del Olmo Lete 1999: 88–89, which needlessly minimizes the rural nature of this text.
27. For text and translation of KTU 4.182, see McGeough 2011: 130–133. For detailed analysis, see Clemens 2001: 356–370.

28. See Matoïan and Vita 2014, 2009 on the vital importance of wool production for the economy of Ugarit, as well as McGeough 2007: 119–121, 168–169, 210–211. See too Rowe 1995 on the *maqqadu* "grazing tax" paid (in sheep and goats) to the king for use of royal pasture land. For sorting out what can be known about the varied and confusing textile terminology used at Ugarit, see Vita 2010.
29. Rarely have past scholars nominated ʿAthtartu as this Mistress of Animals, yet see Pope 1965a: 251.
30. For bibliography on Figure C.2, see Lewis 2005a: 72 and Cornelius 2004: 110–111.
31. For bibliography on Figure C.3, see Cornelius 2004: 109.
32. Bloch-Smith (2014: 179) mentions the military presence at the shrine to Astarte at Mitzpe Yammim, a sixth-/fifth-century BCE Tyrian outpost in northern Israel (with a fortified watchtower). Astarte is mentioned in a secondary inscription on a bronze situla originally made in Egypt (see Berlin and Frankel 2012: 46, 50, 59, 61–64 and Frankel and Ventura 1998: 46–49). An individual presents this votive offering due to the goddess "hearing his voice."

    Should one desire an explicitly articulated Phoenician military deity, see Baʿal ʿOz (the Lord of Might) in fourth-century BCE Kition. This appropriately named deity gives "[po]wer and military victory" ([ʿ]z wnṣḥt) to his chosen king and people over their enemies. See KAI 288 and Mosca 2009.
33. For a full list of independent occurrences of the name ʿAštart in the epigraphic record as well as in onomastica, see Bonnet 1996: 165–169. For archaeological summaries with additional bibliography, see Bloch-Smith 2014 and Esteban and Pellin 2016.
34. For the primary text, see Dupont-Sommer 1970: 15 and Yon 2004: 188, 193, 212–213 (#1100 = D21; figure 17). For additional discussion, see Karageorghis 1976: 105; Markoe 2000: 120–121; and Bloch-Smith 2014: 170.

    The description of the offering for the individual in lines 2–3 is broken: [ʾ]yt PN š wk[bš ʾt š]ʿr z. Yet the mention of the tonsure ritual is clear: PN šʿr z glb. For similar tonsure rituals together with hair offerings, compare *De Dea Syria*, 60, as noted already by Karageorghis (1976: 105) and Bloch-Smith (2014: 170). On tonsure regulations for Aaronid priests and Nazirites, see Chapter Ten, pp. 630–631, 634.

    The *realia* of sacrifice at the Kition Kathari Temple I include, according to Bloch-Smith (2014: 172), "large numbers of sheep and lamb bones (some carbonized), plus cattle, fallow deer, fish, and birds."
35. For alternative readings of this most difficult text, see Peckham 2014: 134–135, which sees personal vows being offered along with ritual weeping.
36. Actually there are two texts here—the so-called temple tariff inscriptions—with differing scribal hands. See KAI 37 A and B.
37. Peckham (1968: 324) suggests that the occasion "commemorates the building of the temple of Astarte and implicitly describes a ritual, which may or may not have been celebrated annually, associated with that event." On gendered roles in Phoenician cult, see Ackerman 2013: 173–178.
38. Another (amuletic, silver) text, though unprovenanced, describes an ʿAštart cult at sixth-century BCE Byblos involving an individual's familial vows for his ancestral house (bt ʾbyʾ) together with the provisions of cult (an altar, animal sacrifices,

and money) to be carried out by a named "chief priest of the temple of the goddess ʿAštart" (*rb khnm bt ʾlm ʿštrt*). The Byblian king Šipitbaʿal is listed as "the guarantor" (*hnṣr*) of the vow. See Peckham 2014: 382–383, following Lemaire.
39. Alternatively, Ackerman (2013: 172) suggests that ʾUmmîʿaštart "may have come into the title 'priestess' by virtue of her marriage to the 'priest,' Tabnit."
40. If the priestly office was hereditary, then perhaps Eshmunazor II was also a "priest of ʿAštart" like his grandfather and father, and yet his mother chose to keep quiet about it on his coffin inscription!
41. See Puech 1994: 52–61, 71 and Bonnet 1996: 30–31, 157.
42. See Aufrecht 1989: 145–148. I am indebted to Smith (2014b: 79) and Bloch-Smith (2014: 183 n. 59), who previously noted this inscription.
43. See Mitzpe Yammim in note 32.
44. Granted, there is no explicit reference to Manasseh and Amon worshipping ʿAštart, with the DtrH instead concentrating on the goddess Asherah (2 Kgs 21:3, 7; cf. 2 Chr 33:3, 19).
45. On the two Taanach cult stands, see Chapter Seven, pp. 315–317, 323–325, 411–415. Smith (2014a: 196, 205–208; 2014b: 56, 73–74, 78) also notes the goddess's name (written in hieroglyphics) in a Late Bronze Age seal from Bethel, and he suggests that the goddess is being referenced in Old Canaanite arrowheads mentioning "the servant of the Lion."
46. As noted in Chapter Nine, note 6, Emar provides the exception to the rule. And yet while the Emar king has a limited active cultic role in the *zukru*, the festival nonetheless underscores royal patronage and benevolence.
47. See Ackerman 1989: 109–124 (= 1999: 21–32); 1992: 5–35; 2003: 461–463; 2008a: 141–145; cf. 2013.
48. Though Jeremiah's response in Jer 44:25 is addressed to men and women (cf. 44:19–20), note the series of third-person feminine plural verbs in Jer 44:25 (*tĕdabbērnâ, tāqîmnâ, taʿăśênâ*).
49. See Chapter Six, pp. 261–262, on how different genres (myths, deities lists, ritual texts) give us different pictures of the "mythological" (or "narrative") pantheon, the "canonical" (or "synthetic") pantheon, and the "functional" pantheon.
50. Generalizations such as what we find in Cogan and Tadmor 1988: 294 need to be better nuanced: "Josiah's act of cultic reform . . . [is] presented in terms and style almost identical to that of Deuteronomy."

    As the reader will see, on the Deuteronomy material, I am indebted to earlier insightful studies by Delcor (1974) and Hadley (1996, 2007).
51. A possible exception is the mention of "[the] Baal of Peor" (*baʿal-pĕʿôr*) in Deut 4:3, on which see Hadley (2007: 173–174). Deut 32:6b–9 constitutes a special case, as any older (El-)Elyon traditions have been fused with those of Yahweh (cf. Ps 82). See Chapter Four, pp. 90–95, and Chapter Nine, pp. 565–569.
52. The rhetoric used in these anti-image polemics has been well studied (e.g., analyses of the *Bilderverbot* by Dohmen [1987, 2012] and others), and especially in light of the *mīs pî* image texts from Mesopotamia (Dick 1999b; Walker and Dick 2001). See Chapters Five and Seven.

NOTES 903

53. For a listing of all the passages regarding "detestation" (*šiqqûṣ*), "abomination" (*tôʿēbâ*), "filth" (*gillul*), and "man-made" (*maʿăśēh yĕdê ʾādām*) in Deuteronomy and the DtrH that Weinfeld labels "Deuteronomic phraseology," see Weinfeld 1972b: 323-324.
54. The word *šāwʾ* can designate worthlessness (being inconsequential, next to nothing) or falsity (that which is empty or lacks substance; Hos 10:4) as well as something that results in nothingness (Hos 12:12; Job 15:31b) or is done for no reason (in vain), as seen in Jer 2:30; 4:30; 6:29; 46:11.
55. Using Deuteronomy 6:13 ("Yahweh your deity you must fear, and him you must serve, and by his name you must swear"), Propp (2006: 174) astutely observes: "A deity is acknowledged and reified by invocation and imprecation no less than by sacrifice." Thus the inability to invoke a deity by name negates any conceptual reification.
56. See too McClellan's (2011: 73-75, 78-79) study of deity in LXX Deuteronomy, where he argues (especially due to LXX Deut 4:19, 17:3 and 32:43) for a de-deification process whereby astral deities become "non-sentient astral bodies." For the LXX translator, Yahweh possesses "ontological uniqueness," with "the sons of the gods" lowered to the "entirely separate and derivative class" of angels.
57. Such rhetoric is similar to how the eighth-century BCE Hosea asserts that Yahweh (and not Canaanite Baal) is Israel's true lord (*baʿal*), who provided agricultural bounty (grain, wine, oil, flax) as well as sheep and goats (wool) that Israel mistakenly used in the Baal cult (Hosea 2:10-11 [Eng 2:8-9]; cf. Hosea 2:18-19 [Eng 2:16-17]).
58. An exception might be studies (e.g., Darby 2014: 367-397, 404-405) of the way in which Judean pillar figurines were used in healing rituals and apotropaically. Though past missteps of analyzing the figurines included an "Astarte Phase" (Darby 2014: 35-36), the goddess may hypothetically have been associated with healing and protection. Yet at present we have no explicit textual material to support this hypothesis.
59. For the primary texts, see Cammarosano 2018.
60. In addition to combining divine attributes, the mourner's Kaddish (in Aramaic) contains beautiful alliteration and assonance, so it is no surprise that it is used elsewhere in daily prayer books:

> *yitbārak wĕyištabbaḥ wĕyitpāʾar wĕyitrômam wĕyitnaśśēʾ wĕyithaddār wĕyitʿalleh wĕyithallāl šĕmēh dĕqudšāʾ bĕrik hûʾ lĕʿēllāʾ min kol birkātāʾ wĕšîrātāʾ tušbĕḥātāʾ wĕneḥĕmātāʾ daʾ ămîrān bĕʿālmāʾ wĕʾimrûʾ ʾāmēn*

> Blessed, praised, glorified, exalted, extolled, mighty, upraised, and lauded be the Name of the Holy One. Blessed is He. Beyond any blessing and song, praise and consolation that are uttered in the world. Now say: Amen.

The Lord's Prayer (used corporately and privately due to Jesus' directive in Matthew 6:9//Luke 11:2) also combines attributes, notably starting with divine parentage before turning to divine kingship:

> Our Father, who art in heaven, hallowed be thy name; thy kingdom come; thy will be done; on earth as it is in heaven. Give us this day our daily bread. And

forgive us our trespasses, as we forgive those who trespass against us. And lead us not into temptation; but deliver us from evil. [For thine is the kingdom, the power and the glory, for ever and ever. Amen.]

Note how both of these prayers continue the long-standing use of the divine Name to encapsulate divine essence. (See the discussion of Deuteronomic/Deuteronomistic Name Theology in Chapter Seven.)

Works Cited

Abba, R. 1977. "Priests and Levites in Deuteronomy." *Vetus Testamentum* 27 (3): 257–267.
Aberbach, M., Smolar, L. 1967. "Aaron, Jeroboam, and the Golden Calves." *Journal of Biblical Literature* 86 (2): 129–140.
Abernethy, A. T. 2015. "God as Teacher in Psalm 25." *Vetus Testamentum* 65: 1–13.
Abou-Assaf, A. 1990. *Der Temple von 'Ain Dara*. Mainz am Rhein: Philip von Zabern.
Abou-Assaf, A. n.d. *The Temple of 'Ain Dara*. Aleppo: Aleppo Museum.
Achenbach, R. 1999. "Levitische Priester und Leviten im Deuteronomium: Überlegungen zur sog. 'Levitisierung' des Priestertums." *Zeitschrift für altorientalische und biblische Rechtsgeschichte* 5: 285–309.
Ackerman, R. 1991. *The Myth and Ritual School: J. G. Frazer and the Cambridge Ritualists*. New York: Garland.
Ackerman, R. 2002. *The Myth and Ritual School: J. G. Frazer and the Cambridge Ritualists*. 2nd ed. New York: Routledge.
Ackerman, S. 1989. "'And the Women Knead Dough': The Worship of the Queen of Heaven in Sixth-Century Judah." In *Gender and Difference in Ancient Israel*, edited by Day, P. L., 109–124. Minneapolis: Fortress.
Ackerman, S. 1992. *Under Every Green Tree: Popular Religion in Sixth-Century Judah*. Atlanta: Scholars Press.
Ackerman, S. 1993. "The Queen Mother and the Cult in Ancient Israel." *Journal of Biblical Literature* 112 (3): 385–401.
Ackerman, S. 1998a. *Warrior, Dancer, Seductress, Queen: Women in Judges and Biblical Israel*. New York: Doubleday.
Ackerman, S. 1998b. "Isaiah." In *Women's Bible Commentary*, expanded ed., edited by Newsom, C. A., Ringe, S. H., 169–177. Louisville: Westminster John Knox.
Ackerman, S. 2003. "At Home with the Goddess." In *Symbiosis, Symbolism, and the Power of the Past: Canaan, Ancient Israel, and Their Neighbors from the Late Bronze Age Through Roman Palaestina*, edited by Dever, W. G., Gitin, S., 455–468. Winona Lake: Eisenbrauns.
Ackerman, S. 2006. "Women and the Worship of Yahweh in Ancient Israel." In *Confronting the Past: Archaeological and Historical Essays on Ancient Israel in Honor of William G. Dever*, edited by Gitin, S., Wright, J. E., Dessel, J. P., 189–197. Winona Lake: Eisenbrauns.
Ackerman, S. 2008a. "Household Religion, Family Religion, and Women's Religion in Ancient Israel." In *Household and Family Religion in Antiquity*, edited by Bodel, J. P., Olyan, S. M., 127–158. Malden: Blackwell.
Ackerman, S. 2008b. "Asherah, the West Semitic Goddess of Spinning and Weaving?" *Journal of Near Eastern Studies* 67 (1): 1–30.
Ackerman, S. 2013. "The Mother of Eshmunazor, Priest of Astarte: A Study of Her Cultic Role." *Die Welt des Orients* 43 (2): 158–178.
Ackerman, S. 2016. "Women in Ancient Israel and the Hebrew Bible." In *Oxford Research Encyclopedia of Religion*, 1–26.

Ackerman, S., Carter, CE., Nakhai, B. A., eds. 2015. *Celebrate Her for the Fruit of Her Hands: Essays in Honor of Carol L. Meyers*. Winona Lake: Eisenbrauns.

Adamthwaite, M. R. 2001. *Late Hittite Emar: The Chronology, Synchronisms, and Sociopolitical Aspects of a Late Bronze Age Fortress Town*. Louvain: Peeters.

Adrom, F., Müller, M. 2017. "The Tetragrammaton in Egyptian Sources—Facts and Fiction." In *The Origins of Yahwism*, edited by van Oorschot, J., Witte, M., 93–113. Berlin: de Gruyter.

Aharoni, M. 1993. "Arad: The Israelite Citadels." In *New Encyclopedia of Archaeological Excavations in the Holy Land*, edited by Stern, E., Vol. 1, 82–87. Jerusalem: Israel Exploration Society and Carta.

Aharoni, M., Rainey, A. F. 1985. "On 'The Israelite Fortress at Arad.'" *Bulletin of the American Schools of Oriental Research* 258: 73–74.

Aharoni, Y. 1966. "Hebrew Ostraca from Tel Arad." *Israel Exploration Journal* 16 (1): 1–7.

Aharoni, Y. 1967. "Excavations at Tel Arad: Preliminary Report on the Second Season, 1963." *Israel Exploration Journal* 17: 233–249.

Aharoni, Y. 1968. "Arad: Its Inscriptions and Temple." *Biblical Archaeologist* 31 (1): 1–32.

Aharoni, Y. 1982. *The Archaeology of the Land of Israel: From the Prehistoric Beginnings to the End of the First Temple Period*. Philadelphia: Westminster.

Aharoni, Y., Naveh, J. 1981. *Arad Inscriptions*. Jerusalem: Israel Exploration Society.

Aḥituv, S. 1984. *Canaanite Toponyms in Ancient Egyptian Documents*. Jerusalem: Magnes Press.

Aḥituv, S. 1992. *Handbook of Ancient Hebrew Inscriptions* [Hebrew]. Jerusalem: Bialik.

Aḥituv, S. 2005. *HaKetav VeHaMiktav: Handbook of Ancient Inscriptions from the Land of Israel and the Kingdoms Beyond the Jordan from the Period of the First Commonwealth*. Jerusalem: Mosad Byalik.

Aḥituv, S. 2008. *Echoes from the Past: Hebrew and Cognate Inscriptions from the Biblical Period*. Jerusalem: Carta.

Aḥituv, S. 2012. "A Rejoinder to Nadav Na'aman's 'A New Appraisal of the Silver Amulets from Ketef Hinnom.'" *Israel Exploration Journal* 62 (2): 223–232.

Aḥituv, S. 2014. "Notes on the Kuntillet 'Ajrud Inscriptions." In *"See, I Will Bring a Scroll Recounting What Befell Me" (Ps 40:8): Epigraphy and Daily Life from the Bible to the Talmud: Dedicated to the Memory of Professor Hanan Eshel*, edited by Eshel, E., Levin, Y., 29–38. Göttingen: Vandenhoeck & Ruprecht.

Aḥituv, S., Eshel, E., Meshel, Z. 2012. "The Inscriptions." In *Kuntillet 'Ajrud (Horvat Teman): An Iron Age II Religious Site on the Judah-Sinai Border*, by Meshel, Z., 73–142. Jerusalem: Israel Exploration Society.

Ahlström, G. W. 1970–1971. "An Israelite God Figurine from Hazor." *Orientalia Suecana* 19–20: 54–62.

Ahlström, G. W. 1975. "An Israelite God Figurine, Once More." *Vetus Testamentum* 25: 106–109.

Ahlström, G. W. 1984. "The Travels of the Ark: A Religio-Political Composition." *Journal of Near Eastern Studies* 43 (2): 141–149.

Ahlström, G. W. 1986. *Who Were the Israelites?* Winona Lake: Eisenbrauns.

Ahlström, G. W. 1990. "The Bull Figurine from Dhahrat et-Tawileh." *Bulletin of the American Schools of Oriental Research* 280: 77–82.

Ahlström, G. W. 1991. "The Role of Archaeological and Literary Remains in Reconstructing Israel's History." In *The Fabric of History: Text, Artifact and Israel's Past*, edited by Edelman, D. V., 116–141. Sheffield: JSOT Press.

Ahlström, G. W. 1993. *The History of Ancient Palestine from the Palaeolithic Period to Alexander's Conquest*. Sheffield: JSOT Press.
Akkermans, P. M. M. G., Schwartz, G. M. 2003. *The Archaeology of Syria: From Complex Hunter-Gatherers to Early Urban Societies (c. 16,000–300 BC)*. Cambridge: Cambridge University.
Albertz, R. 1978. *Persönliche Frömmigkeit und offizielle Religion: Religionsinterner Pluralismus in Israel und Babylon*. Stuttgart: Calwer Verlag.
Albertz, R. 1994. *A History of Israelite Religion in the Old Testament Period*. London: SCM Press.
Albertz, R. 2008. "Family Religion in Ancient Israel and Its Surroundings." In *Household and Family Religion in Antiquity*, edited by Bodel, J. P., Olyan, S. M., 89–112. Malden: Blackwell.
Albertz, R., Schmitt, R. 2012. *Family and Household Religion in Ancient Israel and the Levant*. Winona Lake: Eisenbrauns.
Albrektson, B. 1968. "On the Syntax of ʾehyeh ʾăšer ʾehyeh in Exodus 3:14." In *Words and Meanings: Essays Presented to David Winton Thomas*, edited by Ackroyd, P. R., Lindars, B., 15–28. Cambridge: Cambridge University.
Albright, W. F. 1920. "The Babylonian Temple-Tower and the Altar of Burnt-Offering." *Journal of Biblical Literature* 39: 137–142.
Albright, W. F. 1924. "Contributions to Biblical Archaeology and Philology." *Journal of Biblical Literature* 43 (3): 363–393.
Albright, W. F. 1933. *The Archaeology of Palestine and the Bible*. 2nd ed. New York: Fleming H. Revell Co.
Albright, W. F. 1935. "The Names Shaddai and Abram." *Journal of Biblical Literature* 54 (4): 173–204.
Albright, W. F. 1940. *From the Stone Age to Christianity: Monotheism and the Historical Process*. Baltimore: Johns Hopkins Press.
Albright, W. F. 1944. "The Oracles of Balaam." *Journal of Biblical Literature* 63: 207–233.
Albright, W. F. 1948. Review of B. N. Wambacq, *L'épithète divine Jahvé Sebaʾôt: Étude philologique, historique et exégétique*. *Journal of Biblical Literature* 67 (4): 377–381.
Albright, W. F. 1950–1951. "A Catalogue of Early Hebrew Lyric Poems (Psalm LXVIII)." *Hebrew Union College Annual* 23 (1): 1–39.
Albright, W. F. 1950a. "The Judicial Reforms of Jehoshaphat." In *Alexander Marx: Jubilee Volume on the Occasion of His Seventieth Birthday*, edited by Lieberman, S., 61–81. New York: Jewish Theological Seminary of America.
Albright, W. F. 1950b. "The Psalm of Habakkuk." In *Studies in Old Testament Prophecy*, edited by Rowley, H. H., 1–18. Edinburgh: T. & T. Clark.
Albright, W. F. 1957. *From the Stone Age to Christianity. Monotheism and the Historical Process*. 2nd ed. Garden City: Doubleday.
Albright, W. F. 1959. "Some Remarks on the Song of Moses in Deuteronomy XXXII." *Vetus Testamentum* 9: 339–346.
Albright, W. F. 1961. "The Role of the Canaanites in the History of Civilization." In *The Bible and the Ancient Near East: Essays in Honor of William Foxwell Albright*, edited by Wright, G. E., 438–487. Garden City: Doubleday.
Albright, W. F. 1963. "Jethro, Hobab and Reuel in Early Hebrew Tradition." *Catholic Biblical Quarterly* 25 (1): 1–11.
Albright, W. F. 1966a. *The Proto-Sinaitic Inscriptions and Their Decipherment*. Cambridge: Harvard University.

Albright, W. F. 1966b. *Archaeology, Historical Analogy and Early Biblical Tradition*. Baton Rouge: Louisiana State University.
Albright, W. F. 1968a. *Yahweh and the Gods of Canaan: A Historical Analysis of Two Contrasting Faiths*. Garden City: Doubleday.
Albright, W. F. 1968b. *Archaeology and the Religion of Israel*. 5th ed. Garden City: Doubleday.
Albright, W. F. 2006. *Archaeology and the Religion of Israel with New Introduction by Theodore J. Lewis*. Louisville: Westminster John Knox.
Allen, L. C. 1983. *Psalms 101–150*. Waco: Word Books.
Allen, L. C. 1994. *Ezekiel 1–19*. Waco: Word Books.
Allen, S. L. 2015. *The Splintered Divine*. Berlin: de Gruyter.
Alster, B. 1999. "Tiamat/Tehom." In *Dictionary of Deities and Demons in the Bible*, edited by van der Toorn, K., Becking, B., van der Horst, P. W., 867–869. 2nd ed. Leiden: Brill.
Alt, A. 1968. *Essays on Old Testament History and Religion*. New York: Anchor Books.
Altenmüller, H. 1975. "Bes." In *Lexikon der Ägyptologie*, edited by Otto, E., Helck, W., Westendorf, W., 720–724. Wiesbaden: Harrassowitz.
Altmann, P. 2011. "What Do the 'Levites in Your Gates' Have to Do with the 'Levitical Priests'? An Attempt at European-North American Dialogue on the Levites in the Deuteronomic Law Corpus." In *Levites and Priests in Biblical History and Tradition*, edited by Leuchter, M., Hutton, J. M., 135–154. Atlanta: Society of Biblical Literature.
Altmann, P. 2013. "Diet, Bronze and Iron Age." In *The Oxford Encyclopedia of the Bible and Archaeology*, 286–296. Oxford: Oxford University.
Amiet, P. 1960. "Notes sur le répertoire iconographique de Mari a l'époque du Palais." *Syria* 37 (3): 215–232.
Amiet, P. 1980. *Art of the Ancient Near East*. New York: H. N. Abrams.
Amiet, P. 1983. "Observations sur les 'Tablettes magiques' d'Arslan Tash." *Aula Orientalis* 1: 109.
Amiran, R. 1976. "The Lion Statue and the Libation Tray from Tell Beit Mirsim." *Bulletin of the American Schools of Oriental Research* 222: 29–40.
Amit, Y. 2000. *Hidden Polemics in Biblical Narrative*. Leiden: Brill.
Andersen, F. I. 1966. "The Socio-Juridical Background of the Naboth Incident." *Journal of Biblical Literature* 85: 46–57.
Andersen, F. I. 2001. *Habakkuk: A New Translation with Introduction and Commentary*. New York: Doubleday.
Andersen, F. I., Freedman, D. N. 1980. *Hosea: A New Translation with Introduction and Commentary*. Garden City: Doubleday.
Andersen, F. I., Freedman, D. N. 1989. *Amos: A New Translation with Introduction and Commentary*. New York: Doubleday.
Andersen, F. I., Freedman, D. N. 2000. *Micah: A New Translation with Introduction and Commentary*. New York: Doubleday.
Anderson, B. W. 1986. *Understanding the Old Testament*. Englewood Cliffs: Prentice-Hall.
Anderson, B. W. 1994. "The Slaying of the Fleeing, Twisting Serpent: Isaiah 27:1 in Context." In *Uncovering Ancient Stones: Essays in Memory of H. Neil Richardson*, edited by Hopfe, L. M., 3–15. Winona Lake: Eisenbrauns.
Anderson, G. A. 1987. *Sacrifices and Offerings in Ancient Israel: Studies in Their Social and Political Importance*. Atlanta: Scholars Press.
André, G. 1995. "kābas." In *Theological Dictionary of the Old Testament*, edited by Botterweck, G. J., Ringgren, H., Fabry, H., Vol. VII, 40–42. Grand Rapids: Eerdmans.

Anthonioz, S. 2014. "Astarte in the Bible and Her Relation to Asherah." In *Transformation of a Goddess: Ishtar, Astarte, Aphrodite*, edited by Sugimoto, D. T., 125–139. Fribourg: Academic Press Fribourg.
Ap-Thomas, D. 1966. "An Appreciation of Sigmund Mowinckel's Contribution to Biblical Studies." *Journal of Biblical Literature* 85 (3): 315–325.
Arav, R., Freund, R. A., Shroder, J. F. 2000. "Bethsaida Rediscovered. Long-Lost City Found North of Galilee Shore." *Biblical Archaeology Review* 26 (1): 44–56.
Archi, A. 1979. "The Epigraphic Evidence from Ebla and the Old Testament." *Biblica* 60 (4): 556–566.
Archi, A. 1981. "Further Concerning Ebla and the Bible." *Biblical Archaeologist* 44 (3): 145–154.
Archi, A. 1995. "Hittite and Hurrian Literatures: An Overview." In *Civilizations of the Ancient Near East*, edited by Sasson, J. M., Vol. IV, 2367–2377. New York: Scribner's.
Arnaud, D. 1986. *Recherches au pays d'Ashtata. Emar VI.3: Textes sumériens et accadiens*. Paris: Editions Recherche sur les Civilisations.
Arnaud, D. 1991. *Textes syriens de l'âge du bronze recent: sceaux hieroglyphiques Anatoliens de Syrie*. Sabadell: AUSA.
Arnold, B. T., Strawn, B. A. 2003. "*Beyāh šemô* in Psalm 68,5: A Hebrew Gloss to an Ugaritic Epithet?" *Zeitschrift für die alttestamentliche Wissenschaft* 115 (3): 428–432.
Asher-Greve, J., Westenholz, J. G. 2013. *Goddesses in Context: On Divine Powers, Roles, Relationships and Gender in Mesopotamian Textual and Visual Sources*. Fribourg: Academic Press.
Assante, J. 1998. "The kar.kid/ḫarimtu, Prostitute or Single Woman: A Reconsideration of the Evidence." *Ugarit-Forschungen* 30: 5–96.
Assante, J. 2003. "From Whore to Hierodule: The Historiographic Invention of Mesopotamian Sex Professionals." In *Ancient Art and Its Historiography*, edited by Donahue, A. A., Fullerton, M. D., 13–47. Cambridge: Cambridge University.
Assmann, J. 1983. *Sonnenhymnen in thebanischen Gräbern*. Mainz am Rhein: P. von Zabern.
Assmann, J. 1992. *Akhanyati's Theology of Light and Time*. Jerusalem: Israel Academy of Sciences and Humanities.
Assmann, J. 1997. *Moses the Egyptian: The Memory of Egypt in Western Monotheism*. Cambridge: Harvard University.
Assmann, J. 2008. *Of God and Gods: Egypt, Israel, and the Rise of Monotheism*. Madison: University of Wisconsin.
Aster, S. Z. 2006. "The Phenomenon of Divine and Human Radiance in the Hebrew Bible and in Northwest Semitic and Mesopotamian Literature: A Philological and Comparative Study." University of Pennsylvania.
Aster, S. Z. 2012. *The Unbeatable Light: Melammu and Its Biblical Parallels*. Münster: Ugarit-Verlag.
Aster, S. Z. 2015. "Ezekiel's Adaptation of Mesopotamien 'Melammu.'" *Die Welt des Orients* 45 (1): 10–21.
Astour, M. C. 1979. "Yahweh in Egyptian Topographic Lists." In *Festschrift Elmar Edel*, edited by Görg, M., Pusch, E. B., 17–34. Bamberg: M. Görg.
Athas, G. 2003. *The Tel Dan Inscription: A Reappraisal and a New Interpretation*. Sheffield: Sheffield Academic Press.
Attridge, H. W., Oden, R. A. 1981. *The Phoenician History*. Washington: Catholic Biblical Association of America.

Aufrecht, W. E. 1989. *A Corpus of Ammonite Inscriptions*. Lewiston: Mellen Press.
Aufrecht, W. E. 1999. "The Religion of the Ammonites." In *Ancient Ammon*, edited by MacDonald, B., Younker, R. W., 152–162. Leiden: Brill.
Avalos, H. 1995a. *Illness and Health Care in the Ancient Near East: The Role of the Temple in Greece, Mesopotamia, and Israel*. Atlanta: Scholars Press.
Avalos, H. 1995b. "Legal and Social Institutions in Canaan and Ancient Israel." In *Civilizations of the Ancient Near East*, edited by Sasson, J. M., Vol. I, 615–631. New York: Scribner's.
Avigad, N. 1987. "The Contribution of Hebrew Seals to an Understanding of Israelite Religion and Society." In *Ancient Israelite Religion: Essays in Honor of Frank Moore Cross*, edited by Miller, P. D., Hanson, P. D., McBride, S. D., 195–208. Philadelphia: Fortress.
Avigad, N., Sass, B. 1997. *Corpus of West Semitic Stamp Seals*. Jerusalem: Israel Exploration Society.
Avishur, Y. 1979. "Psalm 29: Canaanite or Hebrew?" In *Sefer Ben-Tsiyon Luria*, edited by Shazar, Z., 247–274. Jerusalem: Kiryat Sepher.
Avishur, Y. 1989. *Studies in Hebrew and Ugaritic Psalms*. Jerusalem: Magnes Press.
Avishur, Y. 1994. *Studies in Hebrew and Ugaritic Psalms*. 2nd ed. Jerusalem: Magnes Press.
Avishur, Y. 2000. *Phoenician Inscriptions and the Bible: Select Inscriptions and Studies in Stylistic and Literary Devices Common to the Phoenician Inscriptions and the Bible*. Tel Aviv–Jaffa: Archaeological Center Publication.
Avner, U. 1984. "Ancient Cult Sites in the Negev and Sinai Deserts." *Tel Aviv* 11: 115–131.
Avner, U. 1993. "Massebot Sites in the Negev and Sinai and Their Significance." In *Biblical Archaeology Today, 1990*, edited by Biran, A., Aviram, J., 166–181. Jerusalem: Israel Exploration Society.
Avner, U. 1996. "Masseboth in the Negev and Sinai and Their Interpretation" [Hebrew]. Hebrew University.
Avner, U. 2018. "Protohistoric Developments of Religion and Cult in the Negev Desert." *Tel Aviv* 45 (1): 23–62.
Avner, U., Arav, R., Filin, S., Nadel, D. 2016. "Three-Dimensional Documentation of Masseboth Sites in the 'Uvda Valley Area, Southern Negev, Israel." *Digital Applications in Archaeology and Cultural Heritage* 3 (1): 9–21.
Axelsson, L. E. 1987. *The Lord Rose Up from Seir: Studies in the History and Traditions of the Negev and Southern Judah*. Stockholm: Almquist & Wiksell.
Ayali-Darshan, N. 2010. "'The Bride of the Sea': The Traditions About Astarte and Yamm in the Ancient Near East." In *A Woman of Valor: Jerusalem Ancient Near Eastern Studies in Honor of Joan Goodnick Westenholz*, edited by Horowitz, W., 19–33. Madrid: Consejo Superior de Investigaciones Científicas.
Ayali-Darshan, N. 2014. "The Question of the Order of Job 26, 7–13 and the Cosmogonic Tradition of Zaphon." *Zeitschrift für die alttestamentliche Wissenschaft* 126 (3): 402–417.
Ayali-Darshan, N. 2015. "The Other Version of the Story of the Storm-God's Combat with the Sea in the Light of Egyptian, Ugaritic, and Hurro-Hittite Texts." *Journal of Ancient Near Eastern Religions* 15 (1): 20–51.
Ayalon, E. 1995. "The Iron Age II Pottery Assemblage from Ḥorvat Teiman (Kuntillet ʿAjrud)." *Tel Aviv* 22: 141–205.
Ayalon, E. 2012. "The Pottery Assemblage." In *Kuntillet ʿAjrud (Horvat Teman): An Iron Age II Religious Site on the Judah-Sinai Border*, by Meshel, Z., 205–274. Jerusalem: Israel Exploration Society.

Bach, A. 1993. "Reading Allowed: Feminist Biblical Criticism Approaching the Millennium." *Currents in Research* 1: 191–215.
Bach, A. 1997. *Women, Seduction, and Betrayal in Biblical Narrative*. Cambridge: Cambridge University.
Bach, A. 1999. *Women in the Hebrew Bible: A Reader*. New York: Routledge.
Baden, J. S. 2009. *J, E, and the Redaction of the Pentateuch*. Tübingen: Mohr Siebeck.
Baden, J. S. 2012. *The Composition of the Pentateuch*. New Haven: Yale University.
Bahrani, Z. 2003. *The Graven Image: Representation in Babylonia and Assyria*. Philadelphia: University of Pennsylvania.
Bailey, L. R. 1968. "Israelite 'Ēl Šadday and Amorite Bêl Šadê." *Journal of Biblical Literature* 87 (4): 434–438.
Bailey, L. R. 1971. "The Golden Calf." *Hebrew Union College Annual* 42: 97–115.
Baines, J. 1998. "Ancient Egyptian Kingship: Official Forms, Rhetoric, Context." In *King and Messiah in Israel and the Ancient Near East*, edited by Day, J., 16–53. Sheffield: Sheffield Academic Press.
Baker, D. W. 2003. "Gods, Names of." In *Dictionary of the Old Testament: Pentateuch*, edited by Alexander, T. D., Baker, D. W., 359–368. Downers Grove: InterVarsity Press.
Bal, M. 1987. *Lethal Love: Feminist Readings of Biblical Love Stories*. Bloomington: Indiana University.
Ballentine, D. S. 2015. *The Conflict Myth and the Biblical Tradition*. Oxford: Oxford University.
Baltzer, K. 1987. "Liberation from Debt Slavery After the Exile in Second Isaiah and Nehemiah." In *Ancient Israelite Religion: Essays in Honor of Frank Moore Cross*, edited by Miller, P. D., Hanson, P. D., McBride, S. D., 477–484. Philadelphia: Fortress.
Baltzer, K. 2001. *Deutero-Isaiah: A Commentary on Isaiah 40–55*. Minneapolis: Fortress.
Barkay, G. 1989. "The Priestly Benediction on the Ketef Hinnom Plaques" [Hebrew]. *Cathedra* 52: 37–76.
Barkay, G. 1992. "The Priestly Benediction on Silver Plaques from Ketef Hinnom in Jerusalem." *Tel Aviv* 19: 139–192.
Barkay, G., Lundberg, M. J., Vaughn, A. G., Zuckerman, B. 2004. "The Amulets from Ketef Hinnom: A New Edition and Evaluation." *Bulletin of the American Schools of Oriental Research* 334: 41–71.
Barkay, G., Vaughn, A. G. 1996a. "New Readings of Hezekian Official Seal Impressions." *Bulletin of the American Schools of Oriental Research* 304: 29–54.
Barkay, G., Vaughn, A. G. 1996b. "*Lmlk* and Official Seal Impressions from Tel Lachish." *Tel Aviv* 23: 61–74.
Barnett, R. D., Bleibtreu, E., Turner, G. 1998. *Sculptures from the Southwest Palace of Sennacherib at Nineveh*. London: British Museum Press.
Barr, J. 1974. "Philo of Byblos and His 'Phoenician History.'" *Bulletin of the John Rylands Library* 57: 17–68.
Barr, J. 1989. "'Determination' and the Definite Article in Biblical Hebrew." *Journal of Semitic Studies* 34 (2): 307–335.
Barr, J. 2000. *History and Ideology in the Old Testament: Biblical Studies at the End of a Millennium*. Oxford: Oxford University.
Barré, M. L. 1988. "Seven Epithets of Zion in Ps 48, 2–3." *Biblica*: 557–563.
Barta, W. 1975. *Untersuchungen zur Göttlichkeit des regierenden Königs*. Munich: Deutscher Kunstverlag.

Barth, J. 1894. "Zur vergleichenden semitischen Grammatik." *Zeitschrift der Deutschen Morgenländischen Gesellschaft* 48 (1): 1–21.
Barthélemy, D. 1986. *Critique textuelle de l'Ancien Testament, Vol. 2.* Göttingen: Vandenhoeck & Ruprecht.
Batten, A. J. 2010. "Clothing and Adornment." *Biblical Theology Bulletin* 40 (3): 148–159.
Batto, B. F. 1983. "The Reed Sea: Requiescat in Pace." *Journal of Biblical Literature* 102 (1): 27–35.
Batto, B. F. 1992. *Slaying the Dragon: Mythmaking in the Biblical Tradition.* Louisville: Westminster John Knox.
Bauer, H., Leander, P. 1922. *Historische Grammatik der hebräischen Sprache des Alten Testamentes.* Tübingen: M. Niemeyer.
Baumgarten, A. I. 1992. "Philo of Byblos." In *The Anchor Bible Dictionary*, edited by Freedman, D. N., Vol. 5, 342–344. New York: Doubleday.
Bean, A.L. Forthcoming. "Local Cults and National Gods: Divine Identity in Levantine Religions." Johns Hopkins University.
Bean, A.L., Rollston, C.A., McCarter, P.K., Wimmer, S.J. 2019. "An Inscribed Altar from the Khirbat Ataruz Moabite Sanctuary." *Levant* DOI: 10.1080/00758914.2019.1619971
Beaulieu, P. 2002. "W. F. Albright and Assyriology." *Near Eastern Archaeology* 65 (1): 11–16.
Beaulieu, P. 2005. "The God Amurru as Emblem of Ethnic and Cultural Identity." In *Ethnicity in Ancient Mesopotamia*, edited by van Soldt, W. H., 31–46. Leiden: Nederlands Instituut voor het Nabije Oosten.
Beaulieu, P. 2006. "Official and Vernacular Languages: The Shifting Sands of Imperial and Cultural Identities in First-Millennium B.C. Mesopotamia." In *Margins of Writing, Origins of Cultures*, edited by Sanders, S. L., 187–216. Chicago: Oriental Institute of the University of Chicago.
Beck, P. 1982. "The Drawings from Horvat Teiman (Kuntillet 'Ajrud)." *Tel Aviv* 9: 3–68.
Beck, P. 1989. "Stone Ritual Artifacts and Statues from Areas A and H." In *Hazor III–IV = The James A. de Rothschild Expedition at Hazor: An Account of the Third and Fourth Seasons of Excavation, 1957–1958*, edited by Ben-Tor, A., Shulamit, G., 322–338. Jerusalem: Israel Exploration Society.
Beck, P. 1994. "The Cult-Stands from Taanach: Aspects of the Iconographic Tradition of Early Iron Age Cult Objects in Palestine." In *From Nomadism to Monarchy: Archaeological and Historical Aspects of Early Israel*, edited by Finkelstein, I., Na'aman, N., 352–381. Jerusalem: Israel Exploration Society.
Beck, P. 2012. "The Drawings and Decorative Designs." In *Kuntillet 'Ajrud (Horvat Teman): An Iron Age II Religious Site on the Judah-Sinai Border*, by Meshel, Z., 143–203. Jerusalem: Israel Exploration Society.
Becking, B. 1997. "Assyrian Evidence for Iconic Polytheism in Ancient Israel?" In *The Image and the Book: Iconic Cults, Aniconism, and the Rise of Book Religion in Israel and the Ancient Near East*, edited by van der Toorn, K., 157–171. Leuven: Peeters.
Becking, B. 2006. "The Return of the Deity: Iconic or Aniconic?" In *Essays on Ancient Israel in Its Near Eastern Context: A Tribute to Nadav Na'aman*, edited by Amit, Y., Ben Zvi, E., Finkelstein, I., Lipschits, O., 53–62. Winona Lake: Eisenbrauns.
Becking, B. 2011. "Yehudite Identity in Elephantine." In *Judah and the Judeans in the Achaemenid Period: Negotiating Identity in an International Context*, edited by Lipschitz, O., Knoppers, G. N., Oeming, M., 403–419. Winona Lake: Eisenbrauns.
Beckman, G. M. 1989. "The Religion of the Hittites." *Biblical Archaeologist* 52 (2): 98–108.

Beckman, G. M. 1993–1997. *Mythologie. A. II. Bei den Hethitern*, edited by Edzard, D., et al., Vol. 8, *Meek–Mythologie*. Reallexicon der Assyriologie und Vorderasiatischen Archäologie. Berlin: de Gruyter.
Beckman, G. M. 1995. "Royal Ideology and State Administration in Hittite Anatolia." In *Civilizations of the Ancient Near East*, edited by Sasson, J. M., 529–543. New York: Scribner's.
Beckman, G. M. 1997. "Elkunirša and Ašertu." In *The Context of Scripture 1: Canonical Compositions from the Biblical World*, edited by Hallo, W. W., Younger, K. L., 149. Leiden: Brill.
Beckman, G. M. 2006. "Annals of Ḫattušili I." In *The Ancient Near East: Historical Sources in Translation*, edited by Chavalas, M. W., 219–221. Malden: Blackwell.
Beckman, G. M. 2011. "Blood in Hittite Ritual." *Journal of Cuneiform Studies* 63: 95–102.
Beckman, G. M., Lewis, T. J., eds. 2006. *Text, Artifact, and Image: Revealing Ancient Israelite Religion*. Providence, R.I.: Brown Judaic Studies.
Bediako, G. M. 1997. *Primal Religion and the Bible: William Robertson Smith and His Heritage*. Sheffield: Sheffield Academic Press.
Beidelman, T. O. 1975. *W. Robertson Smith and the Sociological Study of Religion*. Chicago: University of Chicago.
Bell, C. M. 1992. *Ritual Theory, Ritual Practice*. New York: Oxford University.
Bell, C. M. 1997. *Ritual: Perspectives and Dimensions*. New York: Oxford University.
Bell, C. M. 2007. "Response: Defining the Need for a Definition." In *The Archaeology of Ritual*, edited by Kyriakidis, E., 289–308. Los Angeles: Cotsen Institute of Archaeology.
Bellow, S. 1953. *The Adventures of Augie March*. New York: Viking Press.
Ben Zvi, E. 2003. *The Signs of Jonah: Reading and Rereading in Ancient Yehud*. London: Sheffield Academic Press.
Ben-Ami, D. 2006. "Early Iron Age Cult Places—New Evidence from Tel Hazor." *Tel Aviv* 33: 121–133.
Ben-Dov, J. 2011. "The Elohistic Psalter and the Writing of Divine Names at Qumran." In *The Dead Sea Scrolls and Contemporary Culture*, edited by Roitman, A. D., Schiffman Lawrence, H., Tzoref, S., 79–104. Leiden: Brill.
Ben-Tor, A. 1995. "Notes and News: Tel Hazor, 1995." *Israel Exploration Journal* 45: 283–287.
Ben-Tor, A. 1996. "Notes and News: Tel Hazor, 1996." *Israel Exploration Journal* 46: 262–269.
Ben-Tor, A. 1997. "Hazor." In *The Oxford Encyclopedia of Archaeology in the Near East*, edited by Meyers, E. M., Vol. 3, 1–5. New York: Oxford University.
Ben-Tor, A. 1998. "The Fall of Canaanite Hazor—The 'Who' and 'When' Questions." In *Mediterranean Peoples in Transition: Thirteenth to Early Tenth Centuries BCE*, edited by Gitin, S., Mazar, A., Stern, E., 456–467. Jerusalem: Israel Exploration Society.
Ben-Tor, A. 2006. "The Sad Fate of Statues and the Mutilated Statues of Hazor." In *Confronting the Past: Archaeological and Historical Essays on Ancient Israel in Honor of William G. Dever*, edited by Gitin, S., Wright, J. E., Dessel, J. P., 3–16. Winona Lake: Eisenbrauns.
Ben-Tor, A. 2013. "The Ceremonial Precinct in the Upper City of Hazor." *Near Eastern Archaeology* 76 (2): 81–91.
Ben-Tor, A. 2016. *Hazor: Canaanite Metropolis, Israelite City*. Jerusalem: Israel Exploration Society.
Ben-Tor, A., ed. 1992. *The Archaeology of Ancient Israel*. New Haven: Yale University.
Ben-Tor, A., Rubiato, M. T. 1999. "Excavating Hazor, Part Two: Did the Israelites Destroy the Canaanite City?" *Biblical Archaeological Review* 25 (3): 22–39.

Ben-Tor, A., Yadin, Y. 1989. *Hazor III–IV: The James A. de Rothschild Expedition at Hazor. An Account of the Third and Fourth Seasons of Excavation, 1957–1958*. Jerusalem: Hebrew University of Jerusalem.

Ben-Yosef, E., Levy, T. E., Higham, T., Najjar, M., Tauxe, L. 2010. "The Beginning of Iron Age Copper Production in the Southern Levant: New Evidence from Khirbat al-Jariya, Faynan, Jordan." *Antiquity* 84: 724–746.

Bergmann, C. 2010. "'Like a Warrior' and 'Like a Woman Giving Birth': Expressing Divine Immanence and Transcendence in Isaiah 42:10–17." In *Bodies, Embodiment, and Theology of the Hebrew Bible*, edited by Kamionkowski, S. T., Kim, W., 38–56. New York: T. & T. Clark.

Berlejung, A. 1997. "Washing the Mouth: The Consecration of Divine Images in Mesopotamia." In *The Image and the Book: Iconic Cults, Aniconism, and the Rise of Book Religion in Israel and the Ancient Near East*, edited by van der Toorn, K., 45–72. Leuven: Peeters.

Berlejung, A. 2009. "Twisting Traditions: Programmatic Absence-Theology for the Northern Kingdom in 1 Kgs 12:26–33* (the 'Sin of Jeroboam')." *Journal of Northwest Semitic Languages* 35: 1–42.

Berlejung, A. 2010. "There Is Nothing Better than More! Texts and Images on Amulet 1 from Arslan Tash." *Journal of Northwest Semitic Languages* 36: 1–42.

Berlejung, A. 2016. "Family Ties: Constructed Memories About Aram and the Aramaeans in the Old Testament." In *In Search for Aram and Israel: Politics, Culture, and Identity*, edited by Sergi, O., Oeming, M., de Hulster, I. J., 355–377. Tübingen: Mohr Siebeck.

Berlejung, A. 2017. "The Origins and Beginnings of the Worship of Yhwh: The Iconographic Evidence." In *The Origins of Yahwism*, edited by van Oorschot, J., Witte, M., 67–92. Berlin: de Gruyter.

Berlejung, A., Maeir, A. M., Schüle, A., eds. 2017. *Wandering Arameans: Arameans Outside Syria: Textual and Archaeological Perspectives*. Wiesbaden: Harrassowitz.

Berlin, A. M., Frankel, R. 2012. "The Sanctuary at Mizpe Yammim: Phoenician Cult and Territory in the Upper Galilee During the Persian Period." *Bulletin of the American Schools of Oriental Research* 366: 25–78.

Berman, J. 2014a. "Diachronic Study of the Hebrew Bible: A Field in Crisis." *HIPHIL Novum* 1 (1): 59–65.

Berman, J. 2014b. "The History of Legal Theory and the Study of Biblical Law." *Catholic Biblical Quarterly* 76 (1): 19–39.

Berman, J. 2016. "Supersessionist or Complementary? Reassessing the Nature of Legal Revision in the Pentateuchal Law Collections." *Journal of Biblical Literature* 135 (2): 201–222.

Berner, C. 2017. "'I Am Yhwh Your God, Who Brought You Out of the Land of Egypt' (Exod. 20:2): Reflections on the Status of the Exodus Creed in the History of Israel and the Literary History of the Hebrew Bible." In *The Origins of Yahwism*, edited by van Oorschot, J., Witte, M., 181–206. Berlin: de Gruyter.

Bernett, M., Keel, O. 1998. *Mond, Stier und Kult am Stadttor: Die Stele von Betsaida (et-Tell)*. Freiburg: Universitätsverlag.

Bernhardt, K.-H. 1978. "*Hāyāh*." In *Theological Dictionary of the Old Testament, Vol. III*, edited by Botterweck, G. J., Ringgren, H., 369–381. Grand Rapids: Eerdmans.

Berquist, J. L., Camp, C. V. 2007. *Constructions of Space I: Theory, Geography, and Narrative*. New York: T. & T. Clark.

Berquist, J. L., Camp, C. V. 2008. *Constructions of Space II: The Biblical City and Other Imagined Spaces*. New York: T. & T. Clark.
Bertram, G. 1958. "Hikanos in den griechischen Übersetzungen des ATs als Wiedergabe von schaddaj." *Zeitschrift für die alttestamentliche Wissenschaft* 70: 20–31.
Bertram, G. 1959. "Zur Prägung der biblischen Gottesvorstellung in der griechischen Übersetzung des Alten Testaments. Die Wiedergabe von schadad und schaddaj im Griechischen." *Die Welt des Orients* 2 (5): 502–513.
Beyerlin, W. 1965. *Origins and History of the Oldest Sinaitic Traditions*. Oxford: Blackwell.
Bickel, S. 2002. "Aspects et functions de la déification d'Amenhotep III." *Bulletin de l'Institut français d'archéologie orientale* 102: 63–90.
Bienkowski, P. A. 2000. "Mitanni." In *Dictionary of the Ancient Near East*, edited by Bienkowski, P. A., Millard, A. R., 200. Philadelphia: University of Pennsylvania.
Bietak, M. 2001. "Hyksos." In *The Oxford Encyclopedia of Ancient Egypt*, edited by Redford, D. B., 136–143. Oxford: Oxford University.
Bietak, M. 2010. "From Where Came the Hyksos and Where Did They Go?" In *The Second Intermediate Period (Thirteenth-Seventeenth Dynasties): Current Research, Future Prospects*, edited by Marée, M., 139–181. Leuven: Peeters.
Bietak, M. 2016. "The Egyptian Community in Avaris During the Hyksos Period." *Ägypten und Levante/Egypt and Levant* 26: 263–274.
Biezais, H. 1979. *Religious Symbols and Their Functions*. Stockholm: Almqvist & Wiksell.
Biggs, R. D. 1992. "Ebla Texts." In *The Anchor Bible Dictionary*, edited by Freedman, D. N., Vol. 2, 263–270. New York: Doubleday.
Billings, R. M. 2004. "The Problem of the Divine Presence: Source-Critical Suggestions for the Analysis of Exodus XXXIII 12–23." *Vetus Testamentum* 54: 427–444.
Binford, L. R. 1962. "Archaeology as Anthropology." *American Antiquity* 29: 217–225.
Binford, L R. 1989. *Debating Archaeology*. San Diego: Academic Press.
Binger, T. 1997. *Asherah: Goddesses in Ugarit, Israel and the Old Testament*. Sheffield: Sheffield Academic Press.
Bintliff, J. L. 1991. *The Annales School and Archaeology*. New York: New York University.
Biran, A. 1994. *Biblical Dan*. Jerusalem: Israel Exploration Society.
Biran, A. 1998. "Sacred Spaces: Of Standing Stones, High Places and Cult Objects at Tel Dan." *Biblical Archaeology Review* 24 (5): 38–45.
Biran, A., Ilan, D., Greenberg, R. 1996. *Dan I: A Chronicle of the Excavations, the Pottery Neolithic, the Early Bronze Age and the Middle Bronze Age Tombs*. Jerusalem: Nelson Glueck School of Biblical Archaeology, Hebrew Union College–Jewish Institute of Religion.
Birch, B. C. 2006. "Ark of the Covenant." In *The New Interpreter's Dictionary of the Bible*, edited by Sakenfeld, K. D., Vol. 1, 263–269. Nashville: Abingdon.
Bird, P. A. 1987. "The Place of Women in the Israelite Cultus." In *Ancient Israelite Religion: Essays in Honor of Frank Moore Cross*, edited by Miller, P. D., Hanson, P. D., McBride, S. D., 397–419. Philadelphia: Fortress.
Bird, P. A. 1989. "'To Play the Harlot': An Inquiry into an Old Testament Metaphor." In *Gender and Difference in Ancient Israel*, edited by Day, P. L., 75–94. Minneapolis: Fortress.
Bird, P. A. 1991. "Israelite Religion and the Faith of Israel's Daughters: Reflections on Gender and Religious Definition." In *The Bible and the Politics of Exegesis*, edited by Jobling, D., Day, P. L., Sheppard, G. T., 97–108. Cleveland: Pilgrim.

Bird, P. A. 1997a. *Missing Persons and Mistaken Identities: Women and Gender in Ancient Israel*. Minneapolis: Fortress.

Bird, P. A. 1997b. "The End of the Male Cult Prostitute: A Literary-Historical and Sociological Analysis of Hebrew *qādēš-qědēšîm*." In *Congress Volume, Cambridge 1995*, edited by Emerton, J. A., 37–80. Leiden: Brill.

Bird, P. A. 2015. "Of Whores and Hounds: A New Interpretation of the Subject of Deuteronomy 23:19." *Vetus Testamentum* 65: 352–364.

Black, J. A. 1981. "The New Year Ceremonies in Ancient Babylon: 'Taking Bel by the Hand' and a Cultic Picnic." *Religion* 11 (1): 39–59.

Black, J. A., Cunningham, G., Robson, E., Zólyomi, G. 2006. *The Literature of Ancient Sumer*. Oxford: Oxford University.

Black, J. A., Green, A., Rickards, T. 1992. *Gods, Demons, and Symbols of Ancient Mesopotamia: An Illustrated Dictionary*. London: British Museum.

Blake, W. 1875. *Blake's Illustrations of the Book of Job. With Descriptive Letterpress, and a Sketch of the Artist's Life and Works*, edited by Norton, C. E. Boston: James R. Osgood and Co.

Blau, J. 2010. *Phonology and Morphology of Biblical Hebrew: An Introduction*. Winona Lake: Eisenbrauns.

Blenkinsopp, J. 1983. *A History of Prophecy in Israel*. Philadelphia: Westminster.

Blenkinsopp, J. 1992. *The Pentateuch: An Introduction to the First Five Books of the Bible*. New York: Doubleday.

Blenkinsopp, J. 1996. *A History of Prophecy in Israel*. 2nd ed. Philadelphia: Westminster.

Blenkinsopp, J. 1998. "The Judaean Priesthood During the Neo-Babylonian and Achaemenid Periods: A Hypothetical Reconstruction." *Catholic Biblical Quarterly* 60: 25–43.

Blenkinsopp, J. 2000. *Isaiah 1–39: A New Translation with Introduction and Commentary*. New York: Doubleday.

Blenkinsopp, J. 2002. *Isaiah 40–55: A New Translation with Introduction and Commentary*. New York: Doubleday.

Blenkinsopp, J. 2003. *Isaiah 56–66: A New Translation with Introduction and Commentary*. New York: Doubleday.

Blenkinsopp, J. 2006. "Bethel in the Neo-Babylonian Period." In *Judah and the Judeans in the Neo-Babylonian Period*, edited by Lipschits, O., Blenkinsopp, J., 93–107. Winona Lake: Eisenbrauns.

Blenkinsopp, J. 2008. "The Midianite-Kenite Hypothesis Revisited and the Origins of Judah." *Journal for the Study of the Old Testament* 33 (2): 131–153.

Bloch, Y. 2012. "The Third-Person Masculine Plural Suffixed Pronoun *-mw* and Its Implications for the Dating of Biblical Hebrew Poetry." In *Diachrony in Biblical Hebrew*, edited by Miller-Naudé, C. L., Zevit, Z., 147–170. Winona Lake: Eisenbrauns.

Bloch-Smith, E. 1992a. *Judahite Burial Practices and Beliefs About the Dead*. Sheffield: JSOT Press.

Bloch-Smith, E. 1992b. "The Cult of the Dead in Judah: Interpreting the Material Remains." *Journal of Biblical Literature* 111 (2): 213–224.

Bloch-Smith, E. 1994. "'Who Is the King of Glory?' Solomon's Temple and Its Symbolism." In *Scripture and Other Artifacts: Essays on the Bible and Archaeology in Honor of Philip J. King*, edited by Coogan, M. D., Exum, J. C., Stager, L. E., 18–31. Louisville: Westminster John Knox.

Bloch-Smith, E. 1997. Review of Thomas L. Thompson, *Early History of the Israelite People: From the Written and Archaeological Sources. Journal of Near Eastern Studies* 56 (1): 65–67.
Bloch-Smith, E. 2005. "*Maṣṣēbôt* in the Israelite Cult: An Argument for Rendering Implicit Cultic Criteria Explicit." In *Temple and Worship in Biblical Israel*, edited by Day, J., 28–39. London: T. & T. Clark.
Bloch-Smith, E. 2006. "Will the Real Massebot Please Stand Up: Cases of Real and Mistakenly Identified Standing Stones in Ancient Israel." In *Text, Artifact, and Image: Revealing Ancient Israelite Religion*, edited by Beckman, G. M., Lewis, T. J. 64–79. Providence: Brown Judaic Studies.
Bloch-Smith, E. 2014. "Archaeological and Inscriptional Evidence for Phoenician Astarte." In *Transformation of a Goddess: Ishtar, Astarte, Aphrodite*, edited by Sugimoto, D. T., 167–194. Fribourg: Academic Press Fribourg.
Bloch-Smith, E. 2015. "Massebot Standing for Yhwh: The Fall of a Yhwistic Cult Symbol." In *Worship, Women, and War: Essays in Honor of Susan Niditch*, edited by Collins, J. J., 99–115. Providence: Brown Judaic Studies.
Block, D. I. 1997. *The Book of Ezekiel: Chapters 1–24*. Grand Rapids: Eerdmans.
Block, D. I. 1998. *The Book of Ezekiel: Chapters 25–48*. Grand Rapids: Eerdmans.
Blomquist, T. H. 1999. *Gates and Gods: Cults in the City Gates of Iron Age Palestine: An Investigation of the Archaeological and Biblical Sources*. Stockholm: Almqvist & Wiksell.
Blum, E. 1990. *Studien zur Komposition des Pentateuch*. Berlin: de Gruyter.
Blum, E. 2012. "Der historische Mose und die Frühgeschichte Israels." *Hebrew Bible and Ancient Israel* 1: 37–63.
Blum, E. 2013. "Die Wandinschriften 4.2 und 4.6 sowie die Pithos-Inschrift 3.9 aus Kuntillet ʿAǧrūd." *Zeitschrift des Deutschen Palästina-Vereins* 129: 21–54.
Bodel, J. P., Olyan, S. M., eds. 2008. *Household and Family Religion in Antiquity*. Malden: Blackwell.
Bodi, D. 1991. *The Book of Ezekiel and the Poem of Erra*. Freiburg: Universitätsverlag.
Boecker, H. J. 1980. *Law and the Administration of Justice in the Old Testament and Ancient East*. Minneapolis: Augsburg.
Bokser, B. 1985. "Approaching Sacred Space." *Harvard Theological Review* 78: 279–299.
Boling, R. G. 1982. *Joshua*. Garden City: Doubleday.
Bonanno, A. 1986. *Archaeology and Fertility Cult in the Ancient Mediterranean*. Amsterdam: B. R. Grüner.
Bonfil, R. 1997. "Analysis of the Temple." In *Hazor V: An Account of the Fifth Season of Excavation, 1968: Text and Illustrations*, edited by Ben-Tor, A., Bonfil, R., Arensburg, B., Paris, A., 85–101. Jerusalem: Israel Exploration Society.
Bonhême, M. 2001. "Divinity." In *The Oxford Encyclopedia of Ancient Egypt*, edited by Redford, D. B., 401–406. Oxford: Oxford University.
Bonnet, C. 1996. *Astarte: Dossier documentaire et perspectives historiques*. Rome: Consiglio nazionale delle richerche.
Bordreuil, P. 1986. *Catalogue des sceaux ouest-sémitiques inscrits de la Bibliothèque nationale, du Musée du Louvre et du Musée biblique de Bible et Terre Sainte*. Paris: Bibliothèque nationale.
Bordreuil, P. 1992. "Flèches phéniciennes inscrites: 1981–1991." *Revue Biblique* 99: 205–213, plates II–III.
Bordreuil, P. 2014. "On the Authenticity of Iron Age Northwest Semitic Inscribed Seals." In *"An Eye for Form": Epigraphic Essays in Honor of Frank Moore Cross*, edited by Hackett, J. A., Aufrecht, W. E., 127–140. Winona Lake: Eisenbrauns.

Bordreuil, P., Hawley, R., Pardee, D. 2010. "Données nouvelles sur le déchiffrement de l'alphabet et sur les scribes d'Ougarit." *Comptes rendus de l'Académie des inscriptions et belles-lettres* 4: 1623–1635.

Bordreuil, P., Israel, F., Pardee, D. 1996. "Deux ostraca paléo-hebreux de la Collection Sh. Moussaieff." *Semitica* 46: 49–76, Pls.7–8.

Bordreuil, P., Israel, F., Pardee, D. 1998. "King's Command and Widow's Plea: Two New Hebrew Ostraca of the Biblical Period." *Near Eastern Archaeology* 61 (1): 2–13.

Bordreuil, P., Pardee, D. 1993. "Le combat de Ba'lu avec Yammu d'après les textes ougaritiques." *Mari* 7: 63–70.

Bordreuil, P., Pardee, D. 2001. "10. Lettres (nos 49–51)." In *Études Ougaritiques: 1. Travaux, 1985–1995 Ras Shamra-Ougarit XIV*, edited by Yon, M., Arnaud, D., 371–386. Paris: Editions Recherche sur les civilisations.

Bordreuil, P., Pardee, D. 2009. *A Manual of Ugaritic*. Winona Lake: Eisenbrauns.

Borowski, O. 2007. "Horse." In *The New Interpreter's Dictionary of the Bible*, edited by Sakenfeld, K. D., Vol. 2, 891–893. Nashville: Abingdon.

Bottéro, J., Kramer, S. N. 1989. *Lorsque les dieux faisaient l'homme: mythologie mésopotamienne*. Paris: Gallimard.

Bourdillon, M. F. C., Fortes, M., eds. 1980. *Sacrifice*. London: Royal Anthropological Institute of Great Britain and Ireland.

Bourke, S. 2012. "The Six Canaanite Temples of Ṭabaqāt Faḥil: Excavating Pella's 'Fortress' Temple (1994–2009)." In *Temple Building and Temple Cult*, edited by Kamlah, J., 159–201. Wiesbaden: Harrassowitz.

Bovati, P. 1994. *Re-establishing Justice: Legal Terms, Concepts and Procedures in the Hebrew Bible*. Sheffield: JSOT Press.

Brandl, B. 2012. "Scarabs, Scaraboids, Other Stamp Seals, and Seal Impressions." In *Excavations at the City of David 1978–1985 Directed by Yigal Shiloh, Vol. VIIB*, edited by De Groot, A., Bernick-Greenberg, H., 377–396. Jerusalem: Institute of Archaeology, Hebrew University.

Brandl, B. 2014. "Three Canaanite Design Scarabs, One Egyptian Obsidian Scarab and One Syrian Cylinder Seal from a Burial Cave Near Ras 'Ali, in Naḥal Ẓippori." *'Atiqot* 78: 1–11.

Brandon, S. G. F. 1958. "The Myth and Ritual Position Critically Examined." In *Myth, Ritual, and Kingship: Essays on the Theory and Practice of Kingship in the Ancient Near East and in Israel*, edited by Hooke, S. H., 261–291. Oxford: Clarendon Press.

Branham, J. 1993. "Sacred Space in Ancient Jewish and Early Medieval Christian Architecture." Emory University.

Braun-Holzinger, E. 1993. "Die Ikonographie des Mondgottes in der Glyptik des III. Jahrtausends v. Chr." *Zeitschrift für Assyriologie und vorderasiatische Archäologie* 83: 119–133.

Bregstein, L. B. 1993. "Seal Use in Fifth Century B.C. Nippur, Iraq: A Study of Seal Selection and Sealing Practices in the Murasû Archive." University of Pennsylvania.

Brekelmans, C. H. W. 1959. *De Herem in het Oude Testament*. Nijmegen: Centrale Drukkerij.

Brenner, A. 1985. *The Israelite Woman: Social Role and Literary Type in Biblical Narrative*. Sheffield: JSOT Press.

Brenner, A., Fontaine, C. R. 1997. *A Feminist Companion to Reading the Bible: Approaches, Methods and Strategies*. Sheffield: Sheffield Academic Press.

Bretschneider, J. 1991. *Architekturmodelle in Vorderasien und der östlichen Ägäis vom Neolithikum bis in das 1. Jahrtausend*. Kevelaer: Butzon & Bercker.

Brettler, M. Z. 1989. *God Is King: Understanding an Israelite Metaphor.* Sheffield: JSOT Press.
Brettler, M. Z. 1995. *The Creation of History in Ancient Israel.* London: Routledge.
Brettler, M. Z. 2000. "A 'Literary Sermon' in Deuteronomy 4." In *"A Wise and Discerning Mind": Essays in Honor of Burke O. Long,* edited by Culley, R. C., Olyan, S. M., 33–50. Providence: Brown Judaic Studies.
Bright, J. 1981. *A History of Israel.* 3d ed. Philadelphia: Westminster.
Broida, M. W. 2014. *Forestalling Doom: "Apotropaic Intercession" in the Hebrew Bible and the Ancient Near East.* Münster: Ugarit-Verlag.
Brongers, H. A. 1965. "Bemerkungen zum Gebrauch des adverbialen *we'attāh* im Alten Testament (Ein Lexikologischer Beitrag)." *Vetus Testamentum* 15 (3): 289–299.
Brooke, G. J., Curtis, A., Healey, J. F. 1994. *Ugarit and the Bible: Proceedings of the International Symposium on Ugarit and the Bible, Manchester, September 1992.* Münster: Ugarit-Verlag.
Bryan, B. 2000. "The 18th Dynasty Before the Amarna Period (c. 1550–1352 BC)." In *The Oxford History of Ancient Egypt,* edited by Shaw, I., 218–271. Oxford: Oxford University.
Budde, K. 1899. *The Religion of Israel to the Exile.* London: G. P. Putnam's Sons.
Budin, S. L. 2015. "Qedešet: A Syro-Anatolian Goddess in Egypt." *Journal of Ancient Egypt Interconnections* 7 (4): 1–20.
Bultmann, R. 1957. "Ist voraussetzungslose Exegese möglich?" *Theologische Zeitschrift* 13: 409–417.
Bunnens, G. 2006. *A New Luwian Stele and the Cult of the Storm-God at Til Barsib-Masuwari.* Louvain: Peeters.
Burke, A. A. 2014. "Introduction to the Levant During the Middle Bronze Age." In *The Oxford Handbook of the Archaeology of the Levant: c. 8000–332 BCE,* edited by Steiner, M. L., Killebrew, A. E., 403–413. Oxford: Oxford University.
Burkert, W. 1996. *Creation of the Sacred: Tracks of Biology in Early Religions.* Cambridge: Harvard University.
Burnett, J. S. 2001. *A Reassessment of Biblical Elohim.* Atlanta: Society of Biblical Literature.
Burnett, J. S. 2006. "Forty-Two Songs for Elohim: An Ancient Near Eastern Organizing Principle in the Shaping of the Elohistic Psalter." *Journal for the Study of the Old Testament* 31 (1): 81–101.
Burney, C. F. 1970. *The Book of Judges, with Introduction and Notes, and Notes on the Hebrew Text of the Books of Kings, with an Introduction and Appendix.* New York: KTAV.
Butler, T. C. 1983. *Joshua.* Nashville: Thomas Nelson.
Calaway, J. C. 2010. "Heavenly Sabbath, Heavenly Sanctuary: The Transformation of Priestly Sacred Space and Sacred Time in the Songs of the Sabbath Sacrifice and the Epistle to the Hebrews." Columbia University.
Callaway, R. 1999. "The Name Game: Onomastic Evidence and Archaeological Reflections on Religion in Late Judah." *Jian Dao: A Journal of Bible and Theology* 11: 15–36.
Callot, O. 1983. *Une maison à Ougarit: Études d'architecture domestique.* Paris: Editions Recherche sur les civilisations.
Callot, O. 1994. *La tranchée "Ville Sud": Études d'architecture domestique.* Paris: Editions Recherche sur les civilisations.
Cammarosano, M. 2018. *Hittite Local Cults,* edited by van den Hout, T. Atlanta: SBL Press.
Campbell, A. F. 1975. *The Ark Narrative (1 Sam 4–6; 2 Sam 6): A Form-Critical and Traditio-Historical Study.* Missoula: Scholars Press.

Campbell, A. F. 1979. "Yahweh and the Ark." *Journal of Biblical Literature* 98: 31–43.
Campbell, E. F., Jr. 1965a. "Field VII—The Fifth Campaign at Balâtah (Shechem)." *Bulletin of the American Schools of Oriental Research* 180: 17–26.
Campbell, E. F., Jr. 1965b. "Shechem." *Biblical Archaeologist* 28: 18–22.
Campbell, E. F., Jr. 1983. "Judges 9 and Biblical Archaeology." In *The Word of the Lord Shall Go Forth: Essays in Honor of David Noel Freedman in Celebration of His Sixtieth Birthday*, edited by Meyers, C. L., O'Connor, M. P., 263–271. Winona Lake: Eisenbrauns.
Campbell, E. F., Jr. 2002. *Shechem III: The Stratigraphy and Architecture of Shechem/Tell Balâtah, Vol. 1, Text*. Boston: American Schools of Oriental Research.
Campbell, E. F., Jr., Wright, G. E. 1970. "Excavations at Shechem During the Years 1956–1969." *Qadmoniyot* 3: 126–133.
Caquot, A. 1970. "Le psaume 68." *Revue de l'histoire des religions* 177: 147–182.
Caquot, A. 1995. "Une contribution ougaritique à la préhistorie du titre divin *Shadday*." In *Congress Volume: Paris, 1992. Supplements to Vetus Testamentum LXI*, edited by Emerton, J. A., 1–12. Leiden: Brill.
Caquot, A., Sznycer, M. 1980. *Ugaritic Religion*. Leiden: Brill.
Caquot, A., Sznycer, M., Herdner, A. 1974. *Textes ougaritiques: introduction, traduction, commentaire*. Paris: Éditions du Cerf.
Carasik, M. 1999. "To See a Sound: A Deuteronomic Rereading of Exodus 20:15." *Prooftexts* 19: 257–265.
Carena, O. 1989. *History of the Near Eastern Historiography and Its Problems, 1852–1985*. Kevelaer: Butzon & Bercker.
Carmi, I., Segal, D. 1996. "14C Dating of an Israelite Biblical Site at Kuntillet ʿAjrud (Horvat Teman): Correction, Extension and Improved Age Estimate." *Radiocarbon* 38: 385–386.
Carmi, I., Segal, D. 2012. "14C Dates from Kuntillet ʿAjrud." In *Kuntillet ʿAjrud (Horvat Teman): An Iron Age II Religious Site on the Judah-Sinai Border*, by Meshel, Z., 61–63. Jerusalem: Israel Exploration Society.
Carr, D. M. 1996. *Reading the Fractures of Genesis: Historical and Literary Approaches*. Louisville: Westminster John Knox.
Carr, D. M. 2007. "The Rise of Torah." In *The Pentateuch as Torah: New Models for Understanding Its Promulgation and Acceptance*, edited by Knoppers, G. N., Levinson, B. M., 39–56. Winona Lake: Eisenbrauns.
Carr, D. M. 2008. "The Tel Zayit Abecedary in (Social) Context." In *Literate Culture and Tenth-Century Canaan: The Tel Zayit Abecedary in Context*, edited by Tappy, R. E., McCarter, P. K., 113–129. Winona Lake: Eisenbrauns.
Carr, D. M. 2011. *The Formation of the Hebrew Bible*. Oxford: Oxford University.
Cartledge, T. W. 1989. "Were Nazirite Vows Unconditional?" *Catholic Biblical Quarterly* 51: 409–422.
Cartledge, T. W. 1992. *Vows in the Hebrew Bible and the Ancient Near East*. Sheffield: JSOT Press.
Casadio, G. 1987. "El and Cosmic Order: Is the Ugaritic Supreme God a *deus otiosus*?" *Studia Fennica* 32: 45–58.
Cassin, E. 1968. *La splendeur divine. Introduction à l'étude de la mentalité mésopotamienne*. Paris: Mouton & Co.
Cassuto, U. 1926. "Il. cap. 33 del Deuteronomio e la festa del Capo d'anno nell'antico Israele." *Rivista Degli Studi Orientali* 11: 233–253.

Cassuto, U. 1967. *A Commentary on the Book of Exodus*. Jerusalem: Magnes Press.
Cassuto, U. 1973. *Biblical and Oriental Studies*. Jerusalem: Magnes Press.
Caubet, A. 1995. "Art and Architecture in Canaan and Ancient Israel." In *Civilizations of the Ancient Near East*, edited by Sasson, J. M., Vol. IV, 2671–2691. New York: Scribner's.
Cecil, L. 1989–1996. *Wilhelm II*. Chapel Hill: University of North Carolina.
Chalmers, R. S. 2008. *The Struggle of Yahweh and El for Hosea's Israel*. Sheffield: Sheffield Phoenix Press.
Chapman, C. R. 2016. *The House of the Mother: The Social Roles of Maternal Kin in Biblical Hebrew Narrative and Poetry*. New Haven: Yale University.
Charlesworth, J. H. 2004. "Bashan, Symbology, Haplography, and Theology in Psalm 68." In *David and Zion: Biblical Studies in Honor of J. J. M. Roberts*, edited by Batto, B. F., Roberts, K. L., 351–372. Winona Lake: Eisenbrauns.
Chase, D. A. 1982. "A Note on an Inscription from Kuntillet ʿAjrūd." *Bulletin of the American Schools of Oriental Research* 246: 63–67.
Chase, D. A. 1994. "Baʿl Šamêm: A Study of the Early Epigraphic Sources." Harvard University.
Chavalas, M. W. 2007. *The Ancient Near East: Historical Sources in Translation*. Malden: Blackwell.
Chavalas, M. W., ed. 2014. *Women in the Ancient Near East*. London: Routledge.
Chazan, R., Hallo, W. W., Schiffman, L. H. 1999. *Ki Baruch Hu: Ancient Near Eastern, Biblical, and Judaic Studies in Honor of Baruch A. Levine*. Winona Lake: Eisenbrauns.
Chesterton, G. K. 1908. *Orthodoxy*. London: Collins.
Chidester, D. 1994. "The Poetics and Politics of Sacred Space: Towards a Critical Phenomenology of Religion." *Analecta Husserliana* 43: 211–231.
Childs, B. S. 1970a. "A Traditio-Historical Study of the Reed Sea Tradition." *Vetus Testamentum* 20 (4): 406–418.
Childs, B. S. 1970b. *Biblical Theology in Crisis*. Philadelphia: Westminster.
Childs, B. S. 1974. *The Book of Exodus. A Critical, Theological Commentary*. Philadelphia: Westminster.
Chirichigno, G. 1993. *Debt Slavery in Israel and the Ancient Near East*. Sheffield: JSOT Press.
Christensen, D. L. 2009. *Nahum: A New Translation with Introduction and Commentary*. New Haven: Yale University.
Christian, M. A., Schmitt, R., eds. 2013a. "Permutations of ʿAstarte." *Die Welt des Orients* 43 (2): 150–242.
Christian, M. A., Schmitt, R. 2013b. "Permutations of ʿAštarte: Introduction." *Die Welt des Orients* 43 (2): 150–152.
Civil, M. 1995. "Ancient Mesopotamian Lexicography." In *Civilizations of the Ancient Near East*, edited by Sasson, J., Vol. IV, 2305–2314. New York: Scribner's.
Clemens, D. M. 2001. *Sources for Ugaritic Ritual and Sacrifice*. Münster: Ugarit-Verlag.
Clements, R. E. 1965a. "Deuteronomy and the Jerusalem Cult Tradition." *Vetus Testamentum* 15 (3): 300–312.
Clements, R. E. 1965b. *God and Temple*. Philadelphia: Fortress.
Clements, R. E. 1975. "The Purpose of the Book of Jonah." In *Congress Volume Edinburgh 1974*, edited by Emerton, J. A., 16–28. Leiden: Brill.
Clements, R. E. 1976. *One Hundred Years of Old Testament Interpretation*. Philadelphia: Westminster.
Clements, R. E. 2004. "Qṭr." In *Theological Dictionary of the Old Testament*, edited by Botterweck, G. J., Ringgren, H., Fabry, H., Vol. XIII, 9–16. Grand Rapids: Eerdmans.

Clifford, R. J. 1972. *The Cosmic Mountain in Canaan and the Old Testament*. Harvard Semitic Monographs, Vol. 4. Cambridge: Harvard University.

Clifford, R. J. 1980. "Psalm 89: A Lament over the Davidic Ruler's Continued Failure." *Harvard Theological Review* 73 (1): 35–47.

Clifford, R. J. 1990. "Phoenician Religion." *Bulletin of the American Schools of Oriental Research* 279: 55–64.

Clifford, R. J. 1994. *Creation Accounts in the Ancient Near East and the Bible*. Washington: Catholic Biblical Association.

Clines, D. J. A. 1989. *Job 1–20*. Dallas: Word.

Clines, D. J. A. 2011. *Job 38–42*. Nashville: Thomas Nelson.

Coats, G. W. 1987. "The Golden Calf in Psalm 22." *Horizons in Biblical Theology* 9 (1): 1–12.

Cody, A. 1969. *A History of Old Testament Priesthood*. Rome: Pontifical Biblical Institute.

Cogan, M. 1974. *Imperialism and Religion: Assyria, Judah and Israel in the Eighth and Seventh Centuries B.C.E.* Missoula: Scholars Press.

Cogan, M. 1999. "Ashima." In *Dictionary of Deities and Demons in the Bible*, edited by van der Toorn, K., Becking, B., van der Horst, P. W., 105–106. 2nd ed. Leiden: Brill.

Cogan, M. 2000a. "Sennacherib: The Capture and Destruction of Babylon." In *The Context of Scripture 2: Monumental Inscriptions from the Biblical World*, edited by Hallo, W. W., Younger, K. L., 305. Leiden: Brill.

Cogan, M. 2000b. "Sennacherib's Siege of Jerusalem." In *The Context of Scripture 2: Monumental Inscriptions from the Biblical World*, edited by Hallo, W. W., Younger, K. L., 302–303. Leiden: Brill.

Cogan, M. 2001. *1 Kings: A New Translation with Introduction and Commentary*. New York: Doubleday.

Cogan, M., Tadmor, H. 1988. *II Kings: A New Translation with Introduction and Commentary*. Garden City: Doubleday.

Cohen, R., Westbrook, R. 2008. *Isaiah's Vision of Peace in Biblical and Modern International Relations: Swords into Plowshares*. New York: Palgrave Macmillan.

Cohen, S. L. 2002. *Canaanites, Chronologies, and Connections: The Relationship of Middle Bronze IIA Canaan to Middle Kingdom Egypt*. Winona Lake: Eisenbrauns.

Cohn, R. L. 1981. *The Shape of Sacred Space: Four Biblical Studies*. Chico: Scholars Press.

Colbow, G. 1997. "More Insights into Representations of the Moon God in the Third and Second Millennium B.C." In *Sumerian Gods and Their Representations*, edited by Finkel, I. L., Geller, M. J., 19–31. Groningen: STYX.

Collins, B. J. 2005. "A Statue for the Deity: Cult Images in Hittite Anatolia." In *Cult Image and Divine Representation in the Ancient Near East*, edited by Walls, N. H., 13–42. Boston: American Schools of Oriental Research.

Collins, J. J. 1987. *The Apocalyptic Imagination: An Introduction to the Jewish Matrix of Christianity*. New York: Crossroad.

Collins, J. J. 1993. *Daniel*. Minneapolis: Fortress.

Collins, J. J. 2005. *The Bible After Babel: Historical Criticism in a Postmodern Age*. Grand Rapids: Eerdmans.

Collon, D. 1972. "The Smiting God: A Study of a Bronze in the Pomerance Collection in New York." *Levant* 4 (1): 111–134.

Collon, D. 1997. "Moon, Boats and Battle." In *Sumerian Gods and Their Representations*, edited by Finkel, I. L., Geller, M. J., 11–17. Groningen: STYX.

Collon, D. 2001. *Catalogue of the Western Asiatic Seals in the British Museum: Cylinder Seals V. Neo-Assyrian and Neo-Babylonian Periods*. London: British Museum.

Conklin, B. W. 2003. "Arslan Tash I and Other Vestiges of a Particular Syrian Incantatory Thread." *Biblica* 84: 89–101.
Conrad, J. 2001. "*Pl'*." In *Theological Dictionary of the Old Testament*, edited by Botterweck, G. J., Ringgren, H., Fabry, H., Vol. XI, 533–546. Grand Rapids: Eerdmans.
Coogan, M. D. 1978. "A Structural and Literary Analysis of the Song of Deborah." *Catholic Biblical Quarterly* 40 (2): 143–166.
Coogan, M. D. 1987a. "Canaanite Origins and Lineage: Reflections on the Religion of Ancient Israel." In *Ancient Israelite Religion: Essays in Honor of Frank Moore Cross*, edited by Miller, P. D., Hanson, P. D., McBride, S. D., 115–124. Philadelphia: Fortress.
Coogan, M. D. 1987b. "Of Cults and Cultures: Reflections on the Interpretation of Archaeological Evidence." *Palestine Exploration Quarterly* 119: 1–8.
Coogan, M. D., ed. 1998. *The Oxford History of the Biblical World*. New York: Oxford University.
Coogan, M. D., Smith, M. S. 2012. *Stories from Ancient Canaan*. Louisville: Westminster John Knox.
Cook, S. L. 1992. "Apocalypticism and the Psalter." *Zeitschrift für die alttestamentliche Wissenschaft* 104 (1): 82–99.
Cook, S. L. 2004. *The Social Roots of Biblical Yahwism*. Leiden: Brill.
Cook, S. L. 2011. "Those Stubborn Levites: Overcoming Levitical Disenfranchisement." In *Levites and Priests in Biblical History and Tradition*, edited by Leuchter, M., Hutton, J. M., 155–170. Atlanta: Society of Biblical Literature.
Cooke, G. A. 1903. *A Textbook of North-Semitic Inscriptions: Moabite, Hebrew, Phoenician, Aramaic, Nabataean, Palmyrene, Jewish*. Oxford: Clarendon Press.
Cooke, G. A. 1918. *The Book of Joshua*. Cambridge: Cambridge University.
Cooke, G. A. 1936. *A Critical and Exegetical Commentary on the Book of Ezekiel*. Edinburgh: T. & T. Clark.
Cooper, A. 1987. "MLK 'LM: 'Eternal King' or 'King of Eternity'?" In *Love and Death in the Ancient Near East: Essays in Honor of Marvin H. Pope*, edited by Marks, J. H., Good, R. M., 1–7. Guilford: Four Quarters.
Cooper, J. S. 1978. *The Return of Ninurta to Nippur: An-gim dím-ma*. Analecta orientalia, Vol. 52. Rome: Pontificium institutum biblicum.
Cooper, J. S. 2008. "Divine Kingship in Mesopotamia, A Fleeting Phenomenon." In *Religion and Power: Divine Kingship in the Ancient World and Beyond*, edited by Brisch, N. M., 261–264. Chicago: Oriental Institute.
Cooper, J. S., Schwartz, G. M. 1996. *The Study of the Ancient Near East in the Twenty-First Century: The William Foxwell Albright Centennial Conference*. Winona Lake: Eisenbrauns.
Coote, R. B. 1990. *Early Israel: A New Horizon*. Minneapolis: Fortress.
Coote, R. B., Whitelam, K. W. 1987. *The Emergence of Early Israel in Historical Perspective*. Sheffield: Almond Press.
Copan, P. 2006. "Divine Narcissism? A Further Defense of God's Humility." *Philosophia Christi* 8 (2): 313–325.
Cordwell, J. M., Schwarz, R. A., eds. 1979. *The Fabrics of Culture: The Anthropology of Clothing and Adornment*. The Hague: Mouton.
Cornelius, I. 1994. *The Iconography of the Canaanite Gods Reshef and Ba'al: Late Bronze and Iron Age I Periods (c. 1500–1000 BCE)*. Fribourg: University Press.

Cornelius, I. 1997. "The Many Faces of God: Divine Images and Symbols in Ancient Near Eastern Traditions." In *The Image and the Book: Iconic Cults, Aniconism, and the Rise of Book Religion in Israel and the Ancient Near East*, edited by van der Toorn, K., 21–43. Leuven: Peeters.

Cornelius, I. 1999. "The Iconography of Ugarit." In *Handbook of Ugaritic Studies*, edited by Watson, W. G. E., Wyatt, N., 586–602. Boston: Brill.

Cornelius, I. 2004. *The Many Faces of the Goddess: The Iconography of the Syro-Palestinian Goddesses Anat, Astarte, Qedeshet, and Asherah, c. 1500-1000 BCE*. Fribourg: Academic Press.

Cornelius, I., Niehr, H. 2004. *Götter und Kulte in Ugarit: Kultur und Religion einer nordsyrischen Königsstadt in der Spätbronzezeit*. Mainz am Rhein: Von Zabern.

Cornell, C. R. 2012. "God and the Sea in Job 38." *Journal of Hebrew Scriptures* 12: 1–15.

Craigie, P. C. 1972. "Psalm 29 in the Hebrew Poetic Tradition." *Vetus Testamentum* 22: 143–151.

Craigie, P. C. 1983. *Psalms 1-50*. Waco: Word Books.

Cranz, I. 2017. *Atonement and Purification: Priestly and Assyro-Babylonian Perspectives on Sin and Its Consequences*. Tübingen: Mohr Siebeck.

Crawford, S. W. 2008. *Rewriting Scripture in Second Temple Times*. Grand Rapids: Eerdmans.

Crenshaw, J. L. 1995. *Joel: A New Translation with Introduction and Commentary*. New York: Doubleday.

Cross, F. M. 1962a. "Yahweh and the God of the Patriarchs." *Harvard Theological Review* 55 (4): 225–259.

Cross, F. M. 1962b. "An Archaic Inscribed Seal from the Valley of Aijalon." *Bulletin of the American Schools of Oriental Research* 168: 12–18.

Cross, F. M. 1970. "The Cave Inscriptions from Khirbet Beit Lei." In *Near Eastern Archaeology in the Twentieth Century: Essays in Honor of Nelson Glueck*, edited by Sanders, J. A., 299–306. Garden City: Doubleday.

Cross, F. M. 1973. *Canaanite Myth and Hebrew Epic: Essays in the History of the Religion of Israel*. Cambridge: Harvard University.

Cross, F. M. 1974a. "'ēl." In *Theological Dictionary of the Old Testament, Vol. I*, edited by Botterweck, G. J., Ringgren, H., 242–261. Grand Rapids: Eerdmans.

Cross, F. M. 1974b. "Leaves from an Epigraphist's Notebook." *Catholic Biblical Quarterly* 36 (4): 486–494.

Cross, F. M. 1979. "Two Offering Dishes with Phoenician Inscriptions from the Sanctuary of 'Arad." *Bulletin of the American Schools of Oriental Research* 235: 75–78.

Cross, F. M. 1980. "Newly Found Inscriptions in Old Canaanite and Early Phoenician Scripts." *Bulletin of the American Schools of Oriental Research* 238: 1–20.

Cross, F. M. 1982. "Alphabets and Pots: Reflections on Typological Method in the Dating of Human Artifacts." *Maarav* 3 (2): 121–136.

Cross, F. M. 1983a. "The Seal of Miqneyaw, Servant of Yahweh." In *Ancient Seals and the Bible*, edited by Gorelick, L., Williams-Forte, E., 55–63, plates IX–X. Malibu: Undena.

Cross, F. M. 1983b. "The Epic Traditions of Early Israel: Epic Narrative and the Reconstruction of Early Israelite Institutions." In *The Poet and the Historian: Essays in Literary and Historical Biblical Criticism*, edited by Friedman, R. E., 13–39. Chico: Scholars Press.

Cross, F. M. 1988. "Reuben, First-Born of Jacob." *Zeitschrift für die alttestamentliche Wissenschaft* 100 (3): 46–65.

Cross, F. M. 1989. "The Contributions of W. F. Albright to Semitic Epigraphy and Palaeography." In *The Scholarship of William Foxwell Albright: An Appraisal*, edited by Van Beek, G. W., 17–31. Atlanta: Scholars Press.

Cross, F. M. 1998. *From Epic to Canon: History and Literature in Ancient Israel.* Baltimore: Johns Hopkins University.

Cross, F. M. 2003a. "Notes on the Forged Plaque Recording Repairs to the Temple." *Israel Exploration Journal* 53: 119–123.

Cross, F. M. 2003b. *Leaves from an Epigrapher's Notebook: Collected Papers in Hebrew and West Semitic Palaeography and Epigraphy.* Winona Lake: Eisenbrauns.

Cross, F. M. 2009. "Telltale Remnants of Oral Epic in the Older Sources of the Tetrateuch: Double and Triple Proper Names in Early Hebrew Sources, and in Homeric and Ugaritic Epic Poetry." In *Exploring the Longue Durée: Essays in Honor of Lawrence E. Stager*, edited by Schloen, J. D., 83–88. Winona Lake: Eisenbrauns.

Cross, F. M., Freedman, D. N. 1947. "A Note on Deuteronomy 33:26." *Bulletin of the American Schools of Oriental Research* 108: 6–7.

Cross, F. M., Freedman, D. N. 1948. "The Blessing of Moses." *Journal of Biblical Literature* 67 (3): 191–210.

Cross, F. M., Freedman, D. N. 1952. *Early Hebrew Orthography. A Study of the Epigraphic Evidence.* New Haven: American Oriental Society.

Cross, F. M., Freedman, D. N. 1955. "The Song of Miriam." *Journal of Near Eastern Studies* 14 (4): 237–250.

Cross, F. M., Freedman, D. N. 1972. "Some Observations on Early Hebrew." *Biblica* 53: 413–420.

Cross, F. M., Freedman, D. N. 1975. *Studies in Ancient Yahwistic Poetry.* Atlanta: Society of Biblical Literature.

Cross, F. M., Freedman, D. N. 1997. *Studies in Ancient Yahwistic Poetry.* 2nd ed. Grand Rapids, MI: Eerdmans.

Cross, F. M., Saley, R. J. 1970. "Phoenician Incantations on a Plaque of the Seventh Century B.C. from Arslan Tash in Upper Syria." *Bulletin of the American Schools of Oriental Research* 197: 42–49.

Cross, F. M., Saley, R. J. 2003. "Phoenician Incantations on a Plaque of the Seventh Century BCE from Arslan Tash in Upper Syria." In *Leaves from an Epigrapher's Notebook: Collected Papers in Hebrew and West Semitic Palaeography and Epigraphy* by Frank Moore Cross, 265–269. Winona Lake: Eisenbrauns.

Crouch, C. L. 2012. "The Threat to Israel's Identity in Deuteronomy: Mesopotamian or Levantine?" *Zeitschrift für die alttestamentliche Wissenschaft* 124 (4): 541–554.

Crouch, C. L. 2014. *The Making of Israel: Cultural Diversity in the Southern Levant and the Formation of Ethnic Identity in Deuteronomy.* Leiden: Brill.

Crouch, C. L. 2015. "What Makes a Thing Abominable? Observations on the Language of Boundaries and Identity Formation from a Social Scientific Perspective." *Vetus Testamentum* 65 (4): 516–541.

Crow, L. D. 1996. *The Songs of Ascents (Psalms 120–134): Their Place in Israelite History and Religion.* Atlanta: Scholars Press.

Curtis, A. H. W. 1990. "Some Observations on 'Bull' Terminology in the Ugaritic Texts and the Old Testament." In *In Quest of the Past: Studies on Israelite Religion, Literature and Prophetism*, edited by van der Woude, A. S. 17–31. Leiden: Brill.

Curtis, J. 1988. *Bronzeworking Centres of Western Asia, c. 1000–539 B.C.* London: Kegan Paul.

Dahmen, U. 1996. *Leviten und Priester im Deuteronomium: literarkritische und redaktionsgeschichtliche Studien*. Bodenheim: Philo.
Dahood, M. 1964. "Hebrew-Ugaritic Lexicography II." *Biblica* 45 (3): 393–412.
Dahood, M. 1965. *Psalms I 1–50*. Garden City: Doubleday.
Dahood, M. 1968a. *Psalms II 51–100*. Garden City: Doubleday.
Dahood, M. 1968b. "The Name *yišmā'' ēl* in Genesis 16,11." *Biblica* 49 (1): 87–88.
Dahood, M. 1978. "Ebla, Ugarit and the Old Testament." In *Congress Volume Göttingen 1977*, edited by Emerton, J. A., 81–112. Leiden: Brill.
Dahood, M. 1981. "Ebla, Ugarit, and the Bible." Afterword to Giovanni Pettinato, *The Archives of Ebla: An Empire Inscribed in Clay*, 271–321. Garden City: Doubleday.
Dalix, A. 1997a. "Iloumilkou, scribe d'Ougarit au XIIIe siècle avant J.C." Institut Catholique de Paris et Université de Paris.
Dalix, A. 1997b. "Ougarit au XIIIe siècle av. J.-C.: Nouvelles perspectives historiques." *Comptes rendus de l'Académie des inscriptions et belles-lettres*: 819–824.
Dalley, S. 1990. "Yahweh in Hamath in the 8th Century BC: Cuneiform Material and Historical Deductions." *Vetus Testamentum* 40 (1): 21–32.
Dalley, S. 2008. *Myths from Mesopotamia: Creation, the Flood, Gilgamesh, and Others*. Oxford: Oxford University.
Daly, M. F. 1973. *Beyond God the Father: Toward a Philosophy of Women's Liberation*. Boston: Beacon Press.
Daniels, D. R. 1987. "Is There a 'Prophetic Lawsuit' Genre?" *Zeitschrift für die alttestamentliche Wissenschaft* 99 (3): 339–360.
Danrey, V. 2004. "Winged Human-Headed Bulls of Nineveh: Genesis of an Iconographic Motif." *Iraq*. 66: 133–139.
Darby, E. 2014. *Interpreting Judean Pillar Figurines: Gender and Empire in Judean Apotropaic Ritual*. Tübingen: Mohr Siebeck.
Darr, K. P. 1987. "Like Warrior, Like Woman: Destruction and Deliverance in Isaiah 42:10–17." *Catholic Biblical Quarterly* 49 (4): 560–571.
Darr, K. P. 1994. *Isaiah's Vision and the Family of God*. Louisville: Westminster John Knox.
Daviau, P. M. M. 2001. "Family Religion: Evidence for the Paraphernalia of the Domestic Cult." In *The World of the Aramaeans II*, edited by Daviau, P. M. M., Wevers, J. W., Weigl, M., 199–229. Sheffield: Sheffield Academic Press.
Davies, G. H. 1962. "Glory." In *The Interpreter's Dictionary of the Bible*, edited by Buttrick, G. A., 401–403. New York: Abingdon.
Davies, G. I. 1991. *Ancient Hebrew Inscriptions: Corpus and Concordance*. Cambridge: Cambridge University.
Davies, N. 1943. *The Tomb of Rekh-mi-Rē at Thebes*. New York: Metropolitan Museum of Art.
Davies, P. R. 1992. *In Search of "Ancient Israel."* Sheffield: JSOT Press.
Davies, P. R. 1994. "'House of David' Built on Sand: The Sin of the Biblical Maximizers." *Biblical Archaeology Review* 20: 54–55.
Davies, P. R. 1995. "Method and Madness: Some Remarks on Doing History with the Bible." *Journal of Biblical Literature* 114 (4): 699–705.
Davies, P. R. 2011. "Reading the Bible Intelligently." *Releger: Studies in Religion and Reception* 1: 145–164.
Davila, J. R., Zuckerman, B. 1993. "The Throne of 'Ashtart Inscription." *Bulletin of the American Schools of Oriental Research* 289: 67–80.

Davis, A. R. 2013. *Tel Dan in Its Northern Cultic Context*. Atlanta: Society of Biblical Literature.

Davis, A. R. 2019. *Reconstructing the Temple: The Royal Rhetoric of Temple Renovation in the Ancient Near East and Israel*. Oxford: Oxford University.

Davis, T. W. 2004. *Shifting Sands: The Rise and Fall of Biblical Archaeology*. Oxford: Oxford University.

Day, J. 1985. *God's Conflict with the Dragon and the Sea: Echoes of a Canaanite Myth in the Old Testament*. Cambridge: Cambridge University.

Day, J. 1986. "Asherah in the Hebrew Bible and Northwest Semitic Literature." *Journal of Biblical Literature* 105 (3): 385–408.

Day, J. 1989. *Molech: A God of Human Sacrifice in the Old Testament*. Cambridge: Cambridge University.

Day, J. 1994. "Ugarit and the Bible: Do They Presuppose the Same Canaanite Mythology and Religion?" In *Ugarit and the Bible*, edited by Brooke, G. J., Curtis, A. H. W., Healey, J. F., 35–52. Münster: Ugarit-Verlag.

Day, J. 1995. *William Robertson Smith, Lectures on the Religion of the Semites: Second and Third Series Edited with an Introduction and Appendix by John Day*. Sheffield: Sheffield Academic Press.

Day, J. 1998. "The Canaanite Inheritance of the Israelite Monarchy." In *King and Messiah in Israel and the Ancient Near East*, edited by Day, J., 72–90. Sheffield: Sheffield Academic Press.

Day, J. 2000. *Yahweh and the Gods and Goddesses of Canaan*. Sheffield: Sheffield Academic Press.

Day, J. 2004. "Does the Old Testament Refer to Sacred Prostitution and Did It Actually Exist in Ancient Israel?" In *Biblical and Near Eastern Essays: Studies in Honour of Kevin J. Cathcart*, edited by McCarthy, C., Healey, J. F., 2–21. London: T. & T. Clark.

Day, P. L. 1992. "Anat: Ugarit's 'Mistress of Animals.'" *Journal of Near Eastern Studies* 51 (3): 181–190.

Day, P. L. 1995. "The Personification of Cities as Female in the Hebrew Bible." In *Reading from This Place: Social Location and Biblical Interpretation in Global Perspective, Vol. 2*, edited by Segovia, F. F., Tolbert, M. A., 283–302. Minneapolis: Fortress.

Day, P. L., ed. 1989. *Gender and Difference in Ancient Israel*. Minneapolis: Fortress.

Dayagi-Mendels, M. 1986. *Treasures of the Holy Land: Ancient Art from the Israel Museum*. New York: Metropolitan Museum of Art.

Dearman, J. A. 2006. "Canaan, Canaanites." In *The New Interpreter's Dictionary of the Bible*, edited by Sakenfeld, K. D., Vol. 1, 532–535. Nashville: Abingdon.

DeGrado, J. 2018. "The *qdesha* in Hosea 4:14: Putting the (Myth of the) Sacred Prostitute to Bed." *Vetus Testamentum* 68: 8–40.

DeGrado, J., Richey, M. 2017. "An Aramaic-Inscribed Lamaštu Amulet from Zincirli." *Bulletin of the American Schools of Oriental Research* 377: 107–133.

Delcor, M. 1974. "Astarté et la fécondité des troupeaux en Deut. 7, 13 et parallèles." *Ugarit-Forschungen* 6: 7–14.

Delitzsch, F. 1986. "Psalms." In *Commentary on the Old Testament in Ten Volumes by Carl Keil and Franz Delitzsch*. Grand Rapids: Eerdmans.

Della Vida, G. L. 1944. "El 'Elyon in Genesis 14:18–20." *Journal of Biblical Literature* 63 (1): 1–9.

Démare-Lafont, S., et al. Forthcoming. *Judicial Decisions in Mesopotamia*. Atlanta: SBL Press.

de Pury, A. 1999a. "El-Roi." In *Dictionary of Deities and Demons in the Bible*, edited by van der Toorn, K., Becking, B., van der Horst, P. W., 291–292. 2nd ed. Leiden: Brill.

de Pury, A. 1999b. "El-Olam." In *Dictionary of Deities and Demons in the Bible*, edited by van der Toorn, K., Becking, B., van der Horst, P. W., 288–291. 2nd ed. Leiden: Brill.

De Roche, M. 1983. "Yahweh's Rîb Against Israel: A Reassessment of the So-Called 'Prophetic Lawsuit' in the Preexilic Prophets." *Journal of Biblical Literature* 102 (4): 563–574.

Dessel, J. P. 1997. "Jaffa." In *The Oxford Encyclopedia of Archaeology in the Near East*, edited by Meyers, E. M., Vol. 3, 206–207. New York: Oxford University.

Deutsch, R., Heltzer, M. 1994. *Forty New Ancient West Semitic Inscriptions*. Tel Aviv: Archaeological Center Publication.

De Valerio, K. 1994. *Altes Testament und Judentum im Frühwerk Rudolf Bultmanns*. Berlin: de Gruyter.

Dever, W. G. 1969–1970. "Iron Age Epigraphic Material from the Area of Khirbet el-Kôm." *Hebrew Union College Annual* 40/41: 139–204.

Dever, W. G. 1974. *Gezer II: Report of the 1967–70 Seasons in Fields I and II*. Jerusalem: Hebrew Union College.

Dever, W. G. 1983. "Material Remains and the Cult in Ancient Israel: An Essay in Archeological Systematics." In *The Word of the Lord Shall Go Forth: Essays in Honor of David Noel Freedman in Celebration of His Sixtieth Birthday*, edited by Meyers, C. L., O'Connor, M. P., 571–587. Winona Lake: Eisenbrauns.

Dever, W. G. 1984. "Asherah, Consort of Yahweh? New Evidence from Kuntillet ʿAjrûd." *Bulletin of the American Schools of Oriental Research* 255: 21–37.

Dever, W. G. 1985. "Syro-Palestinian Archaeology." In *The Hebrew Bible and Its Modern Interpreters*, edited by Knight, D. A., Tucker, G. M., 31–74. Chico: Scholars Press.

Dever, W. G. 1987. "The Contribution of Archaeology to the Study of Canaanite and Early Israelite Religion." In *Ancient Israelite Religion: Essays in Honor of Frank Moore Cross*, edited by Miller, P. D., Hanson, P. D., McBride, S. D., 209–247. Philadelphia: Fortress.

Dever, W. G. 1990. *Recent Archaeological Discoveries and Biblical Research*. Seattle: University of Washington.

Dever, W. G. 1991. "Unresolved Issues in the Early History of Israel: Toward a Synthesis of Archaeological and Textual Reconstructions." In *The Bible and the Politics of Exegesis*, edited by Jobling, D., Day, P. L., Sheppard, G. T., 195–208, 344–348. Cleveland: Pilgrim.

Dever, W. G. 1994. "Ancient Israelite Religion: How to Reconcile the Differing Textual and Artifactual Portraits." In *Ein Gott allein? JHWH-Verehrung und biblischer Monotheismus im Kontext der israelitischen und altorientalischen Religionsgeschichte*, edited by Dietrich, W., Klopfenstein, M. A., 105–125. Freiburg: Universitätsverlag.

Dever, W. G. 1995. "'Will the Real Israel Please Stand Up?' Archaeology and Israelite Historiography: Part I." *Bulletin of the American Schools of Oriental Research* 297: 61–80.

Dever, W. G. 1996a. "Archaeology and the Current Crisis in Israelite Historiography." *Eretz-Israel: Archaeological, Historical and Geographical Studies* 25: 18*–27*.

Dever, W. G. 1996b. "Revisionist Israel Revisited: A Rejoinder to Niels Peter Lemche." *Currents in Research: Biblical Studies* 4: 35.

Dever, W. G. 1997. "Qom, Khirbet el-." In *The Oxford Encyclopedia of Archaeology in the Near East*, edited by Meyers, E. M., Vol. 4, 391–392. New York: Oxford University.

Dever, W. G. 1999. "Archaeology and the Ancient Israelite Cult: How the Kh. el-Qôm and Kuntillet ʿAjrûd 'Asherah' Texts Have Changed the Picture." *Eretz-Israel: Archaeological, Historical and Geographical Studies (Cross Volume)* 26: 9*–15*.

Dever, W. G. 2005. *Did God Have a Wife? Archaeology and Folk Religion in Ancient Israel.* Grand Rapids: Eerdmans.
Dever, W. G. 2006. "Were There Temples in Ancient Israel? The Archaeological Evidence." In *Text, Artifact, and Image: Revealing Ancient Israelite Religion,* edited by Beckman, G. M., Lewis, T. J., 300–316. Providence: Brown Judaic Studies.
Dever, W. G. 2014. "The Middle Bronze Age 'High Place' at Gezer." *Bulletin of the American Schools of Oriental Research* 371: 17–57.
Dever, W. G. 2017. *Beyond the Texts: An Archaeological Portrait of Ancient Israel and Judah.* Atlanta: SBL Press.
Dever, W. G., Gitin, S., eds. 2003. *Symbiosis, Symbolism, and the Power of the Past: Canaan, Ancient Israel, and Their Neighbors from the Late Bronze Age Through Roman Palaestina.* Winona Lake: Eisenbrauns.
De Vries, P. 2016. *The Kābôd of YHWH in the Old Testament with Particular Reference to the Book of Ezekiel.* Leiden: Brill.
DeVries, S. J. 1985. *1 Kings.* Waco: Word.
Dewrell, H. D. 2017. *Child Sacrifice in Ancient Israel.* Winona Lake: Eisenbrauns.
Dhorme, É. 1926. "Les Chérubins. I: Le Nom." *Revue Biblique* 35: 328–339.
Dhorme, É. 1967. *A Commentary on the Book of Job.* Nashville: Thomas Nelson.
Di Vito, R. A. 1993. *Studies in Third Millennium Sumerian and Akkadian Personal Names: The Designation and Conception of the Personal God.* Rome: Editrice Pontificio Istituto Biblico.
Diamond, E. 1997. "An Israelite Self-Offering in the Priestly Code: A New Perspective on the Nazirite." *Jewish Quarterly Review* 88 (1): 1–18.
Diamond, J. A. 2017. "The Difference Between a Biblical Scholar and a Philosopher." MosaicMagazine.com, January 23.
Dick, M. B, ed. 1999b. *Born in Heaven, Made on Earth: The Making of the Cult Image in the Ancient Near East.* Winona Lake: Eisenbrauns.
Dick, M. B. 1977. "Job 31: A Form-Critical Study." Johns Hopkins University.
Dick, M. B. 1979. "The Legal Metaphor in Job 31." *Catholic Biblical Quarterly* 41: 37–50.
Dick, M. B. 1983. "Job 31, the Oath of Innocence, and the Sage." *Zeitschrift für die alttestamentliche Wissenschaft* 95: 31–53.
Dick, M. B. 1999a. "Prophetic Parodies of Making the Cult Image." In *Born in Heaven, Made on Earth: The Making of the Cult Image in the Ancient Near East,* edited by Dick, M. B., 1–53. Winona Lake: Eisenbrauns.
Dick, M. B. 2006. "The Neo-Assyrian Royal Lion Hunt and Yahweh's Answer to Job." *Journal of Biblical Literature* 125 (2): 243–270.
Dietrich, M. 1973. *Ugarit-Bibliographie.* Kevelaer: Butzon & Bercker.
Dietrich, M. 1989. "Das Einsetzungsritual der Entu von Emar (Emar VI/3, 369)." *Ugarit-Forschungen* 21: 47–100.
Dietrich, M., Loretz, O. 1967. "Zur ugaritischen Lexikographie, II." *Orientalische Literaturzeitung* 62: 533–552.
Dietrich, M., Loretz, O. 1992. *"Jahwe und seine Aschera": Anthropomorphes Kultbild in Mesopotamien, Ugarit und Israel: das biblische Bilderverbot.* Ugaritisch-biblische Literatur, Vol. 9. Münster: Ugarit-Verlag.
Dietrich, M., Loretz, O. 1996. *Analytic Ugaritic Bibliography, 1972–1988.* Kevelaer: Butzon & Bercker.
Dietrich, M., Loretz, O., Mayer, W. 1989. "Sikkanum 'Betyle.'" *Ugarit-Forschungen* 21: 133–139.

van Dijk, J. 1992. "The Authenticity of the Arslan Tash Amulets." *Iraq* 54: 65–68.
Dijkstra, M. 1983. "Notes on Some Proto-Sinaitic Inscriptions Including an Unrecognized Inscription from Wadi Roḍ El-ʿAîr." *Ugarit-Forschungen* 15: 33–38.
Dijkstra, M. 1987. "El ʿolam in the Sinai." *Zeitschrift für die alttestamentliche Wissenschaft* 99 (2): 249–250.
Dijkstra, M. 1993. "The Ugaritic-Hurrian Sacrificial Hymn to El." *Ugarit-Forschungen* 25: 157–162.
Dijkstra, M. 1997. "Semitic Worship at Serabit el-Khadim (Sinai)." *Zeitschrift für Althebraistik* 10: 89–97.
Dijkstra, M. 2013. "Let Sleeping Gods Lie?" In *Reflections on the Silence of God: A Discussion with Marjo Korpel and Johannes De Moor*, edited by Becking, B., 71–87. Leiden: Brill.
Dion, P. E. 1981. "Did Cultic Prostitution Fall into Oblivion During the Postexilic Era? Some Evidence from Chronicles and the Septuagint." *Catholic Biblical Quarterly* 43 (1): 41–48.
Dion, P. E. 1995. "Aramaean Tribes and Nations of First-Millennium Western Asia." In *Civilizations of the Ancient Near East*, edited by Sasson, J. M., Vol. III, 1281–1294. New York: Scribner's.
Dirksen, P. B., van der Kooij, A. W. 1993. *Abraham Kuenen (1828–1891): His Major Contributions to the Study of the Old Testament*. Leiden: Brill.
Dobbs-Allsopp, F. W. 1993. *Weep, O Daughter of Zion: A Study of the City-Lament Genre in the Hebrew Bible*. Rome: Editrice Pontificio Istituto Biblico.
Dobbs-Allsopp, F. W. 1994. "The Genre of the Meṣad Ḥashavyahu Ostracon." *Bulletin of the American Schools of Oriental Research* 295: 49–55.
Dobbs-Allsopp, F. W. 2015. *On Biblical Poetry*. Oxford: Oxford University.
Dobbs-Allsopp, F. W., Roberts, J. J. M., Seow, C. L., Whitaker, R. E. 2005. *Hebrew Inscriptions: Texts from the Biblical Period of the Monarchy with Concordance*. New Haven: Yale University.
Dohmen, C. 1985. *Das Bilderverbot: Seine Entstehung und seine Entwicklung im Alten Testament*. Königstein: Hanstein.
Dohmen, C. 1987. *Das Bilderverbot: Seine Entstehung und seine Entwicklung im Alten Testament*. 2nd ed. Königstein: Hanstein.
Dohmen, C. 2012. *Studien zu Bilderverbot und Bildtheologie des Alten Testaments*. Stuttgart: Verlag Katholisches Bibelwerk.
Doty, W. G. 1986. *Mythography: The Study of Myths and Rituals*. Tuscaloosa: University of Alabama.
Douglas, M. 1966. *Purity and Danger: An Analysis of Concepts of Pollution and Taboo*. New York: Praeger.
Douglas, M. 1993. "The Forbidden Animals in Leviticus." *Journal for the Study of the Old Testament* 59: 3–23.
Doumet-Serhal, C. 2017. "Sidon: Canaan's Firstborn." *Biblical Archaeology Review* 43 (4): 20–29, 58–59.
Dozeman, T. B. 1989. *God on the Mountain: A Study of Redaction, Theology, and Canon in Exodus 19–24*. Atlanta: Scholars Press.
Dozeman, T. B. 2015. *Joshua 1–12: A New Translation with Introduction and Commentary*. New Haven: Yale University.
Dozeman, T. B. 2017. *The Pentateuch: Introducing the Torah*. Minneapolis: Fortress.
Dozeman, T. B., Römer, T., Schmid, K., eds. 2011. *Pentateuch, Hexateuch, or Enneateuch? Identifying Literary Works in Genesis Through Kings*. Atlanta: Society of Biblical Literature.

Dozeman, T. B., Schmid, K., eds. 2006. *A Farewell to the Yahwist? The Composition of the Pentateuch in Recent European Interpretation*. Atlanta: Society of Biblical Literature.

Dozeman, T. B., Schmid, K., Schwartz, B. J., eds. 2011. *The Pentateuch: International Perspectives on Current Research*. Tübingen: Mohr Siebeck.

Driver, S. R. 1895. *A Critical and Exegetical Commentary on Deuteronomy*. Edinburgh: T. & T. Clark.

Driver, S. R., Gray, G. B. 1950. *A Critical and Exegetical Commentary on the Book of Job*. Edinburgh: T. & T. Clark.

du Mesnil du Buisson, C. 1939. "Une tablette magique de la région du Moyen Euphrate." In *Mélanges syriens offerts à Monsieur René Dussaud*, Vol. 1, 421–434. Paris: Geuthner.

Duke, R. K. 1987. "The Portion of the Levite: Another Reading of Deuteronomy 18:6–8." *Journal of Biblical Literature* 106: 193–201.

Duke, R. K. 1988. "Punishment or Restoration? Another Look at the Levites of Ezekiel 44:6–16." *Journal for the Study of the Old Testament* 40: 61–81.

Dumortier, J. 1972. "Un rituel d'intronisation: le Ps. LXXXIX 2–38." *Vetus Testamentum* 22 (2): 176–196.

Duncan, J. A. 1995. "New Readings for the 'Blessing of Moses' from Qumran." *Journal of Biblical Literature* 114 (2): 273–290.

Duncan, J. A. 2003. "4QDeutj." In *Qumran Cave 4: IX: Deuteronomy, Joshua, Judges, Kings*, edited by Ulrich, E., Cross, F. M., Crawford, S. W., Duncan, J. A., Skehan, P. W., Tov, E., Trebolle Barrera, J., 75–91. Oxford: Clarendon Press.

Dupont-Sommer, A. 1970. *Une inscription phénicienne archaïque récemment trouvée à Kition (Chypre)*. Mémoires de l'Académie des Inscriptions et Belles-Lettres, Extrait des Mémoires de l'Académie, Vol. XLIV. Paris: Imprimerie Nationale, C. Klincksieck.

Durand, J. 1990. Review of D. Arnaud, *Recherches au Pays d'Aštata, Emar VI. Revue d'assyriologie et d'archéologie orientale* 84 (1): 49–85.

Durand, J. 1993. "Le mythologème du combat entre le dieu de l'orage et la mer en Mésopotamie." *Mari* 7: 41–61.

Durham, J. I. 1987. *Exodus*. Waco: Word.

Durkheim, É. 1912. *Les formes élémentaires de la vie religieuse: le système totémique en Australie*. Paris: Quadrige.

Dutcher-Walls, P. 2002. "The Circumscription of the King: Deuteronomy 17:16–17 in Its Ancient Social Context." *Journal of Biblical Literature* 121 (4): 601–616.

Dvorjetski, E. 2016. "From Ugarit to Madaba: Philological and Historical Functions of the *marzēaḥ*." *Journal of Semitic Studies* 61 (1): 17–39.

Eaton, J. H. 1964. "The Origin and Meaning of Habakkuk 3." *Zeitschrift für die alttestamentliche Wissenschaft* 76: 144–171.

Ebeling, E. 1916. "Ein Fragment aus dem Mythos der grossen Schlange." *Orientalistische Literaturzeitung* 19: 106–108.

Ebeling, E. 1931. *Tod und Leben nach den vorstellungen der Babylonier*. Berlin: de Gruyter.

Ebeling, J. R. 2010. *Women's Lives in Biblical Times*. London: T. & T. Clark.

Eberhart, C. A. 2002. *Studien zur Bedeutung der Opfer im Alten Testament: die Signifikanz von Blut- und Verbrennungsriten im kultischen Rahmen*. Neukirchen: Neukirchener Verlag.

Eberhart, C. A. 2011. "Sacrifice? Holy Smokes! Reflections on Cult Terminology for Understanding Sacrifice in the Hebrew Bible." In *Ritual and Metaphor: Sacrifice in the Bibl*, edited by Eberhart, C. A., 17–32. Atlanta: Society of Biblical Literature.

Edelman, D. V. 1992. "Abinadab." In *The Anchor Bible Dictionary*, edited by Freedman, D. N., Vol. 1, 22–23. New York: Doubleday.

Edelman, D. V. 1995. "Edom: A Historical Geography." In *You Shall Not Abhor an Edomite for He Is Your Brother: Edom and Seir in History and Tradition*, edited by Edelman, D. V., 1–11. Atlanta: Scholars Press.
Edelman, D. V., ed. 1996a. *The Triumph of Elohim: From Yahwisms to Judaisms*. 2nd ed. Grand Rapids: Eerdmans.
Edelman, D. V. 1996b. "Tracking Observance of the Aniconic Tradition Through Numismatics." In *The Triumph of Elohim: From Yahwisms to Judaisms*, edited by Edelman, D. V., 185–225. Grand Rapids: Eerdmans.
Edzard, D. 1976. "Il." *Reallexicon der Assyriologie und Vorderasiatischen Archäologie* 5: 46–48. Berlin: de Gruyter.
Edzard, D., et al., eds. 1997. *Reallexicon der Assyriologie und Vorderasiatischen Archäologie*. Berlin: de Gruyter.
Eichrodt, W. 1961. *Theology of the Old Testament*. Philadelphia: Westminster.
Eilberg-Schwartz, H. 1990. *The Savage in Judaism*. Indianapolis: Indiana University.
Eising, H. 1998. "Nōgah." In *Theological Dictionary of the Old Testament*, edited by Botterweck, G. J., Ringgren, H., Fabry, H., Vol. IX, 186–187. Grand Rapids: Eerdmans.
Eissfeldt, O. 1951. *El im ugaritischen Pantheon*. Berlin: Akademie-Verlag.
Eissfeldt, O. 1966a. "Jahwes Verhältnis zu 'Elyon und Schaddaj nach Ps 91." In *Kleine Schriften. Dritter Band*, edited by Sellheim, R., Maass, F., 441–447. Tübingen: J. C. B. Mohr.
Eissfeldt, O. 1966b. "Sohnespflichten im Alten Orient." *Syria* 43: 39–47.
Eliade, M. 1949. *Patterns in Comparative Religion*. New York: Meridian.
Ellis, T. A. 2009. "Jeremiah 44: What if 'the Queen of Heaven' Is YHWH?" *Journal for the Study of the Old Testament* 33 (4): 465–488.
Elnes, E. E., Miller, P. D. 1999. "Elyon." In *Dictionary of Deities and Demons in the Bible*, edited by van der Toorn, K., Becking, B., van der Horst, P. W., 293–299. 2nd ed. Leiden: Brill.
Emerton, J. A. 1962. "Priests and Levites in Deuteronomy: An Examination of Dr. G. E. Wright's Theory." *Vetus Testamentum* 12 (2): 129–138.
Emerton, J. A. 1966. "Spring and Torrent' in Psalm lxxiv 15." In *Volume du Congrès: Genève 1965*. Vetus Testamentum Supplement 15: 122–133. Leiden: Brill.
Emerton, J. A. 1982. "New Light on Israelite Religion: The Implications of the Inscriptions from Kuntillet 'Ajrud." *Zeitschrift für die alttestamentliche Wissenschaft* 94 (1): 2–20.
Emerton, J. A. 1993. "The 'Mountain of God' in Psalm 68:16." In *History and Traditions of Early Israel*, edited by Lemaire, A., 24–37. Leiden: Brill.
Emerton, J. A. 1997. Review of D. Edelman, ed., *The Triumph of Elohim: From Yahwisms to Judaisms. Vetus Testamentum* 47 (3): 393–400.
Emerton, J. A. 1999. "'Yahweh and His Asherah': The Goddess or Her Symbol?" *Vetus Testamentum* 49 (3): 315–337.
Emerton, J. A. 2002. "The Value of the Moabite Stone as an Historical Source." *Vetus Testamentum* 52 (4): 483–492.
Engnell, I. 1943. 1969. *A Rigid Scrutiny: Critical Essays on the Old Testament*. Nashville: Abingdon.
Engnell, I. 1943. *Studies in Divine Kingship in the Ancient Near East*. Uppsala: Almqvist & Wiksell.
Eph'al, I. 1999. "The Bukan Aramaic Inscription: Historical Considerations." *Israel Exploration Journal* 49: 116–121.

Eph'al, I., Naveh, J. 1998. "Remarks on the Recently Published Moussaieff Ostraca." *Israel Exploration Journal* 48 (3): 269–273.
Erisman, A. R. 2013. "The Pentateuch: International Perspectives on Current Research." *Journal of the American Oriental Society* 133 (3): 551–553.
Esteban, C., Pellín, D. I. 2016. "Temples of Astarte Across the Mediterranean." *Mediterranean Archaeology and Archaeometry* 16 (4): 161–166.
Evans, C. D. 1995. "Cult Images, Royal Policies and the Origins of Aniconism." In *The Pitcher Is Broken: Memorial Essays for Gösta W. Ahlström*, edited by Holloway, S. W., Handy, L. K., 192–212. Sheffield: Sheffield Academic Press.
Evans-Pritchard, E. E. 1956. *Nuer Religion*. Oxford: Clarendon Press.
Exum, J. C. 1993. *Fragmented Women: Feminist (Sub)versions of Biblical Narratives*. Sheffield: JSOT Press.
Exum, J. C. 1996. *Plotted, Shot, and Painted: Cultural Representations of Biblical Women*. Sheffield: Sheffield Academic Press.
Fabry, H. 2003. "Ṣûr." In *Theological Dictionary of the Old Testament*, edited by Botterweck, G. J., Ringgren, H., Fabry, H., Vol. XII, 311–321. Grand Rapids: Eerdmans.
Fales, F. M. 2008. "On *Pax Assyriaca* in the Eighth-Seventh Centuries BCE and Its Implications." In *Isaiah's Vision of Peace in Biblical and Modern International Relations: Swords into Plowshares*, edited by Cohen, R., Westbrook, R., 17–35. New York: Palgrave Macmillan.
Fales, F. M. 2011. "Old Aramaic." In *The Semitic Languages: An International Handbook*, edited by Weninger, S., Khan, G., Streck, M. P., Watson, J. C. E., 555–573. Berlin: de Gruyter.
Fales, F. M., Grassi, G. F. 2016. *L'aramaico antico. Storia, grammatica, testi commentate*. Udine: Forum.
Fantalkin, A., Finkelstein, I. 2017. "The Date of Abandonment and Territorial Affiliation of Khirbet Qeiyafa: An Update." *Tel Aviv* 44 (1): 53–60.
Faulkner, R. O. 1955. "The Installation of the Vizier." *Journal of Egyptian Archaeology* 41: 18–29.
Faust, A. 2000. "Ethnic Complexity in Northern Israel During Iron Age II." *Palestine Exploration Quarterly* 132: 2–27.
Faust, A. 2006. *Israel's Ethnogenesis: Settlement, Interaction, Expansion and Resistance*. London: Equinox.
Faust, A. 2012. *The Archaeology of Israelite Society in Iron Age II*. Winona Lake: Eisenbrauns.
Faust, A. 2014. "Highlands or Lowlands? Reexamining Demographic Processes in Iron Age Judah." *Ugarit-Forschungen* 45: 111–142.
Faust, A. 2015a. "The Bible, Archaeology, and the Practice of Circumcision in Israelite and Philistine Societies." *Journal of Biblical Literature* 134 (2): 273–290.
Faust, A. 2015b. "The Emergence of Iron Age Israel: On Origins and Habitus." In *Israel's Exodus in Transdisciplinary Perspective: Text, Archaeology, Culture, and Geoscience*, edited by Levy, T. E., Schneider, T., Propp, W. H. C., 467–482. Heidelberg: Springer.
Faust, A. 2017. "The Bounded Landscape: Archaeology, Language, Texts, and the Israelite Perception of Space." *Journal of Mediterranean Archaeology* 30 (1): 3–32.
Faust, A. 2019. "Israelite Temples: Where Was Israelite Cult Not Practiced, and Why." *Religions* 10: 1–26.
Faust, A., Lev-Tov, J. 2014. "Philistia and the Philistines in the Iron Age I: Interaction, Ethnic Dynamics and Boundary Maintenance." *HIPHIL, Novum* 1 (1): 1–24.

Feder, Y. 2011. *Blood Expiation in Hittite and Biblical Ritual*. Writings from the Ancient World Supplements, Vol. 2. Atlanta: Society of Biblical Literature.

Feder, Y. 2013. "The Aniconic Tradition, Deuteronomy 4, and the Politics of Israelite Identity." *Journal of Biblical Literature* 132 (2): 251–274.

Feigin, S. 1920. "The Meaning of Ariel." *Journal of Biblical Literature* 39: 131–136.

Fensham, F. C. 1962. "Widow, Orphan, and the Poor in Ancient Near Eastern Legal and Wisdom Literature." *Journal of Near Eastern Studies* 21 (2): 129–139.

Fensham, F. C. 1971. "Father and Son as Terminology for Treaty and Covenant." In *Near Eastern Studies in Honor of William Foxwell Albright*, edited by Goedicke, H., 121–135. Baltimore: Johns Hopkins Press.

Finet, A. 1993. "Yahvé au royaume Mari." In *Circulation des monnaies, des marchandises et des biens*, edited by Gyselen, R., 15–22. Res orientales, Vol. 5. Bures-sur-Yvette: Groupe pour l'étude de la civilisation du Moyen-orient.

Finkel, I. L., Geller, M. J., eds. 1997. *Sumerian Gods and Their Representations*. Groningen: STYX Publications.

Finkelstein, I. 1988. *The Archaeology of the Israelite Settlement*. Jerusalem: Israel Exploration Society.

Finkelstein, I. 1998. "Two Notes on Northern Samaria: The 'Einun Pottery' and the Date of the 'Bull Site.'" *Palestine Exploration Quarterly* 130: 94–98.

Finkelstein, I. 2003. "City-States to States: Polity Dynamics in the 10th–9th Centuries B.C.E." In *Symbiosis, Symbolism, and the Power of the Past: Canaan, Ancient Israel, and Their Neighbors from the Late Bronze Age Through Roman Palaestina*, edited by Dever, W. G., Gitin, S., 75–83. Winona Lake: Eisenbrauns.

Finkelstein, I., Fantalkin, A. 2012. "Khirbet Qeiyafa: An Unsensational Archaeological and Historical Interpretation." *Tel Aviv* 39 (1): 38–63.

Finkelstein, J. J. 1958. "Bible and Babel: A Comparative Study of the Hebrew and Babylonian Religious Spirit." *Commentary* 26 (5): 431–444.

Finnegan, R. H. 1977. *Oral Poetry: Its Nature, Significance, and Social Context*. Cambridge: Cambridge University.

Finsterbusch, K. 2002. *JPS Bible Commentary: Haftarot*. Philadelphia: Jewish Publication Society.

Finsterbusch, K. 2005. *Weisung für Israel: Studien zu religiösem Lehren und Lernen im Deuteronomium und in seinem Umfeld*. Tübingen: Mohr Siebeck.

Finsterbusch, K. 2007. *JHWH als Lehrer der Menschen: ein Beitrag zur Gottesvorstellung der Hebräischen Bibel*. Neukirchen-Vluyn: Neukirchener Verlag.

Fishbane, M. A. 1985. *Biblical Interpretation in Ancient Israel*. Oxford: Clarendon Press.

Fitzgerald, A. 1974. "A Note on Psalm 29." *Bulletin of the American Schools of Oriental Research* 215: 61–63.

Fitzmyer, J. A. 1967. *The Aramaic Inscriptions of Sefire*. Rome: Pontifical Biblical Institute.

Fitzmyer, J. A. 1995. *The Aramaic Inscriptions of Sefire*. 2nd ed. Rome: Pontifical Biblical Institute.

Flanagan, J. 1999. "Ancient Perceptions of Space/Perceptions of Ancient Space." *Semeia* 87: 15–43.

Flebbe, J., ed. 2016. *Holy Places in Biblical and Extrabiblical Traditions: Proceedings of the Bonn-Leiden-Oxford Colloquium on Biblical Studies*. Bonn: Bonn University.

Fleming, D. E. 1992a. *The Installation of Baal's High Priestess at Emar: A Window on Ancient Syrian Religion*. Atlanta: Scholars Press.

Fleming, D. E. 1992b. "A Limited Kingship: Late Bronze Age Emar in Ancient Syria." *Ugarit-Forschungen* 24: 59–71.

Fleming, D. E. 1992c. "The Rituals from Emar: Evolution of an Indigenous Tradition in Second-Millennium Syria." In *New Horizons in the Study of Ancient Syria*, edited by Chavalas, M. W., Hayes, J. L., 51–61. Malibu: Undena.

Fleming, D. E. 1997a. "The Installation of the Storm God's High Priestess." In *The Context of Scripture 1: Canonical Compositions from the Biblical World*, edited by Hallo, W. W., Younger, K. L., 427–431. Leiden: Brill.

Fleming, D. E. 1997b. "The *Zukru* Festival." In *The Context of Scripture 1: Canonical Compositions from the Biblical World*, edited by Hallo, W. W., Younger, K. L., 431–436. Leiden: Brill.

Fleming, D. E. 1998. "The Biblical Tradition of Anointing Priests." *Journal of Biblical Literature* 117: 401–414.

Fleming, D. E. 1999a. "If El Is a Bull, Who Is a Calf? Reflections on Religion in Second-Millennium Syria-Palestine." *Eretz-Israel* (Frank Moore Cross Volume) 26: 23*–27*.

Fleming, D. E. 1999b. "The Seven Day Siege of Jericho." In *Ki Baruch Hu: Ancient Near Eastern, Biblical, and Judaic Studies in Honor of Baruch A. Levine*, edited by Chazan, R., Hallo, W. W., Schiffman, L. H., 209–222. Winona Lake: Eisenbrauns.

Fleming, D. E. 2000. *Time at Emar: The Cultic Calendar and the Rituals from the Diviner's Archive*. Winona Lake: Eisenbrauns.

Fleming, D. E. 2008. "The Integration of Household and Community Religion." In *Household and Family Religion in Antiquity*, edited by Bodel, J. P., Olyan, S. M., 37–59. Malden: Blackwell.

Fleming, D. E. 2012. *The Legacy of Israel in Judah's Bible: History, Politics, and the Reinscribing of Tradition*. New York: Cambridge University.

Fleming, D. E. Forthcoming. *Yahweh Before Israel: Glimpses of History in a Divine Name*. Cambridge: Cambridge University.

Fleming, E. E. 2013. "The Politics of Sexuality in the Story of King David." Johns Hopkins University.

Fleming, E. E. 2016. "Political Favoritism in Saul's Court: ḥpṣ, n'm, and the Relationship Between David and Jonathan." *Journal of Biblical Literature* 135 (1): 19–34.

Flint, P. W. 1997. "A Form of Psalm 89." In *The Dead Sea Scrolls: Hebrew, Aramaic, and Greek Texts with English Translations: Pseudepigraphic and Non-Masoretic Psalms and Prayers*, edited by Charlesworth, J. H., Vol. 4A, 40–45. Tübingen: J. C. B. Mohr Paul Siebeck.

Fohrer, G. 1972. *History of Israelite Religion*. Nashville: Abingdon.

Fokkelman, J. P. 1990. "The Structure of Psalm LXVIII." In *In Quest of the Past: Studies on Israelite Religion, Literature and Prophetism*, edited by van der Woude, A. S., 72–83. Leiden: Brill.

Fontenrose, J. E. 1966. *The Ritual Theory of Myth*. Berkeley: University of California.

Forti, T., Glatt-Gilad, D. 2015. "The Function of the Root *śkl* in Shaping the Ideal Figure of David in 1 Samuel 18." *Vetus Testamentum* 65 (3): 390–400.

Foster, B. R. 1993. *Before the Muses: An Anthology of Akkadian Literature*. Bethesda: CDL Press.

Foster, B. R. 1997. "Epic of Creation." In *The Context of Scripture 1: Canonical Compositions from the Biblical World*, edited by Hallo, W. W., Younger, K. L., 390–402. Leiden: Brill.

Foster, B. R. 2005. *Before the Muses: An Anthology of Akkadian Literature*. 2nd ed. Bethesda: CDL Press.

Foster, J. L. 1995. "The Hymn to Aten: Akhenaten Worships the Sole God." In *Civilizations of the Ancient Near East*, edited by Sasson, J. M., Vol. III, 1751–1761. New York: Scribner's.

Foster, J. L. 2001. *Ancient Egyptian Literature: An Anthology*. Austin: University of Texas.

Fowler, J. D. 1988. *Theophoric Personal Names in Ancient Hebrew: A Comparative Study*. Sheffield: JSOT Press.

Fox, M. V. 1977. "Frame-Narrative and Composition in the Book of Qohelet." *Hebrew Union College Annual* 48: 83–106.

Fox, M. V. 1981. "Job 38 and God's Rhetoric." *Semeia* 19: 53–61.

Fox, M. V. 1989. *Qohelet and His Contradictions*. Sheffield: Almond Press.

Fox, M. V. 1999. *A Time to Tear Down and a Time to Build Up: A Rereading of Ecclesiastes*. Grand Rapids: Eerdmans.

Fox, M. V. 2000. *Proverbs 1–9: A New Translation with Introduction and Commentary*. New York: Doubleday.

Fox, M. V. 2009. *Proverbs 10–31: A New Translation with Introduction and Commentaryy*. New Haven: Yale University.

Frahm, E. 1997. *Einleitung in die Sanherib-Inschriften*. Vienna: Institut für Orientalistik der Universität.

Frandsen, J. P. 2008. "Aspects of Kingship in Ancient Egypt." In *Religion and Power: Divine Kingship in the Ancient World and Beyond*, edited by Brisch, N. M., 47–73. Chicago: Oriental Institute.

Frankel, D. 1994. "The Destruction of the Golden Calf: A New Solution." *Vetus Testamentum* 44 (3): 330–339.

Frankel, D. 2010. "El as the Speaking Voice in Psalm 82:6–8." *Journal of Hebrew Scriptures* 10: 2–24.

Frankel, R., Ventura, R. 1998. "The Mişpe Yamim Bronzes." *Bulletin of the American Schools of Oriental Research* 311: 39–55.

Frankfort, H. 1946. *The Intellectual Adventure of Ancient Man: An Essay on Speculative Thought in the Ancient Near East*. Chicago: University of Chicago.

Frankfort, H. 1951. *The Problem of Similarity in Ancient Near Eastern Religions*. Oxford: Clarendon Press.

Frankfort, H., Groenewegen-Frankfort, H. A. 1949. *Before Philosophy. The Intellectual Adventure of Ancient Man. An Essay on Speculative Thought in the Ancient Near East*. Baltimore: Penguin Books.

Freedman, D. N. 1960. "The Name of the God of Moses." *Journal of Biblical Literature* 79 (2): 151–156.

Freedman, D. N. 1963. "The Original Name of Jacob." *Israel Exploration Journal* 13 (2): 125–126.

Freedman, D. N. 1975. "Early Israelite History in the Light of Early Israelite Poetry." In *Unity and Diversity*, edited by Goedicke, H., Roberts, J. J. M., 3–35. Baltimore: Johns Hopkins University.

Freedman, D. N. 1976. "Divine Names and Titles in Early Hebrew Poetry." In *Magnalia Dei, the Mighty Acts of God: Essays on the Bible and Archaeology in Memory of G. Ernest Wright*, edited by Cross, F. M., Lemke, W. E., Miller, P. D., 55–107. Garden City: Doubleday.

Freedman, D. N. 1977. "Pottery, Poetry, and Prophecy: An Essay on Biblical Poetry." *Journal of Biblical Literature* 96: 5–26.

Freedman, D. N. 1978. "Psalm 113 and the Song of Hannah." *Eretz-Israel: Archaeological, Historical and Geographical Studies* (H. L. Ginsberg Volume) 14: 56*–69*.

Freedman, D. N. 1980. *Pottery, Poetry, and Prophecy: Studies in Early Hebrew Poetry.* Winona Lake: Eisenbrauns.

Freedman, D. N. 1987. "'Who Is Like Thee Among the Gods?' The Religion of Early Israel." In *Ancient Israelite Religion: Essays in Honor of Frank Moore Cross*, edited by Miller, P. D., Hanson, P. D., McBride, S. D., 315–335. Philadelphia: Fortress.

Freedman, D. N. 1989. "W. F. Albright as an Historian." In *The Scholarship of William Foxwell Albright: An Appraisal*, edited by Van Beek, G. W., 33–45. Atlanta: Scholars Press.

Freedman, D. N. 1997. *Divine Commitment and Human Obligation: Selected Writings of David Noel Freedman, Vol. 1: Ancient Israelite History*, edited by Huddlestun, J. R. Grand Rapids: Eerdmans.

Freedman, D. N., ed. 1992. *The Anchor Bible Dictionary*. New York: Doubleday.

Freedman, D. N., O'Connor, M. P. 1986. "*YHWH*." In *Theological Dictionary of the Old Testament*, edited by Botterweck, G. J., Ringgren, H., Vol. V, 500–521. Grand Rapids: Eerdmans.

Frei, H. W. 1974. *The Eclipse of Biblical Narrative: A Study in Eighteenth and Nineteenth Century Hermeneutics*. New Haven: Yale University.

Frerichs, E. S. 1987. "Ancient Israel's Scripture and Its Religion: The Achievement of Helmer Ringgren." In *Judaic Perspectives on Ancient Israel*, edited by Neusner, J., Levine, B. A., Frerichs, E. S., 27–30. Philadelphia: Fortress.

Fretheim, T. E. 1968. "The Ark in Deuteronomy." *Catholic Biblical Quarterly* 30: 1–14.

Frevel, C. 1995. *Aschera und der Ausschliesslichkeitsanspruch YHWHs*. Weinheim: Beltz Athenäum.

Friedman, R. E. 1981. *The Exile and Biblical Narrative: The Formation of the Deuteronomistic and Priestly Works*. Chico: Scholars Press.

Friedman, R. E. 2001. *Commentary on the Torah: With a New English Translation*. San Francisco: Harper.

Friedman, R. E. 2005. *The Bible with Sources Revealed: A New View into the Five Books of Moses*. San Francisco: HarperCollins.

Fritz, V. 1979. "Kadesch-Barnea." *Biblische Notizen* 9: 45–50.

Fritz, V. 1990. *Kinneret: Ergebnisse der Ausgrabungen auf dem Tell el-`Oreme am See Gennesaret, 1982–1985*. Wiesbaden: Harrassowitz.

Fritz, V. 1993. "Chinnereth, Tel." In *The New Encyclopedia of Archaeological Excavations in the Holy Land*, edited by Stern, E., Levinzon-Gilboa, A., Aviram, J., Vol. 1, 299–301. Jerusalem: Israel Exploration Society & Carta.

Fritz, V. 2003. *1 & 2 Kings*. Minneapolis: Fortress.

Frye, J. B. 1973. "The Legal Language of the Book of Job." University of London.

Frymer-Kensky, T. 1981. "Patriarchal Family Relationships and Near Eastern Law." *Biblical Archaeologist* 44: 209–214.

Frymer-Kensky, T. 1983. "Pollution, Purification, and Purgation in Biblical Israel." In *The Word of the Lord Shall Go Forth: Essays in Honor of David Noel Freedman in Celebration of His Sixtieth Birthday*, edited by Meyers, C. L., O'Connor, M. P., 399–414. Winona Lake: Eisenbrauns.

Frymer-Kensky, T. 1989. "The Ideology of Gender in the Bible and the Ancient Near East." In *Dumu-e2-Dub-Ba-a: Studies in Honor of Åke W. Sjöberg*, edited by Behrens, H., Loding, D., Roth, M. T., 185–191. Philadelphia: University Museum.

Frymer-Kensky, T. 1992. *In the Wake of the Goddesses: Women, Culture, and the Biblical Transformation of Pagan Myth*. New York: Free Press.

Frymer-Kensky, T. 2003. "Israel." In *A History of Ancient Near Eastern Law*, edited by Westbrook, R., 975–1046. Leiden: Brill.

Fuchs, E. 1985. "The Literary Characterization of Mothers and Sexual Politics in the Hebrew Bible." In *Feminist Perspectives on Biblical Scholarship*, edited by Collins, A. Y., 117–136. Chico: Scholars Press.

Fuchs, E. 2000. *Sexual Politics in the Biblical Narrative: Reading the Hebrew Bible as a Woman*. Sheffield: Sheffield Academic Press.

Fuchs, E. 2008. "Reclaiming the Hebrew Bible for Women: The Neoliberal Turn in Contemporary Feminist Scholarship." *Journal of Feminist Studies in Religion* 8: 45–65.

Furman, N. 1989. "His Story Versus Her Story: Male Genealogy and Female Strategy in the Jacob Cycle." In *Narrative Research on the Hebrew Bible*, edited by Amihai, M., Coats, G. W., Solomon, A. M., 141–149. Atlanta: Scholars Press.

Gafney, W. 2017. *Womanist Midrash: A Reintroduction to the Women of the Torah and the Throne*. Louisville: Westminster John Knox.

Gallagher, W. R. 1999. *Sennacherib's Campaign to Judah: New Studies*. Leiden: Brill.

Gammie, J. G. 1989. *Holiness in Israel*. Minneapolis: Fortess.

Gammie, J. G. 2005. *Holiness in Israel*. 2nd ed. Eugene: Wipf & Stock.

Gansell, A., Shafer, A., eds. 2020. *Testing the Canon of Ancient Near Eastern Art and Archaeology*. Oxford: Oxford University.

Garbini, G. 1988. *History and Ideology in Ancient Israel*. New York: Crossroad.

Garfein, S. 2004. "Temple-Palace Conflict in Pre-exilic Judah." Johns Hopkins University.

Garfinkel, S. P. 1983. "Studies in Akkadian Influences in Ezekiel." Columbia University.

Garfinkel, Y. 2017. "Khirbet Qeiyafa in the Shephela: Data and Interpretations." In *Khirbet Qeiyafa in the Shephelah*, edited by Schroer, S., Münger, S., 5–59. Fribourg: Academic Press Fribourg.

Garfinkel, Y., Golub, M. R., Misgav, H., Ganor, S. 2015. "The ʾIšbaʿal Inscription from Khirbet Qeiyafa." *Bulletin of the American Schools of Oriental Research* 373: 217–233.

Garr, W. R. 1985. *Dialect Geography of Syria-Palestine, 1000–586 B.C.E.* Philadelphia: University of Pennsylvania.

Garr, W. R. 2003. *In His Own Image and Likeness: Humanity, Divinity, and Monotheism*. Leiden: Brill.

Garr, W. R., Fassberg, S. E. 2016. *A Handbook of Biblical Hebrew*. Winona Lake: Eisenbrauns.

Garroway, K. H. 2014. *Children in the Ancient Near Eastern Household*. Winona Lake: Eisenbrauns.

Gaster, T. H. 1942. "A Canaanite Magical Text." *Orientalia* 11: 41–79.

Gaster, T. H. 1961. *Thespis: Ritual, Myth and Drama in the Ancient Near East*. New York: Norton.

Gaster, T. H. 1969. *Myth, Legend, and Custom in the Old Testament*. New York: Harper & Row.

Gaster, T. H. 1973. "A Hang-Up for Hang-Ups: The Second Amuletic Plaque from Arslan Tash." *Bulletin of the American Schools of Oriental Research* 209: 18–26.

Gelb, I. J. 1961. *Old Akkadian Writing and Grammar*. Chicago: University of Chicago.

Gelb, I. J. 1980. *Computer-Aided Analysis of Amorite*. Assyriological Studies, Vol. 21. Chicago: Oriental Institute of the University of Chicago.

Gelinas, M. M. 1995. "United Monarchy—Divided Monarchy: Fact or Fiction?" In *The Pitcher Is Broken: Memorial Essays for Gösta W. Ahlström*, edited by Holloway, S. W., Handy, L. K., 227–237. Sheffield: Sheffield Academic Press.
Geller, S. A. 1985. "Wellhausen and Kaufmann." *Midstream* 31 (10): 39–48.
Geller, S. A. 1996. *Sacred Enigmas: Literary Religion in the Hebrew Bible*. London: Routledge.
Gemser, B. 1955. "The rīb- or Controversy Pattern in Hebrew Mentality." In *Wisdom in Israel and in the Ancient Near East*, edited by Noth, M., Thomas, D. W., 120–137. Leiden: Brill.
George, A. R. 2003. *The Babylonian Gilgamesh Epic*. Oxford: Oxford University.
George, M. K. 2007. "Space and History: Siting Critical Space for Biblical Studies." In *Constructions of Space I: Theory, Geography, and Narrative*, edited by Berquist, J. L., Camp, C. V., 15–31. New York: T. &. T. Clark.
George, M. K. 2009. *Israel's Tabernacle as Social Space*. Atlanta: SBL Press.
Gerstenberger, E. S. 1996a. *Yahweh the Patriarch: Ancient Images of God and Feminist Theology*. Minneapolis: Augsburg Fortress.
Gerstenberger, E. S. 1996b. *Leviticus: A Commentary*. Louisville: Westminster John Knox.
Gerstenberger, E. S. 2001. *Psalms, Part 2 and Lamentations*. Grand Rapids: Eerdmans.
Gerstenberger, E. S. 2002. *Theologies in the Old Testament*. Minneapolis: Fortress.
Gertz, J. C., Levinson, B. M., Rom-Shiloni, D., Schmid, K., eds. 2016. *The Formation of the Pentateuch: Bridging the Academic Cultures of Europe, Israel, and North America*. Forschungen zum Alten Testament, Vol. 111. Tübingen: Mohr Siebeck.
Gertz, J. C., Schmid, K., Witte, M., eds. 2002. *Abschied vom Jahwisten: Die Komposition des Hexateuch in der jüngsten Diskussion*. Beihefte zur Zeitschrift für die alttestamentliche Wissenschaft, Vol. 315. Berlin: de Gruyter.
Gesenius, W., Kautzsch, E., Cowley, A. E. 1976. *Gesenius' Hebrew Grammar*. Oxford: Clarendon Press.
Gevirtz, S. 1961. "West-Semitic Curses and the Problem of the Origins of Hebrew Law." *Vetus Testamentum* 11 (2): 137–158.
Gibson, J. C. L. 1978. *Canaanite Myths and Legends*. Edinburgh: Clark.
Gibson, J. C. L. 1994. "The Kingship of Yahweh Against Its Canaanite Background." In *Ugarit and the Bible*, edited by Brooke, G. J., 101–112. Münster: Ugarit-Verlag.
Gilan, A. 2011. "Hittite Religious Rituals and the Ideology of Kingship." *Religious Compass* 5/7: 276–285.
Gilbert-Peretz, D. 1996. "Ceramic Figurines." In *Excavations at the City of David 1978–1985, Vol.4. Qedem 35*, edited by Ariel, D. T., De Groot, A., 42–84. Jerusalem: Institute of Archaeology, Hebrew University of Jerusalem.
Gilders, W. K. 2004. *Blood Ritual in the Hebrew Bible: Meaning and Power*. Baltimore: Johns Hopkins University.
Gilders, W. K. 2013. "Ancient Israelite Sacrifice as a Symbolic Action: Theoretical Reflections." *Svensk Exegetisk Årsbok* 78: 1–25.
Gilibert, A. 2011. *Syro-Hittite Monumental Art and the Archaeology of Performance: The Stone Reliefs at Carchemish and Zincirli in the Earlier First Millennium BCE*. New York: de Gruyter.
Gilmour, G. H. 1995. "The Archaeology of Cult in the Southern Levant in the Early Iron Age: An Analytical and Comparative Approach." University of Oxford.
Gilmour, G. H. 2009. "An Iron Age II Pictorial Inscription from Jerusalem Illustrating Yahweh and Asherah." *Palestine Exploration Quarterly* 141 (2): 87–103.

Gilula, M. 1979. "To Yahweh Shomron and His Asherah." *Shnaton* 3: 129–137, xv–xvi.
Ginsberg, H. L. 1936. *Kitve Ugarit*. Jerusalem: Mosad Byalik.
Ginsberg, H. L. 1938a. "Ba'l and 'Anat." *Orientalia* 7: 1–11.
Ginsberg, H. L. 1938b. "A Ugaritic Parallel to 2 Sam 1:21." *Journal of Biblical Literature* 57 (2): 209–213.
Ginsberg, H. L. 1939. "Two Religious Borrowings in Ugaritic Literature: I. A Hurrian Myth in Semitic Dress." *Orientalia* 8: 317–327.
Ginsberg, H. L. 1950. "Interpreting Ugaritic Texts." *Journal of the American Oriental Society* 70: 156–160.
Gitin, S. 2012. "Temple Complex 650 at Ekron: The Impact of Multi-Cultural Influences on Philistine Cult in the Late Iron Age." In *Temple Building and Temple Cult: Architecture and Cultic Paraphernalia of Temples in the Levant (2.-1. Mill. B.C.E.)*, edited by Kamlah, J., Michelau, H., 223–256. Wiesbaden: Harrassowitz.
Gitin, S., Aḥituv, S. 2015. "Two New Cultic Inscriptions from Seventh-Century B.C.E. Ekron." In *Marbeh Ḥokmah: Studies in the Bible and the Ancient Near East in Loving Memory of Victor Avigdor Hurowitz*, edited by Yona, S., Greenstein, E. L., Gruber, M. I., Machinist, P., Paul, S. M., 221–227. Winona Lake: Eisenbrauns.
Gitin, S., Wright, J. E., Dessel, J. P., eds. 2006. *Confronting the Past: Archaeological and Historical Essays on Ancient Israel in Honor of William G. Dever*. Winona Lake: Eisenbrauns.
Gittlen, B. M., ed. 2002. *Sacred Time, Sacred Place: Archaeology and the Religion of Israel*. Winona Lake: Eisenbrauns.
Giveon, R. 1964. "'The Cities of Our God' (II Sam 10:12)." *Journal of Biblical Literature* 83 (4): 415–416.
Giveon, R. 1965. "Two Egyptian Documents Concerning Bashan from the Time of Ramses II." *Rivista Degli Studi Orientali* 40 (3): 197–202.
Giveon, R. 1971. *Les Bédouins Shosou des documents égyptiens*. Leiden: Brill.
Gnuse, R. K., Knight, D. A. 1992. Foreword to S. Mowinckel, *The Psalms in Israel's Worship*. Sheffield: JSOT Press.
Godbey, A. H. 1924. "Ariel or David-Cultus." *American Journal of Semitic Languages* 41: 253–266.
Godley, A. D. 1957. *Herodotus*. Cambridge: Harvard University.
Goetze, A. 1969. "Daily Prayer for a King." In *Ancient Near Eastern Texts Relating to the Old Testament*, edited by Pritchard, J. B., 396–397. Princeton: Princeton University.
Gogel, S. L. 1998. *A Grammar of Epigraphic Hebrew*. Atlanta: Scholars Press.
Goitein, S. D. 1956. "YHWH the Passionate: The Monotheistic Meaning and Origin of the Name YHWH." *Vetus Testamentum* 6 (1): 1–9.
Golani, A. 2013. *Jewelry from the Iron Age II Levant*. Fribourg: Academic Press Fribourg.
Golub, M. R. 2014. "The Distribution of Personal Names in the Land of Israel and Transjordan During the Iron II Period." *Journal of the American Oriental Society* 134: 621–642.
Golub, M. R. 2017. "Personal Names in Judah in the Iron Age II." *Journal of Semitic Studies* 62 (1): 19–58.
Goodfriend, E. A. 1992. "Prostitution." In *The Anchor Bible Dictionary*, edited by Freedman, D. N., Vol. 5, 505–510. New York: Doubleday.
Gordon, C. H. 1965. *Ugaritic Textbook*. Rome: Pontifical Biblical Institute.
Gordon, R. P. 2007. *The God of Israel*. Cambridge: Cambridge University.

Gorman, F. H. 1990. *The Ideology of Ritual: Space, Time and Status in the Priestly Theology.* Sheffield: JSOT Press.

Goshen-Gottstein, A. 2001. "God the Father in Rabbinic Judaism and Christianity: Transformed Background or Common Ground?" *Journal of Ecumenical Studies* 38 (4): 470–504.

Goshen-Gottstein, M. 1979. "The Aleppo Codex and the Rise of the Masoretic Bible Text." *Biblical Archaeologist* 42 (3): 145–163.

Gottwald, N. K. 1979. *The Tribes of Yahweh: A Sociology of the Religion of Liberated Israel, 1250–1050 B.C.E.* Maryknoll: Orbis Books.

Gottwald, N. K. 1993. *The Hebrew Bible in Its Social World and in Ours.* Atlanta: Scholars Press.

Grabbe, L. L. 1994. "'Canaanite': Some Methodological Observations in Relation to Biblical Study." In *Ugarit and the Bible*, edited by Brooke, G. J., Curtis, A. H. W., Healey, J. F., 113–122. Münster: Ugarit-Verlag.

Grabbe, L. L. 1995. *Priests, Prophets, Diviners, Sages: A Socio-Historical Study of Religious Specialists in Ancient Israel.* Valley Forge: Trinity Press International.

Grabbe, L. L. 2003. "The Priests in Leviticus—Is the Medium the Message?" In *The Book of Leviticus: Composition and Reception*, edited by Rendtorff, R., Kugler, R. A., 207–224. Leiden: Brill.

Grabbe, L. L. 2004. *A History of the Jews and Judaism in the Second Temple Period, Volume 1. Yehud: A History of the Persian Province of Judah.* London: T. &. T. Clark.

Grabbe, L. L. 2010. "'Many Nations Will Be Joined to Yhwh in That Day': The Question of Yhwh Outside Judah." In *Religious Diversity in Ancient Israel and Judah*, edited by Stavrakopoulou, F., Barton, J., 175–187. London: T. & T. Clark.

Grabbe, L. L. 2017. *Ancient Israel: What Do We Know and How Do We Know It?* London: Bloomsbury T. &. T. Clark.

Graesser, C. F. 1969. "Studies in *Massebôt*." Harvard University.

Graesser, C. F. 1972. "Standing Stones in Ancient Palestine." *Biblical Archaeologist* 35: 34–63.

Grant, E., Wright, G. E. 1931. *Ain Shems Excavations (Palestine), Part 1.* Haverford: Haverford College.

Grant, E., Wright, G. E. 1939. *Ain Shems Excavations (Palestine), Part 5 (Text).* Haverford: Haverford College.

Gras, M., Rouillard, P., Teixidor, J. 1991. "The Phoenicians and Death." *Berytus* 39: 127–176.

Gray, G. B. 1971. *Sacrifice in the Old Testament: Its Theory and Practice with prolegomenon by Baruch A. Levine.* New York: KTAV.

Gray, J. 1953. "The God Yw in the Religion of Canaan." *Journal of Near Eastern Studies* 12 (4): 278–283.

Gray, J. 1965. *The Legacy of Canaan: The Ras Shamra Texts and Their Relevance to the Old Testament.* Leiden: Brill.

Gray, J. 1970. *I & II Kings: A Commentary.* Philadelphia: Westminster.

Gray, J. 1977. "Cantata of the Autumn Festival." *Journal of Semitic Studies* 22: 2–26.

Grayson, A. K. 1976. *Assyrian Royal Inscriptions, Part 2.* Weisbaden: Harrassowitz.

Grayson, A. K. 1991. *Assyrian Rulers of the Early First Millennium BC I (1114–859 BC).* Toronto: University of Toronto.

Grayson, A. K. 1996. *Assyrian Rulers of the Early First Millennium BC II (858–745 BC).* Toronto: University of Toronto.

Grayson, A. K., Novotny, J. R. 2012. *The Royal Inscriptions of Sennacherib, King of Assyria (704–681 BC)*. Winona Lake: Eisenbrauns.
Green, A. 1994. "Mischwesen. B. Archälogie." *Reallexikon der Assyriologie*, Vol. 8, 246–264. Berlin: de Gruyter.
Green, A. 1995. "Ancient Mesopotamian Religious Iconography." In *Civilizations of the Ancient Near East*, edited by Sasson, J. M., Vol. III, 1837–1855. New York: Scribner's.
Green, A. 2003. *The Storm-God in the Ancient Near East*. Winona Lake: Eisenbrauns.
Greenberg, M. 1964. "Kaufmann on the Bible: An Appreciation." *Judaism* 13 (1): 77–89.
Greenberg, M. 1969. *Understanding Exodus: The Heritage of Biblical Israel*. New York: Jewish Theological Seminary of America.
Greenberg, M. 1983. *Ezekiel 1–20: A New Translation with Introduction and Commentary*. Garden City: Doubleday.
Greenberg, M. 1997. *Ezekiel 21–37: A New Translation with Introduction and Commentary*. Garden City: Doubleday.
Greenfield, J. C. 1976. "The Aramean God Rammān/Rimmōn." *Israel Exploration Journal* 26 (4): 195–198.
Greenfield, J. C. 1985. "Baʿal's Throne and Isa. 6:1." In *Mélanges bibliques et orientaux en l'honneur de M. Mathias Delcor*, edited by Caquot, A., 193–198. Kevelaer: Butzon & Bercker.
Greenfield, J. C. 1987a. "Aspects of Aramean Religion." In *Ancient Israelite Religion: Essays in Honor of Frank Moore Cross*, edited by Miller, P. D., Hanson, P. D., McBride, S. D., 67–78. Philadelphia: Fortress.
Greenfield, J. C. 1987b. "The Hebrew Bible and Canaanite Literature." In *The Literary Guide to the Bible*, edited by Alter, R., Kermode, F., 545–560. Cambridge: Harvard University.
Greenfield, J. C. 1999. "Hadad." In *Dictionary of Deities and Demons in the Bible*, edited by van der Toorn, K., Becking, B., van der Horst, P. W., 377–382. 2nd ed. Leiden: Brill.
Greenspahn, F. E. 1987. "Biblical Scholars, Medieval and Modern." In *Judaic Perspectives on Ancient Israel*, edited by Neusner, J., Levine, B. A., Frerichs, E. S., 245–258. Philadelphia: Fortress.
Greenstein, E. L. 1982. "The Snaring of Sea in the Baal Epic." *Maarav* 3 (2): 195–216.
Greenstein, E. L. 1992. "Yhwh's Lightning in Psalm 29:7." *Maarav* 8: 49–57.
Greenstein, E. L. 1996. "A Forensic Understanding of the Speech from the Whirlwind." In *Texts, Temples, and Traditions: A Tribute to Menahem Haran*, edited by Fox, M. V., 241–258. Winona Lake: Eisenbrauns.
Greenstein, E. L. 1997. "Kirta." In *Ugaritic Narrative Poetry*, edited by Parker, S. B., 9–48. Atlanta: Society of Biblical Literature.
Greenstein, E. L. 2016. "Verbal Art and Literary Sensibilities in Ancient Near Eastern Context." In *The Wiley Blackwell Companion to Ancient Israel*, edited by Niditch, S., 457–475. Chichester: John Wiley & Sons.
Greer, J. S. 2007. "A Marzeaḥ and a Mizraq: A Prophet's Mêlée with Religious Diversity in Amos 6.4–7." *Journal for the Study of the Old Testament* 32 (2): 243–261.
Greer, J. S. 2017. "The Cult at Tel Dan: Aramean or Israelite?" In *Wandering Arameans: Arameans Outside Syria: Textual and Archaeological Perspectives*, edited by Berlejung, A., Maeir, A. M., Schüle, A., 3–18. Wiesbaden: Harrassowitz.
Grelot, P. 1998. "GALGAL (Ezéchiel 10, 2.6.13 et Daniel 7, 9)." *Transeuphratène* 15: 137–147.
Gressmann, H. 1909. *Altorientalische Texte und Bilder zum Alten Testamente, in Verbindung mit A. Ungnad und H. Ranke*. Tübingen: J. C. B. Mohr.

Gressmann, H. 1913. *Mose und seine Zeit, ein Kommentar zu den Mose-Sagen.* Göttingen: Vandenhoeck & Ruprecht.
Gressmann, H. 1914. *Albert Eichhorn und die religionsgeschichtliche Schule.* Göttingen: Vandenhoeck & Ruprecht.
Gröndahl, F. 1967. *Die Personennamen der Texte aus Ugarit.* Rome: Pontifical Biblical Institute.
Gropp, D. M. 1997. "Nerab Inscriptions." In *The Oxford Encyclopedia of Archaeology in the Near East*, edited by Meyers, E. M., Vol. 4, 127–129. New York: Oxford University.
Gropp, D. M., Lewis, T. J. 1985. "Notes on Some Problems in the Aramaic Text of the Hadd-Yithʿi Bilingual." *Bulletin of the American Schools of Oriental Research* 259: 45–61.
Grossfeld, B. 1988. *The Targum Onqelos to Genesis. Translated, with a Critical Introduction, Apparatus, and Notes.* The Aramaic Bible, Vol. 6. Wilmington: M. Glazier.
Gruber, M. I. 1983. "The Motherhood of God in Second Isaiah." *Revue Biblique* 90 (3): 351–359.
Gruber, M. I. 1986. "Hebrew *qĕdēšāh* and Her Canaanite and Akkadian Cognates." *Ugarit-Forschungen* 18: 133–148.
Gubel, E. 1987. *Phoenician Furniture: A Typology Based on Iron Age Representations with Reference to the Iconographical Context.* Studia Phoenicia, Vol. 7. Leuven: Peeters.
Guinn-Villareal, E. L. 2018. "Biblical Hebrew *Qinʾâ* and the Maintenance of Social Integrity in Ancient Israelite Literature." Johns Hopkins University.
Gunkel, H. 1895. *Schöpfung und Chaos in Urzeit und Endzeit.* Göttingen: Vandenhoeck und Ruprecht.
Gunkel, H. 1901. *Genesis übersetzt und erklärt.* Handkommentar zum Alten Testament, Vol. 1.1. Göttingen: Vandenhoeck & Ruprecht.
Gunkel, H. 1997. *Genesis.* 3rd ed. Macon: Mercer.
Gunkel, H. 2006. *Creation and Chaos in the Primeval Era and the Eschaton.* Grand Rapids: Eerdmans.
Gunneweg, A. 1965. *Leviten und Priester: Hauptlinien der Traditionsbildung und Geschichte des israelitisch-jüdischen Kultpersonals.* Göttingen: Vandenhoeck & Ruprecht.
Gutman, J. 1971. "The History of the Ark." *Zeitschrift für die alttestamentliche Wissenschaft* 87: 22–30.
Gzella, H. 2015. *A Cultural History of Aramaic: From the Beginnings to the Advent of Islam.* Leiden: Brill.
Gzella, H. 2017. "New Light on Linguistic Diversity in Pre-Achaemenid Aramaic: Wandering Arameans or Language Spread?" In *Wandering Arameans: Arameans Outside Syria: Textual and Archaeological Perspectives*, edited by Berlejung, A., Maeir, A. M., Schüle, A., 19–37. Wiesbaden: Harrassowitz.
Haas, V. 1994. *Geschichte der hethitischen Religion.* Leiden: Brill.
Habachi, L. 1969. *Features of the Deification of Ramesses II.* Glückstadt: J. J. Augustin.
Habel, N. C. 1976. "Appeal to Ancient Tradition as a Literary Form." *Zeitschrift für die alttestamentliche Wissenschaft* 88 (2): 253–272.
Habel, N. C. 1985. *The Book of Job.* Philadelphia: Westminster.
Hackett, J. A. 1980. *The Balaam Text from Deir ʿAllā.* Harvard Semitic Monographs, Vol. 31. Chico: Scholars Press.
Hackett, J. A. 1987. "Religious Traditions in Israelite Transjordan." In *Ancient Israelite Religion: Essays in Honor of Frank Moore Cross*, edited by Miller, P. D., Hanson, P. D., McBride, S. D., 125–136. Philadelphia: Fortress.

Hackett, J. A. 1989. "Can a Sexist Model Liberate Us? Ancient Near Eastern 'Fertility' Goddesses." *Journal of Feminist Studies in Religion* 5 (1): 65–76.

Hackett, J. A. 1997. "Defusing Pseudo-Scholarship: The Siloam Inscription Ain't Hasmonean." *Biblical Archaeology Review* 23 (2): 41–50,68.

Hadley, J. M. 1987. "Some Drawings and Inscriptions on Two Pithoi from Kuntillet 'Ajrud." *Vetus Testamentum* 37 (2): 180–213.

Hadley, J. M. 1993. "Kuntillet 'Ajrud: Religious Centre or Desert Way Station?" *Palestine Exploration Quarterly* 125 (2): 115–124.

Hadley, J. M. 1994. "Yahweh and 'His Asherah': Archaeological and Textual Evidence for the Cult of the Goddess." In *Ein Gott allein? JHWH-Verehrung und biblischer Monotheismus im Kontext der israelitischen und altorientalischen Religionsgeschichte*, edited by Dietrich, W., Klopfenstein, M. A., 235–268. Fribourg: Universitätsverlag.

Hadley, J. M. 1996. "The Fertility of the Flock? The De-personalization of Astarte in the Old Testament." In *On Reading Prophetic Texts: Gender-Specific and Related Studies in Memory of Fokkelien Van Dijk-Hemmes*, edited by Becking, B., Dijkstra, M., 115–133. Leiden: Brill.

Hadley, J. M. 2000. *The Cult of Asherah in Ancient Israel and Judah: Evidence for a Hebrew Goddess*. Cambridge: Cambridge University.

Hadley, J. M. 2007. "The De-Deification of Deities in Deuteronomy." In *The God of Israel*, edited by Gordon, R. P., 157–174. Cambridge: Cambridge University.

Hahn, J. 1981. *Das "Goldene Kalb": Die Jahwe-Verehrung bei Stierbildern in der Geschichte Israels*. Frankfurt am Main: Lang.

Halayqa, I. 2008. *A Comparative Lexicon of Ugaritic and Canaanite*. Münster: Ugarit-Verlag.

Halbertal, M., Margalit, A. 1992. *Idolatry*. Cambridge: Harvard University.

Halkes, C. 1981. "The Themes of Protest in Feminist Theology Against God the Father." In *God as Father? Concilium: International Journal for Theology*, edited by Metz, J., Schillebeeckx, E., 103–112. Edinburgh: T. & T. Clark.

Hallo, W. W. 1983. "Cult Statue and Divine Image: A Preliminary Study." In *Scripture in Context II: More Essays on the Comparative Method*, edited by Hallo, W. W., Moyer, J. C., Perdue, L. G., 1–17. Winona Lake: Eisenbrauns.

Hallo, W. W. 1988. "Texts, Statues and the Cult of the Divine King." In *Congress Volume: Jerusalem 1986*, edited by Emerton, J. A., 54–66. Leiden: Brill.

Hallo, W. W., Younger, K. L., eds. 1997. *The Context of Scripture 1: Canonical Compositions from the Biblical World*. Leiden: Brill.

Hallo, W. W., Younger, K. L., eds. 2000. *The Context of Scripture 2: Monumental Inscriptions from the Biblical World*. Leiden: Brill.

Hallo, W. W., Younger, K. L., eds. 2002. *The Context of Scripture 3: Archival Documents from the Biblical World*. Leiden: Brill.

Halpern, B. 1976. "Levitic Participation in the Reform Cult of Jeroboam I." *Journal of Biblical Literature* 95 (1): 31–42.

Halpern, B. 1983. "The Resourceful Israelite Historian: The Song of Deborah and Israelite Historiography." *Harvard Theological Review* 76 (4): 379–401.

Halpern, B. 1992. "Kenites." In *The Anchor Bible Dictionary*, edited by Freedman, D. N., Vol. 4, 17–22. New York: Doubleday.

Halpern, B. 1995. "Erasing History: The Minimalist Assault on Ancient Israel." *Bible Review* 11 (6): 26–35.

Halpern, B. 2001. *David's Secret Demons: Messiah, Murderer, Traitor, King*. Grand Rapids: Eerdmans.

Hamilton, G. J. 2006. *The Origins of the West Semitic Alphabet in Egyptian Scripts*. Washington: Catholic Biblical Association of America.
Hamilton, M. W. 1998. "The Past as Destiny: Historical Visions in Sam'al and Judah Under Assyrian Hegemony." *Harvard Theological Review* 91 (3): 215–250.
Hamilton, V. P. 1990. *The Book of Genesis: Chapters 1–17*. Grand Rapids: Eerdmans.
Hamilton, V. P. 1995. *The Book of Genesis: Chapters 18–50*. Grand Rapids: Eerdmans.
Hamori, E. J. 2008. *"When Gods Were Men": The Embodied God in Biblical and Near Eastern Literature*. Berlin: de Gruyter.
Hamori, E. J. 2015. *Women's Divination in Biblical Literature: Prophecy, Necromancy, and Other Arts of Knowledge*. New Haven: Yale University.
Handy, L. K. 1994. *Among the Host of Heaven: The Syro-Palestinian Pantheon as Bureaucracy*. Winona Lake: Eisenbrauns.
Hansen, D. P. 1957. "A Bronze in the Semitic Museum of Harvard University." *Bulletin of the American Schools of Oriental Research* 146: 13–19.
Hansen, K. T. 2004. "The World in Dress: Anthropological Perspectives on Clothing, Fashion, and Culture." *Annual Review of Anthropology* 33: 369–392.
Hanson, P. D. 1984. "War and Peace in the Hebrew Bible." *Interpretation* 38 (4): 341–362.
Haran, M. 1959. "The Ark and the Cherubim: Their Symbolic Significance in Biblical Ritual." *Israel Exploration Journal* 9: 30–38.
Haran, M. 1962a. "Shiloh and Jerusalem: The Origin of the Priestly Tradition in the Pentateuch." *Journal of Biblical Literature* 81 (1): 14–24.
Haran, M. 1962b. "Kehunnah (Priesthood)" [Hebrew]. *Encyclopedia Miqrait* 4: 14–45.
Haran, M. 1978. *Temples and Temple-Service in Ancient Israel: An Inquiry into the Character of Cult Phenomena and the Historical Setting of the Priestly School*. Oxford: Clarendon.
Haran, M. 1983. "Priesthood, Temple, Divine Service: Some Observations on Institutions and Practices of Worship." *Hebrew Annual Review* 7: 121–135.
Haran, M. 1985. *Temples and Temple-Service in Ancient Israel: An Inquiry into the Character of Cult Phenomena and the Historical Setting of the Priestly School*. 2nd ed. Winona Lake: Eisenbrauns.
Harrelson, W. J. 1962. "Calf, Golden." In *The Interpreter's Dictionary of the Bible*, edited by Buttrick, G. A., 448–449. New York: Abingdon.
Harrison, R. K. 1969. *Introduction to the Old Testament*. Grand Rapids: Eerdmans.
Hartenstein, F. 1995. "Der Beitrag der Ikonographie zu einer Religionsgeschichte Kanaans und Israels." *Verkündigung und Forschung* 40: 74–85.
Hartenstein, F. 2007. "Cherubim and Seraphim in the Bible and in the Light of Ancient Near Eastern Sources." In *Angels: The Concept of Celestial Beings: Origins, Development and Reception*, edited by Reiterer, F. V., Nicklas, T., Schöpflin, K., 155–188. Berlin: de Gruyter.
Hartman, L. F. 1971. "God, Names of." *Encyclopedia Judaica* 7: 674–682.
Harvey, J. 1962. "Le 'rib-pattern,' réquisitoire prophétique sur la rupture de l'alliance." *Biblica* 43: 172–196.
Hasegawa, S., Paz, Y. 2015. "Tel Rekhesh—2013. Preliminary Report." *Hadashot Arkheologiyot* 127 (December 31).
Hasel, M. G. 1994. "Israel in the Merneptah Stela." *Bulletin of the American Schools of Oriental Research* 296: 45–61.
Hasel, M. G. 2003. "Merenptah's Inscription and Reliefs and the Origin of Israel." In *The Near East in the Southwest: Essays in Honor of William G. Dever*, edited by Nakhai, B. A., 19–44. Boston: American Schools of Oriental Research.

Havice, H. K. 1978. "The Concern for the Widow and the Fatherless in the Ancient Near East: A Case Study in Old Testament Ethics." Yale University.
Hawkins, J. D. 2015. "The Soul in the Stele?" In *Tradition and Innovation in the Ancient Near East: Proceedings of the 57th Rencontre Assyriologique Internationale at Rome, 4–8 July 2011*, edited by Archi, A., Bremanti, A., 49–56. Winona Lake: Eisenbrauns.
Hayes, C. 2015. *What's Divine About Divine Law?* Princeton: Princeton University.
Hayes, J. H. 1963. "The Tradition of Zion's Inviolability." *Journal of Biblical Literature* 82 (4): 419–426.
Hayes, J. H., ed. 1999. *Dictionary of Biblical Interpretation*. Nashville: Abingdon.
Hayes, J. H., Prussner, F. C. 1985. *Old Testament Theology: Its History and Development*. Atlanta: John Knox.
Hays, C. B. 2014. *Hidden Riches: A Sourcebook for the Comparative Study of the Hebrew Bible and Ancient Near East*. Louisville: Westminster John Knox.
Hecker, K. 1974. *Untersuchungen zur akkadischen Epik*. Kevelaer: Butzon & Bercker.
Heidel, A. 1951. *The Babylonian Genesis: The Story of Creation*. Chicago: University of Chicago.
Heider, G. C. 1985. *The Cult of Molek: A Reassessment*. Sheffield: JSOT Press.
Helck, W. 1966. "Zum Auftreten fremder Götter in Ägypten." *Oriens Antiquus* 5: 1–14.
Held, M. 1962. "The *yqtl-qtl* (*qtl-yqtl*) Sequence of Identical Verbs in Biblical Hebrew and in Ugaritic." In *Studies and Essays in Honor of Abraham A. Neuman*, edited by Ben-Horin, M., 281–290. Leiden: Brill.
Held, M. 1965. "The Action-Result (Factitive-Passive) Sequence of Identical Verbs in Biblical Hebrew and Ugaritic." *Journal of Biblical Literature* 84 (3): 272–282.
Heltzer, M. 1976. *The Rural Community in Ancient Ugarit*. Wiesbaden: Reichert.
Heltzer, M. 1978. *Goods, Prices and the Organization of Trade in Ugarit*. Wiesbaden: Reichert.
Heltzer, M. 1999. "The Economy of Ugarit." In *Handbook of Ugaritic Studies*, edited by Watson, W. G. E., Wyatt, N., 423–454. Leiden: Brill.
Hendel, R. S. 1985. "'The Flame of the Whirling Sword': A Note on Genesis 3:24." *Journal of Biblical Literature* 104 (4): 671–674.
Hendel, R. S. 1988. "The Social Origins of the Aniconic Tradition in Early Israel." *Catholic Biblical Quarterly* 50 (3): 365–382.
Hendel, R. S. 1989. "Sacrifice as a Cultural System: The Ritual Symbolism of Exodus 24:3–8." *Zeitschrift für die alttestamentliche Wissenschaft* 101 (3): 366–390.
Hendel, R. S. 1992. "Worldmaking in Ancient Israel." *Journal for the Study of the Old Testament* 56: 3–18.
Hendel, R. S. 1995. Review of Jon Levenson, *The Death and Resurrection of the Beloved Son*. *Bible Review* 11 (1): 14–15.
Hendel, R. S. 1996. "The Date of the Siloam Inscription: A Rejoinder to Rogerson and Davies." *Biblical Archaeologist* 59 (4): 233–237.
Hendel, R. S. 1997. "Aniconism and Anthropomorphism in Ancient Israel." In *The Image and the Book: Iconic Cults, Aniconism, and the Rise of Book Religion in Israel and the Ancient Near East*, edited by van der Toorn, K., 205–228. Leuven: Peeters.
Henshaw, R. A. 1994. *Female and Male: The Cultic Personnel: The Bible and the Rest of the Ancient Near East*. Allison Park: Pickwick.
Herder, J. G. 1833. *The Spirit of Hebrew Poetry*. Burlington: E. Smith.
Herion, G. A. 1986. "The Impact of Modern and Social Science Assumptions on Reconstructions of Israelite History." *Journal for the Study of the Old Testament* 34: 3–33.

Herr, L. G. 1999. "Tall al-'Umayri and the Reubenite Hypothesis." *Eretz-Israel: Archaeological, Historical and Geographical Studies* (Frank Moore Cross Volume) 26: 64*–77*.
Herr, L. G., Clark, D. R. 2001. "Excavating the Tribe of Reuben." *Biblical Archaeology Review* 27 (2): 36–47, 64–66.
Herrmann, C. 1994. *Ägyptische Amulette aus Palästina/Israel I. Mit einem Ausblick auf ihre Rezeption durch das Alte Testament*. Freiburg: Universitätsverlag.
Herrmann, C. 2002. *Ägyptische Amulette aus Palästina/Israel II*. Freiburg: Universitätsverlag.
Herrmann, C. 2006. *Ägyptische Amulette aus Palästina/Israel III*. Freiburg: Universitätsverlag.
Herrmann, C. 2016. *Ägyptische Amulette aus Palästina/Israel: mit einem Ausblick auf ihre Rezeption durch das Alte Testament, Band IV*. Göttingen: Vandenhoeck & Ruprecht.
Herrmann, S. 1973. *Israel in Egypt*. Naperville: Allenson.
Herrmann, S. 1981. *A History of Israel in Old Testament Times*. Philadelphia: Fortress.
Herrmann, V. R., Schloen, J. D., eds. 2014. *In Remembrance of Me: Feasting with the Dead in the Ancient Middle East*. Oriental Institute Museum Publications, Vol. 37. Chicago: Oriental Institute.
Herrmann, W. 1999. "El." In *Dictionary of Deities and Demons in the Bible*, edited by van der Toorn, K., Becking, B., van der Horst, P. W., 274–280. 2nd ed. Leiden: Brill.
Herzog, Z. 1987. "The Stratigraphy of Israelite Arad: A Rejoinder." *Bulletin of the American Schools of Oriental Research* 267: 77–79.
Herzog, Z. 1997a. "Arad: Iron Age Period." In *The Oxford Encyclopedia of Archaeology in the Near East*, edited by Meyers, E. M., Vol. I, 174–176. New York: Oxford University.
Herzog, Z. 1997b. "The Arad Fortresses." In *ARAD Ancient Arad—An Early Bronze Age Community on the Desert Fringe ('Arad Ha-kena'anit: 'ir Sha'ar La-Midbar)*, edited by Amiran, R., Ilan, O., Sebanne, M., Herzog, Z., 113–296. Tel Aviv: Israel Exploration Society.
Herzog, Z. 2001. "The Date of the Temple at Arad: Reassessment of the Stratigraphy and the Implications for the History of Religion in Judah." In *Studies in the Archaeology of the Iron Age in Israel and Jordan*, edited by Mazar, A., 156–178. Sheffield: Sheffield Academic Press.
Herzog, Z. 2002. "The Fortress Mound at Tell Arad: An Interim Report." *Tel Aviv* 29: 3–109.
Herzog, Z. 2006. "Arad." In *The New Interpreter's Dictionary of the Bible*, edited by Sakenfeld, K. D., Vol. 1, 221. Nashville: Abingdon.
Herzog, Z. 2010. "Perspectives on Southern Israel's Cult Centralization: Arad and Beer-sheba." In *One God, One Cult, One Nation: Archaeological and Biblical Perspectives*, edited by Kratz, R. G., Spieckermann, H., 169–199. Berlin: de Gruyter.
Herzog, Z. 2013. "Arad." In *The Oxford Encyclopedia of the Bible and Archaeology*, edited by Master, D. M., 36–42. Oxford: Oxford University.
Herzog, Z., Aharoni, M., Rainey, A. F. 1987. "Arad—An Ancient Israelite Fortress with a Temple to Yahweh." *Biblical Archaeology Review* 13: 16–35.
Herzog, Z., Aharoni, M., Rainey, A. F., Moshkovitz, S. 1984. "The Israelite Fortress at Arad." *Bulletin of the American Schools of Oriental Research* 254: 1–34.
Hess, R. S. 1989. "Cultural Aspects of Onomastic Distribution in the Amarna Texts." *Ugarit-Forschungen* 21: 209–216.
Hess, R. S. 1991. "The Divine Name Yahweh in Late Bronze Age Sources?" *Ugarit-Forschungen* 23: 181–188.
Hess, R. S. 1993. *Amarna Personal Names*. Winona Lake: Eisenbrauns.
Hess, R. S. 1994. "One Hundred Fifty Years of Comparative Studies on Genesis 1–11: An Overview." In *I Studied Inscriptions from Before the Flood: Ancient Near Eastern, Literary,*

and Linguistic Approaches to Genesis 1–11, edited by Hess, R. S., Tsumura, D. T., 3–26. Winona Lake: Eisenbrauns.

Hess, R. S. 1999. "The Onomastics of Ugarit." In *Handbook of Ugaritic Studies*, edited by Watson, W. G. E., Wyatt, N., 499–528. Leiden: Brill.

Hess, R. S. 2002. "Leviticus 10:1: Strange Fire and an Odd Name." *Bulletin for Biblical Research* 12 (2): 187–198.

Hess, R. S. 2007a. "Aspects of Israelite Personal Names and Pre-Exilic Israelite Religion." In *New Seals and Inscriptions, Hebrew, Idumean and Cuneiform*, edited by Lubetski, M., 301–313. Sheffield: Sheffield Phoenix Press.

Hess, R. S. 2007b. *Israelite Religions: An Archaeological and Biblical Survey*. Grand Rapids: Baker Academic.

Hess, R. S. 2007c. "Arrowheads from Iron Age I: Personal Names and Authenticity." In *Ugarit at Seventy-Five*, edited by Younger, K. L., 113–129. Winona Lake: Eisenbrauns.

Hess, R. S. 2009. *Studies in the Personal Names of Genesis 1–11*. Winona Lake: Eisenbrauns.

Hess, R. S. 2015. "Personal Names in the Hebrew Bible with Second-Millennium B.C. Antecedents." *Bulletin for Biblical Research* 25 (1): 5–12.

Hesse, K. J. 2008. "Contacts and Trade at Late Bronze Age Hazor: Aspects of Intercultural Relationships and Identity in the Eastern Mediterranean." Umea University.

Hestrin, R. 1987. "The Cult Stand from Ta'anach and Its Religious Background." In *Phoenicia and the East Mediterranean in the First Millennium B.C.*, edited by Lipiński, E., 61–77. Leuven: Peeters.

Hestrin, R. 1991. "Understanding Asherah: Exploring Semitic Iconography." *Biblical Archaeology Review* 17 (5): 50–59.

Hiebert, T. 1986. *God of My Victory: The Ancient Hymn in Habakkuk 3*. Harvard Semitic Monographs, Vol. 38. Atlanta: Scholars Press.

Higginbotham, C. 1996. "Elite Emulation and Egyptian Governance in Ramesside Canaan." *Tel Aviv* 23 (2): 154–169.

Hill, A. E. 1998. *Malachi: A New Translation with Introduction and Commentary*. New York: Doubleday.

Hillers, D. R. 1964. "Amos 7, 4 and Ancient Parallels." *Catholic Biblical Quarterly* 26: 221–225.

Hillers, D. R. 1968. "Ritual Procession of the Ark and Ps 132." *Catholic Biblical Quarterly* 30: 48–55.

Hillers, D. R. 1985. "Analyzing the Abominable: Our Understanding of Canaanite Religion." *Jewish Quarterly Review* 75 (3): 253–269.

Himbaza, I. 2002. "Dt 32, 8, une correction tardive des scribes: essai d'interprétation et de datation." *Biblica* 83 (4): 527–548.

Hodder, I. 1985. "Post-processual Archaeology." *Advances in Archaeological Method and Theory* 8: 1–26.

Hodder, I. 1989. "Post-modernism, Post-structuralism, and Post-processual Archaeology." In *The Meanings of Things: Material Culture and Symbolic Expression*, edited by Hodder, I., 64–78. London: Unwin Hyman.

Hodder, I. 1992a. *Reading the Past: Current Approaches to Interpretation in Archaeology*. Cambridge: Cambridge University.

Hodder, I. 1992b. *Archaeology: Theory and Practice*. Routledge: London.

Hoffman, Y. 1994. "The Conception of 'Other Gods' in Deuteronomistic Writings." *Israel Oriental Studies* 14: 103–118.

Hoffman, Y. 1996. *A Blemished Perfection: The Book of Job in Context.* Sheffield: Sheffield Academic Press.
Hoffman, Y. 2007. "The Book of Job as Trial: A Perspective from a Comparison to Some Relevant Ancient Near Eastern Texts." In *Das Buch Hiob und seine Interpretationen*, edited by Krüger, T., 21–31. Zürich: Theologischer Verlag Zürich.
Hoffmeier, J. K. 1996. *Israel in Egypt: The Evidence for the Authenticity of the Exodus Tradition.* New York: Oxford University.
Hoffmeier, J. K., Kitchen, K. A. 2007. "Reshep and Astarte in North Sinai: A Recently Discovered Stela from Tell el-Borg." *Ägypten und Levante/Egypt and the Levant* 17: 127–136.
Hoffner, H. A. 1965. "The Elkunirsa Myth Reconsidered." *Revue Hittite et Asianique* 23: 5–16.
Hoffner, H. A. 1990. *Hittite Myths.* Writings from the Ancient World, Vol. 2. Atlanta: Scholars Press.
Hoffner, H. A. 2006. "The Royal Cult in Hatti." In *Text, Artifact, and Image: Revealing Ancient Israelite Religion*, edited by Beckman, G. M., Lewis, T. J., 132–151. Providence: Brown Judaic Studies.
Hoftijzer, J. 1967. "Das sogenannte Feueropfer." In *Hebräische Wortforschung: Festschrift zum 80. Geburtstag von Walter Baumgartner*, edited by Anderson, G. W., de Boer, P. A. H., 114–134. Leiden: Brill.
Hoftijzer, J., van der Kooij, G. 1976. *Aramaic Texts from Deir 'Alla.* Leiden: Brill.
Hogue, T. 2019. "Abracadabra, or 'I Create as I Speak': A Reanalysis of the First Verb in the Katumuwa Inscription in Light of Northwest Semitic and Hieroglyphic Luwian Parallels." *Bulletin of the American Schools of Oriental Research* 381: 193–202.
Holladay, J. S. 1987. "Religion in Israel and Judah Under the Monarchy: An Explicitly Archaeological Approach." In *Ancient Israelite Religion: Essays in Honor of Frank Moore Cross*, edited by Miller, P. D., Hanson, P. D., McBride, S. D., 249–299. Philadelphia: Fortress.
Holladay, J. S. 1992. "Kom, Khirbet el-." In *The Anchor Bible Dictionary*, edited by Freedman, D. N., Vol. 4, 97–99. New York: Doubleday.
Holladay, J. S. 1995. "The Kingdoms of Israel and Judah: Political and Economic Centralization in the Iron IIA-B (ca. 1000–750 BCE)." In *The Archaeology of Society in the Holy Land*, edited by Levy, T. E., 368–398. New York: Facts on File.
Holladay, W. L. 1986. *Jeremiah 1.* Philadelphia: Fortress.
Holladay, W. L. 1989. *Jeremiah 2.* Minneapolis: Fortress.
Holm, T. 2013. *Of Courtiers and Kings: The Biblical Daniel Narratives and Ancient Story-Collections.* Winona Lake: Eisenbrauns.
Holm, T. Forthcoming. *Aramaic Literary Texts.* Writings from the Ancient World. Atlanta: SBL Press.
Holmgren, F. 1974. "Yahweh the Avenger: Isaiah 63:1–6." In *Rhetorical Criticism: Essays in Honor of James Muilenburg*, edited by Jackson, J. J., Martin, M., 133–148. Eugene: Pickwick.
Holt, J. C. 1996. "Introduction." In *Patterns in Comparative Religion* by Mircea Eliade, xvi. Lincoln: University of Nebraska.
Hooke, S. H. 1933. *Myth and Ritual. Essays on the Myth and Ritual of the Hebrews in Relation to the Culture Pattern of the Ancient East.* London: Oxford University.
Hooke, S. H. 1935. *The Labyrinth. Further Studies in the Relation Between Myth and Ritual in the Ancient World.* London: SPCK.

Hooke, S. H. 1938. *The Origins of Early Semitic Ritual*. London: Oxford University.
Hooke, S. H. 1958. *Myth, Ritual, and Kingship: Essays on the Theory and Practice of Kingship in the Ancient Near East and in Israel*. Oxford: Clarendon Press.
Hooke, S. H. 1963. *Middle Eastern Mythology*. New York: Penguin.
Hoop, R. de. 2007. *Genesis 49 in Its Literary and Historical Context*. Atlanta: Society of Biblical Literature.
Hopkins, D. C. 1993. "Pastoralists in Late Bronze Age Palestine: Which Way Did They Go?" *Biblical Archaeologist* 56 (4): 200–211.
Horn, S. H. 1965. "Shechem, History and Excavations of a Palestinian City." *Jahrbericht ex Oriente Lux* 18: 284–306.
Hornkohl, A. 2013. "Biblical Hebrew: Periodization." In *Encyclopedia of Hebrew Language and Linguistics*, edited by Khan, G. Leiden: Brill.
Hornung, E., 1967. "Der Mensch als 'Bild Gottes' in Ägypten." In *Die Gottebenbildlichkeit des Menschen*, edited by Loretz, O., 123–156. Munich: Kösel-Verlag.
Hornung, E. 1995. "Ancient Egyptian Religious Iconography." In *Civilizations of the Ancient Near East*, edited by Sasson, J. M., Vol. III, 1711–1730. New York: Scribner's.
Horowitz, W., Oshima, T., Sanders, S. L. 2006. *Cuneiform in Canaan: Cuneiform Sources from the Land of Israel in Ancient Times*. Jerusalem: Israel Exploration Society.
Horowitz, W., Shaffer, A. 1992. "An Administrative Tablet from Hazor: A Preliminary Edition." *Israel Exploration Journal* 42: 21–33.
Horwitz, L. K. 2015. "Animal Representation in the Yavneh Cult Stands." In *Yavneh II: The "Temple Hill" Repository Pit*, edited by Kletter, R., Ziffer, I., Zwickel, W. Fribourg: Academic Press Fribourg.
Hossfeld, F. 1982. *Der Dekalog: Seine späten Fassungen, die originale Komposition und seine Vorstufen*. Freiburg: Universitätsverlag.
Hossfeld, F., Zenger, E. 2003. "The So-Called Elohistic Psalter: A New Solution for an Old Problem." In *A God So Near: Essays on Old Testament Theology in Honor of Patrick D. Miller*, edited by Strawn, B. A., Bowen, N. R., 35–51. Winona Lake: Eisenbrauns.
Hossfeld, F., Zenger, E. 2005. *Psalms 2: A Commentary on Psalms 51-100*. Minneapolis: Fortress.
Houston, W. 1993. *Purity and Monotheism: Clean and Unclean Animals in Biblical Law*. Sheffield: JSOT Press.
Houtman, C. 1992. "On the Function of the Holy Incense (Exodus XXX 34-8) and the Sacred Anointing Oil (Exodus XXX 22-33)." *Vetus Testamentum* 42 (4): 458–465.
Houtman, C. 1993. *Exodus, Volume 1*. Leuven: Peeters.
Houtman, C. 1996. *Exodus, Volume 2, Chapters 7:14-19:25*. Leuven: Peeters.
Houtman, C. 1999. "Queen of Heaven." In *Dictionary of Deities and Demons in the Bible*, edited by van der Toorn, K., Becking, B., van der Horst, P. W., 678–680. 2nd ed. Leiden: Brill.
Houtman, C. 2000. *Exodus, Volume 3, Chapters 20-40*. Leuven: Peeters.
Huddlestun, J. R. 2002. "Divestiture, Deception, and Demotion: The Garment Motif in Genesis 37-39." *Journal for the Study of the Old Testament* 98: 47–62.
Huehnergard, J. 1983. "Asseverative *la and Hypothetical *lu/law in Semitic." *Journal of the American Oriental Society* 103: 569–593.
Huehnergard, J. 1987. *Ugaritic Vocabulary in Syllabic Transcription*. Atlanta: Scholars Press.
Huehnergard, J. 1995. "What Is Aramaic?" *Aram* 7: 261–282.
Huffmon, H. B. 1959. "The Covenant Lawsuit in the Prophets." *Journal of Biblical Literature* 78 (4): 285–295.

Huffmon, H. B. 1965. *Amorite Personal Names in the Mari Texts: A Structural and Lexical Study*. Baltimore: Johns Hopkins Press.

Huffmon, H. B. 1987. "Babel und Bible: The Encounter Between Babylon and the Bible." In *Backgrounds for the Bible*, edited by O'Connor, M. P., Freedman, D. N., 125–136. Winona Lake: Eisenbrauns.

Hulster, I. J. de, Strawn, B. A., Bonfiglio, R. P. 2015. *Iconographic Exegesis of the Hebrew Bible—Old Testament: An Introduction to Its Method and Practice*. Gottingen: Vandenhoeck & Ruprecht.

Hundley, M. 2009. "To Be or Not to Be: A Reexamination of Name Language in Deuteronomy and the Deuteronomistic History." *Vetus Testamentum* 59 (4): 533–555.

Hurowitz, V. A. 1992. *I Have Built You an Exalted House: Temple Building in the Bible in the Light of Mesopotamian and Northwest Semitic Writings*. Sheffield: JSOT Press.

Hurowitz, V. A. 1995. "Solomon's Golden Vessels (1 Kings 7:48–50) and the Cult of the First Temple." In *Pomegranates and Golden Bells: Studies in Biblical, Jewish, and Near Eastern Ritual, Law, and Literature in Honor of Jacob Milgrom*, edited by Wright, D. P., Freedman, D. N., Hurvitz, A., 151–164. Winona Lake: Eisenbrauns.

Hurowitz, V. A. 1997. "Picturing Imageless Deities: Iconography in the Ancient Near East." *Biblical Archaeology Review* 23 (3): 69.

Hurowitz, V. A. 1999. "'bn mśkyt—A New Interpretation." *Journal of Biblical Literature* 118 (2): 201–208.

Hurowitz, V. A. 2000. "The 'Sun Disk' Tablet of Nabû-Apla-Iddina." In *The Context of Scripture 2: Monumental Inscriptions from the Biblical World*, edited by Hallo, W. W., Younger, K. L., 364–368. Leiden: Brill.

Hurowitz, V. A. 2004–2005. Review of S. Richter, *The Deuteronomistic History and the Name Theology: lĕšakkēn šĕmô šām in the Bible and the Ancient Near East*. *Journal of Hebrew Scriptures* 5.

Hurowitz, V. A. 2005. "Hammurabi in Mesopotamian Tradition." In *"An Experienced Scribe Who Neglects Nothing": Ancient Near Eastern Studies in Honor of Jacob Klein*, edited by Sefati, Y., 497–532. Bethesda: CDL Press.

Hurowitz, V. A. 2006. "What Goes In Is What Comes Out: Materials for Creating Cult Statues." In *Text, Artifact, and Image: Revealing Ancient Israelite Religion*, edited by Beckman, G. M., Lewis, T. J., 3–23. Providence: Brown Judaic Studies.

Hurowitz, V. A. 2007. "Yhwh's Exalted House—Aspects of the Design and Symbolism of Solomon's Temple." In *Temple and Worship in Biblical Israel*, edited by Day, J., 63–110. London: T. & T. Clark.

Hutton, J. M. 2006. "Mahanaim, Penuel, and Transhumance Routes: Observations on Genesis 32–33 and Judges 8." *Journal of Near Eastern Studies* 65 (3): 161–178.

Hutton, J. M. 2009a. *The Transjordanian Palimpsest: The Overwritten Texts of Personal Exile and Transformation in the Deuteronomistic History*. Berlin: de Gruyter.

Hutton, J. M. 2009b. "The Levitical Diaspora (I): A Sociological Comparison with Morocco's Ahansal." In *Exploring the Longue Durée: Essays in Honor of Lawrence E. Stager*, edited by Schloen, J. D., 223–234. Winona Lake: Eisenbrauns.

Hutton, J. M. 2010a. "Southern, Northern and Transjordanian Perspectives." In *Religious Diversity in Ancient Israel and Judah*, edited by Stavrakopoulou, F., Barton, J., 149–174. London: T. & T. Clark.

Hutton, J. M. 2010b. "Local Manifestations of Yahweh and Worship in the Interstices: A Note on Kuntillet 'Ajrud." *Journal of Ancient Near Eastern Religions* 10 (2): 177–210.

Hutton, J. M. 2011a. "The Levitical Diaspora (II): Modern Perspectives on the Levitical Cities Lists (A Review of Opinions)." In *Levites and Priests in Biblical History and Tradition*, edited by Leuchter, M., Hutton, J. M., 45–81. Atlanta: Society of Biblical Literature.

Hutton, J. M. 2011b. "All the King's Men: The Families of the Priests in Cross-Cultural Perspective." In *"Seitenblicke": Literarische und historische Studien zu Nebenfiguren im zweiten Samuelbuch*, edited by Dietrich, W., 121–151. Fribourg and Göttingen: Academic Press and Vandenhoeck & Ruprecht.

Hyatt, J. P. 1939. "The Deity Bethel and the Old Testament." *Journal of the American Oriental Society* 59 (1): 81–98.

Hyatt, J. P. 1967. "Was Yahweh Originally a Creator Deity?" *Journal of Biblical Literature* 86 (4): 369–377.

Iggers, G. G. 1968. *The German Conception of History: The National Tradition of Historical Thought from Herder to the Present*. Middletown: Wesleyan University.

Ilan, D. 1999. "Northeastern Israel in the Iron Age I: Cultural, Socioeconomic and Political Perspectives." Tel Aviv University.

Iwry, S. 1957. "*Massebah* and *Bamah* in 1Q Isaiah[A] 6:13." *Journal of Biblical Literature* 76 (3): 225–232.

Jackson, K. P. 1989. "The Language of the Mesha῾ Inscription." In *Studies in the Mesha Inscription and Moab*, edited by Dearman, J. A., 96–130. Atlanta: Scholars Press.

Jackson, K. P., Dearman, J. A. 1989. "The Text of the Mesha῾ Inscription." In *Studies in the Mesha Inscription and Moab*, edited by Dearman, J. A., 93–95. Atlanta: Scholars Press.

Jacobsen, T. 1932. "The Chief God of Eshnunna." In *Tell Asmar and Khafaje*, edited by Frankfort, H., Jacobsen, T., Preusser, C., 55–59. Chicago: University of Chicago.

Jacobsen, T. 1949. "Mesopotamia." In *Before Philosophy: The Intellectual Adventure of Ancient Man: An Essay on Speculative Thought in the Ancient Near East*, edited by Frankfort, H., Groenewegen-Frankfort, H. A., 137–234. Baltimore: Penguin Books.

Jacobsen, T. 1976. *The Treasures of Darkness: A History of Mesopotamian Religion*. New Haven: Yale University.

Jacobsen, T. 1997. "The Eridu Genesis." In *The Context of Scripture 1: Canonical Compositions from the Biblical World*, edited by Hallo, W. W., Younger, K. L., 513–515. Leiden: Brill.

Jacobson, J. R. 2017. *Chanting the Hebrew Bible, Second, Expanded Edition: The Art of Cantillation*. Philadelphia: Jewish Publication Society.

Jacobson, R. A. 2014a. "Psalm 103: God Is Good!" In *The Book of Psalms*, by DeClaissé-Walford, N. L., Jacobson, R. A., Tanner, B. L., 759–768. Grand Rapids: Eerdmans.

Jacobson, R. A. 2014b. "Psalm 29: Ascribe to the Lord." In *The Book of Psalms*, by DeClaissé-Walford, N. L., Jacobson, R. A., Tanner, B. L., 281–288. Grand Rapids: Eerdmans.

James, T. G. H. 1984. *Pharaoh's People: Scenes from Life in Imperial Egypt*. Chicago: University of Chicago.

Janzen, J. G. 1987. "The Place of the Book of Job in the History of Israel's Religion." In *Ancient Israelite Religion: Essays in Honor of Frank Moore Cross*, edited by Miller, P. D., Hanson, P. D., McBride, S. D., 523–537. Philadelphia: Fortress.

Janzen, J. G. 1989. "Another Look at God's Watch over Job (7:12)." *Journal of Biblical Literature* 108 (1): 109–114.

Janzen, J. G. 1990. "The Character of the Calf and Its Cult in Exodus 32." *Catholic Biblical Quarterly* 52: 597–607.

Japhet, S. 1993. *I & II Chronicles*. Louisville: Westminster John Knox.
Japhet, S. 1998. "Some Biblical Concepts of Sacred Space." In *Sacred Space: Shrine, City, Land: Proceedings of the International Conference in Memory of Joshua Prawer*, edited by Kedar, B., Werblowsky, R., 55–72. Jerusalem: Israel Academy of Sciences and Humanities.
Jasnow, R. L., Zauzich, K. 2005. *The Ancient Egyptian Book of Thoth: A Demotic Discourse on Knowledge and Pendant to the Classical Hermetica*. Wiesbaden: Harrassowitz.
Jasnow, R. L., Zauzich, K. 2014. *Conversations in the House of Life: A New Translation of the Ancient Egyptian Book of Thoth*. Wiesbaden: Harrassowitz.
Jeffers, A. 1996. *Magic and Divination in Ancient Palestine and Syria*. Leiden: Brill.
Jenni, E. 1952. "Das Wort 'ōlām im Alten Testament." *Zeitschrift für die alttestamentliche Wissenschaft* 64 (3–4): 197–248.
Jenni, E. 1953. "Das Wort 'ōlām im Alten Testament." *Zeitschrift für die alttestamentliche Wissenschaft* 65 (1–2): 1–35.
Jenni, E. 1984. "'Ōlām Ewigkeit." *Theologisches Handwörterbuch zum Alten Testament* 2: 228–243.
Jenson, P. P. 1992. *Graded Holiness: A Key to the Priestly Conception of the World*. Sheffield: Sheffield Academic Press.
Jeon, J. 2017. "The Visit of Jethro (Exodus 18): Its Composition and Levitical Reworking." *Journal of Biblical Literature* 136 (2): 289–306.
Jeremias, J. 1965. *Theophanie: Die Geschichte einer alttestamentlichen Gattung*. Neukirchen-Vluyn: Neukirchener Verlag.
Jeremias, J. 1966. *Abba: Studien zur neutestamentlichen Theologie und Zeitgeschichte*. Göttingen: Vandenhoeck & Ruprecht.
Jeremias, J. 1993. "Thron oder Wagen? Eine außergewöhnliche Terrakotte aus der späten Eisenzeit in Juda." In *Biblische Welten: Festschrift für Martin Metzger zu seinem 65. Geburtstag*, edited by Zwickel, W., 40–59. Freiburg/Göttingen: Universitätsverlag/Vandenhoeck & Ruprecht.
Ji, C. 2012. "The Early Iron Age II Temple at Ḥirbet ʿAṭārūs and Its Architecture and Selected Cultic Objects." In *Temple Building and Temple Cult*, edited by Kamlah, J., 203–221. Wiesbaden: Harrassowitz.
Ji, C., Bates, R. D. 2014. "Khirbat ʿAtaruz 2011–2012: A Preliminary Report." *Andrews University Seminary Studies* 52 (1): 47–91.
Jindo, J. Y., Sommer, B. D., Staubli, T., eds. 2017. *Yehezkel Kaufmann and the Reinvention of Jewish Biblical Scholarship*. Fribourg: Academic Press Fribourg.
Joffe, L. 2001. "The Elohistic Psalter: What, How and Why?" *Scandinavian Journal of the Old Testament* 15 (1): 142–169.
Joffe, L. 2002. "The Answer to the Meaning of Life, the Universe and the Elohistic Psalter." *Journal for the Study of the Old Testament* 27 (2): 223–235.
Johanning, K. 1988. *Der Bibel-Babel-Streit: eine forschungsgeschichtliche Studie*. Frankfurt am Main: Lang.
Johnson, A. R. 1935. "The Role of the King in the Jerusalem Cultus." In *The Labyrinth: Further Studies in the Relation Between Myth and Ritual in the Ancient World*, edited by Hooke, S. H., 71–111. London: SPCK.
Johnson, A. R. 1955. *Sacral Kingship in Ancient Israel*. Cardiff: University of Wales.
Johnson, E. 1974. "'Anaph, 'Aph." In *Theological Dictionary of the Old Testament*, edited by Botterweck, G. J., Ringgren, H., Vol. I, 350–360. Grand Rapids: Eerdmans.

Johnston, S. I., ed. 2004. *Religions of the Ancient World: A Guide.* Cambridge: Harvard University.
Johnstone, W. 1995. *William Robertson Smith: Essays in Reassessment.* Sheffield: Sheffield Academic Press.
Jones, P. 2005. "Divine and Non-Divine Kingship." In *A Companion to the Ancient Near East,* edited by Snell, D. C., 330–342. Malden: Blackwell.
Joosten, J. 2007. "A Note on the Text of Deuteronomy xxxii 8." *Vetus Testamentum* 57 (4): 548–555.
Joosten, J. 2012. Review of I. Young, R. Rezetko and M. Ehrensvärd, *Linguistic Dating of Biblical Texts.* In *Babel und Bibel 6,* edited by Kogan, L., Koslova, N., Loesov, S., Tischchenko, S., 535–542. Winona Lake: Eisenbrauns.
Joüon, P., Muraoka, T. 1991. *A Grammar of Biblical Hebrew.* Rome: Pontificio Istituto Biblico.
Kang, S. 1989. *Divine War in the Old Testament and in the Ancient Near East.* Beiheft zur Zeitschrift für die alttestamentliche Wissenschaft, Vol. 177. Berlin: de Gruyter.
Kang, S. I. 2008. "Creation, Eden, Temple and Mountain: Textual Presentations of Sacred Space in the Hebrew Bible." Johns Hopkins University.
Kant, I. 1959. *Foundations of the Metaphysics of Morals and What Is Enlightenment,* edited by Beck, L.W. Indianapolis: Bobbs-Merrill.
Kapelrud, A. S. 1967. "Sigmund Mowinckel and Old Testament Study." *Annual of the Swedish Theological Institute* 5: 4–29.
Kapelrud, A. S. 1974. "'Abhir." In *Theological Dictionary of the Old Testament,* edited by Botterweck, G. J., Ringgren, H., Vol. I, 42–44. Grand Rapids: Eerdmans.
Kaplan, J., Ritter-Kaplan, H. 1993. "Jaffa." In *The New Encyclopedia of Archaeological Excavations in the Holy Land,* edited by Stern, E., Levinzon-Gilboa, A., Aviram, J., Vol. 2, 655–659. Jerusalem: Israel Exploration Society & Carta.
Karageorghis, K. 1976. *View from the Bronze Age: Mycenaean and Phoenician Discoveries at Kition.* New York: Dutton.
Kaufman, S. A. 1980. Review of J. Hoftijzer and G. van der Kooij, *The Aramaic Texts from Deir ʿAllā. Bulletin of the American Schools of Oriental Research* 239: 71–74.
Kaufmann, Y. 1951. "The Bible and Mythological Polytheism." *Journal of Biblical Literature* 70 (3): 179–197.
Kaufmann, Y. 1956. *Toledot ha-ʾemunah ha-yisrʾaelit me-yeme qedem ʿad sof bayit sheni.* Tel Aviv: Mosad Bialik.
Kaufmann, Y. 1960. *The Religion of Israel: From Its Beginnings to the Babylonian Exile.* Chicago: University of Chicago.
Kaufmann, Y. 1972. *The Religion of Israel: From Its Beginnings to the Babylonian Exile.* 2nd ed. New York: Schocken.
Keel, O. 1973. "Das Vergraben der 'fremden Götter' in Genesis XXXV 4b." *Vetus Testamentum* 23: 305–336.
Keel, O. 1977. *Jahwe-Visionen und Siegelkunst: Eine neue Deutung der Majestätsschilderungen in Jes 6, Ez 1 und 10 und Sach 4.* Stuttgart: Verlag Katholisches Bibelwerk.
Keel, O. 1986. Review of *Ancient Seals and the Bible. Journal of the American Oriental Society* 106 (2): 307–311.
Keel, O. 1992. "Iconography and the Bible." In *The Anchor Bible Dictionary,* edited by Freedman, D. N., Vol. 3, 358–374. New York: Doubleday.
Keel, O. 1997. *The Symbolism of the Biblical World: Ancient Near Eastern Iconography and the Book of Psalms.* Winona Lake: Eisenbrauns. Originally published 1972.

Keel, O. 1998. *Goddesses and Trees, New Moon and Yahweh: Ancient Near Eastern Art and the Hebrew Bible*. Sheffield: Sheffield Academic Press.

Keel, O. 2001. "Warum im Jerusalemer Tempel kein anthropomorphes Kultbild gestanden haben dürfte." In *Homo Pictor*, edited by Boehm, G., Hauser, S. E., 244–282. Munich: K. G. Saur.

Keel, O. 2012a. "Glyptic Material." In *Hazor VI: The 1990–2009 Excavations. the Iron Age*, edited by Ben-Tor, A., Ben-Ami, D., Sandhaus, D., 568–577. Jerusalem: Israel Exploration Society and Institute of Archaeology, Hebrew University of Jerusalem.

Keel, O. 2012b. "Paraphernalia of Jerusalem Sanctuaries and Their Relation to Deities Worshiped Therein During the Iron Age IIA-C." In *Temple Building and Temple Cult: Architecture and Cultic Paraphernalia of Temples in the Levant (2.–1. Mill. B.C.E.)*, edited by Kamlah, J., Michelau, H., 317–342. Wiesbaden: Harrassowitz.

Keel, O. 2017. *Jerusalem and the One God: A Religious History*. Minneapolis: Fortress.

Keel, O., Uehlinger, C. 1992. *Göttinnen, Götter und Gottessymbole: neue Erkenntnisse zur Religionsgeschichte Kanaans und Israels aufgrund bislang unerschlossener ikonographischer Quellen*. Freiburg: Herder.

Keel, O., Uehlinger, C. 1996. *Altorientalische Miniaturkunst: die ältesten visuellen Massenkommunikationsmittel: ein Blick in die Sammlungen des Biblischen Instituts der Universität Freiburg Schweiz*. Freiburg: Universitätsverlag.

Keel, O., Uehlinger, C. 1998. *Gods, Goddesses, and Images of God in Ancient Israel*. Minneapolis: Fortress.

Keil, C. 1986. *Exodus*. In *Commentary on the Old Testament in Ten Volumes by Carl Keil and Franz Delitzsch*. Grand Rapids: Eerdmans.

Keller, M. 1996. *Untersuchungen zur deuteronomisch-deuteronomistischen Namenstheologie*. Bonner biblische Beiträge, Vol. 105. Weinheim: Beltz Athenäum Verlag.

Kellermann, D. 1970. *Die Priesterschrift von Numeri 1,1 bis 10,10: literarkritisch und traditionsgeschichtlich untersucht*. Berlin: de Gruyter.

Kennedy, A. R. S. 1901. "Calf, Golden Calf." In *Hastings' Dictionary of the Bible*, edited by Hastings, J., Vol. 1, 340–345. Edinburgh: T. & T. Clark.

Kimbrough, S. T. 1972. "A Non-Weberian Sociological Approach to Israelite Religion." *Journal of Near Eastern Studies* 31 (3): 195–202.

King, P. J. 1983. *American Archaeology in the Mideast: A History of the American Schools of Oriental Research*. Philadelphia: American Schools of Oriental Research.

King, P. J., Stager, L. E. 2001. *Life in Biblical Israel*. Louisville: Westminster John Knox.

Kirk, G. S. 1970. *Myth: Its Meaning and Functions in Ancient and Other Cultures*. Berkeley: University of California.

Kisilevitz, S. 2015. "The Iron IIA Judahite Temple at Tel Moẓa." *Tel Aviv* 42: 147–164.

Kitchen, K. A. 1982. *Ramesside Inscriptions: Historical and Biographical*. Oxford: Blackwell.

Kitchen, K. A. 1986. *The Third Intermediate Period in Egypt, 1100–650 B.C.* Warminster: Aris & Phillips.

Kitchen, K. A. 1992. "The Egyptian Evidence on Ancient Jordan." In *Early Edom and Moab: The Beginning of the Iron Age in Southern Jordan*, edited by Bienkowski, P., 21–34. Sheffield: Collis.

Kitchen, K. A. 1993. "The Tabernacle—A Bronze Age Artifact." *Eretz-Israel* (Avraham Malamat Volume) 24: 119*–129*.

Kitchen, K. A. 2003. *On the Reliability of the Old Testament*. Grand Rapids: Eerdmans.

Kitz, A. M. 1994. "Ṣāra'at Accusations and the Sociology of Exclusion." Johns Hopkins University.

Kitz, A. M. 2003. "Prophecy as Divination." *Catholic Biblical Quarterly* 65 (1): 22–42.
Kitz, A. M. 2014. *Cursed Are You! The Phenomenology of Cursing in Cuneiform and Hebrew Texts*. Winona Lake: Eisenbrauns.
Kitz, A. M. 2019. "The Verb *yahway*." *Journal of Biblical Literature* 138 (1): 39–62.
Klatt, W. 1969. *Hermann Gunkel. Zu seiner Theologie der Religionsgeschichte und zur Entstehung der formgeschichtlichen Methode*. Goettingen: Vandenhoeck und Ruprecht.
Klawans, J. 2000. *Impurity and Sin in Ancient Judaism*. Oxford: Oxford University.
Klawans, J. 2006. *Purity, Sacrifice, and the Temple: Symbolism and Supersessionism in the Study of Ancient Judaism*. New York: Oxford University.
Klawans, J. 2011. "Symbol, Function, Theology, and Morality in the Study of Priestly Ritual." In *Ancient Mediterranean Sacrifice*, edited by Knust, J. W., Várhelyi, Z., 106–122. New York: Oxford University.
Klein, J. 2006. "Sumerian Kingship and the Gods." In *Text, Artifact, and Image: Revealing Ancient Israelite Religion*, edited by Beckman, G. M., Lewis, T. J., 115–131. Providence: Brown Judaic Studies.
Kletter, R. 1996. *The Judean Pillar-figurines and the Archaeology of Asherah*. Oxford: Tempus Reparatum.
Kletter, R., Ziffer, I., Zwickel, W. 2010. *Yavneh I: The Excavation of the "Temple Hill" Repository Pit and the Cult Stands*. Fribourg: Academic Press Fribourg.
Kletter, R., Ziffer, I., Zwickel, W. 2015. *Yavneh II: The "Temple Hill" Repository Pit*. Fribourg: Academic Press Fribourg.
Klingbeil, G. A. 1997. "Ritual Time in Leviticus 8 with Special Reference to the Seven Day Period in the Old Testament." *Zeitschrift für die alttestamentliche Wissenschaft* 109: 500–513.
Klingbeil, G. A. 1998. *A Comparative Study of the Ritual of Ordination as Found in Leviticus 8 and Emar 369*. Lewiston: Edwin Mellon.
Klingbeil, G. A. 2000. "The Anointing of Aaron: A Study of Lev 8:12 in Its OT and ANE Contexts." *Andrews University Seminary Studies* 38: 231–243.
Klingbeil, G. A. 2007. *Bridging the Gap: Ritual and Ritual Texts in the Bible*. Winona Lake: Eisenbrauns.
Klingbeil, M. 1999. *Yahweh Fighting from Heaven: God as Warrior and as God of Heaven in the Hebrew Psalter and Ancient Near Eastern Iconography*. Fribourg: University Press.
Kloos, C. 1986. *Yhwh's Combat with the Sea: A Canaanite Tradition in the Religion of Ancient Israel*. Amsterdam: G. A. van Oorschot.
Knafl, A. K. 2014. *Forming God: Divine Anthropomorphism in the Pentateuch*. Winona Lake: Eisenbrauns.
Knapp, A. 2015. *Royal Apologetic in the Ancient Near East*. Atlanta: SBL Press.
Knauf, E. A. 1984. "Yahwe." *Vetus Testamentum* 34 (4): 467–472.
Knauf, E. A. 1985. "El Šaddai—der Gott Abrahams?" *Biblische Zeitschrift* 29: 97–103.
Knauf, E. A. 1988. *Midian: Untersuchungen zur Geschichte Palästinas und Nordarabiens am Ende des 2. Jahrtausends v. Chr*. Wiesbaden: Harrassowitz.
Knauf, E. A. 1992. "Reuel." In *The Anchor Bible Dictionary*, edited by Freedman, D. N., Vol. 5, 693–694. New York: Doubleday.
Knauf, E. A. 1999. "Shadday." In *Dictionary of Deities and Demons in the Bible*, edited by van der Toorn, K., Becking, B., van der Horst, P. W., 749–753. 2nd ed. Leiden: Brill.
Knauf, E. A. 2006. "Bethel The Israelite Impact on Judean Language and Literature." In *Judah and the Judeans in the Persian Period*, edited by Lipschitz, O., Oeming, M., 291–349. Winona Lake: Eisenbrauns.

Knight, D. A. 1973. *Rediscovering the Traditions of Israel: The Development of the Traditio-historical Research of the Old Testament, with Special Consideration of Scandinavian Contributions*. Missoula: Society of Biblical Literature for the Form Criticism Seminar.

Knight, D. A. 2011. *Law, Power, and Justice in Ancient Israel*. Louisville: Westminster John Knox.

Knobel, A. 1847. *Kurzgefasstes exegetisches handbuch zum Alten Testament. Die bücher Exodus und Leviticus*. Leipzig: S. Hirzel.

Knohl, I. 1995. *The Sanctuary of Silence: The Priestly Torah and the Holiness School*. Minneapolis: Fortress.

Knohl, I. 1996. "Between Voice and Silence: The Relationship Between Prayer and Temple Cult." *Journal of Biblical Literature* 115 (1): 17–30.

Knoppers, G. N. 1992a. "'There Was None Like Him': Incomparability in the Books of Kings." *Catholic Biblical Quarterly* 54 (3): 411–431.

Knoppers, G. N. 1992b. "'The God in His Temple': The Phoenician Text from Pyrgi as a Funerary Inscription." *Journal of Near Eastern Studies* 51 (2): 105–120.

Knoppers, G. N. 1993. *Two Nations Under God: The Deuteronomistic History of Solomon and the Dual Monarchies*. Atlanta: Scholars Press.

Knoppers, G. N. 1994. "Jehoshaphat's Judiciary and 'The Scroll of Yhwh's Torah.'" *Journal of Biblical Literature* 113 (1): 59–80.

Knoppers, G. N. 1995a. "Prayer and Propaganda: Solomon's Dedication of the Temple and the Deuteronomist's Program." *Catholic Biblical Quarterly* 57: 229–254.

Knoppers, G. N. 1995b. "Aaron's Calf and Jeroboam's Calves." In *Fortunate the Eyes That See: Essays in Honor of David Noel Freedman in Celebration of His Seventieth Birthday*, edited by Beck, A. B., 92–104. Grand Rapids: Eerdmans.

Knoppers, G. N. 1996. "The Deuteronomist and the Deuteronomic Law of the King: A Reexamination of a Relationship." *Zeitschrift für die alttestamentliche Wissenschaft* 108 (3): 329–346.

Knoppers, G. N. 1997. "The Vanishing Solomon: The Disappearance of the United Monarchy from Recent Histories of Ancient Israel." *Journal of Biblical Literature* 116 (1): 19–44.

Knoppers, G. N. 1999. "Hierodules, Priests, or Janitors? The Levites in Chronicles and the History of the Israelite Priesthood." *Journal of Biblical Literature* 118 (1): 49–72.

Knoppers, G. N. 2000. "Prayer and Propaganda: Solomon's Dedication of the Temple and the Deuteronomist's Program." In *Reconsidering Israel and Judah: Recent Studies on the Deuteronomistic History*, edited by Knoppers, G. N., McConville, J. G., 370–396. Winona Lake: Eisenbrauns.

Knoppers, G. N. 2001. "Rethinking the Relationship Between Deuteronomy and the Deuteronomistic History: The Case of Kings." *Catholic Biblical Quarterly* 63 (3): 393–415.

Knoppers, G. N. 2003a. *I Chronicles 1–9*. New Haven: Yale University.

Knoppers, G. N. 2003b. "The Relationship of the Priestly Geneaologies to the History of the High Priesthood in Jerusalem." In *Judah and Judeans in the Neo-Babylonian Period*, edited by Lipschits, O., Blenkinsopp, J., 109–133. Winona Lake: Eisenbrauns.

Knoppers, G. N. 2004. *1 Chronicles, 10–29*. New York: Doubleday.

Knoppers, G. N., Levinson, B. M., eds. 2007. *The Pentateuch as Torah: New Models for Understanding Its Promulgation and Acceptance*. Winona Lake: Eisenbrauns.

Knoppers, G. N., McConville, J. G., eds. 2000. *Reconsidering Israel and Judah: Recent Studies on the Deuteronomistic History*. Winona Lake: Eisenbrauns.

Knott, K. 2005. *The Location of Religion: A Spatial Analysis.* London: Equinox.
Koch, K. 1964. *Was ist Formgeschichte?* Neukirchen-Vluyn: Neukirchener Verlag.
Koch, K. 1976. "Šaddaj: Zum Verhältnis zwischen israelitischer Monolatrie und nordwestsemitischem Polytheismus." *Vetus Testamentum* 26 (3): 299–332.
Koch, K. 1988. "Aschera als Himmelskönigin in Jerusalem." *Ugarit-Forschungen* 20: 97–120.
Koenen, K. 1988. "Wer sieht wen? Zur Textgeschichte von Genesis XVI 13." *Vetus Testamentum* 38 (4): 468–474.
Köhler, L. 1956. *Hebrew Man.* London: SCM Press.
Kohlmeyer, K. 2000. *Der Tempel des Wettergottes von Aleppo.* Münster: Rhema.
Kohlmeyer, K. 2009. "The Temple of the Storm God in Aleppo During the Late Bronze and Early Iron Ages." *Near Eastern Archaeology* 72 (4): 190–202.
Koppen, F. van., van der Toorn, K. 1999. "Holy One *qdwš*." In *Dictionary of Deities and Demons in the Bible*, edited by van der Toorn, K., Becking, B., van der Horst, P. W., 415–418. 2nd ed. Leiden: Brill.
Kornfeld, W. 2003. "*Qdš*." In *Theological Dictionary of the Old Testament*, edited by Botterweck, G. J., Ringgren, H., Fabry, H., Vol. XII, 521–526. Grand Rapids: Eerdmans.
Korpel, M. C. A. 1990. *A Rift in the Clouds: Ugaritic and Hebrew Descriptions of the Divine.* Ugaritisch-biblische Literatur, Vol. 8. Münster: Ugarit-Verlag.
Korpel, M. C. A. 1999a. "Stone." In *Dictionary of Deities and Demons in the Bible*, edited by van der Toorn, K., Becking, B., van der Horst, P. W., 818–820. 2nd ed. Leiden: Brill.
Korpel, M. C. A. 1999b. "Rock." In *Dictionary of Deities and Demons in the Bible*, edited by van der Toorn, K., Becking, B., van der Horst, P. W., 709–710. 2nd ed. Leiden: Brill.
Kort, W. 2007. "Sacred/Profane and Adequate Theory of Human Place-Relations." In *Constructions of Space I: Theory, Geography, and Narrative*, edited by Berquist, J. L., Camp, C. V., 32–50. New York: T. &. T. Clark.
Kottsieper, I. 1997. "El—ferner oder naher Gott?" In *Religion und Gesellschaft: Studien zu ihrer Wechselbeziehung in den Kulturen des antiken Vorderen Orients*, edited by Albertz, R., 25–74. Münster: Ugarit-Verlag.
Kraus, H.-J. 1962. *Gottesdienst in Israel: Grundriss einer Geschichte des alttestamentlichen Gottesdienstes.* 2nd ed. Munich: C. Kaiser.
Kraus, H.-J. 1969. *Geschichte der historisch-kritischen Erforschung des Alten Testaments von der Reformatio bis zur Gegenwart.* Neukirchen-Vluyn: Neukirchener.
Kraus, H.-J. 1986. *Theology of the Psalms.* Minneapolis: Augsburg.
Kraus, H.-J. 1988. *Psalms 1–59.* Minneapolis: Augsburg.
Kraus, H.-J. 1989. *Psalms 60–150.* Minneapolis: Augsburg.
Krebernik, M. 1996. "The Linguistic Classification of Eblaite: Methods, Problems and Results." In *The Study of the Ancient Near East in the Twenty-First Century: The William Foxwell Albright Centennial Conference*, edited by Cooper, J. S., Schwartz, G. M., 233–249. Winona Lake: Eisenbrauns.
Krebernik, M. 2017. "The Beginnings of Yahwism from an Assyriological Perspective." In *The Origins of Yahwism*, edited by van Oorschot, J., Witte, M., 45–66. Berlin: de Gruyter.
Krüger, T. 2004. *Qoheleth: A Commentary.* Minneapolis: Fortress.
Kselman, J. S. 2016. Review of T. R. Wardlaw, *Elohim Within the Psalms: Petitioning the Creator to Order Chaos in Oral-Derived Literature. Review of Biblical Literature* 07.
Kuan, J. K. 1995. *Neo-Assyrian Historical Inscriptions and Syria-Palestine: Israelite/Judean-Tyrian-Damascene Political and Commercial Relations in the Ninth-Eighth Centuries BCE.* Eugene: Wipf & Stock.

Kugel, J. L. 2011. *In the Valley of the Shadow: On the Foundations of Religious Belief (and Their Connection to a Certain, Fleeting State of Mind)*. New York: Free Press.

Kugler, R. A. 1997. "Holiness, Purity, the Body, and Society: The Evidence for Theological Conflict in Leviticus." *Journal for the Study of the Old Testament* 76: 3–27.

Kuhn, T. S. 1970. *The Structure of Scientific Revolutions*. Chicago: University of Chicago.

Kuhrt, A. 1995. *The Ancient Near East: c. 3000–330 B.C.* London: Routledge.

Kunin, S. 1998. *God's Place in the World: Sacred Space and Sacred Place in Judaism*. London: Cassell.

Kutsch, E. 1963. *Salbung als Rechtsakt im Alten Testament und im Alten Orient*. Berlin: Töpelmann.

Kvale, D., Rian, D. 1988. "Professor Sigmund Mowinckel: A Bibliography." *Scandinavian Journal of the Old Testament* 2: 93–168.

Kwasman, T., Parpola, S. 1991. *Legal Transactions of the Royal Court of Nineveh, Part I: Tiglath-Pileser III Through Esarhaddon*. Helsinki: Helsinki University.

L'Heureux, C. E. 1979. *Rank Among the Canaanite Gods: El, Baal, and the Rephaim*. Harvard Semitic Monographs, Vol. 21. Missoula: Scholars Press.

Lambdin, T. O. 1953. "Egyptian Loan Words in the Old Testament." *Journal of the American Oriental Society* 73 (3): 145–155.

Lambert, W. G. 1960. *Babylonian Wisdom Literature*. Oxford: Clarendon.

Lambert, W. G. 1965. "A New Look at the Babylonian Background of Genesis." *Journal of Theological Studies* 16 (2): 287–300.

Lambert, W. G. 1988. "Old Testament Mythology in Its Ancient Near Eastern Context." In *Congress Volume: Jerusalem, 1986*, edited by Emerton, J. A., 124–143. Leiden: Brill.

Landsberger, B. 1976. *The Conceptual Autonomy of the Babylonian World*. Malibu: Undena.

Lang, B. 1993. "Kult." In *Handbuch Religionswissenschaftlicher Grundbegriffe*, Vol. 3, 474–488. Stuttgart: Kohlhammer.

Langhe, R. de. 1958. "Myth, Ritual, and Kingship in the Ras Shamra Tablets." In *Myth, Ritual, and Kingship*, edited by Hooke, S. H., 122–148. Oxford: Clarendon Press.

Lapp, P. W. 1969. "The 1968 Excavations at Tell Ta'annek." *Bulletin of the American Schools of Oriental Research* 195: 2–49.

LaRocca-Pitts, E. 2001. *"Of Wood and Stone": The Significance of Israelite Cultic Items in the Bible and Its Early Interpreters*. Harvard Semitic Monographs, Vol. 61. Winona Lake: Eisenbrauns.

Larsen, M. T. 1995. "The 'Babel/Bible' Controversy and Its Aftermath." In *Civilizations of the Ancient Near East*, edited by Sasson, J. M., 95–106. New York: Scribner's.

Larson, E. J. 1997. *Summer for the Gods. The Scopes Trial and America's Continuing Debate over Science and Religion*. New York: Basic Books.

Lasine, S. 1989. "The Riddle of Solomon's Judgment and the Riddle of Human Nature in the Hebrew Bible." *Journal for the Study of the Old Testament* 45: 61–86.

Lasine, S. 2002. "Divine Narcissism and Yahweh's Parenting Style." *Biblical Interpretation* 10 (1): 36–56.

Laughlin, J. C. H. 2007. "Dan, Tell." In *The New Interpreter's Dictionary of the Bible*, edited by Sakenfeld, K. D., Vol. 2, 10–12. Nashville: Abingdon.

Lauinger, J. 2012. "Esarhaddon's Succession Treaty at Tell Tayinat: Text and Commentary." *Journal of Cuneiform Studies* 64: 87–123.

Lauinger, J. 2019. "Literary Connections and Social Contexts: Approaches to Deuteronomy in Light of the Assyrian *adê*-Tradition." *Hebrew Bible and Ancient Israel* 8: 87–100.

Layton, S. C. 1988. "Literary Sources for the History of Palestine and Syria: Old Aramaic Inscriptions." *Biblical Archaeologist* 51 (3): 172–189.

Layton, S. C. 1990. *Archaic Features of Canaanite Personal Names in the Hebrew Bible*. Harvard Semitic Monographs, Vol. 47. Atlanta: Scholars Press.

Layton, S. C. 1996. "Leaves from an Onomastician's Notebook." *Zeitschrift für die alttestamentliche Wissenschaft* 108 (4): 608–620.

Leeuw, G. van der. 1938. *Religion in Essence and Manifestation: A Study in Phenomenology*. London: G. Allen & Unwin.

Lefebvre, H. 1974. "La production de l'espace." *L'Homme et la Societé* 31: 15–32.

Lefebvre, H. 1991. *The Production of Space*. Cambridge: Blackwell.

Lehmann, R. G. 1994. *Friedrich Delitzsch und der Babel-Bibel-Streit*. Freiburg: Universitätsverlag.

Leitz, C. 2002. *Lexikon der ägyptischen Götter und Götterbezeichnungen Band VII*. Leuven: Peeters.

Lemaire, A. 1976. "Prières en temps de crise: les inscriptions de Khirbet Beit Lei." *Revue Biblique* 83 (4): 558–568.

Lemaire, A. 1977. "Les inscriptions de Khirbet el-Qom et l'asherah de YHWH." *Revue Biblique* 84 (4): 595–608.

Lemaire, A. 1984. "Who or What Was Yahweh's Asherah?" *Biblical Archaeology Review* 10 (6): 42–51.

Lemaire, A. 1985. "L'inscription de Balaam trouvée à Deir 'Alla." In *Biblical Archaeology Today: Proceedings of the International Congress on Biblical Archaeology*, 313–325. Jerusalem: Israel Exploration Society.

Lemaire, A. 1994. "'House of David' Restored in Moabite Inscription." *Biblical Archaeology Review* 20 (3): 30–37.

Lemaire, A. 1997. "Arad Inscriptions." In *The Oxford Encyclopedia of Archaeology in the Near East*, edited by Meyers, E. M., Vol. 1, 176–177. New York: Oxford University.

Lemaire, A. 1998. "Une inscription araméenne du viiie s. av. J.-C. trouvée à Bukân (Azerbaïdjan iranien)." *Studia Iranica* 27: 15–30.

Lemaire, A. 1999. "Le ḥérem dans le monde nord-ouest sémitique." In *Guerre et conquête dans le Proche-Orient ancien*, edited by Nehmé, L., 79–92. Paris: J. Maisonneuve.

Lemaire, A. 2006. "Khirbet el-Qôm and Hebrew and Aramaic Epigraphy." In *Confronting the Past: Archaeological and Historical Essays on Ancient Israel in Honor of William G. Dever*, edited by Gitin, S., Wright, J. E., Dessel, J. P., 231–238. Winona Lake: Eisenbrauns.

Lemaire, A. 2013. "Remarques sur les inscriptions phéniciennes de Kuntillet 'Ajrud." *Semitica* 55: 83–99.

Lemaire, A. 2014. "A History of Northwest Semitic Epigraphy." In *"An Eye for Form": Epigraphic Essays in Honor of Frank Moore Cross*, edited by Hackett, J. A., Aufrecht, W. E., 5–29. Winona Lake: Eisenbrauns.

Lemaire, A., Sass, B. 2013. "The Mortuary Stele with Sam'alian Inscription from Ördekburnu Near Zincirli." *Bulletin of the American Schools of Oriental Research* 369: 57–136.

Lemche, N. P. 1985. *Early Israel: Anthropological and Historical Studies on the Israelite Society Before the Monarchy*. Leiden: Brill.

Lemche, N. P. 1991a. *The Canaanites and Their Land: The Tradition of the Canaanites*. Sheffield: JSOT Press.

Lemche, N. P. 1991b. "The Development of the Israelite Religion in the Light of Recent Studies on the Early History of Israel." In *Congress Volume: Leuven, 1989*, edited by Emerton, J. A., 97–115. Leiden: Brill.
Lemche, N. P. 1993. "The Old Testament—A Hellenistic Book?" *Scandinavian Journal of the Old Testament* 7: 163–193.
Lemche, N. P. 1996a. "Early Israel Revisited." *Currents in Research* 4: 9–34.
Lemche, N. P. 1996b. "Where Should We Look for Canaan? A Reply to Nadav Na'aman." *Ugarit-Forschungen* 28: 767–772.
Lemche, N. P. 1998. "Greater Canaan: The Implications of a Correct Reading of EA 151:49–67." *Bulletin of the American Schools of Oriental Research* 310: 19–24.
LeMon, J. M., Strawn, B. A. 2013. "Once More, Yhwh and Company at Kuntillet 'Ajrud." *Maarav* 20 (1): 83–114.
Lenzi, A. 2008. *Secrecy and the Gods: Secret Knowledge in Ancient Mesopotamia and Biblical Israel*. State Archives of Assyria Studies, Volume XIX. Helsinki: Neo-Assyrian Text Corpus Project.
Lenzi, A. 2011. "An OB Ikribu-Like Prayer to Shamash and Adad." In *Reading Akkadian Prayers and Hymns: An Introduction*, edited by Lenzi, A., 85–104. Atlanta: Society of Biblical Literature.
Leuchter, M. 2007. "'The Levite in Your Gates': The Deuteronomic Redefinition of Levitical Authority." *Journal of Biblical Literature* 126 (3): 417–436.
Leuchter, M. 2012. "The Fightin' Mushites." *Vetus Testamentum* 62 (4): 479–500.
Leuchter, M., Hutton, J. M., eds. 2011. *Levites and Priests in Biblical History and Tradition*. Atlanta: Society of Biblical Literature.
Leuenberger, M. 2015. "Noch einmal: Jhwh aus dem Süden. Methodische und religionsgeschichtliche Überlegungen in der jüngsten Debatte." In *Gott und Geschichte*, edited by Meyer-Blanck, M., 267–287. Leipzig: Evangelische Verlagsanstalt.
Leuenberger, M. 2017. "Yhwh's Provenance from the South: A New Evaluation of the Arguments Pro and Contra." In *The Origins of Yahwism*, edited by van Oorschot, J., Witte, M., 157–179. Berlin: de Gruyter.
Levenson, J. D. 1976. *Theology of the Program of Restoration of Ezekiel 40–48*. Atlanta: Scholars Press.
Levenson, J. D. 1985. *Sinai and Zion: An Entry into the Jewish Bible*. Minneapolis: Winston Press.
Levenson, J. D. 1987. "Why Jews are Not Interested in Biblical Theology." In *Judaic Perspectives on Ancient Israel*, edited by Neusner, J., Levine, B. A., Frerichs, E. S., 281–307. Philadelphia: Fortress.
Levenson, J. D. 1993. *The Death and Resurrection of the Beloved Son: The Transformation of Child Sacrifice in Judaism and Christianity*. New Haven: Yale University.
Levenson, J. D. 2017. "Is the Torah a Work of Philosophy?" MosaicMagazine.com, February 16.
Levin, C. 2010. "Source Criticism: The Miracle at the Sea." In *Method Matters: Essays on the Interpretation of the Hebrew Bible in Honor of David L. Petersen*, edited by LeMon, J. M., Richards, K. H., 39–61. Leiden: Brill.
Levin, Y. 2014. "Baal Worship in Early Israel: An Onomastic View in Light of the 'Eshbaal' Inscription from Khirbet Qeiyafa." *Maarav* 21: 203–222.
Levine, B. A. 1965. "The Descriptive Tabernacle Texts of the Pentateuch." *Journal of the American Oriental Society* 85: 307–318.

Levine, B. A. 1985. "The Balaam Inscriptions from Deir ʿAlla: Historical Aspects." In *Biblical Archaeology Today: Proceedings of the International Congress on Biblical Archaeology*, 326–339. Jerusalem: Israel Exploration Society.

Levine, B. A. 1987. "The Language of Holiness: Perceptions of the Sacred in the Hebrew Bible." In *Backgrounds for the Bible*, edited by O'Connor, M. P., Freedman, D. N., 241–255. Winona Lake: Eisenbrauns.

Levine, B. A. 1989. *Leviticus = Va-yikra: The Traditional Hebrew Text with the New JPS Translation*. Philadelphia: Jewish Publication Society.

Levine, B. A. 1991. "The Plaster Inscriptions from Deir ʿAlla: General Interpretation." In *The Balaam Text from Deir ʿAlla Re-evaluated: Proceedings of the International Symposium Held at Leiden, 21–24 August 1989*, edited by Hoftijzer, J., Van der Kooij, G., 58–72. Leiden: Brill.

Levine, B. A. 1993. *Numbers 1–20*. New York: Doubleday.

Levine, B. A. 1997. "Mythic and Ritual Projections of Sacred Space in Biblical Literature." *Journal of Jewish Thought and Philosophy* 6: 59–70.

Levine, B. A. 2000a. *Numbers 21–36*. New York: Doubleday.

Levine, B. A. 2000b. "The Deir ʿAlla Plaster Inscriptions." In *The Context of Scripture 2: Monumental Inscriptions from the Biblical World*, edited by Hallo, W. W., Younger, K. L., 140–145. Leiden: Brill.

Levine, B. A., Tarragon, J. de. 1988. "'Shapshu Cries Out in Heaven': Dealing with Snake-Bites at Ugarit (KTU 1.100, 1.107)." *Revue Biblique* 95: 481–518.

Levine, B. A., Tarragon, J. de. 1993. "The King Proclaims the Day: Ugaritic Rites for the Vintage (KTU 1.41//1.87)." *Revue Biblique* 100 (1): 76–115.

Levine, É. 2002. "Justice in Judaism: The Case of Jonah." *Review of Rabbinic Judaism* 5 (2): 170–197.

Levinson, B. M. 1997. *Deuteronomy and the Hermeneutics of Legal Innovation*. New York: Oxford University.

Levinson, B. M. 2001. "The Reconceptualization of Kingship in Deuteronomy and the Deuteronomistic History's Transformation of Torah." *Vetus Testamentum* 51 (4): 511–534.

Levinson, B. M. 2003. "You Must Not Add Anything to What I Command You: Paradoxes of Canon and Authorship in Ancient Israel." *Numen* 50: 1–51.

Levinson, B. M. 2005. "Deuteronomy's Conception of Law as an 'Ideal Type': A Missing Chapter in the History of Constitutional Law." *Maarav* 12: 83–119.

Levinson, B. M. 2008. *"The Right Chorale": Studies in Biblical Law and Interpretation*. Forschungen zum Alten Testament, Vol. 54. Tübingen: Mohr Siebeck.

Levy, T. E. 2005. "Iron Age Burial in the Lowlands of Edom." *Annual of the Department of Antiquities of Jordan* 49: 443–487.

Levy, T. E. 2009a. "Ethnic Identity in Biblical Edom, Israel, and Midian: Some Insights from Mortuary Contexts in the Lowlands of Edom." In *Exploring the Longue Durée Essays in Honor of Lawrence E. Stager*, edited by Schloen, J. D., 251–261. Winona Lake: Eisenbrauns.

Levy, T. E. 2009b. "Pastoral Nomads and Iron Age Metal Production in Ancient Edom." In *Nomads, Tribes, and the State in the Ancient Near East.*, edited by Szuchman, J., 147–176. Chicago: University of Chicago.

Levy, T. E., Adams, R. B., Muniz, A. 2004. "Archaeology and the Shasu Nomads: Recent Excavations in the Jabal Hamrat Fidan, Jordan." In *Le-David Maskil: A Birthday Tribute for David Noel Freedman*, edited by Propp, W. H. C., Friedman, R. E., 63–89. Winona Lake: Eisenbrauns.

Levy, T. E., Adams, R. B., Shafiq, R. 1999. "The Jabal Hamrat Fidan Project: Excavations at the Wadi Fidan 40 Cemetery, Jordan (1997)." *Levant* 31 (1): 293–308.

Levy, T. E., ed. 1995. *The Archaeology of Society in the Holy Land*. New York: Facts on File.

Levy, T. E., Holl, A. F. C. 1995. "Social Change and the Archaeology of the Holy Land." In *The Archaeology of Society in the Holy Land*, edited by Levy, T. E., 3–8. New York: Facts on File.

Lewis, C. S. 1955. "De Descriptione Temporum: Inaugural Lecture from the Chair of Mediaeval and Renaissance Literature at Cambridge University, 1954." https://archive.org/details/DeDescriptioneTemporum/mode/2up.

Lewis, T. J. 1985. "The Songs of Hannah and Deborah: ḤDL-II ('Growing Plump')." *Journal of Biblical Literature* 104 (1): 105–108.

Lewis, T. J. 1989. *Cults of the Dead in Ancient Israel and Ugarit*. Harvard Semitic Monographs, Vol. 39. Atlanta: Scholars Press.

Lewis, T. J. 1991. "The Ancestral Estate (*naḥalat 'elohim*) in 2 Samuel 14:16." *Journal of Biblical Literature* 110 (4): 597–612.

Lewis, T. J. 1992a. "Dead, Abode of the." In *The Anchor Bible Dictionary*, edited by Freedman, D. N., Vol. 2, 101–105. New York: Doubleday.

Lewis, T. J. 1992b. "Mot." In *The Anchor Bible Dictionary*, edited by Freedman, D. N., Vol. 4, 922–924. New York: Doubleday.

Lewis, T. J. 1994. "The Textual History of the Song of Hannah: 1 Samuel II 1–10." *Vetus Testamentum* 44 (1): 18–46.

Lewis, T. J. 1996a. "The Identity and Function of El/Baal Berith." *Journal of Biblical Literature* 115 (3): 401–423.

Lewis, T. J. 1996b. "CT 13.33–34 and Ezekiel 32: Lion-Dragon Myths." *Journal of the American Oriental Society* 116 (1): 28–47.

Lewis, T. J. 1997. "The Birth of the Gracious Gods." In *Ugaritic Narrative Poetry*, edited by Parker, S. B., 205–214. Writings from the Ancient World, Vol. 9. Atlanta: Scholars Press.

Lewis, T. J. 1998. "Divine Images and Aniconism in Ancient Israel." *Journal of the American Oriental Society* 118 (1): 36–53.

Lewis, T. J. 1999. "Teraphim." In *Dictionary of Deities and Demons in the Bible*, edited by van der Toorn, K., Becking, B., van der Horst, P. W., 844–850. 2nd ed. Leiden: Brill.

Lewis, T. J. 2002. "How Far Can Texts Take Us? Evaluating Textual Sources for Reconstructing Ancient Israelite Beliefs About the Dead." In *Sacred Time, Sacred Place: Archaeology and the Religion of Israel*, edited by Gittlen, B. M., 169–217. Winona Lake: Eisenbrauns.

Lewis, T. J. 2005a. "Syro-Palestinian Iconography and Divine Images." In *Cult Image and Divine Representation in the Ancient Near East*, edited by Walls, N. H., 69–107. Boston: American Schools of Oriental Research.

Lewis, T. J. 2005b. "The Mysterious Disappearance of Zerubbabel." In *Seeking Out the Wisdom of the Ancients: Essays Offered to Honor Michael V. Fox on the Occasion of His Sixty-Fifth Birthday*, edited by Troxel, R. L., Friebel, K. G., Magary, D. R., 301–314. Winona Lake: Eisenbrauns.

Lewis, T. J. 2006a. "Covenant and Blood Rituals: Understanding Exodus 24:3–8 Against Its Ancient Near Eastern Backdrop." In *Confronting the Past: Archaeological and Historical Essays on Ancient Israel in Honor of William G. Dever*, edited by Gitin, S., Wright, J. E., Dessel, J. P., 341–350.

Lewis, T. J. 2006b. "Introduction to William Foxwell Albright." In W. F. Albright, *Archaeology and the Religion of Israel*, xiii–xlix. Louisville: Westminster John Knox.

Lewis, T. J. 2007. "Death." In *The New Interpreter's Dictionary of the Bible*, edited by Sakenfeld, K. D., Vol. 2, 66–69. Nashville: Abingdon.
Lewis, T. J. 2008a. "Family, Household, and Local Religion at Late Bronze Age Ugarit." In *Household and Family Religion in Antiquity*, edited by Bodel, J. P., Olyan, S. M., 60–88. Malden: Blackwell.
Lewis, T. J. 2008b. "'You Have Heard What the Kings of Assyria Have Done': Disarmament Passages vis-à-vis Assyrian Rhetoric of Intimidation." In *Isaiah's Vision of Peace in Biblical and Modern International Relations: Swords into Plowshares*, edited by Cohen, R., Westbrook, R., 75–100. New York: Palgrave Macmillan.
Lewis, T. J. 2011. "ʿAthtartu's Incantations and the Use of Divine Names as Weapons." *Journal of Near Eastern Studies* 70 (2): 207–227.
Lewis, T. J. 2012. "Job 19 in the Light of the Ketef Hinnom Inscriptions and Amulets." In *Puzzling Out the Past: Studies in Northwest Semitic Languages and Literatures in Honor of Bruce Zuckerman*, edited by Lundberg, M., Fine, S., Pitard, W. T., 99–113, 319–320. Leiden: Brill.
Lewis, T. J. 2013a. "The Shaʿtiqatu Narrative from the Ugaritic Story About the Healing of King Kirta." *Journal of Ancient Near Eastern Religions* 13 (2): 188–211.
Lewis, T. J. 2013b. "Divine Fire in Deuteronomy 33:2." *Journal of Biblical Literature* 132 (4): 791–803.
Lewis, T. J. 2014a. "The Identity and Function of Ugaritic Shaʿtiqatu: A Divinely Made Apotropaic Figure." *Journal of Ancient Near Eastern Religions* 14 (1): 1–28.
Lewis, T. J. 2014b. Review of Rainer Albertz and Rüdiger Schmitt, *Family and Household Religion in Ancient Israel and the Levant*. *Near Eastern Archaeology* 77 (2): 154–156.
Lewis, T. J. 2015. "Egyptian Divinity in the Divine Speech in Job 38:36." In *Joyful in Thebes: Egyptological Studies in Honor of Betsy M. Bryan*, edited by Jasnow, R., Cooney, K. M., 343–356. Atlanta: Lockwood Press.
Lewis, T. J. 2016. "Art and Iconography: Representing Yahwistic Divinity." In *The Wiley Blackwell Companion to Ancient Israel*, edited by Niditch, S., 510–533. Chichester: John Wiley & Sons.
Lewis, T. J. 2017. "Piercing God's Name: A Mythological Subtext of Deicide Underlying Blasphemy in Leviticus 24." In *Le-maʿan Ziony: Essays in Honor of Ziony Zevit*, edited by Greenspahn, F. E., Rendsburg, G. A., 213–238. Eugene: Wipf & Stock.
Lewis, T. J. 2019. "Bar-Rakib's Legitimation and The Problem of a Missing Corpse: The End of the Panamuwa Inscription in Light of the Katumuwa Inscription" *ARAM Periodical* 31. 2: 349–374.
Lewis, T. J. 2020. "A Holy Warrior at Kuntillet ʿAjrud? Kuntillet ʿAjrud Plaster Inscription 4.2." In *The Bible in the Ancient Near East: Essays in Honor of P. Kyle McCarter*, edited by Rollston, C. Atlanta: SBL Press.
Lewis, T. J. Forthcoming a. "God (ʾIlu) and King in RS 2.002 [KTU 1.23]." In *"Like ʾIlu Are You Wise": Studies in Northwest Semitic Languages and Literatures in Honor of Dennis G. Pardee*, edited by Hardy, H. H., Lam, J., Reymond, E. D. Chicago: Oriental Institute, University of Chicago.
Lewis, T. J. Forthcoming b. "Gift Giving, Generosity and the Etymology of Manna." In *One Who Loves Knowledge: Studies in Honor of Richard Jasnow*. Atlanta: Lockwood Press.
Lichtheim, M. 1976. *Ancient Egyptian Literature*. Berkeley: University of California.

Lichtheim, M. 1997. "Instruction of Amenemope." In *The Context of Scripture 1: Canonical Compositions from the Biblical World*, edited by Hallo, W. W., Younger, K. L., 115–122. Leiden: Brill.
Liddell, H. G., Scott, R. 1996. *A Greek-English Lexicon with a Revised Supplement*. Oxford: Clarendon Press.
Liebermann, R. R. 2019. "'Hearts of Flesh': Collective Identity and the Body in the Book of Ezekiel." Johns Hopkins University.
Lieven, A. von. 2004. "Kinder, Schreiber, Könige—vergöttliche Menschen im alten Ägypten. Ein Arbeitsbericht." *Mitteilungen der Berliner Gesellschaft für Anthropologie, Ethnologie und Urgeschichte* 25: 47–62.
Lieven, A. von. 2010. "Deified Humans." *UCLA Encyclopedia of Egyptology*, Open Version, https://uee.cdh.ucla.edu.
Lieven, A. von. 2014. "Father of the Fathers, Mother of the Mothers. God as Father (and Mother) in Ancient Egypt." In *The Divine Father: Religious and Philosophical Concepts of Divine Parenthood in Antiquity*, edited by Albrecht, F., Feldmeier, R., 19–36. Leiden: Brill.
Limburg, J. 1969. "The Root *ryb* and the Prophetic Lawsuit Speeches." *Journal of Biblical Literature* 88: 291–304.
Linafelt, T. 1999. "Stanton, Elizabeth Cady." In *A Dictionary of Biblical Interpretation*, edited by Hayes, J., 503–504. Nashville: Abingdon.
Lincoln, B. 2008. "The Role of Religion in Achaemenian Imperialism." In *Religion and Power: Divine Kingship in the Ancient World and Beyond*, edited by Brisch, N. M., 221–241. Chicago: Oriental Institute.
Lind, M. 1980. *Yahweh Is a Warrior: The Theology of Warfare in Ancient Israel*. Scottdale: Herald Press.
Lindblom, J. 1964. "Noch einmal die Deutung des Jahwe-Namens in Ex. 3, 14." *Annual of the Swedish Theological Institute* 3: 4–15.
Lindenberger, J. M. 2003. *Ancient Aramaic and Hebrew Letters*. 2nd ed. Writings from the Ancient World, Vol. 14. Leiden: Brill.
Lipiński, E. 1967. "Juges 5:4–5 et Psaume 68:8–11." *Biblica* 48: 185–206.
Lipiński, E. 1971a. "El's Abode: Mythological Traditions Related to Mt. Hermon and the Mountains of Armenia." *Orientalia Lovaniensia Periodica* 2: 13–69.
Lipiński, E. 1971b. "An Israelite King of Hamat?" *Vetus Testamentum* 21 (3): 371–373.
Lipiński, E. 1971c. "Etymological and Exegetical Notes on the Meša' Inscription." *Orientalia* 40 (3): 325–340.
Lipiński, E. 1971d. "Psalm 68:7 and the Role of the Košarot." *Annali dell'Istituto Orientale di Napoli* 21: 532–537.
Lipiński, E. 1983. "The 'Phoenician History' of Philo of Byblos." *Bibliotheca Orientalis* 40: 305–310.
Lipiński, E. 1987. *Phoenicia and the East Mediterranean in the First Millennium B.C.* Orientalia Lovaniensia Analecta, Vol. 5. Leuven: Peeters.
Lipiński, E. 1988. "The Socio-Economic Condition of the Clergy in the Kingdom of Ugarit." In *Society and Economy in the Eastern Mediterranean, c. 1500–1000 B.C.*, edited by Heltzer, M., Lipinski, E., 125–150. Leuven: Peeters.
Lipiński, E. 1994. *Studies in Aramaic Inscriptions and Onomastics II*. Orientalia Lovaniensia Analecta, Vol. 57. Leuven: Leuven University.
Lipiński, E. 1999. "Nāqam." In *Theological Dictionary of the Old Testament*, edited by Botterweck, G. J., Ringgren, H., Fabry, H., Vol. X, 1–9. Grand Rapids: Eerdmans.

Lipiński, E. 2000. *The Aramaeans: Their Ancient History, Culture, Religion.* Leuven: Peeters.
Lipiński, E. 2006. *On the Skirts of Canaan in the Iron Age: Historical and Topographical Researches.* Leuven: Peeters.
Lipiński, E. 2013. "The Aramaeans in the West (13th–8th centuries)." In *Arameans, Chaldeans, and Arabs in Babylonia and Palestine in the First Millennium B.C.*, edited by Berlejung, A., Streck, M. P., 123–147. Wiesbaden: Harrassowitz.
Liss, H. 2006. "The Imaginary Sanctuary: The Priestly Code as an Example of Fictional Literature in the Hebrew Bible." In *Judah and the Judeans in the Persian Period*, edited by Lipschitz, O., 663–690. Winona Lake: Eisenbrauns.
Liverani, M. 1979a. "The Ideology of the Assyrian Empire." In *Power and Propaganda: A Symposium on Ancient Empires*, edited by Larsen, M. T., 297–317. Copenhagen: Akademisk Forlag.
Liverani, M. 1979b. *Three Amarna Essays.* Malibu: Undena.
Liverani, M. 1995. "The Deeds of Ancient Mesopotamian Kings." In *Civilizations of the Ancient Near East*, edited by Sasson, J. M., 2353–2366. New York: Scribner's.
Loewenstamm, S. E. 1969. "Ugaritic Formulas of Greeting." *Bulletin of the American Schools of Oriental Research* 194: 52–54.
Loewenstamm, S. E. 1992. *From Babylon to Canaan: Studies in the Bible and Its Oriental Background.* Jerusalem: Magnes Press.
Loretz, O. 1976. "Repointing und Redivision in Genesis 16, 11." *Ugarit-Forschungen* 8: 452–453.
Loretz, O. 1980. "Der kanaanäische Ursprung des biblischen Gottesnamens El Šaddaj." *Ugarit-Forschungen* 12: 420–421.
Loretz, O. 1984. *Psalm 29: Kanaanäische El- und Baaltraditionen in jüdischer Sicht.* Altenberge: CIS-Verlag.
Loretz, O. 1989. "Der Wohnort Els nach ugaritischen Texten und Ez 28, 1–2.6–10." *Ugarit-Forschungen* 21: 259–267.
Loretz, O. 2002. "Der ugaritisch-hebräische Parallelismus *rkb 'rpt*//*rkb b 'rbwt* in Psalm 68, 5." *Ugarit-Forschungen* 34: 521–526.
Lorton, D. 1971–1972. Review of Rafael Giveon, *Les bédouins Shosou des documents égyptiens. Journal of the American Research Center in Egypt* 9: 147–150.
Lorton, D. 1999. "The Theology of Cult Statues in Ancient Egypt." In *Born in Heaven, Made on Earth: The Making of the Cult Image in the Ancient Near East*, edited by Dick, M. B., 123–210. Winona Lake: Eisenbrauns.
Lowery, R. H. 1991. *The Reforming Kings: Cults and Society in First Temple Judah.* Sheffield: JSOT Press.
Luckenbill, D. D. 1926–1927. *Ancient Records of Assyria and Babylonia.* Chicago: University of Chicago.
Lundbom, J. R. 1999. *Jeremiah 1–20.* New York: Doubleday.
Lundbom, J. R. 2004. *Jeremiah 37–52.* New York: Doubleday.
Lundbom, J. R. 2013. *Deuteronomy.* Grand Rapids: Eerdmans.
Lutzky, H. 1998. "Shadday as a Goddess Epithet." *Vetus Testamentum* 48 (1): 15–36.
Lyke, L. L. 2009. "Zion, Daughter of." In *The New Interpreter's Dictionary of the Bible*, edited by Sakenfeld, K. D., Vol. 5, 988–989. Nashville: Abingdon.
Maas, A. J. 1910. "Jehova (Yahweh)." In *Catholic Encyclopedia*, edited by Herbermann, C., Vol. 8. New York: Robert Appleton Company.
MacDonald, B. 1994. "Early Edom: The Relation Between the Literary and Archaeological Evidence." In *Scripture and Other Artifacts: Essays on the Bible and Archaeology in*

Honor of Philip J. King, edited by Coogan, M. D., Exum, J. C., Stager, L. E., 230–246. Louisville: Westminster John Knox.

MacDonald, B., Younker, R. W. 1999. *Ancient Ammon*. Leiden: Brill.

Machinist, P. 1991. "The Question of Distinctiveness in Ancient Israel: An Essay." In *Ah, Assyria . . . Studies in Assyrian History and Ancient Near Eastern Historiography Presented to Hayim Tadmor*, edited by Cogan, M., Eph'al, I., 196–212. Jerusalem: Magnes Press.

Machinist, P. 1996. "William Foxwell Albright: The Man and His Work." In *The Study of the Ancient Near East in the Twenty-First Century: The William Foxwell Albright Centennial Conference*, edited by Cooper, J. S., Schwartz, G. M., 385–402. Winona Lake: Eisenbrauns.

Machinist, P. 2006. "Kingship and Divinity in Imperial Assyria." In *Text, Artifact, and Image: Revealing Ancient Israelite Religion*, edited by Beckman, G. M., Lewis, T. J., 152–188. Providence: Brown Judaic Studies.

Machinist, P. 2011. "How Gods Die, Biblically and Otherwise: A Problem of Cosmic Restructuring." In *Reconsidering the Concept of Revolutionary Monotheism*, edited by Pongratz-Leisten, B., 189–240. Winona Lake: Eisenbrauns.

Macholz, G. C. 1972. "Die Stellung des Königs in der israelitischen Gerichtsverfassung." *Zeitschrift für die alttestamentliche Wissenschaft* 84: 157–182.

Mack, J. 2007. *The Art of Small Things*. London: British Museum.

Maeir, A. M. 2017. "Can Material Evidence of Aramean Influences and Presence in Iron Age Judah and Israel be Found?" In *Wandering Arameans: Arameans Outside Syria: Textual and Archaeological Perspectives*, edited by Berlejung, A., Maeir, A. M., Schüle, A., 53–67. Wiesbaden: Harrassowitz.

Magdalene, F. R. 2007a. *On the Scales of Righteousness: Law and Story in the Book of Job: Neo-Babylon-ian Trial Law and the Book of Job*. Providence: Brown University.

Magdalene, F. R. 2007b. "The ANE Legal Origins of Impairment as Theological Disability and the Book of Job." *Perspectives in Religious Studies*: 23–59.

Maier, W. A. 1987. *Asherah: Extrabiblical Evidence*. Atlanta: Scholars Press.

Malaise, M. 2001. "Bes." In *The Oxford Encyclopedia of Ancient Egypt*, edited by Redford, D. B., 179–181. Oxford: Oxford University.

Malamat, A. 1962. "Mari and the Bible: Some Patterns of Tribal Organization and Institutions." *Journal of the American Oriental Society* 82 (2): 143–150.

Malamat, A. 1966. "The Ban in Mari and the Bible." In *Proceedings of the 9th Meeting of Die Ou-Testamentiese Werkgemeenskap in Suid-Afrika*, edited by van Zijl, A. H., 40–49. Potchefstroom: Potchefstroom Herald.

Malamat, A. 1992. "The Divine Nature of the Mediterranean Sea in the Foundation Inscription of Yaḫdunlim." In *Mari in Retrospect: Fifty Years of Mari and Mari Studies*, edited by Young, G. D., 211–215. Winona Lake: Eisenbrauns.

Malamat, A. 1997. "The Exodus: Egyptian Analogies." In *Exodus: The Egyptian Evidence*, edited by Frerichs, E. S., Lesko, L. H., 15–26. Winona Lake: Eisenbrauns.

Malamat, A. 1998. "The Amorite Background of Psalm 29." *Zeitschrift für die alttestamentliche Wissenschaft* 100: 156–160.

Malamat, A. 2002. "Weapons Deposited in a Sanctuary by Zimri-Lim of Mari and David and Saul of Israel." In *Ex Mesopotamia et Syria Lux*, edited by Loretz, O., Metzler, K. A., Schaudig, H., 325–327. Münster: Ugarit-Verlag.

Malina, B. J. 1996. "Mediterranean Sacrifice: Dimenions of Domestic and Political Religion." *Biblical Theology Bulletin* 26: 26–44.

Mandell, A. 2012. "'I Bless You to Yhwh and His Asherah'—Writing and Performativity at Kuntillet ʿAjrud." *Maarav* 19 (1–2): 131–162.
Mandell, A. 2013. "Biblical Hebrew, Archaic." In *The Encyclopedia of Hebrew Language and Linguistics*, edited by Khan, G. Leiden: Brill.
Mandell, A., Smoak, J. D. 2016. "Reconsidering the Function of Tomb Inscriptions in Iron Age Judah: Khirbet Beit Lei as a Test Case." *Journal of Ancient Near Eastern Religions* 16 (2): 192–245.
Mandell, A., Smoak, J. D. 2017a. "Reading and Writing in the Dark at Khirbet el-Qom: The Literacies of Ancient Subterranean Judah." *Near Eastern Archaeology* 80 (3): 188–195.
Mandell, A., Smoak, J. D. 2017b. "Reading Beyond Literacy, Writing Beyond Epigraphy: Multimodality and the Monumental Inscriptions at Ekron and Tel Dan." *Maarav* 22 (1–2): 77–110.
Mandell, S. R. 1996. "Reading Samuel as Saul and Vice Versa." In *Approaches to Ancient Judaism*, edited by Neusner, J., Vol. 9, 13–32. Atlanta: Scholars Press.
Manor, D. W., Herion, G. A. 1992. "Arad." In *The Anchor Bible Dictionary*, edited by Freedman, D. N., Vol. 1, 331–336. New York: Doubleday.
Mansoor, M. 1961. *The Thanksgiving Hymns*. Leiden: Brill.
March, W. E. 1974. "Prophecy." In *Old Testament Form Criticism*, edited by Hayes, J., 141–177. San Antonio: Trinity University Press.
Marchel, W. 1963. *Abba, Père: La prière du Christ et des chrétiens: Etude éxégétique sur les origines et la signification de l'invocation à la divinité comme père, avant et dans le Nouveau Testament*. Rome: Institut Biblique Pontifical.
Margalit, B. 1983. "Lexicographical Notes on the Aqht Epic." *Ugarit-Forschungen* 15: 65–103.
Margalit, B. 1990. "The Meaning and Significance of Asherah." *Vetus Testamentum* 40: 264–297.
Margulis, B. 1970. "The Canaanite Origin of Psalm 29 Reconsidered." *Biblica* 51: 332–348.
Markoe, G. 2000. *Phoenicians*. London: British Museum.
Marsden, G. M. 1994. *The Soul of the American University: From Protestant Establishment to Established Nonbelief*. New York: Oxford University.
Marsman, H. J. 2003. *Women in Ugarit and Israel: Their Social and Religious Position in the Context of the Ancient Near East*. Leiden: Brill.
Martens, K. 2001. "'With a Strong Hand and an Outstretched Arm': The Meaning of the Expression *byd ḥzqh wbzrwʿ nṭwyh*." *Scandinavian Journal of the Old Testament* 15 (1): 123–141.
Mastin, B. A. 2004. "Yahweh's Asherah: Inclusive Monotheism and the Question of Dating." In *In Search of Pre-Exilic Israel: Proceedings of the Oxford Old Testament Seminar*, edited by Day, J., 326–351. London: T. & T. Clark.
Mastin, B. A. 2005. "A Note on Some Inscriptions and Drawings from Kuntillet ʿAjrud." *Palestine Exploration Quarterly* 137 (1): 31–32.
Mastin, B. A. 2009. "The Inscriptions Written on Plaster at Kuntillet ʿAjrud." *Vetus Testamentum* 59: 99–115.
Mathys, H. 2008. *Das Astarte-Quadrat*. Zürich: Theologischer Verlag Zürich.
Matoïan, V., Vita, J. P. 2009. "Les textiles à Ougarit: Perspectives de la recherche." *Ugarit-Forschungen* 41: 469–504.
Matoïan, V., Vita, J. P. 2014. "Wool Production and Economy at Ugarit." In *Wool Economy in the Ancient Near East and the Aegean: From the Beginnings of Sheep Husbandry*

to *Institutional Textile Industry*, edited by Breniquet, C., Michel, C., 310–339. Oxford: Oxbow Books.

Matthews, V. H. 1995. "The Anthropology of Clothing in the Joseph Narrative." *Journal for the Study of the Old Testament* 65: 25–36.

Mattila, R. 2002. *Legal Transactions of the Royal Court of Nineveh, Part II: Assurbanipal Through Sin-šarru-iškun*. Helsinki: Helsinki University.

May, N. N. 2014. "Gates and Their Functions in Mesopotamia and Ancient Israel." In *The Fabric of Cities: Aspects of Urbanism, Urban Topography and Society in Mesopotamia, Greece, and Rome*, edited by May, N. N., Steinert, U., 77–121. Leiden: Brill.

Mayer, G. 1998. "*Nzr, nēzer, nāzîr*." In *Theological Dictionary of the Old Testament*, edited by Botterweck, G. J., Ringgren, H., Fabry, H., Vol. IX, 306–311. Grand Rapids: Eerdmans.

Mayer, W. 2003. "Sennacherib's Campaign of 701 BCE: The Assyrian View." In *"Like a Bird in a Cage": The Invasion of Sennacherib in 701 BCE*, edited by Grabbe, L. L., 168–200. Sheffield: Sheffield Academic Press.

Mayer-Opificius, R. 1984. "Die geflügelte Sonne. Himmels- und Regendarstellungen im alten Vorderasien." *Ugarit-Forschungen* 16: 189–236.

Mays, J. L. 1969. *Hosea: A Commentary*. Philadelphia: Westminster.

Mazar, A. 1982. "The 'Bull Site': An Iron Age I Open Cult Place." *Bulletin of the American Schools of Oriental Research* 247: 27–42.

Mazar, A. 1983. "Bronze Bull Found in Israelite 'High Place' from the Time of the Judges." *Biblical Archaeology Review* 9: 34–40.

Mazar, A. 1988. "On Cult Places and Early Israelites: A Response to Michael Coogan." *Biblical Archaeology Review* 14 (4): 85.

Mazar, A. 1990. *Archaeology of the Land of the Bible, 10,000–586 B.C.E.* New York: Doubleday.

Mazar, A. 1993. "'Bull' Site." In *The New Encyclopedia of Archaeological Excavations in the Holy Land*, edited by Stern, E., Levinzon-Gilboa, A., Aviram, J., Vol. 1, 266–267. Jerusalem: Israel Exploration Society & Carta.

Mazar, A. 1999. "The 'Bull Site' and the 'Einun Pottery' Reconsidered." *Palestine Exploration Quarterly* 131: 144–148.

Mazar, A. 2003. "Remarks on Biblical Traditions and Archaeological Evidence Concerning Early Israel." In *Symbiosis, Symbolism, and the Power of the Past: Canaan, Ancient Israel, and Their Neighbors from the Late Bronze Age Through Roman Palaestina*, edited by Dever, W. G., Gitin, S., 85–98. Winona Lake: Eisenbrauns.

Mazar, A., Ahituv, S. 2011. "Tel Reḥov in the Assyrian Period: Squatters, Burials, and a Hebrew Seal." In *The Fire Signals of Lachish: Studies in the Archaeology and History of Israel in the Late Bronze Age, Iron Age, and Persian Period in Honor of David Ussishkin*, edited by Finkelstein, I., Na'aman, N., 265–280.

Mazar, A., Netzer, E. 1986. "On the Israelite Fortress at Arad." *Bulletin of the American Schools of Oriental Research* 263: 87–91.

Mazar, B. 1965. "The Sanctuary of Arad and the Family of Hobab the Kenite." *Journal of Near Eastern Studies* 24 (3): 297–303.

Mazar, B. 1981. "Yahweh Came Out from Sinai." In *Temples and High Places in Biblical Times*, edited by Biran, A., 5–9. Jerusalem: Nelson Glueck School of Biblical Archaeology of Hebrew Union College–Jewish Institute of Religion.

McBride, S. D. 1969. "The Deuteronomic Name Theology." Harvard University.

McBride, S. D. 2009. "Jeremiah and the Levitical Priests of Anathoth." In *Thus Says the Lord: Essays on the Former and Latter Prophets in Honor of Robert R. Wilson*, edited by Cook, S. L., Ahn, J. J., 179–196. London: T. & T. Clark.

McCarter, P. K. 1980a. *1 Samuel*. Garden City: Doubleday.

McCarter, P. K. 1980b. "The Balaam Texts from Deir 'Allā: The First Combination." *Bulletin of the American Schools of Oriental Research* 239: 49–60.

McCarter, P. K. 1980c. "The Apology of David." *Journal of Biblical Literature* 99: 489–504.

McCarter, P. K. 1984. *II Samuel*. Garden City: Doubleday.

McCarter, P. K. 1987. "Aspects of the Religion of the Israelite Monarchy: Biblical and Epigraphic Data." In *Ancient Israelite Religion: Essays in Honor of Frank Moore Cross*, edited by Miller, P. D., Hanson, P. D., McBride, S. D., 137–155. Philadelphia: Fortress.

McCarter, P. K. 1991. "The Dialect of the Deir 'Alla Texts." In *The Balaam Text from Deir 'Alla Re-Evaluated*, edited by Hoftijzer, J., van der Kooij, G., 87–99. Leiden: Brill.

McCarter, P. K. 1992. "The Origins of Israelite Religion." In *The Rise of Ancient Israel*, edited by Shanks, H., 119–141. Washington: Biblical Archaeology Society.

McCarter, P. K. 1996. *Ancient Inscriptions: Voices from the Biblical World*. Washington: Biblical Archaeology Society.

McCarter, P. K. 1999. "Zion." In *Dictionary of Deities and Demons in the Bible*, edited by Toorn, K. van der, Becking, B., van der Horst, P. W., 940–941. 2nd ed. Leiden: Brill.

McCarter, P. K. 2000a. "Kuntillet 'Ajrud." In *The Context of Scripture 2: Monumental Inscriptions from the Biblical World*, edited by Hallo, W. W., Younger, K. L., 171–173. Leiden: Brill.

McCarter, P. K. 2000b. "The Khirbet Beit Lei Cave Inscriptions." In *The Context of Scripture 2: Monumental Inscriptions from the Biblical World*, edited by Hallo, W. W., Younger, K. L., 179–180. Leiden: Brill.

McCarter, P. K. 2000c. "An Amulet from Arslan Tash." In *The Context of Scripture 2: Monumental Inscriptions from the Biblical World*, edited by Hallo, W. W., Younger, K. L., 222–223. Leiden: Brill.

McCarter, P. K. 2000d. "Khirbet El-Qom." In *The Context of Scripture 2: Monumental Inscriptions from the Biblical World*, edited by Hallo, W. W., Younger, K. L., 179. Leiden: Brill.

McCarter, P. K. 2008a. "When Gods Lose Their Temper: Divine Rage in Ugaritic Myth and the Hypostasis of Anger in Iron Age Religion." In *Divine Wrath and Divine Mercy in the World of Antiquity*, edited by Kratz, R. G., Spieckermann, H., 78–91. Tübingen: Mohr Siebeck.

McCarter, P. K. 2008b. "Paleographic Notes on the Tel Zayit Abecedary." In *Literate Culture and Tenth-Century Canaan: The Tel Zayit Abecedary in Context*, edited by Tappy, R. E., McCarter, P. K., 45–59. Winona Lake: Eisenbrauns.

McCarthy, D. J. 1963. *Treaty and Covenant: A Study in Form in the Ancient Oriental Documents and in the Old Testament*. Rome: Pontifical Biblical Institute.

McCarthy, D. J. 1978. "Exod 3:14: History, Philology and Theology." *Catholic Biblical Quarterly* 40 (3): 311–322.

McClellan, D. O. 2011. "What Is Deity in LXX Deuteronomy?" *Studia Antiqua* 10: 67–79.

McConville, J. G. 1998. "King and Messiah in Deuteronomy and the Deuteronomistic History." In *King and Messiah in Israel and the Ancient Near East*, edited by Day, J., 271–295. Sheffield: Sheffield Academic Press.

McConville, J. G. 1999. "Priesthood in Joshua to Kings." *Vetus Testamentum* 49: 73–87.

McGeough, K. M. 2003. "Locating the *Marziḥu* Archaeologically." *Ugarit-Forschungen* 35: 408–420.

McGeough, K. M. 2007. *Exchange Relationships at Ugarit.* Ancient Near Eastern Studies Supplement, Vol. 26. Leuven: Peeters.

McGeough, K. M. 2011. *Ugaritic Economic Tablets: Text, Translation and Notes*, edited by Smith, M. S. Ancient Near Eastern Studies Supplement, Vol. 32. Leuven: Peeters.

McGinnis, C. M. 1995. *Defending Zion: Edom's Desolation and Jacob's Restoration (Isaiah 34–35) in Context.* Berlin: de Gruyter.

McGovern, P. E. 1985. *Late Bronze Palestinian Pendants: Innovation in a Cosmopolitan Age.* Sheffield: JSOT Press.

McKane, W. A. 1979. *Studies in the Patriarchal Narratives.* Edinburgh: Handsel Press.

McKenzie, D. A. 1964. "Judicial Procedure at the Town Gate." *Vetus Testamentum* 14: 100–104.

McKenzie, S. L. 1986. "1 Kings 8: A Sample Study into the Texts of Kings Used by the Chronicler and Translated by the Old Greek." *Bulletin of the International Organization of Septuagint and Cognate Studies* 19: 15–34.

McLaughlin, J. L. 1991. "The *Marzēaḥ* at Ugarit, a Textual and Contextual Study." *Ugarit-Forschungen* 23: 265–281.

McLaughlin, J. L. 2001. *The Marzēaḥ in the Prophetic Literature: References and Allusions in Light of the Extra-biblical Evidence.* Leiden: Brill.

McMahon, G. 1997. "Instructions to Commanders of Border Garrisons." In *The Context of Scripture 1: Canonical Compositions from the Biblical World*, edited by Hallo, W. W., Younger, K. L., 221–225. Leiden: Brill.

Medill, K. Forthcoming. "You Will Know Me by My Writing." Johns Hopkins University.

Meek, T. J. 1950. *Hebrew Origins.* New York: Harper.

Meier, S. A. 2007. "Granting God a Passport: Transporting Deities Across International Boundaries." In *Moving Across Borders: Foreign Relations, Religion, and Cultural Interactions in the Ancient Mediterranean*, edited by Kousoulis, P., Magliveras, K., 185–208. Leuven: Peeters.

Melugin, R. F. 1974. "The Conventional and the Creative in Isaiah's Judgment Oracles." *Catholic Biblical Quarterly* 36 (3): 301–311.

Mendenhall, G. E. 1973. *The Tenth Generation: The Origins of the Biblical Tradition.* Baltimore: Johns Hopkins University.

Mendenhall, G. E. 1987. "The Nature and Purpose of the Abraham Narratives." In *Ancient Israelite Religion: Essays in Honor of Frank Moore Cross*, edited by Miller, P. D., Hanson, P. D., McBride, S. D., 337–356. Philadelphia: Fortress.

Merlo, P., Xella, P. 1999. "The Ugaritic Cultic Texts." In *Handbook of Ugaritic Studies*, edited by Watson, W. G. E., Wyatt, N., 287–358. Leiden: Brill.

Meshel, N. S. 2013. "The Form and Function of a Biblical Blood Ritual." *Vetus Testamentum* 63: 276–289.

Meshel, Z. 1978. "Kuntillet 'Ajrud: An Israelite Religious Center in Northern Sinai." *Expedition* [University of Pennsylvania Museum] 20 (4): 50–54.

Meshel, Z. 1979. "Did Yahweh Have a Consort? The New Religious Inscriptions from the Sinai." *Biblical Archaeology Review* 5 (2): 24–35.

Meshel, Z. 1992. "Kuntillet 'Ajrud." In *The Anchor Bible Dictionary*, edited by Freedman, D. N., Vol. 4, 103–109. New York: Doubleday.

Meshel, Z. 1993. "Teman, Ḥorvat." In *The New Encyclopedia of Archaeological Excavations in the Holy Land*, edited by Stern, E., Levinzon-Gilboa, A., Aviram, J., Vol. 4, 1458–1464, 1476. Jerusalem: Israel Exploration Society & Carta.

Meshel, Z. 1997. "Kuntillet 'Ajrud." In *The Oxford Encyclopedia of Archaeology in the Near East, Vol. 3*, edited by Meyers, E. M., 310–312. New York: Oxford University.

Meshel, Z. 2012. *Kuntillet 'Ajrud (Horvat Teman): An Iron Age II Religious Site on the Judah-Sinai Border*. Jerusalem: Israel Exploration Society.

Meshorer, Y. 1982. *Ancient Jewish Coinage*. New York: Amphora Books.

Mettinger, T. N. D. 1976. *King and Messiah: The Civil and Sacral Legitimation of the Israelite Kings*. Lund: Gleerup.

Mettinger, T. N. D. 1979. "The Veto on Images and the Aniconic God in Ancient Israel." In *Religious Symbols and Their Functions*, edited by Biezais, H., 15–29. Stockholm: Almqvist & Wiksell.

Mettinger, T. N. D. 1982a. "Yhwh Sabaoth: The Heavenly King on the Cherubim Throne." In *Studies in the Period of David and Solomon and Other Essays*, edited by Ishida, T., 109–138. Winona Lake: Eisenbrauns.

Mettinger, T. N. D. 1982b. *The Dethronement of Sabaoth: Studies in the Shem and Kabod Theologies*. Lund: Gleerup.

Mettinger, T. N. D. 1988. *In Search of God: The Meaning and Message of the Everlasting Names*. Philadelphia: Fortress.

Mettinger, T. N. D. 1994. "Aniconism—A West Semitic Context for the Israelite Phenomenon." In *Ein Gott allein? JHWH-Verehrung und biblischer Monotheismus im Kontext der israelitischen und altorientalischen Religionsgeschichte*, edited by Dietrich, W., Klopfenstein, M. A., 159–178. Göttingen: Vandenhoeck & Ruprecht.

Mettinger, T. N. D. 1995. *No Graven Image? Israelite Aniconism in Its Ancient Near Eastern Context*. Stockholm: Almqvist & Wiksell.

Mettinger, T. N. D. 1997a. "The Roots of Aniconism: An Israelite Phenomenon in Comparative Perspective." In *Congress Volume Cambridge 1995*, edited by Emerton, J. A., 219–233. Leiden: Brill.

Mettinger, T. N. D. 1997b. "Israelite Aniconism: Developments and Origins." In *The Image and the Book: Iconic Cults, Aniconism, and the Rise of Book Religion in Israel and the Ancient Near East*, edited by van der Toorn, K., 173–204. Louvain: Peeters.

Mettinger, T. N. D. 1998. "The Name and the Glory: The Zion-Sabaoth Theology and Its Exilic Successors." *Journal of Northwest Semitic Languages* 24: 1–24.

Mettinger, T. N. D. 1999. "Seraphim." In *Dictionary of Deities and Demons in the Bible*, edited by van der Toorn, K., Becking, B., van der Horst, P. W., 742–744. 2nd ed. Leiden: Brill.

Mettinger, T. N. D. 2001. *The Riddle of Resurrection: "Dying and Rising Gods" in the Ancient Near East*. Stockholm: Almqvist & Wiksell.

Mettinger, T. N. D. 2003. Review of S. Richter, *The Deuteronomistic History and the Name Theology: lĕšakkēn šĕmô šām in the Bible and the Ancient Near East*. *Journal of Biblical Literature* 122 (4): 753–755.

Mettinger, T. N. D. 2006. "A Conversation with My Critics: Cultic Image or Aniconism in the First Temple?" In *Essays on Ancient Israel in Its Near Eastern Context: A Tribute to Nadav Na'aman*, edited by Amit, Y., Ben Zvi, E., Finkelstein, I., Lipschits, O., 273–296. Winona Lake: Eisenbrauns.

Metzger, M. 1985. *Königsthron und Gottesthron: Thronformen und Throndarstellungen in Ägypten und im Vorderen Orient im dritten und zweiten Jahrtausend vor Christus und*

deren Bedeutung für das Verständnis von Aussagen über den Thron im Alten Testament. Kevelaer: Butzon & Bercker.
Meyers, C. L. 1979. "Was There a Seven Branched Lampstand in Solomon's Temple?" *The Biblical Archaeology Review* 5 (5): 47–57.
Meyers, C. L. 1983. "Procreation, Production, and Protection: Male-Female Balance in Early Israel." *Journal of the American Academy of Religion* 51 (4): 569–593.
Meyers, C. L. 1988. *Discovering Eve: Ancient Israelite Women in Context.* New York: Oxford University.
Meyers, C. L. 1991. "To Her Mother's House—Considering a Counterpart to the Israelite Bêt 'āb." In *The Bible and the Politics of Exegesis*, edited by Jobling, D., Day, P. L., Sheppard, G. T., 39–52. Cleveland: Pilgrim Press.
Meyers, C. L. 1992a. "Temple, Jerusalem." In *The Anchor Bible Dictionary*, edited by Freedman, D. N., Vol. 6, 350–369. New York: Doubleday.
Meyers, C. L. 1992b. "Cherubim." In *The Anchor Bible Dictionary*, edited by Freedman, D. N., Vol. 1, 899–900. New York: Doubleday.
Meyers, C. L. 1998. "Everyday Life: Women in the Period of the Hebrew Bible." In *Women's Bible Commentary*, expanded ed., edited by Newsom, C. A., Ringe, S. H., 251–259. Louisville: Westminster John Knox.
Meyers, C. L. 2002. "From Household to House of Yahweh: Women's Religious Culture in Ancient Israel." In *Congress Volume: Basel 2001*, edited by Lemaire, A., 277–303. Leiden: Brill.
Meyers, C. L. 2003a. "Material Remains and Social Relations: Women's Culture in Agrarian Households of the Iron Age." In *Symbiosis, Symbolism, and the Power of the Past: Canaan, Ancient Israel, and Their Neighbors from the Late Bronze Age Through Roman Palestina*, edited by Dever, W. G., Gitin, S., 425–444. Winona Lake: Eisenbrauns.
Meyers, C. L. 2003b. "Engendering Syro-Palestinian Archaeology: Reasons and Resources." *Near Eastern Archaeology* 66 (4): 185–197.
Meyers, C. L. 2005. *Households and Holiness: The Religious Culture of Israelite Women.* Minneapolis: Fortress.
Meyers, C. L. 2010. "Household Religion." In *Religious Diversity in Ancient Israel and Judah*, edited by Stavrakopoulou, F., Barton, J., 118–134. London: T. & T. Clark.
Meyers, C. L. 2013a. *Rediscovering Eve: Ancient Israelite Women in Context.* Oxford: Oxford University.
Meyers, C. L. 2013b. Review of Douglas A. Knight, *Law, Power, and Justice in Ancient Israel. Interpretation* 67: 299–301.
Meyers, C. L., Craven, T., Kraemer, R. S. 2000. *Women in Scripture: A Dictionary of Named and Unnamed Women in the Hebrew Bible, the Apocryphal/Deuterocanonical Books, and the New Testament.* Boston: Houghton Mifflin.
Meyers, C. L., Meyers, E. M. 1987. *Haggai, Zechariah 1-8. A New Translation with Introduction and Commentary.* Garden City: Doubleday.
Meyers, C. L., Meyers, E. M. 1993. *Zechariah 9-14: A New Translation with Introduction and Commentary.* New York: Doubleday.
Meyers, E. M., ed. 1997. *The Oxford Encyclopedia of Archaeology in the Near East.* New York: Oxford University.
Michalowski, P. 2008. "The Mortal Kings of Ur: A Short Century of Divine Rule in Ancient Mesopotamia." In *Religion and Power: Divine Kingship in the Ancient World and Beyond*, edited by Brisch, N. M., 33–45. Chicago: Oriental Institute.

Michel, P. M. 2013. "Ritual in Emar." In *Approaching Rituals in Ancient Cultures*, edited by Ambos, C., Verderame, L., 187–196. Pisa: Fabrizio Serra Editore.

Middlemas, J. A. 2014. *The Divine Image: Prophetic Aniconic Rhetoric and Its Contribution to the Aniconism Debate*. Tübingen: Mohr Siebeck.

Mierse, W. E. 2012. *Temples and Sanctuaries from the Early Iron Age Levant: Recovery After Collapse*. Winona Lake: Eisenbrauns.

Mihelič, J. L. 1948. "The Concept of God in the Book of Nahum." *Interpretation* 2 (2): 199–207.

Milgrom, J. 1970. *Studies in Levitical Terminology, I: The Encroacher and the Levite, The Term ʿAboda*. Berkeley: University of California.

Milgrom, J. 1990. *Numbers: The Traditional Hebrew Text with the New JPS Translation*. Philadelphia: Jewish Publication Society.

Milgrom, J. 1991. *Leviticus 1–16*. New York: Doubleday.

Milgrom, J. 1992. "Priestly ('P') Source." In *The Anchor Bible Dictionary*, edited by Freedman, D. N., Vol. 5, 454–461. New York: Doubleday.

Milgrom, J. 2000. *Leviticus 17–22*. New York: Doubleday.

Milgrom, J. 2001. *Leviticus 23–27*. New York: Doubleday.

Milgrom, J. 2007. "Holy, Holiness, OT." In *The New Interpreter's Dictionary of the Bible*, edited by Sakenfeld, K. D., Vol. 2, 850–858. Nashville: Abingdon.

Milgrom, J., Block, D. I. 2012. *Ezekiel's Hope: A Commentary on Ezekiel 38–48*. Eugene: Cascade.

Milik, J. T. 1956. "An Unpublished Arrow-Head with Phoenician Inscription of the 11th–10th Century B.C." *Bulletin of the American Schools of Oriental Research* 143: 3–6.

Millard, A. R. 1978. "Saul's Shield Not Anointed with Oil." *Bulletin of the American Schools of Oriental Research* 230: 70–70.

Millard, A. R. 1997. "The Babylonian Chronicle." In *The Context of Scripture 1: Canonical Compositions from the Biblical World*, edited by Hallo, W. W., Younger, K. L., 467–468. Leiden: Brill.

Millard, M. 1994. *Die Komposition des Psalters: Ein formgeschichtlicher Ansatz*. Tübingen: J. C. B. Mohr.

Millard, M. 1998. "Zum Problem des elohistischen Psalters: Überlegungen zum Gebrauch von *yhwh* und *ʾĕlōhîm* im Psalter." In *Der Psalter in Judentum und Christentum*, edited by Zenger, E., 75–110. Freiburg im Breisgau: Herder.

Miller, J. L. 2004. *Studies in the Origins, Development and Interpretation of the Kizzuwatna Rituals*. Wiesbaden: Harrassowitz.

Miller, J. L. 2013. *Royal Hittite Instructions and Related Administrative Texts*. Writings from the Ancient World 31. Atlanta: SBL Press.

Miller, P. D. 1964. "Two Critical Notes on Psalm 68 and Deuteronomy 33." *Harvard Theological Review* 57 (3): 240–243.

Miller, P. D. 1965. "Fire in the Mythology of Canaan and Israel." *Catholic Biblical Quarterly* 27: 256–261.

Miller, P. D. 1967. "El the Warrior." *Harvard Theological Review* 60 (4): 411–431.

Miller, P. D. 1970a. "Animal Names as Designations in Ugaritic and Hebrew." *Ugarit-Forschungen* 2: 177–186.

Miller, P. D. 1970b. "Ugaritic *ġzr* and Hebrew *ʿzr* II." *Ugarit-Forschungen* 2: 159–175.

Miller, P. D. 1973. *The Divine Warrior in Early Israel*. Harvard Semitic Monographs, Vol. 5. Cambridge: Harvard University.

Miller, P. D. 1980. "El, Creator of the Earth." *Bulletin of the American Schools of Oriental Research* 239: 43–46.

Miller, P. D. 1981. "Psalms and Inscriptions." In *Congress Volume, Vienna, 1980*, edited by Emerton, J. A., 311–332. Leiden: Brill.

Miller, P. D. 1983. "Wellhausen and the History of Israel's Religion." In *Julius Wellhausen and His Prolegomena to the History of Israel: Semeia 25 (1982)*, edited by Knight, D. A., 61–83. Chico: Scholars Press.

Miller, P. D. 1984. "Sin and Judgment in Jeremiah 34:17–19." *Journal of Biblical Literature* 103 (4): 611–613.

Miller, P. D. 1985. "Israelite Religion." In *The Hebrew Bible and Its Modern Interpreters*, edited by Knight, D. A., Tucker, G. M., 201–237. Chico: Scholars Press.

Miller, P. D. 2000. *The Religion of Ancient Israel*. London/Louisville: SPCK/Westminster John Knox.

Miller, P. D., Hanson, P. D., McBride, S. D., eds. 1987. *Ancient Israelite Religion: Essays in Honor of Frank Moore Cross*. Philadelphia: Fortress.

Miller, P. D., Roberts, J. J. M. 1977. *The Hand of the Lord: A Reassessment of the "Ark Narrative" of 1 Samuel*. Baltimore: Johns Hopkins University.

Miller, R. D. 2010. "The Zion Hymns as Instruments of Power." *Ancient Near Eastern Studies* 47: 218–240.

Miller, R. D. 2011. *Oral Tradition in Ancient Israel*. Eugene: Cascade.

Miller-Naudé, C. L., Zevit, Z., eds. 2012. *Diachrony in Biblical Hebrew*. Linguistic Studies in Ancient West Semitic, Vol. 8. Winona Lake: Eisenbrauns.

Milstein, S. 2018. "Making a Case: The Repurposing of 'Israelite Legal Fictions' as Post-Deuteronomic Law." In *Supplementation and the Study of the Hebrew Bible*, edited by Olyan, S. M., Wright, J., 161–181. Providence: Brown Judaic Studies.

Mittmann, S. 1981. "Die Grabinschrift des Sängers Uriahu." *Zeitschrift des Deutschen Palästina-Vereins* 97 (2): 139–152.

Moberly, R. W. L. 1983. *At the Mountain of God: Story and Theology in Exodus 32–34*. Sheffield: Journal for the Study of the Old Testament.

Monroe, L. 2007. "Israelite, Moabite and Sabaean War-ḥērem Traditions and the Forging of National Identity: Reconsidering the Sabaean Text RES 3945 in Light of Biblical and Moabite Evidence." *Vetus Testamentum* 57 (3): 318–341.

Monroe, L. 2012. "Phinehas' Zeal and the Death of Cozbi: Unearthing a Human Scapegoat Tradition in Numbers 25:1–18." *Vetus Testamentum* 62 (2): 211–231.

Monroe, L., Fleming, D. 2019. "Earliest Israel in Highland Company." *Near Eastern Archaeolgy* 82 (1): 16–23.

Monson, J. 2000. "The New 'Ain Dara Temple—Closest Solomonic Parallel." *Biblical Archaeology Review* 26 (3): 20–35, 67.

Monson, J. 2006. "The 'Ain Dara Temple and the Jerusalem Temple." In *Text, Artifact, and Image: Revealing Ancient Israelite Religion*, edited by Beckman, G. M., Lewis, T. J., 273–299. Providence: Brown Judaic Studies.

Moor, J. C. de. 1970. "The Semitic Pantheon of Ugarit." *Ugarit-Forschungen* 2: 187–228.

Moor, J. C. de. 1971. *The Seasonal Pattern in the Ugaritic Myth of Baʻlu, According to the Version of Ilimilku*. Kevelaer: Butzon & Bercker.

Moor, J. C. de. 1979. "Contributions to the Ugaritic Lexicon." *Ugarit-Forschungen* 11: 639–653.

Moor, J. C. de. 1980. "El, the Creator." In *The Bible World: Essays in Honor of Cyrus H. Gordon*, edited by Rendsburg, G. A., 171–187. New York: KTAV.

Moor, J. C. de. 1987. *An Anthology of Religious Texts from Ugarit*. Leiden: Brill.
Moor, J. C. de. 1990. *The Rise of Yahwism: The Roots of Israelite Monotheism*. Leuven: Peeters.
Moor, J. C. de. 1995a. "Standing Stones and Ancestor Worship." *Ugarit-Forschungen* 27: 1–20.
Moor, J. C. de. 1995b. "Ugarit and Israelite Origins." In *Congress Volume Paris, 1992*, edited by Emerton, J. A., 205–238. Leiden: Brill.
Moor, J. C. de. 1995c. *The Rise of Yahwism: The Roots of Israelite Monotheism*. 2nd ed. Leuven: Peeters.
Moor, J. C. de. 1997. *The Rise of Yahwism: The Roots of Israelite Monotheism*. 3rd ed. Leuven: Peeters.
Moore, G. F. 1958. *A Critical and Exegetical Commentary on Judges*. Edinburgh: T. & T. Clark.
Moorey, P. R. S. 1971. "A Bronze Statuette of a Bull." *Levant* 3: 90–91.
Moorey, P. R. S. 1992. *A Century of Biblical Archaeology*. Louisville: Westminster John Knox.
Moorey, P. R. S. 2003. *Idols of the People: Miniature Images of Clay in the Ancient Near East*. Oxford: Oxford University.
Moorey, P. R. S., Fleming, S. 1984. "Problems in the Study of the Anthropomorphic Metal Statuary from Syro-Palestine Before 330 B.C." *Levant* 16: 67–90, plates XXI–XXVII.
Moran, W. L. 1960. *The Assyrian Dictionary of the Oriental Institute of the University of Chicago (CAD), Volume I–J*. Chicago: Oriental Institute of the University of Chicago.
Moran, W. L. 1963. "The Ancient Near Eastern Background of the Love of God in Deuteronomy." *Catholic Biblical Quarterly* 25 (1): 77–87.
Moran, W. L. 1970. "The Creation of Man in Atrahasis I 192–248." *Bulletin of the American Schools of Oriental Research* 200: 48–56.
Moran, W. L. 1992. *The Amarna Letters*. Baltimore: Johns Hopkins University.
Moran, W. L. 1995. "The Gilgamesh Epic: A Masterpiece from Ancient Mesopotamia." In *Civilizations of the Ancient Near East*, edited by Sasson, J. M., Vol. IV, 2327–2336. New York: Scribner's.
Morgan, R., Barton, J. 1988. *Biblical Interpretation*. Oxford: Oxford University.
Morgenstern, J. 1911. "Biblical Theophanies." *Zeitschrift für Assyriologie und vorderasiatische Archäologie* 25 (1–2): 139–193.
Morgenstern, J. 1914. "Biblical Theophanies." *Zeitschrift für Assyriologie und vorderasiatische Archäologie* 28 (1): 15–60.
Morgenstern, J. 1917. "Two Ancient Israelite Agricultural Festivals." *Jewish Quarterly Review* 8 (1): 31–54.
Morgenstern, J. 1938a. "A Chapter in the History of the High-Priesthood." *American Journal of Semitic Languages and Literatures* 55 (1): 1–24.
Morgenstern, J. 1938b. "A Chapter in the History of the High-Priesthood (Continued)." *American Journal of Semitic Languages and Literatures* 55 (2): 183–197.
Morgenstern, J. 1938c. "A Chapter in the History of the High-Priesthood (Concluded)." *American Journal of Semitic Languages and Literatures* 55 (4): 360–377.
Mosca, P. G. 2009. "Facts or Factoids? Some Historical Observations on the Trophy Inscription from Kition (KAI 288)." In *Exploring the Longue Durée: Essays in Honor of Lawrence E. Stager*, edited by Schloen, J. D., 345–350. Winona Lake: Eisenbrauns.
Mouton, A. 2014. Review of Y. Feder, *Blood Expiation in Hittite and Biblical Ritual*. *Journal of the American Oriental Society* 134 (3): 527–529.

Mowinckel, S. 1952. "Die vermeintliche 'Passahlegende' Ex. 1–15." *Studia Theologica* 5: 66–88.
Mowinckel, S. 1956. *He That Cometh*. New York: Abingdon.
Mowinckel, S. 1961. "The Name of the God of Moses." *Hebrew Union College Annual* 32: 121–133.
Mowinckel, S. 1962. *The Psalms in Israel's Worship*. New York: Abingdon.
Muhly, J. D. 1980. "Bronze Figurines and Near Eastern Metalwork." *Israel Exploration Journal* 3–4 (30): 148–161.
Muilenburg, J. 1966. "A Liturgy on the Triumphs of Yahweh." In *Studia Biblica et Semitica. Theodoro Christiano Vriezen Qui Munere Professoris Theologiae Per XXV Annos Functus Est, Ab Amicis, Collegis, Discipulis Dedicata.*, 233–251. Wageningen: H. Veenman.
Mulder, M. J. 1998. *1 Kings*. Leuven: Peeters.
Mullen, E. T. 1980. *The Divine Council in Canaanite and Early Hebrew Literature*. Harvard Semitic Monographs, Vol. 24. Chico: Scholars Press.
Müller, H. 1980. "Gab es in Ebla einen Gottesnamen Ja?" *Zeitschrift für Assyriologie und vorderasiatische Archäologie* 70 (1): 70–92.
Müller, H. 1981. "Der Jahwename und seine Deutung Ex 3,14 im Licht der Textpublikationen aus Ebla." *Biblica* 62 (3): 305–327.
Müller, H. 1997. "Qdš Holy." In *Theological Lexicon of the Old Testament*, edited by Jenni, E., Vol. 3, 1103–1118. Peabody: Hendrickson.
Müller, H. 2004. "Rěʾēm." In *Theological Dictionary of the Old Testament*, edited by Botterweck, G. J., Ringgren, H., Fabry, H., Vol. XIII, 243–247. Grand Rapids: Eerdmans.
Muntingh, L. M. 1988. "Second Thoughts on Ebla and the Old Testament." In *Text and Context: Old Testament and Semitic Studies for F. C. Fensham*, edited by Claassen, W. T., 157–175. Sheffield: JSOT Press.
Murnane, W. J., Van Siclen, C. C. 1993. *The Boundary Stelae of Akhenaten*. London: Kegan Paul.
Murphy, R. E. 1985. "Wisdom Literature in the Old Testament." In *Harper's Bible Dictionary*, edited by Achtemeier, P. J., 1135. San Francisco: Harper & Row.
Murtonen, A. 1951. *The Appearance of the Name YHWH Outside Israel*. Studia Orientalia. Edidit Societas Orientalis Fennica XVI:3. Helsinki: Suomalaisen Kirjallisuuden Seuran Kirjapainon Oy.
Mykytiuk, L. J. 2004. *Identifying Biblical Persons in Northwest Semitic Inscriptions of 1200–539 B.C.E.* Leiden: Brill.
Mykytiuk, L. J. 2009. "Corrections and Updates to 'Identifying Biblical Persons in Northwest Semitic Inscriptions of 1200–539 B.C.E.'" *Maarav* 16 (1): 49–132.
Naʾaman, N. 1974. "Sennacherib's 'Letter to God' on His Campaign to Judah." *Bulletin of the American Schools of Oriental Research* 214: 25–39.
Naʾaman, N. 1981. "The Recycling of a Silver Statue." *Journal of Near Eastern Studies* 40 (1): 47–48.
Naʾaman, N. 1987. "Beth-aven, Bethel and Early Israelite Sanctuaries." *Zeitschrift des Deutschen Palästina-Vereins* 103: 13–21.
Naʾaman, N. 1988. "Biryawaza of Damascus and the Date of the Kāmid el-Lōz ʿApiru Letters." *Ugarit-Forschungen* 20: 179–194.
Naʾaman, N. 1992. "Israel, Edom and Egypt in the 10th Century B.C.E." *Tel Aviv* 19: 71–93.
Naʾaman, N. 1994a. "The Canaanites and Their Land—A Rejoinder." *Ugarit-Forschungen* 26: 397–418.

Na'aman, N. 1994b. "The 'Conquest of Canaan' in the Book of Joshua and in History." In *From Nomadism to Monarchy: Archaeological and Historical Aspects of Early Israel*, edited by Na'aman, N., Finkelstein, I., 218–281. Jerusalem: Israel Exploration Society.

Na'aman, N. 1997. "Cow Town or Royal Capital: Evidence for Iron Age Jerusalem." *Biblical Archaeology Review* 23 (4): 43–47,67.

Na'aman, N. 1999a. "No Anthropomorphic Graven Image: Notes on the Assumed Anthropomorphic Cult Statues in the Temples of YHWH in the Pre-exilic Period." *Ugarit-Forschungen* 31: 391–415.

Na'aman, N. 1999b. "Lebo-Hamath, Ṣūbat-Hamath and the Northern Boundary of the Land of Canaan." *Ugarit-Forschungen* 31: 417–441.

Na'aman, N. 2006a. *Ancient Israel's History and Historiography. The First Temple Period*. Winona Lake: Eisenbrauns.

Na'aman, N. 2006b. *Ancient Israel and Its Neighbors: Interaction and Counteraction: Collected Essays*. Winona Lake: Eisenbrauns.

Na'aman, N. 2008. "Sojourners and Levites in the Kingdom of Judah in the Seventh Century BCE." *Zeitschrift für altorientalische und biblische Rechtsgeschichte* 14: 237–279.

Na'aman, N. 2011a. "The 'Discovered Book' and the Legitimation of Josiah's Reform." *Journal of Biblical Literature* 130 (1): 47–62.

Na'aman, N. 2011b. "The Inscriptions of Kuntillet 'Ajrud Through the Lens of Historical Research." *Ugarit-Forschungen* 43: 299–324.

Na'aman, N., Lissovsky, N. 2008. "Kuntillet 'Ajrud, Sacred Trees and the Asherah." *Tel Aviv* 35 (2): 186–208.

Naccache, A. F. H. 1996. "El's Abode in His Land." In *Ugarit, Religion and Culture: Proceedings of the International Colloquium on Ugarit, Religion and Culture, Edinburgh, July 1994: Essays Presented in Honour of Professor John C. L. Gibson*, edited by Wyatt, N., Watson, W. G. E., Lloyd, J. B., 249–271. Münster: Ugarit-Verlag.

Nakhai, B. A. 2001. *Archaeology and the Religions of Canaan and Israel*. Boston: American Schools of Oriental Research.

Naveh, J. 1963. "Old Hebrew Inscriptions in a Burial Cave." *Israel Exploration Journal* 13 (2): 74–92.

Naveh, J. 1979. "Graffiti and Dedications." *Bulletin of the American Schools of Oriental Research* 235: 27–30.

Naveh, J. 1982. "Some Recently Forged Inscriptions." *Bulletin of the American Schools of Oriental Research* 247: 53–58.

Naveh, J. 2001. "Hebrew Graffiti from the First Temple Period." *Israel Exploration Journal* 51 (2): 194–207.

Naveh, J. 2009. *Studies in West-Semitic Epigraphy: Selected Papers*. Jerusalem: Magnes Press.

Naveh, J., Shaked, S. 1993. *Magic Spells and Formulae: Aramaic Incantations of Late Antiquity*. Jerusalem: Magnes Press.

Naveh, J., Shaked, S. 1998. *Amulets and Magic Bowls: Aramaic Incantations of Late Antiquity*. Jerusalem: Magnes Press.

Negbi, O. 1976. *Canaanite Gods in Metal: An Archaeological Study of Ancient Syro-Palestinian Figurines*. Tel Aviv: Tel Aviv University Institute of Archaeology.

Negbi, O. 1989. "The Metal Figurines." In *Hazor III–IV = The James A. de Rothschild Expedition at Hazor: An Account of the Third and Fourth Seasons of Excavation, 1957–1958*, edited by Ben-Tor, A., Shulamit, G., 348–362. Jerusalem: Israel Exploration Society.

Negev, A. 1971. "A Nabatean Epitaph from Trans-Jordan." *Israel Exploration Journal* 21 (1): 50–52.
Nelson, R. D. 1991. "The Role of the Priesthood in the Deuteronomistic History." In *Congress Volume: Leuven, 1989*, edited by Emerton, J. A., 132–147. Leiden: Brill.
Nelson, R. D. 1993. *Raising up a Faithful Priest: Community and Priesthood in Biblical Theology*. Louisville: Westminster John Knox.
Nestor, D. 2010. *Cognitive Perspectives on Israelite Identity*. New York: T. & T. Clark.
Newsom, C. A., Ringe, S. H. 1992. *The Women's Bible Commentary*. Louisville: Westminster John Knox.
Newsom, C. A., Ringe, S. H. 1998. *The Women's Bible Commentary*. Expanded ed. Louisville: Westminster John Knox.
Newsom, C. A., Ringe, S. H., Lapsley, J. E. 2012. *Women's Bible Commentary*. 3rd ed. Louisville: Westminster John Knox.
Nicholson, E. W. 1998. *The Pentateuch in the Twentieth Century: The Legacy of Julius Wellhausen*. New York: Oxford University.
Nicholson, E. W. 2003. *The Pentateuch in the Twentieth Century: The Legacy of Julius Wellhausen*. Revised ed. New York: Oxford University.
Niditch, S. 1993. *Folklore and the Hebrew Bible*. Minneapolis: Fortress.
Niditch, S. 1996. *Oral World and Written Word: Ancient Israelite Literature*. Louisville: Westminster John Knox.
Niditch, S. 1997. *Ancient Israelite Religion*. New York: Oxford University.
Niditch, S. 2015. *The Responsive Self*. New Haven: Yale University.
Niebuhr, H. R. 1960. *Radical Monotheism and Western Culture*. Louisville: Westminster John Knox.
Niehr, H. 1990. *Der höchste Gott: alttestamentlicher JHWH-Glaube im Kontext syrisch-kanaanäischer Religion des 1. Jahrtausends v. Chr.* Berlin: de Gruyter.
Niehr, H. 1996. "The Rise of YHWH in Judahite and Israelite Religion: Methodological and Religio-Historical Aspects." In *The Triumph of Elohim: From Yahwisms to Judaisms*, edited by Edelman, D. V., 45–72. Grand Rapids: Eerdmans.
Niehr, H. 1997. "In Search of YHWH's Cult Statue in the First Temple." In *The Image and the Book: Iconic Cults, Aniconism, and the Rise of Book Religion in Israel and the Ancient Near East*, edited by van der Toorn, K., 73–95. Leuven: Peeters.
Niehr, H. 2003. "Götterbilder und Bildverbot." In *Der eine Gott und die Götter: Polytheismus und Monotheismus im antiken Israel*, edited by Oeming, M., Schmid, K., 227–247. Zürich: Theologischer Verlag Zürich.
Niehr, H. 2013. "The Religion of the Aramaeans in the West: The Case of Sam'al." In *Arameans, Chaldeans, and Arabs in Babylonia and Palestine in the First Millennium B.C.*, edited by Berlejung, A., Streck, M. P., 183–221. Wiesbaden: Harrassowitz.
Niehr, H. 2014a. "Religion." In *The Aramaeans in Ancient Syria*, edited by Niehr, H., 127–203. Leiden: Brill.
Niehr, H., ed. 2014b. *The Aramaeans in Ancient Syria*. Leiden: Brill.
Niehr, H., Steins, G. 2004. "Šadday." In *Theological Dictionary of the Old Testament Vol. XIV*, edited by Botterweck, G. J., Ringgren, H., Fabry, H., 418–446. Grand Rapids: Eerdmans.
Nielsen, K. 1978. *Yahweh as Prosecutor and Judge: An Investigation of the Prophetic Lawsuit (Rîb-Pattern)*. Sheffield: JSOT Press.
Nihan, C. 2007. *From Priestly Torah to Pentateuch: A Study in the Composition of the Book of Leviticus*. Tübingen: Mohr Siebeck.

Nihan, C. 2012. "The Literary Relationship Between Deuteronomy and Joshua: A Reassessment." In *Deuteronomy in the Pentateuch, Hexateuch, and the Deuteronomistic History*, edited by Schmid, K., Person, R. F., 79–114. Tübingen: Mohr Siebeck.

Nissinen, M. 1998. *References to Prophecy in Neo-Assyrian Sources*. Helsinki: Neo-Assyrian Text Corpus Project.

Nissinen, M. 2003. "Fear Not: A Study on an Ancient Near Eastern Phrase." In *The Changing Face of Form Criticism for the Twenty-First Century*, edited by Sweeney, M. A., Ben Zvi, E., 122–161. Grand Rapids: Eerdmans.

Nissinen, M. 2008. "From Holy War to Holy Peace: Biblical Alternatives to Belligerent Rhetoric." In *Isaiah's Vision of Peace in Biblical and Modern International Relations: Swords into Plowshares*, edited by Cohen, R., Westbrook, R., 181–197. New York: Palgrave Macmillan.

Nissinen, M. 2015. "(How) Does the Book of Ezekiel Reveal Its Babylonian Context?" *Die Welt des Orients* 45: 85–98.

Nissinen, M., Seow, C. L., Ritner, R. K. 2003. *Prophets and Prophecy in the Ancient Near East*. Writings from the Ancient World, Vol. 12. Atlanta: Society of Biblical Literature.

Nissinen, M., Seow, C. L., Ritner, R. K., Melchert, H. C. 2019. *Prophets and Prophecy in the Ancient Near East*. 2nd ed. Writings from the Ancient World, Vol. 41. Atlanta: SBL Press.

Noll, M. A. 1992. *A History of Christianity in the United States and Canada*. Grand Rapids: Eerdmans.

Nongbri, B. 2013. *Before Religion*. New Haven: Yale University.

Noth, M. 1928. *Die israelitischen Personennamen im Rahmen der gemeinsemitischen Namengebung*. Beiträge zur Wissenschaft vom Alten und Neuen Testament, Vol. III, 10. Hildesheim: Gg Olms.

Noth, M. 1962. *Exodus*. Philadelphia: Westminster.

Noth, M. 1981. *A History of Pentateuchal Traditions*. Translated with an introduction by Bernhard W. Anderson. Chico: Scholars Press.

Noth, M. 1984. *The Laws in the Pentateuch and Other Studies*. London: SCM. Originally published in German in 1957.

Nötscher, F. 1953. "Zum emphatischen Lamed." *Vetus Testamentum* 3: 372–380.

Nunnally, W. E. 1992. "The Fatherhood of God at Qumran." Hebrew Union College–Jewish Institute of Religion.

Nurmela, R. 1998. *The Levites: Their Emergence as a Second Class Priesthood*. Atlanta: Scholars Press.

Nyberg, K. 2008. "Sacred Prostitution in the Biblical World?" In *Sacred Marriages: The Divine-Human Sexual Metaphor from Sumer to Early Christianity*, edited by Nissinen, M., Uro, R., 305–320. Winona Lake: Eisenbrauns.

O'Connor, K. M. 1998. "Jeremiah" and "Lamentations." In *Women's Bible Commentary*, expanded ed., edited by Newsom, C. A., Ringe, S. H., 178–186, 187–191. Louisville: Westminster John Knox.

O'Connor, M. P. 1980. *Hebrew Verse Structure*. Winona Lake: Eisenbrauns.

O'Connor, M. P. 2004. "The Onomastic Evidence for Bronze-Age West Semitic." *Journal of the American Oriental Society* 124 (3): 439–470.

O'Neill, J. C. 1995. "Gunkel Versus Wellhausen: The Unfinished Task of the Religionsgeschichtliche Schule." *Journal of Higher Criticism* 2: 115–121.

Obbink, H. T. 1929. "Jahwebilder." *Zeitschrift für die alttestamentliche Wissenschaft* 47: 264–274.

Oden, R. A. 1977. "Baʿal Šamēm and ʾĒl." *Catholic Biblical Quarterly* 39 (4): 457–473.

Oden, R. A. 1987. *The Bible Without Theology: The Theological Tradition and Alternatives to It.* San Francisco: Harper & Row.
Oden, R. A. 1992. "Mythology." In *The Anchor Bible Dictionary*, edited by Freedman, D. N., Vol. 4, 946–956. New York: Doubleday.
Oldenburg, U. 1969. *The Conflict Between El and Baʿal in Canaanite Religion.* Leiden: Brill.
Olmo Lete, G. del. 1999. *Canaanite Religion: According to the Liturgical Texts of Ugarit.* Bethesda: CDL.
Olyan, S. M. 1982. "Zadok's Origins and the Tribal Politics of David." *Journal of Biblical Literature* 101 (2): 177–193.
Olyan, S. M. 1987a. "The Cultic Confessions of Jer 2, 27a." *Zeitschrift für die alttestamentliche Wissenschaft* 99 (2): 254–259.
Olyan, S. M. 1987b. "Some Observations on the Identity of the Queen of Heaven." *Ugarit-Forschungen* 19: 161–174.
Olyan, S. M. 1988. *Asherah and the Cult of Yahweh in Israel.* Atlanta: Scholars Press.
Olyan, S. M. 1993. *A Thousand Thousands Served Him: Exegesis and the Naming of Angels in Ancient Judaism.* Tübingen: J. C. B. Mohr.
Olyan, S. M. 2000. *Rites and Rank: Hierarchy in Biblical Representations of Cult.* Princeton: Princeton University.
Olyan, S. M. 2010. "What Do We Really Know About Women's Rites in the Israelite Family Context?" *Journal of Ancient Near Eastern Religions* 10 (1): 55–67.
Olyan, S. M., ed. 2015. *Ritual Violence in the Hebrew Bible: New Perspectives.* New York: Oxford University.
Oorschot, J. van., Witte, M., eds. 2017. *The Origins of Yahwism.* Berlin: de Gruyter.
Oppenheim, A. L. 1943. "Akkadian *pul(u)h(t)u* and *melammu*." *Journal of the American Oriental Society* 63 (1): 31–34.
Oppenheim, A. L. 1964. *Ancient Mesopotamia: Portrait of a Dead Civilization.* Chicago: University of Chicago.
Oppenheim, A. L. 1969. "Babylonian and Assyrian Historical Texts." In *Ancient Near Eastern Texts Relating to the Old Testament*, edited by Pritchard, J. B., 265–317. Princeton: Princeton University.
Oren, E. D. 1997. *The Hyksos: New Historical and Archaeological Perspectives.* Philadelphia: University of Pennsylvania.
Ornan, T. 2001. "The Bull and Its Two Masters: Moon and Storm Deities in Relation to the Bull in Ancient Near Eastern Art." *Israel Exploration Journal* 51: 1–26.
Ornan, T. 2005a. *The Triumph of the Symbol: Pictorial Representation of Deities in Mesopotamia and the Biblical Image Ban.* Fribourg: Academic Press Fribourg.
Ornan, T. 2005b. "A Complex System of Religious Symbols: The Case of the Winged-Disc in Near Eastern Imagery of the First Millennium BCE." In *Crafts and Images in Contact: Studies on Eastern Mediterranean Art of the First Millennium BCE*, edited by Suter, C. E., Uehlinger, C., 207–241. Fribourg: Academic Press Fribourg.
Ornan, T. 2006. "The Lady and the Bull: Remarks on the Bronze Plaque from Tel Dan." In *Essays on Ancient Israel in Its Near Eastern Context: A Tribute to Nadav Naʾaman*, edited by Amit, Y., Ben Zvi, E., Finkelstein, I., Lipschits, O., 297–312. Winona Lake: Eisenbrauns.
Ornan, T. 2011. "'Let Baʿal Be Enthroned': The Date, Identification, and Function of a Bronze Statue from Hazor." *Journal of Near Eastern Studies* 70 (2): 253–280.
Ornan, T. 2012. "Member in the Entourage of Yahweh: A Uraeus Seal from the Western Wall Plaza Excavations." *ʿAtiqot* 72: 15*–20*.

Ornan, T. 2016. "Sketches and Final Works of Art: The Drawings and Wall Paintings of Kuntillet 'Ajrud Revisited." *Tel Aviv* 43 (1): 3–26.

Ornan, T. 2019. "The Throne and the Enthroned: On the Conceived Human Image of Yahweh in Iron II Jerusalem." *Tel Aviv* 46: 198–210.

Ornan, T., Weksler-Bdolah, S., Kisilevitz, S., Sass, B. 2012. "'The Lord Will Roar from Zion' (Amos 1:2): The Lion as a Divine Attribute on a Jerusalem Seal and Other Hebrew Glyptic Finds from the Western Wall Plaza Excavations." *'Atiqot* 72: 1*–13*.

Osborne, J. F. 2014. "Monuments and Monumentality." In *Approaching Monumentality in Archaeology*, edited by Osborne, J. F., 1–19. Albany: State University of New York Press.

Oswalt, J. 1986. *The Book of Isaiah: Chapters 1–39*. Grand Rapids: Eerdmans.

Otto, R. 1952. *The Idea of the Holy: An Inquiry into the Non-rational Factor in the Idea of the Divine and Its Relation to the Rational.* 2nd ed. London: Oxford University.

Ouellette, J. 1969. "More on 'Ēl Šadday and Bêl Šadê." *Journal of Biblical Literature* 88 (4): 470–471.

Overholt, T. W. 1989. *Channels of Prophecy: The Social Dynamics of Prophetic Activity*. Minneapolis: Fortress.

Overholt, T. W. 1996. *Cultural Anthropology and the Old Testament*. Minneapolis: Fortress.

Pakkala, J. 2008. "Jeroboam without Bulls." *Zeitschrift für die alttestamentliche Wissenschaft* 120 (4): 501–525.

Pals, D. L. 1996. *Seven Theories of Religion*. New York: Oxford University.

Pals, D. L. 2006. *Eight Theories of Religion*. New York: Oxford University.

Pals, D. L. 2015. *Nine Theories of Religion*. New York: Oxford University.

Pardee, D. 1976. "The Preposition in Ugaritic." *Ugarit-Forschungen* 8: 215–322.

Pardee, D. 1982. *Handbook of Ancient Hebrew Letters*. Chico: Scholars Press.

Pardee, D. 1988a. *Les textes para-mythologiques de la 24e campagne (1961)*. Ras Shamra–Ougarit, Vol. 77. Paris: Editions Recherche sur les civilisations.

Pardee, D. 1988b. "An Evaluation of the Proper Names from Ebla from a West Semitic Perspective: Pantheon Distribution According to Genre." In *Eblaite Personal Names and Semitic Name Giving*, edited by Archi, A., 119–151. Rome: Missione Archeologica Italiana in Siria.

Pardee, D. 1988c. "Ṭukamuna Wa Šunama." *Ugarit-Forschungen* 20: 195–199.

Pardee, D. 1989–1990. "Ugaritic Proper Nouns." *Archiv für Orientforschung* 36/37: 390–513.

Pardee, D. 1996. "Marziḥu, Kispu, and the Ugaritic Funerary Cult: A Minimalist View." In *Ugarit, Religion and Culture: Proceedings of the International Colloquium on Ugarit, Religion and Culture, Edinburgh, July 1994: Essays Presented in Honour of Professor John C. L. Gibson*, edited by Wyatt, N., Watson, W. G. E., Lloyd, J. B., 273–287. Münster: Ugarit-Verlag.

Pardee, D. 1997a. "The Kirta Epic." In *The Context of Scripture 1: Canonical Compositions from the Biblical World*, edited by Hallo, W. W., Younger, K. L., Vol. 1, 333–343. Leiden: Brill.

Pardee, D. 1997b. "'Ilu on a Toot." In *The Context of Scripture 1: Canonical Compositions from the Biblical World*, edited by Hallo, W. W., Younger, K. L., Vol. 1, 302–305. Leiden: Brill.

Pardee, D. 1997c. "The Ba'lu Myth." In *The Context of Scripture 1: Canonical Compositions from the Biblical World*, edited by Hallo, W. W., Younger, K. L., 241–274. Leiden: Brill.

Pardee, D. 1997d. "Ugaritic Prayer for a City Under Siege." In *The Context of Scripture 1: Canonical Compositions from the Biblical World*, edited by Hallo, W. W., Younger, K. L., 283–285. Leiden: Brill.

Pardee, D. 1997e. "Dawn and Dusk." In *The Context of Scripture 1: Canonical Compositions from the Biblical World*, edited by Hallo, W. W., Younger, K. L., 274–283. Leiden: Brill.

Pardee, D. 1997f. "Lachish Inscriptions." In *The Oxford Encyclopedia of Archaeology in the Near East*, edited by Meyers, E. M., Vol. 3, 323–324. New York: Oxford University.

Pardee, D. 1997g. Review of *Ugarit and the Bible*. *Journal of the American Oriental Society* 117 (2): 376–377.

Pardee, D. 1997h. "The Ugaritic." In *The Oxford Encyclopedia of Archaeology in the Near East*, edited by Meyers, E. M., Vol. 5, 262–263. New York: Oxford University.

Pardee, D. 1998. "Les documents d'Arslan Tash: authentiques ou faux?" *Syria* 75: 15–54.

Pardee, D. 1999. "Kosharoth." In *Dictionary of Deities and Demons in the Bible*, edited by van der Toorn, K., Becking, B., van der Horst, P. W., 491–492. Leiden: Brill.

Pardee, D. 2000. *Les textes rituels*. Paris: Editions Recherche sur les civilisations.

Pardee, D. 2002a. *Ritual and Cult at Ugarit*. Writings from the Ancient World, Vol. 10. Atlanta: Society of Biblical Literature.

Pardee, D. 2002b. "Double Letter, from ʾAzzīʾiltu to His Parents, from Same to His Sister." In *The Context of Scripture 3: Archival Documents from the Biblical World*, edited by Hallo, W. W., Younger, K. L., 112. Leiden: Brill.

Pardee, D. 2002c. "The Meṣad Ḥashavyahu (Yavneh Yam) Ostracon." In *The Context of Scripture 3: Archival Documents from the Biblical World*, edited by Hallo, W. W., Younger, K. L., 77–78. Leiden: Brill.

Pardee, D. 2002d. "The Widow's Plea." In *The Context of Scripture 3: Archival Documents from the Biblical World*, edited by Hallo, W. W., Younger, K. L., 86–87. Leiden: Brill.

Pardee, D. 2002e. "Arad Ostraca." In *The Context of Scripture 3: Archival Documents from the Biblical World*, edited by Hallo, W. W., Younger, K. L., 81–85. Leiden: Brill.

Pardee, D. 2002f. "Lachish Ostraca." In *The Context of Scripture 3 Archival Documents from the Biblical World*, edited by Hallo, W. W., Younger, K. L., 78–81. Leiden: Brill.

Pardee, D. 2005. "On Psalm 29: Structure and Meaning." In *The Book of Psalms: Composition and Reception*, edited by Flint, P. W., Miller, P. D., Brunell, A., Roberts, R., 153–183. Leiden: Brill.

Pardee, D. 2007a. "Preliminary Presentation of a New Ugaritic Song to ʿAthtartu (RIH 98/02)." In *Ugarit at Seventy-Five*, edited by Younger, K. L., 27–39. Winona Lake: Eisenbrauns.

Pardee, D. 2007b. "The Ugaritic Alphabetic Cuneiform Writing System in the Context of Other Alphabetic Systems." In *Studies in Semitic and Afroasiatic Linguistics Presented to Gene B. Gragg*, edited by Miller, C. L., 181–200. Chicago: Oriental Institute of the University of Chicago.

Pardee, D. 2008. "Deux tablettes ougaritiques de la main d'un même scribe, trouvées sur deux sites distincts: RS 19.039 et RIH 98/02." *Semitica et Classica* 1: 9–38.

Pardee, D. 2009. "A New Aramaic Inscription from Zincirli." *Bulletin of the American Schools of Oriental Research* 356: 51–71.

Pardee, D. 2012a. "On the Edge." In *The Perfumes of Seven Tamarisks: Studies in Honour of Wilfred G. E. Watson*, edited by Olmo Lete, G. del, Vidal, J., Wyatt, N., 177–195. Münster: Ugarit-Verlag.

Pardee, D. 2012b. *The Ugaritic Texts and the Origins of West Semitic Literary Composition*. 2007 Schweich Lectures. Oxford: Oxford University.

Pardee, D., Bordreuil, P. 1992. "Ugarit: Texts and Literature." *The Anchor Bible Dictionary*, edited by Freedman, D. N., Vol. 6, 706–721. New York: Doubleday.

Parker, H. D. D. 2013. "The Levant Comes of Age: The Ninth Century BCE Through Script Traditions." Johns Hopkins University.

Parker, K. I. 1992. "Solomon as Philosopher King? The Nexus of Law and Wisdom in 1 Kings 1–11." *Journal for the Study of the Old Testament* 53: 75–91.

Parker, S. B. 1977. "Historical Composition of KRT and the Cult of El." *Zeitschrift für die alttestamentliche Wissenschaft* 89 (2): 161–175.

Parker, S. B. 1988. "The Birth Announcement." In *Ascribe to the Lord: Biblical and Other Studies in Memory of Peter C. Craigie*, edited by Eslinger, L. M., Taylor, J. G., 133–149. Sheffield: JSOT Press.

Parker, S. B. 1989a. "KTU 1.16 III, the Myth of the Absent God and 1 Kings 18." *Ugarit-Forschungen* 21: 283–296.

Parker, S. B. 1989b. *The Pre-biblical Narrative Tradition: Essays on the Ugaritic Poems Keret and Aqhat*. Atlanta: Scholars Press.

Parker, S. B. 1997. "The Mare and Horon." In *Ugaritic Narrative Poetry*, edited by Parker, S. B., 219–223. Writings from the Ancient World, Vol. 9. Atlanta: Scholars Press.

Parker, S. B. 2006. "Divine Intercession in Judah?" *Vetus Testamentum* 56 (1): 76–91.

Parpola, S. 1997. *Assyrian Prophecies*. Helsinki: Helsinki University.

Parpola, S., Watanabe, K. 1988. *Neo-Assyrian Treaties and Loyalty Oaths*. State Archives of Assyria, Vol. 2. Helsinki: Helsinki University.

Parr, P. J. 1988. "Pottery of the Late Second Millennium B.C. from North West Arabia and Its Historical Implications." In *Araby the Blest: Studies in Arabian Archaeology*, edited by Potts, D. T., 73–89. Copenhagen: Carsten Niebuhr Institute of Ancient Near Eastern Studies.

Parr, P. J. 1992. "Qurayya." In *The Anchor Bible Dictionary*, edited by Freedman, D. N., Vol. 5, 594–596. New York: Doubleday.

Pat-El, N., Wilson-Wright, A. 2013. "Features of Archaic Biblical Hebrew and the Linguistic Dating Debate." *Hebrew Studies* 54: 387–410.

Pat-El, N., Wilson-Wright, A. 2015. "Deir ʿAllā as a Canaanite Dialect: A Vindication of Hackett." In *Epigraphy, Philology, and the Hebrew Bible: Methodological Perspectives on Philological and Comparative Study of the Hebrew Bible in Honor of Jo Ann Hackett*, edited by Hutton, J. M., Rubin, A. D., 13–23. Atlanta: SBL Press.

Paul, S. M. 1970. *Studies in the Book of the Covenant in the Light of Cuneiform and Biblical Law*. Leiden: Brill.

Paul, S. M. 1979–1980. "Adoption Formulae: A Study of Cuneiform and Biblical Legal Clauses." *Maarav* 2: 173–185.

Paul, S. M. 2012. *Isaiah 40–66: Translation and Commentary*. Grand Rapids: Eerdmans.

Payne, A. 2012. *Iron Age Hieroglyphic Luwian Inscriptions*. Writings from the Ancient World, Vol. 29. Atlanta: Society of Biblical Literature.

Pearce, L. E., Wunsch, C. 2014. *Documents of Judean Exiles and West Semites in Babylonia in the Collection of David Sofer*. Bethesda: CDL Press.

Peckham, B. 1968. "Notes on a Fifth-Century Phoenician Inscription from Kition, Cyprus (CIS 86)." *Orientalia* 37 (3): 304–324.

Peckham, B. 1987. "Phoenicia and the Religion of Israel: The Epigraphic Evidence." In *Ancient Israelite Religion: Essays in Honor of Frank Moore Cross*, edited by Miller, P. D., Hanson, P. D., McBride, S. D., 79–99. Philadelphia: Fortress.

Peckham, B. 2014. *Phoenicia: Episodes and Anecdotes from the Ancient Mediterranean*. Winona Lake: Eisenbrauns.

Pedersen, J. 1926. *Israel: Its Life and Culture I–II*. London: Geoffrey Cumberlege.

Perlitt, L. 1965. *Vatke und Wellhausen: geschichtsphilosophische Vorausetzungen und historiographische Motive für die Darstellung der Religion und Geschichte Israels durch Wilhelm Vatke und Julius Wellhausen*. Berlin: A. Töpelmann.

Péter-Contesse, R. 2003. "La sacerdoce." In *The Book of Leviticus: Composition and Reception*, edited by Rendtorff, R., Kugler, R. A., 189–206. Atlanta: Society of Biblical Literature.

Petersen, D. L. 2002. *The Prophetic Literature: An Introduction*. Louisville: Westminster John Knox.

Petter, T. D. 2014. *The Land Between the Two Rivers: Early Israelite Identities in Central Transjordan*. Winona Lake: Eisenbrauns.

Pettinato, G. 1976. "The Royal Archives of Tell Mardikh-Ebla." *Biblical Archaeologist* 39 (2): 44–52.

Pettinato, G. 1980. "Ebla and the Bible." *Biblical Archaeologist* 43 (4): 203–216.

Petzold, H. 1969. "Die Bedeutung von Ariel im AT und auf der Mescha-Stele." *Theologia*: 372–415.

Pfeiffer, H. 2005. *Jahwes Kommen von Süden: Jdc 5, Hab 3, Dtn 33, und Ps 68 in ihrem literatur- und theologiegeschichtlichen Umfeld*. Göttingen: Vandenhoeck & Ruprecht.

Pfeiffer, H. 2017. "The Origin of Yhwh and Its Attestation." In *The Origins of Yahwism*, edited by van Oorschot, J., Witte, M., 115–144. Berlin: de Gruyter.

Philip, T. S. 2006. *Menstruation and Childbirth in the Bible: Fertility and Impurity*. New York: Peter Lang.

Pike, D. M. 1990. "Israelite Theophoric Personal Names in the Bible and Their Implications for Religious History." University of Pennsylvania.

Pinch, G. 1994. *Magic in Ancient Egypt*. London: British Museum.

Pitard, W. T. 1987. *Ancient Damascus: A Historical Study of the Syrian City-State from Earliest Times Until Its Fall to the Assyrians in 732 B.C.E*. Winona Lake: Eisenbrauns.

Pitard, W. T. 1997. "Arameans." In *The Oxford Encyclopedia of Archaeology in the Near East*, edited by Meyers, E. M., Vol. 1, 184–187. New York: Oxford University.

Pitard, W. T. 1998. "The Binding of Yamm: A New Edition of the Ugaritic Text KTU 1.83." *Journal of Near Eastern Studies* 57 (4): 261–280.

Pitard, W. T. 2000. "The Melqart Stela." In *The Context of Scripture 2: Monumental Inscriptions from the Biblical World*, edited by Hallo, W. W., Younger, K. L., 152–153. Leiden: Brill.

Pitard, W. T. 2002. "Tombs and Offerings: Archaeological Data and Comparative Methodology in the Study of Death in Israel." In *Sacred Time, Sacred Place: Archaeology and the Religion of Israel*, edited by Gittlen, B. M., 145–167. Winona Lake: Eisenbrauns.

Plaskow, J. 1990. *Standing Again at Sinai: Judaism from a Feminist Perspective*. San Francisco: Harper & Row.

Ploeg, J. P. M. van der. 1950. "Les chefs du peuple d'Israel et leurs titres." *Revue Biblique* 57: 40–61.

Polak, F. 1989. "Epic Formulas in Biblical Narrative: Frequency and Distribution." In *Actes du second colloque international Bible et informatique: Méthodes, outils, résultats*, edited by Poswick, R. et al., 437–489. Paris: Champion.

Polak, F. 2006. "Linguistic and Stylistic Aspects of Epic Formulae in Ancient Semitic Poetry and Biblical Narrative." In *Biblical Hebrew in Its Northwest Semitic*

Setting: Typological and Historical Perspectives, edited by Fassberg, S. E., Hurvitz, A., 285–304. Jerusalem: Magnes Press.

Pongratz-Leisten, B. 2011. *Reconsidering the Concept of Revolutionary Monotheism*. Winona Lake: Eisenbrauns.

Pope, M. H. 1955. *El in the Ugaritic Texts*. Leiden: Brill.

Pope, M. H. 1965a. "'Aṭtart, Astart, Astarte." In *Wörterbuch der Mythologie*, edited by Haussig, H. W., Vol. 1, 250–252. Stuttgart: E. Klett.

Pope, M. H. 1965b. *Job*. Garden City: Doubleday.

Pope, M. H. 1973. *Job*. 2nd ed. Garden City: Doubleday.

Pope, M. H. 1979. "Ups and Downs of El's Amours." *Ugarit-Forschungen* 11: 701–708.

Pope, M. H. 1987. "The Status of El at Ugarit." *Ugarit-Forschungen* 19: 219–230.

Pope, M. H. 1994. *Probative Pontificating in Ugaritic and Biblical Literature: Collected Essays*, edited by Smith, M. S. Münster: Ugarit-Verlag.

Porten, B. 1969. "The Religion of the Jews of Elephantine in Light of the Hermopolis Papyri." *Journal of Near Eastern Studies* 28 (2): 116–121.

Porten, B., Yardeni, A. 1986. *Textbook of Aramaic Documents from Ancient Egypt*. Winona Lake: Eisenbrauns.

Porteous, N. 1965. *Daniel*. Philadelphia: Westminster.

Porter, A., Schwartz, G. M., eds. 2012. *Sacred Killing: The Archaeology of Sacrifice in the Ancient Near East*. Winona Lake: Eisenbrauns.

Posener, G. 1960. *De la divinité du pharaon*. Paris: Imprimerie nationale.

Postgate, N. 1995. "Royal Ideology and State Administration in Sumer and Akkad." In *Civilizations of the Ancient Near East*, edited by Sasson, J. M., 395–411. New York: Scribner's.

Preucel, R. W. 1991. *Processual and Postprocessual Archaeologies: Multiple Ways of Knowing the Past*. Carbondale: Center for Archaeological Investigations, Southern Illinois University.

Preuss, H. D. 1995. *Old Testament Theology*. Louisville: Westminster John Knox.

Pritchard, J. B., ed. 1969a. *Ancient Near Eastern Texts Relating to the Old Testament*. Princeton: Princeton University.

Pritchard, J. B., ed. 1969b. *The Ancient Near East in Pictures Relating to the Old Testament*. Princeton: Princeton University.

Propp, W. H. C. 1999. *Exodus 1–18*. New York: Doubleday.

Propp, W. H. C. 2004. "Symbolic Wounds: Applying Anthropology to the Bible." In *Le-David Maskil: A Birthday Tribute for David Noel Freedman*, edited by Friedman, R. E., Propp, W. H. C., 17–24. Winona Lake: Eisenbrauns.

Propp, W. H. C. 2006. *Exodus 19–40*. New York: Doubleday.

Prouser, O. H. 1996. "Suited to the Throne: The Symbolic Use of Clothing in the David and Saul Narratives." *Journal for the Study of the Old Testament* 71: 27–37.

Puech, E. 1985. "L'inscription sur plâtre de Tell Deir 'Alla." In *Biblical Archaeology Today: Proceedings of the International Congress on Biblical Archaeology*, 354–365. Jerusalem: Israel Exploration Society.

Puech, E. 1989. Review of Pierre Bordreuil, *Catalogue des sceaux ouest-sémitiques inscrits de la Bibliothèque nationale, du Musée du Louvre et du Musée biblique de Bible et Terre Sainte*. *Revue Biblique* 96: 588–592.

Puech, E. 1992. "Palestinian Funerary Inscriptions." In *The Anchor Bible Dictionary*, edited by Freedman, D. N., Vol. 5, 126–135. New York: Doubleday.

Puech, E. 1994. "Un cratère phénicien inscrit: rites et croyances." *Transeuphratène* 8: 47–73.
Puech, E. 2014. "Les inscriptions hébraïques de Kuntillet ʿAjrud (Sinaï)." *Revue Biblique* 121: 161–194.
Puhvel, J. 1987. *Comparative Mythology*. Baltimore: Johns Hopkins University.
Quinn, J. C. 2018. *In Search of the Phoenicians*. Princeton: Princeton University.
von Rad, G. 1953. *Studies in Deuteronomy*. London: SCM Press.
von Rad, G. 1962. *Old Testament Theology, Vol. I, The Theology of Israel's Historical Traditions*. New York: Harper and Row.
von Rad, G. 1966a. *The Problem of the Hexateuch and Other Essays*. London: SCM.
von Rad, G. 1966b. *Deuteronomy: A Commentary*. Philadelphia: Westminster.
Rainey, A. F. 1967. *The Social Structure of Ugarit* [Hebrew]. Jerusalem: Bialik.
Rainey, A. F. 1963. "A Canaanite at Ugarit." *Israel Exploration Journal* 13: 43–45.
Rainey, A. F. 1964. "Ugarit and Canaanites Again." *Israel Exploration Journal* 14: 101.
Rainey, A. F. 1965. "Family Relationships in Ugarit." *Orientalia* 34 (1): 10–22.
Rainey, A. F. 1973. "*Ilānu rēṣūtnī lillikū!*" In *Orient and Occident. Essays Presented to Cyrus H. Gordon*, edited by Hoffner, H. A., 139–142. Kevelaer: Butzon & Bercker.
Rainey, A. F. 1975. "Notes on Some Proto-Sinaitic Inscriptions." *Israel Exploration Journal* 25 (2): 106–116.
Rainey, A. F. 1977. "Rainey on Ebla." *Biblical Archaeology Review* 3 (1): 38.
Rainey, A. F. 1978. "The Barth-Ginsberg Law in the Amarna Tablets." *Eretz-Israel: Archaeological, Historical and Geographical Studies* 14: 8*–13*.
Rainey, A. F. 1991. "Can You Name the Panel with the Israelites? Rainey's Challenge." *Biblical Archaeology Review* 17 (6): 56–60,93.
Rainey, A. F. 1992. "Anson F. Rainey Replies." *Biblical Archaeology Review* 18 (2): 73–74.
Rainey, A. F. 1996a. *Canaanite in the Amarna Tablets: A Linguistic Analysis of the Mixed Dialect Used by the Scribes from Canaan*. 4 Vols. Handbuch der Orientalistik. Leiden: Brill.
Rainey, A. F. 1996b. "Who Is a Canaanite? A Review of the Textual Evidence." *Bulletin of the American Schools of Oriental Research* 304: 1–15.
Rainey, A. F. 2001a. "Israel in Merenptah's Inscriptions and Reliefs." *Israel Exploration Journal* 51 (1): 57–75.
Rainey, A. F. 2001b. "Mesha and Syntax." In *The Land That I Will Show You: Essays on the History and Archaeology of the Ancient Near East in Honor of J. Maxwell Miller*, edited by Dearman, J. A., Graham, M. P., 291–311. Sheffield: Sheffield Academic Press.
Rainey, A. F. 2015. *The El-Amarna Correspondence: A New Edition of the Cuneiform Letters from the Site of El-Amarna Based on Collations of All Extant Tablets*. Handbook of Oriental Studies Vol. 110/1–2, edited by Schniedewind, W., Cochavi-Rainey, Z. Leiden: Brill.
Rainey, A. F., Notley, R. S. 2006. *The Sacred Bridge: Carta's Atlas of the Biblical World*. Jerusalem: Carta.
Ramsey, G. W. 1992. "Zadok." In *The Anchor Bible Dictionary*, edited by Freedman, D. N., Vol. 6, 1034–1036. New York: Doubleday.
Rappaport, R. A. 1999. *Ritual and Religion in the Making of Humanity*. Cambridge Studies in Social and Cultural Anthropology, Vol. 110. Cambridge: Cambridge University.
Ratner, R., Zuckerman, B. 1986. "A Kid in Milk? New Photographs of KTU 1.23, Line 14." *Hebrew Union College Annual* 57: 15–60.

Rechenmacher, H. 1997. *Personennamen als theologische Aussagen: Die syntaktischen und semantischen Strukturen der satzhaften theophoren Personennamen in der hebraischen Bibel.* St. Ottilien: EOS-Verlag.

Rechenmacher, H. 2012. *Althebräische Personennamen.* Münster: Ugarit-Verlag.

Redford, D. B. 1984. *Akhenaten, the Heretic King.* Princeton: Princeton University.

Redford, D. B. 1986. "The Ashkelon Relief at Karnak and the Israel Stela." *Israel Exploration Journal* 36 (3): 188–200.

Redford, D. B. 1987. "An Egyptological Perspective on the Exodus Narrative." In *Egypt, Israel, Sinai: Archaeological and Historical Relationships in the Biblical Period,* edited by Rainey, A. F., 137–161. Tel Aviv: Tel Aviv University.

Redford, D. B. 1992. *Egypt, Canaan, and Israel in Ancient Times.* Princeton: Princeton University.

Redford, D. B. 2013. "Akhenaten: New Theories and Old Facts." *Bulletin of the American Schools of Oriental Research* 369: 9–34.

Reed, W. J. 2018. "Yahweh's 'Cruel Sword': The Manifestation of Punishment and the Trauma of Exile." Johns Hopkins University.

Rehm, M. D. 1992. "Levites and Priests." In *The Anchor Bible Dictionary,* edited by Freedman, D. N., Vol. 4, 297–310. New York: Doubleday.

Reindl, J. 1998. "Nṣb/yṣb." In *Theological Dictionary of the Old Testament,* edited by Botterweck, G. J., Ringgren, H., Fabry, H., Vol. IX, 519–529. Grand Rapids: Eerdmans.

Rendsburg, G. A. 2006. "Moses as Equal to Pharaoh." In *Text, Artifact, and Image: Revealing Ancient Israelite Religion,* edited by Beckman, G. M., Lewis, T. J., 201–219. Providence: Brown Judaic Studies.

Rendtorff, R. 1963. "Die Offenbarungsvorstellungen im Alten Israel." In *Offenbarung als Geschichte,* edited by Pannenberg, W., Rendtorff, R., 21–41. Göttingen: Vandenhoeck & Ruprecht.

Rendtorff, R. 1966. "El, Baʿal und Jahwe: Erwägungen zum Verhältnis von kanaanäischer und israelitischer Religion." *Zeitschrift für die alttestamentliche Wissenschaft* 78 (3): 277–292.

Rendtorff, R. 1967. "The Background of the Title ʾl ʿlywn in Gen XIV." *Fourth World Congress of Jewish Studies* 1: 167–170.

Rendtorff, R. 1993a. "Some Observations on the Use of ʾl in the Hebrew Bible." *Eretz-Israel: Archaeological, Historical and Geographical Studies* (Avraham Malamat Volume) 24: 192–196.

Rendtorff, R. 1993b. "The Paradigm Is Changing: Hopes—and Fears." *Biblical Interpretation* 1: 34–53.

Rendtorff, R. 1994. "'El als israelitische Gottesbezeichnung mit einem Appendix: Beobachtungen zum Gebrauch von hāʾĕlōhîm." *Zeitschrift für die alttestamentliche Wissenschaft* 106 (1): 4–21.

Rendtorff, R. 2004. *Leviticus 1. Teilband Leviticus 1,1–10,20.* Neukirchen-Vluyn: Neukirchner Verlag.

Renfrew, C. 1985. *The Archaeology of Cult: The Sanctuary at Phylakopi.* London: British School of Archaeology at Athens.

Renfrew, C., Bahn, P. G. 1991. *Archaeology: Theories, Methods, and Practice.* New York: Thames and Hudson.

Renfrew, C., Bahn, P. G. 2000. *Archaeology: Theories, Methods, and Practice.* 2nd ed. New York: Thames and Hudson.

Renz, J., Röllig, W. 1995. *Handbuch der althebräischen Epigraphik*. Band I. Darmstadt: Wissenschaftliche Buchgesellschaft.
Renz, J., Röllig, W. 2003. *Handbuch der althebräischen Epigraphik*. Band II/2. Darmstadt: Wissenschaftliche Buchgesellschaft.
Reuss, E. 1879. *La Bible*. Paris: Librairie Sandoz et Fischbacher.
Reventlow, H. G. 2010. *History of Biblical Interpretation, Vol. 4, From the Enlightenment to the Twentieth Century*. Atlanta: Society of Biblical Literature.
Rezetko, R., Young, I. 2014. *Historical Linguistics and Biblical Hebrew: Steps Toward an Integrated Approach*. Atlanta: SBL Press.
Ribichini, S. 1997. "Beliefs and Religious Life." In *The Phoenicians*, edited by Moscati, S., 120–144. New York: Rizzoli.
Ribichini, S. 1999. "Baetyl." In *Dictionary of Deities and Demons in the Bible*, edited by van der Toorn, K., Becking, B., van der Horst, P. W., 157–159. 2nd ed. Leiden: Brill.
Richardson, H. N. 1966. "A Critical Note on Amos 7:14." *Journal of Biblical Literature* 85 (1): 89–89.
Richter, H. 1959. *Studien zu Hiob*. Berlin: Evangelische Verlaganstalt.
Richter, S. L. 2002. *The Deuteronomistic History and the Name Theology: lešakken šemô šam in the Bible and the Ancient Near East*. Berlin: de Gruyter.
Richter, S. L. 2007. "The Place of the Name in Deuteronomy." *Vetus Testamentum* 57 (3): 342–366.
Ringgren, H. 1966. *Israelite Religion*. Philadelphia: Fortress.
Ringgren, H. 1972. "Israel's Place Among the Religions of the Ancient Near East." In *Studies in the Religion of Ancient Israel*, edited by Anderson, G. W., et al., 1–8. Leiden: Brill.
Ringgren, H. 1977. "The Impact of the Ancient Near East on Israelite Religion." In *Tradition and Theology in the Old Testament*, edited by Knight, D. A., 31–46. Philadelphia: Fortress.
Ringgren, H. 1980. "*Chāyāh*." In *Theological Dictionary of the Old Testament*, edited by Botterweck, G. J., Ringgren, H., Vol. IV, 324–344. Grand Rapids: Eerdmans.
Ritner, R. K. 1997a. "Daily Ritual of the Temple of Amun-Re at Karnak." In *The Context of Scripture 1: Canonical Compositions from the Biblical World*, edited by Hallo, W. W., Younger, K. L., 55–57. Leiden: Brill.
Ritner, R. K. 1997b. "The Legend of Astarte and the Tribute of the Sea." In *The Context of Scripture 1: Canonical Compositions from the Biblical World*, edited by Hallo, W. W., Younger, K. L., Vol. 1, 35–36. Leiden: Brill.
Ritter, N. C. Forthcoming. "Human-Headed Winged Bull." *Iconography of Deities and Demons*.
Roach, M. E., Eicher, J. B., eds. 1965. *Dress, Adornment, and the Social Order*. New York: John Wiley & Sons.
Roberts, J. J. M. 1973a. "The Davidic Origin of the Zion Tradition." *Journal of Biblical Literature* 92 (3): 329–344.
Roberts, J. J. M. 1973b. "Job's Summons to Yahweh: The Exploitation of a Legal Metaphor." *Restoration Quarterly* 16: 159–165.
Roberts, J. J. M. 1991. *Nahum, Habakkuk, and Zephaniah*. Louisville: Westminster John Knox.
Roberts, J. J. M. 1997. "Whose Child Is This? Reflections on the Speaking Voice in Isaiah 9:5." *Harvard Theological Review* 90 (2): 115–129.

Roberts, J. J. M. 2002. *The Bible and the Ancient Near East: Collected Essays.* Winona Lake: Eisenbrauns.
Robertson Smith, W. 1885. *Kinship and Marriage in Early Arabia.* Cambridge: Cambridge University.
Robertson Smith, W. 1889. *Lectures on the Religion of the Semites.* Burnett Lectures [Aberdeen University, 1888–89]. New York: Appleton.
Robertson Smith, W. 1972. *Religion of the Semites: The Fundamental Institutions.* New York: Schocken.
Robertson, D. A. 1972. *Linguistic Evidence in Dating Early Hebrew Poetry.* Missoula: Society of Biblical Literature.
Robins, G. 2005. "Cult Statues in Ancient Egypt." In *Cult Image and Divine Representation in the Ancient Near East,* edited by Walls, N. H., 1–12. Boston: American Schools of Oriental Research.
Robinson, T. H. 1933. "Hebrew Myths." In *Myth and Ritual. Essays on the Myth and Ritual of the Hebrews in Relation to the Culture Pattern of the Ancient East,* edited by Hooke, S. H., 172–196. London: Oxford University.
Rodd, C. S. 1981. "On Applying a Sociological Theory to Biblical Studies." *Journal for the Study of the Old Testament* 19: 95–106.
Rofé, A. 1988. *The Prophetical Stories: The Narratives About the Prophets in the Hebrew Bible: Their Literary Types and History.* Jerusalem: Magnes Press.
Rogerson, J. W. 1974. *Myth in Old Testament Interpretation.* Berlin: de Gruyter.
Rogerson, J. W. 1985. "The Use of Sociology in Old Testament Studies." In *Congress Volume: Salamanca, 1983,* edited by Emerton, J. A., 245–256. Leiden: Brill.
Rogerson, J. W. 1992. *W. M. L. de Wette, Founder of Modern Biblical Criticism: An Intellectual Biography.* Sheffield: Sheffield Academic Press.
Rohland, E. 1956. *Die Bedeutung der Erwählungstraditionen Israels für die Eschatologie der alttestamentlichen Propheten.* Heidelberg: Ruprecht-Karl Universität.
Rollefson, G. O. 2006. "Desert/*midbār*." In *The New Interpreter's Dictionary of the Bible,* edited by Sakenfeld, K. D., Vol. 2, 102–103. Nashville: Abingdon.
Röllig, W. 1999a. "El-Creator-of-the-Earth." In *Dictionary of Deities and Demons in the Bible,* edited by van der Toorn, K., Becking, B., van der Horst, P. W., 280–281. 2nd ed. Leiden: Brill.
Röllig, W. 1999b. "Bethel." In *Dictionary of Deities and Demons in the Bible,* edited by van der Toorn, K., Becking, B., van der Horst, P. W., 173–175. 2nd ed. Leiden: Brill.
Rollston, C. 1998. "Are They Genuine?" *Near Eastern Archaeology* 61 (1): 8–9.
Rollston, C. 2003. "Non-Provenanced Epigraphs I: Pillaged Antiquities, Northwest Semitic Forgeries, and Protocols for Laboratory Tests." *Maarav* 10: 135–193.
Rollston, C. 2004. "Non-Provenanced Epigraphs II: The Status of Non-Provenanced Epigraphs Within the Broader Corpus of Northwest Semitic." *Maarav* 11: 57–79.
Rollston, C. 2006. "Scribal Education in Ancient Israel: The Old Hebrew Epigraphic Evidence." *Bulletin of the American Schools of Oriental Research* 344: 47–74.
Rollston, C. 2008. "The Phoenician Script of the Tel Zayit Abecedary and Putative Evidence for Israelite Literacy." In *Literate Culture and Tenth-Century Canaan: The Tel Zayit Abecedary in Context,* edited by Tappy, R. E., McCarter, P. K., 61–96. Winona Lake: Eisenbrauns.
Rollston, C. 2013a. "Forgeries of Hebrew Texts." In *Encyclopedia of Hebrew Language and Linguistics,* edited by Khan, G., Vol. 1, 904–906. Leiden: Brill.

Rollston, C. 2013b. "Ad Nomen Argumenta: Personal Names as Pejorative Puns in Ancient Texts." In *In the Shadow of Bezalel: Aramaic, Biblical, and Ancient Near Eastern Studies in Honor of Bezalel Porten*, edited by Botta, A. F., 367–386. Leiden: Brill.

Rollston, C. 2014. "Forging History: From Antiquity to the Modern Period." In *Archaeologies of Text: Archaeology, Technology, and Ethics*, edited by Rutz, M. T., Kersel, M. M., 176–197. Oxford: Oxbow Books.

Rollston, C. 2015a. "The Incised Ishba'l Inscription from Khirbet Qeiyafa: Some Things That Can and Cannot Be Said." *Zwinglius Redivivus* (blog), June 21, https://zwingliusredivivus.wordpress.com/2015/06/21/christopher-rollston-on-the-ishbal-inscription-a-guest-post.

Rollston, C. 2015b. "The Ivory Pomegranate: The Anatomy of a Probable Modern Forgery." In *Epigraphy, Philology and the Hebrew Bible: Methodological Perspectives on Philological and Comparative Study of the Hebrew Bible in Honor of Jo Ann Hackett*, edited by Hutton, J. M., Rubin, A. D., 237–252. Atlanta: SBL Press.

Rollston, C., Vaughn, A. G. 2005. "The Antiquities Market, Sensationalized Textual Data, and Modern Forgeries." *Near Eastern Archaeology* 68: 61–68.

Romano, J. F. 1980. "The Origin of the Bes-Image." *Bulletin of the Egyptological Seminar* 2: 39–56.

Römer, T. 2005. *The So-Called Deuteronomistic History: A Sociological, Historical, and Literary Introduction.* London: T. & T. Clark.

Römer, T. 2007. *The So-Called Deuteronomistic History: A Sociological, Historical, and Literary Introduction.* 2nd ed. London: T. & T. Clark.

Römer, T. 2015. *The Invention of God.* Cambridge: Harvard University.

Römer, T. 2017. "How Jeroboam II Became Jeroboam I." *Hebrew Bible and Ancient Israel* 6: 372–382.

Rom-Shiloni, D. 2011. "From Ezekiel to Ezra-Nehemiah: Shifts of Group Identities Within Babylonian Exilic Ideology." In *Judah and the Judeans in the Achaemenid Period: Negotiating Identity in an International Context*, edited by Lipschits, O., Knoppers, G. N., Oeming, M., 127–151. Winona Lake: Eisenbrauns.

Rooke, D. W. 1998. "Kingship as Priesthood: The Relationship Between the High Priesthood and the Monarchy." In *King and Messiah in Israel and the Ancient Near East*, edited by Day, J., 187–208. Sheffield: Sheffield Academic Press.

Rooke, D. W. 2000. *Zadok's Heirs: The Role and Development of the High Priesthood in Ancient Israel.* Oxford: Oxford University.

Rooke, D. W. 2007. *Zadok's Heirs: The Role and Development of the High Priesthood in Ancient Israel.* 2nd ed. Oxford: Oxford University.

Rooke, D. W., ed. 2009. *Embroidered Garments: Priests and Gender in Biblical Israel.* Sheffield: Sheffield Phoenix Press.

Rose, M. 1978. *Jahwe: zum Streit um den alttestamentlichen Gottesnamen.* Zürich: Theologischer Verlag.

Rösel, C. 1999. *Die messianische Redaktion des Psalters: Studien zu Entstehung und Theologie der Sammlung Psalm 2–89.* Stuttgart: Calwer Verlag.

Roth, M. T. 1995. "Mesopotamian Legal Traditions and the Laws of Hammurabi." *Chicago-Kent Law Review* 71: 13–39.

Rothenberg, B. 1998. "Who Were the 'Midianite' Copper Miners of the Arabah?" In *Metallurgica Antiqua: In Honour of Hans-Gert Bachmann and Robert Maddin*, edited by Rehren, T., et al., 197–212. Bochum: Selbstverlag des Deutschen Bergbau-Museums.

Rothenberg, B. 1999a. "Archaeo-Metallurgical Researches in the Southern Arabah 1959–1990. Part I: Late Pottery Neolithic to Early Bronze IV." *Palestine Exploration Quarterly* 131 (1): 68–89.

Rothenberg, B. 1999b. "Archaeo-Metallurgical Researches in the Southern Arabah 1959–1990. Part 2: Egyptian New Kingdom (Ramesside) to Early Islam." *Palestine Exploration Quarterly* 131 (2): 149–175.

Rouillard, H. 1999. "Rephaim." In *Dictionary of Deities and Demons in the Bible*, edited by van der Toorn, K., Becking, B., van der Horst, P. W., 692–700. 2nd ed. Leiden: Brill.

Rowe, I. M. 1995. "More Evidence of the Grazing Tax in Ugarit." *Ugarit-Forschungen* 27: 317–331.

Rowley, H. H. 1939. "Zadok and Nehushtan." *Journal of Biblical Literature* 58: 113–141.

Rowley, H. H. 1950. *From Joseph to Joshua: Biblical Traditions in the Light of Archaeology*. The Schweich Lectures. London: Oxford University.

Ruane, N. J. 2007. "Bathing, Status and Gender in Priestly Ritual." In *A Question of Sex? Gender and Difference in the Hebrew Bible and Beyond*, edited by Rooke, D. W., 66–81. Sheffield: Sheffield Phoenix Press.

Russell, B. D. 2007. *The Song of the Sea: The Date and Significance of Exodus 15:1–21*. New York: Peter Lang.

Russell, S. C. 2009. *Images of Egypt in Early Biblical Literature: Cisjordan-Israelite, Transjordan-Israelite, and Judahite Portrayals*. Berlin: de Gruyter.

Rüterswörden, U. 1999. "King of Terrors." In *Dictionary of Deities and Demons in the Bible*, edited by van der Toorn, K., Becking, B., van der Horst, P. W., 486–488. 2nd ed. Leiden: Brill.

Ruwe, A. 2003. "The Structure of the Book of Leviticus in the Narrative Outline of the Priestly Sinai Story (Exod 19:1–Num 10:10)." In *The Book of Leviticus: Composition and Reception*, edited by Rendtorff, R., Kugler, R. A., Bartel, S. S., 55–78. Leiden: Brill.

Ryholt, K. S. B. 1997. *The Political Situation in Egypt During the Second Intermediate Period, c. 1800–1550 B.C.* Copenhagen: Museum Tusculanum Press.

Sader, H. S. 1987. *Les états araméens de Syrie depuis leur fondation jusqu'à leur transformation en provinces assyriennes*. Wiesbaden: Franz Steiner Verlag.

Sader, H. S. 2014. "History." In *The Aramaeans in Ancient Syria*, edited by Niehr, H., 11–36. Leiden: Brill.

Said, E. 1991. *Orientalism*. London: Penguin.

Sakenfeld, K. D., et al. 2006. *The New Interpreter's Dictionary of the Bible, Vol. 1, A–C*. Nashville: Abingdon.

Sakenfeld, K. D., et al. 2007. *The New Interpreter's Dictionary of the Bible, Vol. 2, D–H*. Nashville: Abingdon.

Sakenfeld, K. D., et al. 2008. *The New Interpreter's Dictionary of the Bible, Vol. 3, I–Ma*. Nashville: Abingdon.

Sakenfeld, K. D., et al. 2009a. *The New Interpreter's Dictionary of the Bible, Vol. 4, Me–R*. Nashville: Abingdon.

Sakenfeld, K. D., et al. 2009b. *The New Interpreter's Dictionary of the Bible, Vol. 5, S–Z*. Nashville: Abingdon.

Samuel, H. 2014. *Von Priestern zum Patriarchen: Levi und die Leviten im Alten Testament*. Berlin: de Gruyter.

Samuelsson, K. 1964. *Religion and Economic Action: A Critique of Max Weber*. New York: Harper & Row.

Sanders, J. A. 1998. "'Spinning' the Bible: The Hebrew Bible and the Old Testament Contain the Same Basic Books." *Bible Review* 14 (3): 22.
Sanders, P. 1996. *The Provenance of Deuteronomy 32*. Leiden: Brill.
Sanders, S. L. 2009. *The Invention of Hebrew*. Urbana: University of Illinois.
Sanders, S. L. 2014. "'The Mutation Peculiar to Hebrew Religion': Monotheism, Pantheon Reduction, or Royal Adoption of Family Religion." *Journal of Ancient Near Eastern Religions* 14: 217–227.
Sanders, S. L. 2015. "When the Personal Became Political: An Onomastic Perspective on the Rise of Yahwism." *Hebrew Bible and Ancient Israel* 4: 59–86.
Sanderson, J. E. 1998. "Micah." In *Women's Bible Commentary*, expanded ed., edited by Newsom, C. A., Ringe, S. H., 229–231. Louisville: Westminster John Knox.
Sandman, M. 1938. *Texts from the Time of Akhenaten*. Bibliotheca Aegyptiaca, Vol. 8. Brussels: Édition de la Fondation égyptologique reine Élisabeth.
Sandmel, S. 1961. "Genesis 4:26b." *Hebrew Union College Annual* 32: 19–29.
Sandmel, S. 1962. "Parallelomania." *Journal of Biblical Literature* 81 (1): 1–13.
Sanmartín, J. 1995. "Das Handwerk in Ugarit: Eine lexikalische Studie." *Studi Epigrafici e Linguistici* 12: 169–190.
Sarna, N. M. 1986. *Exploring Exodus: The Heritage of Biblical Israel*. New York: Schocken Books.
Sarna, N. M. 1989. *Genesis = Bereshit: The Traditional Hebrew Text with New JPS Translation*. Philadelphia: Jewish Publication Society.
Sarna, N. M. 1991. *Exodus = Shemot: The Traditional Hebrew Text with the New JPS Translation*. Philadelphia: Jewish Publication Society.
Sarna, N. M. 1999. "Israel in Egypt. The Egyptian Sojourn and the Exodus." In *Ancient Israel. From Abraham to the Roman Destruction of the Temple*, edited by Shanks, H., 33–54. Washington: Biblical Archaeology Society.
Sass, B. 1993. "The Pre-exilic Hebrew Seals: Iconism vs. Aniconism." In *Studies in the Iconography of Northwest Semitic Inscribed Seals*, edited by Sass, B., Uehlinger, C., 194–256. Fribourg: University Press.
Sass, B. 2005. *The Alphabet at the Turn of the Millennium*. Tel Aviv: Emery and Claire Yass Publications in Archaeology.
Sass, B., Uehlinger, C., eds. 1993. *Studies in the Iconography of Northwest Semitic Inscribed Seals: Proceedings of a Symposium Held in Fribourg on April 17–20, 1991*. Orbis biblicus et orientalis, Vol. 125. Fribourg: University Press.
Sasson, J. M. 1968. "Bovine Symbolism in the Exodus Narrative." *Vetus Testamentum* 18: 380–387.
Sasson, J. M. 1990. *Jonah: A New Translation with Introduction, Commentary, and Interpretation*. New York: Doubleday.
Sasson, J. M. 2014. *Judges 1–12: A New Translation with Introduction and Commentary*. New Haven: Yale University.
Sasson, J. M., ed. 1995. *Civilizations of the Ancient Near East*. New York: Scribner's.
Savran, G. 2005. *Encountering the Divine: Theophany in Biblical Narrative*. London: T. &. T. Clark.
Sawyer, J. F. A., Clines, D. J. A., eds. 1983. *Midian, Moab and Edom: The History and Archaeology of Late Bronze and Iron Age Jordan and North-West Arabia*. Sheffield: JSOT Press.
Schaeffer, C. F. A. 1966. "Nouveaux témoignages du culte de El et de Baal a Ras Shamra-Ugarit et ailleurs en Syrie-Palestine." *Syria* 43: 1–19.

Schäfer-Lichtenberger, C. 1991. "The Pariah: Some Thoughts on the Genesis and Presuppositions of Max Weber's Ancient Judaism." *Journal for the Study of the Old Testament* 16 (51): 85–113.

Schaper, J. 2000. *Priester und Leviten im achämenidischen Juda: Studien zur Kult- und Sozialgeschichte Israels in persischer Zeit.* Tübingen: Mohr Siebeck.

Schaper, J. 2007. "The 'Publication' of Legal Texts in Ancient Judah." In *The Pentateuch as Torah: New Models for Understanding Its Promulgation and Acceptance*, edited by Knoppers, G. N., Levinson, B. M., 225–236. Winona Lake: Eisenbrauns.

Schild, E. 1954. "On Exodus III 14: 'I Am That I Am.'" *Vetus Testamentum* 4 (3): 296–302.

Schloen, J. D. 1993a. "Caravans, Kenites and Casus Belli: Enmity and Alliance in the Song of Deborah." *Catholic Biblical Quarterly* 55 (1): 18–38.

Schloen, J. D. 1993b. "The Exile of Disinherited Kin in KTU 1.12 and KTU 1.23." *Journal of Near Eastern Studies* 52 (3): 209–220.

Schloen, J. D. 2001. *The House of the Father as Fact and Symbol: Patrimonialism in Ugarit and the Ancient Near East.* Winona Lake: Eisenbrauns.

Schloen, J. D. 2002. "W. F. Albright and the Origins of Israel." *Near Eastern Archaeology* 65 (1): 57–62.

Schloen, J. D. 2016. "Economy and Society in Iron Age Israel and Judah: An Archaeological Perspective." In *The Wiley Blackwell Companion to Ancient Israel*, edited by Niditch, S., 433–453. Chichester: John Wiley & Sons.

Schloen, J. D., ed. 2009. *Exploring the Longue Durée: Essays in Honor of Lawrence E. Stager* Winona Lake: Eisenbrauns.

Schloen, J. D., Fink, A. S. 2009. "New Excavations at Zincirli Höyük in Turkey (Ancient Sam'al) and the Discovery of an Inscribed Mortuary Stele." *Bulletin of the American Schools of Oriental Research* 356: 1–13.

Schlögl, H. A. 2001. "Aten." In *The Oxford Encyclopedia of Ancient Egypt*, edited by Redford, D. B., 156–158. Oxford: Oxford University.

Schmidt, B. B. 1996. "The Aniconic Tradition: On Reading Images and Viewing Texts." In *The Triumph of Elohim: From Yahwisms to Judaisms*, edited by Edelman, D. V., 75–105. Grand Rapids: Eerdmans.

Schmidt, B. B. 2002. "The Iron Age Pithoi Drawings from Horvat Teman or Kuntillet 'Ajrud: Some New Proposals." *Journal of Ancient Near Eastern Religions* 2 (1): 91–125.

Schmidt, B. B. 2013. "Kuntillet 'Ajrud's Pithoi Inscriptions and Drawings: Graffiti or Scribal-Artisan Drafts?" *Maarav* 20 (1): 53–81.

Schmidt, B. B. 2016. *The Materiality of Power: Explorations in the Social History of Early Israelite Magic.* Forschungen zum Alten Testament, Vol. 105. Tübingen: Mohr Siebeck.

Schmidt, B. B., ed. 2015. *Contextualizing Israel's Sacred Writing: Ancient Literacy, Orality, and Literary Production.* Atlanta: SBL Press.

Schmidt, W. H. 1962. "Wo hat die Aussage: Jahwe 'der Heilige' ihren Ursprung?" *Zeitschrift für die alttestamentliche Wissenschaft* 74 (1): 62–66.

Schmidt, W. H. 1983. *The Faith of the Old Testament: A History.* Philadelphia: Westminster.

Schmitt, J. J. 1985. "The Motherhood of God and Zion as Mother." *Revue Biblique* 92 (4): 557–569.

Schmitt, R. 2008. "Ashdod and the Material Remains of Domestic Cults in the Philistine Coastal Plain." In *Household and Family Religion in Antiquity*, edited by Bodel, J. P., Olyan, S. M., 159–170. Malden: Blackwell.

Schmitt, R. 2013. "Astarte, Mistress of Horses, Lady of the Chariot: The Warrior Aspect of Astarte." *Die Welt des Orients* 43 (2): 213–225.
Schmitz, P. C. 1992. "Phoenician Religion." In *The Anchor Bible Dictionary*, edited by Freedman, D. N., Vol. 5, 357–363. New York: Doubleday.
Schmitz, P. C. 2004. "Phoenician-Punic Grammar and Lexicography in the New Millennium." *Journal of the American Oriental Society* 124 (3): 533–547.
Schneider, T. 1992. *Asiatische Personennamen in ägyptischen Quellen des Neuen Reiches*. Freiburg: Universitätsverlag.
Schneider, T. 2003. "Foreign Egypt: Egyptology and the Concept of Cultural Appropriation." *Ägypten und Levante/Egypt and the Levant* 13: 155–161.
Schneider, T. 2004. "Sacred Kingship." In *Egypt: The World of the Pharaohs*, edited by Schulz, R., Seidel, M., 322–329. Königswinter: Könemann.
Schneider, T. 2006. "Akkulturation—Identität—Elitekultur: Eine Positionsbestimmung zur Frage der Existenz und des Status von Ausländern in der Elite des Neuen Reiches." In *Der ägyptische Hof des Neuen Reiches: seine Gesellschaft und Kultur im Spannungsfeld zwischen Innen- und Aussenpolitik*, edited by Gundlach, R., Klug, A., 201–216. Wiesbaden: Harrassowitz.
Schneider, T. 2007. "The First Documented Occurrence of the God Yahweh? (Book of the Dead Princeton 'Roll 5')." *Journal of Ancient Near Eastern Religions* 7 (2): 113–120.
Schniedewind, W. M. 1999. *Society and the Promise to David: The Reception History of 2 Samuel 7:1–17*. New York: Oxford University.
Schniedewind, W. M. 2000. "Orality and Literacy in Ancient Israel." *Religious Studies Review* 26 (4): 327–332.
Schniedewind, W. M. 2004. *How the Bible Became a Book: The Textualization of Ancient Israel*. Cambridge: Cambridge University.
Schniedewind, W. M. 2013. *A Social History of Hebrew: Its Origins Through the Rabbinic Period*. New Haven: Yale University.
Schniedewind, W. M. 2014. "Understanding Scribal Education in Ancient Israel: A View from Kuntillet 'Ajrud." *Maarav* 21: 271–293.
Schniedewind, W. M. 2017. "An Early Iron Age Phase to Kuntillet 'Ajrud?" In *Le-ma'an Ziony: Essays in Honor of Ziony Zevit*, edited by Greenspahn, F. E., Rendsburg, G. A., 134–146. Eugene: Wipf & Stock.
Schniedewind, W. M. Forthcoming. "'And Now': A Transition Particle in Epigraphic Hebrew." In *"Like 'Ilu Are You Wise": Studies in Northwest Semitic Languages and Literatures in Honor of Dennis G. Pardee*, edited by Hardy, H. H., Lam, J., Reymond, E. D. Chicago: Oriental Institute, University of Chicago.
Schniedewind, W. M., Sivan, D. 1997. "The Elijah-Elisha Narratives: A Test Case for the Northern Dialect of Hebrew." *Jewish Quarterly Review* 87 (3): 303–337.
Scholnick, S. H. 1975. "Lawsuit Drama in the Book of Job." Brandeis University.
Scholnick, S. H. 1982. "The Meaning of *mišpat* in the Book of Job." *Journal of Biblical Literature* 101 (4): 521–529.
Scholnick, S. H. 1987. "Poetry in the Courtroom: Job 38–41." In *Directions in Biblical Hebrew Poetry*, edited by Follis, E. R., 185–204. Sheffield: JSOT Press.
Scholz, S., ed. 2013–2017. *Feminist Interpretation of the Hebrew Bible in Retrospect, Vol. I, Biblical Books; Vol II, Social Locations; Vol. III, Methods*. Sheffield: Sheffield Phoenix Press.
Schoors, A. 2013. *Ecclesiastes*. Leuven: Peeters.

Schottroff, L., Wacker, M., eds. 2012. *Feminist Biblical Interpretation: A Compendium of Critical Commentary on the Books of the Bible and Related Literature*. Grand Rapids: Eerdmans.

Schroer, S. 1983. "Zur Deutung der Hand unter der Grabinschrift von Chirbet el Qôm." *Ugarit-Forschungen* 15: 191–199.

Schroer, S. 1987. *In Israel gab es Bilder: Nachrichten von darstellender Kunst im Alten Testament*. Orbis biblicus et orientalis, Vol. 74. Freiburg: Universitätsverlag.

Schroer, S. 2005–2018. *Die Ikonographie Palästinas/Israels und der Alte Orient: eine Religionsgeschichte in Bildern*, Vols. 1–4. Fribourg/Basel: Academic Press Fribourg/ Schwabe Verlag.

Schüle, A. 2017. "Balaam from Deir Allā—A Peripheral Aramean?" In *Wandering Arameans: Arameans Outside Syria: Textual and Archaeological Perspectives*, edited by Berlejung, A., Maeir, A. M., Schüle, A., 69–80. Wiesbaden: Harrassowitz.

Schuller, E. M., Newsom, C. A. 2012. *The Hodayot (Thanksgiving Psalms)*. Atlanta: Society of Biblical Literature.

Schwartz, G. M. 1989. "The Origins of the Aramaeans in Syria and Northern Mesopotamia: Research Problems and Potential Strategies." In *To the Euphrates and Beyond: Archaeological Studies in Honour of Maurits N. Van Loon*, edited by Haex, O. M. C., Curvers, H. H., Akkermans, P. M. M. G., 275–291. Rotterdam: Balkema.

Schwartz, H. 2010. "Does God Have a Body? The Problem of Metaphor and Literal Language in Biblical Interpretation." In *Bodies, Embodiment, and Theology of the Hebrew Bible*, edited by Kamionkowski, S. T., Kim, W. 201–237. New York: T. & T. Clark.

Schwartz, J. H., Houghton, F. D., Bondioli, L., Macchiarelli, R. 2012. "Bones, Teeth and Estimating Age of Perinates: Carthaginian Infant Sacrifice Revisited." *Antiquity* 86: 738–745.

Schwarz, R. A. 1979. "Uncovering the Secret Vice: Toward an Anthropology of Clothing and Adornment." In *The Fabrics of Culture: The Anthropology of Clothing and Adornment*, edited by Cordwell, J. M., Schwarz, R. A., 23–45. The Hague: Mouton.

Schwemer, D. 2001. *Die Wettergottgestalten Mesopotamiens und Nordsyriens im Zeitalter der Keilschriftkulturen: Materialien und Studien nach den schriftlichen Quellen*. Wiesbaden: Harrassowitz.

Schwemer, D. 2007. "The Storm-Gods of the Ancient Near East: Summary, Synthesis, Recent Studies Part I." *Journal of Ancient Near Eastern Religions* 7 (2): 121–168.

Schwemer, D. 2008a. "The Storm-Gods of the Ancient Near East: Summary, Synthesis, Recent Studies Part II." *Journal of Ancient Near Eastern Religions* 8 (1): 1–44.

Schwemer, D. 2008b. "Fremde Götter in Ḫatti. Die hethitische Religion im Spannungsfeld von Synkretismus und Abgrenzung." In *Ḫattuša-Boğazköy das Hethiterreich im Spannungsfeld des Alten Orients*, edited by Wilhelm, G., 137–157. Wiesbaden: Harrassowitz.

Schwemer, D. 2016. "Quality Assurance Managers at Work: The Hittite Festival Tradition." In *Liturgie oder Literatur? Die Kultrituale der Hethiter im transkulturellen Vergleich*, edited by Müller, G. G. W., 1–29. Wiesbaden: Harrassowitz.

Schwemer, D. 2019. "Hittite Prayers to the Sun-God for Appeasing an Angry Personal God: A Critical Edition of CTH 372–374." https://www.academia.edu/21864375/ Hittite_Prayers_to_the_Sun-god_for_Appeasing_an_Angry_Personal_God_A_ Critical_Edition_of_CTH_372_74.

Scott, J., Simpson-Housley, P., eds. 1991. *Sacred Places and Profane Spaces: Essays in the Geographies of Judaism, Christianity, and Islam*. New York: Greenwood Press.

Scurlock, J. A., Beal, R. H., eds. 2013. *Creation and Chaos: A Reconsideration of Hermann Gunkel's Chaoskampf Hypothesis*. Winona Lake: Eisenbrauns.
Seeden, H. 1980. *The Standing Armed Figurines in the Levant*. Prähistorische Bronzefunde, Abteilung I, Vol. 1. Munich: C. H. Beck.
Seeden, H. 1982. "Peace Figurines from the Levant." In *Archéologie au Levant: Recueil à la mémoire de Roger Saidah*, edited by Yon, M., 107–121. Lyon: Maison de l'Orient.
Selms, A. van. 1954. *Marriage and Family Life in Ugaritic Literature*. London: Luzac.
Seow, C. L. 1984. "The Syro-Palestinian Context of Solomon's Dream." *Harvard Theological Review* 77 (2): 141–152.
Seow, C. L. 1985. "The Designation of the Ark in Priestly Theology." *Hebrew Annual Review* 8: 185–198.
Seow, C. L. 1989. *Myth, Drama, and the Politics of David's Dance*. Harvard Semitic Monographs, Vol. 44. Atlanta: Scholars Press.
Seow, C. L. 1992. "Ark of the Covenant." In *The Anchor Bible Dictionary*, edited by Freedman, D. N., Vol. 1, 386–393. New York: Doubleday.
Seow, C. L. 1997. *Ecclesiastes: A New Translation with Introduction and Commentary*. New York: Doubleday.
Seow, C. L. 2013. *Job 1–21: Interpretation and Commentary*. Grand Rapids: Eerdmans.
Sergi, O. 2019. "The Formation of Israelite Identity in the Central Canaanite Highlands in the Iron Age I–IIA." *Near Eastern Archaeology* 82 (1): 42–51.
Sergi, O., Oeming, M., de Hulster, I. J., eds. 2016. *In Search for Aram and Israel: Politics, Culture, and Identity*. Tübingen: Mohr Siebeck.
Shanks, H. 1997a. "The Biblical Minimalists: Expunging Ancient Israel's Past." *Bible Review* 13 (3): 32–39, 50–52.
Shanks, H. 1997b. "Face to Face but Not Eye to Eye: Biblical Minimalists Meet Their Challengers." *Biblical Archaeology Review* 23 (4): 26–42,66.
Shanks, H. 1997c. "Three Shekels for the Lord: Ancient Inscription Records Gift to Solomon's Temple." *Biblical Archaeology Review* 23 (6): 28–32.
Shanks, M., Tilley, C. Y. 1987. *Re-constructing Archaeology: Theory and Practice*. Cambridge: Cambridge University.
Shea, W. H. 1990. "The Khirbet el-Qom Tomb Inscription Again." *Vetus Testamentum* 40 (1): 110–116.
Shectman, S. 2009. *Women in the Pentateuch: A Feminist and Source-Critical Analysis*. Sheffield: Sheffield Phoenix Press.
Shedletsky, L., Levine, B. A. 1999. "The *mšr* of the Sons and Daughters of Ugarit (KTU$_2$ 1.40)." *Revue Biblique* 106 (3): 321–344.
Shiloh, Y. 1979. "Iron Age Sanctuaries and Cult Elements in Palestine." In *Symposia: Celebrating the Seventy-Fifth Anniversary of the Founding of the American Schools of Oriental Research (1900–1975)*, edited by Cross, F. M., 147–157. Cambridge: American Schools of Oriental Research.
Shiloh, Y. 1993. "Megiddo: The Iron Age." In *The New Encyclopedia of Archaeological Excavations in the Holy Land*, edited by Stern, E., Levinzon-Gilboa, A., Aviram, J., Vol. 3, 1012–1024. Jerusalem: Israel Exploration Society & Carta.
Shupak, N. 1989. "New Light on Shamgar ben 'Anath." *Biblica* 70 (4): 517–525.
Silberman, N. A. 1982. *Digging for God and Country: Exploration, Archeology, and the Secret Struggle for the Holy Land, 1799–1917*. New York: Knopf.
Simone, M. 2015. "On Fire: Preternatural and Hypostatic Fire in Ancient Israelite Religion." Johns Hopkins University.

Singer, I. 2002. *Hittite Prayers*. Writings from the Ancient World, Vol. 11. Atlanta: SBL Press.

Singer, I. 2007. "The Origins of the 'Canaanite' Myth of Elkunirša and Ašertu Reconsidered." In *Tabularia Hethaeorum: Hethitologische Beiträge: Silvin Košak zum 65.Geburtstag*, edited by Groddek, D., Zorman, M., 632–642. Wiesbaden: Harrassowitz.

Singer-Avitz, L. 2002. "The Iron Age Pottery Assemblages." *Tel Aviv* 29: 110–214.

Sivan, D. 2001. *A Grammar of the Ugaritic Language*. Leiden: Brill.

Ska, J. L. 2006. *Introduction to Reading the Pentateuch*. Winona Lake: Eisenbrauns.

Ska, J. L. 2009. *The Exegesis of the Pentateuch: Exegetical Studies and Basic Questions*. Forschungen zum Alten Testament, Vol. 66. Tübingen: Mohr Siebeck.

Smend, R. 1893. *Lehrbuch der alttestamentlichen Religionsgeschichte*. Freiburg: J. C. B. Mohr.

Smend, R. 1995. "William Robertson Smith and Julius Wellhausen." In *William Robertson Smith: Essays in Reassessment*, edited by Johnstone, W., 226–242. Sheffield: Sheffield Academic Press.

Smith, G. 1873. "The Chaldean Account of the Deluge." *Transactions of the Society of Biblical Archaeology* 2: 213–234.

Smith, J. Z. 1969. "The Glory, Jest and Riddle: James George Frazer and The Golden Bough." Yale University.

Smith, J. Z. 1978. *Map Is Not Territory: Studies in the History of Religions*. Chicago: University of Chicago.

Smith, J. Z. 1987a. "Dying and Rising Gods." In *The Encyclopedia of Religion*, edited by Eliade, M., Vol. 4, 521–527. New York: Macmillan.

Smith, J. Z. 1987b. *To Take Place: Toward Theory in Ritual*. Chicago: University of Chicago.

Smith, J. Z. 1993. *Map Is Not Territory: Studies in the History of Religions*. 2nd ed. Chicago: University of Chicago.

Smith, M. S. 1986. "Interpreting the Baal Cycle." *Ugarit-Forschungen* 18: 313–339.

Smith, M. S. 1988. "Divine Form and Size in Ugaritic and Pre-exilic Israelite Religion." *Zeitschrift für die alttestamentliche Wissenschaft* 100: 424–427.

Smith, M. S. 1990. *The Early History of God. Yahweh and the Other Deities in Ancient Israel*. San Francisco: Harper & Row.

Smith, M. S. 1994a. "Yahweh and the Other Deities in Ancient Israel: Observations on Old Problems and Recent Trends." In *Ein Gott allein? JHWH-Verehrung und biblischer Monotheismus im Kontext der israelitischen und altorientalische Religionsgeschichte*, edited by Dietrich, W., Klopfenstein, M. A., 197–234. Göttingen: Vandenhoeck & Ruprecht.

Smith, M. S. 1994b. *The Ugaritic Baal Cycle*. Leiden: Brill.

Smith, M. S. 1994c. "Mythology and Myth-Making in Ugaritic and Israelite Literatures." In *Ugarit and the Bible*, edited by Brooke, G. J., Curtis, A., Healey, J. F., 293–341. Münster: Ugarit-Verlag.

Smith, M. S. 1995. "The God Athtar in the Ancient Near East and His Place in KTU 1.6 I." In *Solving Riddles and Untying Knots: Biblical, Epigraphic, and Semitic Studies in Honor of Jonas C. Greenfield*, edited by Zevit, Z., Gitin, S., Sokoloff, M., 627–640. Winona Lake: Eisenbrauns.

Smith, M. S. 1996. Review of D. Edelman, ed., *The Triumph of Elohim: From Yahwisms to Judaisms*. *Jewish Quarterly Review* 86 (3): 504–507.

Smith, M. S. 1997. "The Baal Cycle." In *Ugaritic Narrative Poetry*, edited by Parker, S. B., 81–180. Writings from the Ancient World, Vol. 9. Atlanta: Scholars Press.

Smith, M. S. 2001a. *Untold Stories: The Bible and Ugaritic Studies in the Twentieth Century*. Peabody: Hendrickson.

Smith, M. S. 2001b. *The Origins of Biblical Monotheism: Israel's Polytheistic Background and the Ugaritic Texts*. Oxford: Oxford University.

Smith, M. S. 2002a. *The Early History of God: Yahweh and the Other Deities in Ancient Israel*. 2nd ed. San Francisco: Harper & Row.

Smith, M. S. 2002b. "Ugaritic Studies and Israelite Religion: A Retrospective View." *Near Eastern Archaeology* 65 (1): 17–29.

Smith, M. S. 2004. *The Memoirs of God: History, Memory, and the Experience of the Divine in Ancient Israel*. Minneapolis: Fortress.

Smith, M. S. 2006. *The Rituals and Myths of the Feast of the Goodly Gods of KTU/CAT 1.23: Royal Constructions of Opposition, Intersection, Integration, and Domination*. Leiden: Brill.

Smith, M. S. 2008. *God in Translation: Deities in Cross-Cultural Discourse in the Biblical World*. Forschungen zum Alten Testament, Vol. 57. Tübingen: Mohr Siebeck.

Smith, M. S. 2012. "Why Was 'Old Poetry' Used in Hebrew Narrative? Historical and Cultural Considerations About Judges 5." In *Puzzling Out the Past: Studies in the Northwest Semitic Languages and Literature in Honor of Bruce Zuckerman*, edited by Lundberg, M. J., Fine, S., Pitard, W. T., 197–212. Leiden: Brill.

Smith, M. S. 2014a. *Poetic Heroes: Literary Commemorations of Warriors and Warrior Culture in the Early Biblical World*. Grand Rapids: Eerdmans.

Smith, M. S. 2014b. "'Athtart in Late Bronze Age Syrian Texts." In *Transformation of a Goddess: Ishtar, Astarte, Aphrodite*, edited by Sugimoto, D. T., 33–85. Fribourg: Academic Press Fribourg.

Smith, M. S. 2016. *Where the Gods Are. Spatial Dimensions of Anthropomorphism in the Biblical World*. New Haven: Yale University.

Smith, M. S. 2017. "Yhwh's Original Character: Questions About an Unknown God." In *The Origins of Yahwism*, edited by van Oorschot, J., Witte, M., 23–44. Berlin: de Gruyter.

Smith, M. S., Parker, S. B., Greenstein, E. L., Lewis, T. J., Marcus, D. 1997. *Ugaritic Narrative Poetry*, edited by Parker, S. B. Writings from the Ancient World, Vol. 9. Atlanta: Scholars.

Smith, M. S., Pitard, W. T. 2009. *The Ugaritic Baal Cycle, Volume II, Introduction with Text, Translation and Commentary of KTU/CAT 1.3–1.4*. Leiden: Brill.

Smith, P., Avishai, G., Greene, J. A., Stager, L. E. 2011. "Aging Cremated Infants: The Problem of Sacrifice at the Tophet of Carthage." *Antiquity* 85: 859–874.

Smoak, J. D. 2015. *The Priestly Blessing in Inscription and Scripture: The Early History of Numbers 6:24–26*. New York: Oxford University.

Smoak, J. D., Schniedewind, W. 2019. "Religion at Kuntillet ʿAjrud." *Religions* 10 (3): 211.

Snaith, N. H. 1965. "*ym-swp*: The Sea of Reeds: The Red Sea." *Vetus Testamentum* 15 (3): 395–398.

Soden, W. von. 1965. "Jahwe 'Er ist, Er erweist sich.'" *Die Welt des Orients* 3: 177–187.

Soggin, J. A. 1972. *Joshua: A Commentary*. Philadelphia: Westminster.

Soggin, J. A. 1981. *Judges: A Commentary*. Philadelphia: Westminster.

Soggin, J. A. 1993. "Levites." In *The Oxford Companion to the Bible*, edited by Metzger, B., Coogan, M. D., 434–435. Oxford: Oxford University.

Soja, E. W. 1989. *Postmodern Geographies: The Reassertion of Space in Critical Social Theory*. London: Verso.

Soja, E. W. 1996. *Thirdspace: Journeys to Los Angeles and Other Real-and-Imagined Places.* Cambridge: Blackwell.

Sokoloff, M. 1999. "The Old Aramaic Inscription from Bukan: A Revised Interpretation." *Israel Exploration Journal* 49: 105–115.

Soldt, W. H. 1989. "ʾAtn Prln, ʿAttā/ēnu the Diviner.'" *Ugarit-Forschungen* 21: 365–368.

Sommer, B. D. 2001. "Conflicting Constructions of Divine Presence in the Priestly Tabernacle." *Biblical Interpretation* 9 (1): 41–63.

Sommer, B. D. 2009. *The Bodies of God and the World of Ancient Israel.* Cambridge: Cambridge University.

Sommer, B. D. 2011. "Dating Pentateuchal Texts and the Perils of Pseudo-Historicism." In *The Pentateuch: International Perspectives on Current Research*, edited by Dozeman, T. B., Schmid, K., Schwartz, B. J., 85–108. Tübingen: Mohr Siebeck.

Sommer, B. D. 2017. "Kaufmann and Recent Scholarship: Toward a Richer Discourse of Monotheism." In *Yehezkel Kaufmann and the Reinvention of Jewish Biblical Scholarship*, edited by Jindo, J. Y., Sommer, B. D., Staubli, T., 204–239. Fribourg: Academic Press Fribourg.

Sparks, K. L. 1998. *Ethnicity and Identity in Ancient Israel: Prolegomena to the Study of Ethnic Sentiments and Their Expression in the Hebrew Bible.* Winona Lake: Eisenbrauns.

Sparks, K. L. 2002. *The Pentateuch: An Annotated Bibliography.* Grand Rapids: Baker.

Speiser, E. A. 1964. *Genesis.* Garden City: Doubleday.

Sperling, S. D. 1982. "An Arslan Tash Incantation: Interpretations and Implications." *Hebrew Union College Annual* 53: 1–10.

Stackert, J. 2007. *Rewriting the Torah: Literary Revision in Deuteronomy and the Holiness Legislation.* Forschungen zum Alten Testament, Vol. 52. Tübingen: Mohr Siebeck.

Stackert, J. 2011. "The Cultic Status of the Levites in the Temple Scroll: Between History and Hermeneutics." In *Levites and Priests in Biblical History and Tradition*, edited by Leuchter, M., Hutton, J. M., 199–214. Atlanta: Society of Biblical Literature.

Stade, B. 1887. *Geschichte der Volkes Israel*, Vol. 1. Berlin: G. Grote.

Stadelmann, R. 1967. *Syrisch-palästinensische Gottheiten in Ägypten.* Probleme der Ägyptologie, Vol. 5. Leiden: Brill.

Stager, L. E. 1985a. "The Archaeology of the Family in Ancient Israel." *Bulletin of the American Schools of Oriental Research* 260: 1–35.

Stager, L. E. 1985b. "Merenptah, Israel and Sea Peoples: New Light on an Old Relief." *Eretz-Israel: Archaeological, Historical and Geographical Studies* (Nahman Avigad Volume) 18: 56*–64*.

Stager, L. E. 1988. "Archaeology, Ecology, and Social History: Background Themes to the Song of Deborah." In *Congress Volume: Jerusalem, 1986*, edited by Emerton, J. A., 229–232. Leiden: Brill.

Stager, L. E. 1998. "Forging an Identity: The Emergence of Ancient Israel." In *The Oxford History of the Biblical World*, edited by Coogan, M. D., 123–173. New York: Oxford University.

Stager, L. E. 1999. "The Fortress-Temple at Shechem and the 'House of El, Lord of the Covenant.'" In *Realia Dei: Essays in Archaeology and Biblical Interpretation in Honor of Edward F. Campbell, Jr. at His Retirement*, edited by Williams, P. H., Hiebert, T., 228–249. Atlanta: Scholars Press.

Stager, L. E. 2000. "Jerusalem as Eden." *Biblical Archaeology Review*: 36–47.

Stager, L. E. 2003. "The Shechem Temple—Where Abimelech Massacred a Thousand." *Biblical Archaeology Review* 29 (4): 265–66–69.

Stager, L. E. 2008. "The Canaanite Silver Calf." In *Ashkelon 1: Introduction and Overview (1985-2006)*, edited by Stager, L. E., Schloen, J. D., Master, D. M., 577-580. Winona Lake: Eisenbrauns.

Stager, L. E., Wolff, S. R. 1981. "Production and Commerce in Temple Courtyards: An Olive Press in the Sacred Precinct at Tel Dan." *Bulletin of the American Schools of Oriental Research* 243: 95-102.

Stamm, J. J. 1939. *Die akkadische Namengebung*. Leipzig: J. C. Hinrichs.

Stanton, E. C. 1895-1902. *The Woman's Bible*. Boston: Northeastern University.

Stavrakopoulou, F. 2004. *King Manasseh and Child Sacrifice: Biblical Distortions of Historical Realities*. Berlin: de Gruyter.

Stavrakopoulou, F., Barton, J., eds. 2010. *Religious Diversity in Ancient Israel and Judah*. London: T. & T. Clark.

Steck, O. H. 1991. *Studien zu Tritojesaja*. Berlin: de Gruyter.

Stein, B. 1939. *Der Begriff Kebod Jahweh und seine Bedeutung für die alttestamentliche Gotteserkenntnis*. Emsdetten i. Westf.: H. & J. Lechte.

Steiner, R. C. 1992. "Northwest Semitic Incantations in an Egyptian Medical Papyrus of the Fourteenth Century B.C.E." *Journal of Near Eastern Studies* 51 (3): 191-200.

Steiner, R. C. 1996. "*Dāt* and *'ên*: Two Verbs Masquerading as Nouns in Moses' Blessing (Deuteronomy 33:2, 28)." *Journal of Biblical Literature* 115 (4): 693-698.

Steiner, R. C. 1997a. "The Aramaic Text in Demotic Script." In *The Context of Scripture 1: Canonical Compositions from the Biblical World*, edited by Hallo, W. W., Younger, K. L., 309-327. Leiden: Brill.

Steiner, R. C. 1997b. "The London Medical Papyrus." In *The Context of Scripture 1: Canonical Compositions from the Biblical World*, edited by Hallo, W. W., Younger, K. L., 328-329. Leiden: Brill.

Steiner, R. C. 2011. *Early Northwest Semitic Serpent Spells in the Pyramid Texts*. Harvard Semitic Studies, Vol. 61. Winona Lake: Eisenbrauns.

Steiner, R. C., Leiman, S. Z. 2009. "The Lost Meaning of Deuteronomy 33:2 as Preserved in the Palestinian Targum to the Decalogue." In *Mishneh Todah: Studies in Deuteronomy and Its Cultural Environment in Honor of Jeffrey H. Tigay*, edited by Fox, N. S., Glatt-Gilad, D. A., Williams, M. J., 157-166. Winona Lake: Eisenbrauns.

Steiner, R. C., Nims, C. F. 2017. "The Aramaic Text in Demotic Script: Text, Translation, and Notes." https://www.academia.edu/31662776/The_Aramaic_Text_in_Demotic_Script_Text_Translation_and_Notes.

Stephens, F. J. 1969. "Hymn to the Moon God." In *Ancient Near Eastern Texts Relating to the Old Testament*, edited by Pritchard, J. B., 385-386. Princeton: Princeton University.

Stern, P. D. 1991. *The Biblical Herem: A Window on Israel's Religious Experience*. Atlanta: Scholars Press.

Stockton, E. D. 1972. "Sacred Pillars in the Bible." *Australian Bible Review* 20: 16-32.

Stökl, J. 2012. *Prophecy in the Ancient Near East: A Philological and Sociological Comparison*. Leiden: Brill.

Stökl, J. 2015a. "Schoolboy Ezekiel: Remarks on the Transmission of Learning." *Die Welt des Orients* 45: 50-61.

Stökl, J. 2015b. "A Youth Without Blemish, Handsome, Proficient in All Wisdom, Knowledgeable and Intelligent: Ezekiel's Access to Babylonian Culture." In *Exile and Return: The Babylonian Context*, edited by Stökl, J., Waerzeggars, C., 223-252. Berlin: de Gruyter.

Stolz, F. 1980. "Monotheismus in Israel." In *Monotheismus im alten Israel und seiner Umwelt*, edited by Keel, O., 143–189. Fribourg: Verlag Schweizerisches Katholisches Bibelwerk.
Strauss, H. 1999. "Juridisches im Buch Hiob." *Recht und Ethos im Alten Testament—Gestalt und Wirkung: Festschrift für Horst Seebass zum 65. Geburtstag*, edited by Beyerle, S., Mayer, G., Strauss, H., 83–89. Neukirchen-Vluyn: Neukirchener.
Strawn, B. A. 2002. "*Wenilā(h)*, 'O Victorious One,' in Psalm 68:10." *Ugarit-Forschungen* 34: 785–798.
Strawn, B. A. 2005. *What Is Stronger than a Lion? Leonine Image and Metaphor in the Hebrew Bible and the Ancient Near East*. Fribourg: Academic Press.
Strawn, B. A. 2009. "Yahweh's Outstretched Arm Revisited Iconographically." In *Iconography and Biblical Studies*, edited by de Hulster, I. J., Schmitt, R., 163–211. Münster: Ugarit-Verlag.
Streck, M. P. 2000. *Das amurritische Onomastikon der altbabylonischen Zeit*. Alter Orient und Altes Testament, Vol. 271. Münster: Ugarit-Verlag.
Strine, C. A. 2014. "Ezekiel's Image Problem: The Mesopotamian Cult Statue Induction Ritual and the Imago Dei: Anthropology in the Book of Ezekiel." *Catholic Biblical Quarterly* 76 (2): 252–272.
Struble, E. J., Herrmann, V. R. 2009. "An Eternal Feast at Sam'al: The New Iron Age Mortuary Stele from Zincirli in Context." *Bulletin of the American Schools of Oriental Research* 356: 15–49.
Stuart, D. K. 1987. *Hosea-Jonah*. Waco: Word Books.
Sugimoto, D. T., ed. 2014. *Transformation of a Goddess: Ishtar, Astarte, Aphrodite*. Orbis biblicus et orientalis, Vol. 263. Fribourg: Academic Press Fribourg.
Suriano, M. J. 2013. "Tetragrammaton." In *Encyclopedia of Hebrew Language and Linguistics*, edited by Khan, G., Vol. 3, 751–755. Leiden: Brill.
Suriano, M. J. 2014. "Breaking Bread with the Dead: Katumuwa's Stele, Hosea 9:4, and the Early History of the Soul." *Journal of the American Oriental Society* 134 (3): 385–405.
Suriano, M. J. 2018. *A History of Death in the Hebrew Bible*. New York: Oxford University.
Süssenbach, C. 2005. *Der elohistische Psalter: Untersuchungen zur Komposition und Theologie von Ps 42–83*. Tübingen: Mohr Siebeck.
Sweeney, M. A. 2001. *King Josiah: The Lost Messiah of Israel*. Oxford: Oxford University.
Sweeney, M. A. 2007. *I and II Kings*. Louisville: Westminster John Knox.
Sweeney, M. A., Ben Zvi, E., eds. 2003. *The Changing Face of Form Criticism for the Twenty-First Century*. Grand Rapids: Eerdmans.
Tadmor, H. 1961. "Azriyau of Yaudi." In *Studies in the Bible: Scripta Hierosolymitana 8*, edited by Rabin, C., 232–271. Jerusalem: Magnes Press.
Taggar-Cohen, A. 2015. "Between Herem, Ownership, and Ritual: Biblical and Hittite Perspectives." In *Current Issues in Priestly and Related Literature: The Legacy of Jacob Milgrom and Beyond*, edited by Gane, R., Taggar-Cohen, A., 419–434. Atlanta: SBL Press.
Tainter, J. A. 1977. "Modeling Change in Prehistoric Social Systems." In *For Theory Building in Archaeology*, edited by Binford, L. R., 327–352. New York: Academic Press.
Tallqvist, K. L. 1906. *Neubabylonisches Namenbuch zu den Geschäftsurkunden aus der Zeit des Šamaššumukin bis Xerxes*. Helsingfors: Finnish Society of Sciences and Letters.
Tallqvist, K. L. 1966. *Assyrian Personal Names*. Hildesheim: Georg Olms.
Talmon, S. 1978a. "*Har*." In *Theological Dictionary of the Old Testament*, Vol. III, edited by Botterweck, G. J., Ringgren, H., 427–447. Grand Rapids: Eerdmans.

Talmon, S. 1978b. "The 'Comparative Method' in Biblical Interpretation: Principles and Problems." In *Congress Volume: Göttingen, 1977*, edited by Emerton, J. A., 320–356. Leiden: Brill.
Tappy, R. E. 1992. *The Archaeology of Israelite Samaria, Vol. 1, Early Iron Age Through the Ninth Century BCE*. Atlanta: Scholars Press.
Tappy, R. E. 2001. *The Archaeology of Israelite Samaria, Vol. 2, The Eighth Century BCE*. Winona Lake: Eisenbrauns.
Tappy, R. E., McCarter, P. K., eds. 2008. *Literate Culture and Tenth-Century Canaan: The Tel Zayit Abecedary in Context*. Winona Lake: Eisenbrauns.
Tappy, R. E., McCarter, P. K., Lundberg, M. J., Zuckerman, B. 2006. "An Abecedary of the Mid-Tenth Century B.C.E. from the Judaean Shephelah." *Bulletin of the American Schools of Oriental Research* 344: 5–46.
Tarragon, J. de. 1980. *Le Culte à Ugarit: d'après les textes de la pratique en cunéiformes alphabétiques*. Paris: J. Gabalda.
Tasker, D. R. 2004. *Ancient Near Eastern Literature and the Hebrew Scriptures About the Fatherhood of God*. New York: P. Lang.
Tasker, D. R. 2008. "Divine Fatherhood: Re-Examining the Paradigm." *Journal of Asia Adventist Seminary* 11 (2): 109–127.
Tate, M. E. 1990. *Psalms 51–100*. Dallas: Word.
Tate, M. E. 2000. *Psalms 51–100*. Waco: Word.
Tawil, H. 1976. "Hebrew ṣlḥ/hṣlḥ, Akkadian ešēru/šūšuru: A Lexicographical Note." *Journal of Biblical Literature* 95 (3): 405–413.
Taylor, J. G. 1988. "The Two Earliest Known Representations of Yahweh." In *Ascribe to the Lord: Biblical and Other Studies in Memory of Peter C. Craigie*, edited by Eslinger, L. M., Taylor, J. G., 557–566. Sheffield: JSOT Press.
Taylor, J. G. 1993. *Yahweh and the Sun: Biblical and Archaeological Evidence for Sun Worship in Ancient Israel*. Sheffield: JSOT Press.
Taylor, J. G. 1994. "Was Yahweh Worshipped as the Sun?" *Biblical Archaeology Review* 20 (3): 91.
Tazawa, K. 2009. *Syro-Palestinian Deities in New Kingdom Egypt: The Hermeneutics of Their Existence*. Oxford: British Archaeological Reports.
Tazawa, K. 2014. "Astarte in New Kingdom Egypt: Reconsideration of Her Role and Function." In *Transformation of a Goddess: Ishtar—Astarte—Aphrodite*, edited by Sugimoto, D. T., 103–123. Fribourg: Academic Press Fribourg.
Teixidor, J. 1983. "Les tablettes d'Arslan Tash au Musée d'Alep." *Aula Orientalis* 1: 105–108.
Tellenbach, H. 1976. *Das Vaterbild in Mythos und Geschichte: Ägypten, Griechenland, Altes Testament, Neues Testament*. Stuttgart: Kohlhammer.
Testen, D. 1994. "The I-w Verbal Class and the Reconstruction of the Early Semitic Preradical Vocalism." *Journal of the American Oriental Society* 114 (3): 426–434.
Thames, J. T. 2016. "Ritual Revision and the Influence of Empire: The Politics of Change in the *Zukru* Festival of Late Bronze Age Emar." Johns Hopkins University.
Thareani, Y. 2016. "Enemy at the Gates? The Archaeological Visiblity of the Aramaeans at Dan." In *In Search for Aram and Israel: Politics, Culture, and Identity*, edited by Sergi, O., Oeming, M., de Hulster, I. J., 169–197. Tübingen: Mohr Siebeck.
Thiessen, M. 2004. "The Form and Function of the Song of Moses (Deuteronomy 32:1–43)." *Journal of Biblical Literature* 123 (3): 401–424.
Thomas, C. N. 2014. "Reconceiving the House of the Father: Royal Women at Ugarit." Harvard University.

Thomas, R. 2019. "The God Gad." *Journal of the American Oriental Society* 139 (2): 307–316.
Thompson, H. O. 1992. "Yahweh." In *The Anchor Bible Dictionary*, edited by Freedman, D. N., Vol. 6, 1011–1012. New York: Doubleday.
Thompson, S. 1965. "Myths and Folktales." In *Myth: A Symposium*, edited by Sebeok, T. A., 169–180. Bloomington: Indiana University.
Thompson, T. L. 1974. *The Historicity of the Patriarchal Narratives: The Quest for the Historical Abraham*. Berlin: de Gruyter.
Thompson, T. L. 1992. *Early History of the Israelite People from the Written and Archaeological Sources*. Leiden: Brill.
Thompson, T. L. 1995. "How Yahweh Became God: Exodus 3 and 6 and the Heart of the Pentateuch." *Journal for the Study of the Old Testament* 68: 57–74.
Thompson, T. L. 1999. *The Mythic Past: Biblical Archaeology and the Myth of Israel*. New York: Basic Books.
Tiele, C. P. 1872. *Vergelijkende Geschiedenis van der Egyptische en Mesopotamische Godsdiensten*. Amsterdam: Van Kampen.
Tigay, J. H. 1982. *The Evolution of the Gilgamesh Epic*. Philadelphia: University of Pennsylvania.
Tigay, J. H. 1986. *You Shall Have No Other Gods: Israelite Religion in the Light of Hebrew Inscriptions*. Harvard Semitic Studies, Vol. 31. Atlanta: Scholars Press.
Tigay, J. H. 1987. "Israelite Religion: The Onomastic Evidence." In *Ancient Israelite Religion: Essays in Honor of Frank Moore Cross*, edited by Miller, P. D., Hanson, P. D., McBride, S. D., 157–194. Philadelphia: Fortress.
Tigay, J. H. 1996. *Deuteronomy = Devarim: The Traditional Hebrew Text with the New JPS Translation*. Philadelphia: Jewish Publication Society.
Tilley, C., ed. 1993. *Interpretive Archaeology*. Berg: Providence.
Toews, W. I. 1993. *Monarchy and Religious Institution in Israel under Jeroboam I*. Atlanta: Scholars Press.
van der Toorn, K. 1985. *Sin and Sanction in Israel and Mesopotamia: A Comparative Study*. Assen: Van Gorcum.
van der Toorn, K. 1986. "Herem-Bethel and Elephantine Oath Procedure." *Zeitschrift für die alttestamentliche Wissenschaft* 98 (2): 282–285.
van der Toorn, K. 1989. "Female Prostitution in Payment of Vows in Ancient Israel." *Journal of Biblical Literature* 108: 193–205.
van der Toorn, K. 1991a. "Funerary Rituals and Beatific Afterlife in Ugaritic Texts and in the Bible." *Bibliotheca Orientalis* 48: 40–66.
van der Toorn, K. 1991b. "The Babylonian New Year Festival: New Insights from the Cuneiform Texts and Their Bearing on Old Testament Study." In *Congress Volume: Leuven, 1989*, edited by Emerton, J. A., 331–344. Leiden: Brill.
van der Toorn, K. 1992a. "Anat-Yahu, Some Other Deities, and the Jews of Elephantine." *Numen* 39 (1): 80–101.
van der Toorn, K. 1992b. "Cultic Prostitution." In *The Anchor Bible Dictionary*, edited by Freedman, D. N., Vol. 5, 510–513. New York: Doubleday.
van der Toorn, K. 1993. "Ilib and the 'God of the Father.'" *Ugarit-Forschungen* 25: 379–387.
van der Toorn, K. 1995. "Ritual Resistance and Self-assertion: The Rechabites in Early Israelite Religion." In *Pluralism and Identity: Studies in Ritual Behaviour*, edited by Platvoet, J., van der Toorn, K., 229–259. Leiden: Brill.

van der Toorn, K. 1996a. "Ancestors and Anthroponyms: Kinship Terms as Theophoric Elements in Hebrew Names." *Zeitschrift für die alttestamentliche Wissenschaft* 108 (1): 1–11.
van der Toorn, K. 1996b. *Family Religion in Babylonia, Syria, and Israel: Continuity and Changes in the Forms of Religious Life*. Leiden: Brill.
van der Toorn, K. 1997b. "The Iconic Book: Analogies Between the Babylonian Cults of Images and the Veneration of the Torah." In *The Image and the Book: Iconic Cults, Aniconism, and the Rise of Book Religion in Israel and the Ancient Near East*, edited by van der Toorn, K., 229–248. Leuven: Peeters.
van der Toorn, K. 1999a. "God (I)." In *Dictionary of Deities and Demons in the Bible*, edited by van der Toorn, K., Becking, B., van der Horst, P. W., 352–365. 2nd ed. Leiden: Brill.
van der Toorn, K. 1999b. "Yahweh." In *Dictionary of Deities and Demons in the Bible*, edited by van der Toorn, K., Becking, B., van der Horst, P. W., 910–919. 2nd ed. Leiden: Brill.
van der Toorn, K. 2000. "Mesopotamian Prophecy Between Immanence and Transcendence: A Comparison of Old Babylonian and Neo-Assyrian Prophecy." In *Prophecy in Its Ancient Near Eastern Context: Mesopotamian, Biblical, and Arabian Perspectives*, edited by Nissinen, M., 71–87. Atlanta: Society of Biblical Literature.
van der Toorn, K. 2002. "Israelite Figurines: A View from the Texts." In *Sacred Time, Sacred Place: Archaeology and the Religion of Israel*, edited by Gittlen, B. M., 45–62. Winona Lake: Eisenbrauns.
van der Toorn, K. 2007. *Scribal Culture and the Making of the Hebrew Bible*. Cambridge: Harvard University.
van der Toorn, K. 2008. "Family Religion in Second Millennium West Asia (Mesopotamia, Emar, Nuzi)." In *Household and Family Religion in Antiquity*, edited by Bodel, J. P., Olyan, S. M., 20–36. Malden: Blackwell.
van der Toorn, K. 2018a. *Papyrus Amherst 63*. Münster: Ugarit-Verlag.
van der Toorn, K. 2018b. *God in Context: Selected Essays on Society and Religion in the Early Middle East*. Tübingen: Mohr Siebeck.
van der Toorn, K. 2019. *Becoming Diaspora Jews. Behind the Story of Elephantine*. New Haven: Yale University.
van der Toorn, K., ed. 1997a. *The Image and the Book: Iconic Cults, Aniconism, and the Rise of Book Religion in Israel and the Ancient Near East*. Leuven: Peeters.
van der Toorn, K., Becking, B., van der Horst, P. W., eds. 1995. *Dictionary of Deities and Demons in the Bible*. Leiden: Brill.
van der Toorn, K., Becking, B., van der Horst, P. W., eds. 1999. *Dictionary of Deities and Demons in the Bible*. 2nd ed. Leiden: Brill.
Tournay, R. J. 1959. "Le Psaume 68 et le livre des Juges." *Revue Biblique* 66: 358–368.
Tov, E. 1992. *Textual Criticism of the Hebrew Bible*. Minneapolis: Fortress.
Treves, M. 1988. *The Dates of the Psalms: History and Poetry in Ancient Israel*. Pisa: Giardini.
Trible, P. 1978. *God and the Rhetoric of Sexuality*. Overtures to Biblical Theology. Philadelphia: Fortress.
Trible, P. 1984. *Texts of Terror: Literary-feminist Readings of Biblical Narratives*. Philadelphia: Fortress.
Tropper, J. 1994. "Is Ugaritic a Canaanite Language?" In *Ugarit and the Bible*, edited by Brooke, G. J., 343–353. Münster: Ugarit-Verlag.

Tropper, J. 2000. *Ugaritische Grammatik*. Münster: Ugarit-Verlag.
Tropper, J. 2001. "Der Gottesname *Yahwa." *Vetus Testamentum* 51: 81–106.
Trotter, J. M. 2012. "Death of the 'lhym in Psalm 82." *Journal of Biblical Literature* 131 (2): 221–239.
Tsevat, M. 1992. "Was Samuel a Nazirite?" In *Shaʻarei Talmon: Studies in the Bible, Qumran, and the Ancient Near East Presented to Shemaryahu Talmon*, edited by Fishbane, M. A., Tov, E., 199–204. Winona Lake: Eisenbrauns.
Tsumura, D. T. 2007. *The First Book of Samuel*. Grand Rapids: Eerdmans.
Tubb, J. N. 1998. *Canaanites*. London: British Museum.
Tucker, G. M. 1971. *Form Criticism of the Old Testament*. Philadelphia: Fortress.
Tweed, T. A. 2006. *Crossing and Dwelling: A Theory of Religion*. Cambridge: Harvard University.
Uehlinger, C. 1993. "Northwest Semitic Inscribed Seals, Iconography and Syro-Palestinian Religions of Iron Age II: Some Afterthoughts and Conclusions." In *Studies in the Iconography of Northwest Semitic Inscribed Seals*, edited by Sass, B., Uehlinger, C., 257–288. Fribourg: University Press.
Uehlinger, C. 1996. "Israelite Aniconism in Context." *Biblica* 77: 540–549.
Uehlinger, C. 1997. "Anthropomorphic Cult Statuary in Iron Age Palestine and the Search for Yahweh's Cult Images." In *The Image and the Book: Iconic Cults, Aniconism, and the Rise of Book Religion in Israel and the Ancient Near East*, edited by van der Toorn, K., 97–155. Leuven: Peeters.
Uehlinger, C. 1998. "'... und wo sind die Götter von Samarien?' Die Wegführung syrisch-palästinischer Kultstatuen auf einem Relief Sargons II in Ḥorsābād/Dūr-Šarrukīn." In *"Und Mose schrieb dieses Lied auf": Studien zum Alten Testament und zum Alten Orient: Festschrift für Oswald Loretz zur Vollendung seines 70. Lebensjahres*, edited by Dietrich, M., Kottsieper, I., 739–776. Münster: Ugarit-Verlag.
Uehlinger, C. 2003. "Clio in a World of Pictures—Another Look at the Lachish Reliefs from Sennacherib's Southwest Palace at Nineveh." In *"Like a Bird in a Cage": The Invasion of Sennacherib in 701 BCE*, edited by Grabbe, L. L., 221–305. Sheffield: Sheffield Academic Press.
Uehlinger, C. 2006. "Arad, Qitmit—Judahite Aniconism vs. Edomite Iconic Cult? Questioning the Evidence." In *Text, Artifact, and Image: Revealing Ancient Israelite Religion*, edited by Beckman, G. M., Lewis, T. J., 80–112. Providence: Brown Judaic Studies.
Uehlinger, C., Trufaut, S. M. 2001. "Babylonian Cosmological Scholarship and Iconography: Attempts at Further Refinement." *Theologische Zeitschrift* 57: 140–171.
Ussishkin, D. 1988. "The Date of the Judaean Shrine at Arad." *Israel Exploration Journal* 38: 142–157.
Ussishkin, D. 2004. *The Renewed Archaeological Excavations at Lachish (1973–1994)*. Tel Aviv: Emery and Claire Yass Publications in Archaeology.
Utzschneider, H., Oswald, W. 2015. *Exodus 1–15*. Stuttgart: Kohlhammer.
Vall, G. 1995. "'From Whose Womb Did the Ice Come Forth?' Procreation Images in Job 38:28–29." *Catholic Biblical Quarterly* 57 (3): 504–513.
Van de Mieroop, M. 2004. *A History of the Ancient Near East, ca. 3000–323 BC*. Malden: Blackwell.
Van den Branden, A. 1990. "Les Dieux des Patriarches." *Bibbia e Oriente* 162: 27–53.
Van der Kooij, G. 1991. "Book and Script at Deir ʻAlla." In *The Balaam Text from Deir ʻAlla Re-Evaluated*, edited by Hoftijzer, J., Van der Kooij, G., 239–262. Leiden: Brill.
Van Seters, J. 1975. *Abraham in History and Tradition*. New Haven: Yale University.

Van Seters, J. 1983. *In Search of History: Historiography in the Ancient World and the Origins of Biblical History*. New Haven: Yale University.
Van Seters, J. 1992. *Prologue to History: The Yahwist as Historian in Genesis*. Louisville: Westminster John Knox.
Van Seters, J. 1994. *The Life of Moses: The Yahwist as Historian in Exodus-Numbers*. Louisville: Westminster John Knox.
Van Seters, J. 2003a. Review of S. Richter, *The Deuteronomistic History and the Name Theology: lĕšakkēn šĕmô šām in the Bible and the Ancient Near East*. *Journal of the American Oriental Society* 123.4 (4): 871–872.
Van Seters, J. 2003b. *A Law Book for the Diaspora: Revision in the Study of the Covenant Code*. Oxford: Oxford University.
Van Seters, J. 2013. *The Yahwist: A Historian of Israelite Origins*. Winona Lake: Eisenbrauns.
Van Zeist, W., Bakker-Heeres, J. 1985. "Archaeobotanical Studies in the Levant, 4. Bronze Age Sites on the North Syrian Euphrates." *Palaeohistoria* 27: 247–316.
Vanderhooft, D. S. 2014. "Ezekiel in and on Babylon." In *Bible et Proche-Orient, Mélanges André Lemaire III*, edited by Elayi, J., Durand, J., 99–119. Paris: Gabalda.
Vaughn, A. G. 1993. "*il ǵzr*—An Explicit Epithet of El as Hero/Warrior." *Ugarit-Forschungen* 25: 423–430.
Vaughn, A. G. 1999. *Theology, History, and Archaeology in the Chronicler's Account of Hezekiah*. Atlanta: Scholars Press.
Vaughn, A. G., Dobler, C. 2006. "A Provenance Study of Hebrew Seals and Seal Impressions: A Statistical Analysis." In *I Will Speak in Riddles of Ancient Times: Archaeological and Historical Studies in Honor of Amihai Mazar on the Occasion of His Sixtieth Birthday*, edited by Maeir, A. M., de Miroschedji, P., 757–774. Winona Lake: Eisenbrauns.
Vaux, R. de. 1961. *Ancient Israel: Its Life and Institutions*. New York: McGraw-Hill.
Vaux, R. de. 1970. "The Revelation of the Divine Name YHWH." In *Proclamation and Presence: Old Testament Essays in Honour of Gwynne Henton Davies*, edited by Durham, J. I., Porter, J. R., 48–75. London: SCM.
Vaux, R. de. 1978. *The Early History of Israel*. Philadelphia: Westminster.
Vawter, B. F. 1955. "The Canaanite Background of Genesis 49." *Catholic Biblical Quarterly* 17 (1): 1–18.
Vawter, B. F. 1980. "Prov 8:22: Wisdom and Creation." *Journal of Biblical Literature* 99 (2): 205–216.
Vawter, B. F. 1986. "Yahweh: Lord of the Heavens and the Earth." *Catholic Biblical Quarterly* 48 (3): 461–467.
Veijola, T. 1996. *Das Deuteronomium und siene Querbeziehungen*. Helsinki: Finnische Exegetische Gesellschaft in Helsinki.
Velde, H. te. 1999. "Bes." In *Dictionary of Deities and Demons in the Bible*, edited by van der Toorn, K., Becking, B., van der Horst, P. W., 173. 2nd ed. Leiden: Brill.
Vermeylen, J. 2007. *Jérusalem centre du monde: développements et contestations d'une tradition biblique*. Paris: Editions du Cerf.
Vern, R. 2011. *Dating Archaic Biblical Hebrew Poetry: A Critique of the Linguistic Arguments*. Piscataway: Gorgias Press.
Virolleaud, C. 1957. *Le Palais d'Ugarit publié sous la direction de Claude F.-A. Schaeffer*. Mission de Ras Shamra, Vol. II. Paris: Imprimerie Nationale.
Vita, J. P. 1999. "The Society of Ugarit." In *Handbook of Ugaritic Studies*, edited by Watson, W. G. E., Wyatt, N., 455–498. Leiden: Brill.

Vita, J. P. 2010. "Textile Terminology in the Ugaritic Texts." In *Textile Terminologies in the Ancient Near East and Mediterranean from the Third to the First Millennia BC*, edited by Michel, C., Nosch, M.-L., 323–337. Oxford: Oxbow Books.
Vleeming, S. P., Wesselius, J. W. 1984. "Betel the Saviour." *Jaarbericht . . . ex Oriente Lux* 28: 110–140.
Vleeming, S. P., Wesselius, J. W. 1985. *Studies in Papyrus Amherst 63: Essays on the Aramaic Texts in Aramaic-Demotic Papyrus Amherst 63*. Amsterdam: Juda Palache Instituut.
Wagenaar, J. A. 2005. *Origin and Transformation of the Ancient Israelite Festival Calendar*. Wiesbaden: Harrassowitz.
Wagner, A. 2010. *Gottes Körper: zur alttestamentlichen Vorstellung der Menschengestaltigkeit Gottes*. Gütersloh: Gütersloher Verlaghaus.
Wagner, A. 2014. *Göttliche Körper—Göttliche Gefühle: Was leisten anthropomorphe und anthropopathische Götterkonzepte im Alten Orient und im Alten Testament?* Freiburg: Academic Press.
Waldman, N. M. 1984. "A Note on Ezekiel 1:18." *Journal of Biblical Literature* 103 (4): 614–618.
Walker, C., Dick, M. B. 1999. "The Induction of the Cult Image in Ancient Mesopotamia: The Mesopotamia *mīs pî* Ritual." In *Born in Heaven, Made on Earth: The Making of the Cult Image in the Ancient Near East*, edited by Dick, M. B., 55–121. Winona Lake: Eisenbrauns.
Walker, C., Dick, M. B. 2001. *The Induction of the Cult Image in Ancient Mesopotamia: The Mesopotamian Mis Pî Ritual*. Helsinki: The Neo-Assyrian Text Corpus Project.
Walls, N. H. 1992. *The Goddess Anat in Ugaritic Myth*. Atlanta: Scholars Press.
Walls, N. H., ed. 2005. *Cult Image and Divine Representation in the Ancient Near East*. Boston: American Schools of Oriental Research.
Waltke, B. K. 2007. *A Commentary on Micah*. Grand Rapids: Eerdmans.
Waltke, B. K., O'Connor, M. P. 1990. *An Introduction to Biblical Hebrew Syntax*. Winona Lake: Eisenbrauns.
Walton, J. H. 2018. *Ancient Near Eastern Thought and the Old Testament: Introducing the Conceptual World of the Hebrew Bible*. Second Edition. Grand Rapids: Baker Academic.
Wanke, G. 1966. *Die Zionstheologie der Korachiten in ihrem traditionsgeschichtlichen Zusammenhang*. Berlin: Töpelmann.
Ward, W. A. 1969. "La déesse nourricière d'Ugarit." *Syria* 46: 225–239.
Ward, W. A. 1972. "The Shasu 'Bedouin': Notes on a Recent Publication." *Journal of the Economic and Social History of the Orient* 15 (1): 35–60.
Ward, W. A. 1974. "The Semitic Biconsonantal Root *SP* and the Common Origin of Egyptian *čwf* and Hebrew *sûp*: 'Marsh(-Plant).'" *Vetus Testamentum* 24 (3): 339–349.
Ward, W. A. 1992. "Shasu." In *The Anchor Bible Dictionary*, edited by Freedman, D. N., Vol. 5, 1165–1167. New York: Doubleday.
Wardlaw, T. R. 2016. *Elohim Within the Psalms: Petitioning the Creator to Order Chaos in Oral-derived Literature*. London: Bloomsbury T. & T. Clark.
Warmuth, G. 1978a. "Hādār." In *Theological Dictionary of the Old Testament*, edited by Botterweck, G. J., Ringgren, H., Vol. III, 335–341. Grand Rapids: Eerdmans.
Warmuth, G. 1978b. "Hôd." In *Theological Dictionary of the Old Testament*, edited by Botterweck, G. J., Ringgren, H., Vol. III, 352–356. Grand Rapids: Eerdmans.
Wason, P. K. 1994. *The Archaeology of Rank*. Cambridge: Cambridge University.
Waters, J. L. 2015. *Threshing Floors in Ancient Israel: Their Ritual and Symbolic Significance*. Minneapolis: Fortress.

Watson, W. G. E. 1999a. "Fire." In *Dictionary of Deities and Demons in the Bible*, edited by van der Toorn, K., Becking, B., van der Horst, P. W. 2nd ed., 331–332. Leiden: Brill.
Watson, W. G. E. 1999b. "Flame." In *Dictionary of Deities and Demons in the Bible*, edited by van der Toorn, K., Becking, B., van der Horst, P. W., 335–336. 2nd ed. Leiden: Brill.
Watson, W. G. E. 2013. "Terms Related to the Family in Ugaritic." *Historiae* 10: 17–50.
Watts, J. D. W. 1957. "The Song of the Sea: Ex. XV." *Vetus Testamentum* 7 (4): 371–380.
Watts, J. D. W. 1985. *Isaiah 1–33*. Waco: Word Books.
Watts, J. W. 1998. "The Legal Characterization of Moses in the Rhetoric of the Pentateuch." *Journal of Biblical Literature* 117 (3): 415–426.
Watts, J. W. 2013. *Leviticus 1–10*. Leuven: Peeters.
Weinfeld, M. 1972a. "The Worship of Molech and of the Queen of Heaven and Its Background." *Ugarit-Forschungen* 4: 133–154.
Weinfeld, M. 1972b. *Deuteronomy and the Deuteronomic School*. Oxford: Clarendon Press.
Weinfeld, M. 1977. "Judge and Officer in Ancient Israel and in the Ancient Near East." *Israel Oriental Studies* 7: 65–88.
Weinfeld, M. 1980. "Diary of Publications" [Hebrew]. *Shnaton* 4: 280–284.
Weinfeld, M. 1983. "Divine Intervention in War in Ancient Israel and in the Ancient Near East." In *History, Historiography, and Interpretation: Studies in Biblical and Cuneiform Literatures*, edited by Tadmor, H., Weinfeld, M., 121–147. Jerusalem: Magnes Press.
Weinfeld, M. 1984. "Kuntillet ʿAjrud Inscriptions and Their Significance." *Studi Epigrafici e Linguistici* 1: 121–130.
Weinfeld, M. 1987. "The Tribal League at Sinai." In *Ancient Israelite Religion: Essays in Honor of Frank Moore Cross*, edited by Miller, P. D., Hanson, P. D., McBride, S. D., 303–314. Philadelphia: Fortress.
Weinfeld, M. 1991. *Deuteronomy 1–11*. New York: Doubleday.
Weinfeld, M. 1992. *Deuteronomy and the Deuteronomic School*. 2nd ed. Winona Lake: Eisenbrauns.
Weinfeld, M. 1995a. "*Kābôd*." In *Theological Dictionary of the Old Testament*, edited by Botterweck, G. J., Ringgren, H., Fabry, H., Vol. VII, 22–38. Grand Rapids: Eerdmans.
Weinfeld, M. 1995b. *Social Justice in Ancient Israel and in the Ancient Near East*. Minneapolis/Jerusalem: Fortress/Magnes.
Weingreen, J. 1976. *From Bible to Mishna: The Continuity of Tradition*. Manchester: Manchester University.
Weippert, H. 1988. *Palästina in vorhellenistischer Zeit*. Munich: C. H. Beck.
Weippert, H., Weippert, M. 1982. "Die 'Bileam'-Inschrift von Tell Dēr 'Allā." *Zeitschrift des Deutschen Palästina-Vereins* 98: 77–103.
Weippert, M. 1961a. "Erwägungen zur Etymologie des Gottesnamens ʾĒl Šaddaj." *Zeitschrift der Deutschen Morgenländischen Gesellschaft* 111 (n.f. 36) (1): 42–62.
Weippert, M. 1961b. "Gott und Stier." *Zeitschrift des Deutschen Palästina-Vereins* 77: 93–103.
Weippert, M. 1971. *The Settlement of the Israelite Tribes in Palestine: A Critical Survey of Recent Scholarly Debate*. Naperville: Allenson.
Weippert, M. 1972. "Heiliger Krieg in Israel und Assyrien: kritische Anmerkungen zu Gerhard von Rads Konzept des Heiligen Krieges im alten Israel." *Zeitschrift für die alttestamentliche Wissenschaft* 84 (4): 460–493.
Weippert, M. 1974a. "Semitische Nomaden des zweiten Jahrtausends: Über die Š3św der ägyptischen Quellen." *Biblica* 55 (2): 265–280.

Weippert, M. 1974b. "Semitische Nomaden des zweiten Jahrtausends: Über die Š3św der ägyptischen Quellen." *Biblica* 55 (3): 427–433.
Weippert, M. 1984. "Šaddaj (Gottesname)." *Theologisches Handwörterbuch zum Alten Testament* 2: 874–881.
Weippert, M. 1991. "The Balaam Text from Deir ʿAlla and the Study of the Old Testament." In *The Balaam Text from Deir ʿAlla Re-Evaluated*, edited by Hoftijzer, J., Van der Kooij, G., 151–184. Leiden: Brill.
Wellhausen, J. 1887. *Reste arabischen Heidentums*. Berlin: G. Reimer.
Wellhausen, J. 1897. *Israelitische und jüdische Geschichte*. Berlin: de Gruyter.
Wellhausen, J. 1957. *Prolegomena to the History of Ancient Israel*. New York: Meridian.
Wellhausen, J. 1965. *Prolegomena to the History of Ancient Israel*. Cleveland: World Pub. Co. Originally published 1878.
Wells, B. 2005. "Law and Practice." In *A Companion to the Ancient Near East*, edited by Snell, D. C., 183–195. Malden: Blackwell.
Wenham, G. J. 1987. *Genesis 1–15*. Waco: Word Books.
Wenham, G. J. 1997. *Numbers*. Sheffield: Sheffield Academic Press.
Wente, E. F. 1990. *Letters from Ancient Egypt*. Writings from the Ancient World, Vol. 1. Atlanta: Scholars Press.
Westbrook, R. 1985. "Biblical and Cuneiform Law Codes." *Revue Biblique* 92: 247–265.
Westbrook, R. 1988. *Studies in Biblical and Cuneiform Law*. Paris: Gabalda.
Westbrook, R. 2009. "Biblical and Cuneiform Law Codes." In *Law from the Tigris to the Tiber: The Writings of Raymond Westbrook*, edited by Wells, B., Magdalene, F. R., 3–20. Winona Lake: Eisenbrauns.
Westbrook, R., ed. 2003. *A History of Ancient Near Eastern Law*. Leiden: Brill.
Westbrook, R., Lewis, T. J. 2008. "Who Led the Scapegoat in Leviticus 16:21?" *Journal of Biblical Literature* 127 (3): 417–422.
Westbrook, R., Wells, B. 2009. *Everyday Law in Biblical Israel: An Introduction*. Louisville: Westminster John Knox.
Westenholz, J. G. 1989. "Tamar, Qĕdēšā, Qadištu, and Sacred Prostitution in Mesopotamia." *Harvard Theological Review* 82 (3): 245–265.
Westenholz, J. G. 1990. "Towards a New Conceptualization of the Female Role in Mesopotamian Society." *Journal of the American Oriental Society* 110 (3): 510–521.
Westermann, C. 1969. *Isaiah 40–66*. Philadelphia: Westminster.
Westermann, C. 1979. *What Does the Old Testament Say About God?* Atlanta: John Knox.
Westermann, C. 1984. *Genesis 1–11*. Minneapolis: Augsburg.
Westermann, C. 1985. *Genesis 12–36*. Minneapolis: Augsburg.
Westermann, C. 1986. *Genesis 37–50*. Minneapolis: Augsburg.
Westermann, C. 1991. *Basic Forms of Prophetic Speech*. Philadelphia: Westminster John Knox.
White, E. 2014. *Yahweh's Council: Its Structure and Membership*. Tübingen: Mohr Siebeck.
White, M. 1990. "The Elohistic Depiction of Aaron: A Study in the Levite-Zadokite Controversy." In *Studies in the Pentateuch*, edited by Emerton, J. A., 149–159. Leiden: Brill.
Whitelam, K. W. 1979. *The Just King: Monarchical Judicial Authority in Ancient Israel*. Sheffield: University of Sheffield.
Whitelam, K. W. 1986. "Recreating the History of Israel." *Journal for the Study of the Old Testament* 35: 45–70.

Whitelam, K. W. 1996. *The Invention of Ancient Israel: The Silencing of Palestinian History*. London: Routledge.
Whitley, C. F. 1975. "Some Remarks on *lû* and *lo'*." *Zeitschrift für die alttestamentliche Wissenschaft* 87: 202–204.
Widdicombe, P. 2000. "Fatherhood and the Conception of God in Early Greek Christian Literature." *Anglican Theological Review* 82 (3): 519–536.
Wifall, W. R. 1980. "El Shaddai or El of the Fields." *Zeitschrift für die alttestamentliche Wissenschaft* 92 (1): 24–32.
Wiggerman, F. A. M. 1989. "Tišpak, His Seal, and the Dragon *Mušḫuššu*." In *To the Euphrates and Beyond: Archaeological Studies in Honour of Maurits N. Van Loon*, edited by Haex, O. M. C., Curvers, H. H., Akkermans, P. M. M. G., 117–133. Rotterdam: Balkema.
Wiggins, S. A. 1991. "The Myth of Asherah: Lion Lady and Serpent Goddess." *Ugarit-Forschungen* 23: 383–394.
Wiggins, S. A. 1993. *A Reassessment of 'Asherah': A Study According to the Textual Sources of the First Two Millennia B.C.E.* Kevelaer: Butzon & Bercker.
Wildberger, H. 1991. *Isaiah 1–12*. Minneapolis: Fortress.
Wildberger, H. 1997. *Isaiah 13–27*. Minneapolis: Fortress.
Wildberger, H. 2002. *Isaiah 28–39*. Minneapolis: Fortress.
Wildung, D. 1973. "Göttlichkeitsstufen des Pharaoh." *Orientalistische Literaturzeitung* 68: 549–565.
Wilhelm, G. 1995. "The Kingdom of Mitanni in the Second-Millennium Upper Mesopotamia." In *Civilizations of the Ancient Near East*, edited by Sasson, J. M., Baines, J., Beckman, G. M., Rubinson, K. S., Vol. II, 1243–1254. New York: Scribner's.
Willi, T. 1971. *Herders Beitrag zum Verstehen des Alten Testaments*. Tübingen: J. C. B. Mohr.
Williams-Forte, E. 1983. "The Snake and the Tree in the Iconography and Texts of Syria During the Bronze Age." In *Ancient Seals and the Bible*, edited by Gorelick, L., Williams-Forte, E., Vol. 2/1, 18–43. Malibu: Undena.
Williamson, H. G. M. 1982. *1 and 2 Chronicles*. Grand Rapids: Eerdmans.
Williamson, H. G. M. 1999. "'From One Degree of Glory to Another': Themes and Theology in Isaiah." In *In Search of True Wisdom: Essays in Old Testament Interpretation in Honour of Ronald E. Clements*, edited by Ball, E., 174–195. Sheffield: Sheffield Academic Press.
Williamson, H. G. M. 2001. "Isaiah and the Holy One of Israel." In *Biblical Hebrew, Biblical Texts: Essays in Memory of Michael P. Weitzman*, edited by Rapoport-Albert, A., Greenberg, G., 22–38. London: Sheffield Academic Press.
Williamson, H. G. M. 2004. "In Search of Pre-exilic Isaiah." In *In Search of Pre-Exilic Israel: Proceedings of the Oxford Old Testament Seminar*, edited by Day, J., 181–206. London: T. & T. Clark.
Williamson, H. G. M. 2005a. "Isaiah, Micah and Qumran." In *Semitic Studies in Honour of Edward Ullendorff*, edited by Khan, G., 203–211. Leiden: Brill.
Williamson, H. G. M. 2005b. "Temple and Worship in Isaiah 6." In *Temple and Worship in Biblical Israel*, edited by Day, J., 123–144. London: T. & T. Clark.
Williamson, H. G. M. 2006. *Isaiah 1–5: A Critical and Exegetical Commentary*. London: T. & T. Clark.
Williamson, H. G. M. 2007. "Temple and Worship in Isaiah 6." In *Temple and Worship in Biblical Israel*, edited by Day, J., 123–144. Revised ed. London: T. & T. Clark.

Willis, J. T. 1997. "Isaiah 2:2–5 and the Psalms of Zion." In *Writing and Reading the Scroll of Isaiah*, edited by Broyles, C. C., Evans, C. A., 295–316. Leiden: Brill.
Wilson, E. J. 1994. *"Holiness" and "Purity" in Mesopotamia*. Neukirchen-Vluyn: Neukirchener Verlag.
Wilson, E. O. 1998. *Consilience: The Unity of Knowledge*. New York: Knopf.
Wilson, G. H. 1985. *The Editing of the Hebrew Psalter*. Chico: Scholars Press.
Wilson, I. 1995. *Out of the Midst of the Fire: Divine Presence in Deuteronomy*. Atlanta: Scholars Press.
Wilson, J. A. 1969a. "Hymns to the Gods as a Single God." In *Ancient Near Eastern Texts Relating to the Old Testament*, edited by Pritchard, J. B., 371–372. Princeton: Princeton University.
Wilson, J. A. 1969b. "Astarte and the Tribute of the Sea." In *Ancient Near Eastern Texts Relating to the Old Testament*, edited by Pritchard, J. B., 17–18. Princeton: Princeton University.
Wilson, R. R. 1980. *Prophecy and Society in Ancient Israel*. Philadelphia: Fortress.
Wilson, R. R. 1983. "Israel's Judicial System in the Preexilic Period." *Jewish Quarterly Review* 74 (2): 229–248.
Wilson, V. 1975. "The Iconography of Bes with Particular Reference to the Cypriot Evidence." *Levant* 7 (1): 77–103.
Wilson-Wright, A. 2015. "Love Conquers All: Song of Songs 8:6b–7a as a Reflex of the Northwest Semitic Combat Myth." *Journal of Biblical Literature* 134 (2): 333–345.
Wilson-Wright, A. 2016. *Athtart: The Transmission and Transformation of a Goddess in the Late Bronze Age*. Forschungen zum Alten Testament. 2. Reihe, Vol. 90. Tübingen: Mohr Siebeck.
Winitzer, A. 2014. "Assyriology and Jewish Studies in Tel Aviv: Ezekiel Among the Babylonian Literati." In *Encounters by the Rivers of Babylon: Scholarly Conversations Between Jews, Iranians and Babylonians in Antiquity*, edited by Gabbay, U., Secunda, S., 163–216. Tübingen: Mohr Siebeck.
Winter, I. J. 1992. "'Idols of the King': Royal Images as Recipients of Ritual Actions in Ancient Mesopotamia." *Journal of Ritual Studies* 6: 13–42.
Winter, I. J. 1994. "Radiance as an Aesthetic Value in the Art of Mesopotamia (With Some Indian Parallels)." In *Art, the Integral Vision: A Volume of Essay in Felicitation of Kapila Vatsyayan*, edited by Saraswati, B. N., Malik, S. C., Khanna, M., 123–132. New Delhi: DK Printworld.
Winter, I. J. 2008. "Touched by the Gods: Visual Evidence for the Divine Status of Rulers in the Ancient Near East." In *Religion and Power: Divine Kingship in the Ancient World and Beyond*, edited by Brisch, N. M., 75–101. Chicago: Oriental Institute.
Winter, N. A. 1996. "The Terracottas." In *The Sanctuary of Apollo Hylates at Kourion: Excavations in the Archaic Precinct*, edited by Buitron-Oliver, D., 33. Göteborg: Paul Åströms förlag.
Winter, U. 1983. *Frau und Göttin: exegetische und ikonographische Studien zum weiblichen Gottesbild im Alten Israel und in dessen Umwelt*. Freiburg: Universitätsverlag.
Wiseman, D. J. 1958. "The Vassal-Treaties of Esarhaddon." *Iraq* 20: 1–99 + plates.
Wolff, H. W. 1974. *Hosea: A Commentary on the Book of the Prophet Hosea*. Philadelphia: Fortress.
Wolff, H. W. 1977. *Joel and Amos: A Commentary on the Books of the Prophets Joel and Amos*. Philadelphia: Fortress.
Wolff, H. W. 1990. *Micah: A Commentary*. Minneapolis: Augsburg.

Wood, A. 2008. *Of Wings and Wheels: A Synthetic Study of the Biblical Cherubim*. Beihefte zur Zeitschrift für die alttestamentliche Wissenschaft, Vol. 385. Berlin: de Gruyter.

Woudstra, M. H. 1965. *The Ark of the Covenant from Conquest to Kingship*. Philadelphia: Presbyterian and Reformed.

Wright, D. P. 1986. "The Gesture of Hand Placement in the Hebrew Bible and in Hittite Literature." *Journal of the American Oriental Society* 106: 433–446.

Wright, D. P. 1995. "David Autem Remansit in Hierusalem: Felix Coniunctio!" In *Pomegranates and Golden Bells: Studies in Biblical, Jewish, and Near Eastern Ritual, Law, and Literature in Honor of Jacob Milgrom*, edited by Wright, D. P., Freedman, D. N., Hurvitz, A., 215–230. Winona Lake: Eisenbrauns.

Wright, D. P. 2004. Review of John Van Seters, *A Law Book for the Diaspora: Revision in the Study of the Covenant Code*. *Journal of the American Oriental Society* 124: 129–131.

Wright, D. P., Freedman, D. N., Hurvitz, A., eds. 1995. *Pomegranates and Golden Bells. Studies in Biblical, Jewish, and Near Eastern Ritual, Law, and Literature in Honor of Jacob Milgrom*. Winona Lake: Eisenbrauns.

Wright, G. E. 1954. "The Levites in Deuteronomy." *Vetus Testamentum* 4 (3): 325–330.

Wright, G. E. 1962. "The Lawsuit of God: A Form-Critical Study of Deuteronomy 32." In *Israel's Prophetic Heritage: Essays in Honor of James Muilenburg*, edited by Anderson, B. W., Harrelson, W., 26–67. New York: Harper.

Wright, G. E. 1964. *Shechem: The Biography of a Biblical City*. New York: McGraw-Hill.

Wright, G. E. 1965. *Shechem: The Biography of a Biblical City*. 2nd ed. New York: McGraw-Hill.

Wright, G. R. H. 2002. *Shechem III: The Stratigraphy and Architecture of Shechem/Tell Balâtah, Vol. 2, The Illustrations*. Boston: American Schools of Oriental Research.

Wright, J. W. 2002. "A Tale of Three Cities: Urban Gates, Squares and Power in Iron Age II, Neo-Babylonian and Achaemenid Judah." In *Second Temple Studies III: Studies in Politics, Class and Material Culture*, edited by Halligan, J. M., Davies, P. R., 19–50. London: Sheffield Academic Press.

Würthwein, E. 1952. "Der Ursprung der prophetischen Gerichtsrede." *Zeitschrift für Theologie und Kirche* 49: 1–16.

Wyatt, N. 1978. "Problem of the 'God of the Fathers.'" *Zeitschrift für die alttestamentliche Wissenschaft* 90 (1): 101–104.

Wyatt, N. 1983. "The Stela of the Seated God from Ugarit." *Ugarit-Forschungen* 15: 271–277.

Wyatt, N. 1992. "Of Calves and Kings: The Canaanite Dimension in the Religion of Israel." *Scandinavian Journal of the Old Testament* 6 (1): 68–91.

Wyatt, N. 1994. "The Meaning of El Roi and the Mythological Dimensions in Genesis 16." *Scandinavian Journal of the Old Testament* 8: 141–151.

Wyatt, N. 1996. *Myths of Power: A Study of Royal Myth and Ideology in Ugaritic and Biblical Tradition*. Ugaritisch-biblische Literatur, Vol. 13. Münster: Ugarit-Verlag.

Wyatt, N. 1998. *Religious Texts from Ugarit: The Words of Ilimilku and His Colleagues*. London: Sheffield Academic Press.

Wyatt, N. 1999a. "Calf 'gl.'" In *Dictionary of Deities and Demons in the Bible*, edited by van der Toorn, K., Becking, B., van der Horst, P. W., 180–182. 2nd ed. Leiden: Brill.

Wyatt, N. 1999b. "The Religion of Ugarit: An Overview." In *Handbook of Ugaritic Studies*, edited by Watson, W. G. E., Wyatt, N., 529–585. Boston: Brill.

Wyatt, N. 1999c. "Asherah." In *Dictionary of Deities and Demons in the Bible*, edited by van der Toorn, K., Becking, B., van der Horst, P. W., 99–105. 2nd ed. Leiden: Brill.

Wyatt, N. 2005. *The Mythic Mind: Essays on Cosmology and Religion in Ugaritic and Old Testament Literature*. London: Equinox.

Xella, P., ed. 2012–2013. *The Tophet in the Phoenician Mediterranean*. Studi epigrafici e linguistici, Vol. 29–30. Verona: Essedue Edizioni.

Xella, P., Quinn, J., Melchiorri, V., van Dommelen, P. 2013. "Phoenician Bones of Contention." *Antiquity* 87: 1199–1207.

Yadin, Y. 1958. *Hazor I: An Account of the First Season of Excavations, 1955*. Jerusalem: Magnes Press.

Yadin, Y. 1961. *Hazor III–IV: An Account of the Third and Fourth Seasons of Excavations, 1957-1958*. Jerusalem: Magnes Press.

Yadin, Y. 1962. *The Scroll of the War of the Sons of Light Against the Sons of Darkness*. Oxford: Oxford University.

Yadin, Y. 1970. "Symbols of Deities at Zinjirli, Carthage and Hazor." In *Near Eastern Archaeology in the Twentieth Century*, edited by Sanders, J. A., 199–231. Garden City: Doubleday.

Yadin, Y. 1972. *Hazor: The Head of All Those Kingdoms (Joshua 11:10) with a Chapter on Israelite Megiddo*. London: Oxford University.

Yadin, Y. 1975. *Hazor: The Rediscovery of a Great Citadel of the Bible*. New York: Random House.

Yadin, Y., Naveh, J. 1989. "The Aramaic and Hebrew Ostraca and Jar Inscriptions." In *Masada I: The Yigael Yadin Excavations 1963-1965: Final Reports*, edited by Yadin, Y., Naveh, J., Meshorer, Y., 1–63, pls. 1–60. Jerusalem: Israel Exploration Society.

Yakubovich, I. 2010. "The West Semitic God El in Anatolian Hieroglyphic Transmission." In *Pax Hethitica: Studies on the Hittites and Their Neighbours in Honour of Itamar Singer*, edited by Cohen, Y., Gilan, A., Miller, J. L., 385–398. Wiesbaden: Harrassowitz.

Yakubovich, I. 2015. "Phoenician and Luwian in Early Iron Age Cilicia." *Anatolian Studies* 65: 35–55.

Yardeni, A. 1991. "Remarks on the Priestly Blessing on Two Ancient Amulets from Jerusalem." *Vetus Testamentum* 41 (2): 176–185.

Yasur-Landau, A., Ebeling, J. R., Mazow, L. B., eds. 2011. *Household Archaeology in Ancient Israel and Beyond*. Leiden: Brill.

Yeivin, S. 1959. "Ya'qob'el." *The Journal of Egyptian Archaeology* 45: 16–18.

Yon, M. 1991. "Stèles de pierre." In *Arts et industries de la pierre. Ras Shamra-Ougarit VI*, edited by Yon, M., Caubet, A., 273–344. Paris: Éditions Recherche sur les Civilisations.

Yon, M. 1992. "The End of the Kingdom of Ugarit." In *The Crisis Years: The 12th Century B.C. from Beyond the Danube to the Tigris*, edited by Ward, W. A., Joukowsky, M., 111–122. Dubuque: Kendall/Hunt.

Yon, M. 1993. "Statue de dieu El." In *Syrie, Mémoire et Civilisation*, edited by Cluzan, S., Delpont, E., Mouliérac, J., 224–225. Paris: Institut du monde arabe.

Yon, M. 1996. "The Temple of the Rhytons at Ugarit." In *Ugarit, Religion and Culture: Proceedings of the International Colloquium on Ugarit, Religion and Culture, Edinburgh, July 1994: Essays Presented in Honour of Professor John C. L. Gibson*, edited by Wyatt, N., Watson, W. G. E., Lloyd, J. B., 405–422. Münster: Ugarit-Verlag.

Yon, M. 1997. *La cité d'Ougarit sur le tell de Ras Shamra*. Paris: Éditions Recherche sur les civilisations.

Yon, M. 2004. *Kition dans les textes: testimonia littéraires et épigraphiques et corpus des inscriptions*. Paris: ADPF-Editions; Éditions Recherche sur les civilisations.

Yon, M. 2006. *The City of Ugarit at Tell Ras Shamra*. Winona Lake: Eisenbrauns.
Yon, M., Arnaud, D., eds. 2001. *Études ougaritiques: 1. Travaux, 1985–1995*. Ras Shamra-Ougarit XIV. Paris: Éditions Recherche sur les civilisations.
Yon, M., Caubet, A., eds. 1991. *Arts et industries de la pierre*. Ras Shamra–Ougarit VI. Paris: Éditions Recherche sur les civilisations.
Yon, M., Gachet, J. 1989. "Une statuette du dieu El à Ougarit." *Syria* 66 (1): 349.
Yonah, S., Greenstein, E. L., Gruber, M. I., Machinist, P., Paul, S. M., eds. 2015. *Marbeh Ḥokmah: Studies in the Bible and the Ancient Near East in Loving Memory of Victor Avigdor Hurowitz*. Winona Lake: Eisenbrauns.
Young, G. D. 1992. *Mari in Retrospect: Fifty Years of Mari and Mari Studies*. Winona Lake: Eisenbrauns.
Young, I. 2005. "Biblical Texts Cannot Be Dated Linguistically." *Hebrew Studies* 46: 341–351.
Young, I., Rezetko, R., Ehrensvärd, M. 2008. *Linguistic Dating of Biblical Texts*. London: Equinox.
Young, J. H., Young, S. H. 1955. *Terracotta Figurines from Kourion in Cyprus*. Philadelphia: University Museum, University of Pennsylvania.
Younger, K. L. 1998. "The Phoenician Inscription of Azatiwada: An Integrated Reading." *Journal of Semitic Studies* 43 (1): 11–47.
Younger, K. L. 2000a. "The Azatiwada Inscription." In *The Context of Scripture 2: Monumental Inscriptions from the Biblical World*, edited by Hallo, W. W., Younger, K. L., 148–150. Leiden: Brill.
Younger, K. L. 2000b. "Sargon II: The Annals." In *The Context of Scripture 2: Monumental Inscriptions from the Biblical World*, edited by Hallo, W. W., Younger, K. L., 293–294. Leiden: Brill.
Younger, K. L. 2016. *A Political History of the Arameans: From Their Origins to the End of Their Polities*. Atlanta: SBL Press.
Younger, K. L. 2019. "Gods at the Gates: A Study of the Identification of the Deities Represented at the Gates of Ancient Sam'al (Zincirli) with Possible Historical Implications." *ARAM Periodical* 31. 2: 317–348.
Younger, K. L., ed. 2017. *The Context of Scripture 4: Supplements*. Leiden: Brill.
Yun, I. A. 2008. "The Aramaic and Akkadian Bilingual Inscription from Tell Fekheriyeh and the Dialects of Old Aramaic." Johns Hopkins University.
Yurco, F. J. 1978. "Merenptah's Palestinian Campaign." *Journal of the Society for the Study of Egyptian Antiquities* 8: 70.
Yurco, F. J. 1986. "Merenptah's Canaanite Campaign." *Journal of the American Research Center in Egypt* 23: 189–215.
Yurco, F. J. 1990. "3,200-Year-Old Picture of the Israelites Found in Egypt." *Biblical Archaeology Review* 16 (5): 20–38.
Yurco, F. J. 1991. "Can You Name the Panel with the Israelites? Yurco's Response." *Biblical Archaeology Review* 17 (6): 61.
Yurco, F. J. 1997. "Merenptah's Canaanite Campaign and Israel's Origins." In *Exodus: The Egyptian Evidence*, edited by Frerichs, E. S., Lesko, L. H., 27–55. Winona Lake: Eisenbrauns.
Zaccagnini, C. 1994. "Feet of Clay at Emar and Elsewhere." *Orientalia* 63 (1): 1–4.
Zadok, R. 1988. *The Pre-Hellenistic Israelite Anthroponymy and Prosopography*. Orientalia Lovaniensia Analecta, Vol. 28. Leuven: Peeters.

Zadok, R. 1997. "Names and Naming." In *The Oxford Encyclopedia of Archaeology in the Near East*, edited by Meyers, E. M., Vol. 4, 91–96. New York: Oxford University.

Zamora, J. Á. 2007. "The Inscription from the First Year of King Bodashtart of Sidon's Reign: CIS I, 4." *Orientalia* 76 (1): 100–113.

Zauzich, K. 1985. "Der Gott des aramäisch-demotischen Papyrus Amherst 63." *Göttinger Miszellen* 85: 89–90.

Zevit, Z. 1977. "A Phoenician Inscription and Biblical Covenant Theology." *Israel Exploration Journal* 27 (2): 110–118.

Zevit, Z. 1984. "The Khirbet el-Qôm Inscription Mentioning a Goddess." *Bulletin of the American Schools of Oriental Research* 255: 39–47.

Zevit, Z. 1991. "Yahweh Worship and Worshippers in 8th-Century Syria." *Vetus Testamentum* 41 (3): 363–366.

Zevit, Z. 2001. *The Religions of Ancient Israel: A Synthesis of Parallactic Approaches*. New York: Continuum.

Zevit, Z. 2004. "The Prophet Versus Priest Antagonism Hypothesis: Its History and Origin." In *The Priests in the Prophets: The Portrayal of Priests, Prophets and Other Religious Specialists in the Latter Prophets*, edited by Grabbe, L. L., Bellis, A. O., 189–217. London: T. &. T. Clark.

Zevit, Z. 2006. "Israel's Royal Cult in the Ancient Near Eastern Kulturkreis." In *Text, Artifact, and Image: Revealing Ancient Israelite Religion*, edited by Beckman, G. M., Lewis, T. J., 189–200. Providence: Brown Judaic Studies.

Zevit, Z. 2012. "Mesha's *ryt* in the Context of Moabite and Israelite Bloodletting." In *Puzzling Out the Past: Studies in the Northwest Semitic Languages and Literature in Honor of Bruce Zuckerman*, edited by Lundberg, M. J., Fine, S., Pitard, W. T., 235–238. Boston: Brill.

Ziffer, I. 2010. "The Iconography of the Cult Stands." In *Yavneh I: The Excavation of the "Temple Hill" Repository Pit and the Cult Stands*, edited by Kletter, R., Ziffer, I., Zwickel, W., 69–73. Fribourg: Academic Press Fribourg.

Zimhoni, O. 1985. "The Iron Age Pottery of Tel 'Eton and Its Relation to the Lachish, Tell Beit Mirsim and Arad Assemblages." *Tel Aviv* 12 (1): 63–90.

Zimmerli, W. 1979a. *Ezekiel 1: A Commentary on the Book of the Prophet Ezekiel*. Philadelphia: Fortress.

Zimmerli, W. 1979b. "The History of Israelite Religion." In *Tradition and Interpretation*, edited by Anderson, G. W., 351–384. Oxford: Clarendon.

Zimmerli, W. 1983. *Ezekiel 2: A Commentary on the Book of the Prophet Ezekiel, Chapters 25–48*. Philadelphia: Fortress.

Zivie-Coche, C. 1994. "Dieux autres, dieux des autres: Identité culturelle et altérité dans l'Égypte ancienne." In *Concepts of the Other in Near Eastern Religions*, edited by Alon, I., Gruenwald, I., 39–80. Leiden: Brill.

Zivie-Coche, C. 2011. "Foreign Deities in Egypt." *UCLA Encyclopedia of Egyptology*, Open Version, https://uee.cdh.ucla.edu.

Zobel, H. 1974. "'Arôn." In *Theological Dictionary of the Old Testament*, edited by Botterweck, G. J., Ringgren, H., Vol. III, 363–374. Grand Rapids: Eerdmans.

Zobel, H. 1990. "Yiśrā'ēl." In *Theological Dictionary of the Old Testament*, edited by Botterweck, G. J., Ringgren, H., Vol. VI, 397–420. Grand Rapids: Eerdmans.

Zuckerman, B. 1991. *Job the Silent: A Study in Historical Counterpoint*. Oxford: Oxford University.

Zuckerman, S. 2011. "Ruin Cults at Iron Age I Hazor." In *The Fire Signals of Lachish: Studies in the Archaeology and History of Israel in the Late Bronze Age, Iron Age, and Persian Period in Honor of David Ussishkin.*, edited by Finkelstein, I., Na'aman, N., 387–394. Winona Lake.: Eisenbrauns.

Zwickel, W. 1994. *Der Tempelkult in Kanaan und Israel: Studien zur Kultgeschichte Palästinas von der Mittelbronzezeit bis zum Untergang Judas.* Tübingen: Mohr Siebeck.

Subject Index

References to boxes, figures, tables, and notes are denoted by an italicized b, f, t, and n. The index of authors' names and their citations is not comprehensive. Readers should use digital searches and consult the Notes and the Works Cited.

Aaron
  anointing rituals for, 625
  cultic activities by, 752*n*191
  Yahweh's anger against, 650
Aaronid priests
  in Chronicles, 659–60
  in handling of Ark, 597
  holiness of, 640–41
  regulations for, in Holiness source, 631–32
  ritual acts required for, 619–29
abcedaries, 764*n*86
Abihu, death of, 370–73
Abijah (biblical figure), 752–53*n*192
Absalom (biblical figure), 513
abstract representations of Yahweh, 336–44, 422–25
  divine fire, 344–58
  divine radiance, 358–79
  in Hebrew Bible, 344–79
  Name Theology, 379–92
  and other deities in ancient Near East, 338–41, 340*f*
  pairing of iconoclasm and aniconism, 341–44
  sacred emptiness, 392–415, 416*f*–17*f*
abuse of justice, prosecution of, 535–38
academic disciplines, 48–49
Ackerman, Susan, 44–46, 84, 502, 667–668, 677, 685, 687, 689–691, 711*n*87, 711*n*92, 781*n*196, 788*n*27, 841*n*240, 842*n*253, 847*n*28, 853*n*83, 866*n*13, 886*n*175, 895*n*277, 896*n*278, 896*n*279, 896*n*280, 896*n*281, 896*n*282, 899*n*8, 901*n*37, 902*n*39, 902*n*47 and passim
active presence, of Yahweh, 218–19
Adad (deity), 266, 268, 439–40, 458, 804–5*n*193

adonay, as substitute for Yahweh, 212, 213
agrarian goddess, ʿAthtartu as, 681–83
agriculture, association of El Shadday with, 103–4
Aharoni, Yohanan, 184, 246, 706*n*52, 710*n*77, 748*n*165, 866*n*12
Ahaz (Judean king), 502–3
Ahijah (biblical figure), 752*n*192
Ahiram of Byblos (Phoenician king), 402, 403*f*
Ahlström, Gösta, 75, 126, 157, 158, 200, 202
Ai, cult stand from, 415, 416*f*
AIAR (W. F. Albright Institute of Archaeological Research), 705–6*n*48
Akitu festival, 28, 259
Akizzi, mayor of Qatna, 132, 133
Akkadian language, 56, 57, 60, 74, 215, 259, 266, 337, 390, 400, 445, 454, 517, 526, 669, 714*n*19, 717*n*6, 719*n*21, 719*n*23, 740*n*86, 748*n*163, 757*n*9, 778*n*172, 798*n*135, 815*n*144, 803*n*179, 817*n*18, 818*n*26, 834*n*162, 838*n*198, 839*n*217 and passim
Alaca Höyük, city gate, 149, 149*f*
aladlammu (lamassu) sculptures, 399–400, 399*f*, 814*n*272
Aladlammu Seal, from Seyrig collection, 305–6, 306*f*
Alalakh, precious metals in, 303–4
Albertz, Rainer, 9, 26–27, 39, 42, 43–44, 50, 56, 57, 58–59, 83, 84, 107, 111, 112, 214, 218, 235, 255, 272, 274, 304, 306, 479, 493–94, 522, 586, 702*n*4, 707*n*56, 711*n*88, 714*n*18, 722*n*50, 723*n*54,

725*n*77, 731*n*136, 732*n*145, 735*n*11, 755*n*1, 756*n*5, 756*n*7, 759*n*35, 837*n*186, 839*n*214, 839*n*215, 843*n*262, 852*n*74, 852*n*75, 886*n*174 and passim
Albright, William F., 31–32, 213–14, 220–21, 270–71, 319, 705–07*nn*48–49, 51–55
Albright-Freedman-Cross hypothesis, on name Yahweh, 220–22, 270–71
Aleppo Citadel, 156*f*
Alt, Albrecht, 84–85
altar, consecration of, 624, 625
Amarna letters (EA)
  El in, 74–75
  exile of statues in, 140
  materials for icons in, 132
  references to Canaanite religion in, 258
  traveling rituals in, 137
Amenhotep II, 679
Amenhotep III, 737*n*51, 761*n*53, 761*n*59, 782*n*210, 798*n*130, 900*n*6
American School of Oriental Research, 705–6*n*48
Ammonites, El worship by, 83
Amorite hypothesis, 108, 717*n*6
Amorite language, "Yahweh" in, 220
Amorites, El Shadday for, 108
Amos, book of
  prosecution of abuse of justice in, 535–36
  twisting of justice in, 550–51
amulets
  deities represented in, 328, 330
  Egyptian, in Israel, 772–73*n*148
anachronisms, 760*n*44
Anat-Astarte, representations of, 324

1020 SUBJECT INDEX

ʿAnatu (deity), 441–42, 462, 819n40
ancient or eternal god, El as, 97–99, 109, 110
Andersen, Francis, 359–60, 452, 535–36
anger, hypostatic use of, 351
aniconism
  of ancient Israel, 119, 155, 156
  in Deuteronomist sources, 291
  divine fire in, 356–58
  iconoclasm and, 341–44
  and Jeroboam I's bull images, 318–20
  and lack of male figurines from Iron Age, 302–4
  material, 333–36, 421–22
  representations of Yahweh in, 333–36, 421–22
anointing rituals, 622–29
anthropomorphic language, in Ezekiel, 374–79
anthropomorphic representations of Yahweh, 287–313, 418–19
  absence of, from Iron Age, 298–304
  as divine images, 290–97
  in material culture, 297–98
  in textual sources, 287–90, 786n5
  and Yahweh as member of divine couple, 304–13
anthroponyms, related to divine names, 59–60
apocalyptic literature
  divine justice in, 532–34
  Yahweh as warrior in, 469–70
apotropaism. *See* protection (apotropaism)
Appollo Hylates, sanctuary of, at Kourion, 308
ʾAqhatu story, 79, 134, 215, 262, 474, 476, 483, 516, 838n200, 840n225
Arad, 41, 55, 296, 576, 750n185, 768n115, 832n149, 866n12
  aniconic representations of Yahweh in, 296
  desacralizing of temple at, 303, 788n32
  masseboth at, 121, 122f, 172, 183–87, 185f–86f, 194, 296, 333, 422, 748n164, 749n175
  material culture in fortress temple at, 463
  name of Yahweh on ostraca from, 246–47, 247f
Aramaic language, use of, 265
Aramean religion, 264–268
  and bull-headed warrior from Bethsaida, 332

El worship in Iron Age, 82–83
  and Yahweh's origin from North, 270–71
archaeology, 710n83 and passim
  data about ʿAštart from, 694
  evidence of empty-space aniconism in, 409–17, 410f, 411f, 413f–17f
  and Israel's ethnogenesis, 710n81
  material culture as source material, 68–69
  processual, 40
  in religious scholarship, 31, 39–41, 706n53
  Yahweh iconography in, 287, 297
archaic biblical Hebrew, 715n27, 782n210, 822n68
Ariel, 197, 315
Ark, 397
  divine radiance in narrative of, 364–65
  El associated with, 805n199
  as focal point for sacred emptiness, 394–97, 425
  hidden allusions to, 812–13n262
  holiness of, 595–99, 604–5, 891n239
  moved to Jerusalem temple, 655–56
  and name as practical presence of Yahweh, 408
Arnuwanda I (Hittite king), 515–16
aroma, consecration with, 622
Arslan Tash
  Canaanite and Aramean religion in, 268, 576
  incantations from, 55, 268, 576, 727n98, 727n102, 742n103, 779n181, 779n183
  stela from, 151f
art, in ancient Israelite religion, 7–8
artisans, in ancient Near East, 133–35
Asherah (deity)
  analysis of, 701n2
  as consort of Yahweh, 237–39, 238f, 239f, 243, 327–28
  divine images of, 120, 122, 125, 167, 168, 326
  and El Shadday, 730–31n132
  image of, in Jerusalem Temple, 292, 294
  and Kuntillet ʿAjrud, 763n78
  as part of divine couple, 304–13, 305f, 307f, 309f, 312f
  representations of, 412
Ashkelon, bull statuette from, 153, 154, 160f, 324

Ashurbanipal, violence done by troops of, 466, 572–73, 572f, 800n156, 814n272, 842n251, 850n51
Ashurnasirpal II, 396, 430, 431f, 573, 814n272
Aššur/Astarte (deity), 97, 157, 231, 265, 268, 344, 365, 368, 375–77, 376f, 396, 797n126, 818n34, 827n99
Assyria, king's association with divinity in, 497
Assyriology, 703–4n22
ʿAštart/Astarte (deity), 675–96
  in ancient Israelite religion, 693–96
  Astarte in Egypt, 679
  Aštartu at Emar, 678–79
  ʿAthtartu at Ugarit, 679–83, 684f
  biblical portrayal of, 676–78, 687–89
  in Deuteronomy, 691–93
  in Phoenicia and its extended world, 576, 668, 676, 684–87
  as Queen of Heaven, 689–91
Astarte (ʿAštart), 679, 680f, 901n32
Aštartu (ʿAštart), 509, 678–79, 899n10
Aster, Shawn, 339, 374, 797n124, 797n125, 797n126, 797n127, 798n135, 798n136, 803n179, 803n180, 805n193, 809n227, 825n81
Ataroth/Ataruz, 172, 193–94, 202–205, 203f, 204f, 205f, 208, 333, 422, 743n122, 749n172, 749n173, 749n175, 750n176, 751n186, 769n125, 792n80
Aten (deity), 339–40, 340f
ʿAthiratu (deity), 475–76, 475f, 738n63
ʿAthtar (deity), 828n108
ʿAthtartu (ʿAštart), 441, 679–83, 684f, 819nn38–39, 900n22
atonement rituals, for kings, 498
attendant beings of fire, for Yahweh, 347–50
auditory experience, of Yahweh's presence, 613
Avalos, Hector, 138
Ayn Dara, Iron Age temple at, 393
  abstract images of divine, 341, 342f, 343f
  invisibility as focal point for, 408–9
  sacred emptiness in, 425, 426

SUBJECT INDEX

and superlative power of gods as kings, 511
ʾAzziʾiltu, 837–38n197

Baal
 iconography of, 202, 206
 in inscriptions at Kuntillet ʿAjrud, 586
Baʿal, divine images of, 151, 152, 160–61, 164f, 165f
Baalam oracles, 89–90, 94
Babel and Bible (Delitzsch), 704n28
"Babel-Bibel" controversy, 24–25
Bahn, Paul, 336–37
Bailey, Lloyd, 318
Baʿlu (deity)
 cosmic warfare in myth of, 440–42, 459, 460–61
 as family god, 474
 and ʾIlu, 80, 82, 118
 as storm god, 267
Barkay, Gabriel, 42–43, 249–250, 710n77, 768n117, 769n120, 769n122, 843n263, 866n12
Beck, Pirhiya, 316, 326, 742n110, 790n49, 793n88, 793n90, 794n98
Becking, Bob, 292–94
Beckman, Gary, 217, 497, 708n64, 721n45, 737n39, 738n69, 750n177, 844n4, 884n158
Bedouin tribalism, 23
belief, in Yahweh as judge, 528–30
Bell, Catherine, 3, 15, 42, 49, 613–614, 640, 704n35, 709n67, 848n38, 876n101, 879n125
Bellow, Saul, 52, 473
Ben-Ami, Doron, 175, 176, 180, 181, 710n77, 742n117, 742n118, 747n157, 747n160
beneficence, of ʾIlu, 79
benevolent protector, El as, 111–13
Ben-Tor, Amnon, 141, 159, 162, 402 and passim
Bes (deity), 120, 325f, 326–30, 329f, 421, 793n89
Beset (deity), 327, 328
Bethel, 2, 59, 85, 99–101, 112, 113, 135, 171, 174, 187, 195, 196, 198, 199, 227, 295, 320, 335, 382, 386, 387, 419, 502, 602, 619, 667, 713n6, 728n116, 737n42, 746n153, 747n156, 753n192, 769n125, 792n73, 847n30, 902n45
Bethsaida gate shrine, 190, 191f, 330–32, 331f, 794–95n101
Beth Shean

bronze figurine from, 165, 168f
cult stand with fenestrations from, 415, 417f
seal from, 166–69, 170f
Beth-Shemesh
 Ark of the Testimony at, 596, 874n77
 bronze figurine at, 163, 164, 166f
Beth ʿOlam, 727n103
Bethsaida, 41, 120, 189, 190, 191f, 264, 267, 302, 330–33, 331f, 742n110, 749n171, 794n101, 831n130
Beya, Moses as, 229
Bible and Orient Museum, University of Fribourg, 306–9, 307f
biblical polemics, 692–93
Bibliothèque Nationale (Paris, France), 305–6, 306f
Biran, Avraham, 187, 189, 710n77, 749n169
Bird, Phyllis, 42, 45, 111, 668–69, 711n85, 711n87, 711n96, 842n249, 889n213
birth narratives, 479
blazing mountain (image), 353–54, 356
Blenkinsopp, Joseph, 446, 470, 533, 537
Blessing of Jacob, 277
blessings, god of family as giver of, 476
Bloch-Smith, Elizabeth, 46, 121, 172, 180, 181, 185, 187, 189, 317, 394, 511, 676, 684–685, 688, 709n76, 710n83, 732n149, 736n36, 748n164, 748n165, 749n175, 798n133, 901n32, 901n33, 901n34, 902n42 and passim
Block, Daniel, 643–44
bloodletting, after divine warfare, 470–71
blood manipulation
 in anointing rituals, 624, 627–29, 881–82n142
 by consecrated priests only, 665
 in study of ancient Israelite religion, 51
Bordreuil, Pierre, 236, 260, 714n14, 718n17, 774n154, 789n35, 899n13
Bourke, Stephen, 205–06
bovine imagery, 754n206–7
breast, association of El Shadday with, 102
Brettler, Marc, 512–13, 521, 802n167, 822n65, 851n67

bribery, 536–38
bronze statuary
 El representations in, 156–65, 166f–70f
 ʾIlu representations in, 142–44, 143f–44f
Buddhas of Bamyan, destruction of, 343
bull-headed warrior, from Bethsaida, 330–32, 331f
the Bull of Jacob, 197–98
bull of Samaria, 320–21
bull riders, divine, 319–20, 319f
Bull Site
 bull representation of Yahweh from, 322
 massebah at, 174–76, 175f
 metal expertise from Iron Age at, 302
 theriomorphic representations of El from, 200, 202, 202f
bull symbolism
 in ancient Near East, 751–51n190
 for El, 116, 197–200, 318
 for ʾIlu, 150–53, 158f–61f, 754–55n210
 on Taanach cult stand, 323–24, 323f, 420–21
 for Yahweh, 317–33, 319f, 321f, 323f, 325f, 329f, 331f, 420
Bull ʾIlu, 76, 78, 117, 588, 720n26, 725n74
burial
 of ancient Near East statues, 141
 of precious metals, 303
Burkert, Walter, 495
burning bush, 345
burnt offerings, 406–7, 501, 502
Byblos, 155f

Cain (biblical figure), 272
Callot, Olivier, 151–52
Campbell, Edward, 301, 301f, 302, 787n24, 787n26
Canaanite Gods in Metal (Negbi), 258
Canaanite religion and culture, 253–64, 286
 and *Chaoskampf* in Hebrew Bible, 459–60
 as construct, 253–54
 El worship in, 74–75
 in Middle Bronze Age, Late Bronze Age, and Iron Age, 256–59
 name of Yahweh in epigraphs from, 252
 Philo of Byblos on, 255–56

Canaanite religion and culture (*cont.*)
  Phoenician epigraphic sources on, 254–55
  pre-Israelite, 253, 773–74n152
  Ugarit and conceptualization of, 259–64
  and Yahweh's origin from North, 270–71
caring father, Yahweh as, 481–82
Carr, David, 53, 448, 714n20, 770n131, 856n111
Chaoskampf traditions, 150
  in ancient Near East, 430–33
  in Hebrew Bible, 443–46, 448, 459–60
  in Levant, 439–42
  royal legitimization in, 454
  royal military might in, 510
  in Ugaritic religion, 262
  use of language in, 817n16
chariot riders, representation of, 308–9
Chemosh (deity), 2, 33, 71, 134, 140, 235, 254, 261, 285, 304, 335, 419, 428, 429, 462, 501, 691, 729n116, 749n172, 755n211, 762n69, 769n125
cherubim
  composite, 320
  as focal point for sacred emptiness, 394f, 397–400, 398f, 399f, 409, 425, 815–16n289
  function of, 813n271
  as thrones for rulers, 400–402, 401f–4f, 814n276
Chesterton, G. K., 8
childbirth, connection of Yahweh to, 489–93
child rearing, by Yahweh, 481–82
children
  humans as rebellious, 482–89
  sacrifice of, 64, 542, 715n25
Chronicles
  cultic activities of king in, 499–500
  David in, 697–98
  and divine image of Yahweh in Jerusalem Temple, 296
  hypostatic use of fire in, 352
  on Jehoshaphat as king of justice, 520–21
  singers and musicians in, 66
  Yahweh alone in battle in, 466
  Yahweh as the Holy One in, 657–65

circumvention, in description of Yahweh, 378–79
city gates, 149, 513, 524, 539, 544, 850n57
City of David
  empty throne in seal from, 405
  striding lion seal from, 314–15, 314f
classical nomenclature (of source criticism), 62, 65, 274
clay
  humans as, 839n217, 841n238
  used for divine images, 739n80
Clines, David, 555–56, 860n156, 860n159, 870n44
clothing
  of ancient Near East icons, 135–36
  as offering to ʿAthtartu, 682–83
  symbolic uses of, 879–80n125
  washing of, for consecration, 611
  of Yahweh in radiance, 454–55
clothing rituals, for Aaronid priests, 619–22
cloud pillar (as symbol), 453
Collins, John, 47, 99, 533, 534, 711n87, 711n92, 725n76, 736n36, 855n102, 855n103
combat myth, in Ugaritic religion, 262
comparanda, ancient Near Eastern, 67, 69–72
compassion, language to express Yahweh's, 492
composite beasts, 433, 434f–36f (see *Mischwesen*)
consecration
  of ancient Near East icons, 135
  with anointing, 622
  for holy war, 464
  of Nazirites, 634
  of priests, in Chronicles, 661–65
  process of, in Exodus, 608–15
  rituals for Aaron and Aaronid priests, 619–29
  of women, 668–70
contrastive approach, to Ugaritic studies, 260
coronation rituals, 512–13
cosmic warfare, 430–61
  in ancient Near East, 430–33, 431f, 432f
  and archaic lore in Israelite religion, 446–48
  in Enuma Elish, 437–39

and legitimization of royalty, 453–60
  in mythology from Ugarit, 439–42
  preternatural dragons in, 433, 434f–37f
  swallowing of death by Yahweh, 460–61
  Yahweh's divine battle at sea, 448–53
  Yahweh's engagement in, 442–61
  and Yahweh's kingship, 510
covenant lawsuits, 539–43
creation myths
  combat myths and, 444, 445
  and gods as parents, 477–78, 481, 838nn202–3
creator
  El as, 109, 110
  Elkunirsha as, 81
  ʾIlu as, 76–77
  Yahweh as, 94–95
crises of everyday life, connection of Yahweh to, 493–94
Cross, Frank Moore, 34–36, 74, 84, 86, 87, 90, 97, 102, 104, 105, 107, 111, 113, 210–11, 220–22, 236, 241, 245, 251, 253, 270, 271, 276–78, 349, 363, 395, 396, 454, 459, 619, 706n52, 708n61, 708n62, 713n8, 716n6, 717n13, 718n18, 719n23, 720n30, 722n50, 723n57, 723n60, 728n105, 728n109, 728n111, 728n113, 729n123, 730n127, 732n156, 752n192, 759n35, 766n98, 767n107, 767n110, 768n111, 769n125, 770n128, 782n205, 782n208, 783n214, 805n195, 812n252, 812n253, 813n269, 820n52, 822n69, 828n106, 828n108, 830n129, 832n145, 866n12, 869n37, 887n183 and passim
Crouch, Carly, 42, 285, 785n233, 785n235, 890n219
CT 13.33-34 (Old Akkadian cuneiform text), 431–33
cultic holiness, 606–15
cultic prostitution, 668–70
cultic status, 612
cult inventories, 696–97
Curtis, A. H. W., 152, 198

Dagan (deity), 677
Dagon (deity), 254, 303
Dahood, Mitchell, 95, 98, 228

SUBJECT INDEX

Dalley, Stephanie, 233–34, 270
dance, in ancient Israelite religion, 7–8
Daniel, book of
  divine images in, 134–35
  God as eschatological judge in, 533–34
Danilu (Ugarit patriarch), 476–77
Darby, Erin, 46, 132, 735n11, 748n164, 789n41, 841n238, 889n210, 903n58
dataset size, of textual sources, 66–67
dating, in iconographic studies, 126–27, 126f–28f
Daughter Zion, 485, 486, 488–89
David (biblical figure)
  abuse of justice by, 534–35
  and attributes of Yahweh, 697–98
  infusing of divinity in kingship of, 505
  as judge, 855n105
  as king of justice, 517–18
  kinship of Yahweh with, 219
  Philistine idols destroyed by, 739n77
  role of, in cultic activities, 499–500, 880n131
  royal legitimization of, 455–58
  Yahweh as supporter of underdog, 465
Davis, Andrew, 196, 712n5, 748n168, 752n190, 791n57, 800n148, 837n187, 841n239, 897n295
Dawn (deity), 77, 474
Day, John, 262, 443, 444, 445, 452, 512, 677, 696, 701n2, 703n22, 718n18, 819n43, 820n45, 821n58, 821n62, 829n111, 849n42, 889n213 and passim
Day, Peggy, 837n189, 841n240
Day of Atonement/Purgation, 498, 621, 622, 646, 808n218, 875n85
death
  of Abihu and Nadab, 370–73
  of gods, 758n23
  lethal God hearings, 355, 367
  lethal God sightings, 296–97, 355, 557
  lethal holiness of Yahweh, 494
  swallowing of, by Yahweh, 460–61
Deborah (biblical figure), 13, 273, 411, 524, 667, 781n196, 853n83

Decalogue, Ark as storage place for, 408
de facto traditions, of aniconism, 333
DeGrado, Jessie, 45, 669, 896n288
Deir 'Alla
  Canaanite and Aramean religion in, 268–69
  El Shadday in, 105, 113
  El worship in, 90
Delitzsch, Friedrich, 24–25
demonization approach, to Ugaritic studies, 259–60
de Moor, Johannes, 87, 229, 232, 719n20, 721n38, 760n51, 761n52
the Destroyer, El Shadday as, 104–5
destruction, of ancient Near East statues, 141
Deuteronomic Law of the King, 503
Deuteronomistic History (DtrH)
  'Aštart in, 676–77, 691–92
  cultic activities of kings in, 501, 502
  divine fire in, 353
  divine radiance in, 366
  holiness in, 651–53, 660–61
  holy personnel in, 651–53, 651–57
  human involvement in warfare in, 464–65
  lack of singers and musicians in, 66
  Name Theology and, 379
  priestly personnel in, 651–57
  throne imagery in, 405
  of Yahweh as the Holy One in, 651–53
Deuteronomistic sources
  active presence of Yahweh in, 218–19
  aniconism in, 291
  anthropomorphic representations of Yahweh in, 288–89
  Asherah images in Jerusalem Temple in, 294–95
  bull images of Jeroboam I in, 198–99
  David as king of justice in, 518
  destruction/mutilation of statues in, 141
  divine fire in, 353–56
  divine radiance in, 366
  hypostatic use of name in, 388
  kings of justice in, 519
  on masseboth, 173–74, 335
  superlative quality of Yahweh's kingship in, 509

Deuteronomy, book of
  allusions to geographic origin of Yahweh in, 280
  and aniconic tradition, 357–58
  'Aštart in, 691–93
  creation and fatherhood in, 481
  Dagan, Shagar, and 'Aštart in, 677
  discipline by Yahweh in, 484
  divine fire in, 353–56
  divine law in, 561
  divine radiance in, 361
  El as benevolent protector in, 112
  El as father in, 110
  El Olam in, 98–99
  El Shadday in, 104
  Elyon and Yahweh in, 91–92
  and essence of fire, 358
  fiery attendants of Yahweh in, 348–49
  humans as rebellious children in, 483
  Levites in, 637–39
  limits on judicial power of kings in, 543–45, 561
  love expressed in, 890n219
  Name Theology and, 379–80, 384–86
  origin myths of Israelite judiciaries in, 526–27
  self-identification in, 285
  Yahweh as absolute judge in, 528–29
  Yahweh as the Holy One in, 647–51
Deutero-Isaiah/Second Isaiah, 485, 490, 491, 599, 600, 603, 649, 738n60, 842n245, 875n92
Dever, William, 40–41, 126, 157–158, 163, 202, 232,, 241, 242, 298, 707n56, 709n73, 709n76, 710n81, 710n83, 735n16, 735n18, 742n118, 745n142, 754n203, 762n66, 766n99, 766n100 and passim
de Wette, Wilhelm, 20–21, 702n5, 702n6, 702n8
Dewrell, Heath, 64, 730n129, 733n161, 772n140, 847n31, 857n124, 887n194
Dick, Michael, 133, 554, 556
direct communication, of Moses with God, 562–63
disappearance, of gods, 217–18
disarmament
  rhetoric of, 471–72
  Yahweh as teacher-judge after, 530

discipline, by Yahweh as
    father, 484–86
divination, for decisions about
    battle, 464
divine accessibility, provided by
    Ark, 597–99
divine beings, surrounding
    Yahweh, 863n180
divine council/assembly, 565,
    863n180
    and El worship, 113
    judgment by, 534
    Yahweh's judgment of, 565–67
divine couple
    Asherah as consort of Yahweh,
        237–39, 238f, 239f,
        243, 327–28
    Yahweh as member of, 304–13,
        305f, 307f, 309f, 312f
divine empowerment
    of David, 456–58
    of human troops in
        battle, 464–65
divine figures, representations
    of human figures vs.,
    308, 310
divine fire, 344–58, 423
    and aniconic
        tradition, 356–58
    attendant beings of fire for
        Yahweh, 347–50
    crafting essence of fire, 358
    Deuteronomic/Deuteronomistic
        views of, 353–56
    fire to depict presence of
        Yahweh, 344–47,
        802–3n174
    hypostatic use of fire, 350–53
    and radiance of Yahweh, 370–71
divine images, passim
    anthropomorphic
        representations of Yahweh
        as, 290–97
    criteria for identifying, 142
    materials used for, 739n80
    misidentification of, 121–22
    of Yahweh, 290–97
divine justice
    and apocalyptic
        literature, 532–34
    and ideal of just divine
        judge, 545–57
    in Job, 551–57
    non-royal frameworks
        for, 521–24
    on personal level, 521–23
    proverbial understandings
        of, 547–49
    royal framework for, 513–21

divine kingship, 503–4, 705n40
divine kinsman, El as, 111
divine mercy
    in book of Jonah, 571–74
    Psalms on, 569–71
divine "name," to depict presence of
    Yahweh, 379–80
divine parent, Yahweh as, 477–82
divine radiance, 358–79, 423–24
    in Chronicles, 658
    consecration required to
        mediate, 662–63
    divine *kābôd* in pre-priestly
        cultic settings, 364–68
    in early poetry, 359–62
    and enthronement in Jerusalem
        Temple, 510–11
    kābôd Yahweh in
        Ezekiel, 373–79
    kābôd Yahweh in Priestly
        sources, 368–73
    Moses' request to see *kābôd* of
        Yahweh, 362–63
    radiance to depict presence of
        Yahweh, 358–59
divine speeches, in Job, 555–57
divine traits, overlapping
    of, 590–91
divine visitation, 476–77
divine war, synergism of human
    war and, 462–64
divine warrior(s)
    on cosmic scale, 430–42
    in inscriptions at Kuntillet
        ʿAjrud, 583–87, 584f–85f
    radiance of, 359–61
divinity
    Aramean, 265–66
    conceptualization of, 73, 575
    in Deir ʿAlla, 269
    in environmental context, 2
    female, 675–696
    of kings, 496–98, 504–7
    as organizing principle, 9–10
    in Ugaritic religion, 261–64
Dobbs-Allsopp, F. W., 448, 554 and
    passim
Documentary Hypothesis, 54, 84,
    707n53
domestic religion
    representations of figures in,
        310, 311
    See also family religion
dragons
    allusions to, in Hebrew
        Bible, 443–46
    divine warriors' battles
        with, 431–33
    preternatural, 433, 434f–37f

drawing process, for iconographic
    analysis, 127–28, 129f–32f
dreams and visions
    communication of God with
        Moses vs., 562–63
    El's association with, 81–82, 90,
        100–101
DtrH. *See* Deuteronomistic
    History (DtrH)
Durkheim, Émile, 23, 26, 36, 50,
    704n33, 712n2, 712n4,
    879n125
Dusk (deity), 77, 474

EA. *See* Amarna letters (EA)
Ebal, Mt., 41, 173, 284, 383, 561,
    784n231
Ebla, Yahweh at, 228
Edomites, 285–86
Egypt
    abstract images of divine in,
        339–40, 340f
    ʿAštart (Astarte) in, 679, 680f
    contact between Canaan
        and, 256–58
    El worship in Ramesside
        period, 75
    judicial instructions in, 516
    justice as theme in wisdom
        literature of, 547
    king's association with divinity
        in, 496, 504
    materials for icons in, 130–32
    name Yahweh in, 229–33
Egyptian Papyrus Amherst 322,
    728n116, 739n73, 792n73
Ein Gedi, 245–46, 246f
El
    characteristics of, 722–23n50
    characteristics of Yahweh
        vs., 427
    distinction between Elyon
        and, 87–88
    Elyon traditions associated
        with, 88–90
    epigraphy related to, 54–55
    as family deity, 473, 723n54
    as father, 480–81
    and "the Holy One of
        Israel," 602–3
    identification of Yahweh with,
        209, 868n26
    in inscriptions at Kuntillet
        ʿAjrud, 586
    Iron Age representations
        of, 298
    judicial authority of Yahweh
        over, 565–67
    as mother, 489

SUBJECT INDEX 1025

and Yahweh as "He Who Causes to Be," 221–22
and Yahweh in Hebrew Bible, 427
and Yahweh in Masoretic tradition, 568–69
and Yahweh's origin from the North, 271
El Berith, 85–86, 111, 174, 723–24n60
El Bethel, 99–101
El Elyon, 86–95, 112
  distinction between El and Elyon, 87–88
  Elyon traditions associated with El, 88–90
  Elyon traditions associated with Yahweh, 90–92
  and "the Holy One of Israel," 601–2
  and origin of Yahweh in ethnic self-identification, 285
  Yahweh Elyon traditions and El Elyon motifs, 92–95
El iconography, 10–11, 119–208
  and ancient Near Eastern iconography, 128–41
  Beth Shean seal, 166–69, 170f
  bronze statuary, 156–65, 166f–70f
  and iconography of Ugaritic 'Ilu, 142–55, 156f–61f
  and iconography of Yahweh, 318
  masseboth representations, 169, 171–96, 335, 336
  methodology for studying, 119–28, 129f–32f
  theriomorphic representations, 196–208
Elide priesthood, divine radiance in, 364–65
Elijah (biblical figure)
  fire associated with, 350
  holiness of, 665–67
  as prophet, 5
  as prosecutor of abuse of justice, 535
the Elim, 84–85
Elisha (biblical figure)
  holiness of, 665–67
  as prophet, 5
Elkunirsha and Ashertu, myth of, 81–82
'ĕlōhîm, designation, 344, 509, 568–69, 724n65
Elohistic Psalter, 724n65
  El Elyon motifs from, 92–94
  'ĕlōhîm in, 724n65, 782–83n212, 784n229
  Elyon traditions in, 88–90

Elohist source (E)
  Midianite hypothesis and, 276
  on Moses's father-in-law, 781n197
  revelation of name Yahweh in, 223–26
  use of, 65
El Olam, 97–99, 727n100
  epigraphy related to, 55
  and Yahweh, 210, 217
El Roi, 95–97, 110, 112
El Shadday, 101–9, 489, 729n121
  dating of, 105–7
  as the Destroyer, 104–5
  and El as father, 110
  as God of the Mountain, 102
  as God of the Steppe Lands, 103–4, 108
  place/sanctuary associated with, 108–9
  and revelation of name Yahweh, 225
El worship, 10, 73–118
  characteristics not associated with El, 114–15
  and divine council, 113
  El as benevolent protector, 111–13
  El as divine kinsman, 111
  El as father, 110–11
  El as original god of Israel, 115–18
  El Bethel, 99–101
  El Elyon, 86–95
  El Olam, 97–99
  El Roi, 95–97
  El Shadday, 101–9
  functions of El deities, 109–10
  and the God of the Fathers, 83–85
  and Hittite Elkunirsha myth, 81–82
  in Iron Age, 82–83
  in Late Bronze Age Levant, 74–76, 210
  onomastica in, 59
  and revelation of name Yahweh, 226, 227
  in Shechem, 85–86
  at Ugarit, 76–81
  elders, see town elders
  Emar anointing rituals at, 626–27, 883nn153–54
  'Aštart (Aštartu) at, 678–79
  cultic holiness at, 608
  evidence of indentured slavery from, 486–87, 486f

  zukru festival at, 627–29, 747n156, 876n99, 883n156, 899n10, 902n46
empty space aniconism, 333, 409–17
empty throne, of Yahweh, 405
Enlightenment, religious scholarship during, 18–19
enthroned-benedictory deities, images of
  with animal thrones, 401–5, 401f–4f
  from Israel, 156–57
  Late Bronze Age, 298
  and representation of Yahweh, 298
  from Ugarit, 143–44, 143f, 144f
enthronement
  of Yahweh, 400–401, 405
  of Yahweh in Jerusalem, 510–11
Enuma Elish
  cosmic warfare in, 437–39
  traveling rituals in, 136
epigraphic sources
  on Canaanite religion, 254–55
  of name Yahweh, 234–52
    lack of, from tenth century BCE, 251–52
    from ninth and eighth centuries BCE, 234–43, 234f, 235f, 238f, 239f, 241f–43f
    from seventh and sixth centuries BCE, 243–51, 244f–50f
epigraphy
  related to "the Holy One," 576
  as textual source, 54–55, 709–10n76
Esarhaddon (Neo-Assyrian king), 133, 458, 466, 478, 573, 659, 685, 688, 690, 728n116, 771n138, 850n51
Esarhaddon's Succession Treaty (EST), 54, 716n31, 890n219
eschatological judge, God as, 532–34
Eshmunazor I (Sidonian king), 685–87
Eshmunazor II (Sidonian king), 686, 687
E source See Elohist source (E)
ethnic self-identification, Yahweh as part of, 284–86
European superiority prejudice of, 703n19
Eusebius of Caesarea, 255–56
the existing god, Yahweh as, 217–18

1026 SUBJECT INDEX

Exodus, book of
 anointing rituals in, 622–25
 battle at sea in, 448–50, 452–53
 dating chapter 15 of, 822n69
 divine radiance in, 369, 377–78
 El worship in, 91
 fatherly redemption in, 486
 fiery attendants of Yahweh in, 350
 fire to depict presence of Yahweh in, 345
 handling of Ark in, 598
 hypostatic use of names in, 389
 Levites in, 637
 Midianite hypothesis and, 275–76
 Moses's judicial role in, 562
 name Yahweh in, 214–15, 217, 218
 origin myths of Israelite judiciaries in, 525–26, 528
 praise for Yahweh in, 5
 process of consecration in, 608–15
 revelation of name Yahweh in, 223–24, 225
 self-identification in, 285–86
 Yahweh's holiness in, 578–79
exodus from Egypt, 115–18
expansive holiness
 in Holiness source, 630–31
 in Priestly tradition, 632–36
Ezekiel (biblical figure), 665, 895n275
Ezekiel, book of
 anthropomorphic representations of Yahweh in, 289–90
 apocalyptic battle in, 470
 bull symbolism in, 317
 cherubim in, 400
 discipline by Yahweh in, 484–85
 historical study of, 716n31, 809n225, 841n241, 888n201, 895n275
 holiness in, 897n291
 kābôd of Yahweh in, 373–79, 424
 Yahweh as the Holy One in, 643–47

faithfulness, 657
family
 judicial authority in, 523
 viewing gods as, 474–76, 475f
family language, applied to deities, 718n7
family religion
 ancient Israelite religion as, 5–6

association of Yahweh with, 249–50
and community as holy, 648–49
and divine justice on personal level, 521–23
and El as God of the Fathers, 83–84
and "the Holy One of Israel," 602–3
incantations in, 66, 769n122
and personal piety, 42–44
Queen of Heaven as, 689, 690
women's participation in, 667–68
and Yahweh as divine warrior, 449
fascinans, defined, 337, 870n45
father
 El as, 110–11, 480–81
 'Ilu as, 76
 redemption of humans by, 486–89
 reproving of humans by, 484–86
 Yahweh as, 479–82
fatherless, father to, 482
Faust, Avraham, 232, 473, 672, 710n77, 710n78, 710n81, 762n66, 785n233, 897n295
fear, in stories of Yahweh as divine warrior, 453, 468–69, 825n82, 826n99
feast of Asiph, 28
female divinity, 675, 696
feminist contributions, to Israelite religion scholarship, 44–46 (*see* Ackerman, Bird, Frymer-Kensky, Meyers et al.)
fields, 'Athtartu as goddess of, 681–83
fiery transcendent anthropomorphisms, for Yahweh, 346, 375–78, 799n141, 834n168
Finkelstein, Israel, 232, 710n77, 710n81, 754n203, 762n67
fire
 abstract representation of Yahweh as, 344
 crafting essence of, 358
 depicting presence of Yahweh with, 344–47
 as focal point for sacred emptiness, 405–7, 425–26
 hypostatic use of, 350–53
 See also divine fire
First Isaiah, 599
Fishbane, Michael, 483–84, 833n161, 862n170
flaming torch (symbol), 345

Fleming, Daniel, x, 53, 154, 200, 271, 324–325, 421, 608, 626–628, 678–679, 712–13n6, 713n7, 716n3, 747n156, 761n53, 761n59, 766n104, 780n187, 782n210, 784n227, 785n232, 793n83, 876n99, 883n150, 883n151, 883n152, 883n153, 883n154, 883n156 and passim
Fleming, Stuart, 121, 313
food, consecrated, 624, 632, 654–55
forgeries, of text sources, 55, 236, 713n9, 714n14, 866n12
Foundation Inscription of Yaḥdunlim, King of Mari, 717n7
Fox, Michael V., 7, 547, 550, 555, 556, 673, 701n6, 722n49, 858n133, 858n134, 858n138, 898n298
Freedman, David N., 84, 220–21, 270–71, 349, 535–36
Fribourg school of iconography, 37–38, 128, 129
Friedman, Richard, 406–7
Frymer-Kensky, Tikva, 45, 539, 564, 611, 711n87, 711n96, 877n107
functional pantheon, 261–62

Gad, El and, 83, 720n27, 750n176
Gafney, Wilda, 46, 534, 545, 726n88
Geller, Stephen, 22, 357, 702n13, 707n56, 802n171, 802n174
Genesis, book of
 cherubim in, 397
 El as benevolent protector in, 112, 113
 El Bethel in, 99–100
 El Olam in, 97, 98
 El Roi in, 95–97
 El Shadday in, 102, 106–7
 Elyon associations in, 95
 fiery attendants of Yahweh in, 349
 Hagar in, 726n88
 and revelation of name Yahweh, 224, 226–27
 Yahweh as absolute judge in, 528
Germany, religious scholarship in, 19–23, 702n4
Gezer, misdating of limestone altar from, 126, 127f, 128f
Gideon (biblical figure), 272–73
Gilgamesh Epic, 23, 69, 215, 740n86, 758n22
Gilmour, Garth, 240, 309–11

SUBJECT INDEX

Ginsberg, Harold Louis, 29, 31, 97, 262, 361, 705n45, 706n50, 758–59n28, 774n156, 804n187, 830n128
gittu, 682
Giveon, Raphael, 231, 731n142, 761n53
glory
  and divine radiance, 361–62
  as focal point for sacred emptiness, 407, 426
  "Glory of Yahweh," 368–70
God of seeing, El as, 95–97
God of the Fathers, El as, 83–85
God of the Mountain, El Shadday as, 102
God of the Steppe Lands, El Shadday, 103–4
gods
  as family in Ugarit, 474–76, 475f
  lists of, 776–78nn171–172
  Yahweh's judicial authority over, 565–68
Goliath (biblical figure), 465
Gottwald, Norman, 24, 41
Grabbe, Lester, 211, 230, 233, 256, 625, 627, 717n6, 731n139, 761n53, 879n125, 881n140, 882n146, 885n172
Greenberg, Moshe, 33, 289, 345, 378, 707n56, 708n58, 708n60, 790n53, 808n221, 888n198, 888n202
Greenfield, Jonas, 264, 266, 267, 511, 718n18, 719n19, 733n156, 777n172, 778n176, 798n133, 850n53
Greenstein, Edward, 552, 556–57, 701n7, 738n63, 804n187, 819n38, 837n192, 860n153, 860n154
Gruber, Mayer, 490, 492, 669, 843n259
Gunkel, Hermann, 23–25, 28, 44, 262, 443, 703n21, 703n22, 704n27, 817n16, 819n43, 884n165,

Habakkuk
  allusions to geographic origin of Yahweh in, 280–81
  divine radiance in, 359–61
  fiery attendants in, 348
  Yahweh as divine warrior in, 451–52, 801n164
Hackett, Jo Ann, 45, 105, 269, 709n75, 710n76, 711n96, 724–25n71, 730n129
Hadad (deity), 264, 266, 332, 334, 747–48n163

Hagar (biblical figure), 59, 95, 96, 97, 100, 110, 112, 227, 545, 726n88, 726n92
Hallo, William, 70, 158, 287, 304–5
Halpern, Baruch, 396, 517, 534
Hamath, 233–34
Hammurabi (Babylonian king), 513–15, 514f, 517
Hartman, L. F., 101–2
Hathor, temple to, at Dendera, 328, 329f
Ḥatti, royal cult in, 497
Hazor, xi, 41, 131, 141, 303, 324, 412, 576, 717n6, 739n81, 742n110, 742n115, 743n125, 748n163, 749n175, 750n185, 772n144, 792n77
  cherub carving from, 398, 398f
  cherub throne on scarab from, 402, 404f
  divine images of El from, 159–63, 163f–64f, 168
  masseboth at, 171, 172, 176–83, 177f–79f, 181f–84f, 193, 194, 195, 422
  misidentified figurine from, 126, 126f, 157–58, 162f, 180–81, 183f, 184f, 298, 333
  statue of storm/warrior god from, 149, 154f, 165f
  theriomorphic representations of El from, 197, 200, 201f
healing
  cultic images for, 138, 738n61, 903n58
  and 'Ilu, 78, 79, 89, 475, 720n31
  incantations to gods for, 773n148
healing rituals, 3, 138
Hebrew Bible
  abstract representations of Yahweh in, 344–79, 423
  active presence of Yahweh in, 218–19
  allusions to geographic origin of Yahweh, 279–80, 282
  anthropomorphic representations of Yahweh in, 287–90, 382, 418
  Aramean religion in, 264
  archaic vocalization of name Yahweh, 219–20
  artisans' role in, 134
  bull symbolism for Yahweh in, 317
  Canaanite religion in, 254
  Chaoskampf traditions in, 443–46, 448, 459–60

characterization of Nineveh in, 572, 573
clothing of images in, 136
content edited out of, 560
in context of ancient Near East, 69–70
cultic images in, 293
culture-specific practices in, 263–64
divine fatherhood in, 479
divine "name" in, 379
divine names in, 57–58
encounters with Yahweh in, 171–72
equating of El and Yahweh in, 427
etymology of name Yahweh, 213–14
exile of statues in, 140, 141
Exodus 3:14 on name Yahweh, 214–15
function of El in, 110
ḥērem warfare at, 463
historical study of, 715n27
historicist reductionism of scholars of, 426, 816n297
Judahite revision in, 53
judicial system of Israel in, 523–24
law collections in, 714n23
leonine metaphors and images in, 313
magic use of divine images in, 139, 140
masseboth mentioned in, 169–96, 333–36
materials for icons in, 132–33
meaning of name Yahweh, 210–11
Midianites and Kenites in, 272–79
myth in, 708n63
origin myths of Israelite judiciaries in, 525
origins of Yahweh in, 210–27, 271
pronunciation of name Yahweh, 211
and putative name "Jehovah," 212–13
quickening and consecration rituals in, 135
religious personnel in, 4–5
representations of deities in, 303
revelation of name Yahweh in, 223–27
royal legislation in, 559–61
and source criticism, 61–68
and textual criticism, 61
traveling and pilgrimage in, 137–38

Hebrew Bible (*cont.*)
  Ugaritic religion in themes of, 262–63
  Yahweh as "He Who Causes to Be," 220–23
  Yahweh as "He Who Is," 215–18
  Yahweh as king in, 508–9
  See also specific books
Hebrew language
  in Canaanite family, 253
  personal names attesting to God as divine father in, 480
  "Yahweh" in, 218–22
Hebrew poem, oldest known, 240
Hebron, Yahweh of, 701*n*1, 875*n*90
Hendel, Ronald, 42, 51, 158, 164, 296–97, 349, 355, 376, 423, 733*n*161, 796*n*120, 799*n*141, 801*n*159, 807*n*216, 860*n*159
ḥērem warfare, 55, 462–64, 763*n*70, 832*n*147
hermeneutics, 38–39
Herzog, Ze'ev, 122*f*, 184, 185, 186*f*, 187, 303, 710*n*77, 748*n*166, 788*n*32, 866*n*12 and passim
ḥesed relationships, 542–43
Hess, Richard, 56, 58, 74, 229, 628, 712*n*2, 713*n*11, 714*n*16, 717*n*11, 723*n*53, 741*n*98, 756*n*5, 770*n*129, 808*n*217
He Who Blows, Yahweh as, 223
He Who Causes to Be, Yahweh as, 220–23
He Who Fells with Lightning, Yahweh as, 223
He Who Is, Yahweh as, 215–18
Hezekiah (biblical figure), 335, 466–67, 847*n*27, 893*n*261
Hiebert, Theodore, 359, 452
Hillers, Delbert, 259–260, 346–47
history-of-religion method, of biblical studies, 24, 703*n*21, 819*n*43
Hittites
  Elkunirsha myth of, 81–82
  gods as mother and father for, 478
  judicial instructions for, 515–16
Hobab (biblical figure), 274, 275, 527
Hoffner, Harry, 217, 497, 626, 721*n*45, 844*n*4
holiness
  of Ark, 595–99, 604–5
  as awesome power, 577–78, 582–83
  in book of Joshua, 652–53
  centrality of Yahweh's, 577
  in Chronicles, 658–59
  concept of, 14–15
  of cultic objects, 866*n*12
  early attestations of cultic, 606–15
  in early texts, 578–83
  expansive, 630–36
  expressed with destructive power or benevolence, 593–95
  ideological, 613–15
  lethal (*See* lethal holiness)
  of Levites, 636–43
  management of, in Priestly traditions, 616–43
  management of cultic, 605–6
  Rudolph Otto's approach to understanding, 587–88
  and power, 587–88, 603–4, 645
  in Priestly traditions, 616, 878–79*n*118
  of prophets, 665–67
  Holiness source (H), 786*n*5, 854*n*93, 881*n*136, 884*n*159, 884*n*160, 886*n*162, 887*n*190, 893*n*260
  holy personnel in, 630–32
  Moses viewed in, 618–19
  priesthood in, 660
Holladay, John, 40, 317, 520, 710*n*82, 766*n*100, 790*n*52
holy garments, 619–22
"the Holy One"
  in inscriptions at Kuntillet 'Ajrud, 587
  Northwest Semitic deities referred to as, 575–76
"the Holy One of Israel"
  and ancient Israelite religion, 600–602
  in Isaianic traditions, 599–603
holy personnel, 3–5
  in Chronicles, 659–61
  in Deuteronomist History, 653–57
  Deuteronomistic conceptions of, 651–53
  in Deuteronomy, 647–51
  in different traditions, 15
  in Ezekiel, 643–47
  gradations in, 617
  and gradations of status, 612
  in handling of Ark, 596–97
  in Holiness source, 630–32
  holy prophets as, 665–67
  Nazirites, 632–36
  priestly personnel, 653–57
  in Priestly traditions, 615–43, 629–30
  role of Levites as, 636–43
  in Ugaritic religion, 263
  women as, 667–70
holy spirit, living in Moses, 614–15
holy war, 429–30, 462–64, 655. *See also* warfare
homogegnization, of ancient Near East cultures, 70–71
Horeb, Mt., 109, 282, 356, 666, 753*n*198, 782*n*205, 805*n*196, 879*n*118
horse symbolism, on Taanach cult stand, 323–24, 323*f*, 420
Hosea, book of
  discipline by Yahweh in, 484
  holiness of Yahweh in, 593–95, 615–16, 873*n*75
  humans as rebellious children in, 483
  Jeroboam I's bull images in, 320–21
  revelation of name Yahweh in, 226
  Yahweh as caring father in, 481–82
  Yahweh as mother in, 492–93
House of the Magician-Priest at Ugarit, 123, 124*f*, 144–46, 145*f*
H source. *See* Holiness source (H)
humans
  involvement of, in non-cosmic warfare, 464–66
  as rebellious children, 482–89
  redemption of, by father, 486–89
  representations of divine figures vs., 308, 310
  reproving of, by father, 484–86
  synergism of divine war and war involving, 462–64
human sacrifice, 64, 730*n*129, 733*n*161, 772*n*140, 847*n*31, 857*n*124, 887*n*194
hunting, association of El Shadday with, 103
huntress, 'Athtartu as, 681
Hurowitz, Victor, 121, 133, 364, 391
hypocorism, 760*n*48
hypostasis
  of Bethel, 728–29*n*116
  for fire, 350–53
  of names, 386–90, 407

iconoclasm, aniconism and, 341, 343–44
iconographic studies, 119–28, 129*f*–32*f*
  limitations of, 120–21
  material culture use, lack of, 120
  misdating in, 126–27, 126*f*–28*f*
  misidentifications in, 121–23, 124*f*–25*f*, 125

SUBJECT INDEX

misinterpretations from drawing
process, 127–28, 129f–32f
misuse of material culture
in, 121
iconography
decline in anthropormorphic
representations of gods,
787–88n27
immortality of gods in, 216, 216f
study of, 37–38, 709n71
of ʾAštart, 689
See also El iconography; Yahweh
iconography
ideal just divine judge, 545–57, 564
divine justice for Job, 551–57
and justice as theme in wisdom
literature, 546–47
proverbial understandings of
divine justice, 547–49
and theodicy in
Qoheleth, 549–51
ideal just human judge, 534–45
and covenant lawsuits, 539–43
and judgment oracles, 538–39
as prosecutor of abuse of
justice, 534–38
ideological holiness, 613–15
ʾIl
in Aramean religion, 267
as proper name, 716–17n6
Ildayyi (Ḫasi ruler), 75
ʾIlu
abode of, 718n16
in Baʿlu cycle, 440, 441
characterization of El,
110, 112–14
dependability of, 217
and El Shadday, 103, 104, 108
as family god, 474–75, 477
and healing, 720n31
as holy, 582–83
iconography of, 142–55,
156f–61f
Ugarit statuette of, 127,
129f, 130f
worship of, at Ugarit, 76–81, 118
ilu/ʾel (Semitic word), 73
Ilumilka (Tyrian messenger), 75
image ban texts, 303, 902n52,
796n116
immortality, of Near East
gods, 215–17
impotency, ʾIlu as sufferer of, 78
incantations
in family religion, 66, 769n122
to healing gods, 773n148
on plaques, 779n181
incense
burned by Levites, 639,
894–95n271

burned by priests, 622, 664,
894–95n271
consecration required to
burn, 662
indentured slavery, 486–87, 486f
ineffable, language of, 343–44
injustice, unaddressed, 534
Instructions of Amenemope, 547
interdisciplinary work,
necessary for religious
scholarship, 49–50
intolerance, and El, 115
invisibility, as focal point for sacred
emptiness, 407–9, 426
Iron Age
absence of anthropomorphic
images of male deity from,
298–304
abstract images of divine from,
341, 342f, 343f
Canaanite culture in, 258, 286
El Shadday in, 105–6
El worship in, 73, 82–83, 210
kings in, 495
Yahweh's name in, 210,
229, 270–71
Isaiah, book of
association of Yahweh with
masseboth in, 336
bloodletting after divine warfare
in, 470, 471
cosmic warfare by Yahweh as
king, 510
discipline by Yahweh in, 485
divine combat myth in, 444–46
on divine justice in
future, 530–31
divine radiance in, 366–68, 377
El Elyon in, 87
fatherly redemption in, 487–88
fiery attendants of Yahweh
in, 348
fire to depict Yahweh's presence
in, 346
God as eschatological judge, 533
holiness in, 591–93
holiness of Moses in, 614–15
humans as rebellious children
in, 483
hypostatic use of names in, 387
infusing of divinity in kingship
in, 506–7
inviolability of Jerusalem in, 468
location of El's mountain in, 108
procession of deities in, 137–38
prosecution of abuse of justice
in, 536–37
Yahweh alone in battle in, 466
Yahweh as absolute judge
in, 529

Yahweh as divine parent
in, 477–78
Yahweh as law giver in, 560–61
Yahweh as mother in, 490–92
Isaianic Apocalypse, 460–61
Isaianic traditions, "the Holy One
of Israel" in, 599–603
Ishbaʿl inscription, 234–35, 234f
Ishtar/Mulissu (deity), 401, 401f,
402f, 466, 478–79, 737n51
Israel
aniconic tradition of, 119,
155, 156
discipline of, by Yahweh, 484–86
early Israelite judiciaries, 525–28
El as original god of, 115–18
establishment of, 716n3
geographic location of, 253
iconography of El in, 155–208,
166f–70f, 173f, 175f, 177f–
79f, 181f–86f, 188f–93f,
201f–7f
judicial system of, 523–24
king's role in cultic activities in,
498–503
lack of male divine figures in
Iron Age, 302–4
law writing in, 558–59, 564
as rebellious child, 483
Yahweh as father of, 479, 481–82
Yahweh as mother to, 489–90
Yahweh as national god of, 209–10
Yahweh as redeemer of, 487–88
Israelite religion, ancient
archaic lore in, 446–48
ʾAštart in, 693–96
definitions of, 52–53,
712–13nn6–7
developments in study
of, 50–52
distinctiveness of, 30–31
divine radiance in, 359
and "the Holy One of Israel,"
600–602
literature, music, art, and dance
in, 7–8
and priestly cult, 14
reflection in, 6–7
religious personnel in, 3–5
and royal cult, 13
viewed as primitive, 703n19
Yahweh as divine warrior in,
429–30, 443–46
Israelites, Shasu nomads as,
231–32

Jacob (patriarch of Israel),
73, 99–101
Jacob-El, 112
Jacob-el (as toponym), 75, 717n12

Jacobsen, Thorkild, 338–39
Jael (biblical figure), 273, 277–78
Jahaziel, 658
Jahwist/Yahwist source (J)
   anthropomorphic representations of Yahweh in, 288
   cherubim in, 397
   Midianites and Kenites portrayals in, 272
   on Moses's father-in-law, 276, 781n197
   revelation of name Yahweh in, 224, 226–27
   use of, 65
Jehoiakim, injustice of, 519–20
Jehoida (biblical figure), 895n273
Jehoshaphat (biblical figure)
   acknowledgment of Yahweh by, 658
   as king of justice, 520–21
Jehovah, as putative name, 212–13
Jekke, stela from, 150f
Jeremiah (biblical figure), 665
Jeremiah, book of, 139
   on David as king of justice, 518
   on divine justice in future, 531, 532
   humans as rebellious children in, 483
   on Josiah as king of justice, 519–20
   Name Theology in, 383
   and Yahweh in family religion, 473
Jeremias, Jörg, 306–9
Jericho, 891n238
Jeroboam I
   bull images of, 198–200, 318–21, 420
   cultic activities by, 502, 752–53nn191–193
Jerusalem
   abuse of justice in, 537
   enthronement of Yahweh in, 510–11
   geometric humanoid figures on potsherd from, 309–13, 312f
   inviolability of, 467–69, 511
   as sanctuary in Name Theology, 382–83, 392
   Yahweh of, 701n1
   as Yahweh's daughter, 485, 486
Jerusalem Temple (Solomonic Temple)
   Ark and cherubim as focal points of, 394–95, 398–99
   building of, 500–501
   dedication of, 655–56
   destruction of, and inviolability of Jerusalem, 469
   divine image of Yahweh in, 290–97
   divine radiance in dedication of, 365–66
   enthronement of Yahweh in, 510–11
   fire and glory as focal points in, 406, 407
   name and invisibility as focal points in, 408, 409, 415
   "name" of Yahweh in, 356
   and Name Theology, 381–83, 392
   pragmatic focal points in, 425–26
   sacred emptiness of, 393
   and Yahweh's holiness, 659
Jethro (biblical figure)
   in Midianite hypothesis, 272–76, 781n197
   in origin myth of Israelite judiciary, 525–26
Ji, Chang-ho, 193, 203, 205
Job, book of, 672–73
   divine combat myth in, 445–46, 820–21n57
   divine justice in, 551–57
   divine speeches and theophany in, 555–57
   El Shadday in, 104–5
   filing of Job's legal complaint, 554–55
   Job's imaginary lawsuit in, 553–54, 897–98n297
   remembering archaic lore in, 447–48
   twisting of justice in, 551, 552
Joel, book of
   bloodletting after divine warfare in, 471
   rhetoric of disarmament in, 472
Jonah, book of, 571–74, 864–65n195
Joseph, as Nazirite, 633, 884n165
Joshua, book of, 652–53, 890n227
Josiah (biblical figure), 519–20
JPFs (Judean pillar figurines), 735n11, 748n164, 789n41, 841n238, 889n210, 903n58 (see Darby)
J source. See Jahwist/Yahwist source (J)
Judah
   divine kingship in, 504
   infusing of divinity for kings of, 505–7
   "Kings of Justice" of, 517–21
   lack of male divine figures in Iron Age, 302–4
   royal judicial ideology of, 517
Judean pillar figurines (JPFs), 735n11, 748n164, 789n41, 841n238, 889n210, 903n58 (see Darby)
Judges, book of
   allusions to geographic origin of Yahweh in, 279
   divine radiance in, 377
   fiery attendants of Yahweh in, 350
   human involvement in warfare in, 465
   Kenites in, 273
   Levites in, 637
   support for Midianite hypothesis in, 277–78
judgment oracles, 538–39
judicial authority of Yahweh, 565–69
judicial system, of early Israel, 523–24
justice
   God's twisting of, 550–51
   ideal just divine judge, 545–57
   ideal just human judge, 534–45
   prosecution of abuse of, 535–38

kābôd of Yahweh, 358–379
   as body, 808–9n224
   in Ezekiel, 373–79
   and honoring of Yahweh as parent, 483–84
   Moses' request to see, 362–63
   in pre-priestly cultic settings, 364–68
   in Priestly sources, 368–73
Kant, Immanuel, 18–19
Karnak battle reliefs, 230, 231
kashrut, 63–64
Katumuwa inscription, 333–34, 334f, 407, 722n49, 776n171, 777n171, 778n172, 795n108, 815n286
Kaufmann, Yehezkel, 32–34, 35, 71, 110, 318–20, 707n56, 707n57, 707n58, 708n60, 708n63, 752n192, 876n105
Keel, Othmar, 37–38, 119–120, 147–148, 158, 166–69, 170f, 197, 243, 256–57, 267, 299, 303, 305f, 306, 313, 323,

324, 326 327, 330, 332, 405, 412, 415, 701n2, 709n71, 710n83, 718n16, 738n62, 741n97, 741n98, 743n124, 744n134, 744n136, 744n138, 750n184, 765n90, 772n148, 787n19, 787n22, 787n27, 789n40, 790n51, 792n72, 792n76, 792n77, 794n97, 794n101 and passim
Kenites, in Hebrew Bible, 272–73
Ketef Hinnom
   amulets from, 328, 330, 768n117, 769n120, 769n122
   discoveries at, 42–43
   name of Yahweh in inscriptions from, 247–50, 248f, 249f
Ketiv-Qere practice, Jehovah as result of, 212–13
Khirbet Ataruz (see Ataroth)
   masseboth at, 193, 193f
   theriomorphic representations of El from, 202–5, 203f–5f
Khirbet Beit Lei, 55, 166, 211, 245, 408, 481, 765n93, 767n107, 789n42, 828n108
Khirbet el-Qom, 38, 167, 241–44, 243f, 250, 766n99, 766n101, 769n121
Khirbet Qeiyafa, 60, 234–35, 234f, 252, 762n67, 770n132
kings
   divine election of, 848–49n40
   infusing of, with divinity, 504–7
   limits on judicial power of, 543–45, 561
   religious lives and divinity of, 496–98
   as religious personnel, 3–4
   role of, in cultic activities, 498–503
Kings, book of
   allusions to geographic origin of Yahweh, 282
   Ark in, 408
   'Aštart in, 691
   bull symbolism in, 317
   on cherubim, 398
   and divine image of Yahweh in Jerusalem Temple, 296
   divine images in, 134
   divine radiance in, 365–66
   fire to depict Yahweh's presence in, 347
   Name Theology and, 385, 810–11n243
   on Solomon as king of justice, 519

Yahweh alone in battle in, 466
kingship
   cosmic warfare and Yahweh's, 510
   cultic enactment of Yahweh's, 511–13
   divine, 503–4, 705n40
   and divine speeches of Job, 556
   in El traditions, 95
   enthronement of Yahweh in Jerusalem, 510–11
   for 'Ilu, 80
   and inviolability of Jerusalem, 469
   Judean, 505–7
   superlative quality of Yahweh's, 509
   of Yahweh, in Zion theology, 511
"kings of justice," 517–21, 564
kinship
   El's association with, 111
   of Kenites and Midianites, 272
   and origin of Yahweh in ethnic self-identification process, 285
Kirta (Syrian king), 75, 95, 114, 474–75, 497–98, 516, 517, 738n63, 837n192, 844n9
Kirta Epic, 262, 681
   'Ilu in, 78–79, 81, 82, 95, 497, 870n47
   immortality of gods in, 216–17, 725n79
Kisilevitz, Shua, 195–96
Kition, 'Aštart at, 255, 684–85, 690, 694, 901n34
Klein, Jacob, 496–97
Knohl, Israel, 288, 375, 617, 630, 632, 640, 786n5, 786n6, 786n11, 807n214, 854n93, 875n82, 876n105, 881n136 881n139, 884n159, 884n160, 884n162, 884n164, 887n185, 887n190, 893n260
Knoppers, Gary, 66, 198–99, 366, 385, 386, 395, 519, 520, 521, 655, 658, 665, 709n76, 739n74, 751n190, 752n192, 753n195, 758n23, 781n204, 807n206, 811n245, 811n246, 845n11, 845n13, 846n19, 851n67, 851n69, 851n72, 853n89, 891n236, 892n245, 892n248, 893n253, 893n256, 894n266, 894n269 and passim

Kohathite Levites, 597, 599, 604, 636, 639, 640, 645, 847n25, 887n187, 887n191, 892n242
Korah, 372–73, 640–41
Kotharu-wa-Hasisu (deity), 134, 190, 440, 441, 477, 681, 736n34, 755n1, 818n35
Kraus, Hans-Joachim, 92, 454–55
Krebernik, Manfred, 228, 233, 716n3
Kugel, James, 10
Kuntillet 'Ajrud
   allusions to geographic origin of Yahweh from, 281
   and Asherah, 38, 42, 54–55, 125, 125f, 167, 236, 237, 238f, 239, 239f, 240, 243, 281, 293, 305, 308, 325–28, 330, 409, 411, 701n2, 711n87, 740n82, 763n73, 763n78, 765n88, 765n89, 765n90, 774n154, 794n94, 816n290, 898n1
   bull representations from, 322, 325–30, 325f, 421
   discoveries at, 42, 236–41, 711n87, see Meshel
   empty-space aniconism and pithoi from, 409–11, 410f
   holy warrior in inscriptions at, 583–87, 584f–85f
   iconography from, 325–28, 325f
   name Yahweh in inscriptions from, 222
   name Yahweh in texts from, 236–40, 238f, 239f, 241f, 243
   representations of divine couple from, 305, 325–28
Lachish
   aniconic representations of Yahweh and, 296
   name of Yahweh on ostraca from, 250–51, 250f
"the Lady of Byblos," Phoenician temple of, 154, 161f
Lamentations, book of, 523
lamps, as focal points, 406
Lapp, Paul, 316–17, 316f, 323
Late Bronze Age
   'Athtartu at Ugarit during, 679–84
   Canaanite culture in, 256–59, 261
   El figurines from, 163, 166f–69f
   El worship in, 74–76, 97
   gods as family in, 473–76, 475f

1032 SUBJECT INDEX

Late Bronze Age (cont.)
  male divine figurines in, 298–302, 299f–301f
  Shadday in, 105
Lauinger, Jacob, 716n31, 890n219
lawgiver, God as, 558–61
Laws of Hammurabi, 25, 513–15, 514f, 517, 804n191, 850n58, 853n84, 861n161
lawsuits, covenant, 539–43
law writer, God as, 558–61
legal codes, 558
  biblical law collections as, 714n23, 862n168
  royal appropriation of, 513–17, 861n161
legal fictions, for conflicts of theory and practice, 561
legitimization of royalty
  Ark for, 396–97
  and Yahweh as cosmic warrior, 453–60
Lemaire, André, 245, 306, 713n8, 724n71, 762n69, 763n73, 764n84, 766n94, 766n102, 767n107, 767n110, 768n111, 776n171, 870n42 and passim
Lemche, Niels Peter, 38, 39, 709n74, 709n75, 710n76, 771n134, 774n155
lethal God hearings, 354, 355, 357, 358, 367, 423, 802n171
lethal God sightings, 96, 296–97, 353, 355, 367, 378, 379, 510, 557, 801n159, 802n170, 860n159
lethal holiness, 424, 583, 595–99, 605, 606, 609, 611–12, 621, 625, 642, 654, 656, 666, 667, 891n239
  of Ark, 891n239
  in Exodus, 611–12
  as manifestation of power, 671
  and Yahweh as family god, 494
lethality, of fire and radiance of Yahweh, 370–73, 377–78, 389, 423
Levant
  Chaoskampf myths in, 439–42
  El worship in, 74–76, 83
  inscriptions with images in, 739–40n82
  role of artisans in, 133
Levenson, Jon, 33–34
Levine, Baruch, 14, 89–90, 96, 107, 116, 208, 268–69, 273, 528, 563, 597, 618, 626, 720n31, 725n71, 731n133, 808n217, 808n218, 812n253, 833n155, 874n80, 881n136, 887n185 and passim
Levinson, Bernard, 518, 525–526, 545, 561, 714n21, 714n23, 802n169, 845n13, 849n48, 851n72, 853n91, 854n93, 862n169, 862n170, 863n177, 876n100 and passim
Levites
  and Ark, 874n77
  in Chronicles, 661, 663–64
  cultic privileges of, 641–43
  in Deuteronomy, 649–51, 660–61
  holiness of, 636–43
  intermediary role of, 893–94n262
  modern research on, 885–86n172
  in Priestly tradition, 660
  rebellion of, 639–41
  restrictions on, in book of Ezekiel, 646–47, 889n211
Leviticus, book of
  anointing rituals in, 624
  divine radiance in, 369–72
  ḥērem warfare in, 463
  holiness of community in, 630–31
  holiness of Yahweh in, 615
  priesthood in, 631–32
  sources for, 807n214
Levy, Thomas, 40, 231, 251, 745n144, 780n188
lexicography, 713n12
Lincoln, Bruce, 29, 708n66, 848n38
Lind, Millard, 465, 817n9, 831n140
lions
  at Arad, 750–51n185
  Bes representations as, 326–30, 329f
  as representation of El, 196
  as representation of Yahweh, 313–17, 314f–16f
Lipiński, Edward, 83, 233, 265, 267, 718n18, 722n50, 723n51, 730n130, 741nn91–93, 750n182, 769n125, 778n172, 784n229, 835n176, 868n21 and passim
Lissovsky, Nurit, 237, 240
listen, charge to, 539
literature, in ancient Israelite religion, 7–8, 862nn168–69
Liverani, Mario, 513, 797n127, 875n95

Locus 3283 of Hazor, standing stone in, 180–83, 181f–83f
Lord of the Dream/Sleep, 81–82
Lord's Prayer, 903–4n60
love
  expressed in Deuteronomy, 890n219
  language to express Yahweh's, 492–93
love spells, 311–12, 312f
Lundbom, Jack, 383, 483, 520, 649, 689, 699, 728n114, 840n230, 842n248, 842n251, 849n49, 850n51, 853n89, 861n165, 886n179 and passim
Luwian Karatepe inscription, 81, 98, 479

Maccabees, book of, 465
Machinist, Peter, 69, 71, 497, 505, 706n48, 725n72, 758n23, 807n209, 863n179 and passim
Maeir, Aren, 269, 710n77, 776n169
magic rituals
  icon use, in ancient Near East, 138–39, 139f
  use of potsherds with figures in, 311–12, 312f
Malachi, book of
  creation and fatherhood in, 481
  humans as rebellious children in, 483–84
  retribution in, 550
male deities
  absence of Iron Age images of, 302–4
  fatherhood for, 479–80
  Late Bronze Age figurines of, 298–302, 299f–301f
Manasseh, 134, 292, 294, 559, 688–89
Mandell, Alice, 237, 245, 310, 408, 715n27, 766n101, 766n102, 767n107, 770n131, 789n42, 812n260, 815n287, 816n292
Marduk (deity), in cosmic warfare, 437–39, 454
Mari
  cylinder seal from, 147–48, 148f
  Foundation Inscription from, 717n7
Marsman, Hennie, 42, 44, 45, 46, 479, 711n94
marzeaḥ, 773nn149–150
  and Canaanite culture/religion, 258, 721nn32–33
  enduring of, through millennia, 79, 773n150
  'Ilu at, 79–80

SUBJECT INDEX   1033

Masoretic Text (MT), 57, 59
Masoretic tradition
　El Bethel in, 100
　and hybrid name
　　Jehovah, 212–13
　understanding of Psalm 82
　　in, 568–69
massebah/masseboth, 169–96,
　　333–36, 744–45n141
　attributions of use of, 121,
　　122f, 123f
　in Hebrew Bible, 745n143
　purpose of, 747n157
　as representation of Yahweh, 422
　representations of El on,
　　169, 171–96
　representations of Yahweh
　　on, 333–36
material aniconism,
　　333–36, 421–22
material culture
　aniconism in, 333–36, 421–22
　anthropomorphic
　　representations of Yahweh
　　in, 297–98, 419
　bull representations of Yahweh
　　in, 322–33
　in iconographic analysis, 120–21
　as source material, 68–69
　theriomorphic representations
　　of El in, 200–208, 201f–7f
materiality, 9, 40, 43, 53, 310, 393,
　　407, 408, 697, 767n107,
　　789n42, 816n292
Mazar, Amihai, 120, 175, 175f, 176,
　　200, 202, 710n77, 710n83,
　　742n109, 742n110, 746n154,
　　754n203, 754n204, 843n263
McBride, Dean, 380–82, 386
McCarter, P. Kyle, 218, 219,
　　236, 245, 251–52, 269,
　　283, 322, 326, 351–53,
　　364, 365, 386, 401,
　　465, 535, 586, 657,
　　696, 701n1, 710n83,
　　717n13, 737n49, 739n78,
　　750n184, 754n207,
　　762n69, 764n81, 764n82,
　　765n92, 767n107,
　　767n110, 768n111,
　　770n127, 770n129,
　　770n132, 784n226,
　　785n234, 788n30,
　　788n31, 806n203,
　　811n249, 811n251,
　　823n74, 824n76, 824n79,
　　832n145, 833n154,
　　855n196, 870n48,
　　871n49, 873n76, 874n77,

　　874n79, 885n169 and
　　　passim
McCarthy, Dennis, 214, 218
Meek, James, 275–76
Megiddo
　bronze figurine from, 164,
　　165, 167f
　cult stand with fenestrations
　　from, 415, 417f
　male divine figurines from,
　　298–99, 299f, 300f
　representations of human figures
　　from, 310
　Shemaʿ-servant of Jeroboam (II)
　　seal from, 313
Mekal, 120, 744n133
melammu, 339, 797nn125–27
　and divine radiance in Ezekiel,
　　375–76, 376f
　and divine radiance in
　　Isaiah, 368
Meṣad Ḥashavyahu
　inscription, 554–55
Mesha stela (Moabite stone),
　　235, 235f, 251, 429, 462,
　　749n172
Meshel, Zeʾev, 42, 236–37,
　　325–26, 327,
　　583, 586, 710n77,
　　711n86, 763n73,
　　763n74, 763n75,
　　763n79, 764n83,
　　764n85, 764n86, 765n87,
　　765n88, 766n94,
　　766n95, 866n12, 884n34,
　　868–69n36, 869n37
　and passim
Mesopotamia
　abstract images of divine
　　in, 338–39
　divine kingship in, 504
　justice as theme in wisdom
　　literature of, 546–47
　kings as judges in, 513
　myths in, 708n64
　role of artisans in, 133
Messenger/Angel of Yahweh
　(*malʾak*-Yahweh)
　divine fire associated
　　with, 349–50
　divine radiance associated with,
　　353, 355, 377
　and Name Theology, 389–90
metal figurines, production
　of, 302–3
methodology, 48–72
　academic disciplines for subject
　　study, 48–49
　and comparanda, 69–72

　and definitions of Israelite
　　religion, 52–53
　and definitions of religion, 49–52
　history of, 1–2
　material culture as source
　　material, 68–69
　for studying iconography, 119–
　　28, 129f–32f
　texts as source material, 53–68
Mettinger, Tryggve, 39, 116, 121,
　　169, 171, 194, 219, 220, 226,
　　294, 297, 319, 320, 333, 357,
　　362, 381, 382, 383, 384, 386,
　　395, 408, 415, 421, 495, 510,
　　710n83, 729n119, 758n26,
　　767n106, 791n59, 807n214,
　　810n240 and passim
Meyers, Carol, 42, 44–47, 111, 122,
　　310–311, 400, 406, 494,
　　524, 690, 710n83, 711n87,
　　711n92, 711n93, 711n96,
　　711n97, 711n98, 712n99,
　　756n5, 794n100, 796n118,
　　842n253, 853n84 and passim
Micah, book of
　bloodletting after divine warfare
　　in, 471
　covenant lawsuit in, 539–43
　inviolability of Jerusalem in,
　　467, 468
　prosecution of abuse of justice
　　in, 537–38
Michalowski, Piotr, 497, 504,
　　705n40
Middle Bronze Age, Canaanite
　culture in, 71, 153, 154,
　　160f, 176, 177f, 183, 195,
　　256–59, 447, 740n83,
　　743n124, 772n144,
　　772n147, 820n48
Midianite/Kenite hypothesis,
　　271–82, 780n187
　instruction of Moses and Jethro
　　in, 275–76
　and Midianites vs. Kenites in
　　Hebrew Bible, 272–73
　and Moses' father-in-law in
　　Hebrew Bible, 273–75
　overview, 271–72
　topographic allusions
　　supporting, 279–82
　updated versions of, 276–79
Midianites, in Hebrew
　　Bible, 272–73
"Mighty One of Jacob," 84, 100, 105,
　　174, 197, 199, 287, 318, 420,
　　601–603
Milgrom, Jacob, 14, 51, 107, 370,
　　407, 424, 499, 605–6, 614,

1034 SUBJECT INDEX

Milgrom, Jacob (cont.)
    616, 617, 618, 619, 621,
    625, 626, 629, 635–36, 642,
    786n8, 807n214, 807n215,
    844n8, 864n187, 876n105,
    877n109, 878n112,
    878n118, 879n121, 879n124,
    881n135, 881n140,
    881n142, 882n143,
    882n145, 882n146,
    883n155, 883n158,
    887n185, 887n187,
    887n195, 888n208,
    889n210, 889n211, 892n243
    and passim
militaristic wilderness theophany,
    583–87, 721n44
military camps, holiness in, 647–48
military context, for Name
    Theology, 388–89
military power, of Yahweh,
    600, 603–4
Milkom (deity), 303, 304, 509,
    788n31
Miller, Patrick, 11, 87, 88, 349,
    800n147, 805n199,
    806n204, 817n9, 831n140
Miller, Robert, 448
Minet el Beida, 683
Miqneyaw seal, 241, 242f
miracles, performed by Elijah and
    Elisha, 666
Mischwesen, 149, 150, 157f, 320
    battles with, in *Chaoskampf*
        tradition, 430–31,
        431f, 432f
    cherubim vs., 397
    enthroned deities atop, 401,
        401f, 794n94
    and other composite mythic
        beasts, 433, 434f–37f
Mistress of the Animals, 2, 148,
    683, 683f, 901n29
Moabites, 285–86
modern values, overlaid on
    premodern societies,
    711–12n98
Molten Sea, 173, 317, 419, 511
Monroe, Lauren, 462, 716n3,
    780n188, 780n190,
    832n147, 833n157
Moorey, P. R. S., 121, 153, 164, 313
Moran, William L., 74, 140, 649,
    717n8, 717n9, 737n51,
    758n21, 758n23, 840n229,
    842n247, 875n95, 890n218,
    890n219
Moses (biblical figure)
    as Beya, 229
    father-in-law of, 273–75

holiness of, 614–15
    as holy personnel, 617–19
    as intercessionary, 650
    in Midianite hypothesis, 271–76
    in origin myths of Israelite
        judiciary, 525–27
    request to see *kābôd* of Yahweh
        from, 362–63
    seeing of "human" body parts of
        Yahweh by, 377–78
    special status of, in
        Exodus, 612–13
    in victory at sea against
        Pharaoh, 452–53
    and Yahweh as judge, 561–63
mother, Yahweh as, 489–93
Motu (deity), in cosmic warfare, 57,
    161-62, 262, 365, 440, 442,
    460–61, 720n31, 819n40
mourner's Kaddish, 903n60
Mousseiff Ostraca, 236
Mowinckel, Sigmund, 27, 214, 395,
    504, 512, 704n36
MT (Masoretic Text), 57
murmuring motif, 372–73
Mushite priesthood, 4, 619, 653,
    782n205, 879n123, 887n183
music
    in ancient Israelite religion, 7–8
    lack of textual sources on, 66,
        894n266
mutilation, of ancient Near East
    statues, 141
myth
    as category of religious
        thought, 24
    in Hebrew Bible, 708n63
    Mesopotamian, 708n64
    new definitions of,
        35–37, 709n67
myth-and-ritual approach, to biblical
    studies, 27–29
mythological pantheon (narrative
    pantheon), 261
mythopoeic, 35, 37, 262, 349, 442,
    454, 459, 565-569, 602,
    801n164, 827n103
mythopoetic, 37, 262, 349, 442,
    459, 565–569, 602,
    801n164, 863n183

Na'aman, Nadav, 185, 187, 231,
    237, 240, 260, 293, 294–97,
    303–4, 321, 381, 395,
    595, 651, 702n5, 710n76,
    729n118, 761n55, 761n56,
    762n64, 763n78, 765n89,
    768n117, 774n155, 788n32,
    854n93, 885n172, 890n223,
    890n225 and passim

Nablus, bronze figure from, 164, 170f
Nadab, death of, 370–73
Nahum, book of, 471, 571, 835n179
name(s)
    as focal point for sacred
        emptiness, 407–9, 426
    lack of data about, 56–57
    obliteration of, 692–93
    placement of, to designate divine
        presence, 383–91
    Yahwistic, 756n5
Name of Yahweh, 387–89
Name Theology, 379–92, 424–25,
    672, 809–10n233
    Ark in, 408
    in book of Kings, 810–11n243
    and divine "name" to
        depict presence of
        Yahweh, 379–80
    and divine radiance, 366
    Jerusalem as sanctuary
        in, 382–83
    national catastrophes of 597 and
        586 BCE, 381
    placement of name to designate
        divine presence, 383–91
    reactionary nature of, 381–82
    tenets of, 380–91
    throne imagery and, 405
Nathan (biblical figure), 534–35
national deities, and El, 114–15
nations, gods as warriors on behalf
    of, 428–29
Naveh, Joseph, 244–45, 244f, 245f,
    311–12, 713n9,
    764n86, 765n87,
    766n102, 766n105,
    767n107, 767n110,
    789n42, 817n9, 832n145
    and passim
Nazirites, 884n164, 884n168
    and consecration, 660, 667,
        884n165
    as religious personnel, 4
Nazirite vows, 4, 15, 377, 617,
    632–36, 833n155,
    885n169, 885n171
Near East, ancient, 1, 9–10, 13, 67,
    69–72, 128–41 and passim
    abstract images to depict divine
        in, 338–41, 340f
    artisan's role in, 133–35
    broad cultural continuum
        in, 71–72
    burial of statues, 141
    clothing of icons, 135–36
    as context of Hebrew
        Bible, 69–70
    cosmic warfare in, 430–33,
        431f, 432f

SUBJECT INDEX 1035

destruction/mutilation of
    statues, 141
divine images in, 291, 293, 393
divine kingship in, 503–4
filial duties of children
    in, 482–83
god as mother and father
    in, 478–79
gods as kings in, 507–8
homogenization of cultures
    in, 70–71
icon use in magic
    rituals, 138–39
immortality of gods in, 215–17
justice as theme in wisdom
    literature of, 546–47
king as embodiment of justice
    in, 513
kingship in lore of, 495
law writing in, 558
materials used for icons, 130–33
in myth-and-ritual approach, 28
procession and traveling rituals
    for icons, 136–38
quickening and consecration
    rituals for icons, 135
royal cult in, 496–507
taking divine images in battle
    in, 140–41
warrior gods in, 428–29
worship of ʿAštart in, 694–95
Nebo, Yahweh cult in, 235, 251, 284,
    462, 769–70n125,
    782n205
Nebuchadrezzar, King (biblical
    figure), 134–35, 295–96, 458
Negbi, Ora, 143, 163, 258, 301,
    744n129, 744n133,
    787n20 and passim
Neo-Assyrian Empire
    gods as mother and father
        in, 478–79
    treatment of prisoners of war in,
        572–73, 572f
New Testament, lion references
    in, 313
Niebuhr, H. Richard, 337
Niehr, Herbert, 136, 265, 290, 291,
    292, 294, 321, 394, 405,
    723n51, 743n123, 776n169,
    779n179, 787n13, 787n17,
    791n69, 844n6
Nimrud prisms, 292–95
Nineveh
    in book of Jonah, 571–74
    legal transactions in, 559
Ninurta, temple to, at Kalhu,
    430–31, 431f
Nissinen, Martti, 5, 269, 466,
    778n175, 809n225, 826n98,

830n123, 830n124, 833n153,
    834n162, 839n208, 851n60,
    895n274, 898n300
non-cosmic warfare, 461–70
    apocalyptic battles, 469–70
    inviolability of Zion/Jerusalem
        in, 467–69
    and synergism of human and
        divine war, 462–64
    underdog ideology and human
        involvement in, 464–66
    Yahweh alone in, 466–70
non-cultic understandings, of
    Yahweh, 577–605
non-elite communities
    and family religion, 43–44
    holiness of, 630–31, 640,
        648–49, 660
    Nazirite vows as path to holiness
        for, 634–36
    in study of ancient Israelite
        religion, 51–52
Non-P, 62, 65 and passim
non-static cult, 62–65
the North
    Deir ʿAlla and Arslan
        Tash, 268–69
    origin of Yahweh from, 270–71
    and Yahweh in Aramean
        religion, 264–68
Northwest Semitic deities
    hypostatization of, 387
Northwest Semitic divinity
    onomastic record of, 57–58
    and Yahweh, 575–77
Noth, Martin, 56, 626–27,
    810n236, 883n150,
    890n227
Numbers, book of
    cherubim in, 400
    divine radiance of Yahweh
        in, 372–73
    El Elyon in, 89–90
    El Shadday in, 106, 107
    handling of Ark in, 597
    hypostatic use of name in, 388
    Levite rebellion in, 639–41
    Moses's judicial role in, 562
    origin myths of Israelite
        judiciaries in, 527
    Yahweh as divine warrior
        in, 430
    Yahweh as mother in, 489–90

offspring deities, representations
    of, 324–25
oil, in anointing rituals, 627–29
Olyan, Saul, 15, 43, 44, 138, 635,
    636, 639–640, 641, 647,
    659, 701n2, 722n50,

733n161, 741n101,
    793n89, 795n111, 817n3,
    837n186, 884n164, 899n8
onomastica, as textual source,
    56–60, 714n18 and passim
    See also personal names
    (onomastics)
"On the Proper Distinction
    Between Biblical and
    Dogmatic Theology and the
    Specific Objectives of Each"
    (Gabler), 702n4
opening remarks, covenant
    lawsuit, 540
Ophel, potsherd from, 309–11, 309f
Oppenheim, A. Leo, 51, 129,
    737n38, 797n124
oracles
    Balaam, 89–90, 94
    for decisions about battle, 464
    judgment, 538–39
oral traditions, passing down
    archaic lore via, 447–48
Ornan, Tallay, 46, 148–149, 159,
    160, 161, 164, 237, 313–14,
    326, 327, 328, 330, 332,
    359, 405, 411, 678, 689,
    739n71, 742n110, 742n120,
    743n121, 763n73, 789n44,
    791n61, 791n62, 791n63,
    793n87, 794n98, 795n104,
    796n116, 815n285,
    815n289 and passim
orphans
    abuse of justice against, 536–37
    Yahweh as father for, 482
    Yahweh as redeemer of, 487–88
Otto, Rudolph, 11, 337–338, 355,
    372, 422, 424, 430, 443,
    461, 587–88, 598–599,
    658, 666–667, 796n117,
    796n123, 817n15, 870n45

palladium, Ark as, 595–97
pan-Babylonian school, 25
parallelomania, 70–71
parallelomania approach, to
    Ugaritic studies, 259
Pardee, Dennis, 57–58, 103, 120,
    135–136, 217, 236, 259, 260,
    263, 440, 448, 498, 714n16,
    714n17, 714n18, 714n22,
    718n17, 718n18, 719n22,
    720n29, 720n30, 721n33,
    721n34, 721n37, 721n38,
    722n49, 724n61, 727n98,
    735n19, 738n63, 769n123,
    774n154, 775n157,
    775n159, 775n160,
    775n165, 778n172,

Pardee, Dennis (cont.)
778n178, 795n108,
799n144, 804n187,
804n188, 817n4, 818n36,
818n38, 819n40, 837n192,
837n196, 838n197, 844n7,
844n10, 875n96, 899n6,
899n12, 899n13, 900n15
and passim
parent, divine, 477–82
Parker, Simon, 79, 217, 262, 497,
775n162
Pella (Ṭabaqāt Faḥil), 205–8,
206f–7f
people's retort, covenant
lawsuit, 540–41
perceptive hymns,
Mesopotamian, 546
perpetual flame, as focal point, 407
Persian period coin, 404f, 405
personal gods, and El, 84–85
personal names
(onomastics), 58–59
connection of Yahweh to
childbirth in, 493
connection of Yahweh to crises
in, 493–94
in Hebrew Bible, 479–80, 726n91
and hypocorism, 760n48
indicators of divine justice
in, 522
in texts from Kuntillet 'Ajrud,
763–64n79
view of God as divine father
in, 480
view of Ugaritic gods as family
in, 476
Yahwistic names, 756n5
personal piety
and family religion, 42–44
and holiness, 643
incantations in, 769n122
and onomastica, 58–59
See also holiness
Pettinato, Giovanni, 228
Philo of Byblos
on Canaanite religion, 255–56
Elyon in, 87, 88
Phoenicia, 'Aštart in, 684–87
Phoenicians, epigraphic sources
from, 254–55, 771n138
Phoenician language, 869n40
pilgrimage, 137–38
pillar of fire (symbol), 345
pithoi, name Yahweh on, 237–40,
238f, 239f
plaintiff, speech to accused by, 540

plowshares, from swords,
836nn180–81,
836–37n185
poetic conventions, in Ugaritic
texts, 262
pollution, and consecration, 611
Pope, Marvin, 76, 85, 87, 88, 123,
716n4, 718n16, 719n19,
719n20, 719n24, 721n38,
741n96, 821n57, 901n29
Postgate, Nicholas, 497
pouring, in anointing
rituals, 625–26
power
of Elijah and Elisha, 667
and holiness, 603–4, 645
related to holiness, 577–78,
582–83, 587–88
practice of religion, study of, 3
prayer, votive, 606
precious metals, divine images
of, 303–4
pre-Israelite Canaanite
religion, 253–264
pre-priestly cultic settings, divine
kābôd in, 364–73
preternatural dragons, 433,
434f–37f
priestly cult, 605–665 and passim
and ancient Israelite
religion, 14
in religious scholarship, 4–5
and royal cult, 846n18
priestly personnel, 605–665
and passim
Priestly sources/traditions (P)
Aaronid priests in, 659–60
anointing rituals in, 622–24
anthropomorphic
representations of Yahweh
in, 288, 289
cherubim in, 397
cultic privileges of Levites
in, 641–43
dating of, 21, 65, 107
divine radiance in, 368–73, 375,
382, 424
El Shadday in, 107
on handling of Ark, 598
holy personnel in, 615–43
and humanities in religious
service, 7–8
Levite's rebellion in, 639–41
and Leviticus, 807n214
Midianites and Kenites
portrayals in, 272–73
Moses viewed in, 618–19
Nazirite vows in, 632–36

revelation of name Yahweh,
223–25, 225f
on ritual acts required for
Aaronid priests, 619–29
use of, 65
priests
adjudication by, 528, 529, 538,
563, 854n93
anointing rituals for, 625–26
in Chronicles, 661–65
and cultic activities of kings,
498–500, 502–3
in Deuteronomistic
History, 656–57
in Deuteronomy, 650–51
in Holiness source, 631–32
Nazirites vs., 635–36
and prophets, 5
prophets vs., 895n275
types and ranks of, 4, 653, 885n172
procession ritual
for ancient Near East icons,
136–38, 137f
Ark in, 395–96
processual archaeology, 40
programmatic traditions, of
aniconism, 333
prophecies, about Yahweh as
judge, 530–32
prophets
as holy personnel, 665–67
in Israelite religion, 5
priests vs., 895n275
as prosecutors of abuse of
justice, 534–38
Propp, William, 66–67, 283–84,
317, 345, 350, 405–406,
428, 599, 606, 610, 618, 621,
753n198, 759n39, 780n190,
781n197, 804n191,
813n271, 823n73, 824n75,
825n82, 825n83, 830n127,
876n103, 879n118,
882n146, 890n222, 903n55
and passim
Propp Principle, 66–67, 283
protection (apotropaism)
association of Bes with, 328–30,
329f, 421, 772–73n148
association of Yahweh with,
247–49, 248f, 249f, 328
in family religion, 66
as function of cherubim, 399–400
king as protector, 515
Proverbs, book of
discipline by Yahweh in, 484
on divine justice in future, 532
on holiness of Yahweh, 673

SUBJECT INDEX   1037

on ideal just divine judge, 547–48
Psalms, book of
  allusions to geographic origin of Yahweh, 279–80
  Ark in, 396
  battle at sea in, 450–51
  benediction in, 699
  cherubim in, 400
  on David as king of justice, 518
  divine combat myth in, 443–44
  on divine mercy, 569–70
  divine radiance in, 361, 362, 367–68, 376, 827n103
  El as benevolent protector in, 112
  El Elyon in, 86–90
  El Olam in, 98, 99
  Elyon and Yahweh in, 92
  on enactment of Yahweh's kingship, 511–13
  fiery attendants of Yahweh in, 348, 349
  fire to depict Yahweh's presence in, 345–46
  God as caring judge in, 522–23
  holiness and power of Yahweh in, 605
  hypostatic use of fire in, 351
  hypostatic use of names in, 387–88
  on ideal just divine judge, 548–49
  infusing of divinity in kingship in, 506, 507
  on judicial authority of Yahweh, 565–69
  judicial ideology in, 517
  origin of specific poems in, 804n187
  remembering archaic lore in, 447–48
  royal legitimization in, 454–59
  superlative quality of Yahweh's kingship in, 509
  twisting of justice in, 551
  Yahweh as caring father in, 482
  Yahweh as mother in, 489–90
  Yahweh's holiness in, 579–82
P sources. See Priestly sources/traditions (P)
purification rites
  dangers related to, 882n146
  for kings, 498
  related to military camps, 647–48
  related to warfare, 833n155
purity, consecration and, 611

Qoheleth, book of, 7, 14, 445
  affirmation of God's role as judge in, 549–51, 564, 574
  holiness of Yahweh in, 672–73
Qubbah, stela from, 149, 153f
Qudshu-Astarte-Anat, 122, 124f, 720n30
Queen of Heaven, 509
  ʿAštart as, 688–89, 689–91
  biblical references to, 677–78
quickening ritual, for ancient Near East icons, 135

Rad, Gerhard von, 65, 382, 652, 810n235, 853n89
radiance, 358–379
  abstract representation of Yahweh as, 344
  clothing of Yahweh in, 454–55
  depicting presence of Yahweh with, 358–59
  See also divine radiance
Rainey, Anson, 74, 228, 231–32, 235, 260, 576, 710n76, 717n9, 717n13, 718n17, 759n28, 769n125, 771n134, 772n143, 774n155, 829n117, 866n12, 875n95 and passim
Rakib-El, 196, 266, 309, 722n50, 732–33n156, 750n180, 771n138, 777n171, 848n40
Ramses II, 59, 75, 230, 232, 504, 747n159, 761n53, 761n59
Ramses III, 59, 75, 232, 832n144
Rationalism, 18–19
reactionary nature, of Name Theology, 381–82
realia, for Yahwistic cult, 67–68
rebellion, of Levites, 639–41
redemption
  of humans by father, 486–89
  by Yahweh as judge, 543
Redford, Donald, 230–32, 339, 496
Red/Reed Sea, 448–453, 454, 466, 823–24n75
reflection, in ancient Israelite religion, 6–7
Rekhmire (Egyptian vizier), 516
religion, definitions of, 49–52, 712n2
religious lives, of ancient Near East kings, 496–98
religious personnel. See holy personnel
religious topics, scholarship, 17–47
  by William Foxwell Albright, 31–32

ancient Israel's distinctiveness in, 30–31
  archaeology in, 39–41
  "Babel-Bibel" controversy, 24–25
  by Frank Moore Cross, 34–35
  during Enlightenment, 18–19
  feminist contributions to, 44–46
  Fribourg school of iconography, 37–38
  and hermeneutics, 38–39
  history of, 1–2
  history-of-religion method, 24
  by Yehezkel Kaufmann, 32–34
  by Carol Meyers, 46–47
  myth-and-ritual approach to, 27–29
  and new definitions of myth, 35–37
  in nineteenth century Germany, 19–23
  personal piety and family religion in, 42–44
  by William Robertson Smith, 23–24
  social sciences in, 41–42
  theological approach to, 26–27
  Ugaritic discoveries in, 29–30
Rendtorff, Rolf, 17, 35, 87, 88, 369, 807n213, 807n214
Renfrew, Colin, 336–37
reproof, of humans by father, 484–86
Reshef, divine figurines of, 299, 299f, 300f
resolution, covenant lawsuit, 540–42
retribution
  in Jonah, 574
  and Yahweh as ideal just divine judge, 549–50
Reuel (biblical figure), 274, 276, 781n197
revisionist hermeneutics, 39
rhetoric, by just human judges, 543
Rhyton Sanctuary at Ugarit, 146–47, 146f, 259, 721n33
rîb (covenant/prophetic lawsuit), 539–43
Rib-Adda letters, 606
Ribichini, Sergio, 254
Richter, Sandra, 380, 383, 384, 390–91, 408, 746n149, 784n231, 809n233, 810n235, 812n257, 812n258
Rimmon, Horvat, 312
ritual body, 3, 15, 619-29, 879n125

1038 SUBJECT INDEX

ritual performance, *see* Bell, Catherine
of consecration, 608–10, 620, 625, 629
for ʿAshtart, 685
for Levites, 642
of priests, in Deuteronomistic History, 654
study of, 3, 15, 42, 49, 130, 135, 208, 393, 406, 612,
for Zadokite priests, 646
rituals, study of, 3, *see* Bell, Catherine
Robertson Smith, William, 23–24, 28, 41, 44, 703n16, 703n17, 703n19, 703n20, 703n22, 896n283
Rooke, Deborah, 45, 46, 503, 618, 619, 878n118, 879n120, 880n128, 888n196, 889n209, 890n227, 892n250
Rollston, Christopher, 53, 58, 236, 252, 713n9, 754n207, 762n67, 763n72, 770n132, 866n12
Roth, Martha, 514–515
royal cult
and ancient Israelite religion, 13
in ancient Near East, 496–507
and dedication of Jerusalem Temple, 655–56
and Deuteronomy, 849n48
differing views of, 845n13
and priestly cult, 846n18
Queen of Heaven as, 689, 690
in religious scholarship, 3–4
and worship of ʿAštart, 685–87
and ʿAthtartu, 682
royal entry ritual, for ʿAthtartu, 682–83
royal judicial ideology, of Judah, 517
royal legislation
in Hebrew Bible, 560–61
need for, 558–60
royal status, anointing rituals for, 626–27
royalty
Ark for legitimization of, 396–97
divine images' association with, 134
religious roles of, 880–81n131
royal framework for divine justice, 513–21
Yahweh as cosmic warrior for legitimization of, 453–60

Reuben (biblical figure), 235, 251, 272, 284, 781n204, 782n205, 276–77
ruin cults, 179, 180, 195, 747n158
rulers, as parents, 479

Sabaean texts, ḥērem warfare in, 55, 462, 763n70, 832n147
sacral kingship, 28, 504–5
sacred emptiness, 392–417, 422
and abstract representations of Yahweh, 336–38
archaeological evidence of empty-space aniconism, 409–17, 410f, 411f, 413f–17f
Ark and cherubim as focal points for, 394–405, 394f, 398f, 399f, 401f–4f, 815–16n289
fire and glory as focal points for, 405–7
name and invisibility as focal points for, 407–9
sacred space, 2, 9, 69, 671–72 and passim
delimiting, in Exodus, 611–12
in Deuteronomistic History, 654
exclusion from, 877n108
and gradations of status, 612, 664
holiness of, 607
importance of, 2–3
kings as builders of, 499–501
made holy by Yahweh, 671–72
marked by anointing, 622
on Mt. Sinai, 877–78n109, 878n111
in Name Theology, 379–80
restrictions on Levites in, 643
in Ugaritic religion, 263
for Yahweh the Holy One, 576
sacred time
and consecration, 610–11
importance of, 2–3
sacrifice
child, 64, 542, 715n25
as cultic activity of king, 501–3
of humans, 733n161
Levites as, 642–43
in Ugaritic religion, 263–64
Śahr (deity), 267, 332
Samʾal, inscriptions from, 82, 196, 266, 750n180, 750n181, 752n190, 775n158, 776n171, 869n40
Samaria
bull of, 320–21
divine images of Yahweh in, 295

Yahweh of, 237–39, 238f, 293, 295, 322, 701n1
Samson (biblical figure), 353, 377, 464, 633
Samuel (biblical figure), 172, 559, 633, 634, 645, 657, 884n168
Samuel, book of, 589–90
active presence of Yahweh in, 218–19
cultic activities of king in, 499
on David as king of justice, 518
divine radiance in, 364–65
hypostatic use of name in, 388
Yahweh as supporter of underdog, 465
Zadok prophesied in, 657
sanctuary, Yahweh as, 592–93
Sanders, Seth, 53, 56, 57, 251, 262, 713n7, 713n11, 714n18, 756n5, 762n68, 775n166, 816n295, 832n147
Saphon, Mt. (Mt. Zion), 108–9, 821n58
Sargon II, 140, 292–95, 814n272
śārîm, 525, 526, 537, 856n112
Sarna, Nahum, 97, 197, 218, 467, 730n130, 746n153, 780n189, 799n139, 800n149, 823n75, 826n97, 877n109
Sass, Benjamin, 241, 306, 766n98, 776n171, 789n35, 792n71, 792n72, 832n145, 843n263
Sasson, Jack, 524, 571, 791n57, 853n83, 854n96, 864n195
Saul (biblical figure), 464, 518, 559
and geographic origin of Yahweh, 278–79
role of, in cultic activities, 499
Schaeffer, C. F. A., 29, 123, 127, 130f, 131f, 145f, 159f, 705n43, 742n109
Schloen, David, 43, 80, 272, 277–79, 474, 710n78, 782n205, 782n206, 782n207, 782n208, 795n107
Schmidt, Brian, 42, 47, 291, 292, 327, 328, 409–11, 415, 701n2, 711n87, 725n72, 763n73, 766n101, 769n121, 793n89, 793n90, 794n94
Schmitt, John, 490–91
Schmitt, Rüdiger, 9, 42, 43, 44, 50, 59, 83, 111, 255, 304, 306, 479, 493–94, 679, 701n2, 713n11, 722n50, 723n52, 723n54, 735n11, 756n5, 837n186, 839n214, 852n75, 898n2 and passim

SUBJECT INDEX 1039

Schneider, Thomas, 232–34, 496, 679, 762n62
Schniedewind, William, 53, 236, 237, 251, 258, 715n27, 763n73, 763n74, 765n89, 769n124, 772n144, 781n201, 782n210, 791n64, 794n98, 822n64, 822n67, 849n43
Scholnick, Sylvia, 555, 556
Schwemer, Daniel, 9–10, 266, 267, 738n69, 780n186, 787n20, 817n9, 839n204
Scroll of the Wars of Yahweh, 430
Second Isaiah, *see* Deutero-Isaiah
sea
  in Ba'lu cycle, 440–42
  Marduk's battle against, 437–39
  Yahweh's battle at, 448–53
sea, parting of, 824nn78–79
seeing
  of deities, 96–97
  of "human" body parts of Yahweh by Moses, 377–78
  lethal God sightings, 296–97, 355, 557
Sefire inscriptions, Elyon in, 87–88
Seir, location of, 231, 232
Sellin, Ernst, 26, 315–16, 315f, 575, 670, 744n129, 816n291, 865n1
Sennacherib, 296, 466–67, 571, 573, 599, 739n73, 776n170, 834n164
Seow, C. L., 87, 90, 94, 109, 117, 553, 554, 721n41, 722n46, 722n48, 724n62, 725n80, 726n86, 733n158, 734n168, 805n199, 812n262, 845n16, 858n134, 859n141, 859n142, 897n297, 898n298
Septuagint, El Shadday in, 101–2
Serabit el-Khadim, El worship at, 75–76
seraphim, 349
serpentine stela, 'Ilu depiction on, 144, 144f
seven-headed monsters, 435f–37f
sexuality, rhetoric of, 489, 842n249
Seyrig collection, Bibliothèque Nationale, 305–6, 306f
Shaddayyin deities, 90, 105, 269, 730n129
Shagar, in book of Deuteronomy, 677
Shaked, Shaul, 311–12
Shalmaneser III, 190, 192f
Shamash, 546
  divine image of, 190, 192f
  and King Hammurabi, 513–14, 514f
Shasu nomads, 60, 229–34, 251, 284, 696, 761n53, 761n59, 782n210, 784n227
Sha'tiqatu, 77, 78, 138, 719n21, 720n31
Shechem
  El worship in, 85–86
  masseboth at, 172–74, 173f
Shelby White-Leon Levy Program for Archaeological Publications, 309
Shema'-servant of Jeroboam (II) seal, 313
Shema'yahu son of 'Azaryahu seal, 321–22, 321f
Shiloh, temple at, 364–65, 383, 805–6n199
Sidon, worship of 'Aštart at, 688–89
sikkānu stelae, 628, 745n141, 747n156, 883n157
Sinai, Mt., 109, 225, 271, 278, 279, 280, 283, 284, 345, 357, 369, 370, 424, 542, 608, 609, 610, 612, 613, 616, 782n205, 784n229, 877–78n109, 878n110, 878n111
Singer, Itamar, 81
singers, 66, 894n266
Sippar Tablet of Nabu-apla-iddina II, 190, 192f
slavery, indentured, 486–87, 486f
Smith, Mark, 9–10, 37, 39, 42, 67, 80, 81, 84, 117, 217, 260, 263, 264, 322, 324, 331, 412, 428, 440, 474, 511, 575, 607, 675, 678, 681, 687, 689, 696, 706n50, 706n51, 708n61, 708n62, 709n68, 712n2, 718n16, 718n17, 719n22, 719n23, 720n26, 721n36, 722n50, 723n59, 725n72, 728n109, 730n126, 731n143, 734n168, 755n211, 758n26, 764n82, 773n151, 773n152, 775n161, 775n164, 785n239, 785n240, 792n80, 796n123, 805n199, 822n68, 827n102, 828n108, 830n126, 863n179, 864n184, 883n153, 898n5, 899n8, 900n15, 900n22, 902n42, 902n45 and passim
Smoak, Jeremy, 240, 245, 310, 408, 766n101, 767n107, 768n117, 770n131, 789n42, 815n287
social sciences, in religious scholarship, 41–42
social status
  of Levites, 637
  and mortuary data, 879n125
  and ritual garments, 620
  and sacred space, 612, 877–78n109
sociological approach, to biblical studies, 23–24
Solomon (biblical figure)
  cultic activities of, 500–501, 846n20
  dedication of Jerusalem Temple, 655
  infusing of divinity in kingship of, 505–7
  as king of justice, 518–19
Solomonic Temple. *See* Jerusalem Temple (Solomonic Temple)
Sommer, Benjamin, 32, 34, 65, 324, 337, 372, 375, 384, 422, 426, 598, 701n1, 707n26, 708n58, 715n27, 786n3, 792n78, 806n202, 806n204, 808–809n224, 810n242, 816n297, 817n15, 875n84
Song of Hannah, 588–91, 870–71nn48–50
Song of Moses, 91–92
Song of the Ark, 388–89, 396
šōpār horn, 609, 610, 611, 613, 876n105
source criticism, 18, 21, 24, 44, 61–68 and passim
source material
  material culture as, 68–69
  texts as, 53–68
the South
  and Midianites vs. Kenites in Hebrew Bible, 272–79
  origin of Yahweh from, 271–72, 867n19
  textual allusions to Yahweh's origin in, 279–82
South City Trench of Ugarit, 143–44, 143f, 740n86
sovereignty
  of El, 109–10
  of Yahweh, 507–11
sphinxes, on cult stands from Taanach, 315–17, 315f, 316f
sprinkling, in anointing rituals, 625–26

1040 SUBJECT INDEX

Stager, Lawrence, 84, 121, 172–74, 230, 231, 277, 278, 282, 324, 710n78, 710n83, 742n111, 742n112, 745n147, 746n149, 780n188, 782n208, 798n132, 840n221
standing stones, 169–96, 333–36, 744–45n141 (see *massebah/masseboth*)
Stanton, Elizabeth Cady, 44–45
state formation, god as king prior to, 508
statistical evaluations, on textual sources, 66–67
Steiner, Richard, 256, 322, 349, 739n73, 773n148, 792n73, 792n74, 800n155
steppe lands, ʿAthtartu as goddess of, 681–83
storm imagery, to depict presence of Yahweh, 345–47, 799n144
Strawn, Brent, 197, 313, 327, 711n87, 750n183, 750n84, 751n185, 751n188, 826n94, 834n167
streams of traditions, 62, 64, 65, 224, 274, 379, 393, 424, 426, 461, 464, 604, 816n297
striding figures, in divine images, 298–99, 299f, 300f
sukkôt celebrations, 3, 501, 512, 827n101
Sumer, king's association with divinity in, 496–97
Sumerian King List, 496, 844n3, 845n13
supremacy, of El, 109
Suriano, Matthew, 245, 757n12, 766n101, 767n107, 767n110, 768n117, 795n106, 815n286
Syria, name Yahweh in, 230, 233–34
Syro-Palestinian deities, iconography of, 120, 122

Taanach cult stands
 bull representations of Yahweh on, 323–25, 323f, 420–21
 fenestrations in, 412, 413f–15f
 lions on, 315–17, 315f, 316f
 representation of invisible Yahweh on, 411–15, 411f, 413f–15f
Tabnit, Sidonian king, 686, 686f, 687
Taliban, 343

Targums, anthropomorphism of divine in, 290
Taylor, J. Glen, 324, 411–12, 415, 792n81, 816n290
Tel Dan
 divine bull rider on plaque from, 319–20, 319f, 420
 masseboth at, 187, 188f–92f, 189, 190, 195, 196
 metal working from Iron Age at, 302
Telepinu, disappearance of, 217
Tel Kinneret (Tell el-ʿOreme), bronze figurine from, 164, 169f
Tel Moẓa, *masseboth at*, 195
Tell Ahmar, stela from, 152f, 153f
Tell Asmar, image of seven-headed dragon from, 436f
Tell Balâṭah, divine figurine from, 301–2, 301f
Tell Beit Mirsim, lion heads on libation tray from, 315
Tell Ras Shamra, Canaanite religious culture in artifacts from, 259, 260
Tell Revov, cult stand with fenestrations from, 415, 416f
Teman, Yahweh of, 222, 239–40, 239f, 251, 281, 360, 586, 701n1, 765n92
Tetragrammaton, 59, 210, 213, 756n8, 757n12, 835n173
textile production, goddess of, 690–91
texts, as source material, 53–68. *See also specific texts*
textual criticism, 61
Thanksgiving Hymns at Qumran, 478
theodicy, 49, 469, 564–65, 644, 857n127, 863n178
 and challenges to testify against Yahweh, 545–46
 and divine justice for Job, 447, 551–57
 in Jonah, 573–74
 and justice as theme in wisdom literature, 546–47
 in Qoheleth, 549–51
theological approach, to biblical studies, 26–27, 706–7n53
theophany, in book of Job, 557, 860–61n159
theriomorphic representations
 of El, 196–208
 of ʾIlu, 148–55, 149f–55f
 of Yahweh, 313–33, 419–21

 bull, 317–33, 319f, 321f, 323f, 325f, 329f, 331f
 lion, 313–17, 314f–16f
Thompson, Thomas L., 38, 39, 75, 83, 709n74, 710n75, 717n6
thrones
 cherubim as, 400–402, 401f–4f
 empty throne of Yahweh, 405
 enthronement of Yahweh, 400–401, 405, 510–11
 sizes of, 511, 736n36
Thutmose III, 59, 75, 516
Tiamat (deity), in cosmic warfare, 216, 265, 266, 437–40, 443, 445, 451, 818n29, 818n34, 821n57, 823n75
Tigay, Jeffrey, 57, 58, 349, 478, 648, 708n59, 710n83, 725n73, 725n74, 749n175, 756n5, 758n22, 854n95
Tiglath-Pileser III, 140, 140f, 187, 367, 466, 750n181, 848n40
Tirzah (Tell el-Farʿah North), *masseboth* at, 121, 123f
Tishpak (deity), as divine warrior, 431–33
Toews, Wesley, 78, 116, 320, 752n192
toponyms, related to divine names, 59, 60
town elders, in judicial system, 515, 524, 526, 527, 529, 563, 850n57, 852n82, 853n89, 855n108, 857n127
tradent, 107, 363, 418, 816n295
trade and caravan routes, 4, 11, 42, 176, 230, 236, 237, 277, 278, 279, 283, 284, 782n206
traditional texts, as sources, 227
traditions, streams of, *see* streams of traditions
traveling ritual
 for ancient Near Eastern images, 136–38
 and divine image of Yahweh in Jerusalem Temple, 292, 294
tree and horned animals motif, 160, 164f
tremendum, 337, 828n108, see Otto, Rudolph
Trible, Phyllis, 45, 492, 711n91, 732n147, 842n249, 843n258, 843n259
Tropper, Joseph, 260, 757n9, 757n15, 774n156, 774n157
Trufant, Susanne Müller, 374
Tukulti-Ninurta I and II (Assyrian kings), 375, 376f, 505

SUBJECT INDEX 1041

Tushratta of Mitanni, 132, 737n51, 900n16
typology, 706n52

Uehlinger, Christoph, 38, 119, 120, 166–69, 170f, 197, 243, 256–57, 287, 291, 292, 293, 297, 299, 302, 303, 305f, 306, 307, 308, 313, 323, 324, 326, 327, 328, 330, 374, 412, 709n71, 710n83, 743n124, 744n134, 744n136, 744n138, 744n139, 765n90, 766n101, 772n148, 787n19, 787n22, 787n27, 788n28, 789n35, 789n40, 790n51, 794n94, 794n97, 794n100, 809n227 and passim
Ugarit
  ʿAštart (ʿAthtartu) at, 679–83, 684f
  clothing of divine images in, 135–36
  and conceptualization of Canaanite religion, 258–64
  cosmic warfare in mythology from, 439–42, 444
  cultic holiness at, 606–7
  discoveries from, in religious scholarship, 29–30
  drinking mug from, 123, 124f
  El worship at, 76–81
  god as king in, 80, 161, 508, 719n22
  gods as family in, 473–76, 475f
  ḥērem warfare at, 462
  iconography of ʾIlu, 142–55, 156f–61f
  image use in magic rituals, 138, 139f
  judicial ideal at, 516–17
  king's association with divinity in, 497–98
  ritual processions in, 136–37
  statuette of ʾIlu from, 127, 129f, 130f
  warrior gods in, 428–29
  Yahweh at, 228–29
Ugaritic language
  as Canaanite, 260, 774nn156–157
  as written language, 775n166
Ugaritic texts, discovery of, 29–30
Ultimate Magistrate, Yahweh as, 529
ʾUmmī ʿaštart, 686–87
underdog ideology, in non-cosmic warfare, 464–66

University of Fribourg (Switzerland), 306–9, 307f
unprovenanced objects, use of, 306–8
updating, of textual sources, 63
Urim and Thummim, 5, 499, 621, 624, 637–638, 639, 649, 846n17, 854n93, 880–81n131
Uruk, images of composite beasts from, 433, 434f–35f
Uzzah (biblical figure), 15, 395, 596, 604, 612, 892n242
Uzziah (biblical figure), 661–63

van der Toorn, Karel, 9, 43, 82, 84, 90, 111, 211, 223, 228, 231, 233, 272, 278–79, 291, 292, 293, 294, 322, 337, 422, 668, 713n12, 728n110, 729n116, 731n134, 732n149, 739n73, 757n9, 759n31, 759n36, 780n187, 782n209, 789n43, 792n73, 792n74, 796n123, 817n15, 832n148, 833n153, 837n186, 838n198, 843n261, 879n123, 889n213, 896n285 and passim
van Seters, John, 38, 96, 391, 408, 709n75, 805n196
Vatke, Johan Karl Wilhelm, 20–21
Vaux, Roland de, 108, 215, 218, 219, 222, 558–59, 749n174, 757n13, 758n17, 810n234, 852n82
Victorious Bull, El as, 76, 78, 198
Virolleaud, Charles, 29, 228, 259, 705n43, 705n45, 737n46, 760n50
visitation, divine, 476–77
vocalization, of name Yahweh, 219–20
voice, of Yahweh
  and aniconic tradition, 357–58
  and divine fire, 353–56, 423, 802–3n174
  and transcendent anthropomorphism, 799n144
votive prayer, 606, 607

W. F. Albright Institute of Archaeological Research (AIAR), 705–6n48
Walker, C. B. F., 133, 735n22, 736n31, 736n22, 902n52
warfare
  Ark procession in, 396

bloodletting after, 470–71
cosmic, 430–42
holiness in military camps, 647–48
as holy enterprise, 583
purification related to, 833n155
rhetoric vs. realia of, 835–36n179
synergism of human and divine war, 462–64
taking of images in, 140–41
views of, 470–73
violence done by troops in, 572–73, 572f
warrior goddess, ʿAštart as, 678–79
warrior judges, 464
warrior nature, holiness related to, 578–83
warrior or storm deities
  in ancient Near East, 428–72
  Baʿlu and ʿAnatu, 267, 439–442
  and bull-headed warrior from Bethsaida, 331, 332
  El, 112–13, 115–18
  El Shadday, 104
  Hadad, 266–67
  ʾIlu, 80–81
  images from Israel of, 154f, 165f, 298–301, 299f, 300f, 301f
  images from Syria of, 149, 150f–53f
  Late Bronze and Iron Age images of, 149–156, 298–302, 299f, 300f, 301f
  and representation of Yahweh, 298
  and weapons of Yahweh as divine warrior, 450–51
  Yahweh as, 361–62, 429–430, 442–472
washing, of clothes, 476, 609, 611, 612, 620, 621, 844n8
Weinfeld, Moshe, 231, 345, 356–58, 375, 379, 648, 761n56, 799n144, 833n155, 852n81, 903n53
Wellhausen, Julius, 21–24, 27, 28, 39, 44, 65, 83, 96, 223, 702n10, 702n11, 702–703n13, 703n15, 703n17, 703n22, 704n23, 706–707n53, 753n193, 807n214, 851n72, 888n208, 889n211
Wenham, Gordon, 226–27
Westbrook, Raymond, 524, 527, 558, 780n190, 836n181, 856n112, 861n161, 861n162, 881n133

Westermann, Claus, 87, 97, 112, 114, 600
West Semites
  El worship by, 73–74, 76–81, 111
  epigraphic sources of name Yahweh from, 234–52, 234f, 235f, 238f, 239f, 241f–50f
Whitelam, Keith, 38, 40, 518, 559, 561, 851n67, 861n164, 861n165, 862n167
widows, abuse of justice against, 536–37
Wiggins Steve, 701n2, 720n30, 837n194, 837n195
Wildberger, Hans, 336, 367, 368, 601
Williamson, Hugh, 294, 367–68, 472–73, 483, 511, 599, 601, 602, 797n127, 798n136, 807n210, 836n182, 836n183, 840n227, 847n27, 850n52, 856n111, 857n127, 894n267, 895n271, 895n273
Willis, John, 472, 834n169
Wilson, Ian, 357–58, 384, 810n240, 811n244
Wilson, Robert, 5, 42, 518, 523–24, 527, 538, 703n15, 862n174
Wilson, Veronica, 328
Wilson-Wright, Aaron, 269, 676, 679, 680–82, 695, 715n27, 821n62, 898n3, 899n9, 899n11, 900n15, 900n20, 900n22
Winchester plaque, 122, 124f
Winter, Nancy, 308, 505
wisdom
  and divine council of El, 113
  personification of, 858n133
wisdom literature
  archaic lore in, 447
  divine combat myth in, 445
  holiness of Yahweh in, 672–73
  justice as theme in, 546–47
  reflection in, 6–7
womb imagery, 489–90, 843n259
women
  in biblical scholarship, 44–47
  as holy functionaries, 667–70, 686, 687, 896n282, 902n39
  in legal matters within household, 524, 853n83, 853n84, 853n85
  as Nazirites, 4, 15, 632, 634, 635
  religious life of ancient, 44, see Meyers, Carol and Ackerman, Susan

as royalty, 502, 845n11, 847n28
studies of religion and, 44–47, 711n92, 711n93, 711–12n98
Wyatt, Nick, 116–17, 121, 709n71, 726n90, 727n103, 728n110, 733n162, 734n168, 740n88, 780n187

X mark, in interpretation of potsherd, 310–11

Ya, at Ebla, 228
Yadin, Yigael, 158, 180, 267, 706n52, 710n77, 792n77, 889n215
Yah, land of, 232–33
Yaḥdunlim, King of Mari, Foundation Inscription of, 717n7
Yahô, Temple of, pillars at, 196
Yahweh
  attributes of, 697–99
  challenges to testify against, 545–46
  characteristics of El vs., 114–15, 427
  clothing associated with, 136
  conceptualizations of, 697–99
  data available about, 696–97
  and El in Hebrew Bible, 427
  and El in Masoretic tradition, 568–69
  in Elohistic Psalter, 88–89
  epigraphy related to, 54–55
  Hazor figurine misidentified as, 126, 126f
  identification of, with El, 209, 868n26
  in inscriptions at Kuntillet ʿAjrud, 586
  language for encounters with, 171–72
  as national god of Israel, 209–10
  in non-cosmic warfare alone, 466–70
  onomastica in study of, 59–60
  as potter, 477, 481, 485, 839n217
  as warrior, 117–18, 361–62, 429–430, 442–472
  wrath and benevolence of, 594–95
Yahweh, name of, 210–52
  active presence in Hebrew Bible, 218–19
  archaic vocalization of, 219–20
  and Beya as Moses, 229
  daily use of, 756–57n8
  at Ebla, 228

epigraphic sources, 234–52
etymology of, 213–14
Exodus 3:14 on, 214–15
in Hamath, 233–34
"He Who Blows" interpretation of, 223
"He Who Causes to Be" interpretation of, 220–22
"He Who Is" interpretation of, 215–18
hypostatic function of, 385–90
as marker of ownership, 390–91
as marker of practical presence, 384–85, 408
in material from Shasu (Shosu) nomads, 229–32
meaning of, 210–11
pronunciation of, 211
and putative name "Jehovah," 212–13
revelation of, 223–27
for shepherd from land of Yah, 232–33
as symbol of divine presence, 383–84
at Ugarit, 228–29
Yahweh, origins of, 11, 209–86
  and Aramean religion, 264–68
  and Canaanite religion, 253–64
  in epigraphic sources, 234–52
  in extra-biblical sources, 227–34
  in Hebrew Bible, 210–27
  Midianites and Kenites in Hebrew Bible, 272–79
  from North, 270–71
  from South, 271–72, 867n19
  textual allusions to Southern origin, 279–82
Yahweh as divine warrior, 12, 361–62, 428–73
  on cosmic scale, 442–61
  and legitimization of royalty, 453–60
  in non-cosmic battles, 461–70
  other divine warriors on cosmic scale, 430–42
  and views of warfare, 470–73
  and Yahweh as judge, 530–32
Yahweh as the Holy One, 14–15, 575–673
  in Chronicles, 657–65
  Deuteronomistic conceptions of, 651–53
  in Deuteronomy, 647–51
  early attestations of, 606–15
  in Ezekiel, 643–47

SUBJECT INDEX   1043

holy personnel in Priestly traditions, 615–43
and holy prophets, 665–67
in Joshua, 652–53
non-cultic understandings of, 577–605
and Northwest Semitic holy gods, 575–77
priestly personnel in Deuteronomist History, 653–57
systematic cultic frameworks for, 605–6
and women as holy functionaries, 667–70
Yahweh as judge, 12–14, 513–74
divine justice and apocalyptic literature, 532–34
and early Israelite judiciaries, 525–28
God as law writer and lawgiver, 558–61
and ideal of just divine judge, 545–57
and ideal of just human judge, 534–45
non-royal frameworks for divine justice, 521–24
overarching belief in, 528–30
prophecies about, 530–32
and role of Moses, 561–63
royal framework for divine justice, 513–21
Yahweh as king, 12–13, 495–513
cultic enactment of, 511–13
royal cult in ancient Near East, 496–507
and Yahweh as sovereign, 507–11
Yahweh as parent, 12, 477–493
Yahweh-El-Olam, 97, 99
Yahweh Elyon
and El Elyon motifs, 92–95
El traditions vs., 90–92
Yahweh iconography, 11–12, 287–426
abstract traditions, 336–44, 825n86

anthropomorphic representations, 287–313
divine fire, 344–58
divine radiance, 358–79
masseboth representations, 333–36
and Name Theology, 379–92
and sacred emptiness, 392–415, 416f–17f
theriomorphic representations, 313–33
Yahweh in family religion, 12, 473–94
historical context for, 473–77
humans as rebellious children, 482–89
Yahweh as divine parent, 477–93
Yahweh as mother, 489–93
Yahweh of Hebron, 701n1, 875n90
Yahweh of Hosts, 219, 221–22, 244f, 245, 271, 318, 336, 367, 401, 412, 483, 510, 530, 536, 767n106, 797n127, 817n9
Yahweh of Samaria, 237–39, 238f, 293, 295, 322
Yahweh of Teman, 239–40, 239f, 360, 586
Yahweh Sabaoth (Yahweh of Armies)
cherubim for, 400–401
and focal point for Jerusalem Temple, 395
and inviolability of Jerusalem, 467–69
Yahweh Sebaoth, 221–22, 245, 245f, *see* Yahweh of Hosts
Yahwisms, with divine images, 292–93
Yam/Yammu (deity), in cosmic warfare, 30, 115, 117, 228–29, 261, 262, 360–61, 427, 440–46, 448–453, 456, 457, 459, 681, 772n146, 800n147, 801n164, 818n35, 818–19n38, 819n39,

819n40, 826n92, 828n110, 830n128, 830n129
Yaqub-ilu, 75, 717n12
Yau-bidi, king of Hamath, 233–34
yhwh, pronunciation of, 211
Yon, Marguerite, 30, 123, 144, 146, 147, 151, 705n43, 735n8, 735n13, 735n14, 740n86, 740n88, 741n89, 741n90, 741n94, 741n95, 761n52, 774n154, 901n34
Yurco, Frank, 231–32

Zadok, 645, 646, 653, 656, 657, 660, 894n271
Zadokite priests, 645–46, 660, 888n208
Zevit, Ziony, 2–3, 9, 50, 54, 69, 97, 176, 180, 181f, 185, 187, 236, 240, 245–246, 246f, 257–58, 315f, 319, 327–28, 333–334, 397, 399, 412, 415f, 499, 502–503, 619, 665, 672, 695, 710n83, 712n1, 712n2, 712n3, 713n8, 715n27, 751n190, 755n1, 756n5, 763n77, 764n86, 765n92, 766n103, 767n107
and passim
Zimri-Lim (Mari king)
carrying out of justice by, 515
legitimization of, 266, 439, 458
Zincirli (*see* Samʾal)
masseboth from, 333–34, 334f
reference to ruler as parent from, 479
Zion. *See* Jerusalem
Zion-Sabaoth tradition, 373, 380, 381, 382, 386, 400, 418, 422, 425
Zion theology, 50, 283, 384, 396, 467–69, 511, 513, 834n165, 836–37n185, 888n199
Zuckerman, Sharon, 179, 180, 710n77, 747n158
zukru festival, 627–29, 747n156, 876n99, 883n156, 899n10, 902n46

Citation Index

References to boxes, figures, tables, and notes are denoted by an italicized b, f, t, and n.

HEBREW BIBLE
Genesis
1:11 729n121
1:27 489, 842n249
2:2–3 225
2:7 133, 288, 719n21, 737n40, 839n217
2:8 288
3:8 288
3:14 842n254
3:15 824n75
3:21 288
3:22 215, 727n100
3:24 349, 353, 397, 399, 813n271
4:1 226, 722n49
4:1–7 224
4:1–16 272
4:26 224, 226, 228, 284, 760n43
6:2 477
6:6 288
7:1 224
7:5 224
7:16 288
8:20 224
8:20–21 224
8:21 288, 786n5
9:16–17 225
12:1 224
12:1–3 649
12:4 224
12:7–8 224
12:8 100
12:10 761n55
12:18 227
13:4 224
13:18 224
14 113
14:10 826n92
14:18 507
14:18–22 85, 86, 95, 602
14:19 81, 95, 97
14:19–20 88, 461
14:20 113
14:22 81, 95, 97

15:1 84, 113, 224
15:6–7 224
15:17 345, 354
15:19 272
16 726n88, 726n90
16:1–6 524
16:7 726n92, 733n162
16:11 95, 227, 726n91
16:11–14 96, 110
16:13 85, 95, 227
16:13–14 96
16:14 733n162
17:1 209, 224, 729n121, 730n131
17:1–2 101, 110
17:7 225
17:11 225
18 224
18:9–15 489
18:21 288
18:22–32 288
18:22–33 574
18:25 546, 550
19:24 799n146
19:30–38 285
20:1–18 489
21:1 224
21:1–7 489
21:19 726n92
21:33 85, 97, 98, 99, 210, 758n25
22 733n161
22:2 846n18
22:23 264
24:1 224
24:2–4 265
25:2 272
25:8 732n150
25:17 732n150
25:19–28 489
25:20 264
25:21–23 224
25:25 285
26:12 224
26:24–25 224

26:25 224
27:11 285
28 171
28:3 102, 730n131
28:3–4 102, 110
28:5 264
28:10–22 99
28:11 100
28:12 101, 730n130
28:13 100, 224, 795n109
28:14 100
28:15 100, 101, 240
28:16 224, 227, 795n109
28:18 100, 135, 194, 335
28:18–19 100, 174
28:18–22 745n145
28:19 227
28:20 100, 101
28:22 100, 135, 174, 194, 335, 730n130
28:23 172
29:7 101
29:31–35 224, 489
30:1–8 489
30:22–24 489
30:24 224
30:27 224
31 100, 523, 524
31:1–17 99
31:3 101, 795n109
31:7 100
31:10–11 101
31:13 85, 100, 174, 194, 335, 737n42, 737n42
31:32 524
31:34 137
31:37 524, 528
31:42 84
31:44–49 121, 171, 336
31:49 528, 795n109
31:49–54 524
31:50 528
31:53 84
31:53–54 528
32 289

1046 CITATION INDEX

Genesis (*Cont.*)
32:3   285
32:29-30   215
32:31   100
33:20   73, 85, 100, 111, 174, 226, 287, 723n60
33:23   287
35:1   100
35:1-16   99
35:2   115
35:2-4   303
35:3   100
35:4   100, 141
35:5   100, 113
35:6-15   194, 335
35:7   85, 100, 227, 737n42
35:8   100
35:9-15   99, 176
35:10   99
35:11   99, 102, 110, 730n131
35:14   100, 135, 174, 176, 730n130, 737n42
35:15   737n42
35:17-18   364
35:19   121
35:19-20   171
35:29   732n150
36:3-4   781n203
36:8-9   285
36:9-13   203
37   884n165
37-39   880n125
37:28   272
37:36   272
38   523, 524
38:15   668
38:21-22   668, 669
38:24   668
39:23   224
40-41   884n165
42:2ff   761n55
43:14   729, 730n131
44:5   6, 224, 884n165
44:15   6, 224, 884n165
46:3   85, 111
48:3   730n131
48:15   100, 112, 233
49   84, 112, 270, 731n135, 886n179
49:2-27   822n68
49:3   277
49:4   277
49:6   803n179
49:9   824n75
49:9-10   313
49:24   84, 112, 194, 197, 233, 335, 336, 601
49:24-25   105-106, 174, 197, 318, 602

49:25   100, 102, 106, 107, 110, 112, 225, 730n131, 731n134, 732n152, 733n165
49:25a   730n132
49:25c   730n132
49:26   633
49:29   732n150
49:33   732n150
50:20   633

Exodus
2   275, 276
2:3   823n75
2:5   823n75
2:15b-22   273, 276
2:16   274, 275
2:18   274, 781n197
2:21   274
3   276
3:1   272, 273, 274, 275
3:1-5   891n238
3:1-6   345, 350, 351, 354, 355, 802n168
3:1-8   345
3:1-4:18   798n137
3:2   407
3:2-4   799n140
3:5   607, 617, 672, 891n238
3:6   276
3:12   214, 218, 223, 758n27
3:13   85, 276
3:14   214, 215, 216, 218, 220, 221, 222, 363, 757n16, 758n27, 805n197
3:14-15   214, 223
3:15   214, 216
3:15-16   85, 276
3:16   276
3:18   617, 867n19
4:5   85
4:12   101, 214, 218, 222, 223, 758n27
4:13   758n17
4:14   636
4:14-15   886n176
4:15   214, 218, 222, 758n27
4:16   562, 830n127
4:18   274
4:19   274
4:22   482
4:22-23   486
4:24-26   667, 802n170
5:1   867n19
5:3   617, 867n19
5:8   617
5:17   617
6:2-3   223, 224, 225, 284, 427
6:3   91, 101, 107, 108, 209, 276, 868n20
6:16-25   636

6:20   759n39
7:1   6, 562, 830n127
8:8   617
8:14   216
8:25-29   617
8:27-28   867n19
9:11   596
9:18   804n190
9:23-24   799n142
10:25   617
12:43-50   67
13   642
13:2   887n194
13:3-10   67
13:6-7   610
13:9   563
13:11-13   887n194
13:12a-13   64
13:15   643
13:21   350, 453
13:21-22   345
13:21-14:22   452
14:2   824n79
14:4   671, 827n99
14:7   452
14:9   452
14:10   453
14:13   452, 453
14:13-14   658
14:14   350, 452
14:16   452
14:17-18   452, 671, 827n99
14:19   350
14:19a   453
14:19b   453
14:21   452, 453
14:23   452
14:24   345, 350, 452, 453
14:25   350, 452
14:25-26   452
14:26-27   452
14:27   452, 826n96
14:28   452
14:30   452
14:31   453, 452
15   84, 270, 448, 454, 462, 464, 578, 580, 582, 583, 587, 590, 593, 603, 708n62, 818n33, 822n69
15:1   325, 450, 824n76
15:1-5   734n172
15:1-12   449-50, 825n82
15:1-18   430, 448, 822n68
15:1b-18   824n76
15:2   211, 449, 578-9, 822n70
15:3   288, 389, 429, 825n83
15:4   823n73, 823n75
15:6   288, 449, 450, 452, 578-9
15:7   450

CITATION INDEX   1047

15:7–8 450
15:7b 578–9
15:8 288, 325
15:10 825n82
15:10–11 449
15:11 5, 71, 360, 451, 578,
    582, 583, 589, 615, 803n180,
    825n82, 869n36, 891n239
15:11–18 578–9
15:12 450, 452, 825n82
15:13 449, 576, 578, 588, 593,
    598, 599
15:14–15 588
15:15–16 286
15:16 449, 822n70
15:17 576, 578, 588, 593,
    598, 873n74
15:18 453, 508, 510
15:19 325
15:19–23 64
15:21 325, 430, 823n72
16:10 806n206, 867n19
16:19–21 64
16:22ff 225
16:23 758n17
17:1–7 638
17:14 563
17:15 221
18 273, 275, 276, 525, 526,
    528, 544, 781n198, 853n91,
    879n121
18:1 272, 275
18:1–12 781n198
18:1–27 274
18:8 275
18:8–11 781n198
18:9–11 275
18:9–12 273, 276, 525
18:11 275
18:12 275, 526, 527
18:13–26 273, 525, 562
18:13–27 520, 781n198
18:15b 528
18:15b–16 525
18:16 562, 853n88
18:19 276
18:19b–20 525
18:20 562, 853n88
18:21 276, 528, 856n112, 863n181
18:21–22 526
18:23 276
18:25 528, 856n112, 856n114,
    863n181
18:25–26 526
19 612, 617, 862n175, 876n100,
    877n109, 878n113
19:1–2a 876n100
19:2b–25 876n100
19:3 613

19:5 608
19:7 877n109
19:10 608, 609, 610, 611, 614
19:10–11 607
19:10–15 876n100
19:10–20 876n100
19:10–25 608–10, 612–13, 616,
    876n100, 877n109, 878n112
19:11 609, 610
19:11b 876n100
19:12–13 609, 877n108
19:12–13a 876n100
19:12 609, 611
19:12ab–13 876n100
19:13 612, 616
19:14 608, 609, 611
19:15 609, 610, 611
19:15b 876n100
19:16 610, 804n190
19:16–19 347
19:16aa 876n100
19:17 609, 612
19:18 345, 354, 610, 876n100
19:18–19 608
19:19 611, 613, 617, 876n100
19:20 613
19:20–25 876n100
19:21 355, 609
19:21–22 612
19:21–24 609
19:22 596, 608, 609, 612, 614
19:23 609, 611, 617, 877n108
19:24 596, 609, 612, 613
20:2 226, 408
20:4 287, 356
20:7 692
20:12 483, 484, 524
20:15 613, 802n172
20:15–18 673
20:16 613
20:16–18 614
20:18 347, 613
20:19–23:19 63
20:21 845n12
20:22 463
20:23 133, 287, 303
20:24 381, 382, 392
21:15 524, 840n227, 853n84
22:17 6, 840n227
22:21–24 482
22:27 693
22:28b 542
22:28b–29 64, 887n194
23:10–19 68, 610
23:14–27 501
23:19 63, 714n23
23:20–21 381
23:20–22 389
23:23–24 335

23:24 194, 745n143
23:27 797n127,
    799n143, 826n99
23:37–39 64
24 612, 877n109, 878n110,
    878n111
24–40 805n196
24:1 613
24:2 613
24:2–3 614
24:3–8 121, 171
24:4 563
24:4–8 619, 878n110, 878n111
24:6–8 895n272
24:9 613
24:9–11 370, 371, 613, 807n215,
    838n201, 877n109, 878n111
24:10 136
24:11 838n201
24:12 542, 563
24:15–18 369
24:16 806n206
24:16–17 369
24:17 344, 345, 354, 407,
    799n139
24:17–18 369
25 398, 405
25–31 874n82, 878n109
25:2 598
25:8 369, 598, 874n82
25:8–22 598
25:10 397, 598
25:17–18 598
25:18–22 397
25:20 397, 813n271
25:21–22 598
25:22 397, 598
25:31–40 406
26:1 398
26:28 824n75
26:31 398
27:20–21 406
27:21 629, 641
28–29 619
28:1 622
28:2–3 620, 629, 663
28:6–12 620
28:15 621, 639, 854n93
28:15–30 620
28:29 621, 639, 854n93
28:29–30 621
28:31–35 620
28:35 592
28:36–38 620
28:38 880n130
28:41 637
29 618, 622, 624, 627, 628,
    881n136, 881n140, 882n146
29:1 622

1048 CITATION INDEX

Exodus (*Cont.*)
29:1–6 623
29:1b–3 623
29:4 624, 629, 880*n*126
29:4–5 612
29:5–6 624
29:6 634
29:7 623, 624, 625
29:8–9a 623
29:9 629, 641
29:9–10 629
29:10 623, 624
29:10–14 623
29:12 619, 882*n*145
29:15 623, 624, 629
29:15–18 623
29:16 619, 624
29:19 623, 624, 629
29:19–21 623
29:20 624
29:20–21 619
29:21 623, 624, 625, 627, 628, 629
29:21a 629
29:21b 625
29:22–25 623
29:26–28 623
29:28 629
29:29 637
29:29–30 623, 639
29:31–34 623
29:31–37 624
29:32 629
29:33 624, 637, 844*n*163, 882*n*143
29:33–34 618, 624, 884*n*163
29:35 625, 629
29:35–36a 623
29:36 624, 625, 629, 881*n*140
29:36–37 624, 625, 882*n*143
29:36b–37 623
29:37 622
29:37b 629
29:38–42a 623
29:38–46 881*n*136, 881*n*139
29:42 369
29:43 623, 672
29:43–44 369, 663
29:43–46 369
29:44 369, 371, 623, 629
29:45–46 369
30:7 894*n*271
30:9 808*n*217
30:19 629
30:22–30 629
30:22–38 622
30:26–29 622
30:29 622
30:30 622, 625, 629
30:32–33 622
30:38 622
31:1–11 7
31:3 8
31:4 8
31:12–18 225
31:16–17 225
31:18 289, 542, 563
32 198, 199, 318, 619, 637, 752*n*191, 753*n*195, 886*n*177
32:1 137, 200
32:1–4 736*n*35
32:2–4 304
32:4 116, 132, 753*n*196
32:5 318, 752*n*191, 791*n*58
32:5–6 200
32:5b 752*n*191
32:7–14 351
32:8 116, 736*n*35, 753*n*196
32:16 542
32:19 200, 753*n*196
32:20 141, 200, 736*n*35, 752*n*192, 753*n*196
32:21–24 752*n*191
32:23–24 736*n*35
32:24 753*n*196
32:25–29 637, 886*n*173
32:26–29 638, 886*n*177
32:27 637, 638, 886*n*182
32:29 637, 638, 886*n*182
32:35 753*n*196
33 378, 787*n*14
33:2–3 389
33:7–11 563, 785*n*2
33:11 288, 562, 618
33:17–23 359, 362, 363, 366, 377, 378, 805*n*195, 862*n*173
33:19 381, 758*n*17, 805*n*197
33:20 96, 287, 296, 355, 377, 378, 557, 588, 597, 612, 801*n*159
33:21–22 796*n*111
33:22 379
33:23 287, 289
34:1 563
34:5 172
34:5–6 381
34:6 377, 481
34:6–7 839*n*216
34:9 569
34:11–14 335
34:11–26 63
34:13 194
34:14 221, 335, 733*n*163
34:17–26 64
34:18–26 68, 610
34:19–20 887*n*194
34:26 63
34:27–28 563
34:29 619
34:29–35 791
35–40 874*n*82, 878*n*109
35:5–9 736*n*28
35:30–35 7
35:30–36:1 599
35:31 8
35:32–35 8
36:8 398
36:33 824*n*75
36:35 398
37 398
37:1 397
37:7–9 397, 598
37:17–24 406
37:29 622
38:8 667
39:1–31 619
39:2–7 620
39:8–21 620
39:22–26 620
39:27 629
39:30 634
39:30–31 620
40 622, 881*n*136, 881*n*140
40:2 369
40:9 624
40:9–10 629
40:9–11 881*n*140
40:10 624
40:12 629, 880*n*126
40:12–15 619
40:13 625
40:13–15 626
40:15 620, 626, 629, 635, 641
40:31 629
40:34 369
40:34–35 366, 806*n*206
40:34–38 369
40:35 367
Leviticus
1ff 893*n*262
1–7 643
1–8 619
1:5 619
1:11 619
2:2 894*n*271
2:3 629
2:10 629
3:2 619
3:5 894*n*271
3:8 619
3:13 619
4 598
4:3 625
4:5 625
4:15 642
4:15–20 597
4:18–20 642

4:25 619
4:30 619
4:34 619
5:1 556
6:2 406
6:2–6 406
6:5–6 406
6:6 407
6:9 629
6:13 625
6:15 625
6:16 629
6:20 629, 876n106
7:2 619
7:31 629, 894n271
7:36 626
7:38 867n19
8 618, 624, 625, 627, 628, 878n112, 881n136, 881n140, 882n145, 883n153
8–9 622, 624
8–10 807n217, 882n144
8:1–4 624
8:2 629
8:6 624, 629 880n126
8:7 620, 876n106
8:7–9 612, 624
8:8 620
8:9 620, 634
8:10–11 624, 629, 881n140
8:11 624, 625
8:12 612, 624, 625
8:14 624, 629
8:15 619, 624, 629, 882n145
8:15b 882n143
8:18 624, 629
8:19 619, 624
8:22 624, 629
8:23 612
8:23–24 619, 624
8:24 624
8:29b 618
8:30 619, 620, 624, 625, 627, 628, 629
8:30–33 612
8:30b 625
8:31 629
8:31–35 624
8:33–35 625
8:34 624
8:35 625, 882n146
8:36 629
9 369, 424, 625
9:1 629, 878n109
9:1–14 610
9:1–24 369
9:4 370, 484, 807n215
9:6 370, 484, 806n206, 807n215
9:7 624

9:9 619
9:23 370, 806n206, 807n215
9:23–24 370, 407
9:24 407
9:24a 371
10:1 894n271
10:1–2 640
10:1–3 370, 371, 372, 424, 592, 625, 663, 879n124, 882n144
10:2 371
10:2–3 370
10:3 371
10:7 626
10:10 631, 644
10:11 563, 639
11:1–2a 630
11:25 876n106
11:28 876n106
11:40 876n106
11:42 842n842
11:44–45 605, 615, 630, 670, 884n160
11:47 631
12:1–8 896n277
13:6 876n106
13:34 876n106
13:54–56 876n106
13:58 876n106
14:8 876n106
14:10 806n206
14:47 876n106
15:5–8 876n106
15:10–13 876n106
15:17 876n106
15:19–30 896n277
15:21 876n106
15:27 876n106
16 625, 646, 887n185
16:1–2 372, 808n218
16:2 597, 621, 875n85
16:4 498, 621
16:21 621, 881n133, 881n137
16:22 335
16:23 621
16:23–24 498
16:26 621, 876n106
16:26–28 621
16:28 621, 876n106
16:29–34 622
16:32 620, 622, 626, 641
16:42 806n206
17 845n12
17–26 884n159, 887n190
17:15–16 876n106
18 630, 887n185
18:21 255, 715n25, 888n201
19 630, 635
19:2 605, 630, 660, 661, 670
19:3 403

19:3–36 630
19:10 876n106
19:18 864n187
19:21 876n106
19:26 499
19:30 631
19:37 630
20 630
20:1 630
20:3 888n201
20:6 806n206
20:7 605, 631, 670
20:7–8 630, 631
20:9 840n227
20:24b–26 631
20:26 630, 631
20:27 668
21–22 631
21:1–8 631-2
21:6 888n201
21:7 617
21:7–8 661
21:8 605, 631, 670
21:10 624, 625, 631, 884n163
21:10–15 631
21:11–12 631, 633
21:12 631, 632, 634, 884n163
21:16–23 632
22:1–9 632
22:2 888n201
22:6–7 632
22:10–16 632
22:21 885n170
22:32 888n201
23 610, 876n105
23:4–8 68
23:24 876n105
24 826n91
24:5–9 655
24:9 629
24:11 692
24:14 881n137
24:16 692, 757n8
25:9 876n105
25:39–55 486
26:1 194, 335, 745n143
26:1–13 888n206
26:27 484
26:46 563
27:2 885n170
27:26–27 887n194
27:28–29 463
Numbers
1:1 867n19
1:5–15 59, 65, 106, 107, 731n137, 796n111
1:6 729n124
1:12 105
1:50–51 642

Numbers (*Cont.*)
1:50–53 640
2:3–29 106, 107
2:12 729n124
2:14 106
2:25 105
3 619, 887n190, 887n191
3:3 625
3:5–10 641, 642
3:9 629, 642
3:10 620, 624, 626, 629, 641, 879n124
3:11–13 887n194
3:12 642, 643
3:12–13 642
3:13 643
3:14 867n19
3:35 729n124
3:38 629
3:40–42 642
3:42 643
3:45 642, 643
3:48 629
3:51 629
4 596, 597, 604, 641, 847n25, 887n187, 892n242
4:4–12 597
4:5 629
4:5–6 874n81
4:15 629, 874n80
4:15–20 597
4:16 894n271
4:17–20 597
4:19 629
4:27 629
5:11–31 523
5:23–28 200
6 633, 769n122
6:1 634, 636
6:1–21 633
6:2 635
6:4 633
6:5 633, 636, 660, 661
6:6–8 633
6:6–12 633
6:7 887n182
6:8 633, 634, 636, 660, 661
6:9–12 634, 635
6:10–11 635
6:13 634
6:13–21 634
6:14–15 634
6:16–17 634, 635
6:18 634
6:19–20 635
6:23–27 484
6:24 240
6:24–26 247, 248, 769n122
7:1 624

7:36 729n124
7:41 729n124
7:89 400
8 887n190, 887n194
8:7 642
8:7–10 642
8:10–12 881n137
8:11 642
8:13 642
8:13–14 642
8:14–22 641
8:15 642
8:16 642, 643
8:16–17 642
8:17 643
8:18 643
8:19 629, 642
8:21 642
9:1 867n19
9:1–15 68
9:5 867n19
9:15–16 345
10:9 463
10:10 876n105
10:19 729n124
10:29 274, 275, 781n197
10:29–32 273, 276, 527
10:35 430, 812n252
10:35f 813n267
10:35–36 388, 396, 430
11–12 528, 562
11:4–15 527
11:10–25 527
11:12 490
11:16 527
11:16–25 525, 526, 527, 528, 562, 854n91
11:21 838n203
11:26–30 527
11:29 562
11:31–33 351
12 289
12:1–16 527
12:6 562
12:6–8 562
12:7 892n251
12:7–8 562
12:8 563, 618
12:8b–9 562
13:8–16 759n39
14:9 372
14:11 372
14:12 372
14:14 345
14:14–16 372
14:21 367
15:3 885n170
15:8 885n170
15:31 859n144

15:40 630, 884n160
16 639–41, 659, 887n185
16–17 643
16:1–35 372
16:2–3 639
16:3 639, 640
16:5 660, 849n49
16:5–7 640, 894n271
16:8–11 640
16:9 641, 643
16:10 849n49
16:11 639, 641
16:16–17 640
16:16–18 894n271
16:18 641
16:19–21 372, 641
16:32 372
16:35 372, 639, 641, 662, 894n271
16:42 806n206
17:1–5 641
17:1–15 372
17:5 639, 640, 662
17:7–10 373
17:16–26 887n189
17:27–28 592
18 887n190, 889n211
18:1–7 641
18:2–5 641
18:3 639
18:6 642
18:7 620, 624, 629, 639, 879n124
18:13–18 887n194
18:15–17 642
19 264
20:2–13 638
20:24 732n150
20:26 732n150
21:2 833n150
21:8 138
21:8–9 132, 736n35
21:9 284, 784n230
21:11 887n182
21:14 430, 448
22–24 90, 269
22:4 780n191
22:7 780n191
22:20–22 351
22:22–23 172
22:31 172
22:31–35 351
22:34 172
23–24 84
23:7 780n185
23:7–10 822n68
23:8 116, 733n157
23:18–24 822n68
23:19 288

CITATION INDEX 1051

23:21 850n50
23:21b 509
23:21b–22 318
23:22 116, 198, 733n157, 733n162
24:3–9 822n68
24:4 89, 106, 113, 724n68
24:8 116, 198, 318, 733n157
24:9 197
24:15–19 822n68
24:16 89, 94, 96, 106, 109, 113, 724n68, 726n89
24:20 824n75
25:3–4 351
25:6–18 272
25:13 629, 641
26:58–59 636
26:59 759n39
27:13 732n150
27:21 528, 620, 621
27:27 233
28–29 610
28:2 632
28:16–25 68
31 272, 833n155
31:2 732n150
31:19 833n155
31:20 833n155
31:21–23 833n155
31:24 833n155
32:34 749n172
33 782n205
33:2 563
35:12 528
35:24 528
36:13 563

Deuteronomy
1:2 231
1:5 526, 562, 853n88
1:9–18 520, 525, 526, 527, 544, 562
1:12 526
1:13–17 856n114
1:15 526, 527, 853n89, 856n112, 863n181
1:16 526
1:16–17 526, 560
1:17 521, 526, 531, 562
1:30 137, 385
1:33 345, 353
2:1 286
2:1–6 286
2:5 286
4 802n167, 802n171, 802n172, 802n173, 802n174
4–5 355, 356
4:3 902n51
4:11 345, 353, 354, 357
4:11–12 356, 358, 384

4:12 354, 357, 786n7
4:15 354, 357, 786n7
4:15–16 356, 358, 384
4:19 91, 903n56
4:20 648, 649
4:23–24 358
4:24 344, 353
4:31 481
4:32 824n75
4:32–34 360, 447
4:33 354
4:35 509
4:36 354, 355, 356, 384, 392, 648, 802n174
4:39 509
4:40 766n95
5:1–5 802n172
5:4 354
5:4–5 354
5:6 408
5:8 356
5:11 692
5:12 647
5:16 483, 524, 766n95
5:19 354, 355, 647
5:19–23 354
5:20 357
5:20–21 355
5:21 354, 355, 407
5:22 563
5:23 354, 355
5:26 766n95
6:4 509
6:13 903n55
6:17–18a 865n195
6:18 529
7:1–8 785n236
7:5 194, 335, 353, 801n166
7:6 648, 660, 661
7:7 651
7:8 649, 650
7:9 657
7:12–13 459
7:13 105, 269, 676, 677, 692, 693, 898n6
7:25 141, 353, 801n166
8:5 484
9:3 344, 353, 358
9:6–7 650
9:6–24 650
9:7–21 198
9:8 650
9:10 289, 354, 563
9:12 753n196
9:13–15 650
9:14 650
9:15 345, 353, 354
9:16 753n196
9:19 650

9:20 637, 650, 752n191, 890n222
9:21 353, 753n196
9:24 650
9:26 649
9:26–27 650
9:29 648, 649, 650
10:1–5 408
10:2 563
10:4 354, 563
10:6 650, 890n222
10:8 651
10:9 651
10:17 509, 526, 531
10:17–18 521, 544
10:18 482, 487
12–26 811n244
12:3 194, 335, 353, 693, 801n166
12:5 380
12:5–6 380, 385
12:7 380
12:11 380, 385
12:12 380, 651
12:13–14 380, 385
12:16 499
12:18 380
12:18–19 651
12:25 529, 766n95
12:26 647
12:27 882n142
12:28 529
12:31 715n25
13 716n31, 890n219
13:1 561
13:8 824n75
13:19 529
14:1–2 483
14:2 648, 660, 661
14:21 63, 648, 660, 661
14:23 380
14:27 651
14:29 651
15:19–23 887n194
16–18 544
16:1–8 68
16:1–17 501
16:2 380
16:6 380
16:11 380, 651
16:14 651
16:16–17 610
16:18 526, 850n57
16:18–20 520, 526, 527, 544
16:18–18:22 845n13
16:19 521
16:22 194, 335, 353, 746n150
17:2 544
17:2–3 544

1052 CITATION INDEX

Deuteronomy (*Cont.*)
17:3 903*n*56
17:4 544
17:5 544
17:6–7 544
17:8 544
17:8–12 528
17:8–13 520, 852*n*76
17:9 544, 651
17:10–11 544, 544
17:12 544
17:14–17 518
17:14–20 405, 503, 544, 559, 845*n*13, 849*n*47, 849*n*48
17:15 849*n*49
17:18 651
17:18–19 545
17:18–20 561, 849*n*48
17:19 558
17:20 545
18:1 651
18:1–8 544, 651, 660
18:3 651
18:6–7 651
18:9–22 544
18:11 6
18:15–21 862*n*174
18:16 354, 355
19:12 526
19:15–19 528
19:17 651
20:1 648
20:1–4 464
20:4 137, 385, 464, 648
21:1–9 526, 528
21:5 528, 529, 651
21:6–7 529
21:9 529
21:10 648
21:18–20 526
21:18–21 483, 484, 523, 840*n*227, 840*n*228, 841*n*234
22:7 766*n*95
22:13–21 523
22:15–18 526
23:10 648
23:10–15 654, 655
23:11 889*n*215
23:11–12 464
23:15 385, 464, 583, 647, 810*n*242, 889*n*212
23:17 647
23:18 668, 669
23:18–19 668
24:8 639, 651
25:7–9 526
26:2 380
26:2–4 380, 385
26:5 264
26:12 890*n*226
26:11–12 651
26:11–13 651
26:15 648
26:18–19 648, 660, 661
26:19 725*n*79
27 173, 746*n*150, 746*n*151
27:1–8 173, 383, 784*n*231
27:2 746*n*150
27:3 561
27:5–6 463
27:8 853*n*88
27:9 648, 651
27:9–10 651
27:12 651
27:14 651
27:16 840*n*227
27:19 471
28 716*n*31, 890*n*219
28:1 725*n*79
28:1b 849*n*48
28:4 105, 269, 459, 676, 692, 693
28:9 648, 660, 661
28:18 459, 676, 692, 693
28:38 105, 269
28:51 105, 269, 459, 676, 692, 693, 898*n*6
29:9 531
29:9–14 649
29:11–12 648
29:17 691, 692
29:19 351
31:6 137, 385
31:9 563, 651, 862*n*176
31:19–20 485
31:22 563
31:24 563
31:24–29 598
31:25 651
32 539, 568, 719*n*19, 725*n*72, 857*n*120
32:4 521, 795*n*111
32:6 104, 473, 477, 478, 483, 489, 722*n*49, 822*n*70, 839*n*212, 842*n*250
32:6b 110, 481
32:6b–9 91, 110, 568, 602, 827*n*103, 849*n*44, 902*n*51
32:7 6, 360, 447
32:7–9 285
32:8 88, 91, 791*n*67
32:8–9 479, 483, 649, 725*n*72, 755*n*2
32:10 104
32:11 468
32:13–14 104
32:15 795*n*111, 889*n*212
32:18 110, 473, 477, 478, 483, 489, 732*n*148, 795*n*111, 842*n*250
32:20 824*n*75
32:21 692
32:31 795*n*111
32:35 518
32:37 795*n*111
32:39 509, 692
32:40–42 835*n*174
32:41 800*n*156, 824*n*75
32:41–42 471
32:43 903*n*56
32:43a 725*n*74
32:50 650, 732*n*150
32:50–51 890*n*222
32:51 650
33 270, 728*n*109
33:2 232, 280, 286, 348, 349, 352, 353, 359, 360, 361, 366, 430, 453, 576, 578, 583, 782*n*210, 783*n*214, 800*n*150, 803*n*184, 825*n*80, 835*n*177, 863*n*180, 868*n*24, 889*n*217
33:2–3 580, 648, 812*n*253
33:2–29 822*n*68
33:3 890*n*217
33:5 508
33:6 277
33:8 639, 651, 881*n*131
33:8–11 619, 637–9, 649, 660, 886*n*179, 895*n*271
33:9 886*n*182
33:9–10 638
33:9a 638
33:9b 638
33:11 638
33:16 345, 353, 633, 784*n*229, 799*n*140
33:17 113, 198, 824*n*75
33:23 289
33:26 732*n*156
33:26–27 98–9
33:27 112, 115
33:28 717*n*12
34:10 288, 562, 563
Joshua
1:5 218
1:7 531, 561
1:9 218
3:4–6 891*n*239
3:5 464, 654, 660, 891*n*239
3:10 96, 726*n*93
3:13 824*n*79
3:16 824*n*79
5:10–15 67
5:13–15 463, 891*n*238
5:15 607, 617, 654, 672
6:4 463
6:6 463
6:8 463
6:9 463
6:12 218, 463
6:13 463

CITATION INDEX 1053

6:15 463
6:16 463
6:19 463, 654, 832n149
6:20–21 463
6:24 463, 768n116
7 351, 523
7:13 654, 660
8 832n147
8:30–31 464
8:31–32 563
8:32 561
8:33 527, 528
10:10 826n99
10:24–26 836n179
11:17 231
12:7 231
13:21 780n191
14:1 653
16:5 88
20:1–6 850n57
20:4 524, 526
20:6 528
21 653, 891n233
21:1 653
23:2 527
23:6 561, 563
24 174, 652, 746n152
24:1 527, 653
24:15b 652
24:18b 652
24:19 652
24:19–21 652
24:21–24 653
24:26 561
24:26–27 174, 746n151
24:33 653

Judges
1:16 274
2:16 530, 836n185
3:31 462, 780n194
4 853n83
4:4 781n196
4:4–5 524
4:9 273
4:11 274
4:15 273, 826n99
4:17–22 273
4:18 274
5 84, 270, 272, 273, 277, 708n62, 710n83, 723n59, 853n83
5:2 462, 464, 833n155
5:2–31 822n68
5:3–5 430
5:4 232, 583, 784n229, 835n177
5:4–5 279, 283, 347, 360, 580, 724n65, 783n212, 784n229, 867n17
5:5 784n229
5:6 273, 462
5:6–7 278

5:8 285, 829n115
5:9 462
5:10 278
5:11 829n115
5:12 812n252
5:13 784n227
5:13–16 833n155
5:14b 854n96
5:16 232
5:19 278, 411
5:22 198
5:23 831n139
5:24–26 273
5:30 278
6:1–8:12 272
6:19–24 353
6:21 353
6:22 353
6:22–23 353, 801n159
6:24 221
6:25–32 739n76
6:26 133
6:34 464
6:36–40 464
7 465
7:2 465
7:13 464
8–9 723n60
8:10 465
8:24–27 736n35
8:33 86
9 174, 746n152
9:4 84, 86
9:6 174, 746n152
9:13 79, 744n135
9:46 84, 86, 174
11:10 555
13 378, 379, 389, 424, 489
13–16 464
13:2–23 349, 353, 377
13:4 633
13:5 633
13:6 350, 355, 377
13:7 633
13:8 350, 377
13:10–11 350, 377
13:14 633
13:16 350
13:16–20 407
13:17–18 215, 350
13:18 377
13:19–22 350, 351
13:20 353, 370
13:21–22 350
14:6 464
14:19 464
15:14 464
16:17 633
17–18 84, 619, 637, 737n49, 788n27, 886n174, 886n175

17:1–4 667
17:1–5 132
17:2 764n80
17:3 135, 577, 654, 788n27
17:3–5 637
17:4 134
17:5 637, 639
17:6 521
17:10–12 637
18 637
18:1 521
18:5 464
18:5–6 637, 639
18:14 637, 639
18:17–18 637, 639
18:20 637, 639
18:24 140, 637, 806n204
18:30–31 637
19–21 523
19:1 521
20:9 464
20:26 464
20:27–28 464
20:28 653
21:25 521

1 Samuel
1 284, 713n7
1–6 805n199
1:1–20 489
1:3 653
1:4 896n278
1:7 768n116, 832n149
1:9 653
1:11 633, 884n168, 885n169
1:13–15 885n169
1:20 726n91
1:21–28 667
1:22 633, 884n168
1:25 896n278
1:27–28 726n91
2 593, 603
2:1 590
2:1–2 593
2:1–10 588. 589–90, 670, 822n68
2:2 589, 605, 615, 651, 658
2:3 90
2:4 590
2:4–8 589, 590
2:8 591
2:9 590
2:10 589, 590, 591, 651, 658, 725n82, 871n49
2:12–17 364
2:22 667
2:22–25 364
2:27–36 657
2:28 894n271
2:35 645, 657
2:35–36 653

1054 CITATION INDEX

1 Samuel (Cont.)
3:3 815n282
3:10 172
3:13–14 693
3:20 657
4:1–7:1 364
4:3 595
4:3–4 395
4:4 221, 401
4:6 806n202
4:6–7 648
4:6–8 596
4:7–8 364, 395
4:19 364
4:19–22 364, 366, 407
4:21 364, 805n199
4:22 364
5 138, 254
5:1–4 596
5:1–5 141, 303
5:4 141, 788n30
5:9 596
5:10–11 596
6:4 119
6:4–15 139
6:11 119
6:13–14 596
6:14–15 596, 604
6:15 596, 642
6:20 596, 652
7:1 596, 654, 656, 660, 661
7:5–11 464
7:10 826n99
7:12 336, 746n153
8 405
8–12 849n47
8:5 513
8:11 513, 556
8:11–18 558
8:20 513
9:13 634
10:1 499, 625, 634
10:5–6 7
10:6 464
10:8 634
10:10 464
10:25 559
10:27 836n179
11:6 464
12:5–6 528
13:9 464
13:9–14 499
13:11–14 845n14
13:12 464
14:3 more, 653
14:6 465
14:15 465
14:24 471
14:31–35 499

14:35 499
15:6 273, 782n209
15:7 836n179
15:13 764n80
16:5 654, 660
16:7 289
16:13 499, 882n148
16:13–14 464
16:18 219
17:37 219
17:45 389, 405
17:45–47 465
17:46 465
17:47 389, 833n160
17:50–51 465, 833n160
17:51 836n179
18 531, 851n68
18:5 531
18:14 219, 531
18:15 531
18:17 462
18:27 836n179
18:28 219
18:30 531
20:12 528
21 892n243
21:1 653
21:1–7 648, 654–5, 660
21:2–7 877n107
21:5 655, 848n36
21:6 464, 655
21:7 848n36
21:10 464
22:11–19 653
22:20–23 653
23:1–5 499, 880n131
23:6 653
23:6–12 499, 880n131
23:13 758n17
24 518
24:8–22 556
24:13 518
24:16 518
25:28 462, 657
28 668
28:6 880n131
28:9–10 559
28:13 801n160
30:7–8 464, 499, 880n131
30:25 559
31:1–13 461
31:9 137
31:10 464, 676, 689, 899n7

2 Samuel
1:17–27 461
1:19–27 822n68
1:21 464, 833n154
2:1 880n131
4:7–8 836n179

4:12 836n179
5:10 219
5:17–25 461
5:21 141, 739n77
5:23–24 880n131
6 396, 596, 813n266
6:1–11 596, 604, 652
6:2 383, 401
6:5 396
6:6–7 351
6:7 596, 874n79
6:8 612
6:8–9 596
6:12–16 7
6:13 499
6:14 396
6:16 499
6:16–17 396
6:17 499
6:17–18 655
6:21 396
7:2 813n262
7:4–17 458
7:6 219, 813n262
7:11–16 114, 500
7:11–17 849n43
7:11b–16 534
7:12 218–19
7:13 391, 810n243
7:14 458, 505, 839n212
7:15 505
7:16 657
7:26 391
8:2–6 836n179
8:9–10 233
8:11 463, 654, 891n240
8:15 518, 855n105
8:17 645, 653
8:18 637, 653, 845n11, 891n232
11 535
11–12 892n241
11:4 654, 892n241
11:8–13 655
11:11 464
11:27b–12:14 849n47
12:1 534, 855n106
12:1–15 535
12:7 499, 882n148
12:30 141, 303, 737n49, 739n75
12:31 836n179
14:1–20 518
14:4–11 528, 535
14:16 856n112
14:17 518, 529
15:1–6 513
15:2–4 850n57
15:2–6 849n47
15:3–4 855n105

CITATION INDEX 1055

15:8 264, 331
15:20 758n17
15:24–29 645, 653
15:35 653
15:36 653
18:1–5 513
18:18 121, 171
19:9 513
19:11 653
20:8 860n156
20:26 653
21:19 833n160
22 270, 345, 349, 376, 378, 799n141
22:3 795n111
22:8–11 346, 453
22:8–15 347
22:10–11 400
22:11 809n228, 814n275
22:13–15 346, 453
22:14 92, 602, 732n156
22:15 376, 453, 826n99
22:16 824n78, 834n172
22:29 406
22:32 795n111
22:35 458
22:51 505
23:1 823n74
23:1–7 458
23:5 727n104
23:33 843n263
24 351, 352, 849n47, 855n107
24:1 352
24:10 352
24:14–16 855n107
24:15 352
24:16 352
24:17 352
24:18–25 499
24:25 855n107
1 Kings
1–2 518
1:5 513
1:7 653
1:7–8 645
1:22–39 645, 653
1:37 219
1:38 760n44
2:3 531, 563
2:5 860n156
2:26 596, 604
2:26–27 383, 645, 653
2:35 645, 653
3:2 391, 846n20
3:2–4 500, 655
3:3 519, 847n31
3:3–4 846n20
3:3–15 518
3:4 541, 851n70

3:9 519
3:12 519
3:12–13 846n21
3:13 366, 505
3:15 500, 519, 846n20
3:16–28 519, 851n71
3:28 519, 529
4:2 653
4:5 653
4:12 411
5:5 500
5:15–8:13 501
5:17 500
5:19 380
6 398, 399, 814n274
6:16 654
6:16–36 501, 655
6:19–28 398
6:20 398
6:23 119, 398
6:23–27 398
6:23–28 399, 405
6:27 398
6:29 398
6:32 398
6:35 398
7:13–47 847n22
7:21 119, 196
7:21–26 317
7:25 317
7:27–37 317, 790n49
7:29 315, 317, 398
7:36 315, 317, 398
7:39 317
7:44 317
7:49 406
7:50 654
7:51 891n240
8 365, 366, 385, 386, 392, 396, 655, 807n206, 810n243, 811n245, 847n25
8:1–12 366
8:1–13 366
8:3–11 501, 655, 660
8:4 654, 656
8:5 385, 392, 396, 501, 541, 655
8:5–9 385, 386
8:6 365, 407, 595, 654
8:6–7 656
8:7 397, 405
8:8 654
8:9 408
8:10 654, 656
8:10–11 364, 365, 366, 368, 385, 386, 392, 806n206, 811n244
8:11 367, 407, 656
8:12 366, 806n206
8:13 283, 501
8:16 366

8:16–20 386
8:16–21 408
8:17 366
8:19 366
8:20 366
8:21 408
8:22 384, 390
8:23–53 384
8:27 384, 811n243
8:29 366, 380, 386
8:30 384, 390, 648
8:32 384, 390
8:33 366
8:34 384, 390
8:35 366
8:36 384, 390
8:39 384, 390, 648
8:41–44 386
8:42–44 366
8:43 380, 384, 390, 648
8:45 384, 390
8:48 366, 386
8:49 384, 390, 648
8:54 384, 390
8:58 558
8:62 385, 811n244
8:62–64 396, 501, 541, 655
8:64 654
9:3 654, 659, 672
9:7 654, 659
9:25 501
10:9 519
10:19–20 317
11 661, 689, 846n21
11:1–10 753n193
11:1–11 849n47
11:1–13 518
11:5 509, 676, 684, 688, 691
11:5–8 134
11:7 509, 691
11:7–8 501
11:8 667
11:33 509, 676, 684, 688
11:38 219
12 753n194, 791n57
12:25 199, 752n190
12:25–33 198, 320, 752n190
12:28 134, 200, 753n196
12:28–29 752n190
12:28–33 100, 187, 197, 502
12:29–33 200
12:31 199, 654, 656
12:32 753n196
12:32a 752n190
13:1 502
13:1–10 662, 847n30
13:32 199
13:33 654, 656
13:33–34 657, 847n29

1056 CITATION INDEX

1 Kings (*Cont.*)
14:9 752*n*192, 791*n*66
14:22–24 847*n*31
14:23 194, 335
14:24 668
15:12 668
15:12–13 141, 302
15:13 134, 292, 667
15:14 847*n*31
15:15 654
16:29–34 713*n*6
16:33 134
17:1–7 666
17:8–16 666
17:17–24 666
18 281, 347
18:4 302
18:19 502
18:20–40 666
18:24 347
18:26 845*n*16
18:27 217
18:36 347
18:38 347
18:38–39 370
18:41–45 666
18:46 666
19 281, 283, 347, 805*n*196
19:5–8 666, 801*n*161
19:9–12 666
19:9–13 805*n*196
19:11–12 347, 800*n*149
19:12–13 786*n*7
19:18 136
20:39–40 535
21:1–24 535
21:8 526, 535, 855*n*108
21:10 693
21:13 693
21:16 855*n*108
22 405
22:5ff 464
22:10 513
22:19 289, 294, 405
22:19–22 565
22:19–23 814*n*276
22:22 352
22:39 790*n*48
22:43 847*n*31
22:47 668
23:4–15 302

2 Kings
1:9–16 666
2:11 801*n*162
2:11–12 350, 666
2:19–22 666
2:23–25 666, 667
3:2 132, 134, 141, 171, 194, 335
3:4 769*n*125

3:9–20 666
3:15 7
3:27 255, 715*n*25
4:1 487
4:1–7 666, 667
4:8–17 489
4:8–37 666
4:9 654, 665–7
4:38–41 666
4:42–44 666
5 666
5:17 888*n*203
5:18 266
5:26–27 666
6:1–7 666
6:12 666
6:15–23 466
6:16 466
6:17 350, 739*n*72
6:18 360
6:18–23 666
8:1 758*n*17
9:3 499, 625
9:6 499, 625
10:1 490
10:5 490
10:7–14 836*n*179
10:18–27 713*n*6
10:18–28 752*n*192, 892*n*249
10:20 654
10:26–27 132, 141, 171, 194, 335
10:29 752*n*192
10:31 563
11 502
11–12 503, 653
11:18 141
12:3 847*n*31
12:4 654
12:18 654, 892*n*240
13:20–21 666
14:6 563
15:4 847*n*31
15:5 662
15:35 847*n*31
16:3–4 502
16:7 841*n*242
16:8 296
16:10 264
16:10–11 815*n*288
16:10–16 502, 653, 894*n*270
16:12 849*n*49
16:12–13 882*n*142
16:13 502, 848*n*32, 879*n*122, 895*n*272
16:14 296
16:14–18 502
16:15 848*n*32
16:15–16 502

16:17 296
17:7–23 199, 752*n*192, 791*n*66
17:10 194
17:16 199, 295, 752*n*192, 791*n*66
17:21–23 199, 752*n*192, 791*n*66
17:24–28 295
17:30 387
17:31 715*n*25
17:32 656
18:4 138, 141, 194, 335, 784*n*230, 788*n*32
18:5 496, 519, 846*n*21
18:13–19:37 834*n*163
18:22 335
18:34 295
19:15 400, 401
19:18 353
19:22 652, 658
19:32–38 467
19:35 461
21:1–16 849*n*47
21:3 134, 788*n*29, 902*n*44
21:6 255, 715*n*25
21:7 134, 292, 294, 788*n*29, 902*n*44
22:4 653
22:13 351
23 889*n*210
23:3 558
23:4 653
23:4–6 294
23:5 653
23:6 141, 292
23:7 136, 668, 842*n*253
23:8–9 335
23:10 255, 715*n*25
23:11 324, 353, 412, 421, 792*n*77
23:13 509, 676, 684, 688, 691
23:13–14 325
23:14 171, 194
23:14–15 141
23:15 753*n*192
23:15–20 753*n*192
23:17 351
23:20 653
23:21–23 67
23:25 496, 519, 563, 846*n*21
23:27 391
24:13 296
25:13–17 296
25:18 653

Isaiah
1:2 481, 539
1:2–3 483, 603
1:4 599
1:7–8 486
1:10 856*n*114

CITATION INDEX

1:11 769n125
1:11–17 856n111
1:16–17 856n111
1:16–20 469
1:16b–17 536
1:17 482, 856n114, 857n127
1:17–18a 545
1:21 536, 537
1:21–26 467
1:23 849n47
1:23–24 536
1:24 197, 318, 601
1:26–27 543
2:2–4 472, 530, 532, 836n180
2:4 468, 473, 530
2:6–22 798n136
2:10 344
2:18–19 798n136
2:19 344, 828n108
2:21 344, 828n108
3:3 6
3:14 526
5:4 461
5:14 467, 831n134
5:15–16 671
5:16 577, 600, 601
5:19 599
5:23 537
5:24 563, 599
5:27 860n156
6 367, 511, 600, 813n268
6:1 136, 294, 405, 785n1
6:1–2 289
6:1–2a 510
6:1–4 294
6:1–5 366–8, 407
6:1–7 349, 353
6:1–8 565
6:3 368, 599, 600
6:4 367
6:5 355, 367, 379, 510
6:5–7 406
6:6 349, 801n163
6:13 194, 796n112
7 466
7:1–8:15 367
7:6 591
7:14 219, 476
8:3 667
8:7 368
8:7ff 797n127
8:11 591
8:11–15 591–3
8:12 591
8:12–13 591
8:12b 591
8:13 615
8:14 592
8:14–15 593

8:21–22 693
9:2–7 313
9:3 273
9:5 99, 505
9:5–6 505, 506, 507
9:6 517, 518, 530
10:1–2 536, 559
10:2 482, 856n112
10:5 458
10:5–11 467
10:5–19 368
10:10–12 787n16
10:11 295
10:16 368, 407
10:16–19 368
10:17 344, 406
10:17–21 602
10:20 599
10:21 506
10:26 273
10:27b–34 467
10:33–34 468
11:1–5 531
11:1–9 507
11:1–10 313
11:2–4 517, 518
11:2–5 506, 531
11:3 526
11:6–9 468
11:9 367
12:2 823n74
13:6 104
14 724n63
14:3 731n143, 741n98
14:12–15 505
14:13 108, 113
14:13–14 88
14:14 88, 110
14:24–27 467
14:32 467
16:5 518
17:4 808n224
17:12–13 468
17:12–13a 468
17:12–14 467
17:13 469
19–20 466
19:3 831n135
19:6 823n75
19:18–22 336, 422
19:19 336
19:19–20 194
20:6 466
21:5 464
24–27 460
25:8 460, 461, 489, 825n82
26:4 796n111
27:1 446, 460, 470, 734n172, 835n174

28:16 467
28:29 506
29:1–2 197
29:1–7 467
29:5–6 348, 352, 353
29:6 468, 583
29:7 197
29:18–21 533
29:21 855n101
29:23 601
30 378
30:1–7 466
30:7 820n53
30:9 563
30:11 599
30:12 599
30:15 468, 591, 599
30:15–16 468
30:27 351, 809n230
30:27–28 799n144
30:27–28a 387
30:27–30 346, 354, 377, 405
30:27–33 387, 425, 467, 468
30:28 809n230
30:29 796n111
30:30 799n144, 809n230
30:30b–31 387
30:31 377
31:1 591, 599, 600
31:1–2 468
31:1–3 466
31:1–8 467
31:4 468
31:4–5 468
31:8 468, 835n174
31:9 468
32:10ff 784n221
33:1 104
33:17–24 467
33:22 529, 560, 563, 854n96
34 835n177
34:2–10 471
34:5–6 835n174
34:7 198
35:1–10 820n51
36:1–37:38 834n163
36:20 725n76
37:11 571
37:16 400, 401
37:24 468
37:33–38 467
37:36 461
40–48 470
40–55 487
40:12 858n132
40:19 134
40:19–20 133, 287, 303
40:20 132, 134
40:21–24 447

Isaiah (Cont.)

40:28 99, 758n25
41:5-14 287
41:7 133, 303
41:8-9 649
41:14 599, 603
41:25 812n254
42:1 649
42:6-7 492
42:10 491
42:13 430
42:13-14 12, 471, 697
42:13-16 491, 875n92
42:16 843n258
42:25 351
43:1 488
43:1-7 481, 487-8, 603
43:3 599
43:3b 488
43:5-7 488
43:7 488
43:10 649
43:14 599, 603
43:14-17 897n290
43:15 577
43:20 649
43:26 539, 546
43:28 865n8
44:1-2 649
44:6 509
44:6-22 287
44:8 796n111
44:12 132
44:13-17 132
45:4 649
45:7 873n72
45:9-12 477, 481, 485, 603, 841n236
45:10 477
45:11 599
45:11a 841n239
45:21 210
46:1 138
46:1-7 137
46:6 133, 303
47:4 599, 603
47:9 6
47:12 6
48:17 599, 603
49:7 599, 603, 649
49:14 492
49:14-15 492
49:15b 492
49:23 490
49:26 197, 318, 601
50:1 492, 841n240
51 820n52
51:9 210
51:9ff 728n113
51:9-10 360, 444, 491
51:9-11 444-5, 450, 734n172
51:11 820n51
52:1-2 488
52:10 670
52:11 762n69
52:12 453
54:5 599, 603
56:1-8 571
57:3 668
57:4 831n133
59 470
59:1 644
59:3 470
59:7 470
59:14 470
59:15b-20 835n175
59:16 470
59:17 470
60:5 871n52
60:6 808n217
60:13 409
60:16 197, 318, 601
62:11 489
63:1-3 136, 471
63:1-6 470, 835n175
63:5 470
63:10 615
63:10-12a 614-15
63:11 233, 614, 615, 618, 878n116, 878n117
63:11-12 445
63:12 826n95
63:16 488, 839n212
64:1 470
64:7 481
64:8 839n212
65:6 534
66:13 492
66:15 801n163, 835n172
66:15-16 470
66:16 801n163, 835n174
66:19 843n254

Jeremiah

1:1 383
1:5 473, 489, 649, 665
1:16-17 860n156
2:4-14 539
2:27 483, 732n148, 795n111
2:30 903n54
3:4 839n212
3:12 864n187
3:16-17 813n263
3:17 813n263
3:19 483, 839n212
4:4 351
4:30 903n54
4:31 486
5:28 538
6:1-7 486
6:4 429, 464, 583, 648, 830n118, 895n274
6:20 808n217
6:22-26 486
6:29 903n54
7:1-15 469
7:3 864n195
7:5 538
7:5-6 574, 864n195
7:6 482
7:12 380, 383, 389, 392
7:16-20 509, 667, 677
7:18 677, 689, 690
7:20 351, 677
7:31 64
8:8 532, 563
8:16 198
8:19 386, 400
9:22-23 532
10:1-6 287
10:3-4 133, 134, 303
10:5 138, 139
12:1 546
12:12 104
14:12 835n174
18:6 133
18:11 864n195
19:1-11 471
19:5 64
20:9 665
20:11 828n108
20:18 489
21:12 351
22 519
22:3 518, 519
22:7 895n274
22:13 519
22:15 520, 542, 865n195
22:15-17 519-20
22:16 520, 529, 532
22:17 849n47
23:5 517, 518, 531, 532, 564
23:5-6 313
23:9 665
23:18 565
23:22 565
23:23 697, 699
23:29 665
25:6 104
25:15-17 289
25:30 313
25:31 470, 835n174
26:4-6 469
26:10-11 850n57
26:11 528
26:13 864n195
26:16 528
26:17 526

26:17-19 467
27:16-18 296
28:3 296
30:4 849n49
30:14 484
30:21 507, 849n49
30:22 849n49
31:7-9 842n248
31:9 839n212
31:21 292
31:22 485
31:33 561
31:35 820n57
32:31-35 484
32:33 483
32:35 64
33:14-16 313
34:8-10 559
35:13 484
35:14 484
35:14b 484
35:15b 484
35:16a 484
35:16b 484
35:17-19 484
35:17b 484
35:18-19 484
36:30-31 849n47
38:7 850n57
40:10 99, 758n25
43:13 194, 335, 745n143
44:6 351
44:15-19 139, 667
44:15-30 509, 677
44:17 677, 690
44:17-18 677, 679, 688, 689
44:17-19 136
44:17b 689
44:18 687, 689
44:19 133, 690
44:19-20 902n48
44:25 667, 902n48
46:10 835n174
46:11 903n54
46:18 509
47:3 198
47:4 104
48:1 104
48:7 140, 806n204
48:8 104
48:13 729n116
51:55 104
51:56 104
51:59-64 471
52:17-23 296
52:20 317
Ezekiel
  1 809n229
  1·1 289, 379

1:3 375, 644, 665
1:4 373, 786n9, 808n221, 860n159
1:4-26 400
1:5-25 373, 397
1:7 317, 373
1:10 317, 320, 791n63
1:13 373
1:14 373
1:15-21 400
1:16 373
1:18 373
1:22 136, 373
1:24 104
1:26 136, 373, 378, 401, 405, 511
1:26-28 289, 290, 373, 374, 375, 377, 397, 790n53, 797n126
1:27 373, 786n9, 808n221
1:28 344, 370, 373, 790n53, 806n206
3:12 373
3:23 373
4:14 895n275
6:13 786n5
7:20 133
8 311
8-10 805n199
8:2 289, 374, 378, 808n221
8:2-3 375
8:3 379, 790n53
8:4 373
8:8 644
8:14 646, 668
9:2-3 621
9:3 373, 407
9:4-6 311
9:9 644
9:11 621
10:1 401, 511
10:1-5 400
10:2 374, 621
10:4 344, 373, 374, 379, 407, 806n206
10:5 104
10:6 374
10:12-13 374
10:13 374
10:14 317, 791n63
10:18 373, 407
10:19 373
11:12 373
11:22 407
11:23 373
12:14 829n117
12:25 758n17
13:17-23 668
13:19 644
14:11 646, 889n211
14:21 835n174

16 737n49
16:8 136, 841n240
16:8-14 785n1
16:17 133
16:19 786n5
18 485
18:10 869n37
18:25 485
18:29 485
18:30 538
20:12 644
20:18-21 484
20:20 644
20:25 542, 545
20:25-26 64, 542
20:26 542
20:28 786n5
20:39 644
20:40 644
20:41 645, 786n5, 897n291
20:42 671
21 835n174
21:15 800n156
21:30 538
21:36 351
22:6 888n198
22:8 644
22:21 351
22:26 644
22:31 351
23:37 841n240
24:14 538
26:7 850n51
26:11 335
26:20 727n100
28 722n50
28:2-10 505
28:14 813n271
28:16 813n271
28:22 371, 577, 671
28:22-23 671
28:25 645
28:25-26 671
29:3-5 820n53
30:2-3 104
30:24-25 458
32:2b-8 820n53
34:1-10 849n47
34:17 538
36:19 538
36:20 645, 758n17, 888n202
36:20-22 644
36:20-23 644
36:23 671, 897n291
36:23a 645
36:23b 645
36:27 561
37:26 760n41
37:26-27 645

1060 CITATION INDEX

Ezekiel (*Cont.*)
  37:26–28 888n206
  37:28 644, 645
  38–39 464, 470
  38:4 470
  38:11–13 470
  38:15 470
  38:16 671
  38:18–23 533
  38:19 351
  38:21a 835n174
  38:21b 835n174
  38:22 799n146
  38:23 645, 671
  39:3 470
  39:7 644, 888n197
  39:9–10 470
  39:25 644
  39:25–27 671, 897n291
  39:26 644
  39:27 645
  40–43 644
  40–48 646–7, 660, 888n196
  40:2 644, 790n53
  40:45 888n208
  40:45–46 646, 888n208
  40:46 646
  41:4 644
  41:18–20 398
  41:21 644
  41:23 644
  42:13 644
  42:13–14 644
  42:14 644, 646
  42:20 644
  43:2 373, 374
  43:4–5 373
  43:7 393, 409
  43:7–8 644
  43:12 644
  43:13–27 646, 790n46
  43:15 315, 750n183
  43:15–16 197, 789n46
  43:18 882n142
  43:18–21 646
  43:18–27 625
  43:19 646
  43:26 646
  43:27 646
  44 889n210
  44:1 646
  44:4 373
  44:6–16 889n211
  44:10 646, 647, 889n211
  44:11 647
  44:12 646, 889n211
  44:12b 647
  44:13 644, 646, 647, 660, 889n211
  44:14 647

  44:15 596, 645, 646, 888n208
  44:15–16 646
  44:17–19 646
  44:19 644
  44:20–27 646
  44:23–24 644
  44:24 528
  44:27 644
  45:1–7 644
  45:4 646
  45:18–20 619
  45:18–25 610
  45:21–25 68
  46:19 644
  46:20 644
  47:5 824n76
  48:10 644
  48:11 646, 889n211
  48:12 644
  48:14 644
  48:18 644
  48:20–21 644

Hosea
  1:6 484
  1:7 594
  1:8–9 484
  1:9 214
  2:1 96
  2:1–2 594
  2:10 737n49
  2:10–11 903n57
  2:16–25 594
  2:18 235
  2:18–19 903n57
  3:4 194, 796n112
  4:14 668, 669, 896n288
  4:15 729n118
  5:8 729n118
  5:14 313
  6:1–3 594
  7:12–13 484
  8 198, 320
  8:4 133, 303, 849n47
  8:5–6 198, 320
  8:6 725n74, 753n192, 791n67
  9:10 633, 884n166
  10:1–2 194, 796n112
  10:2 104
  10:4 903n54
  10:5 729n118, 753n197
  10:14–15 873n75
  11:1 226, 482–3
  11:1–4 840n229
  11:1–6 594
  11:2–3 483
  11:3–4 481–2
  11:6–7 873n75
  11:8–9 492–3
  11:9 288, 593–5, 600, 603, 616, 873n75

  11:10 313, 873n75
  12:1 873n75
  12:10 226
  12:12 903n54
  13:1–2 321
  13:2 133, 134, 136, 303, 320
  13:4 226
  13:7–8 313
  14:4 668
  14:4b 482
  14:5–8 594

Joel
  1:15 104
  2:1 784n221
  2:10 784n221
  2:10–11 470
  3:3–4 470
  4:2 532
  4:9 464, 895n274
  4:9–16 471, 472, 836n180
  4:12 532
  4:16 313

Amos
  1:2 313
  1:2–2:16 471
  1:11 864n187
  2:4 563
  2:6–8 535
  2:11–12 633
  3:2 649
  3:8 313
  5 856n110
  5–6 856n110
  5:5 729n118
  5:7 533, 535, 855n101
  5:10–12 533, 535, 850n57, 855n101
  5:12 536
  5:15 542, 865n195
  5:18 534
  5:24 530, 536
  5:26 137
  6:12b 535
  7:4 347, 799n146, 827n105
  7:7 172
  7:11 849n47
  7:13 502, 713n6
  7:14 873n75
  8:4–6 550
  9:1 172, 294

Obadiah
  11–16 471

Jonah
  1:2 571
  2:6 823n75
  3:4 571, 574
  3:8 571
  3:10 571
  4:1 573
  4:2 481

CITATION INDEX   1061

4:4 574
4:11 571
4:11a 574
Micah
1:2 857n121
1:4 583
3:1 538
3:1–4 849n47
3:2–3 538
3:5 895n274
3:9 538
3:9–12 469, 537, 849n47
3:11 528
3:11b 467, 469, 538
3:12 467
4:1–3 472, 530, 532
4:1–4 836n180
4:3 473, 530
4:7 850n56
4:10 486
4:11–13 471, 472, 836n180
5:11 6
5:12 194
6:1–8 539–41, 570
6:1b 857n122
6:2 857n122
6:2a 542
6:3b 541, 545
6:5 541, 542
6:6 541
6:6–7a 769n125
6:7b 542
6:8 542, 865n195
6:8a 542
6:16 559
7:18–20 569
Nahum
1:4 824n78, 826n92, 834n172
1:6 351
3:1 571
3:1–18 471
3:19 571
Habakkuk
1:12 210
2:2 853n88
2:5 461
2:14 367
2:19 133, 134, 303
3 270, 359–60, 448, 734n170, 734n171, 782n210, 822n68, 825n88, 866n14
3:2 359, 451, 578
3:2–3 577, 755n2
3:2–5 359, 366
3:2a 280, 360, 784n221
3:3 117, 427, 576, 586, 825n81, 835n177, 875n88
3:3–5 360, 863n180
3:3–6 347
3:3–7 280–1

3:3–15 430
3:4 803n182
3:5 117, 309, 348, 352, 801n164
3:6 583
3:8 117, 309, 452, 578, 801n164
3:8–9 451
3:8–11 451–2
3:8–15 360, 451
3:9 450
3:9a 825n89
3:9b 825n89
3:11 360, 450, 451, 825n89
3:12 801n164
3:13b–15 451–2
3:15 452
3:16 784n221
3:18 578
3:19 578
Zephaniah
2:11 869n36
3:3 538
3:4 888n198
3:4b 644
3:7 484
3:14 488
3:15 859n147
Haggai
1:13 350, 801n161
2:23 532
Zechariah
2:4–5 470
2:5 407
2:9 406
2:10 489
3 565
4:6 464, 465
9:9 489, 850n56
9:9–10 793n84
9:14 860n159
12:11 266
14:1–2 532
14:1–5 464
14:1–21 461
14:5 576
14:16 827n101
14:16–17 512
Malachi
1:1 350, 801n161
1:6 483, 839n212
1:6–2:9 483
1:14 509
2:10 481, 839n212
2:17 546, 550
3:1 350, 801n161
3:2–3 406
3:5 482
3:13–21 858n137
3:18 550
3.20 139
3:22 563

Psalms
1:2 563
1:5 528
2:7 219, 458, 489, 505
2:12 351
7 522
7:7b 522, 530
7:9 522
7:18 92, 602
8:2 506
9 522
9:2 88
9:2–3 92
9:3 88, 602
9:4–9 837n185
9:5 522, 529
9:8b–10 522, 529
9:12 728n106
10:14 482
10:16 509
16:8 829n117
16:9 808n224
17:15 786n8
18 270, 345, 349, 376, 378, 799n141, 809n229
18:3 795n111
18:7–16 734n172
18:8 583
18:8–11 346, 453
18:8–15 347, 354
18:10 50, 345
18:10–11 400
18:11 349, 377, 814n275
18:13–15 346, 453
18:14 92, 266, 602, 732n156
18:15 376, 453, 826n99
18:16 824n78, 834n172
18:29 406
18:32 795n111
18:35 458
18:51 505
19:8 563
19:15 796n111
20:2 388
20:5 765n93
20:6 388
20:8 388
20:10 388
21:2–3 506
21:4–8 506
21:6 458, 829n117
21:7 506
21:8 92, 95, 505, 602
21:10 351, 831n135
22:2 548
22:10–11 490, 842n254
22:22b 734n169
24 368, 396, 458–60, 813n268
24:1 368
24:3 576

Psalms (*Cont.*)
24:3-4 368, 607
24:7-10 362, 386, 396, 400, 407, 459, 506, 510
24:8 430, 510
24:10 430, 510
25:8 865n195
25:8-10 854n98
25:11 574
26 522
26:1 522, 529
26:6 529
27:9ff 843n254
27:10 492
28:1 796n111
29 84, 270, 359, 361, 366, 430, 443, 448, 454, 460, 568, 734n172, 804n187, 822n68, 827n103, 831n131, 863n183
29:1 361, 568, 827n103, 863n183
29:1-2 565, 869n36
29:2 361, 381, 658, 893n256
29:3 361, 803n176
29:3-5 361
29:5 803n176
29:5-6 753n198
29:6 198, 200, 753n198
29:7 368, 803n176
29:7-8 803n176
29:7-9 361
29:8 867n19
29:9 361
29:10 509, 510, 827n105
31:3-4 796n111
32:8 531
34:4 728n107
34:9 8
35:1 852n78
35:10b 852n78
35:11a 852n78
35:23-24 852n78
35:24 523, 529
36:7 729n123
37 548, 549
37:9 553
37:25-28 548-9
37:30-33 548-9
38:12 827n105
41:1 531
41:14 699
42-83 88, 92, 784n229, 852n80
43 522, 852n79
43:1 523, 529, 566
43:4 724n65
44 447, 822n66
44:2 360, 447, 822n66
44:3 833n160
44:4 465

45 507
45:3-5 507
45:7 13, 507
45:7-8 507
45:8 724n65
46 467, 576
46:2 468
46:2-3 468
46:4 824n76
46:5 93, 467, 576, 601, 875n91
46:5-8 386, 400
46:6 468, 469
46:7-10 836n184
46:8 468
46:9 834n170
46:10 468
46:11 468
46:12 468
47 511
47:3 93, 94, 95, 458, 512, 602
47:6 396
47:7-9 509, 512
47:9 724n65
48 467, 850n56
48:2 467
48:2-3 109
48:3 467, 468, 469, 511, 731n143
48:4 468, 469
48:6-7 469
48:9 467, 469
48:13-14 469
50 539
50:3 348
50:13 198
50:14 93
51:3-7 574
51:19 724n65
54 522
54:3 523, 529
56:9 534
57:3 89, 93, 95, 875n91
58:6 6
60:10 136
65:2 876n105
68 270, 430, 448, 578, 579-81, 588, 593, 602, 603, 604, 733n166, 782n210, 822n68, 867n17, 868n30
68:1 396
68:2-3 580-1, 587
68:3 583
68:5 211, 400, 732n156, 814n275
68:5-9 580-1
68:5b 867n17
68:6 482, 487, 522, 530, 570, 576, 577, 588, 590, 593, 604, 839n212

68:6-7 590
68:7-9 279
68:8 784n229, 867n19
68:8-9 283, 360, 724n65, 783n212
68:8-11 784n229, 867n17
68:9 347, 583, 588, 784n229
68:15-17 102
68:16 602
68:16-17 579
68:17 279
68:18 580-1, 812n253, 863n180
68:18-19 360
68:19 211
68:20 603
68:20-21 580-1, 588
68:20-22 875n88
68:21 588
68:25 509, 580-1, 599, 783n214, 850n50
68:29 582
68:29-30 580-1
68:31 198
68:33-36 580-1
68:34 867n19
68:34-36 582
68:36 601, 804n191
69:31 728n107
71:3 796n111
71:6 490, 843n254
71:22 600
72:1-2 517
72:1-4 529
72:1-14 564
72:4 517
72:12-14 517, 529
72:19 367, 699
73:1 93, 875n91
73:1-2 98
73:11 90, 93, 115, 875n91
74 443, 444, 820n45, 820n46, 827n102
74:1 351
74:1-11 444
74:3 443
74:7 443
74:12 210, 454, 509, 817n13
74:12-14 734n172
74:12-15 510
74:12-17 360, 443, 444, 491
74:13-14 820n49
74:15 820n49
74:16-17 444, 445
74:19 444
74:22 812n252
75:10 98, 728n105
76 467
76:3 386, 400, 467
76:3-4 836n184

CITATION INDEX 1063

76:4 837n185
76:4-7 468
76:6-7 469, 836n184, 837n185
76:8-11 468
77 825n88
77:2 89
77:4 89
77:6 89, 99
77:8-10 697
77:10 112, 732n152
77:10-11 89, 99
77:11-14 93
77:12 360, 450
77:14 89, 605
77:17 451, 605
77:17-21 450
77:19 784n221
77:20 393, 409, 451, 825n86
77:21 450
78 88
78:13 824n79
78:14 88, 345
78:17-18 93
78:21 352
78:31 352
78:34-35 86, 88, 89, 93, 112
78:35 86, 89, 95, 113
78:38-39 569
78:41 600
78:49-50 351, 352, 353
78:52 233
78:54 588, 612
78:56 93, 875n91
78:61 806n205
78:68 467
79:10-12 471
79:11 322
80:1 233
80:2 401
80:11 729n123
82 92, 565-9, 570, 602, 725n78, 756n2, 827n103, 863n179, 863n181, 902n51, 864n184, 869n36
82:1 89, 113, 172
82:1a 567
82:1b 567
82:2-4 567
82:2-5 568
82:5 567
82:6-7 215, 568, 569
82:6-8 89
82:6a 567
82:6b 567
82:7 567, 725n79, 825n82, 863n181
82:7-8 92, 849n44
82:8 567, 568, 812n252, 837n185

83:10 780n191
83:17b 726n83
83:19 93, 94, 875n91
84:3 96
84:4 469, 850n56
86:15 481
87:4 820n53
87:5-6 94, 95, 602
89 454, 455, 448, 578, 582, 583, 587, 590, 593, 603, 812n254, 821n58, 822n68, 828n106, 875n93
89:2 98
89:4-5 456
89:6 576, 582
89:6-8 579, 582, 869n36, 870n46
89:6-9 455, 565
89:6-19 454, 455-6, 458, 510
89:7 583, 869n36
89:7-9 589
89:8 576, 582, 583, 588, 828n108, 875n88
89:8-9 451
89:9 211, 579
89:9-11 734n172
89:11 820n53
89:11a 829n111
89:11b 829n111
89:13 821n58, 829n113
89:15 518, 855n105
89:19 582, 588, 600, 670, 829n114, 869n36
89:20 458, 829n115
89:20-21 457
89:20-25 457
89:20-28 505
89:20-38 455, 456
89:21 219, 499, 882n148
89:22-25 812n254
89:23 830n119
89:26 457, 458, 469
89:27 839n212
89:27-28 219
89:28 458, 505, 849n48
89:28-29 456
89:29-30 456
89:34-37 456
89:35-38 456
89:40 829n117
89:41-45 455
89:47 351
89:50 455, 829n115
89:51 828n107
89:51-52 455
89:52 828n107
89:53 699
90:1-2 99
90:2 99, 109, 217, 843n238

91:1 109, 112
91:4 813n271
91:9 94, 602
91:11 813n271
92:2 94, 602
93 443, 454, 455, 456, 511, 512, 513, 822n68
93:1 512
93:1-4 454-5, 510, 512
93:2 210, 455, 512, 513, 817n13
93:4 826n92, 827n105
94:10-12 854n98
94:12 484
94:20 560, 561
94:22 796n111
95-99 511
95:1 796n111
95:3 509, 512
96:3 512
96:6 804n191
96:8-13 837n185
96:9 605, 615, 658
96:10 512
97 362, 454
97:1 454, 512
97:1-5 348, 510
97:2-6 454
97:3 352, 353
97:5 583
97:6 362
97:7 454
97:9 94, 113, 602
98:1 670
98:5-6 512
98:9 512, 837n185
99:1 512
99:4-5 577
99:6 618, 619, 879n120
102:25b-28 99
103 569
103:3-4 569-70
103:4 570
103:6-7a 570
103:6-14 569-70
103:8 481, 570
103:9 864n187
103:10 570
103:11-12 570
103:13 482, 492, 839n217
103:13-14 570
103:19 570
103:20 831n139
103:22b 570
104 362, 804n193
104:1-2 344
104:1-4 359, 362, 805n193
104:1-9 734n172
104:3 732n156, 814n276
104:4 349, 351, 353, 814n276

Psalms (*Cont.*)
104:26 821*n*60
105:1–2 448
105:3 659
106 117
106:9 824*n*78, 826*n*92
106:19–20 200, 753*n*198
106:20 117
106:21 117
106:47 659
106:48 699
107 94
107:1 94, 602
107:11 90, 94, 113, 602
108:10 136
109:31 859*n*147
110 507
110:1 507
110:4 498, 507
112:5 865*n*195
113 872*n*63
113:8 872*n*64
114:3 451
114:5 451
114:7 451
115:4 133, 134, 303
118:10–11 812*n*254
118:14 823*n*74
118:27 209
119 854*n*98
119:1 563
119:35 865*n*195
119:68 864*n*195
119:73 725*n*73
119:99 531
119:126 859*n*144
120–134 876*n*98
122:3–5 517
122:5 534, 861*n*164
125:4 865*n*195
132 396, 511, 601, 813*n*265, 813*n*266
132:2 197, 318, 396, 601
132:5 197, 318, 601
132:7–8 400, 401
132:8 812*n*252, 813*n*265, 813*n*266, 813*n*267
132:11–18 500
133:2 624
135:15 133, 303
136:2–4 509
136:13–16 570
136:17–20 509
137:4 888*n*203
137:7–9 471
139:13 722*n*49
139:13–15 489
140 522
140:13 522, 529

141:7 831*n*134
143:3 727*n*100
143:5 360
144:1–2 796*n*111
144:5 51, 346
144:5–6 453, 826*n*99
145:5 359
145:8 481
146:9 482, 550–1
146:10 850*n*56
148:1–2 827*n*103
148:13 506
149:2 850*n*56
150:1 209
Proverbs
1:2–3 532
1:3 531
1:8–9 840*n*227
1:12 831*n*134
2:8 872*n*66
2:9 542, 865*n*195
2:21–22 553
3:12 483, 484, 839*n*212
4:1 483
5:21 547
6:20–21 840*n*227
8:15 559
8:15–16 547
8:22 210, 722*n*49
8:22–31 547
8:23 489
9:1–3 7
9:10 6, 673
10:1 840*n*227
10:30 553
11:7 827*n*105
12:8 859*n*140
15:20 840*n*227
15:25 482
16:10–15 518
16:11 858*n*132
16:11–13 547–8
16:18 662
18:12 662
20:26 548
20:28 505, 548
23:10b–11 482, 487
27:20 831*n*134
29:4 548
29:14 548
29:26 548
30:15b–16 831*n*134
Job
1:5 672
1:6 172, 511, 565
1:8 552
2:1 172, 511, 565
2:3 552
3 820*n*55

3:8 6, 445
4:7 552
5:1 576
5:10 478
5:17 104, 484
5:21 104
6:4 104, 734*n*172
6:9 734*n*172
6:10 673, 897*n*297
7:8 726*n*86
7:12 445, 734*n*172
8:2 551
8:3 551, 552
8:8–10 6, 447
8:20 552
9 554, 557
9:2 553
9:3a 859*n*145
9:3b 859*n*145
9:4 557
9:4–5 551
9:4b 553
9:5–8 553
9:8 445
9:13 445, 553, 734*n*172, 820*n*53
9:14–15 553, 557
9:15 553, 859*n*146
9:16 553, 557
9:17–18 553
9:20 553, 859*n*146
9:20–21 553
9:21 553
9:22 552, 553, 557
9:24 553, 556
9:25–31 553
9:32 289, 553, 557
9:33 554, 555, 860*n*150, 873*n*75
10:4–6 289
10:9 133, 719*n*21, 839*n*217
10:11 489
12:15 478
13:1–2 556
13:3 556
13:22 860*n*156
14:2 551
14:15 860*n*156
15:8 565
15:15 576
15:31b 903*n*54
16:4 860*n*150
16:9 289, 554
16:12 554
16:12–14 554
16:17b 554
16:19 554, 555
18:13–14 461
18:14 461, 831*n*137
19:6 551
19:16a 859*n*145

CITATION INDEX

19:26–27 557, 861n159
19:29–31 859n145
21:20 104
21:32–33 898n298
23:4–5 556
23:11–12 897n297
23:15–16 831n137
23:16 104
24:25 859n148
26 821n58
26:1 820n57
26:7 821n58
26:7–13 821n58
26:8 478
26:11–13 835n172
26:12 820n50, 820n53, 820–1n57
26:12–13 445, 820–1n57
26:13 821n57
28:25–26 478
29–31 554, 856n112
30:19–23 554
31 860n154
31:4 555
31:6 555
31:13 860n158
31:35 104, 310, 546, 555
32–37 555
33:6 133, 719n21, 758n24, 839n217
33:13 553, 557, 859n145
34:4 542
34:10–12 551
36:27–28 478
37:5–6 759n38
37:6 759n37
37:10 478
38 478
38–41 555, 859n145
38:1 860n159
38:7 7
38:8–9 843n254
38:8–11 445, 820n55
38:13 826n96
38:28–29 477
38:36 858n130
40:2 555
40:3–5 861n159
40:6 860n159
40:8 552, 556
40:9 734n172
40:9–41:26 445–6
40:10 445
40:14 446
40:19 734n172
40:24–26 826n91
40:25–41:26 820n56
41:10–13 446
41:17 446

41:22–24 446
41:25–26 446, 821n60
42:1–6 861n159
42:3 557
42:5 557, 787n18
42:5–6 564, 574
42:6 860n158
42:6b 557
42:10–17 557
Song of Songs
  8:6b–7a 821n62
Ruth
  2:20 764n80
  4:1–12 524, 526, 850n57
Lamentations
  1:10 486
  1:15 486
  2:1 401
  2:4 351, 486
  2:5 831n135
  2:8 486
  2:13 486
  2:15 486
  2:18 486
  3 522
  3:6 727n100
  3:59 523, 530
  4:7 884n165
  5:19 509
Qohelet
  1:9–10 35
  1:15 551
  3:14 561
  3:16 549
  3:17 549
  7:7b 859n140
  7:15 549
  8:10 898n298
  8:14 549–50, 898n298
  10:11 6
  11:9 549
  12:5 727n100
  12:9–14 858n134
  12:12–13 672
  12:13 858n134
  12:14 549, 858n134
Esther
  1:19 559
  2:7 490
  4:11 719n23
  5:2 719n23
  8:8 559
Daniel
  1:17 101
  1:20 6
  2:27 6
  2:31–32 134
  2:31–36 736n37
  2:37 850n51

2:47 509
3 505
3:1 134
3:1–7 135
3:2–3 135
3:4–7 135
3:12 134
3:14 134
3:18 134
4:4 6
4:5–6 576
4:10 576
4:14–15 576
4:20 576
4:31 99, 110
5:2 778n175
5:3 778n175
5:5 289
5:11 576
5:23 xi, 778n175
7 821n62, 855n102
7:9 136, 289, 511
7:9–10 533
7:10 534, 565
7:13 99, 110, 855n103
7:13–14 464
7:18 576
7:21–22 533, 576
7:25 576
7:27 576
8:13 576
9:9–10 569
9:11 563
9:13 563
10:5 621
10:13 725n76
12:1–3 533
12:7 99, 110
Ezra
  1:7–11 296
  5:14 778n175
  5:15 778n175
  6:1–12 559
  6:5 778n175
  6:12 380
  6:19–22 67
  7:12 850n51
  7:12–26 559
  7:19 778n175
  8:16 197
  9–10 571
  9:14 859n144
Nehemiah
  1:9 380
  5:8 486
  8:1 563
  9:3 563
  9:8 893n261
  9:12 345

Nehemiah (Cont.)
9:13 542, 865n195
9:14 563
9:19 345
9:29–31 569
9:31 481
13:23–25 571
13:26 506

1 Chronicles
2:50–55 782n209
6:1–38 891n236
6:34 662, 664, 894n271
6:39–66 891n233
7:24 724n64
7:25 714n17
9:22 893n261
9:26 893n261
9:31 893n261
13 596, 604, 652
13:2–3 596, 604, 892n242
13:9–10 395
13:10 596
13:11–12 596
14:12 141, 739n77
15:2–15 597
15:11–15 596, 604, 892n242
15:12 663
15:13 596
15:14 663
15:18 241
15:21 241
16:7–36 698
16:10 659
16:14 563
16:27 804n191
16:29 658
16:35 659
17:13 839n212
18:17 845n11
20:5 833n160
21 351, 352, 855n107
21:1 352
21:13–15 855n107
21:15–30 499
21:15–22:1 499
21:27 855n107
21:29 867n19
22:2–5 500
22:7–8 500
22:10 839n212
22:12 563
22:14–16 500
23 500
23:13 662, 664, 894n271
23:25–32 661
24:5 865n8
25:1 500
28:2 401
28:2–3 500
28:6 839n212
28:11–19 500
28:18 405, 814n275
29:1–18 698
29:2–5 500
29:5 662
29:10 839n212
29:14 659
29:16 659
29:23 13, 507
29:25 506

2 Chronicles
1:3 851n70
1:3–6 519
1:8 505
1:12 505
1:13 519
1:18–6:11 501
2:13–16 847n22
3:1 499, 681, 846n18
3:7 398
3:8–10 398
3:8–13 398, 501, 655
3:10–13 405
3:14 398
4:11–18 847n22
5:4–7 501
5:4–11 663
5:6 501, 655
5:7 595
5:7–8 405
5:11 663
6:2 501
6:41 396
7:1 407
7:1–3 811n244
7:3 370, 407
7:5–7 501, 655
7:6 500
7:16 659
7:20 659
8:5 724n64
8:12–13 501
8:13 501
8:14 501
9:8 519
12:1 563
13:4–12 752n192
13:5 752n192
13:8 753n192
13:9 753n192
13:14–15 463
14:2 194
14:2–4 865n195
15:3 661
17–21 893n255
17:7–9 520
17:8 520
17:9 563
18:18 511
19:4b–11 520
19:6 529
19:6–7 521, 529
19:8 520, 528
19:9 529, 893n261
20 658
20:6 658
20:8 659
20:12 658
20:15 428, 658
20:15–17 466
20:17 658
20:21 658
21:12 350
23:6 661, 663, 664, 665
23:18 563
24 503
24:15–16 895n273
25:4 563
25:14–16 136, 140, 296, 806n204
26:10 894n264
26:16 662
26:16–20 640, 847n30
26:16–21 661–3
26:17–18 503, 662
26:18 663, 664, 894–5n271
26:19–20 663
28:22–25 894n270
28:23 136
28:24 296, 895n271
29 663
29–31 847n27
29:5 663, 895n271
29:7 895n271
29:11 665, 894–5n271
29:15 663
29:15–16 661
29:16 664
29:19 663
29:20–24 663
29:22 619, 661, 665
29:24 619, 665
29:25–30 66, 663
29:31 662
29:31–34 663
29:32–34 663
30:1–27 67
30:3 663
30:8 659
30:15 661, 663
30:16 563, 619, 661, 665
30:17 663
30:24 663
31:1 194
31:3–4 563
31:15 893n261
31:16 661

CITATION INDEX

31:18 664, 893n261
31:20 893n261
31:20–21 865n195
32:1 893n261
32:1–22 834n163
32:6 513
33:3 134, 902n44
33:7 134
33:8 563
33:19 902n44
34:14 563, 563
35:1–9 67
35:3 661, 664, 665
35:5 661
35:6 663
35:8–9 661
35:26 563
36:7 296
36:10 296
36:18–19 296

SECOND TEMPLE
   LITERATURE
Tobit
   1:5 792n68
Wisdom of Solomon 215,
   897n297
   15:6–17 736n29
Ben Sira (Sirach,
   Ecclesiasticus) 897n296
   42:4 858n132
   43:25 820n53
   48:17–22 834n163
1 Maccabees
   3:18–19 465
Bel and the Dragon
   7 736n29
1 Enoch
   81 534
   89:70 534
   90:20 534
   103:2 534
Jubilees
   5:12–19 534
   16:9 534
Dead Sea Scrolls
1QHodayot^a
   XVII, lines 29b–31a 838n203
   XVII, lines 35–36 478, 843n255
1QM (War Scroll)
   VII, lines 6–7 890n215
1QIsa^a 445, 796n112, 820n50,
   843n256
1QS
   XI:4–5 215
4Q158 862n170
4Q524 862n170
4QDeut^h 886n180
4QDeut^j 91, 568, 725n74

4QDeut^q 725n74
4QPs89 (=4Q236) 829
4QSam^a 596, 836n179, 871n49,
   871n51, 872n66, 872n67,
   872n69, 884n168, 885n169,
   892n241
4QTestim 886n180
4QQoh^a 859n140
11QT 862n170

WEST SEMITIC INSCRIPTIONS
Adon Papyrus (KAI 266) 779n179
Ahiqar
   TAD 3, C1.1.79 576
Ahiram (KAI 1) 727n100, 771n138
Aladlammu seal (Seyrig
   Collection) 305–6
Arad ostraca 54, 246, 768n115
   16 749n175
   18 749n175
   18.2–3 246
   18.9 246, 832n149
   21 246, 749n175
   21.2 247
   40 749n175
   40.3 247
   41 749n175
   49 749n175
   51 749n175
   56 749n175
   60 749n175
   67 749n175
   68 749n175
   79 749n175
arrowhead inscriptions 723n53,
   770n128, 832n145, 902n45
Arslan Tash 55, 97, 268,
   576, 727n98, 727n102,
   779n181, 865n6
   I, line 2 779n184
   I, lines 8–10 97
   I, lines 11–12 576
   I, line 14 779n183
   II 6
   II, line 1 779n183
   II, lines 1–2 742n103
   II, line 6
   II, line 14 780n183
Bar-Rakib I (KAI 216) 776n171
   lines 5–6 848n40
Bar-Rakib II (KAI 217) 776n171
Batnoam (KAI 11) 845n11
Bod'aštart (KAI 16) 686, 866n8
Bukan (KAI 320) 266, 776n171
CIS
   I, 4 686
CWSS
   205:523 755n1
   107:186 755n1

Deir 'Alla 54, 90, 96, 101, 105,
   113, 116, 268–9, 284, 722n50,
   723n52, 725n70, 727n100,
   728n103, 730n129, 746n149
   I.1–2 90
   I.2 724n71
   I.36 6
   II.6 725n71
   V 724n71
   XV 724n71
Ein Gedi 54, 246
   line 1 768n113
Elephantine Papyri 336, 559,
   729n116
El Khadr arrowhead 832n145
Eshmunazor (KAI 14) 685, 686,
   687, 771n138
   line 9 576, 863n180
   line 14 687
   line 15 686, 687
   lines 15–16 685
   line 16 686
   line 17 865n8
   line 18 681, 685, 686
   lines 21–22 583
   line 22 576
Geniza 18
   §17:9 312
Geniza 22
   §1.8ff. 311–12
Gezer Calendar 610
Hadad Inscription (KAI
   214) 196, 722n50,
   776n171, 789n34
   line 1 739n82
   line 2 750n180
   lines 2–3 82, 732n156, 750n180
   line 11 82, 732n156, 750n180
   line 14 739n82
   line 16 739n82
   line 17 334
   line 18 732n156, 750n180
   lines 18–19 82
   lines 21–22 334
Hatra 54
Hazael inscription (KAI
   311) 776n171
Horvat Rimmon ostracon 312
Ishba'l 54, 234
Jerusalem inscription 54, 81, 166
KAI
   1 727n100, 771n138
   4 771n138
   4.4–5 576, 863n180
   10 771n138
   11 845n11
   13 685, 687, 771n138
   13.1–2 686, 845n11
   14 685, 686, 687, 771n138

KAI (*Cont.*)
14:9 576, 863n180
14.14 687
14.15 686, 687
14.15-16 685
14.16 686
14.17 865n8
14.18 681, 685, 686
14.21-22 583
14.22 576
15 685, 686, 866n8
16 686, 866n8
17 685
24 722n50, 771n138, 870n40
24.10-11 839n209
24.15 681
24.15-16 732n156
25 722n49, 776n171
26 722n50, 771n138
26 A I.3 839n210
26 A III.18 81
26 A III.19 98
26 A IV.2-3 98
27.2 779n184
27.8-10 97
27.11-12 576
27.14 780n183
37 255
37, A 7 685, 865n7
37, A 10 685, 690, 865n7
69 772n138
181 54, 208, 235, 251, 252, 270, 429, 462, 754n207, 762n70, 832n147
181.4 429
181.5 429
181.8 763n69
181.9 429, 755n211
181.10-11 755n211
181.10-13 749n172, 770n125
181.11-12 755n211
181.12 429, 770n125
181.12-13 429
181.14 429
181.14-18 251, 462
181.17 429, 755n211, 770n125
181.17-18 755n211
181.18 429, 762n69, 769n125
181.19 429
181.32 429
181.33 429
200 554, 860n154
200.1 856n11
200.10-12a 860n155
200.12 856n11
201 776n171
201.23 778n172
202 776n171, 779n179
202.4-5 833n158

214 196, 722n50, 776n171, 789n34
214.1 739n82
214.2 750n180
214.2-3 82, 732n156, 750n180
214.11 82, 732n156, 750n180
214.14 739n82
214.16 739n82
214.17 334
214.18 732n156, 750n180
214.18-19 82
214.21-22 334
215 196, 722n50, 815n286
215.22 82, 196, 732n156
215.59 334
216 776n171
216.5-6 848n40
217 776n171
222 722n50
222.8-10 778n172
222.9 88
222.11 87
222.11-12 778n173
222.38 777n172
223.2-3 744n140
223.7 744n140
223.9-10 744n140
224 776n171
225 776n171
225:1 891n235
226 776n171
226:1 891n235
244 722n50
244:3 81
266 779n179
277.8-9 758n23
309 390, 776n171, 784n229
309.5 778n175, 843n259
309.6 778n175
309.10-12 812n257
309.16-17 778n172, 812n257
309.23 778n172
310 709n76, 776n171
311 776n171
320 266, 776n171
Katumuwa 334, 407, 722n49, 776n171, 778n172, 815n286
Karatepe (KAI 26) 54, 81, 95, 479, 722n50, 771n138
A I, line 3 839n210
A III, line 18 81
A III, line 19 98
A IV, lines 2-3 98
Ketef Hinnom (KH) 54, 240, 247, 328
I 769n122
I.10 249
I.14-18 247
II.2-5 249, 769n120

II.5-12 247
Khirbet Beit Lei 54, 166, 211, 245, 408, 765n93, 789n42, 828n108
Khirbet el-Qom 54, 167, 241-3, 244, 250, 769n121
line 3 766n101
Khirbet Qeiyafa 252
Kulamuwa (KAI 24) 479, 722n50, 771n138, 870n40
lines 10-11 839n209
line 15 681
lines 15-16 732n156
Kulamuwa scepter inscription (KAI 25) 722n49, 776n171
Kuntillet ʻAjrud (KA) 54, 113, 167, 236, 248, 250, 251, 279, 293, 305, 308, 360, 576, 701n2, 733n162, 764n80, 764n81, 765n87, 765n88, 774n154, 811n250, 835n177, 866n12, 867n19, 875n90
1.1-1.4 586
1.2 763n79, 869n41
2.1-2.9 586
3.1-3.16 586
3.1 236, 326, 763n79, 869n41
3.6 763n79, 765n85, 784n222, 869n41
3.9 763n79, 766n91, 869n41
3.11-3.14 764n86
4.1-4.5 586
4.1-4.6 766n94
4.1 763n74
4.1.1 240, 281, 586, 763n79, 784n224, 869n41
4.2 4, 240, 281, 381, 583, 585-7, 603, 711n87, 721n44, 722n50, 734n171, 762n67, 763n74, 763n79, 764n83, 782n210, 794n99, 803n184, 816n2, 817n9, 869n36, 869n37, 870n43, 875n88
4.2.2 586
4.2.4 866n12
4.2.5 586
4.2.6 586, 587
4.3 763n74
4.4.1 586, 870n42
Pithos A (3.1-3.5) 125, 237, 239, 409-11
Pithos B (3.6-3.15) 239-40, 281, 409-11, 764n80
Plaster inscriptions (4.1-4.6) 262, 746n149, 765n92, 869n37
Stone basin inscription (1.2) 237
Lachish ewer 739n82
Lachish letters

CITATION INDEX 1069

1-18 769n123
2.2-3 250
2.5 251
3 769n124
3.2-4 250
3.9 250
4.1-2 250
5.1-2 250
5.7-8 250
6.1-2 250
6.12 250
Lachish, Old Canaanite
  inscription 770n129
Leptis Magna 54, 81
Magische Qaudrate 900n14
"Marseilles" Sacrificial Tariff
  (KIA 69) 772n138
Melqart Stela (Bar Hadad; KAI
  201) 776n171
  line 23 778n172
Meṣad Ḥashavyahu (KAI 200)
  554, 860n154
  line 1 856n11
  lines 10-12a 860n155
  line 12 856n11
Mesha stele (Moabite stone;
  KAI 181) 54, 208, 235, 251,
  252, 270, 429, 462, 754n207,
  762n70, 832n147
  line 4 429
  line 5 429
  line 8 763n69
  line 9 429, 755n211
  lines 10-13 749n172, 770n125
  lines 10-11 755n211
  lines 11-12 755n211
  lines 12-13 429
  line 12 429, 770n125
  lines 14-18 251, 462
  line 14 429
  lines 17-18 755n211
  line 17 429, 755n211, 770n125
  line 18 429, 762n69, 769n125
  line 19 429
  line 32 429
  line 33 429
Miqneyaw seal 241
Moabite Ataruz
  inscription 754n207
Moussaieff ostraca 236
Nerab I (KAI 225) 776n171
  line 1 891n235
Nerab II (KAI 226) 776n171
  line 1 891n235
Naveh inscriptions 244-5
Ördekburnu 776n171
Palmyra (KAI 244) 722n50
  line 3 81
Palmyrene votive inscription 196

Panamuwa (KAI 215) 196,
  722n50, 815n286
  line 22 82, 196, 732n156
  line 59 334
Papyrus Amherst 63 322,
  728n116, 792n73
  XII 11-XIII 17 792n74
  XIII 9-17 739n73
  XIV 9-17 739n73
Passover Letter from Elephantine
  (TAD A 4.1=P. Berlin
  13464) 68
  1.A4.7.8-12 750n179
  1.A4.8.7-11 750n179
Proto-Sinaitic Inscriptions 97
Pyrgi inscription (KAI
  277) 758n23
  lines 8-9
Qubūr el-Walaydah 722n50
Samaria ostraca
  41 321, 869n40
Serabit el-Khadim 97
Siloam 709-10n76
Tabnit (KAI 13) 685, 687, 771n138
  lines 1-2 686, 845n11
Tel Zayit abecedary 252, 770n130
Tel Dan inscription (KAI
  310) 709n76, 776n171
Tell el-Kheleifah Ostracon
  6043.1 781n203
Tell Fakhariyah (KAI 309) 390,
  776n171, 784n229
  line 5 778n175, 843n259
  line 6 778n175
  lines 10-12 812n257
  lines 16-17 778n172, 812n257
  line 23 778n172
Tell Qasile ostraca 724n64
Yaḥimilk (KAI 4) 771n138
  lines 4-5 576, 863n180
Yehawmilk (KAI 10) 771n138
Zakkur (KAI 202) 776n171,
  779n179
  lines 4-5 833n158

TEXTS FROM UGARIT
'Aqhatu (KTU 1.17-KTU
  1.19) 134, 215, 262, 483, 516
Ba'lu Cycle (KTU 1.1-KTU
  1.6) 150, 443, 447, 827n102
CTA
  1 iv 819n40
  2 iv 819n40
Kirta (KTU 1.14-KTU 1.16) 262,
  497, 516
KTU
  1.1-1.24 261
  1.1.4 228, 229, 270
  1.1.4.12 78, 754n210

1.1.4.13-14 228-9
1.1.5 719n24
1.2.1.7-8 680, 681, 685
1.2.1.16 78, 754n210
1.2.1.[18] 830n119
1.2.1.20-24 459
1.2.1.21 720n30
1.2.1.27 459
1.2.1.32 800n147
1.2.1.35 830n119
1.2.1.36-37 440, 441
1.2.1.40 680
1.2.3.20 720n30
1.2.4.10 98
1.2.4.11-23 818n35
1.2.4.15-18 440
1.2.4.23-27 441
1.2.4.27 818-19n38
1.2.4.28 824n78
1.2.4.28-30 680, 681
1.2.4.28-39 819n39
1.2.4.34-35 441
1.3 774n154
1.3.1.10-11 744n135
1.3.2.3-41 462, 835n178
1.3.2.5-20 442
1.3.3.38-42 442, 446
1.3.3.38-43 818n35
1.3.3.38-47 819n40
1.3.3.39 826n92
1.3.3.45 800n147
1.3.4.25-27 754n210
1.3.4.54 78, 754n210
1.3.5.8 718n18
1.3.5.10 78, 754n210
1.3.5.24-25 76
1.3.5.30-31 78, 97
1.3.5.35 78, 754n210
1.3.5.35-36 719
1.3.6.11 865n3
1.4.1.4 78, 754n210
1.4.1.29-35 190
1.4.2.2-11 476
1.4.2.3-4 690
1.4.2.10 78, 754n210
1.4.2.11 719n19
1.4.3.32 719n19
1.4.4.2 865n3
1.4.4.8 865n3
1.4.4.13 865n3
1.4.4.16 865n3
1.4.4.24 718n18
1.4.4.29-30 147
1.4.4.38-39 78, 152
1.4.4.41-42 97
1.4.4.41-43 78, 113
1.4.4.47 78, 754n210
1.4.4.48 719n19
1.4.5.3-4 76, 78, 113

1070 CITATION INDEX

KTU(*Cont.*)
1.4.6.38–40 778n177
1.4.6.38–59 474
1.4.6.40–43 755n210
1.4.6.46 475
1.4.6.56–57 511
1.4.7.35–39 778n177
1.4.8.17–20 460
1.5.1.1–3 442, 446, 821n57
1.5.1.19–20 460, 461
1.5.1.22–23 778n177
1.5.2.2–4 460, 461
1.5.2.6–7 461
1.5.2.21–23 778n177
1.5.4.7 778n177
1.5.6.2 718n18
1.6.1.36 718n18
1.6.1.54–63 828n108
1.6.1.56–65 511, 736n36
1.6.1.59–60 147
1.6.2.9–37 819n40
1.6.3.1–21 81
1.6.3.5 719n19
1.6.4.4–5 365
1.6.6.27–29 80, 118, 162
1.6.6.51–53 818n35
1.6.6.55–56 146
1.10.2.1–2 778n177
1.10.2.4–5 778n177
1.10.2.32–33 778n177
1.10.3.5 719n19
1.10.3.5–7 97
1.10.3.6–7 719n18
1.10.3.7–8 778n177
1.10.3.35–36 755n210
1.12.1.40–41 778n177
1.12.2.53–55 778n177
1.12.2.60–61 78
1.12.2.53–55 742n107
1.12.2.54 755n210
1.13 55, 831n143
1.13.3–7 462, 762n70
1.13.5–6 442
1.13.7 831n143
1.14.1.26ff 79, 475
1.14.1.35–1.14.3.51 81
1.14.2.6–26 735n13
1.14.2.9–27 844n9
1.14.3.52–1.14.4.9 844n9
1.14.4.34 720n30
1.14.4.34–43 475
1.15.2.12ff 79, 475
1.15.2.16–28 476
1.15.2.26–28 738n63, 837n192
1.15.2.27 837n192
1.16.1.11 720n30
1.16.1.20–23 216
1.16.1.21–22 720n30
1.16.1.22 725n79

1.16.2.43 216
1.16.3 217
1.16.3.4–8 87, 88
1.16.4.1–2 78
1.16.5.10ff 79, 475
1.16.5.10–1.16.6.14 720n31
1.16.5.25–28 78
1.16.5.25–30 138
1.16.5.25–41 77
1.16.5.29 719n21
1.16.6.44–48 516
1.16.6.45–50 498
1.16.6.54–57 680, 681, 685
1.17–1.19 476
1.17.1.24 719n19
1.17.1.24ff 79
1.17.1.25–34 840n225
1.17.1.31–32 718n18, 721n34
1.17.1.43–48 840n225
1.17.2.1–8 840n225
1.17.2.5–6 721n34
1.17.2.12–23 840n225
1.17.2.19–20 721n34
1.17.2.24–38 476
1.17.5.4–8 476, 498, 840n223
1.17.5.7–8 516
1.17.5.10–11 88
1.17.5.21–31 477
1.18.1.11–12 76
1.19.1.23–25 516
1.20–22 76, 79, 721n41, 900n17
1.22.8–10 832n143
1.23 77–8, 79, 80, 81, 103, 110, 114, 152, 156, 161, 498, 508, 517, 715n24, 719n22, 719n24, 719n25, 721n33, 721n40, 726n90, 732n146, 733n159, 847n28, 870n47
1.23.8–9 162, 460, 831n132
1.23.13 103, 104, 730n126
1.23.23–24 738n63
1.23.24 475
1.23.28 103
1.23.32–33 474, 477, 719n25
1.23.37 719n23
1.23.40 719n23
1.23.44 719n23
1.23.47 719n23
1.23.59 475, 738n63
1.23.61 475, 738n63
1.23.61–62 831n133
1.23.65 867n19
1.23.67b–68 103
1.23.68 103, 900n19
1.24 837n193
1.24.5–7 476
1.28 80
1.39 79
1.39.16 899n6

1.40 76, 263, 498, 517, 718n17, 718n18, 721n33, 844n7, 844n10
1.41 79, 264, 498, 844n7
1.41.21 881n134
1.43 136, 498, 682, 844n7
1.43.4 136
1.43.8 736n34
1.43.22 136, 737n48
1.47 80, 775n159
1.48 682
1.48.8–9 755n210
1.65 80, 718n17, 718n18, 721n33, 775n159
1.65.4 718n17
1.65.9 779n178
1.79 682, 900n24
1.79.8 900n25
1.80 682, 900n24
1.80.2 900n25
1.81.17–19 865n3
1.82.1 819n41
1.82.38 819n41, 821n57
1.83 442, 680, 681
1.83.8–14 442
1.83.13 826n92
1.84 844n10
1.87 498, 844n7
1.91 137, 682
1.91.10 682
1.92 681, 900n15
1.100 720n31, 721n38
1.100.3 76
1.100.20 899n14
1.100.73–76 138
1.101 121
1.101.1–10 511
1.101.6 754n210
1.102 80, 775n159
1.102.9 899n6
1.102.15 778n178
1.102.28 778n178
1.107 721n38
1.107.38' 720n31
1.107.39' 899n14
1.108 55, 103, 105, 870n46
1.108.1 97, 98, 718n18
1.108.12 730n125
1.111.17–18 87
1.112 498, 844n7
1.112.6–8 137, 900n21
1.112.21 896n287
1.114 76, 79–80, 156, 718n18, 721n41, 744n135
1.114.23–24 681
1.114.26'–28' 681
1.116.1 900n17
1.116.1–3 681
1.116.8–10 899n12

CITATION INDEX 1071

1.118 80, 775n159
1.118.18 818n29
1.119 81, 118, 264, 498,
  606, 774n154, 817n4,
  844n7, 875n96
1.119.6 76, 576, 876n97
1.119.13-16 735n13
1.119.14 76
1.119.26'-29' 429
1.119.28' 875n96
1.119.28'-34a' 607
1.119.30'-31' 607
1.119.31' 715n25, 875n96
1.119.33' 576, 876n97
1.121 844n10
1.122 844n10
1.123.20' 865n3
1.123.26' 865n3
1.128.14-15 723n60
1.141 146
1.148 80, 682, 775n159
1.148.6 818n29
1.148.18-22 137, 682, 683
1.148.21 881n134
1.148.41 818n29
1.152 844n10
1.153 844n10
1.154 844n10
1.161.8 727n100
1.162.2 830n126
1.169.18 779n181
1.170.1 844n9
1.179 259
1.179.14 865n4
1.179.17 575
1.179.18 899n14
1.180 (RIH 98/02) 680, 681,
  689, 899n13
2.40.14-17 741n90
2.42 98
2.42.9 727n101
3.1 900n22
4.4.20-24 76
4.96 260
4.149 847n28
4.149.14-15 844n9
4.168 135
4.182 135, 900n27
4.182.55 682-3
4.182.58 682-3
4.219.2 679
4.226.3 730n130
4.623.3 716n3
6.10 146
6.13 76
6.14 76
6.62 735n8
Ras Shamra (RS)
  1.017 775n159

4.474 775n159
6.138 775n159
8.295 (A 4622) 740n88
15.82 737n46
15.115 737n46
17.22+ 899n12
17.87.21-23 899n12
17.227 900n22
17.380 900n22
17.382+ 900n22
20.024 80, 775n159
20.024.18 818n29
20.178 (=*Ugaritica* V
  #55) 838n198
20.182A+B (=*Ugaritica* V
  #36) 260
24.246 775n159
24.264+ 775n159
24.266 817n4, 875n96
24.278 723n60
24.325 146
24.643 775n159
24.643.1-9 775n159
88.70 741n95
86.2230 229
92.2004 775n159
92.2004.29 818n29
92.2005 765n87
92.2010 765n87
92.2016 259, 899n14
92.2016.14 865n4
92.2016.17 575

MESOPOTAMIAN/AKKADIAN/
SUMERIAN SOURCES
A. 1121+ A. 2731
  lines 53-55 515
A. 1968 830n125
  lines 6'-11' 516
Adapa 215
Adad-nirari III inscription
  lines 1-5 805n193
Alalakh VII 303-4
Amarna letters (EA) 258
  17:24-28 840n229
  23 899n14, 900n16
  23:13-17 737n51
  26:41 132
  27:33 132
  53:40-44 840n229
  55 132
  83:51 840n229
  114:59-69 840n229
  121:61-63 840n229
  123:23 840n229
  134 140, 806n204
  137 606
  137:31-32 576
  138:47 840n229

146:6-7 727n101
147:13-15 799n144
149:24ff 727n101
155:6 727n101
155:47 727n101
164 137
175 717n9
175:3 75
151:45 75
252 140, 806n204
255 205
256 205
265:15 75
287:56 103
287:60-61 381
288 762n61
288:5-7 381
288:26 231
Ashur
  418 736n32
Ashurnasirpal II
  inscription 573
Atrahasis 839n217
  1.4.223-226 216
Babylonian Chronicle 296
Bavian Rock inscription of
  Sennacherib 739n73
Chagar Bazar
  inscriptions 717n12
CT
  13.33-34 431-3
  13.33-34:8-13 432
  13.33-34:14-19 432
  13:33-34:20-22 432
  13.33-34: Reverse 5-9 433
Cylinder C (RINAP 3.15)
  iv, lines 6-25, 1'-14' 834n163
Cylinder D (RINAP 3.16)
  iii, line 74—iv, line 37 834n163
Ebla (Tell Mardikh) 228
Emar
  369 883n153
  369.6 608
  369.22 608
  370 678, 883n153
  373 883n156
  373+.15 899n10
  375 883n156
Enki and Ninmah 839n217
Enuma Elish 136, 150, 216,
  437-9, 443, 447, 704n22,
  705n40, 818n33
  Tablet I, lines 1-2 817n13
  Tablet I, lines 92-93 850n53
  Tablet I, lines
    99-100 812n261, 850n53
  Tablet IV, line 1 850n53
  Tablet IV, line 41 821n57
  Tablet VI, line 61-66 850n53

1072 CITATION INDEX

Esarhaddon's Succession Treaty (EST) 715n31, 728n116, 890n219
Esarhaddon's treaty with Baal, king of Tyre 729n116, 771n138
Foundation inscription of Yahdunlim
   I.34–35 717n7
Gilgamesh 215
   Tablet X, 301 [Column VI.10] 215
Gilgamesh Old Babylonian Version
   OB VA + BM (Meisner Fragment) iii, 3–5 758n21
   OB Yale tablet (OB III) column iv, lines 140-143 (= Gilg Y. IV, 5–8) 758n22
GLL A, 28–29 758n22
Flood Story (Eridu Genesis)
   Segment B, lines 6ff. 844n3
Idrimi statue 771n134
Inanna's Descent into the Underworld 736n23
Jerusalem Prism (RINAP 3.23)
   iii, lines 16–42 834n163
KAR
   6 433
Khorsabad annals 294
King Prism (Heidel Prism; RINAP 3.17)
   iii, lines 38–81 834n163
Law of Hammurabi (LH) 513–15, 861n161
   ii 60–62 805n191
   Prologue, vv. 16–19 514
   xlvii 59–78 514–15
   xlviii 3–47 515
   xlviii 41–47 517
   xlviii 59–78 517
   §195 853n84
Laws of Lipit-Ishtar 861n161
Laws of Ur-Nammu 861n161
Mari prophecy 266, 459
"Ninurta's Return to Nibru: A Šir-gida to Ninurta"
   lines 55–63 818n26
Nimrud Prism IV 786n12
Nin A
   I 1–ii 11 830n124
OB administrative text from Hazor 717n6
Oriental Institute/Chicago Prism ("Taylor Prism"; RINAP 3.22)
   iii, lines 18–49 834n163
Rassam Cylinder (RINAP 3.4)
   A III 118-127 801n156
   lines 49–58 834n163

RINAP 3 (Grayson and Novotny 2012)
   4, lines 49–59 (Rassam Cylinder) 834n163
   15 iv, lines 6–25, 1'–14' (Cylinder C) 834n163
   16 iii line 74 through iv line 37 (Cylinder D) 834n163
   17 iii, lines 38–81 (King Prism, Heidel Prism) 834n163
   18 iii, lines 15–31 834n163
   19 i', lines 3'–14' 834n163
   22 iii, lines 18–49 (Oriental Institute/Chicago Prism, "Taylor Prism") 834n163
   23 iii, lines 16–42 (Jerusalem Prism) 834n163
   26 i, lines 12'–13' 834n163
   34, line 15 834n163
SAA 2 (Parpola and Watanabe 1988)
   2 779n180
   5, line r.e.18 685
SAA 9 (Parpola 1997)
   1.4, lines 27–30 834n162
   1.6, line 7' 839n208
   1.6, lines 15'–18' 839n208
   2.5, lines 26'–27' 839n208
Sargon II booty inscriptions (Nimrud prisms) 292, 294–5
Sargon II inscription from Dūr-Šarrukīn 140
Sennacherib inscriptions 573
Sumerian King List 495, 496, 845n13
   line 1 844n3
   line 41 844n3
Tiglath-pileser's annals 233
VAT 17019 839n217
Verse Account of Nabonidus 737n38

ANATOLIAN SOURCES
CTH
   1 831n142
   4 831n142
   61.II 831n142
   261.I §37' 515
   261.I §38' 515, 853n90
   261.I §39' 516, 853n90
   261.I §40' 516, 853n90
   264 831n142
   423 831n142
   481 737n39
Elkunirsha 54, 81–2, 86, 95, 719n19
Hieroglyphic Luwian text 135, 839n210
Hittite prayer to Elkunirsha 81–82

KUB
   29.4 IV 38–40 737n39
Telepinu 217
TÜNP 1 721n45, 723n50

EGYPTIAN SOURCES
Amenophis III geographical lists 230, 761n53
Astarte and the Tribute of the Sea 257, 679, 772n146
"The Destuction of Mankind" 735–6n23
Execration texts 257
Instructions of Amenemope 547, 858n131
Job stone of Ramses II (Sheik Sa'd) 731n142
Legend of the Winged Disk 827n99
London Medical Papyrus 773n148
Papyrus Anastasi I 230
Papyrus Anastasi VI 230, 232, 251
Papyrus Chester Beatty IV 839n205
Papyrus Harris I 232, 251
Rameses II geographical lists 230, 761n53
Serabit el-Khadim 257, 773n146
Seti I Karnak temple 230
Shishak I's topographical list #36 728n103
Tale of Sinuhe 257
Wadi Hammamat 832n144

ANCIENT SOUTH ARABIAN INSCRIPTIONS
DAI Ṣirwāḥ 2005-50 55, 462, 762n70, 832n147
RES
   3945 55, 462, 762n70, 832n147

NEW TESTAMENT
Matthew
   6:9 903n60
Luke
   1:46–55 589
   11:2 903n60
1 Corinthians
   15:54–57 831n133
Galatians
   1:15 842n251
1 Timothy
   6:15 850n51
Revelation
   5:5 313
   7:17 831n133
   19:16 509
   21:4 831n133

CITATION INDEX

RABBINIC WORKS
Genesis Rabbah (Gen Rab)
  V 8 729n121
  XLVI 3 729n121
  XCII 1 729n121
Talmud
  Ḥagigah 12a 102

Mishnah
  Ma'aser Sheni 4:10–11 866n12

GRECO-ROMAN LITERATURE
Eusebius, *Praeparatio Evangelica* 255
Herodotus
  IV, 82 798n133

Josephus, *Antiquities*
  VI, 1 874n77
Philo of Byblos, *The Phoenician History* 255
  1.10.15–30 772n141
Tacitus, *Historiae*
  V, 5 105

CPSIA information can be obtained
at www.ICGtesting.com
Printed in the USA
BVHW030232170722
642202BV00005B/22/J